ESSEX COUNTY

JEFF LEMIRE

Top Shelf Productions
Atlanta / Portland

Other Works by Jeff Lemire:

Sweet Tooth (DC Comics/Vertigo)
The Nobody (DC Comics/Vertigo)
Lost Dogs (Self-Published)

Essex County
ISBN: 978-1-60309-038-4

1. Farm Life
2. Family Drama
3. Hockey
4. Graphic Novels

Essex County © 2009 Jeff Lemire. Introduction © 2009 Darwyn Cooke. Edited by Chris Staros. Published by Top Shelf Productions, P.O. Box 1282, Marietta, GA 30061-1282, USA. Publishers: Chris Staros and Brett Warnock. Top Shelf Productions and the Top Shelf logo are registered trademarks of Top Shelf Productions, Inc. All Rights Reserved. No part of this publication may be reproduced without permission, except for small excerpts for purposes of review. Visit our online catalog at www.topshelfcomix.com. Visit Jeff Lemire at www.jefflemire.com. Second Printing, November 2010. Printed in Canada.

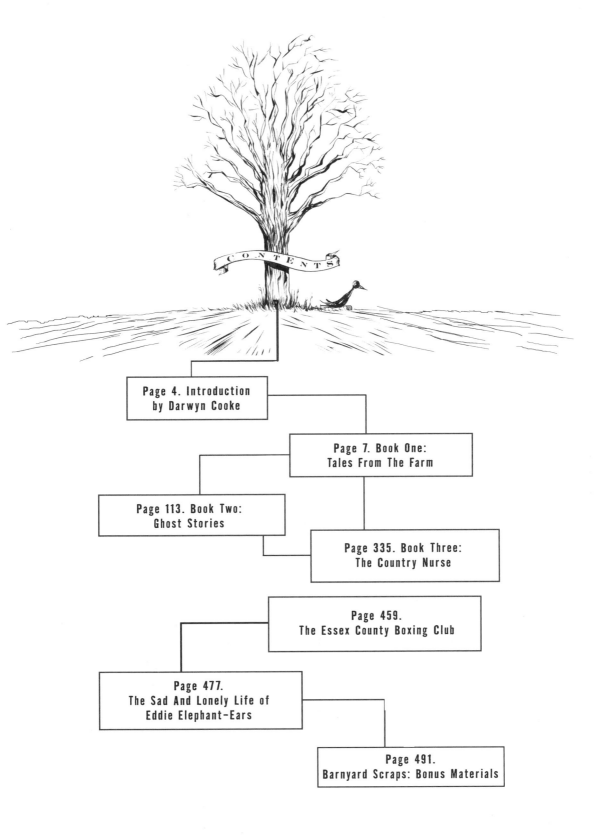

CONTENTS

INTRODUCTION BY
DARWYN COOKE

I think it appropriate to confess a degree of trepidation regarding my qualifications for writing this introduction. Although I've been called upon many times to do just that for a variety of collected comics stories, they usually involve flying men or scheming femme fatales. I am, and probably always will be, a genre entertainer. As such, it is fairly easy work for me to key up an engaging thousand words about the craft displayed in a book of that ilk.

Here we have a somewhat different situation: Jeff Lemire's **Essex County** is more than an engaging afternoon's read; it supersedes the labels "graphic fiction" and even "graphic literature." This is a high watermark in Canadian Literature that can proudly rest beside the Lawrences, Richlers, and Atwoods on the big shelf.

Canadian cartooning has a rich and wildly varied history that calls back to the very beginnings of the form. But by the 1970s it became clear that mass market comics publications aimed at an exclusively Canadian audience weren't viable, and over the next couple of decades we saw the ascendance of the independent cartoonist. With Dave Sim and Gerhard charting the waters and setting an astonishing standard, young Canadian cartoonists began to see that there were alternatives to going to New York and drawing Batman.

The '90s saw the emergence of autobiographical comics, and the trio of Seth, Brown and Matt focused much of the Indy world's attention on Canada. It is early now, but I believe this will one day be seen as Canada's first real golden age of cartooning. It must have been impossible for an art comics connoisseur in the late '90s to think of Canada without thinking autobio.

As we moved into the 21st century, what I have found particularly exciting is the emergence of a new generation that has taken its inspiration from that era, but pushed forward into broader areas of interest. At the crest of this wave are two cartoonists at completely different points on the compass: Bryan Lee O'Malley, the genre-splicing genius behind **Scott Pilgrim** and relative newcomer Jeff Lemire.

It would seem Jeff Lemire is a haunted man. I don't mean this in any melodramatic, ectoplasmic sense. I refer to a more serious condition common amongst many great storytellers. His head and his heart seem to carry remembrances of the quiet beats in which people stand revealed. With a casual grace that would make the late Raymond Carver envious, Lemire's stories build out of innocuous and seemingly unconnected moments that gather and gain weight when viewed in a cumulative light. His instinct for where to start and end a scene, and where to place that scene within the larger tapestry is sublime. The ease with which **Essex County** flows from past to present to future to fantasy shows the kind of mastery that most cartoonists remain incapable of after a lifetime of practice.

While **Essex County** is laced with sentiment, it all seems natural and hard earned. Lemire has either cannily or intuitively avoided the pitfall of many far more celebrated cartoonists; the pitfall of self-pity. Many of our best cartoonists have a conflated sense of their own suffering and isolation, and large passages of their work seem engineered to give this type of self-absorption a heroic context. Lemire's characters weather their lives with resolution and quiet despair. We feel for them because of Lemire's talent for revealing their inner strength, not their outer weakness. In **Tales from the Farm**, our cast are people trapped in a life they didn't ask for or expect. Lester, Kenny and Jimmy are all caught in a stasis brought about by external forces they couldn't foresee or control. It seems their only substantive way forward is to endure and abide. The road out of the woods is laid stone by quiet stone.

Lemire's approach is so devoid of melodrama that when he does go all-in, we're taken aback, and shopworn clichés take on a heartbreaking freshness. When the life of a character that has been so spartanly laid before us ends, we expect yet another moment of quiet despair. Off-panel tapping spurs us to turn the page, however, and we see Lemire dive in with both feet: a hockey team stands before us, offering that most Canadian sign of masculine respect—the quiet clicking of sticks on the ice. It is a moment of melodrama timed so perfectly, it sneaks past our cynicism and floods our hearts with something we forgot we had inside us.

What this all adds up to is a work of unexpected maturity that speaks on a universal level, but holds special rewards for those familiar with life in rural Canada. **Essex County** is a tremendous achievement made all the more incredible when we consider the relative youth of the author. This heartfelt piece of graphic literature surpasses its form to stand as what I'm sure will be an enduring example of the finest in Canadian Literature proper.

Pierre Berton, Farley Mowat, Jeff Lemire. Sounds as natural as the quiet clean of a sharpened blade on fresh ice.

Darwyn Cooke 2009
East of Essex County

Darwyn Cooke is the Eisner Award-winning Canadian cartoonist behind such comics as Catwoman, Will Eisner's The Spirit, *and one of Jeff Lemire's all-time favorites,* DC: The New Frontier. *Cooke is currently hard at work on graphic novel adaptations of Richard Stark's "Parker" crime novels for IDW Publishing.*

BOOK ONE
TALES FROM THE FARM

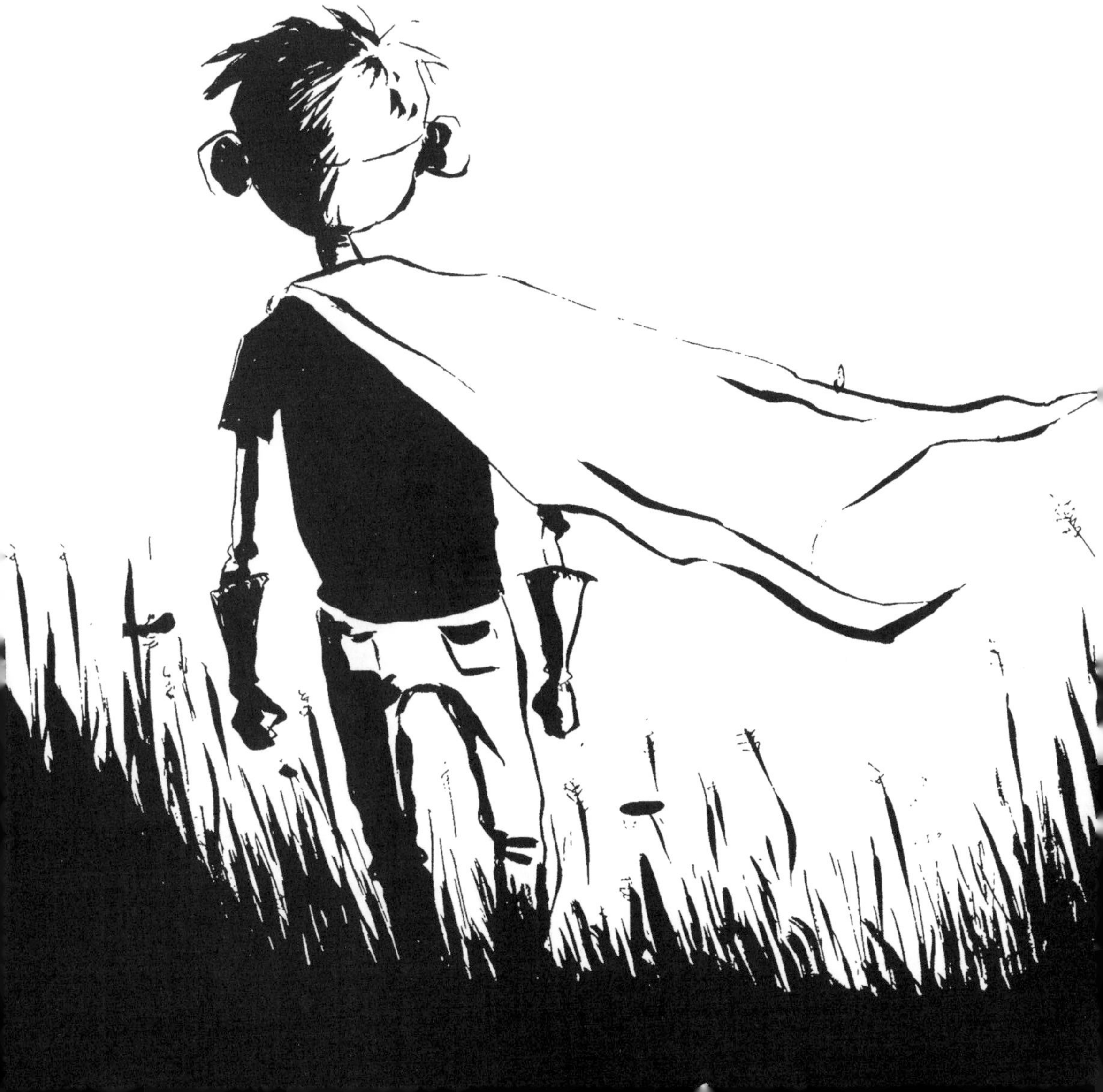

SUMMER

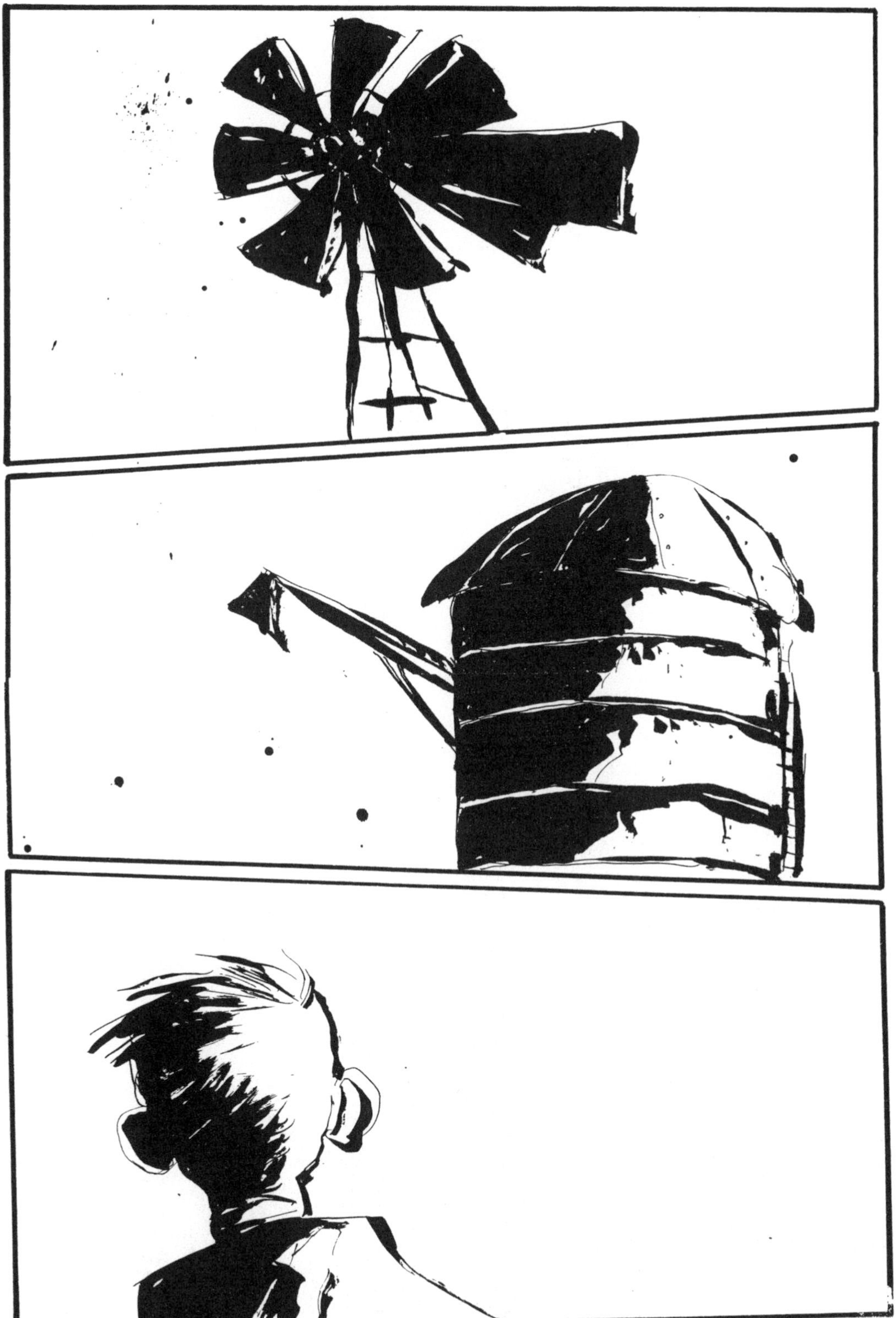

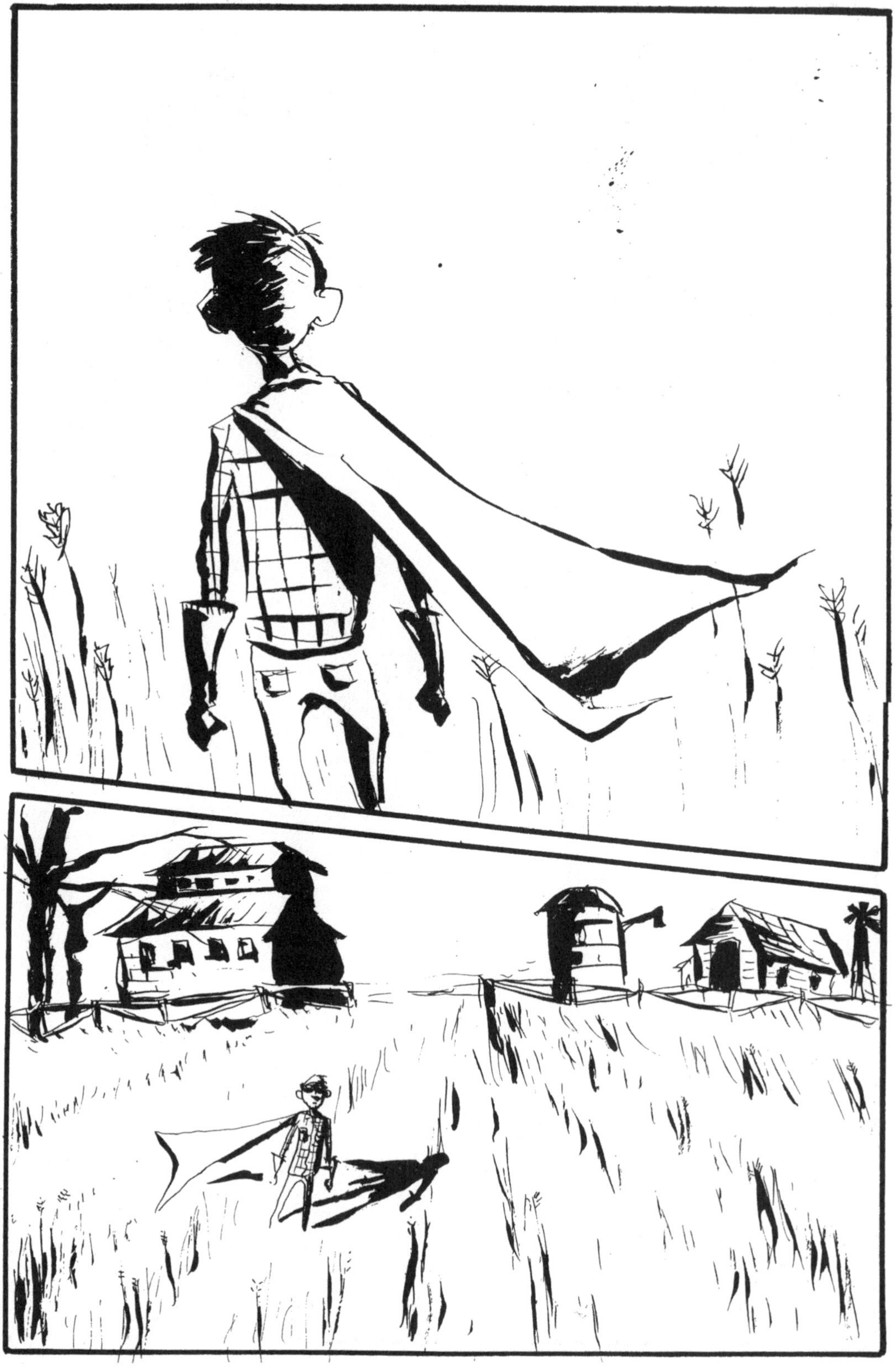

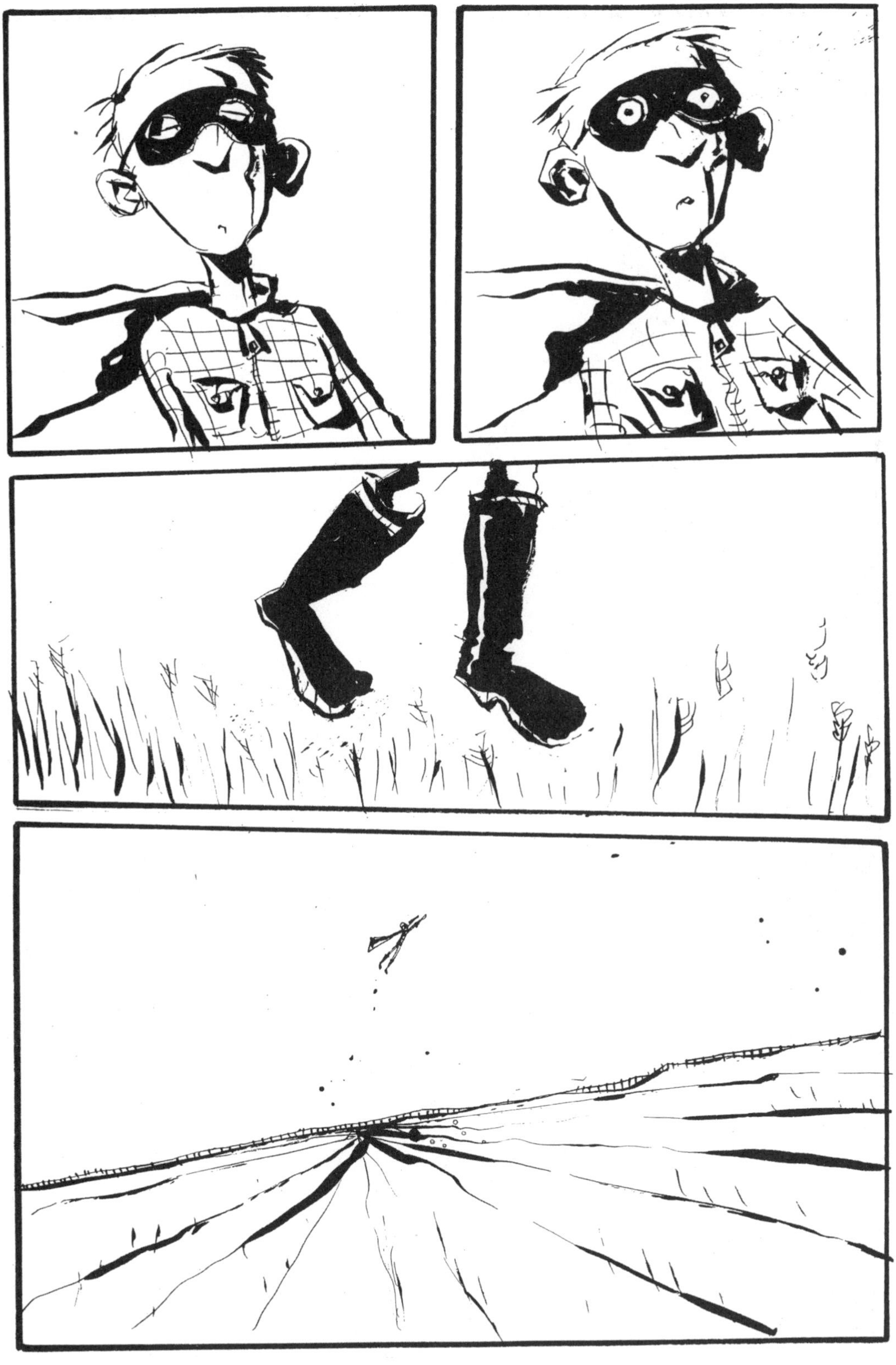

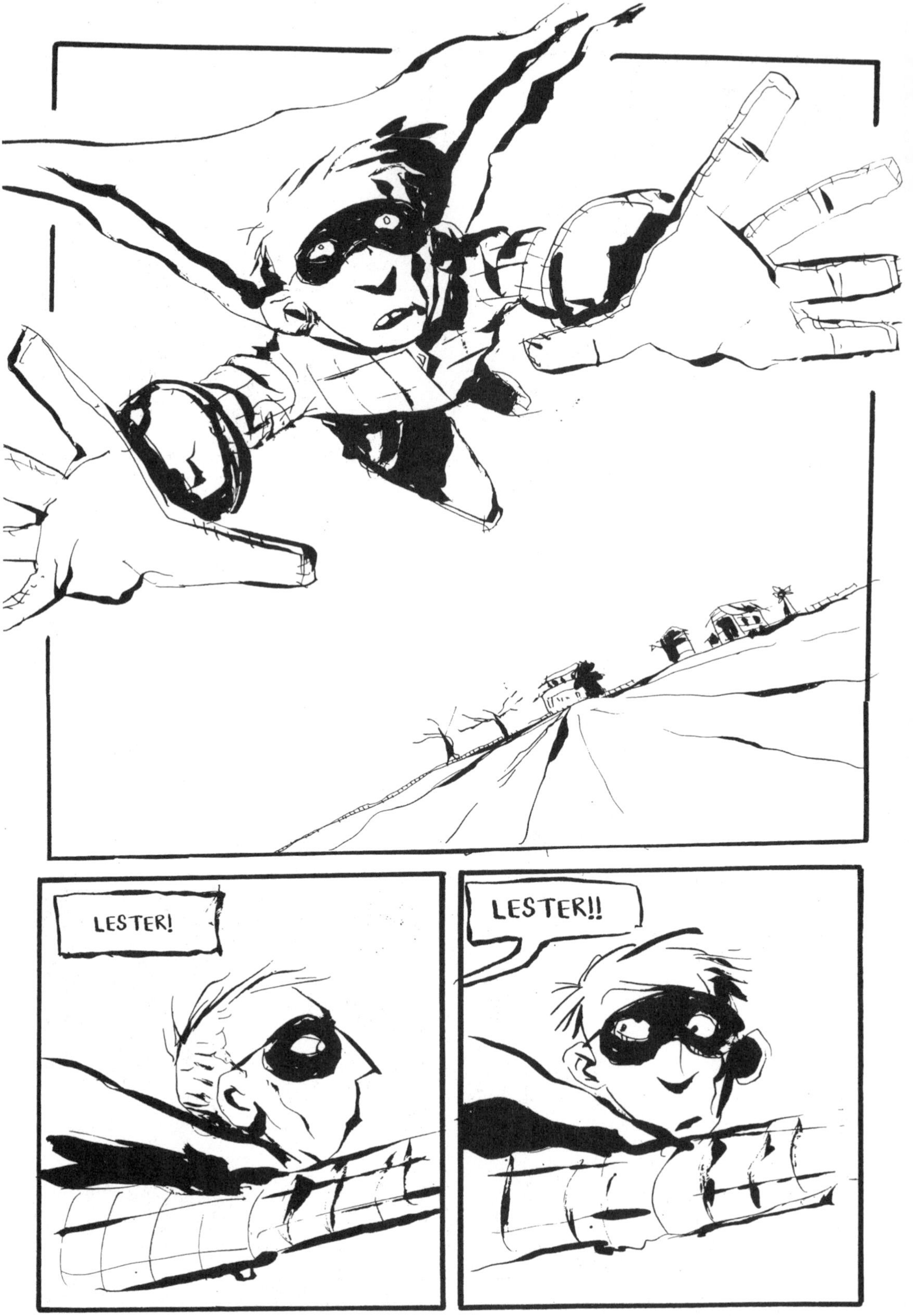
LESTER!
LESTER!!

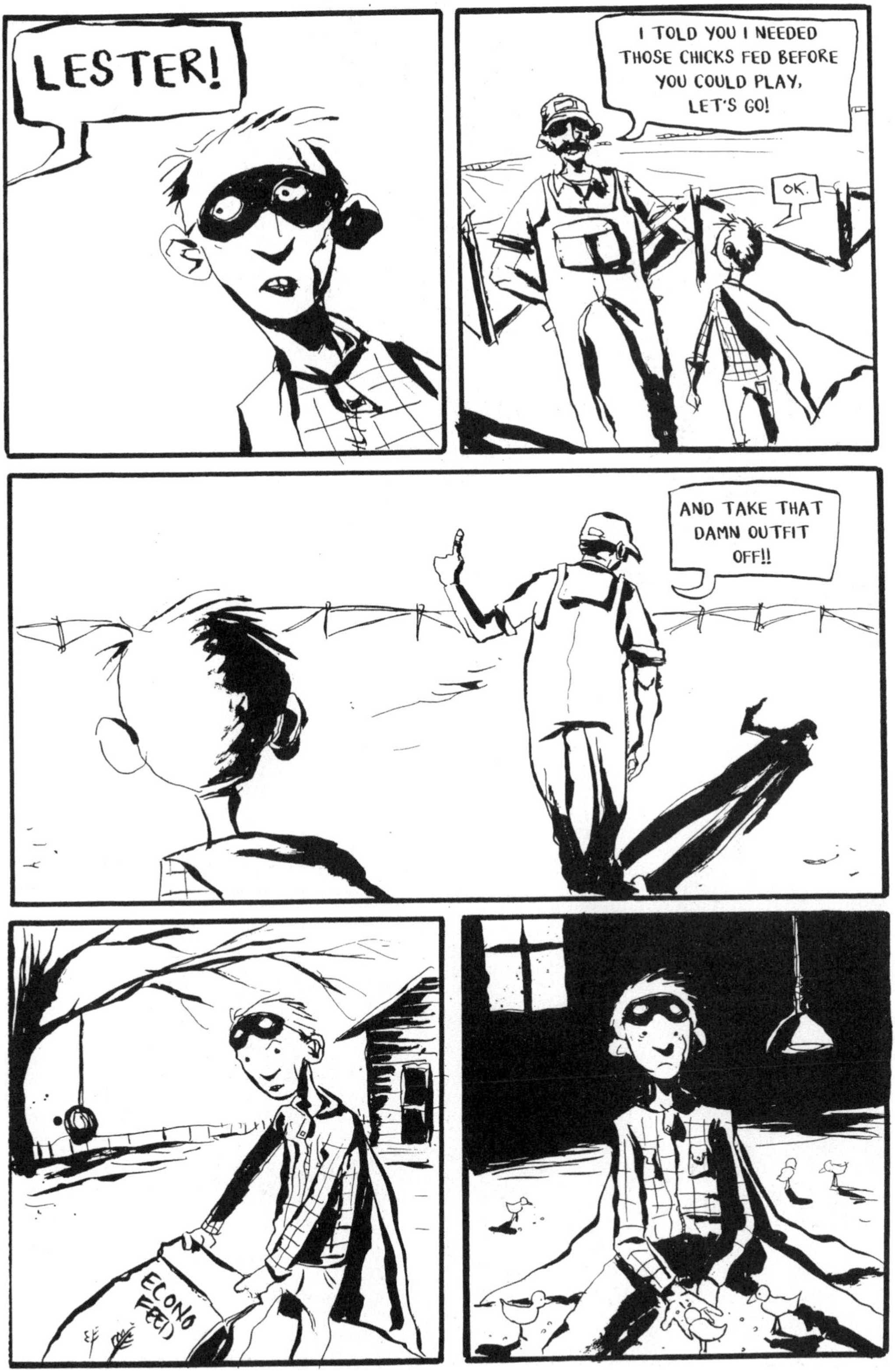
LESTER!
I TOLD YOU I NEEDED THOSE CHICKS FED BEFORE YOU COULD PLAY, LET'S GO!
OK.
AND TAKE THAT DAMN OUTFIT OFF!!
ECONO FEED

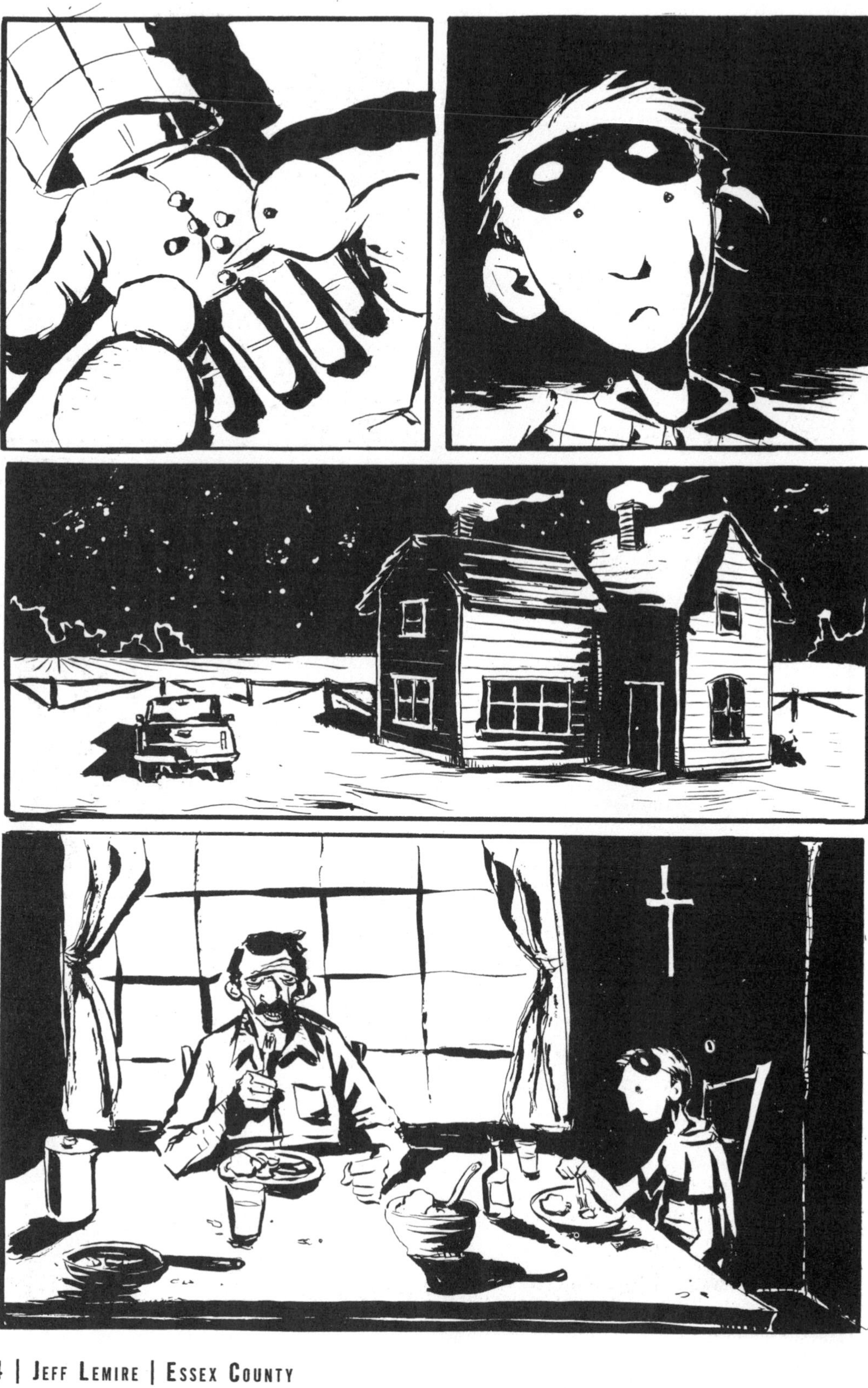

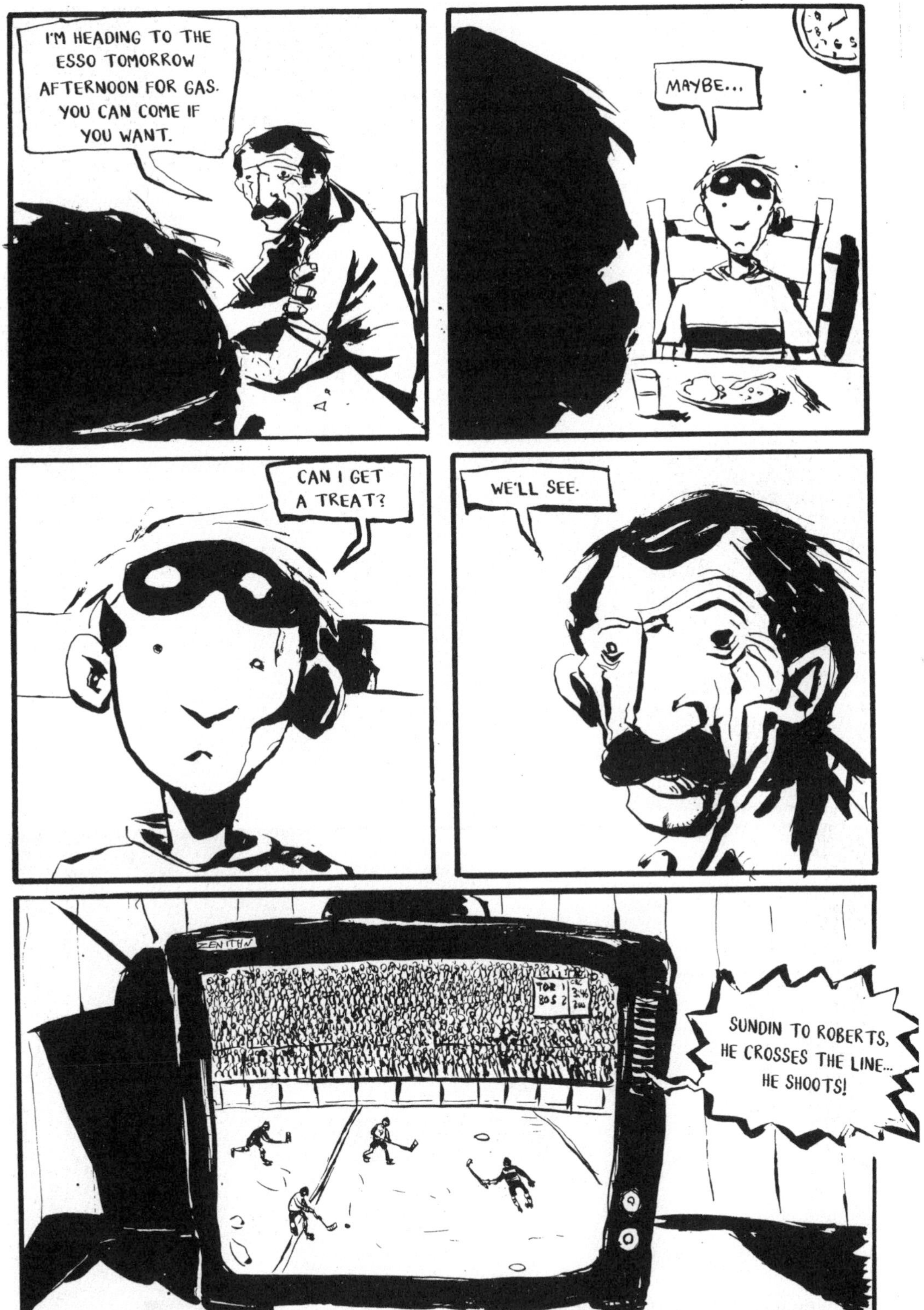
I'M HEADING TO THE ESSO TOMORROW AFTERNOON FOR GAS. YOU CAN COME IF YOU WANT.
MAYBE...
CAN I GET A TREAT?
WE'LL SEE.
ZENITH
SUNDIN TO ROBERTS, HE CROSSES THE LINE... HE SHOOTS!

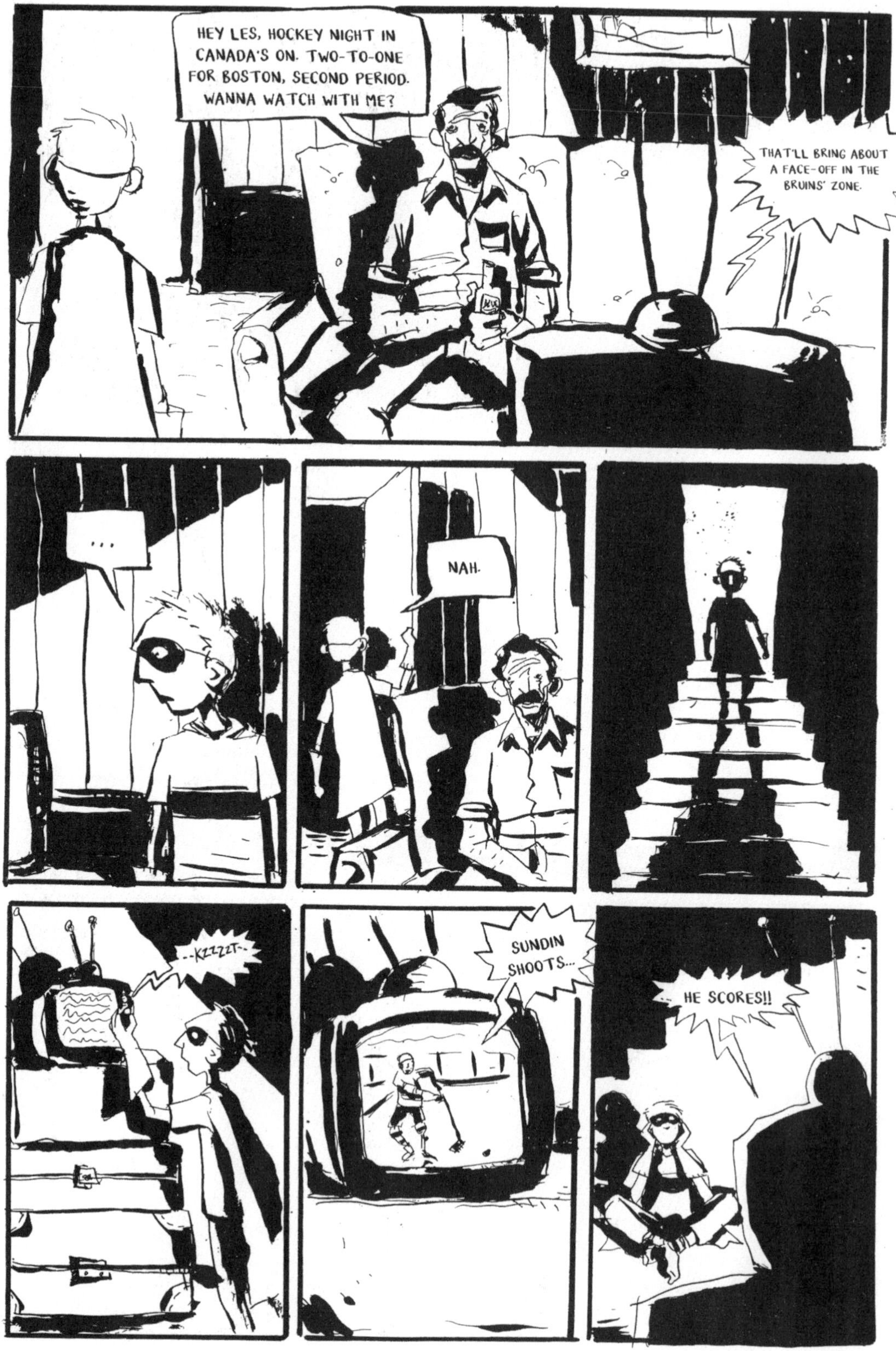
HEY LES, HOCKEY NIGHT IN CANADA'S ON. TWO-TO-ONE FOR BOSTON, SECOND PERIOD. WANNA WATCH WITH ME?
THAT'LL BRING ABOUT A FACE-OFF IN THE BRUINS' ZONE.
...
NAH.
--KZZZZT--
SUNDIN SHOOTS...
HE SCORES!!

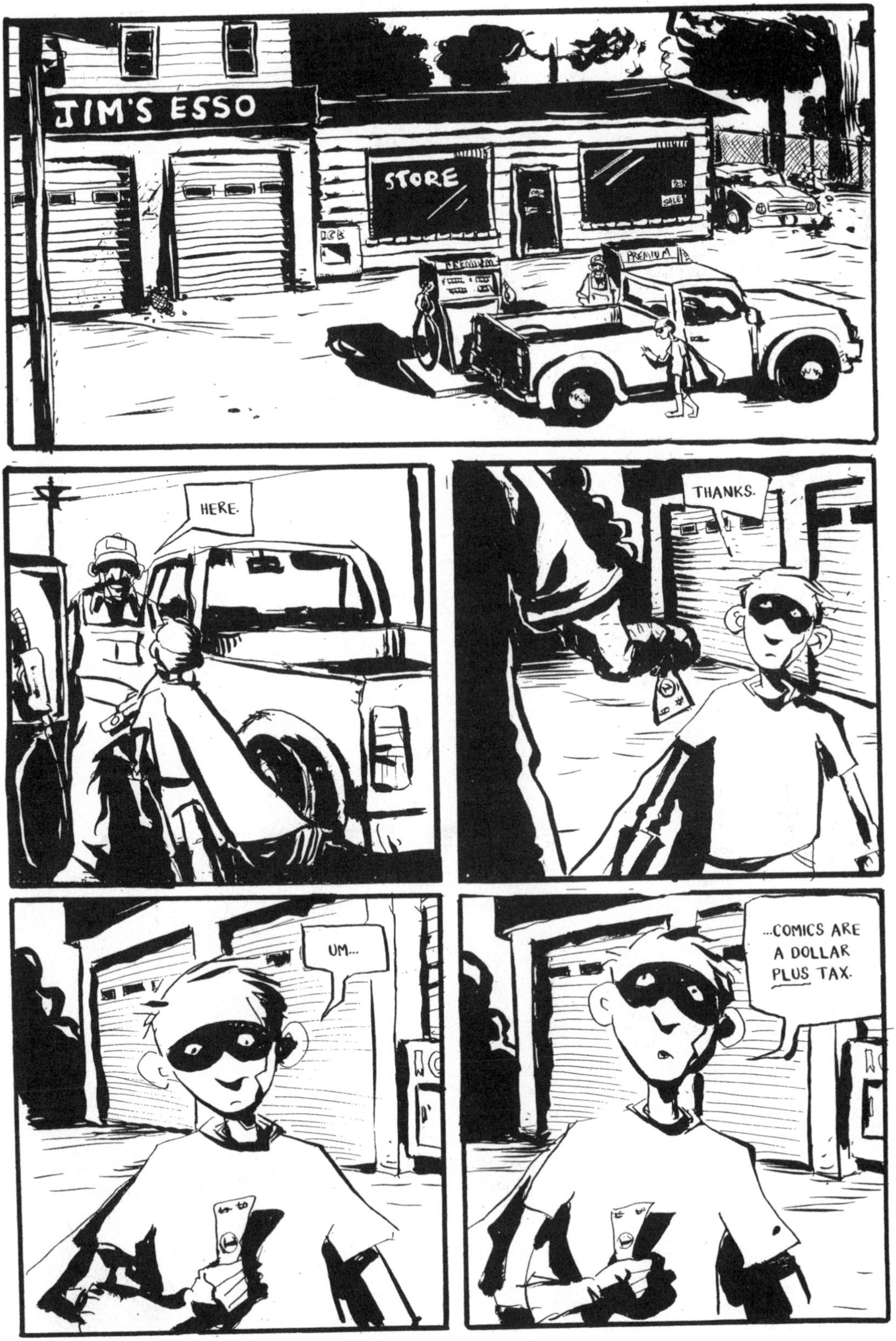
JIM'S ESSO
STORE
SALE
PREMIUM
PREMIUM
HERE.
THANKS.
UM...
...COMICS ARE A DOLLAR PLUS TAX.

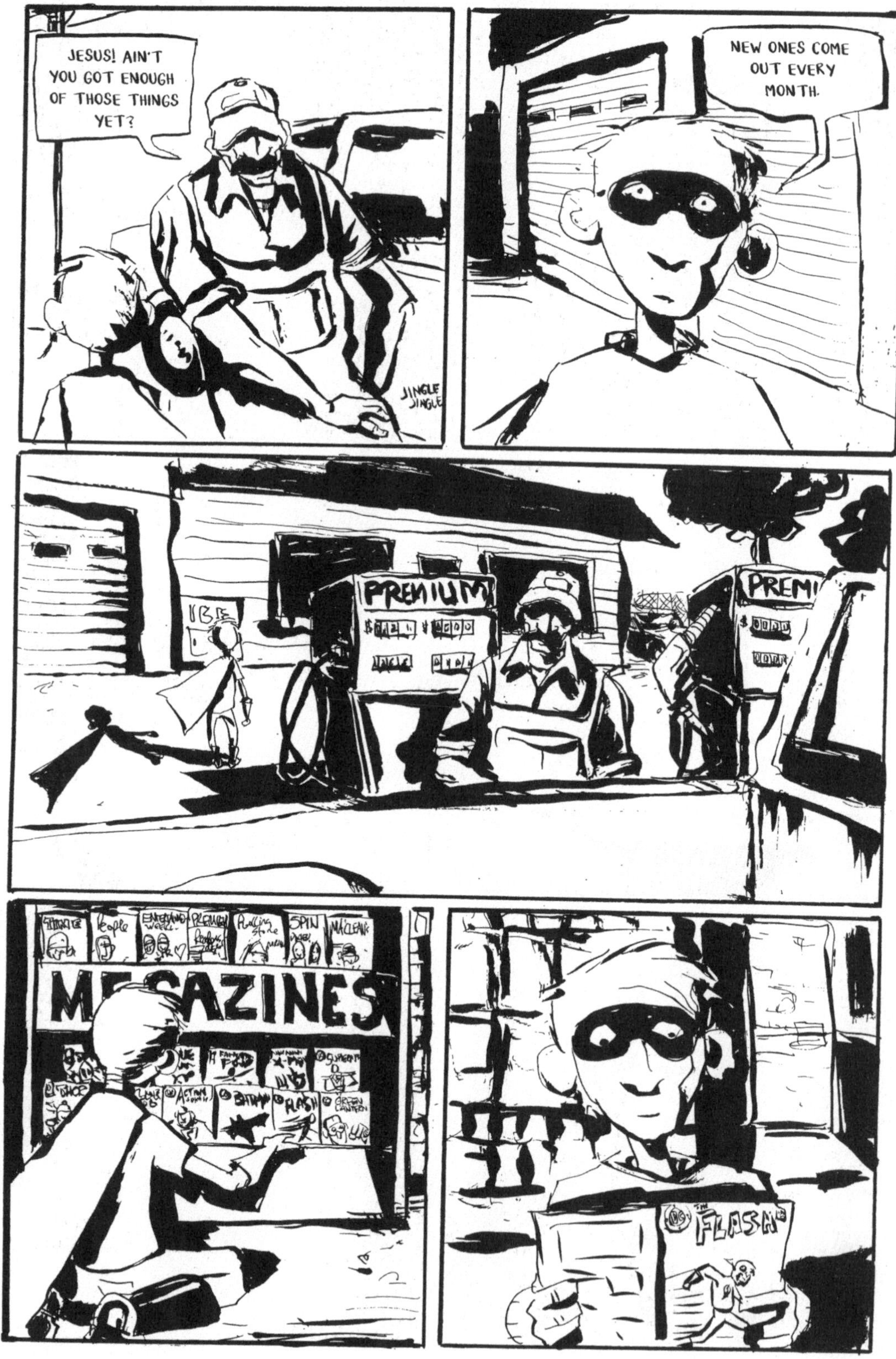
JESUS! AIN'T YOU GOT ENOUGH OF THOSE THINGS YET?
JINGLE JINGLE
NEW ONES COME OUT EVERY MONTH.
PREMIUM
PREMI
MAGAZINES
FLASH
THE FLASH

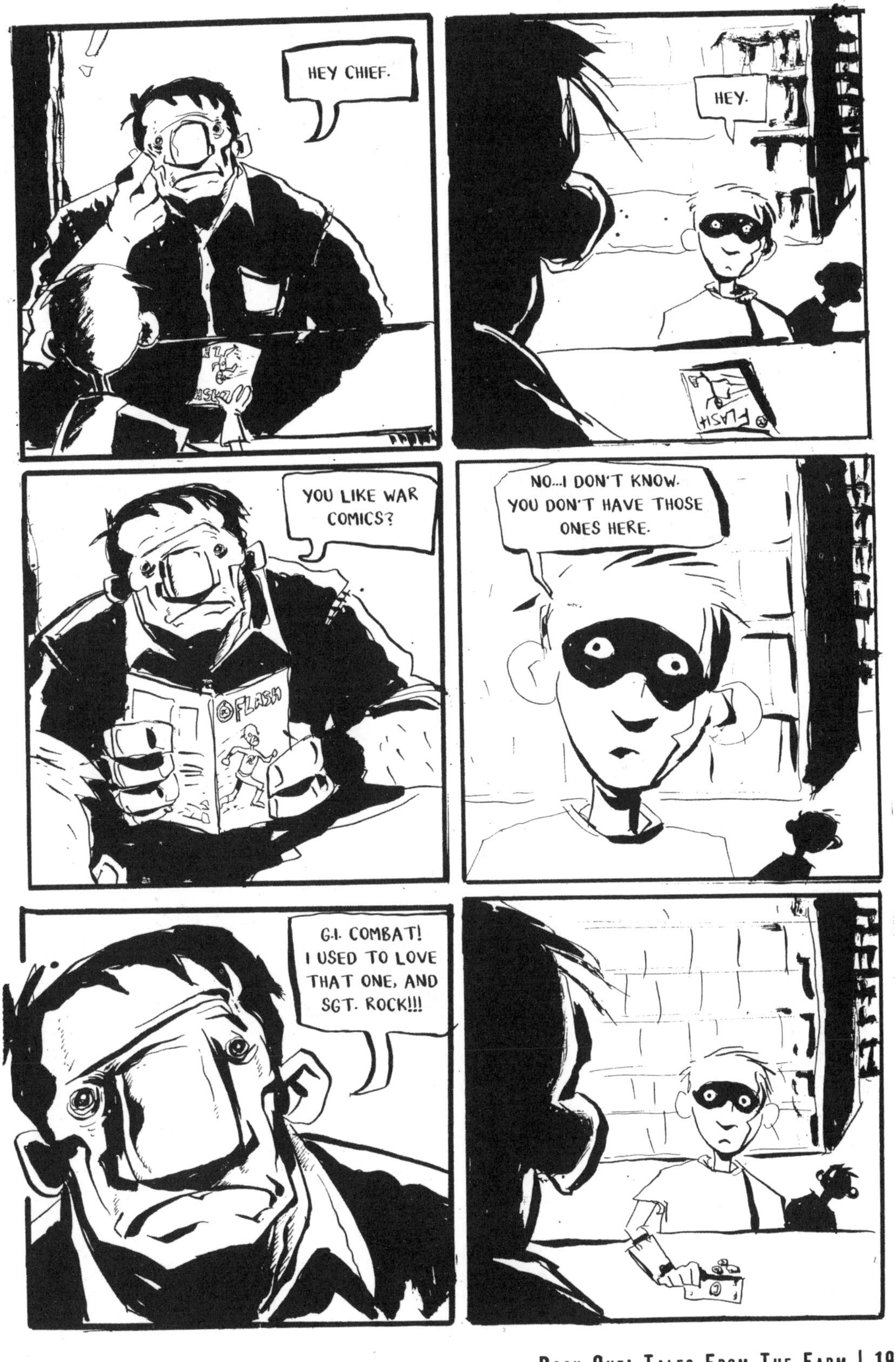
HEY CHIEF.
HEY.
YOU LIKE WAR COMICS?
NO...I DON'T KNOW. YOU DON'T HAVE THOSE ONES HERE.
G.I. COMBAT! I USED TO LOVE THAT ONE, AND SGT. ROCK!!!

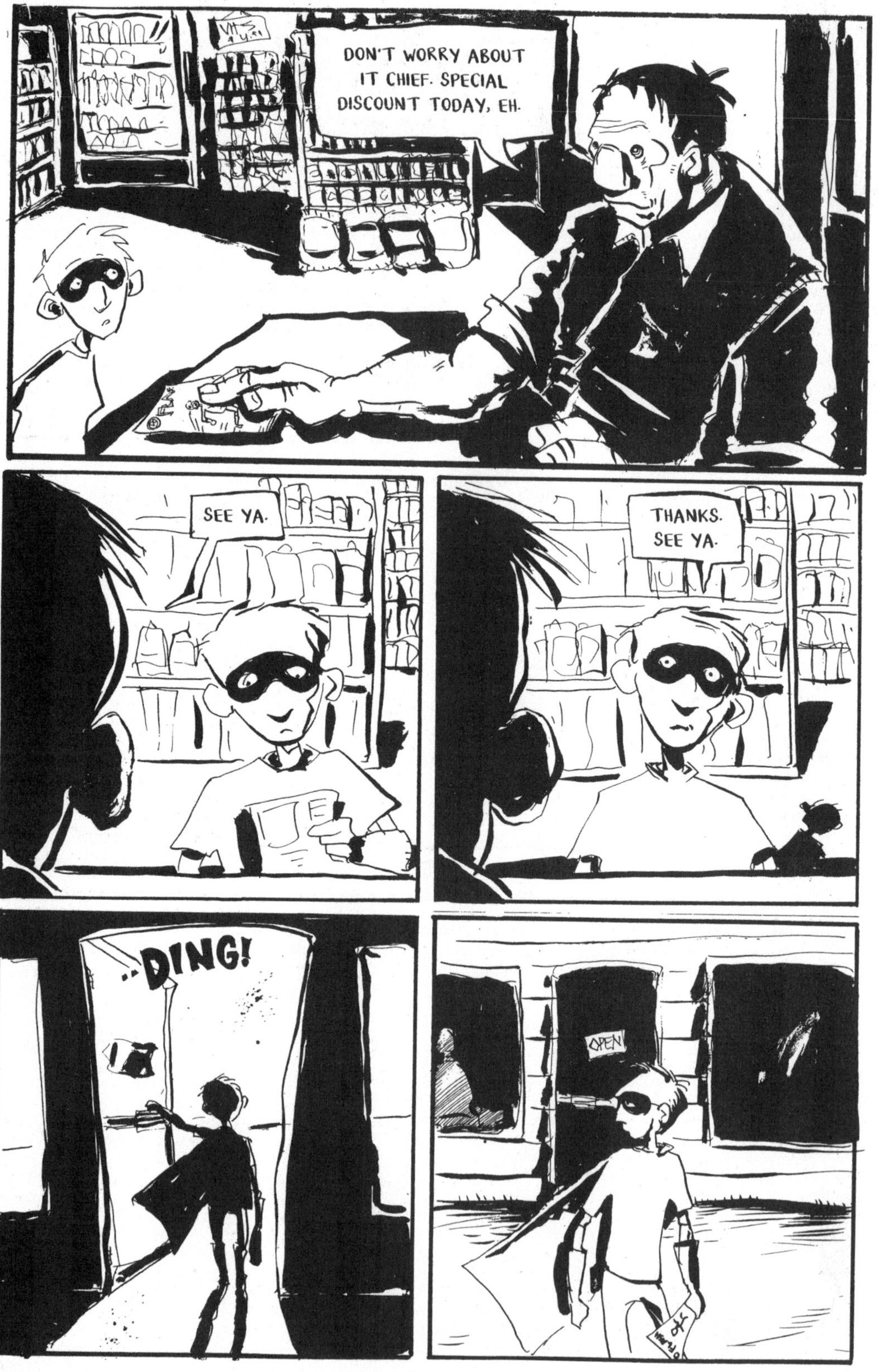
DON'T WORRY ABOUT IT CHIEF. SPECIAL DISCOUNT TODAY, EH.
SEE YA.
THANKS. SEE YA.
..DING!
OPEN

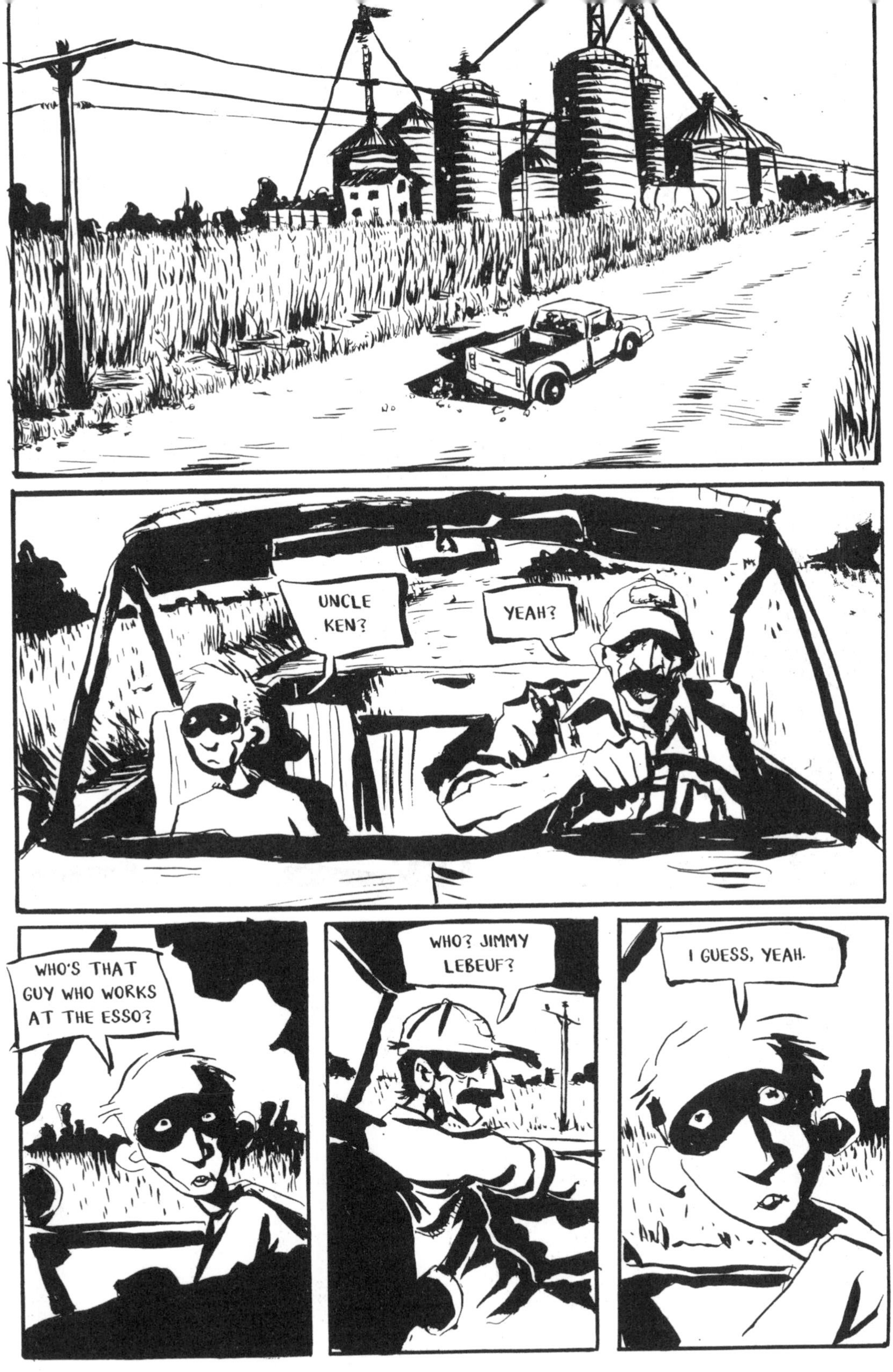
UNCLE KEN?
YEAH?
WHO'S THAT GUY WHO WORKS AT THE ESSO?
WHO? JIMMY LEBEUF?
I GUESS, YEAH.

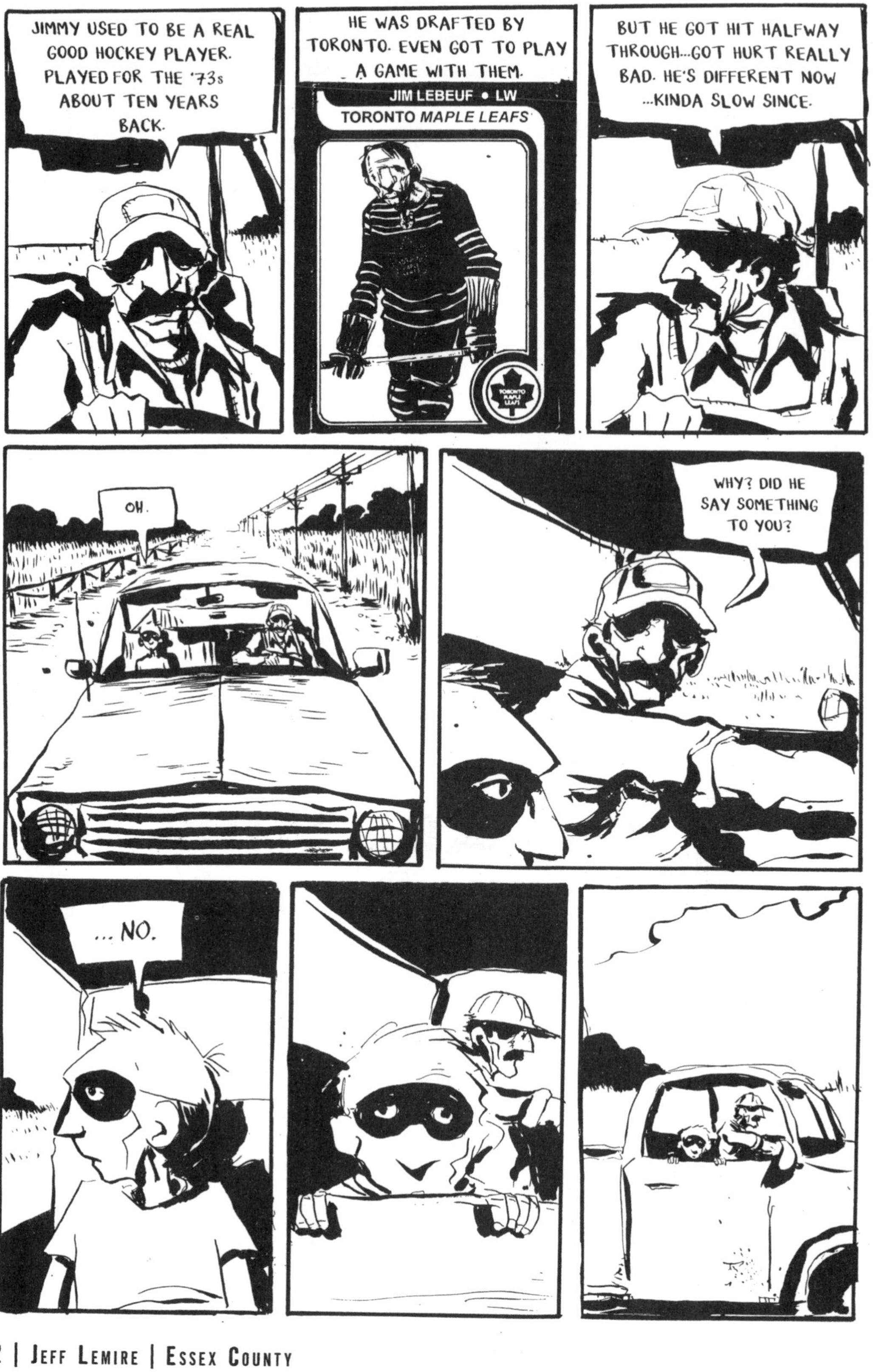
JIMMY USED TO BE A REAL GOOD HOCKEY PLAYER. PLAYED FOR THE '73s ABOUT TEN YEARS BACK.
HE WAS DRAFTED BY TORONTO. EVEN GOT TO PLAY A GAME WITH THEM.
JIM LEBEUF • LW
TORONTO MAPLE LEAFS
BUT HE GOT HIT HALFWAY THROUGH...GOT HURT REALLY BAD. HE'S DIFFERENT NOW ...KINDA SLOW SINCE.
OH.
WHY? DID HE SAY SOMETHING TO YOU?
...NO.

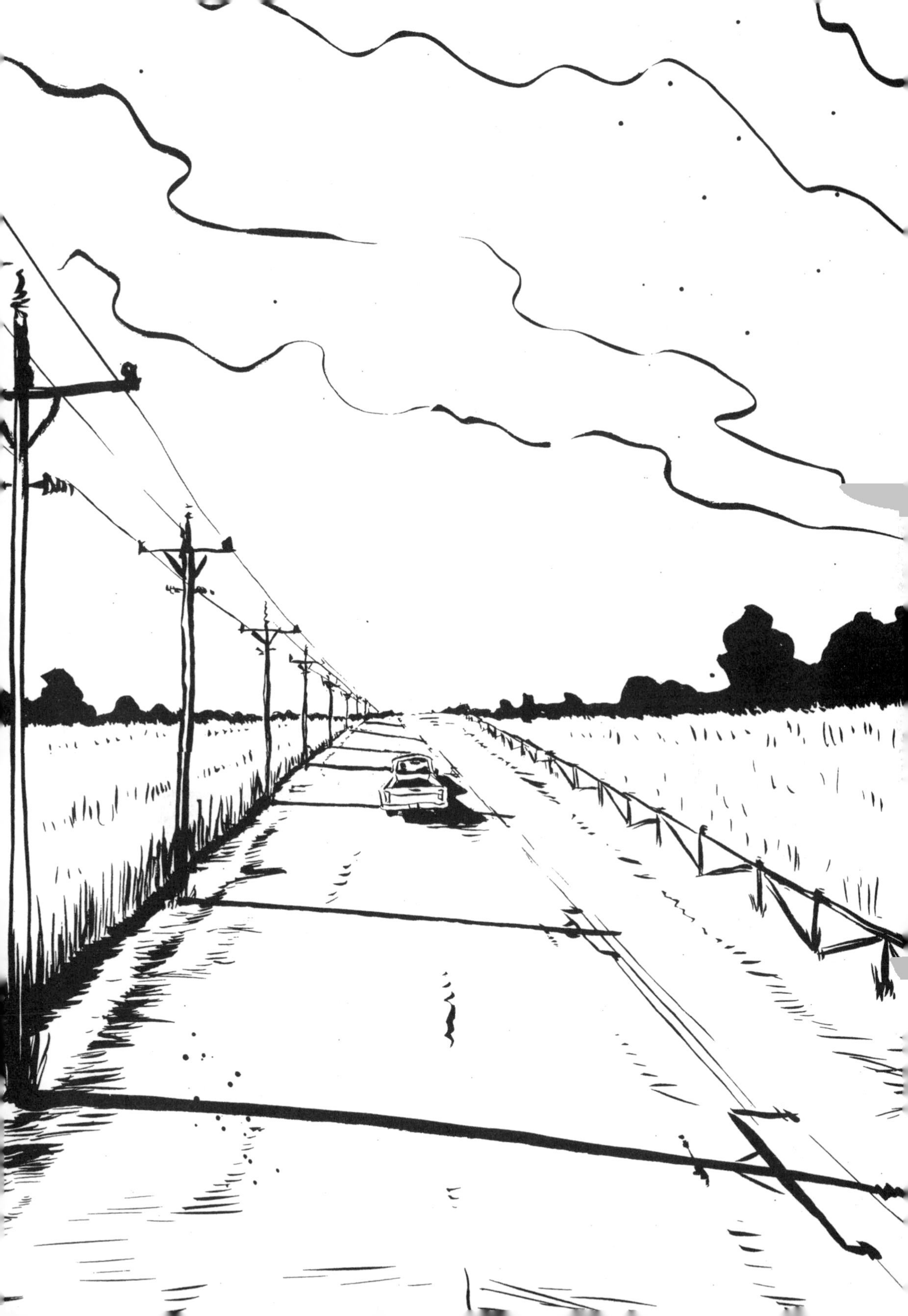

FALL

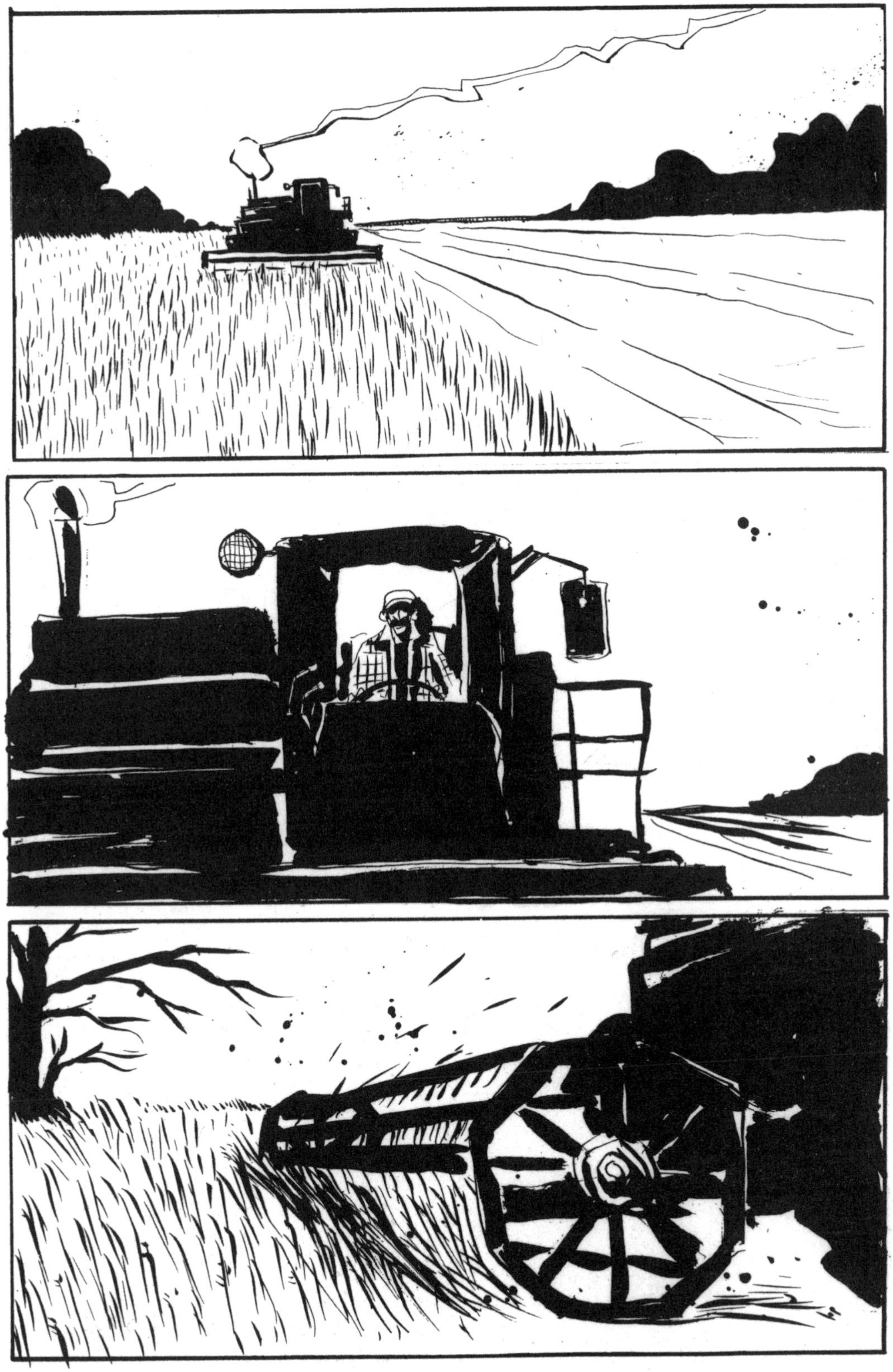

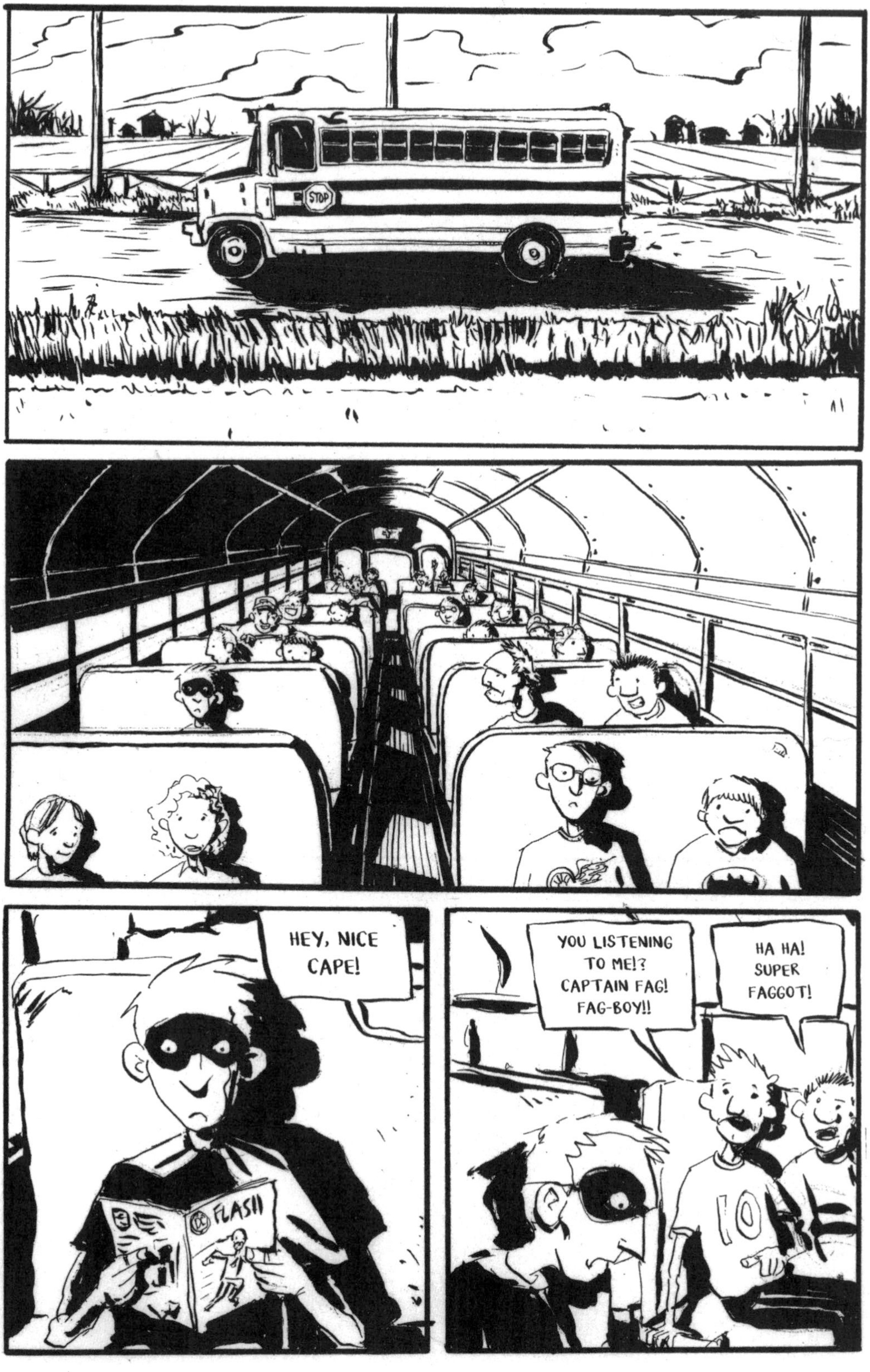
STOP
HEY, NICE CAPE!
FLASH
YOU LISTENING TO ME!? CAPTAIN FAG! FAG-BOY!!
HA HA! SUPER FAGGOT!

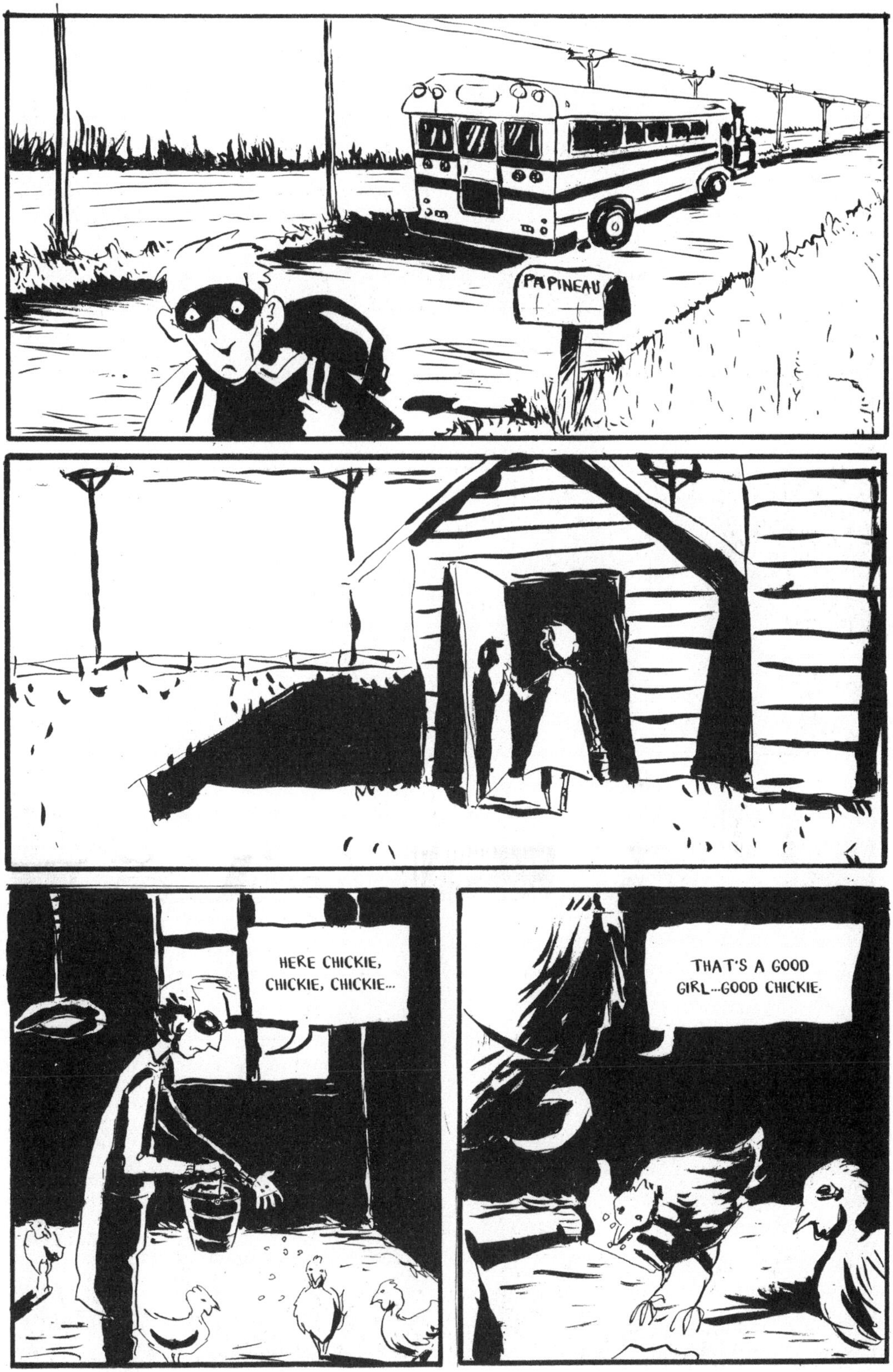
PAPINEAU
HERE CHICKIE, CHICKIE, CHICKIE...
THAT'S A GOOD GIRL...GOOD CHICKIE.

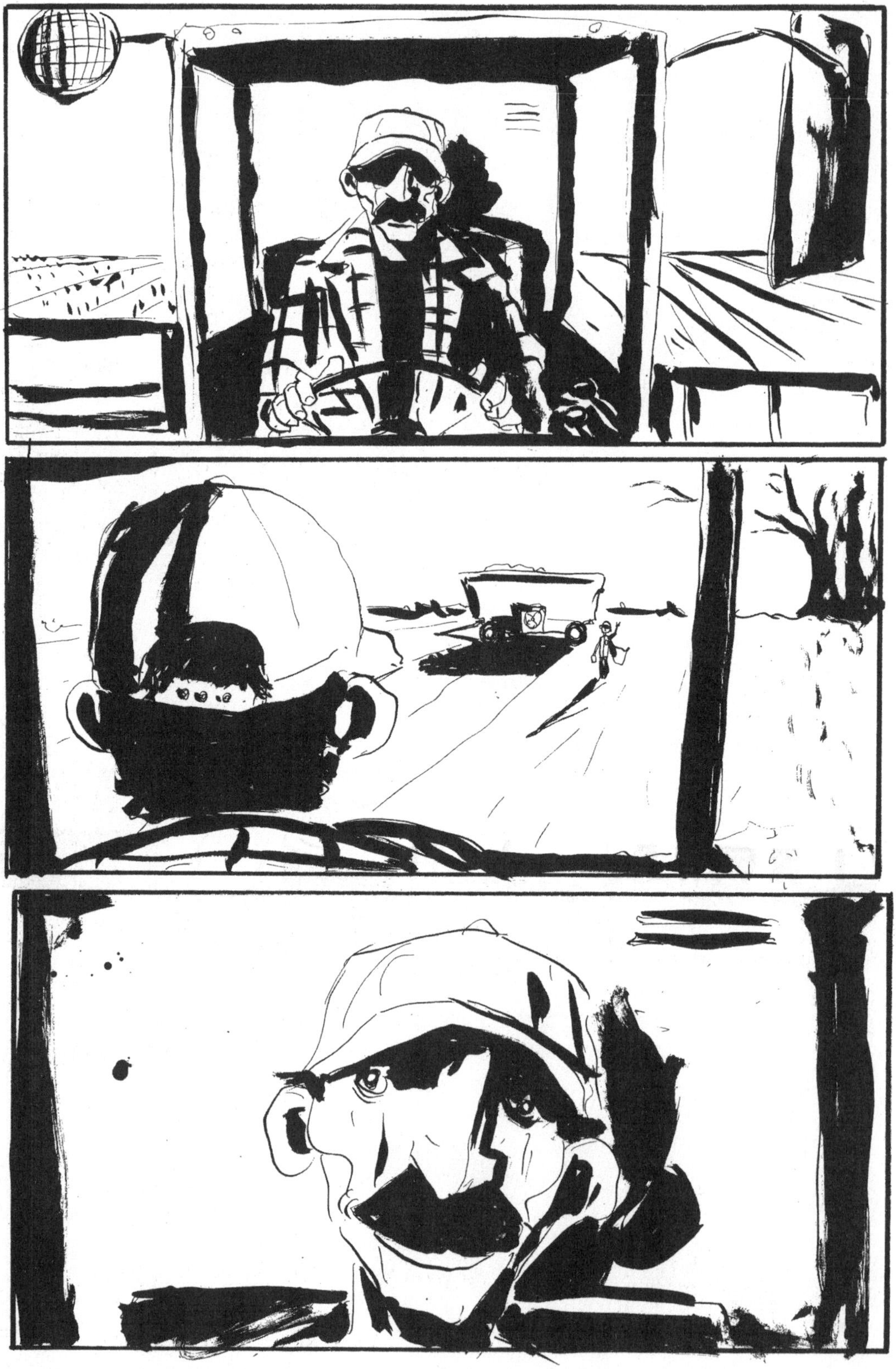

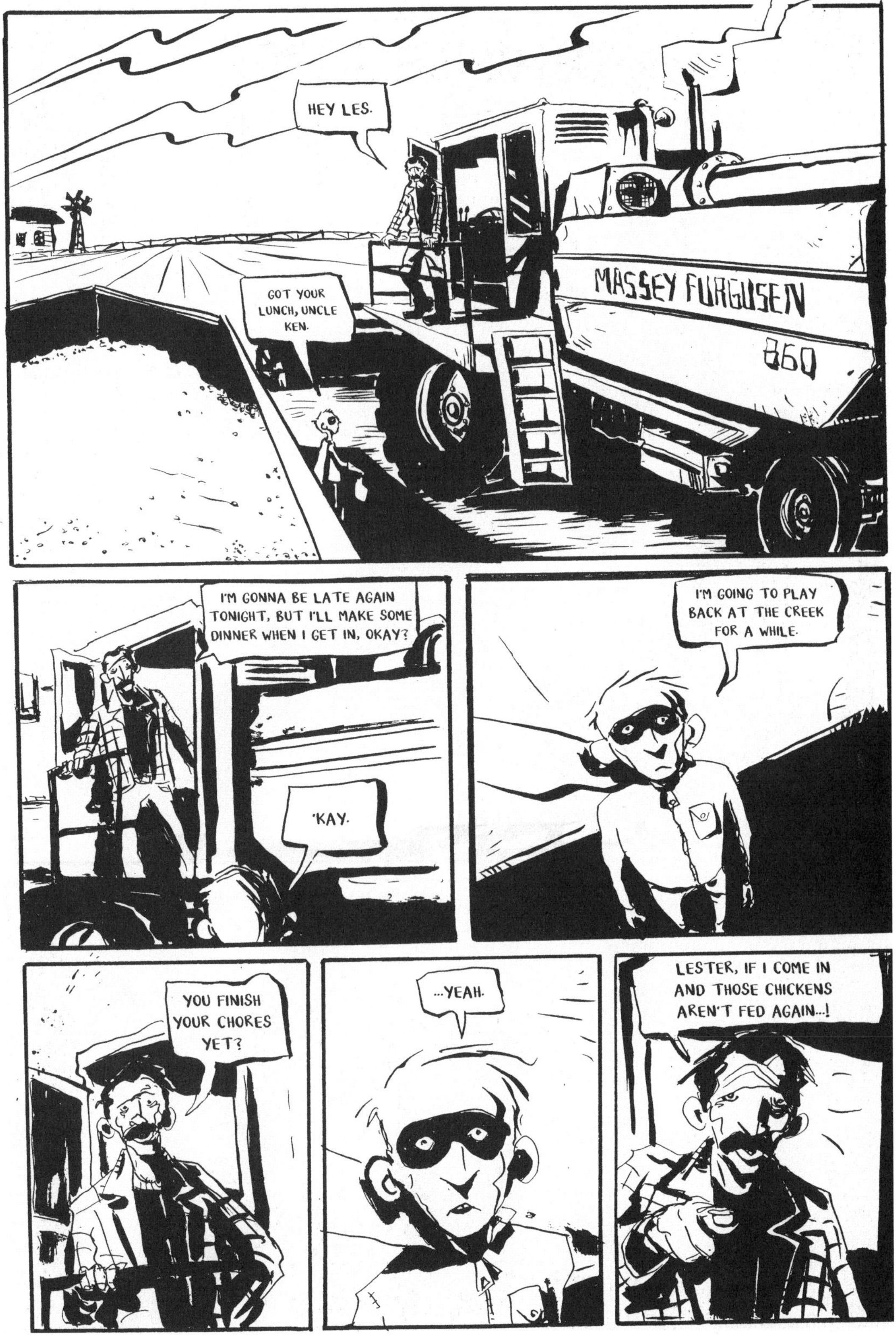
HEY LES.
GOT YOUR LUNCH, UNCLE KEN.
MASSEY FURGUSEN
860
I'M GONNA BE LATE AGAIN TONIGHT, BUT I'LL MAKE SOME DINNER WHEN I GET IN, OKAY?
'KAY.
I'M GOING TO PLAY BACK AT THE CREEK FOR A WHILE.
YOU FINISH YOUR CHORES YET?
...YEAH.
LESTER, IF I COME IN AND THOSE CHICKENS AREN'T FED AGAIN...!

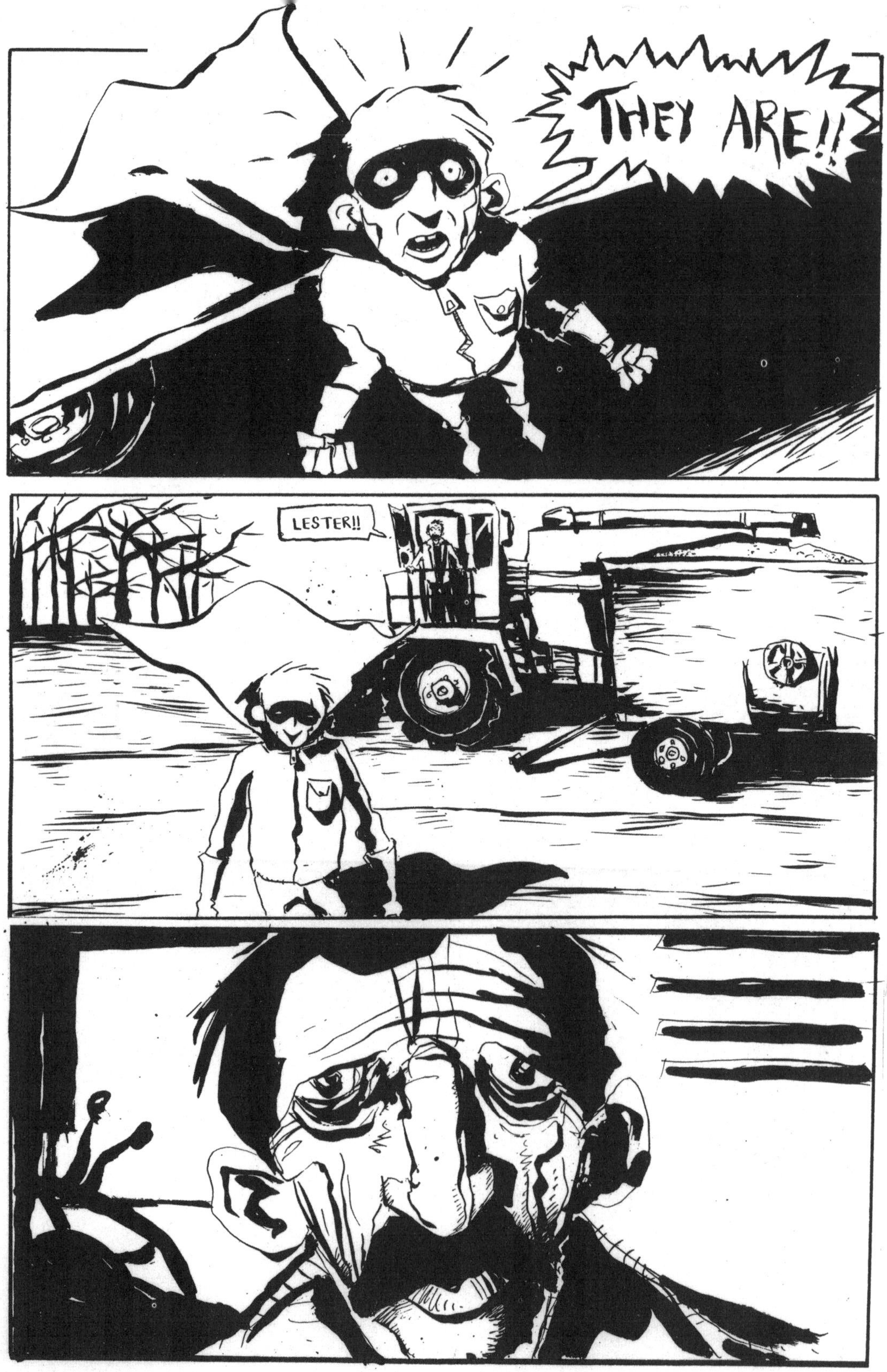
THEY ARE!!
LESTER!!

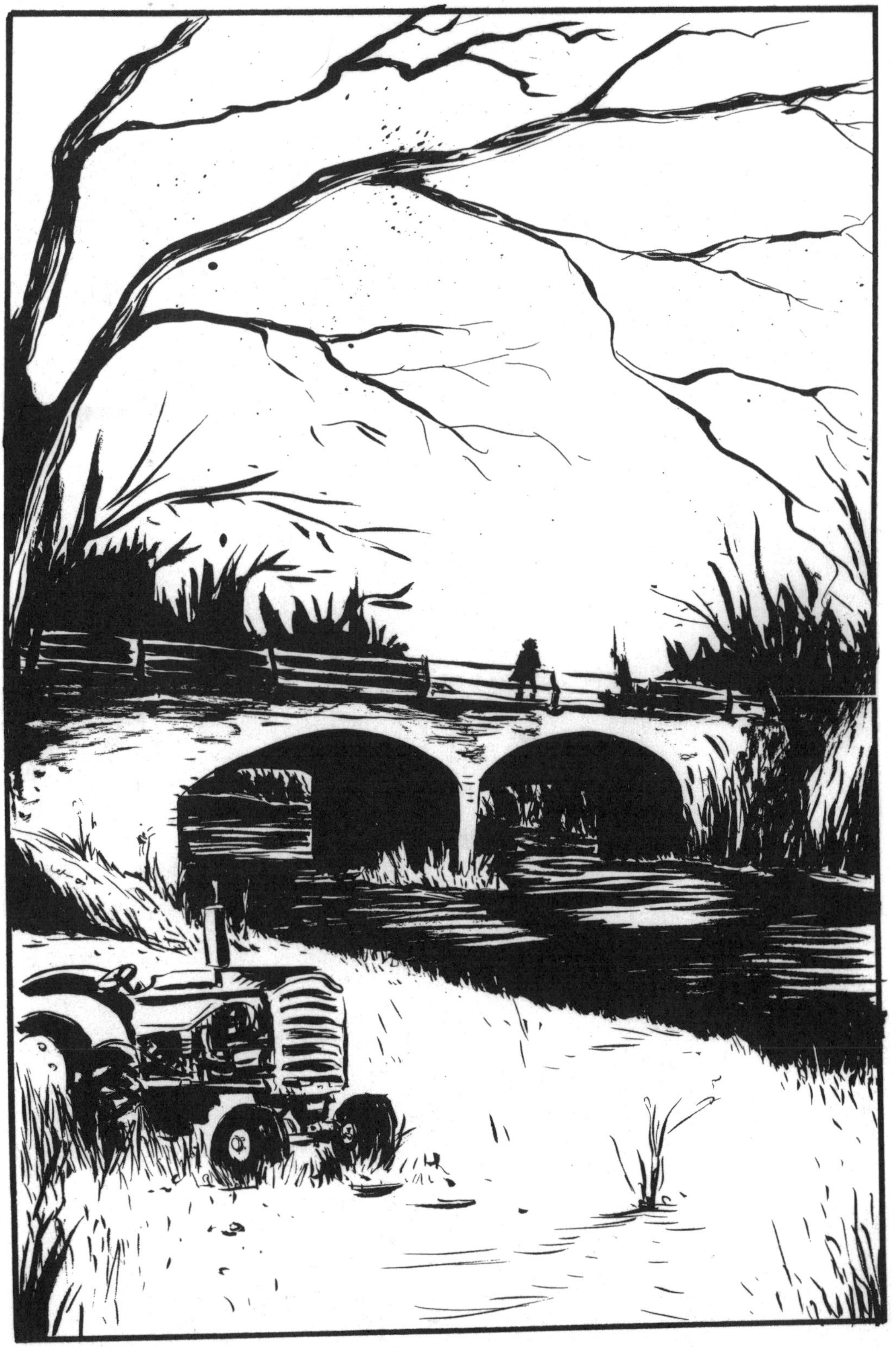

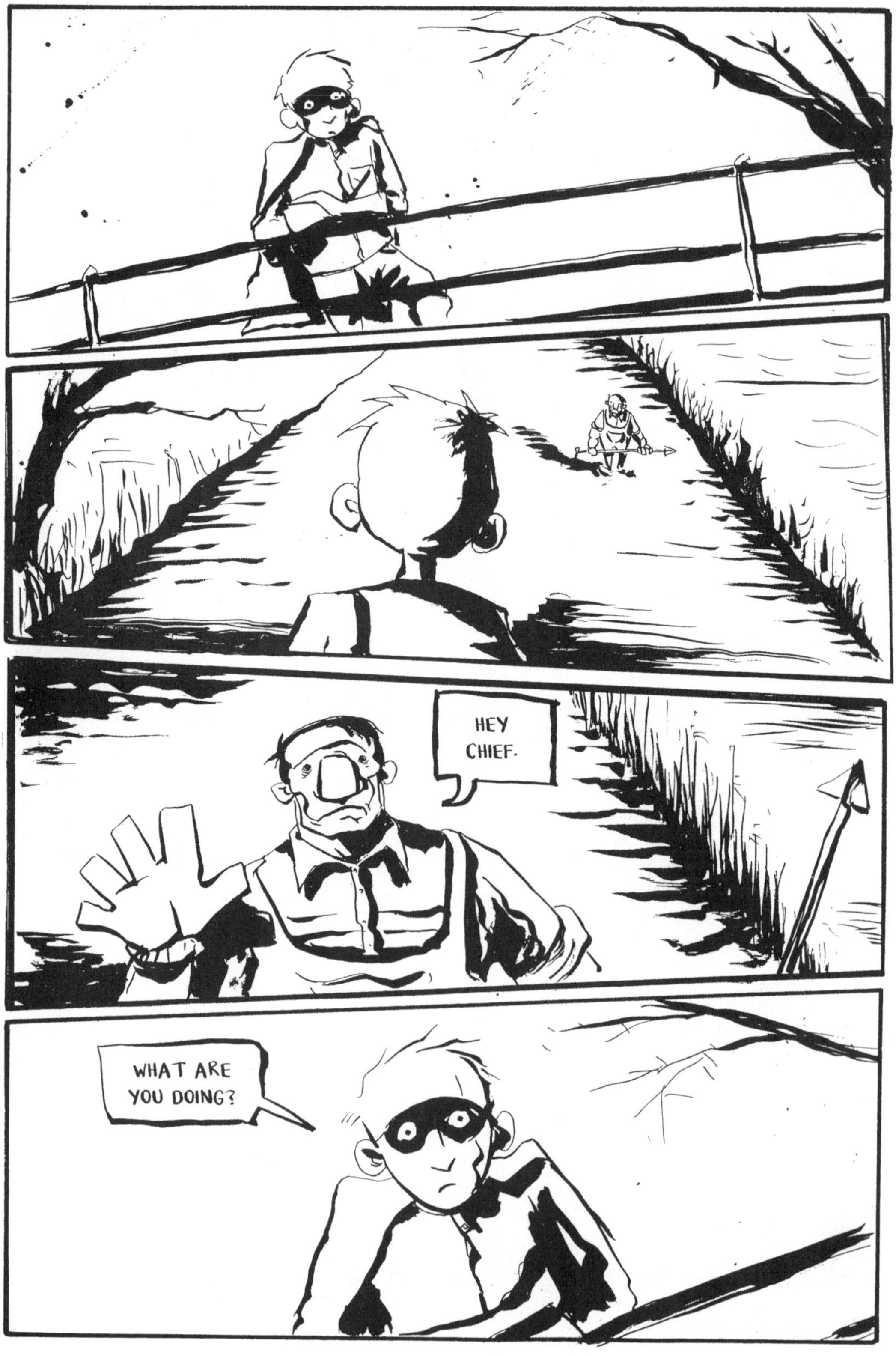
HEY CHIEF.
WHAT ARE YOU DOING?

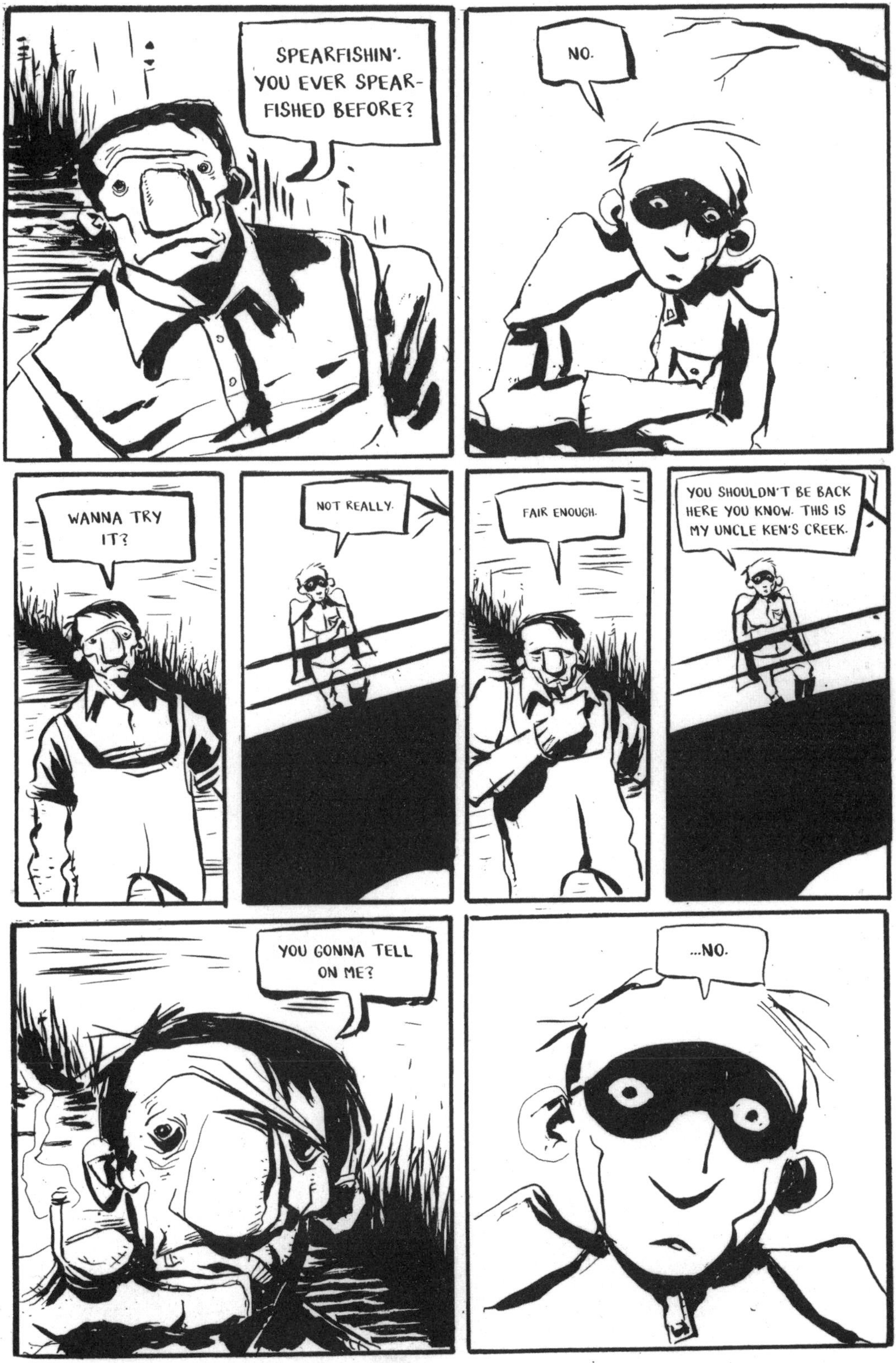
SPEARFISHIN'. YOU EVER SPEAR-FISHED BEFORE?
NO.
WANNA TRY IT?
NOT REALLY.
FAIR ENOUGH.
YOU SHOULDN'T BE BACK HERE YOU KNOW. THIS IS MY UNCLE KEN'S CREEK.
YOU GONNA TELL ON ME?
...NO.

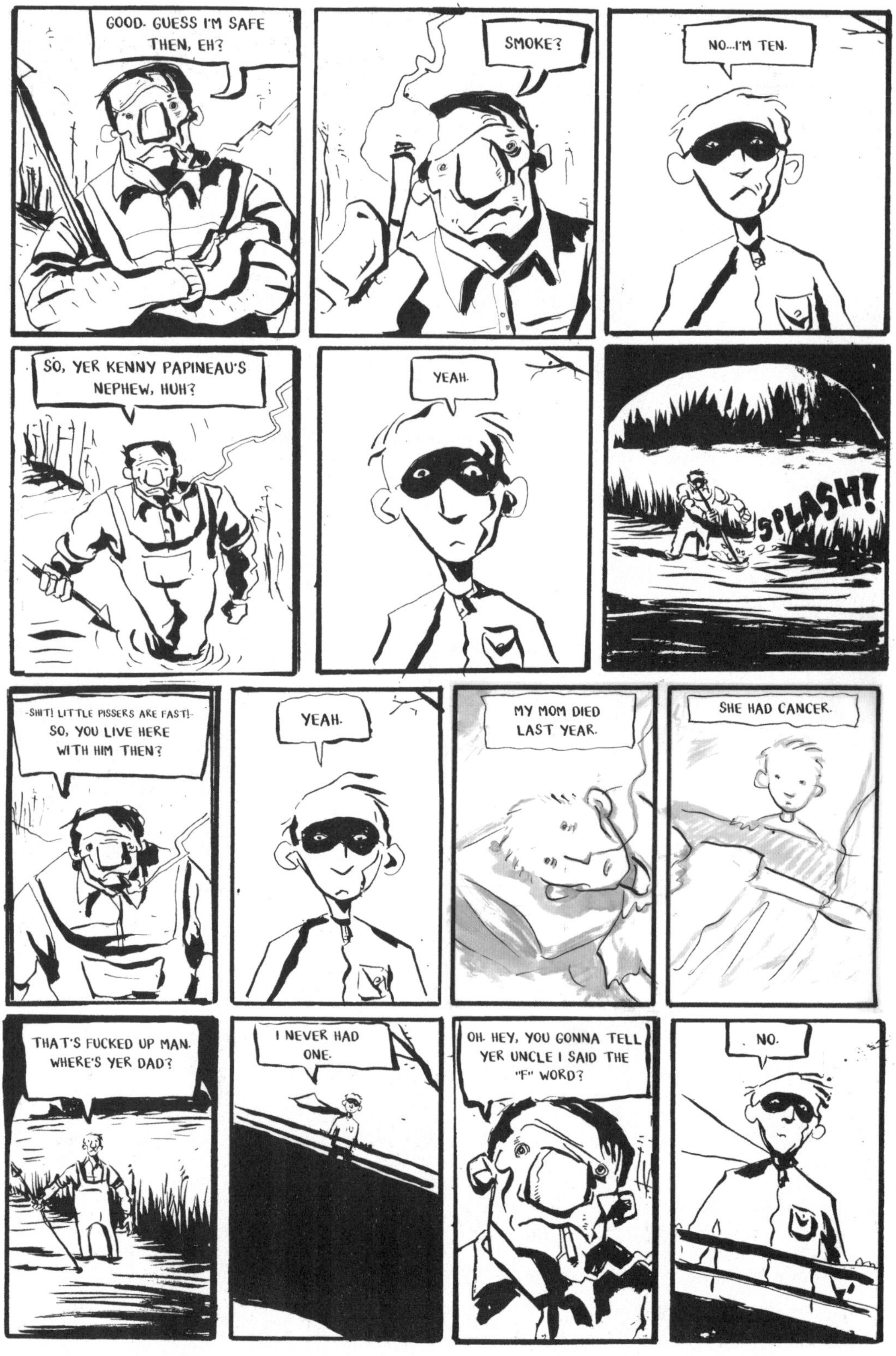
GOOD. GUESS I'M SAFE THEN, EH?
SMOKE?
NO...I'M TEN.
SO, YER KENNY PAPINEAU'S NEPHEW, HUH?
YEAH.
SPLASH!
-SHIT! LITTLE PISSERS ARE FAST!- SO, YOU LIVE HERE WITH HIM THEN?
YEAH.
MY MOM DIED LAST YEAR.
SHE HAD CANCER.
THAT'S FUCKED UP MAN. WHERE'S YER DAD?
I NEVER HAD ONE.
OH. HEY, YOU GONNA TELL YER UNCLE I SAID THE "F" WORD?
NO.

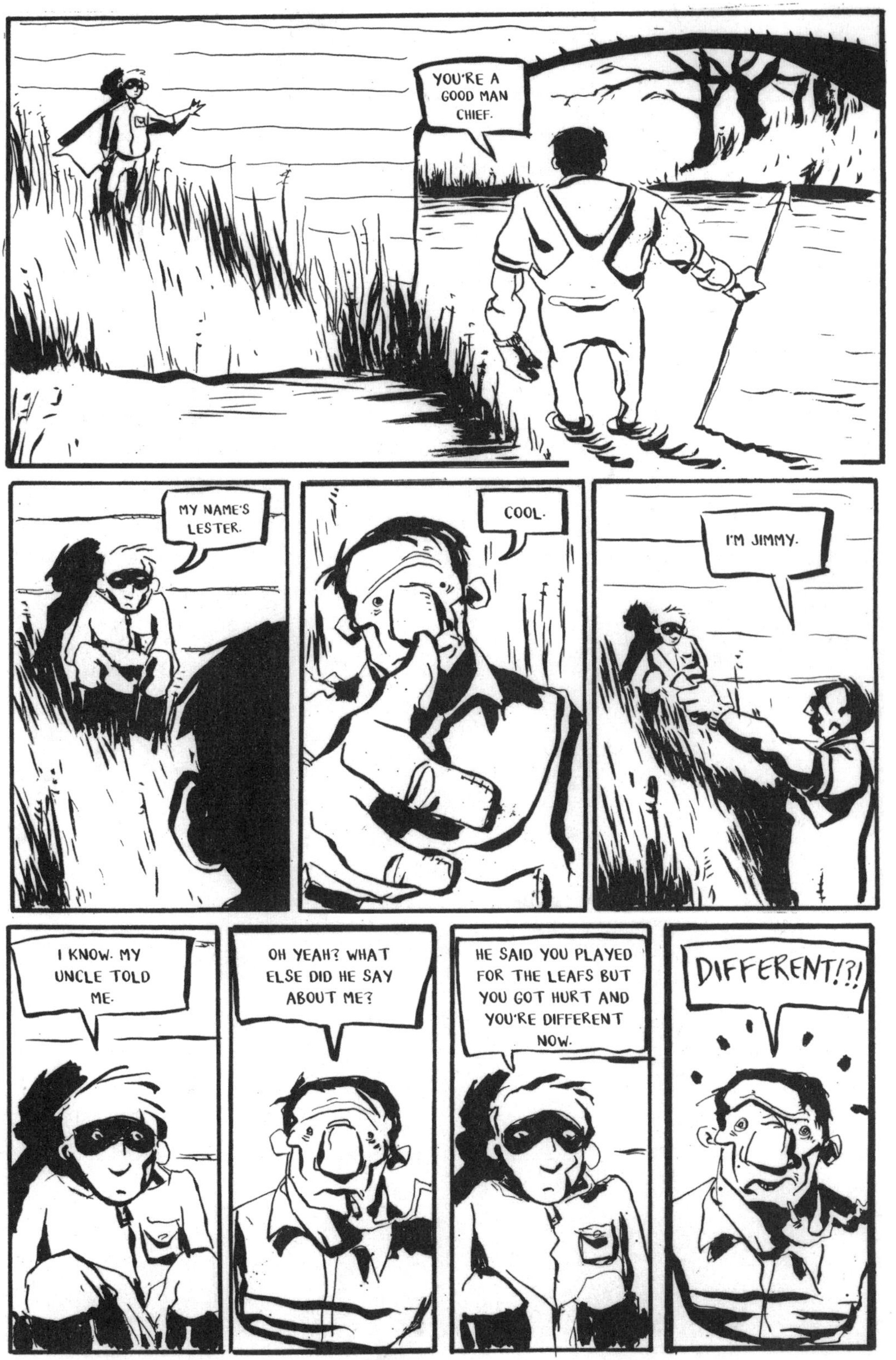
YOU'RE A GOOD MAN CHIEF.
MY NAME'S LESTER.
COOL.
I'M JIMMY.
I KNOW. MY UNCLE TOLD ME.
OH YEAH? WHAT ELSE DID HE SAY ABOUT ME?
HE SAID YOU PLAYED FOR THE LEAFS BUT YOU GOT HURT AND YOU'RE DIFFERENT NOW.
DIFFERENT!?!

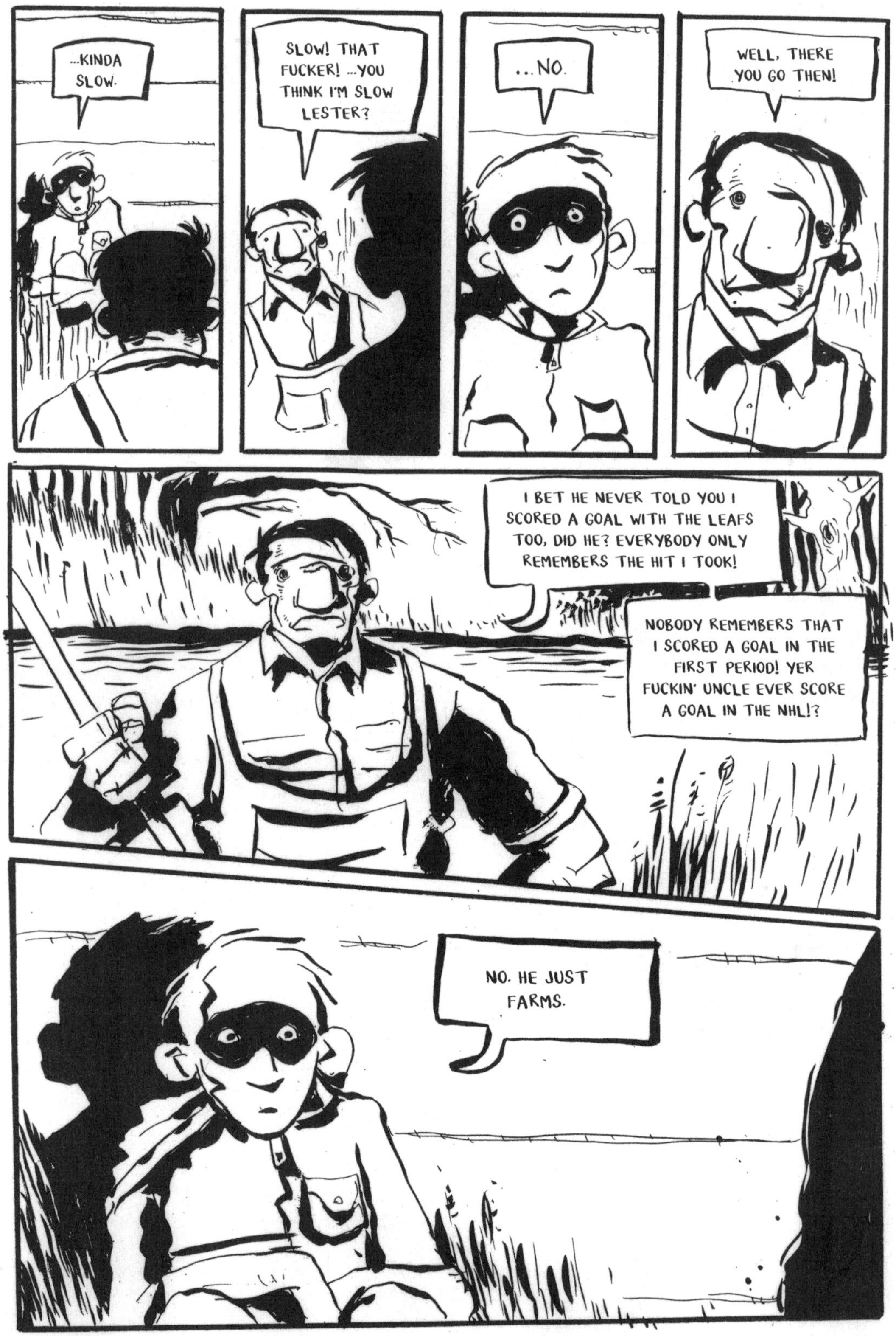
...KINDA SLOW.
SLOW! THAT FUCKER! ...YOU THINK I'M SLOW LESTER?
...NO.
WELL, THERE YOU GO THEN!
I BET HE NEVER TOLD YOU I SCORED A GOAL WITH THE LEAFS TOO, DID HE? EVERYBODY ONLY REMEMBERS THE HIT I TOOK!
NOBODY REMEMBERS THAT I SCORED A GOAL IN THE FIRST PERIOD! YER FUCKIN' UNCLE EVER SCORE A GOAL IN THE NHL!?
NO. HE JUST FARMS.

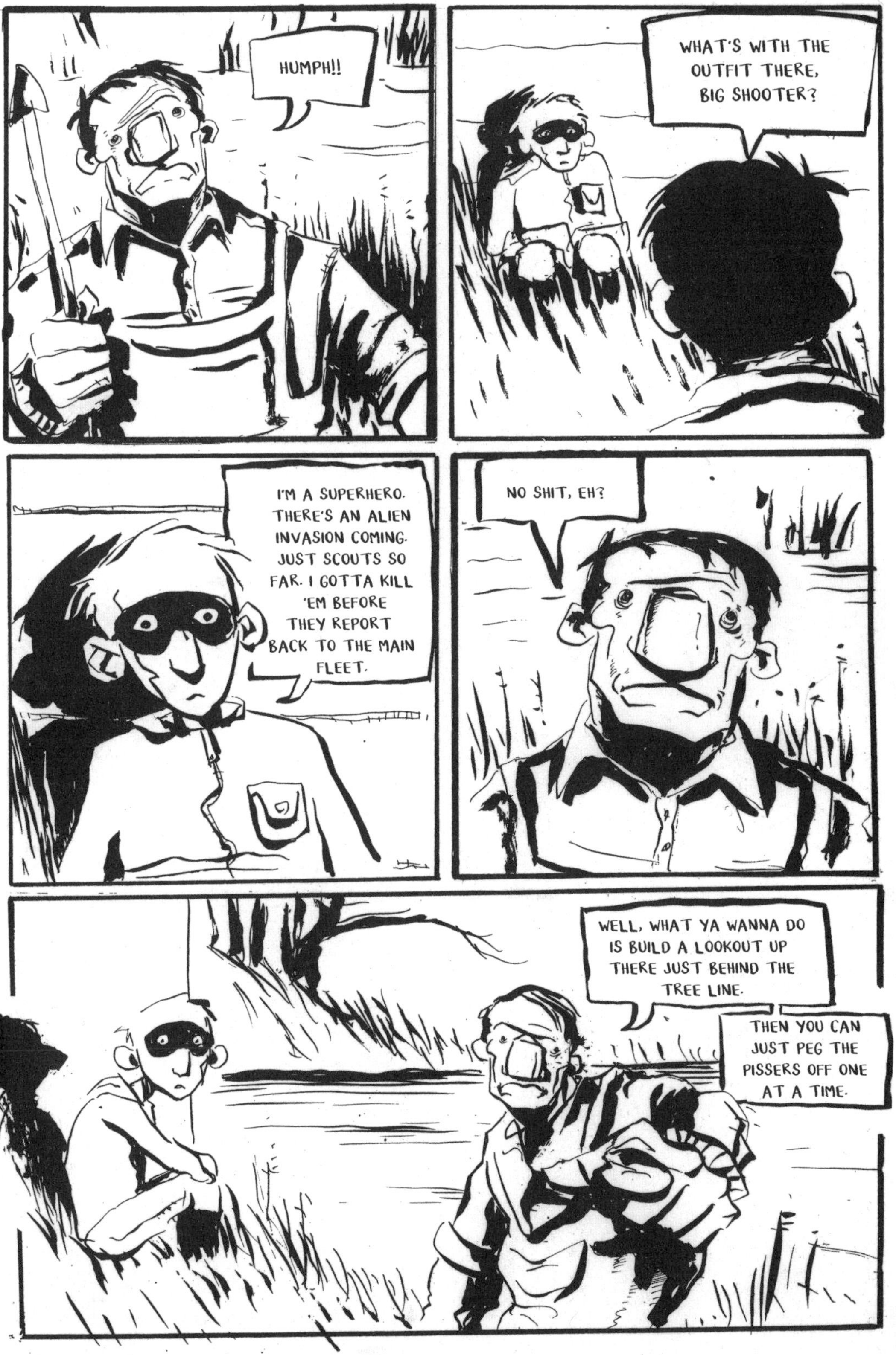
HUMPH!!
WHAT'S WITH THE OUTFIT THERE, BIG SHOOTER?
I'M A SUPERHERO. THERE'S AN ALIEN INVASION COMING. JUST SCOUTS SO FAR. I GOTTA KILL 'EM BEFORE THEY REPORT BACK TO THE MAIN FLEET.
NO SHIT, EH?
WELL, WHAT YA WANNA DO IS BUILD A LOOKOUT UP THERE JUST BEHIND THE TREE LINE.
THEN YOU CAN JUST PEG THE PISSERS OFF ONE AT A TIME.

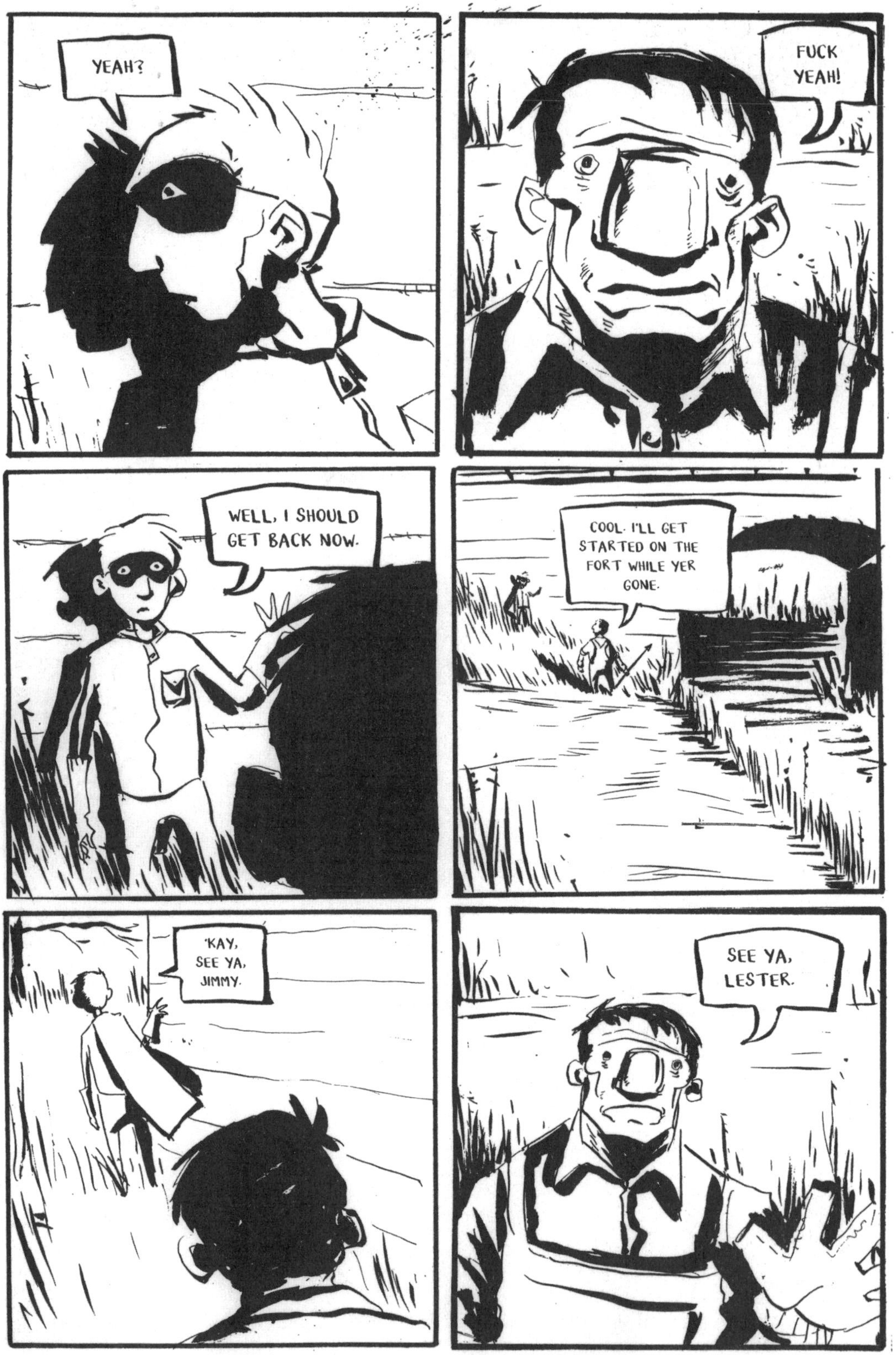
YEAH?
FUCK YEAH!
WELL, I SHOULD GET BACK NOW.
COOL. I'LL GET STARTED ON THE FORT WHILE YER GONE.
'KAY, SEE YA, JIMMY.
SEE YA, LESTER.

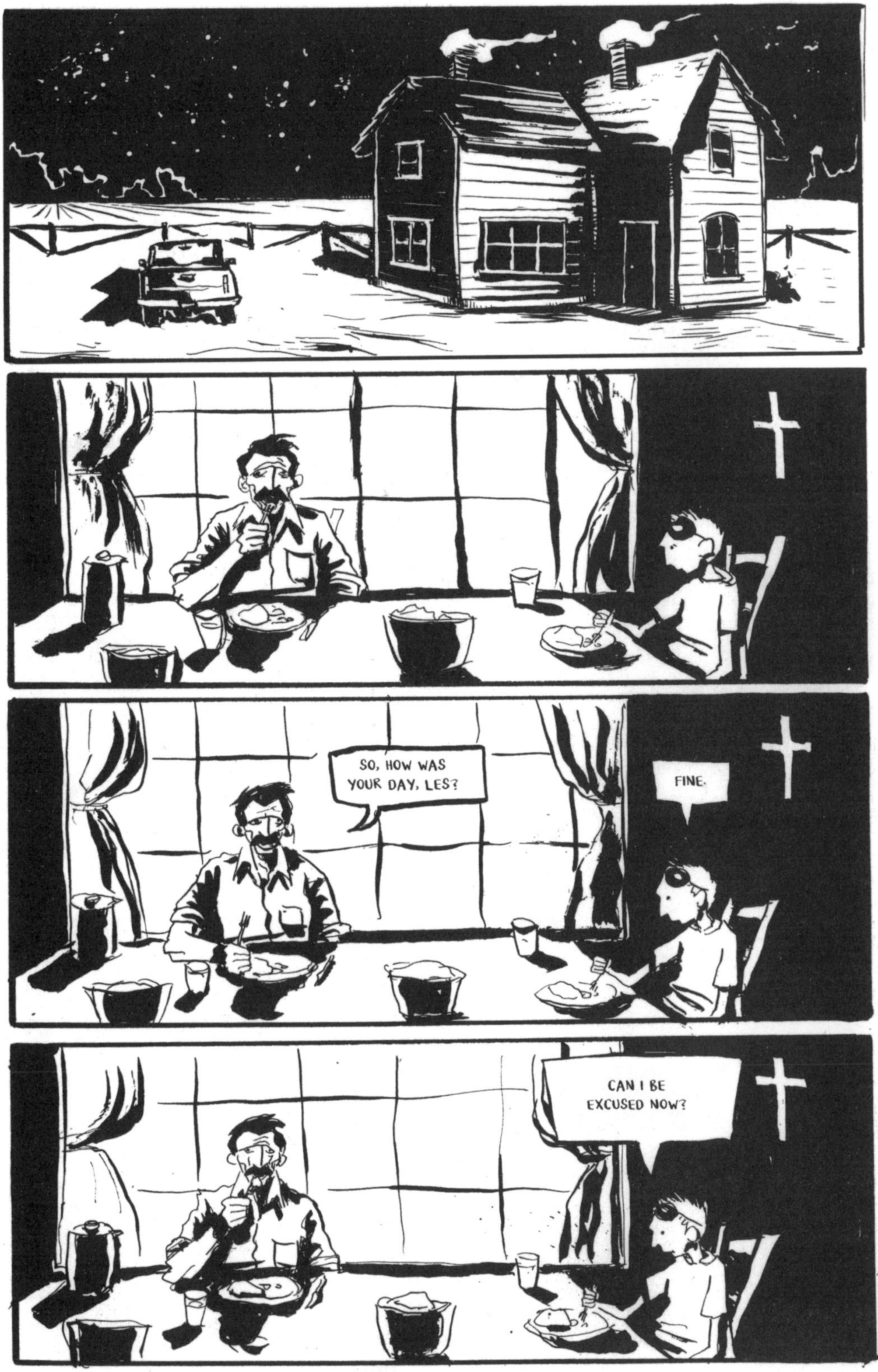
SO, HOW WAS YOUR DAY, LES?
FINE.
CAN I BE EXCUSED NOW?

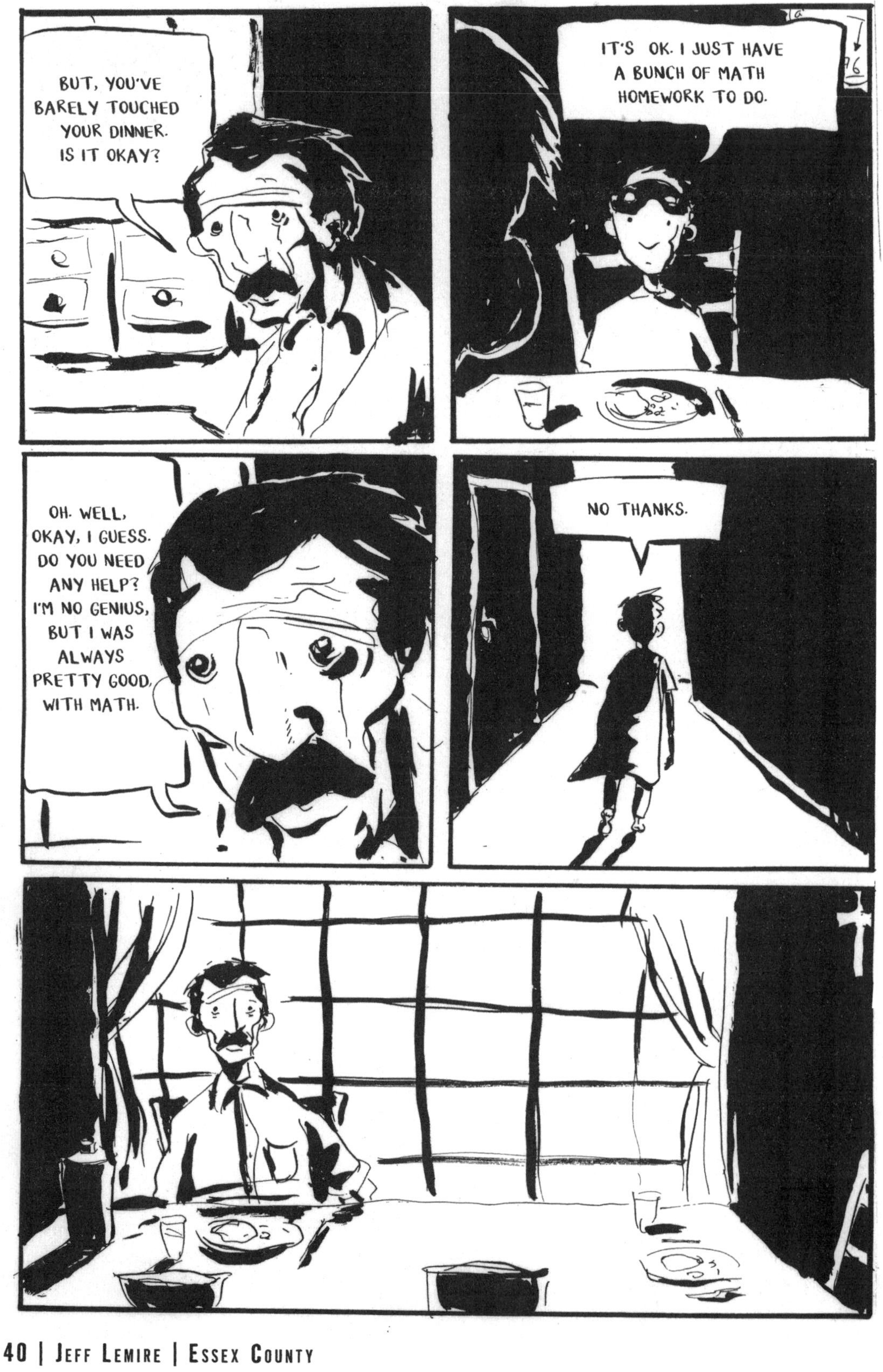
BUT, YOU'VE BARELY TOUCHED YOUR DINNER. IS IT OKAY?
IT'S OK. I JUST HAVE A BUNCH OF MATH HOMEWORK TO DO.
OH. WELL, OKAY, I GUESS. DO YOU NEED ANY HELP? I'M NO GENIUS, BUT I WAS ALWAYS PRETTY GOOD WITH MATH.
NO THANKS.

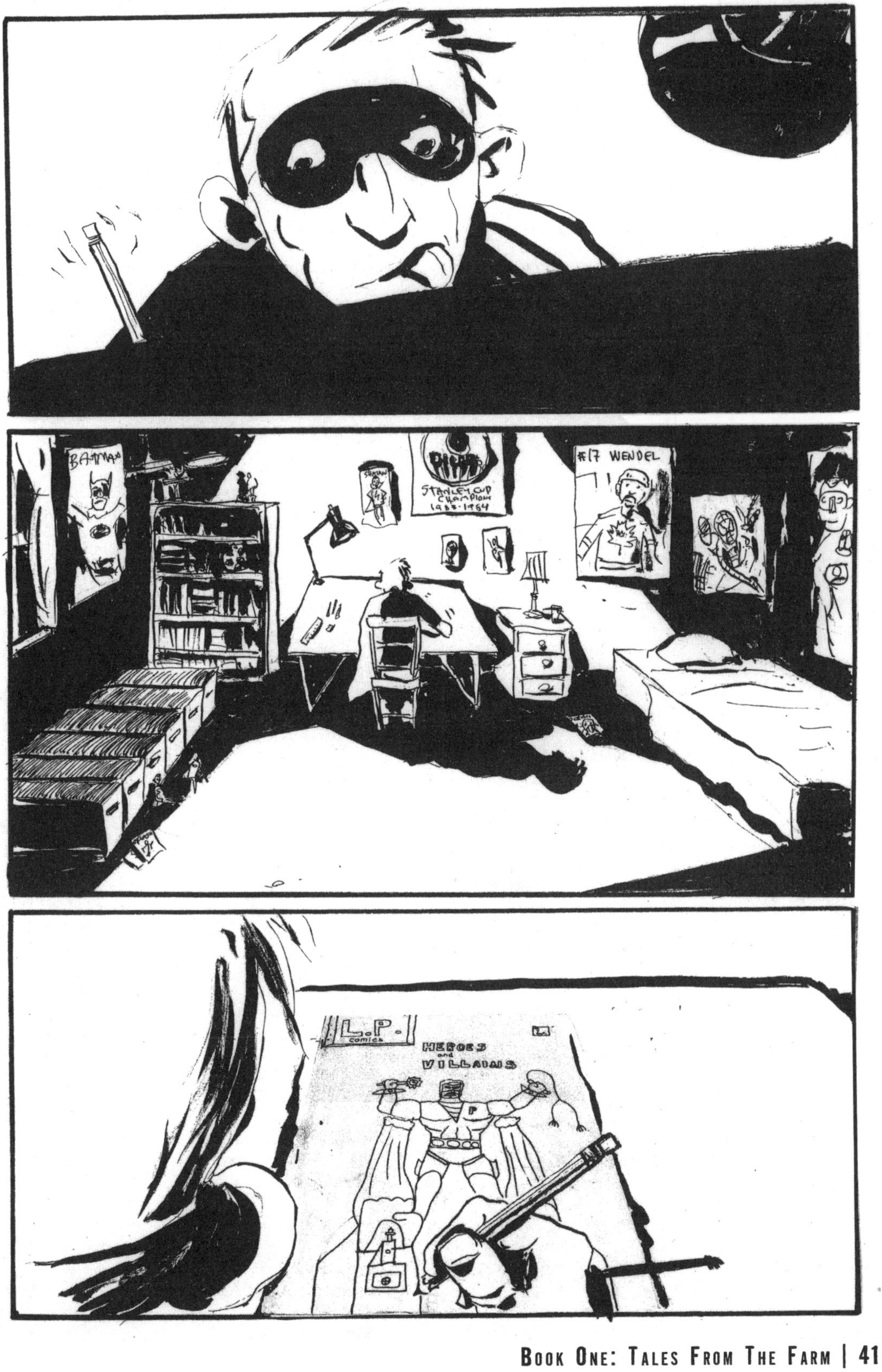

BATMAN
STANLEY CUP CHAMPIONS 1983-1984
#17 WENDEL
L.P. comics
HEROES and VILLAINS

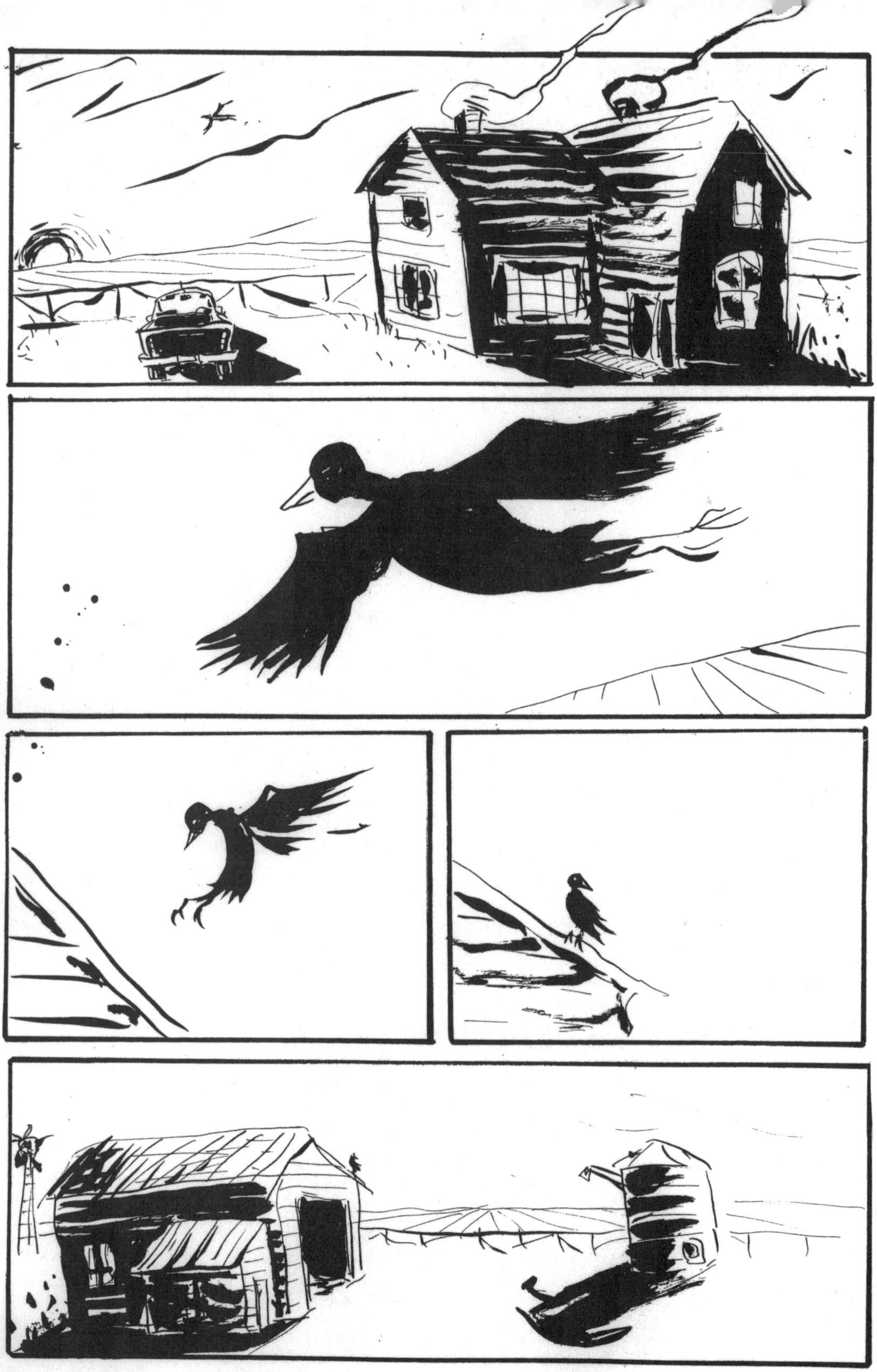

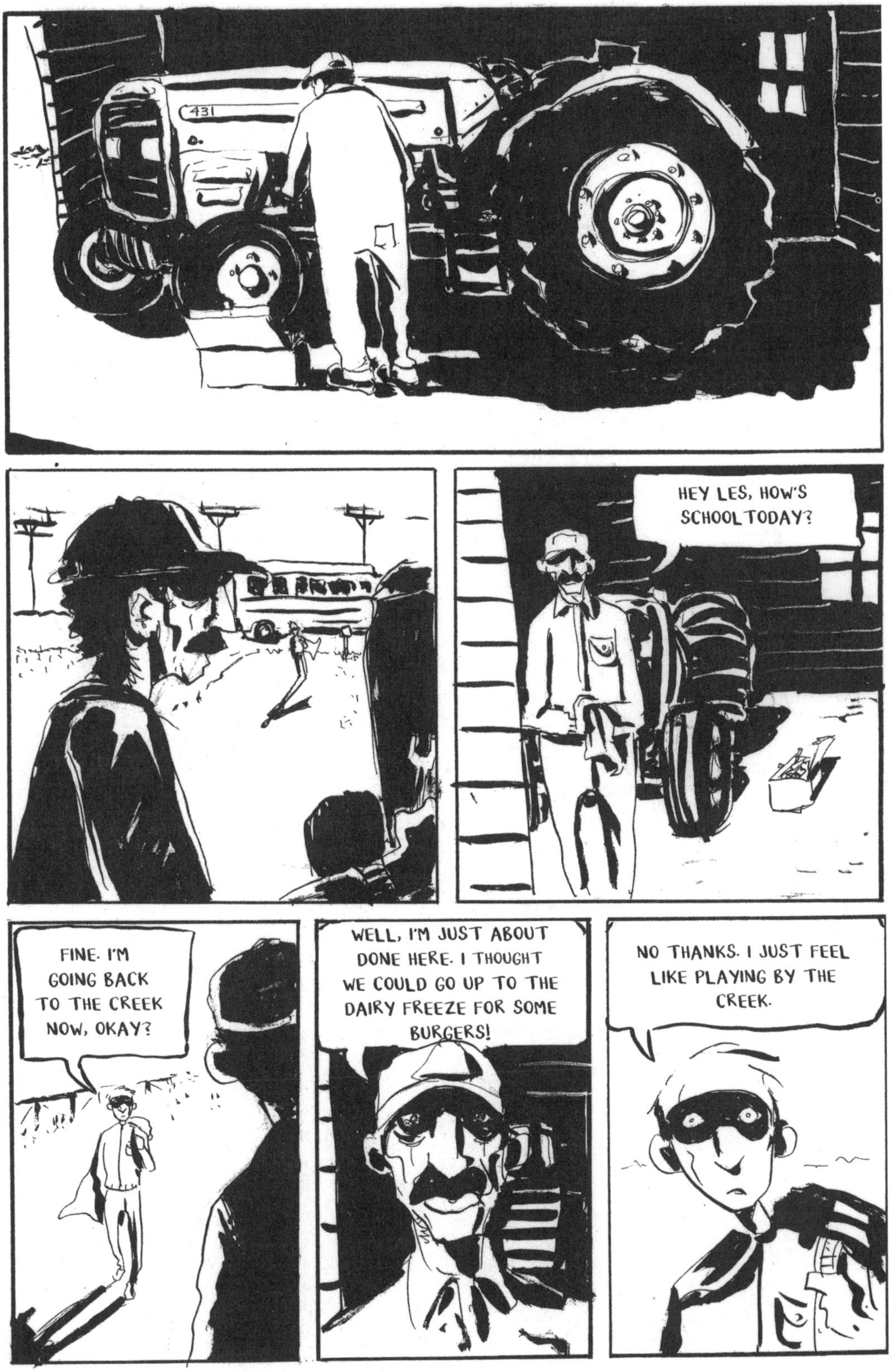
431
HEY LES, HOW'S SCHOOL TODAY?
FINE. I'M GOING BACK TO THE CREEK NOW, OKAY?
WELL, I'M JUST ABOUT DONE HERE. I THOUGHT WE COULD GO UP TO THE DAIRY FREEZE FOR SOME BURGERS!
NO THANKS. I JUST FEEL LIKE PLAYING BY THE CREEK.

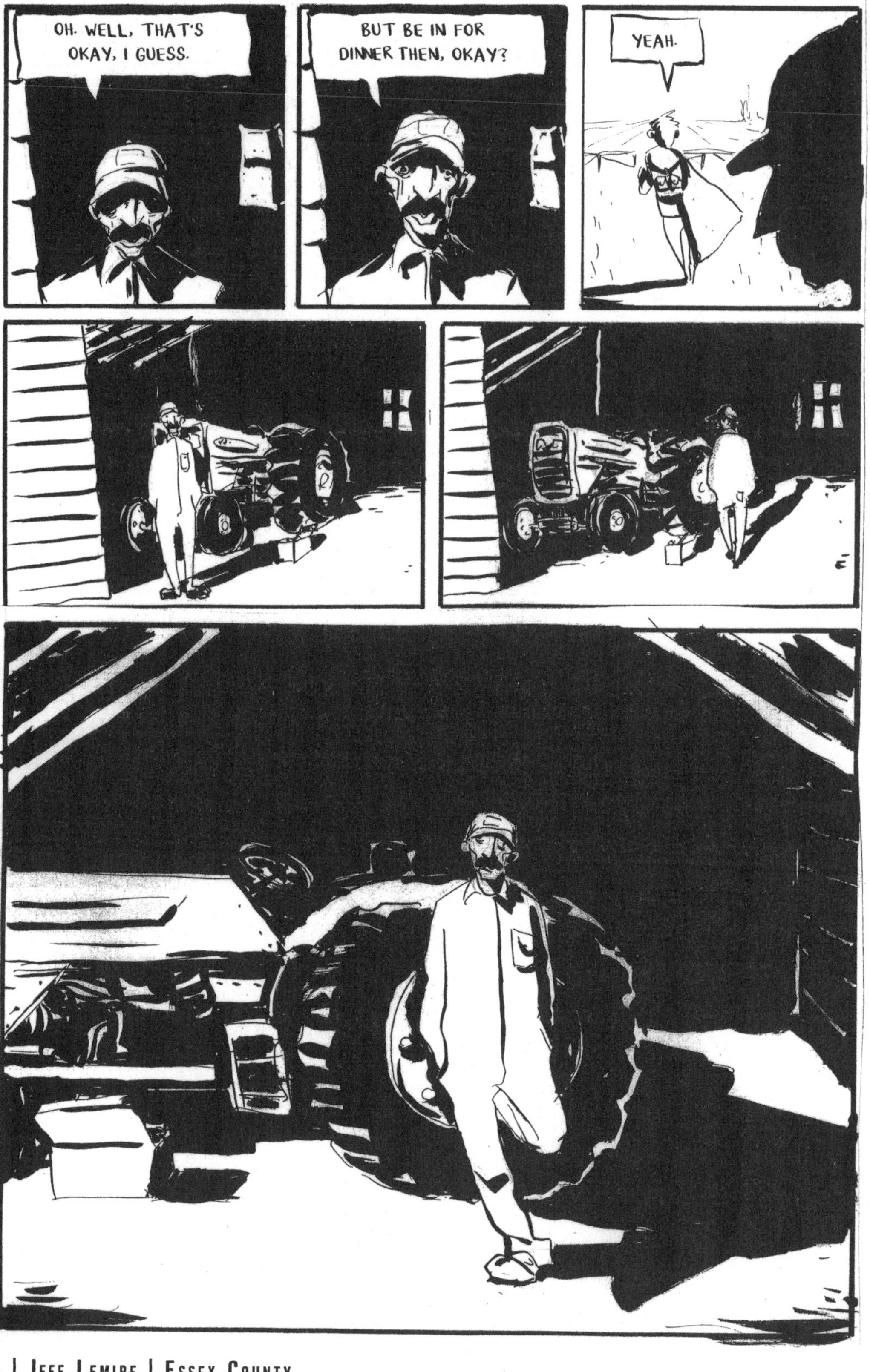
OH. WELL, THAT'S OKAY, I GUESS.
BUT BE IN FOR DINNER THEN, OKAY?
YEAH.

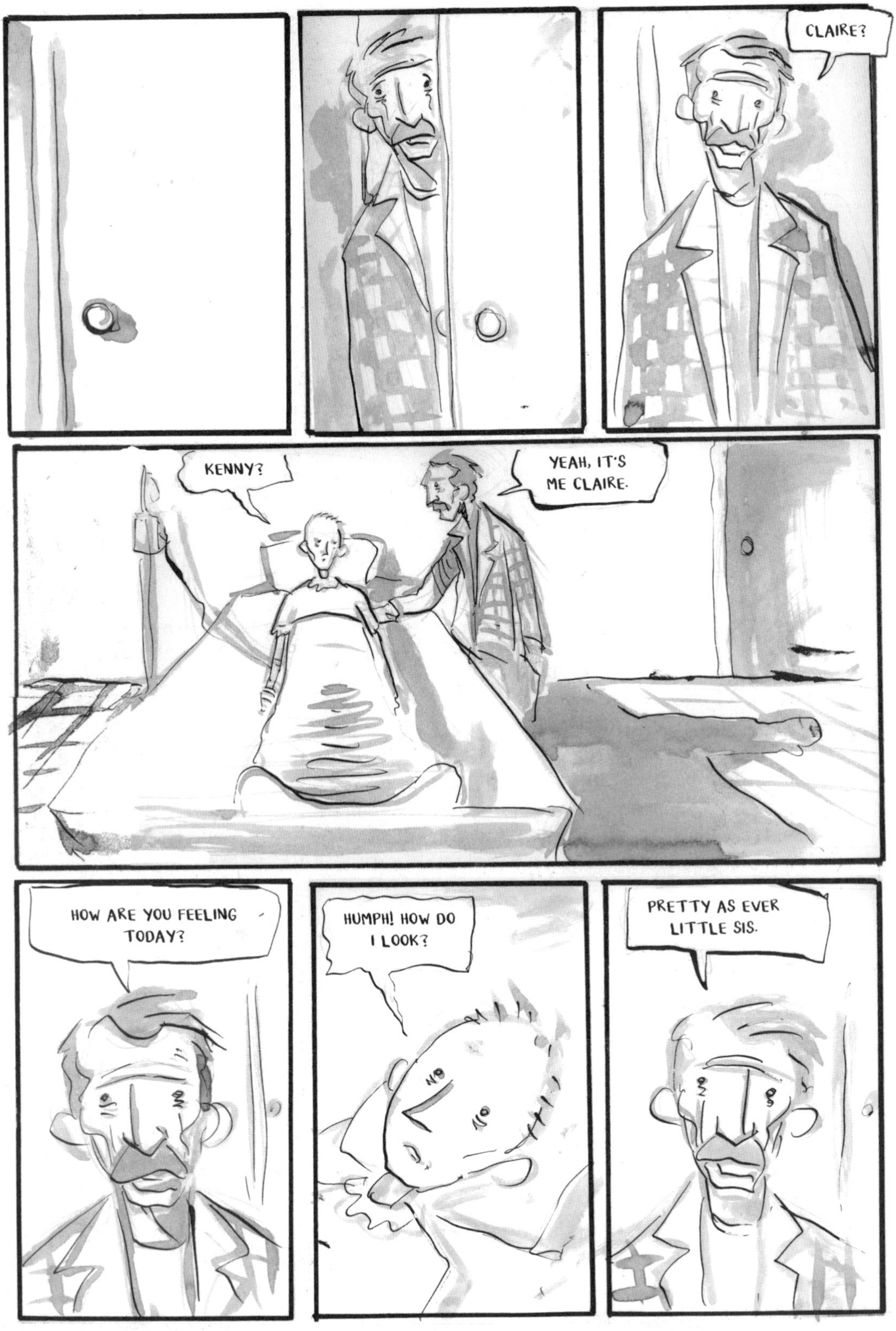
CLAIRE?
KENNY?
YEAH, IT'S ME CLAIRE.
HOW ARE YOU FEELING TODAY?
HUMPH! HOW DO I LOOK?
PRETTY AS EVER LITTLE SIS.

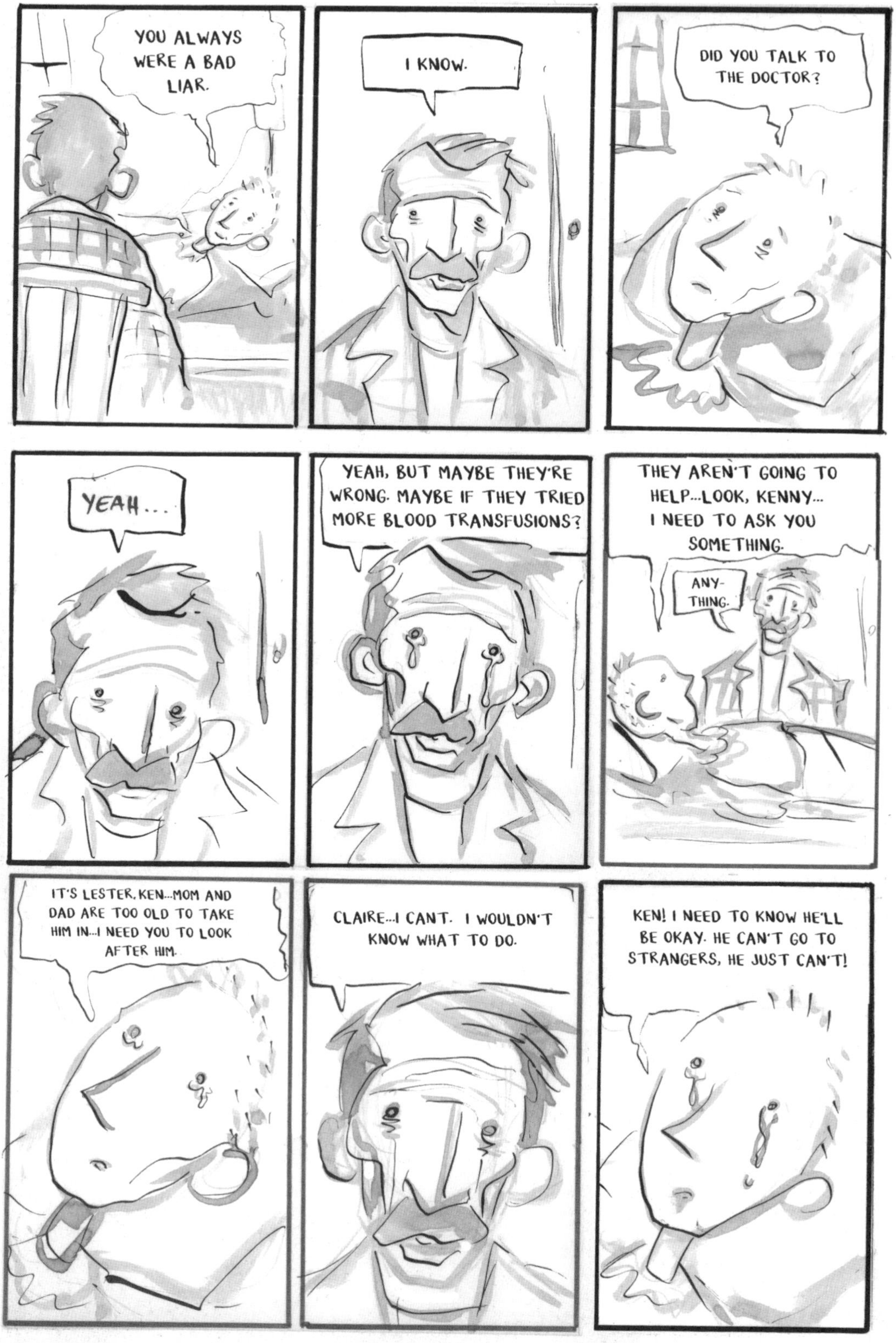
YOU ALWAYS WERE A BAD LIAR.
I KNOW.
DID YOU TALK TO THE DOCTOR?
YEAH...
YEAH, BUT MAYBE THEY'RE WRONG. MAYBE IF THEY TRIED MORE BLOOD TRANSFUSIONS?
THEY AREN'T GOING TO HELP...LOOK, KENNY... I NEED TO ASK YOU SOMETHING.
ANY-THING.
IT'S LESTER, KEN...MOM AND DAD ARE TOO OLD TO TAKE HIM IN...I NEED YOU TO LOOK AFTER HIM.
CLAIRE...I CANT. I WOULDN'T KNOW WHAT TO DO.
KEN! I NEED TO KNOW HE'LL BE OKAY. HE CAN'T GO TO STRANGERS, HE JUST CAN'T!

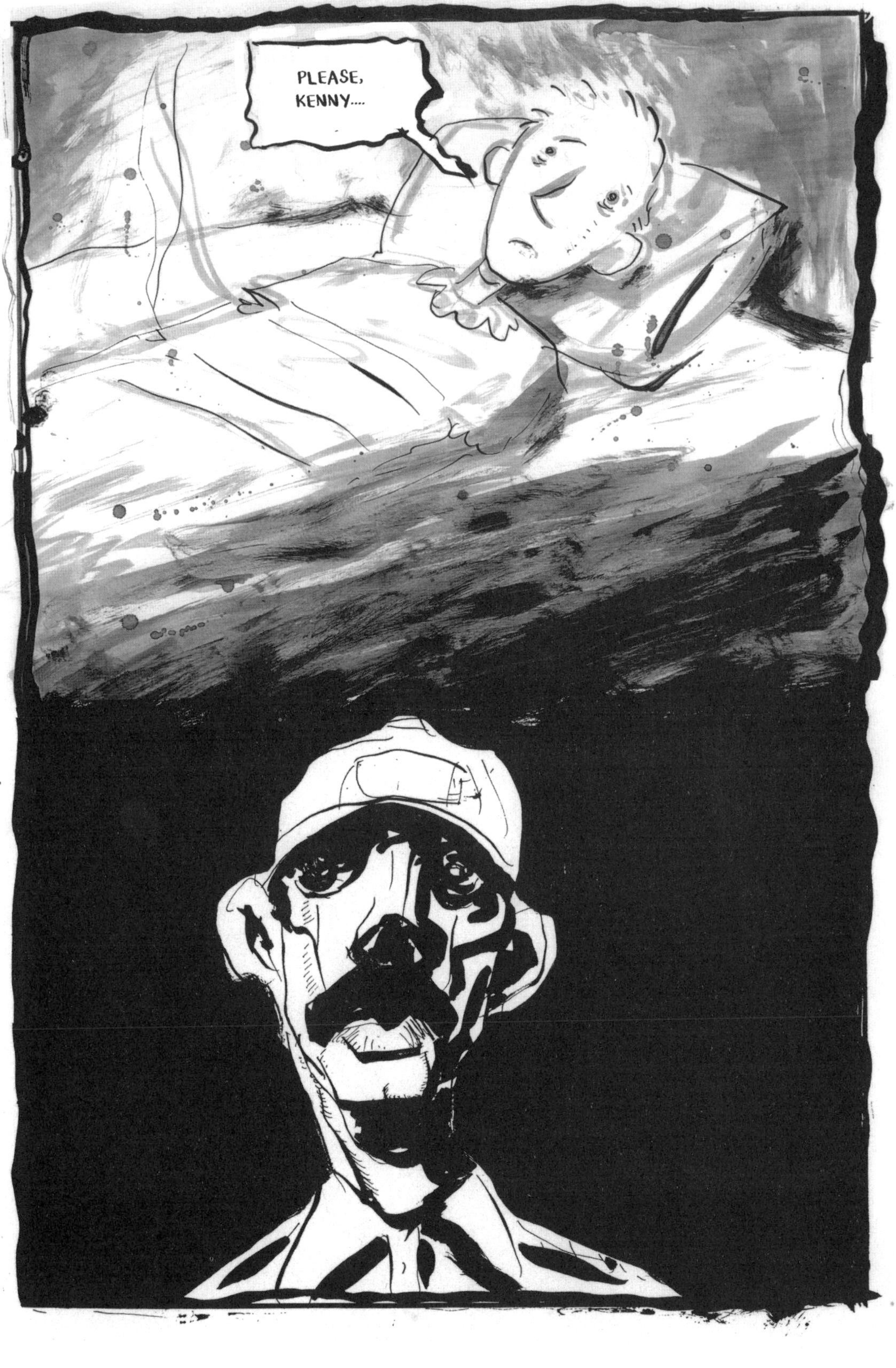
PLEASE, KENNY....

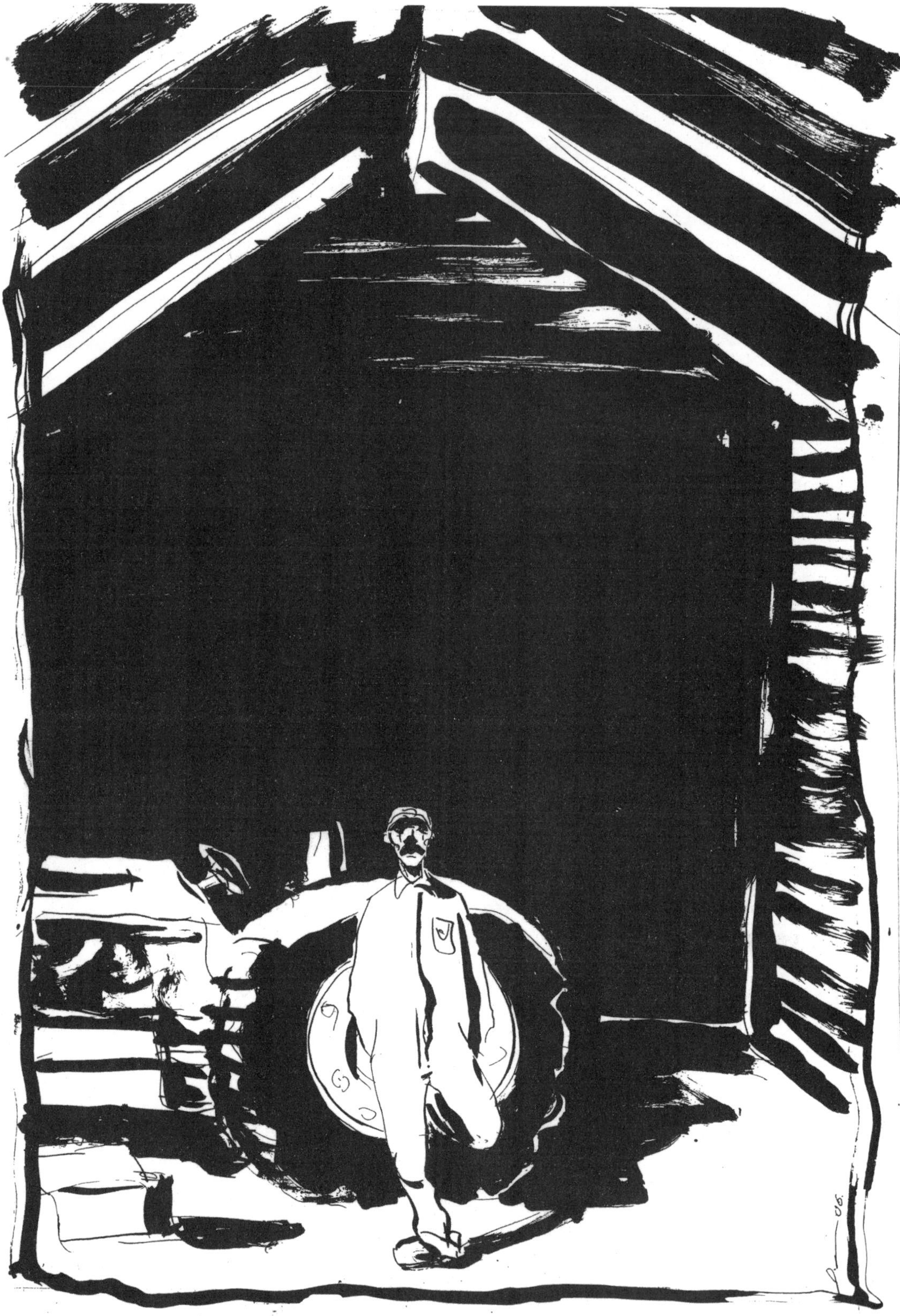

WINTER

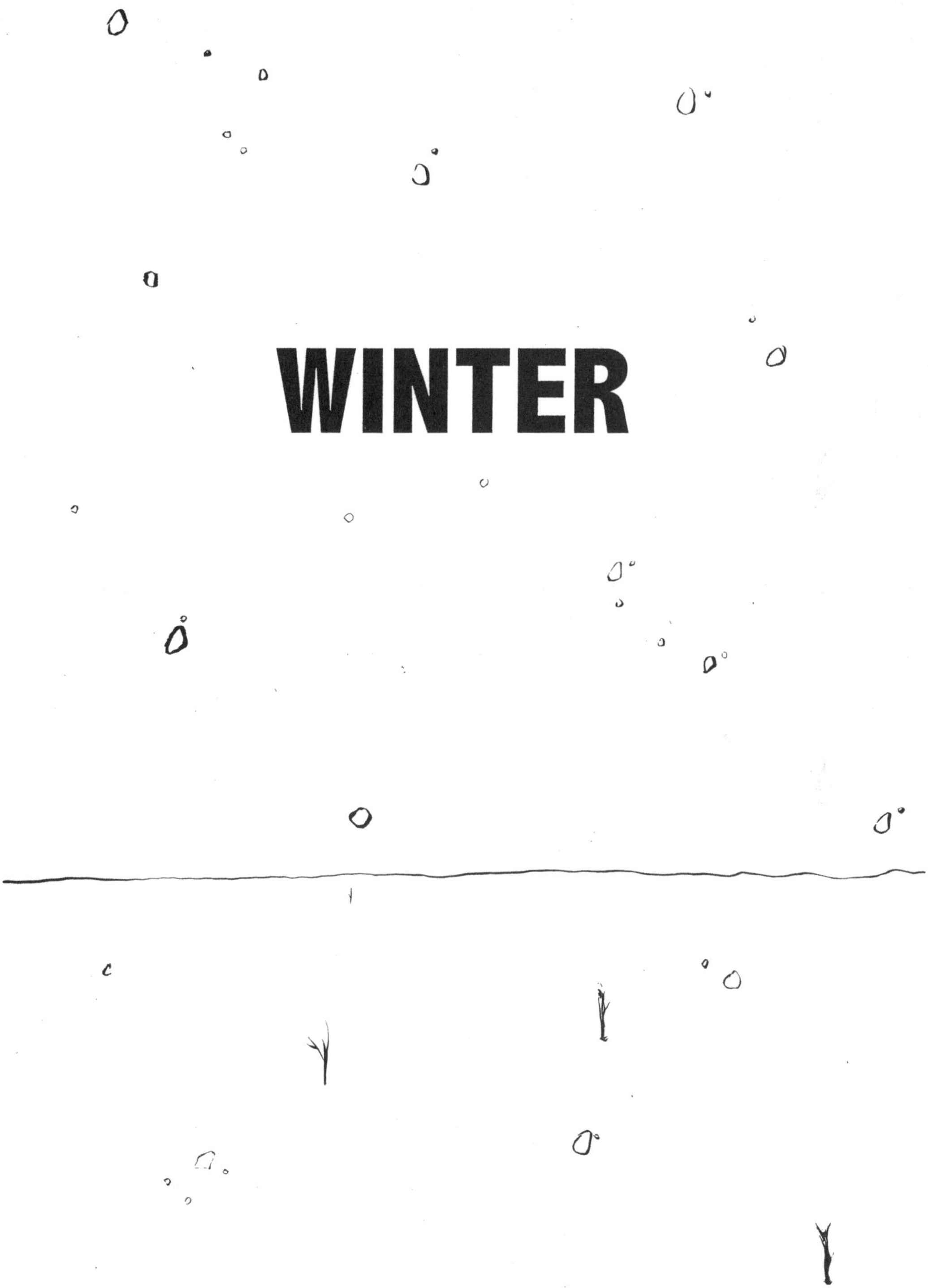

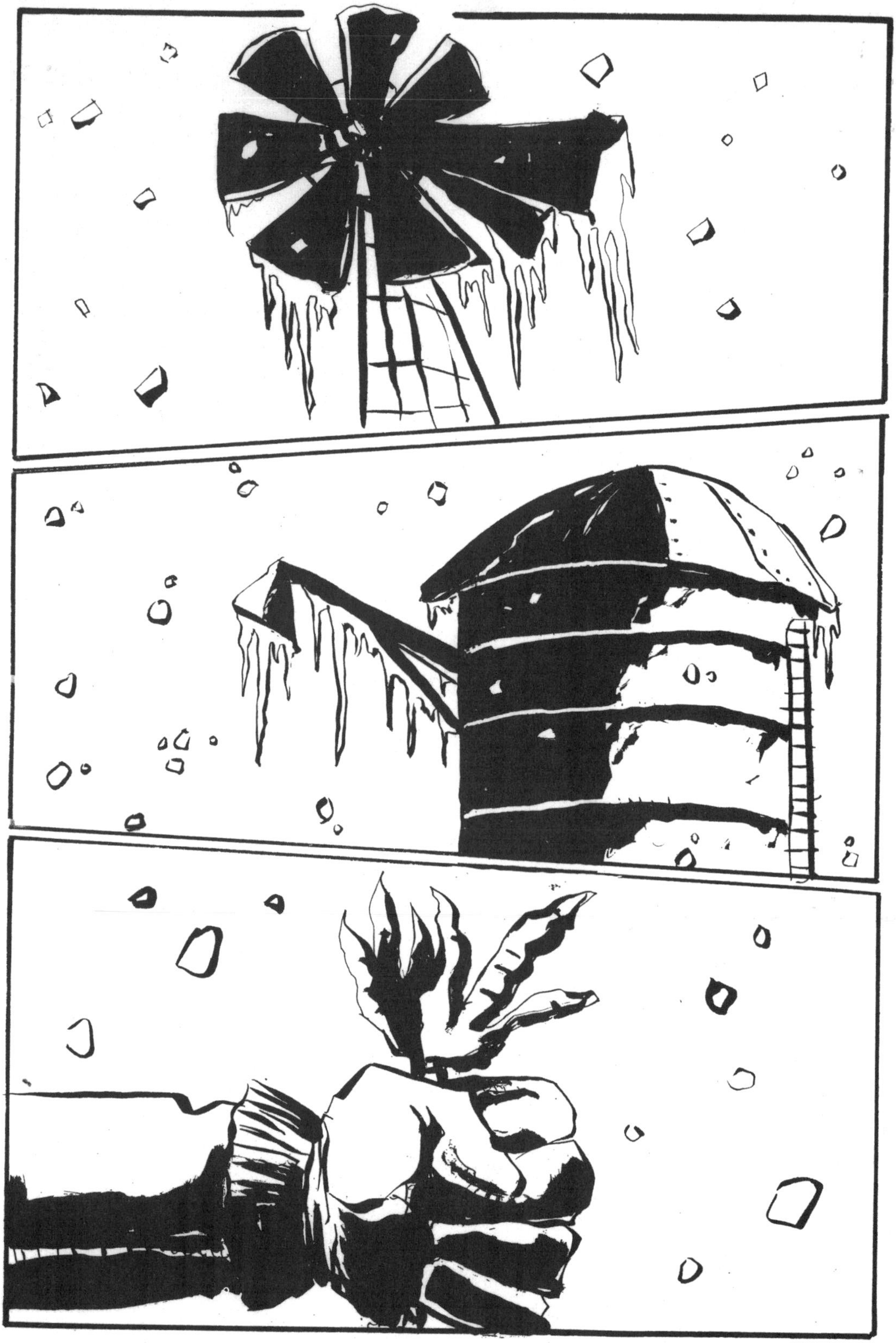

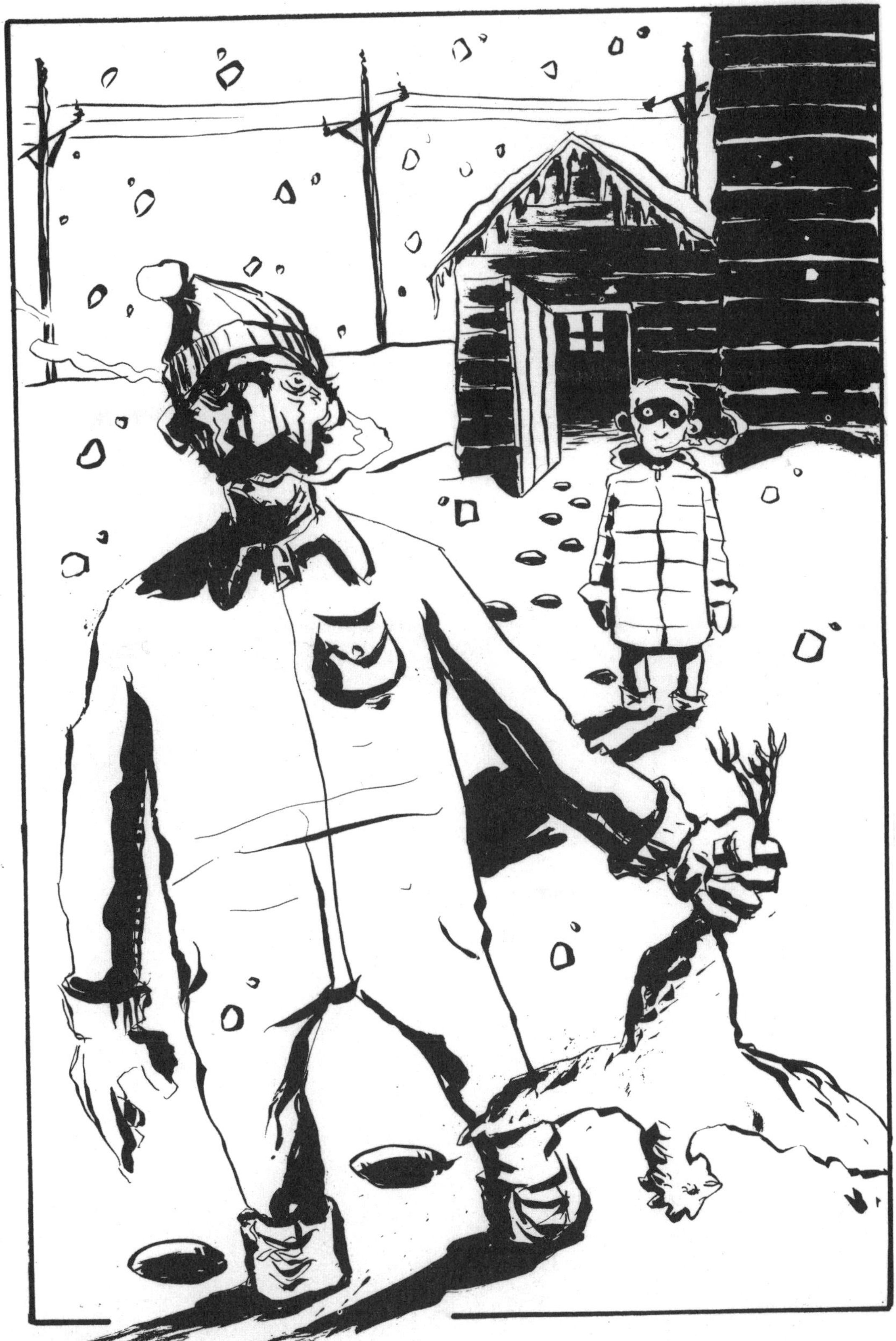

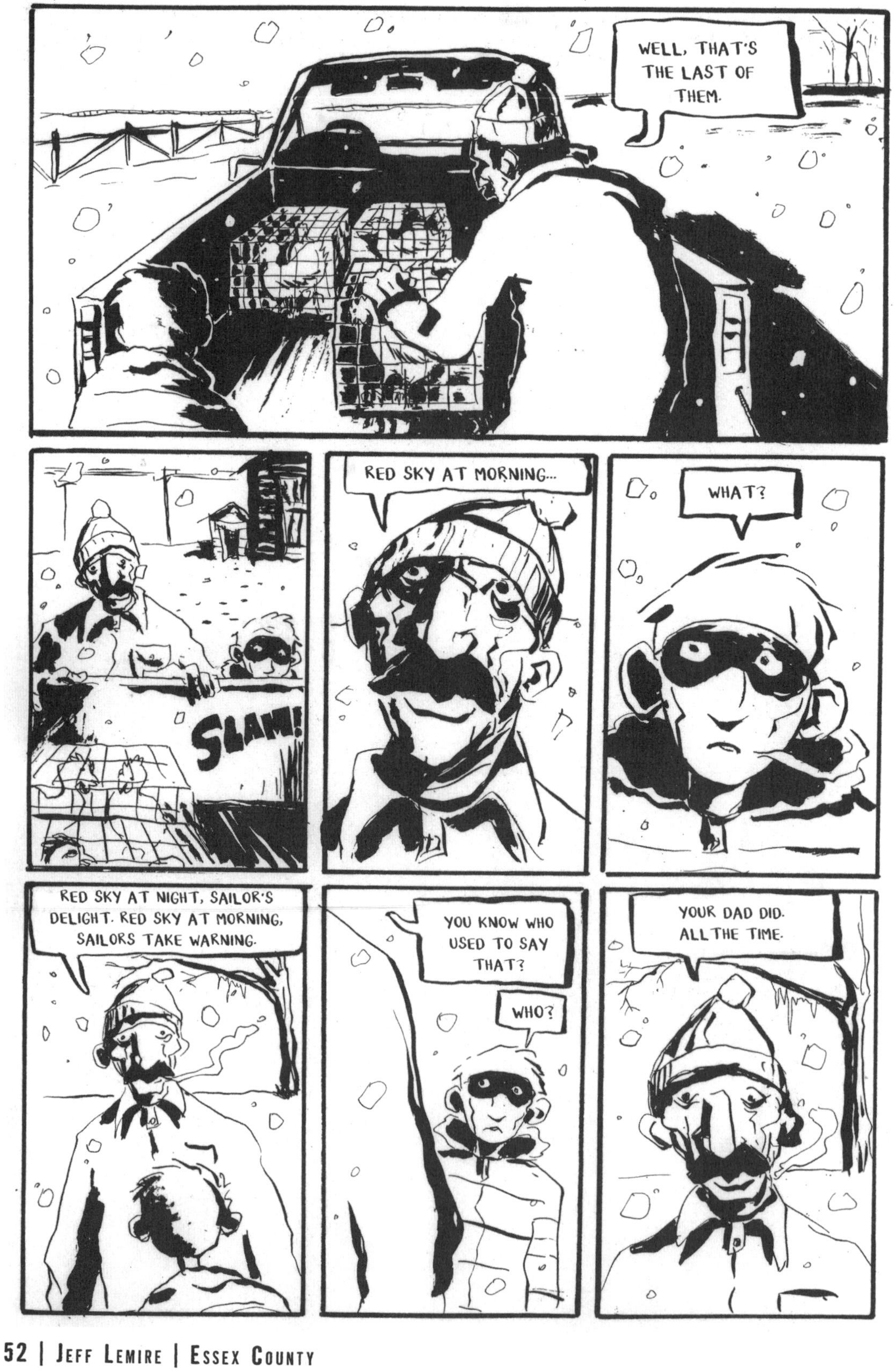
WELL, THAT'S THE LAST OF THEM.
SLAM!
RED SKY AT MORNING...
WHAT?
RED SKY AT NIGHT, SAILOR'S DELIGHT. RED SKY AT MORNING, SAILORS TAKE WARNING.
YOU KNOW WHO USED TO SAY THAT?
WHO?
YOUR DAD DID. ALL THE TIME.

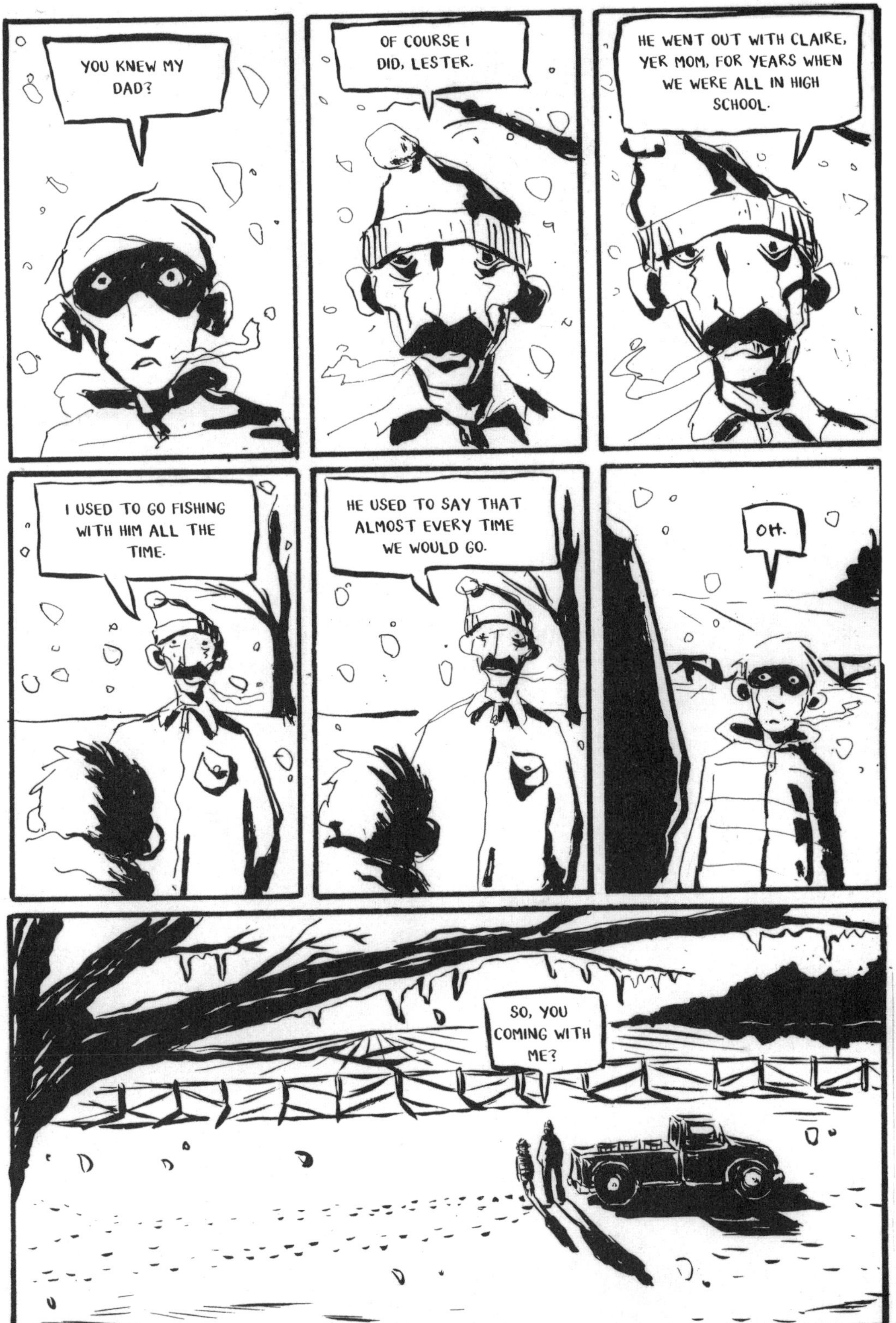
YOU KNEW MY DAD?
OF COURSE I DID, LESTER.
HE WENT OUT WITH CLAIRE, YER MOM, FOR YEARS WHEN WE WERE ALL IN HIGH SCHOOL.
I USED TO GO FISHING WITH HIM ALL THE TIME.
HE USED TO SAY THAT ALMOST EVERY TIME WE WOULD GO.
OH.
SO, YOU COMING WITH ME?

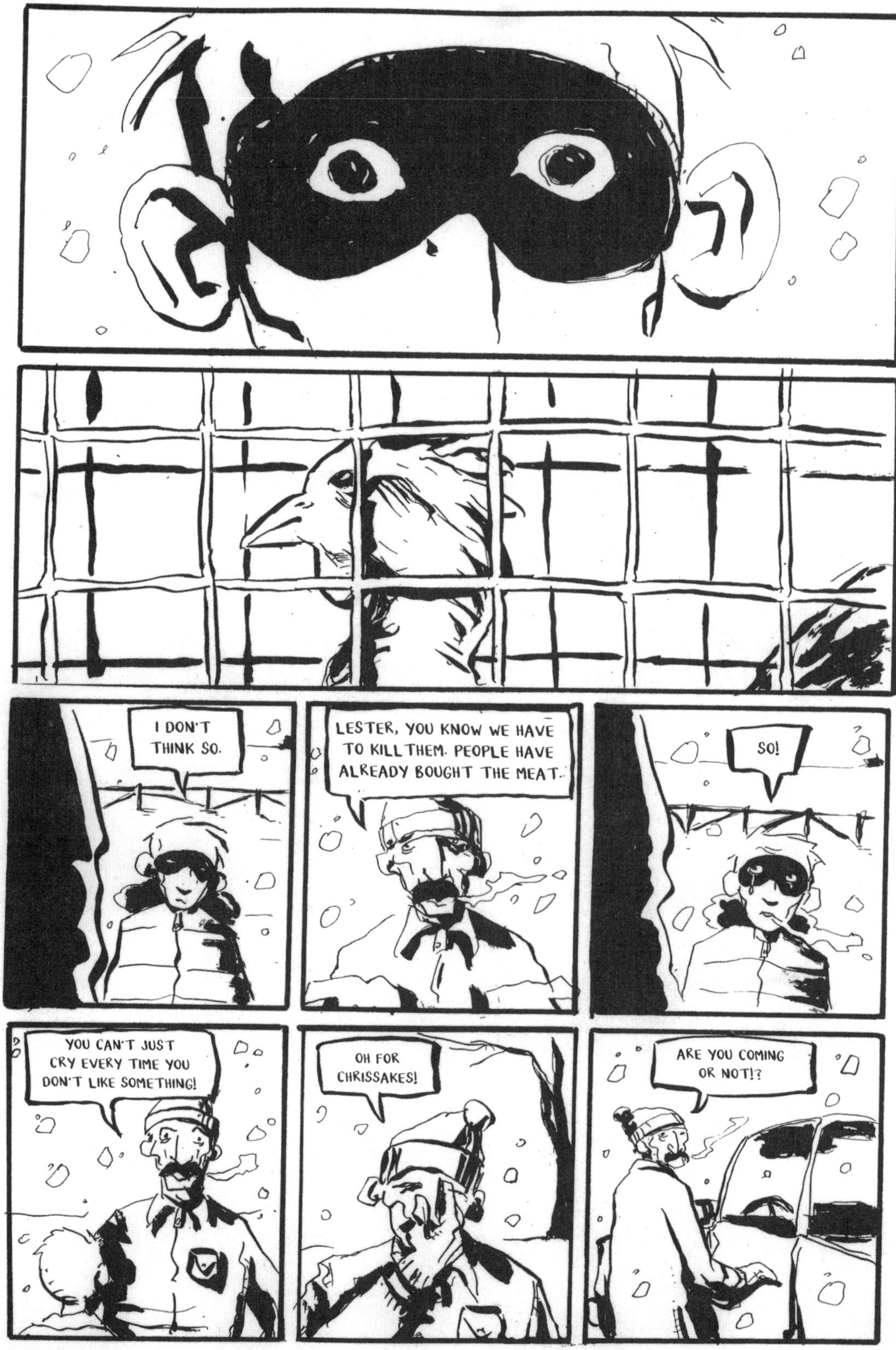
I DON'T THINK SO.
LESTER, YOU KNOW WE HAVE TO KILL THEM. PEOPLE HAVE ALREADY BOUGHT THE MEAT.
SO!
YOU CAN'T JUST CRY EVERY TIME YOU DON'T LIKE SOMETHING!
OH FOR CHRISSAKES!
ARE YOU COMING OR NOT!?

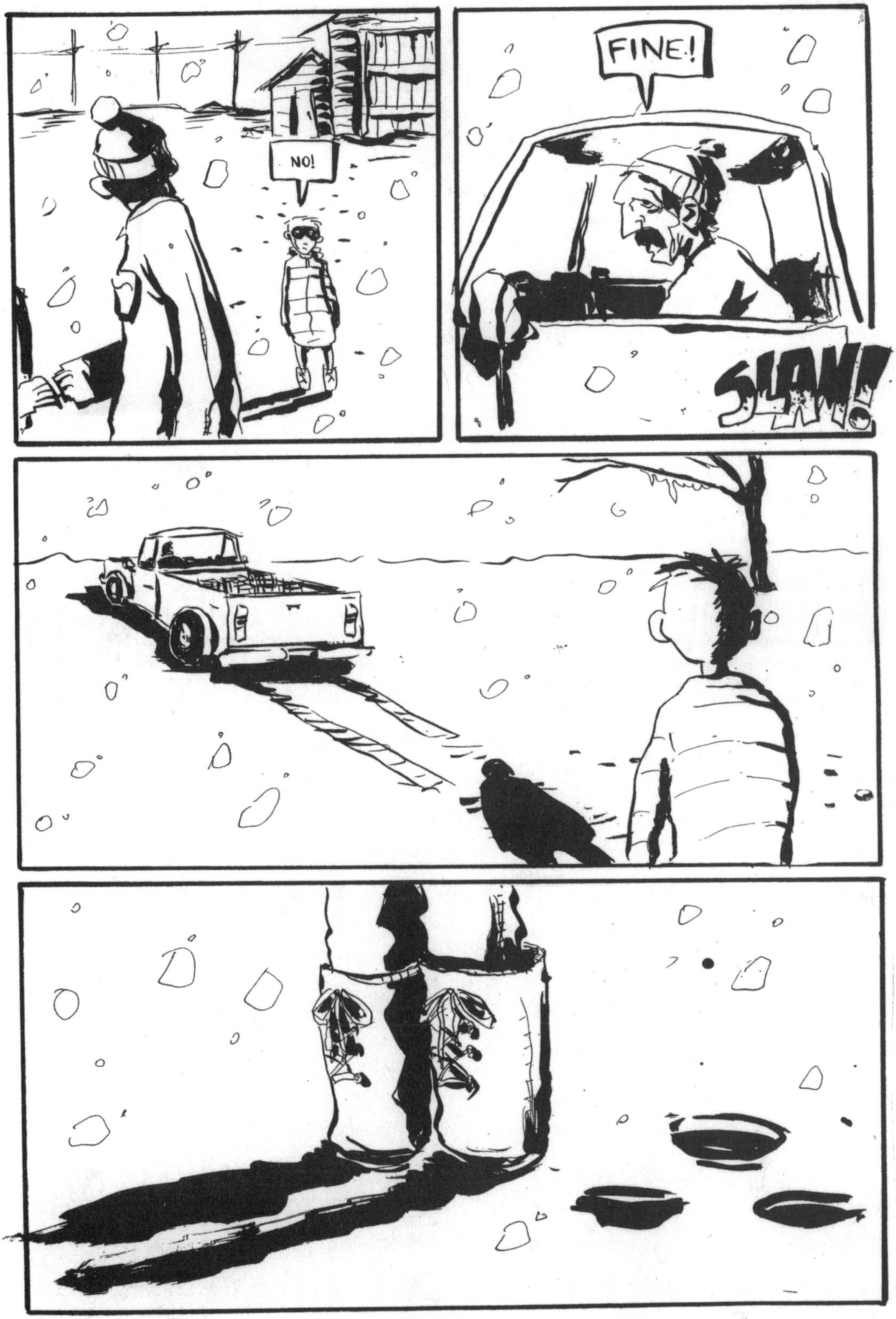
NO!
FINE!
SLAM!

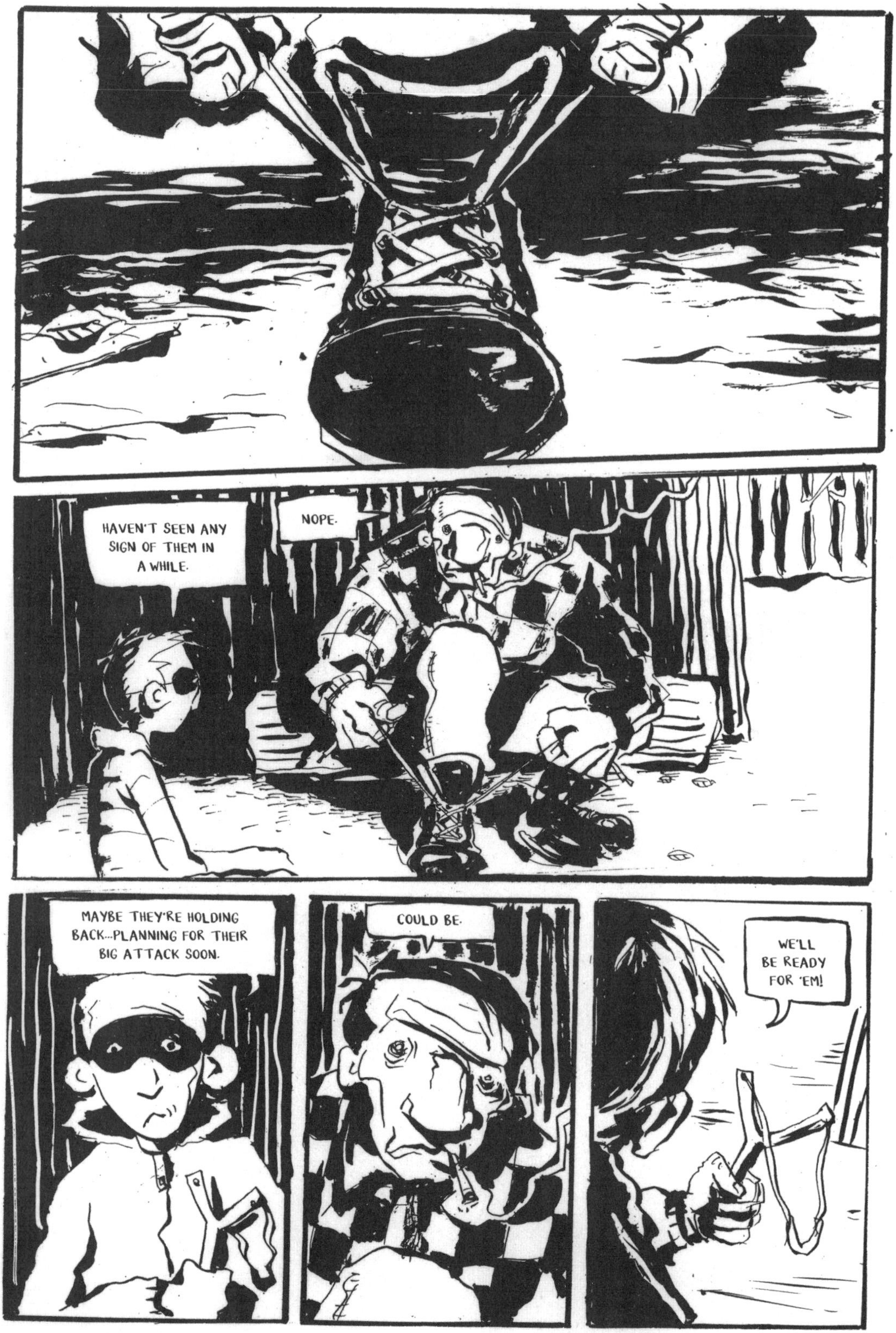
HAVEN'T SEEN ANY SIGN OF THEM IN A WHILE.
NOPE.
MAYBE THEY'RE HOLDING BACK...PLANNING FOR THEIR BIG ATTACK SOON.
COULD BE.
WE'LL BE READY FOR 'EM!

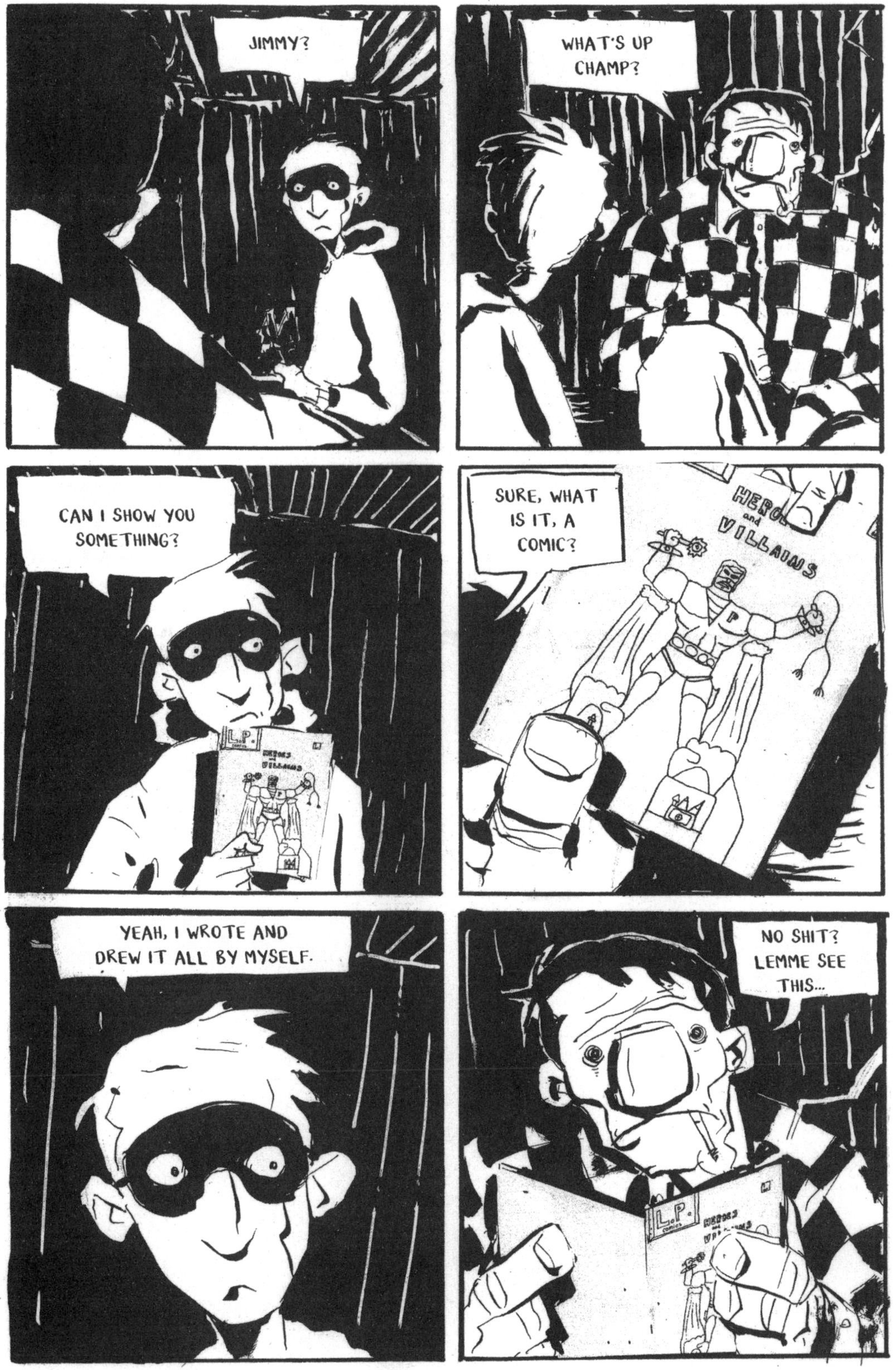
JIMMY?
WHAT'S UP CHAMP?
CAN I SHOW YOU SOMETHING?
SURE, WHAT IS IT, A COMIC?
HEROES and VILLAINS
YEAH, I WROTE AND DREW IT ALL BY MYSELF.
NO SHIT? LEMME SEE THIS...

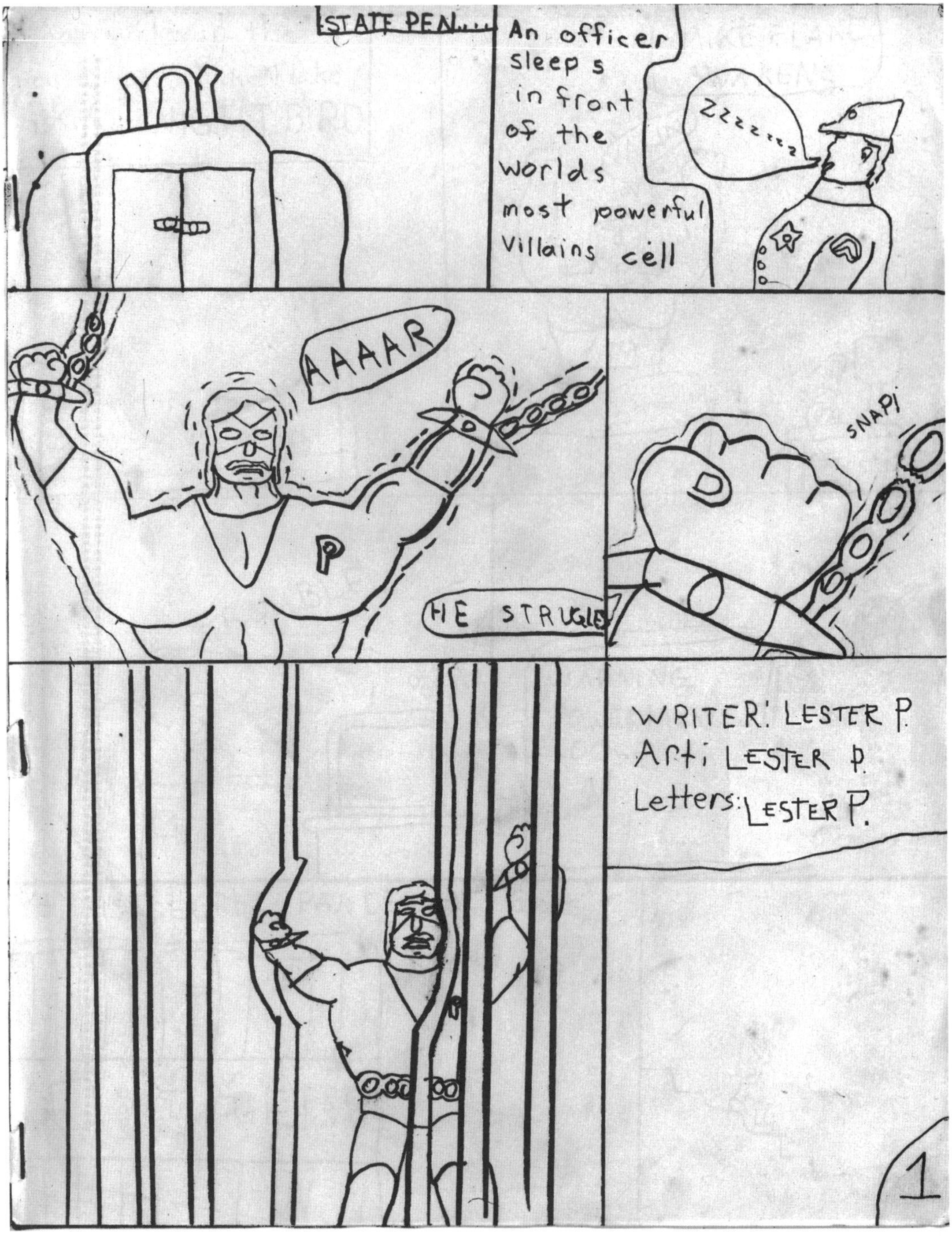
STATE PEN....
An officer sleeps in front of the worlds most powerful villains cell
ZZzzzzzz
AAAAR
HE STRUGLE
SNAP!
WRITER: LESTER P.
Art: LESTER P.
Letters: LESTER P.
1

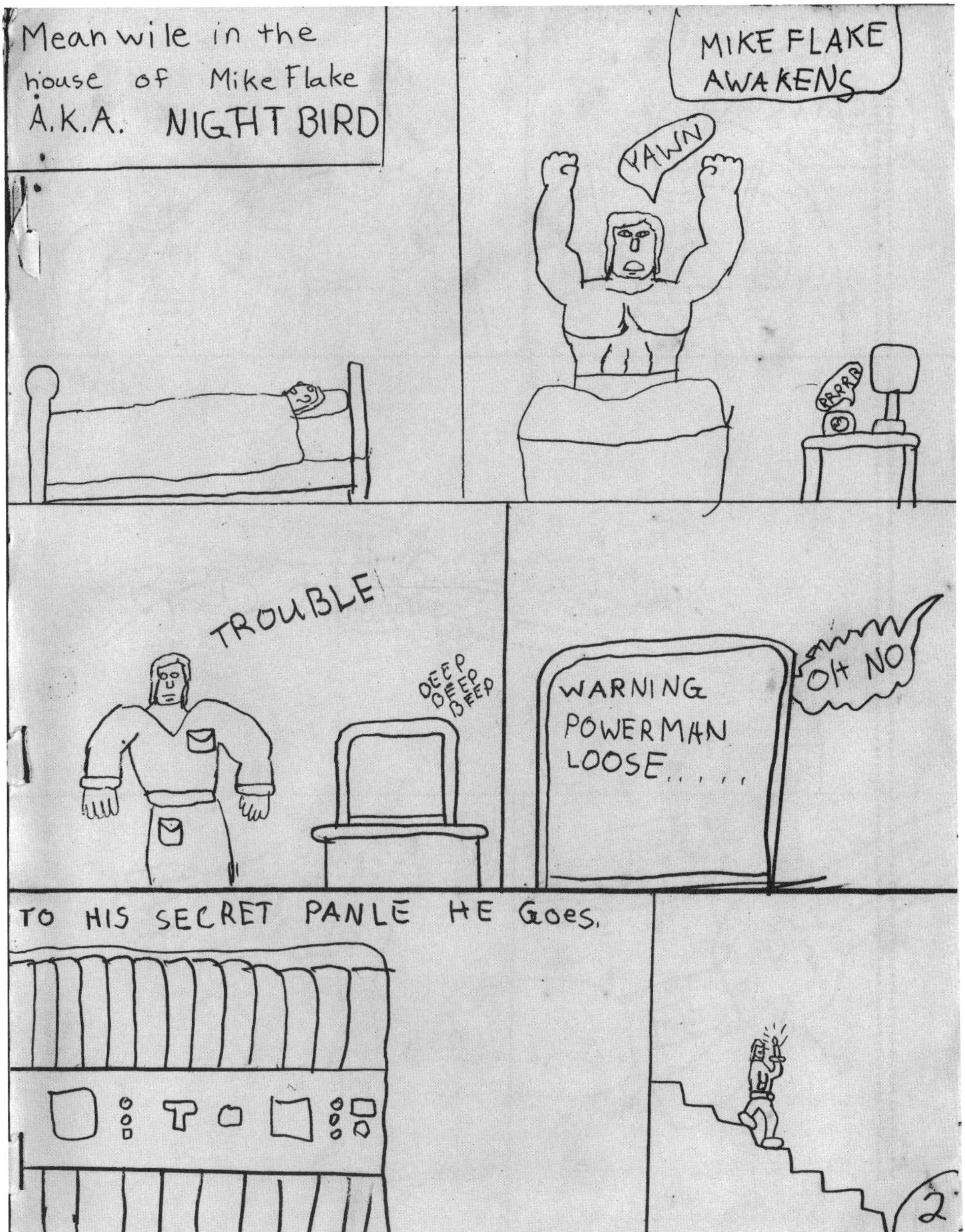
Meanwile in the house of Mike Flake A.K.A. NIGHT BIRD
MIKE FLAKE AWAKENS
YAWN
RRRRR
TROUBLE
DEEP DEEP BEEP
WARNING POWERMAN LOOSE.....
OH NO
TO HIS SECRET PANLE HE Goes.
2

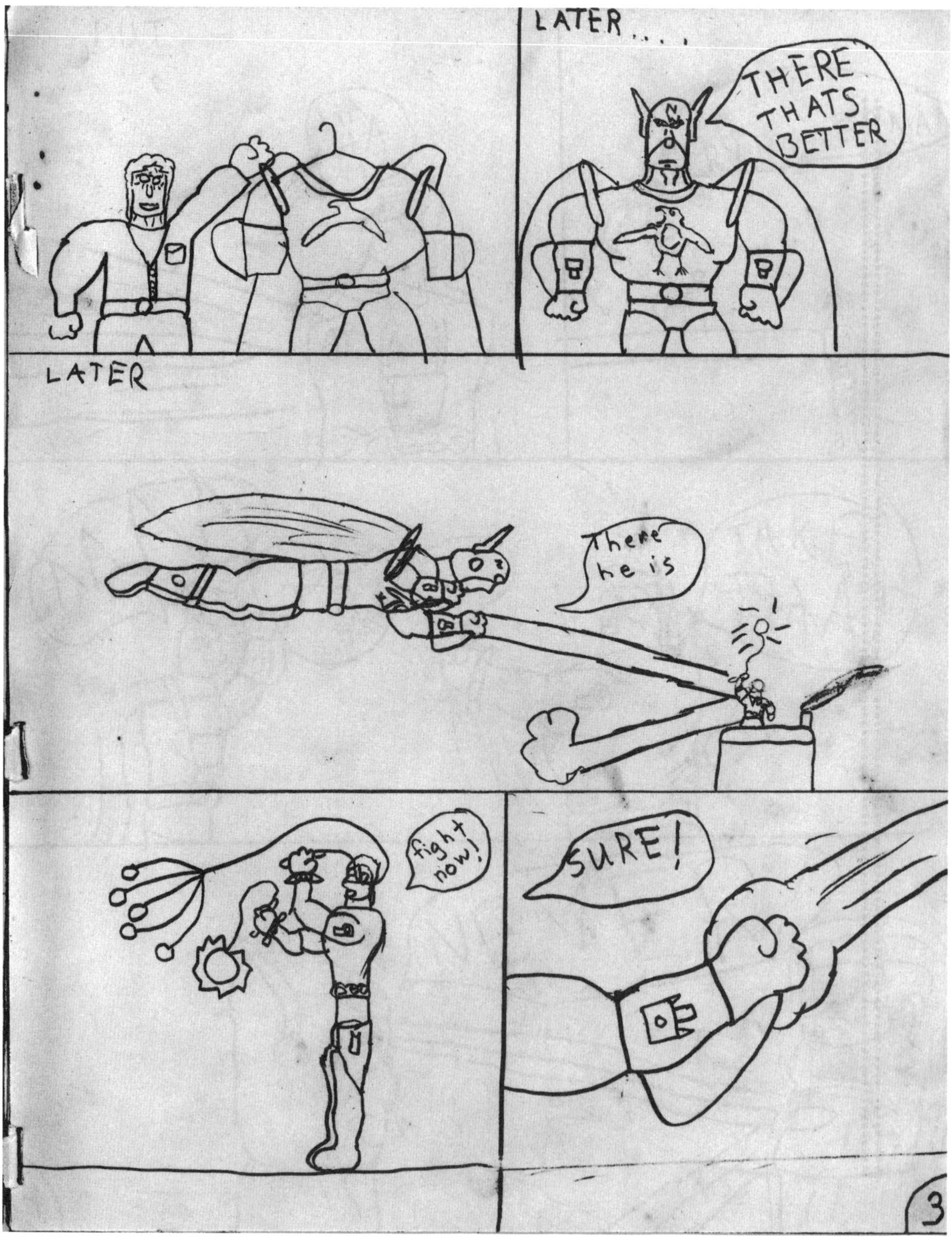
LATER....
THERE THATS BETTER
LATER
There he is
fight now!
SURE!
3

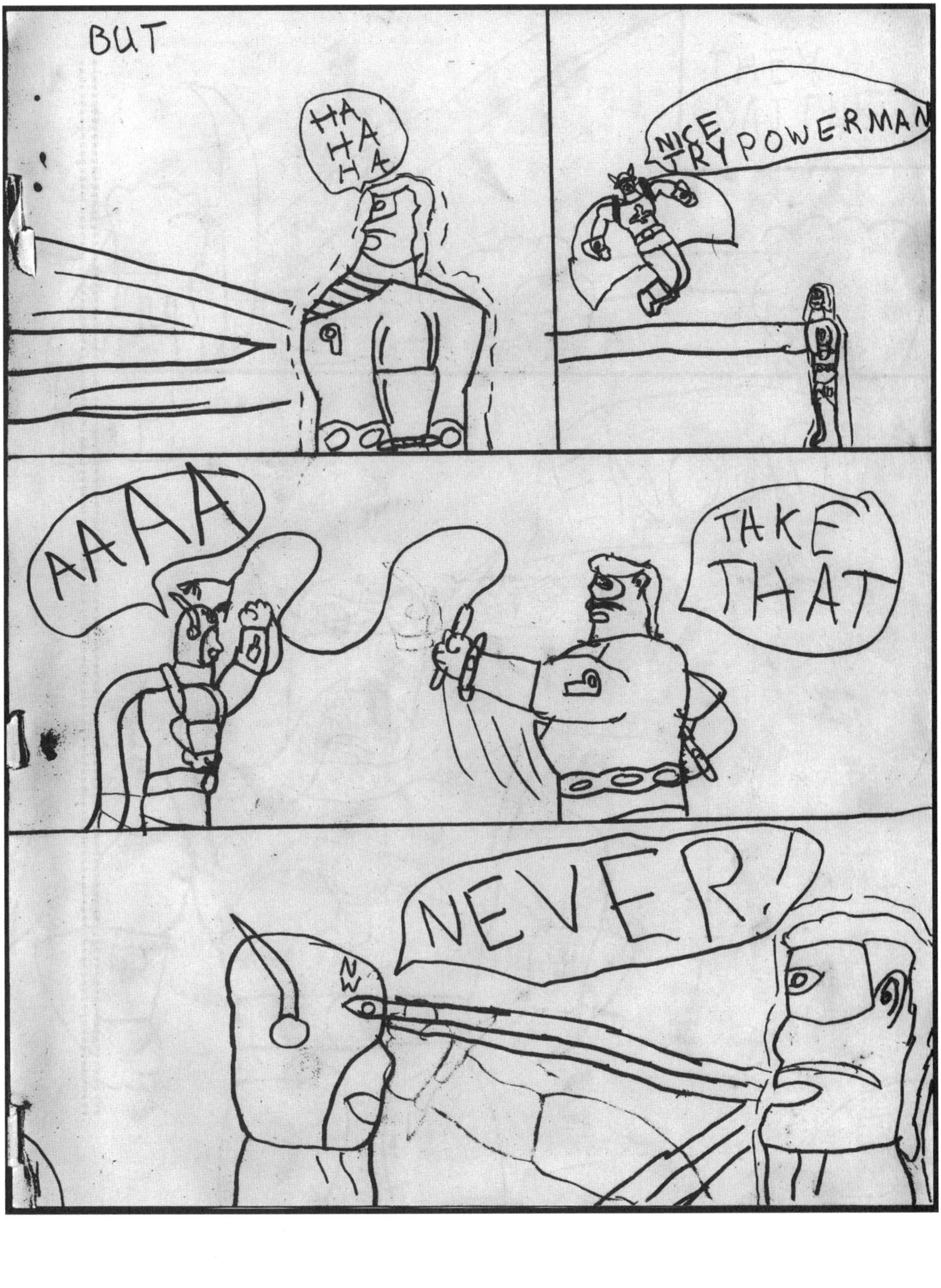
BUT
HA HA HA HA
NICE TRY POWERMAN
AAAA
TAKE THAT
NEVER!
NW

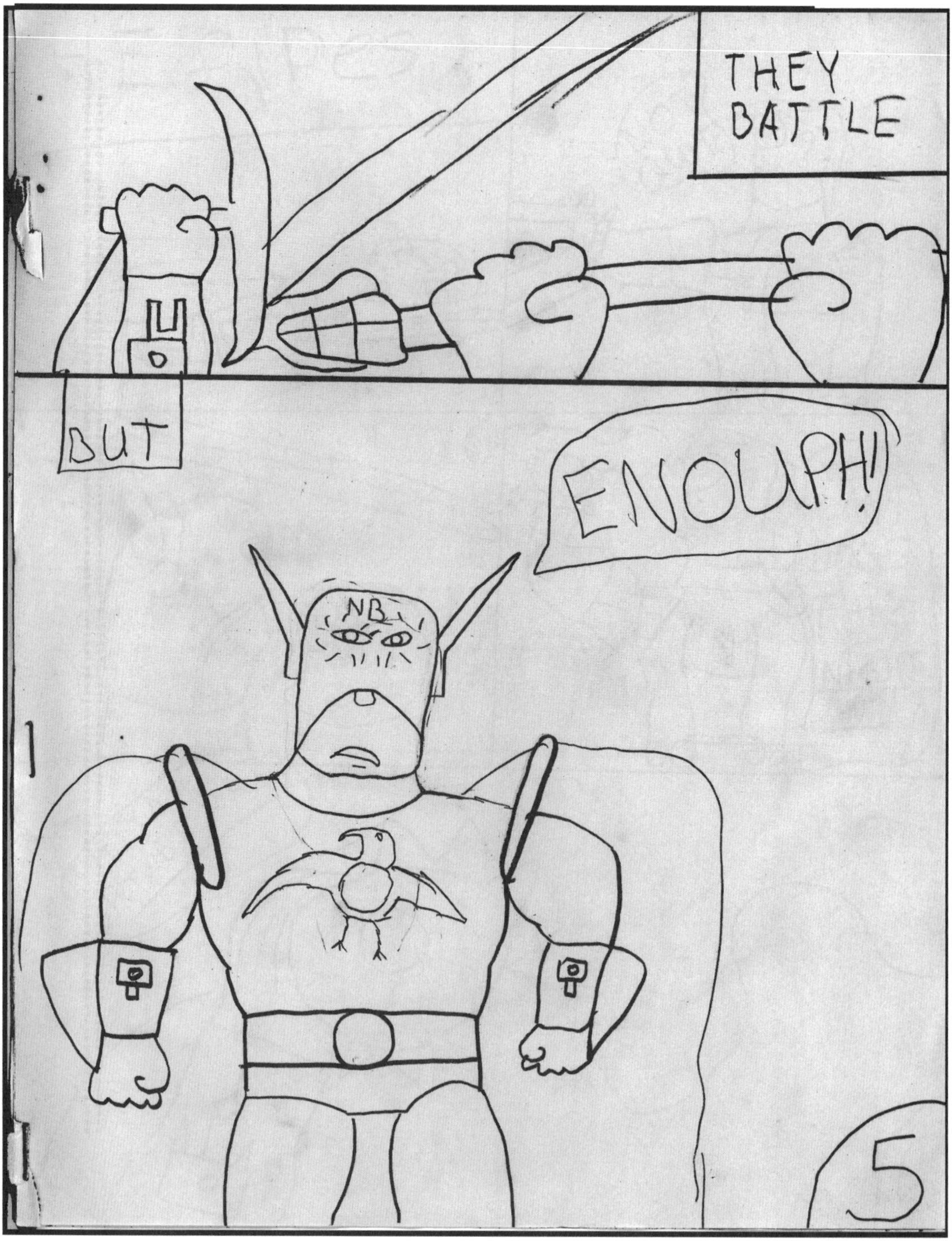
THEY BATTLE
BUT
ENOUPH!
NB
5

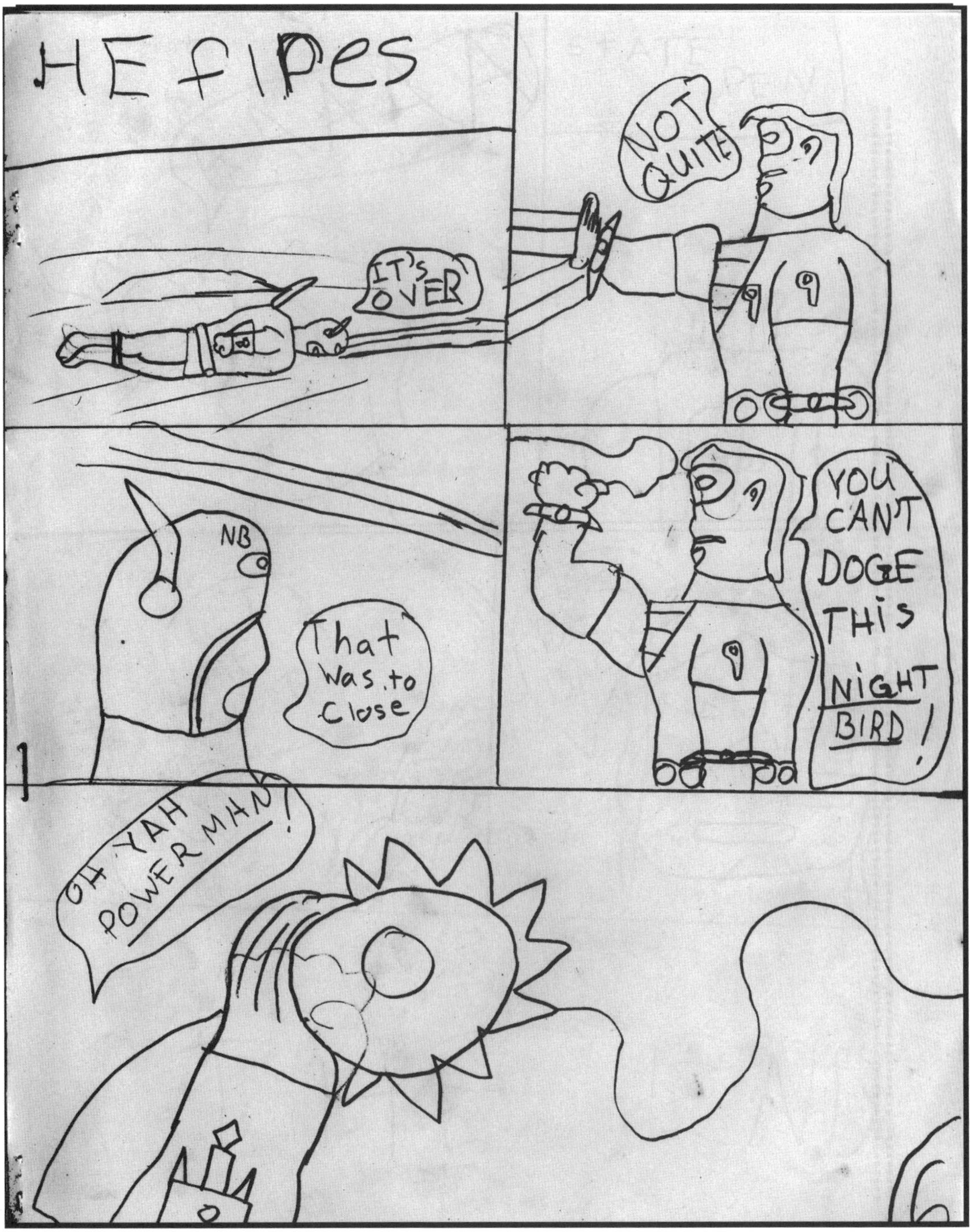
HE fIDes
IT'S OVER
NOT QUITE
NB
That was to Close
YOU CAN'T DOGE THIS NIGHT BIRD!
OH YAH POWERMAN!

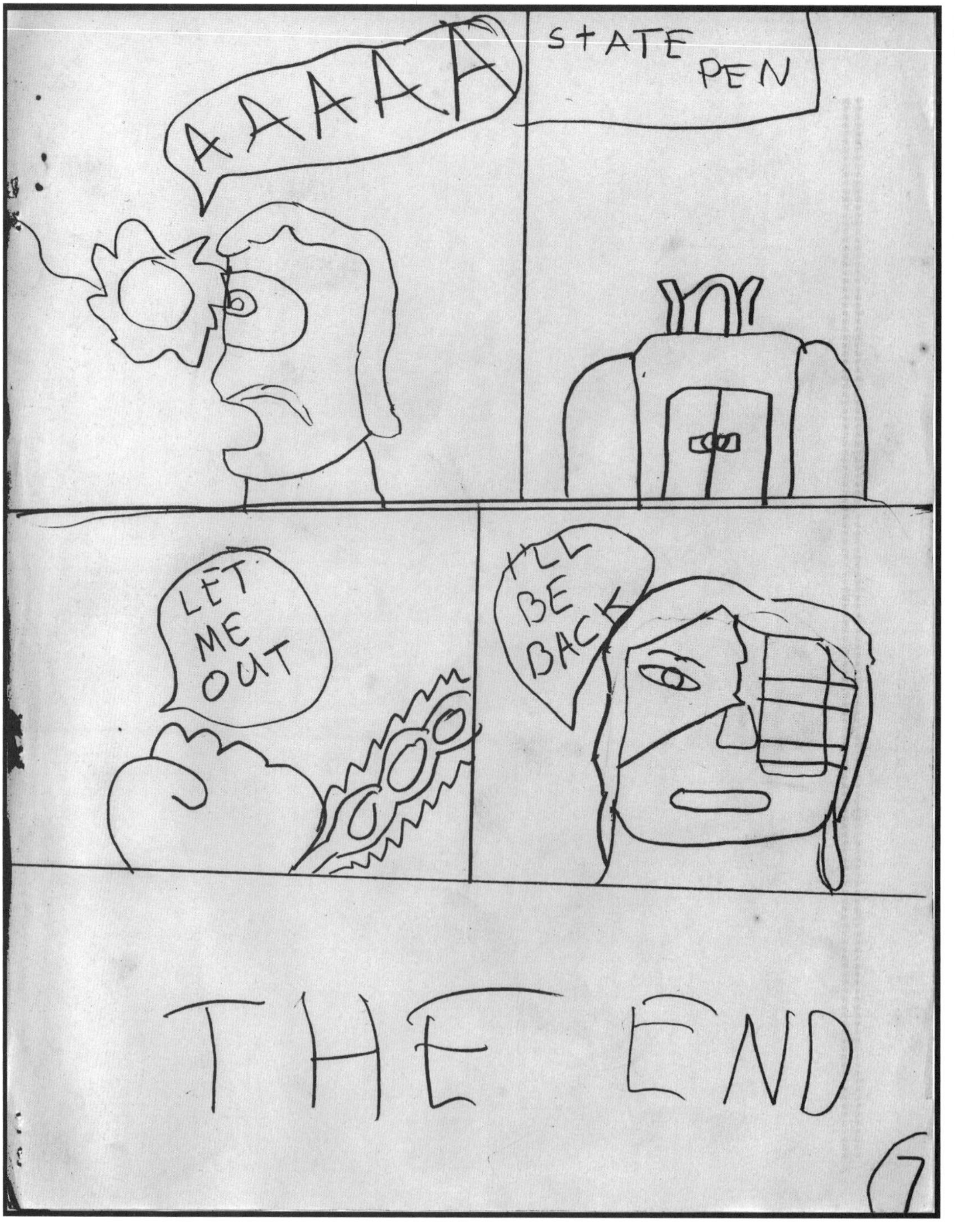
AAAAA
STATE PEN
LET ME OUT
I'LL BE BACK
THE END
7

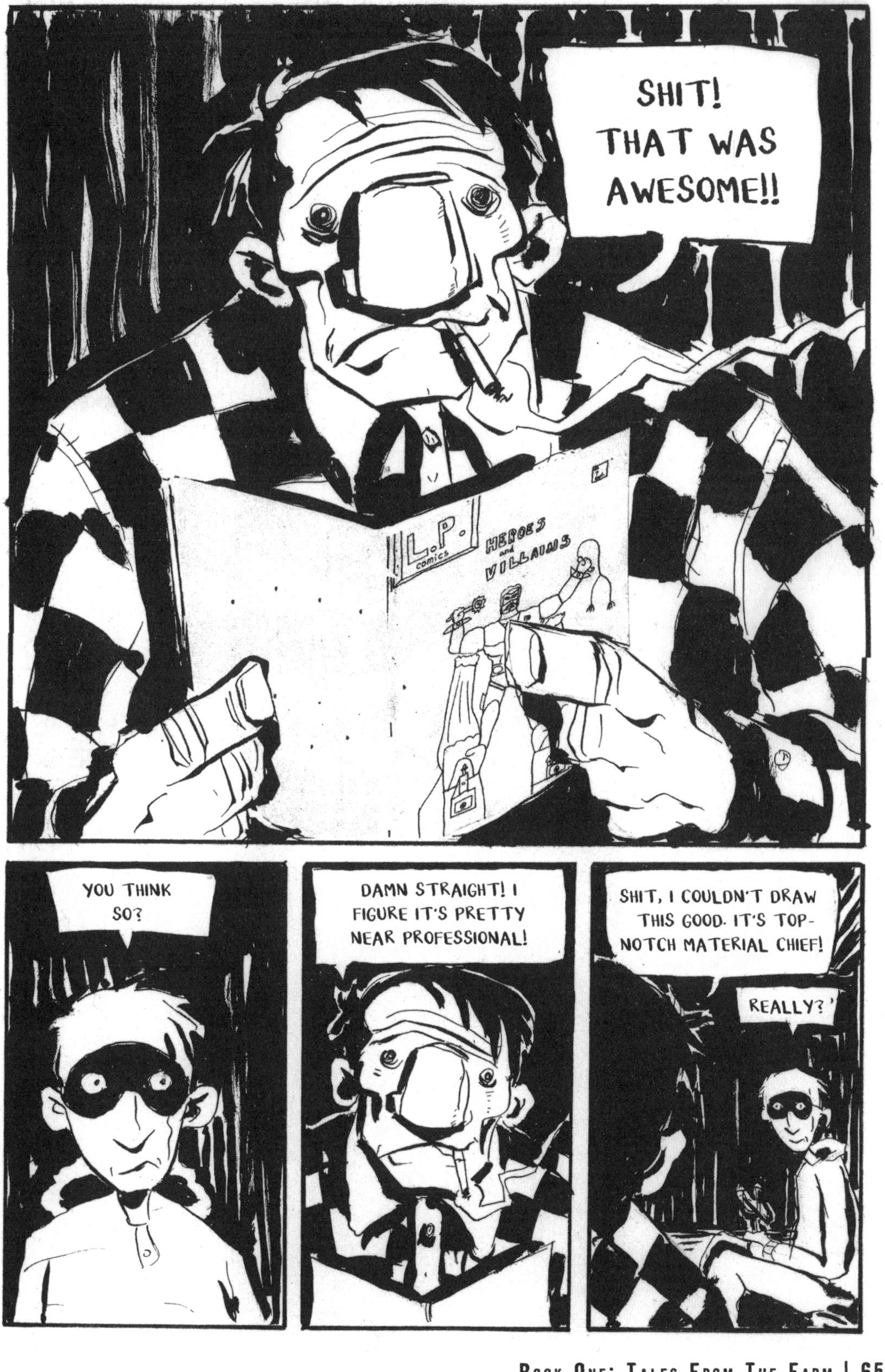
SHIT! THAT WAS AWESOME!!
L.P. comics
HEROES and VILLAINS
YOU THINK SO?
DAMN STRAIGHT! I FIGURE IT'S PRETTY NEAR PROFESSIONAL!
SHIT, I COULDN'T DRAW THIS GOOD. IT'S TOP-NOTCH MATERIAL CHIEF!
REALLY?

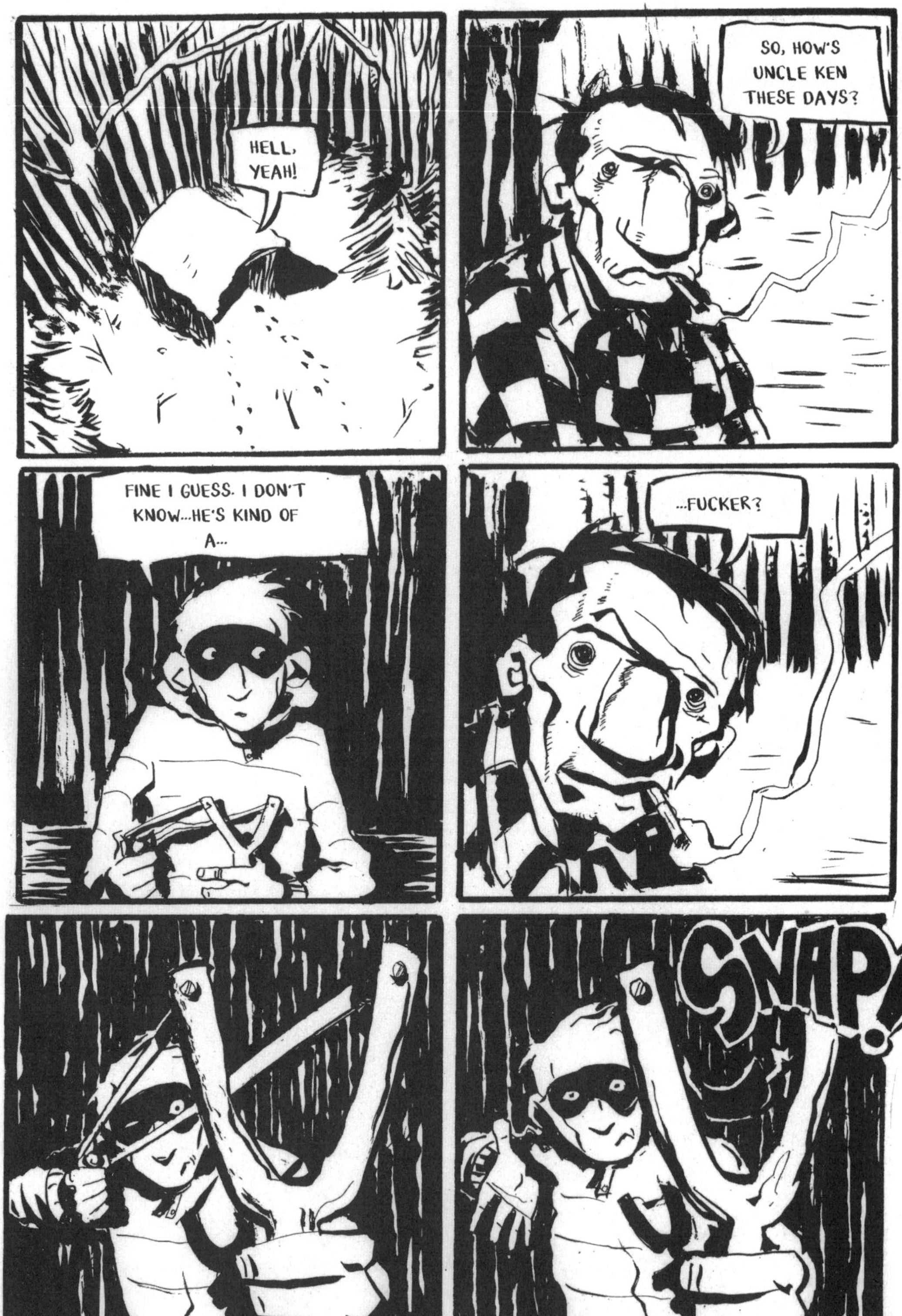
HELL, YEAH!
SO, HOW'S UNCLE KEN THESE DAYS?
FINE I GUESS. I DON'T KNOW...HE'S KIND OF A...
...FUCKER?
SNAP!

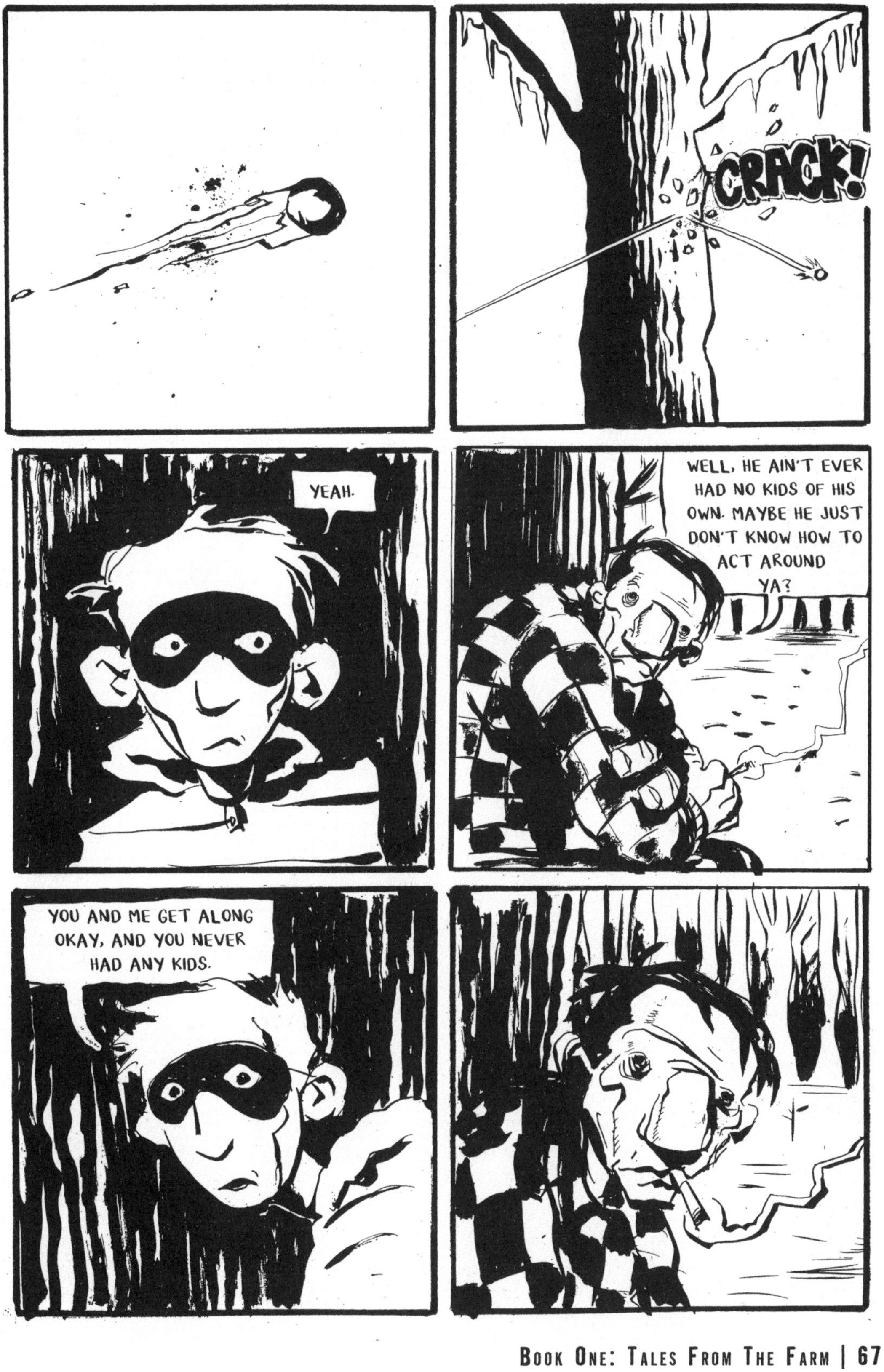
CRACK!
YEAH.
WELL, HE AIN'T EVER HAD NO KIDS OF HIS OWN. MAYBE HE JUST DON'T KNOW HOW TO ACT AROUND YA?
YOU AND ME GET ALONG OKAY, AND YOU NEVER HAD ANY KIDS.

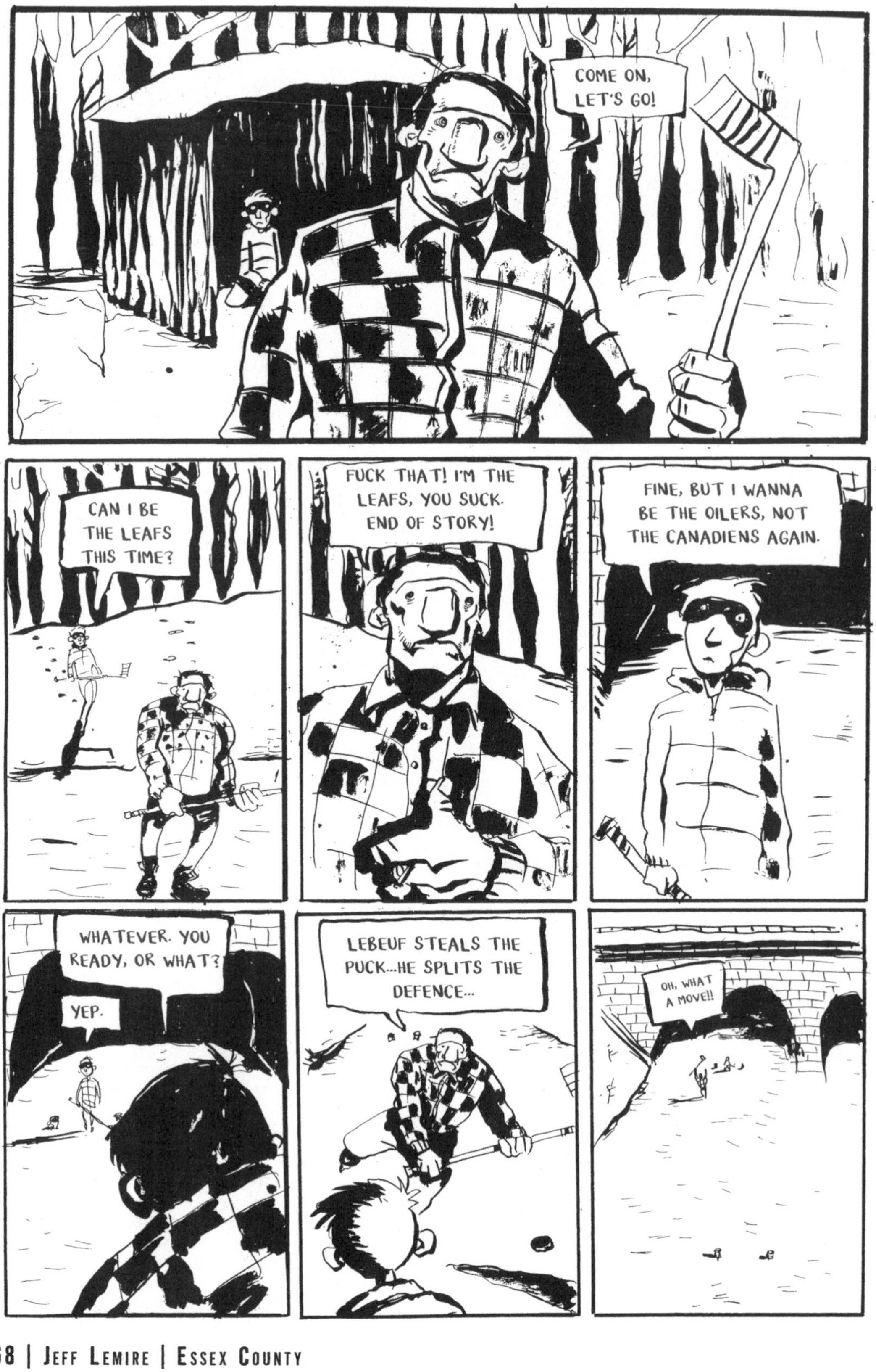
COME ON, LET'S GO!
CAN I BE THE LEAFS THIS TIME?
FUCK THAT! I'M THE LEAFS, YOU SUCK. END OF STORY!
FINE, BUT I WANNA BE THE OILERS, NOT THE CANADIENS AGAIN.
WHATEVER. YOU READY, OR WHAT?
YEP.
LEBEUF STEALS THE PUCK...HE SPLITS THE DEFENCE...
OH, WHAT A MOVE!!

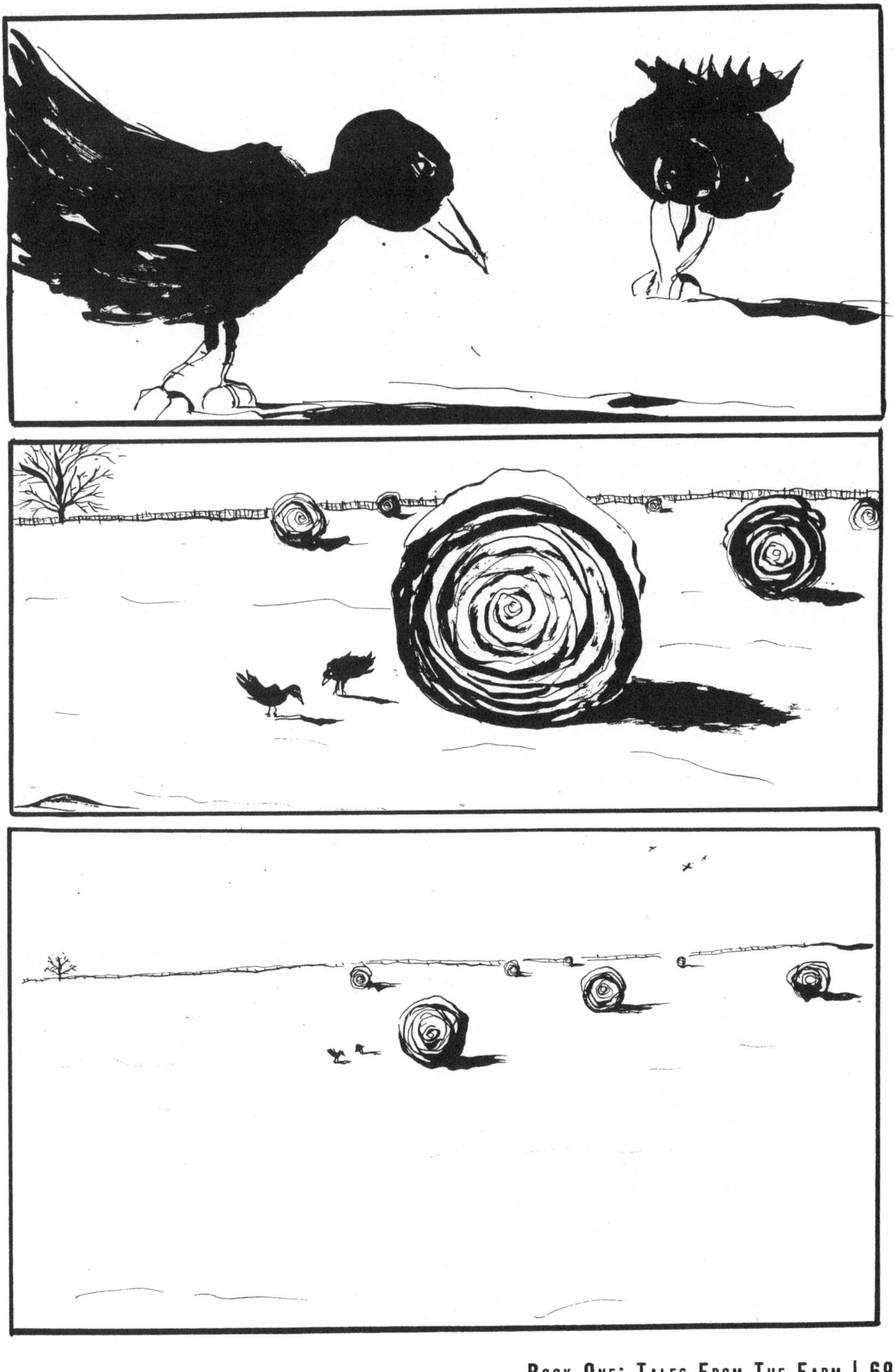

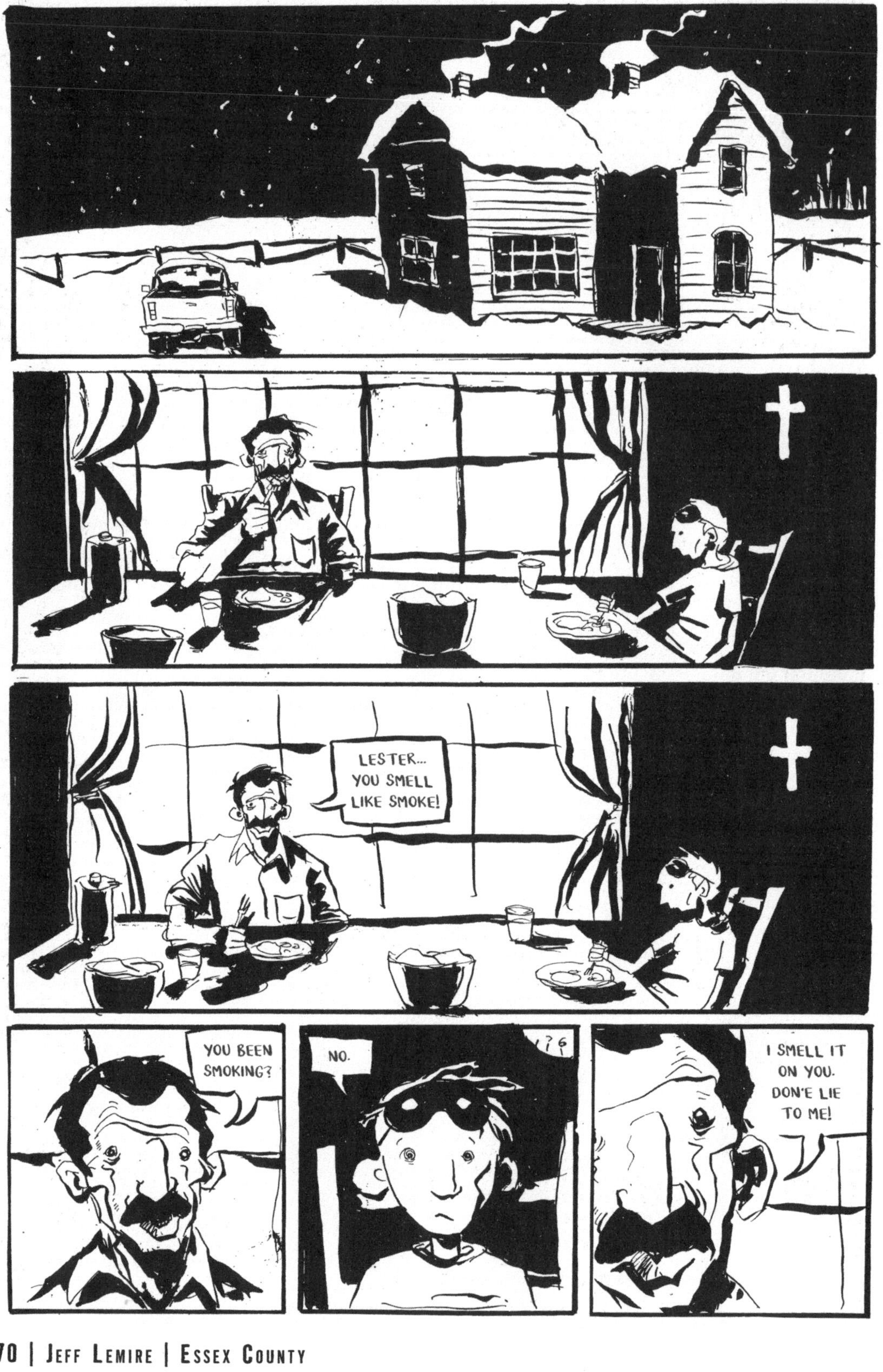
LESTER... YOU SMELL LIKE SMOKE!
YOU BEEN SMOKING?
NO.
I SMELL IT ON YOU. DON'T LIE TO ME!

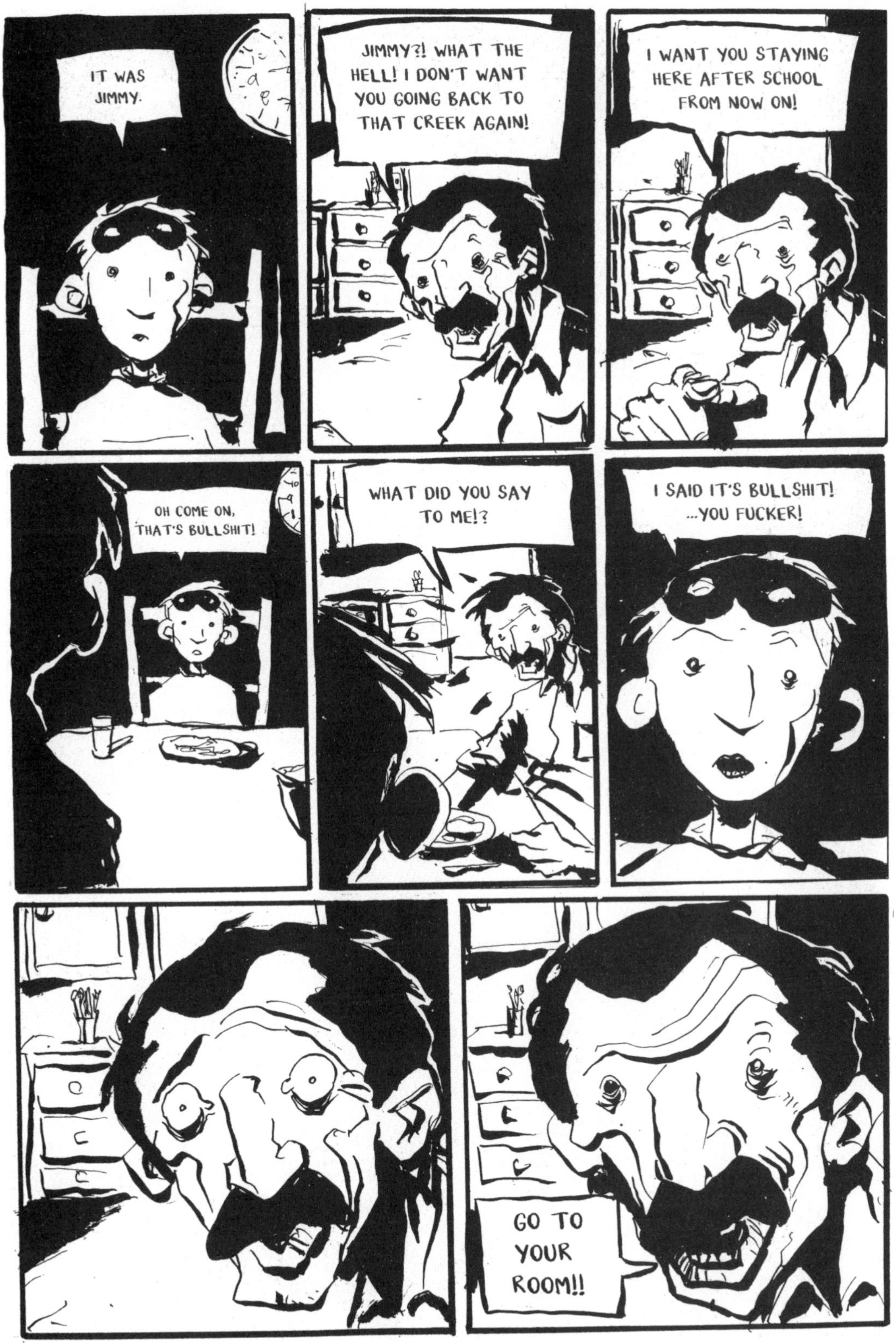
IT WAS JIMMY.
JIMMY?! WHAT THE HELL! I DON'T WANT YOU GOING BACK TO THAT CREEK AGAIN!
I WANT YOU STAYING HERE AFTER SCHOOL FROM NOW ON!
OH COME ON, THAT'S BULLSHIT!
WHAT DID YOU SAY TO ME!?
I SAID IT'S BULLSHIT! ...YOU FUCKER!
GO TO YOUR ROOM!!

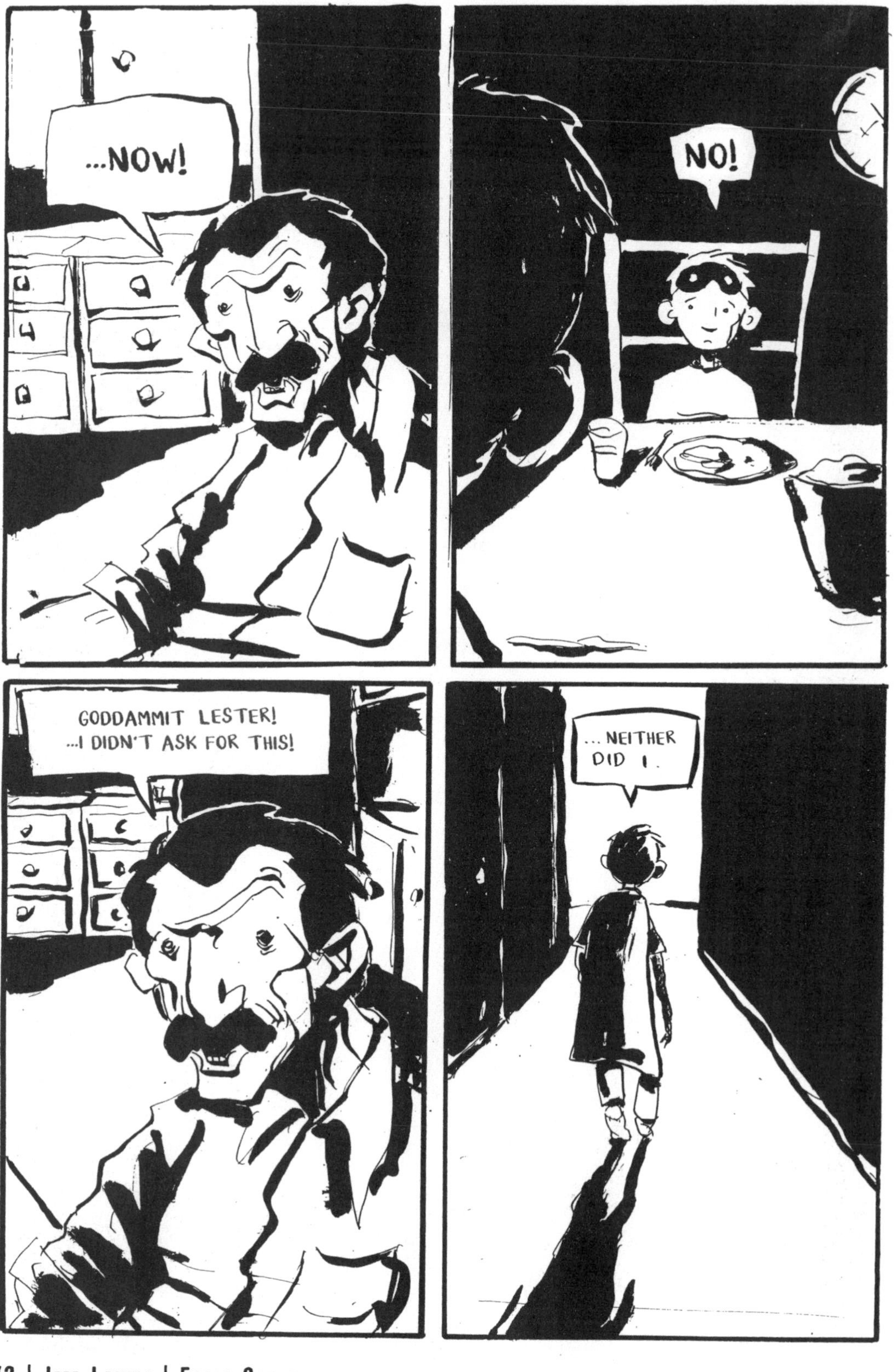
...NOW!
NO!
GODDAMMIT LESTER!
...I DIDN'T ASK FOR THIS!
...NEITHER DID I.

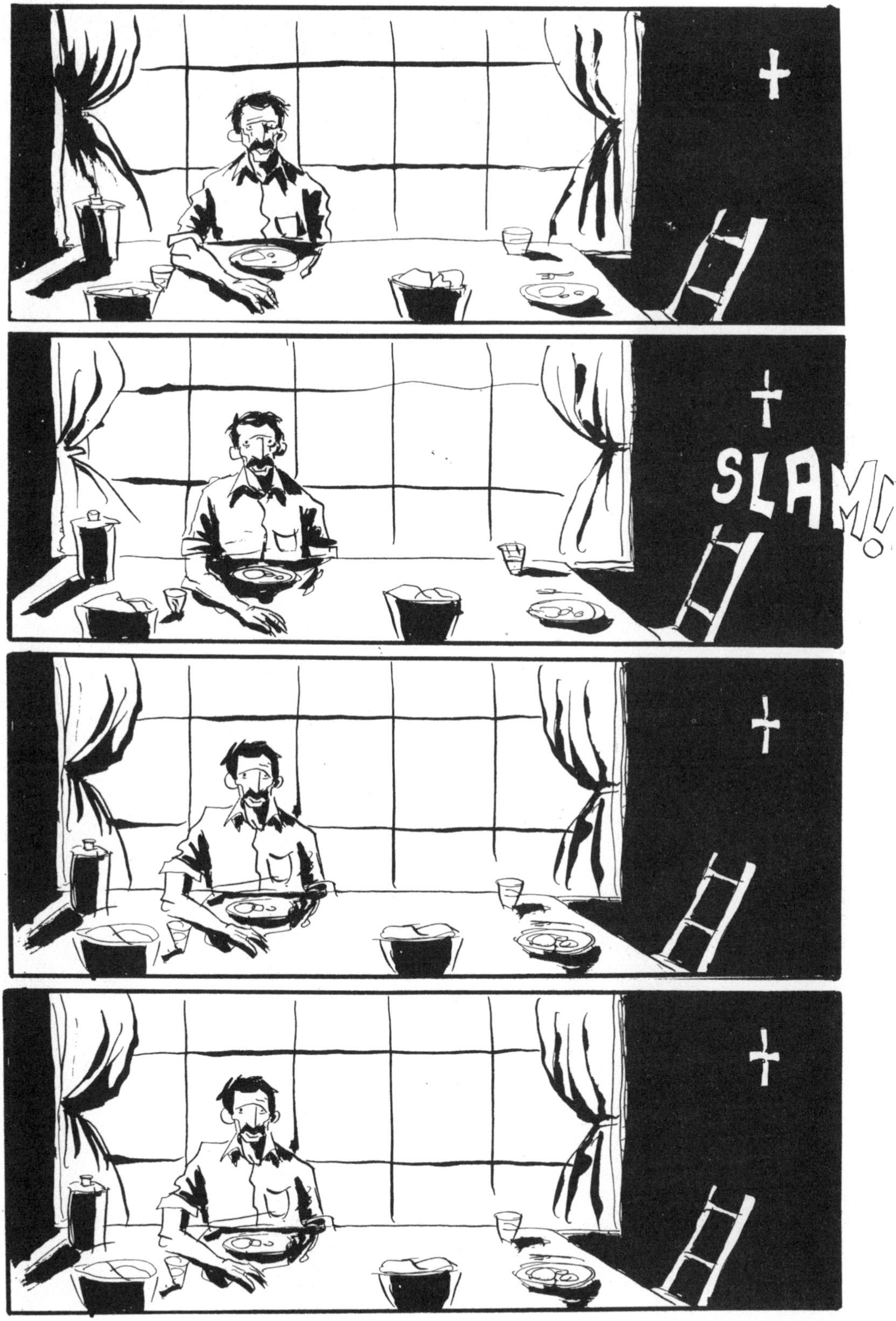
SLAM!

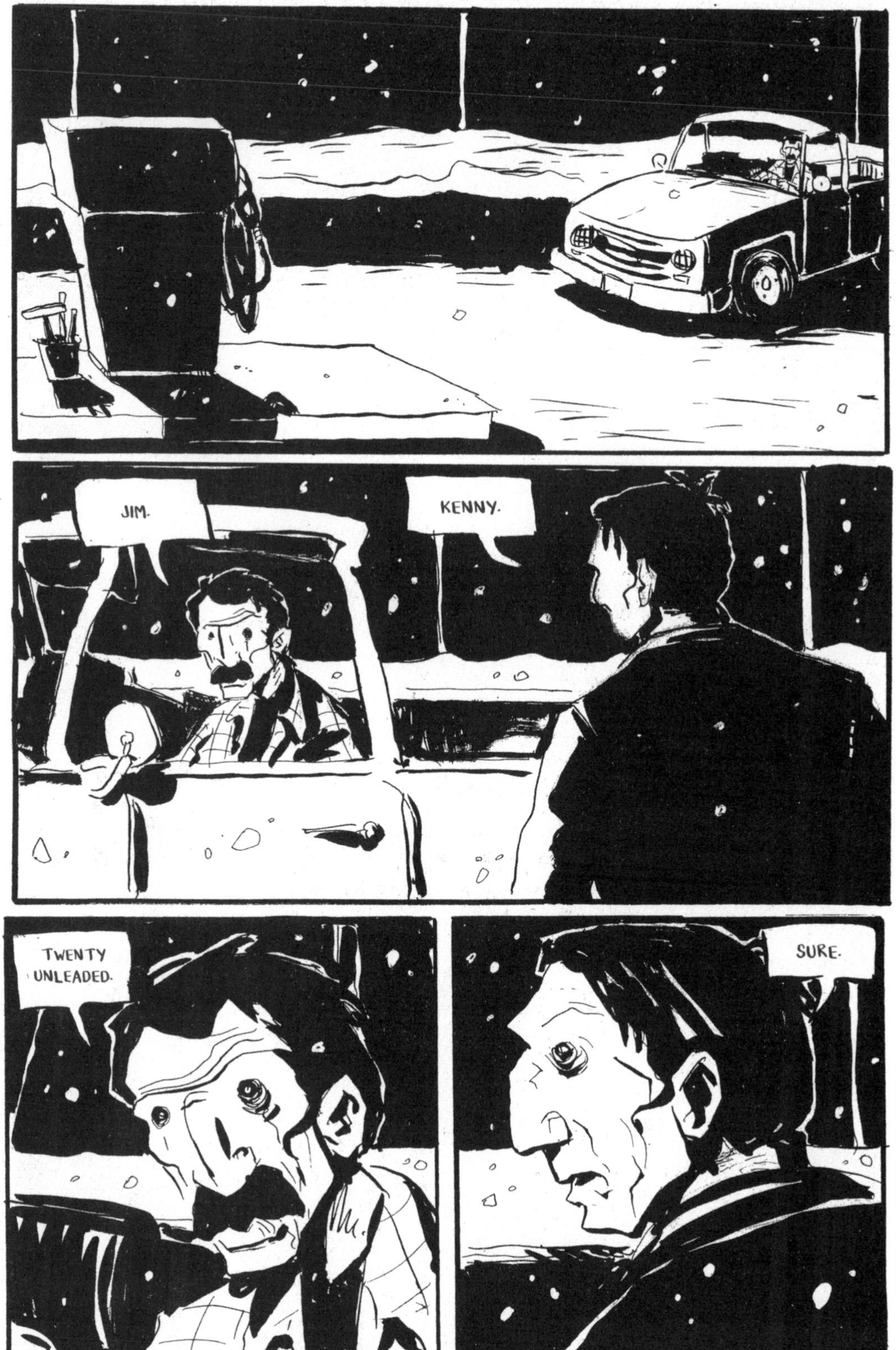
JIM.
KENNY.
TWENTY UNLEADED.
SURE.

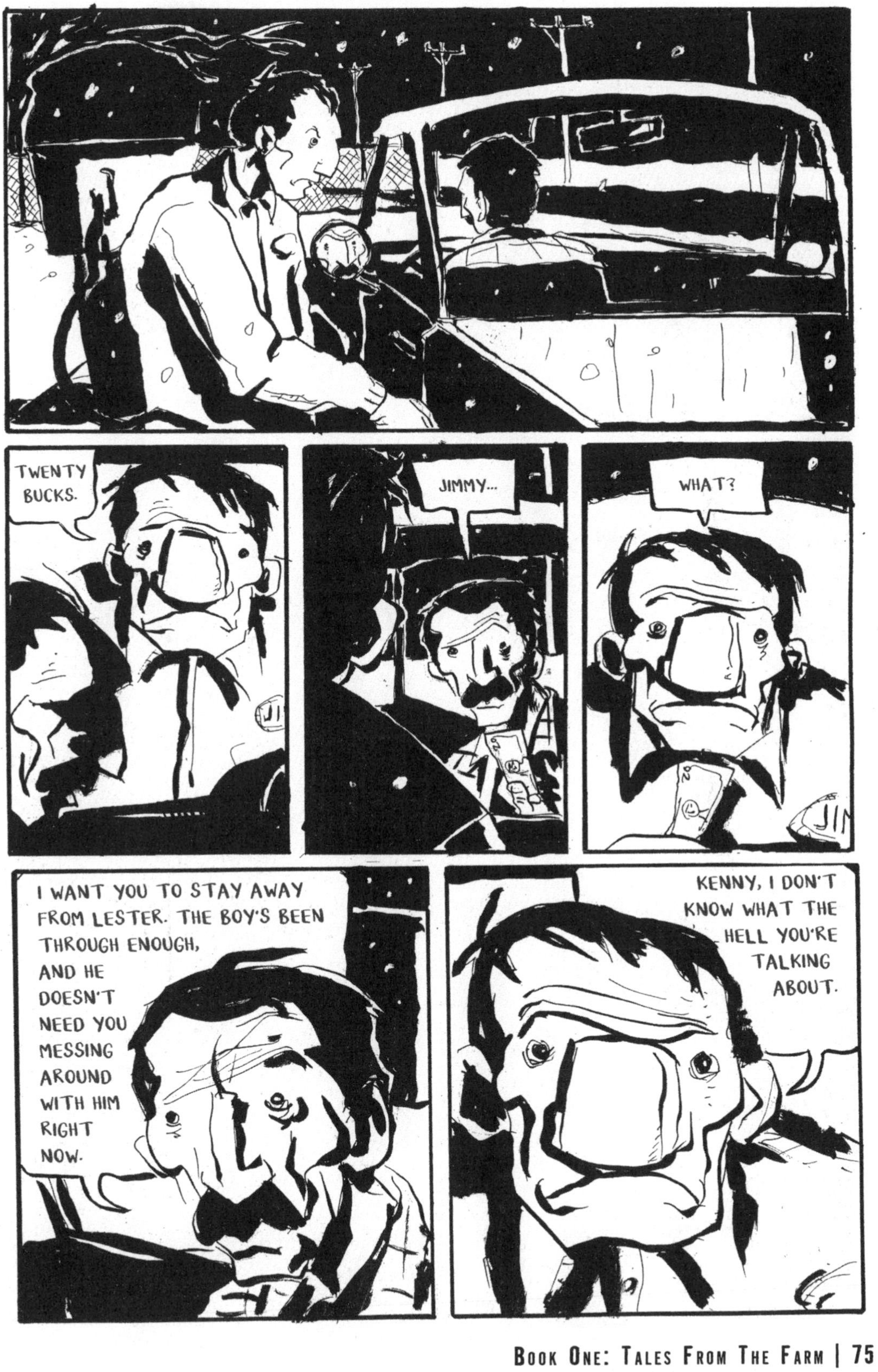
TWENTY BUCKS.
JIMMY...
WHAT?
I WANT YOU TO STAY AWAY FROM LESTER. THE BOY'S BEEN THROUGH ENOUGH, AND HE DOESN'T NEED YOU MESSING AROUND WITH HIM RIGHT NOW.
KENNY, I DON'T KNOW WHAT THE HELL YOU'RE TALKING ABOUT.

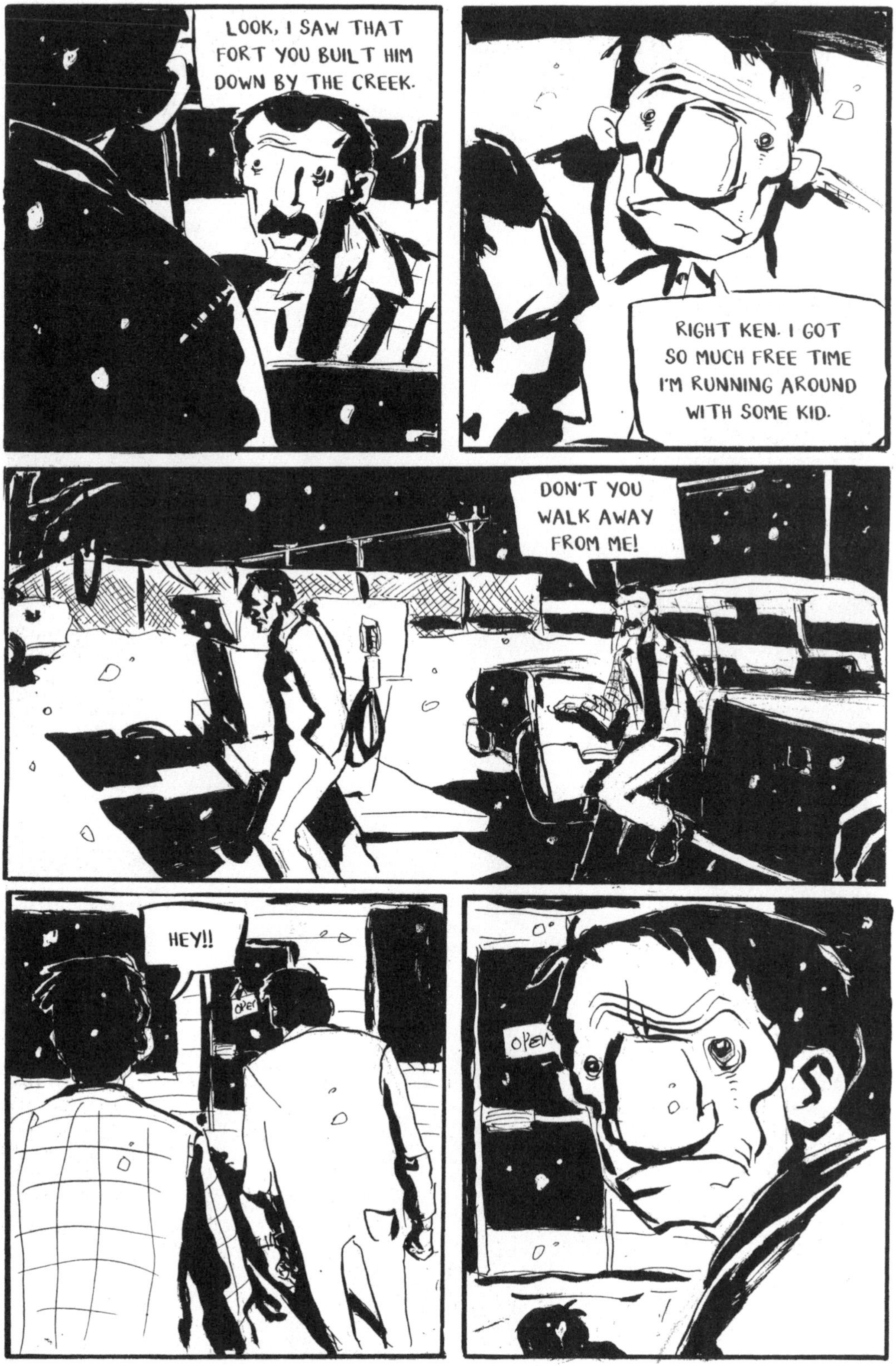
LOOK, I SAW THAT FORT YOU BUILT HIM DOWN BY THE CREEK.
RIGHT KEN. I GOT SO MUCH FREE TIME I'M RUNNING AROUND WITH SOME KID.
DON'T YOU WALK AWAY FROM ME!
HEY!!
OPEN
OPEN

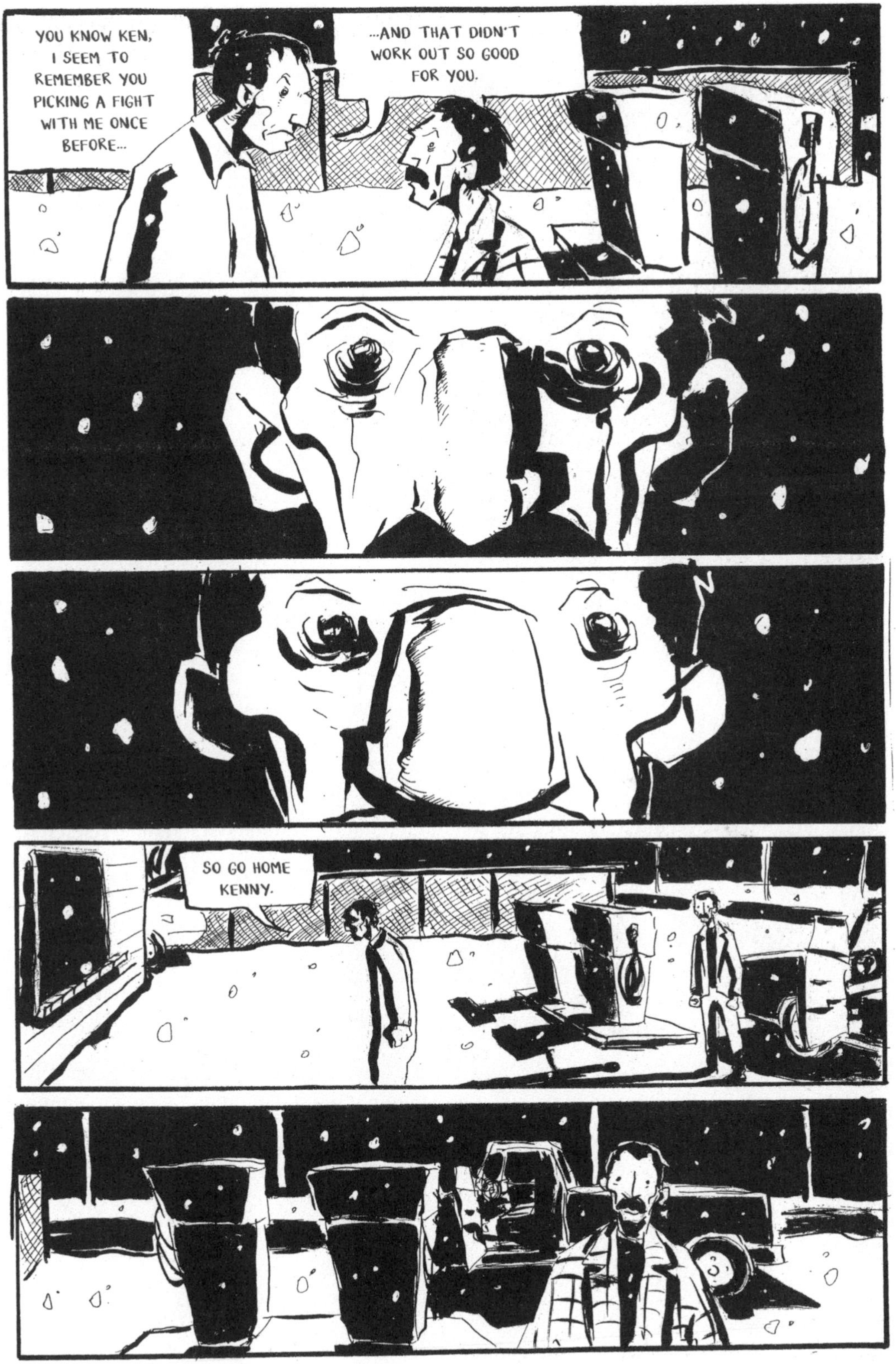
YOU KNOW KEN, I SEEM TO REMEMBER YOU PICKING A FIGHT WITH ME ONCE BEFORE...
...AND THAT DIDN'T WORK OUT SO GOOD FOR YOU.
SO GO HOME KENNY.

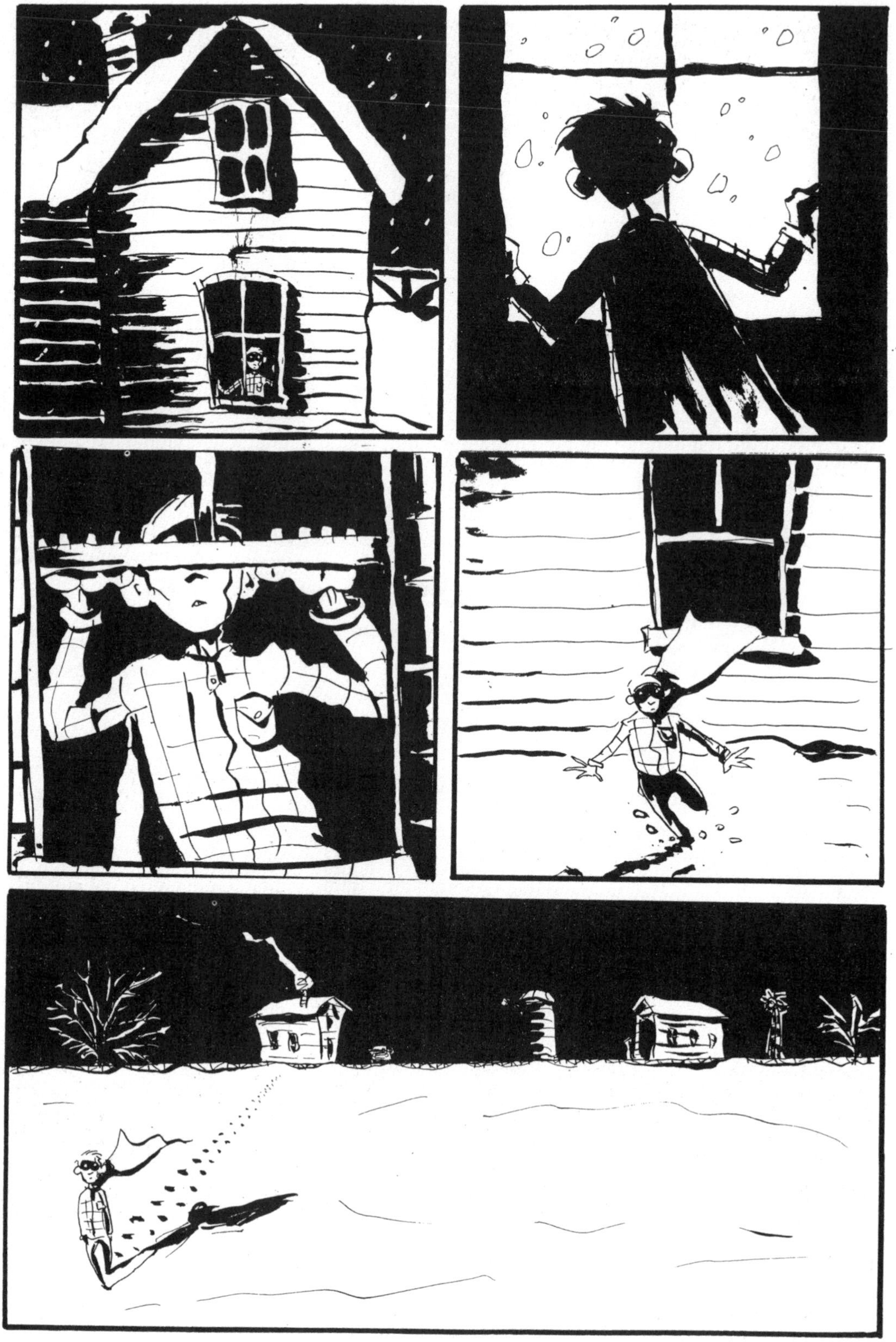

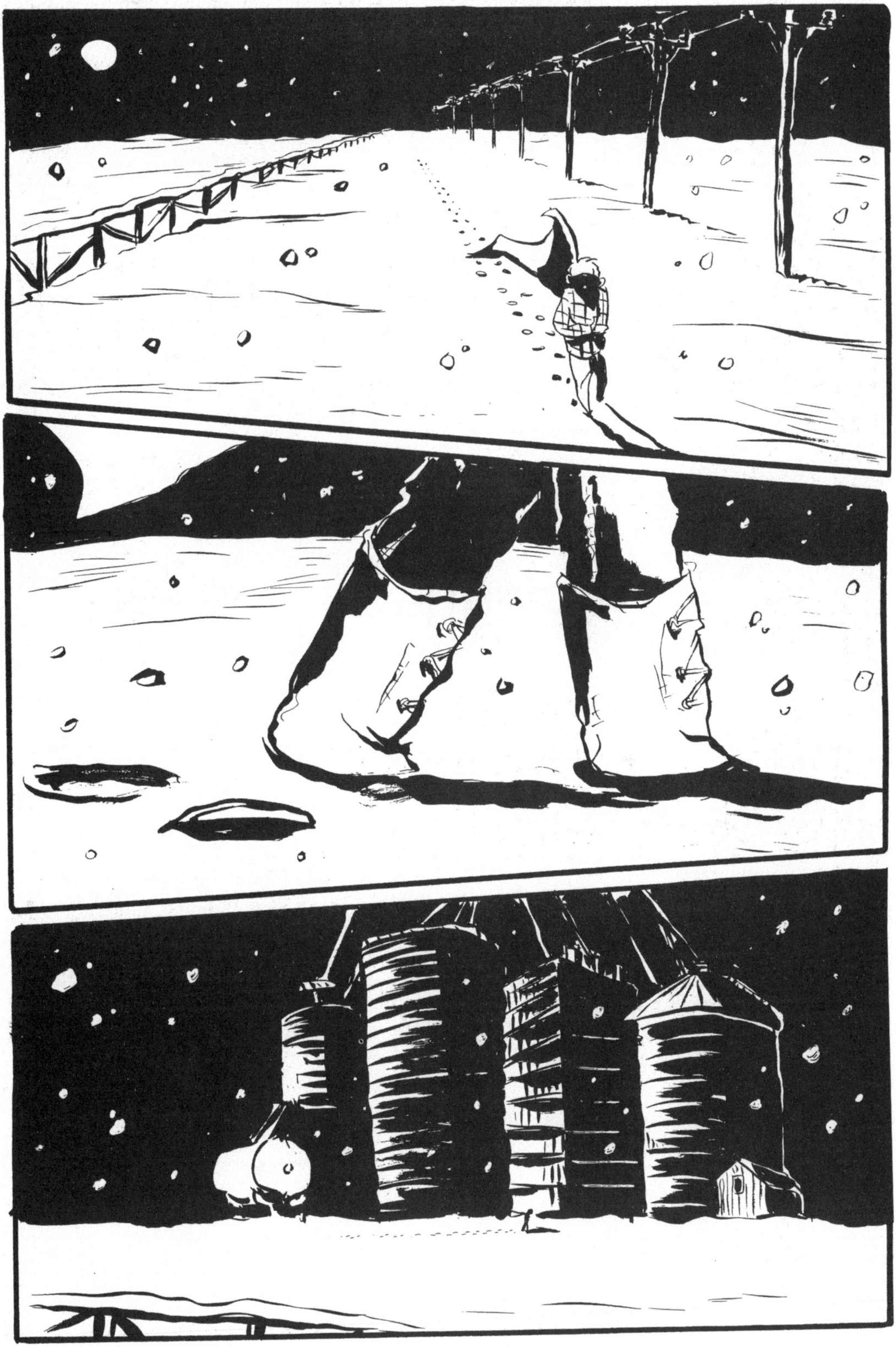

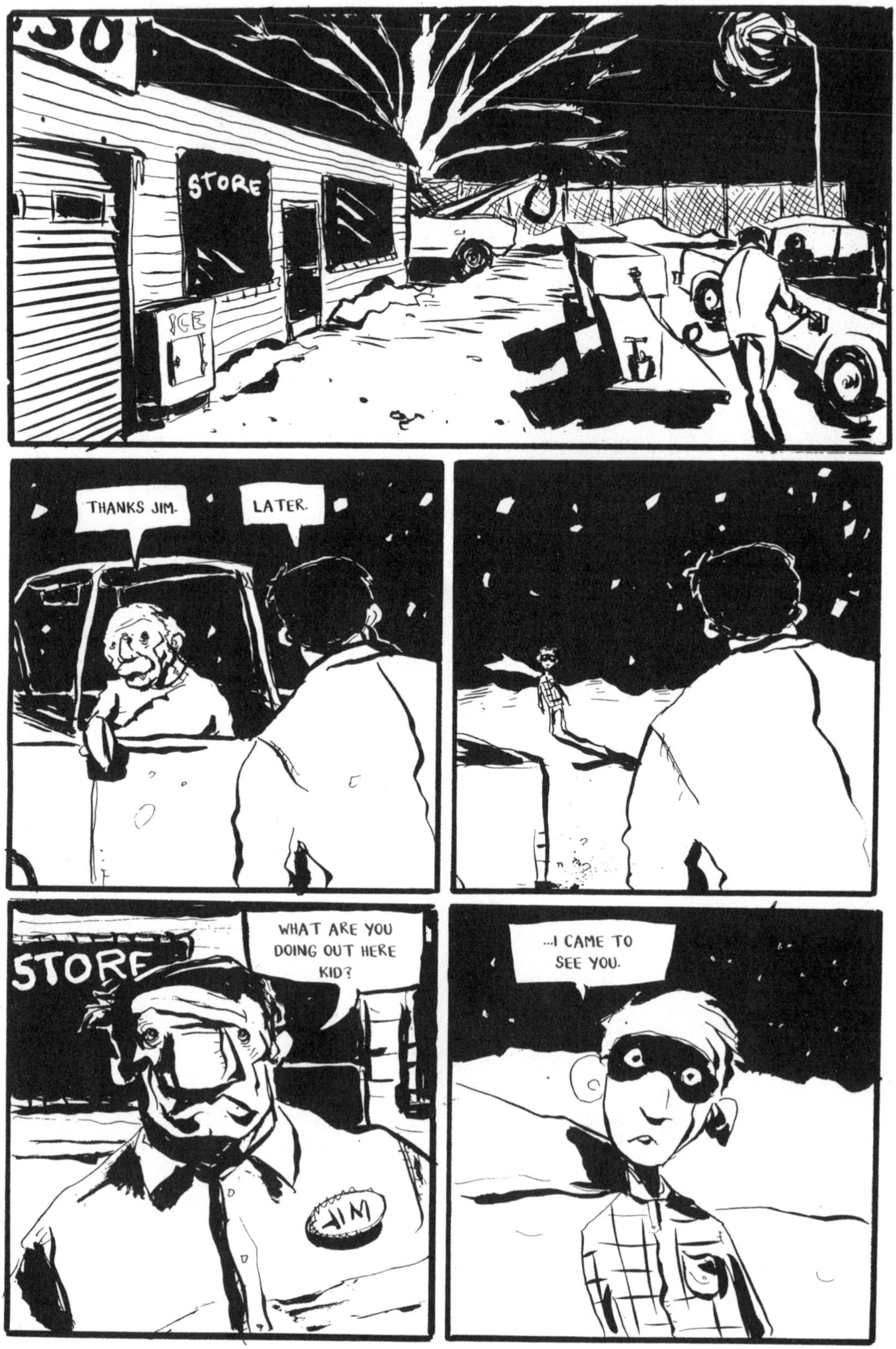

STORE
ICE
THANKS JIM.
LATER.
STORE
WHAT ARE YOU DOING OUT HERE KID?
...I CAME TO SEE YOU.

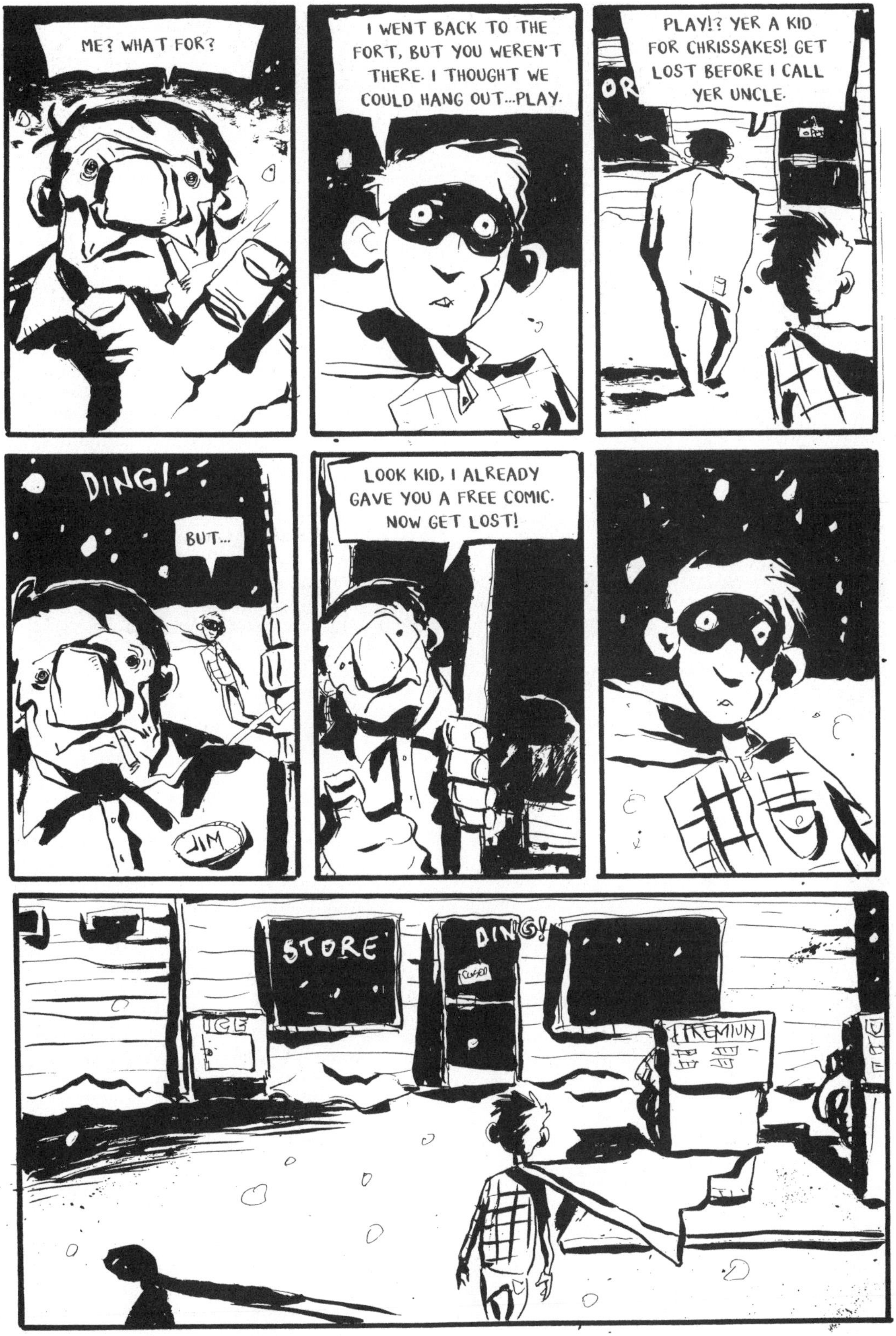

ME? WHAT FOR?
I WENT BACK TO THE FORT, BUT YOU WEREN'T THERE. I THOUGHT WE COULD HANG OUT...PLAY.
PLAY!? YER A KID FOR CHRISSAKES! GET LOST BEFORE I CALL YER UNCLE.
DING!
BUT...
JIM
LOOK KID, I ALREADY GAVE YOU A FREE COMIC. NOW GET LOST!
STORE
DING!
ICE
PREMIUM

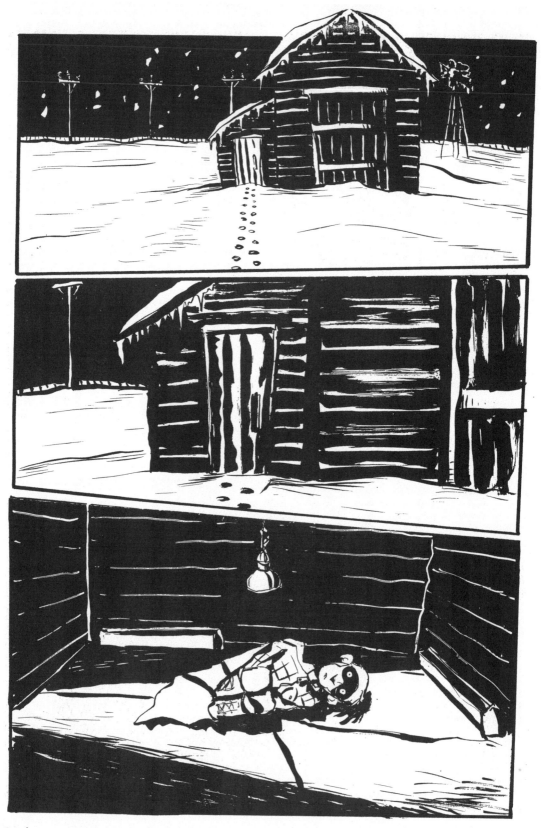

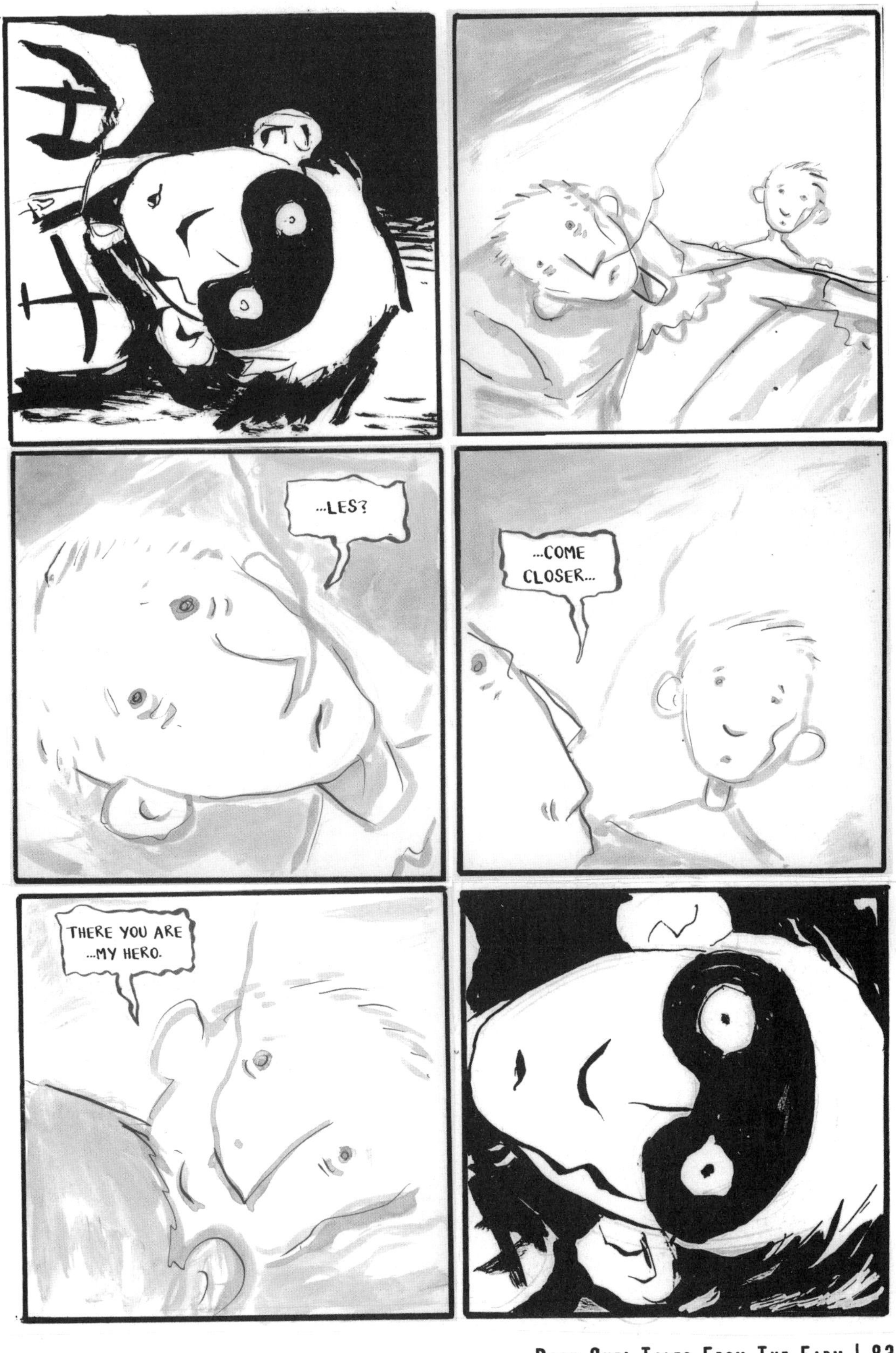
...LES?
...COME CLOSER...
THERE YOU ARE ...MY HERO.

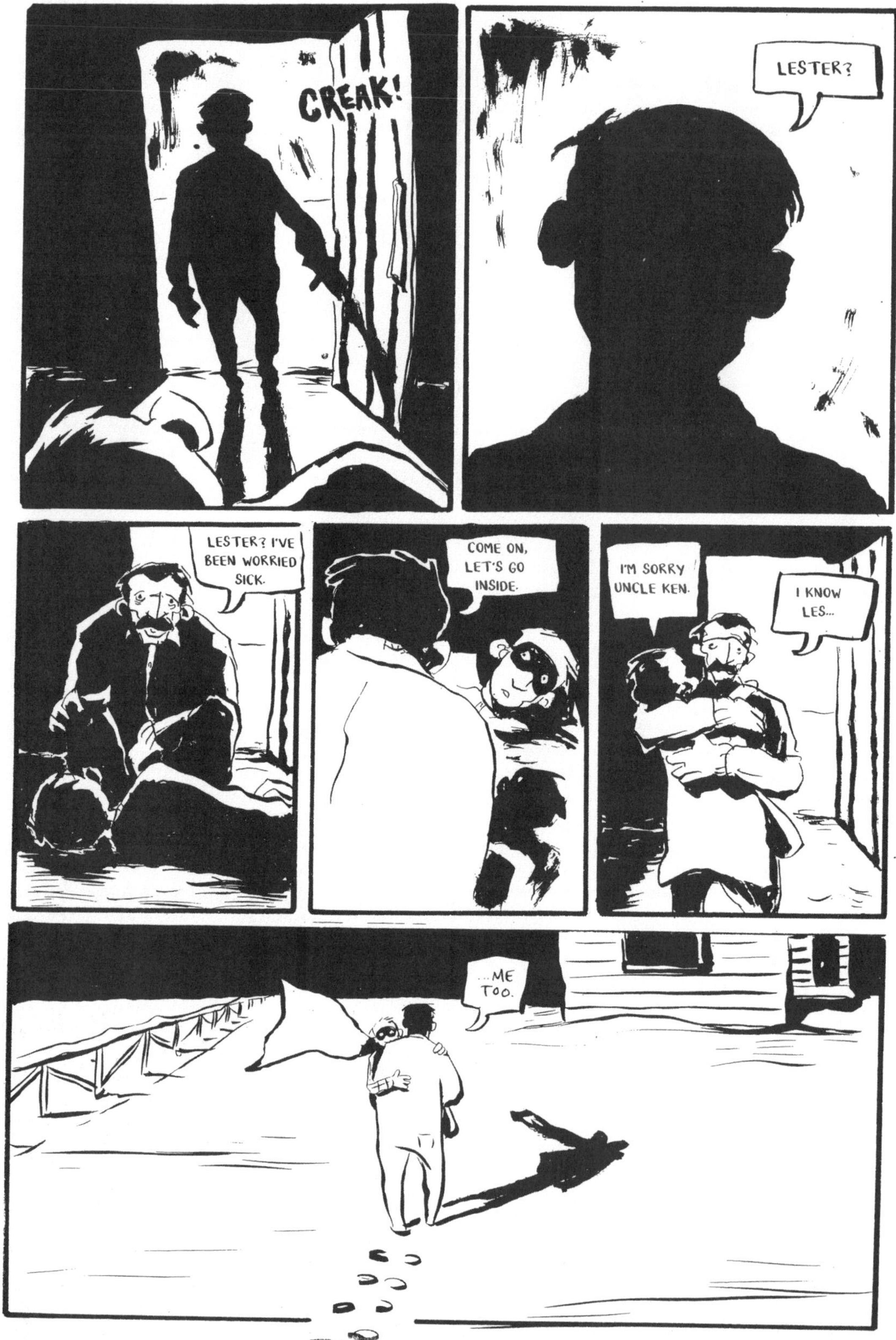
CREAK!
LESTER?
LESTER? I'VE BEEN WORRIED SICK.
COME ON, LET'S GO INSIDE.
I'M SORRY UNCLE KEN.
I KNOW LES...
...ME TOO.

SPRING

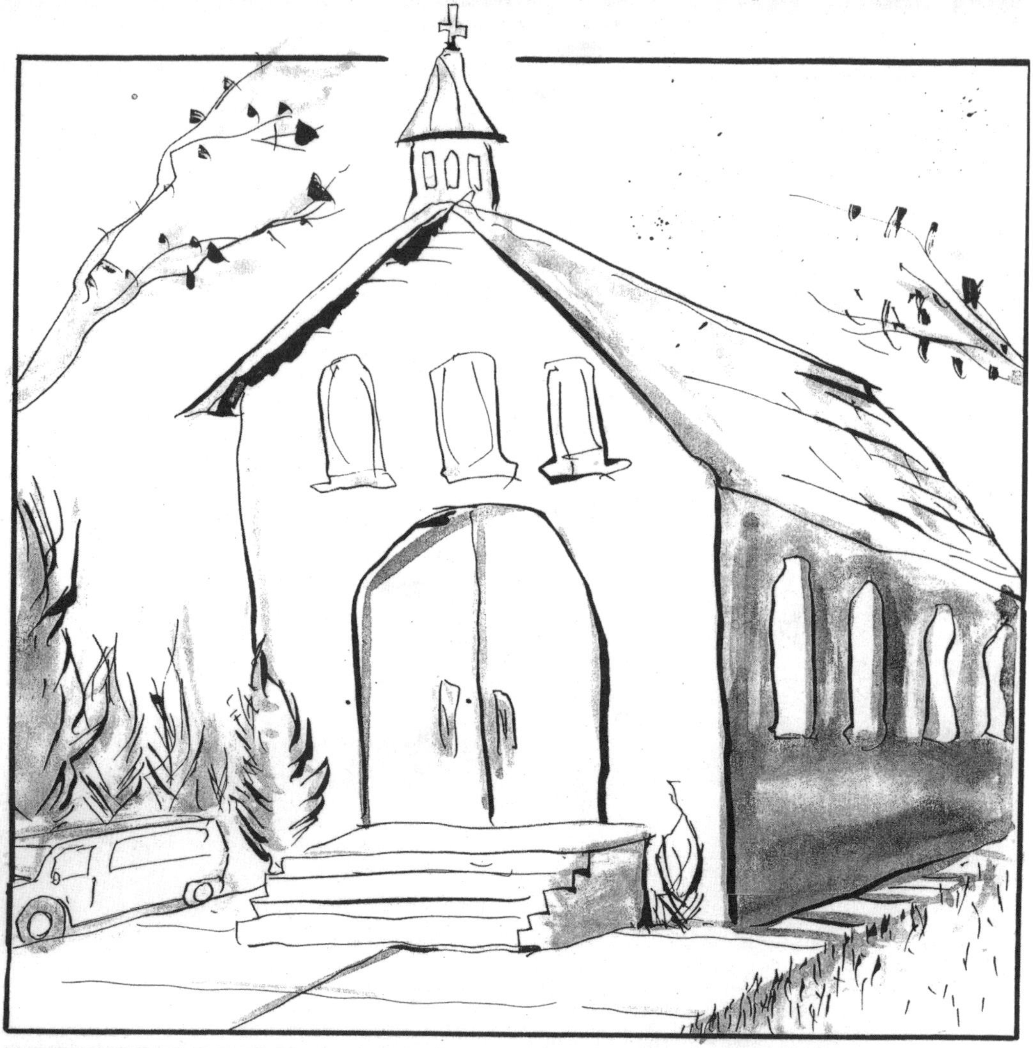

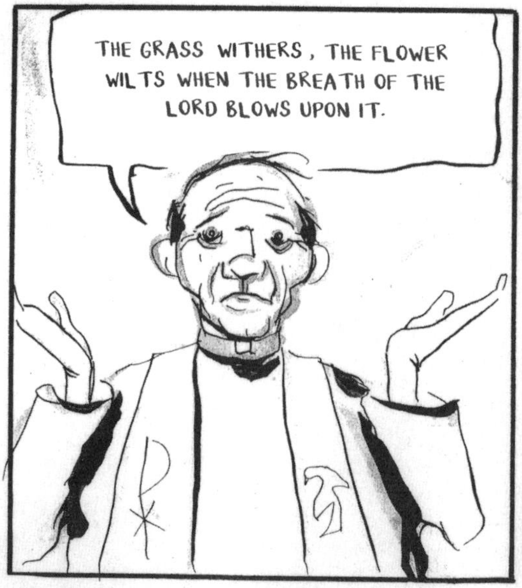
THE GRASS WITHERS, THE FLOWER WILTS WHEN THE BREATH OF THE LORD BLOWS UPON IT.

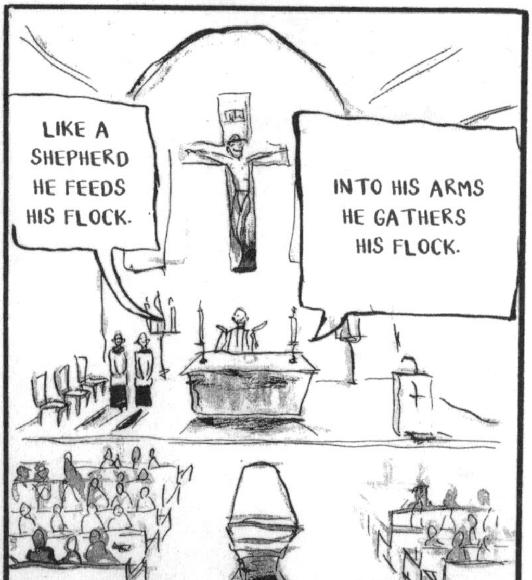
LIKE A SHEPHERD HE FEEDS HIS FLOCK.
INTO HIS ARMS HE GATHERS HIS FLOCK.

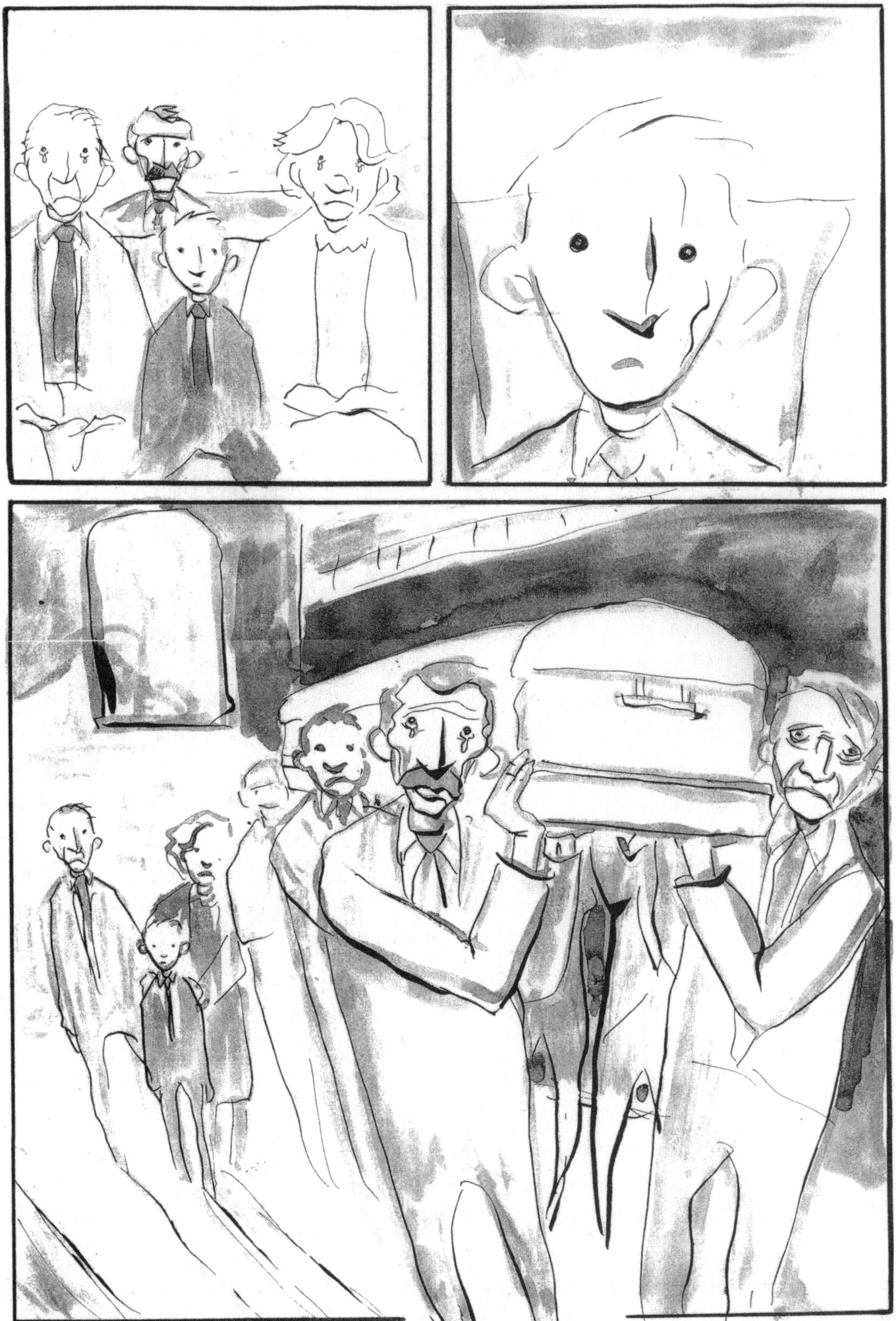

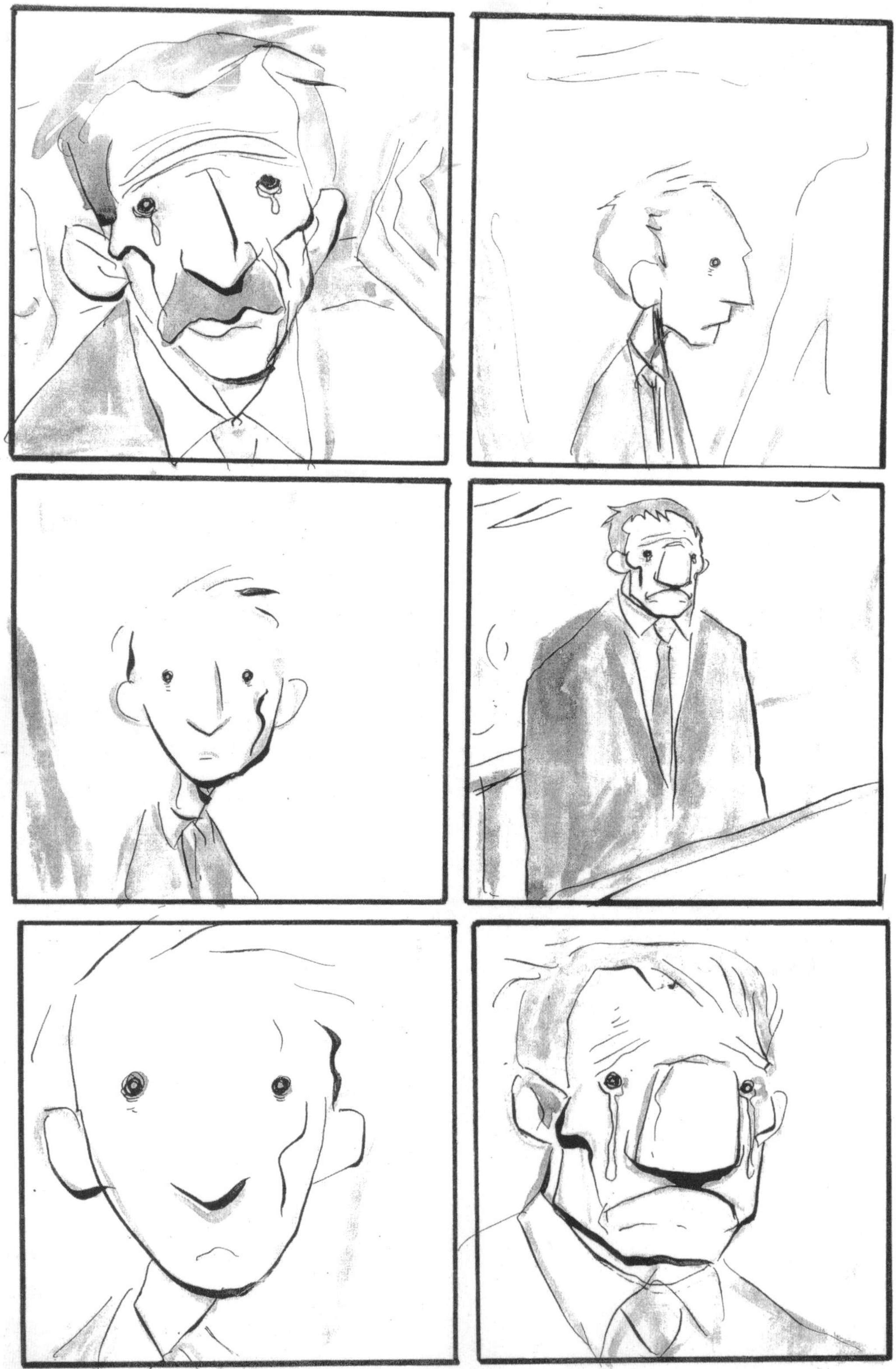

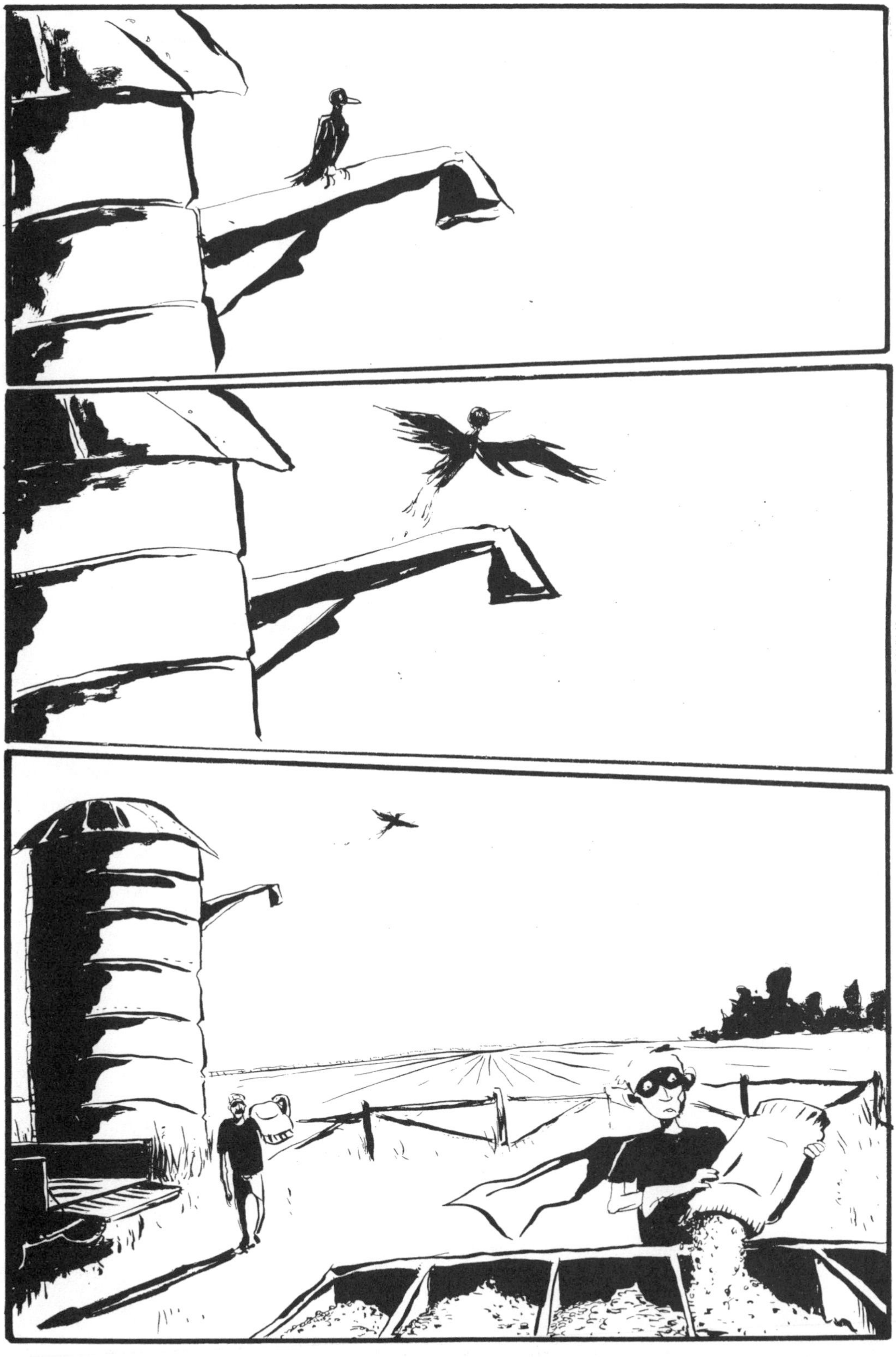

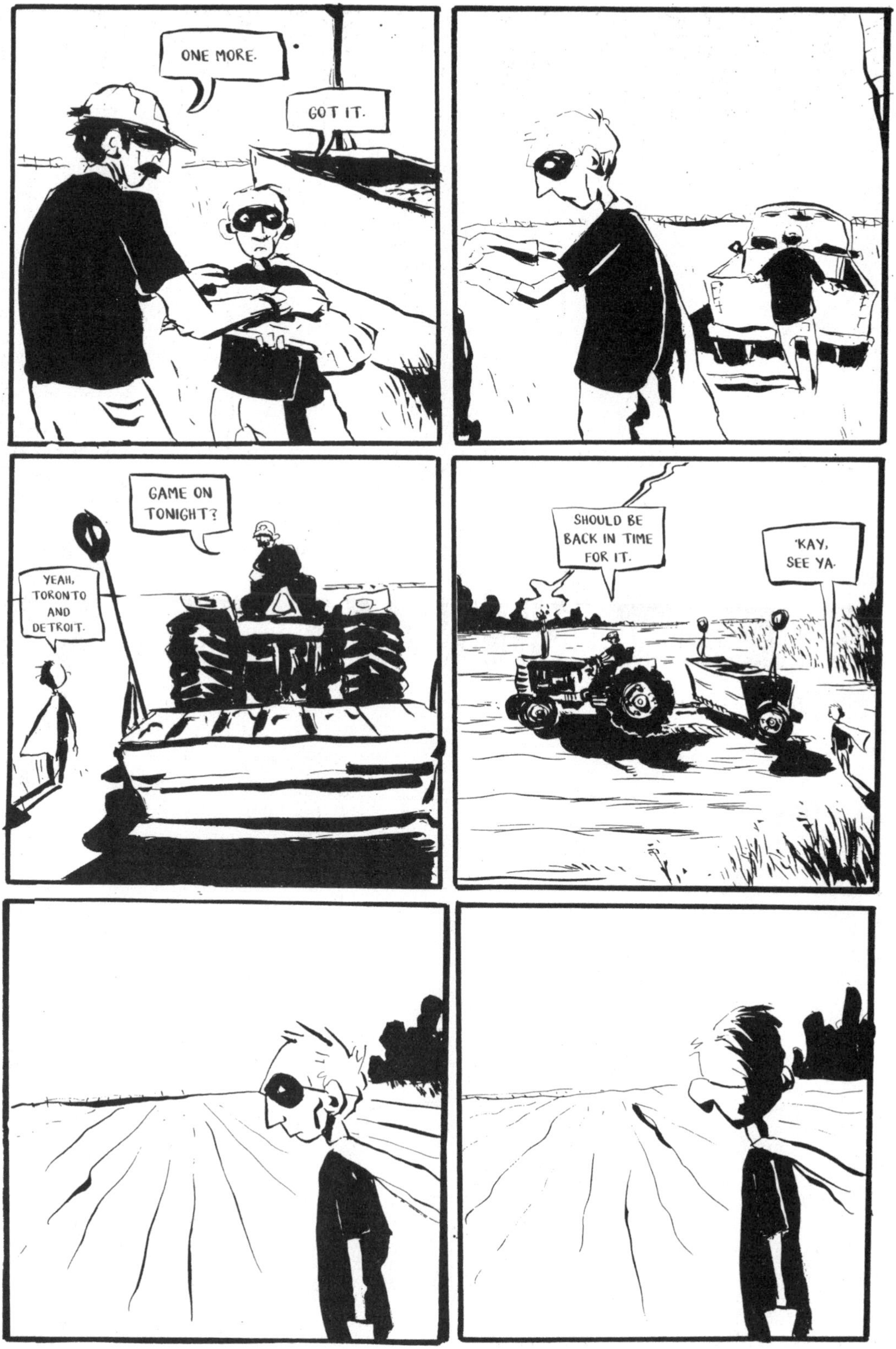
ONE MORE.
GOT IT.
GAME ON TONIGHT?
YEAH, TORONTO AND DETROIT.
SHOULD BE BACK IN TIME FOR IT.
'KAY, SEE YA.

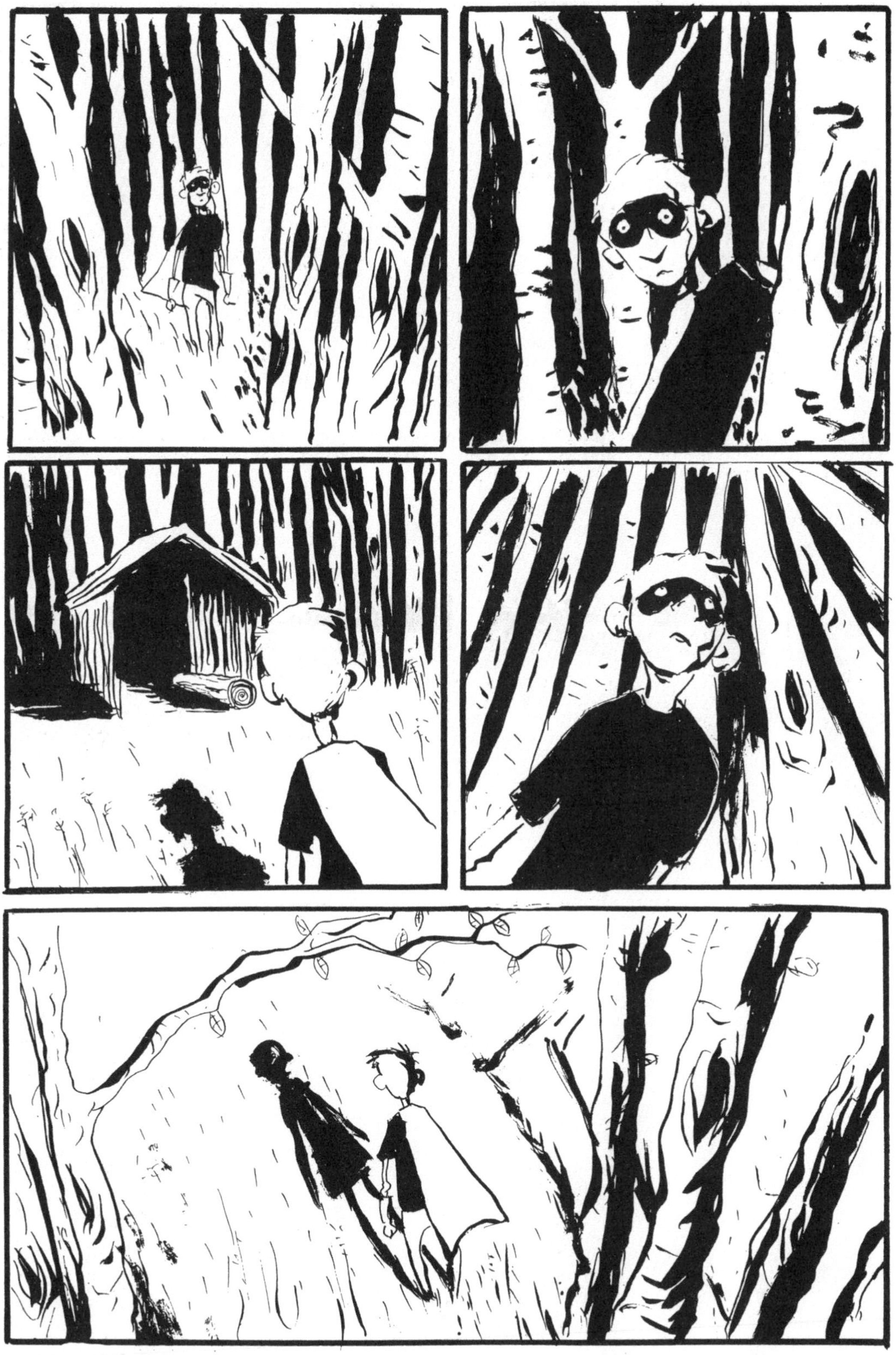

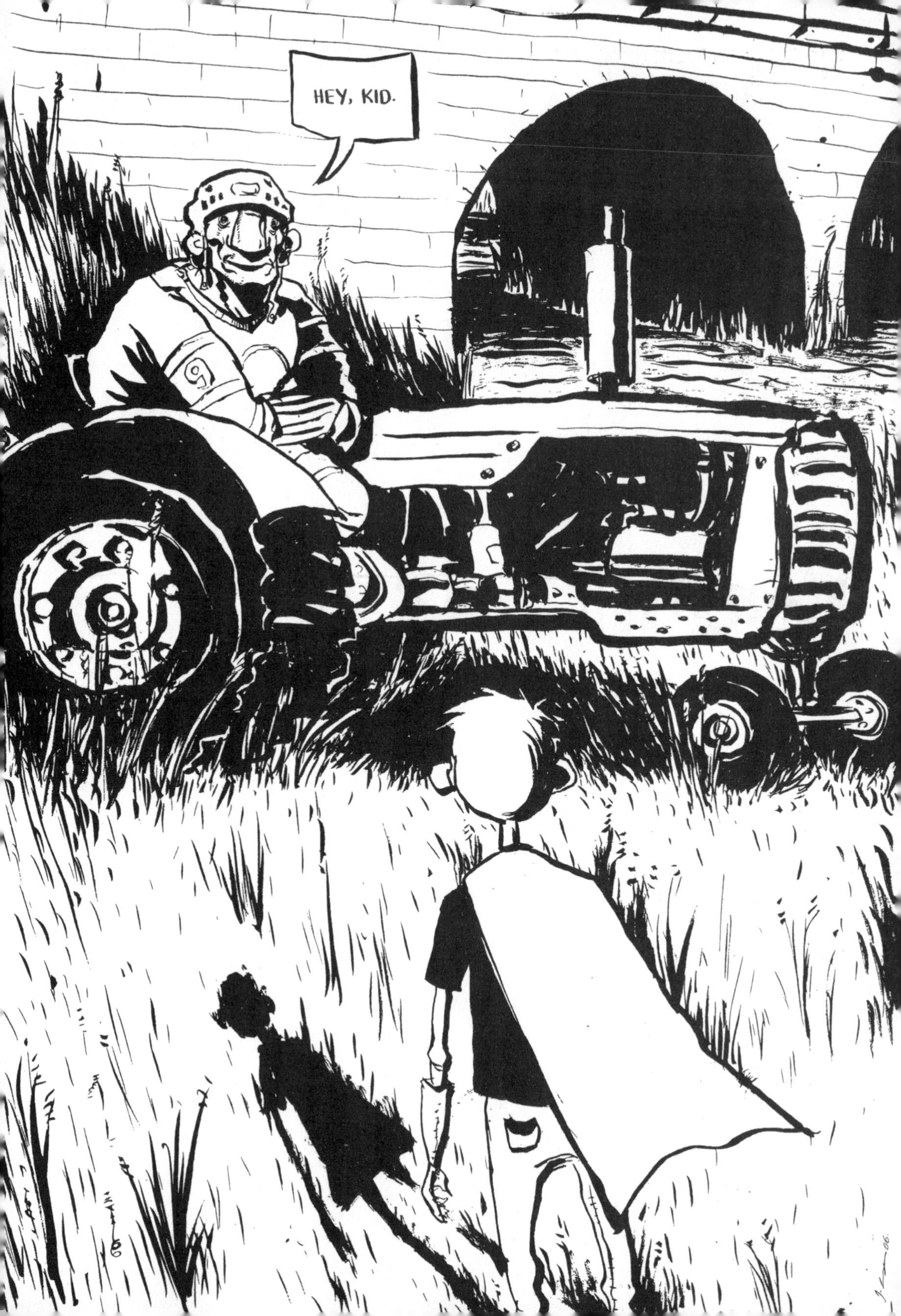
HEY, KID.

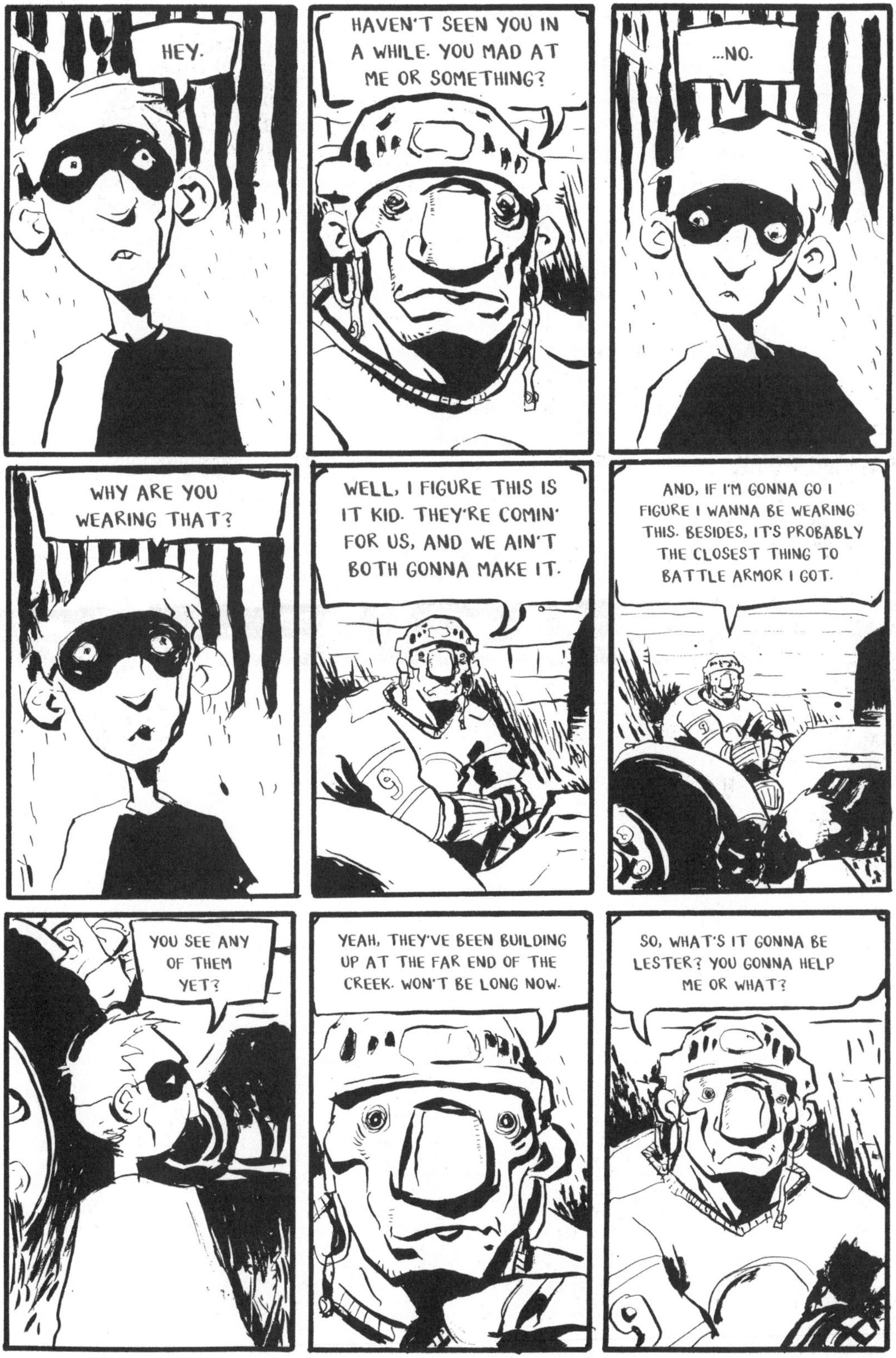
HEY.
HAVEN'T SEEN YOU IN A WHILE. YOU MAD AT ME OR SOMETHING?
...NO.
WHY ARE YOU WEARING THAT?
WELL, I FIGURE THIS IS IT KID. THEY'RE COMIN' FOR US, AND WE AIN'T BOTH GONNA MAKE IT.
AND, IF I'M GONNA GO I FIGURE I WANNA BE WEARING THIS. BESIDES, IT'S PROBABLY THE CLOSEST THING TO BATTLE ARMOR I GOT.
YOU SEE ANY OF THEM YET?
YEAH, THEY'VE BEEN BUILDING UP AT THE FAR END OF THE CREEK. WON'T BE LONG NOW.
SO, WHAT'S IT GONNA BE LESTER? YOU GONNA HELP ME OR WHAT?

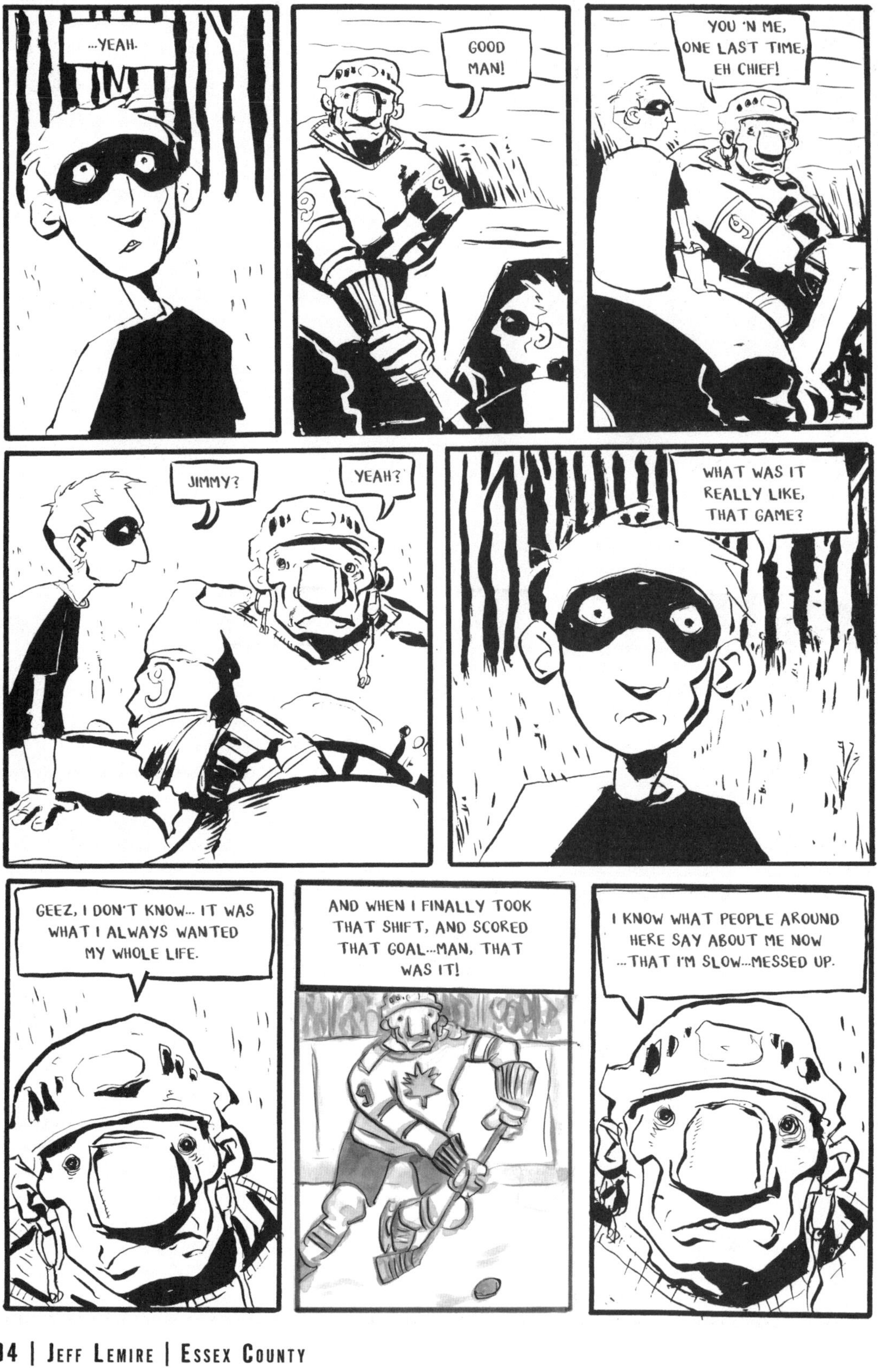
...YEAH.
GOOD MAN!
YOU 'N ME, ONE LAST TIME, EH CHIEF!
JIMMY?
YEAH?
WHAT WAS IT REALLY LIKE, THAT GAME?
GEEZ, I DON'T KNOW... IT WAS WHAT I ALWAYS WANTED MY WHOLE LIFE.
AND WHEN I FINALLY TOOK THAT SHIFT, AND SCORED THAT GOAL...MAN, THAT WAS IT!
I KNOW WHAT PEOPLE AROUND HERE SAY ABOUT ME NOW ...THAT I'M SLOW...MESSED UP.

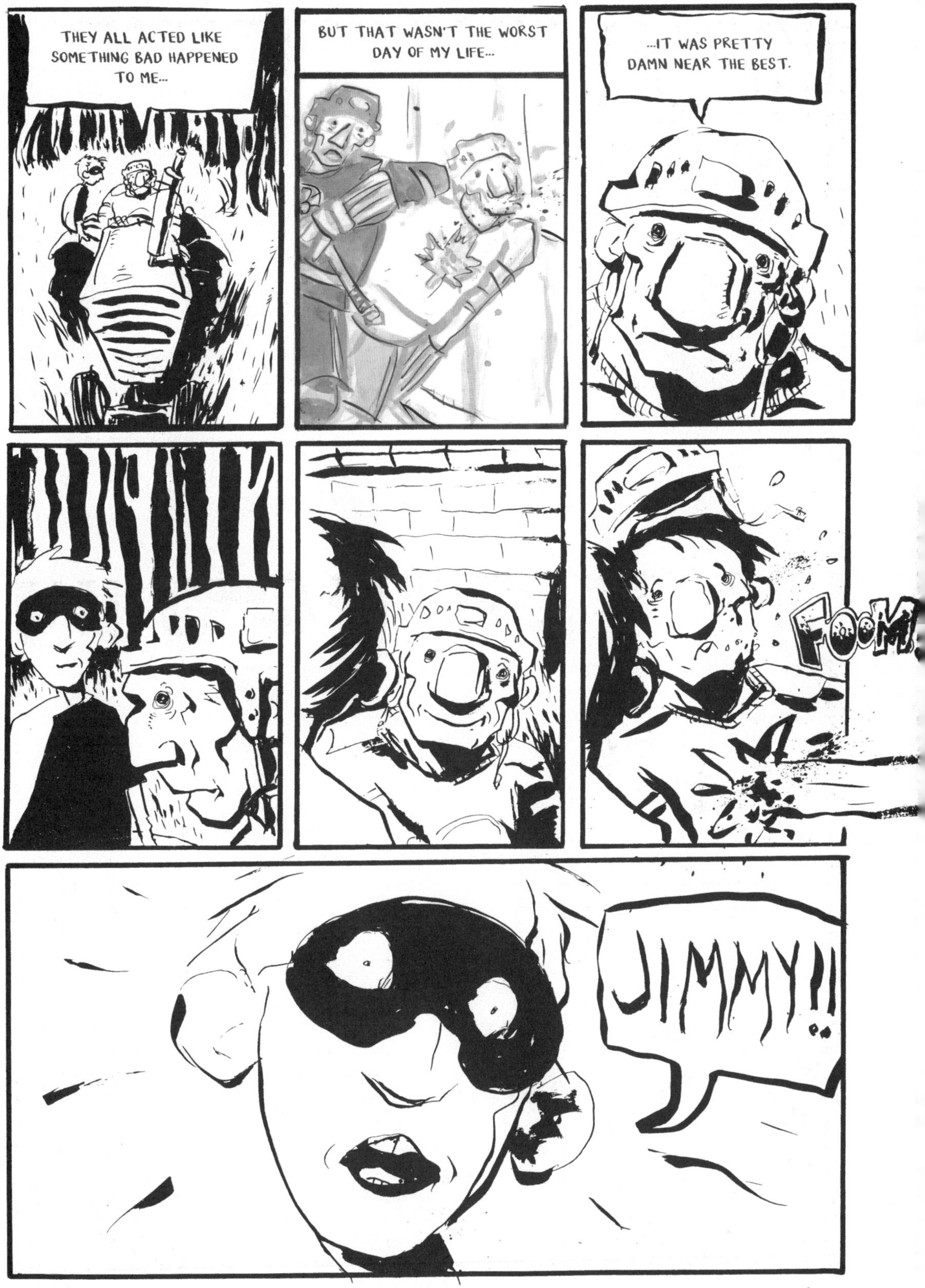
THEY ALL ACTED LIKE SOMETHING BAD HAPPENED TO ME...
BUT THAT WASN'T THE WORST DAY OF MY LIFE...
...IT WAS PRETTY DAMN NEAR THE BEST.
FOOM!
JIMMY!!

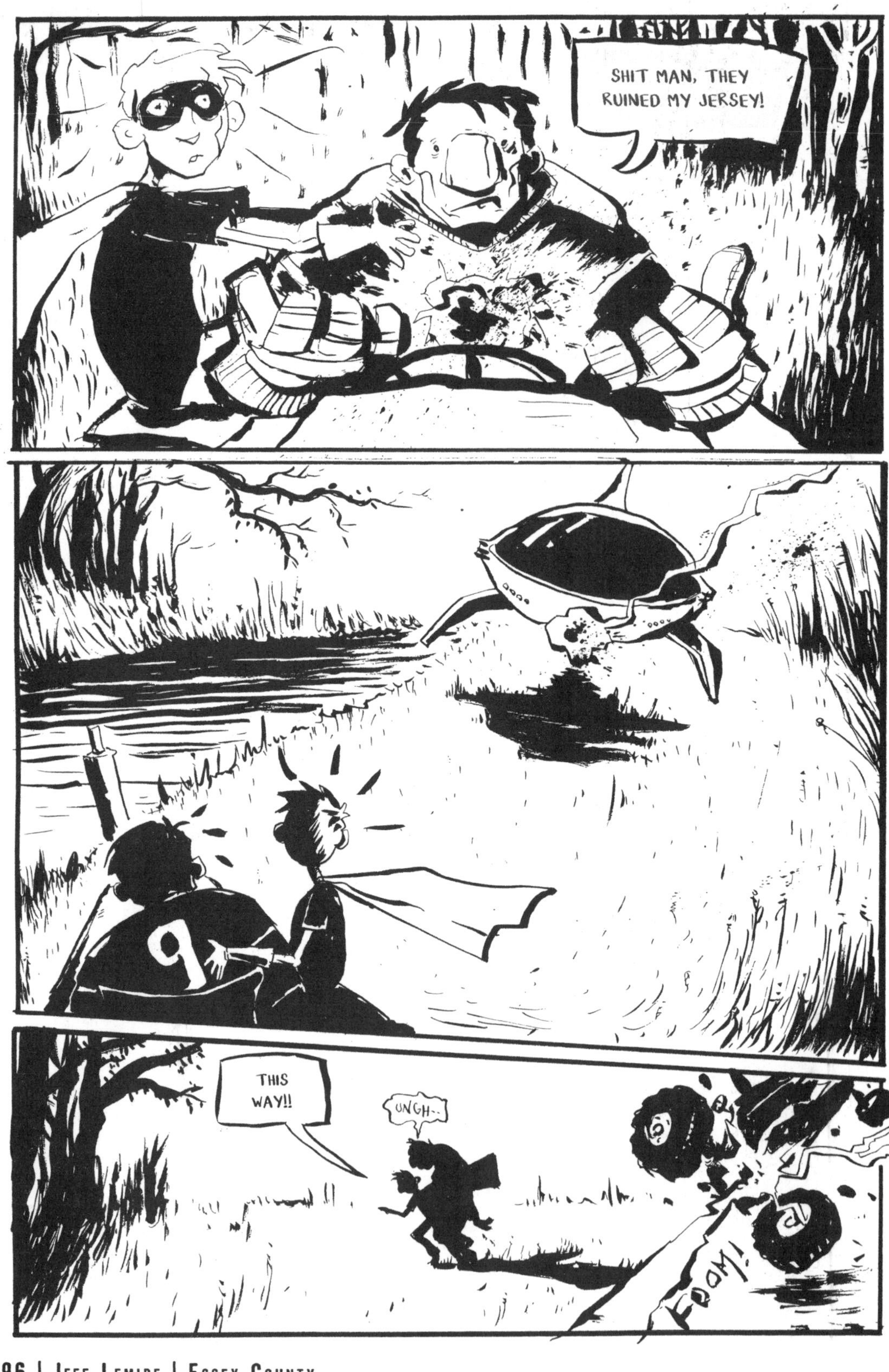

SHIT MAN, THEY RUINED MY JERSEY!
9
THIS WAY!!
UNGH..
FOOM!

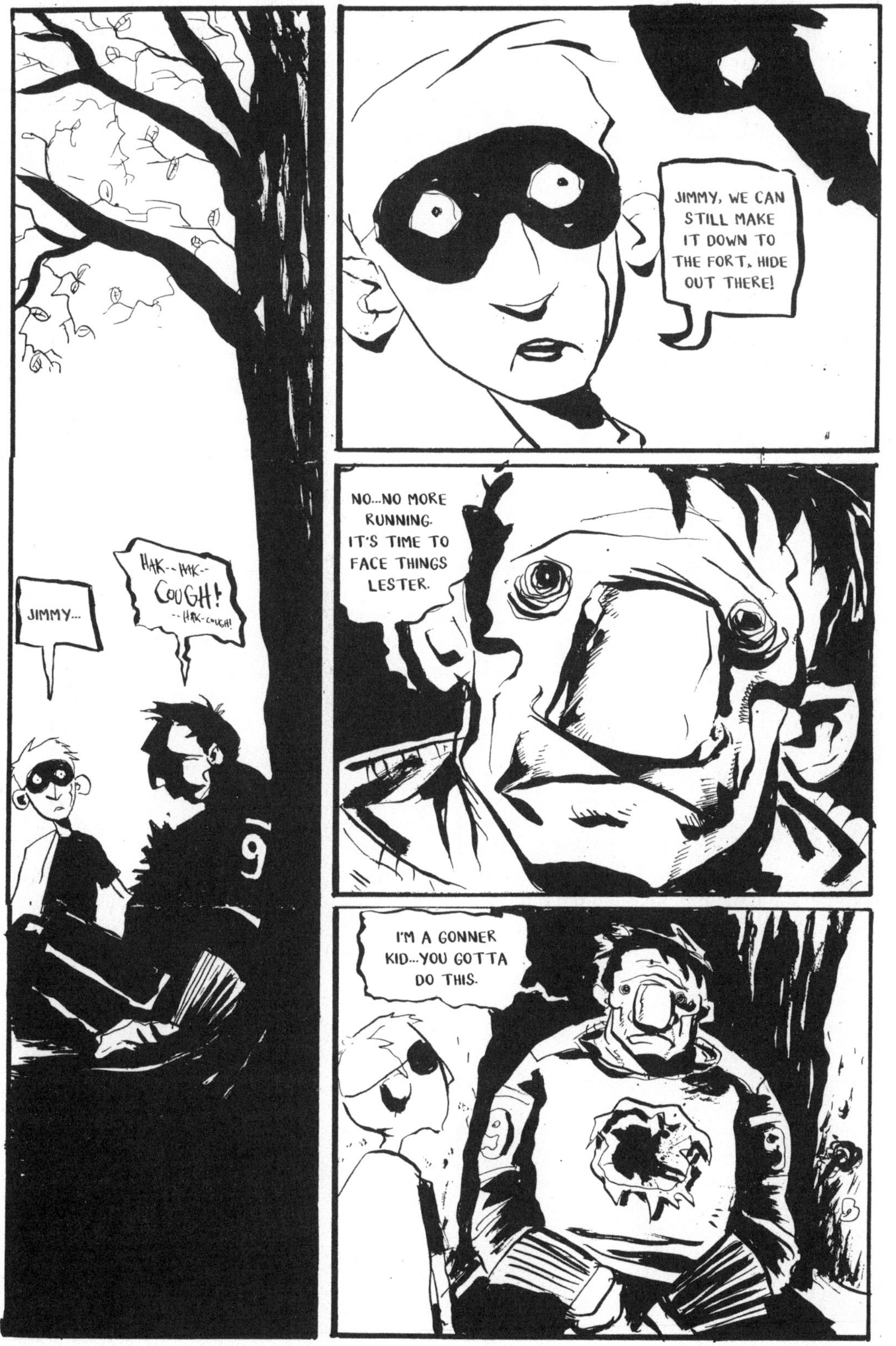
JIMMY, WE CAN STILL MAKE IT DOWN TO THE FORT, HIDE OUT THERE!
JIMMY...
HAK--HAK--COUGH! --HAK-COUGH!
NO...NO MORE RUNNING. IT'S TIME TO FACE THINGS LESTER.
I'M A GONNER KID...YOU GOTTA DO THIS.

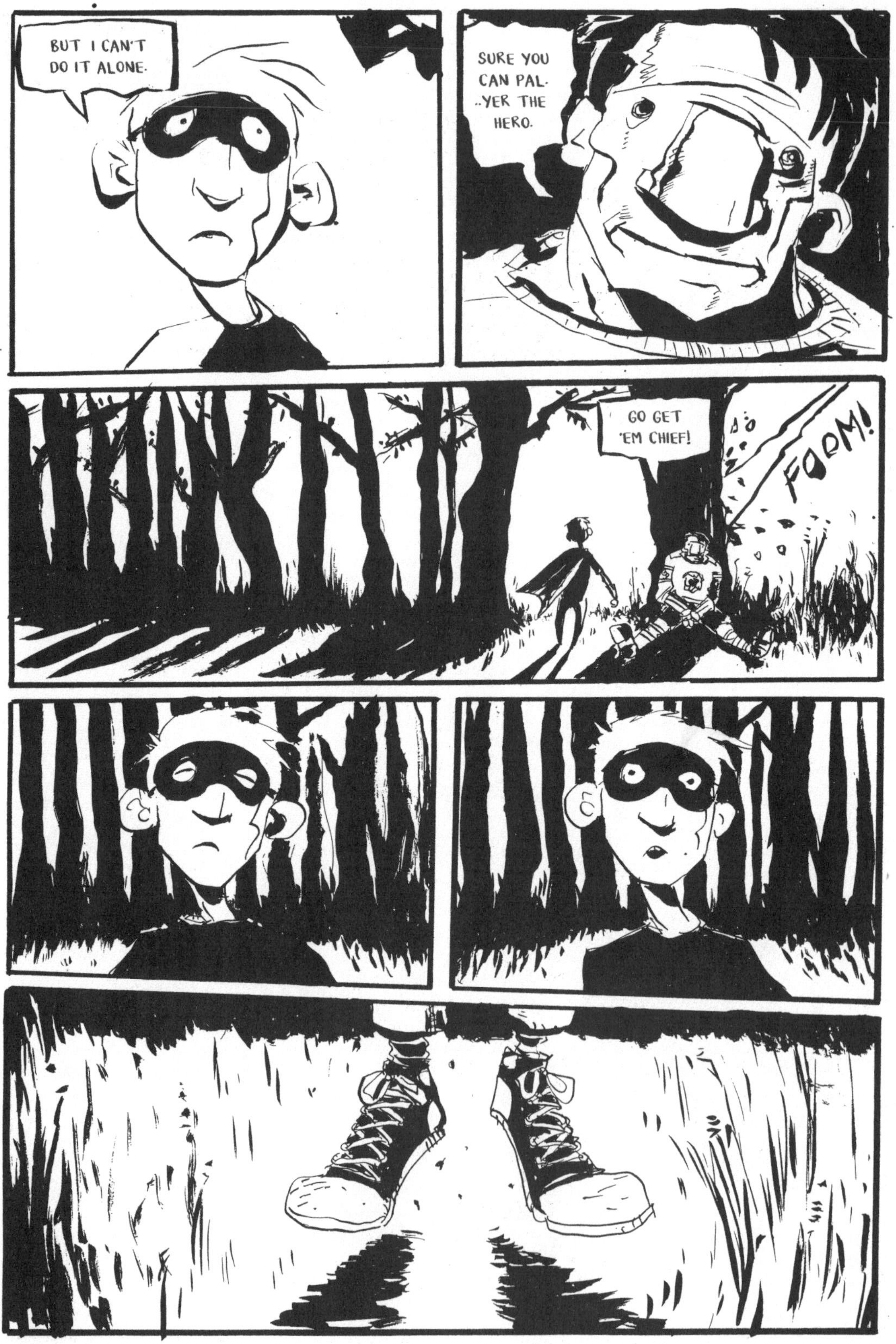
BUT I CAN'T DO IT ALONE.
SURE YOU CAN PAL. ..YER THE HERO.
GO GET 'EM CHIEF!
FOOM!

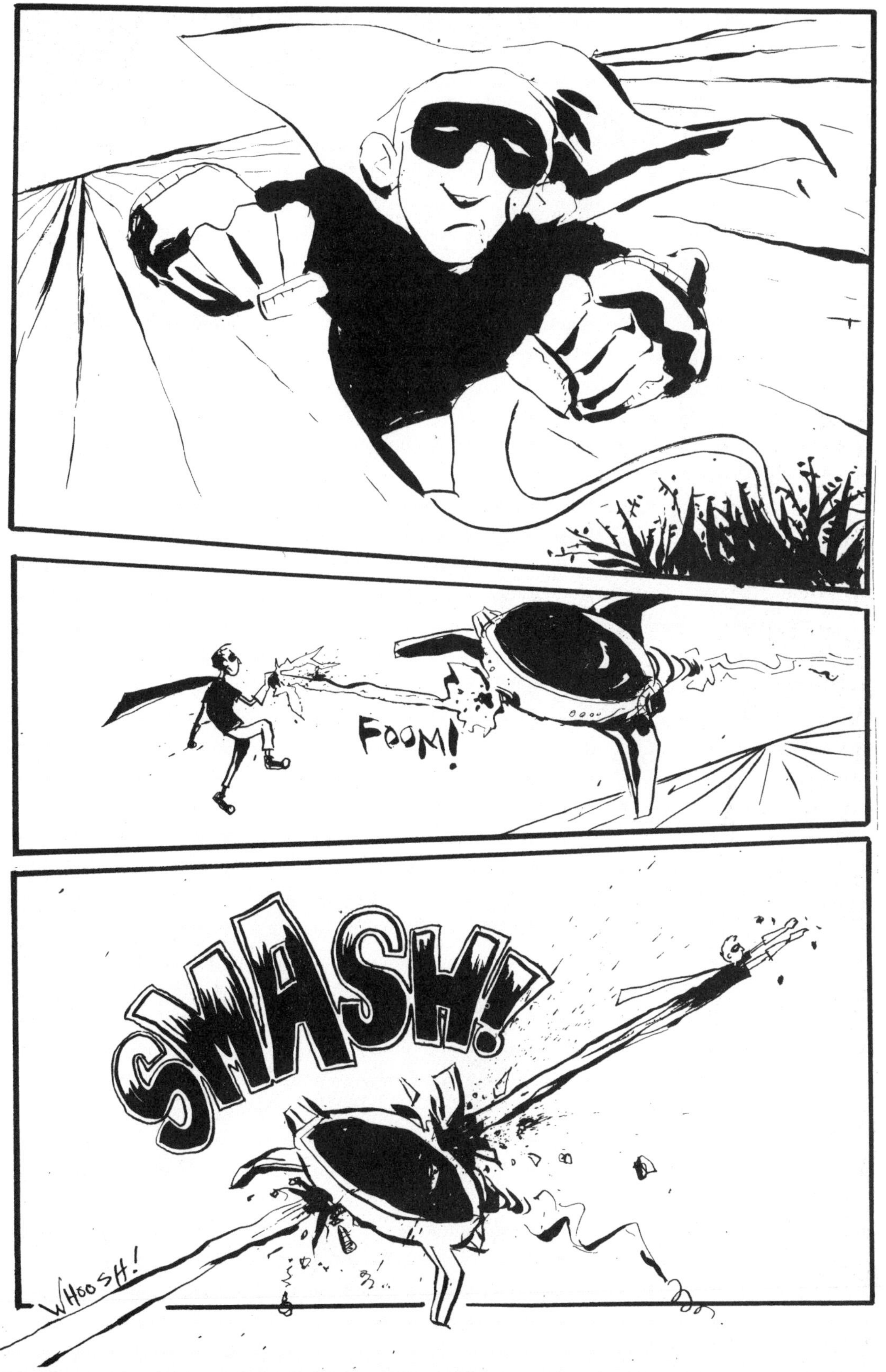
FOOM!
SMASH!
WHOOSH!

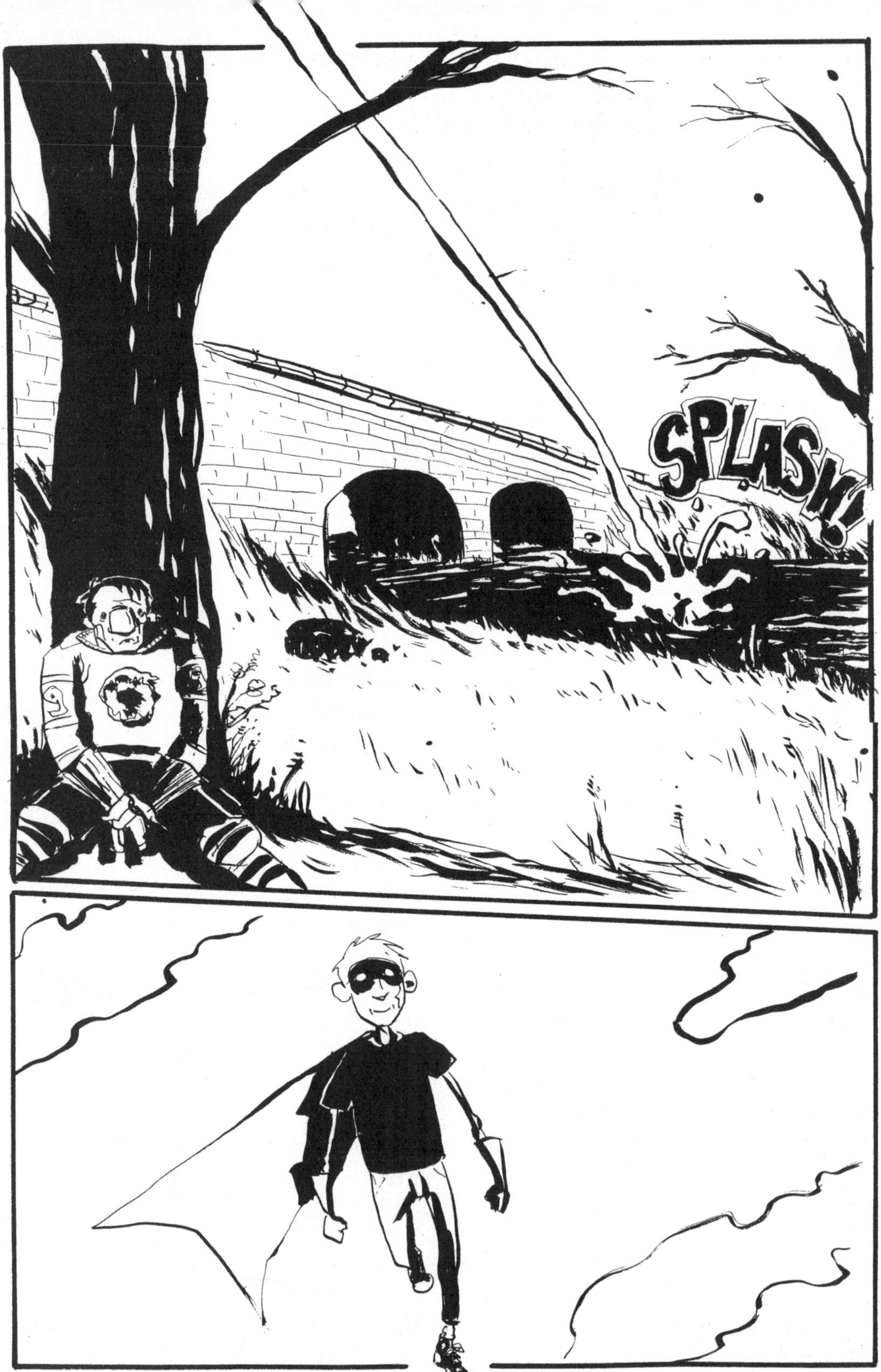
SPLASH!

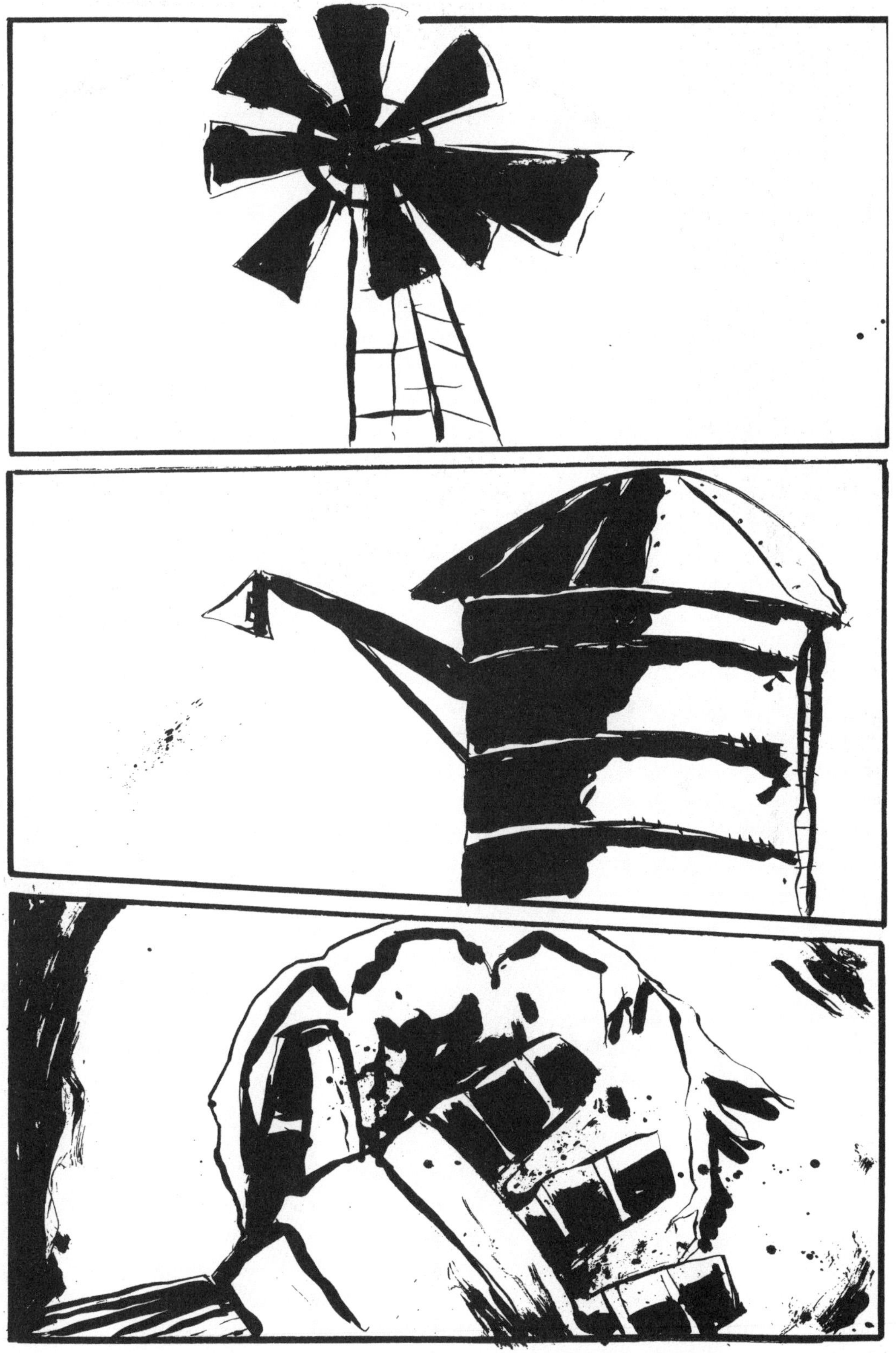

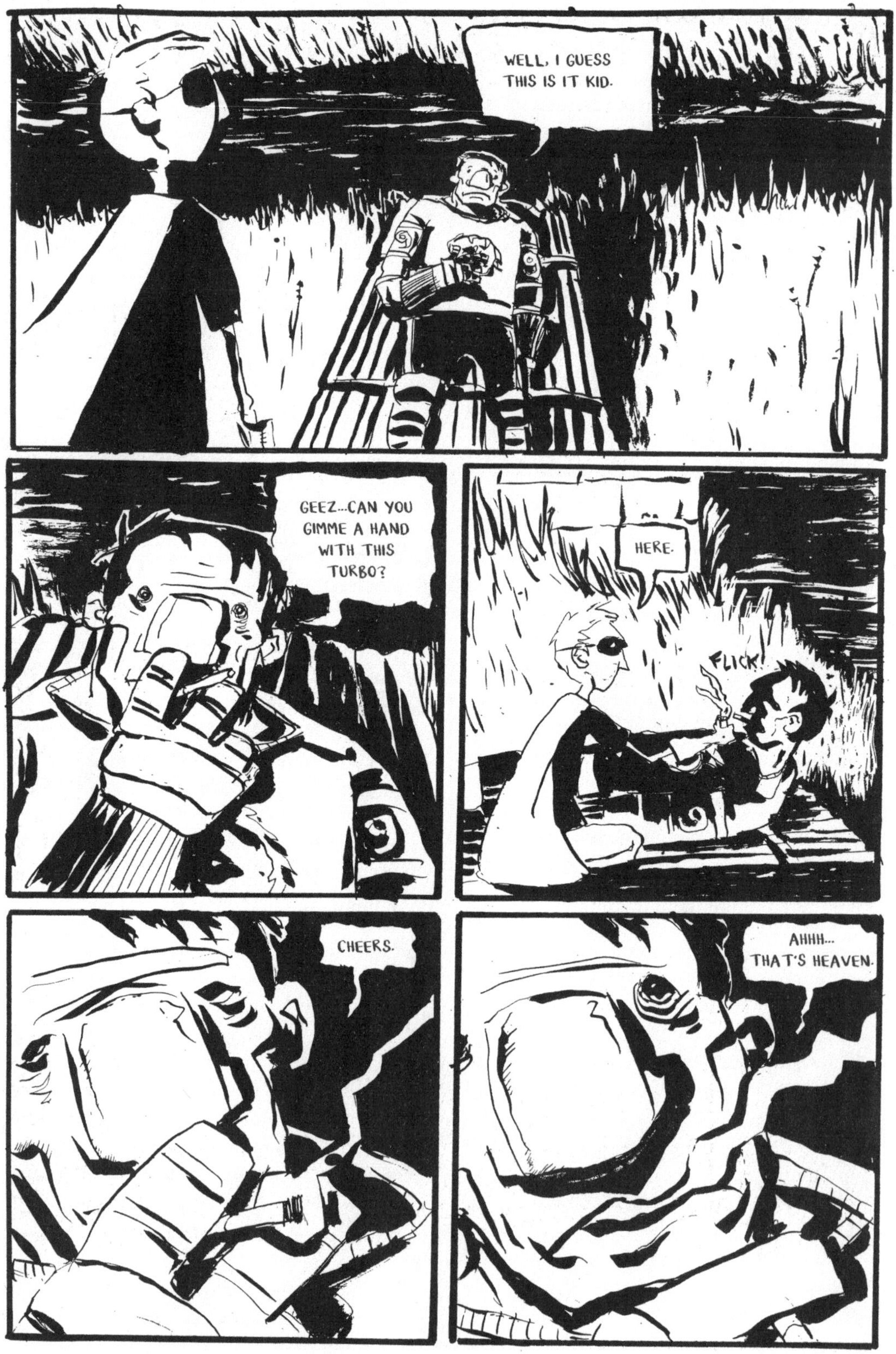
WELL, I GUESS THIS IS IT KID.
GEEZ...CAN YOU GIMME A HAND WITH THIS TURBO?
HERE.
FLICK!
CHEERS.
AHHH... THAT'S HEAVEN.

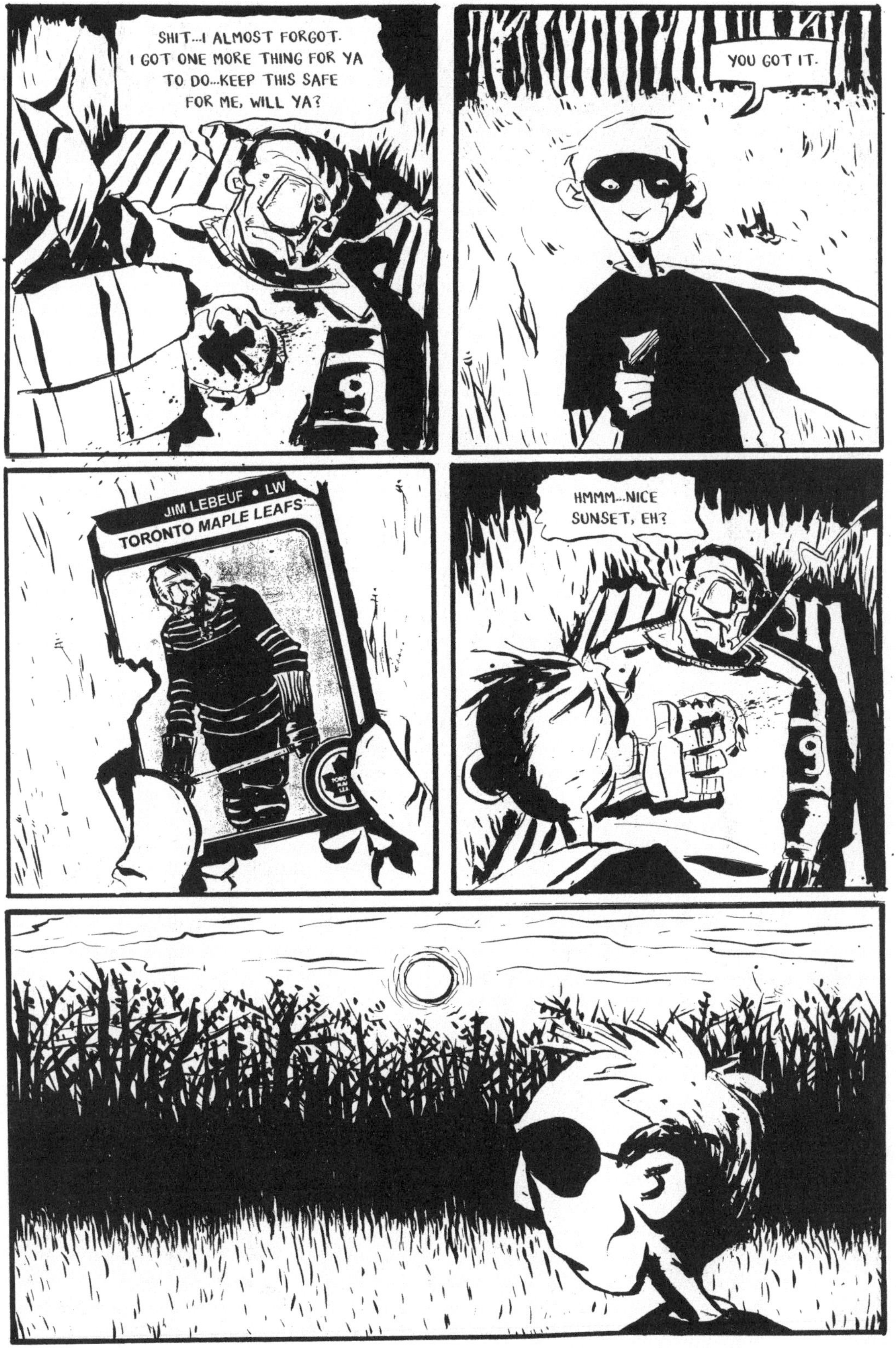
SHIT...I ALMOST FORGOT. I GOT ONE MORE THING FOR YA TO DO...KEEP THIS SAFE FOR ME, WILL YA?
YOU GOT IT.
JIM LEBEUF • LW
TORONTO MAPLE LEAFS
HMMM...NICE SUNSET, EH?

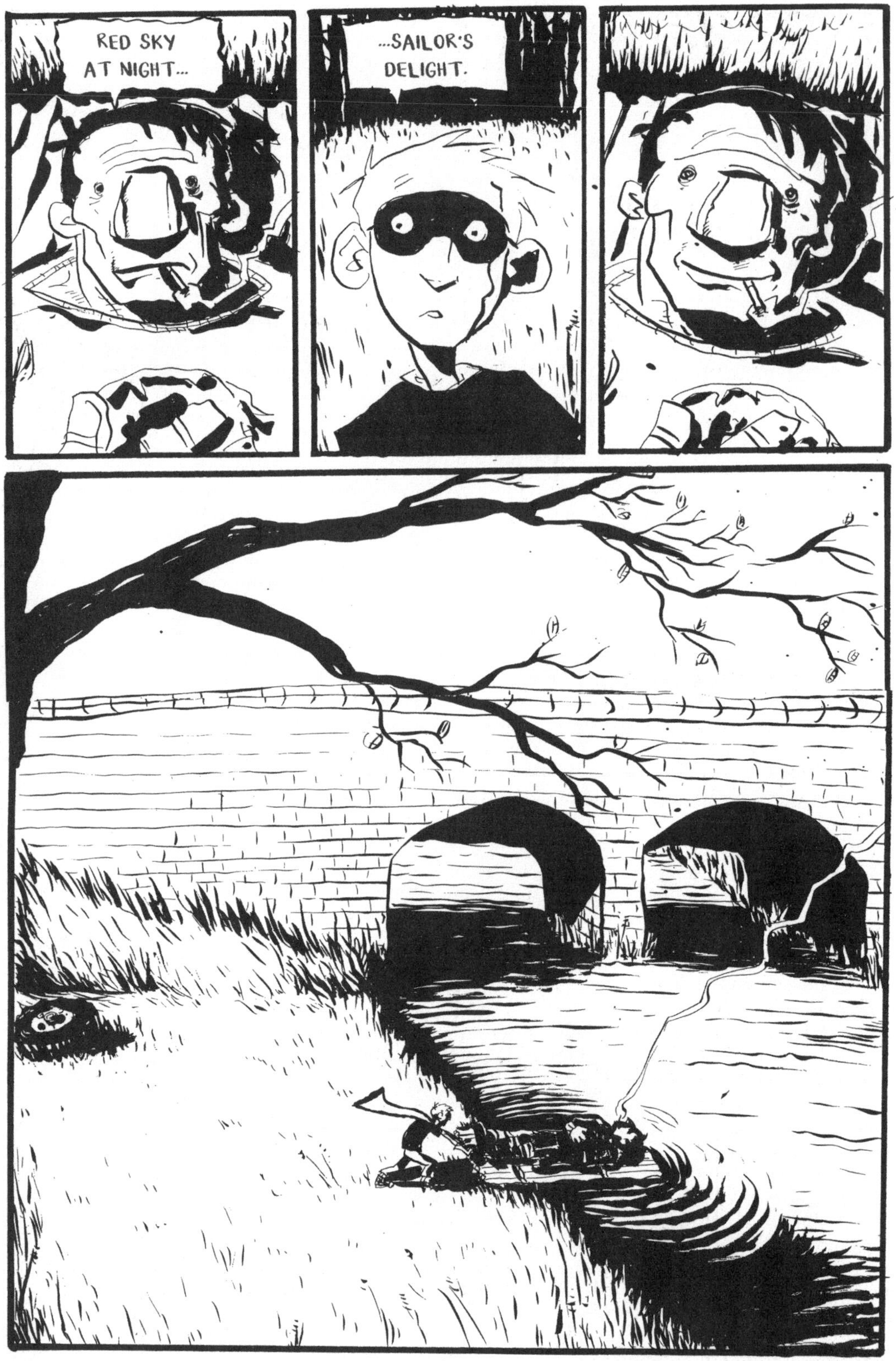
RED SKY AT NIGHT...
...SAILOR'S DELIGHT.

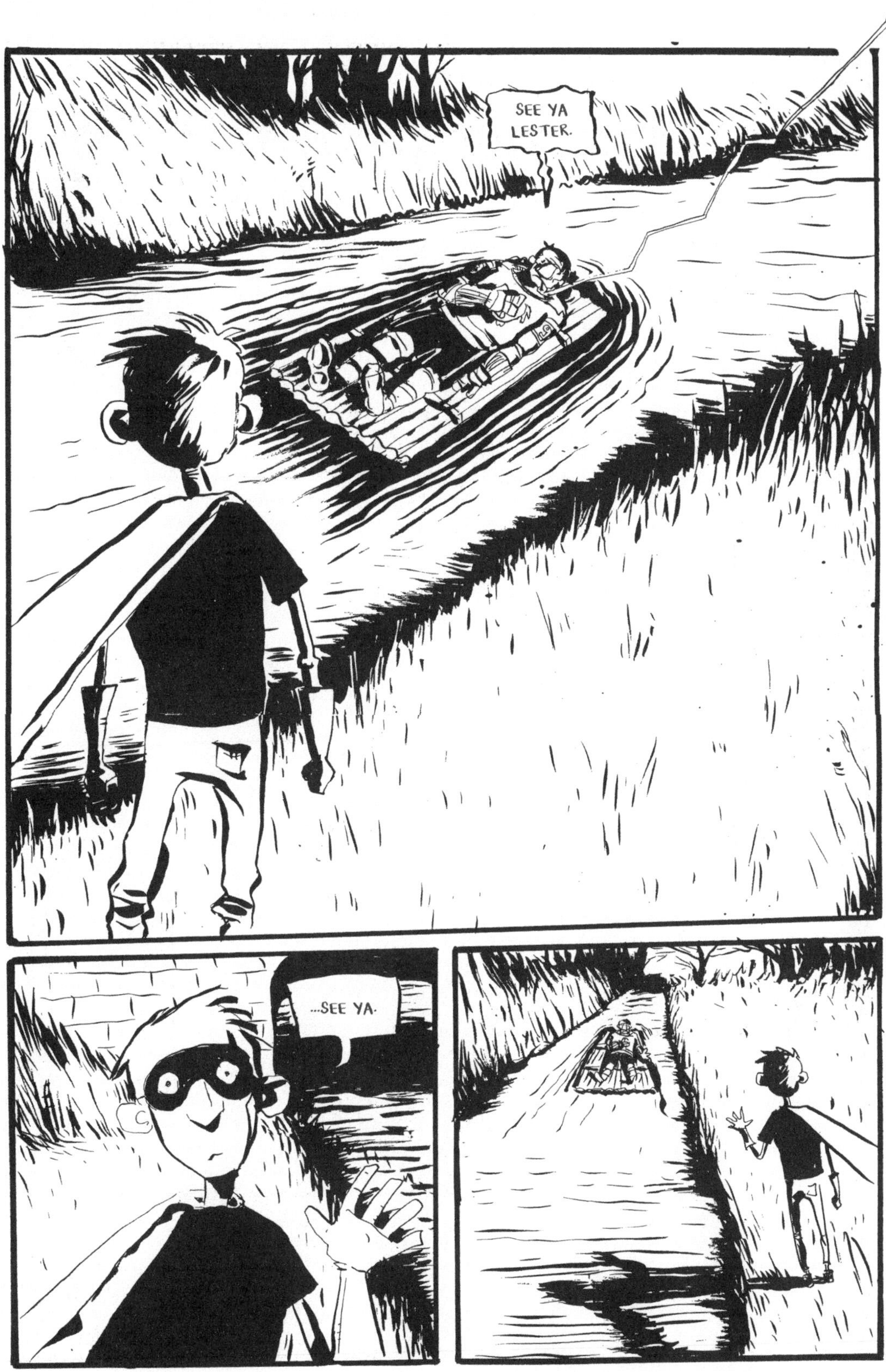
SEE YA
LESTER.
...SEE YA.

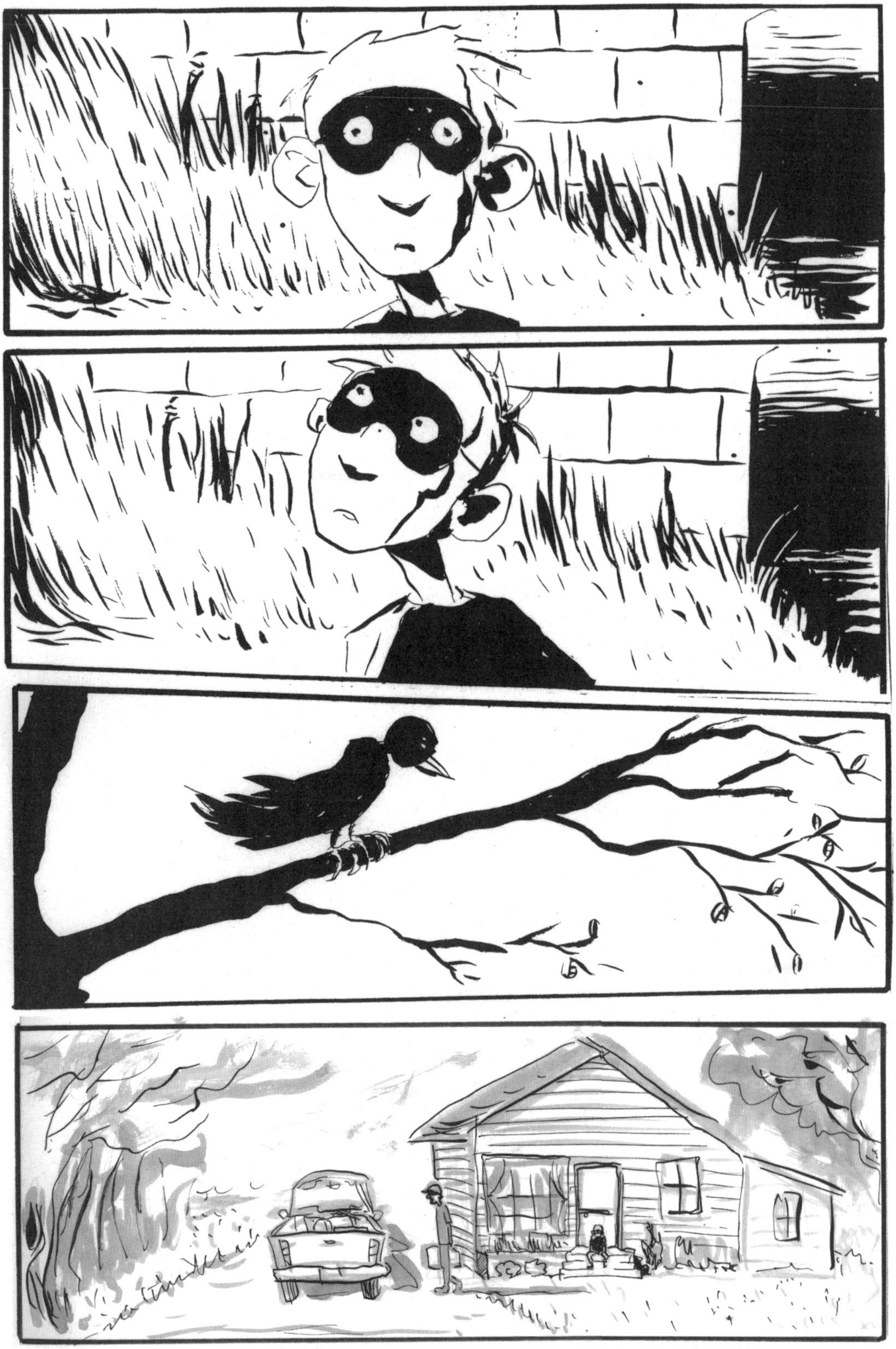

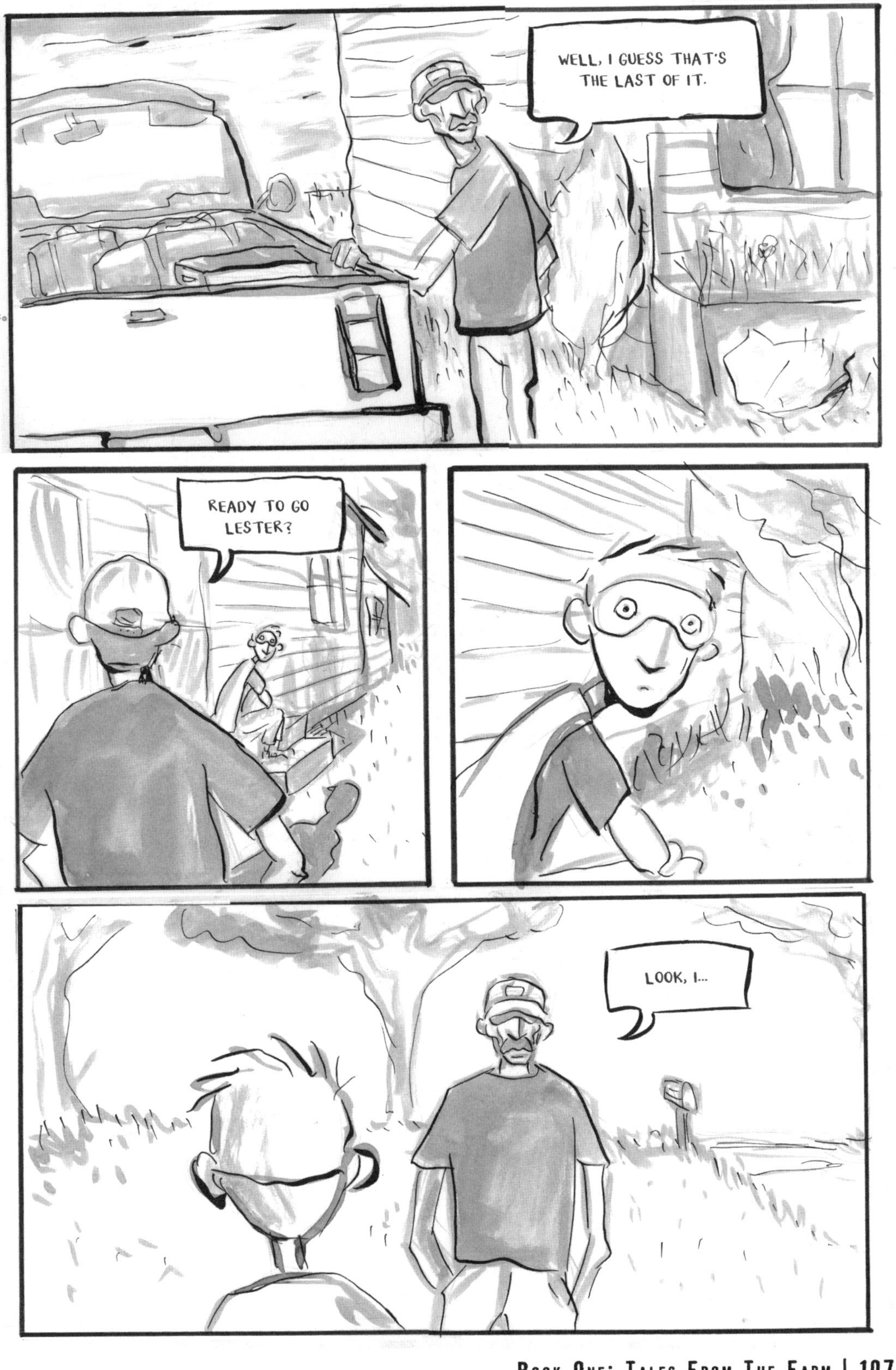
WELL, I GUESS THAT'S THE LAST OF IT.
READY TO GO LESTER?
LOOK, I...

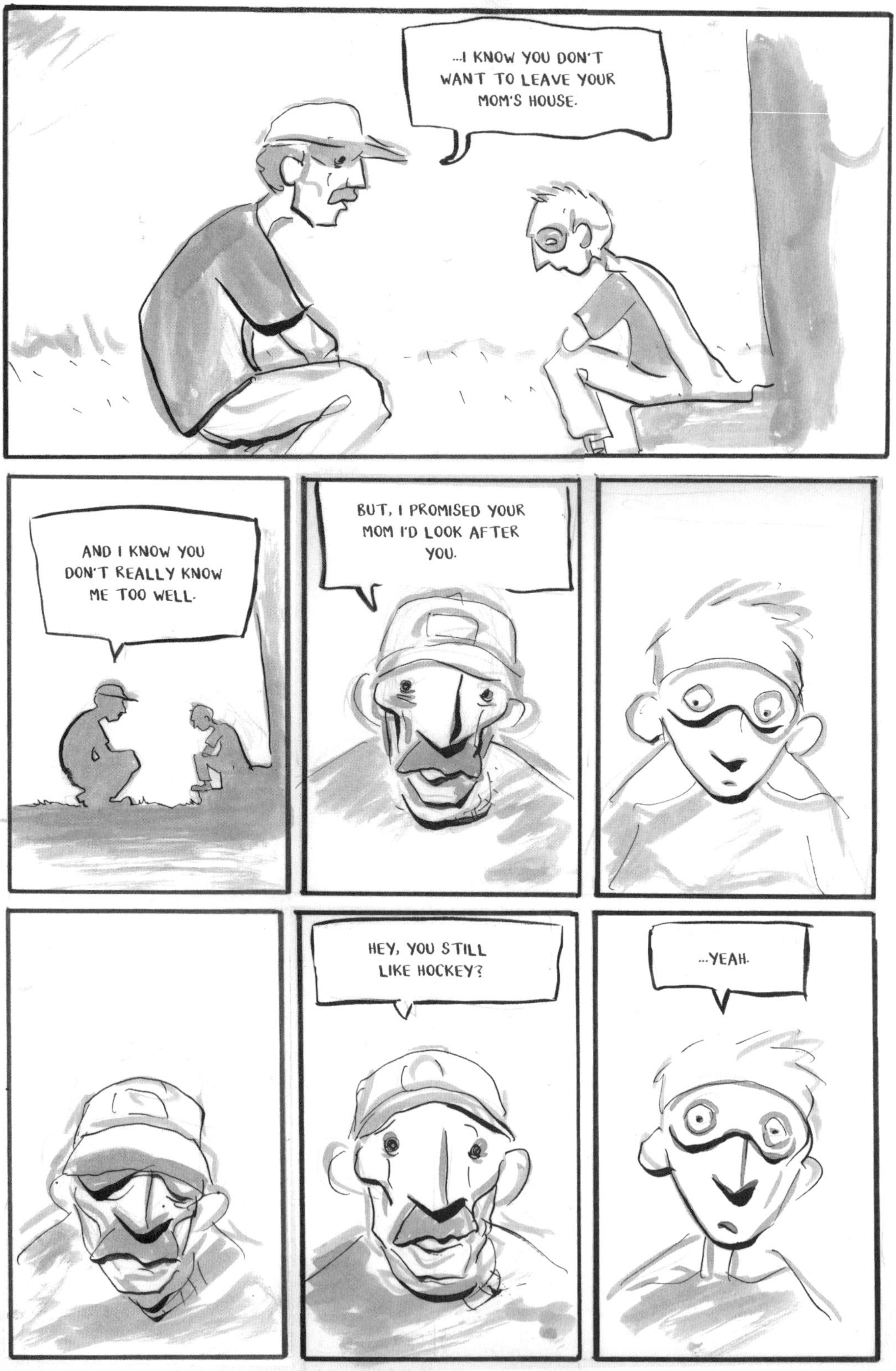
...I KNOW YOU DON'T WANT TO LEAVE YOUR MOM'S HOUSE.
AND I KNOW YOU DON'T REALLY KNOW ME TOO WELL.
BUT, I PROMISED YOUR MOM I'D LOOK AFTER YOU.
HEY, YOU STILL LIKE HOCKEY?
...YEAH.

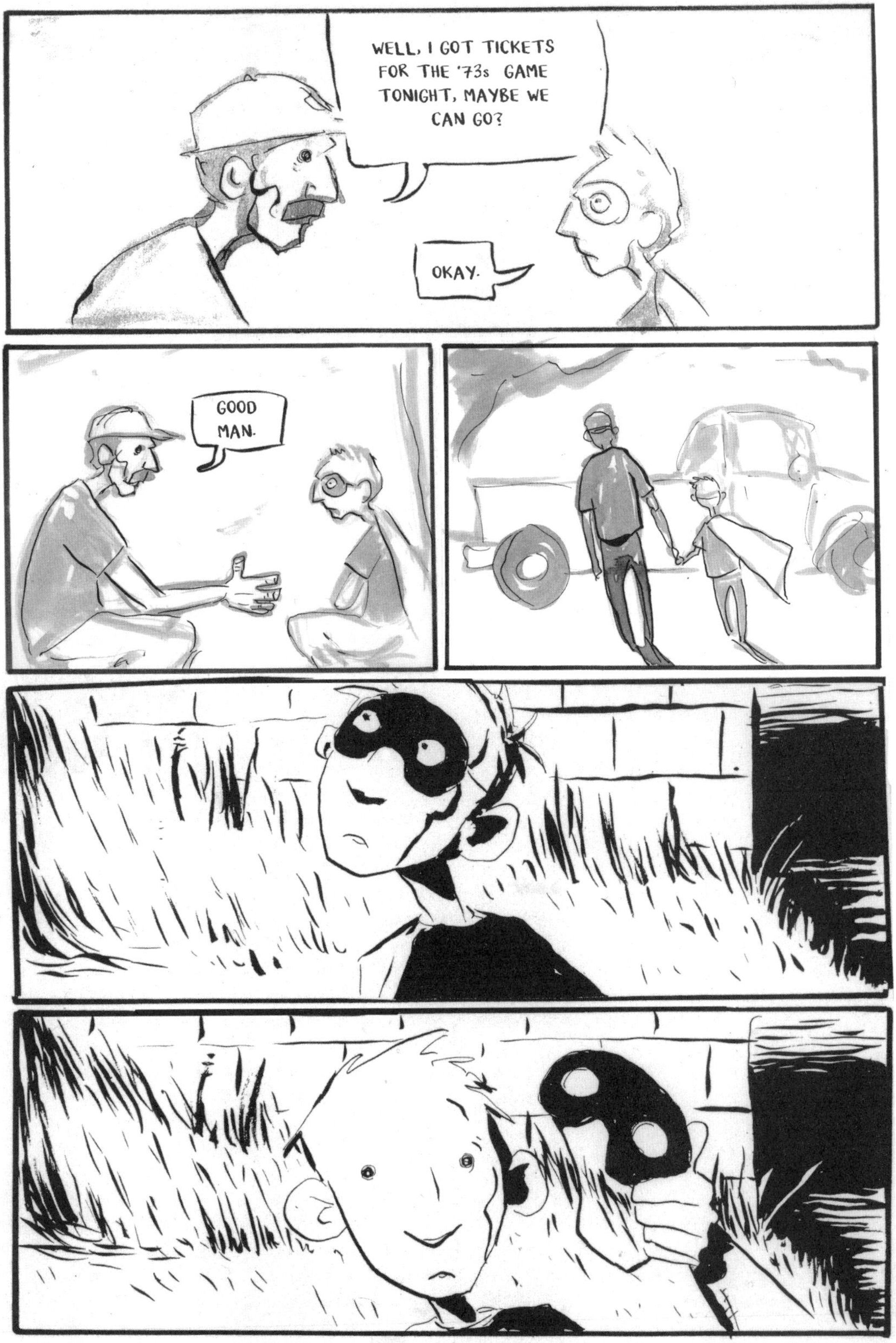
WELL, I GOT TICKETS FOR THE '73s GAME TONIGHT, MAYBE WE CAN GO?
OKAY.
GOOD MAN.

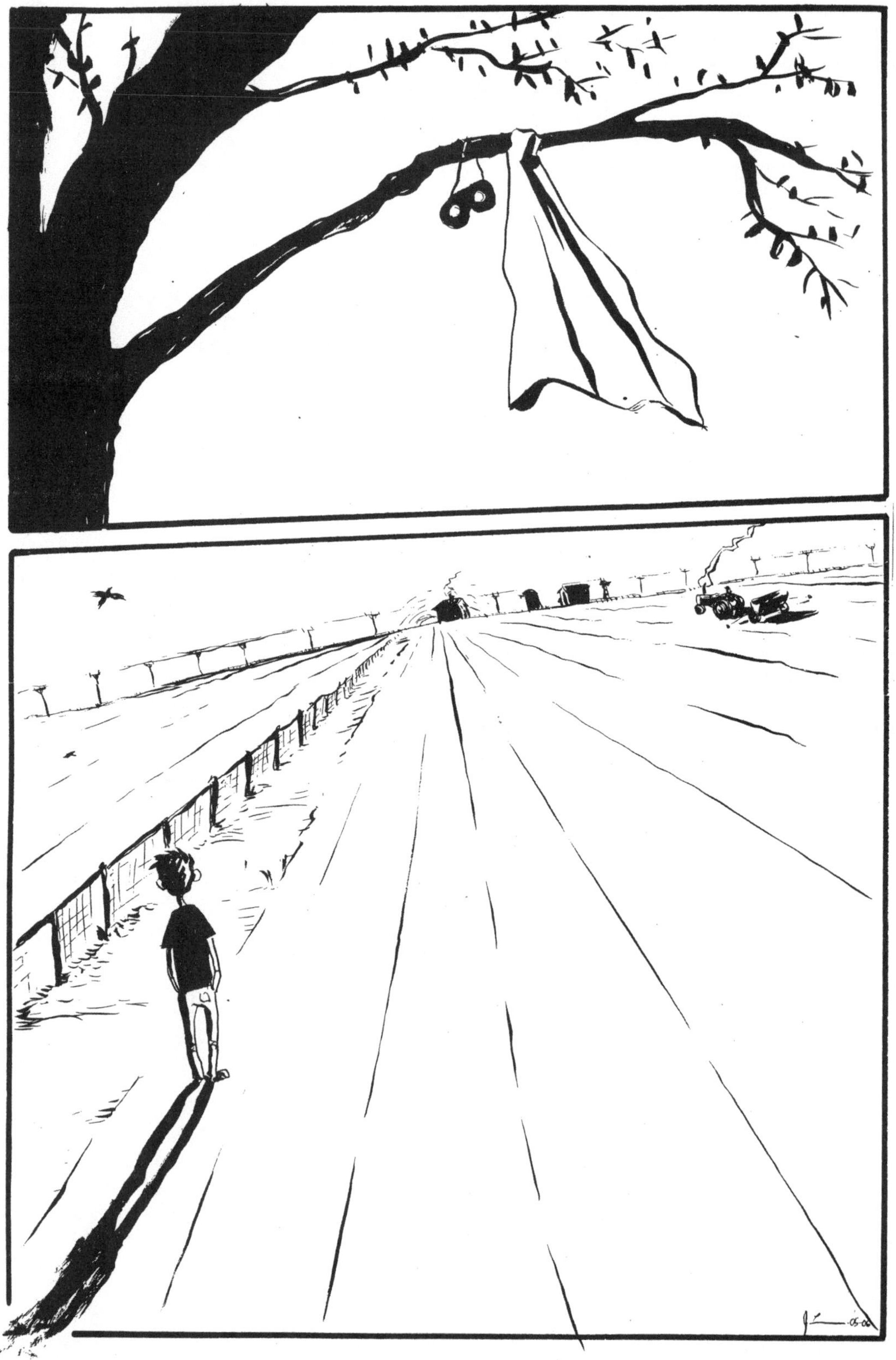

"Hockey captures the essence
of Canadian experience in the New World.
In a land so inescapably and inhospitably cold,
hockey is the chance of life, and
an affirmation that despite the deathly
chill of winter we are alive."
-Stephen Leacock

BOOK TWO
GHOST STORIES

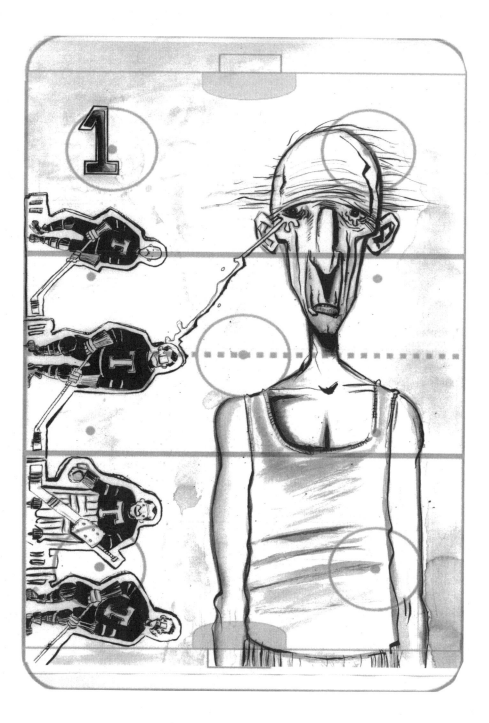

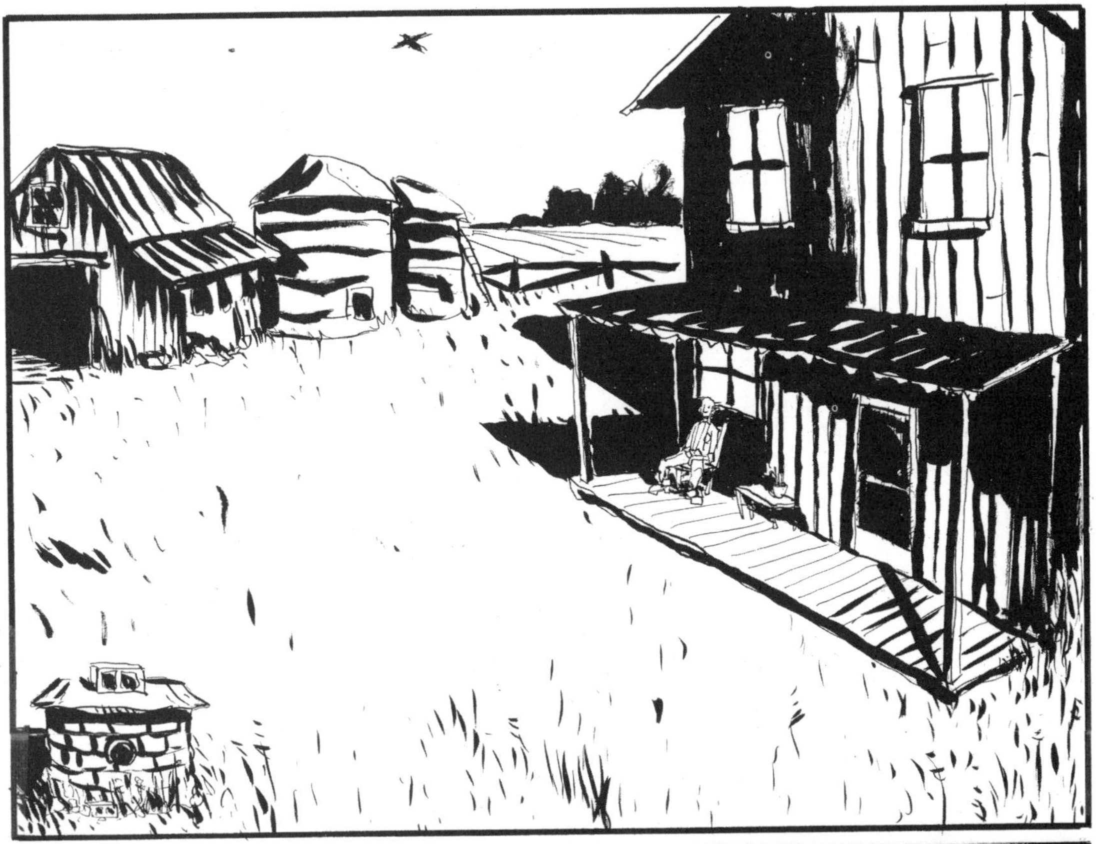

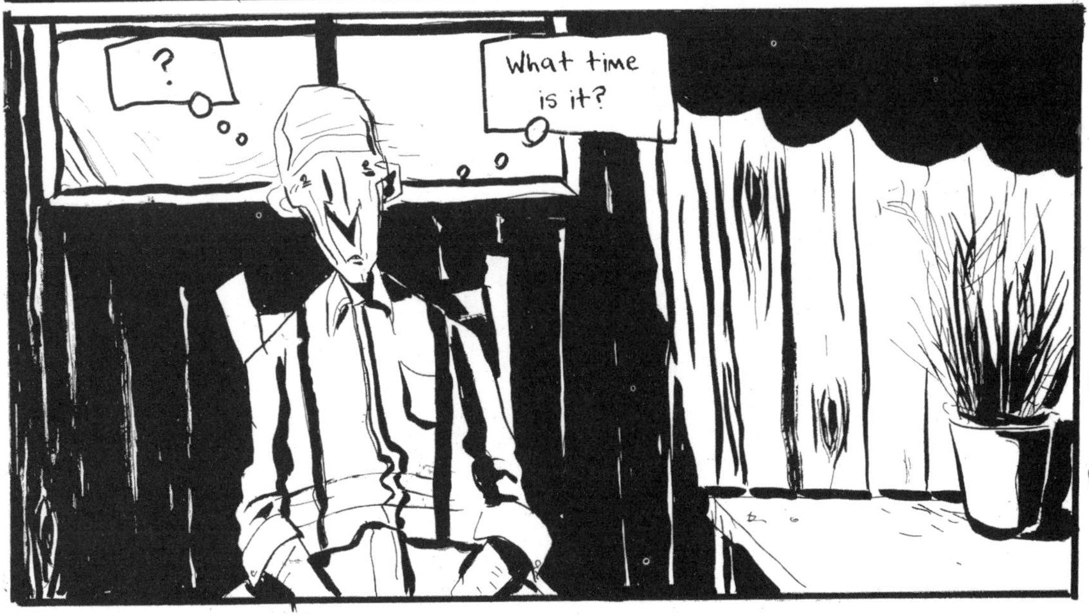
?
What time is it?

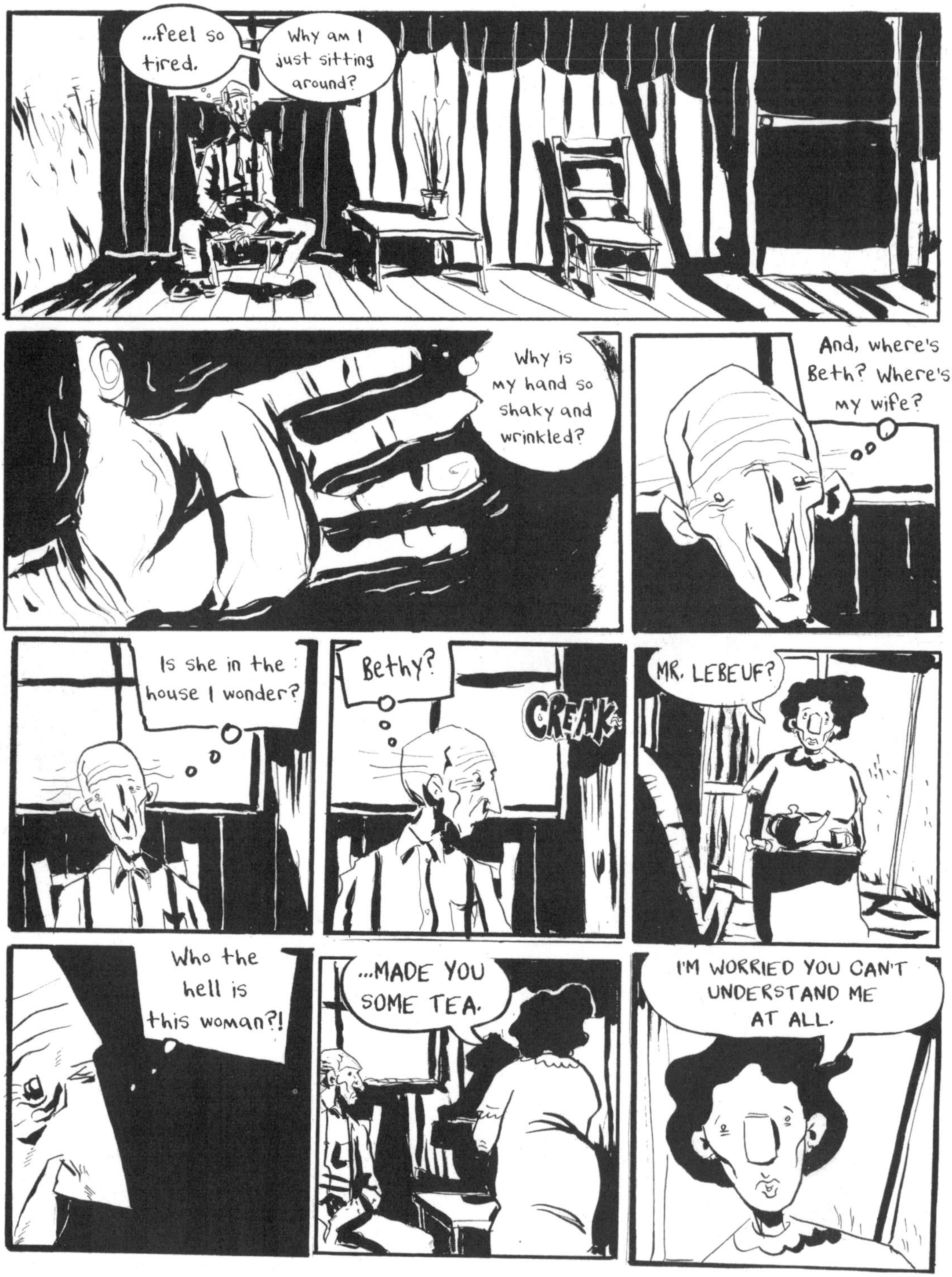

...feel so tired.
Why am I just sitting around?
Why is my hand so shaky and wrinkled?
And, where's Beth? Where's my wife?
Is she in the house I wonder?
Bethy?
CREAK
MR. LEBEUF?
Who the hell is this woman?!
...MADE YOU SOME TEA.
I'M WORRIED YOU CAN'T UNDERSTAND ME AT ALL.

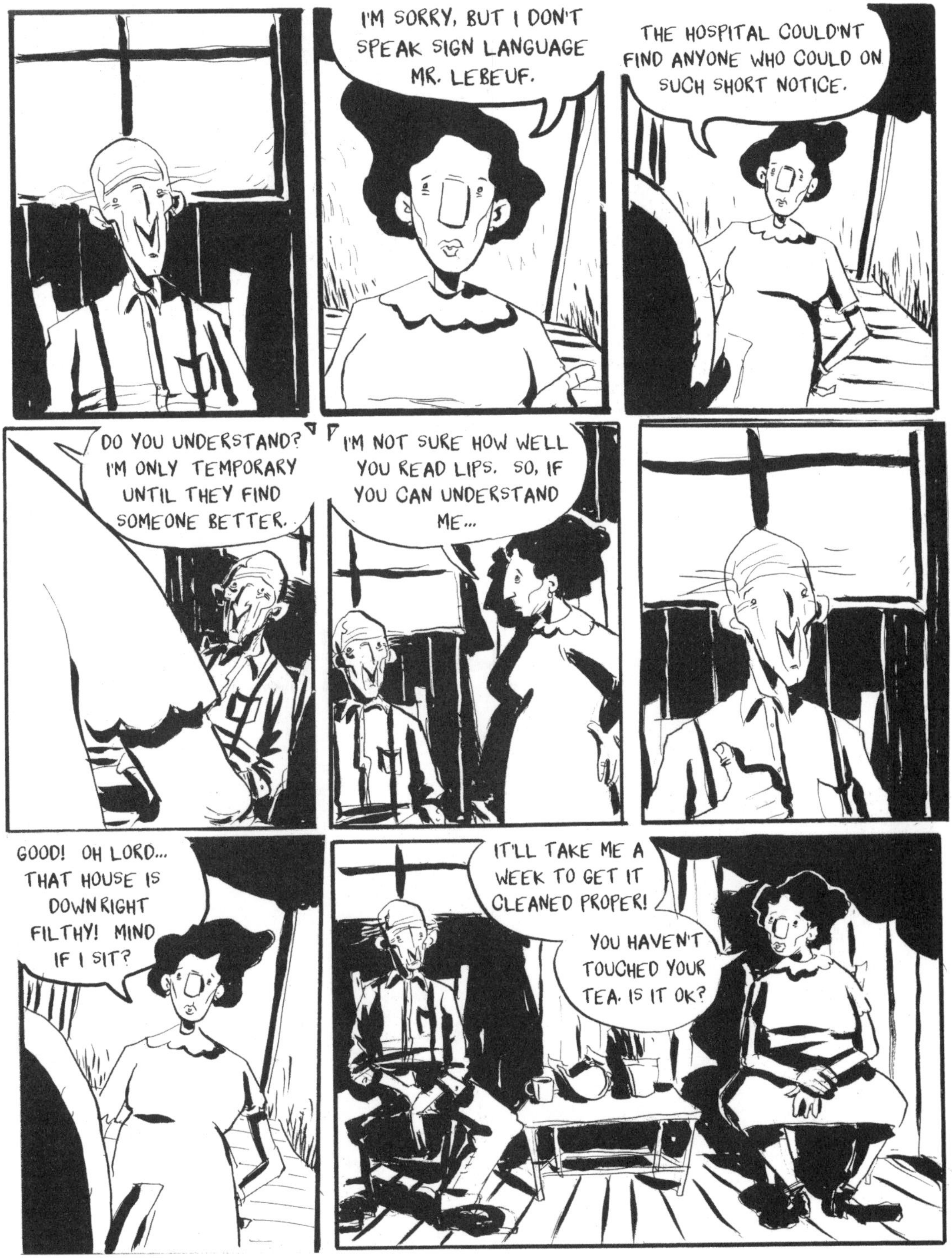
I'M SORRY, BUT I DON'T SPEAK SIGN LANGUAGE MR. LEBEUF.
THE HOSPITAL COULDN'T FIND ANYONE WHO COULD ON SUCH SHORT NOTICE.
DO YOU UNDERSTAND? I'M ONLY TEMPORARY UNTIL THEY FIND SOMEONE BETTER.
I'M NOT SURE HOW WELL YOU READ LIPS. SO, IF YOU CAN UNDERSTAND ME...
GOOD! OH LORD... THAT HOUSE IS DOWNRIGHT FILTHY! MIND IF I SIT?
IT'LL TAKE ME A WEEK TO GET IT CLEANED PROPER!
YOU HAVEN'T TOUCHED YOUR TEA. IS IT OK?

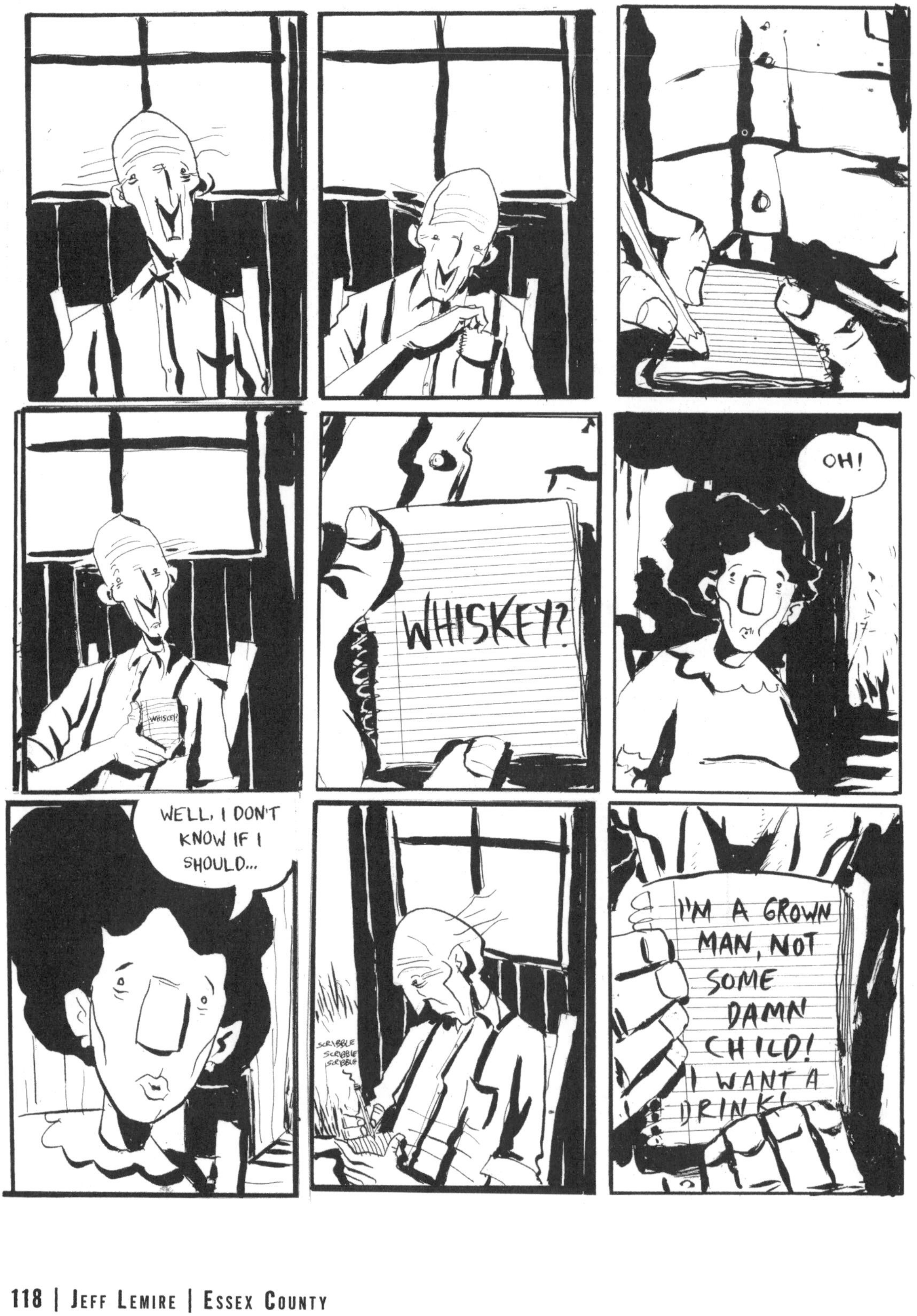
WHISKEY?
WHISKEY?
OH!
WELL, I DON'T KNOW IF I SHOULD...
SCRIBBLE SCRIBBLE SCRIBBLE
I'M A GROWN MAN, NOT SOME DAMN CHILD! I WANT A DRINK!

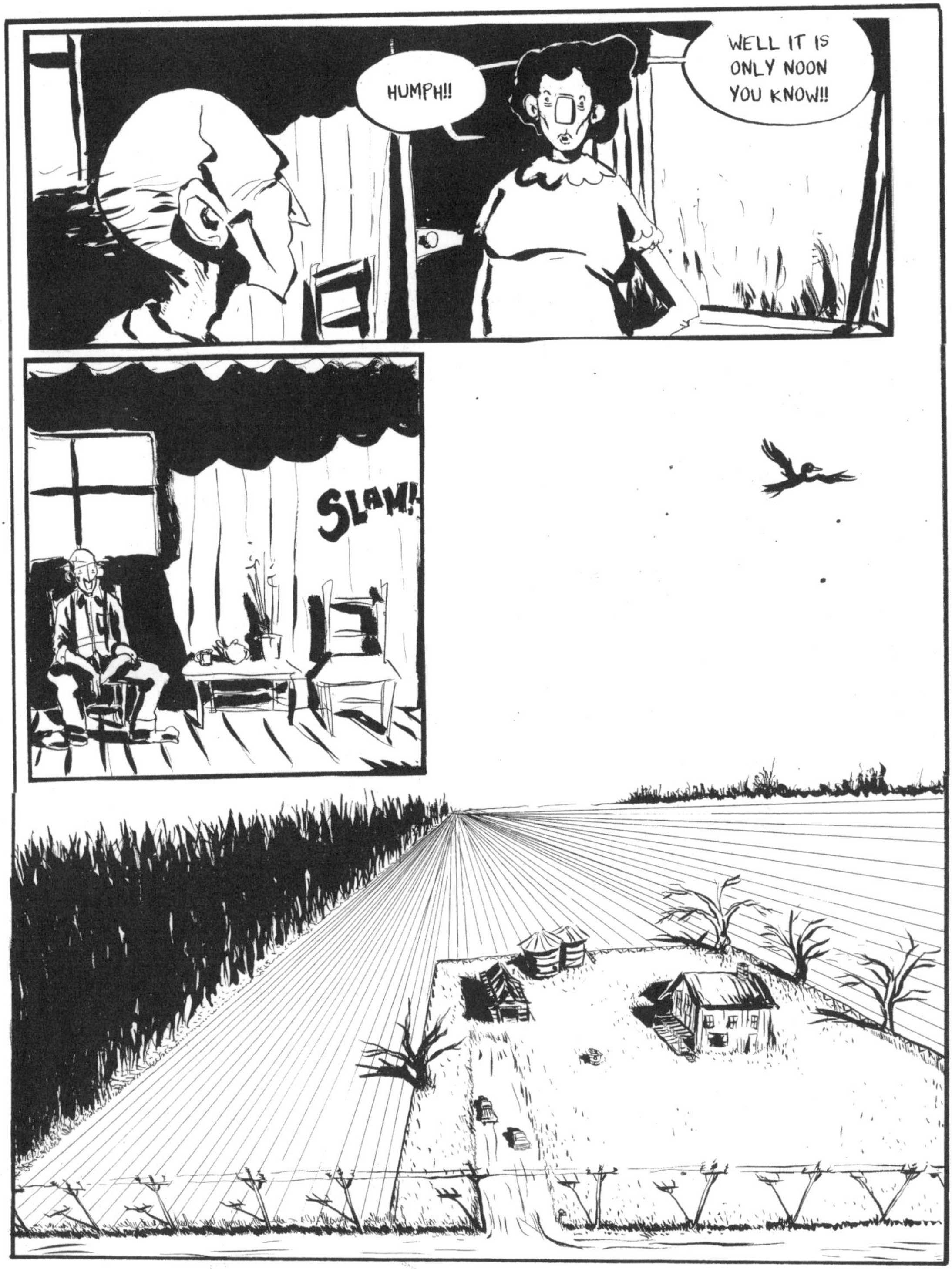
HUMPH!!
WELL IT IS ONLY NOON YOU KNOW!!
SLAM!!

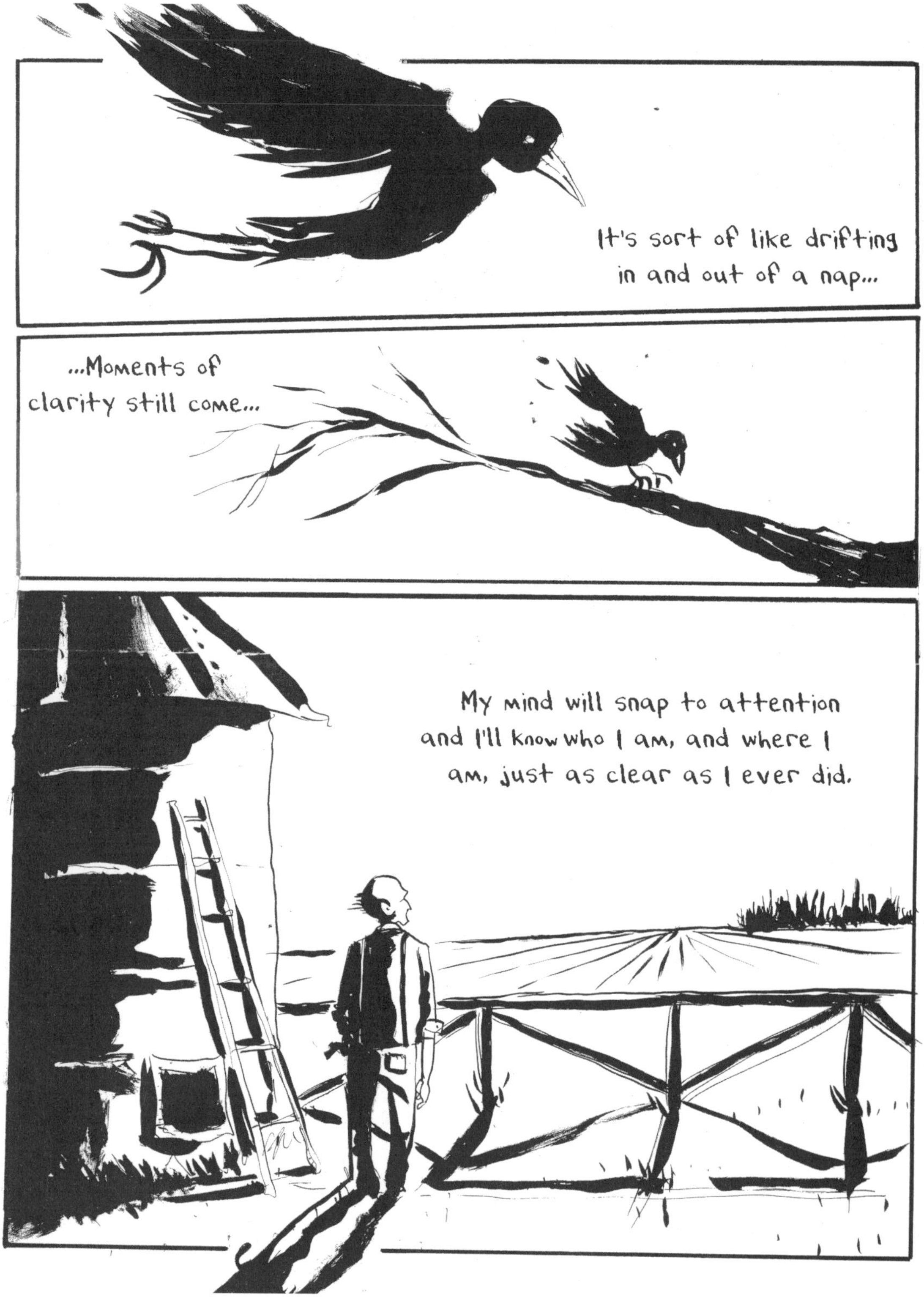
It's sort of like drifting in and out of a nap...
...Moments of clarity still come...
My mind will snap to attention and I'll know who I am, and where I am, just as clear as I ever did.

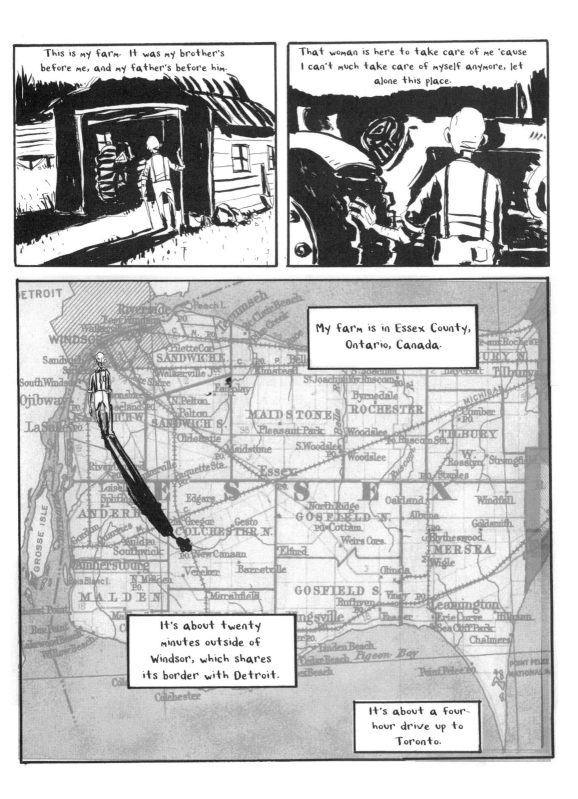

This is my farm. It was my brother's before me, and my father's before him.

That woman is here to take care of me 'cause I can't much take care of myself anymore, let alone this place.

My farm is in Essex County, Ontario, Canada.

It's about twenty minutes outside of Windsor, which shares its border with Detroit.

It's about a four-hour drive up to Toronto.

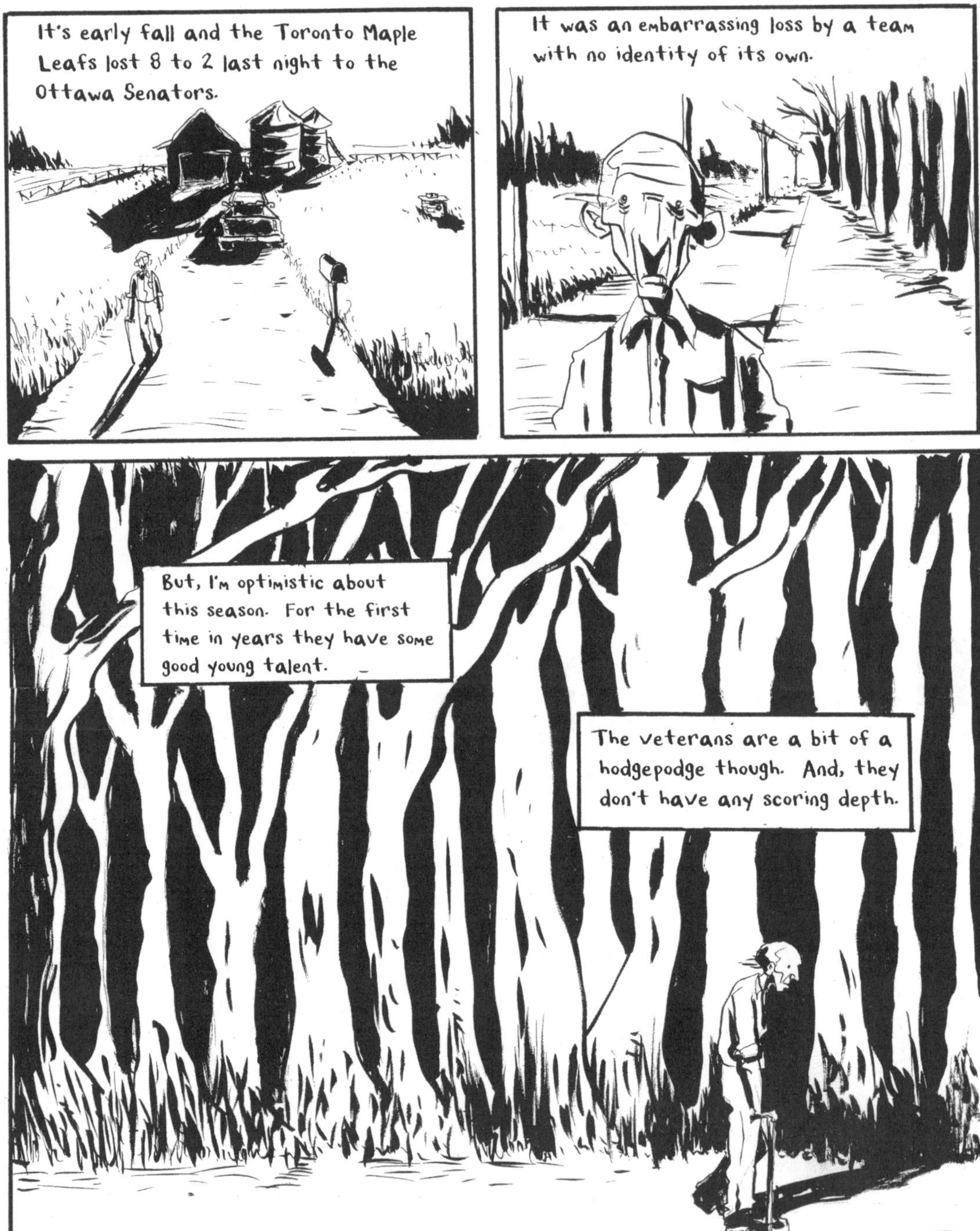

It's early fall and the Toronto Maple Leafs lost 8 to 2 last night to the Ottawa Senators.
It was an embarrassing loss by a team with no identity of its own.
But, I'm optimistic about this season. For the first time in years they have some good young talent.
The veterans are a bit of a hodgepodge though. And, they don't have any scoring depth.

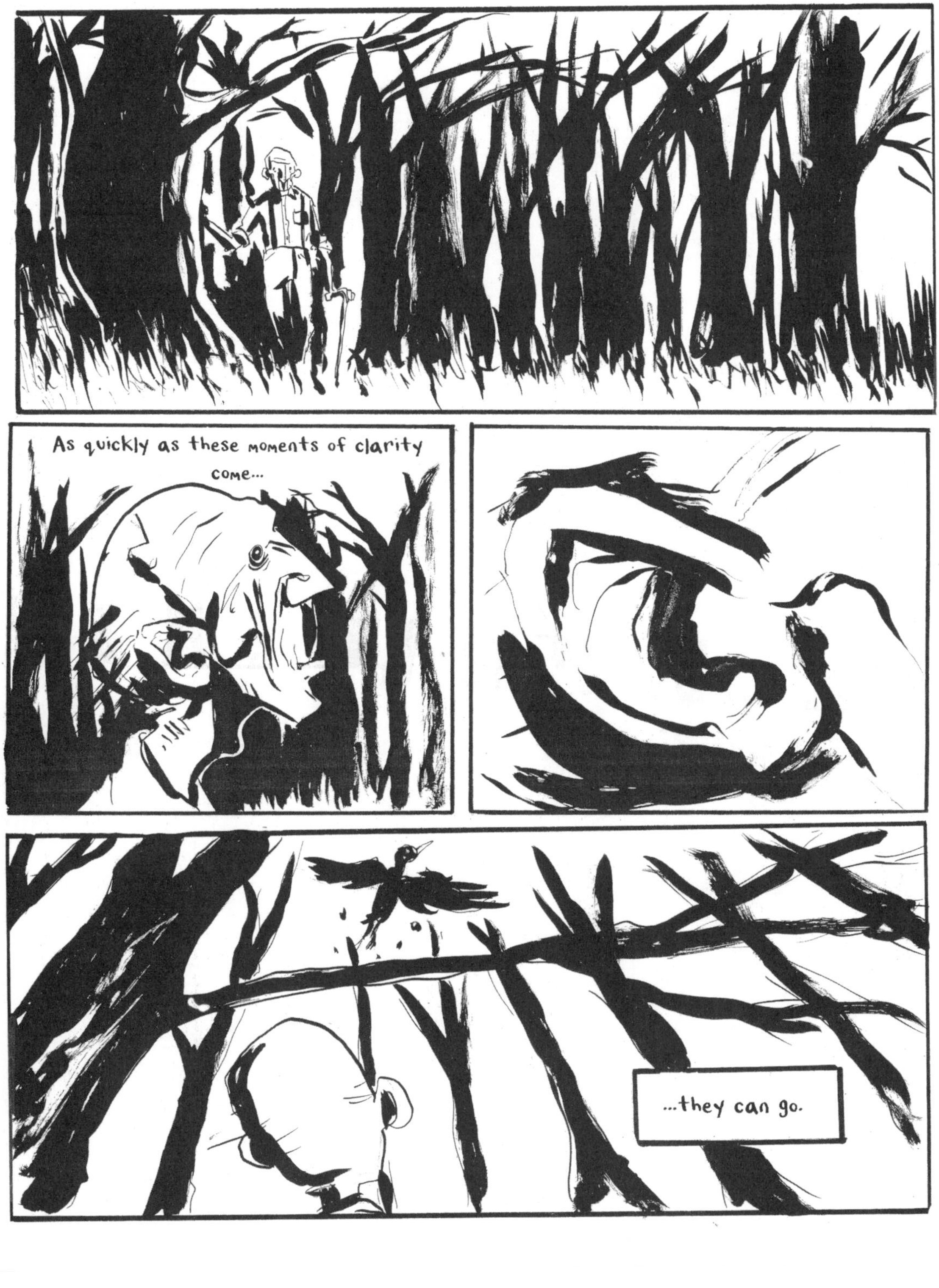
As quickly as these moments of clarity come...
...they can go.

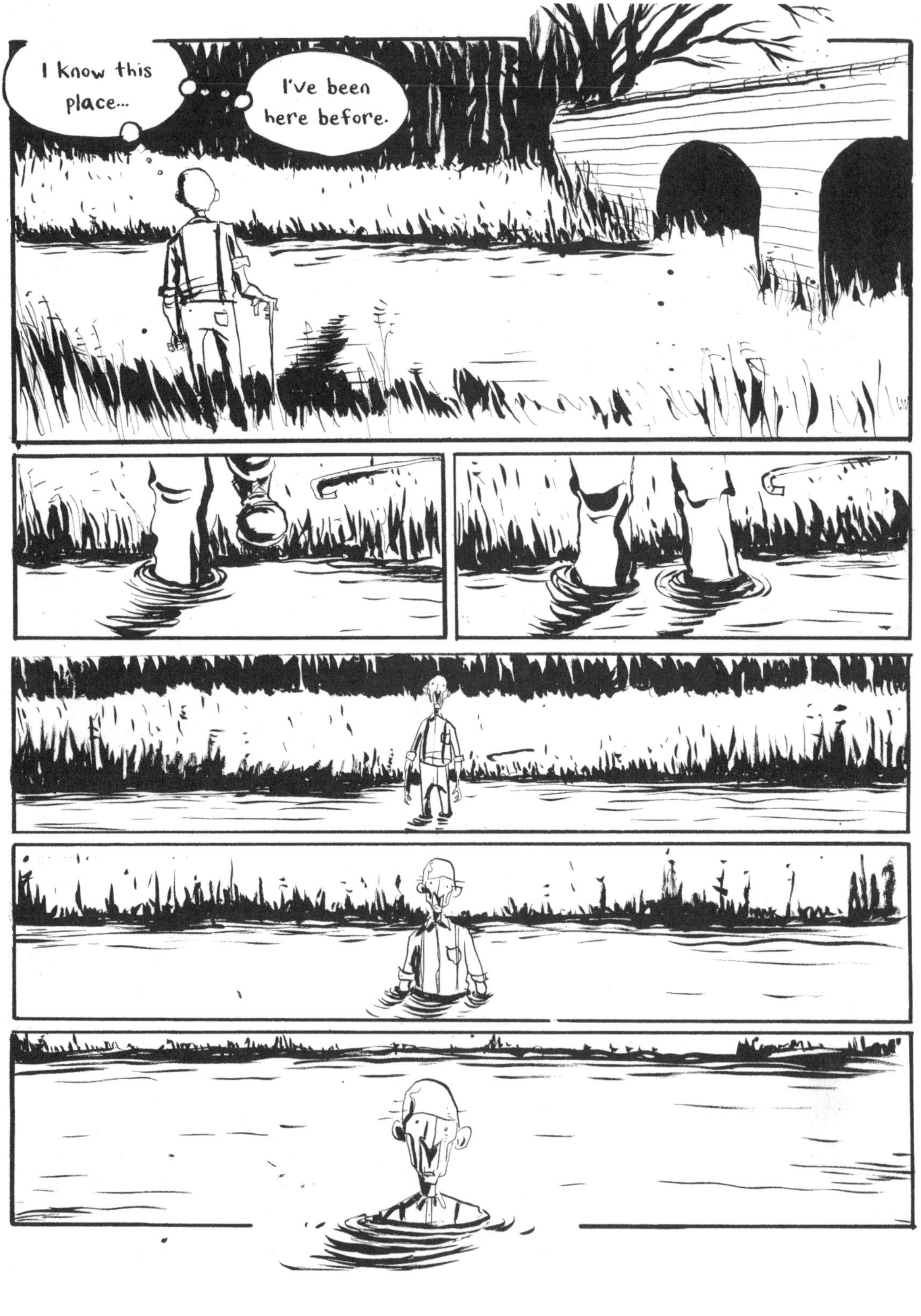
I know this place...
I've been here before.

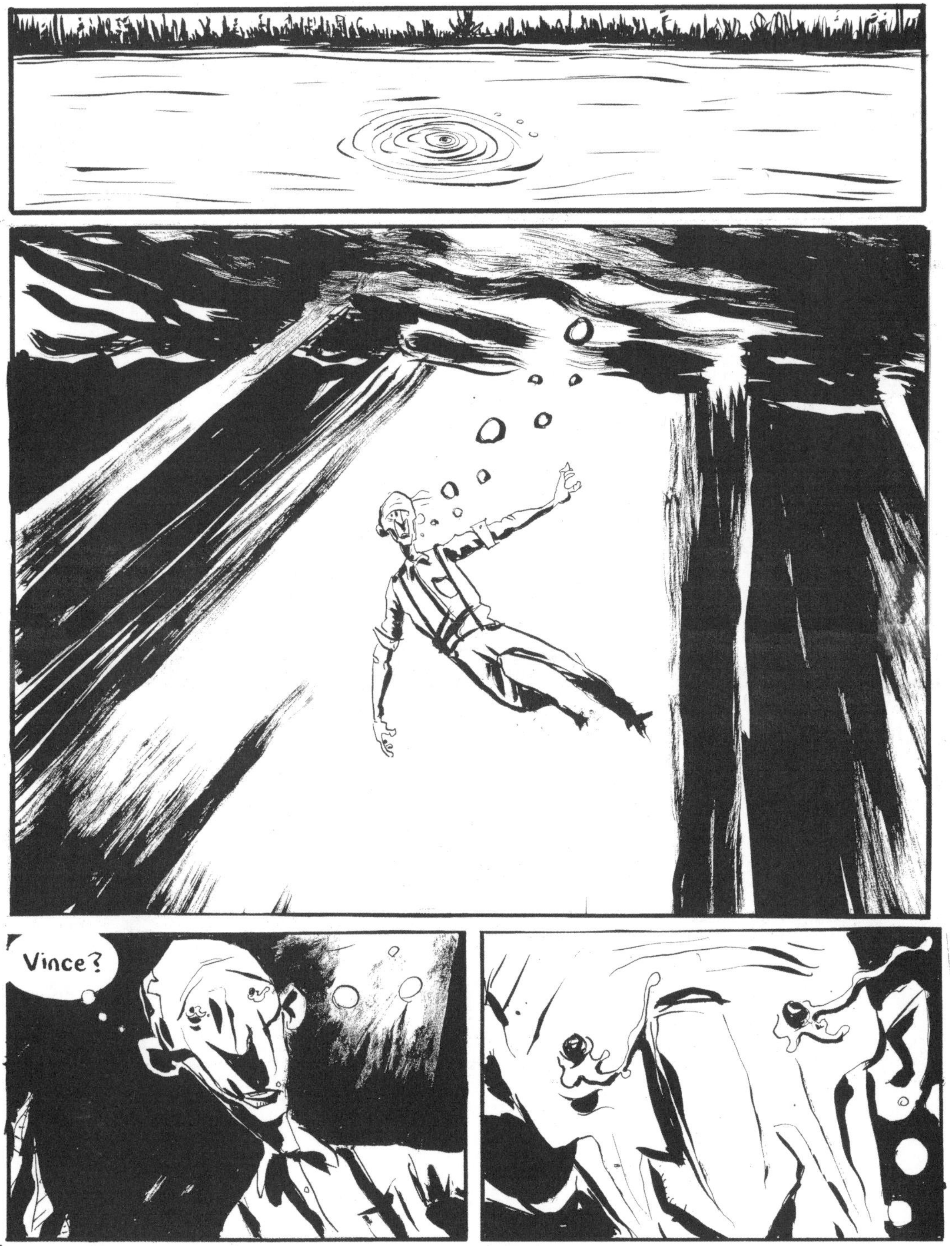
Vince?

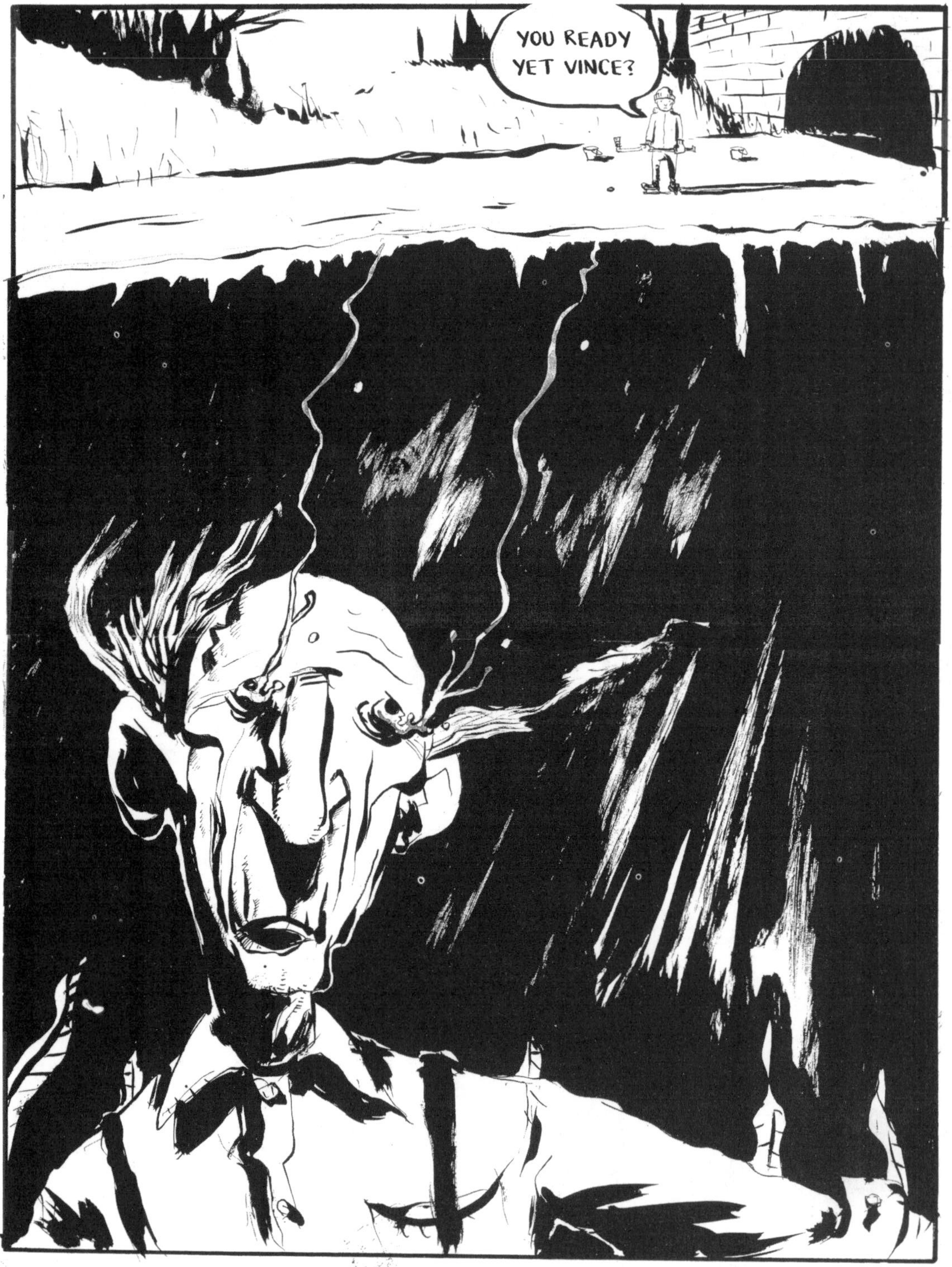
YOU READY YET VINCE?

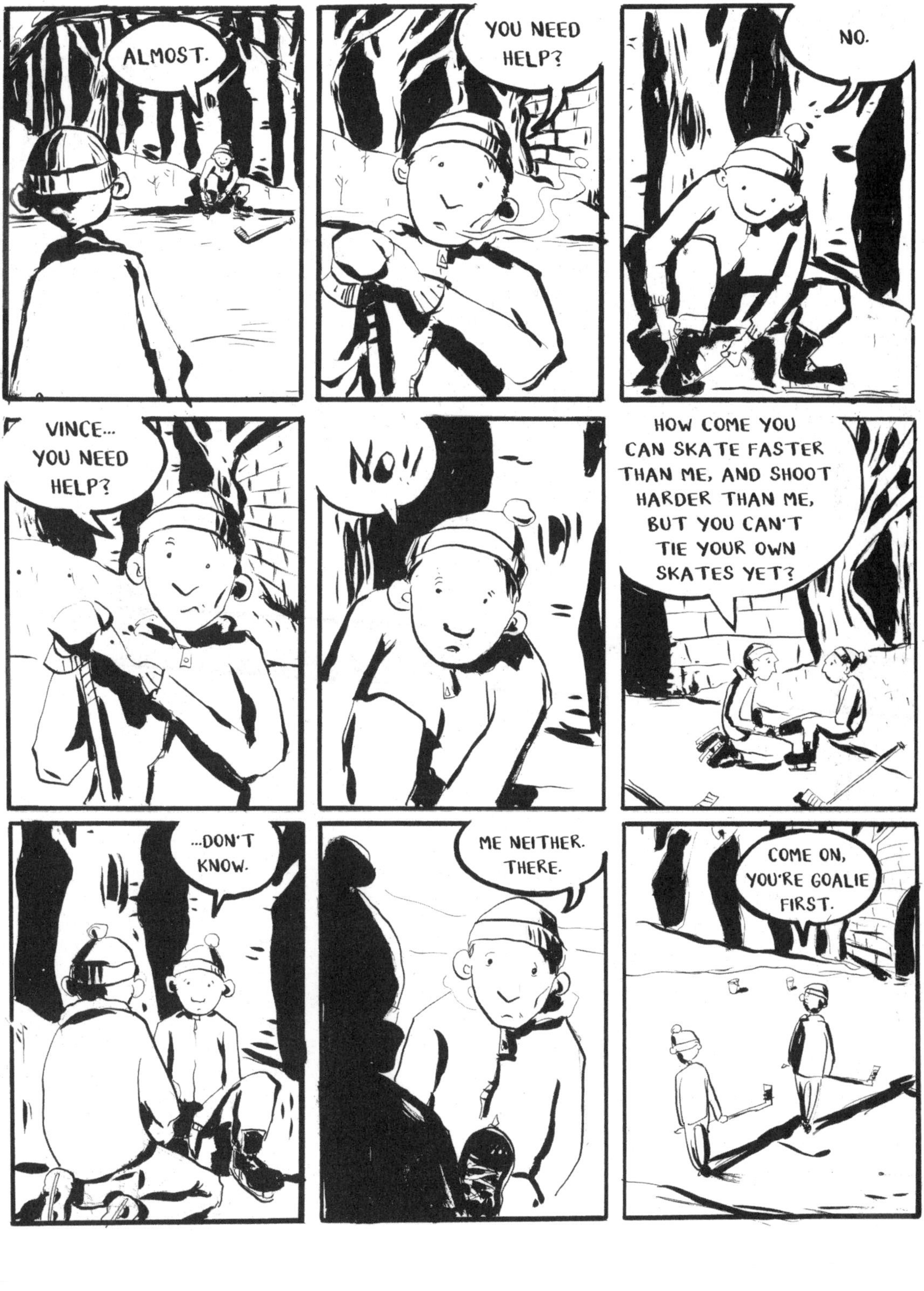
ALMOST.
YOU NEED HELP?
NO.
VINCE... YOU NEED HELP?
NO!!
HOW COME YOU CAN SKATE FASTER THAN ME, AND SHOOT HARDER THAN ME, BUT YOU CAN'T TIE YOUR OWN SKATES YET?
...DON'T KNOW.
ME NEITHER. THERE.
COME ON, YOU'RE GOALIE FIRST.

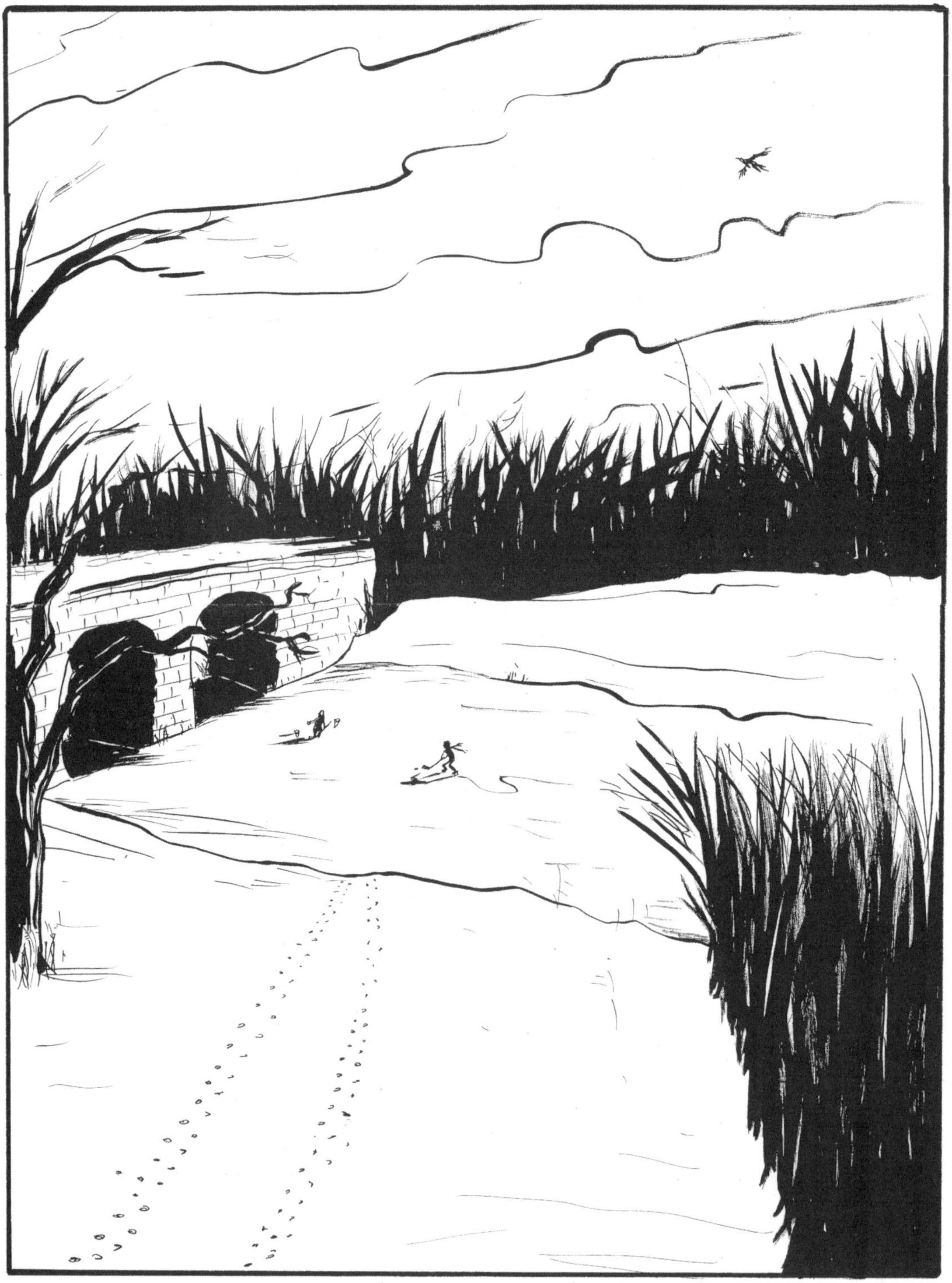

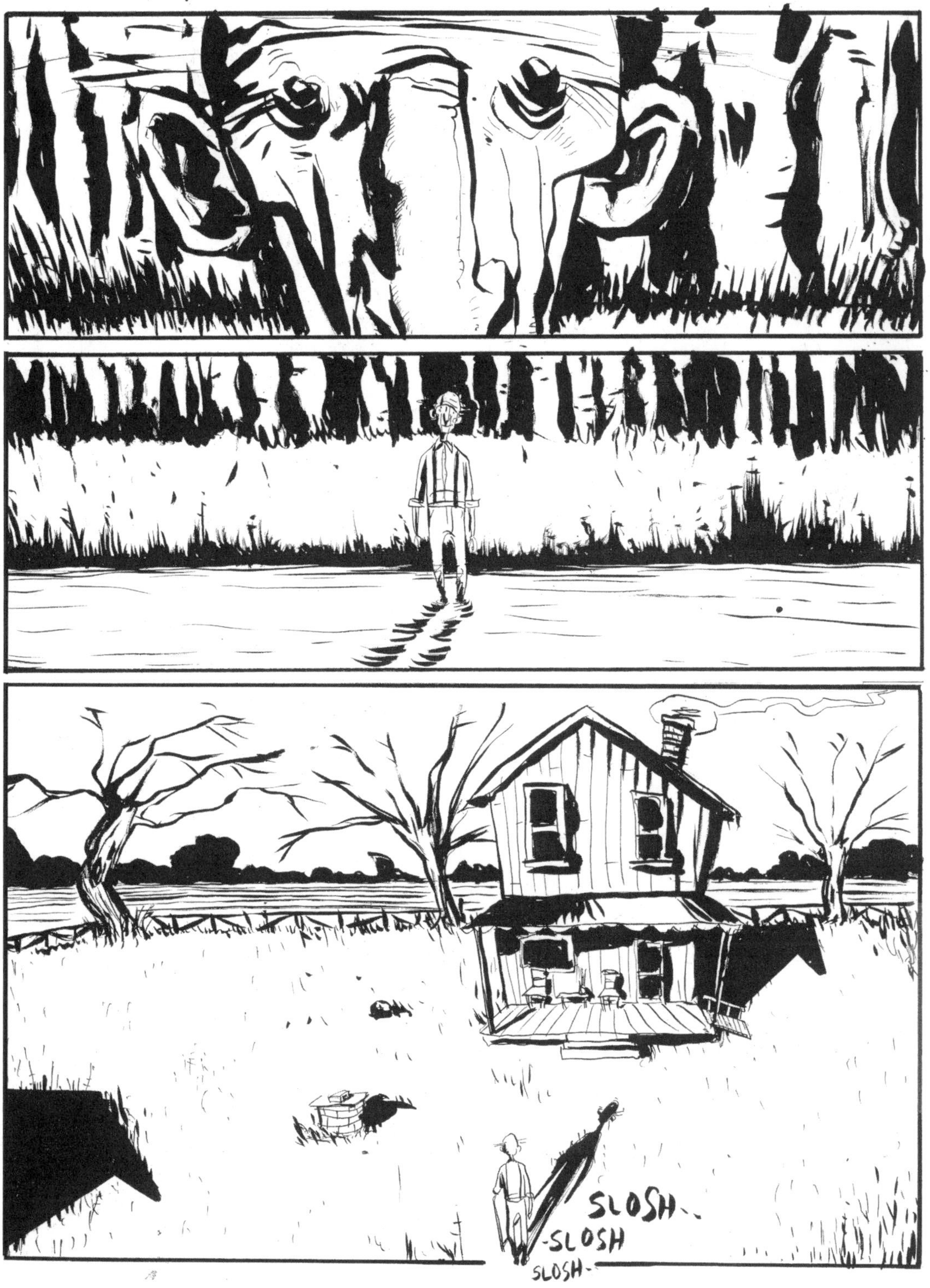
SLOSH..
-SLOSH
SLOSH-

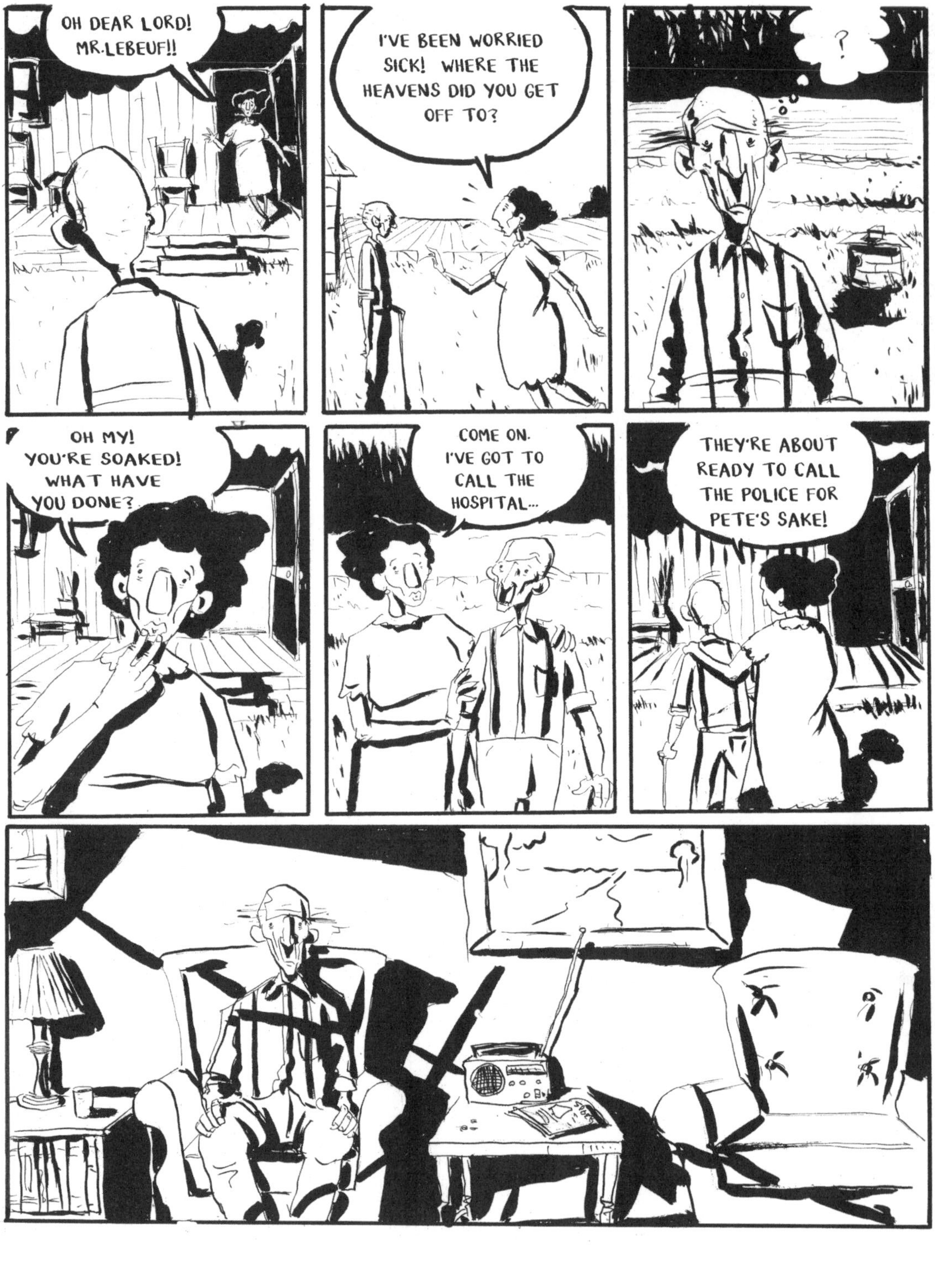

OH DEAR LORD! MR. LEBEUF!!
I'VE BEEN WORRIED SICK! WHERE THE HEAVENS DID YOU GET OFF TO?
?
OH MY! YOU'RE SOAKED! WHAT HAVE YOU DONE?
COME ON. I'VE GOT TO CALL THE HOSPITAL...
THEY'RE ABOUT READY TO CALL THE POLICE FOR PETE'S SAKE!

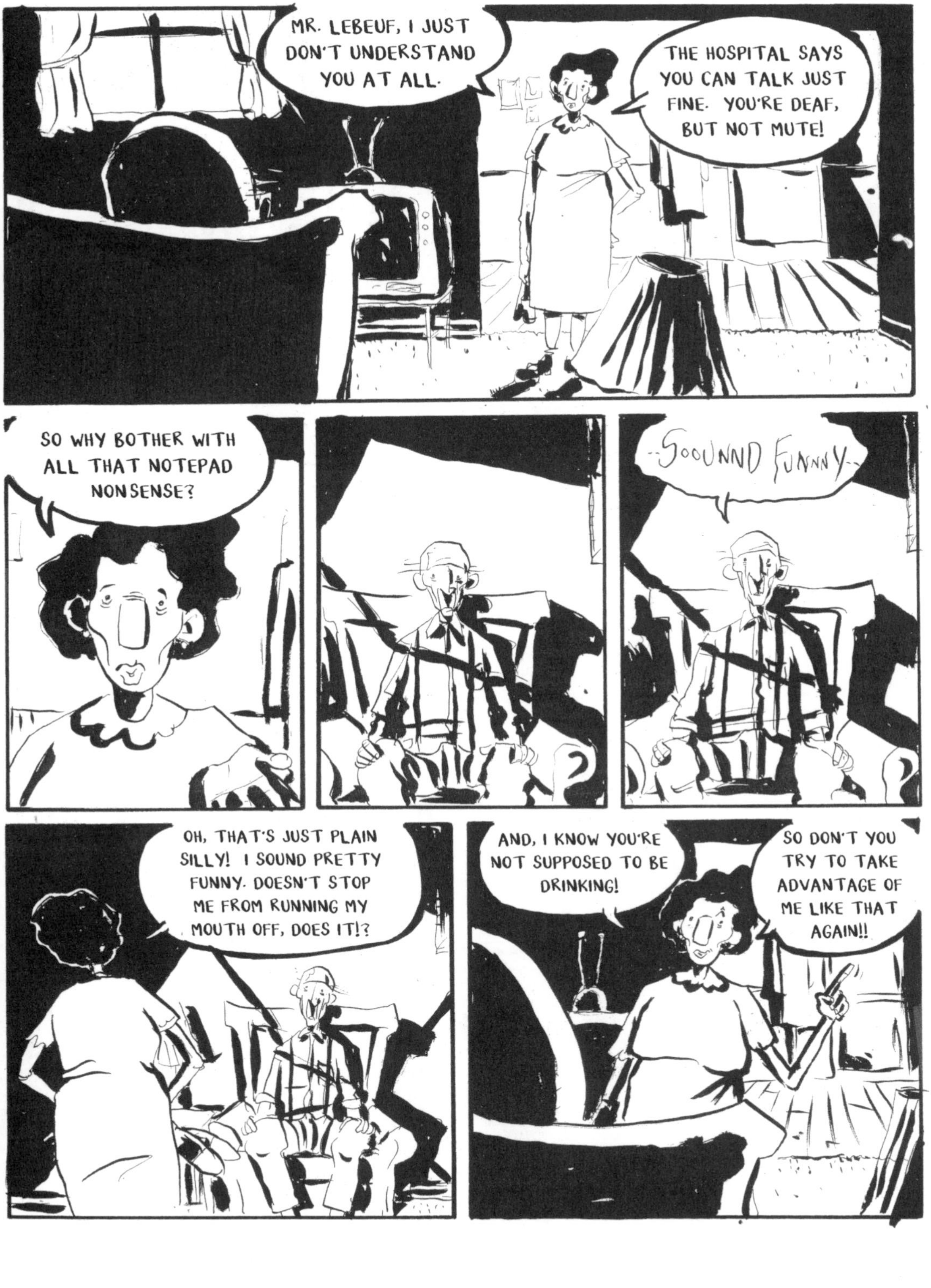
MR. LEBEUF, I JUST DON'T UNDERSTAND YOU AT ALL.
THE HOSPITAL SAYS YOU CAN TALK JUST FINE. YOU'RE DEAF, BUT NOT MUTE!
SO WHY BOTHER WITH ALL THAT NOTEPAD NONSENSE?
--SOOUNND FUNNNY--
OH, THAT'S JUST PLAIN SILLY! I SOUND PRETTY FUNNY. DOESN'T STOP ME FROM RUNNING MY MOUTH OFF, DOES IT!?
AND, I KNOW YOU'RE NOT SUPPOSED TO BE DRINKING!
SO DON'T YOU TRY TO TAKE ADVANTAGE OF ME LIKE THAT AGAIN!!

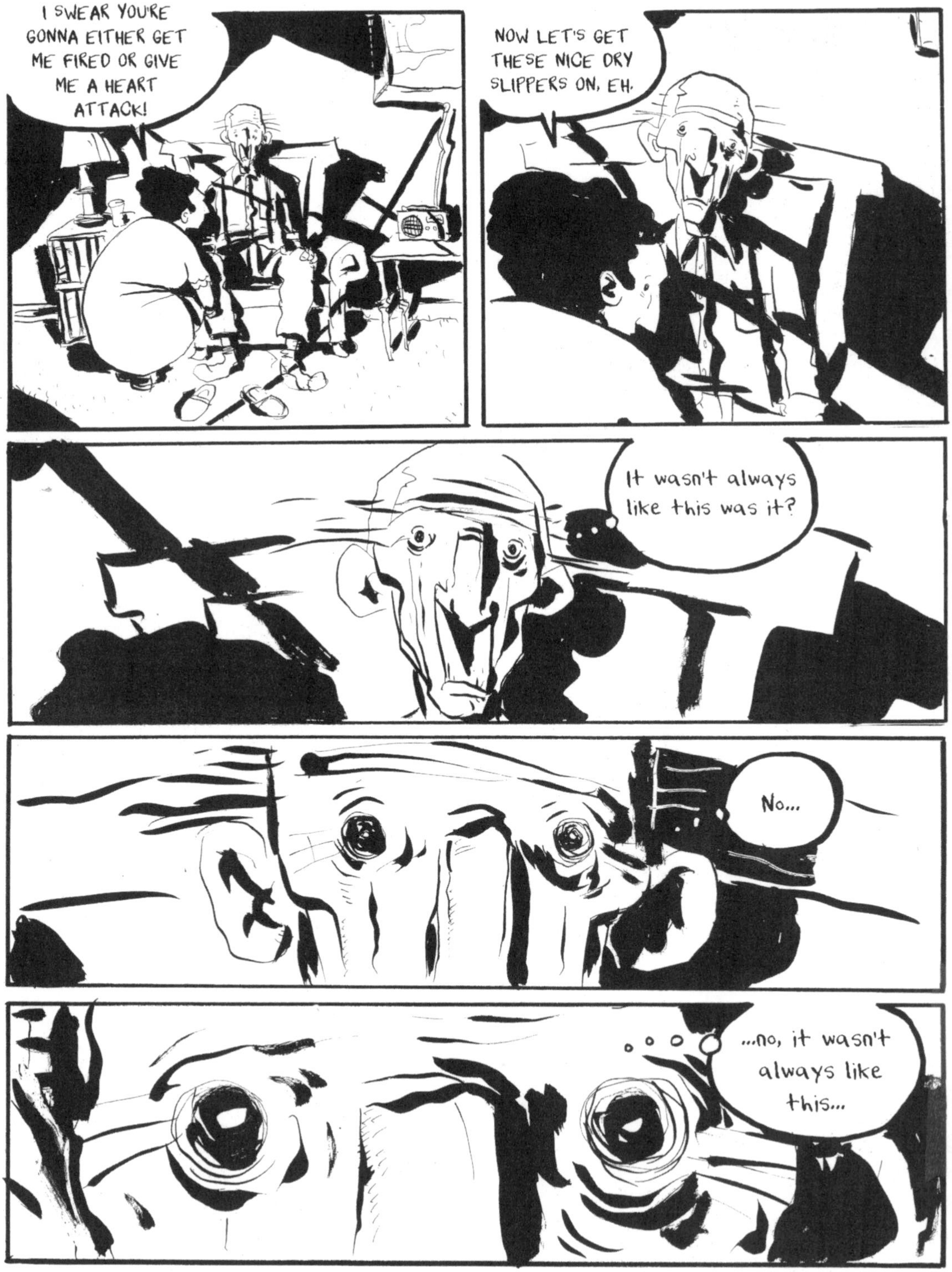
I SWEAR YOU'RE GONNA EITHER GET ME FIRED OR GIVE ME A HEART ATTACK!
NOW LET'S GET THESE NICE DRY SLIPPERS ON, EH.
It wasn't always like this was it?
No...
...no, it wasn't always like this...

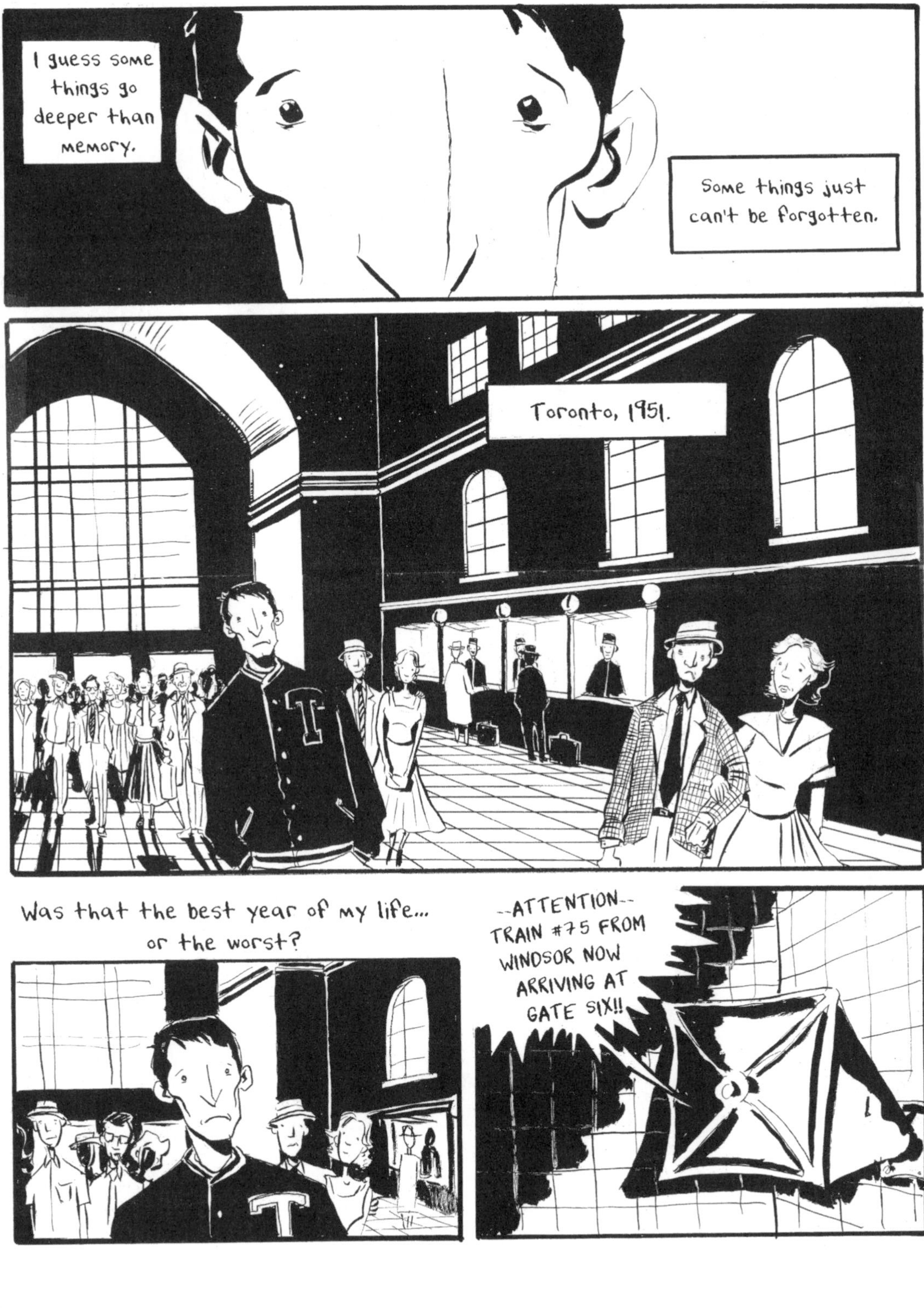
I guess some things go deeper than memory.
Some things just can't be forgotten.
Toronto, 1951.
Was that the best year of my life... or the worst?
--ATTENTION-- TRAIN #75 FROM WINDSOR NOW ARRIVING AT GATE SIX!!

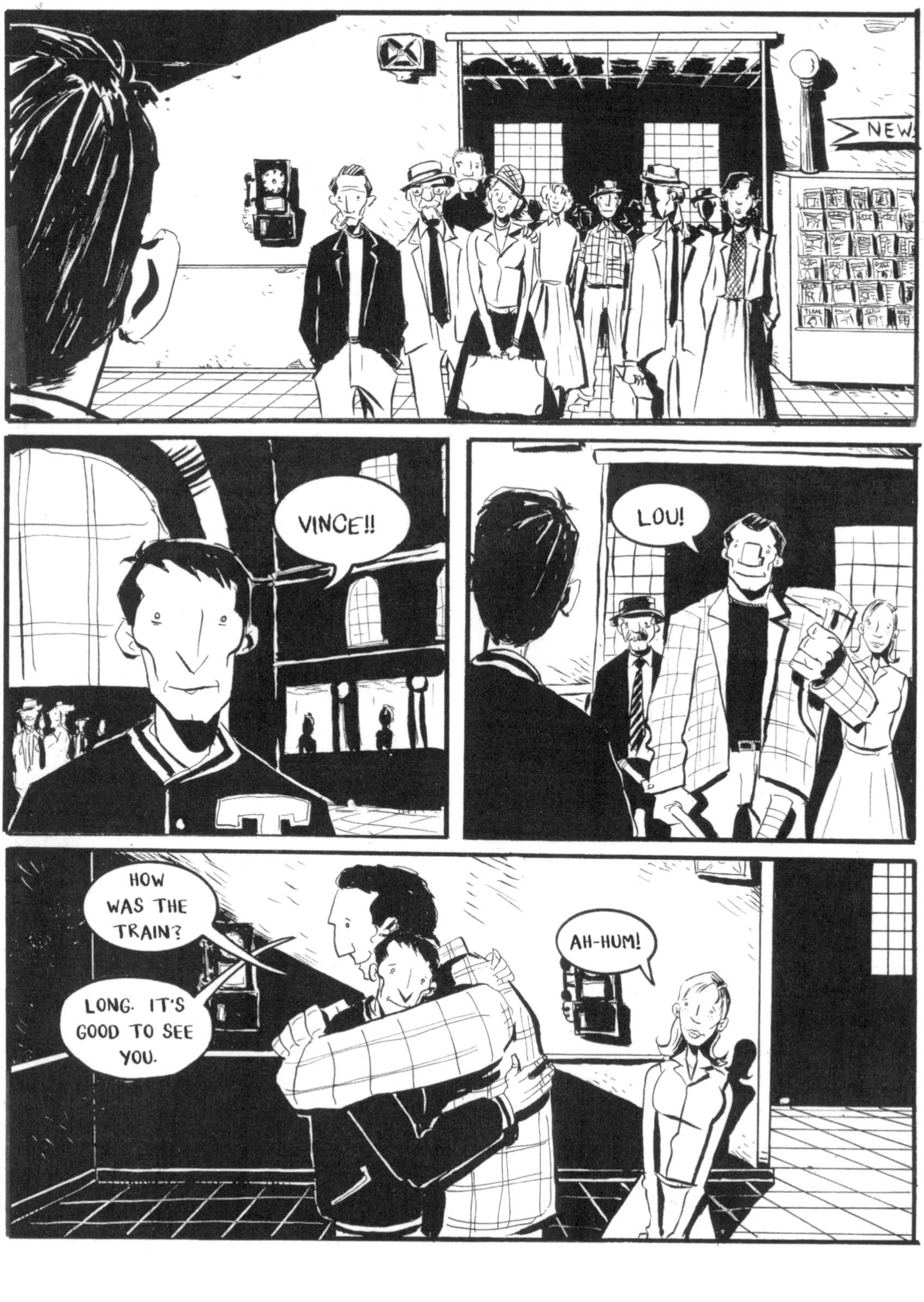
NEWS
TIME
VINCE!!
LOU!
HOW WAS THE TRAIN?
LONG. IT'S GOOD TO SEE YOU.
AH-HUM!

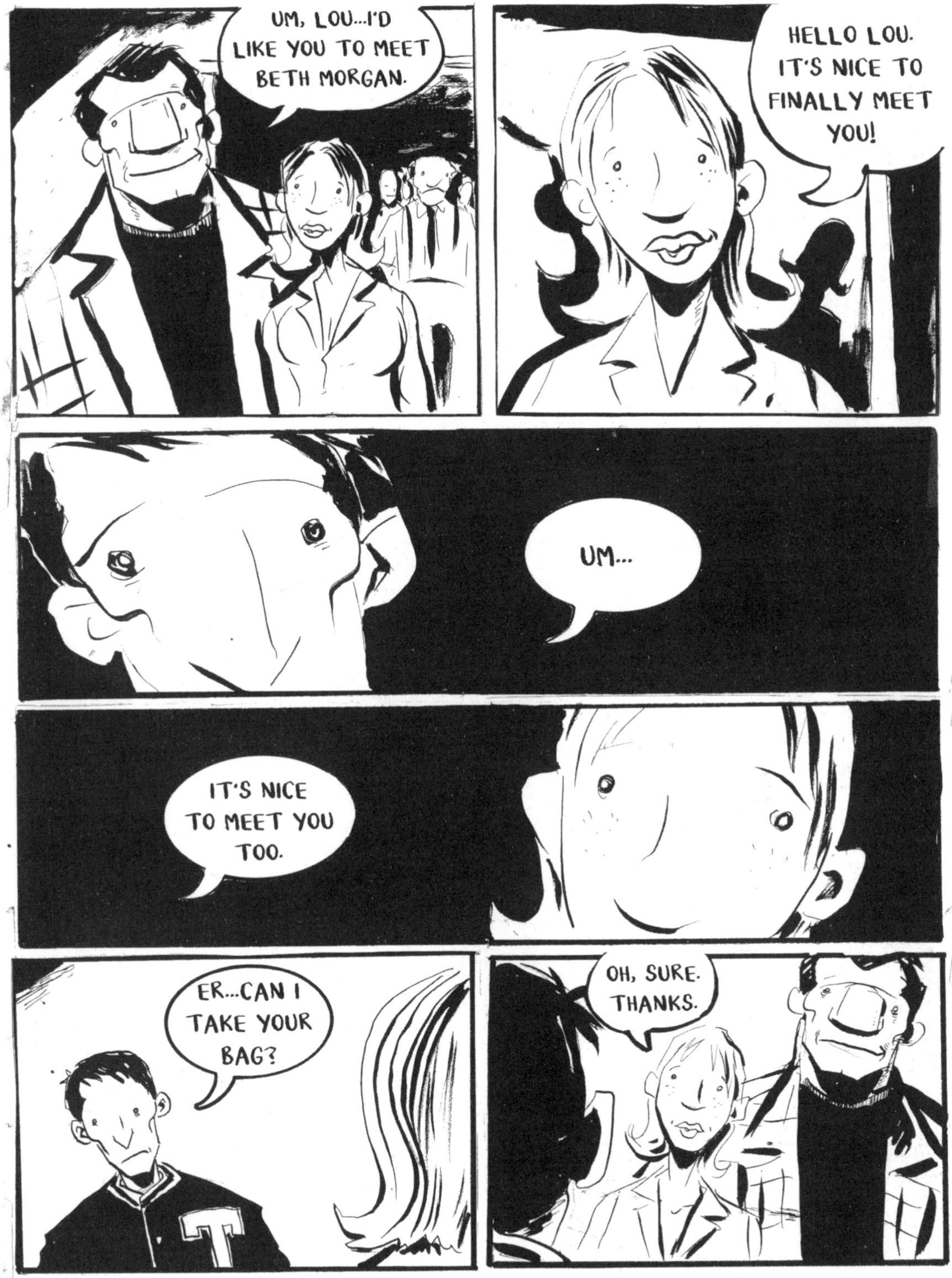
UM, LOU...I'D LIKE YOU TO MEET BETH MORGAN.
HELLO LOU. IT'S NICE TO FINALLY MEET YOU!
UM...
IT'S NICE TO MEET YOU TOO.
ER...CAN I TAKE YOUR BAG?
OH, SURE. THANKS.

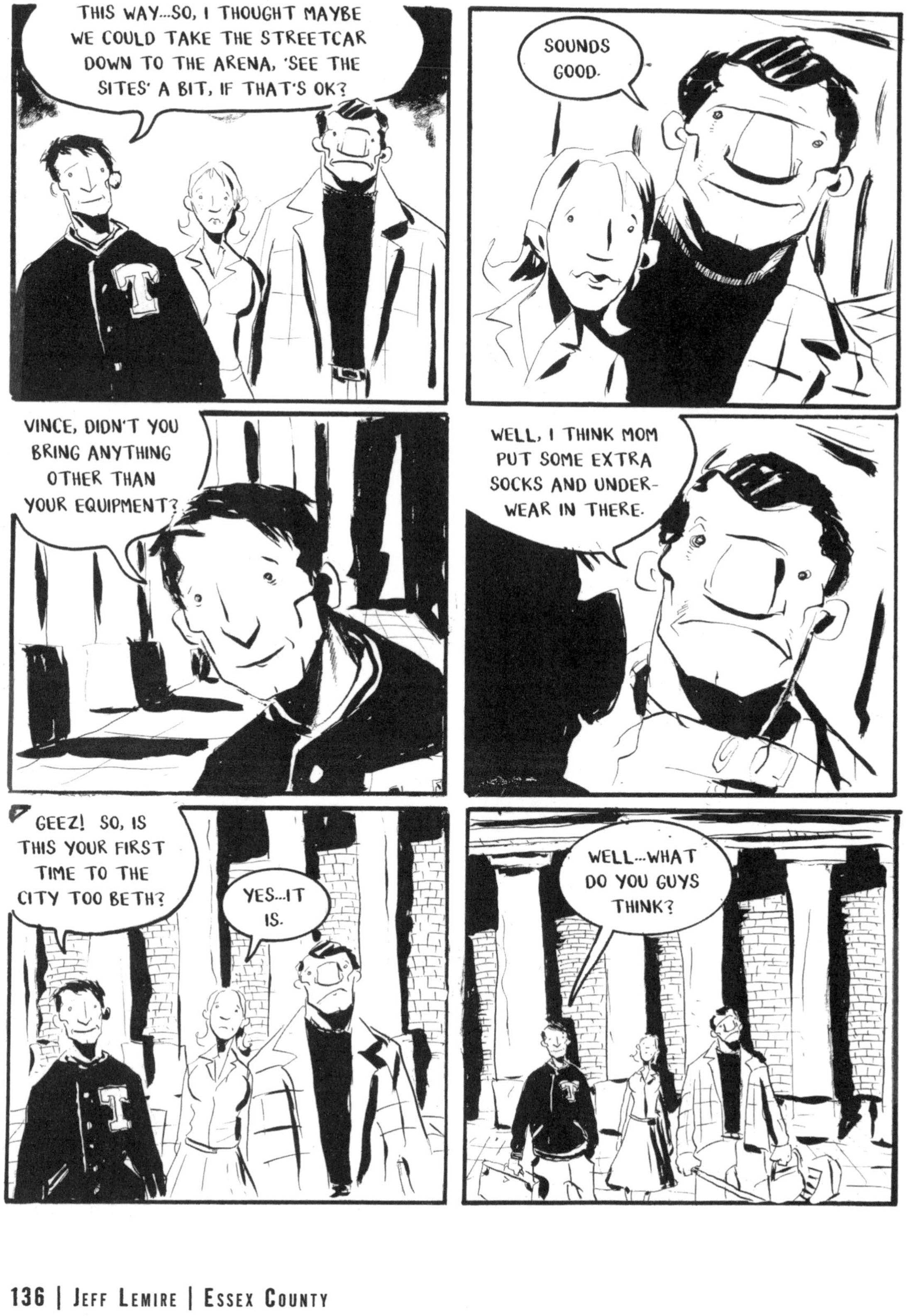
THIS WAY...SO, I THOUGHT MAYBE WE COULD TAKE THE STREETCAR DOWN TO THE ARENA, 'SEE THE SITES' A BIT, IF THAT'S OK?
SOUNDS GOOD.
VINCE, DIDN'T YOU BRING ANYTHING OTHER THAN YOUR EQUIPMENT?
WELL, I THINK MOM PUT SOME EXTRA SOCKS AND UNDER-WEAR IN THERE.
GEEZ! SO, IS THIS YOUR FIRST TIME TO THE CITY TOO BETH?
YES...IT IS.
WELL...WHAT DO YOU GUYS THINK?

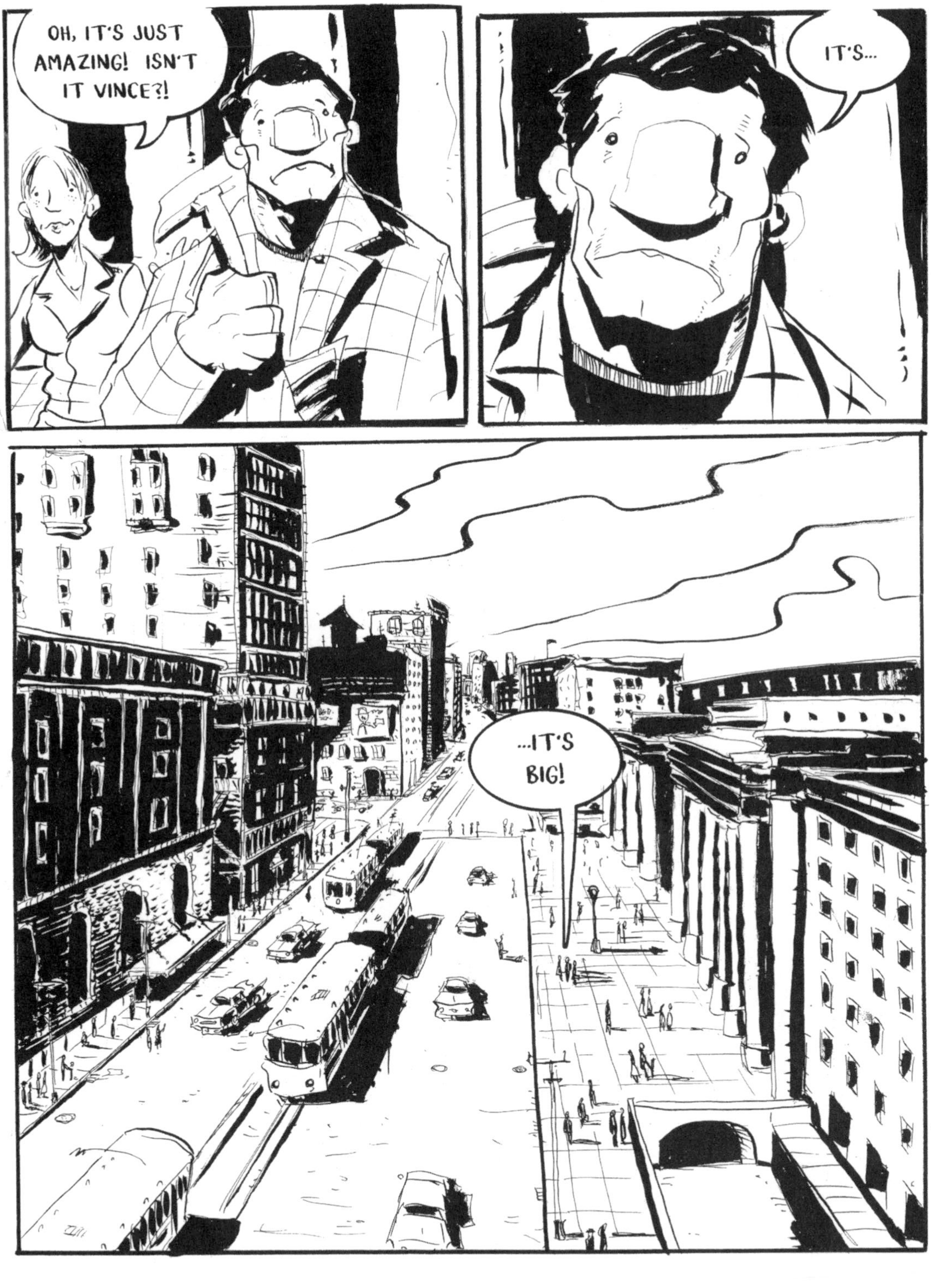
OH, IT'S JUST AMAZING! ISN'T IT VINCE?!
IT'S...
...IT'S BIG!

1951. The year my "little" brother followed me to Toronto to play hockey for a now defunct semiprofessional hockey club called THE GRIZZLIES. We played out of the old Ricoh Coliseum downtown. I was in my third year with the team, and I'd established myself as a reliable third line centerman.

The Grizzlies were struggling to hold on to a playoff spot when the scouts got wind of a young winger from Essex County who had scored thirty goals in his last junior season. The fact that he also happened to be my younger brother only sweetened the deal for them. A day after his 18th birthday they had him on a train to the city...

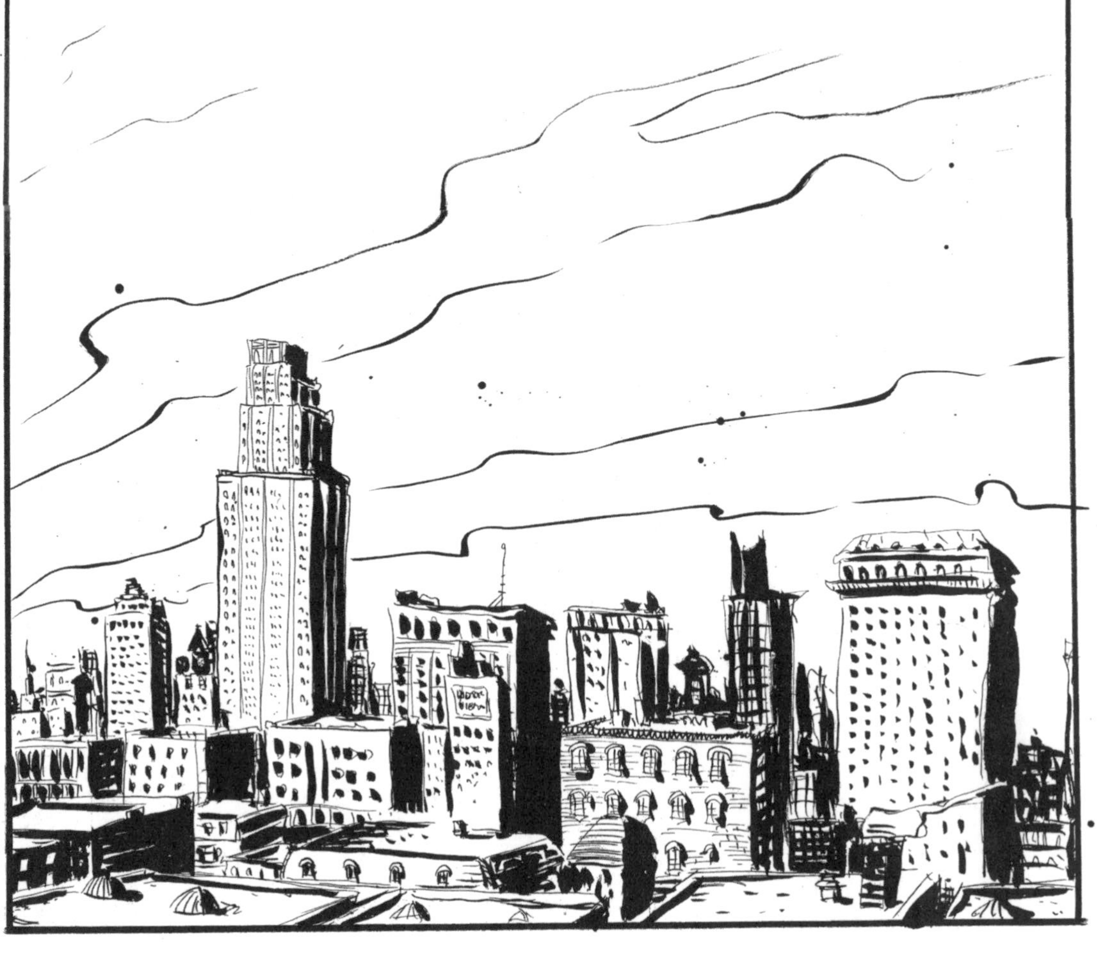

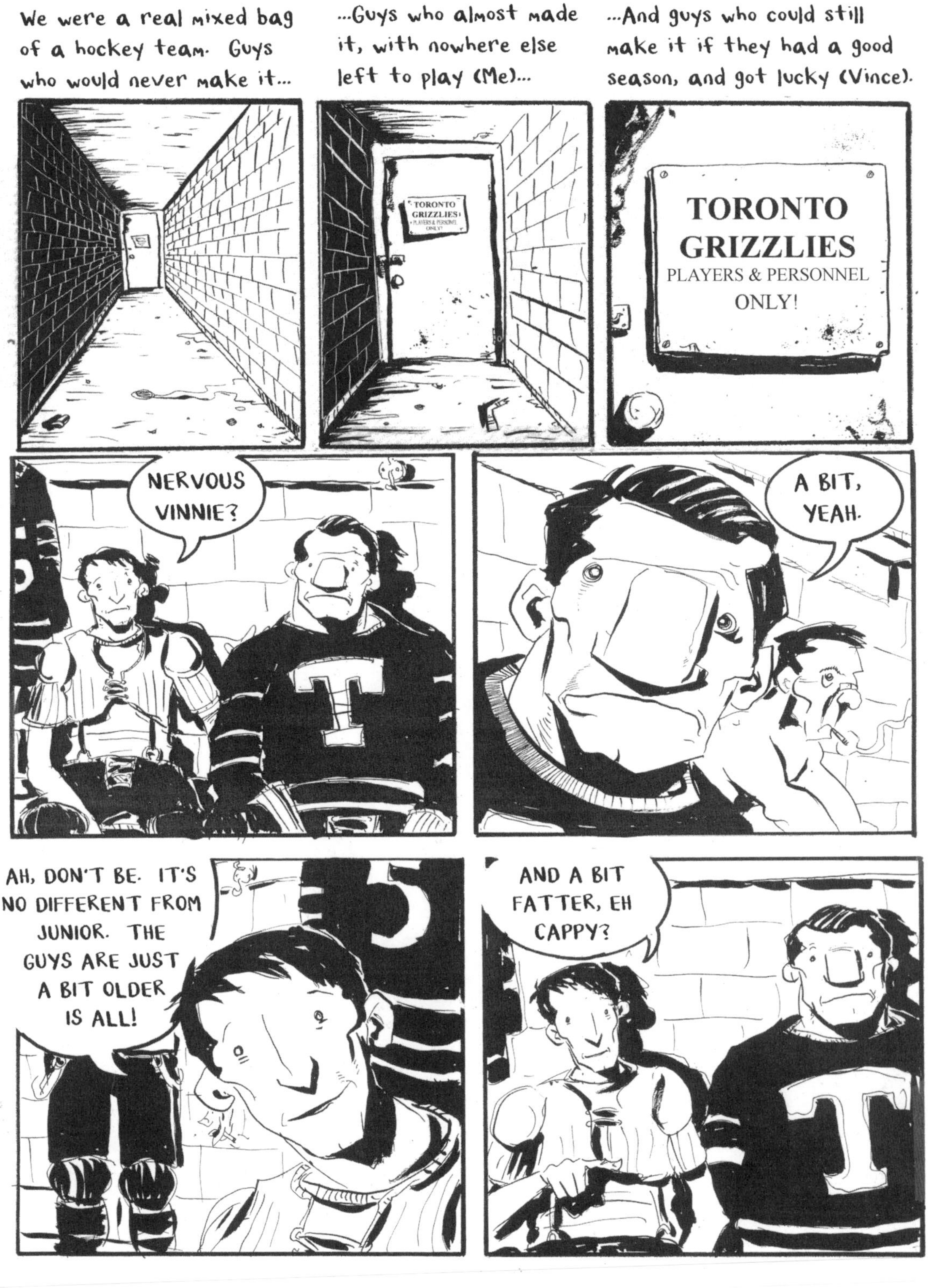
We were a real mixed bag of a hockey team. Guys who would never make it...
...Guys who almost made it, with nowhere else left to play (Me)...
...And guys who could still make it if they had a good season, and got lucky (Vince).
TORONTO GRIZZLIES PLAYERS & PERSONNEL ONLY!
NERVOUS VINNIE?
A BIT, YEAH.
AH, DON'T BE. IT'S NO DIFFERENT FROM JUNIOR. THE GUYS ARE JUST A BIT OLDER IS ALL!
AND A BIT FATTER, EH CAPPY?

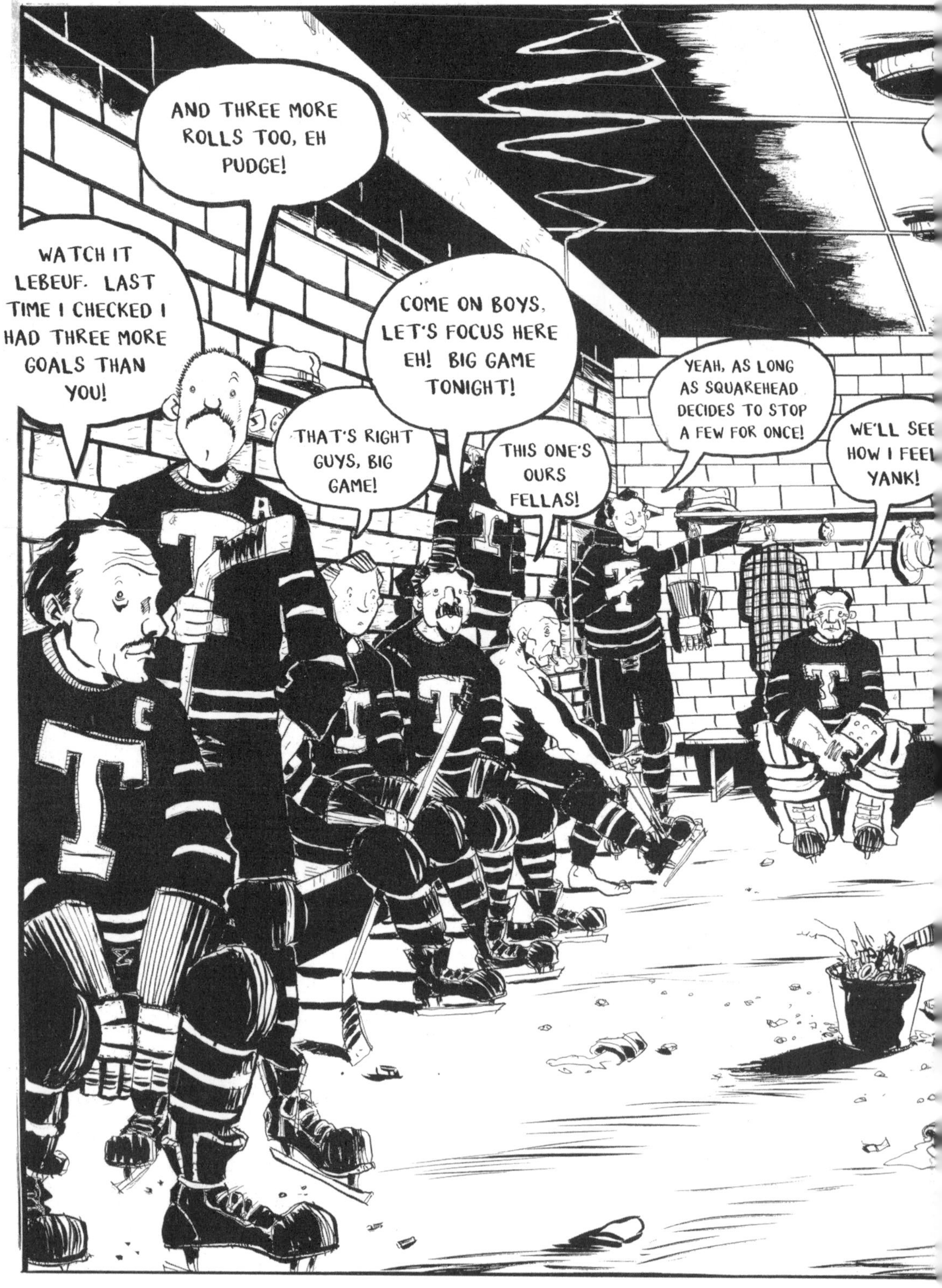
AND THREE MORE ROLLS TOO, EH PUDGE!
WATCH IT LEBEUF. LAST TIME I CHECKED I HAD THREE MORE GOALS THAN YOU!
COME ON BOYS, LET'S FOCUS HERE EH! BIG GAME TONIGHT!
THAT'S RIGHT GUYS, BIG GAME!
THIS ONE'S OURS FELLAS!
YEAH, AS LONG AS SQUAREHEAD DECIDES TO STOP A FEW FOR ONCE!
WE'LL SEE HOW I FEEL YANK!

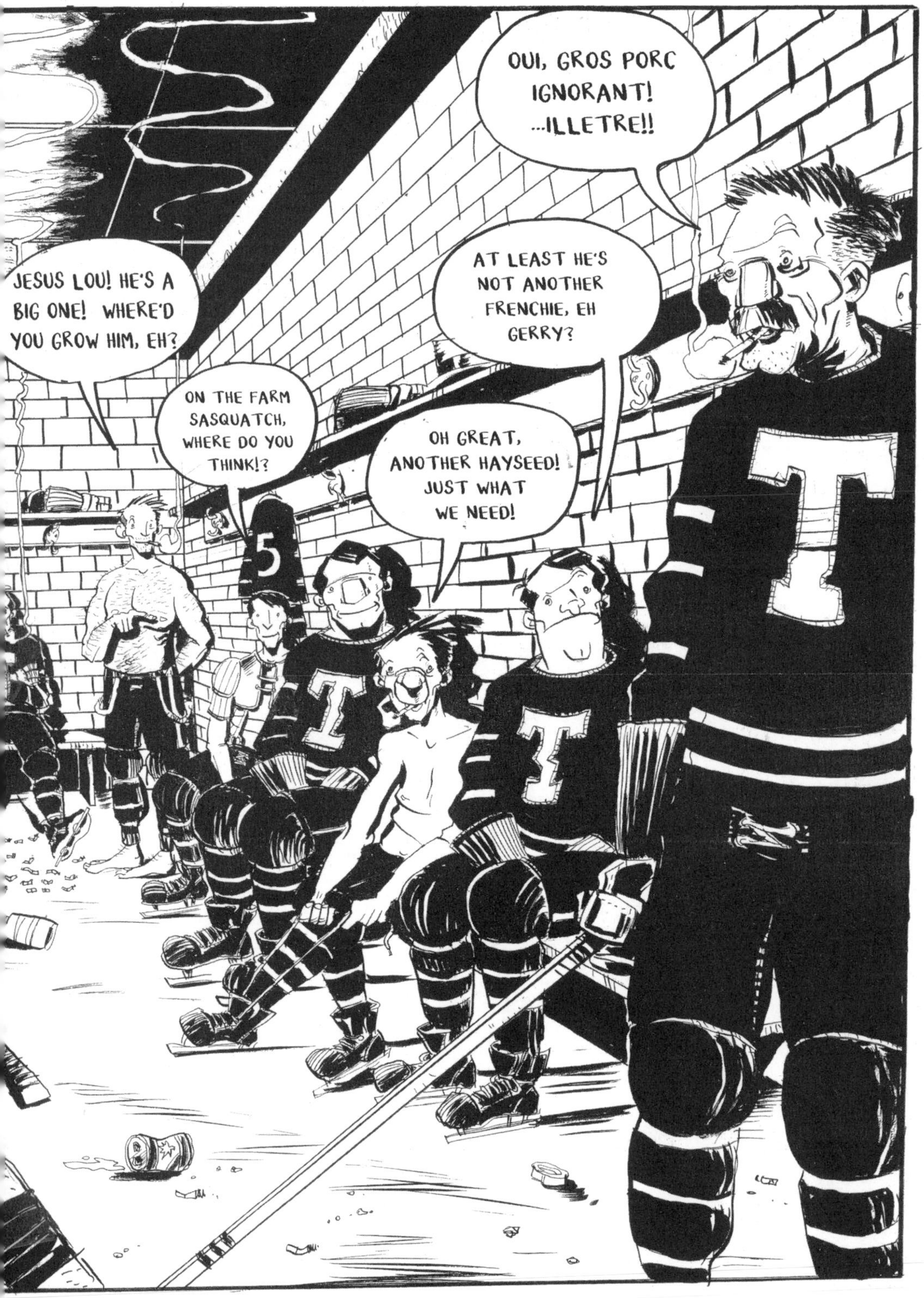
JESUS LOU! HE'S A BIG ONE! WHERE'D YOU GROW HIM, EH?
ON THE FARM SASQUATCH, WHERE DO YOU THINK!?
OH GREAT, ANOTHER HAYSEED! JUST WHAT WE NEED!
AT LEAST HE'S NOT ANOTHER FRENCHIE, EH GERRY?
OUI, GROS PORC IGNORANT! ...ILLETRE!!
5
T

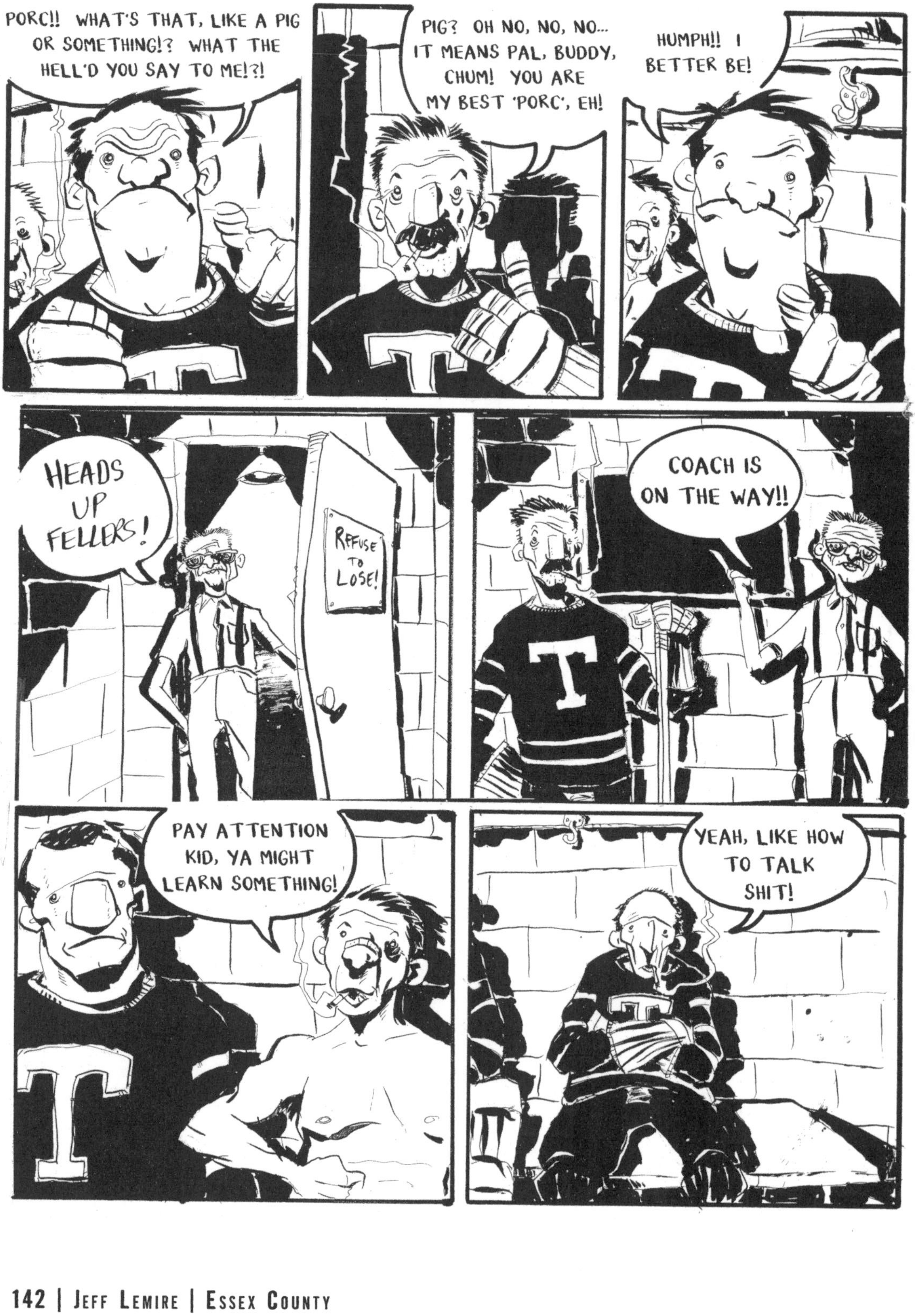
PORC!! WHAT'S THAT, LIKE A PIG OR SOMETHING!? WHAT THE HELL'D YOU SAY TO ME!?!
PIG? OH NO, NO, NO... IT MEANS PAL, BUDDY, CHUM! YOU ARE MY BEST 'PORC', EH!
HUMPH!! I BETTER BE!
HEADS UP FELLERS!
REFUSE TO LOSE!
COACH IS ON THE WAY!!
PAY ATTENTION KID, YA MIGHT LEARN SOMETHING!
YEAH, LIKE HOW TO TALK SHIT!

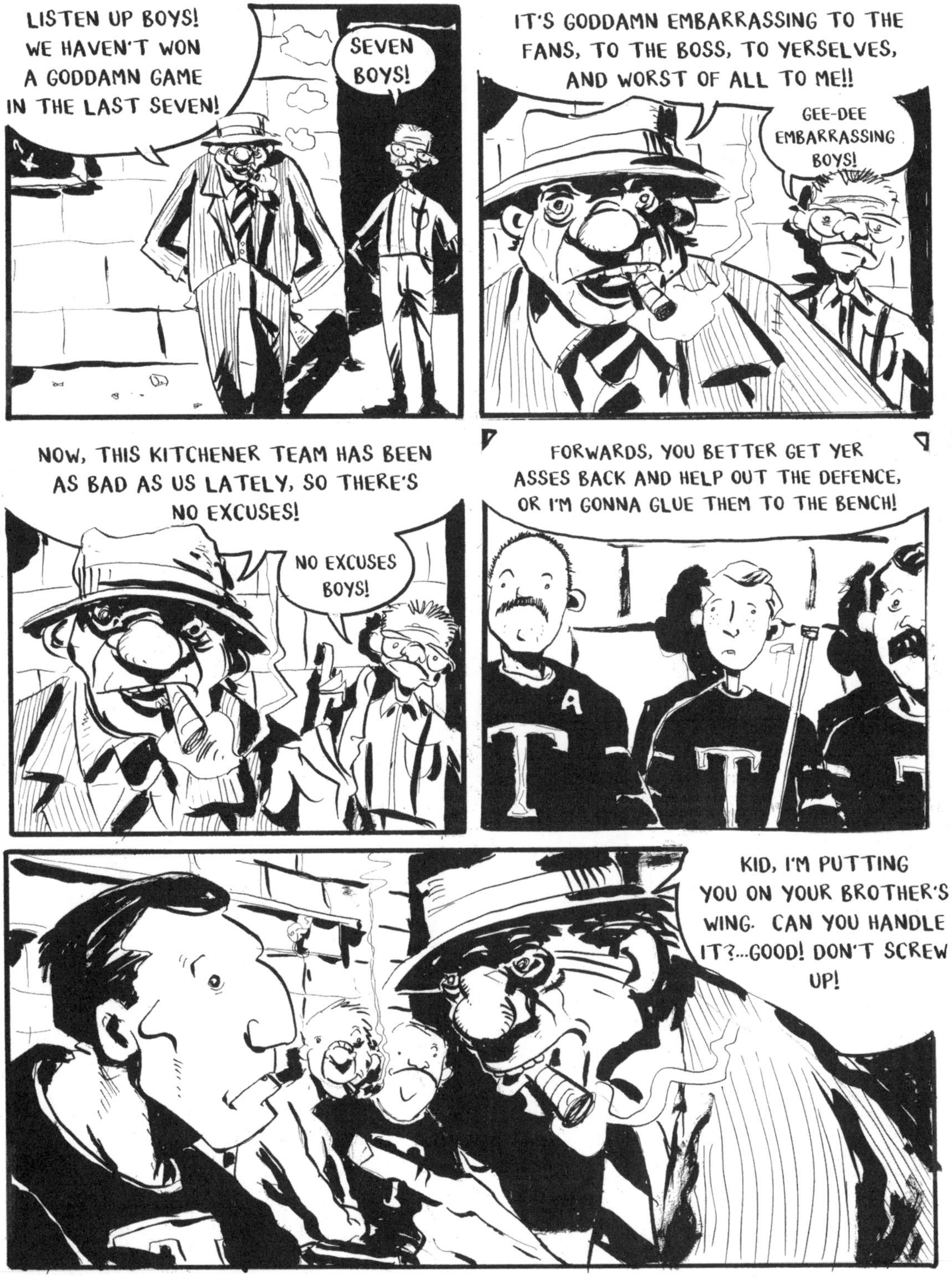
LISTEN UP BOYS! WE HAVEN'T WON A GODDAMN GAME IN THE LAST SEVEN!
SEVEN BOYS!
IT'S GODDAMN EMBARRASSING TO THE FANS, TO THE BOSS, TO YERSELVES, AND WORST OF ALL TO ME!!
GEE-DEE EMBARRASSING BOYS!
NOW, THIS KITCHENER TEAM HAS BEEN AS BAD AS US LATELY, SO THERE'S NO EXCUSES!
NO EXCUSES BOYS!
FORWARDS, YOU BETTER GET YER ASSES BACK AND HELP OUT THE DEFENCE, OR I'M GONNA GLUE THEM TO THE BENCH!
KID, I'M PUTTING YOU ON YOUR BROTHER'S WING. CAN YOU HANDLE IT?...GOOD! DON'T SCREW UP!

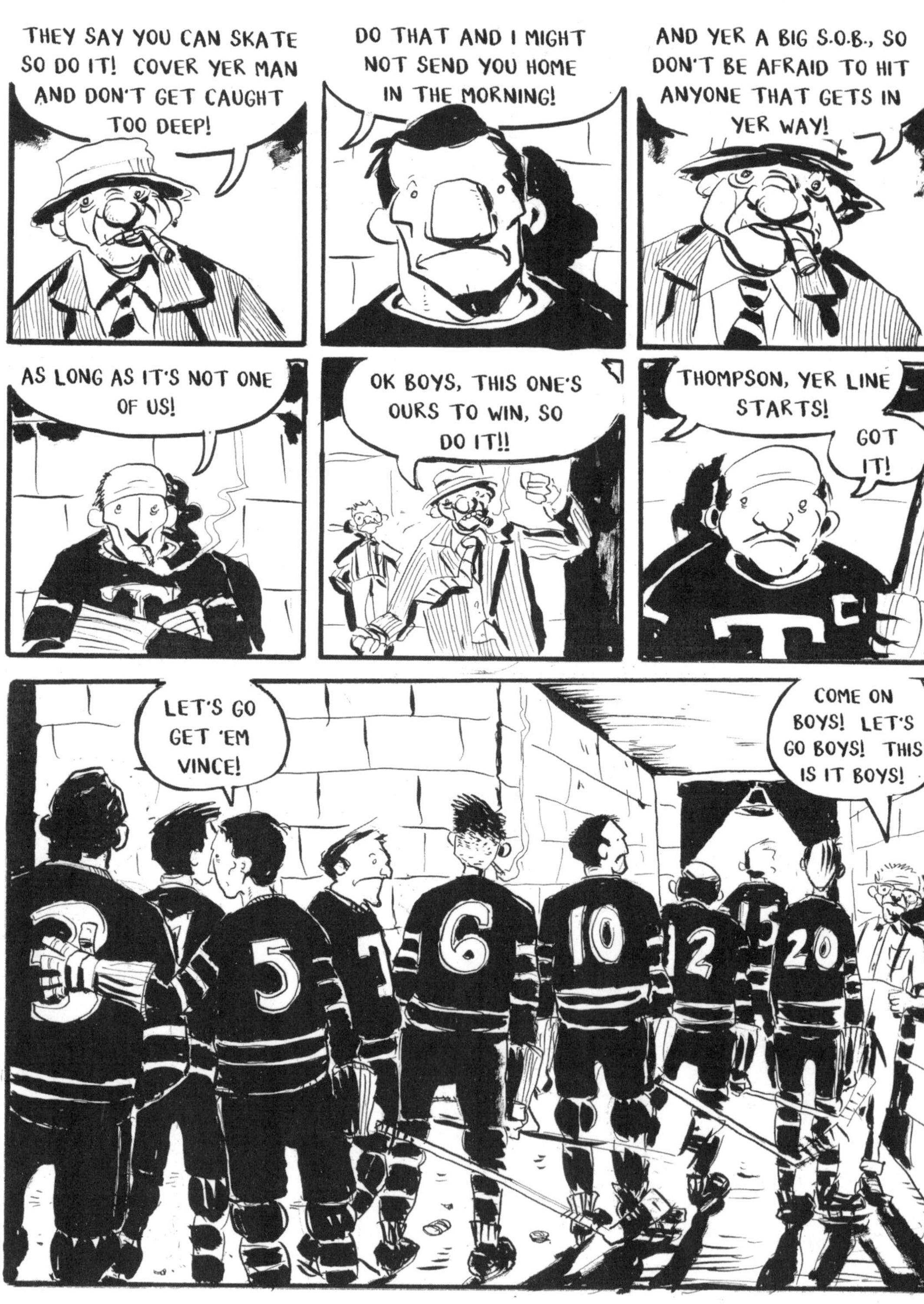
THEY SAY YOU CAN SKATE SO DO IT! COVER YER MAN AND DON'T GET CAUGHT TOO DEEP!
DO THAT AND I MIGHT NOT SEND YOU HOME IN THE MORNING!
AND YER A BIG S.O.B., SO DON'T BE AFRAID TO HIT ANYONE THAT GETS IN YER WAY!
AS LONG AS IT'S NOT ONE OF US!
OK BOYS, THIS ONE'S OURS TO WIN, SO DO IT!!
THOMPSON, YER LINE STARTS!
GOT IT!
LET'S GO GET 'EM VINCE!
COME ON BOYS! LET'S GO BOYS! THIS IS IT BOYS!

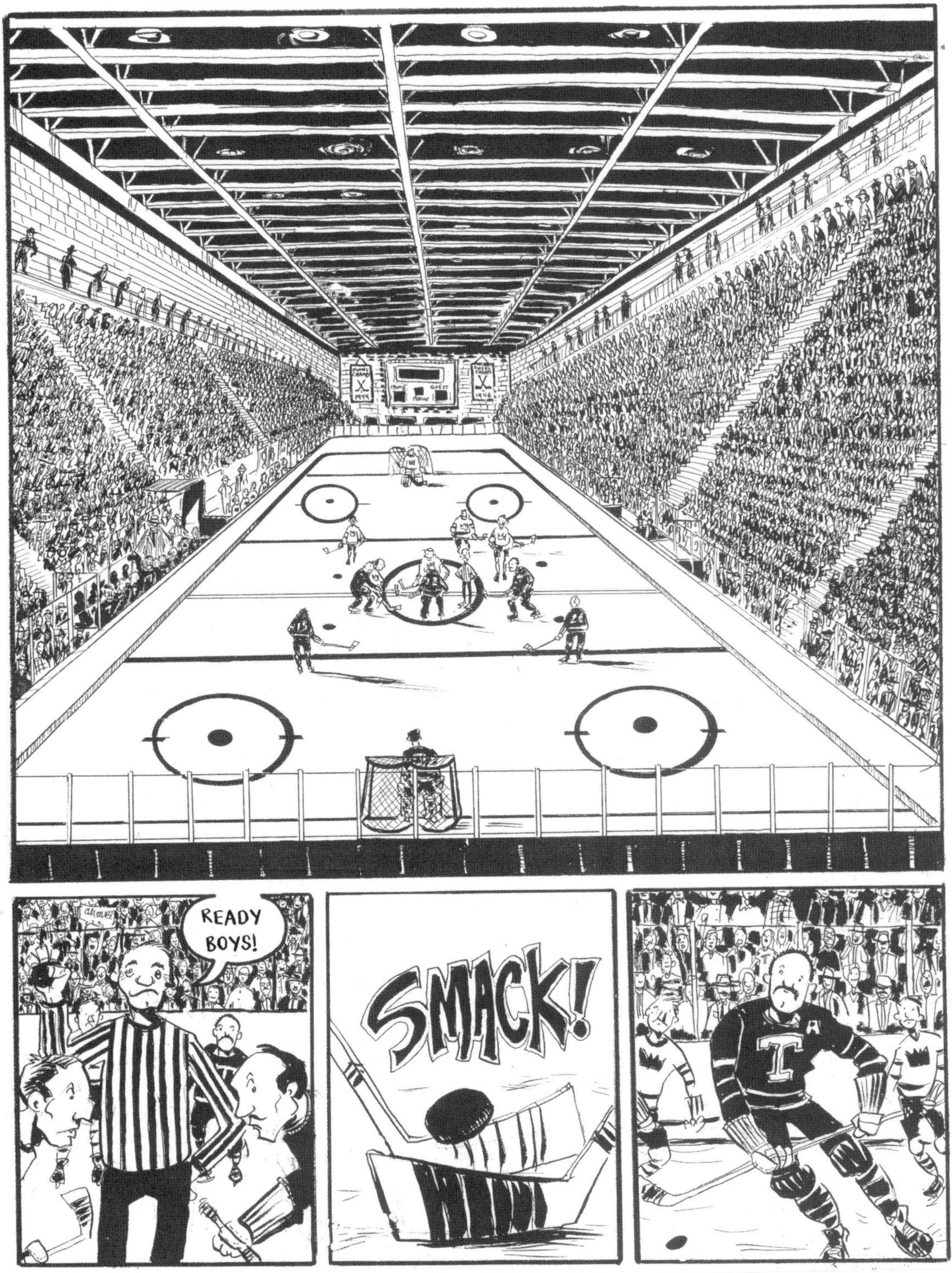
READY BOYS!
SMACK!

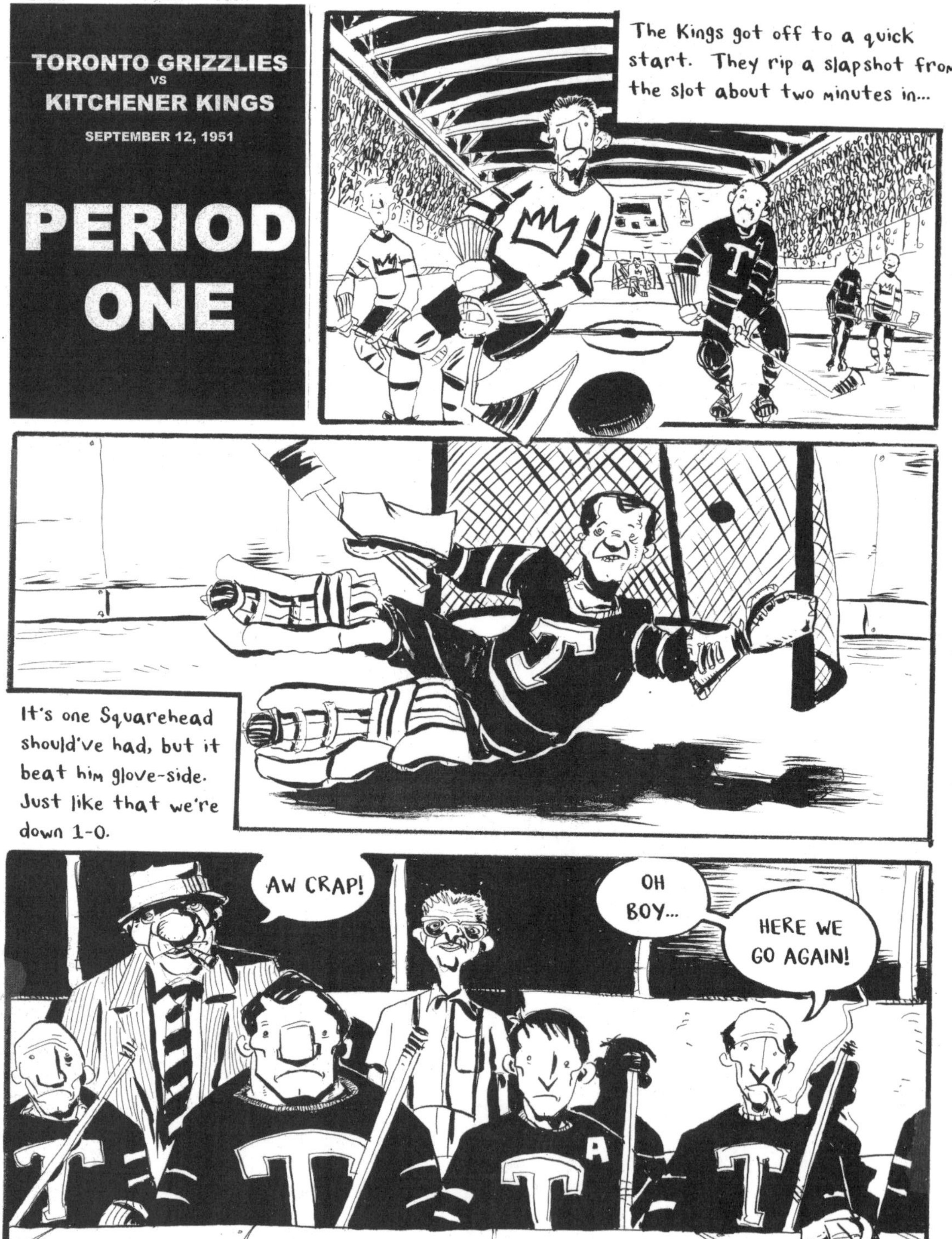
TORONTO GRIZZLIES
VS
KITCHENER KINGS
SEPTEMBER 12, 1951
PERIOD ONE
The Kings got off to a quick start. They rip a slapshot from the slot about two minutes in...
It's one Squarehead should've had, but it beat him glove-side. Just like that we're down 1-0.
AW CRAP!
OH BOY...
HERE WE GO AGAIN!

Vince and I got our first shift right after the goal.

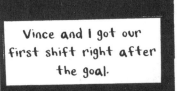

Things got worse quick. Vince missed a check, and the Kings poke another past Squarehead.

We were down 2-0 before we could even catch our breaths.

Things settled down a bit after that. We held them off, and our 'French boys' got one back for us!

My line got out again, but aside from a couple'a nice hits we don't do much.

The first period ended and we were lucky to only be down by a goal.

SLAM!

PERIOD TWO

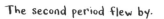

The second period flew by.

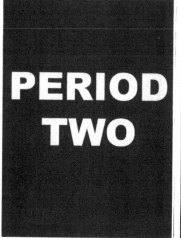

No goals halfway through, but things started to get chippy.

Vince was still playing quiet...almost timid.

His head hadn't caught up with everything yet.

I knew he could take this game and win it by himself if he wanted to.

I just needed to get him going!

So, with about six minutes left in the period I picked a fight...

...and I made sure I lost.

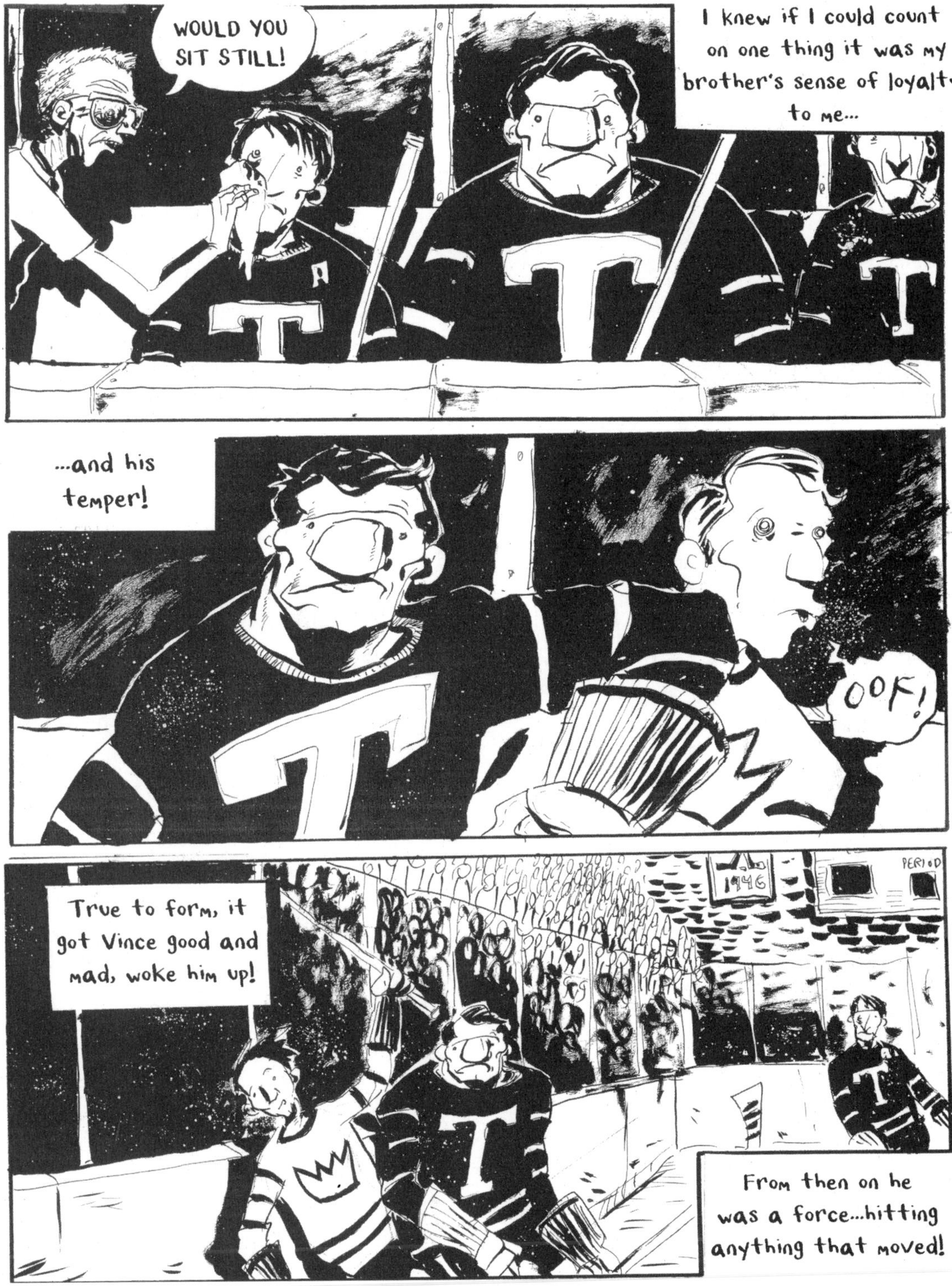
WOULD YOU SIT STILL!
I knew if I could count on one thing it was my brother's sense of loyalty to me...
...and his temper!
OOF!
True to form, it got Vince good and mad, woke him up!
1946
PERIOD
From then on he was a force...hitting anything that moved!

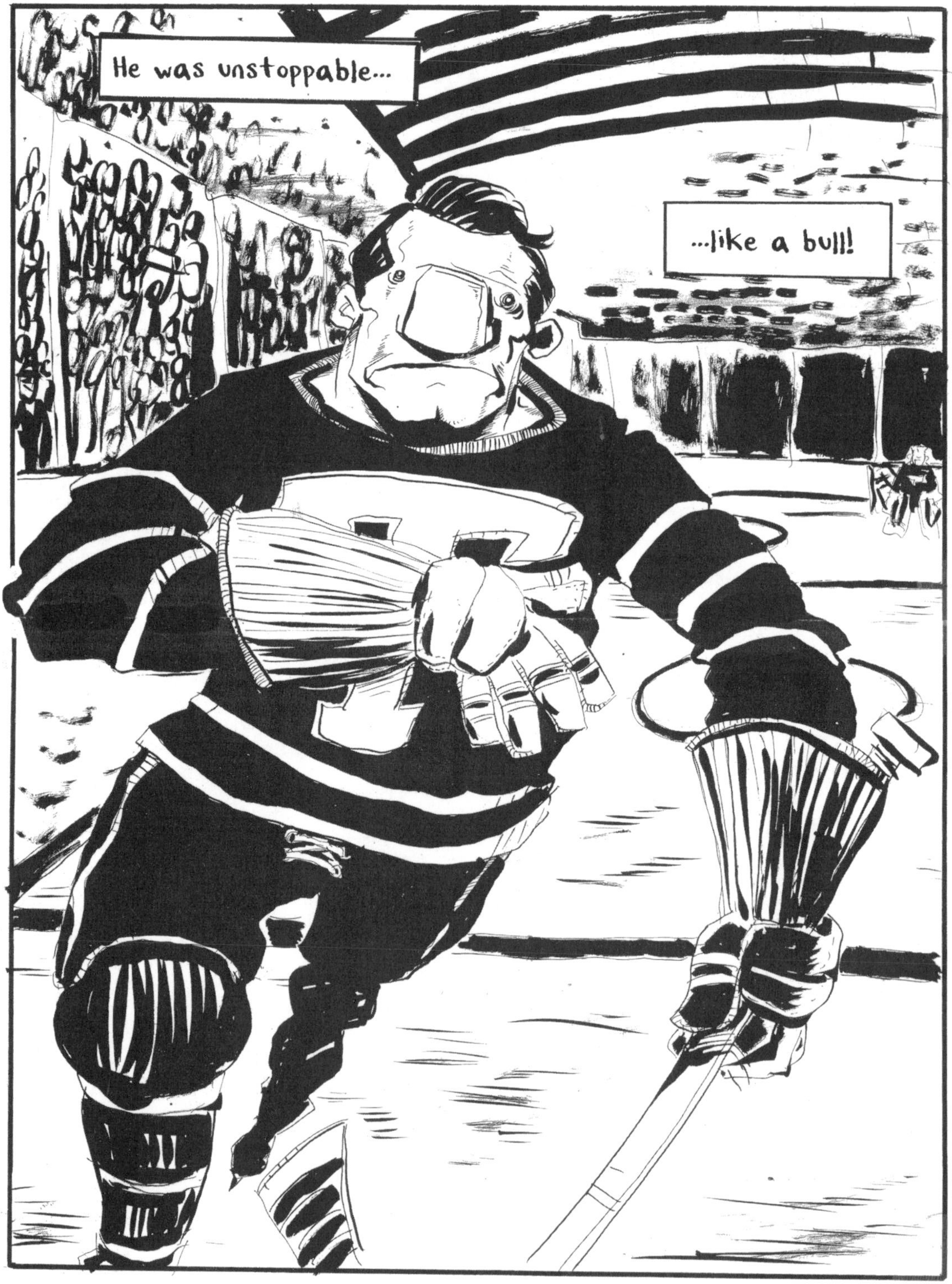
He was unstoppable...
...like a bull!

PERIOD THREE

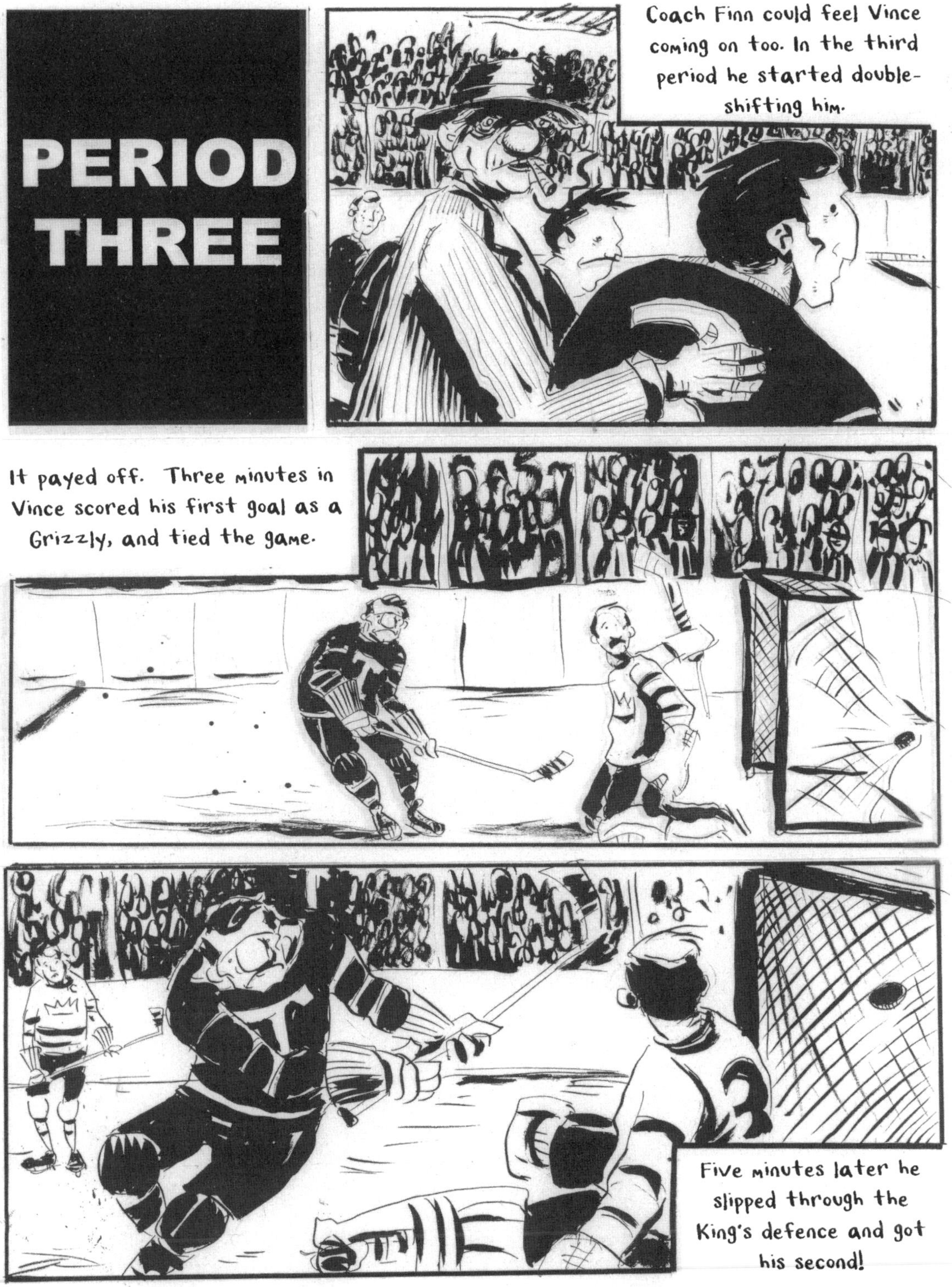
Coach Finn could feel Vince coming on too. In the third period he started double-shifting him.
It payed off. Three minutes in Vince scored his first goal as a Grizzly, and tied the game.
Five minutes later he slipped through the King's defence and got his second!

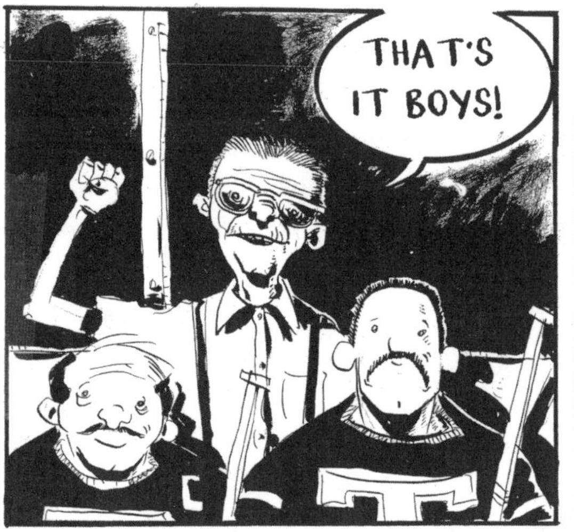
THAT'S IT BOYS!

The Kings didn't know what hit 'em, and we weren't about to let our feet off'a their throats!

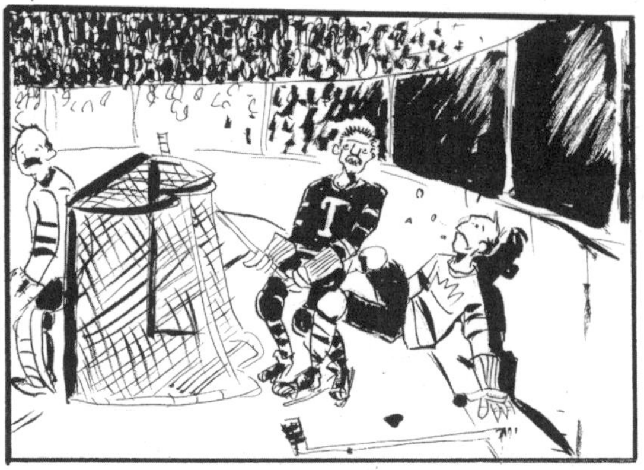

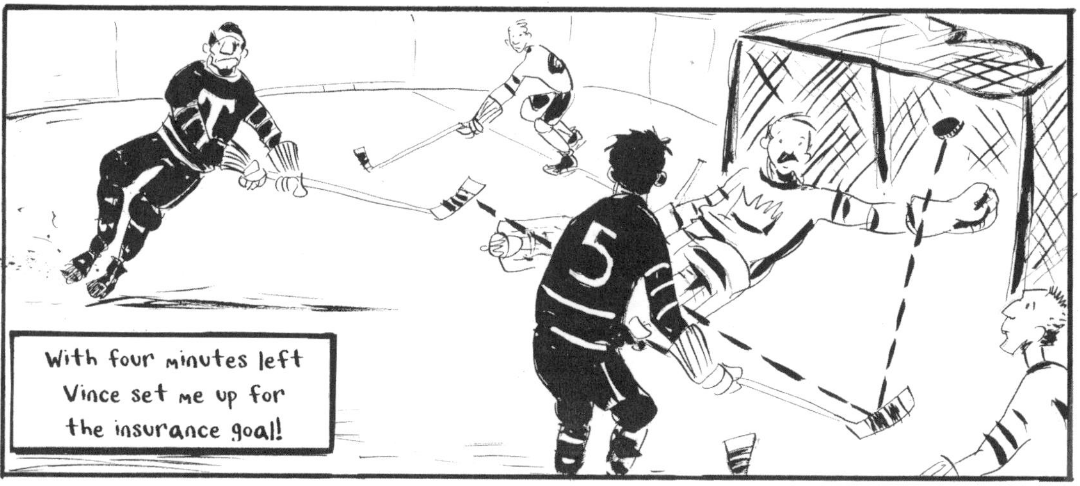
With four minutes left Vince set me up for the insurance goal!

When the final whistle blew, we'd won.

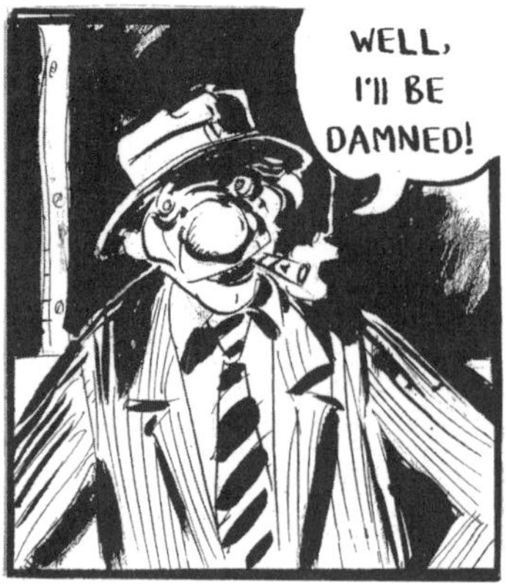
WELL, I'LL BE DAMNED!

The fans had a new hero.

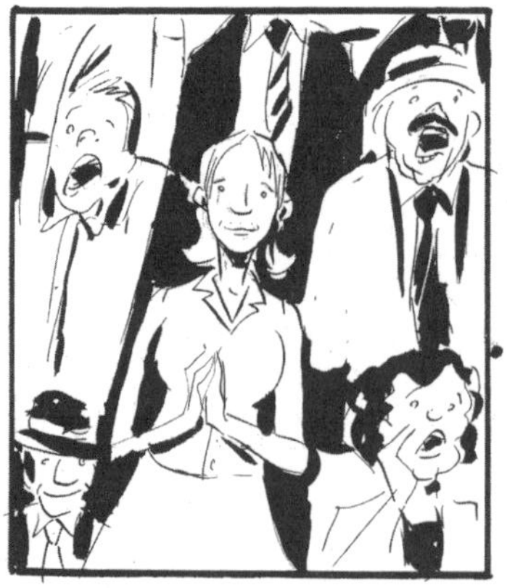

And The Grizzlies had a new star!

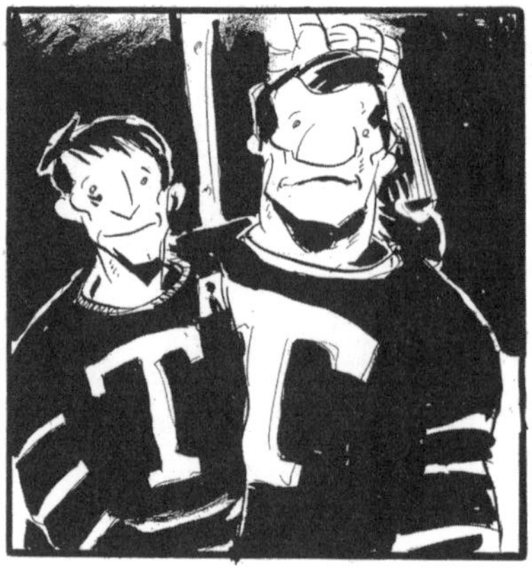

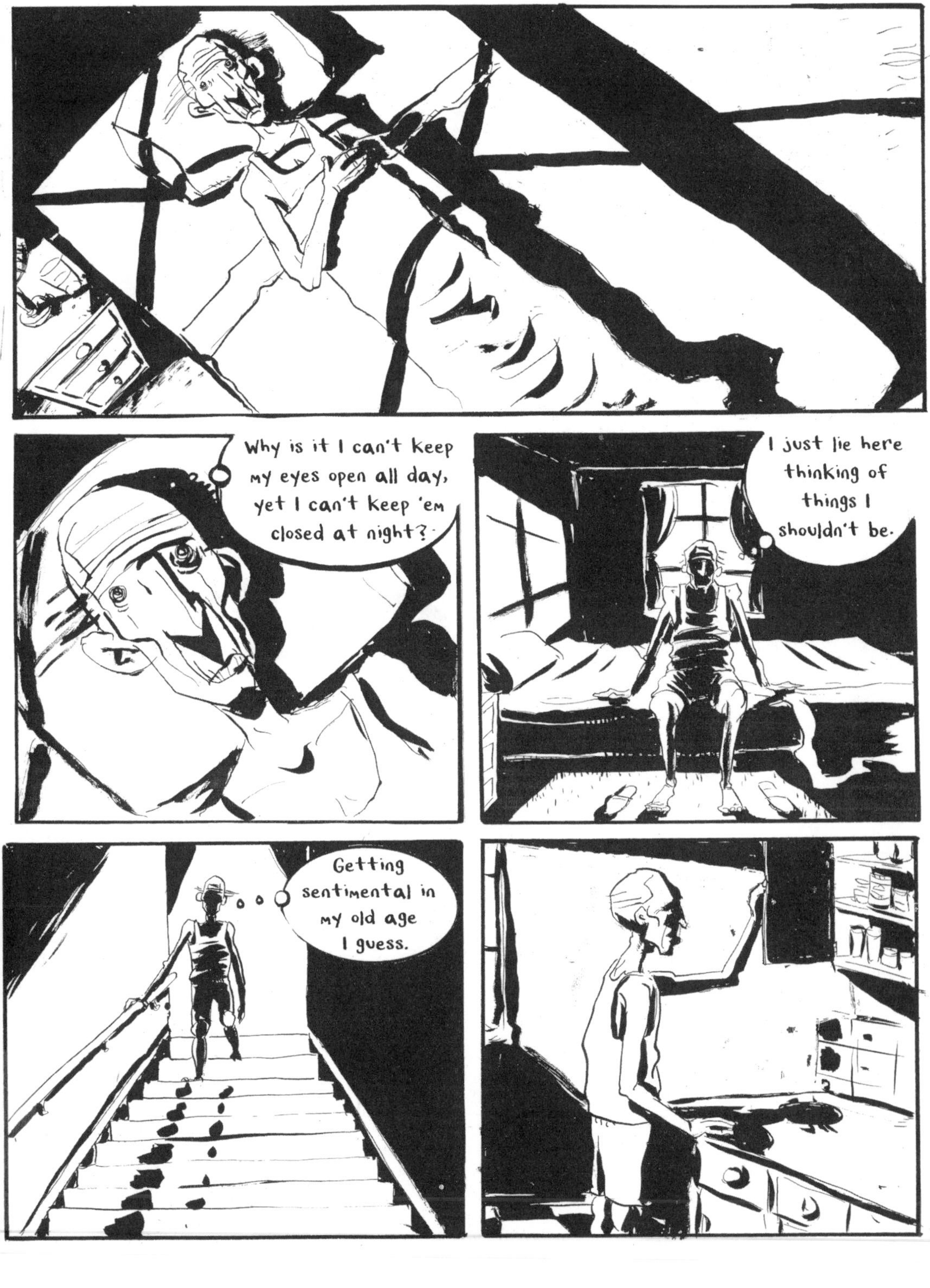
Why is it I can't keep my eyes open all day, yet I can't keep 'em closed at night?
I just lie here thinking of things I shouldn't be.
Getting sentimental in my old age I guess.

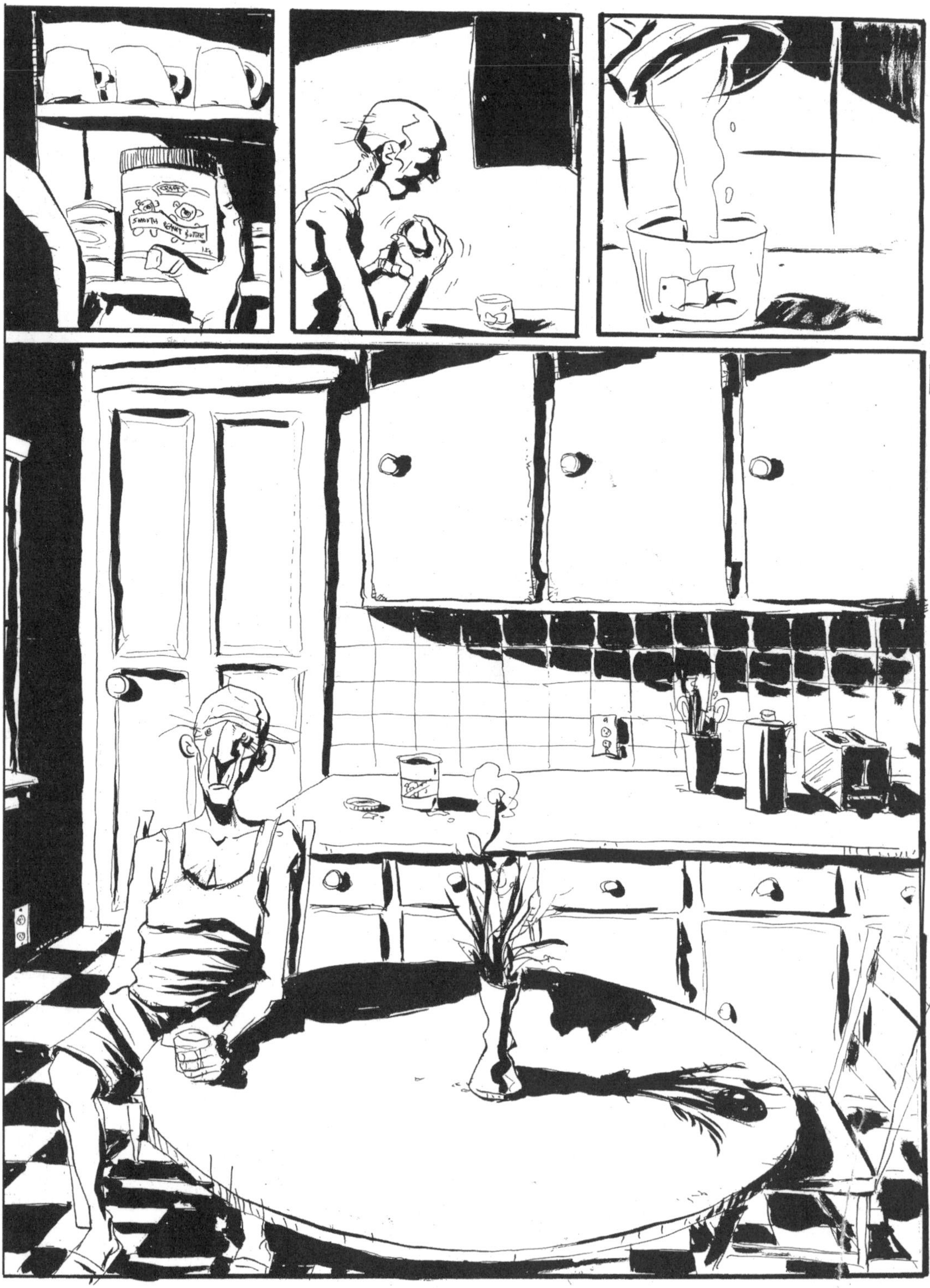

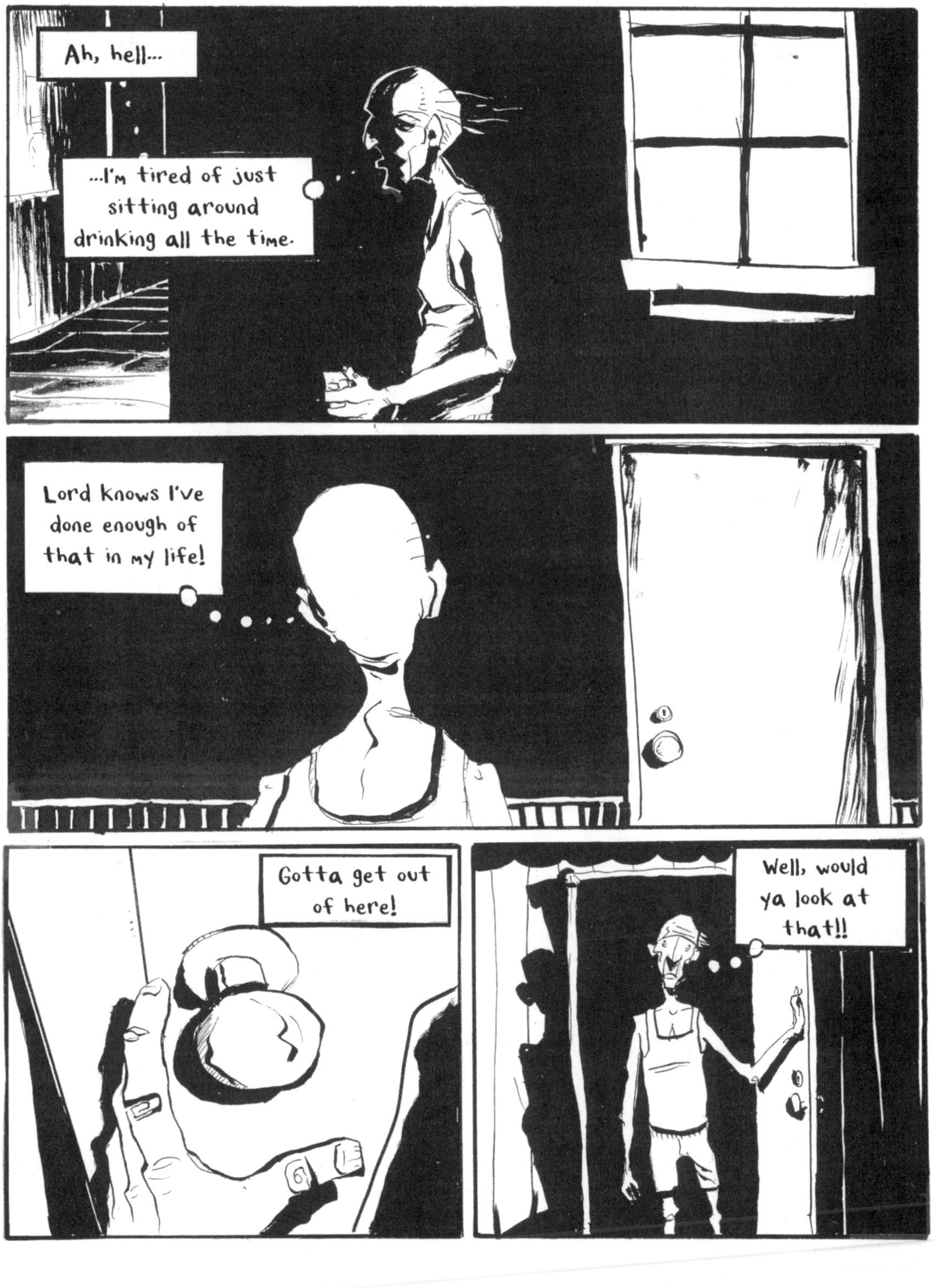
Ah, hell...
...I'm tired of just sitting around drinking all the time.
Lord knows I've done enough of that in my life!
Gotta get out of here!
Well, would ya look at that!!

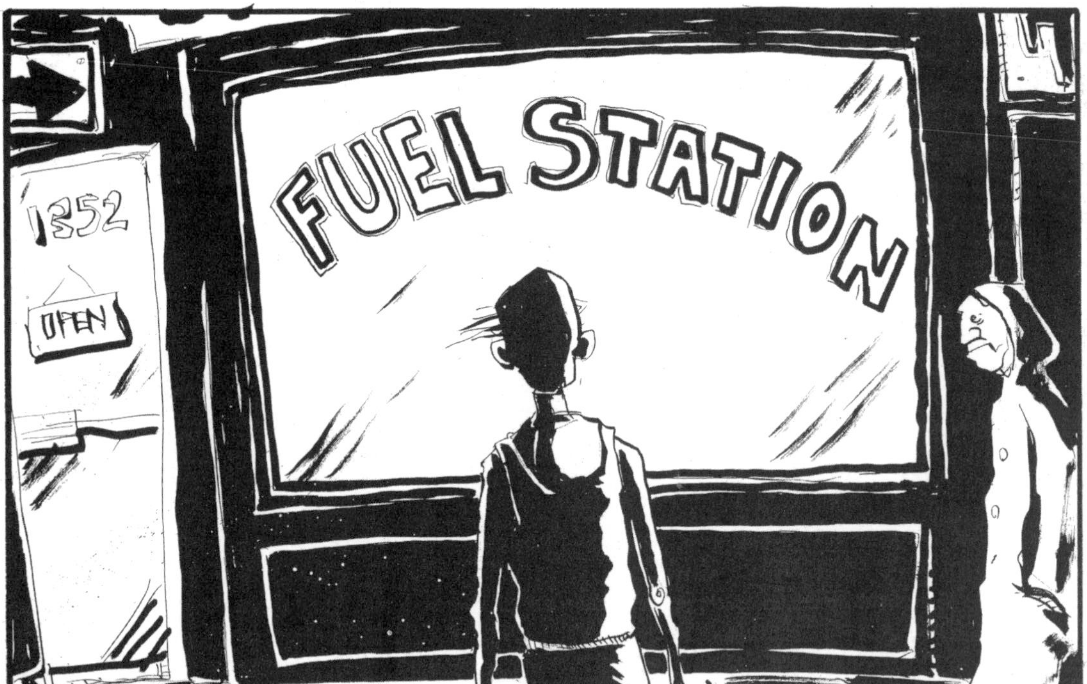
FUEL STATION
1352
OPEN

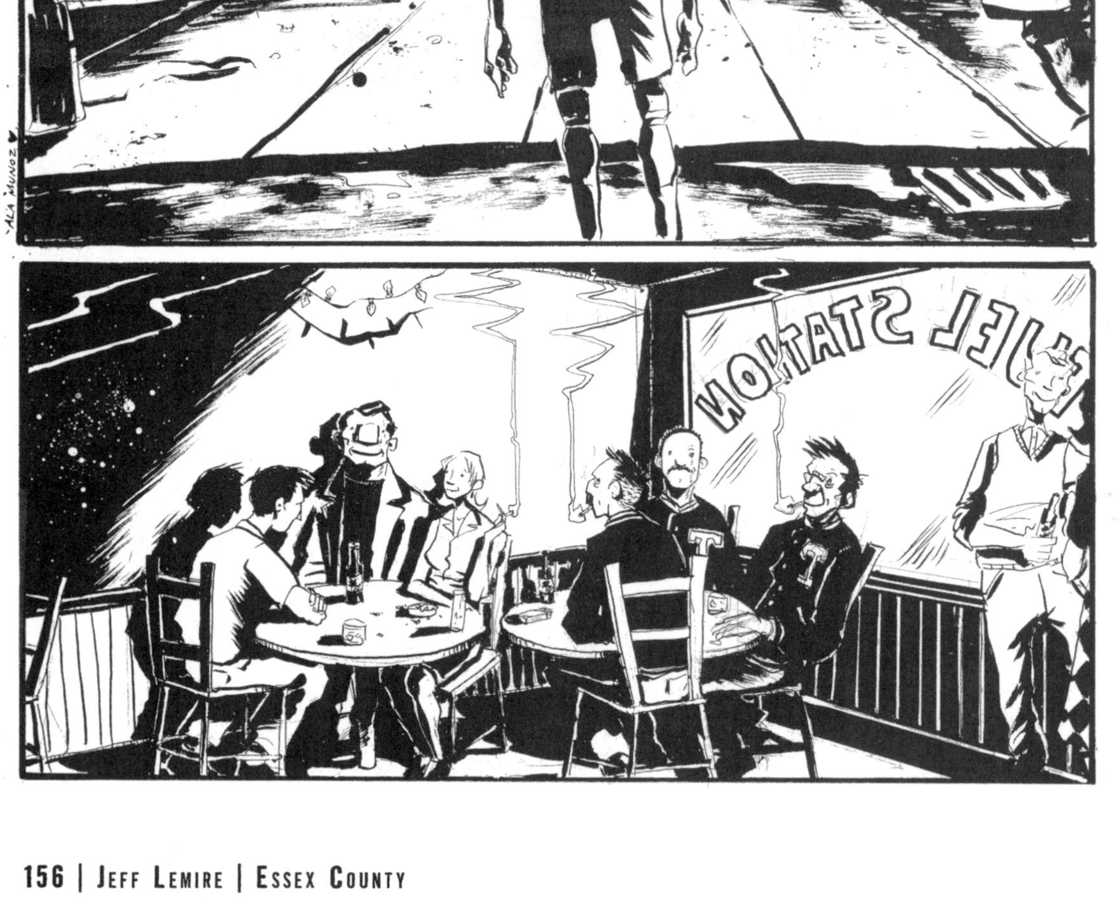

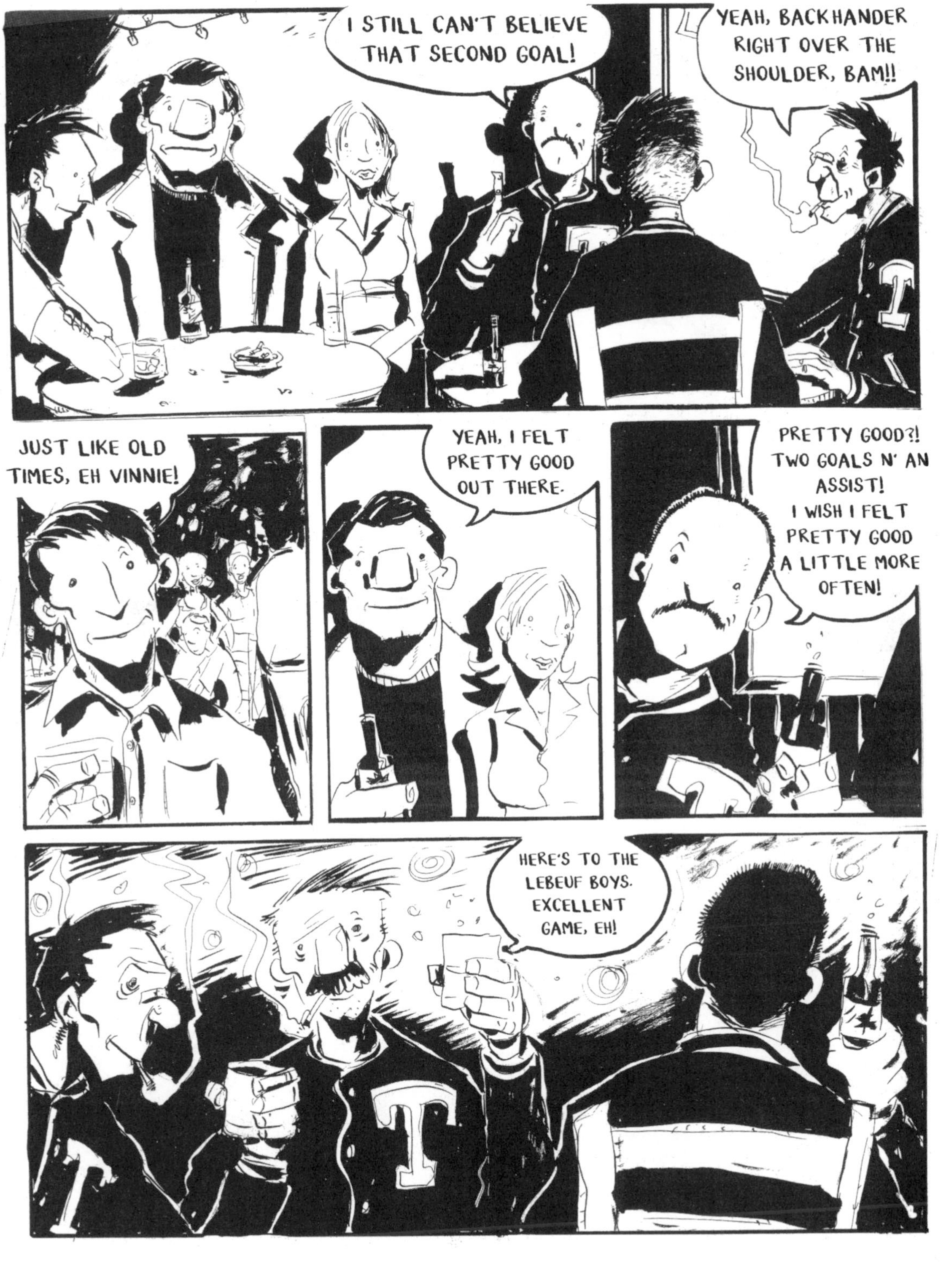
I STILL CAN'T BELIEVE THAT SECOND GOAL!
YEAH, BACKHANDER RIGHT OVER THE SHOULDER, BAM!!
JUST LIKE OLD TIMES, EH VINNIE!
YEAH, I FELT PRETTY GOOD OUT THERE.
PRETTY GOOD?! TWO GOALS N' AN ASSIST! I WISH I FELT PRETTY GOOD A LITTLE MORE OFTEN!
HERE'S TO THE LEBEUF BOYS. EXCELLENT GAME, EH!

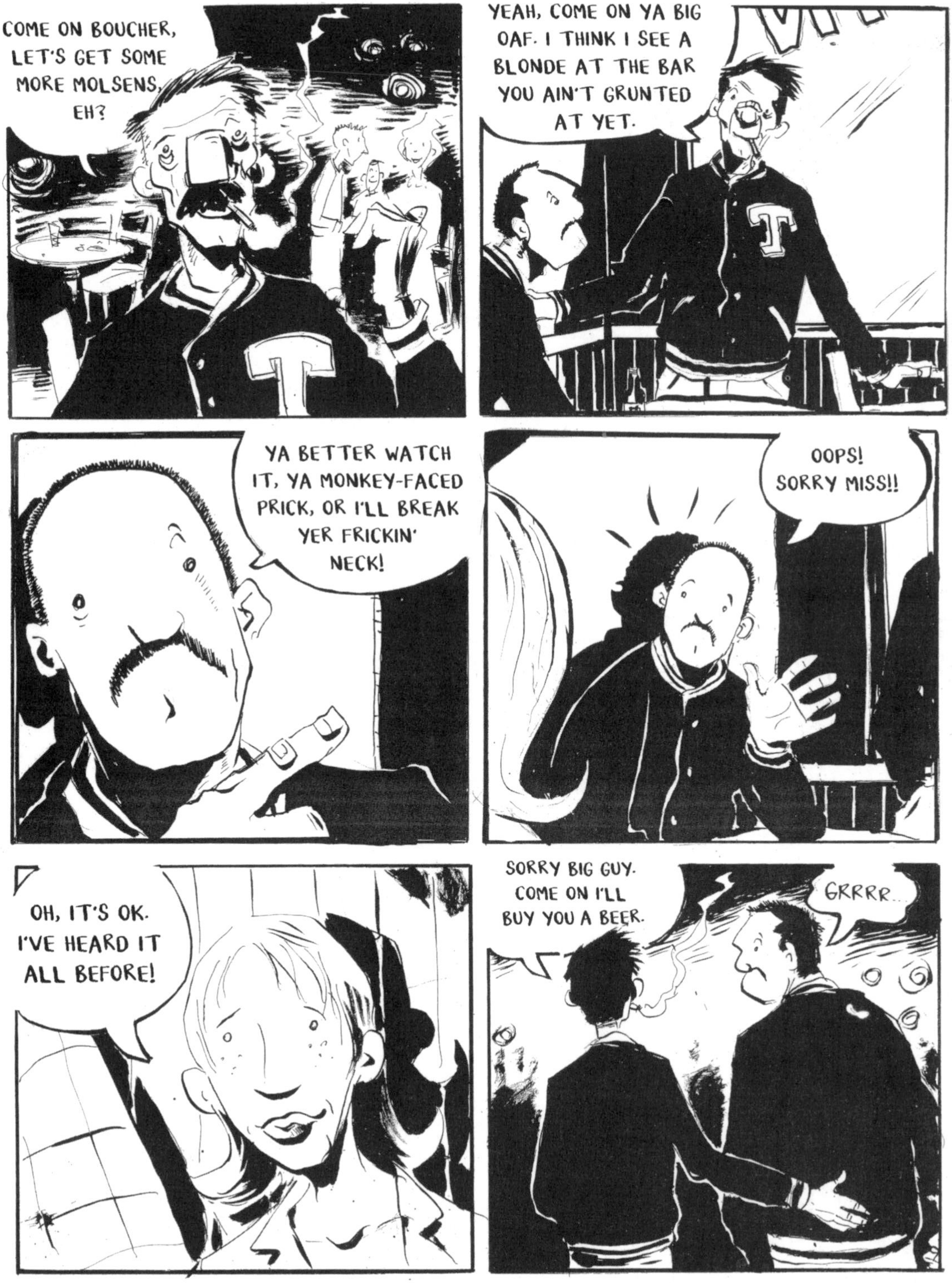
COME ON BOUCHER, LET'S GET SOME MORE MOLSENS, EH?
YEAH, COME ON YA BIG OAF. I THINK I SEE A BLONDE AT THE BAR YOU AIN'T GRUNTED AT YET.
YA BETTER WATCH IT, YA MONKEY-FACED PRICK, OR I'LL BREAK YER FRICKIN' NECK!
OOPS! SORRY MISS!!
OH, IT'S OK. I'VE HEARD IT ALL BEFORE!
SORRY BIG GUY. COME ON I'LL BUY YOU A BEER.
GRRRR...

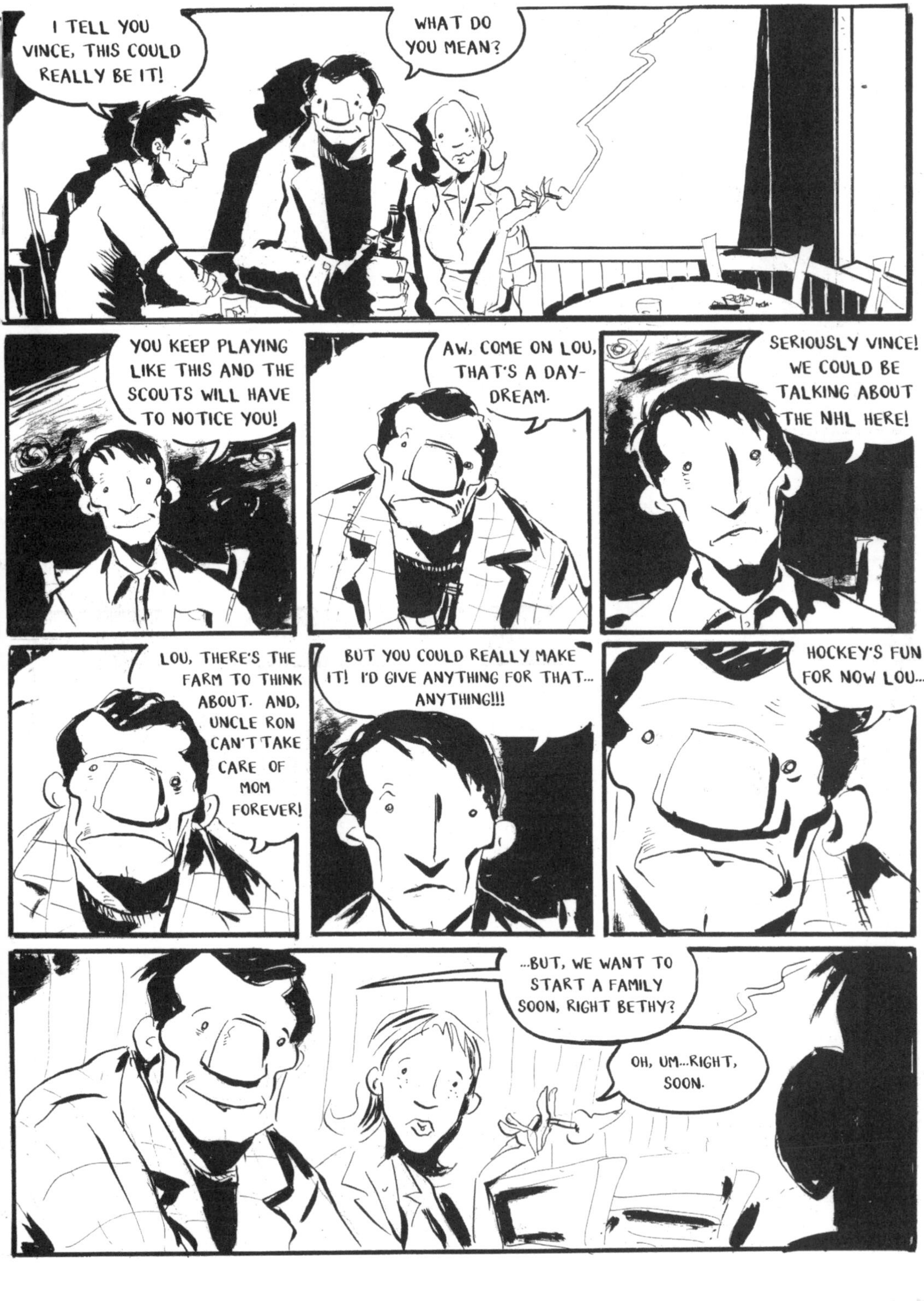
I TELL YOU VINCE, THIS COULD REALLY BE IT!
WHAT DO YOU MEAN?
YOU KEEP PLAYING LIKE THIS AND THE SCOUTS WILL HAVE TO NOTICE YOU!
AW, COME ON LOU, THAT'S A DAY-DREAM.
SERIOUSLY VINCE! WE COULD BE TALKING ABOUT THE NHL HERE!
LOU, THERE'S THE FARM TO THINK ABOUT. AND, UNCLE RON CAN'T TAKE CARE OF MOM FOREVER!
BUT YOU COULD REALLY MAKE IT! I'D GIVE ANYTHING FOR THAT... ANYTHING!!!
HOCKEY'S FUN FOR NOW LOU...
...BUT, WE WANT TO START A FAMILY SOON, RIGHT BETHY?
OH, UM...RIGHT, SOON.

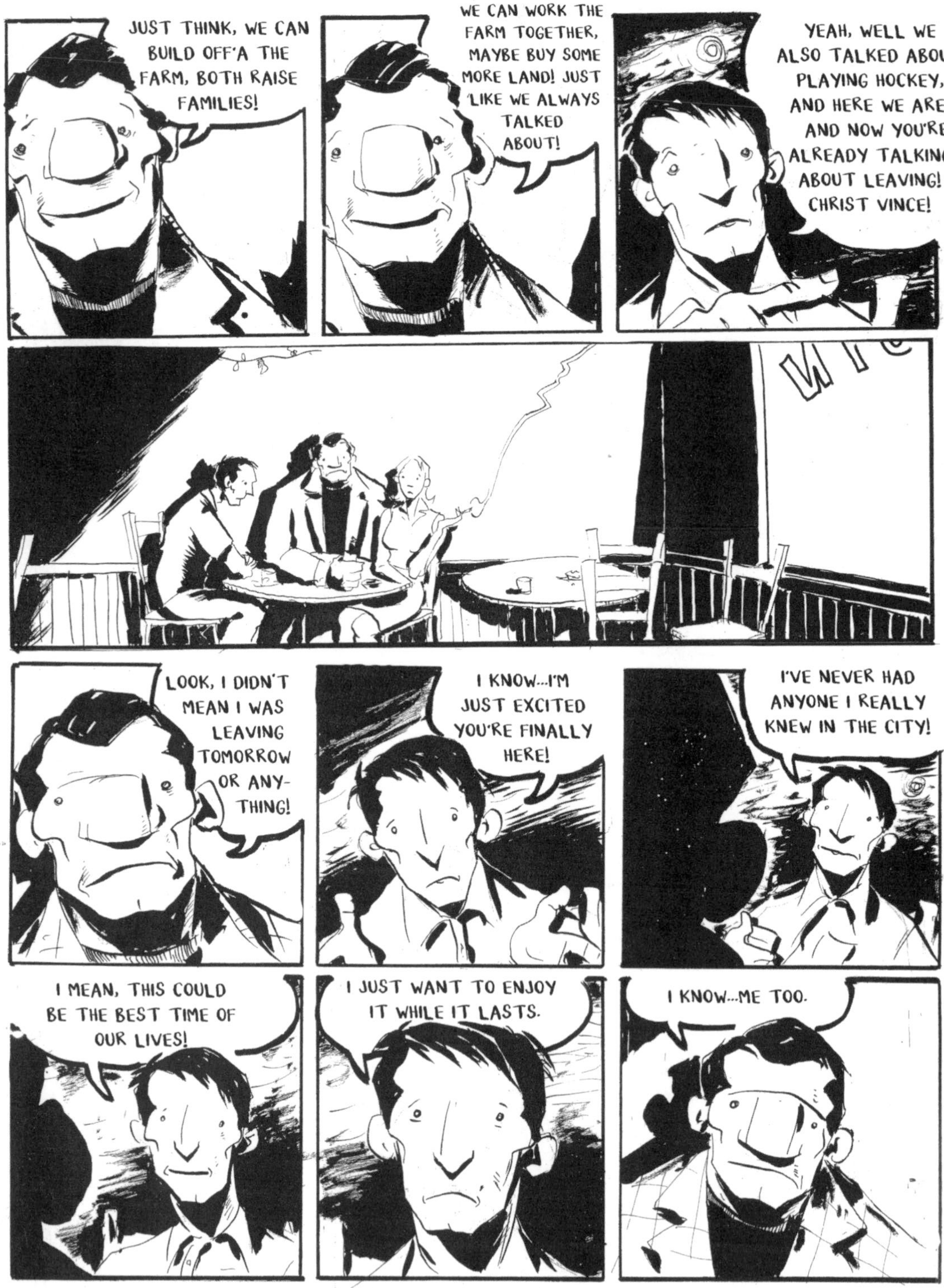
JUST THINK, WE CAN BUILD OFF'A THE FARM, BOTH RAISE FAMILIES!
WE CAN WORK THE FARM TOGETHER, MAYBE BUY SOME MORE LAND! JUST LIKE WE ALWAYS TALKED ABOUT!
YEAH, WELL WE ALSO TALKED ABOUT PLAYING HOCKEY, AND HERE WE ARE! AND NOW YOU'RE ALREADY TALKING ABOUT LEAVING! CHRIST VINCE!
LOOK, I DIDN'T MEAN I WAS LEAVING TOMORROW OR ANY-THING!
I KNOW...I'M JUST EXCITED YOU'RE FINALLY HERE!
I'VE NEVER HAD ANYONE I REALLY KNEW IN THE CITY!
I MEAN, THIS COULD BE THE BEST TIME OF OUR LIVES!
I JUST WANT TO ENJOY IT WHILE IT LASTS.
I KNOW...ME TOO.

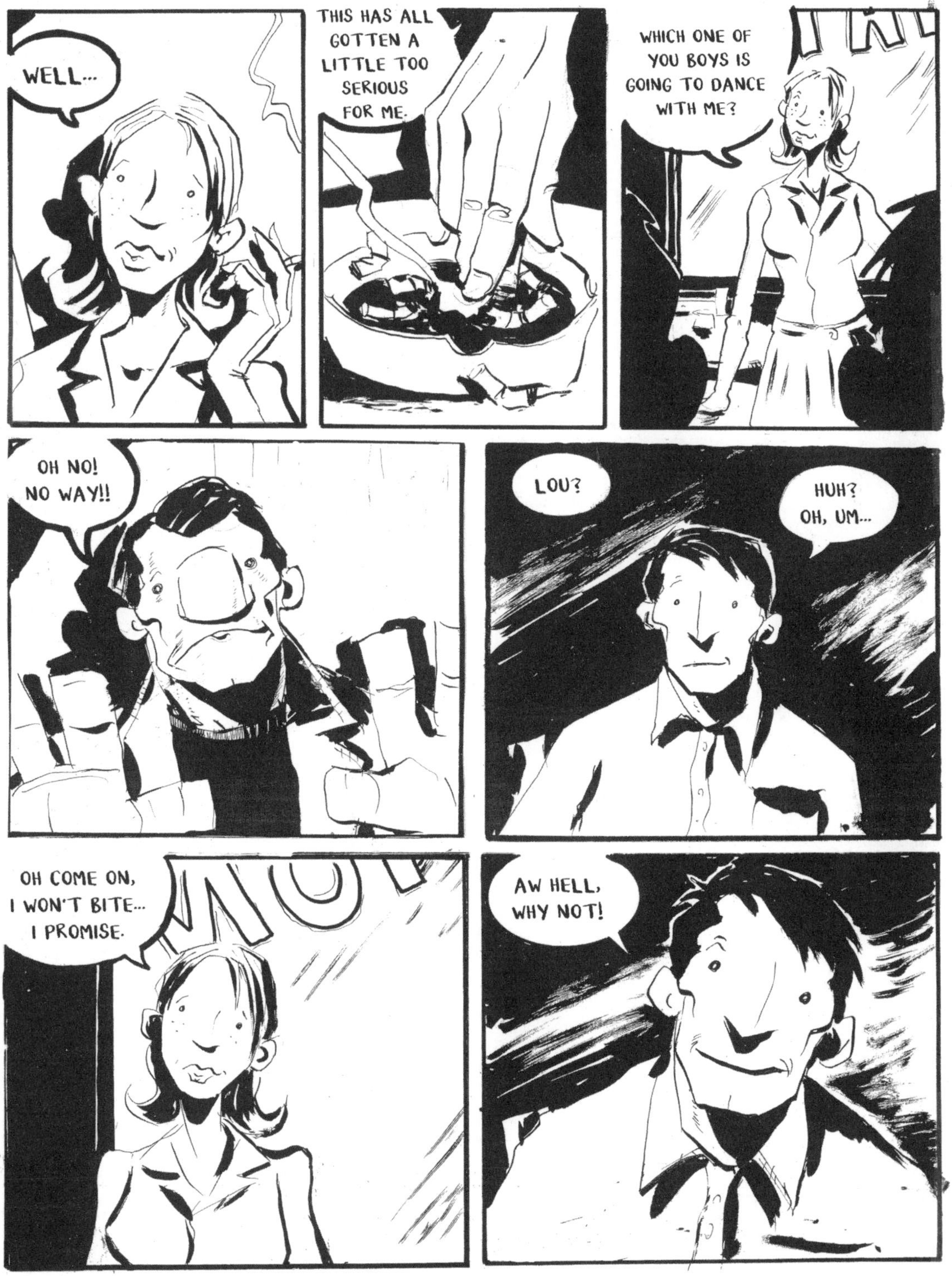
WELL...
THIS HAS ALL GOTTEN A LITTLE TOO SERIOUS FOR ME.
WHICH ONE OF YOU BOYS IS GOING TO DANCE WITH ME?
OH NO! NO WAY!!
LOU?
HUH? OH, UM...
OH COME ON, I WON'T BITE... I PROMISE.
AW HELL, WHY NOT!

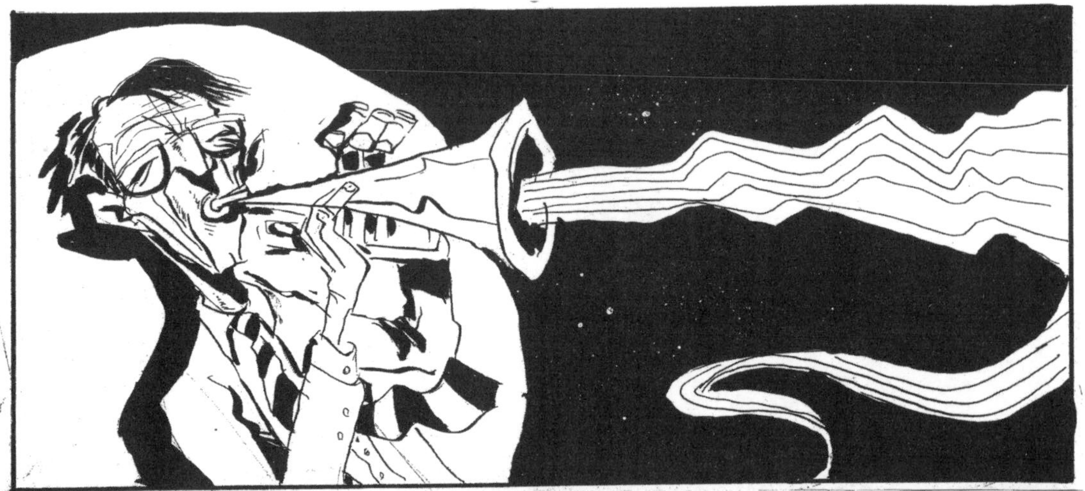

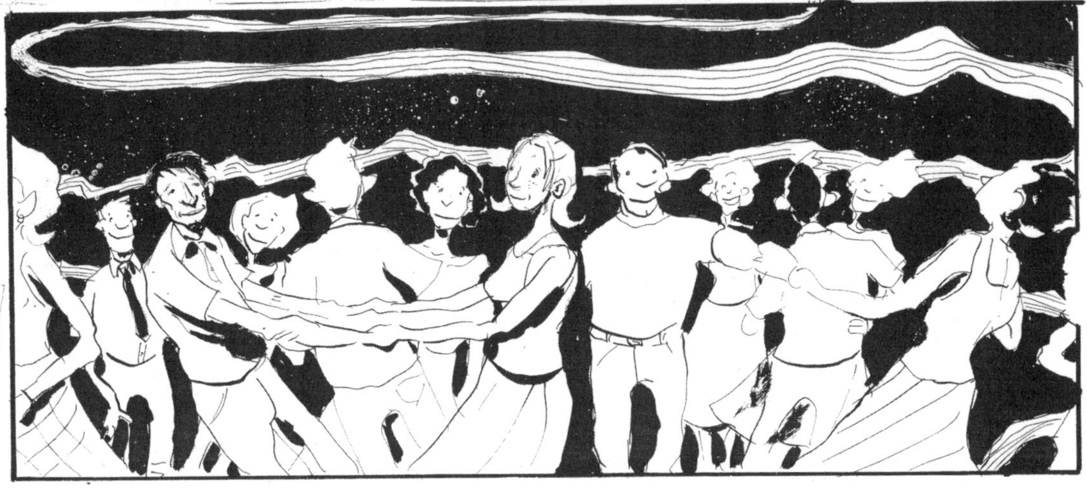

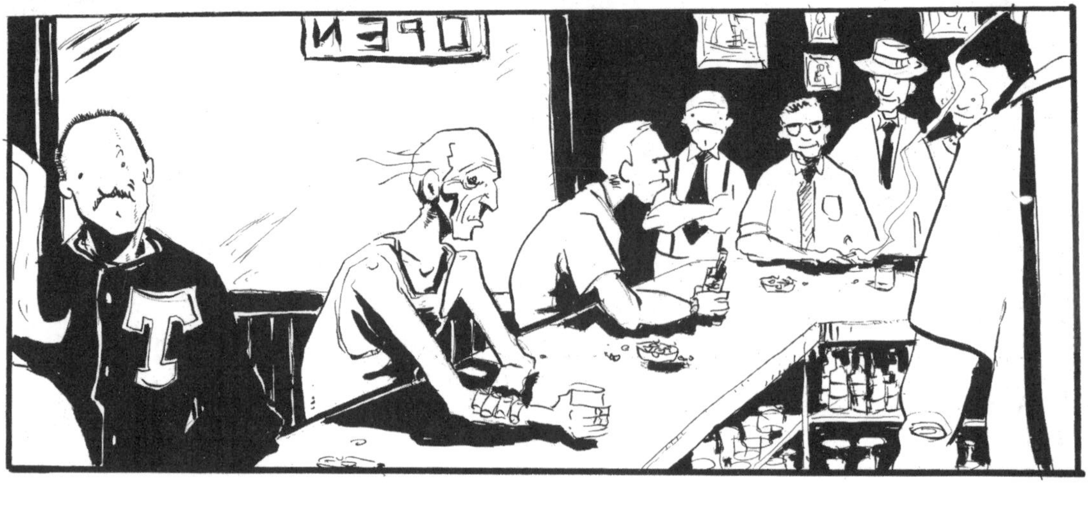

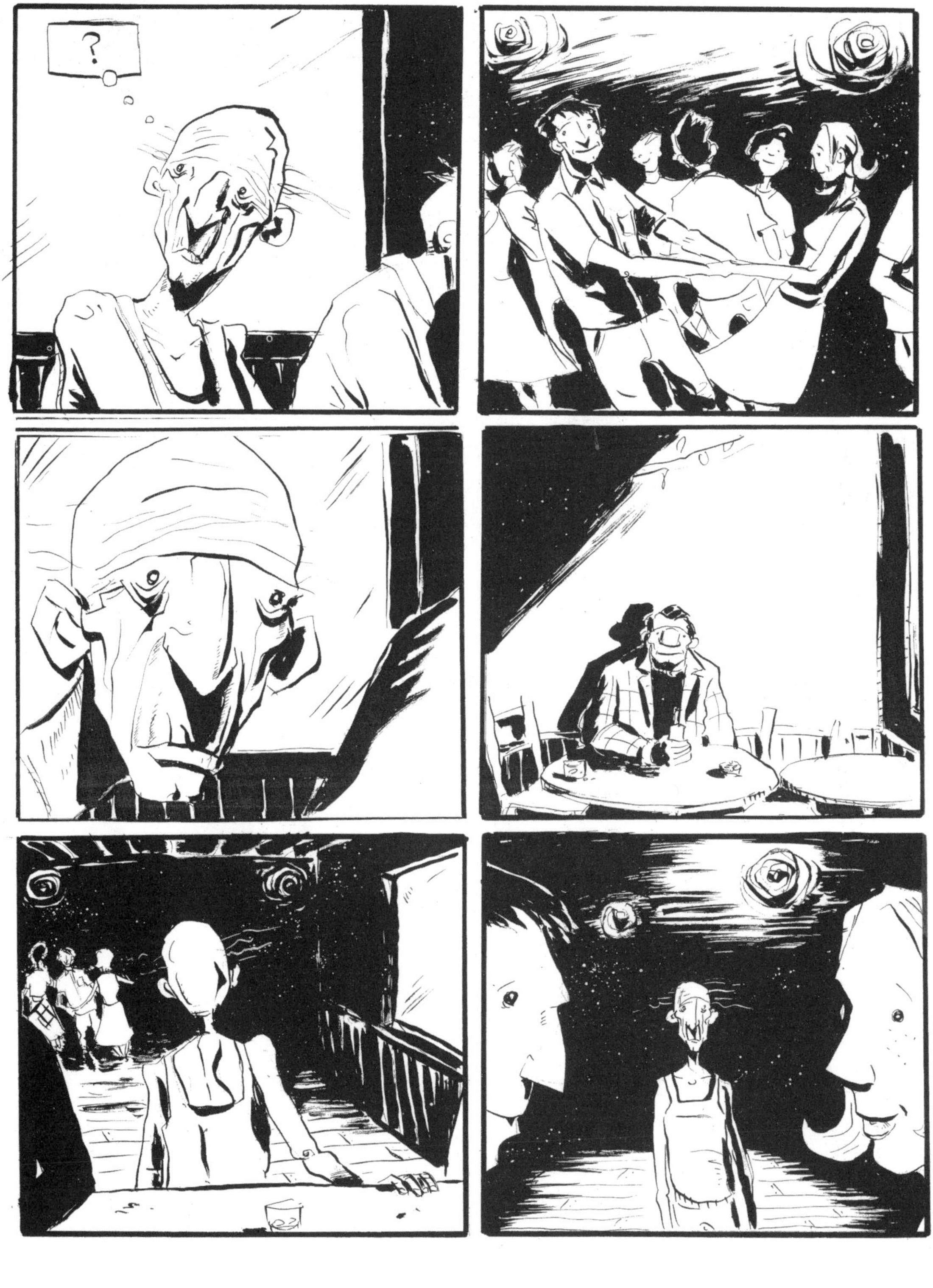
?

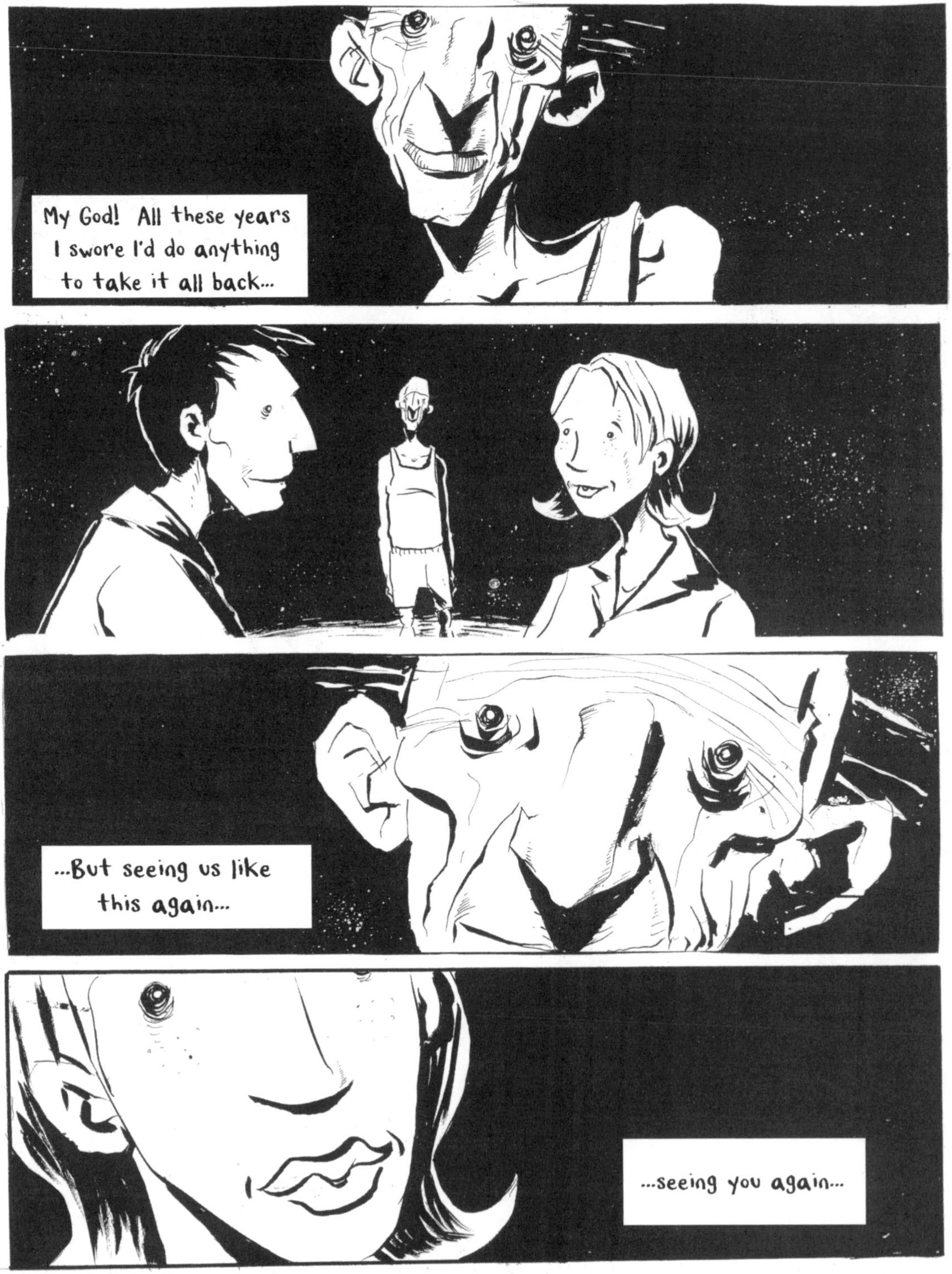
My God! All these years I swore I'd do anything to take it all back...
...But seeing us like this again...
...seeing you again...

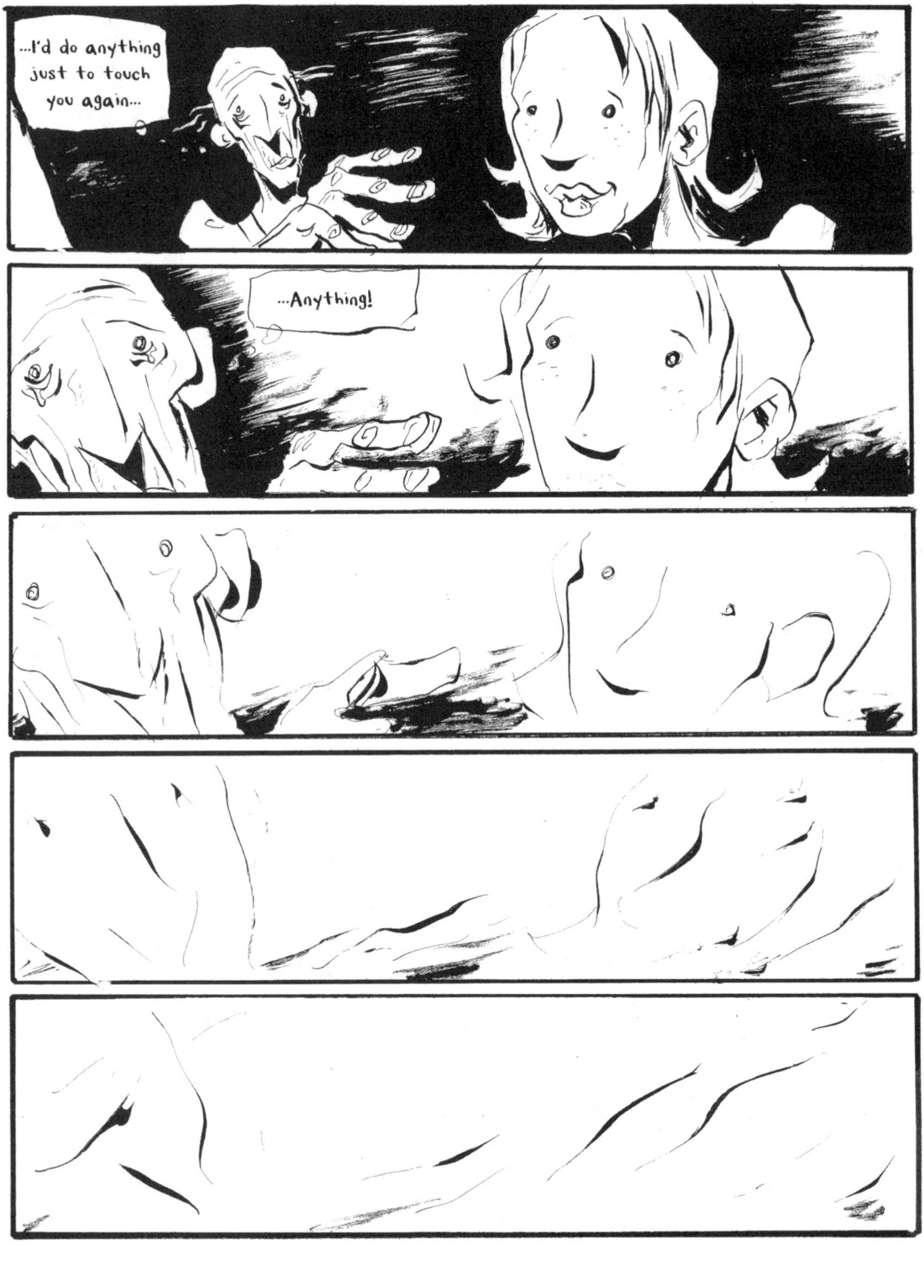
...I'd do anything just to touch you again...
...Anything!

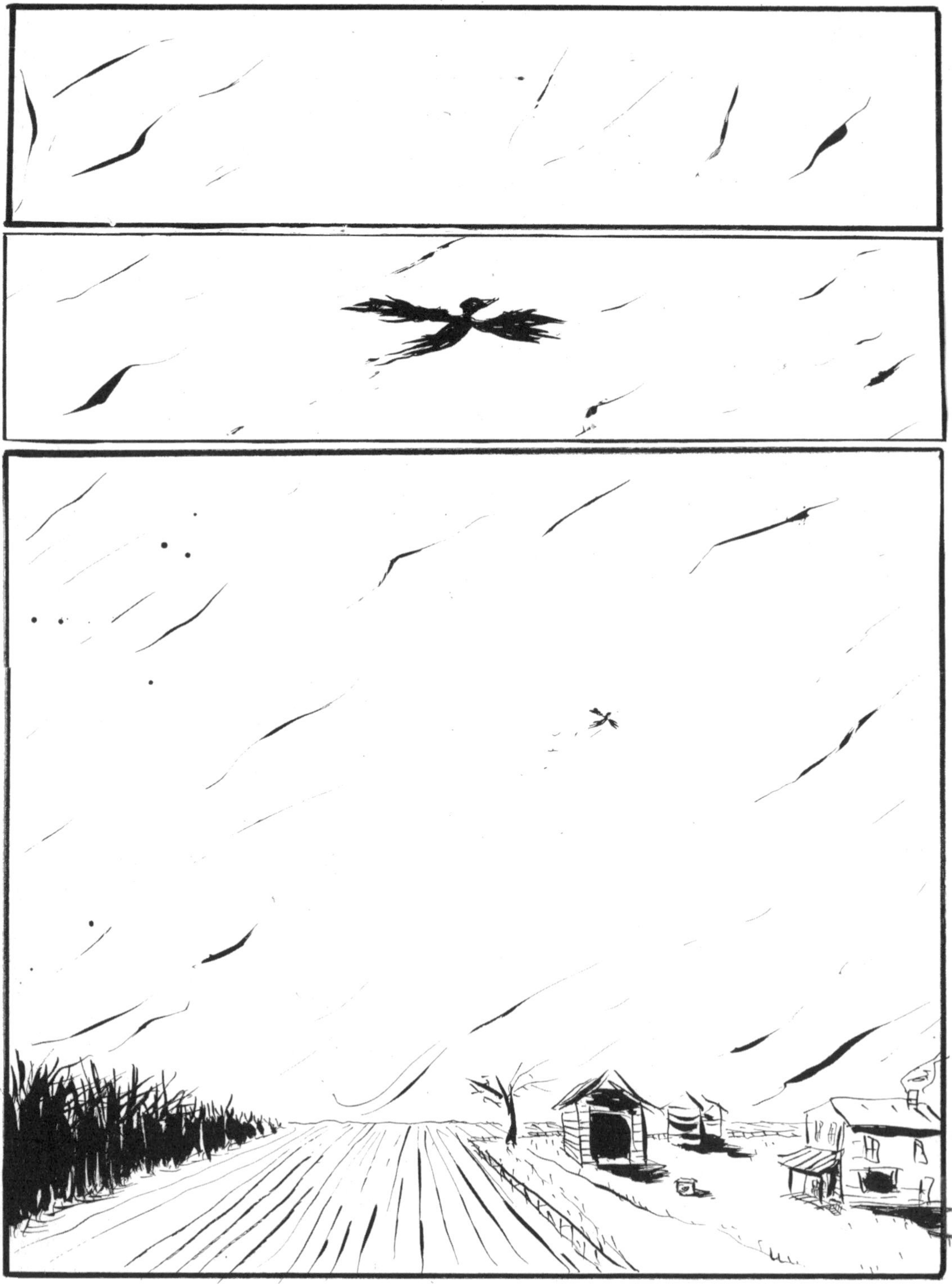

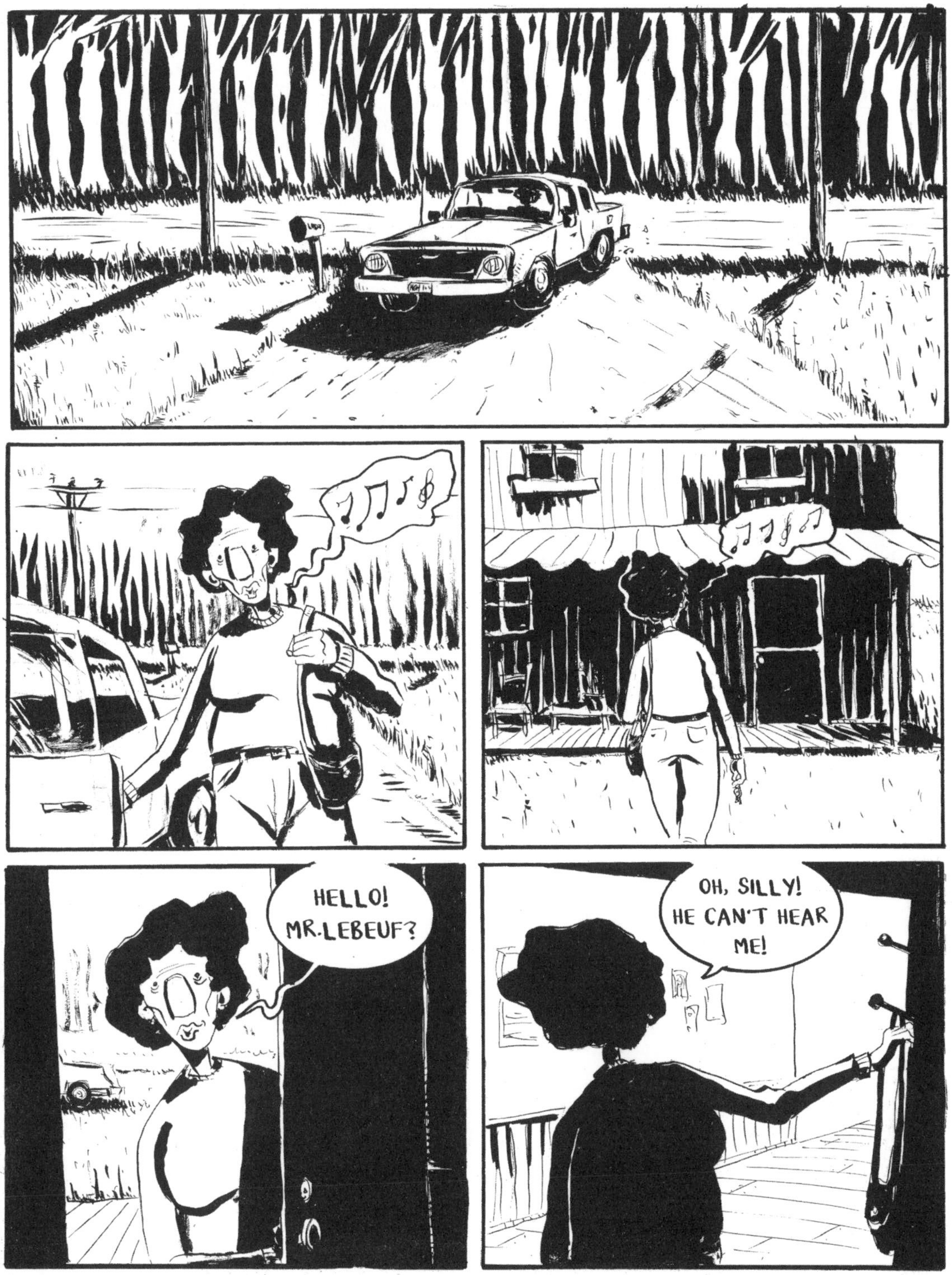
HELLO! MR.LEBEUF?
OH, SILLY! HE CAN'T HEAR ME!

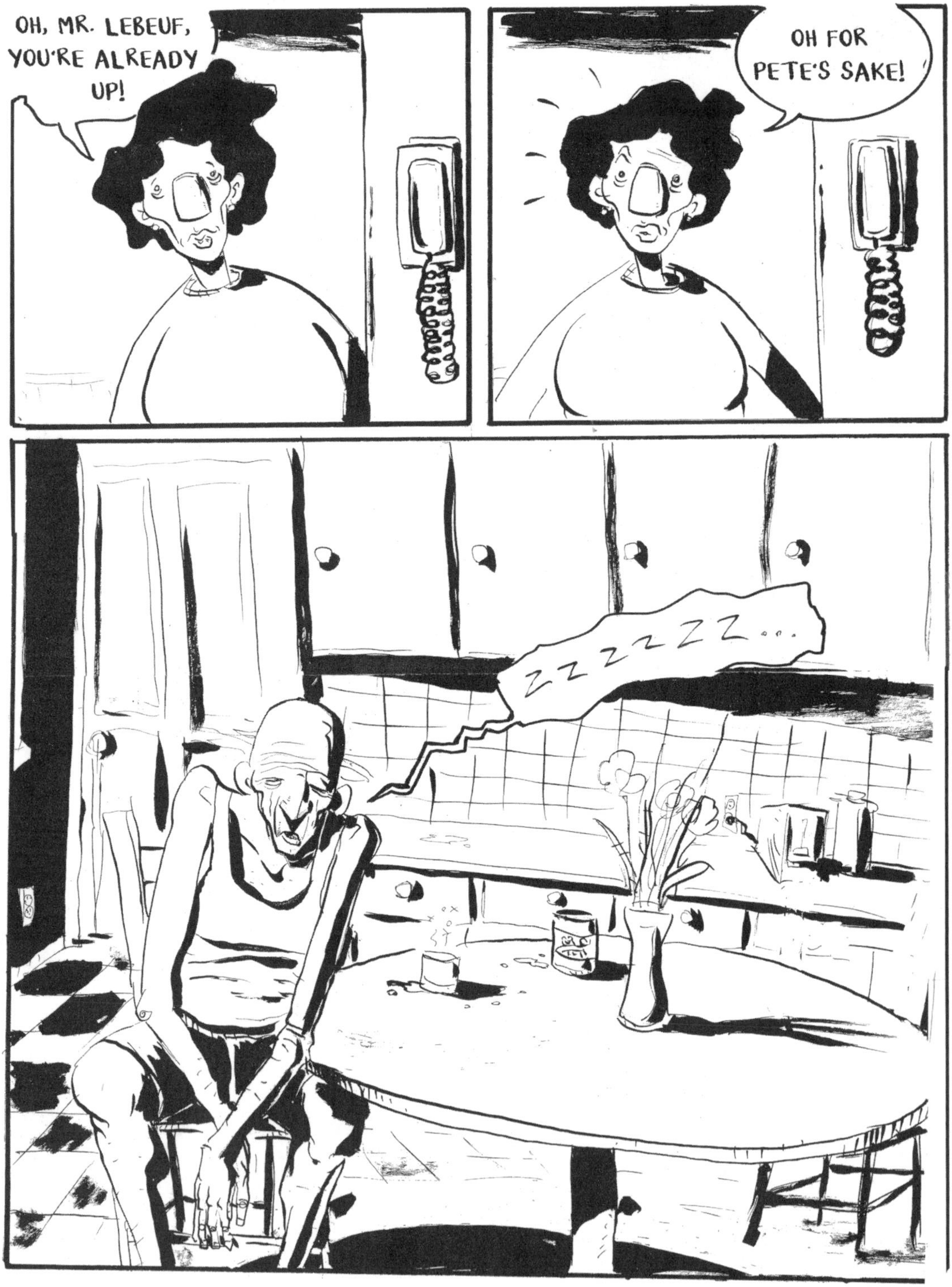
OH, MR. LEBEUF, YOU'RE ALREADY UP!
OH FOR PETE'S SAKE!
ZZZZZZZ...

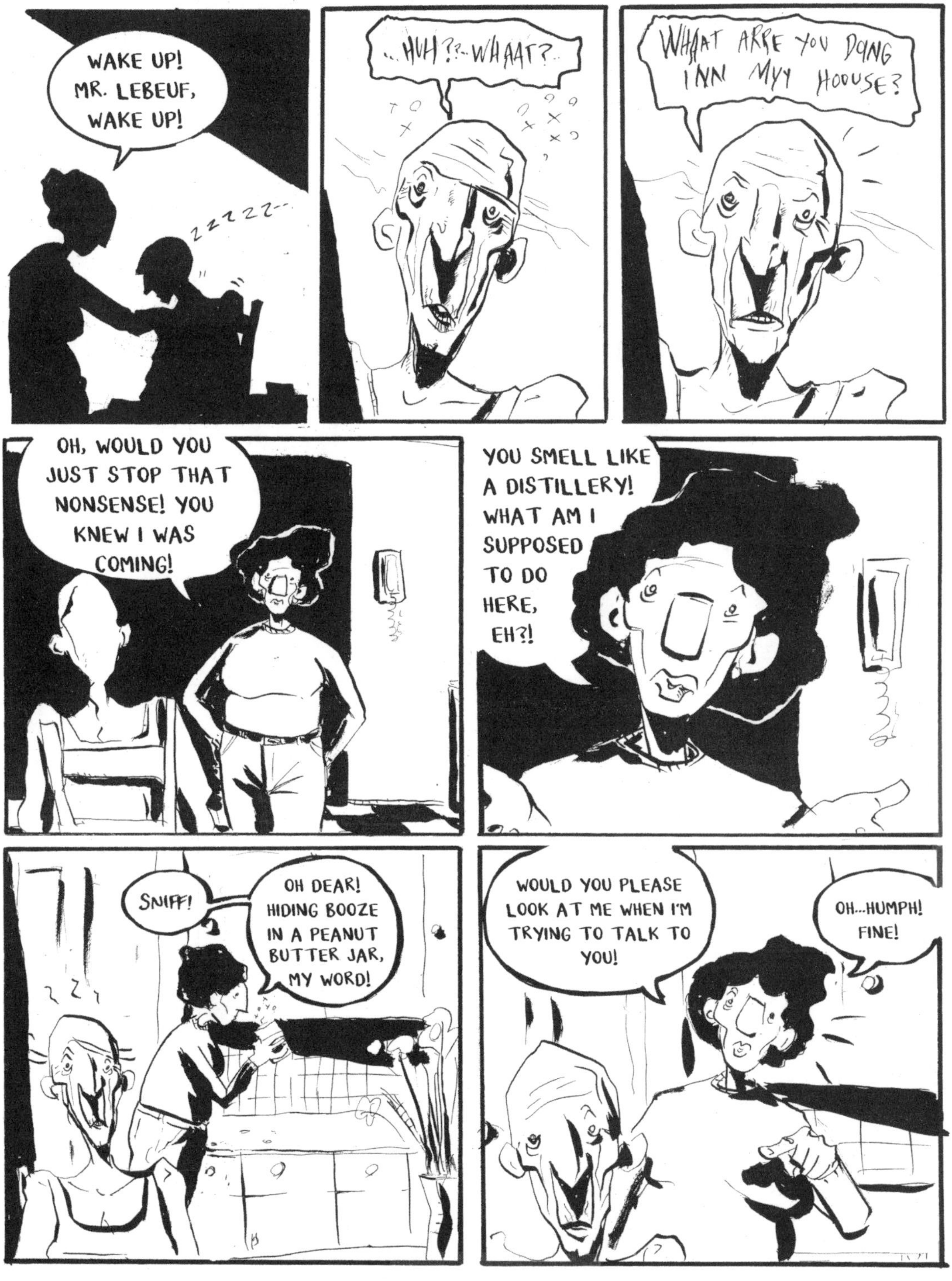
WAKE UP! MR. LEBEUF, WAKE UP!
ZZZZZ...
...HUH??...WHAAT?...
WHAAT ARRE YOU DOING INN MYY HOOUSE?
OH, WOULD YOU JUST STOP THAT NONSENSE! YOU KNEW I WAS COMING!
YOU SMELL LIKE A DISTILLERY! WHAT AM I SUPPOSED TO DO HERE, EH?!
SNIFF!
OH DEAR! HIDING BOOZE IN A PEANUT BUTTER JAR, MY WORD!
WOULD YOU PLEASE LOOK AT ME WHEN I'M TRYING TO TALK TO YOU!
OH...HUMPH! FINE!

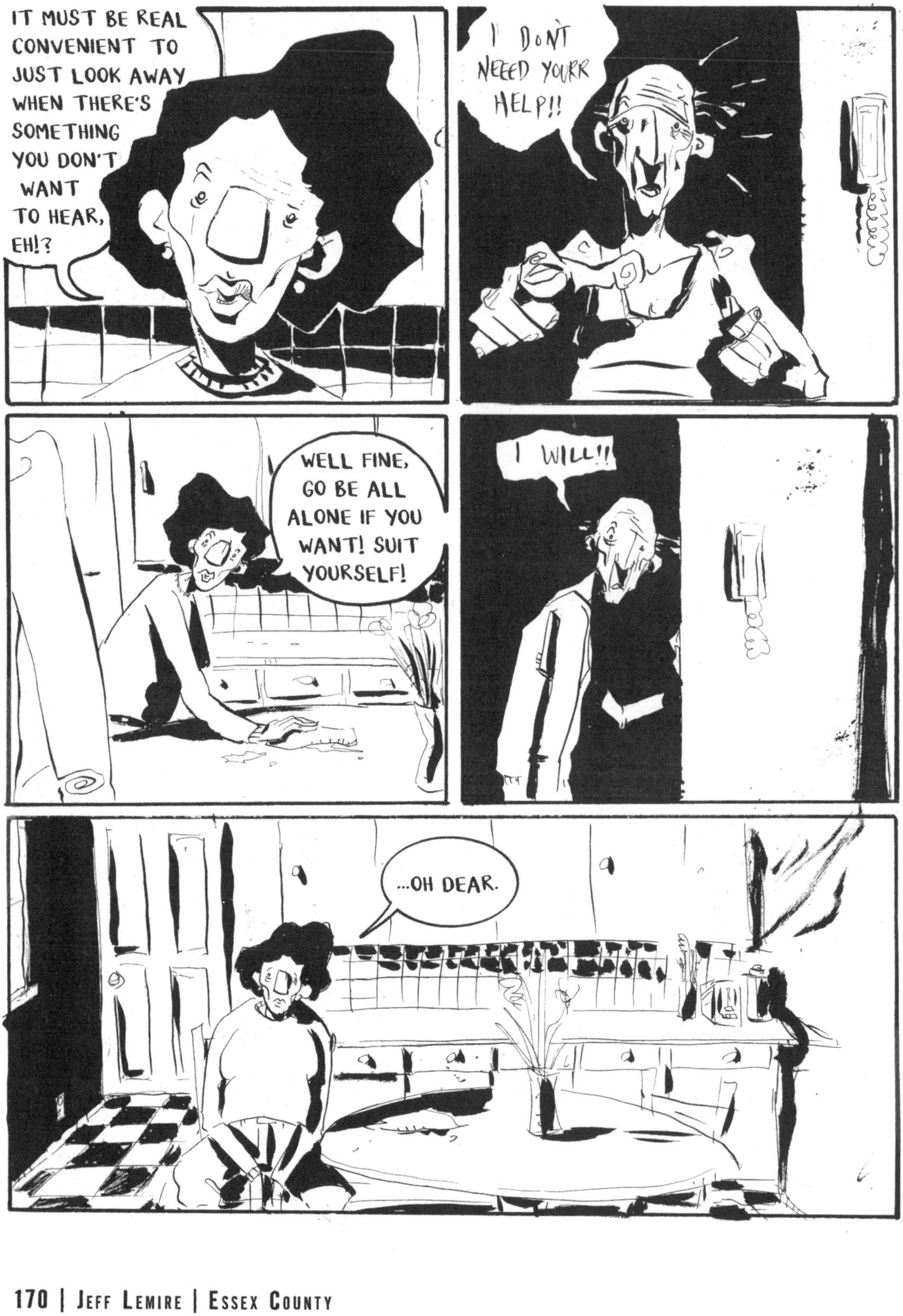
IT MUST BE REAL CONVENIENT TO JUST LOOK AWAY WHEN THERE'S SOMETHING YOU DON'T WANT TO HEAR, EH!?
I DON'T NEEED YOURR HELP!!
WELL FINE, GO BE ALL ALONE IF YOU WANT! SUIT YOURSELF!
I WILL!!
...OH DEAR.

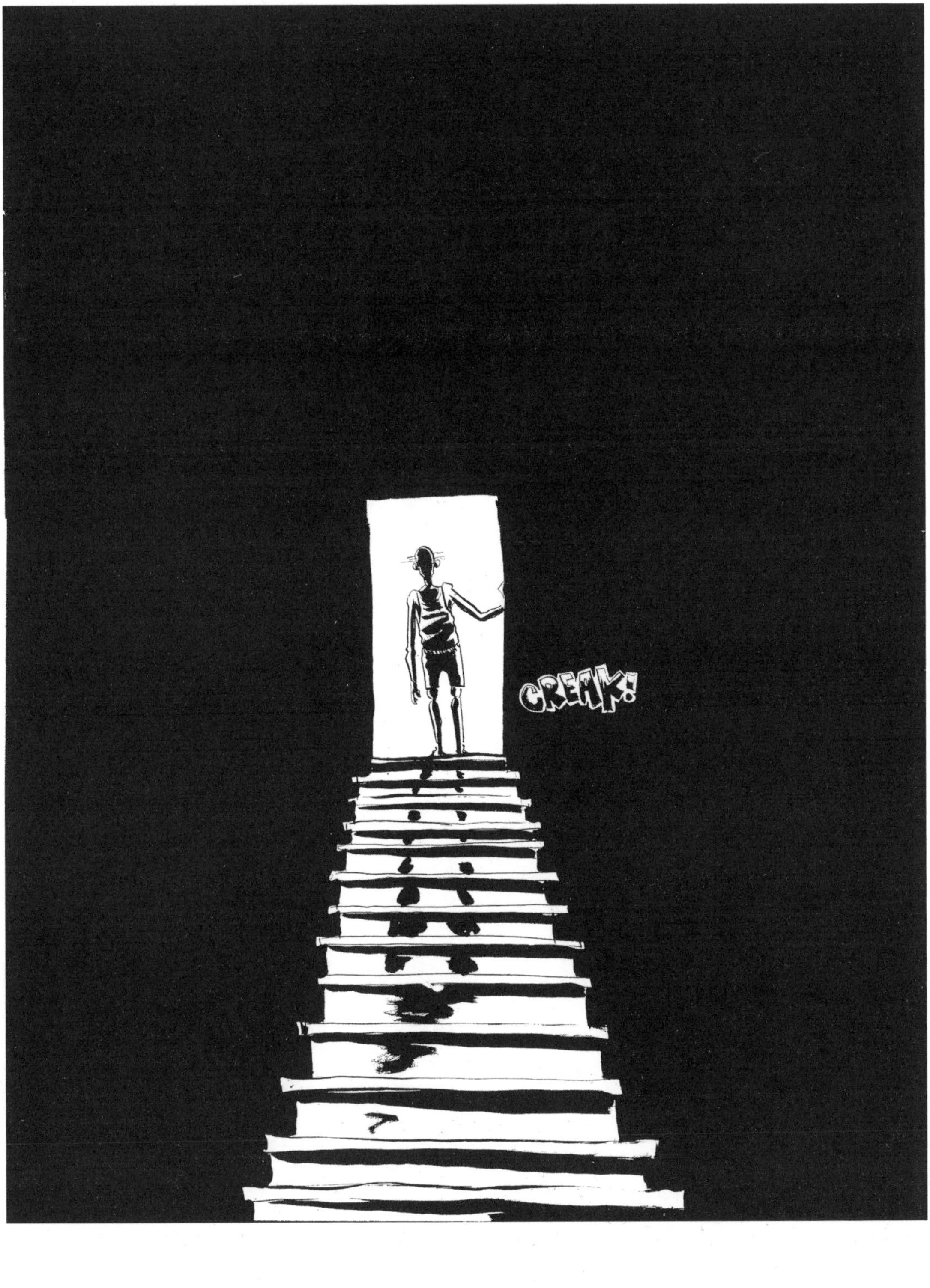
CREAK!

CLICK!
What a mess!
Come on, where is it?

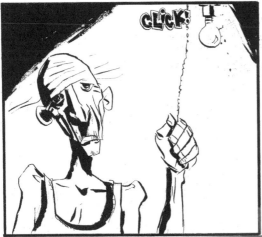

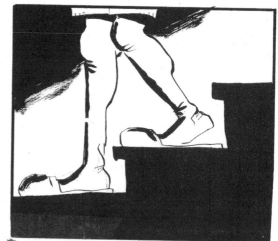

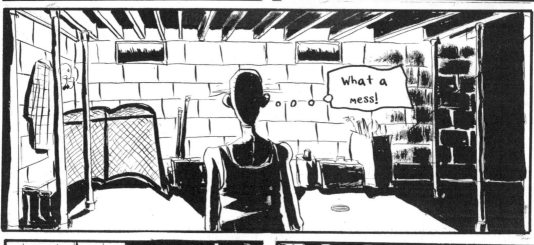

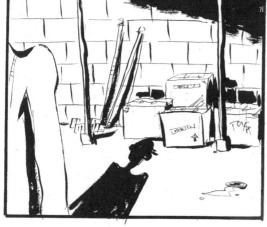

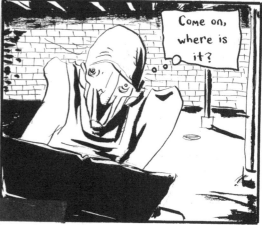

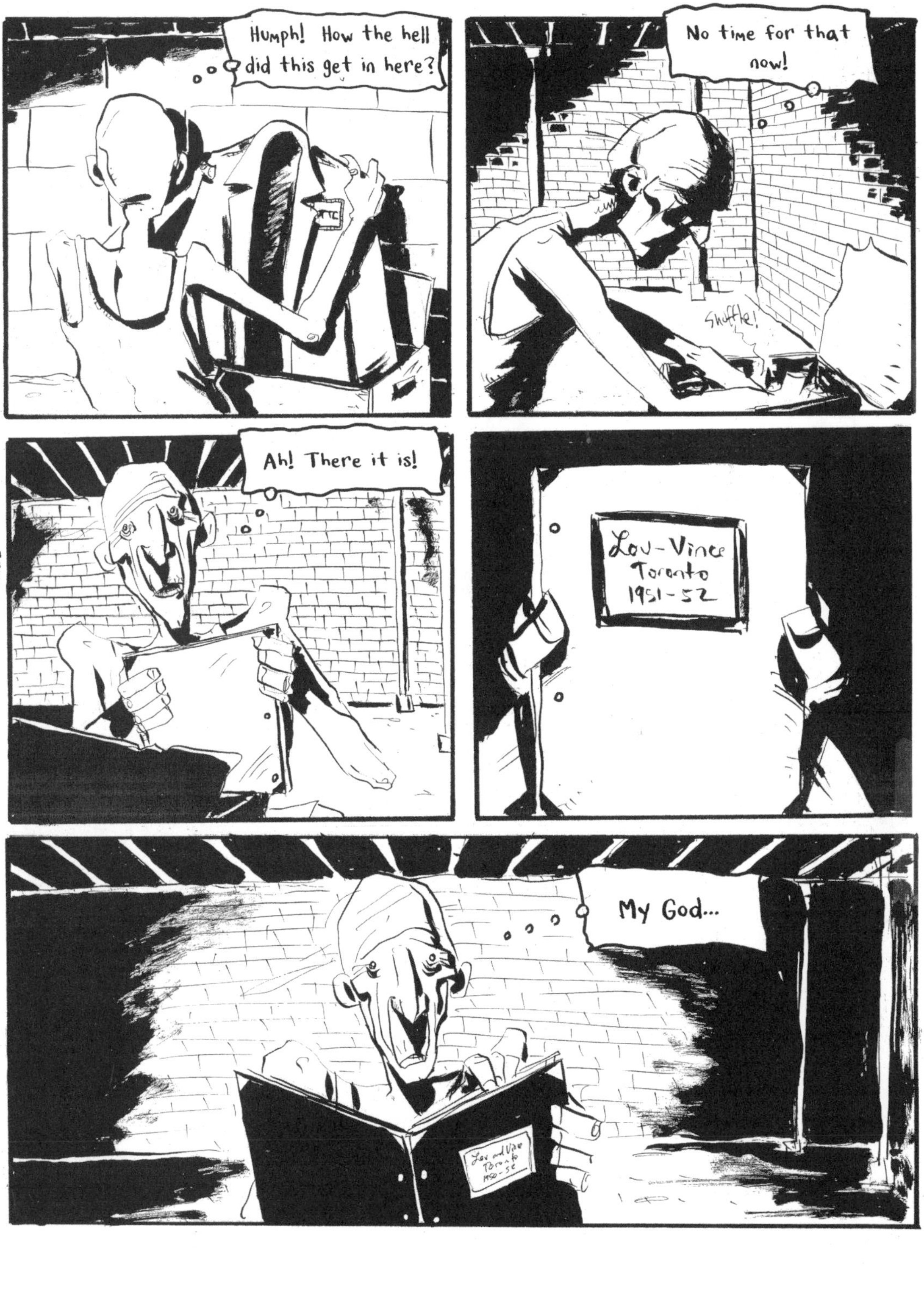
Humph! How the hell did this get in here?
No time for that now!
Shuffle!
Ah! There it is!
Lou-Vince
Toronto
1951-52
My God...

Vince on to team bus '51

GRIZZLIE BROS. DRAW NEW FANS

By NEIL MacCARL

The smashing success of rinks from the Oshawa Curling club in carrying off the two blue-ribbon awards in double rink competition, the Ontario Tankard and the Governor-General's Trophy, should not come as a surprise to the close followers of the curling game.

There have been plenty of tipoffs in the past five years that the Oshawa club was producing some excellent young curlers as shown by their victories in the Ontario Junior Tankard for three successive years, 1947, 1948 and 1949. And all Oshawa victory in the Governor-General's play in 1948 added further to their prestige, although the club had never managed to score in a major event such as the Tankard.

An All-Oshawa Show

But it was an all-Oshawa show yesterday as A. J. Parkhill and Dr. J. Brock scored in the Tankard final at Toronto Curling club while William Minnett and Rev. J. Pereyma were winning the Governor-General's final at Granite club.

It took a strong finish, particularly by Dr. Brock, to give Oshawa its first Tankard victory. After eight ends of play, Dr. Brock was trailing J. G. W. Sands of Kingston 12-3, while Parkhill of Oshawa had a four-shot lead over R. M. Best of Kingston, which gave the Kingston entry a combined lead of six shots.

Dr. Brock was down 10-4 after 11 ends, but Kingston failed to store in the remainder of the game, while Oshawa counted 11 shots to finish one shot behind.

Youngsters Shine

The Oshawa victory in the Tankard adds weight to the theory that curling isn't an old man's game. Shel Moore, who played lead for A. J. Parkhill, is only 19, and probably one of the youngest members ever to play on a Tankard winner. And Allan Morrison, second shot, is only two years older.

Despite their comparative youth, these two lads have been playing for six years, and each played on three junior Tankard winners. Morrison also played on a Governor-General's trophy winner in 1948.

It is the same story with regard

to the Governor-General's winners, W. Minnett and Rev. Pereyma, the winning skips, both played on the Oshawa trophy winner in 1948.

Minnett defeated C. Reswick of Wingham 19-11 for an eight-shot margin which compensated for Rev. Pereyma's 17-11 defeat by J. R. Rae in the final round.

In the consolation play, H. Forsythe and Percy Stutch of Lindsay took the Burden trophy, defeating Kitchener 28-13. Forsythe lost 13-10 to Carl Asmussen, and his 1950 Brier rink from Kitchener, but Stutch trounced J. Lucas 19-4.

Kitchener didn't miss out altogether on the silverware as W. A. Clarke and Allan Sherk took the Globe and Mail trophy by defeating Brockville 42-33. Sherk defeated O. Bigford 17-8 and Clarke beat T. G. Goodison 25-17.

STORY REVERSED THIS TIME
BLUES WIN IN FINAL MINUTE

Queen's University provided a smaller-than-usual Hart House Athletic Night crowd with plenty of thrills before they went down in a heart-breaking 35-34 defeat at the hands of the University of Toronto Blues last night.

A foul shot

LETHBRIDGE LEAFS BEAT AMBRI-PROTTI

Ambri, Italy, Feb. 3—(CP)—Lethbridge Maple Leafs last night walloped the Ambri-Piotta hockey team 13-1.

BAGNATO BUSY GETTING BOUTS FOR NEWSBOYS

Hardly had the welts and bruises subsided on the frames and features of last year's contestants when another Newsboys' boxing show comes along. This latest edition of a program that was instituted about a quarter of a century ago, is scheduled for a week Monday night (Feb. 12) at the Gardens. All proceeds go to the Toronto Newsboys' Welfare fund, and this boxing show is the fund's only source of revenue.

Vic Bagnato is again matchmaking the Newsboys' program, and announces that he has lined up a top team of Montreal scrappers to take on the best from this province in the feature matches.

Star of the Montreal squad is the Quebec bantam champion, Frankie Fitzgerald, who made such a smash hit on last year's show, in besting Oakwood's fiery Maurice Muir. Bagnato hasn't yet decided who should represent Ontario against the capable Montrealer.

LEBEUF BOYS DOMINATE

GRIDDER IN CO

San Franci Radovich, fo Southern Cal has won a pr in his $105,00 the old Natio Federal Ju man yesterday

Oct. 3, 1951

Dear Mom,

Sorry I haven't written in a while. Things have been real busy here. Lou is fine, and says "Hi!" The team is a real good bunch of guys and we've been playing a lot better lately.

We leave for a road trip up North to Parry Sound on Saturday. Should be nice this time of year.

The city sure is busy. So many people, always going. Lou really likes it. I guess it's ok for some people, but it's not for me. I can't wait to come back home this summer. Hope Uncle Ron got the winter wheat off in time.

I'll write soon. Beth is coming up again after we get back. Looking forward to that! Bye Mom.

xoxo Vince

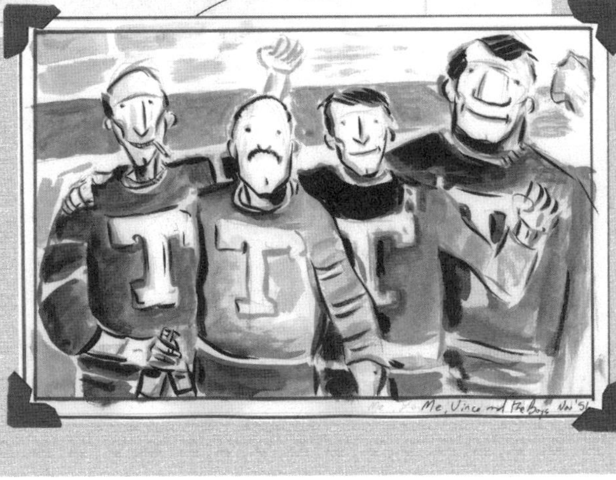
Me, Vince and the Boys Nov '51

TORONTO DAILY STAR
Speaking on Sport
By Milt Dunnell – Sports Editor
Grizzlies Win Fourth In A Row
Wave Goodbye to th
HABITANTS HOP TO THIRD SPOT HOWE NEAR MARK
'CUT
WAR
Vincent Lebeuf
Junior City Fight Entries Close April 16
N.H.L. S
Lou on team bus Oct' 51
TORONTO'S MINOR LEAGUE GRIZZLIES ON A ROLL
STEWART TRIES TIPTOE BUT LEAFS STILL DON'T BEAT GUMP
Phil Might Even Pay For The Privilege
He Decides He Was Screwball On Shutes
One Day, Clancy Dreams of 1st Place The Next, He's Fearful of Cellar
BELIVEAU 1-MAN GANG AS CANADIENS BEAT, TIE BOSTON OVER WEEK-END
Varsity Injuries Take Much of the Joy Out of Romp Over Western Mustangs

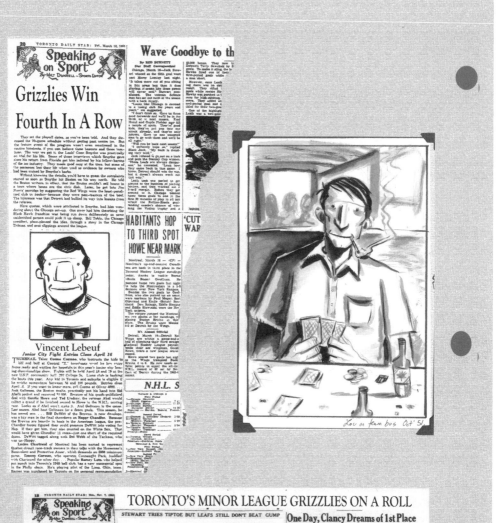

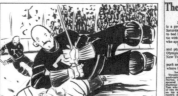

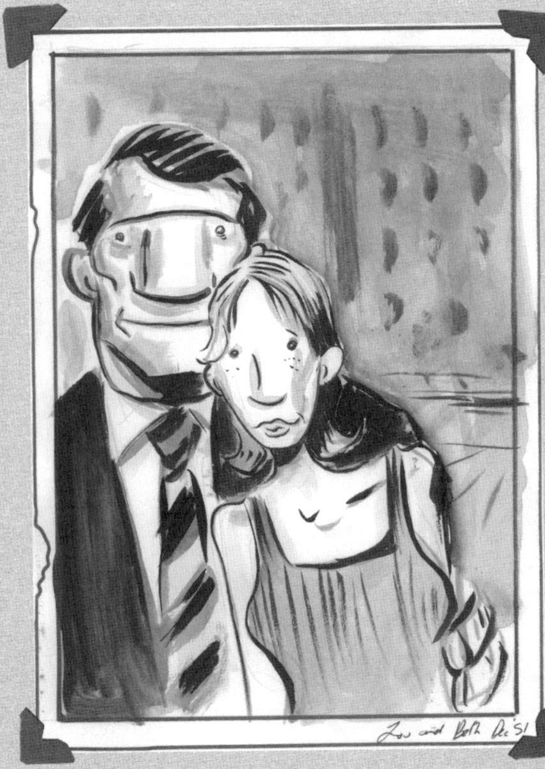
Lou and Beth Dec '51

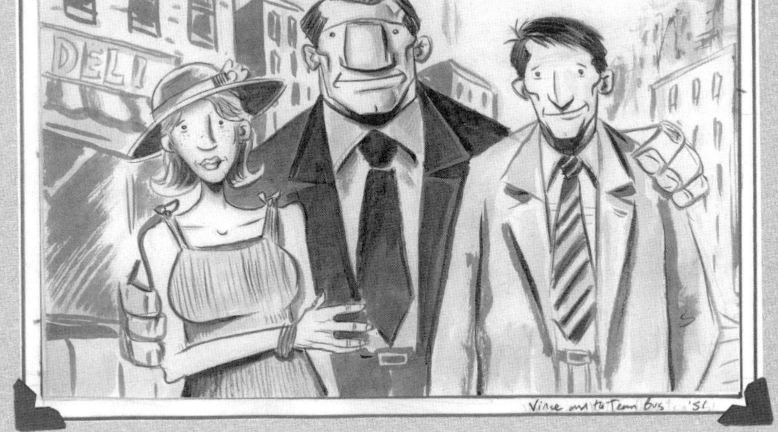
DELI
Vince and the Team Bus '51

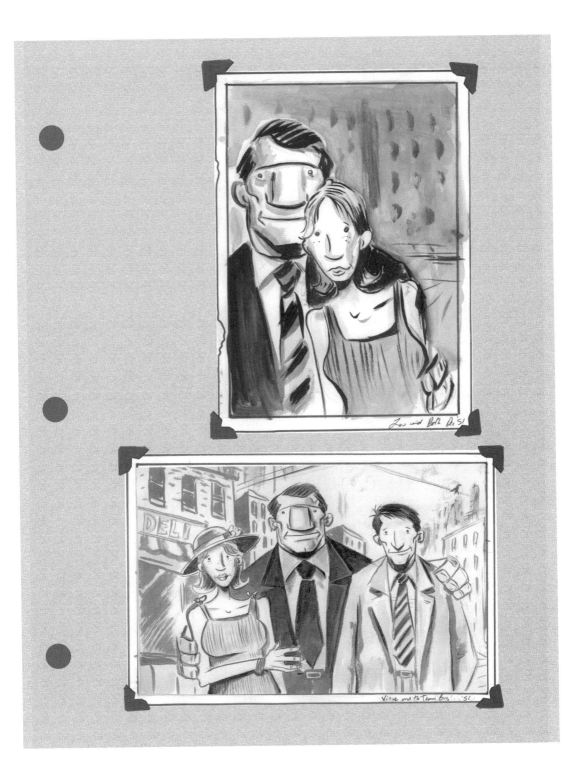

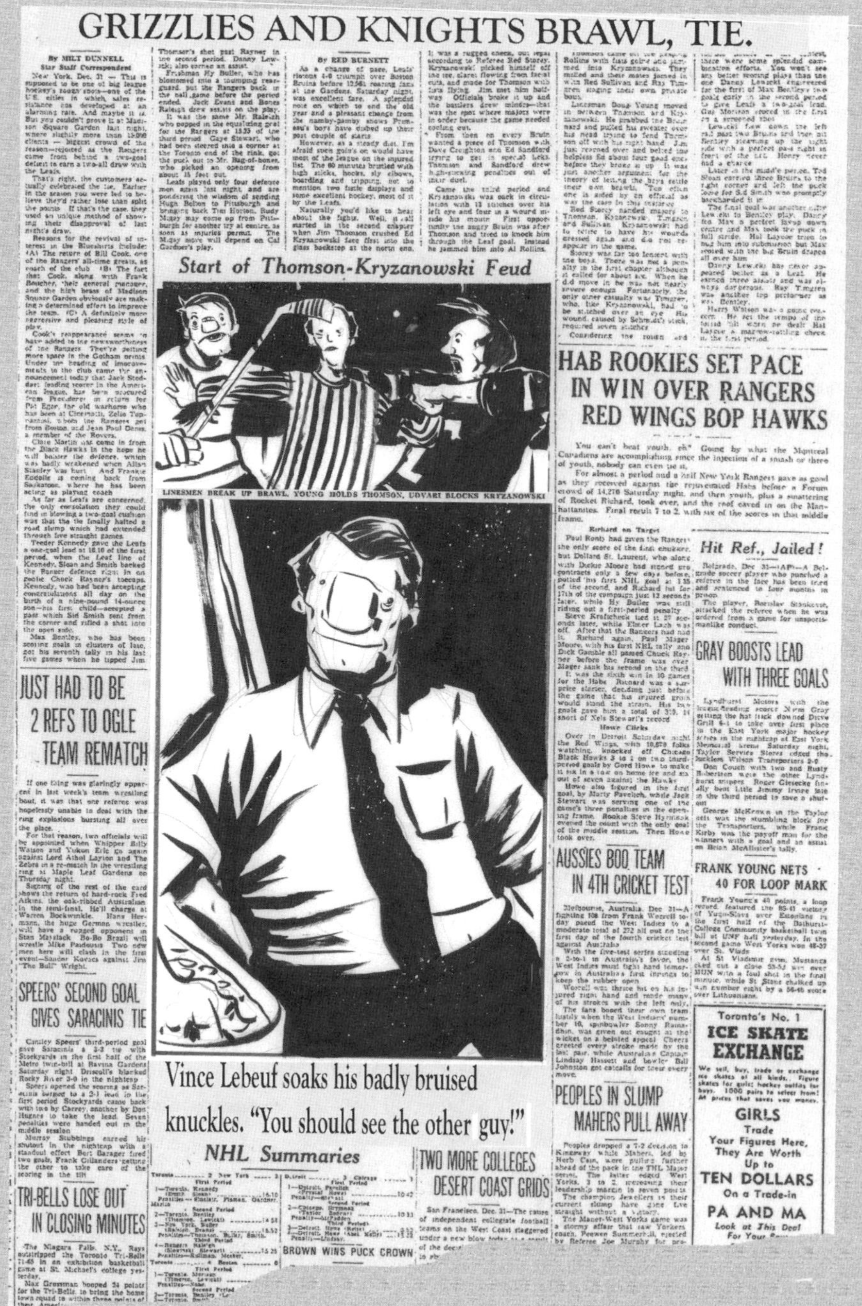
GRIZZLIES AND KNIGHTS BRAWL, TIE.
Start of Thomson-Kryzanowski Feud
LINESMEN BREAK UP BRAWL, YOUNG HOLDS THOMSON, UDVARI BLOCKS KRYZANOWSKI
HAB ROOKIES SET PACE IN WIN OVER RANGERS RED WINGS BOP HAWKS
Hit Ref., Jailed!
GRAY BOOSTS LEAD WITH THREE GOALS
JUST HAD TO BE 2 REFS TO OGLE TEAM REMATCH
AUSSIES BOO TEAM IN 4TH CRICKET TEST
FRANK YOUNG NETS 40 FOR LOOP MARK
SPEERS' SECOND GOAL GIVES SARACINIS TIE
PEOPLES IN SLUMP MAHERS PULL AWAY
Vince Lebeuf soaks his badly bruised knuckles. "You should see the other guy!"
NHL Summaries
TWO MORE COLLEGES DESERT COAST GRIDS
TRI-BELLS LOSE OUT IN CLOSING MINUTES
BROWN WINS PUCK CROWN
Toronto's No. 1
ICE SKATE EXCHANGE
GIRLS
Trade
Your Figures Here,
They Are Worth
Up to
TEN DOLLARS
On a Trade-in
PA AND MA
Look at This Deal

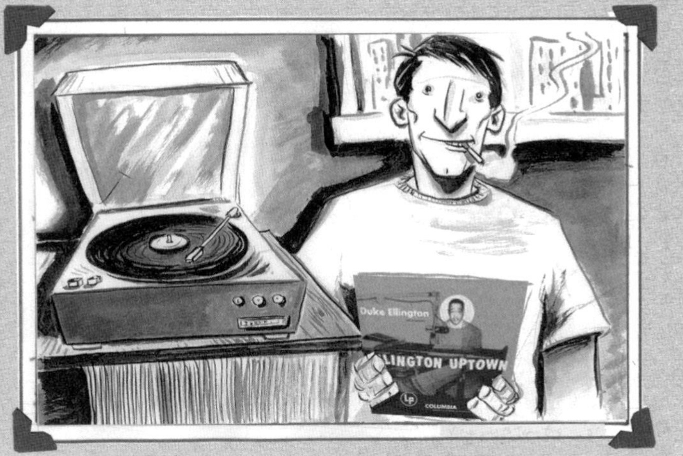
Duke Ellington
LLINGTON UPTOWN
LP
COLUMBIA

Dec 16, 1951.

Dear Mom,

I hope you got that last package of clippings and photographs I sent. Lou bought a new fancy camera and won't stop snapping pictures of us. I guess you'll probably like them though.

We got the care package you sent up with Beth. Thanks. Sorry to hear about Aunt Alma's health. Hopefully she'll pull through.

Only one more week then we'll be off for the holidays! So, we'll be at the train station at 2:30 pm on the 22nd. Don't forget us!

xoxo. Vince

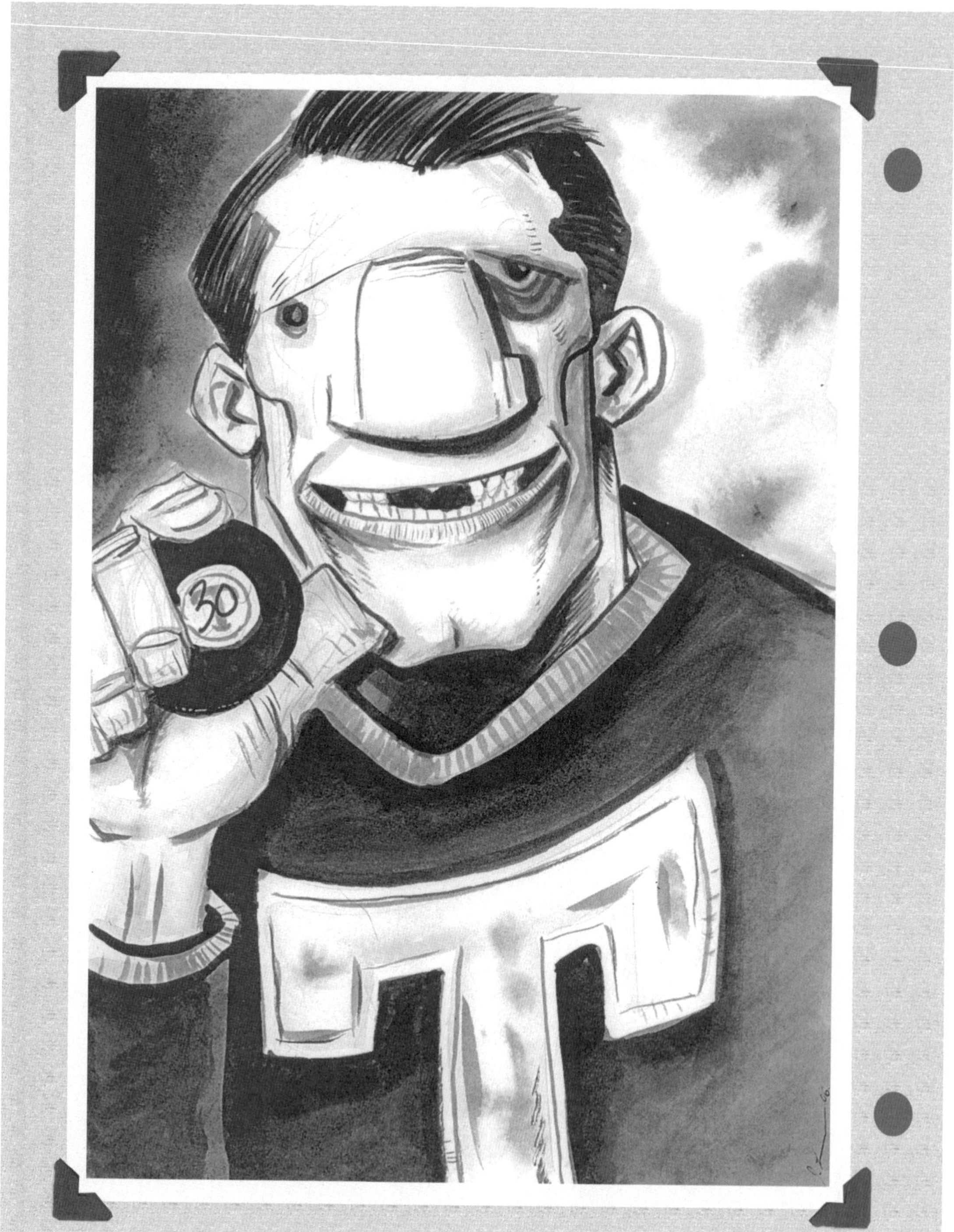
30

Jan 12, 1952.

Dear Mom,

Can you believe it! 30 goals! I asked the newspaper man and he gave me this nice big photograph for you. It's the same one that they ran in the paper on Friday!

We're real close to making the playoffs now. If we do, I won't be home until ~~at the~~ March at the earliest. So, I hope Uncle Ron can get started on the planting if I don't make it home ~~till~~ in time. Have to get going, meeting the boys to celebrate.

xoxo Vince.

LEBEUF GETS 30 AND QUITE A SHINER

DiMaggio Just Can't Get Going

YANKEES

...wood, Calif., March 21—Joe DiMaggio, the New Yankees' $100,000 outfielder, ...g it more difficult than ...round into playing form. ..., who announced shortly ... training season began, ... might be his last year ... qualified it the next ...aving his worst spring. ...nt batting average is only ...esenting two hits in 18 ...ecover. DiMaggio has ...less two straight days ...minor league pitching. ...le, Mickey Mantle, the ... rookie riot, has taken ... stage once held by ...nd is batting a cool .571. ... went hitless for the ...straight day when he ... three trips as the Yan... to the Chicago White Sox, 5 to 0, at Glendale, Calif., yesterday. To make it worse—Glendale is Manager Casey Stengel's home town.

ATHLETICS

Ft. Lauderdale, Fla., March 21—The Philadelphia Athletics gave an old friend an unpleasant afternoon yesterday when the Brooklyn Dodgers sent Bill McCahan to the mound against them. McCahan, who once pitched a no-hitter for the Athletics and now is attempting a comeback after a sore arm, faced only six hitters in his first two innings. But then the roof fell in and the Athletics rushed eight runs over the plate before McCahan could be replaced. The Athletics won, 12 to 1, for their most decisive spring victory.

RED SOX

Sarasota, Fla., March 21—Sore-armer Harry Taylor of the Boston Red Sox seemed ready to fulfill Manager Steve O'Neill's prediction today that he might be the Sox's best pitcher this year. Taylor, after a poor debut, came back yesterday to hold the Boston Braves to three hits and only one run in five innings. The Braves won, 2 to 1, when two singles and Fred Hatfield's error shoved over a run in the sixth inning.

PHILLIES

Miami, Fla., March 21—The Philadelphia Phillies sent Pitcher Bill Fogg and Third-baseman Walt Derucki to Baltimore in the International league today, cutting their roster to 37 players.

LEBEUF SCORES 30 GOALS!

New York, March 21 — Experiments designed to convert outfielder Ralph Kiner of the Pittsburgh Pirates into a first baseman apparently are doomed to failure, just as so many of these attempted switch-overs have been in the past.

One of the few standout hitters who can hold down either job with equal eclat is Stan Musial of the St. Louis Cardinals. Joe DiMaggio is among those who never could get the hang of real bang-up first basing.

Kiner, a superior slugger, does not like the infield spot and that is about as good a reason as any for the club to move him on back to the picket line. He probably would play second rate first base and because of dissatisfaction with such a switch most likely would fall off in his hitting.

Billy Goodman of the Boston Red Sox, the American league batting champion, is the most versatile of them all. He can almost literally play any position and in his younger days did, meaning back in his school days down Carolina way.

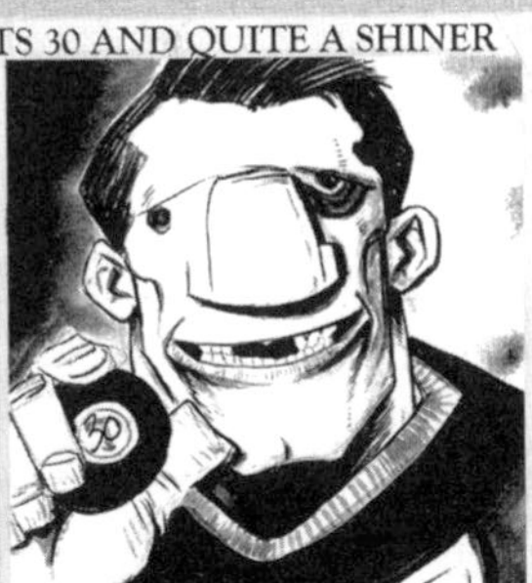

...ON ONE UP ...HEAD STARS ...TING REGENTS

...March 21 — Netminder ...sparked Weston Dukes to a 4-3 victory over Brampton Regents in their best-of-seven O.H.A. Junior "B" series here last night before 1,700 fans. Dukes now lead the series 3 games to 2.

Halifax Team Plays Here

Halifax Sea Gulls Midget hockey team will arrive in Toronto Good Friday morning for a four-day visit in which they will play three games with T.H.L. squads. The 16-man team will be guests of the Toronto Hockey league for their stay and will take in the Boston-Leafs N.H.L. contest here Saturday.

On Friday night they play St. Michael's college minor-midgets at Varsity and Saturday take on Dennis House Bombers as a curtain-raiser to the Major Series playoff game. They wind up at Maple Leaf Gardens against North Toronto Lions Easter Monday.

GRIZZLIES COACH EARNS PRAISE FOR TURNAROUND

TORONTO DAILY STAR: Thurs., Feb. 1, 1951 — 22

Speaking on Sport

By MILT DUNNELL—SPORTS EDITOR

A Bleat From Miss Duddleydumpple

MISS Daisy Duddleydumpple just called to say she and her gals probably will picket the Gardens. Miss Duddleydumpple, it develops, is chairman of the civil rights committee of the Two's the Quota for a Honeymoon league, which has branches in the U.S., Mexico and some sections of Santa Domingo. The league is anxious to gain a foothold in Canada. Miss Duddleydumpple had heard, we suspected, about the case of Johnny McCormack. Miss Duddleydumpple said she had, and that was the reason for the league's indignation. The league had decided that Connie Smythe should be brought to trial, and that was the reason for the pickets. Miss Duddleydumpple was non-plussed to learn that Smythe is in Florida. How, she wondered, could Smythe, who's nearly two thousand miles away, send one of his slaves to a honeymoon nest of Pittsburgh Hornets.

We asked Miss Duddleydumpple if she knew Smythe. She admitted she didn't. That's just the trouble with a lot of the executives in those high-sounding, well-intentioned international organizations. They're not versed in fundamentals. She wouldn't know, for instance, that Smythe intervened, a year ago, when a beloved Turk Broda, decided to show a waistline bulge, as a badge of the success he'd attained in hockey. Or maybe he might even get around to running for alderman.

By the time Smythe and the physical torture specialists got through, the Turkey could have feathered the end of his belt and let it dangle like a highlander's sporran. And then there was the time the Turk got himself a horse and was looking over the condition books for posh parks like Sunshine, San Mateo and Billings, Montana. Turk tore up his application for membership in the Jockey club a few minutes after Smythe read the announcement in the newspapers. There's no evidence that any pressure was brought to bear. Smythe's an old racing man himself—Shoeless Joe, Skating Fool, Blue Ice, remember?—so there's no reason why he should be prejudiced against the turf. You'll find him at Woodbine on King's Plate day—and likely at the daily double cashier's window.

But Miss Duddleydumpple should have some knowledge of things like that before she starts popping off about civil liberties. If they're still in the book, they're in fine type, underneath the clause that says there shall be no assist on a goal for the attacking team, when a defending player boots the disc into his own rigging.

Off-Hours Are Their Own — Almost

YOU see, Miss Duddleydumpple, it's like this: playing hockey for a club like the Leafs is partly punching a clock and partly like being a member of a family—a big happy family. You have to be on the job. If the coach says practice at ten, you're ready to go on the ice at ten. The train leaves for New York at 11.30 from Union Station. So you'd better be aboard. If you're not, you'd better beat that rattler to Sunnyside. Otherwise, there's liable to be a chunk of you know what missing from your next pay envelope. That's the

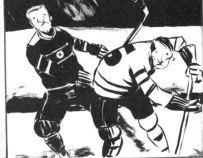

GRIZZLIES CLOSE IN ON PLAYOFFS

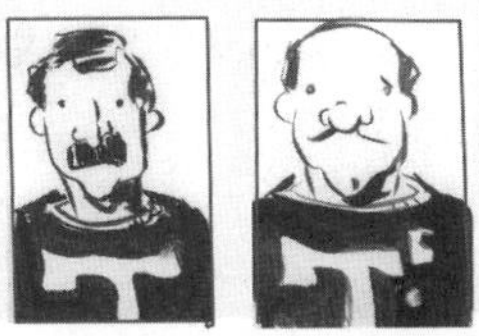

Team Trades Captain, Winger To Barrie

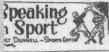

McCOR
LEA

By RED
Those checks
Johnny McCorma
for Pittsburgh
next two weeks
very costly to the
demotion of "Lon
when the Maple
Detroit Red Wing
first place in the
blow to the home
There's no dou
too good for the
no doubt that,
ability and perfo
others on the Le
be spared easier
It could be that
Cormack, the Le
off the nose to
the moment, Co
needs all the b
brains available
place spot. The
going John had
hearts on the clu
a good hockey br
a hockey stick w
tension. He ha
plays than any o
the N.H.L.
The Leaf front
no rule against
mid-season or at
that McCormack's
Hornets was not
This could be, b
able to sell that
Order Fr
Hap Day, Leafs
manager and ho
has been watchin
past few games
lost Rudy Migay
an injured ankle
Smythe in Florid
hum they needed
called back today
said McCormack
take Migay's pl
line.
"The Migay-A
Solinger line is th
goals and they n
take over for Ru
playing very wel
It usually costs
ference between
when he is sent t
a rough jolt to J
days.
Frank Selke
Canadiens will b
McCormack wo
bother them toni
Forum. Selke
as a second F

WON'T TAKE CUT
FOUR CARDS FROM

HOWL DOWN TENNIS HECKLERS ISN'T CRICKET, AUSSIES TOLD

TO DAILY STAR: Fri., March 16, 1951

LEBEUF NAMED CAPTAIN

Speaking on Sport

LT DUNNELL—SPORTS EDITOR

rs Put Stingeroo On Smythe?

rong about wire-tapping, after all. Our feel-
been that once the coppers get the right to
ephone, you might as well return the gadget
Bell's estate. But we'd have given a hatful
in't be money—to tune in on the National
s the other day in New York. That wouldn't
it would be close enough to the real thing.
med, via the jungle drums and the hilltop
of the best shows the N.H.L. has put on
owners keep it to themselves. The rich get

ff dates, as you've been told. And they dis-
hedule without getting past centre ice. But
the program wasn't even mentioned in the
u can believe those beacons and those tom-
t it, the Leafs' Conn Smythe was practically
ome of those interviews which Smythe gave
Florida got him indicted by his fellow-barons
hey made good copy at the time, but some of
lilt when used as evidence by owners who
ythe's barbs.
he details, you'd have to guess the complaints
ythe hit Boston on his way north. He told
effect, that the Bruins couldn't sell beans in
re the civic dish. Later, he got into Jim
gesting the Red Wings were the least-penal-
ecause they were past-masters of the beef.
into breaks from
'm won-

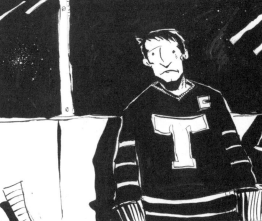

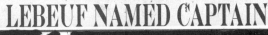

LOU LEBEUF TAKES ON CAPTAIN'S ROLE FOR ALL-IMPORTANT GAME TOMMOROW NIGHT VS. CHATHAM

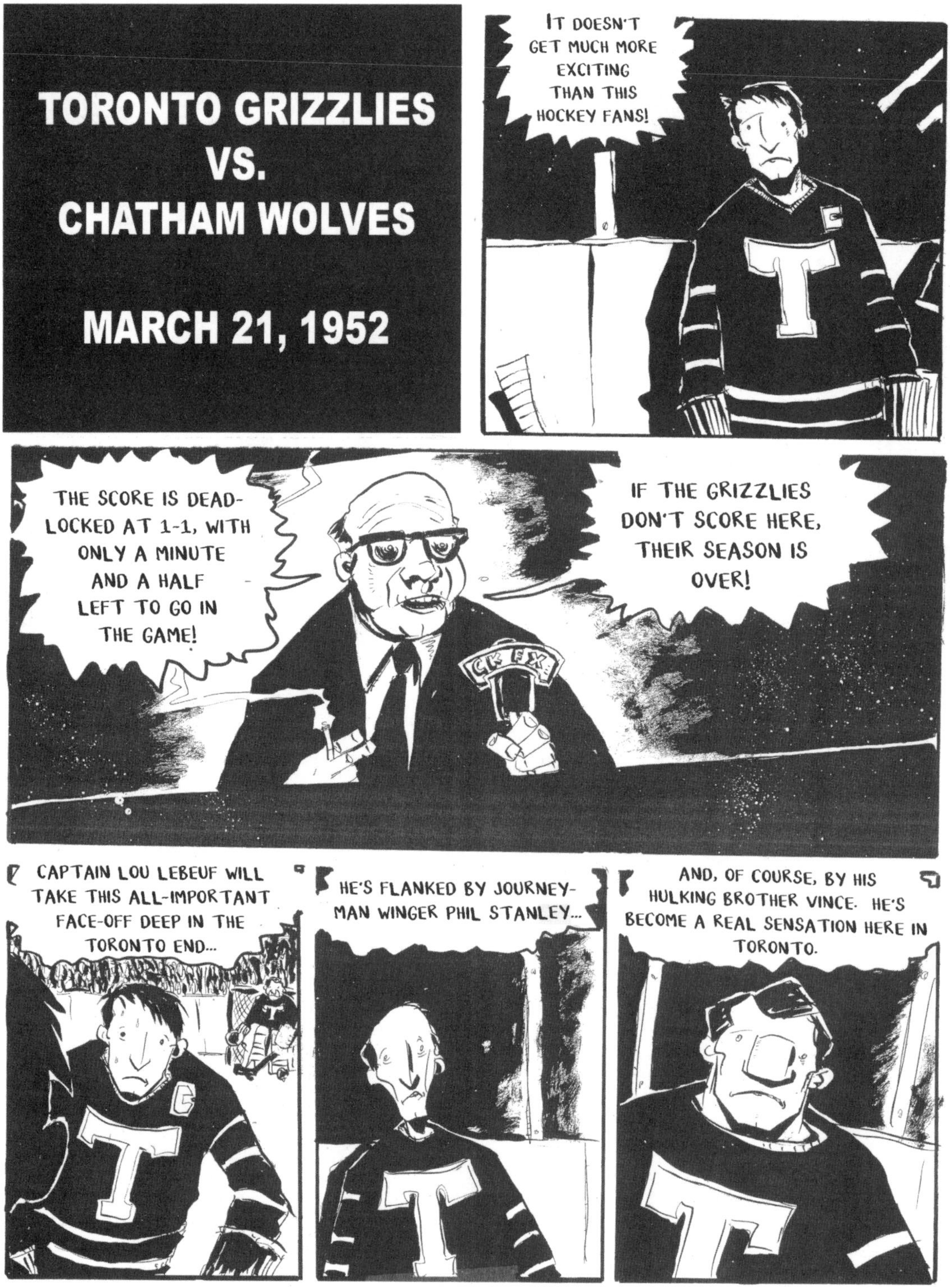
TORONTO GRIZZLIES
VS.
CHATHAM WOLVES
MARCH 21, 1952
IT DOESN'T GET MUCH MORE EXCITING THAN THIS HOCKEY FANS!
THE SCORE IS DEAD-LOCKED AT 1-1, WITH ONLY A MINUTE AND A HALF LEFT TO GO IN THE GAME!
IF THE GRIZZLIES DON'T SCORE HERE, THEIR SEASON IS OVER!
CK FX
CAPTAIN LOU LEBEUF WILL TAKE THIS ALL-IMPORTANT FACE-OFF DEEP IN THE TORONTO END...
HE'S FLANKED BY JOURNEY-MAN WINGER PHIL STANLEY...
AND, OF COURSE, BY HIS HULKING BROTHER VINCE. HE'S BECOME A REAL SENSATION HERE IN TORONTO.

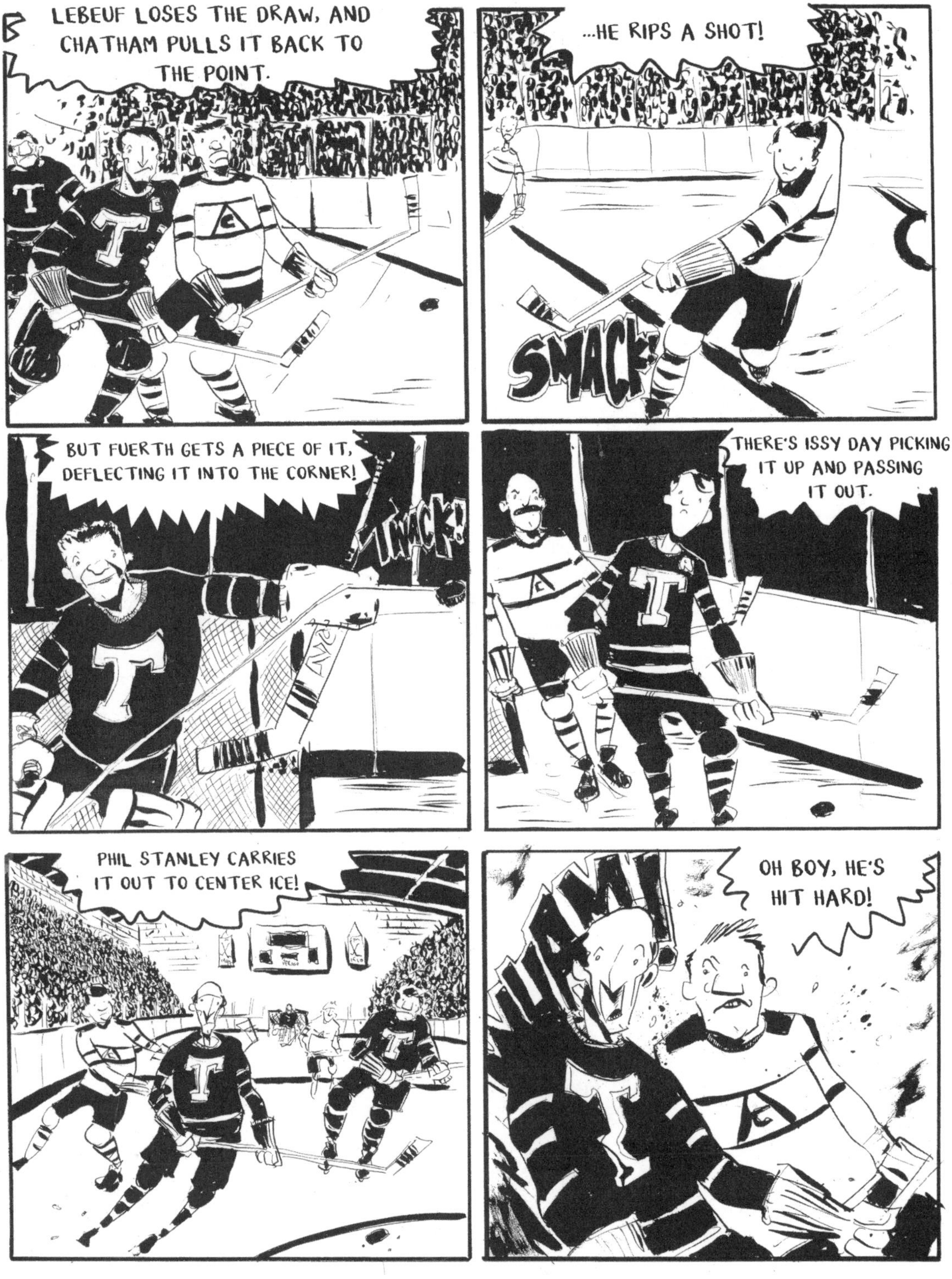
LEBEUF LOSES THE DRAW, AND CHATHAM PULLS IT BACK TO THE POINT.
...HE RIPS A SHOT!
SMACK!
BUT FUERTH GETS A PIECE OF IT, DEFLECTING IT INTO THE CORNER!
TWACK!
THERE'S ISSY DAY PICKING IT UP AND PASSING IT OUT.
PHIL STANLEY CARRIES IT OUT TO CENTER ICE!
WHAM!
OH BOY, HE'S HIT HARD!

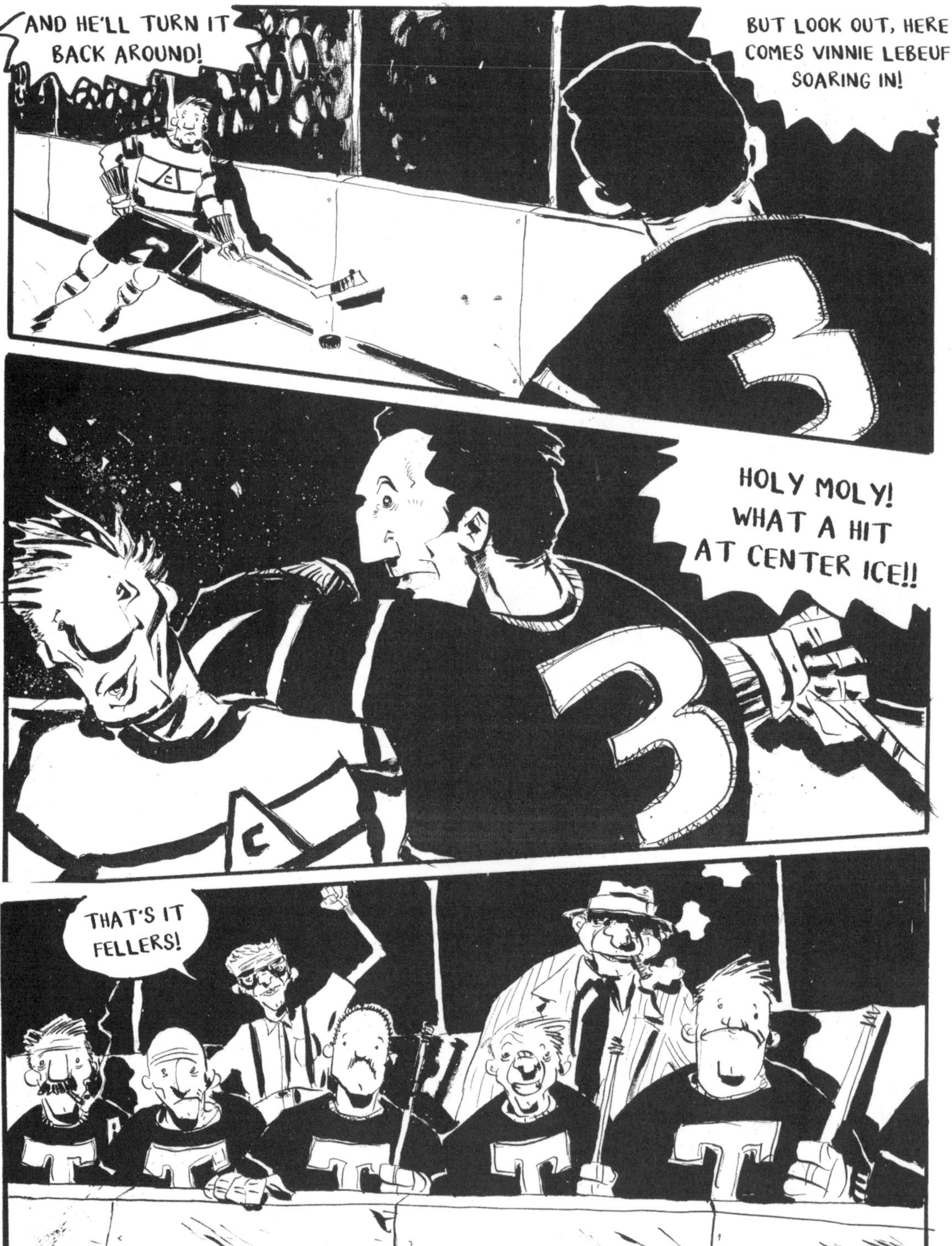
AND HE'LL TURN IT BACK AROUND!
BUT LOOK OUT, HERE COMES VINNIE LEBEUF SOARING IN!
HOLY MOLY! WHAT A HIT AT CENTER ICE!!
THAT'S IT FELLERS!

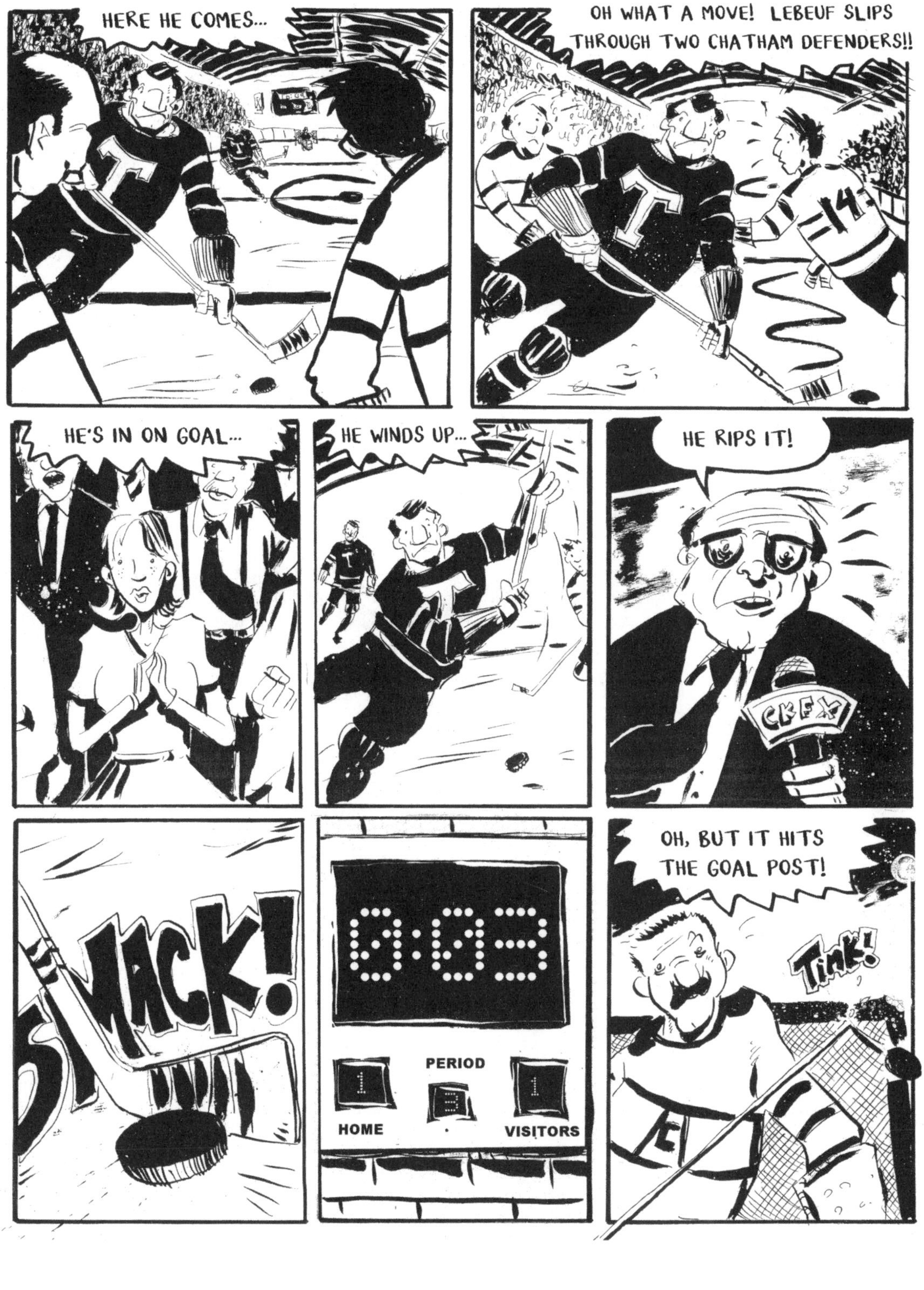
HERE HE COMES...
OH WHAT A MOVE! LEBEUF SLIPS THROUGH TWO CHATHAM DEFENDERS!!
14
HE'S IN ON GOAL...
HE WINDS UP...
HE RIPS IT!
CKFX
SMACK!
0:03
PERIOD
1
3
1
HOME
VISITORS
OH, BUT IT HITS THE GOAL POST!
TINK!

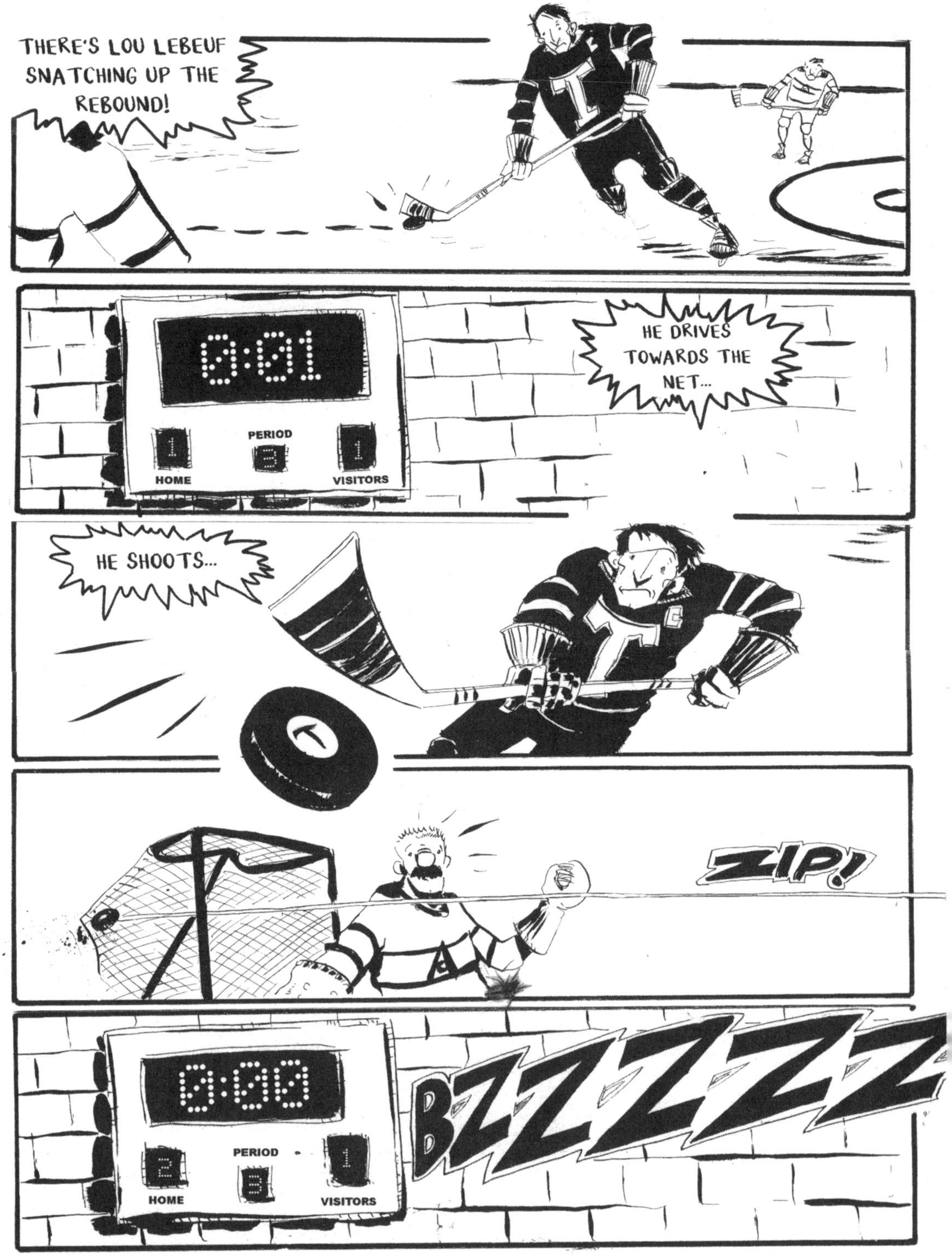
THERE'S LOU LEBEUF SNATCHING UP THE REBOUND!
0:01
PERIOD
1
3
1
HOME
VISITORS
HE DRIVES TOWARDS THE NET...
HE SHOOTS...
ZIP!
0:00
PERIOD
2
3
1
HOME
VISITORS
BZZZZZ

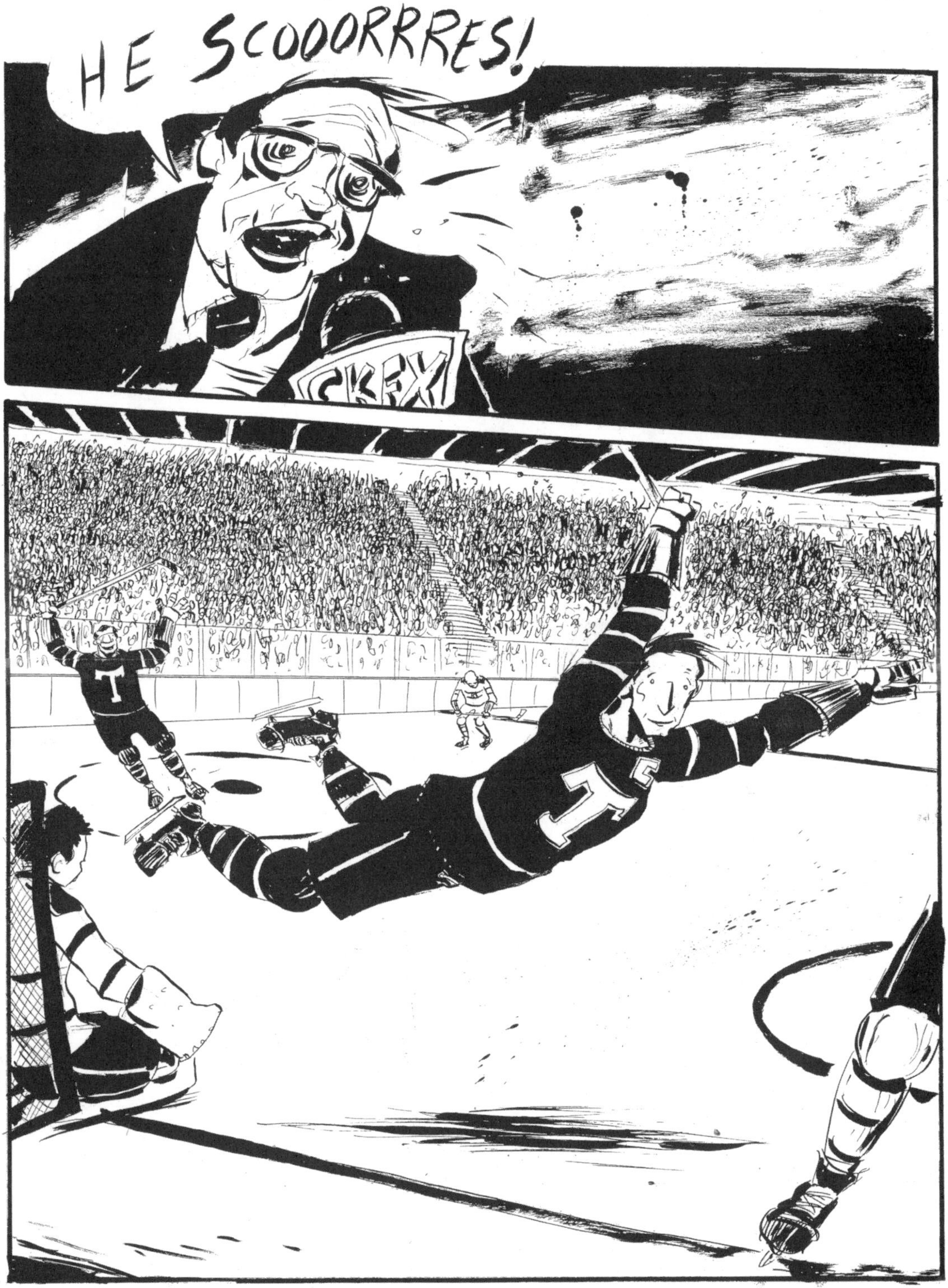
HE SCOOORRRES!
CKFX

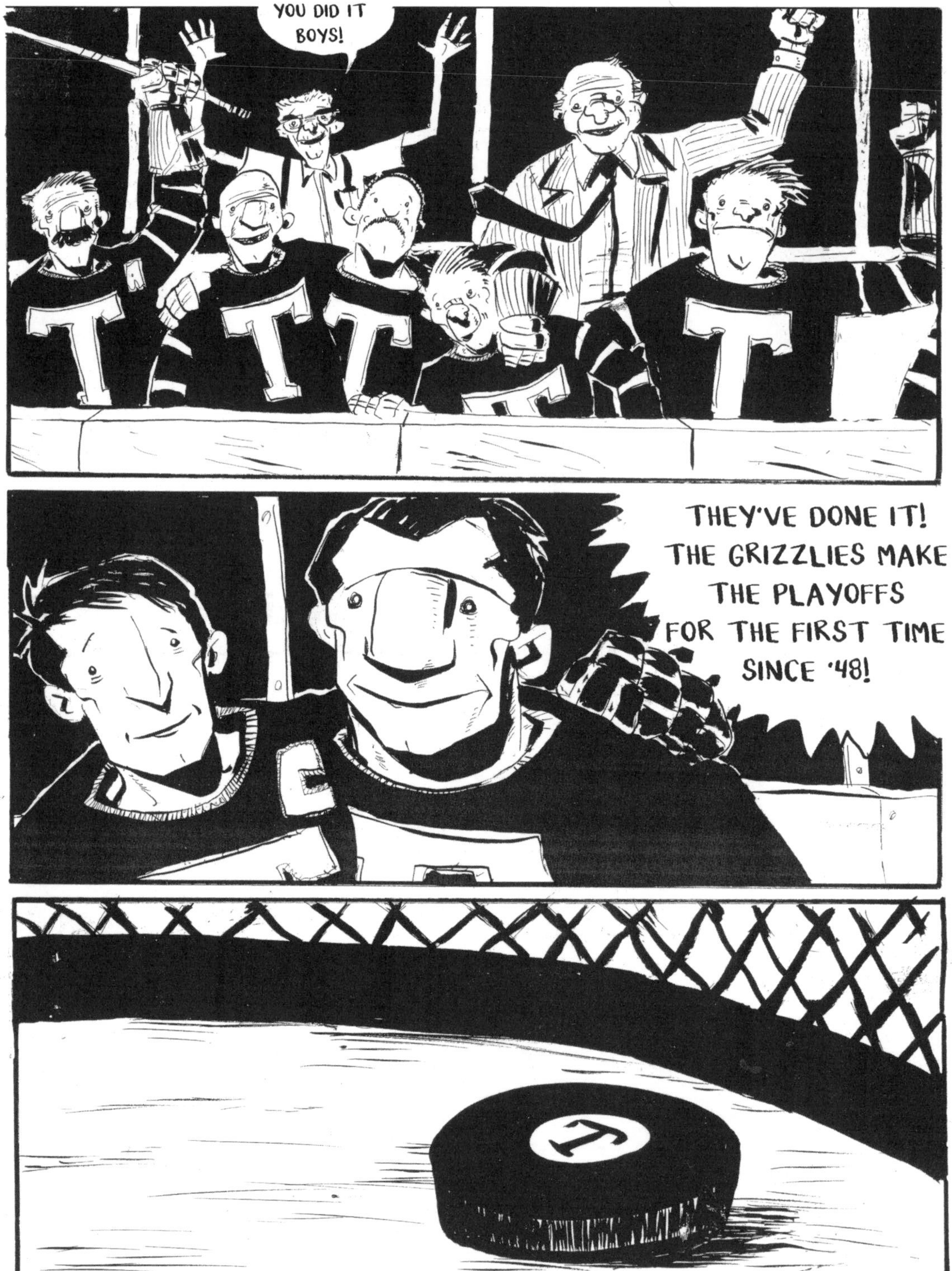
YOU DID IT BOYS!
THEY'VE DONE IT! THE GRIZZLIES MAKE THE PLAYOFFS FOR THE FIRST TIME SINCE '48!

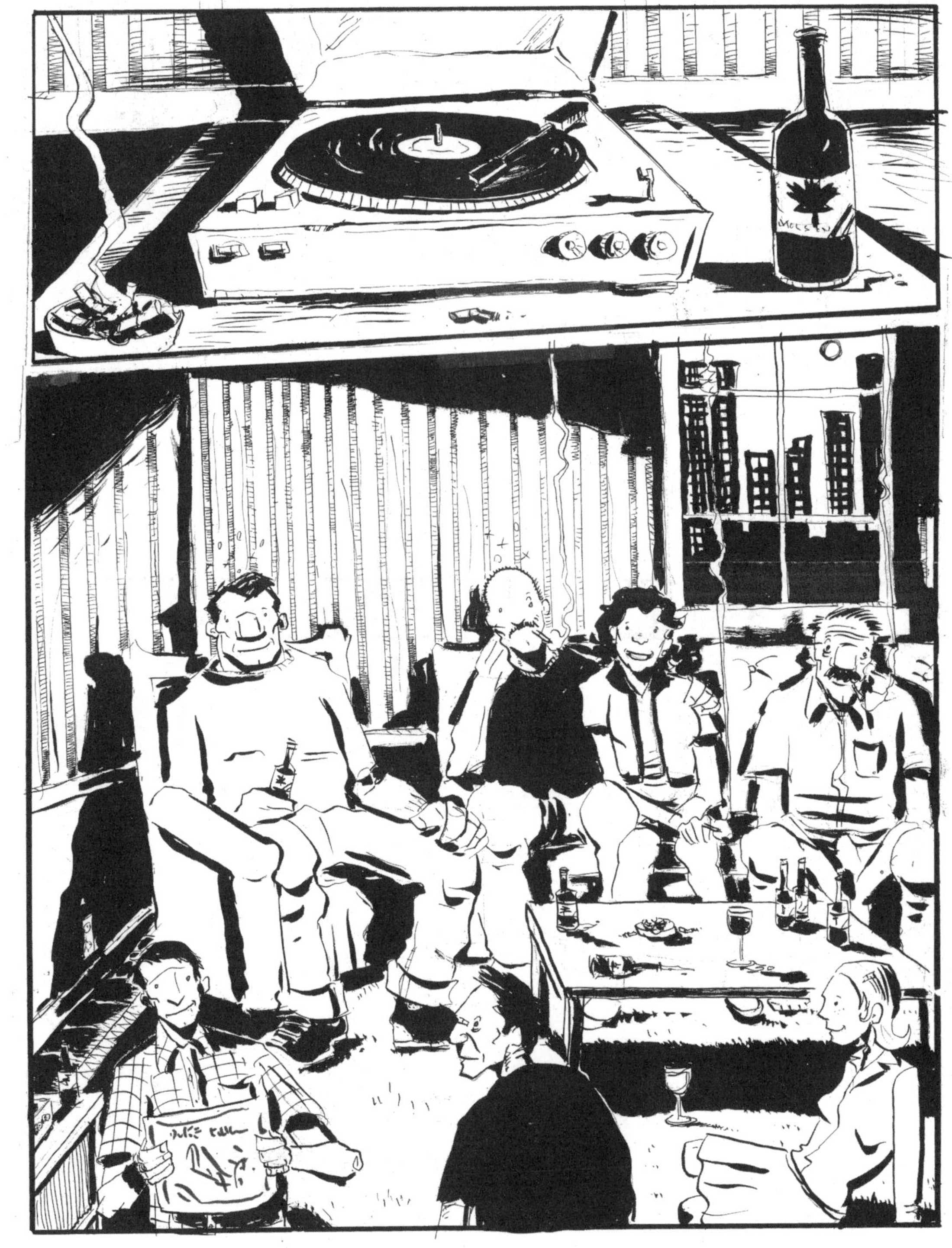
MOLSON

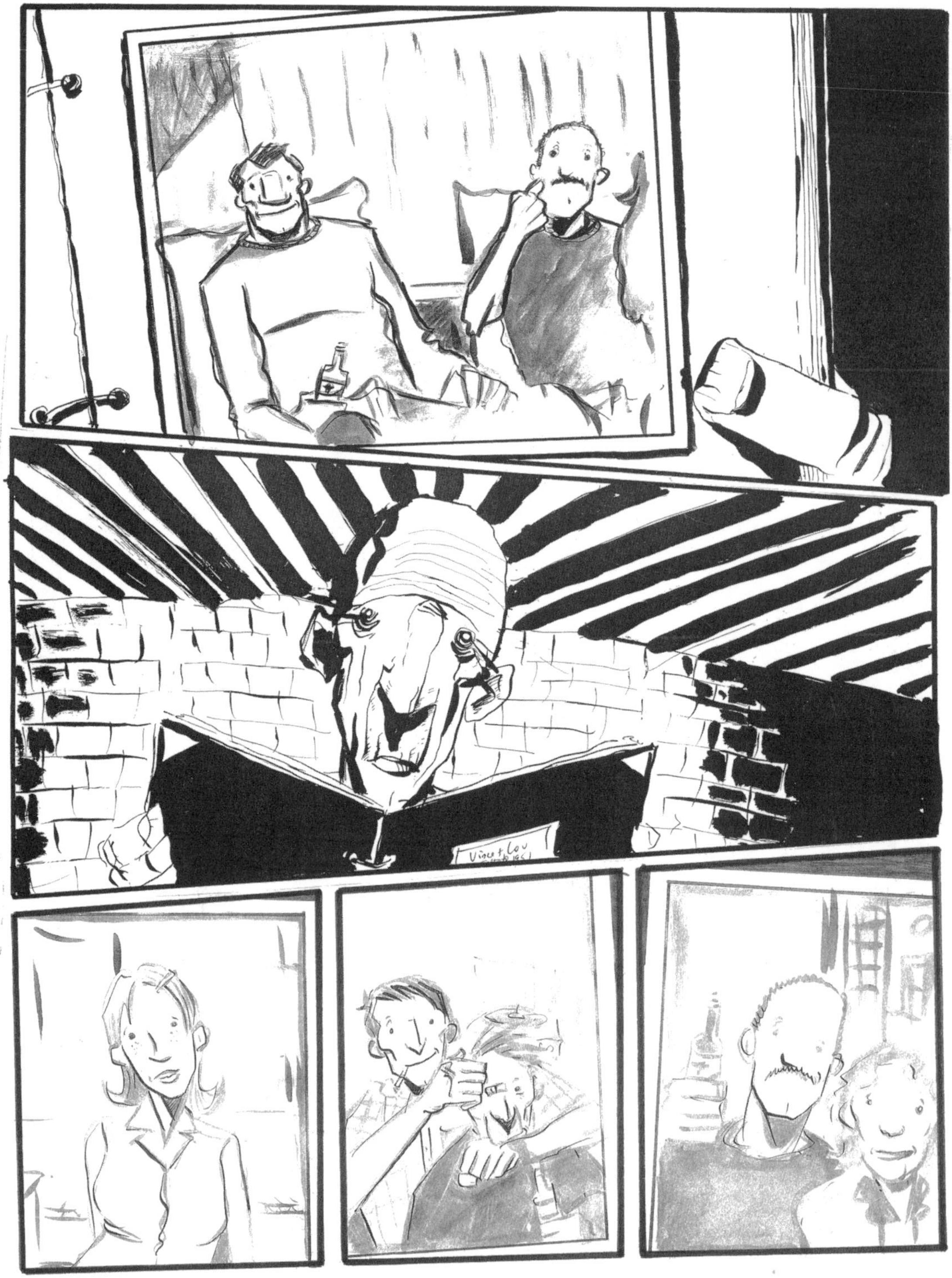
Vince + Lou

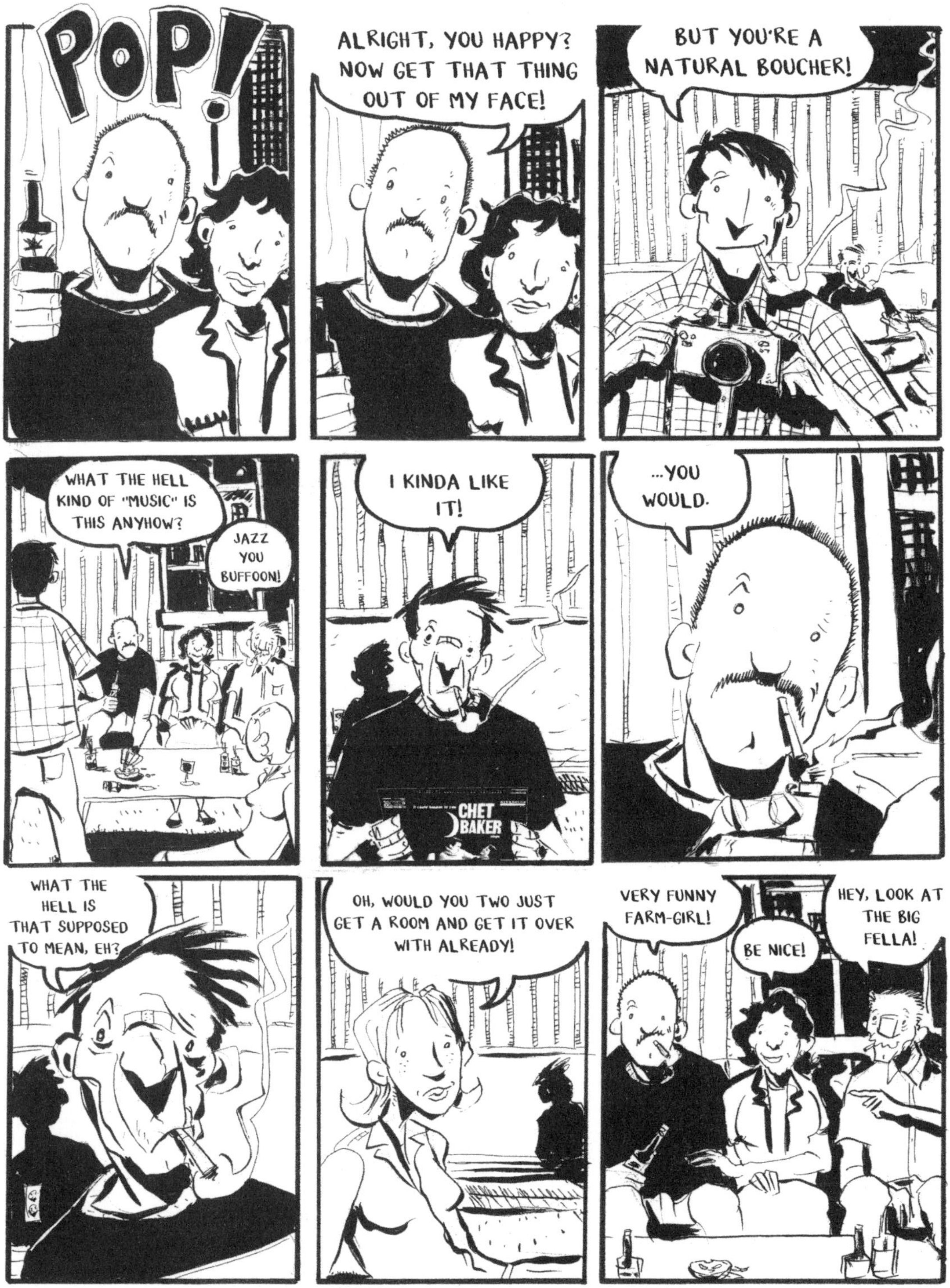
POP!
ALRIGHT, YOU HAPPY? NOW GET THAT THING OUT OF MY FACE!
BUT YOU'RE A NATURAL BOUCHER!
WHAT THE HELL KIND OF "MUSIC" IS THIS ANYHOW?
JAZZ YOU BUFFOON!
I KINDA LIKE IT!
CHET BAKER
...YOU WOULD.
WHAT THE HELL IS THAT SUPPOSED TO MEAN, EH?
OH, WOULD YOU TWO JUST GET A ROOM AND GET IT OVER WITH ALREADY!
VERY FUNNY FARM-GIRL!
BE NICE!
HEY, LOOK AT THE BIG FELLA!

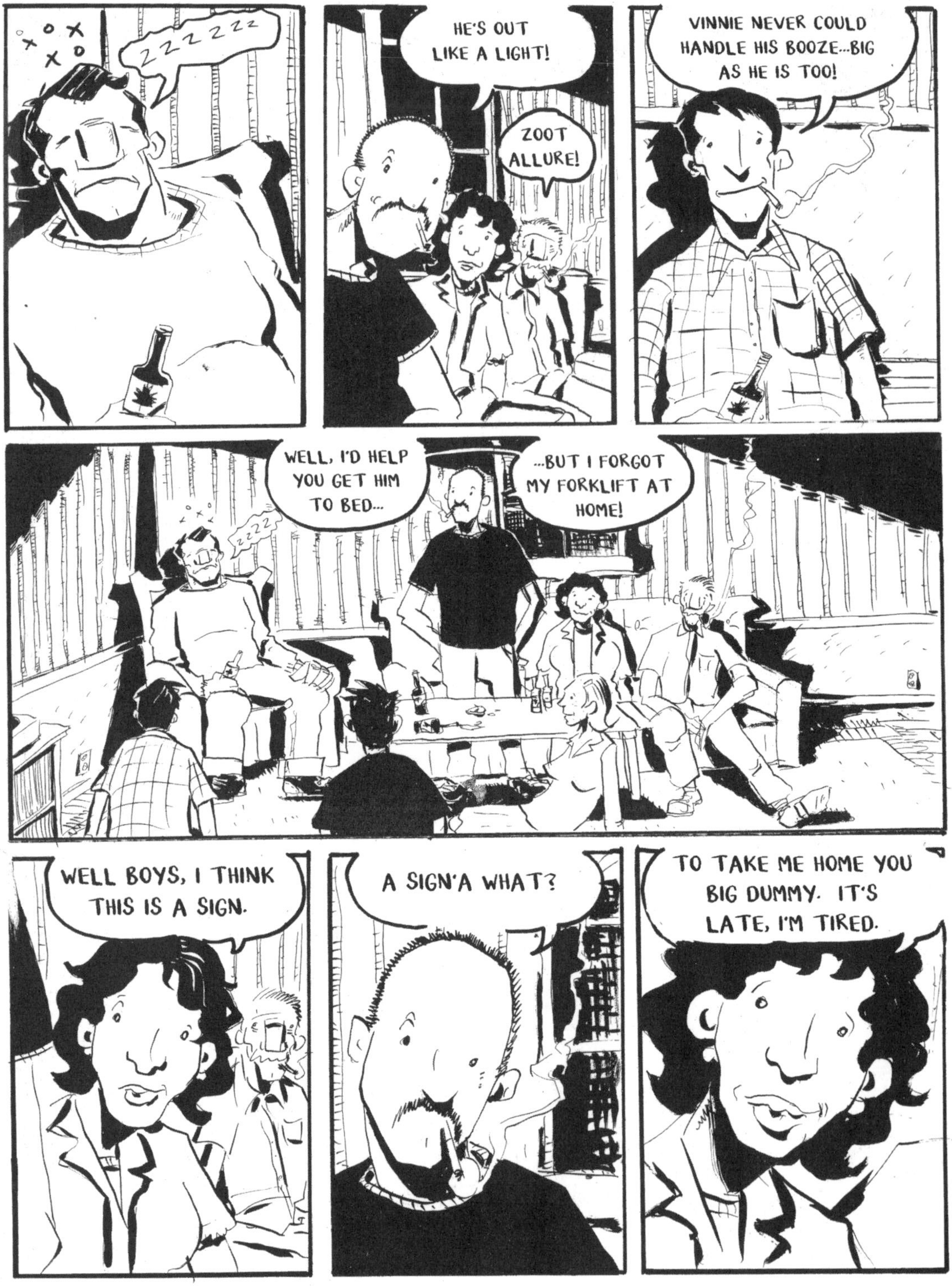
ZZZZZZZ
HE'S OUT LIKE A LIGHT!
ZOOT ALLURE!
VINNIE NEVER COULD HANDLE HIS BOOZE...BIG AS HE IS TOO!
WELL, I'D HELP YOU GET HIM TO BED...
...BUT I FORGOT MY FORKLIFT AT HOME!
WELL BOYS, I THINK THIS IS A SIGN.
A SIGN'A WHAT?
TO TAKE ME HOME YOU BIG DUMMY. IT'S LATE, I'M TIRED.

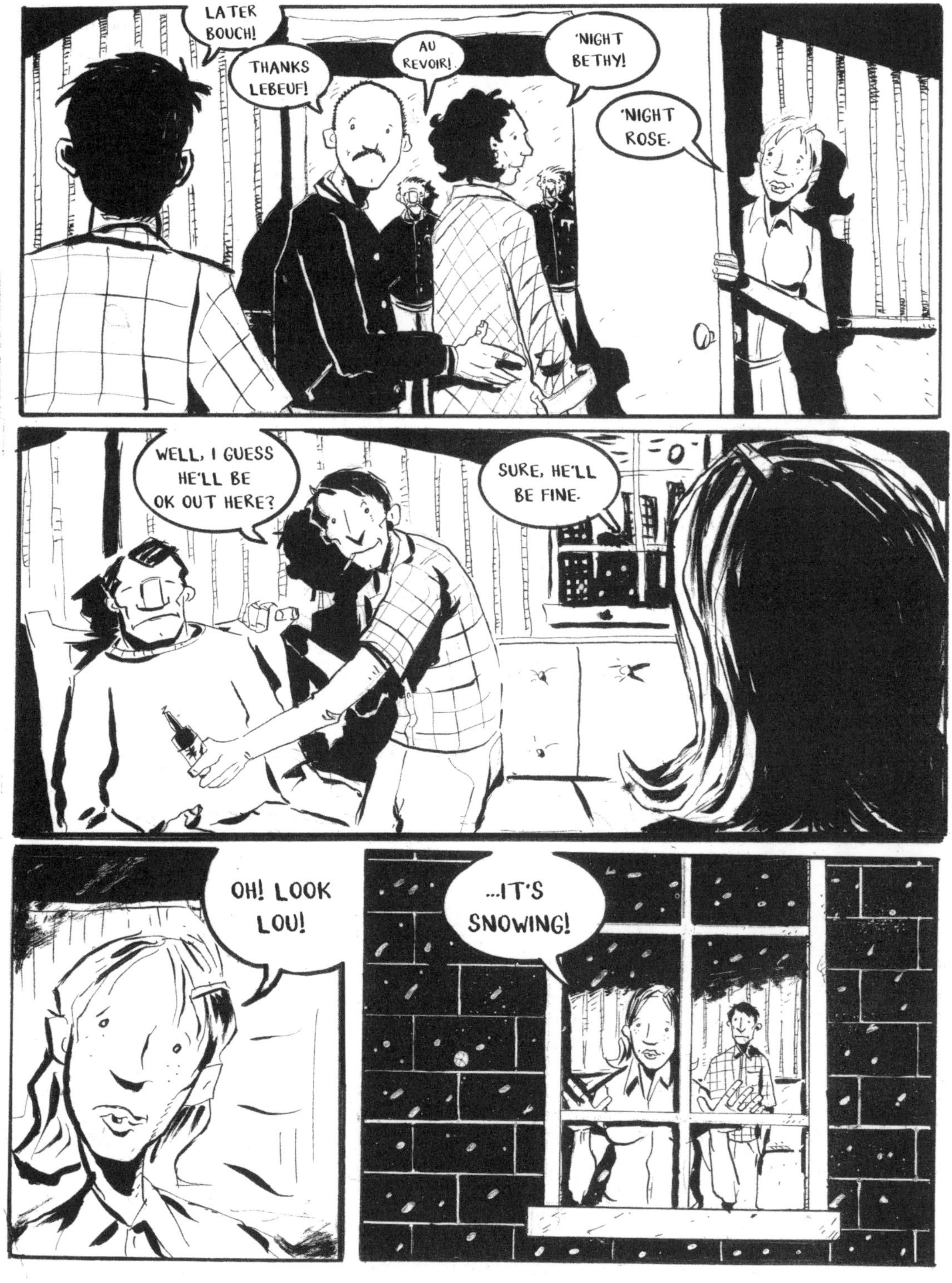
LATER BOUCH!
THANKS LEBEUF!
AU REVOIR!
'NIGHT BETHY!
'NIGHT ROSE.
WELL, I GUESS HE'LL BE OK OUT HERE?
SURE, HE'LL BE FINE.
OH! LOOK LOU!
...IT'S SNOWING!

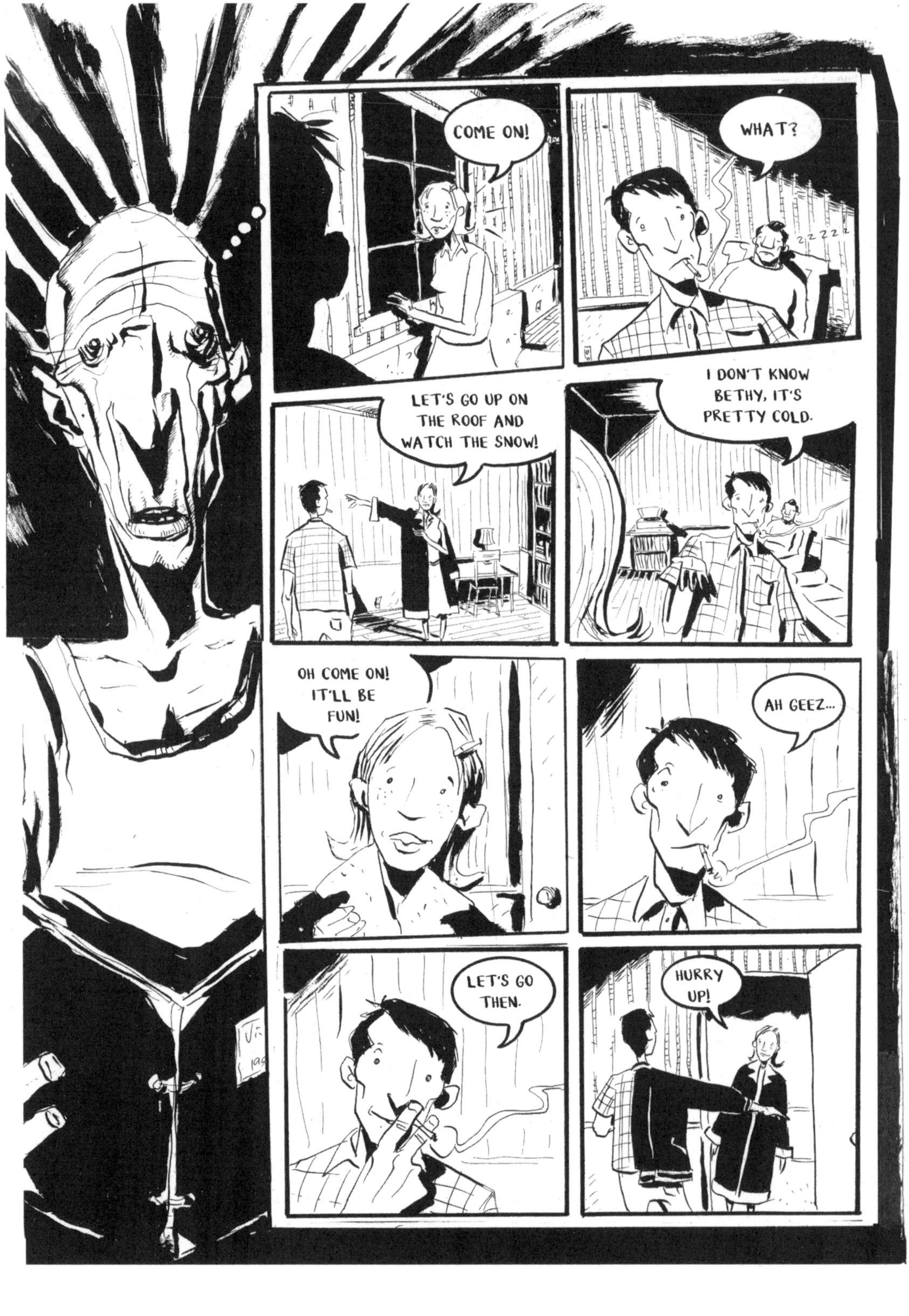
COME ON!
WHAT?
ZZZZZ
LET'S GO UP ON THE ROOF AND WATCH THE SNOW!
I DON'T KNOW BETHY, IT'S PRETTY COLD.
OH COME ON! IT'LL BE FUN!
AH GEEZ...
LET'S GO THEN.
HURRY UP!

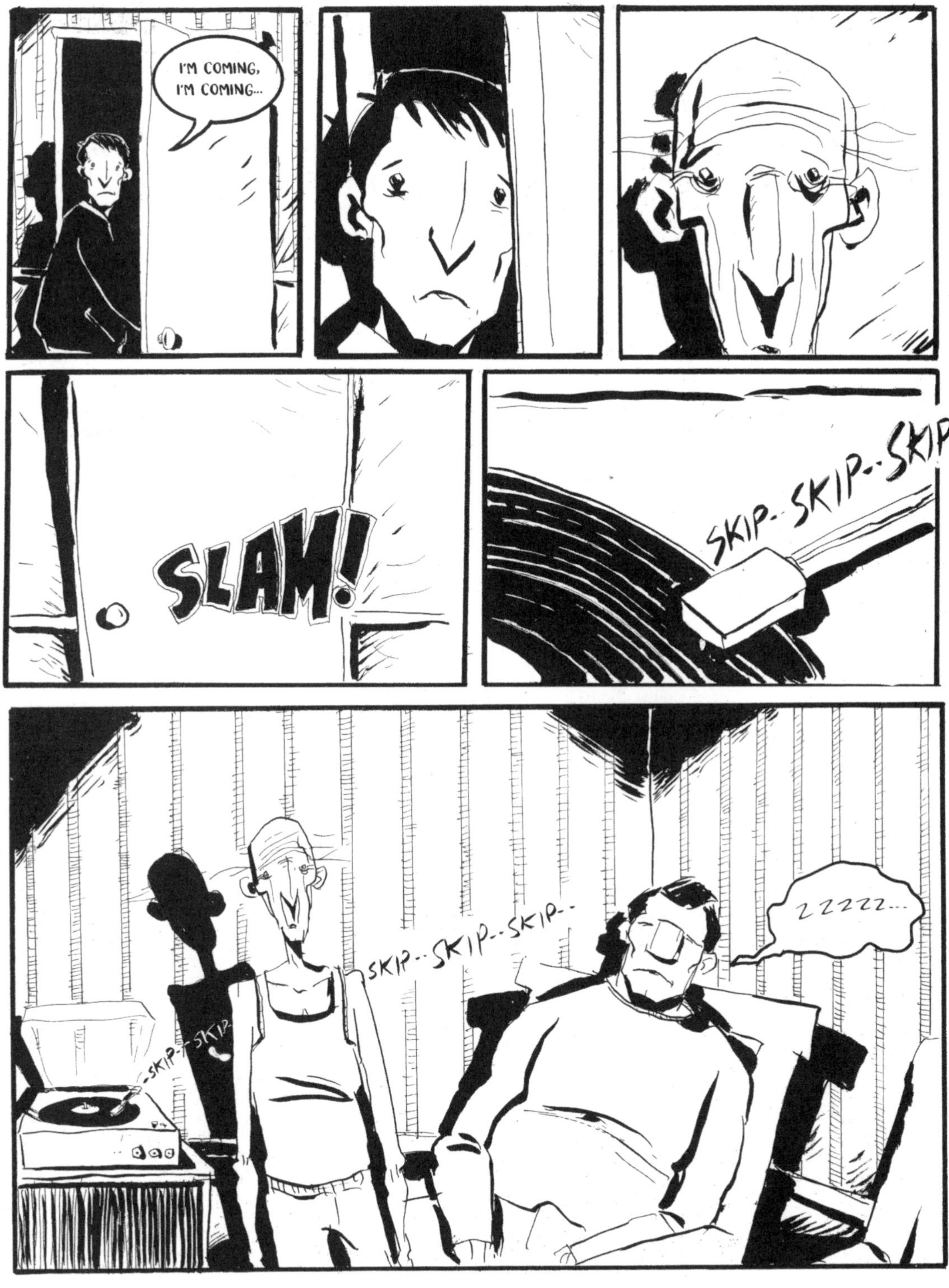
I'M COMING, I'M COMING...
SLAM!
SKIP-SKIP-SKIP
SKIP-SKIP
SKIP-SKIP-SKIP-
ZZZZZ...

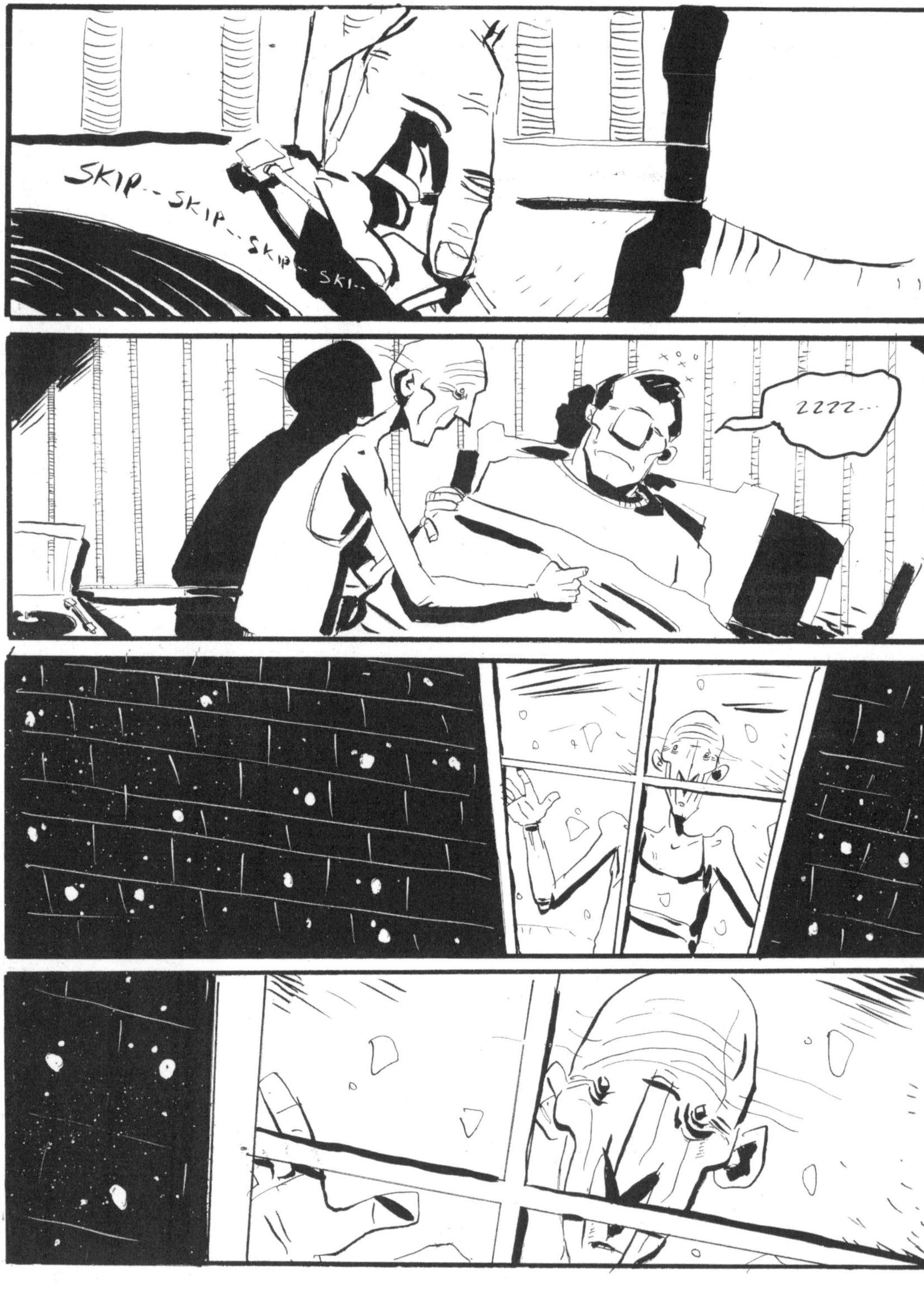
SKIP--SKIP--SKIP--SKI--
ZZZZ...

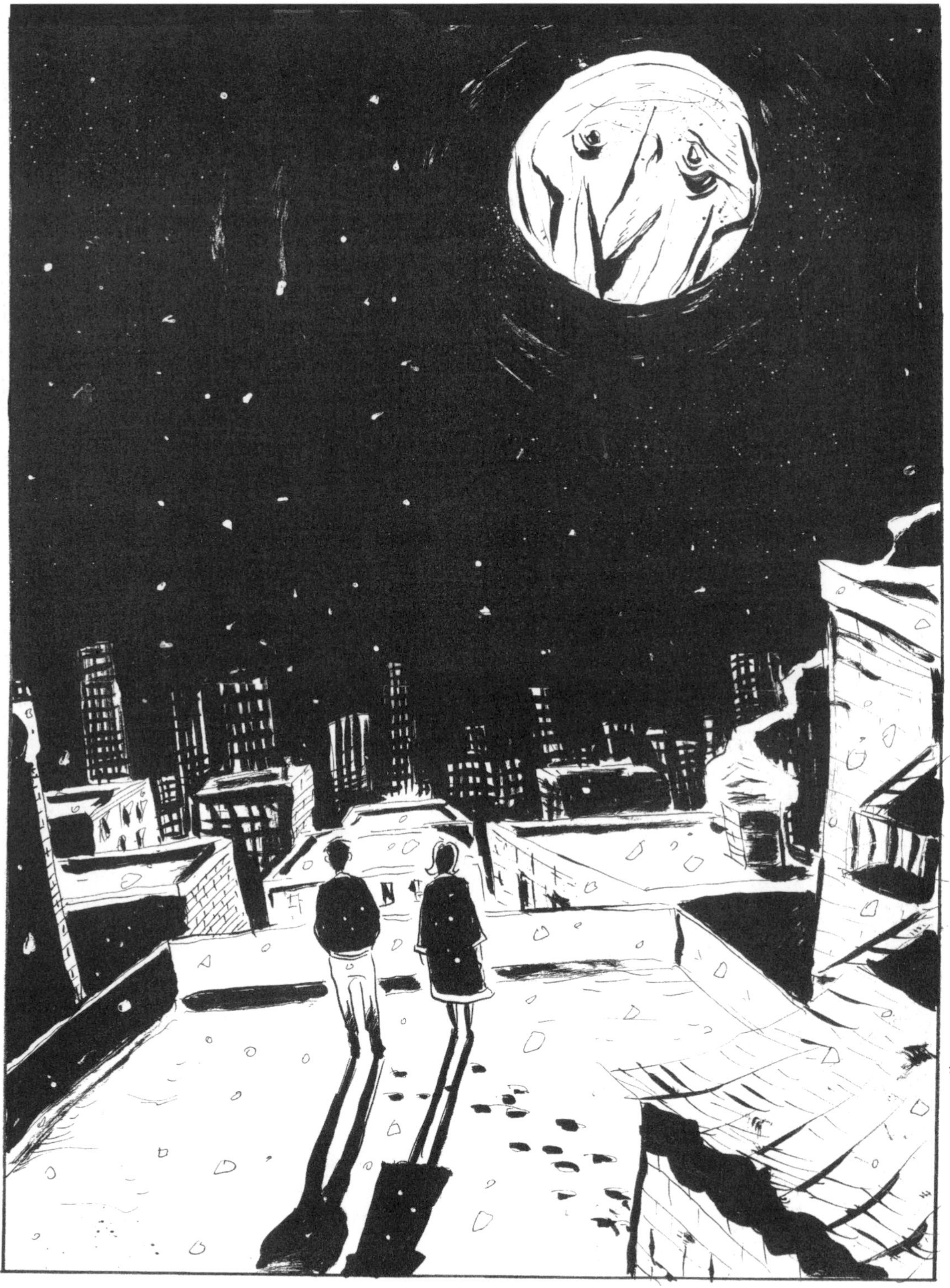

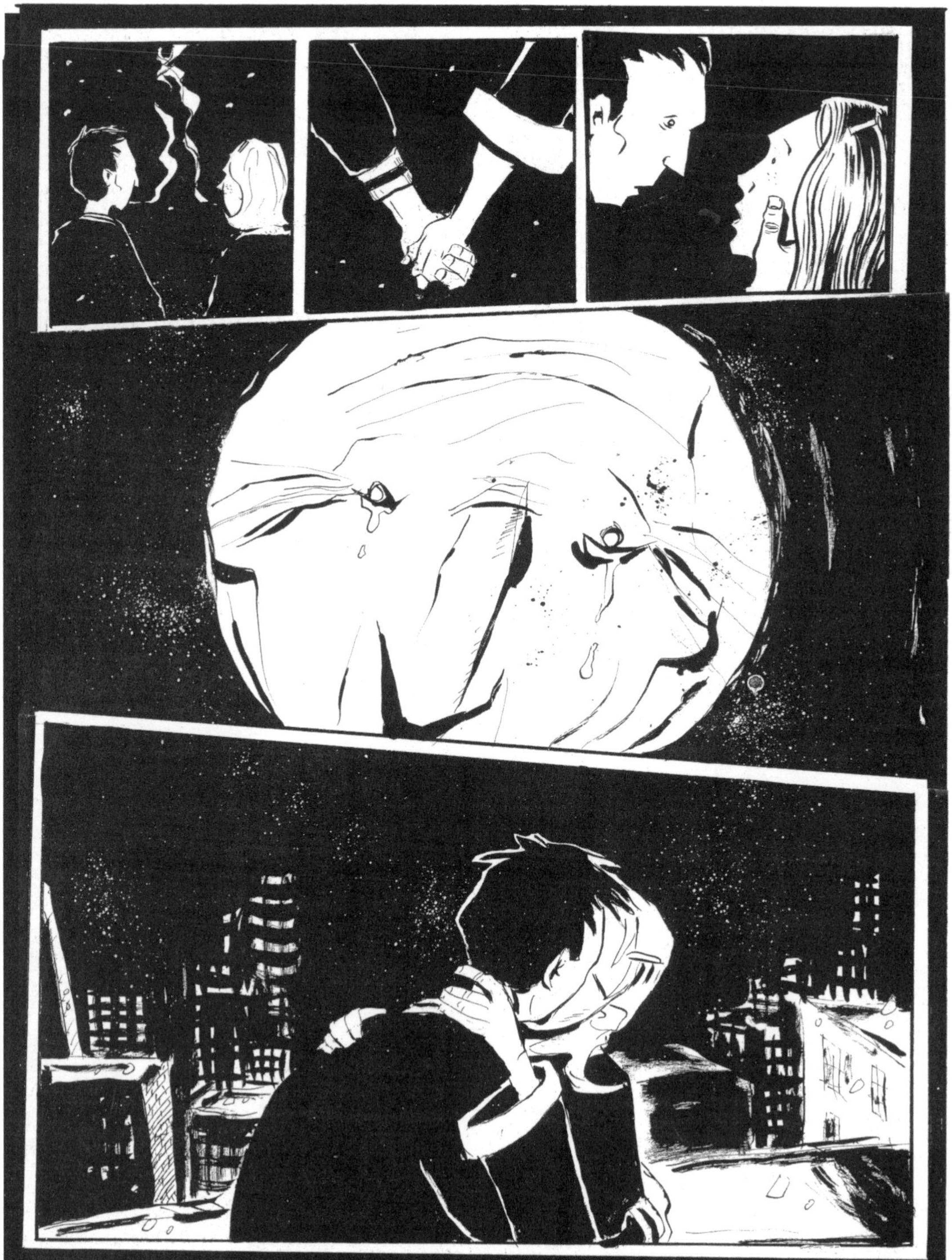

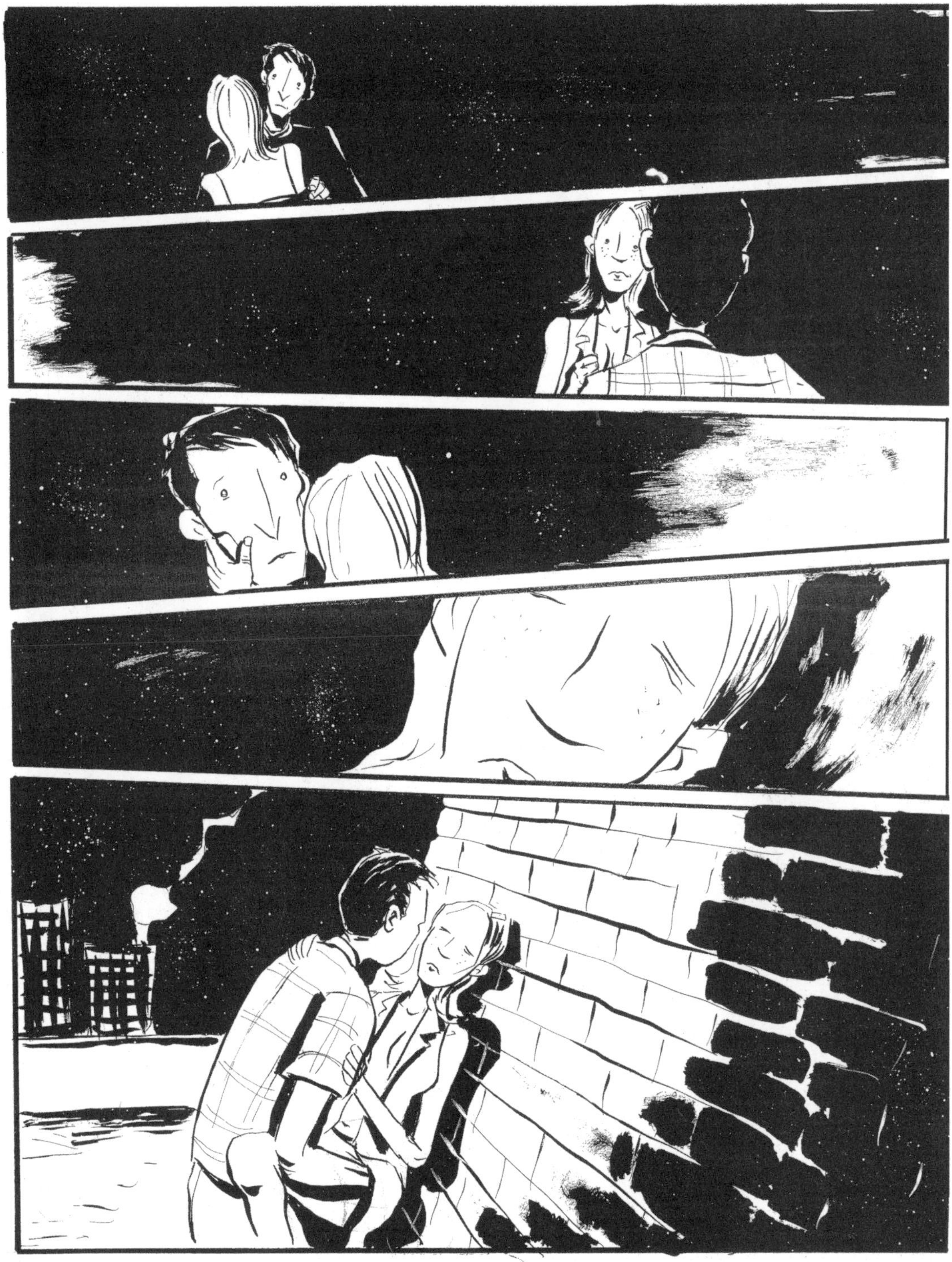

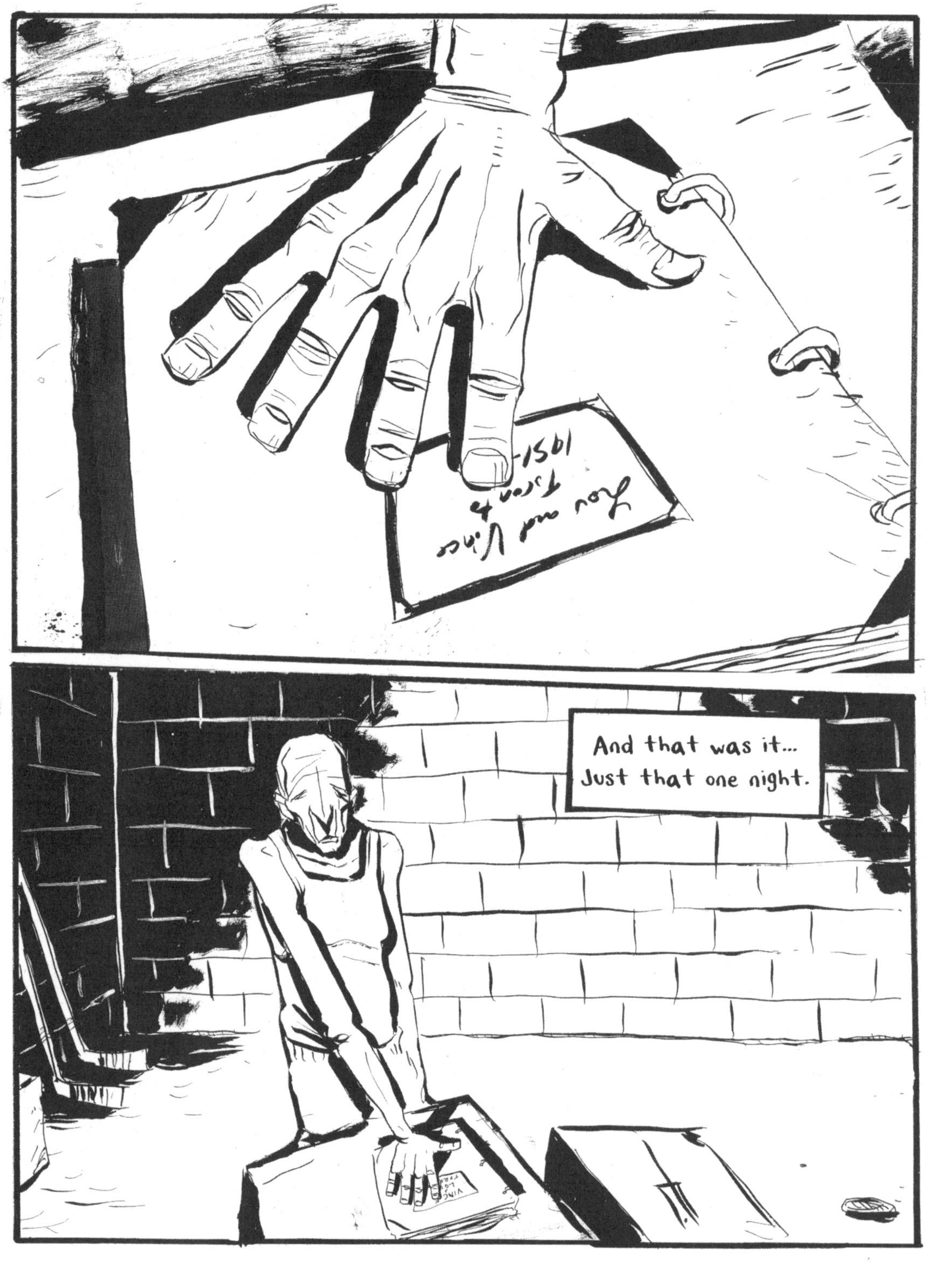
And that was it...
Just that one night.

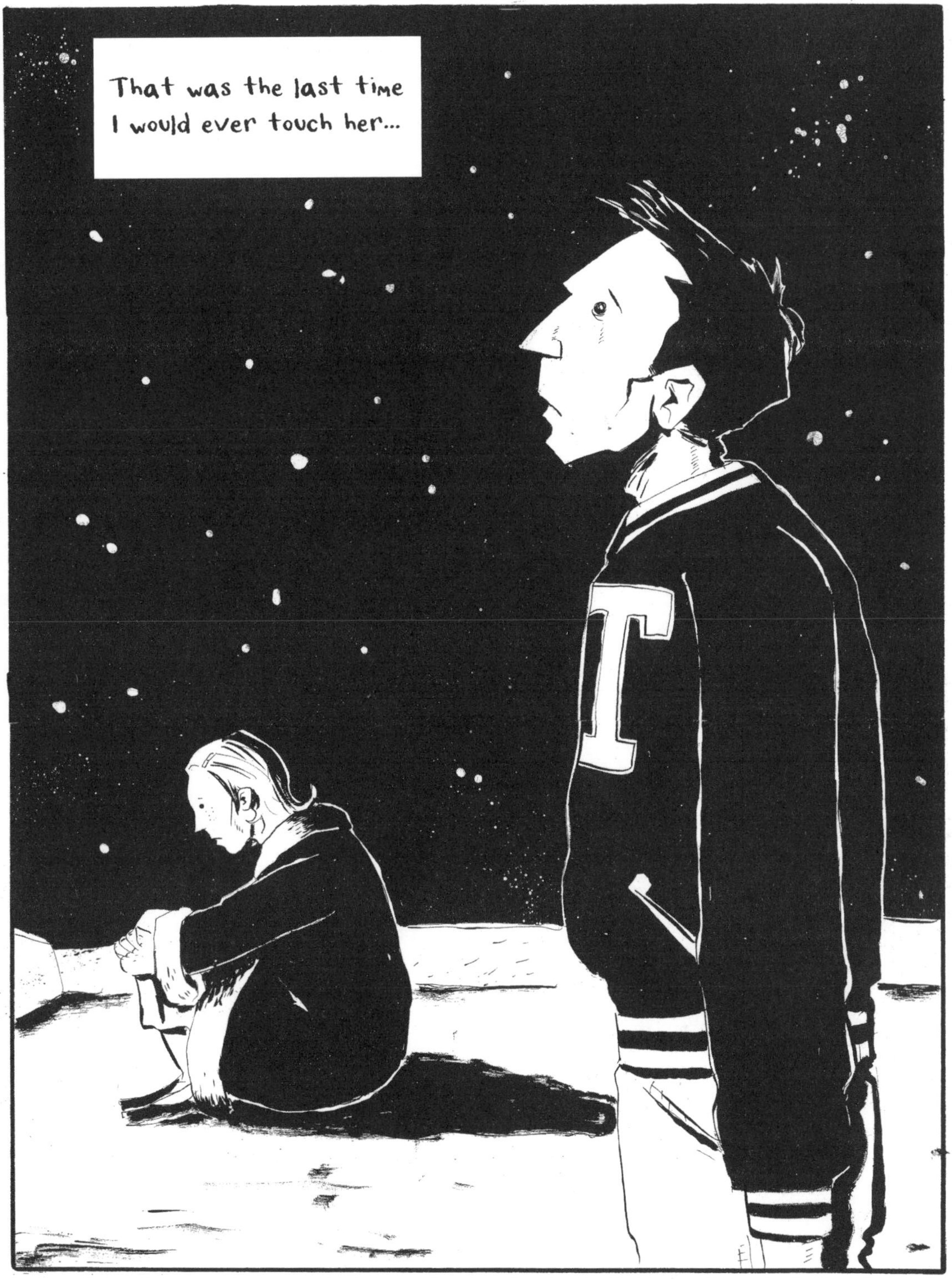
That was the last time
I would ever touch her...

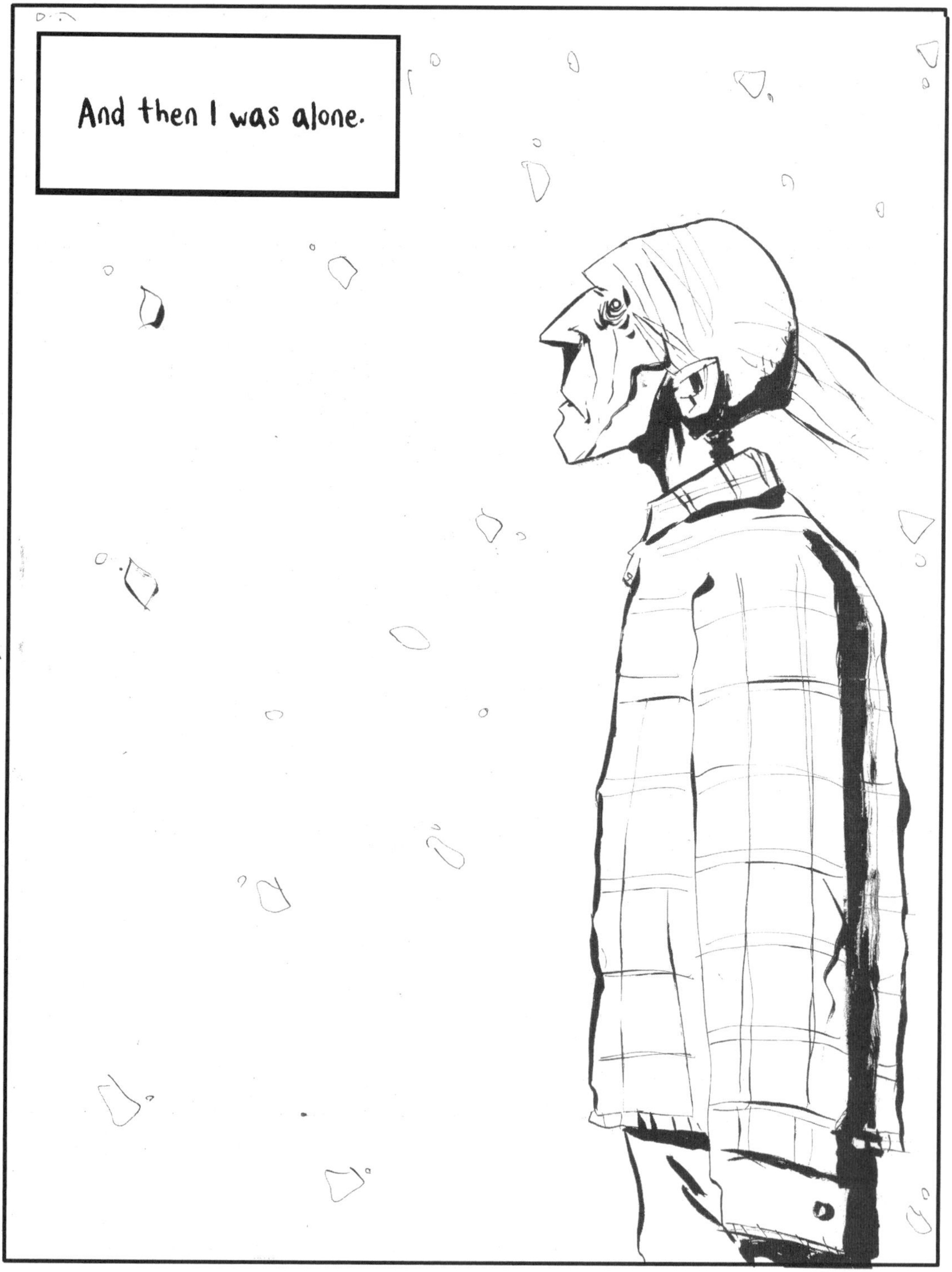
And then I was alone.

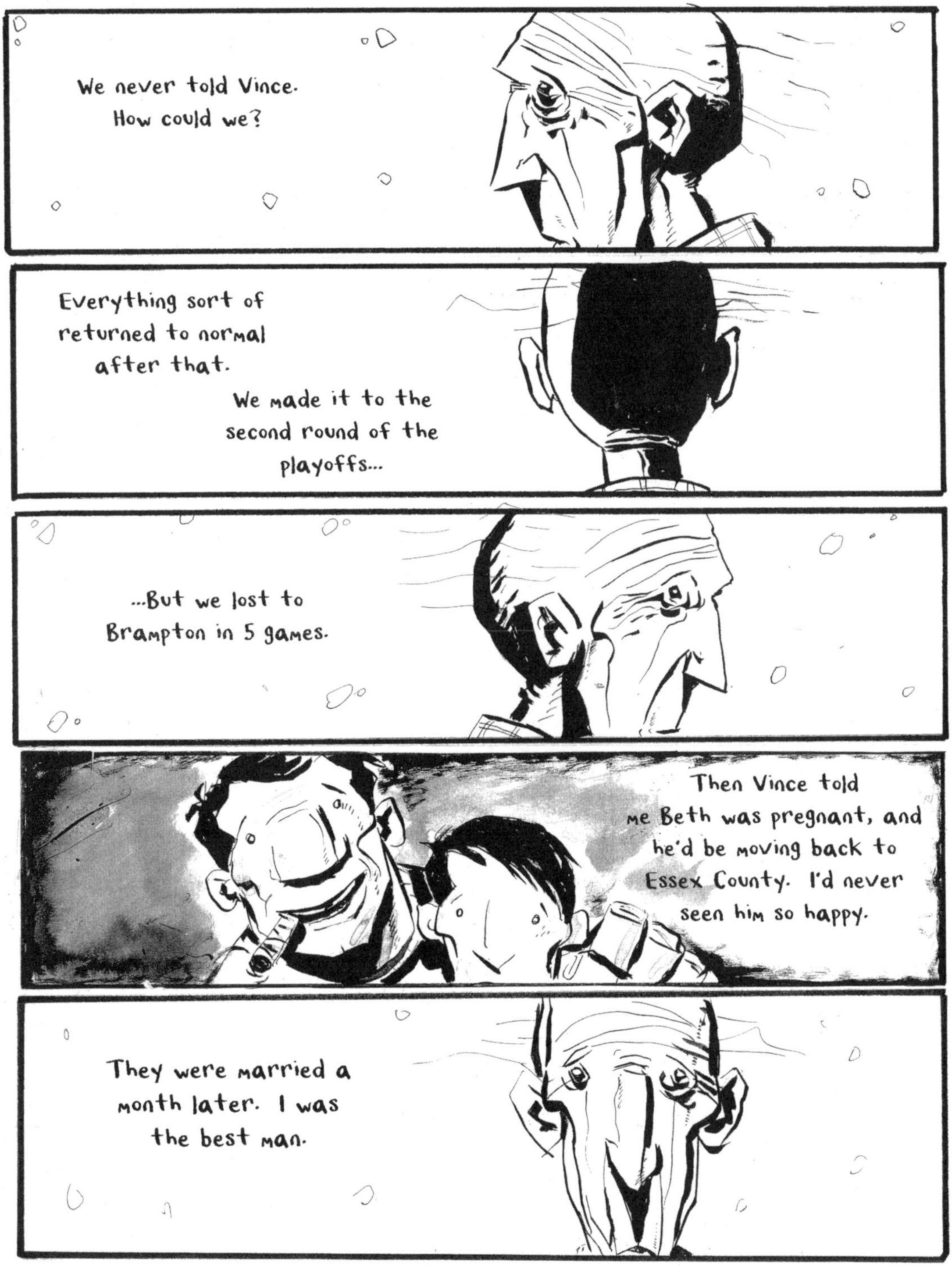
We never told Vince. How could we?
Everything sort of returned to normal after that.
We made it to the second round of the playoffs...
...But we lost to Brampton in 5 games.
Then Vince told me Beth was pregnant, and he'd be moving back to Essex County. I'd never seen him so happy.
They were married a month later. I was the best man.

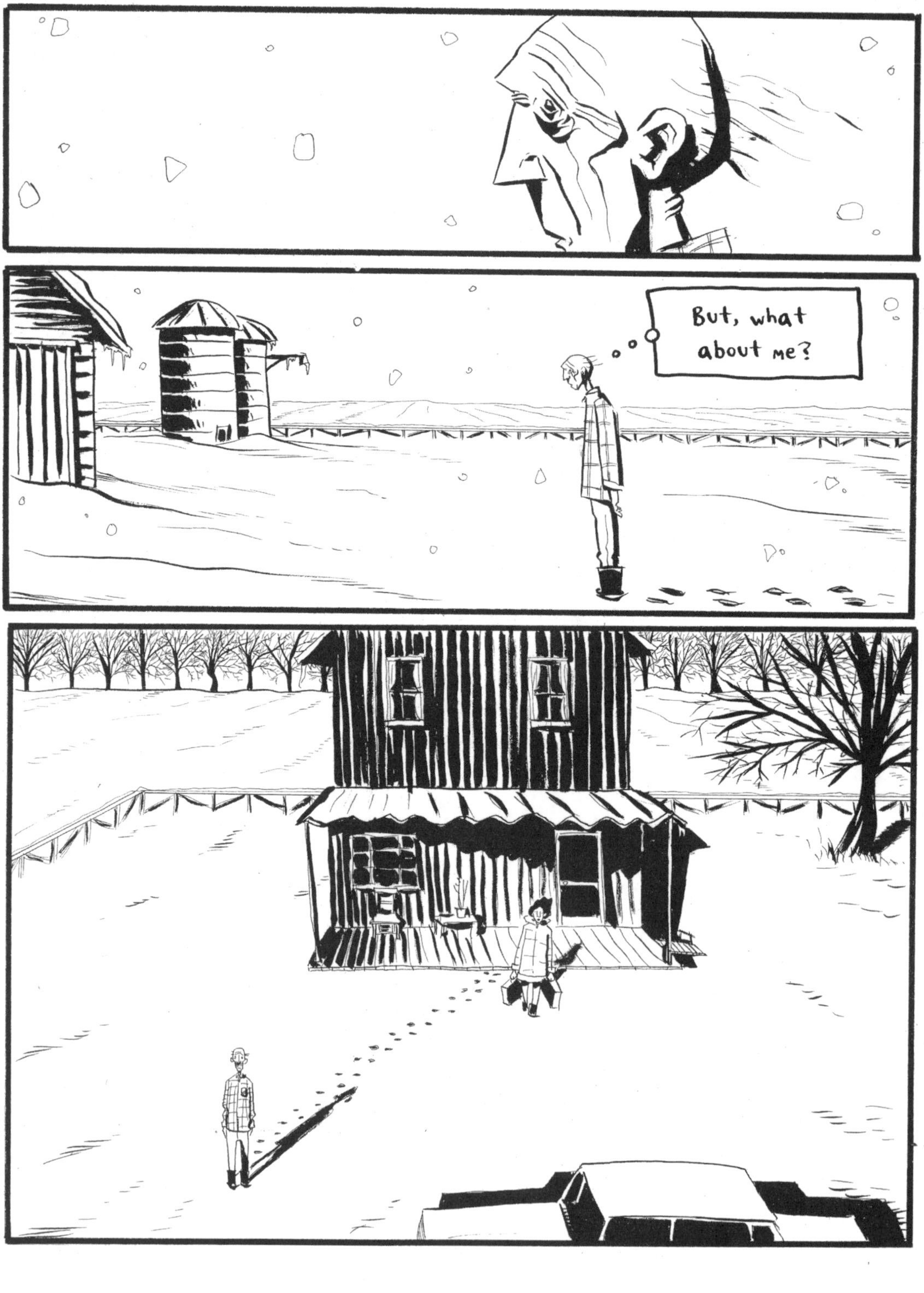
But, what about me?

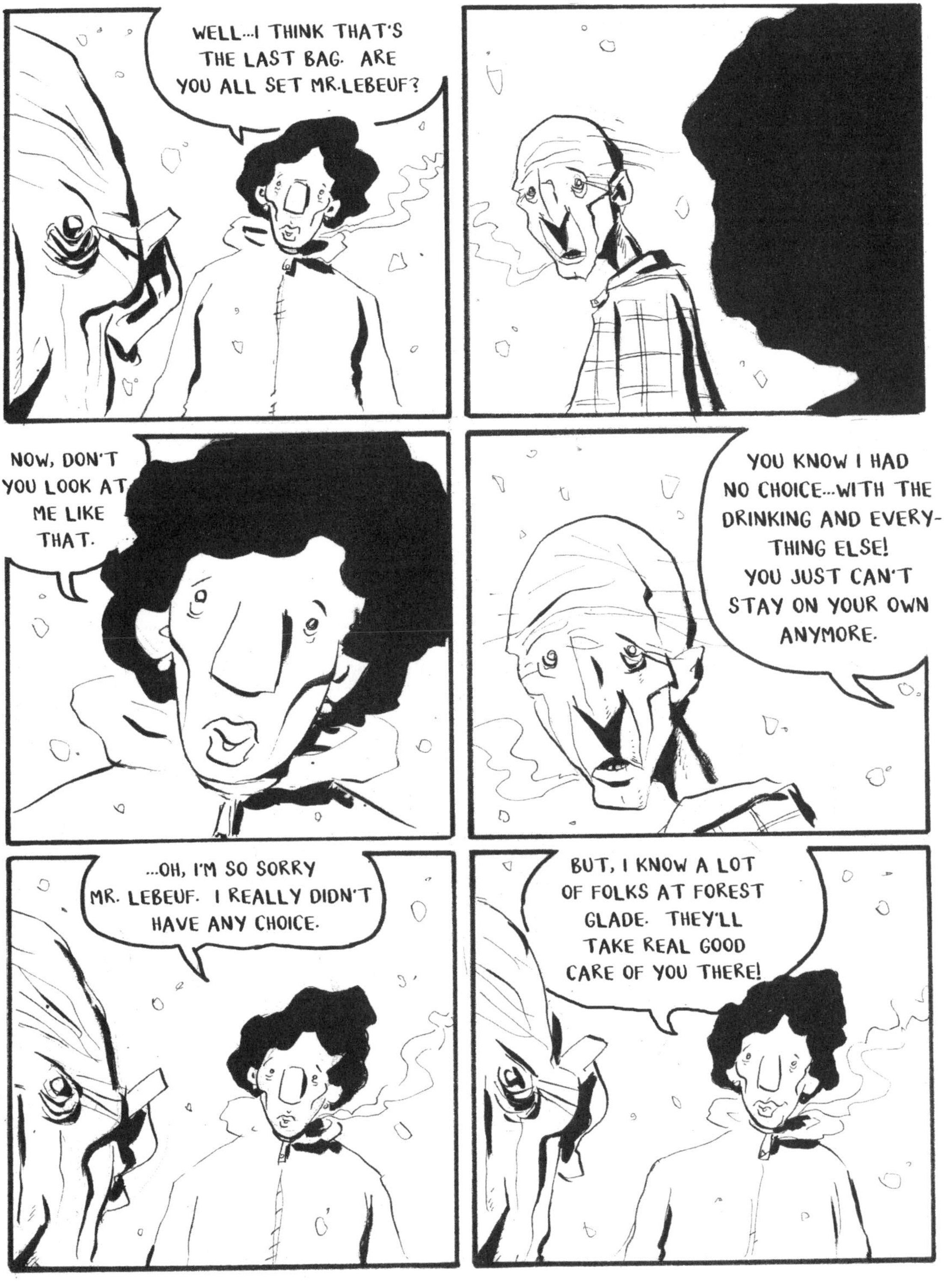
WELL...I THINK THAT'S THE LAST BAG. ARE YOU ALL SET MR.LEBEUF?
NOW, DON'T YOU LOOK AT ME LIKE THAT.
YOU KNOW I HAD NO CHOICE...WITH THE DRINKING AND EVERY-THING ELSE! YOU JUST CAN'T STAY ON YOUR OWN ANYMORE.
...OH, I'M SO SORRY MR. LEBEUF. I REALLY DIDN'T HAVE ANY CHOICE.
BUT, I KNOW A LOT OF FOLKS AT FOREST GLADE. THEY'LL TAKE REAL GOOD CARE OF YOU THERE!

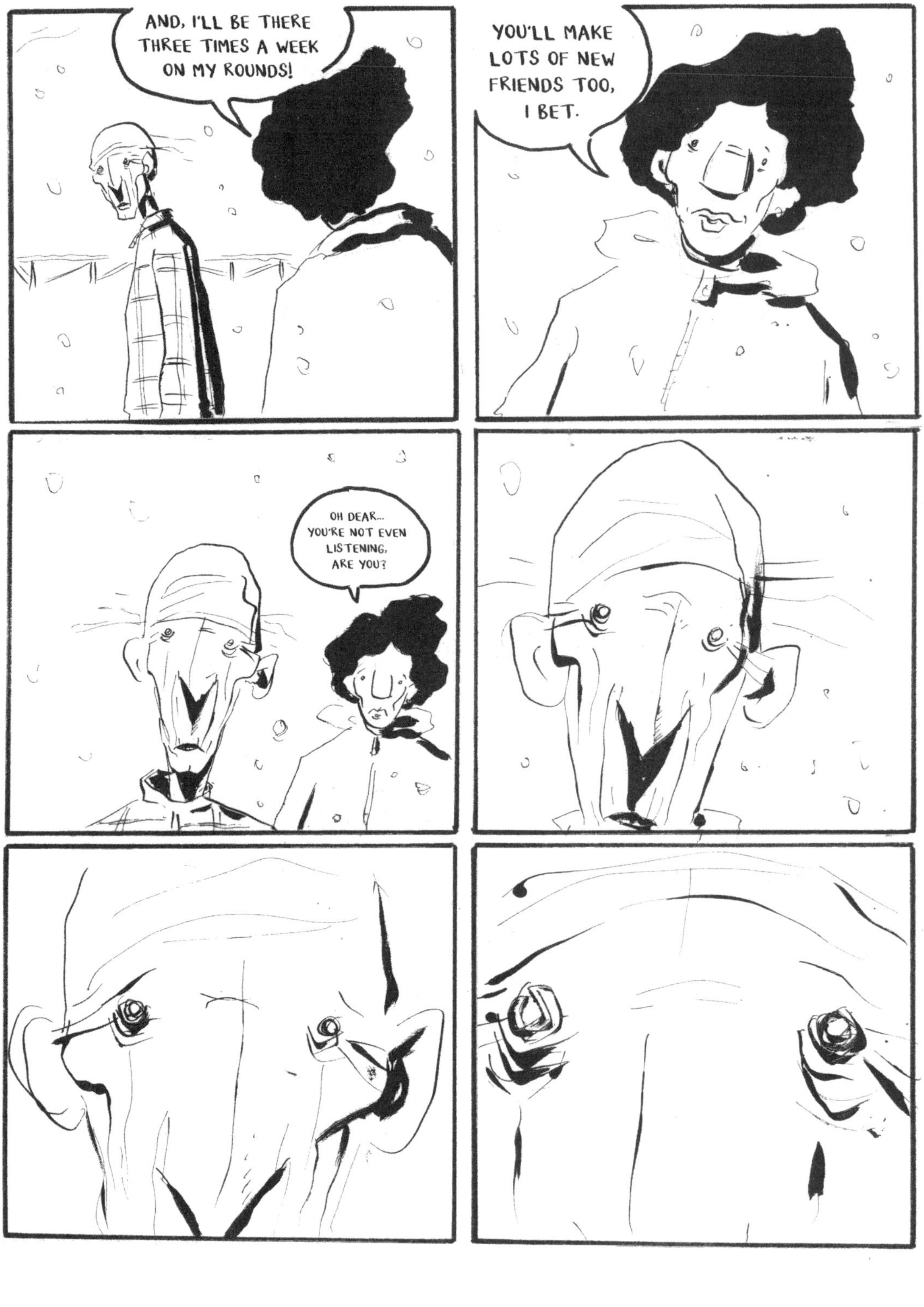
AND, I'LL BE THERE THREE TIMES A WEEK ON MY ROUNDS!
YOU'LL MAKE LOTS OF NEW FRIENDS TOO, I BET.
OH DEAR... YOU'RE NOT EVEN LISTENING, ARE YOU?

I went right back to the city after the wedding.

I knew I had to stay away...let them be happy.

I started a new season with The Grizzlies.

But, it wasn't the same anymore. My lifelong dream of playing pro hockey seemed empty without my brother beside me.

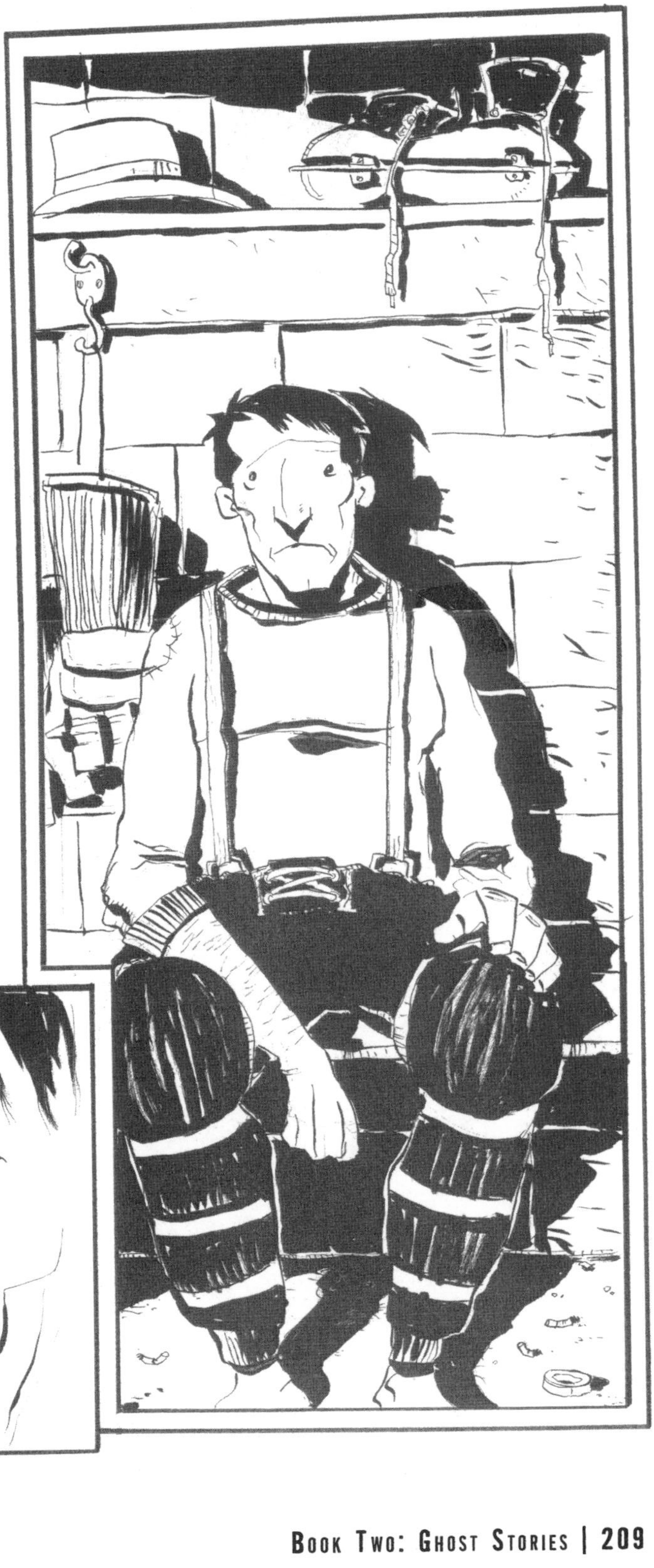

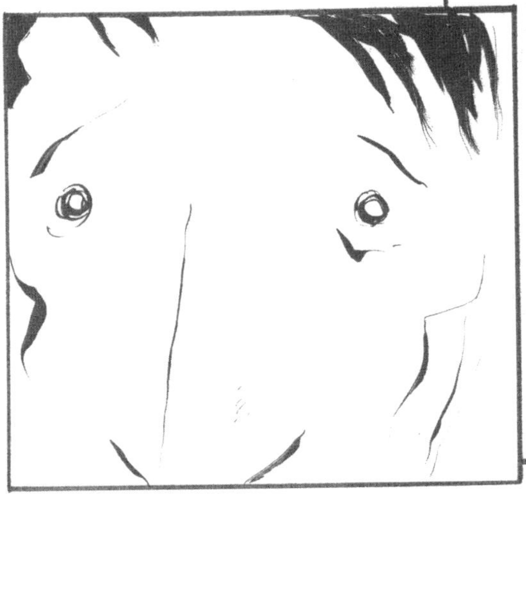

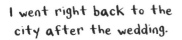

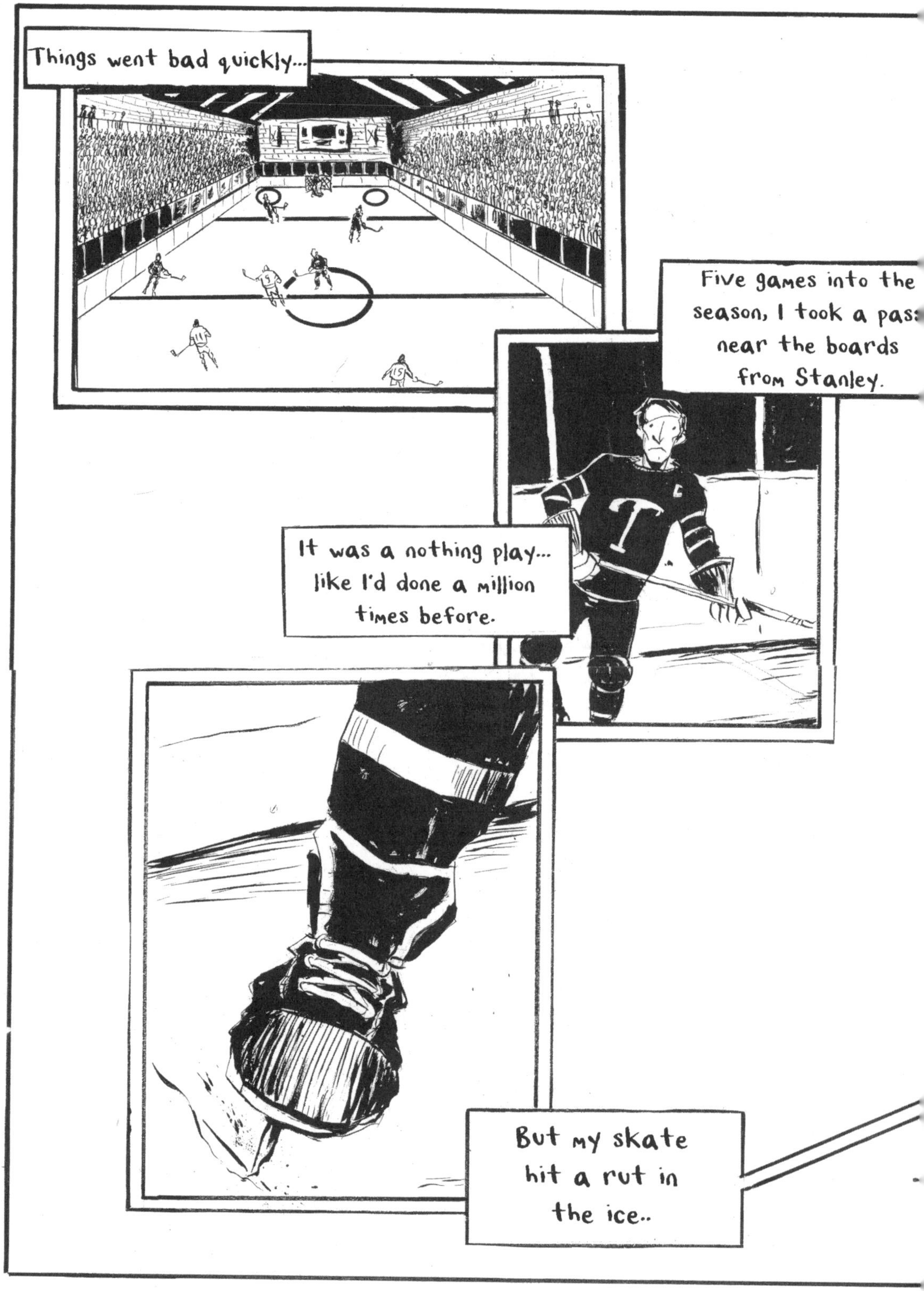

Things went bad quickly...
Five games into the season, I took a pass near the boards from Stanley.
It was a nothing play... like I'd done a million times before.
But my skate hit a rut in the ice..

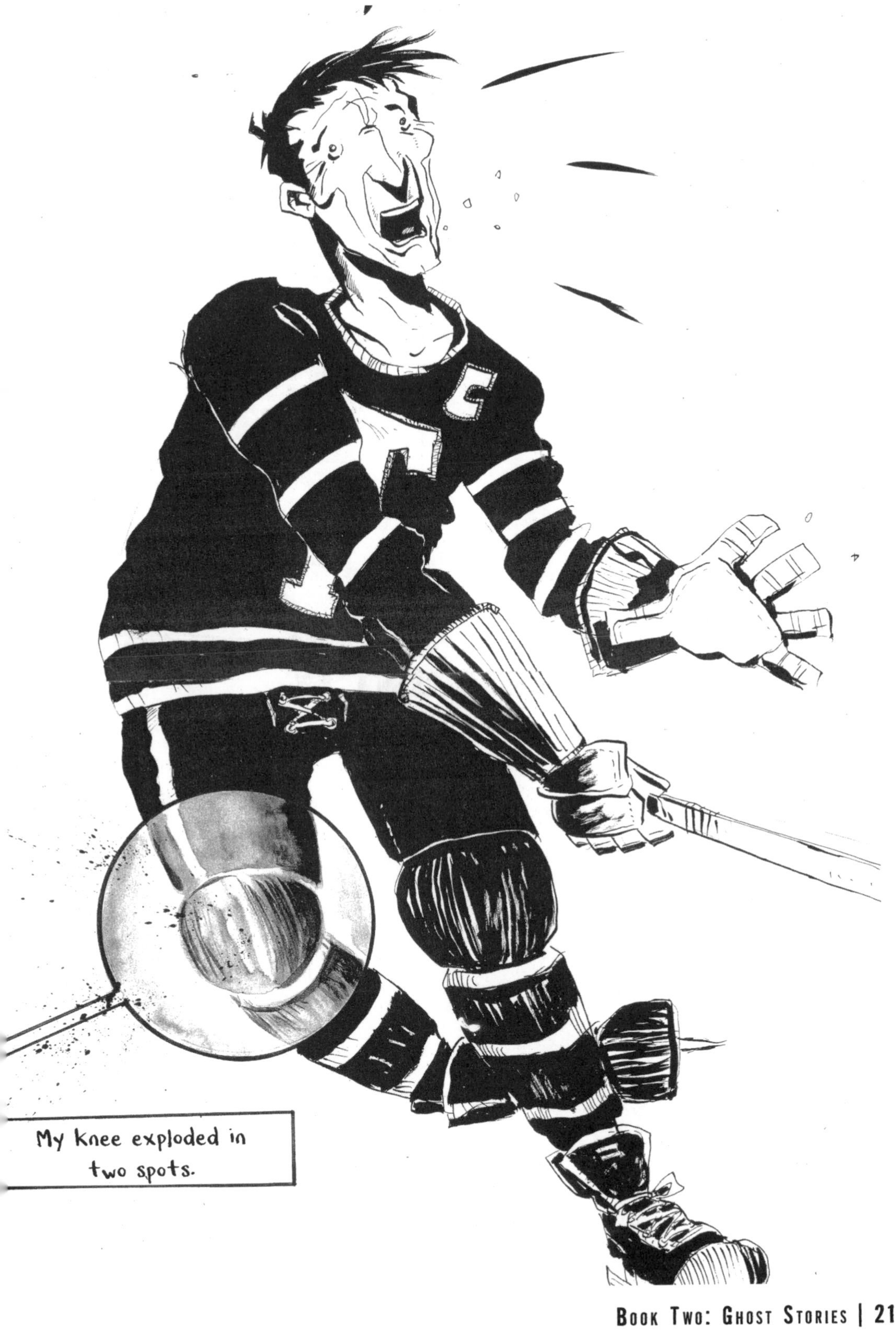
My knee exploded in
two spots.

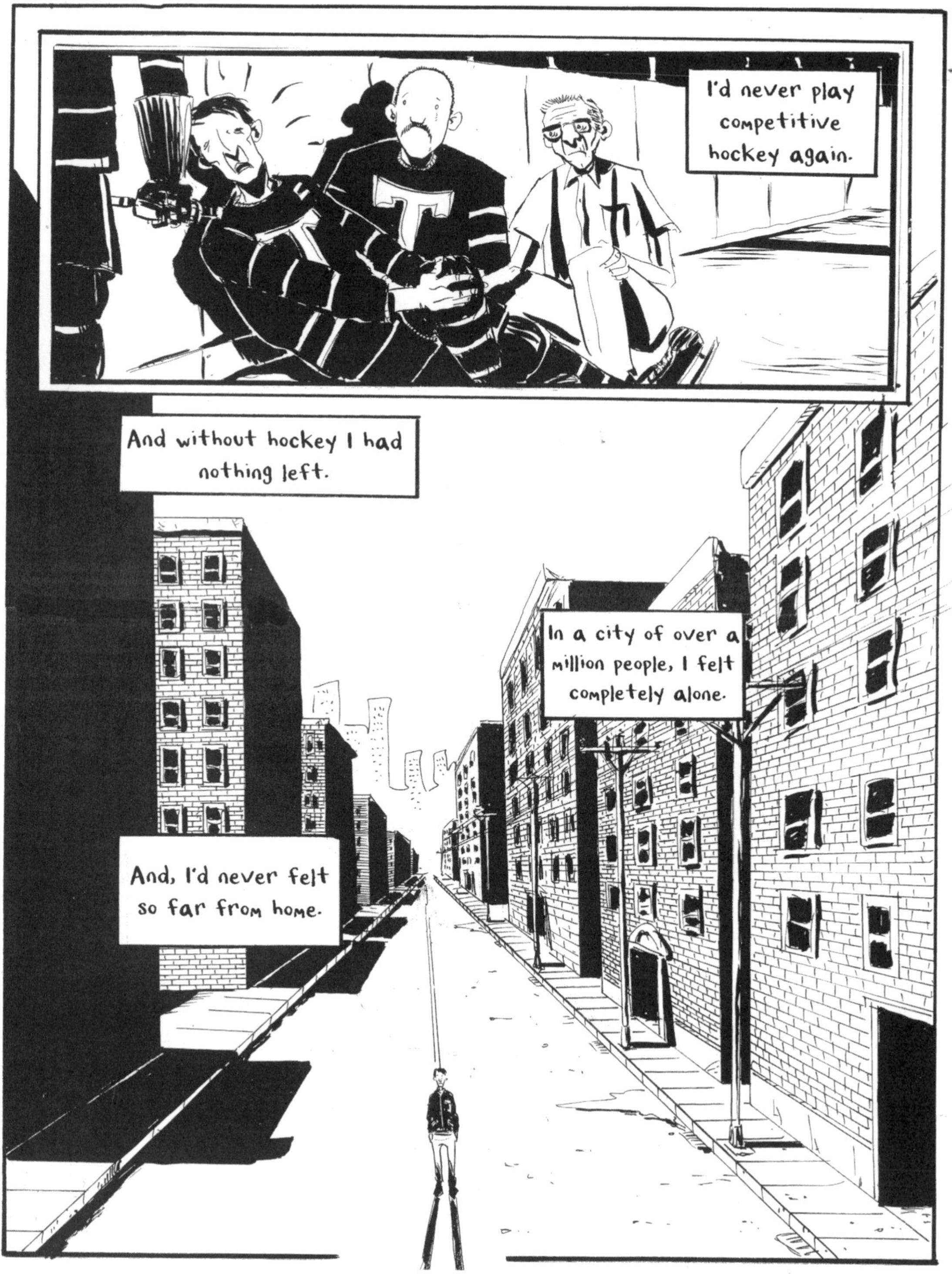

I'd never play competitive hockey again.
And without hockey I had nothing left.
In a city of over a million people, I felt completely alone.
And, I'd never felt so far from home.

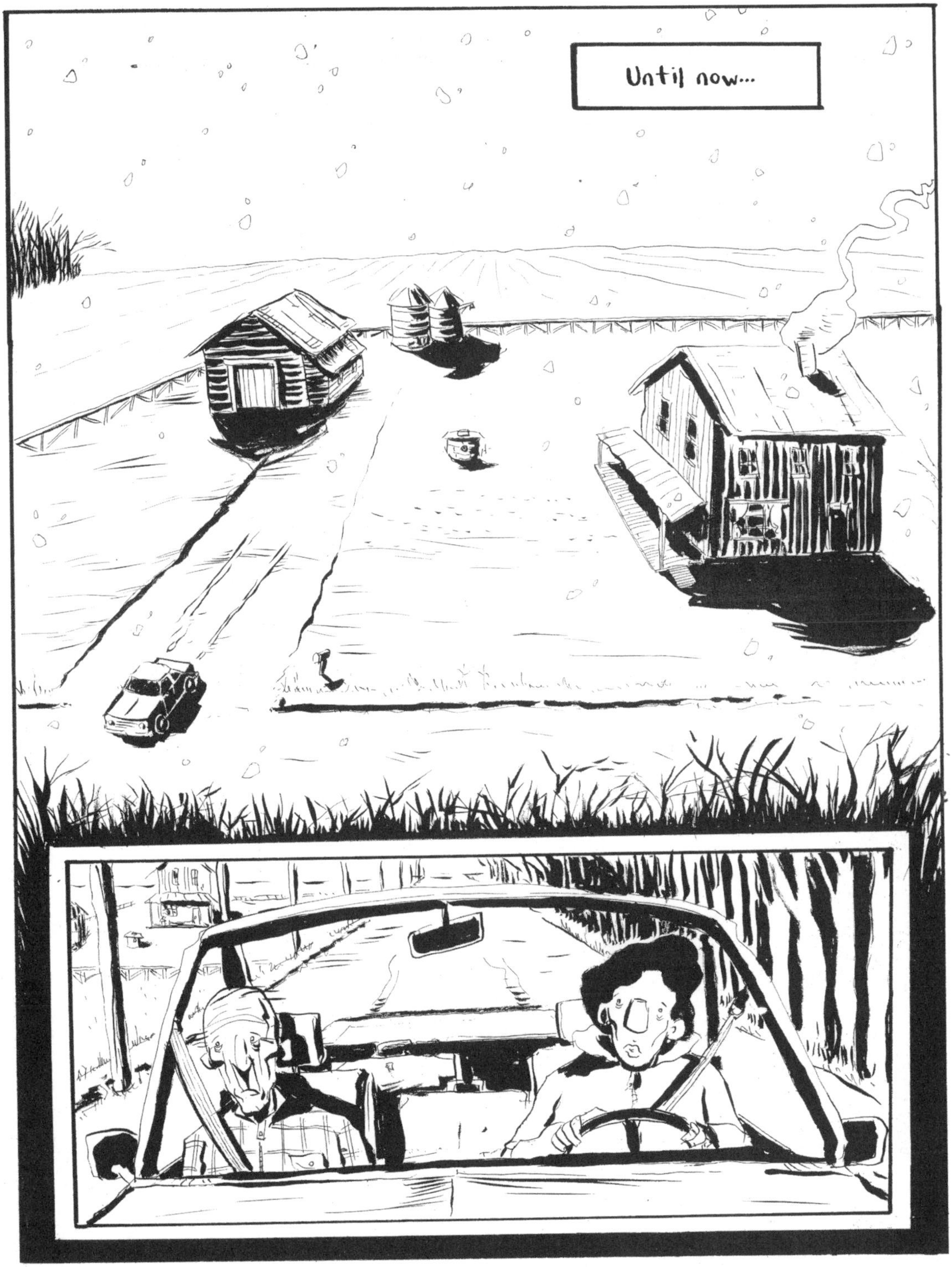
Until now...

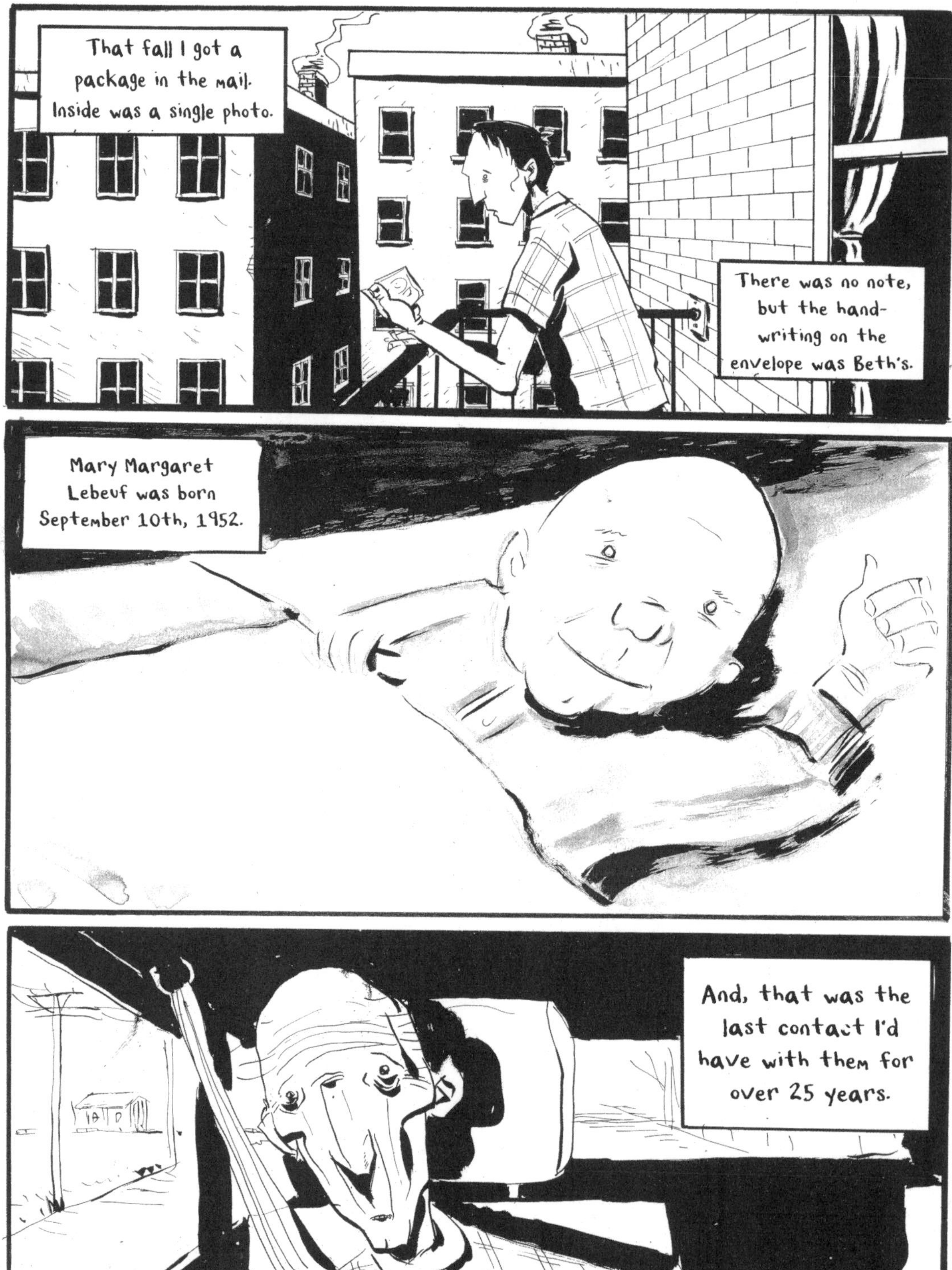
That fall I got a package in the mail. Inside was a single photo.
There was no note, but the handwriting on the envelope was Beth's.
Mary Margaret Lebeuf was born September 10th, 1952.
And, that was the last contact I'd have with them for over 25 years.

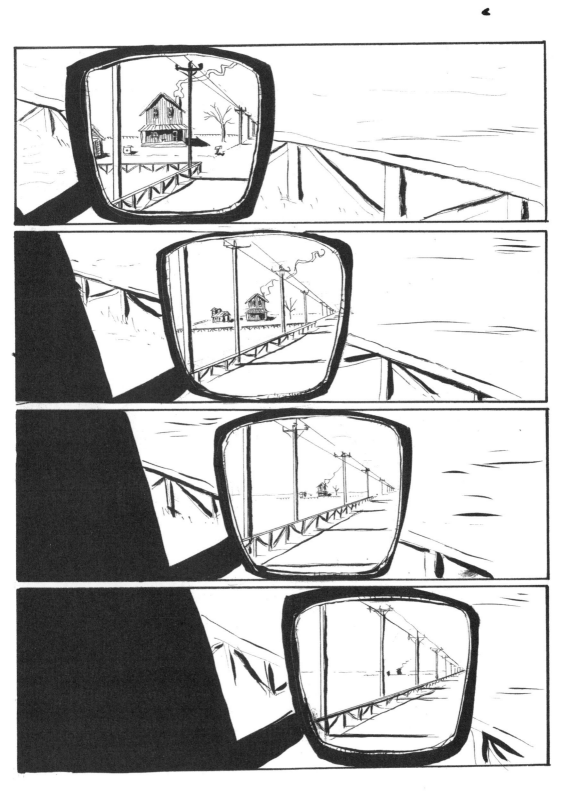

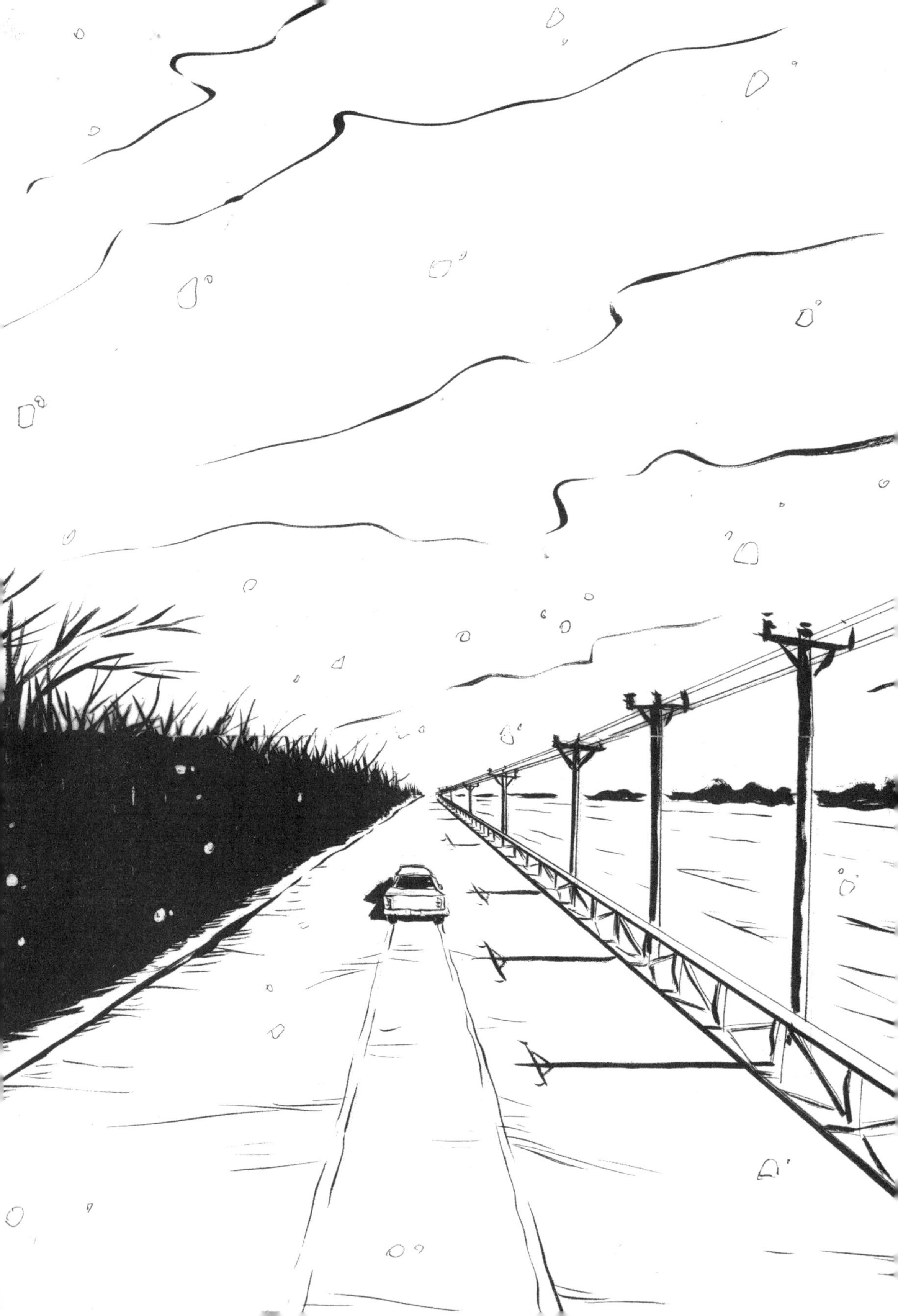

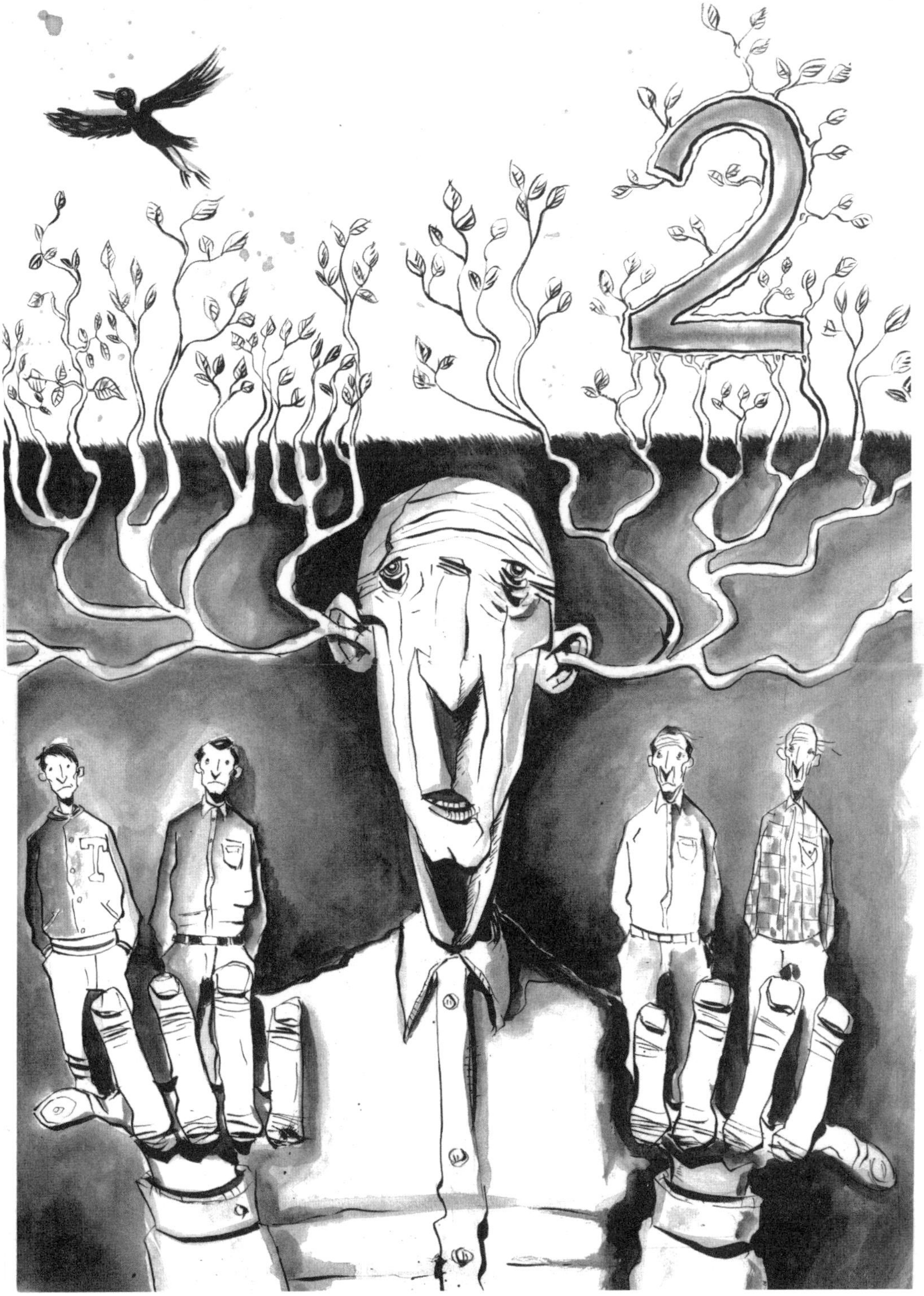

2

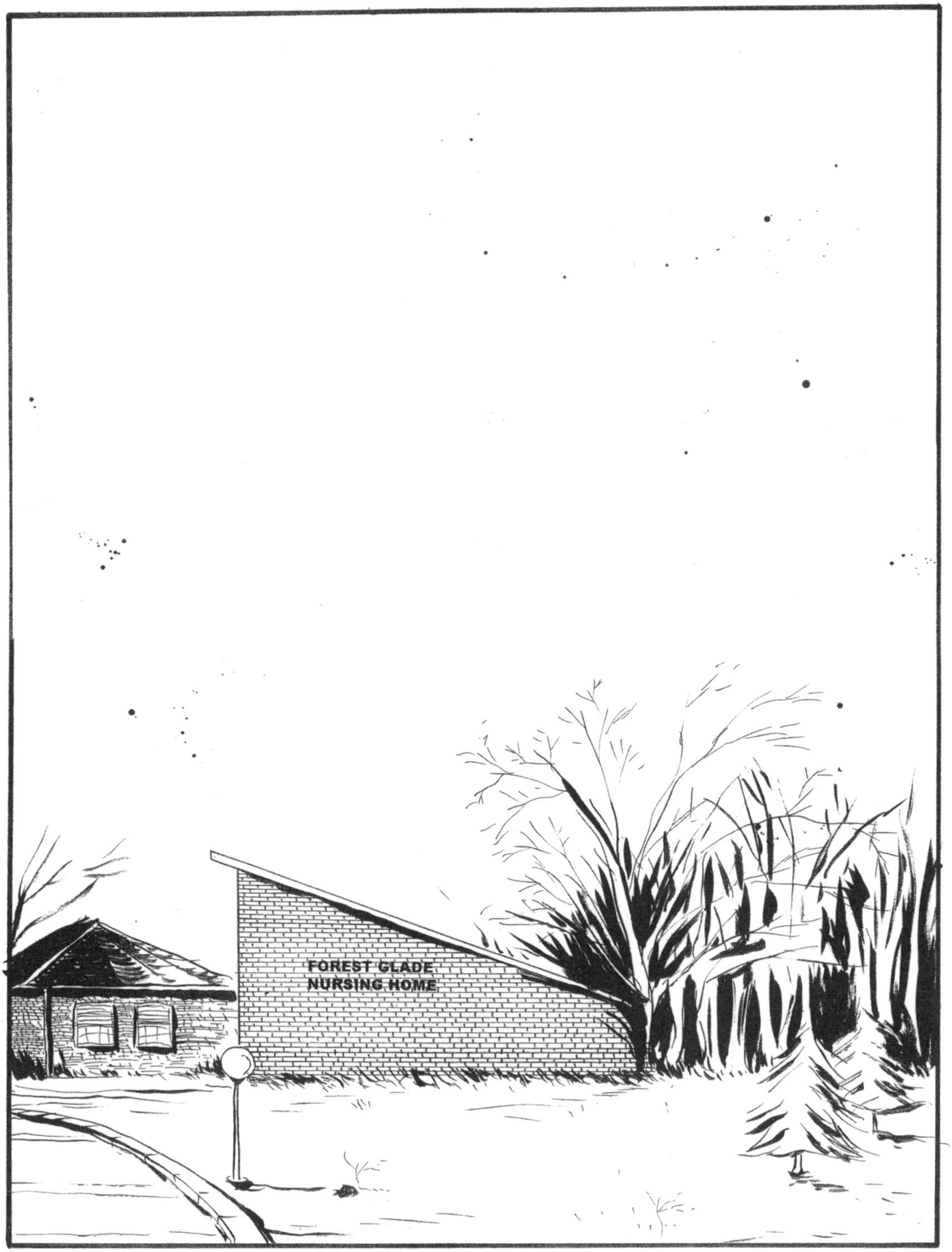
FOREST GLADE
NURSING HOME

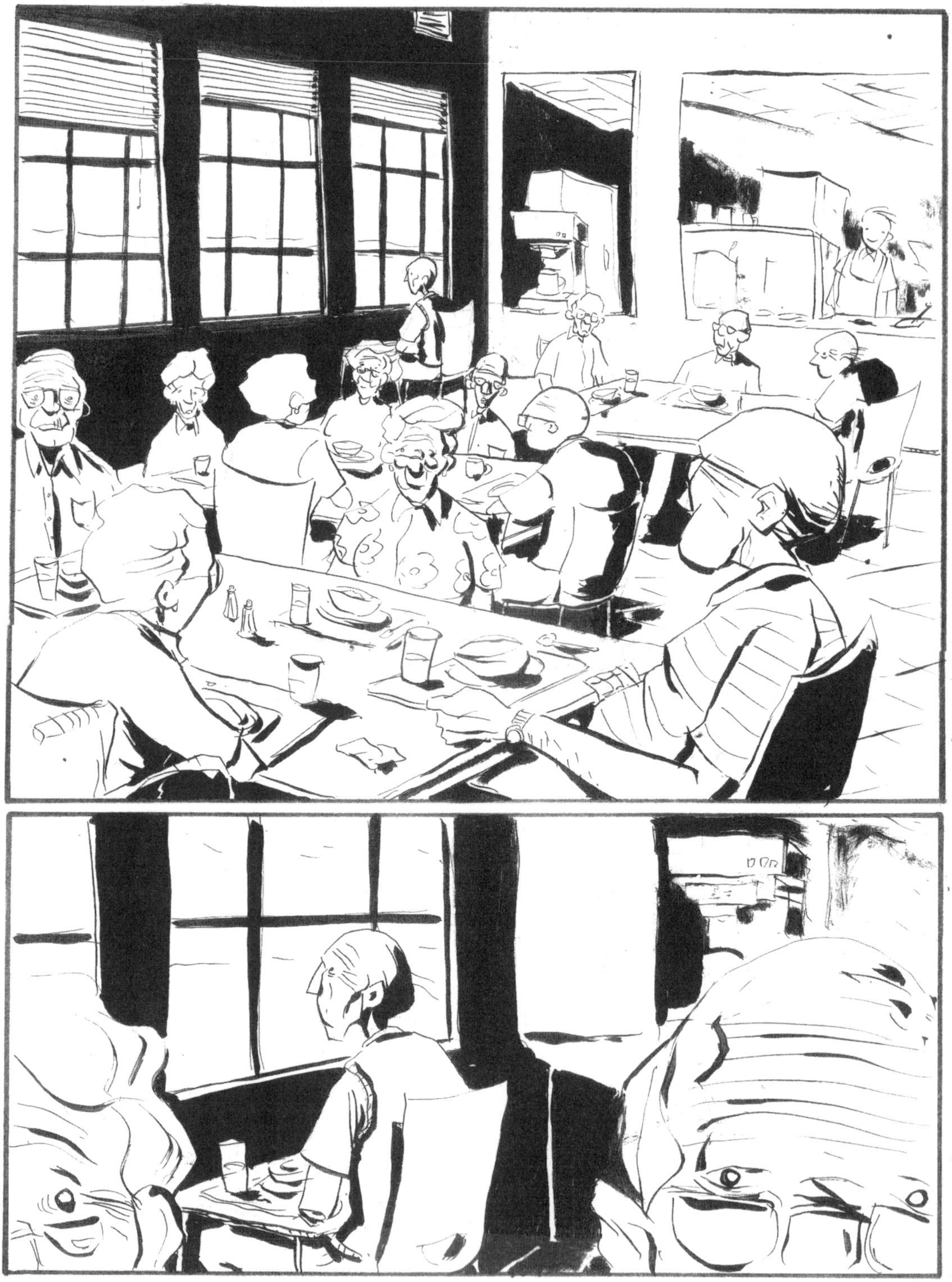

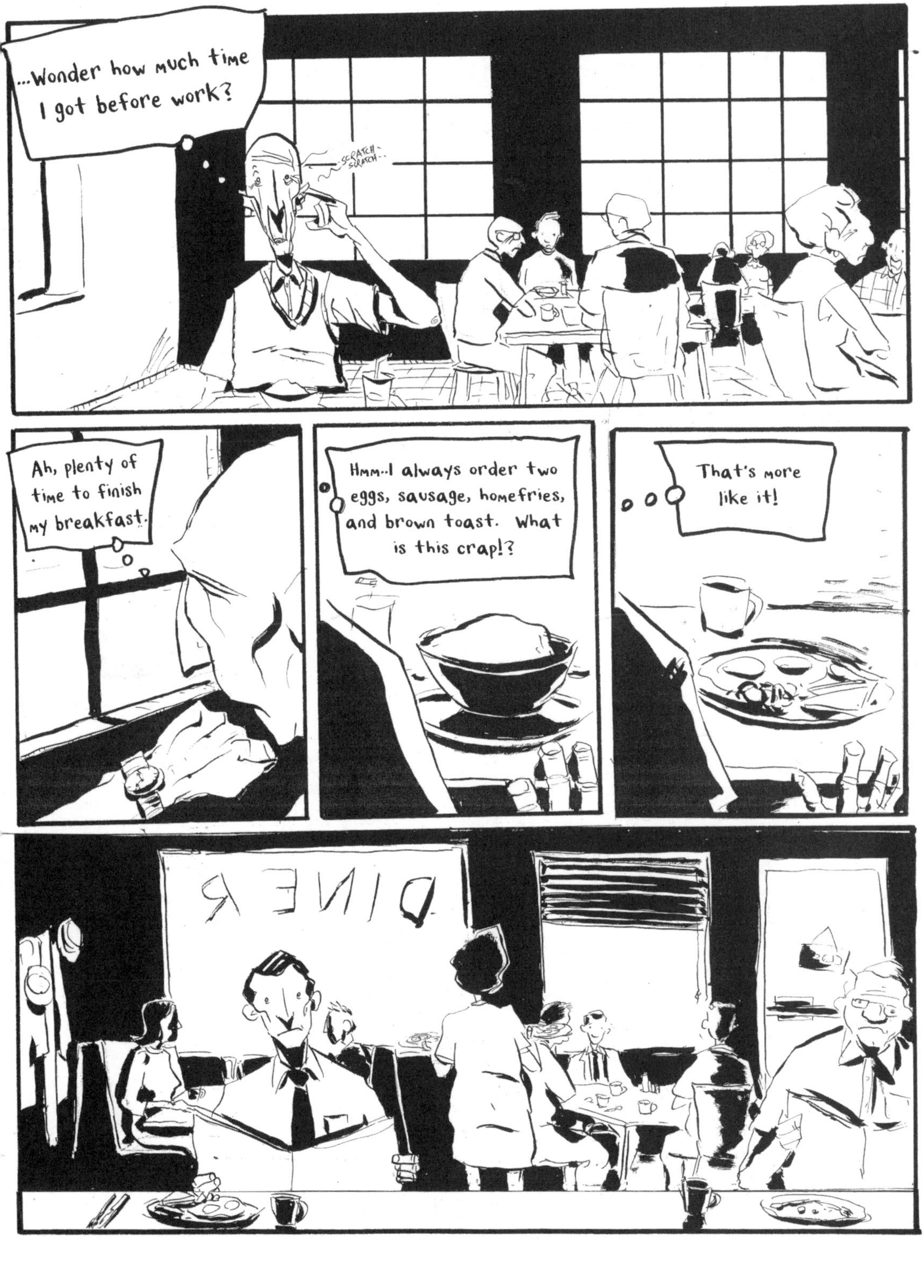
...Wonder how much time I got before work?
SCRATCH SCRATCH
Ah, plenty of time to finish my breakfast.
Hmm..I always order two eggs, sausage, homefries, and brown toast. What is this crap!?
That's more like it!
DINER

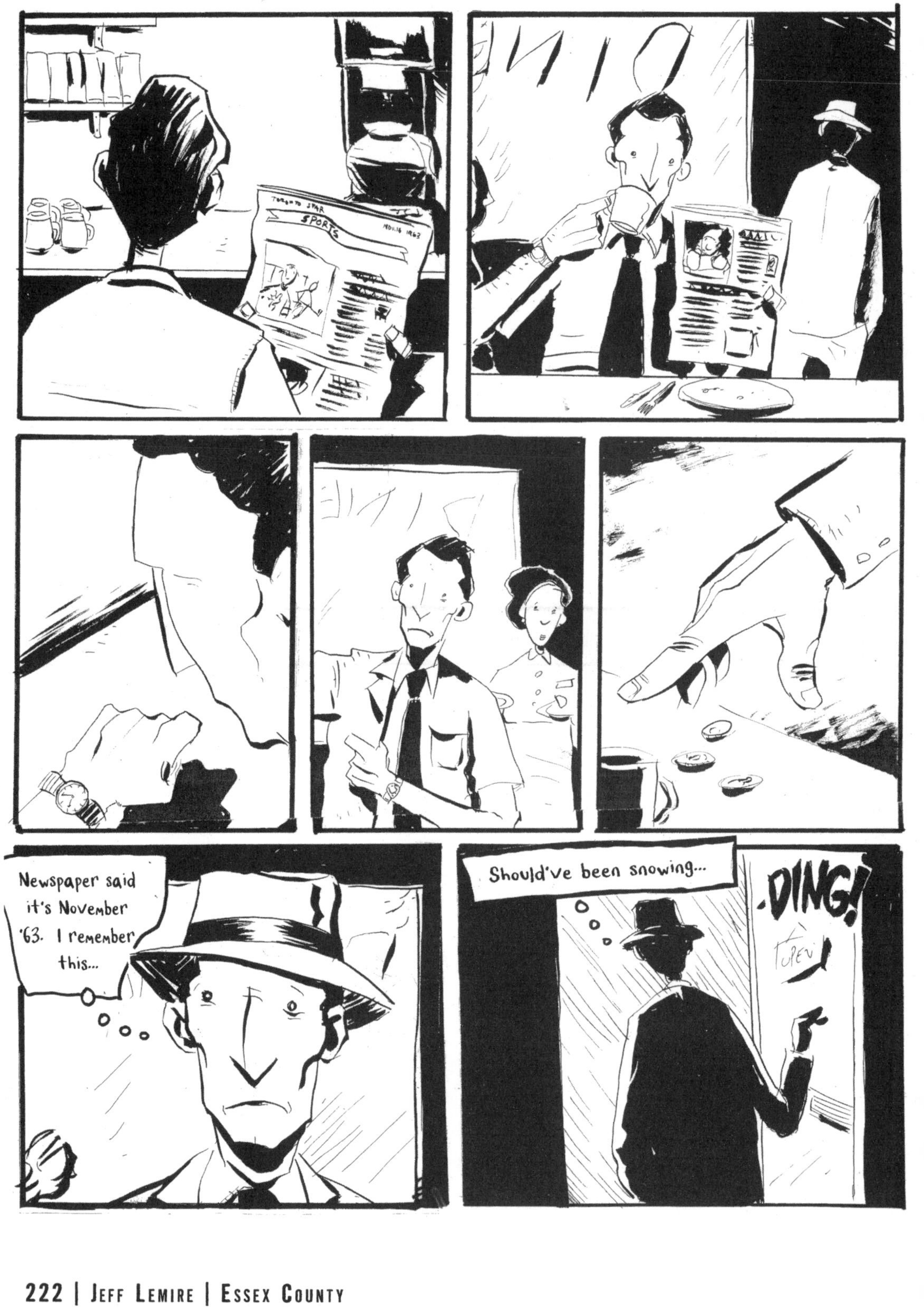
TORONTO STAR
SPORTS
NOV.16 1963
Newspaper said it's November '63. I remember this...
Should've been snowing...
DING!
OPEN

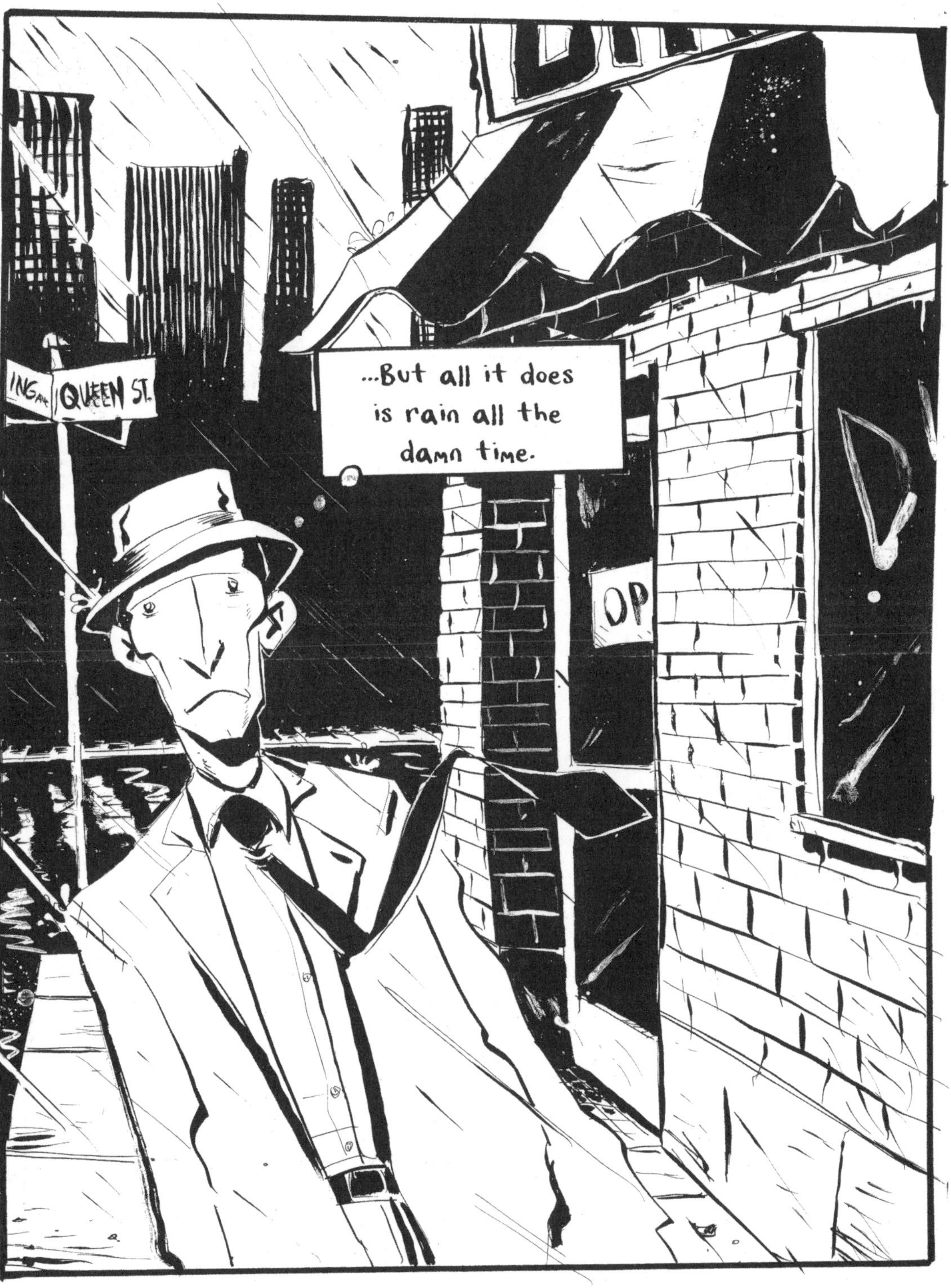

...But all it does is rain all the damn time.
QUEEN ST.
OP

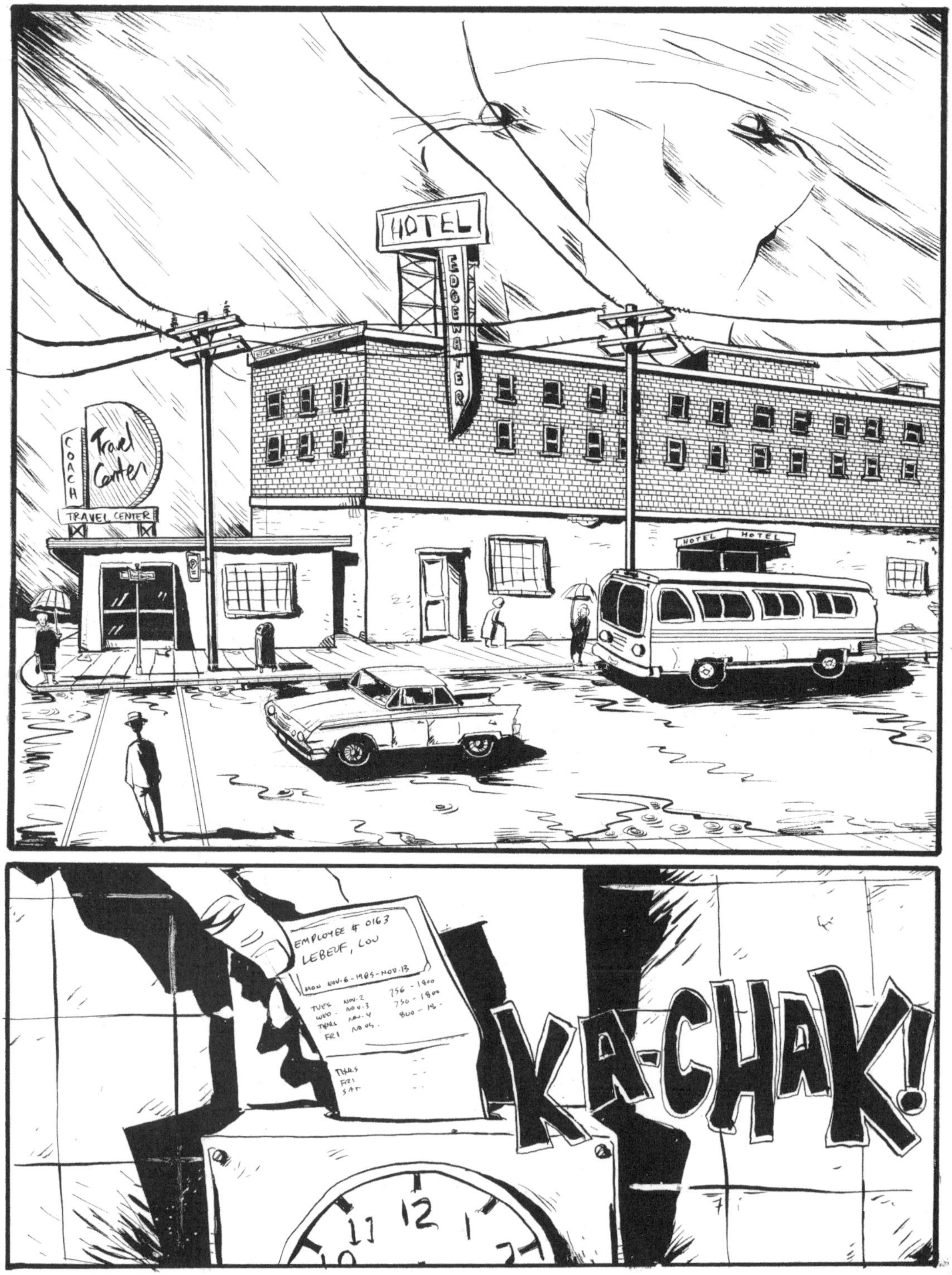
HOTEL
EDGEWATER
Travel Center
COACH
TRAVEL CENTER
HOTEL
HOTEL
EMPLOYEE # 0163
LEBEUF, LOU
KA-CHAK!

When Vince left, and I got hurt, I was kind of lost. I didn't have hockey anymore, and I needed to find a job fast.

Donnie Gill, one of my old Grizzly pals, had gotten a job as a mechanic for the TTC (Toronto's Public Transit).

The city was expanding its transit lines in the late '50s, so he put in a word for me, and I applied to the union.

Before I knew it I was driving a streetcar full-time.

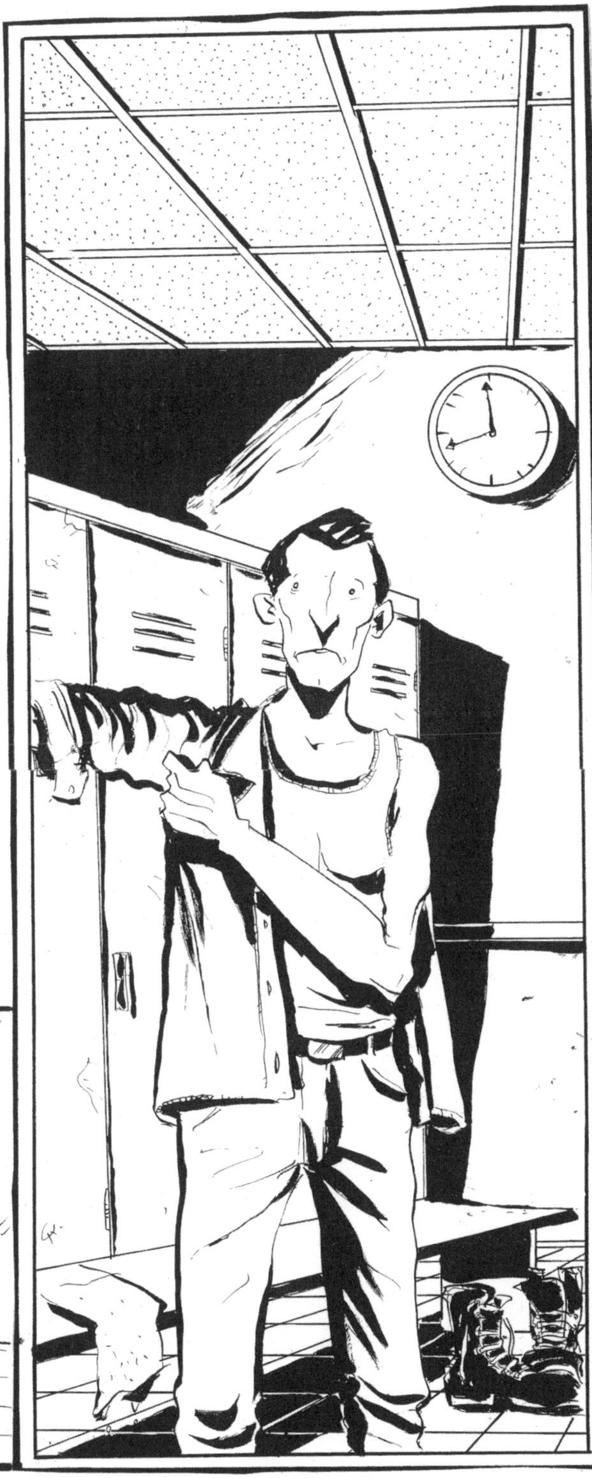

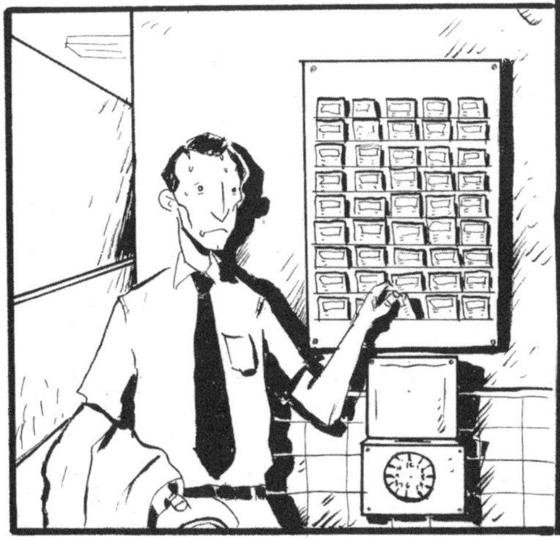

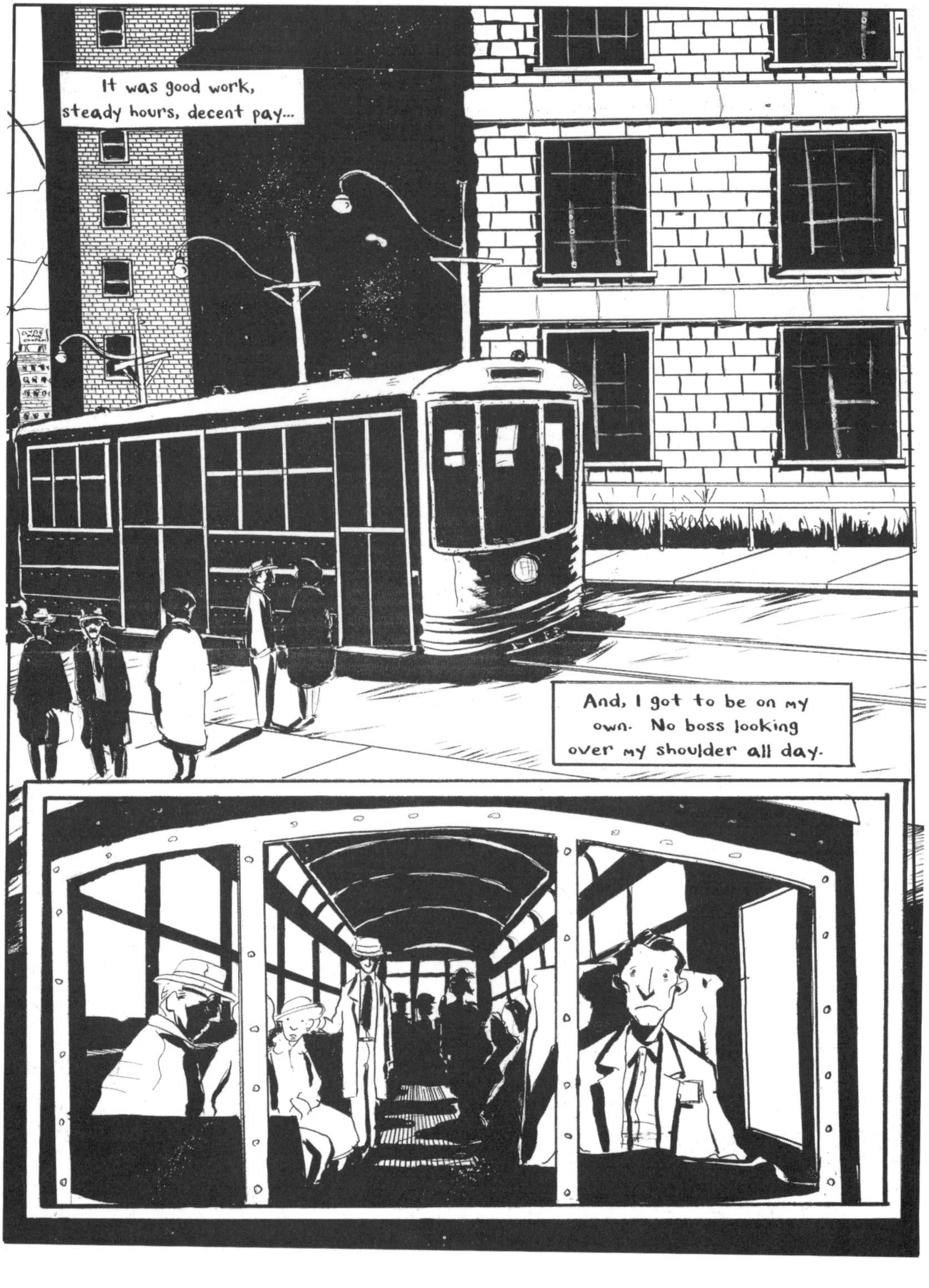
It was good work, steady hours, decent pay...
And, I got to be on my own. No boss looking over my shoulder all day.

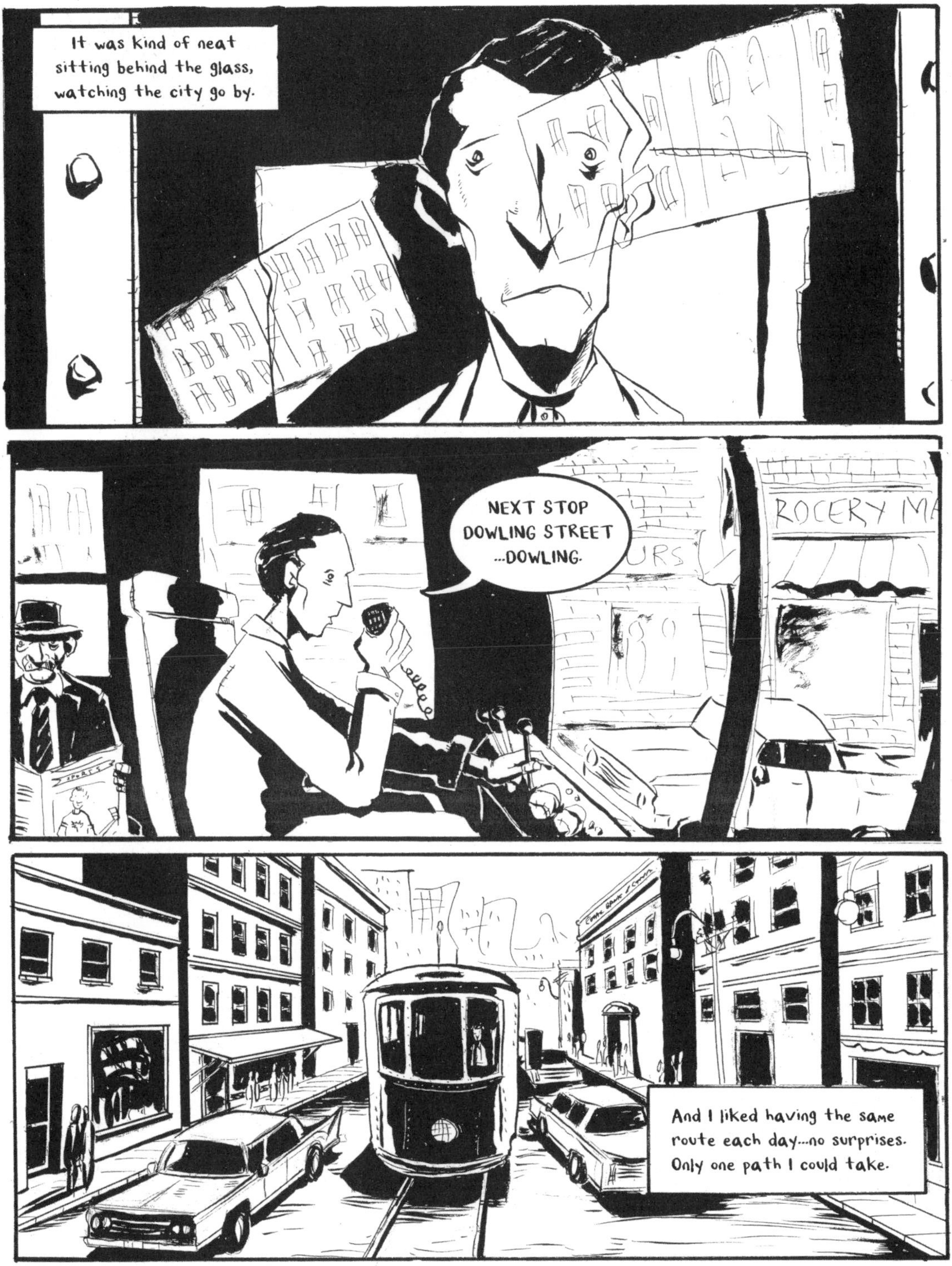
It was kind of neat sitting behind the glass, watching the city go by.
NEXT STOP DOWLING STREET ...DOWLING.
ROCERY MA
And I liked having the same route each day...no surprises. Only one path I could take.

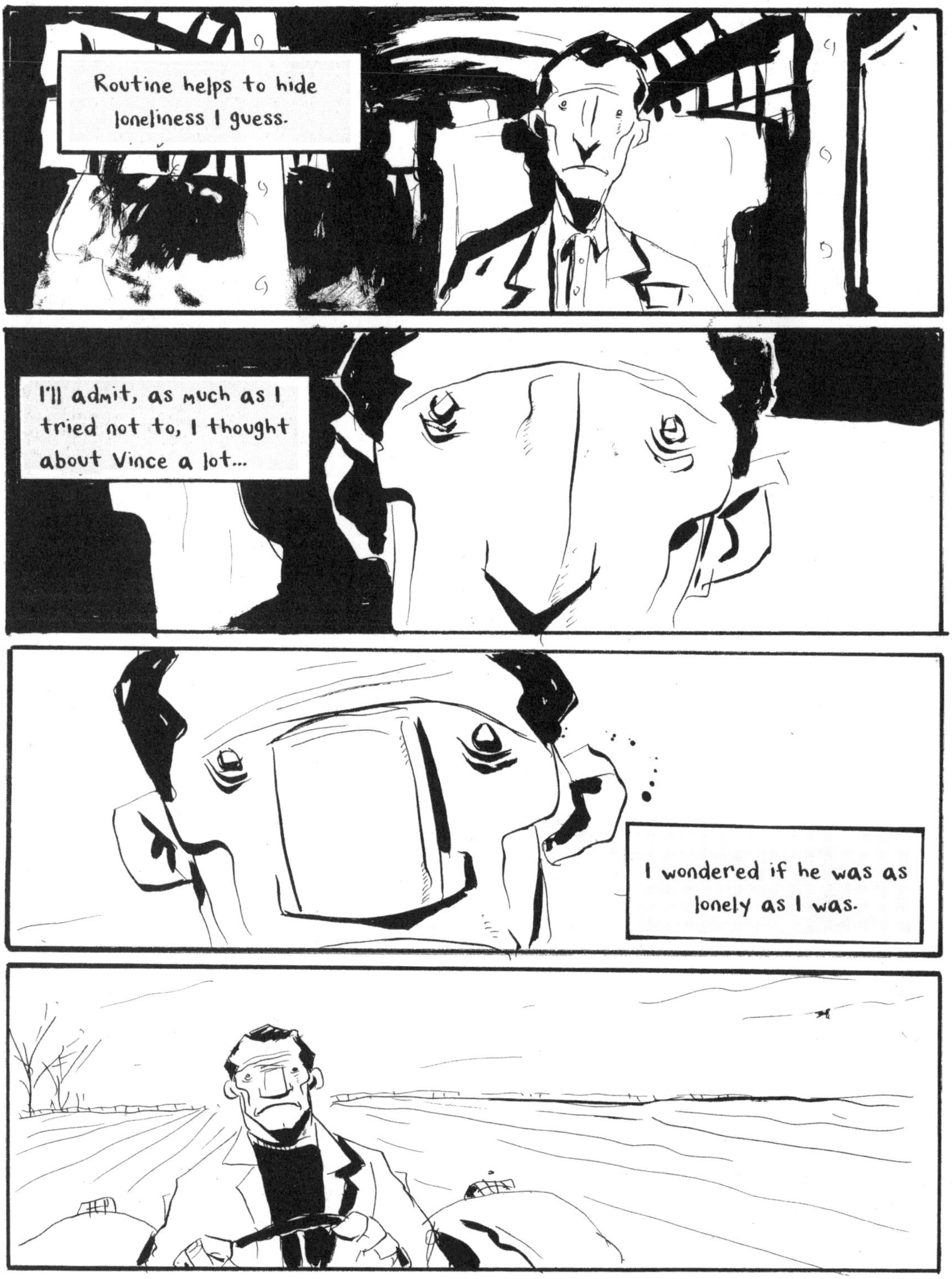
Routine helps to hide loneliness I guess.
I'll admit, as much as I tried not to, I thought about Vince a lot...
I wondered if he was as lonely as I was.

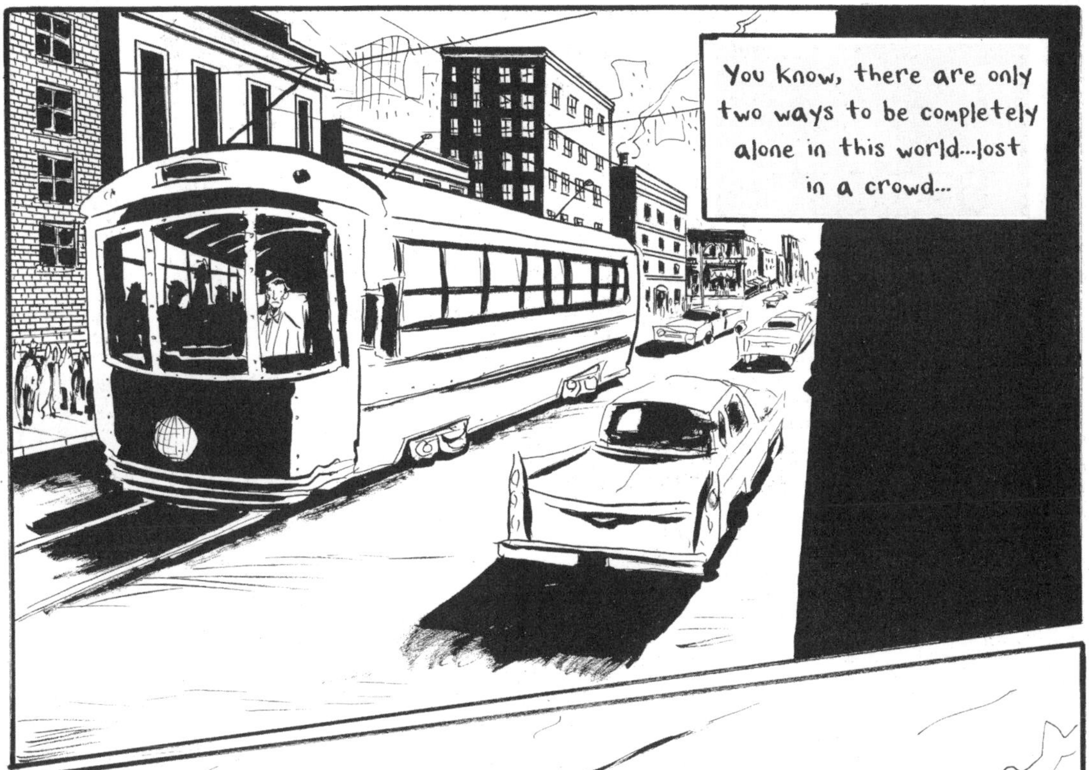
You know, there are only two ways to be completely alone in this world...lost in a crowd...

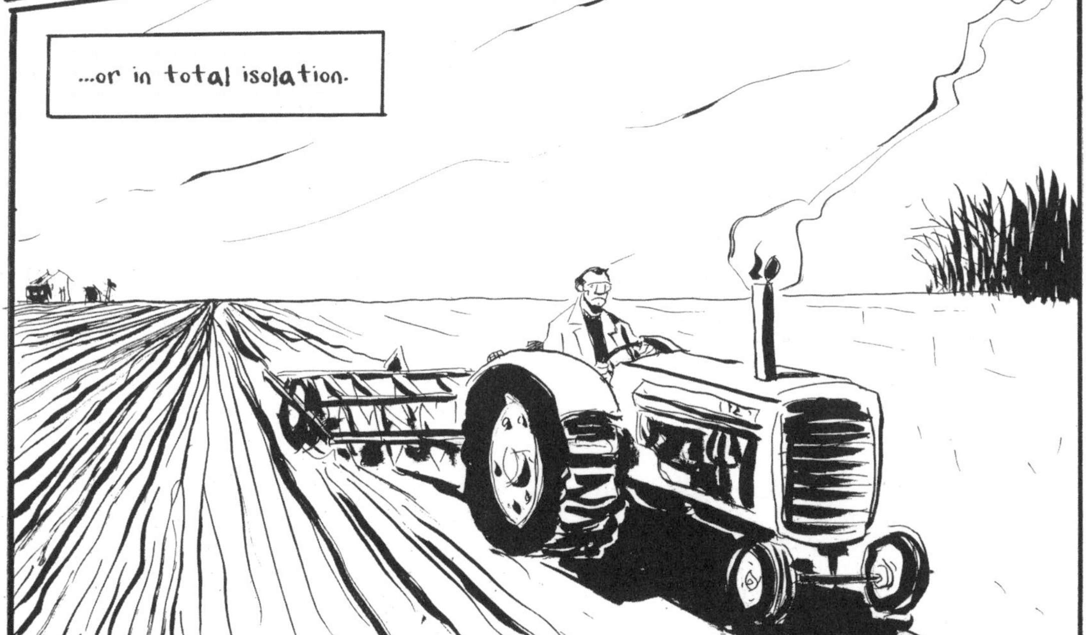
...or in total isolation.

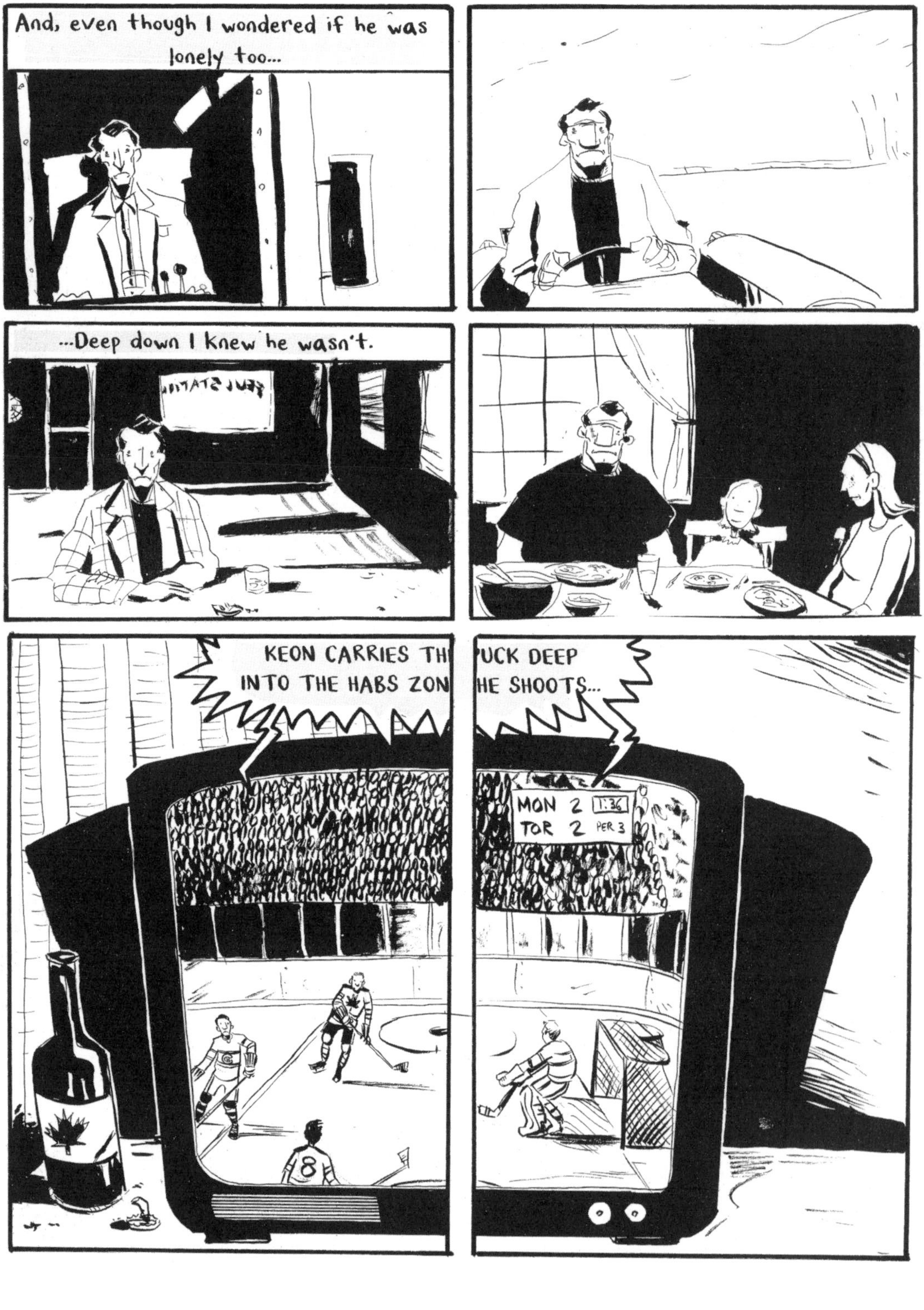
And, even though I wondered if he was lonely too...
...Deep down I knew he wasn't.
KEON CARRIES THE PUCK DEEP INTO THE HABS ZONE HE SHOOTS...
MON 2 1:36
TOR 2 PER 3

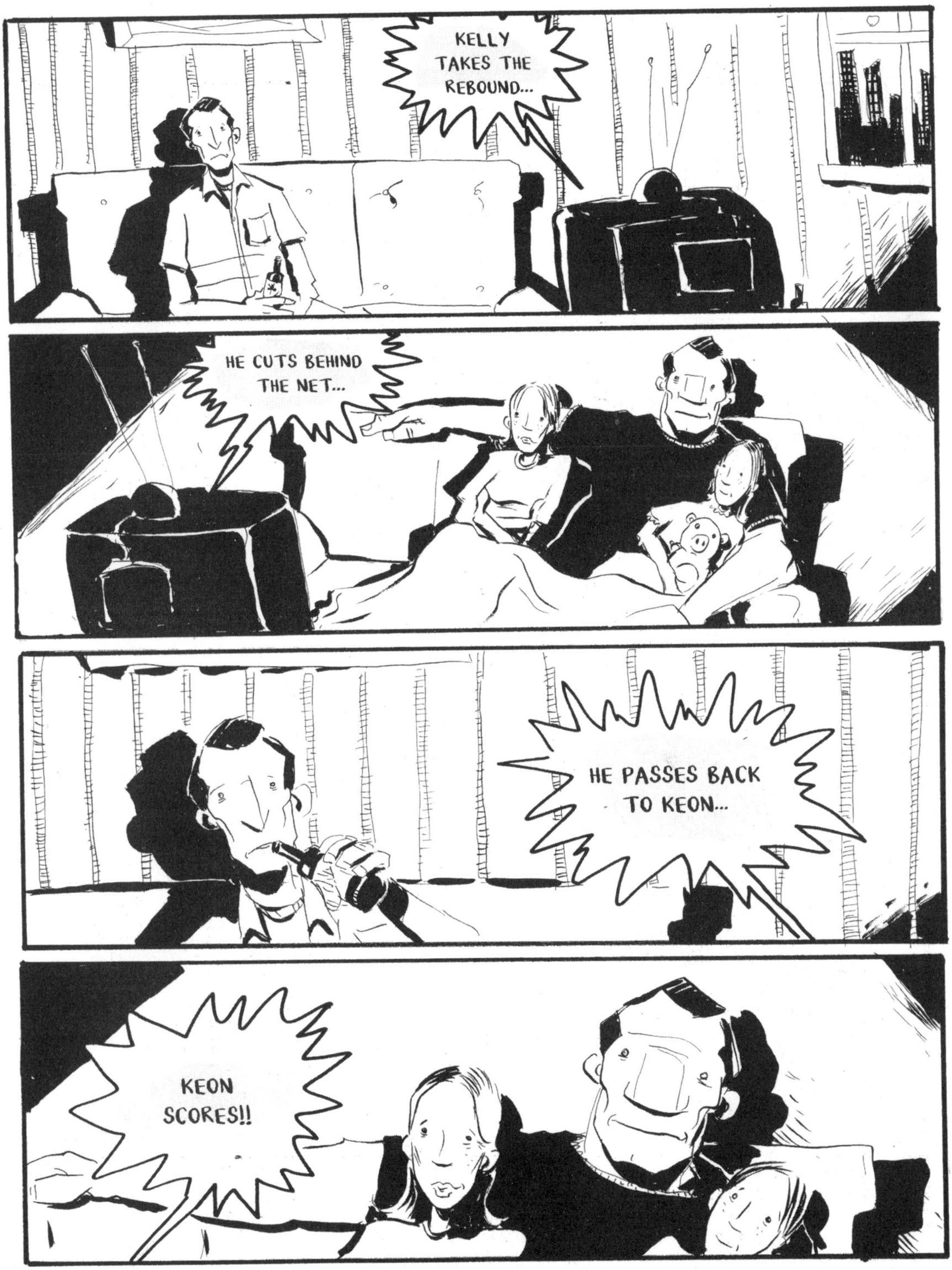
KELLY TAKES THE REBOUND...
HE CUTS BEHIND THE NET...
HE PASSES BACK TO KEON...
KEON SCORES!!

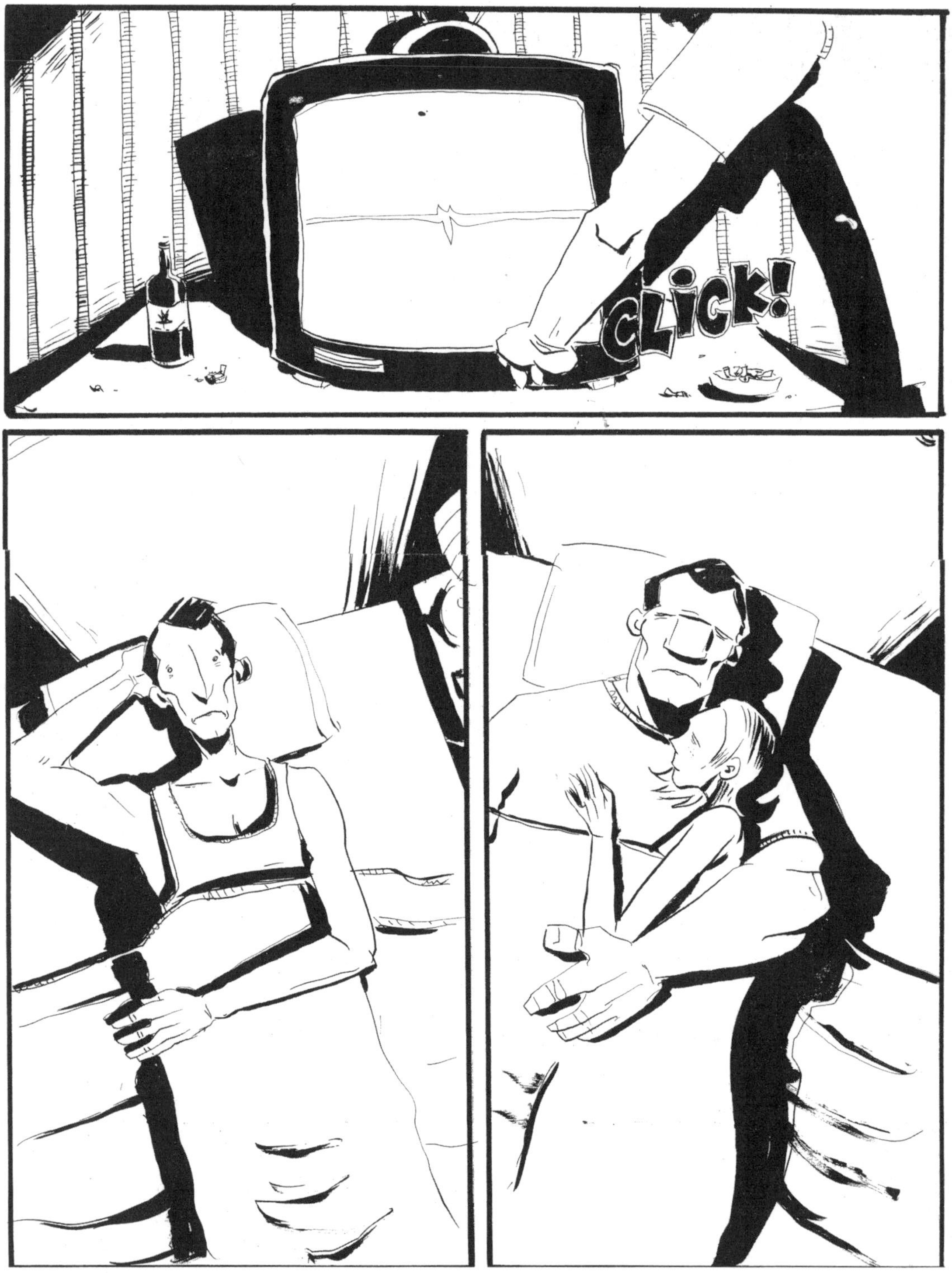
CLICK!

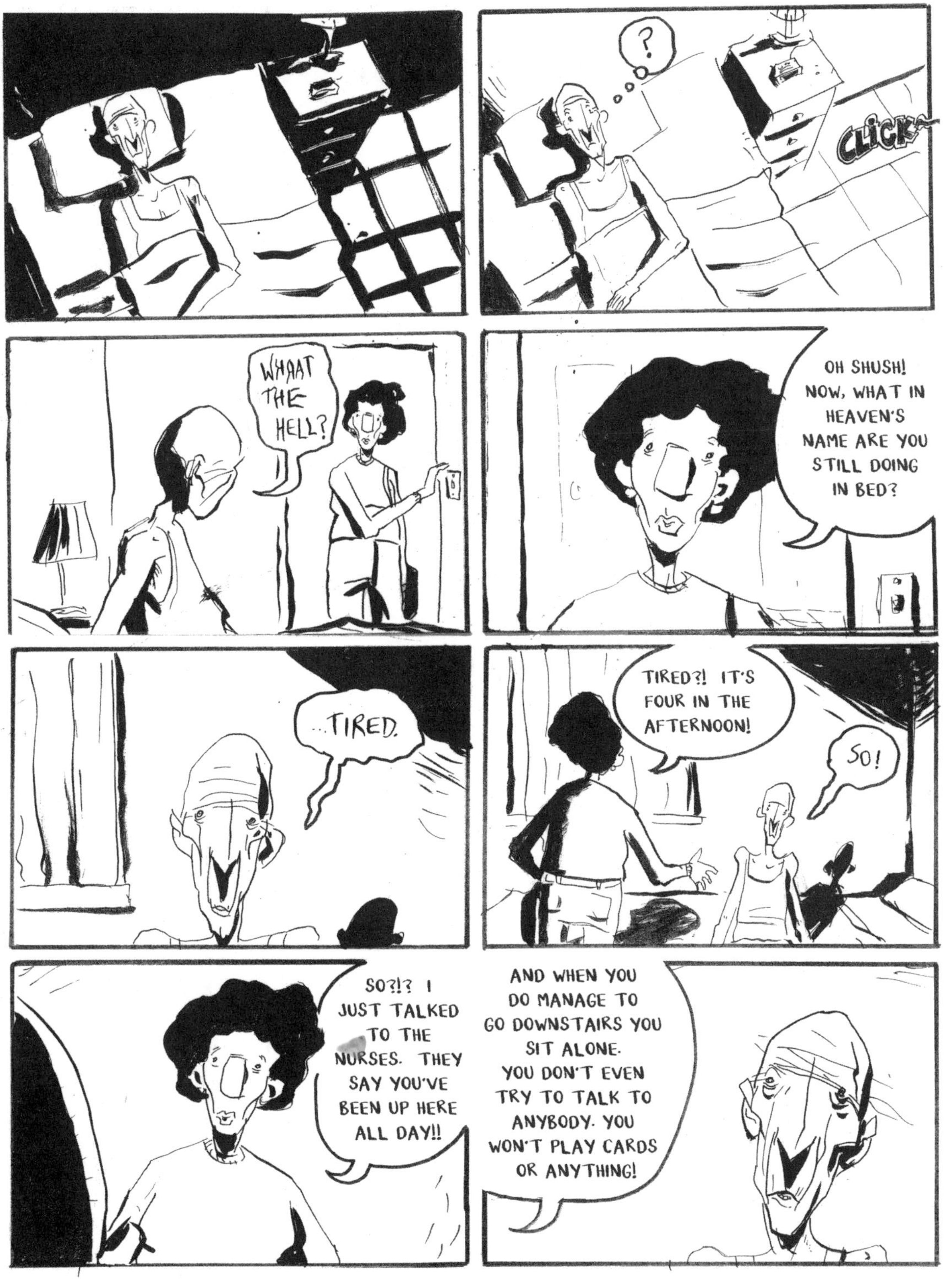
?
CLICK
WHAT THE HELL?
OH SHUSH! NOW, WHAT IN HEAVEN'S NAME ARE YOU STILL DOING IN BED?
...TIRED.
TIRED?! IT'S FOUR IN THE AFTERNOON!
SO!
SO?!? I JUST TALKED TO THE NURSES. THEY SAY YOU'VE BEEN UP HERE ALL DAY!!
AND WHEN YOU DO MANAGE TO GO DOWNSTAIRS YOU SIT ALONE. YOU DON'T EVEN TRY TO TALK TO ANYBODY. YOU WON'T PLAY CARDS OR ANYTHING!

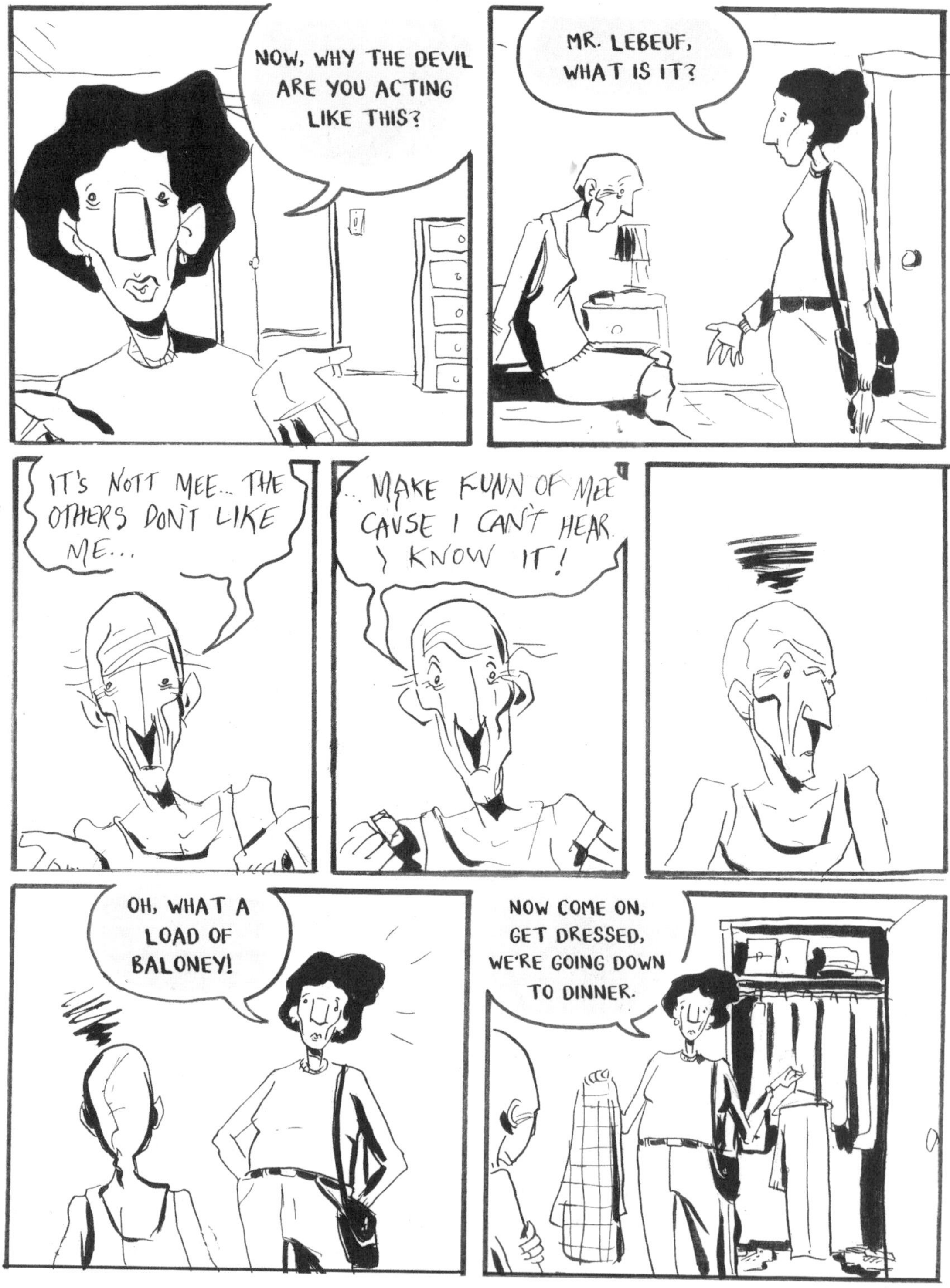
NOW, WHY THE DEVIL ARE YOU ACTING LIKE THIS?
MR. LEBEUF, WHAT IS IT?
IT'S NOTT MEE... THE OTHERS DON'T LIKE ME...
...MAKE FUNN OF MEE CAUSE I CAN'T HEAR. I KNOW IT!
OH, WHAT A LOAD OF BALONEY!
NOW COME ON, GET DRESSED, WE'RE GOING DOWN TO DINNER.

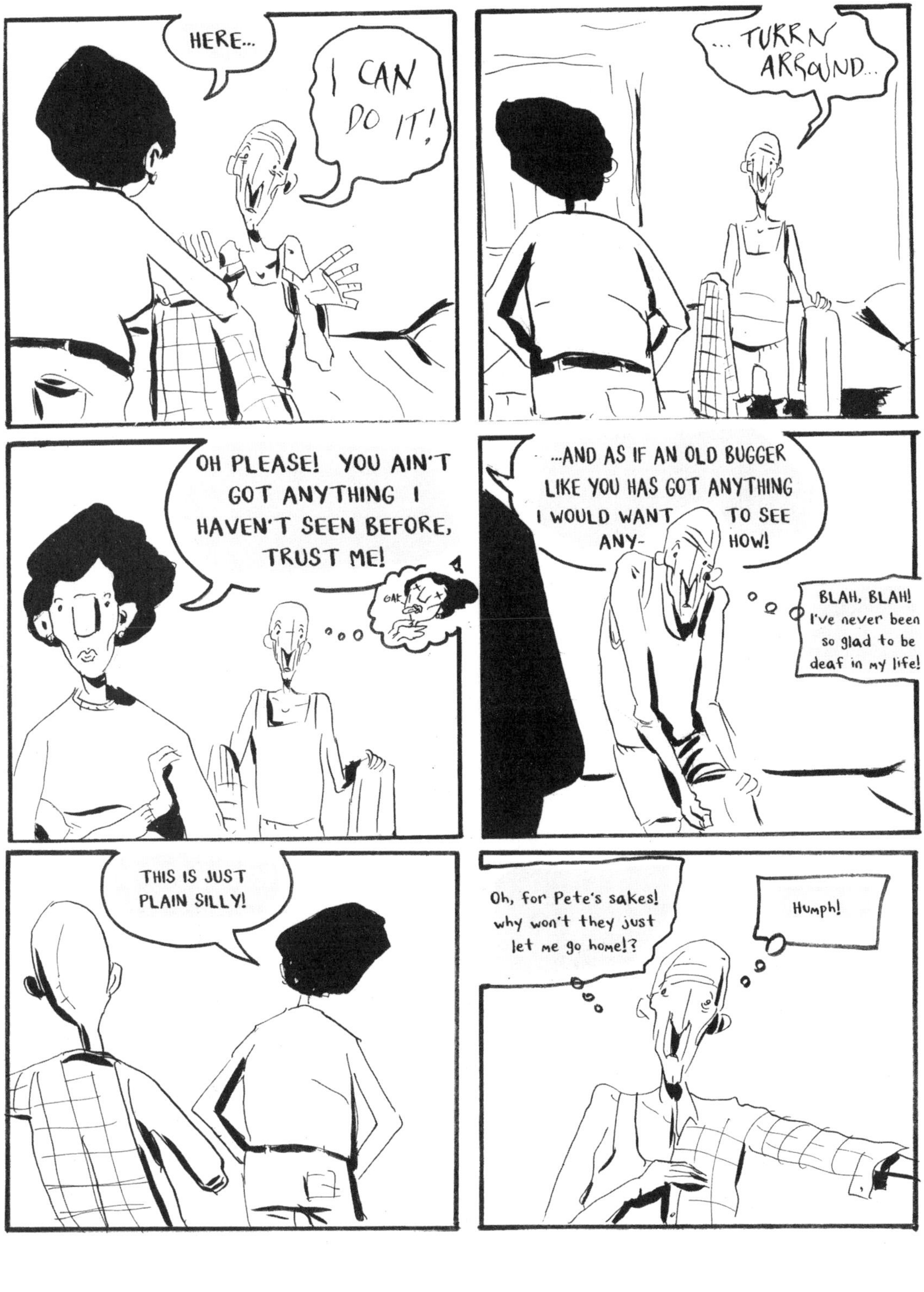
HERE...
I CAN DO IT!
... TURRN ARROUND...
OH PLEASE! YOU AIN'T GOT ANYTHING I HAVEN'T SEEN BEFORE, TRUST ME!
GAK
...AND AS IF AN OLD BUGGER LIKE YOU HAS GOT ANYTHING I WOULD WANT TO SEE ANY-HOW!
BLAH, BLAH! I've never been so glad to be deaf in my life!
THIS IS JUST PLAIN SILLY!
Oh, for Pete's sakes! why won't they just let me go home!?
Humph!

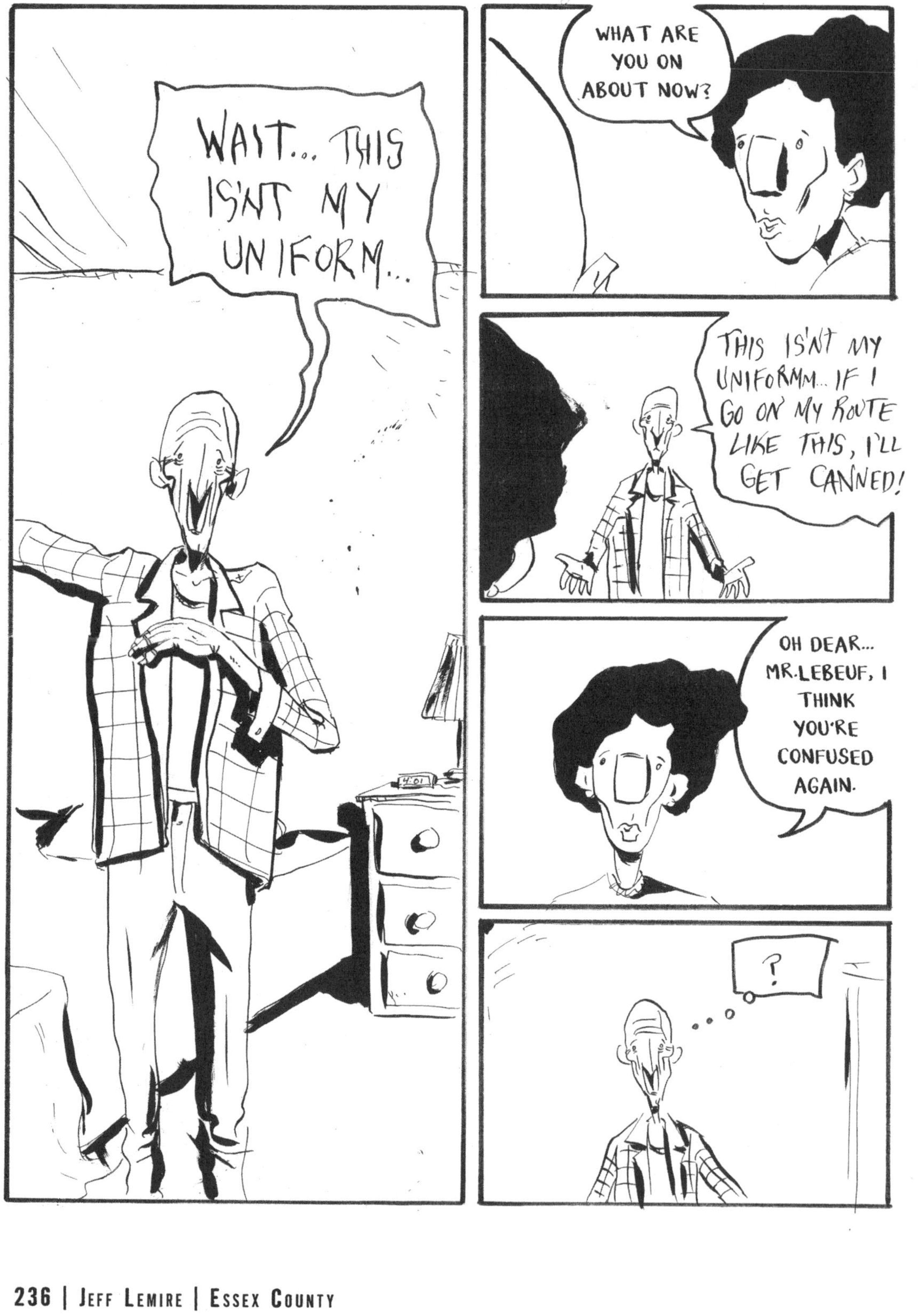
WAIT... THIS IS'NT MY UNIFORM...
WHAT ARE YOU ON ABOUT NOW?
THIS IS'NT MY UNIFORMM... IF I GO ON MY ROUTE LIKE THIS, I'LL GET CANNED!
OH DEAR... MR. LEBEUF, I THINK YOU'RE CONFUSED AGAIN.
?

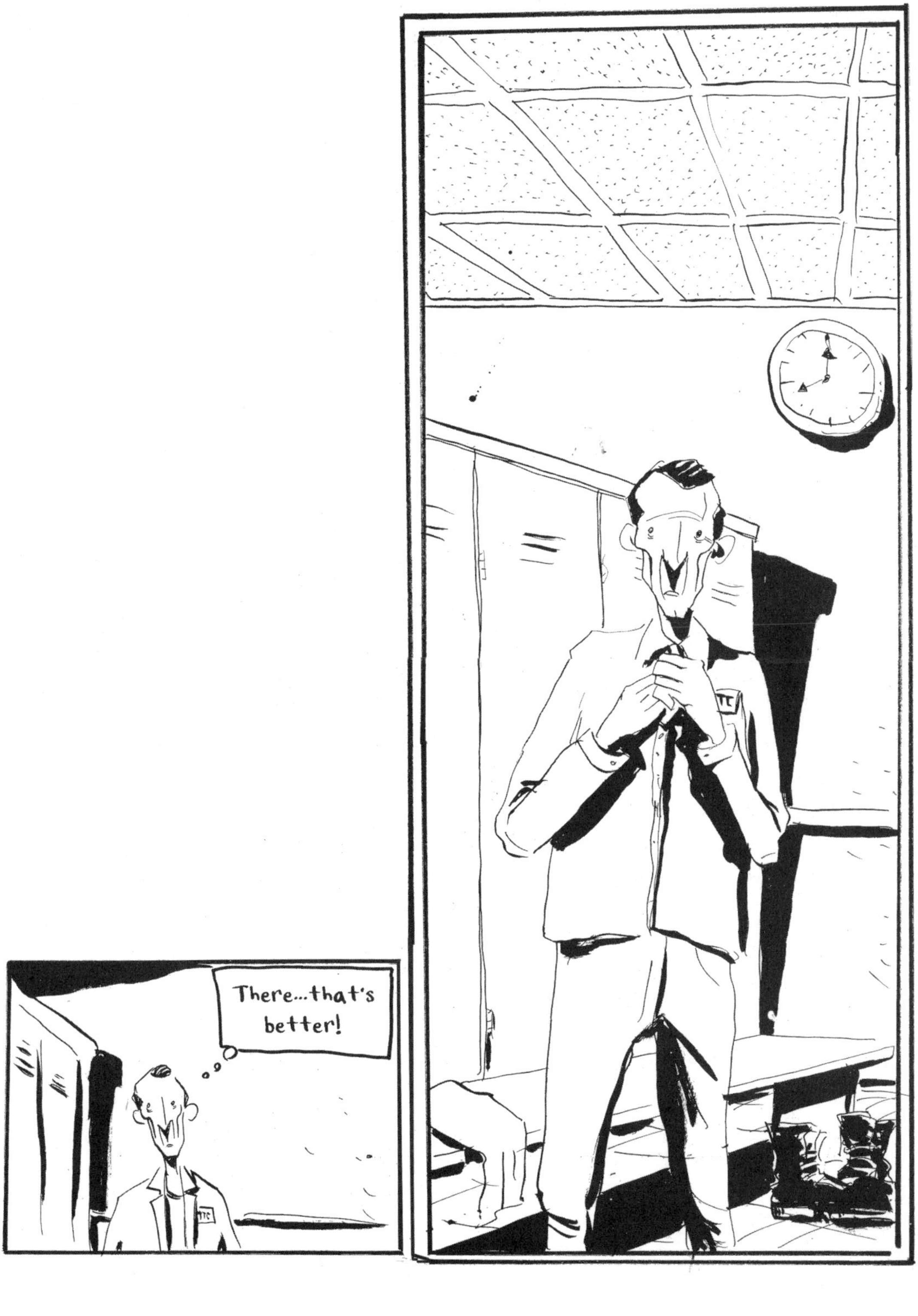
There...that's better!

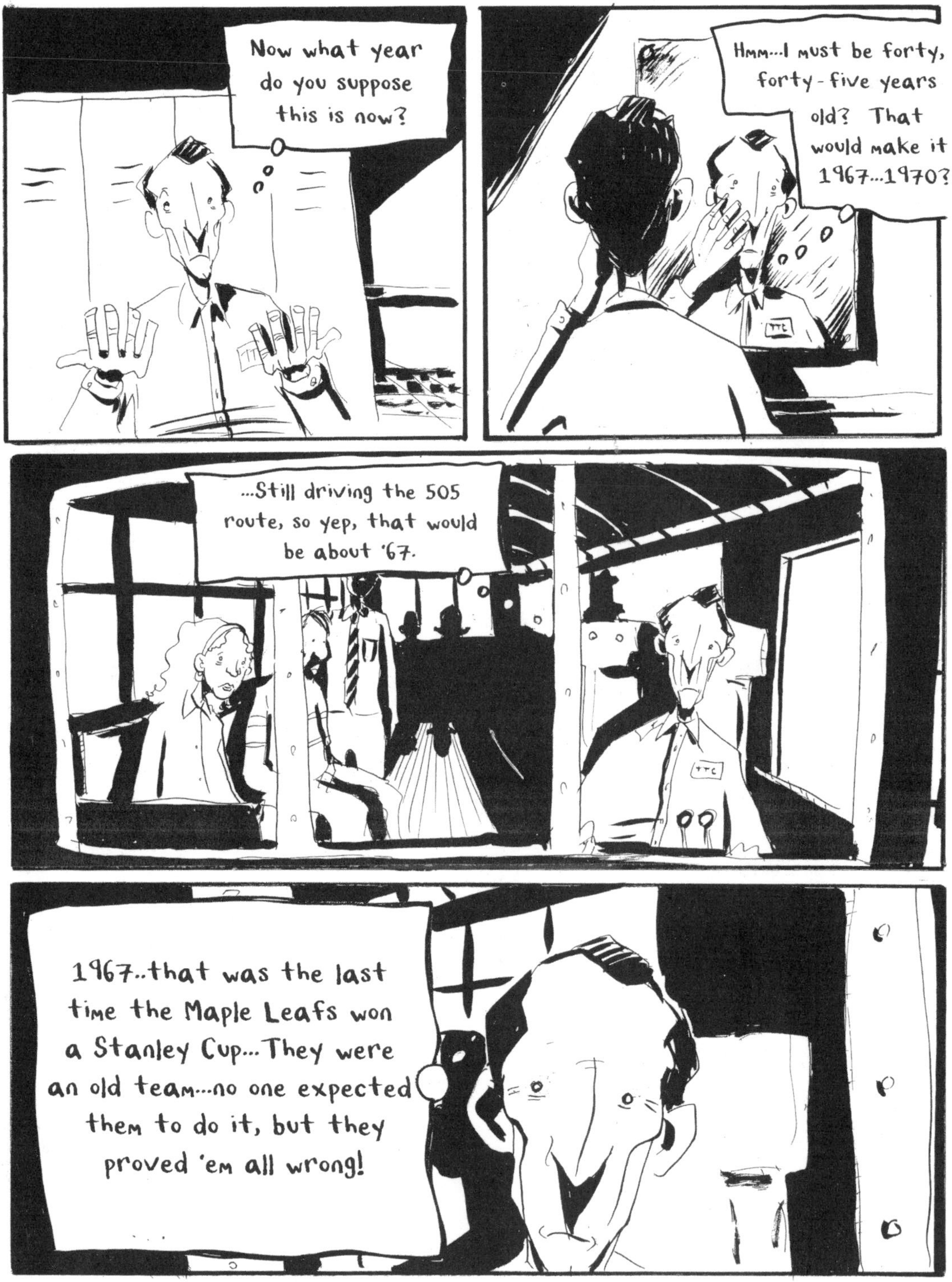
Now what year do you suppose this is now?
Hmm...I must be forty, forty-five years old? That would make it 1967...1970?
...Still driving the 505 route, so yep, that would be about '67.
1967..that was the last time the Maple Leafs won a Stanley Cup...They were an old team...no one expected them to do it, but they proved 'em all wrong!

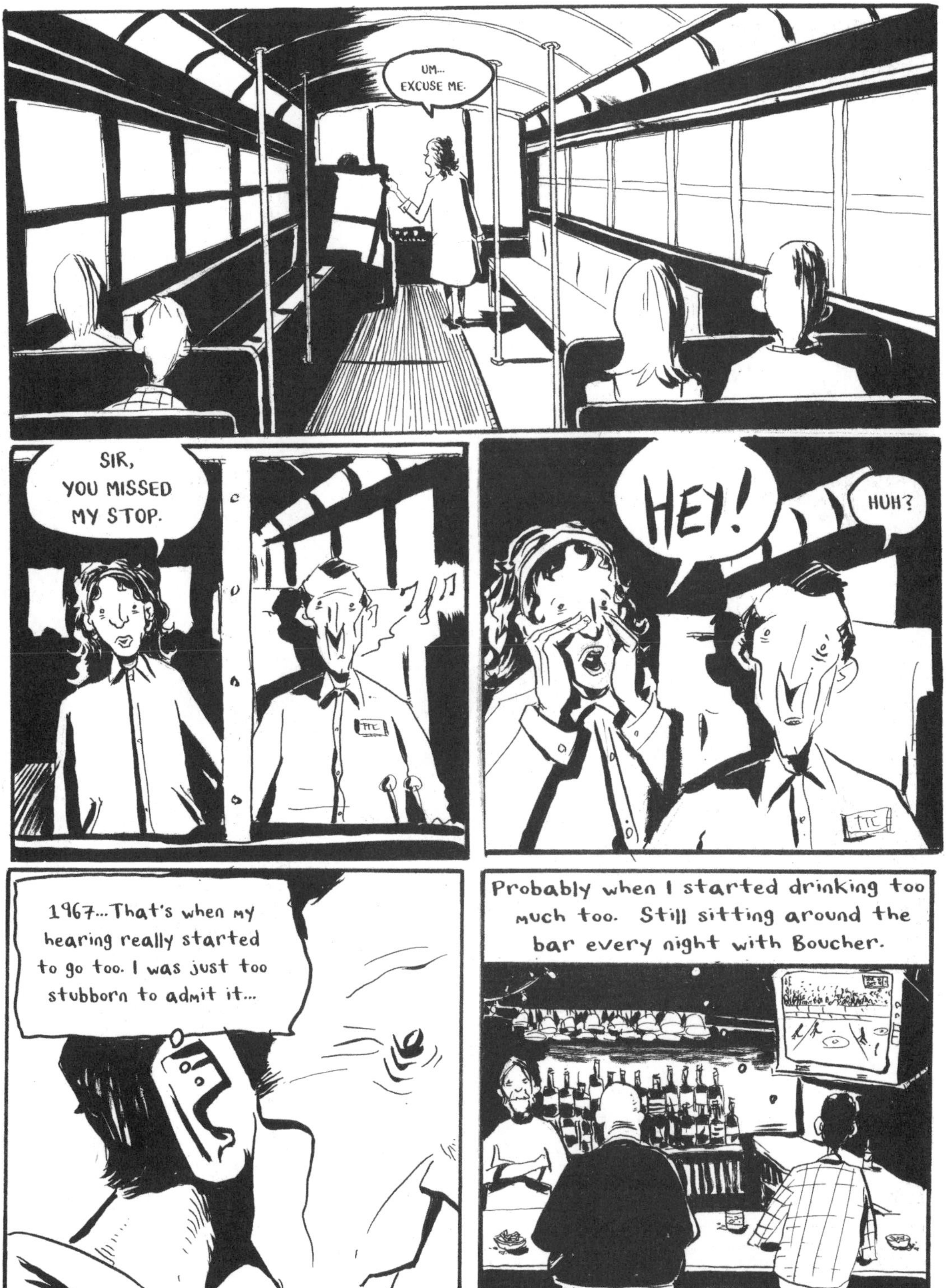
UM... EXCUSE ME.
SIR, YOU MISSED MY STOP.
HEY!
HUH?
1967... That's when my hearing really started to go too. I was just too stubborn to admit it...
Probably when I started drinking too much too. Still sitting around the bar every night with Boucher.

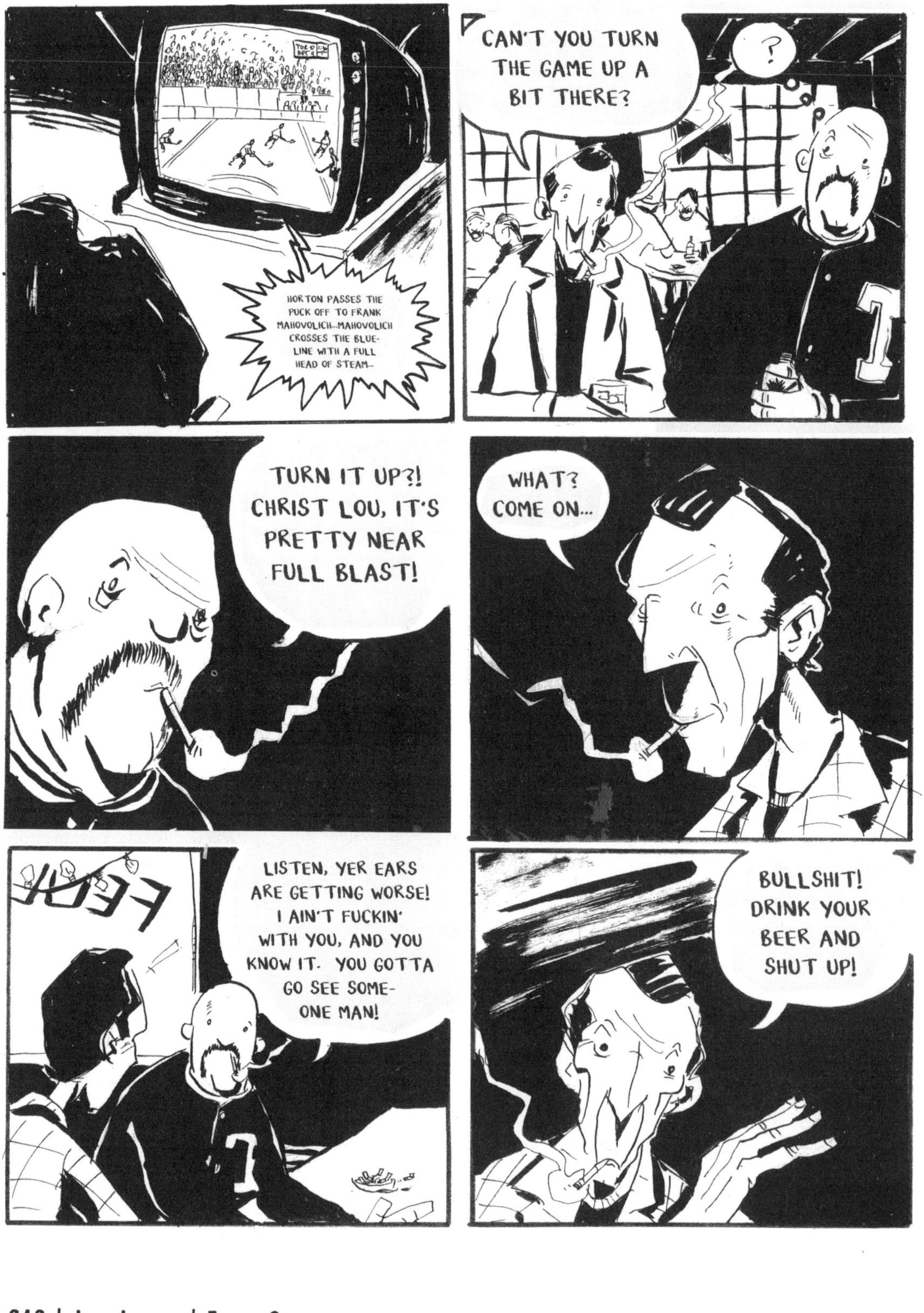
HORTON PASSES THE PUCK OFF TO FRANK MAHOVOLICH...MAHOVOLICH CROSSES THE BLUE-LINE WITH A FULL HEAD OF STEAM...
CAN'T YOU TURN THE GAME UP A BIT THERE?
?
TURN IT UP?! CHRIST LOU, IT'S PRETTY NEAR FULL BLAST!
WHAT? COME ON...
LISTEN, YER EARS ARE GETTING WORSE! I AIN'T FUCKIN' WITH YOU, AND YOU KNOW IT. YOU GOTTA GO SEE SOME-ONE MAN!
BULLSHIT! DRINK YOUR BEER AND SHUT UP!

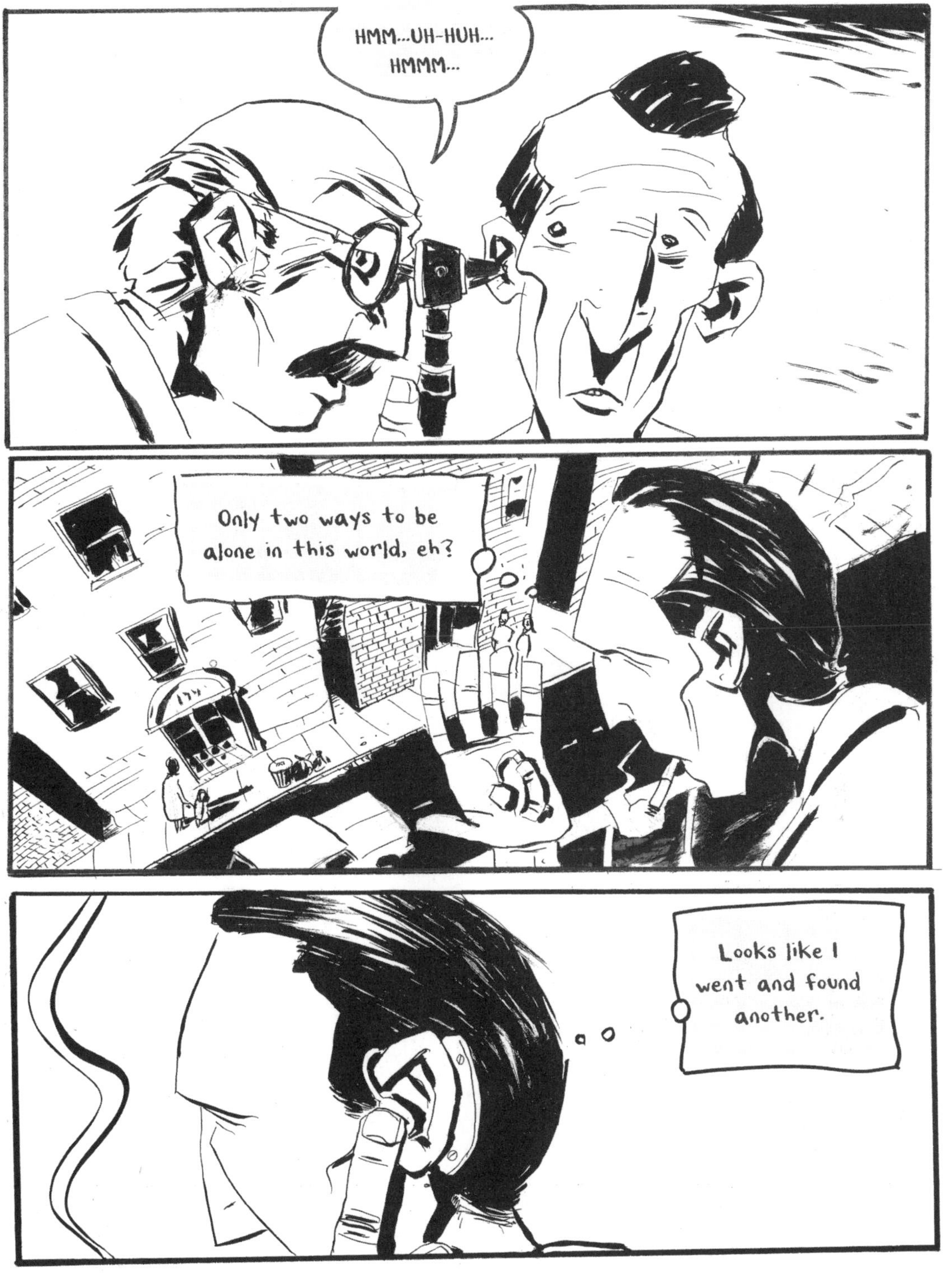
HMM...UH-HUH...
HMMM...
Only two ways to be alone in this world, eh?
Looks like I went and found another.

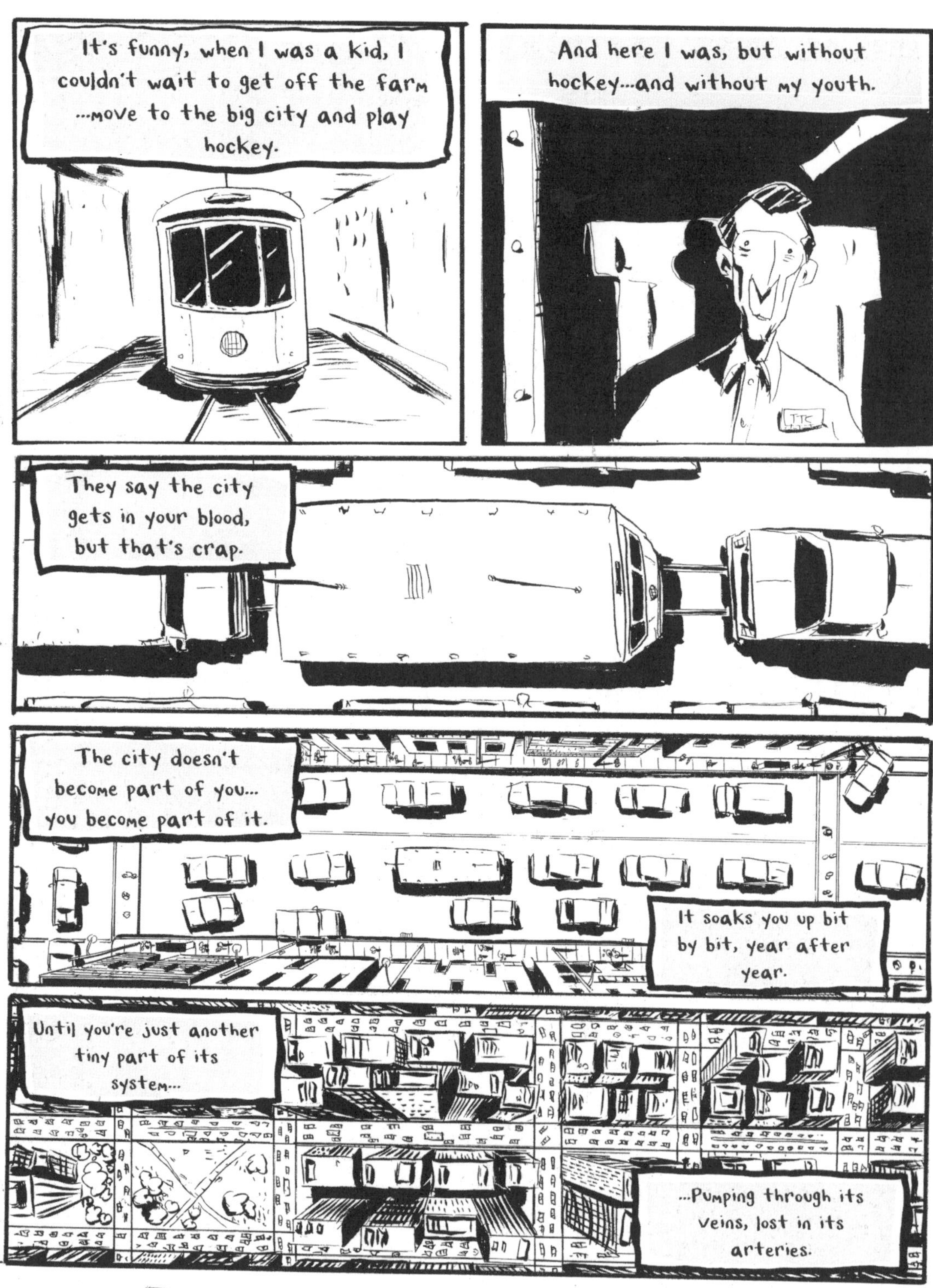
It's funny, when I was a kid, I couldn't wait to get off the farm ...move to the big city and play hockey.
And here I was, but without hockey...and without my youth.
TTC
They say the city gets in your blood, but that's crap.
The city doesn't become part of you... you become part of it.
It soaks you up bit by bit, year after year.
Until you're just another tiny part of its system...
...Pumping through its veins, lost in its arteries.

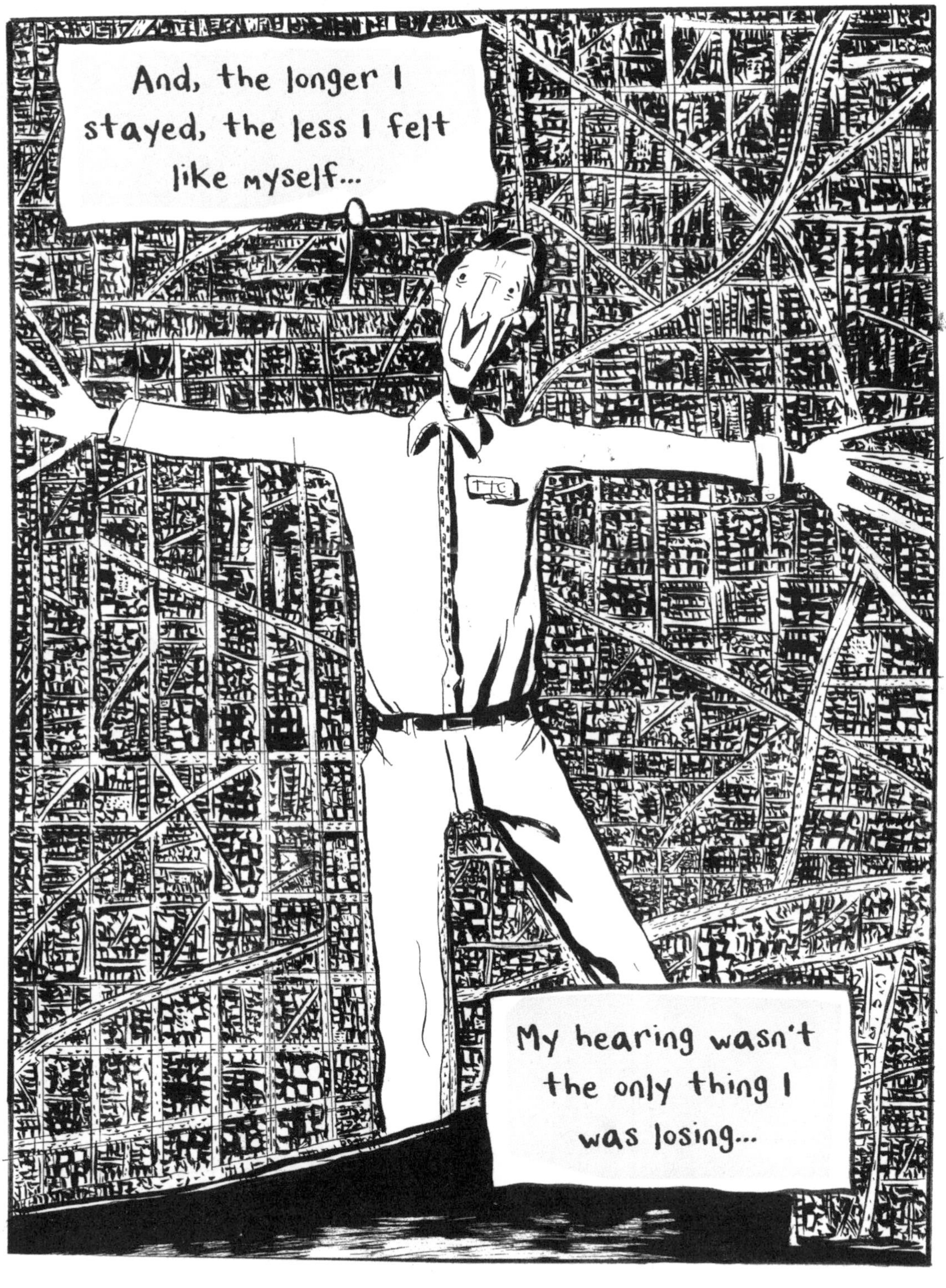
And, the longer I stayed, the less I felt like myself...
My hearing wasn't the only thing I was losing...

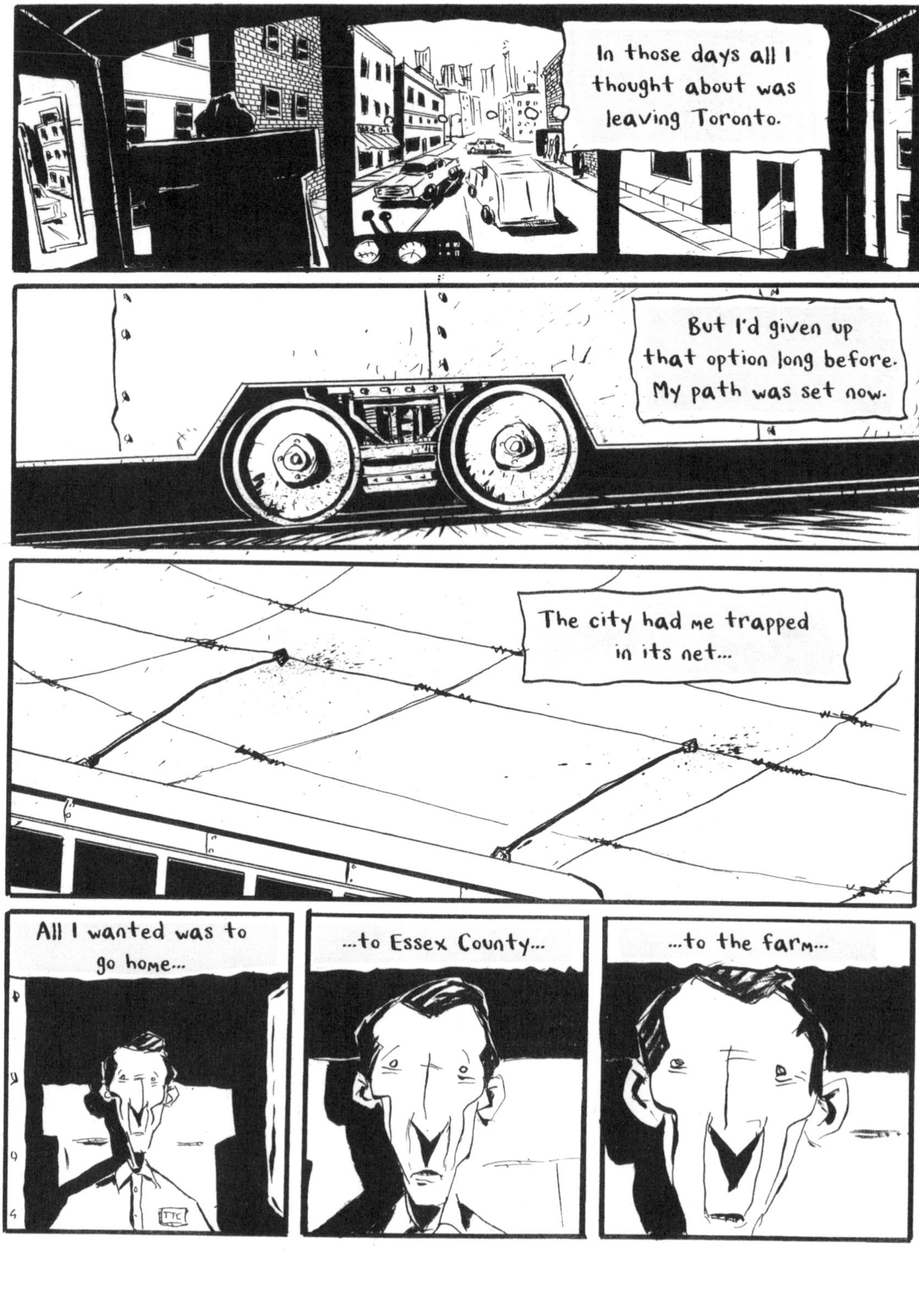
In those days all I thought about was leaving Toronto.
But I'd given up that option long before. My path was set now.
The city had me trapped in its net...
All I wanted was to go home...
...to Essex County...
...to the farm...
TTC

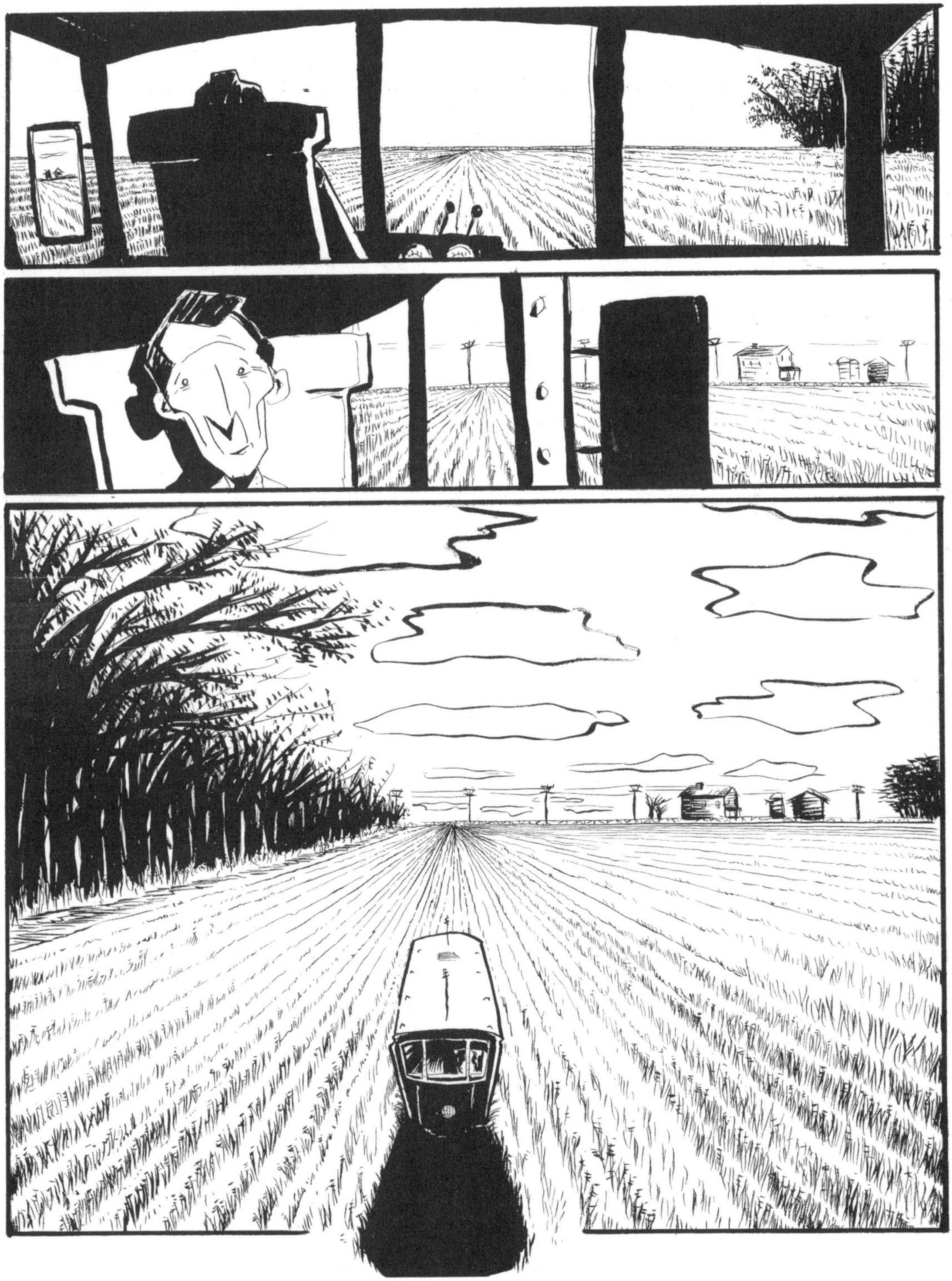

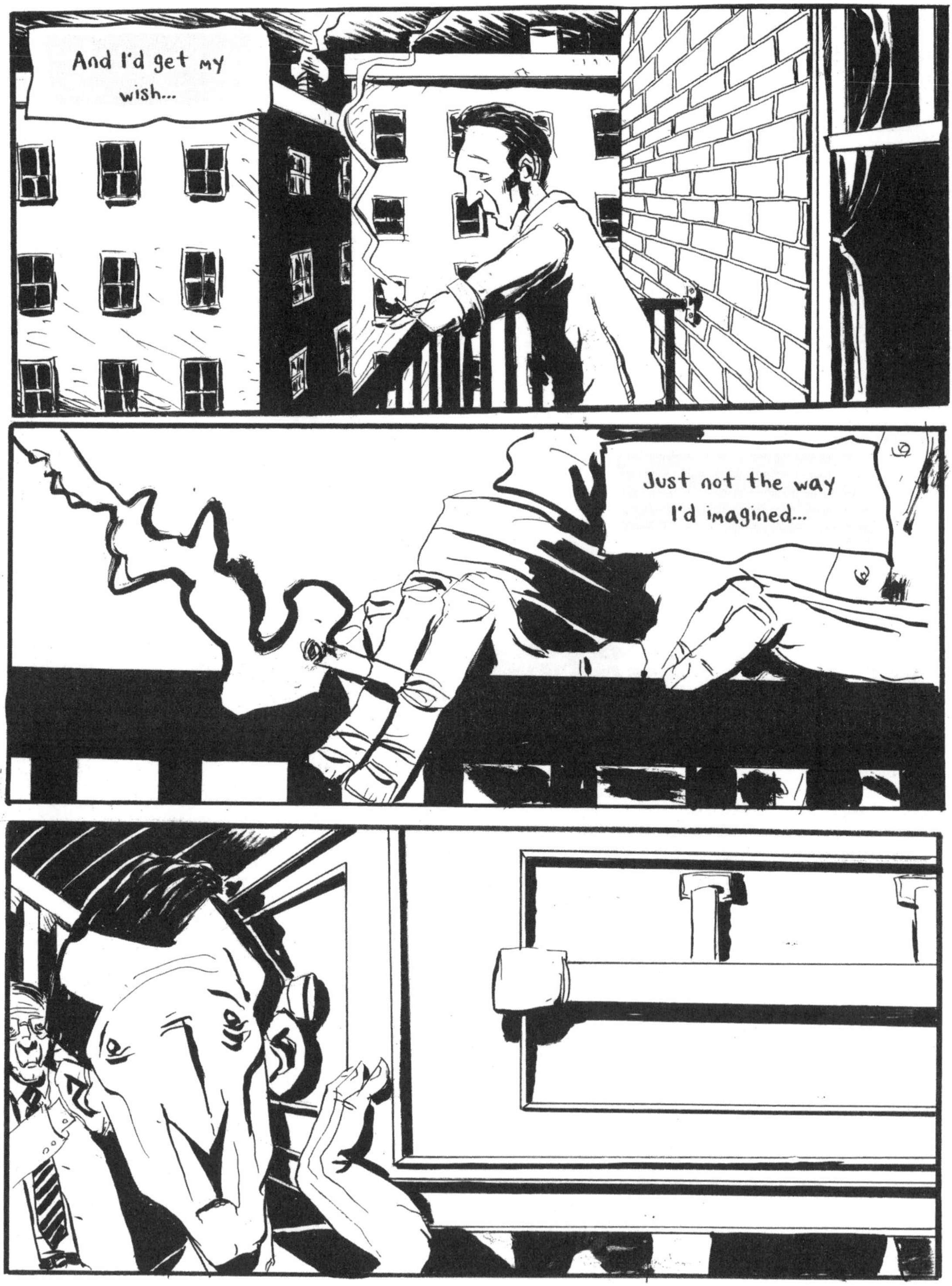
And I'd get my wish...
Just not the way I'd imagined...

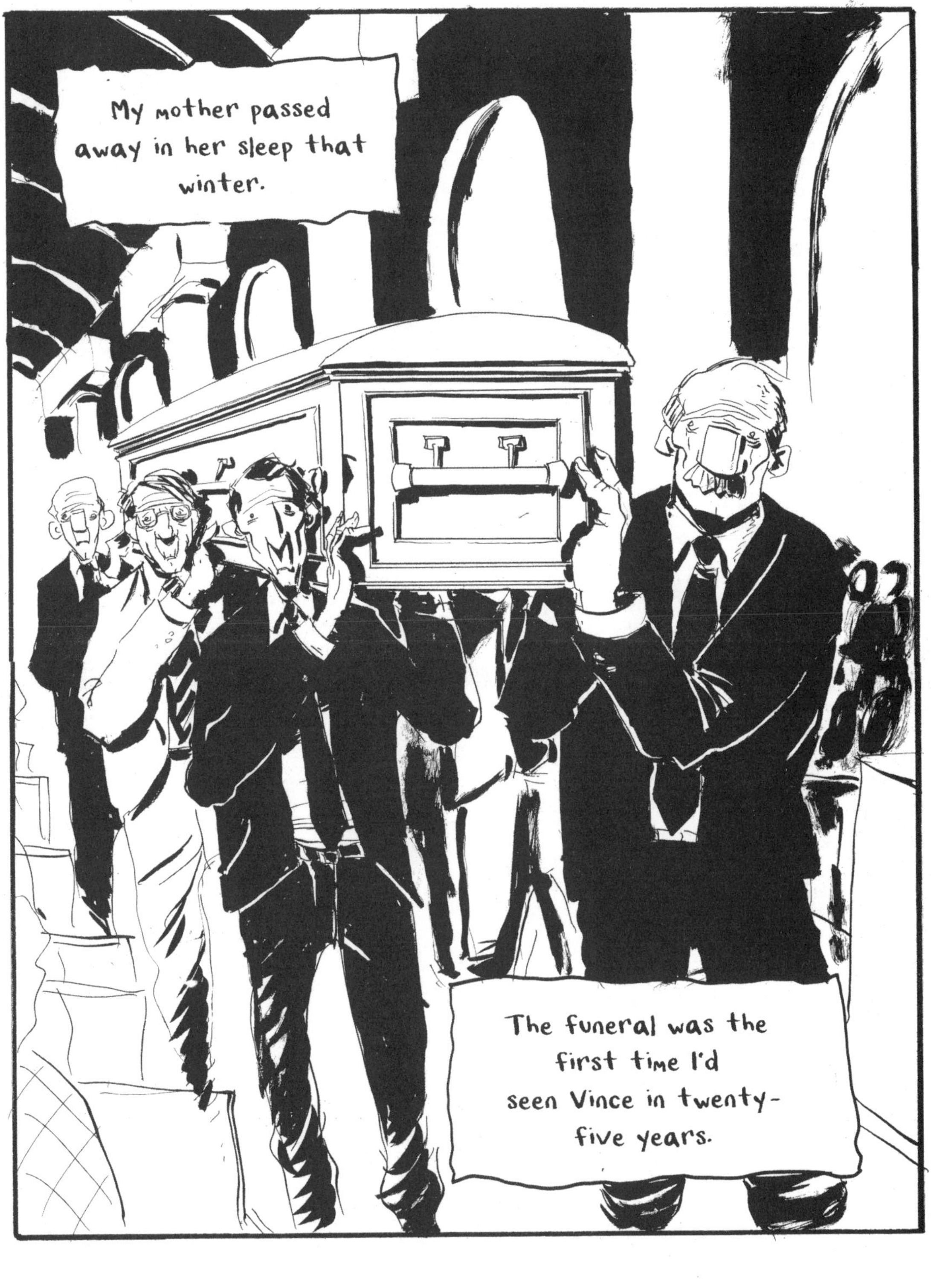
My mother passed away in her sleep that winter.
The funeral was the first time I'd seen Vince in twenty-five years.

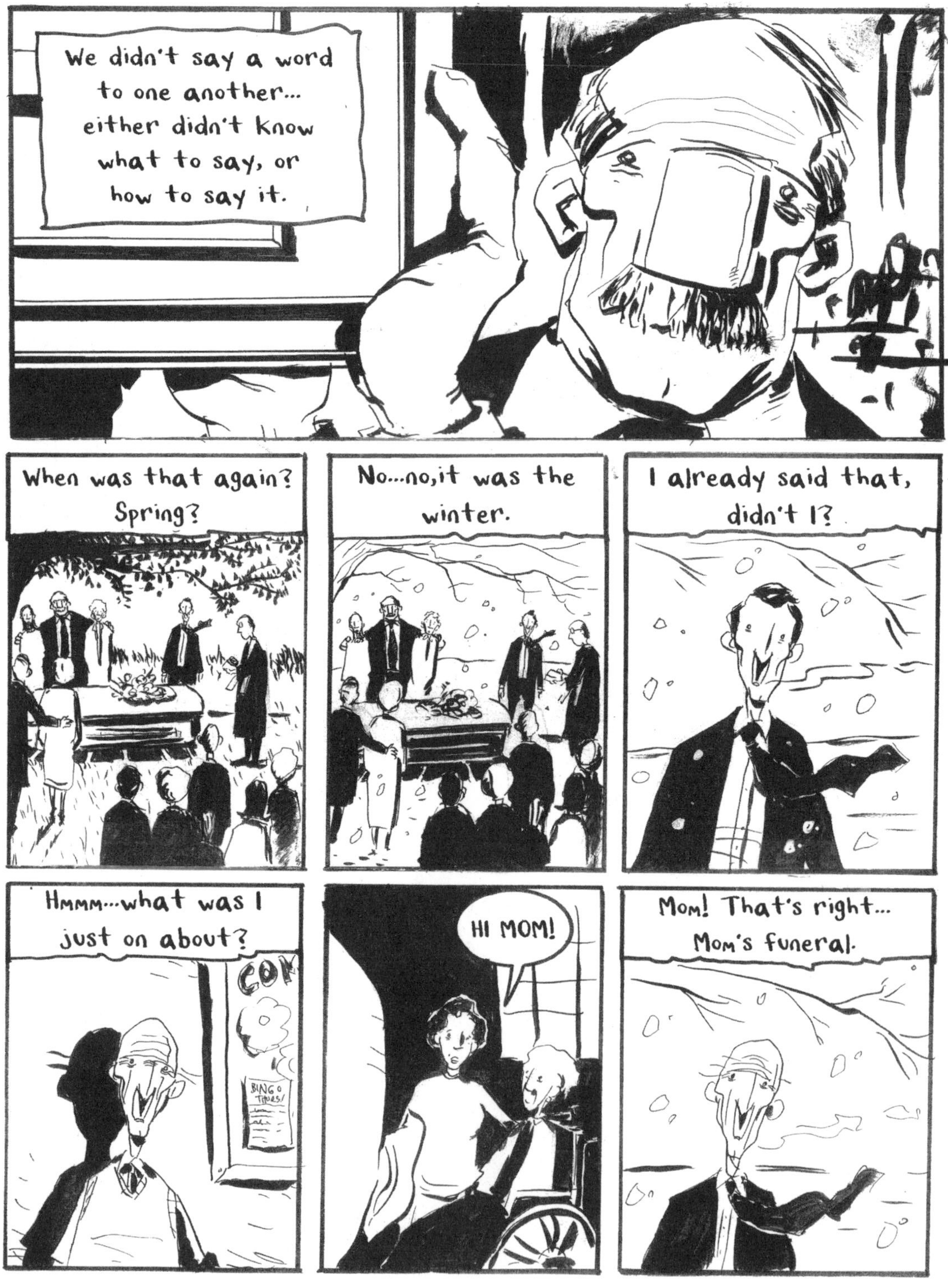
We didn't say a word to one another... either didn't know what to say, or how to say it.
When was that again? Spring?
No...no, it was the winter.
I already said that, didn't I?
Hmmm...what was I just on about?
HI MOM!
Mom! That's right... Mom's funeral.

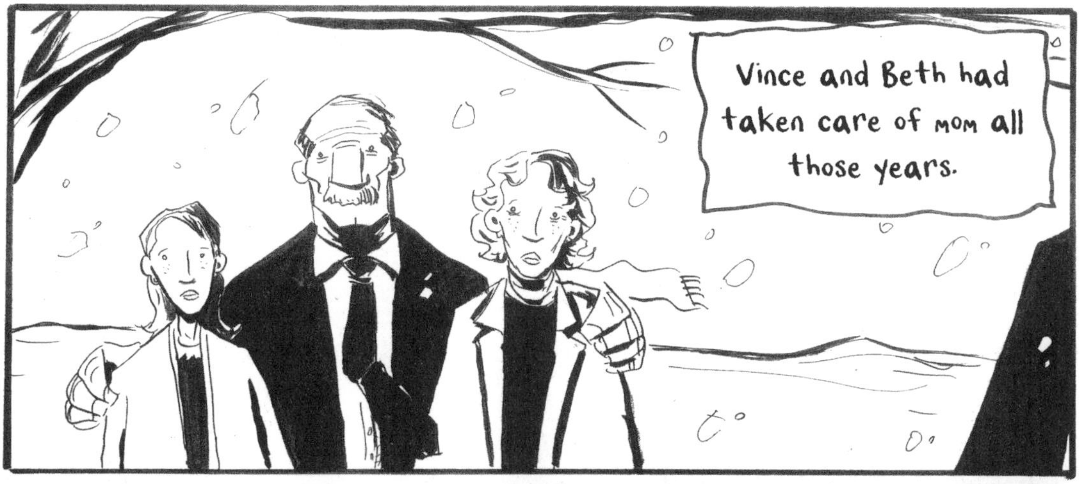
Vince and Beth had taken care of MOM all those years.

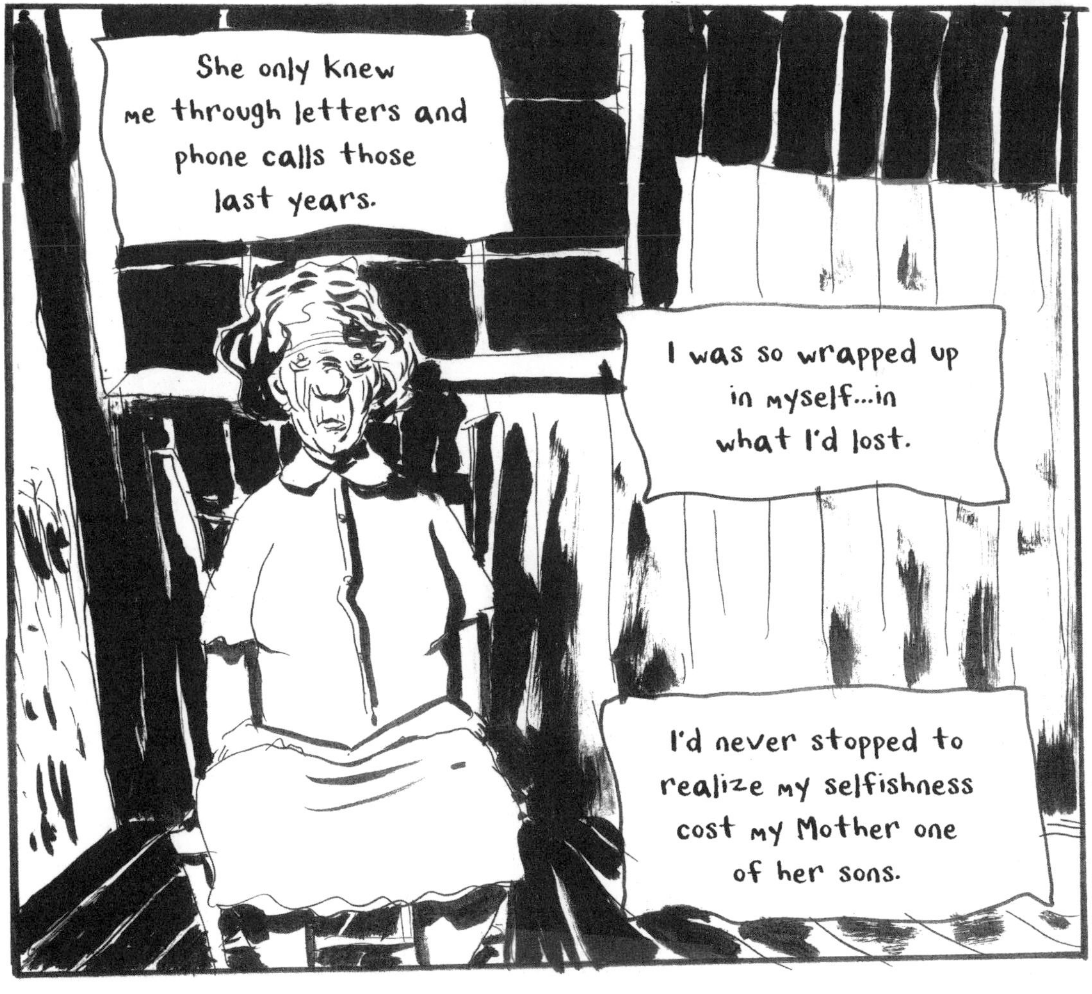
She only knew me through letters and phone calls those last years.
I was so wrapped up in myself...in what I'd lost.
I'd never stopped to realize my selfishness cost my Mother one of her sons.

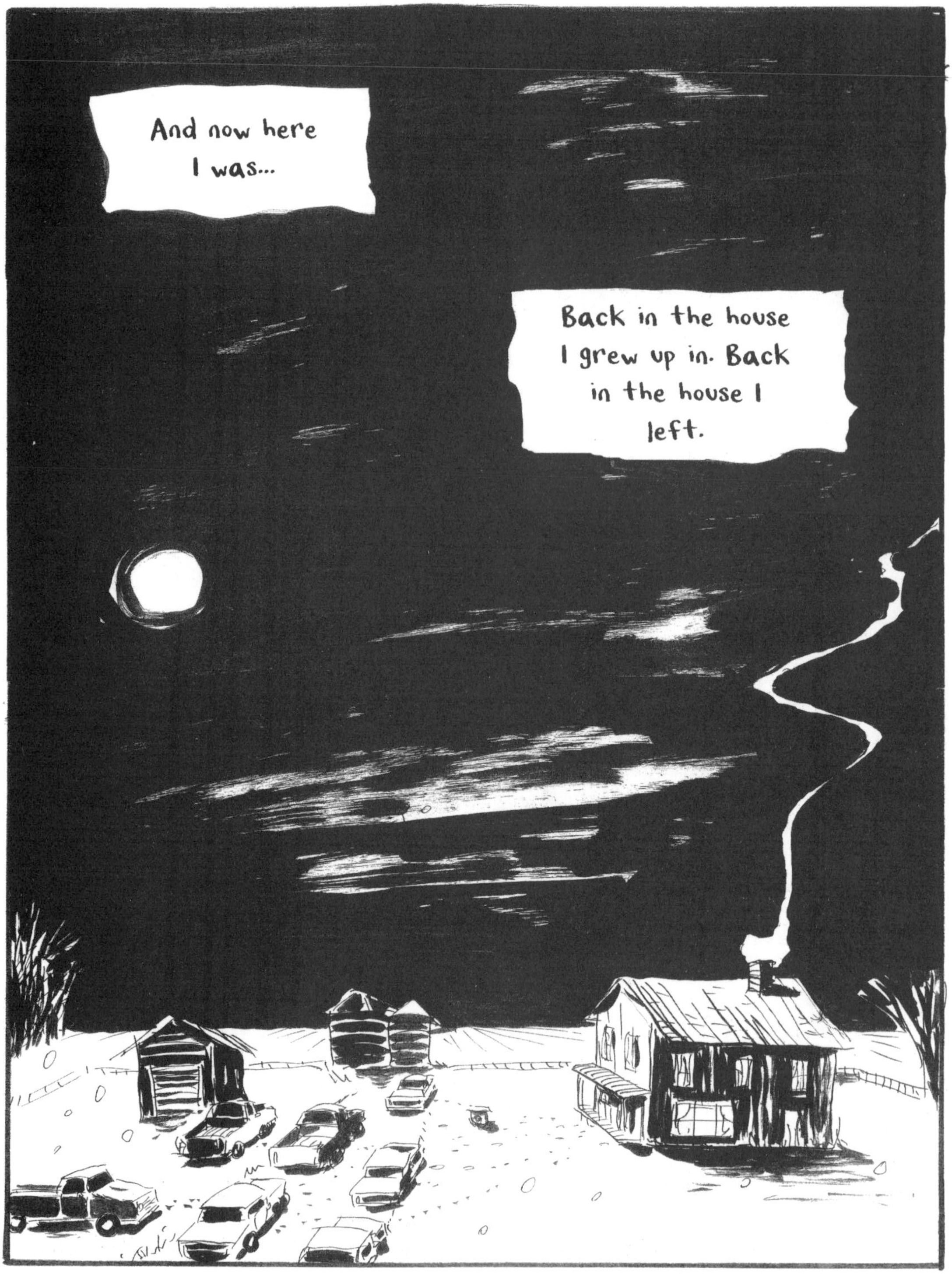
And now here I was...
Back in the house I grew up in. Back in the house I left.

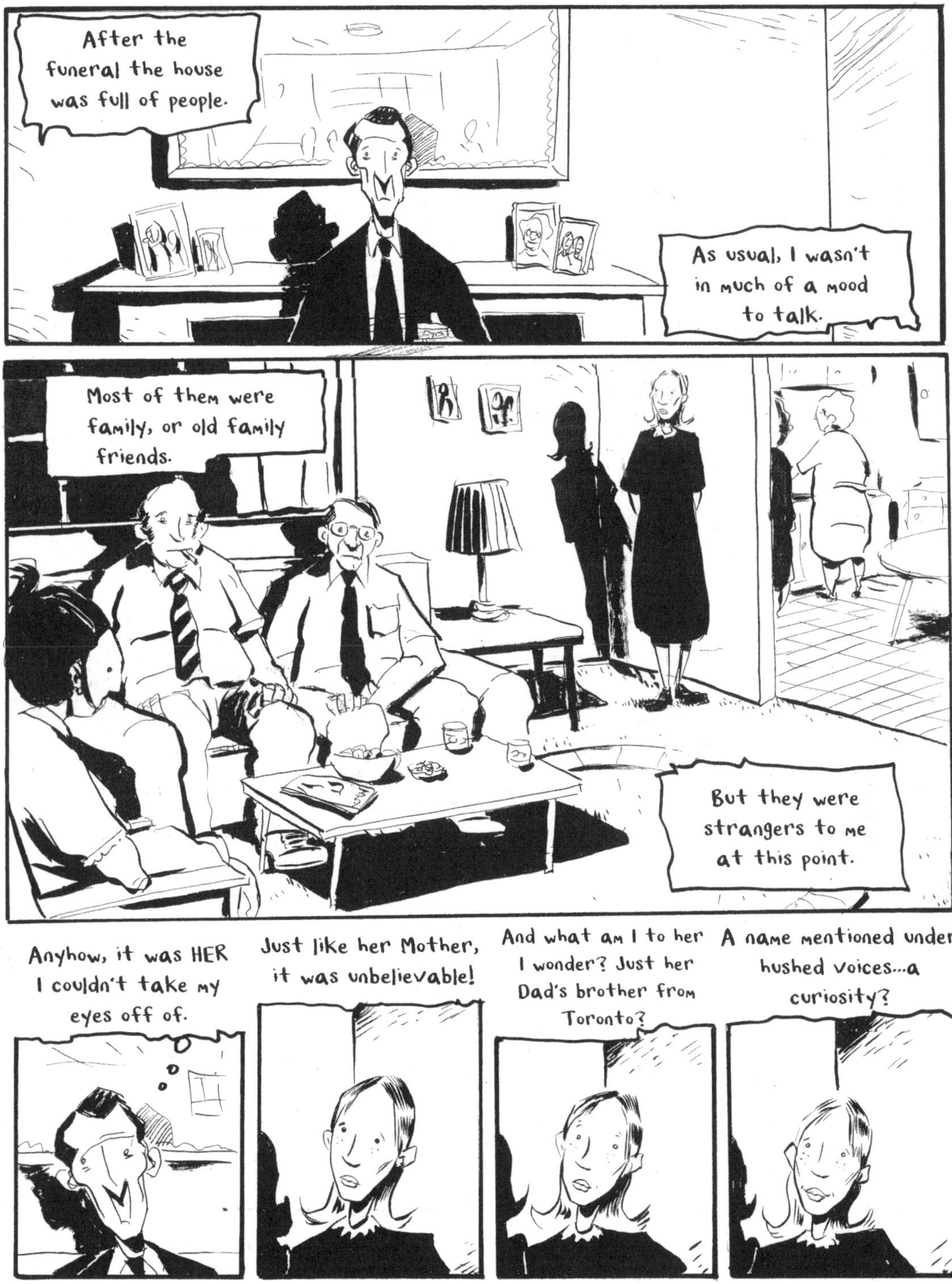
After the funeral the house was full of people.
As usual, I wasn't in much of a mood to talk.
Most of them were family, or old family friends.
But they were strangers to me at this point.
Anyhow, it was HER I couldn't take my eyes off of.
Just like her Mother, it was unbelievable!
And what am I to her I wonder? Just her Dad's brother from Toronto?
A name mentioned under hushed voices...a curiosity?

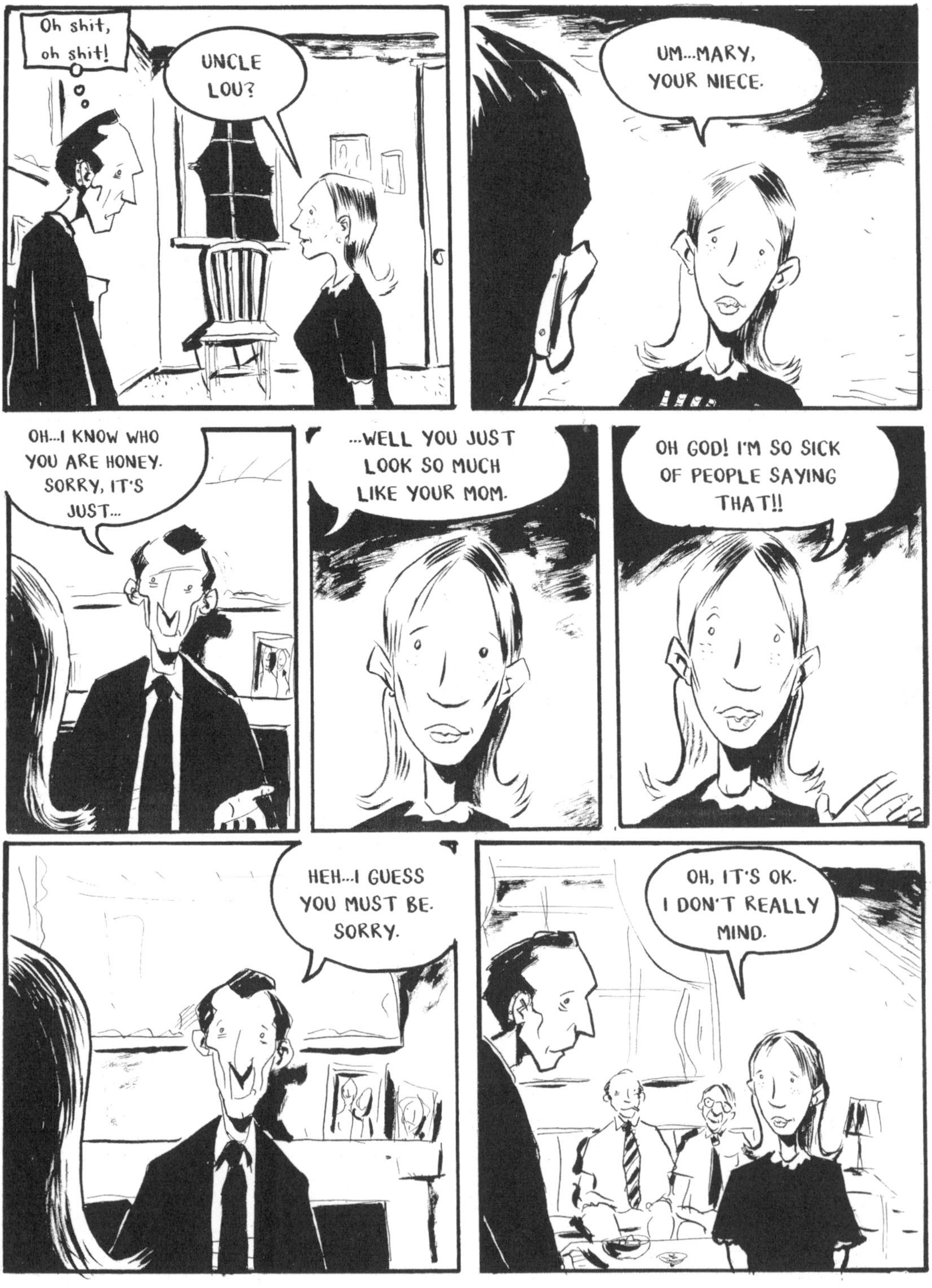
Oh shit,
oh shit!
UNCLE LOU?
UM...MARY, YOUR NIECE.
OH...I KNOW WHO YOU ARE HONEY. SORRY, IT'S JUST...
...WELL YOU JUST LOOK SO MUCH LIKE YOUR MOM.
OH GOD! I'M SO SICK OF PEOPLE SAYING THAT!!
HEH...I GUESS YOU MUST BE. SORRY.
OH, IT'S OK. I DON'T REALLY MIND.

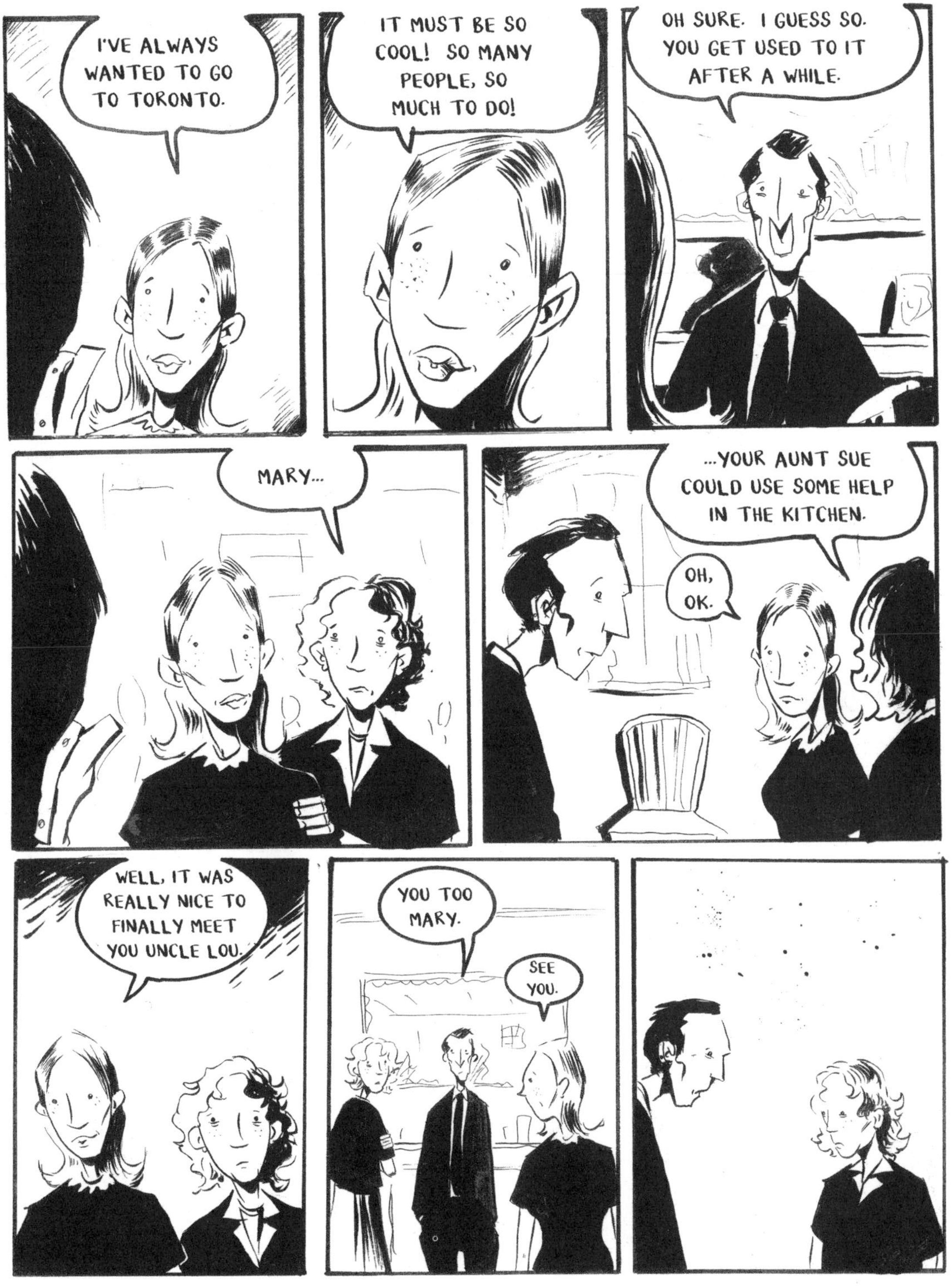
I'VE ALWAYS WANTED TO GO TO TORONTO.
IT MUST BE SO COOL! SO MANY PEOPLE, SO MUCH TO DO!
OH SURE. I GUESS SO. YOU GET USED TO IT AFTER A WHILE.
MARY...
...YOUR AUNT SUE COULD USE SOME HELP IN THE KITCHEN.
OH, OK.
WELL, IT WAS REALLY NICE TO FINALLY MEET YOU UNCLE LOU.
YOU TOO MARY.
SEE YOU.

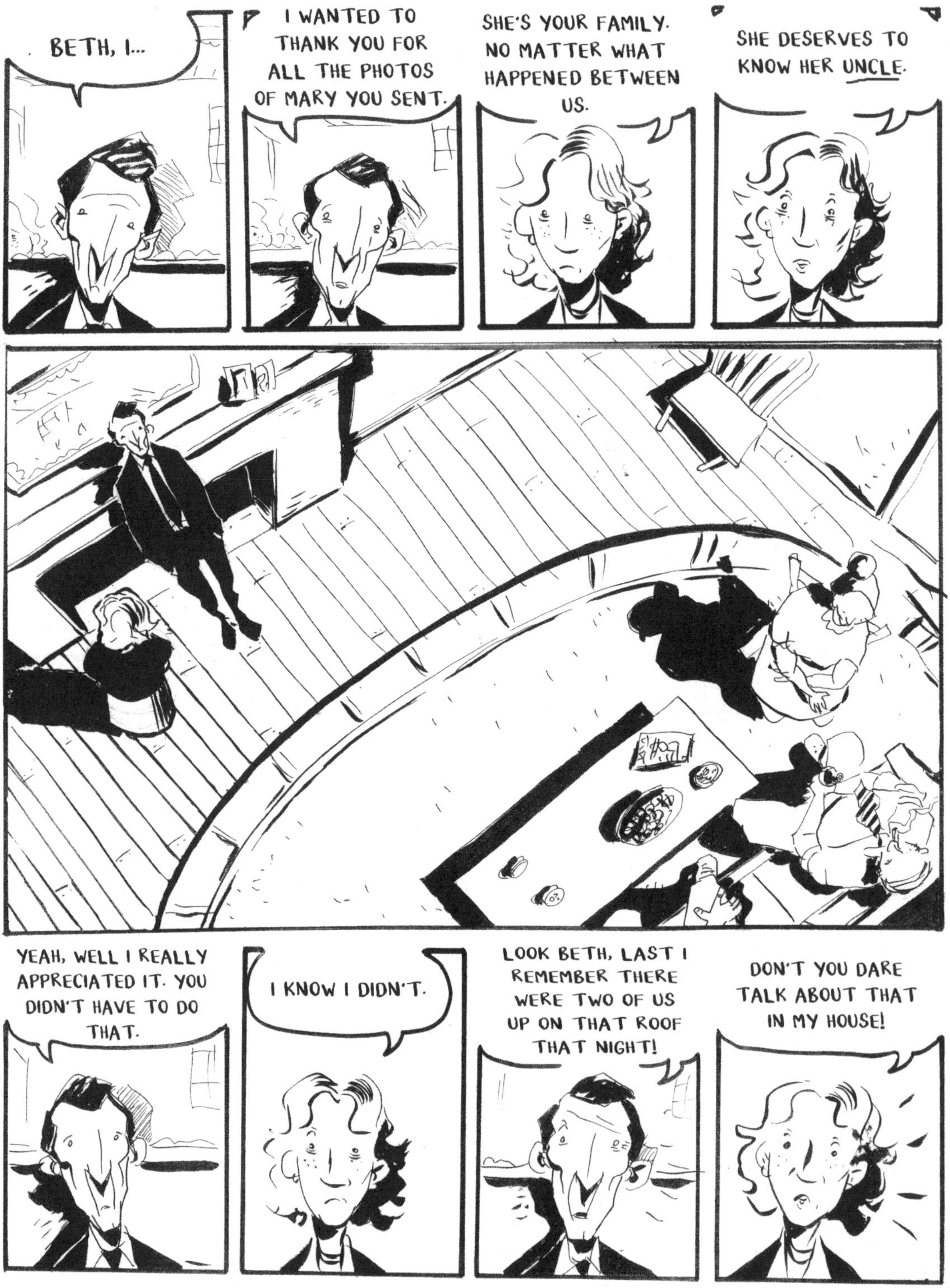
BETH, I...
I WANTED TO THANK YOU FOR ALL THE PHOTOS OF MARY YOU SENT.
SHE'S YOUR FAMILY. NO MATTER WHAT HAPPENED BETWEEN US.
SHE DESERVES TO KNOW HER UNCLE.
YEAH, WELL I REALLY APPRECIATED IT. YOU DIDN'T HAVE TO DO THAT.
I KNOW I DIDN'T.
LOOK BETH, LAST I REMEMBER THERE WERE TWO OF US UP ON THAT ROOF THAT NIGHT!
DON'T YOU DARE TALK ABOUT THAT IN MY HOUSE!

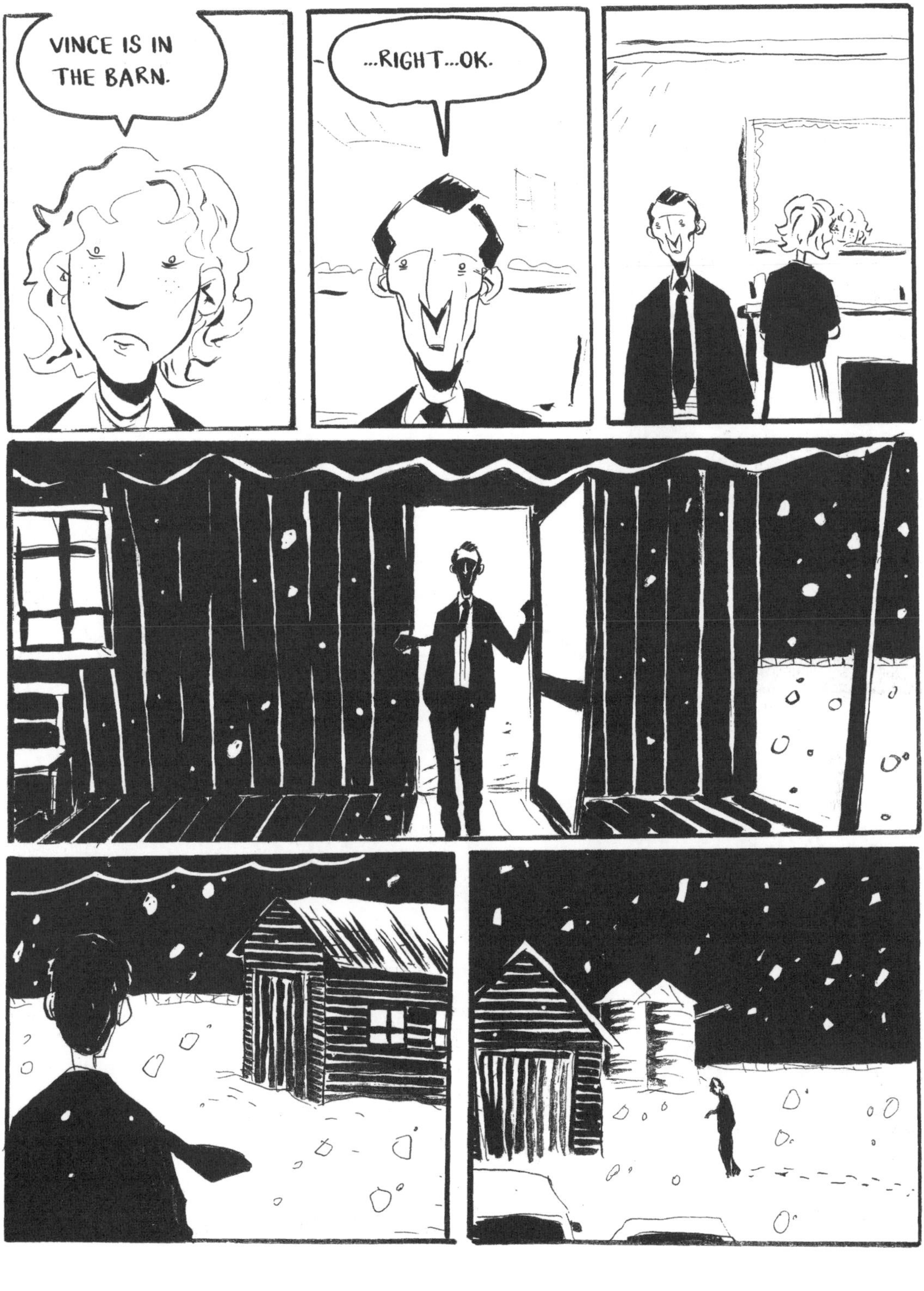
VINCE IS IN THE BARN.
...RIGHT...OK.

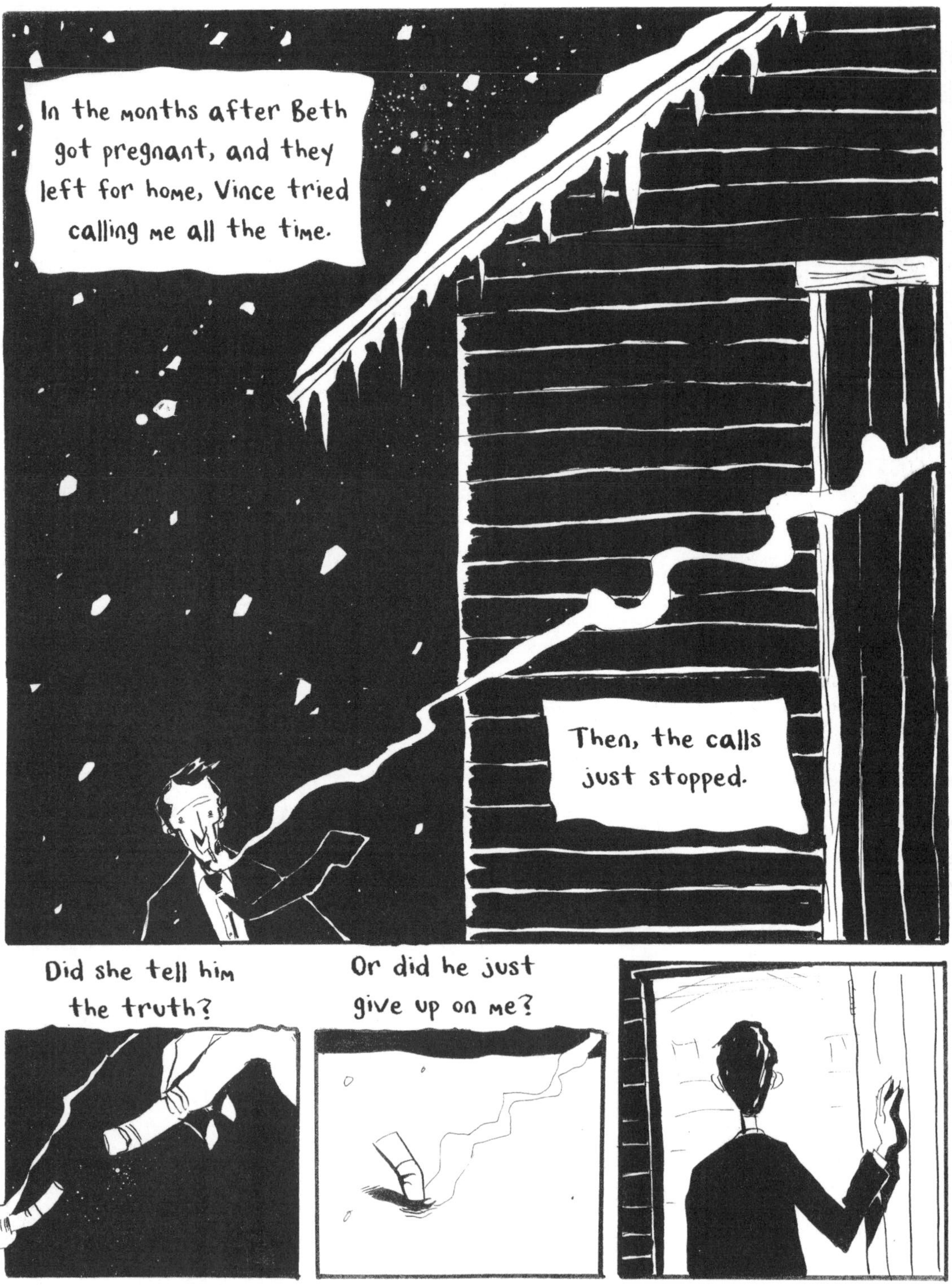
In the months after Beth got pregnant, and they left for home, Vince tried calling me all the time.
Then, the calls just stopped.
Did she tell him the truth?
Or did he just give up on me?

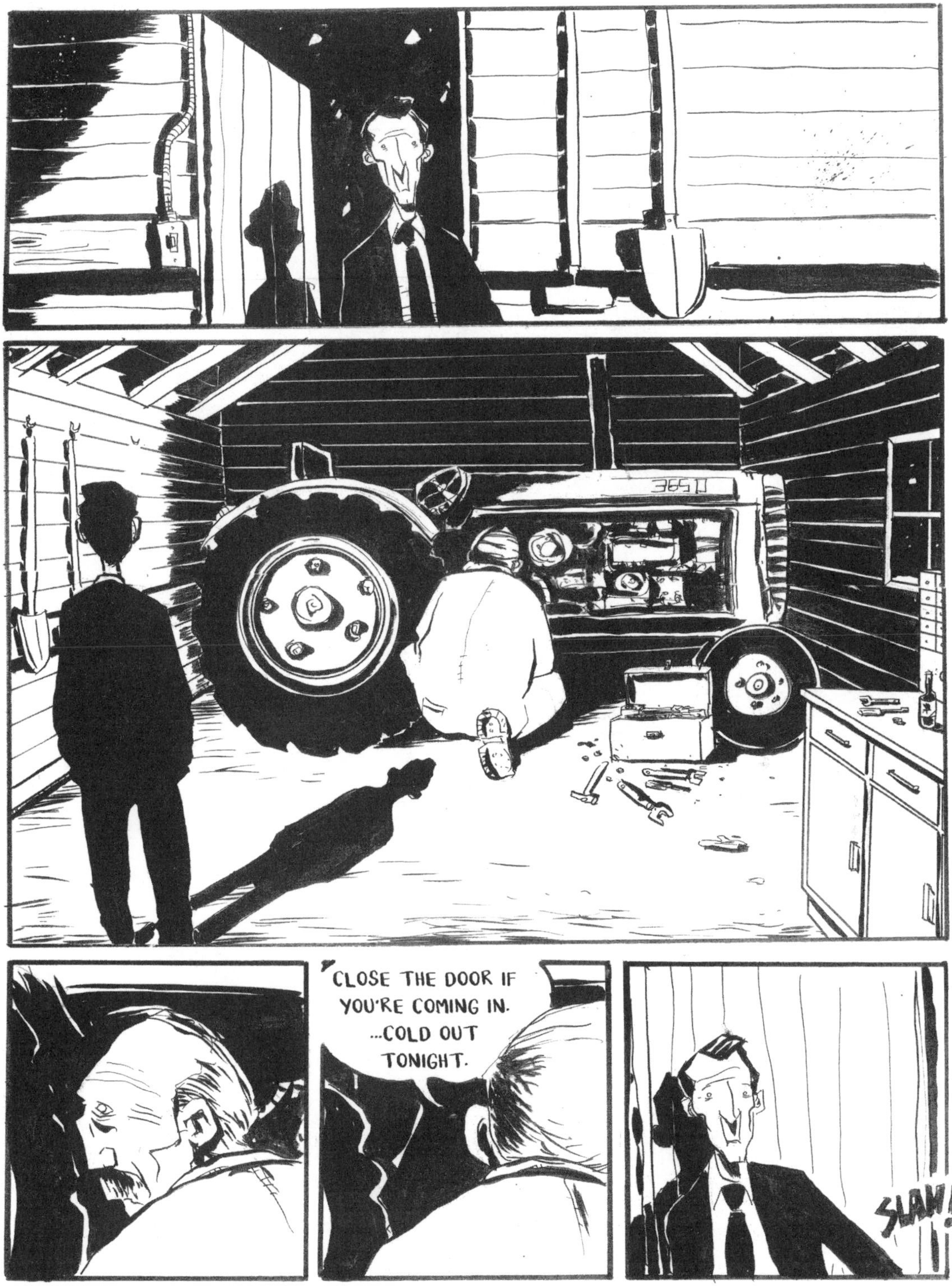
CLOSE THE DOOR IF YOU'RE COMING IN. ...COLD OUT TONIGHT.
SLAM!

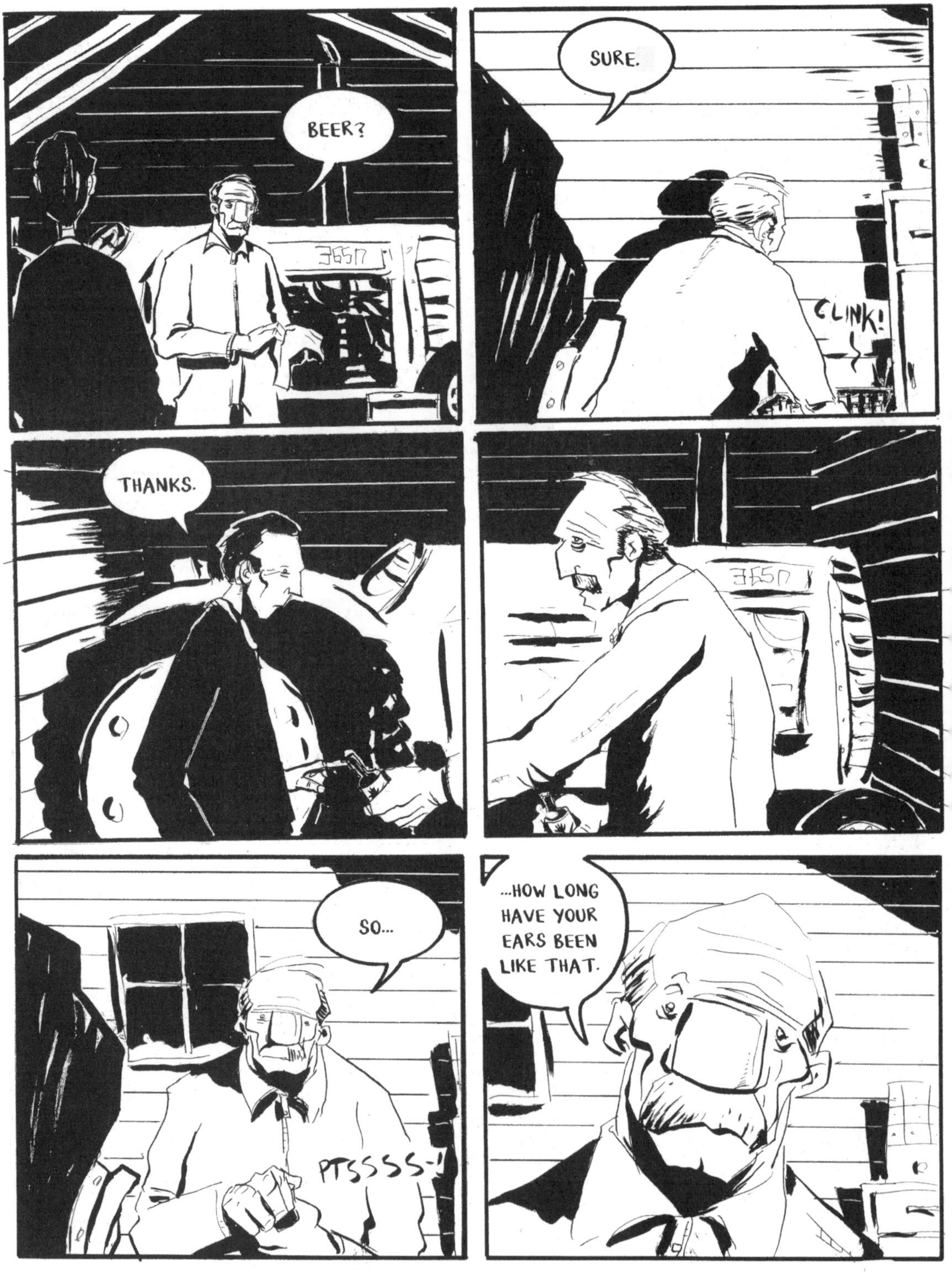
BEER?
SURE.
CLINK!
THANKS.
SO...
PTSSSS-!
...HOW LONG HAVE YOUR EARS BEEN LIKE THAT.

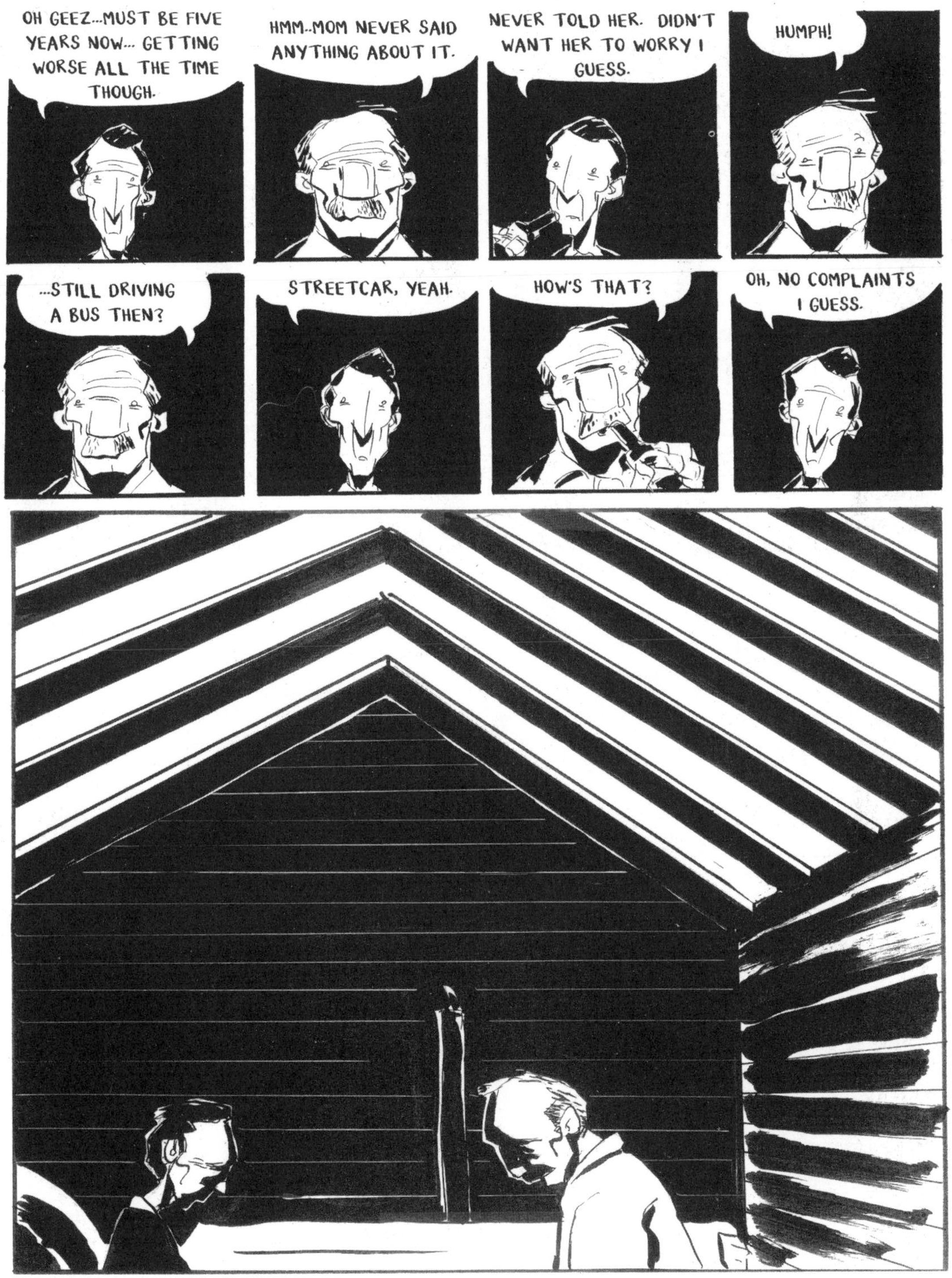
OH GEEZ...MUST BE FIVE YEARS NOW... GETTING WORSE ALL THE TIME THOUGH.
HMM..MOM NEVER SAID ANYTHING ABOUT IT.
NEVER TOLD HER. DIDN'T WANT HER TO WORRY I GUESS.
HUMPH!
...STILL DRIVING A BUS THEN?
STREETCAR, YEAH.
HOW'S THAT?
OH, NO COMPLAINTS I GUESS.

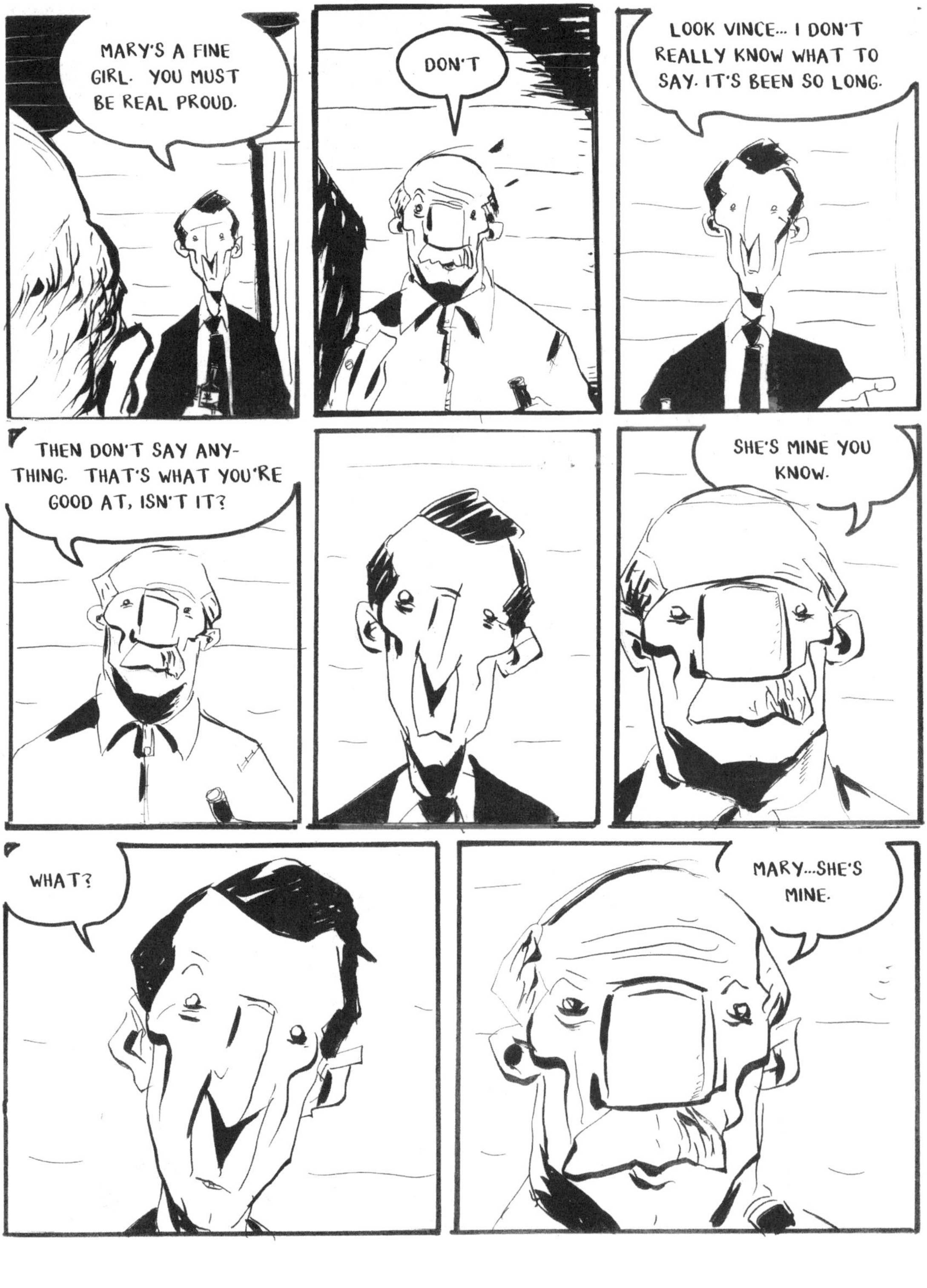
MARY'S A FINE GIRL. YOU MUST BE REAL PROUD.
DON'T
LOOK VINCE... I DON'T REALLY KNOW WHAT TO SAY. IT'S BEEN SO LONG.
THEN DON'T SAY ANY-THING. THAT'S WHAT YOU'RE GOOD AT, ISN'T IT?
SHE'S MINE YOU KNOW.
WHAT?
MARY...SHE'S MINE.

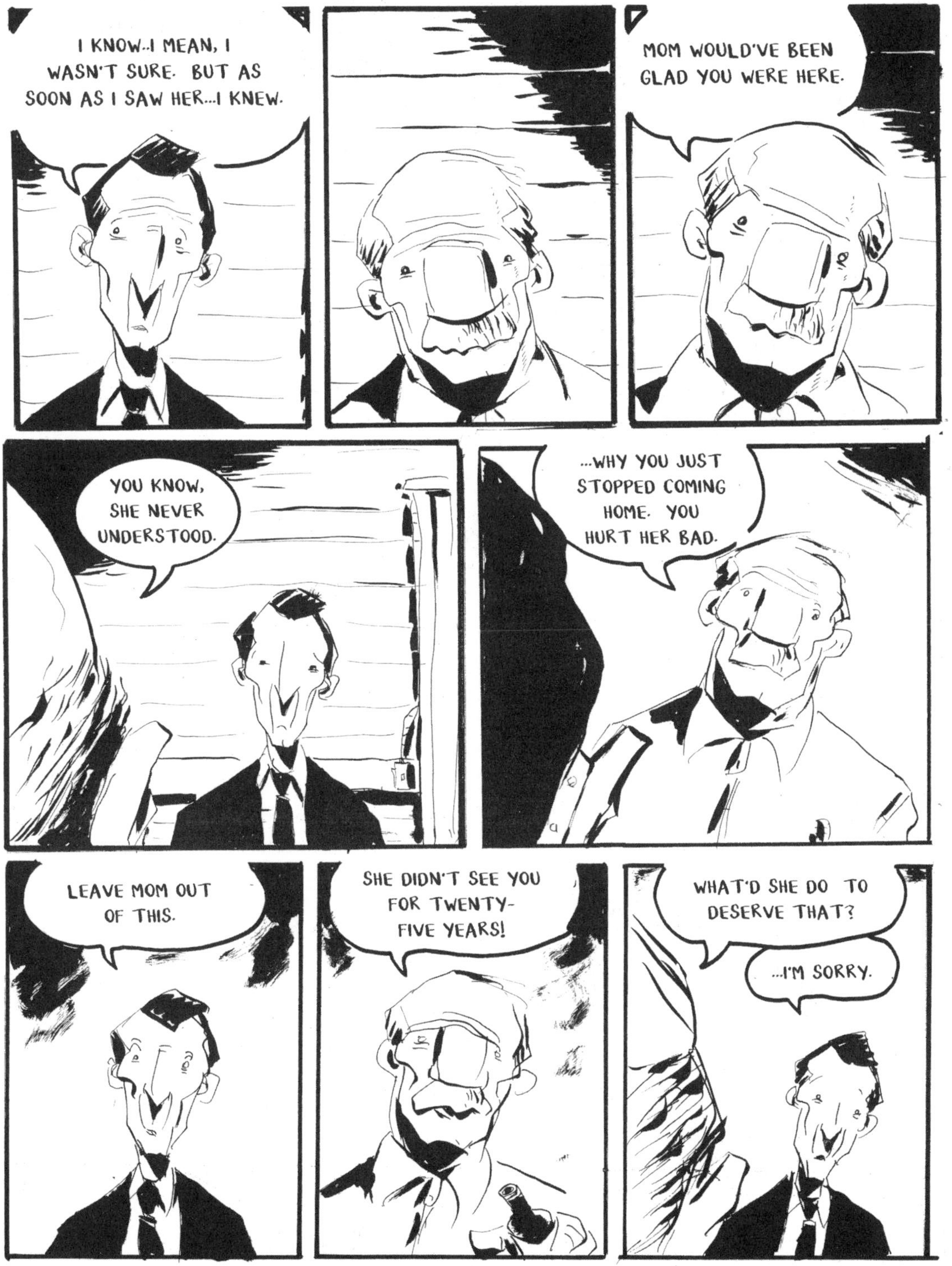
I KNOW..I MEAN, I WASN'T SURE. BUT AS SOON AS I SAW HER...I KNEW.
MOM WOULD'VE BEEN GLAD YOU WERE HERE.
YOU KNOW, SHE NEVER UNDERSTOOD.
...WHY YOU JUST STOPPED COMING HOME. YOU HURT HER BAD.
LEAVE MOM OUT OF THIS.
SHE DIDN'T SEE YOU FOR TWENTY-FIVE YEARS!
WHAT'D SHE DO TO DESERVE THAT?
...I'M SORRY.

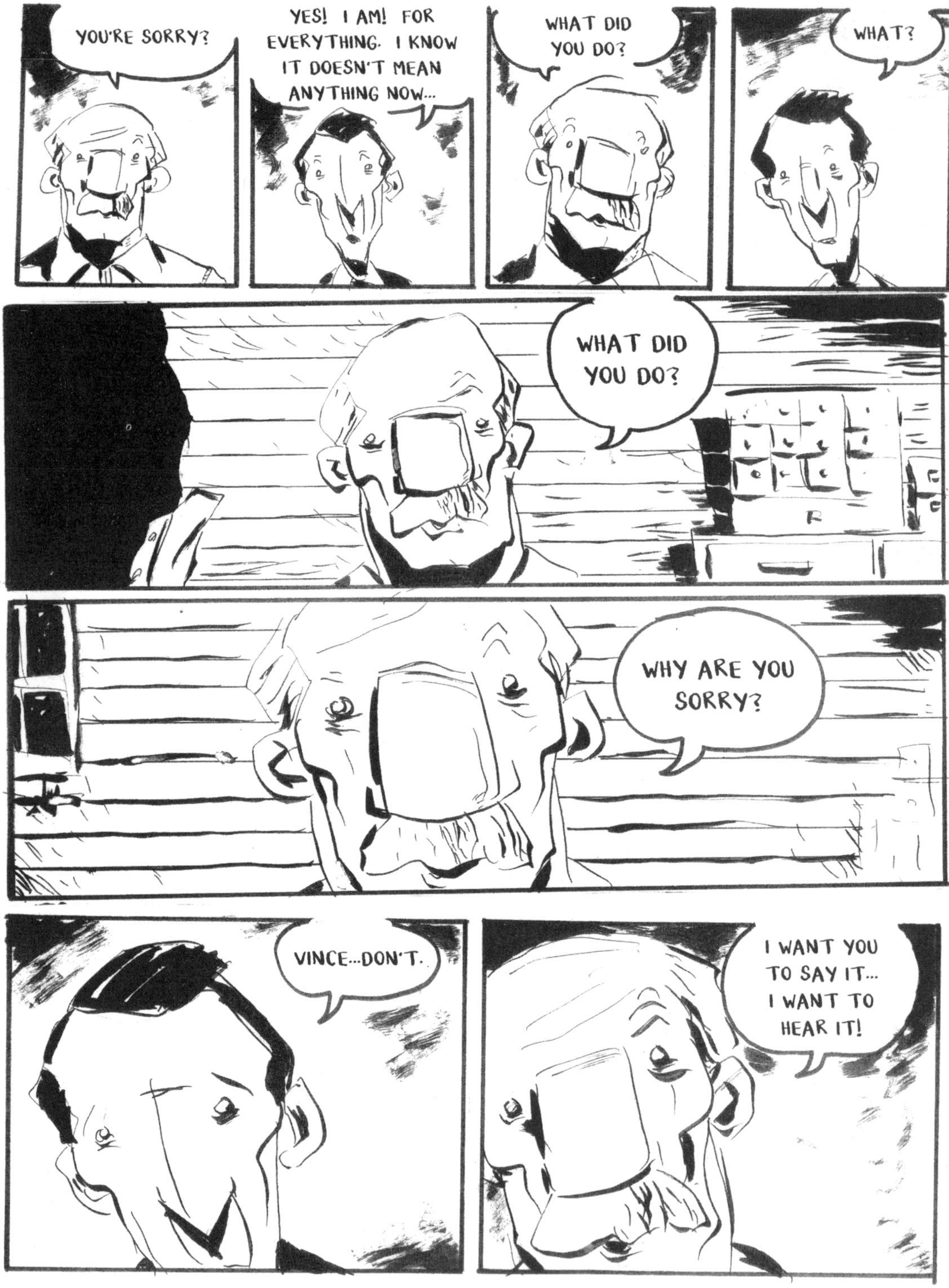
YOU'RE SORRY?
YES! I AM! FOR EVERYTHING. I KNOW IT DOESN'T MEAN ANYTHING NOW...
WHAT DID YOU DO?
WHAT?
WHAT DID YOU DO?
WHY ARE YOU SORRY?
VINCE...DON'T.
I WANT YOU TO SAY IT... I WANT TO HEAR IT!

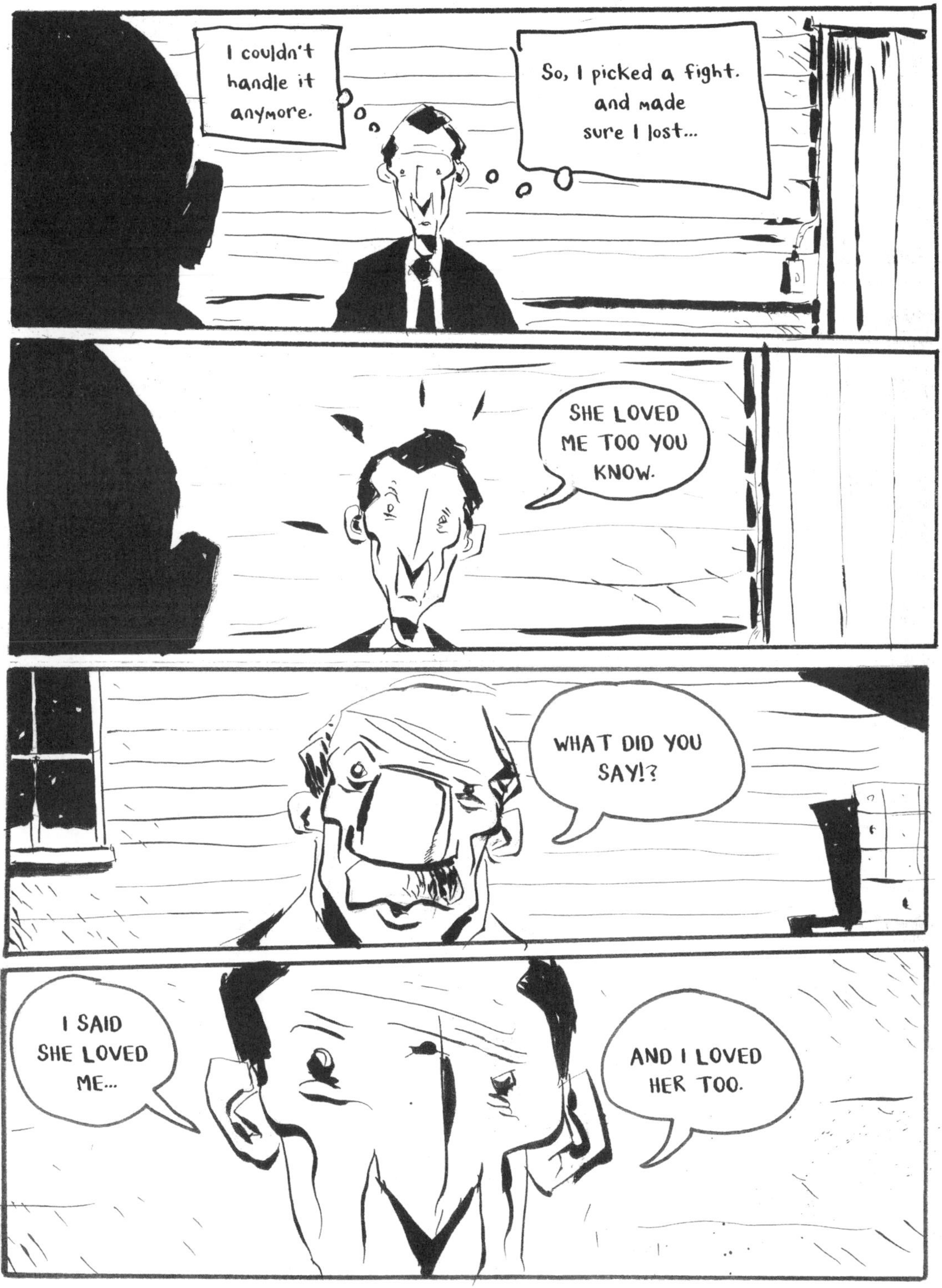
I couldn't handle it anymore.
So, I picked a fight. and made sure I lost...
SHE LOVED ME TOO YOU KNOW.
WHAT DID YOU SAY!?
I SAID SHE LOVED ME...
AND I LOVED HER TOO.

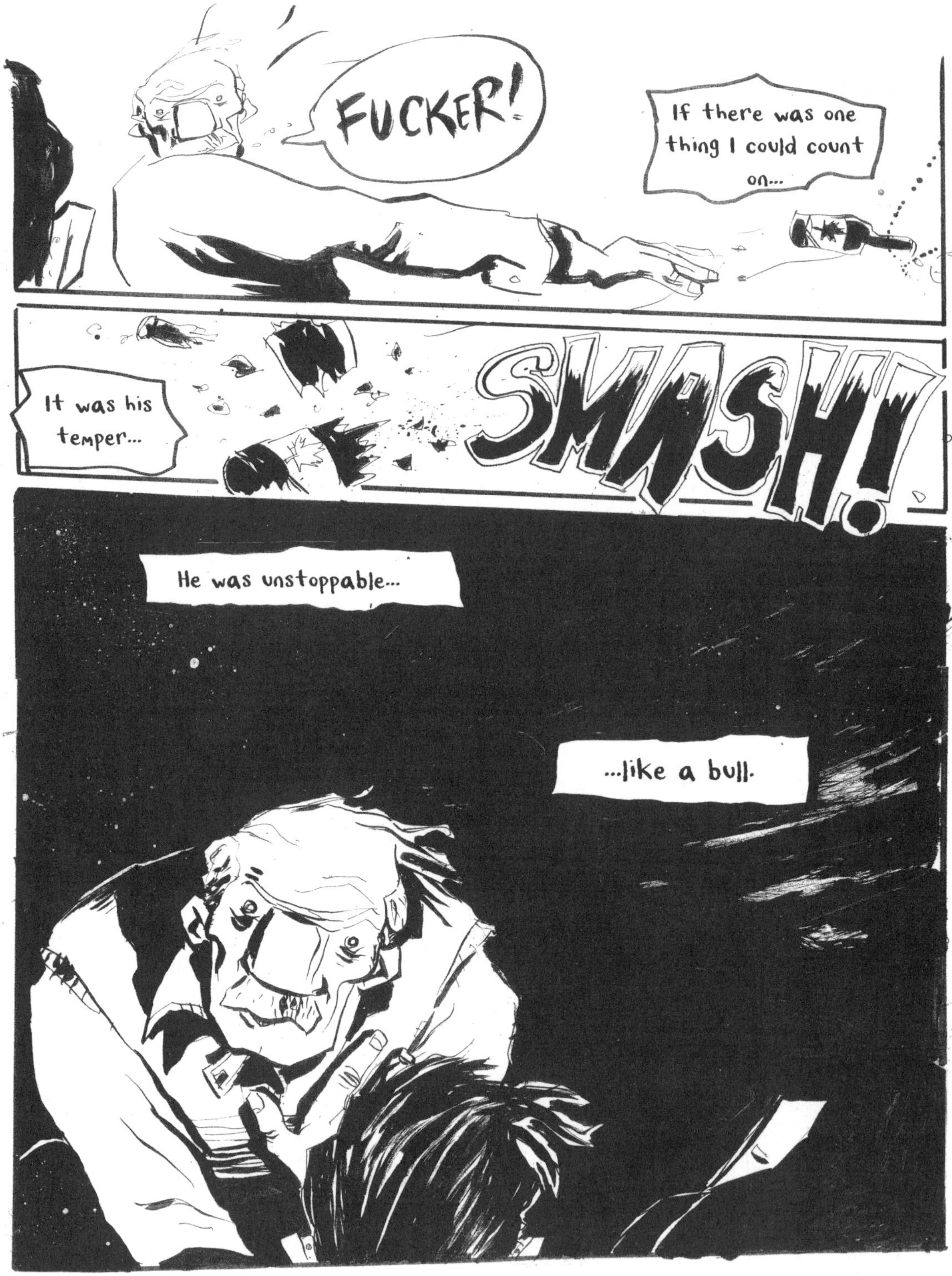
FUCKER!
If there was one thing I could count on...
It was his temper...
SMASH!
He was unstoppable...
...like a bull.

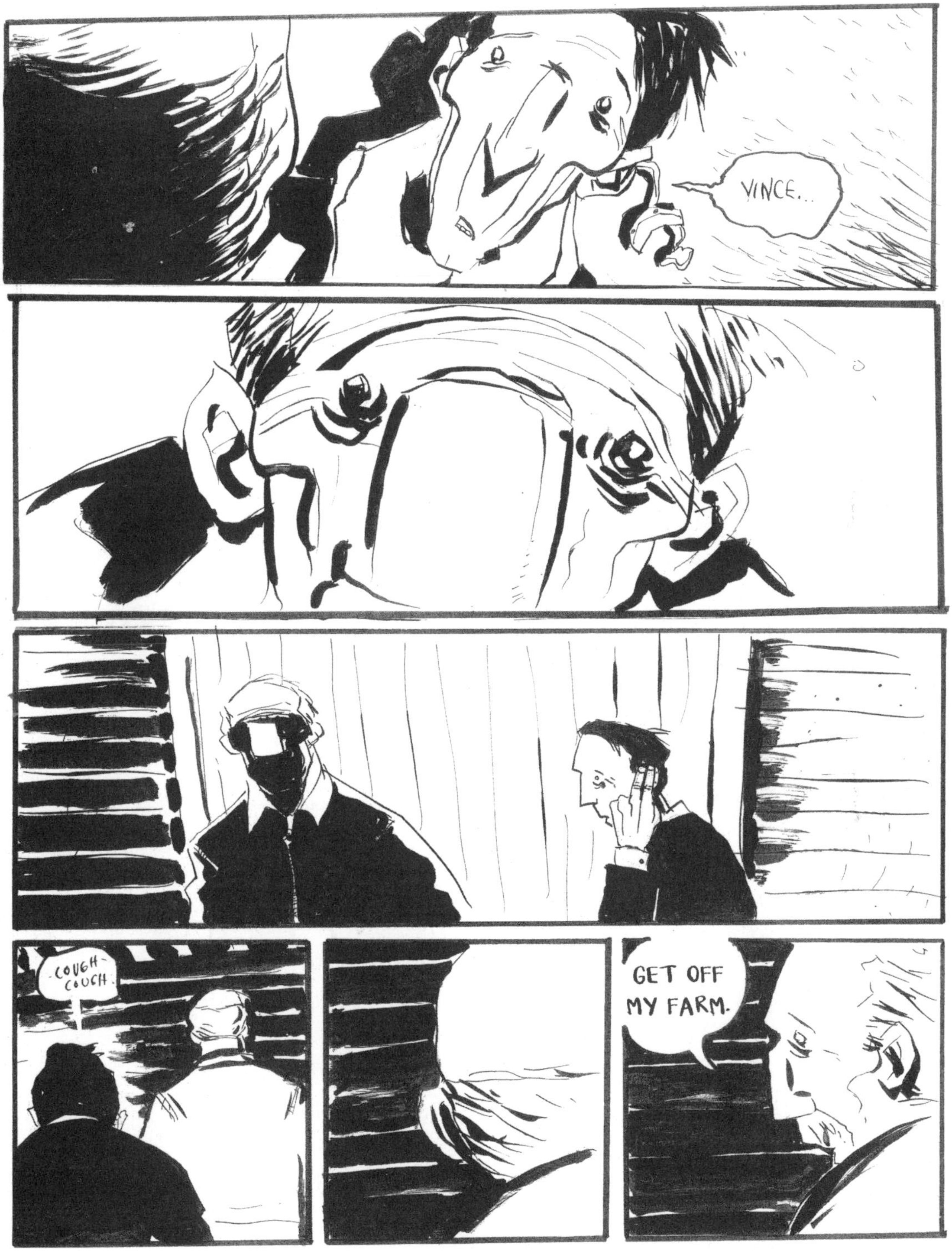
VINCE...
-COUGH-
COUGH-
GET OFF
MY FARM.

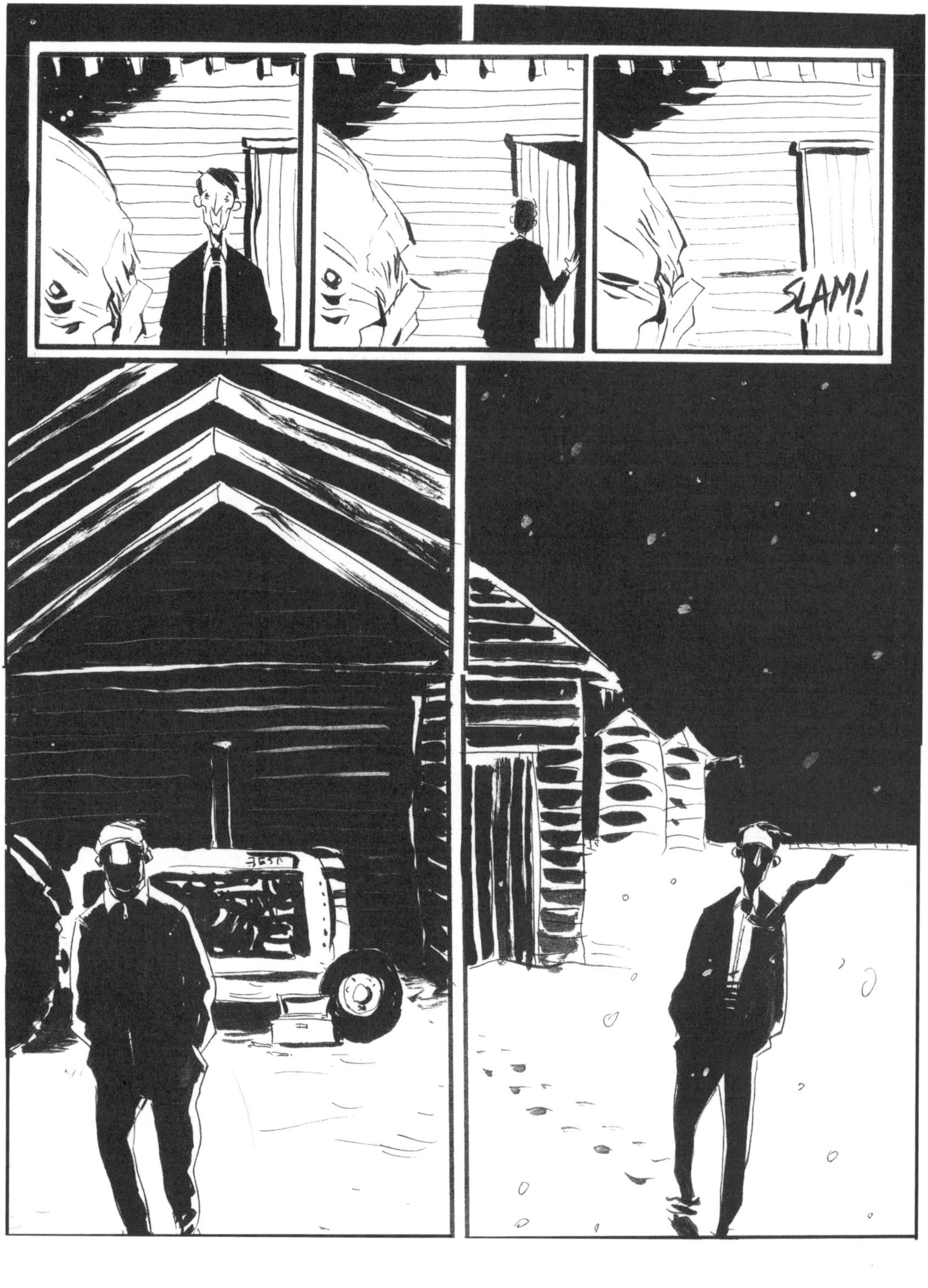
SLAM!

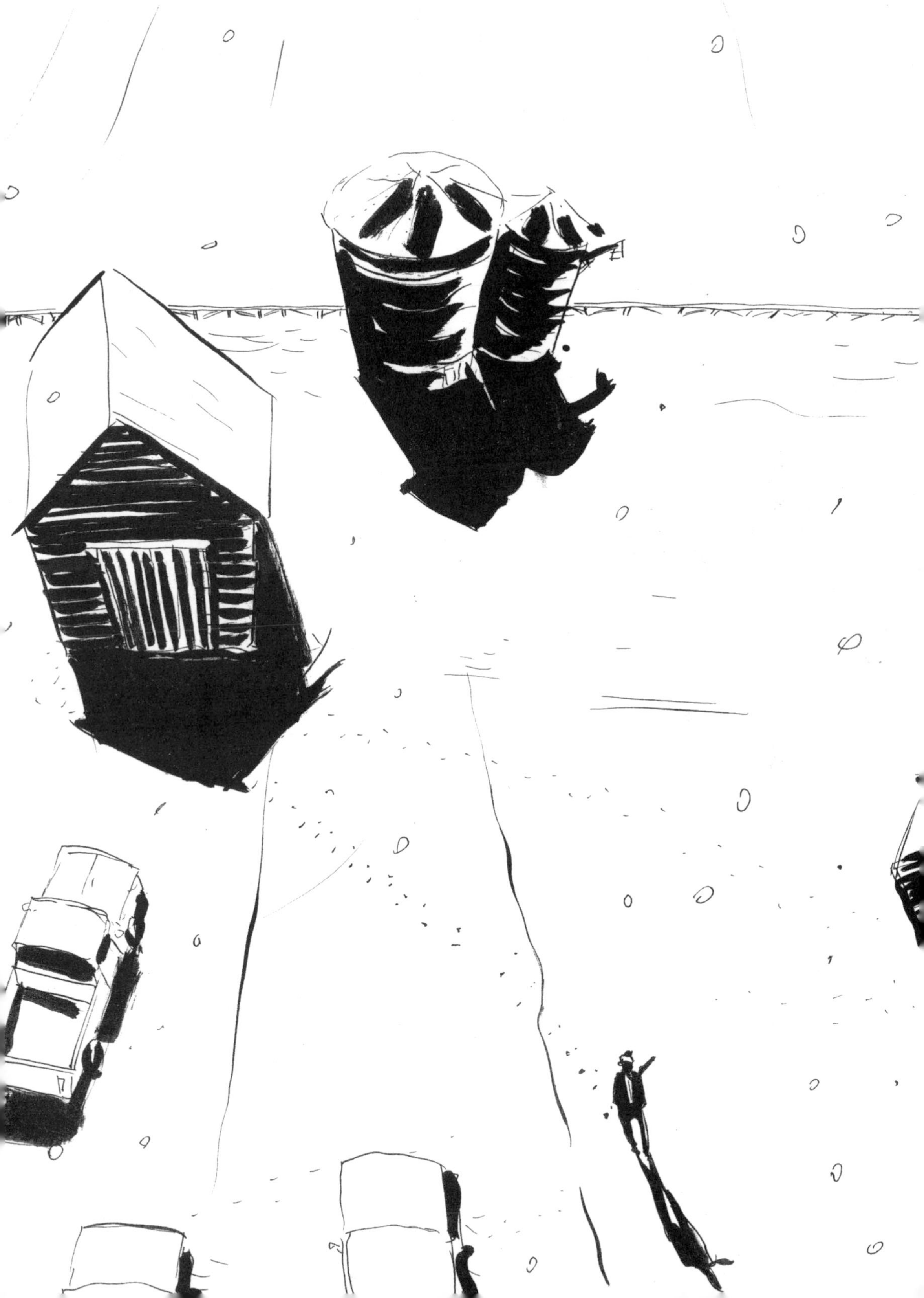

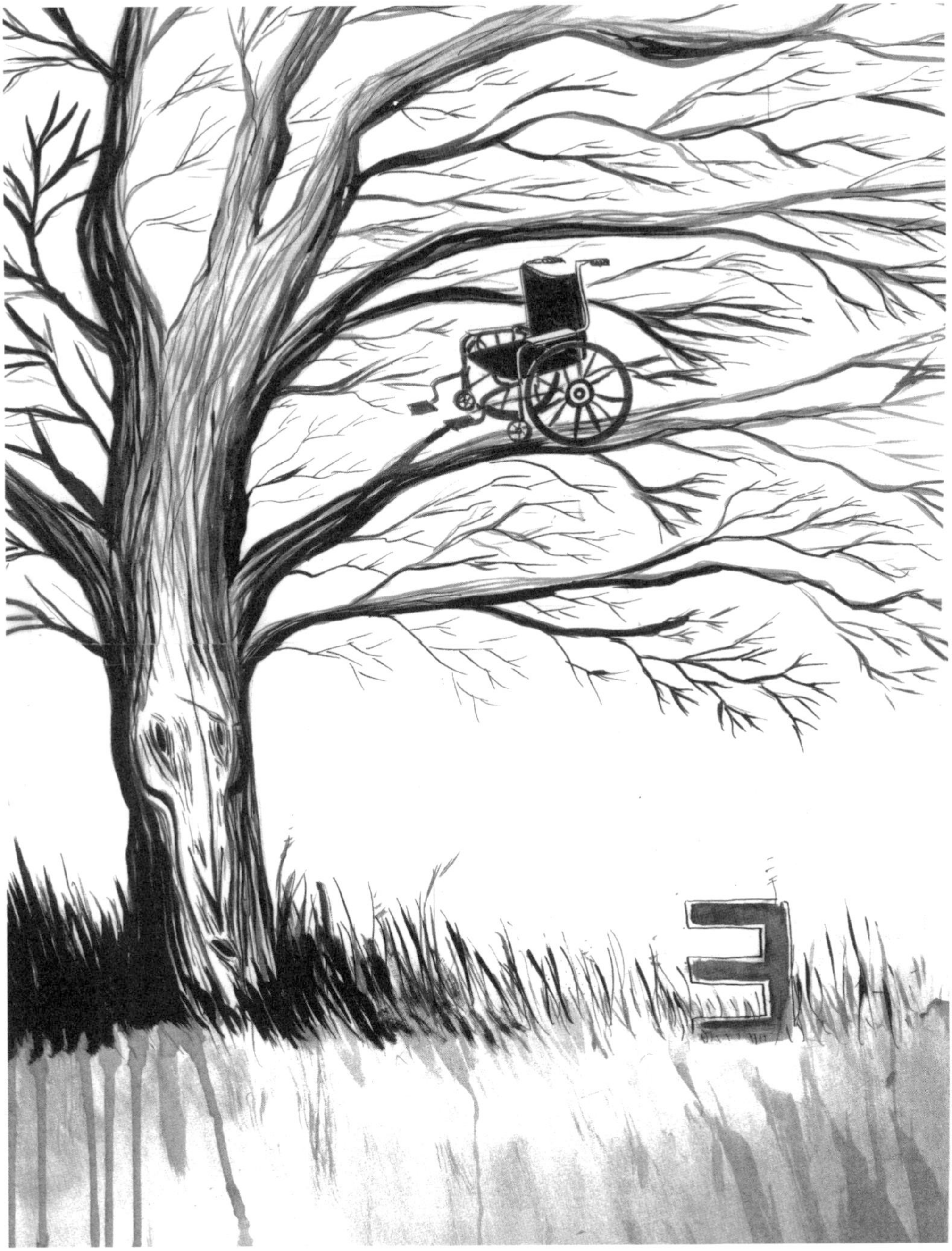
3

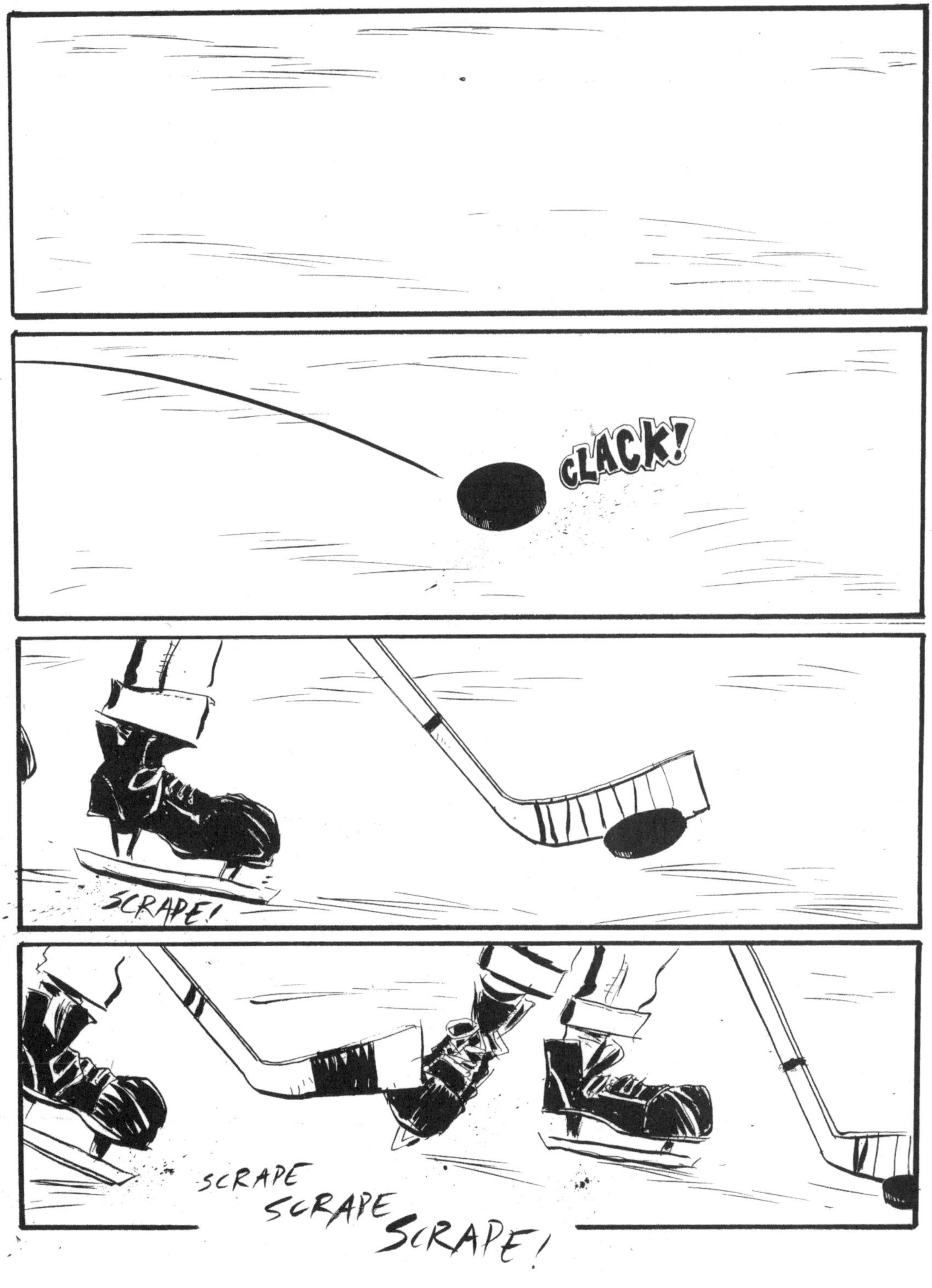
CLACK!
SCRAPE!
SCRAPE
SCRAPE
SCRAPE!

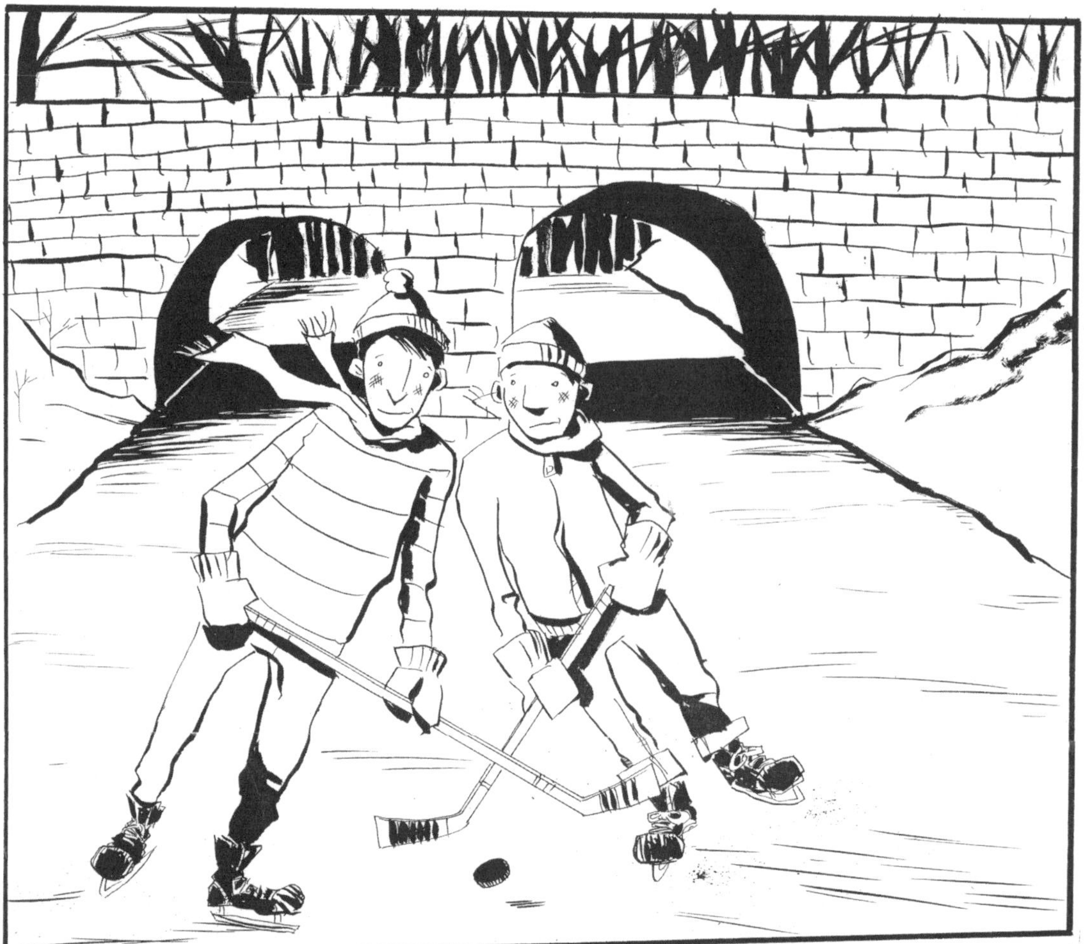

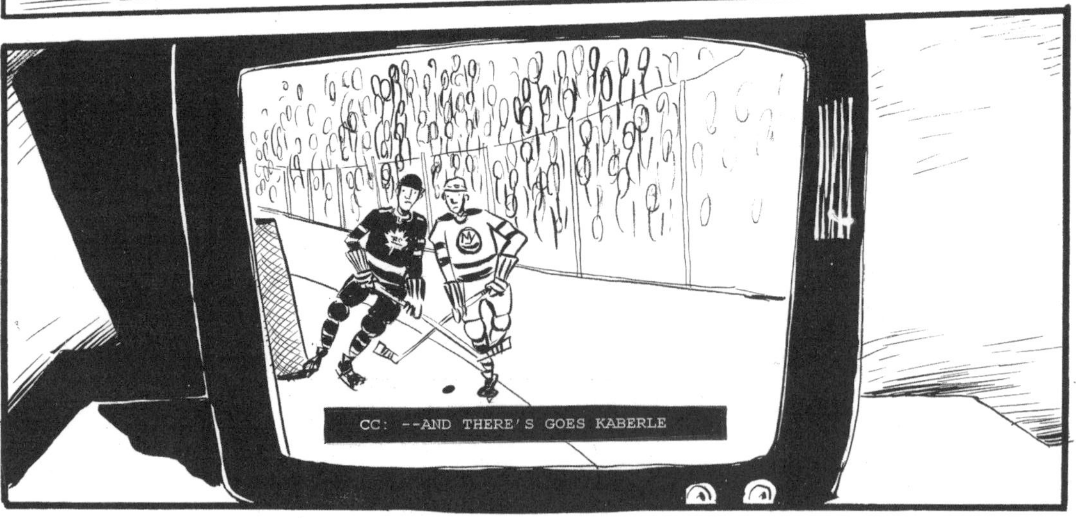
CC: --AND THERE'S GOES KABERLE

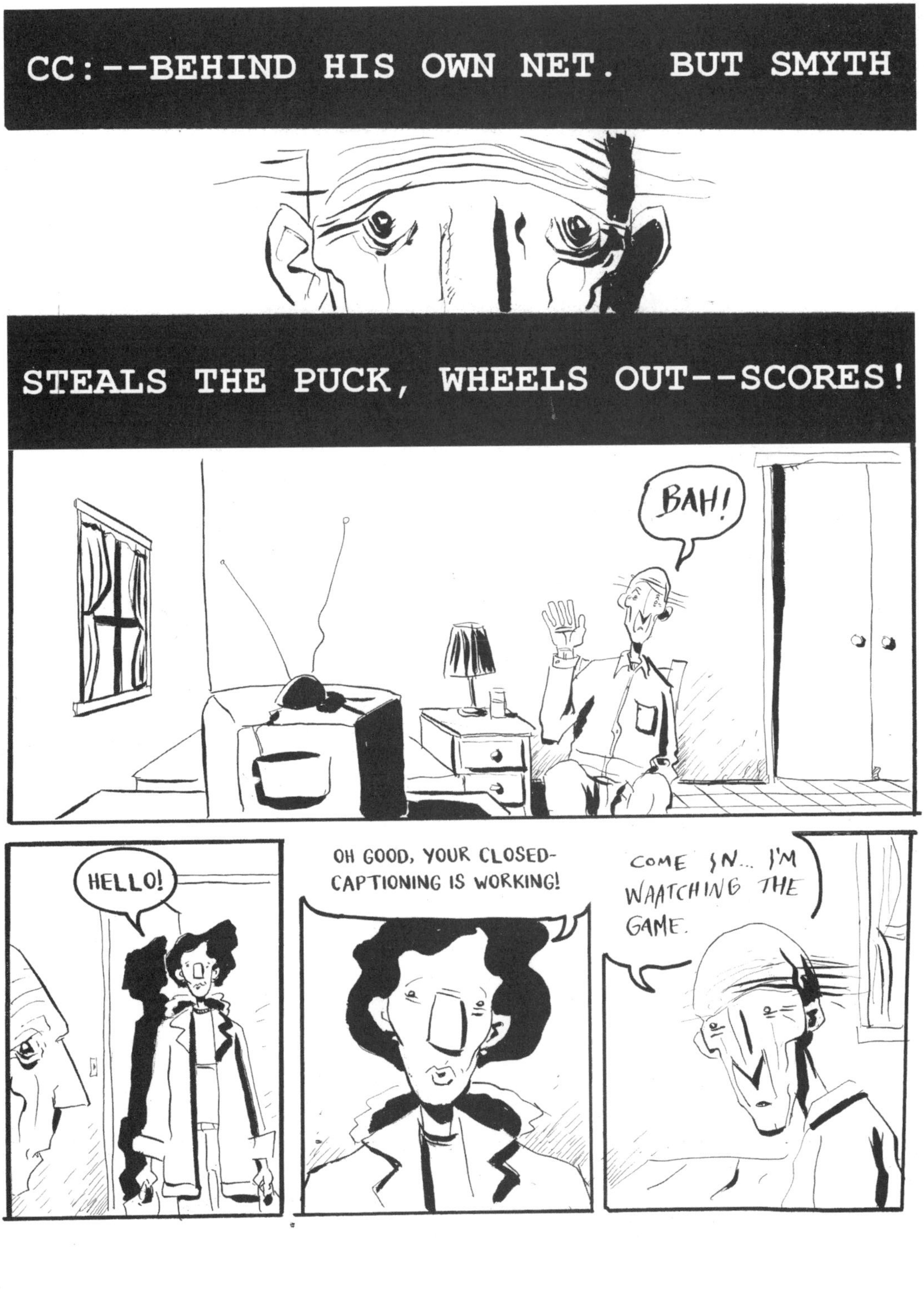
CC:--BEHIND HIS OWN NET. BUT SMYTH
STEALS THE PUCK, WHEELS OUT--SCORES!
BAH!
HELLO!
OH GOOD, YOUR CLOSED-CAPTIONING IS WORKING!
COME IN... I'M WAATCHING THE GAME.

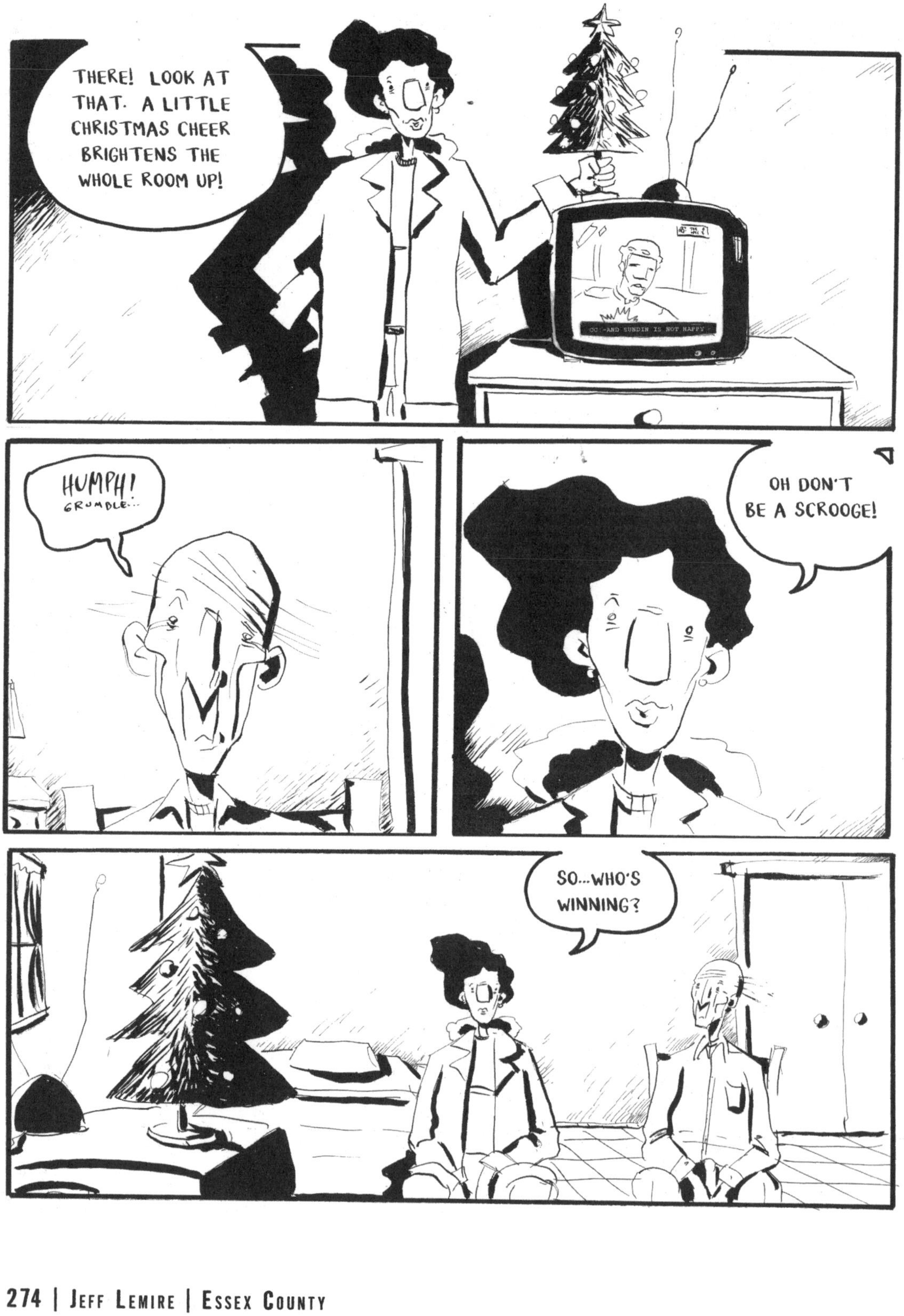
THERE! LOOK AT THAT. A LITTLE CHRISTMAS CHEER BRIGHTENS THE WHOLE ROOM UP!
CC: -AND SUNDIN IS NOT HAPPY -
HUMPH! GRUMBLE...
OH DON'T BE A SCROOGE!
SO...WHO'S WINNING?

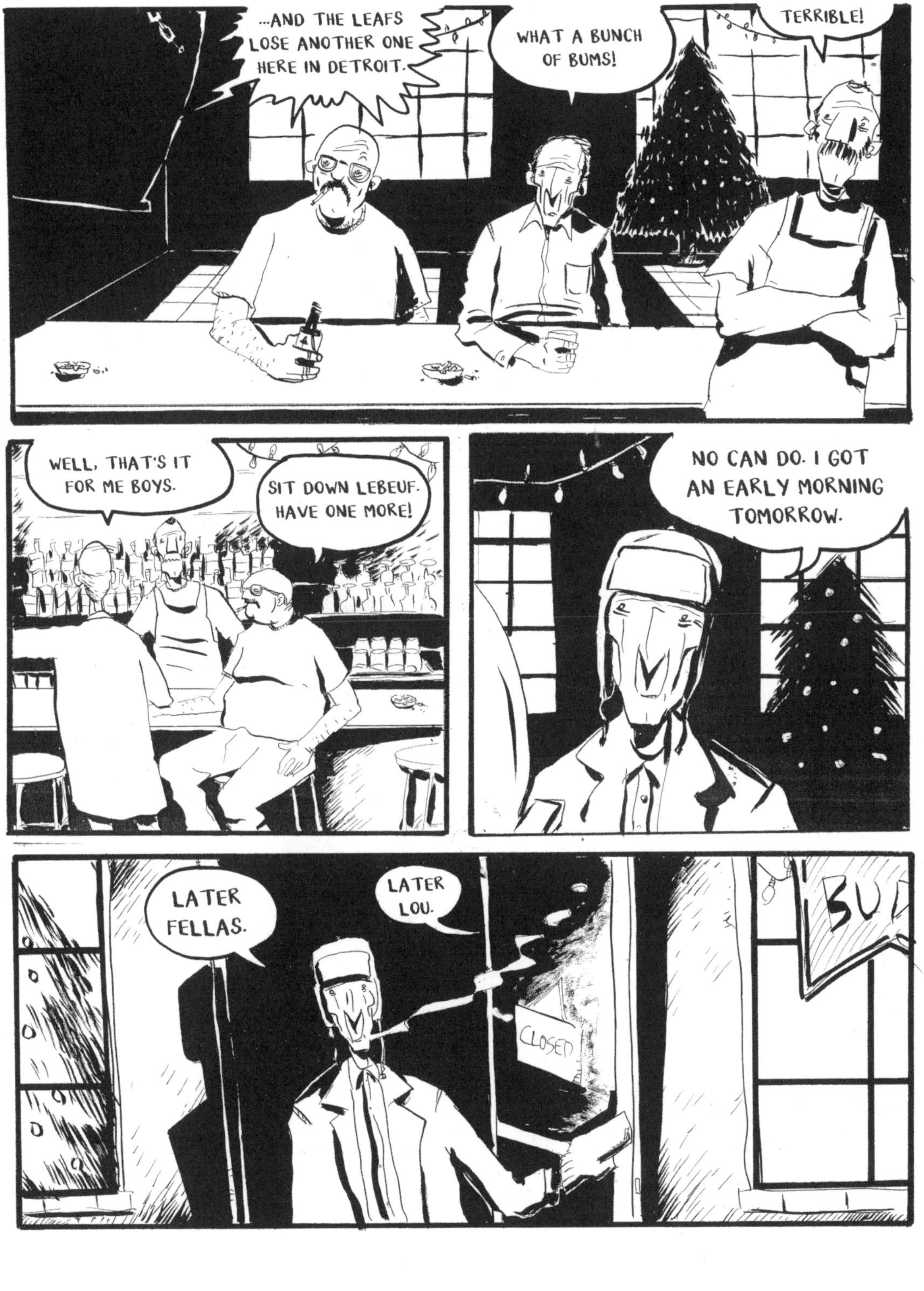
...AND THE LEAFS LOSE ANOTHER ONE HERE IN DETROIT.
WHAT A BUNCH OF BUMS!
TERRIBLE!
WELL, THAT'S IT FOR ME BOYS.
SIT DOWN LEBEUF. HAVE ONE MORE!
NO CAN DO. I GOT AN EARLY MORNING TOMORROW.
LATER FELLAS.
LATER LOU.
CLOSED

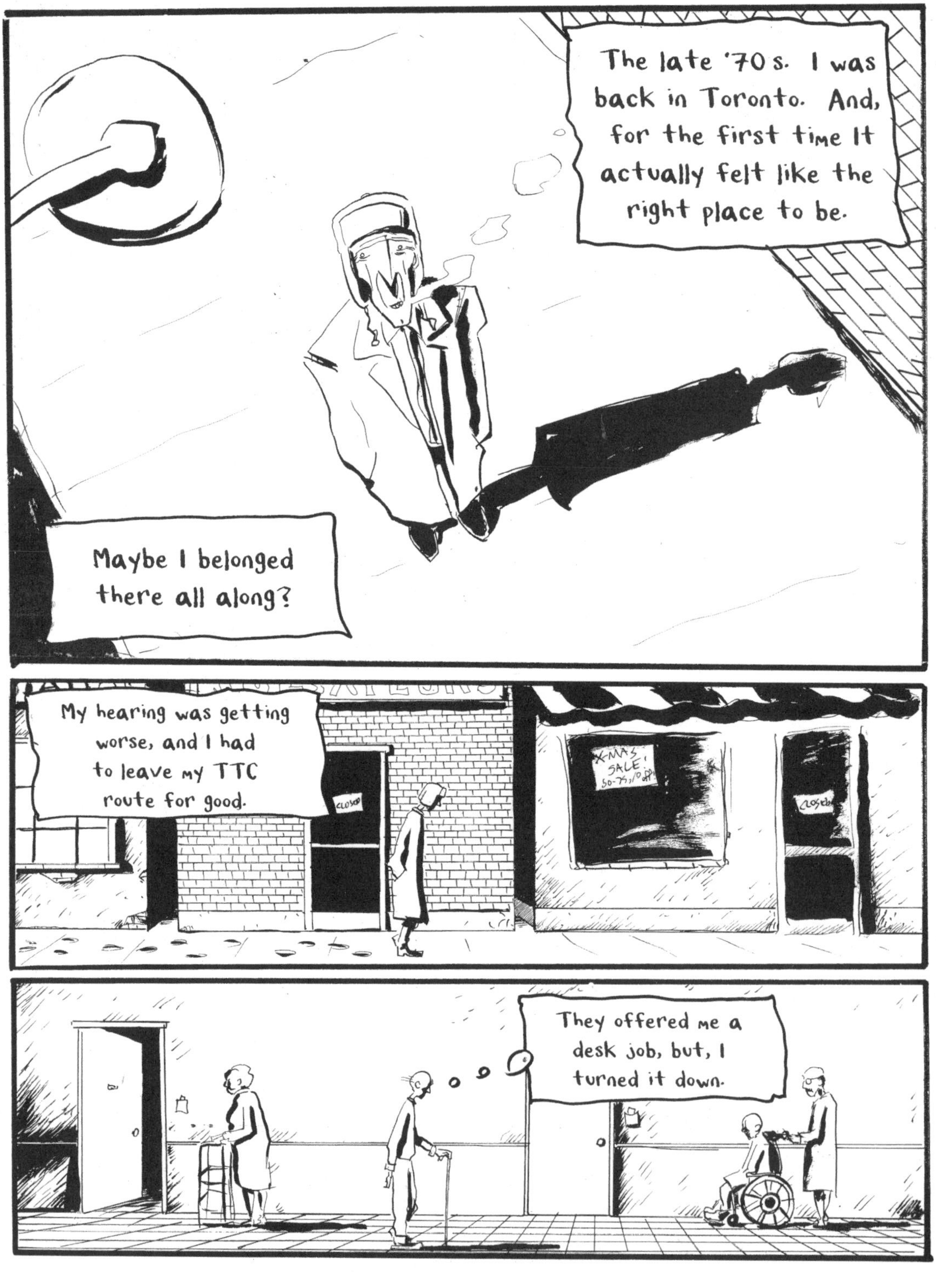
The late '70s. I was back in Toronto. And, for the first time It actually felt like the right place to be.
Maybe I belonged there all along?
My hearing was getting worse, and I had to leave my TTC route for good.
CLOSED
X-MAS SALE!
They offered me a desk job, but, I turned it down.

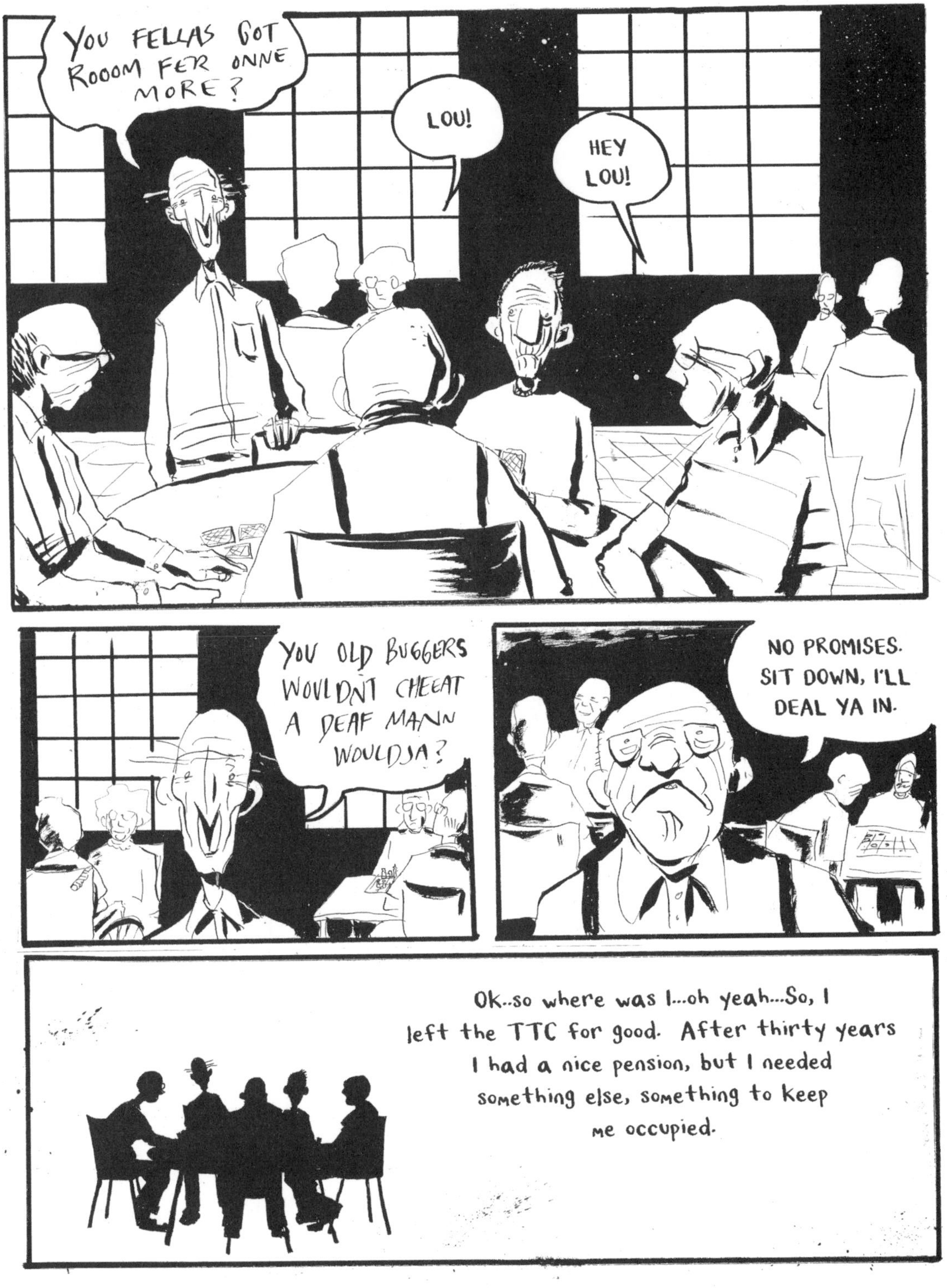
YOU FELLAS GOT ROOOM FER ONNE MORE?
LOU!
HEY LOU!
YOU OLD BUGGERS WOULDN'T CHEEAT A DEAF MANN WOULDJA?
NO PROMISES. SIT DOWN, I'LL DEAL YA IN.
Ok...so where was I...oh yeah...So, I left the TTC for good. After thirty years I had a nice pension, but I needed something else, something to keep me occupied.

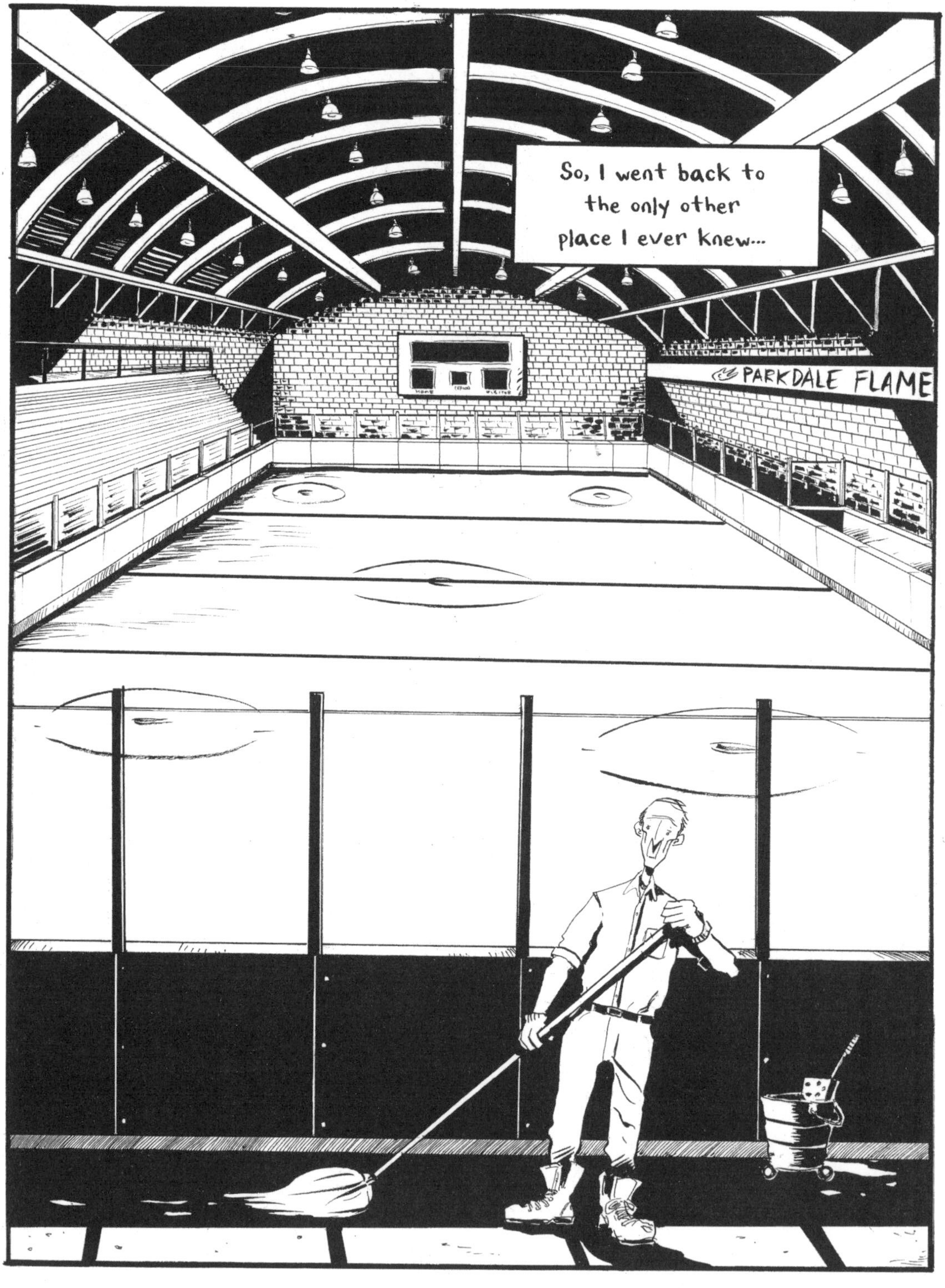
So, I went back to the only other place I ever knew...
PARKDALE FLAME

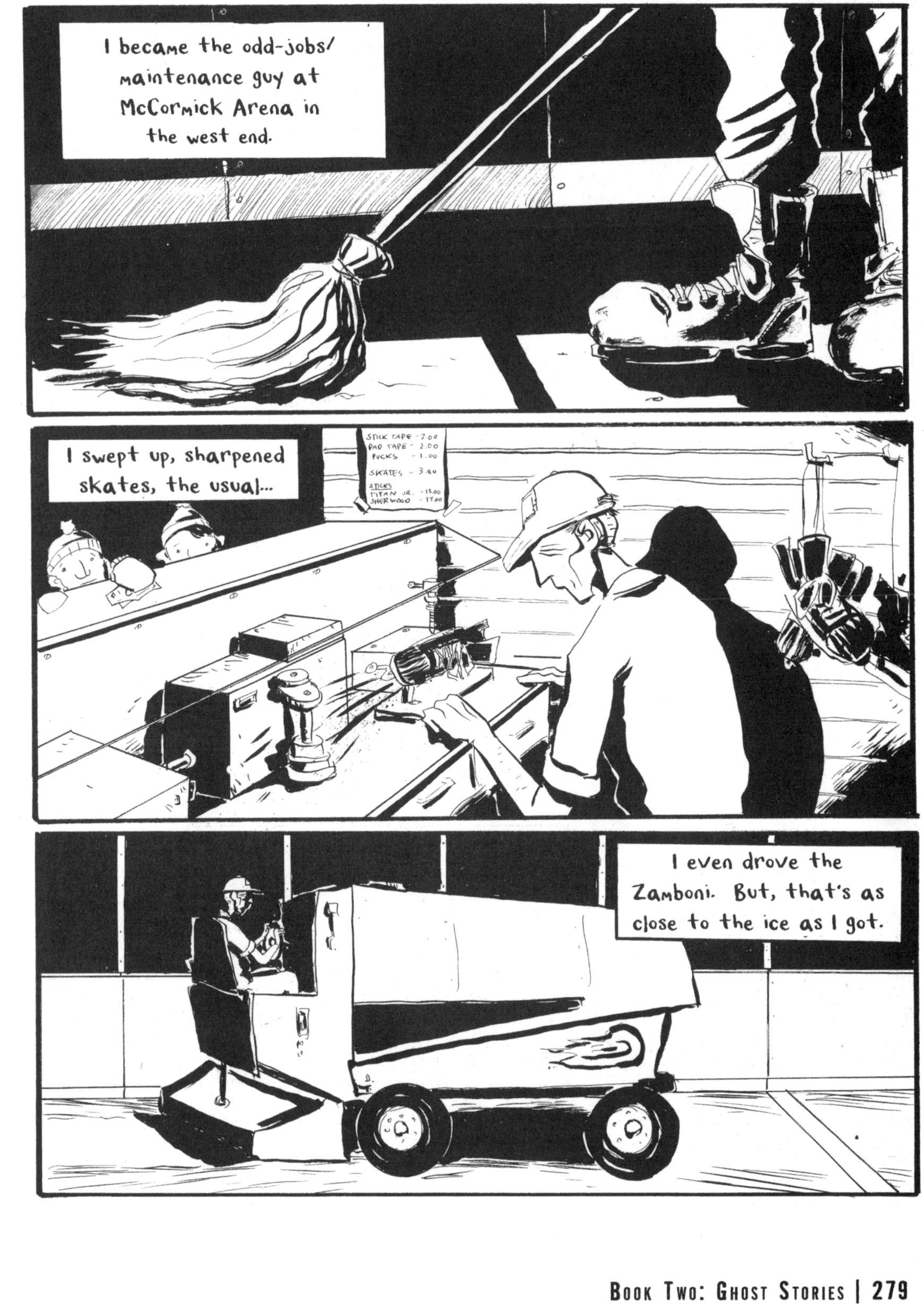
I became the odd-jobs/ maintenance guy at McCormick Arena in the west end.
I swept up, sharpened skates, the usual...
STICK TAPE - 2.00
PAD TAPE - 2.00
PUCKS - 1.00
SKATES - 3.00
STICKS
TITAN JR. - 15.00
SHERWOOD - 17.00
I even drove the Zamboni. But, that's as close to the ice as I got.

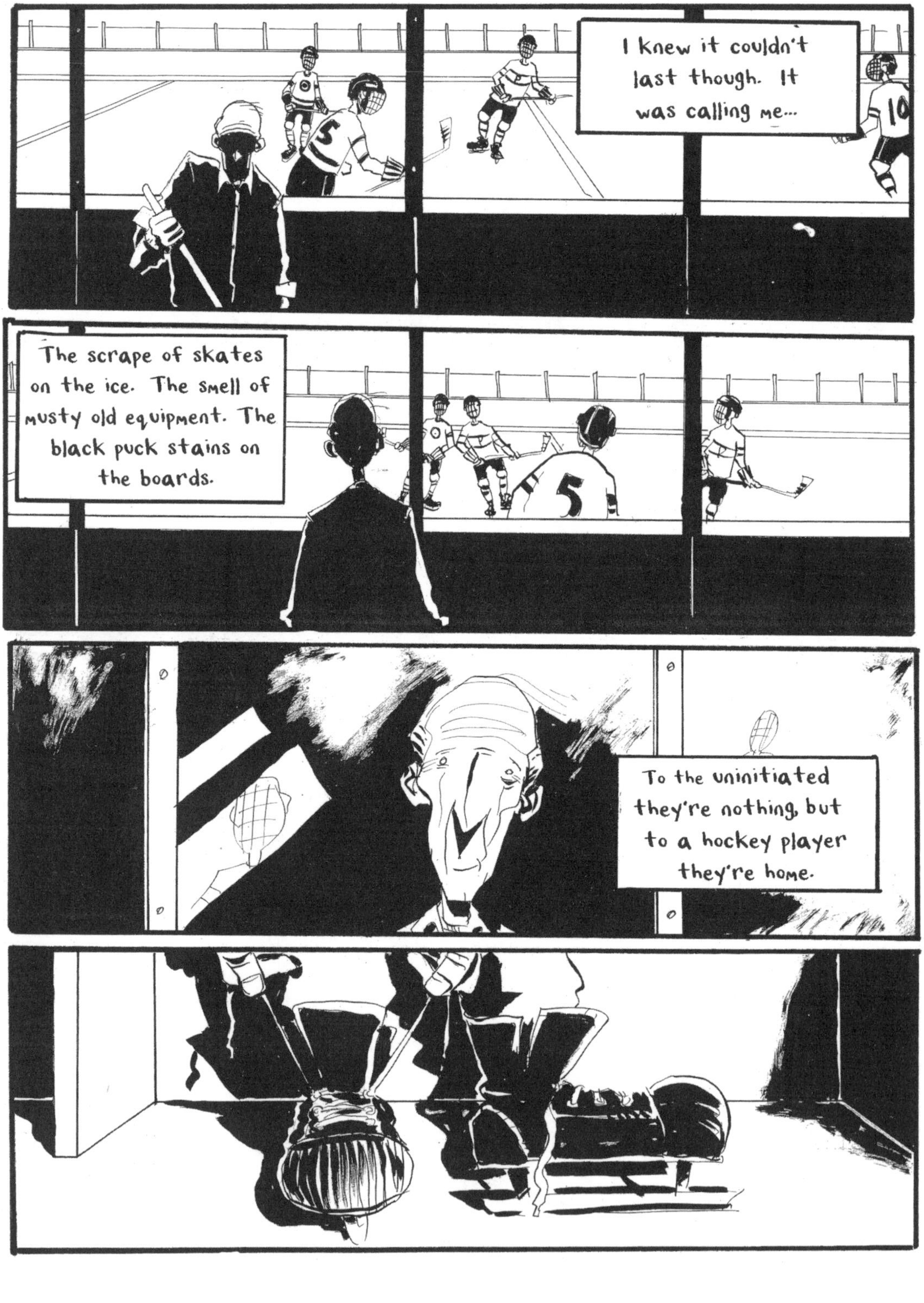
I knew it couldn't last though. It was calling me...
10
5
The scrape of skates on the ice. The smell of musty old equipment. The black puck stains on the boards.
5
To the uninitiated they're nothing, but to a hockey player they're home.

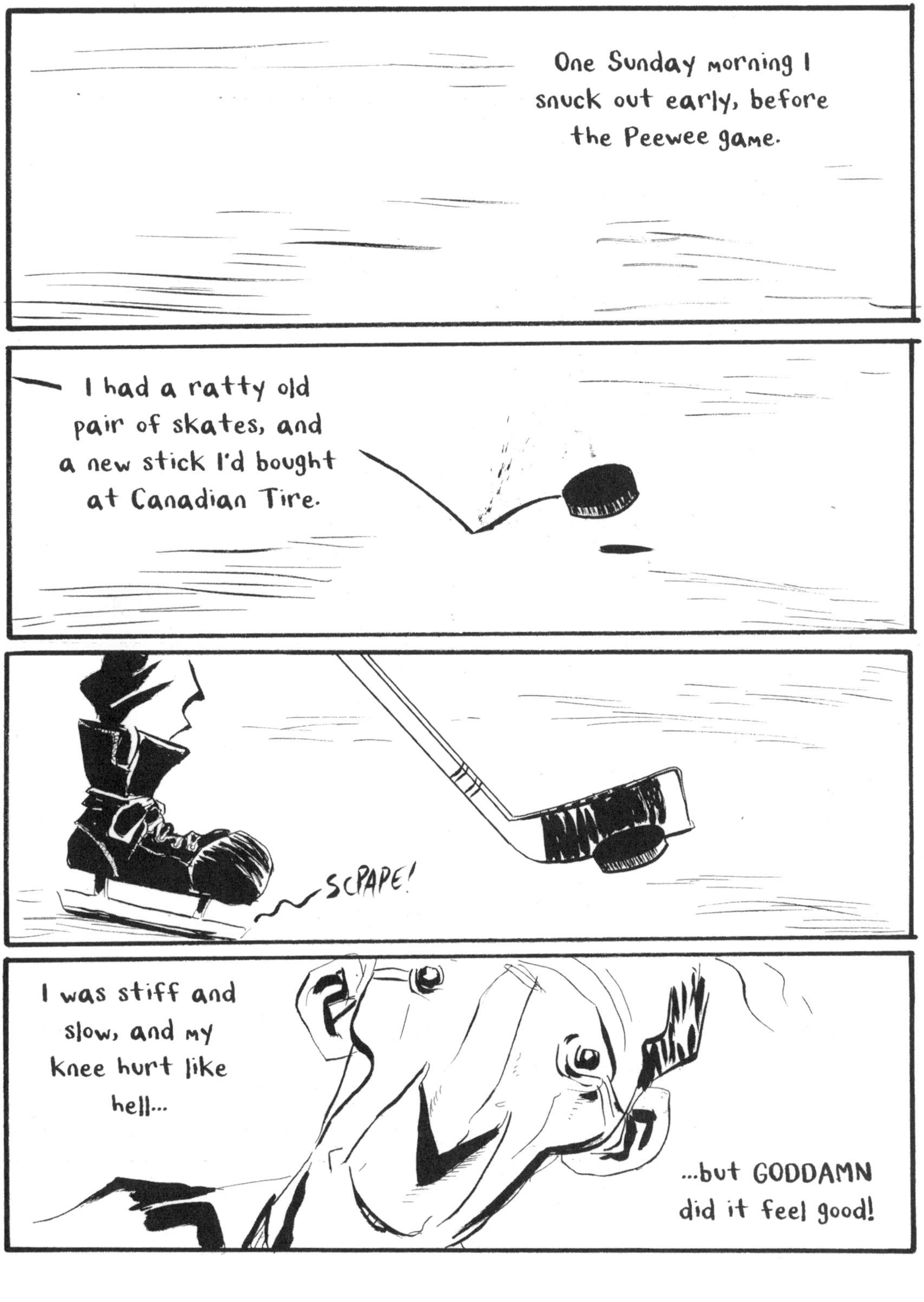
One Sunday morning I snuck out early, before the Peewee game.
I had a ratty old pair of skates, and a new stick I'd bought at Canadian Tire.
SCRAPE!
I was stiff and slow, and my knee hurt like hell...
...but GODDAMN did it feel good!

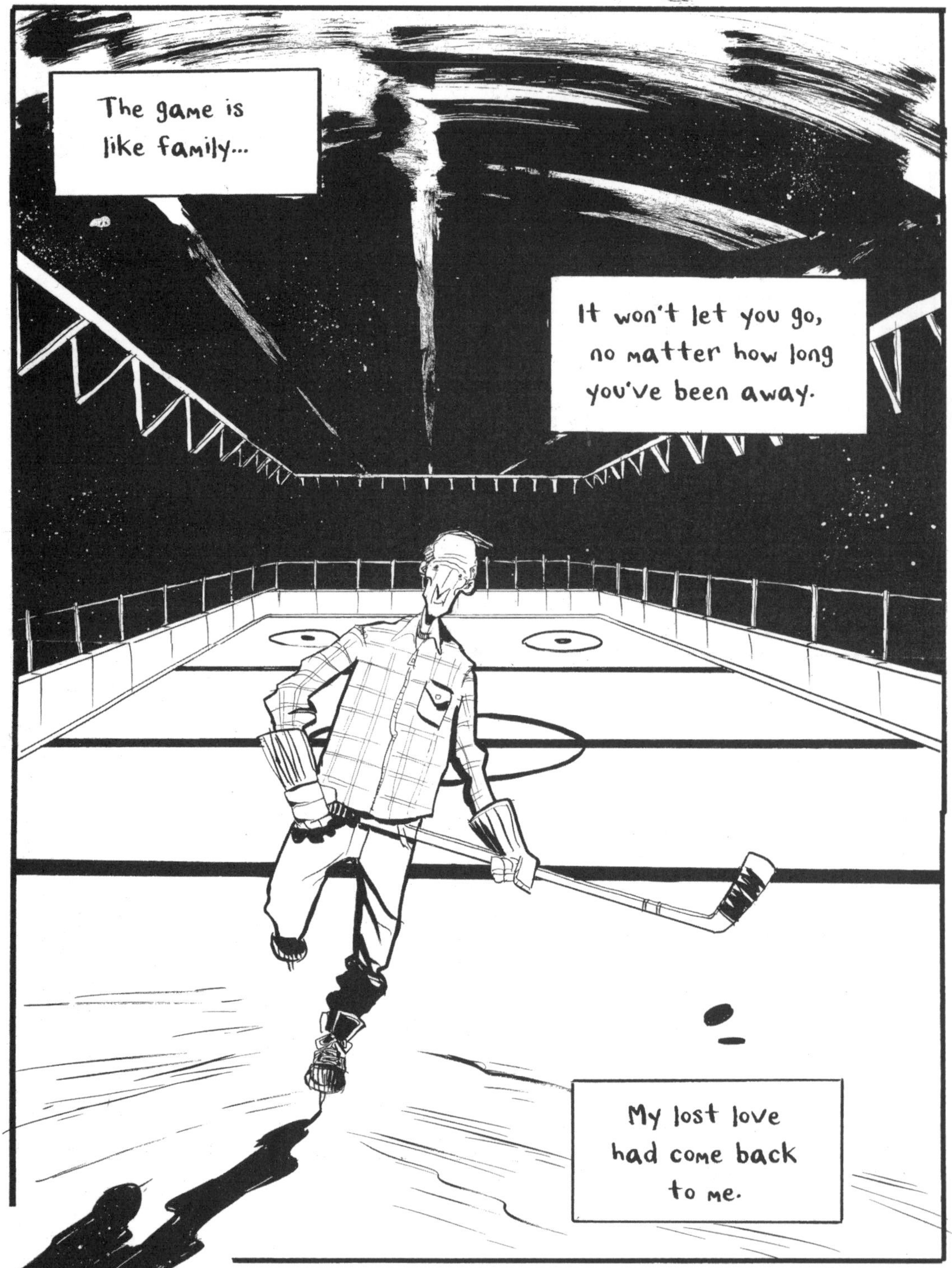
The game is like family...
It won't let you go, no matter how long you've been away.
My lost love had come back to me.

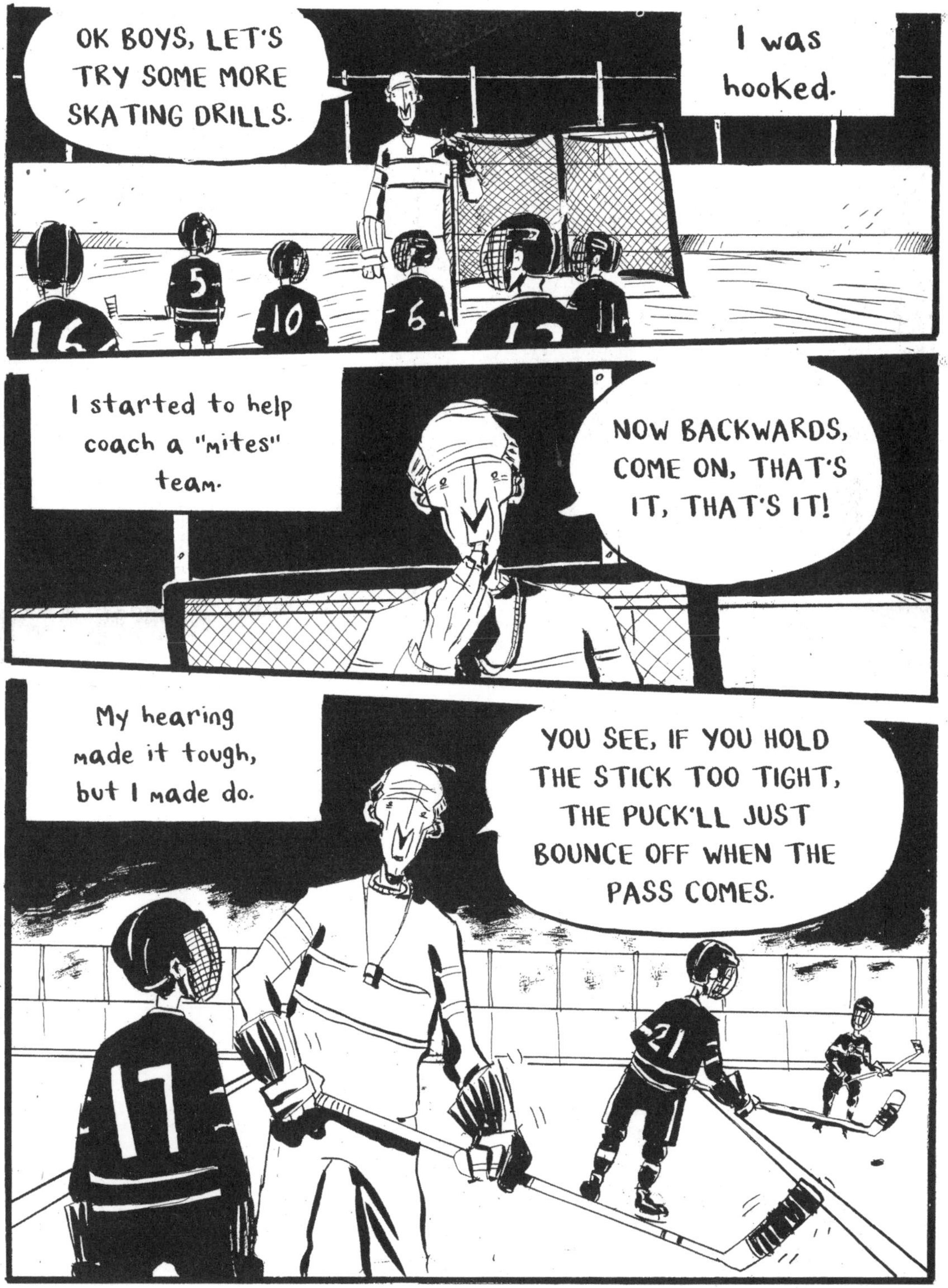
OK BOYS, LET'S TRY SOME MORE SKATING DRILLS.
I was hooked.
5
10
6
I started to help coach a "mites" team.
NOW BACKWARDS, COME ON, THAT'S IT, THAT'S IT!
My hearing made it tough, but I made do.
YOU SEE, IF YOU HOLD THE STICK TOO TIGHT, THE PUCK'LL JUST BOUNCE OFF WHEN THE PASS COMES.
17
21

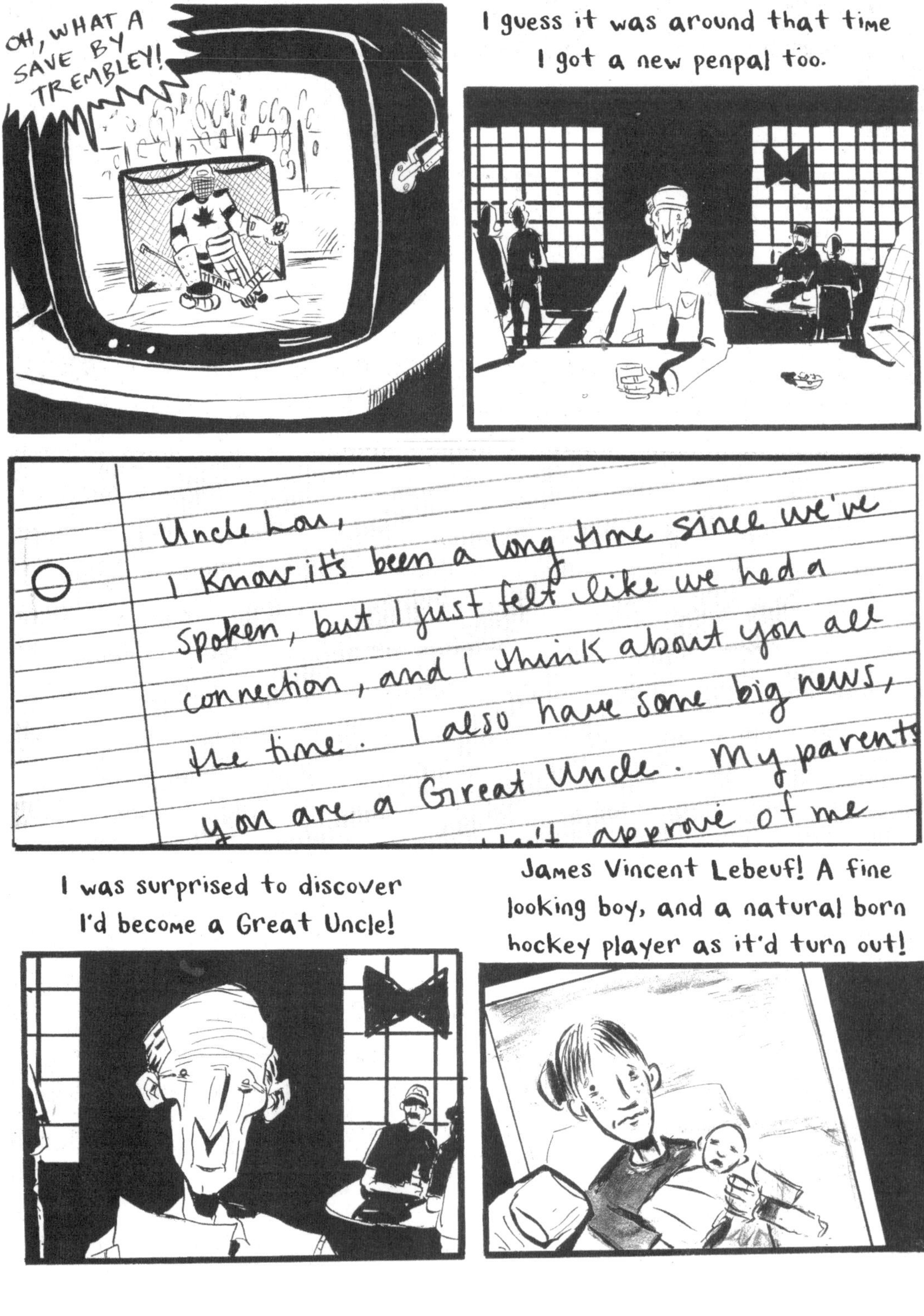
OH, WHAT A SAVE BY TREMBLEY!
I guess it was around that time I got a new penpal too.
Uncle Lou,
I know it's been a long time since we've
spoken, but I just felt like we had a
connection, and I think about you all
the time. I also have some big news,
you are a Great Uncle. My parents
approve of me
I was surprised to discover I'd become a Great Uncle!
James Vincent Lebeuf! A fine looking boy, and a natural born hockey player as it'd turn out!

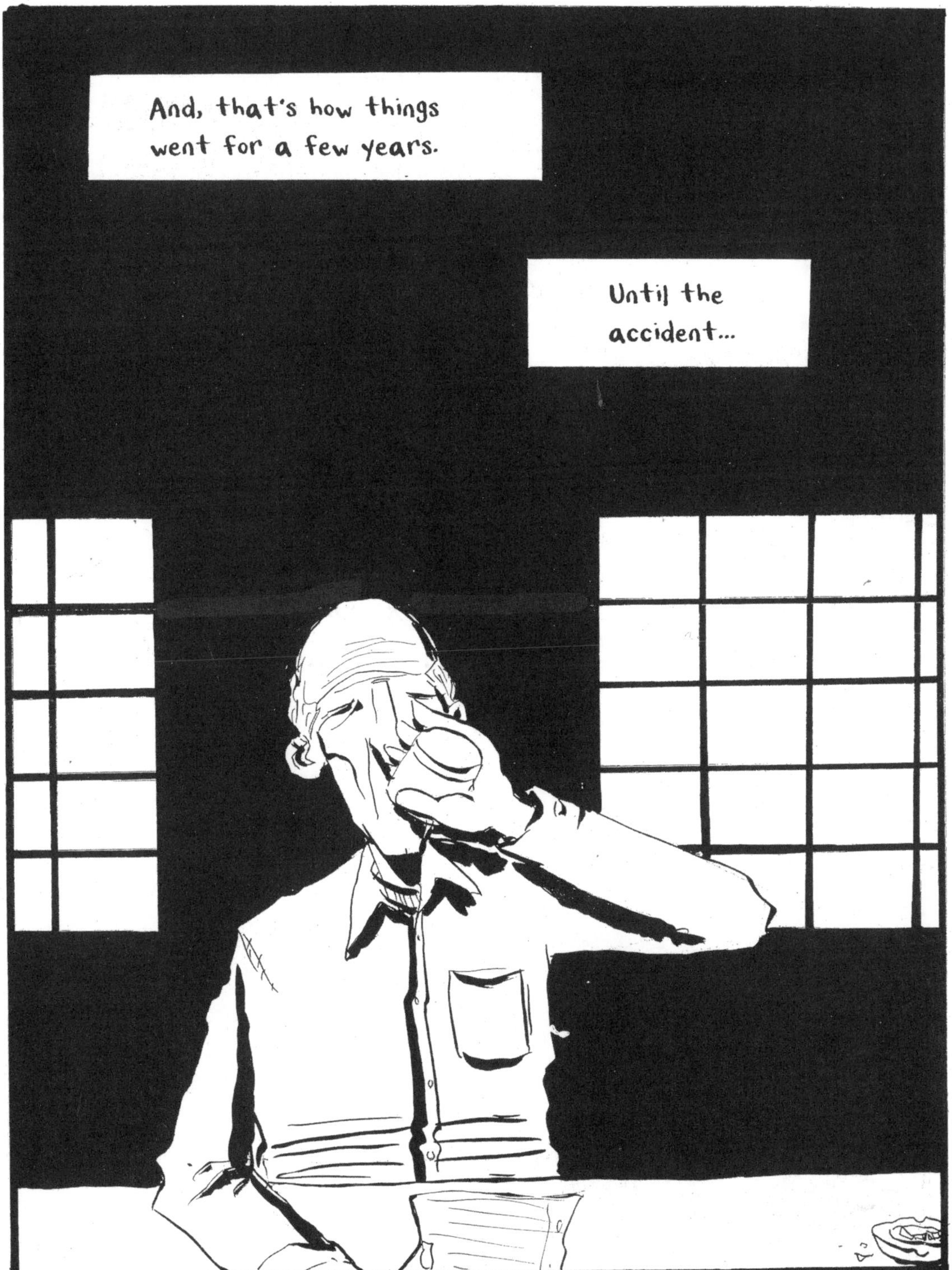
And, that's how things went for a few years.
Until the accident...

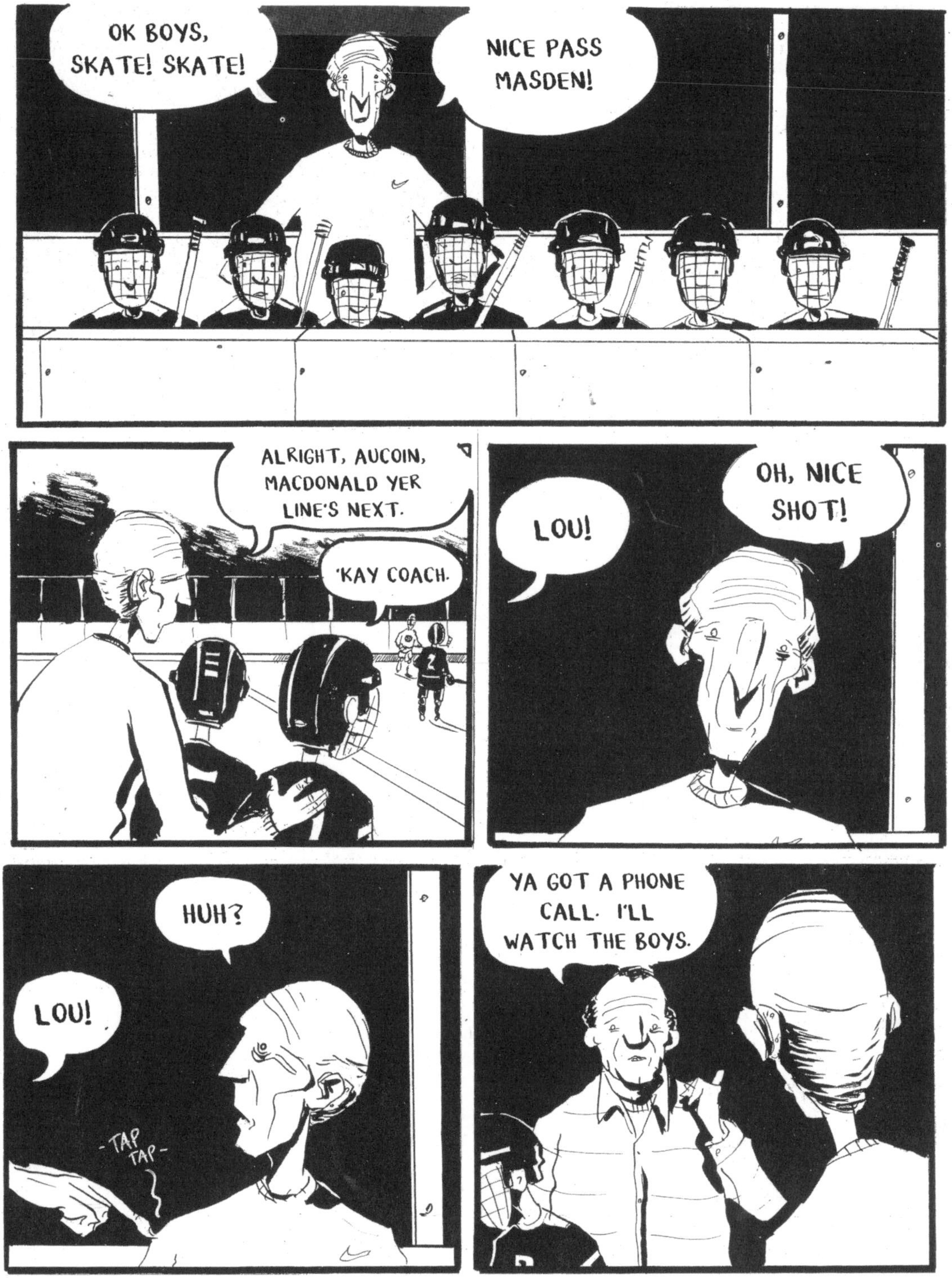
OK BOYS, SKATE! SKATE!
NICE PASS MASDEN!
ALRIGHT, AUCOIN, MACDONALD YER LINE'S NEXT.
'KAY COACH.
OH, NICE SHOT!
LOU!
HUH?
LOU!
-TAP TAP-
YA GOT A PHONE CALL. I'LL WATCH THE BOYS.

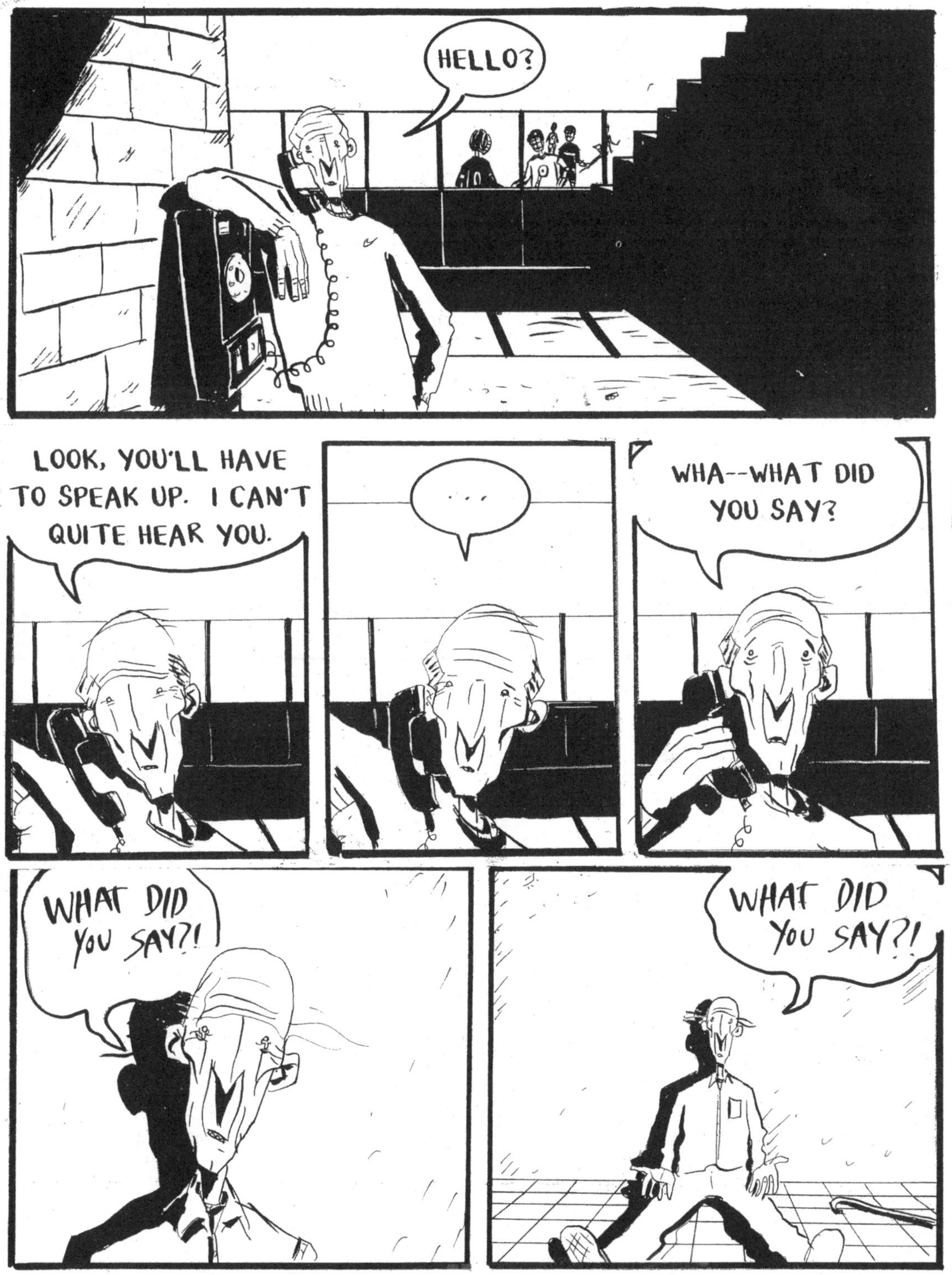
HELLO?
LOOK, YOU'LL HAVE TO SPEAK UP. I CAN'T QUITE HEAR YOU.
. . .
WHA--WHAT DID YOU SAY?
WHAT DID YOU SAY?!
WHAT DID YOU SAY?!

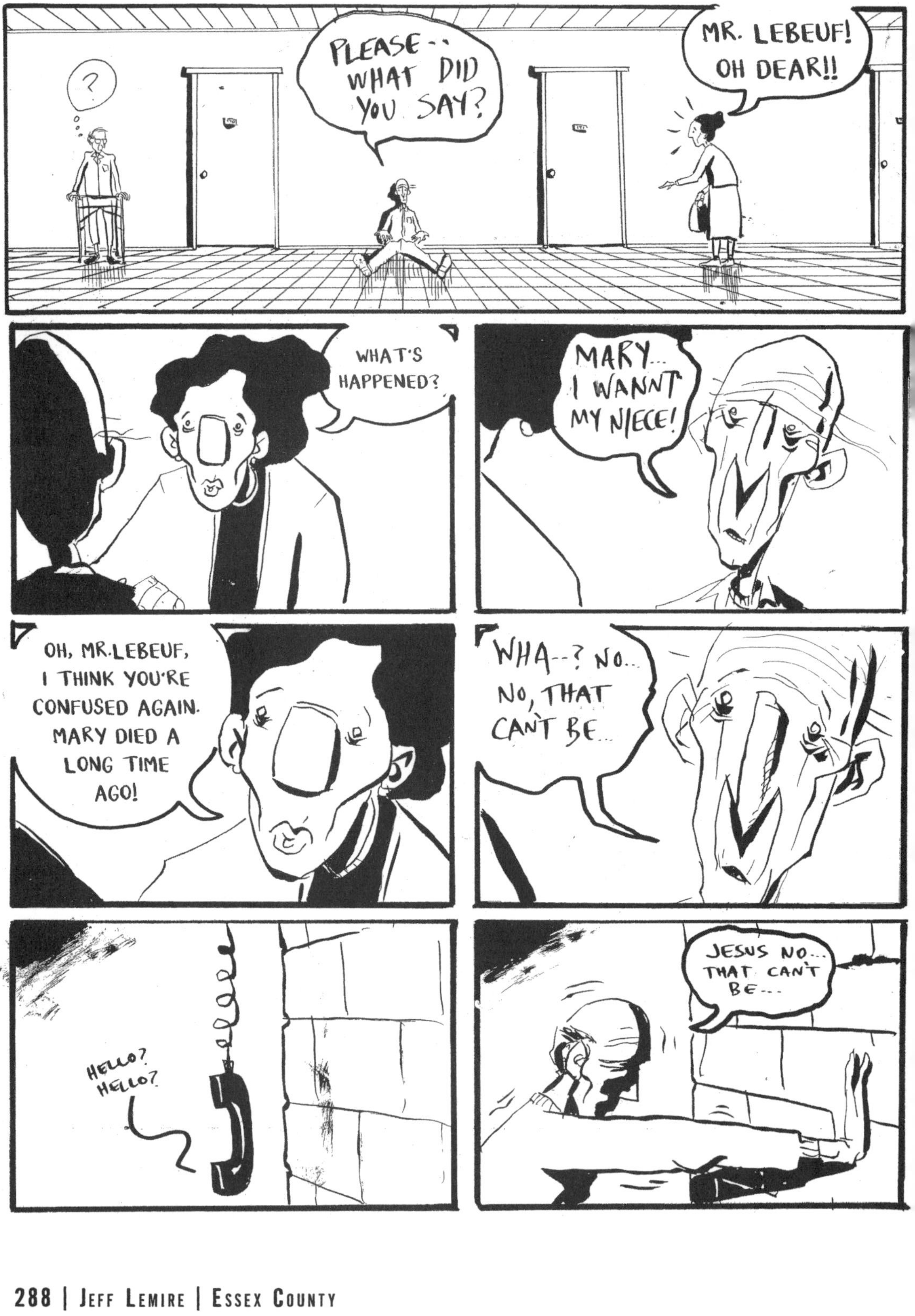
?
PLEASE-- WHAT DID YOU SAY?
MR. LEBEUF! OH DEAR!!
WHAT'S HAPPENED?
MARY... I WANNT MY NIECE!
OH, MR. LEBEUF, I THINK YOU'RE CONFUSED AGAIN. MARY DIED A LONG TIME AGO!
WHA--? NO... NO, THAT CAN'T BE...
HELLO? HELLO?
JESUS NO... THAT CAN'T BE...

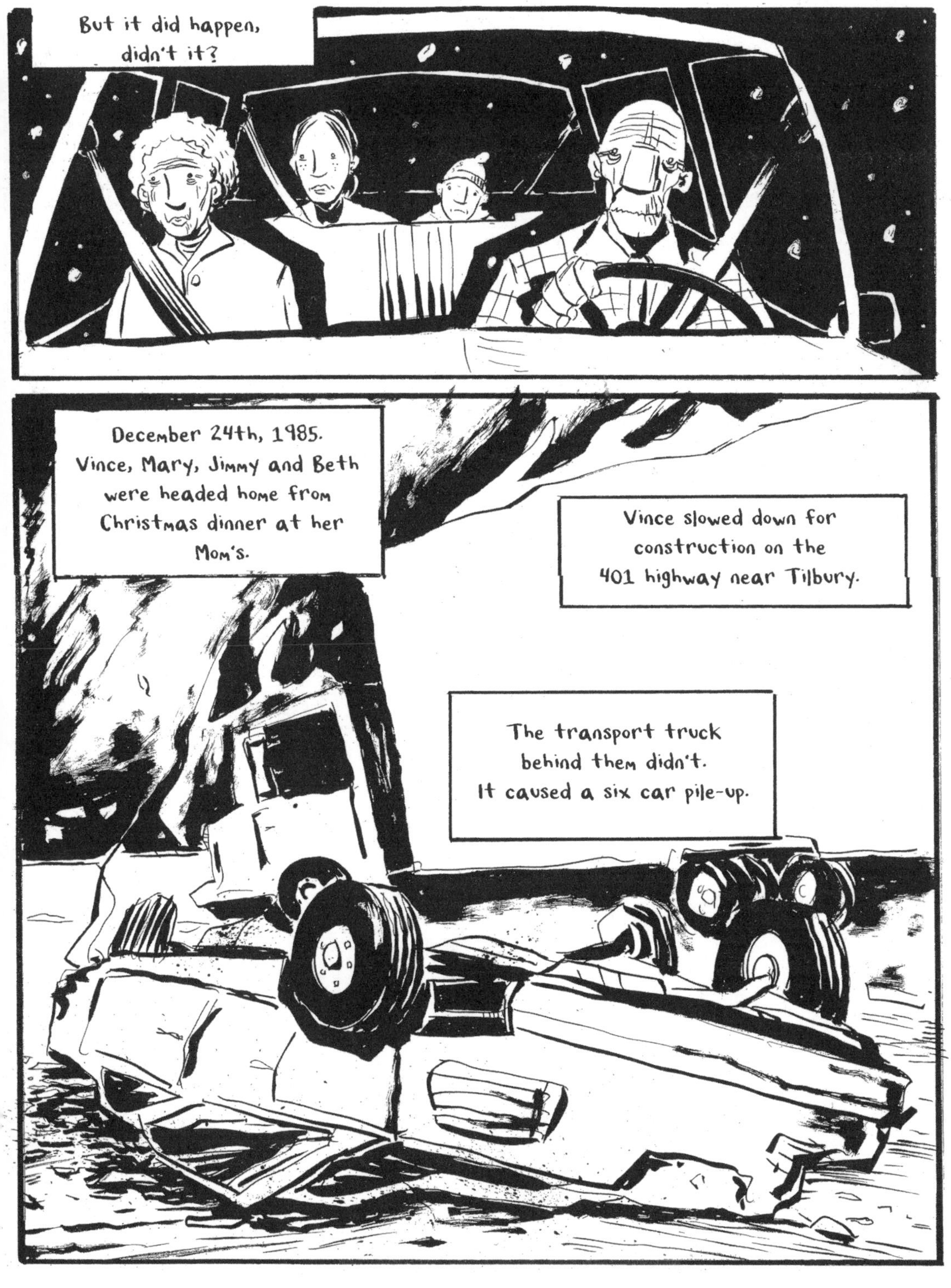
But it did happen, didn't it?
December 24th, 1985. Vince, Mary, Jimmy and Beth were headed home from Christmas dinner at her Mom's.
Vince slowed down for construction on the 401 highway near Tilbury.
The transport truck behind them didn't. It caused a six car pile-up.

Fourteen people were killed that night, including Beth...

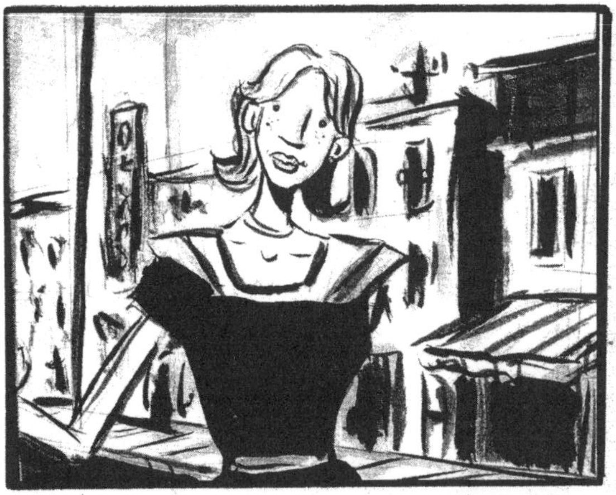

...and Mary.

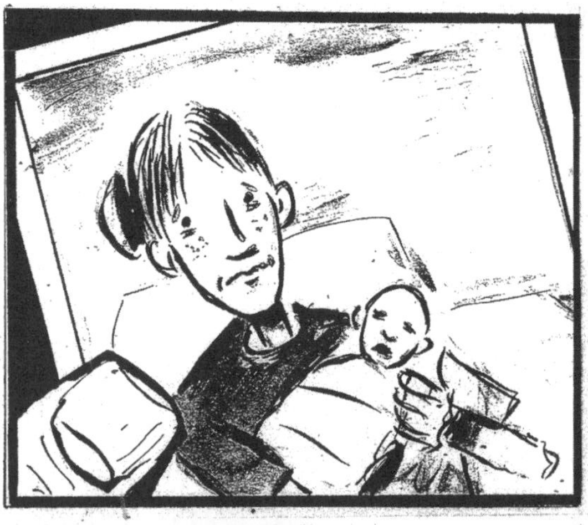

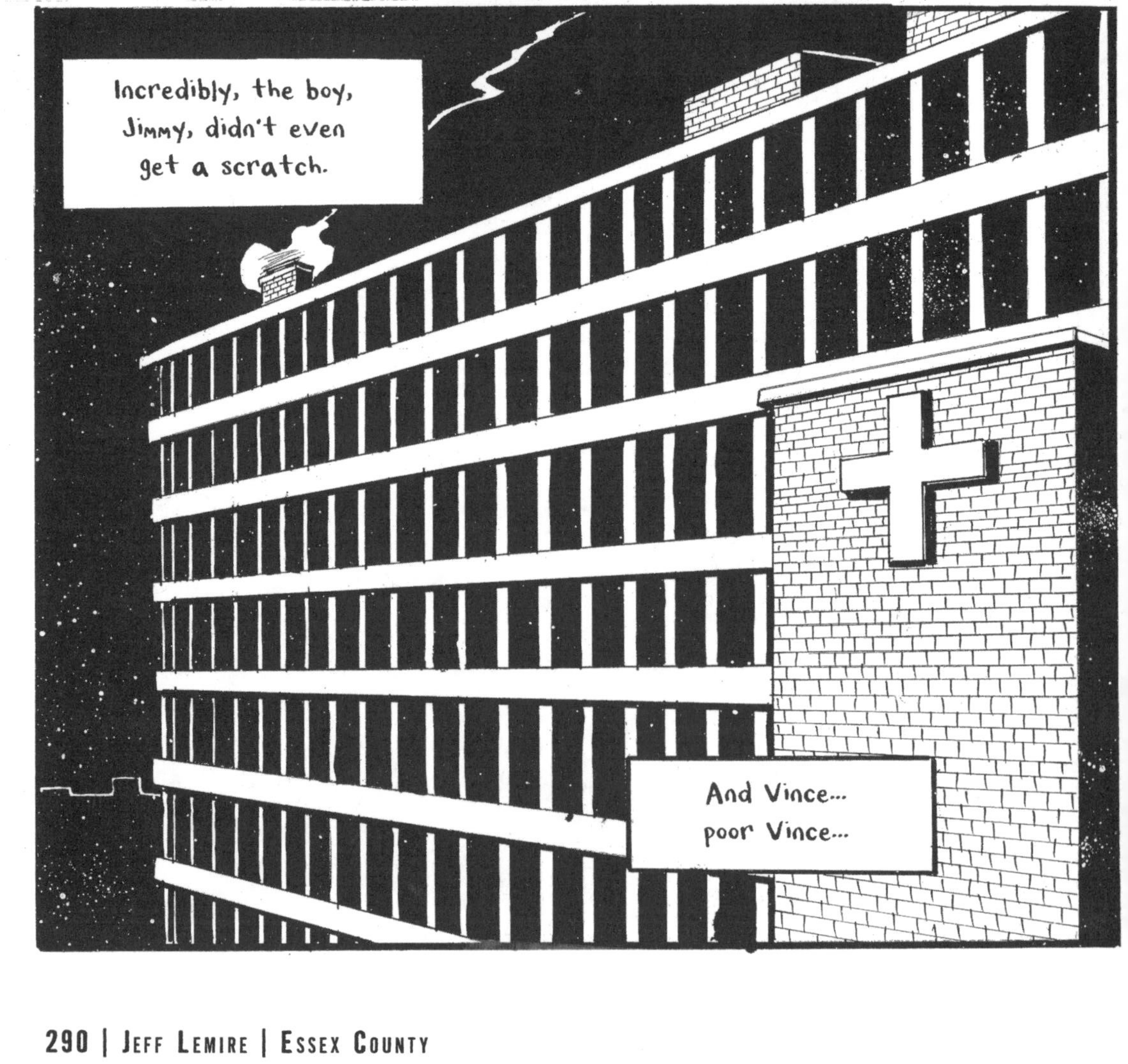
Incredibly, the boy, Jimmy, didn't even get a scratch.
And Vince... poor Vince...

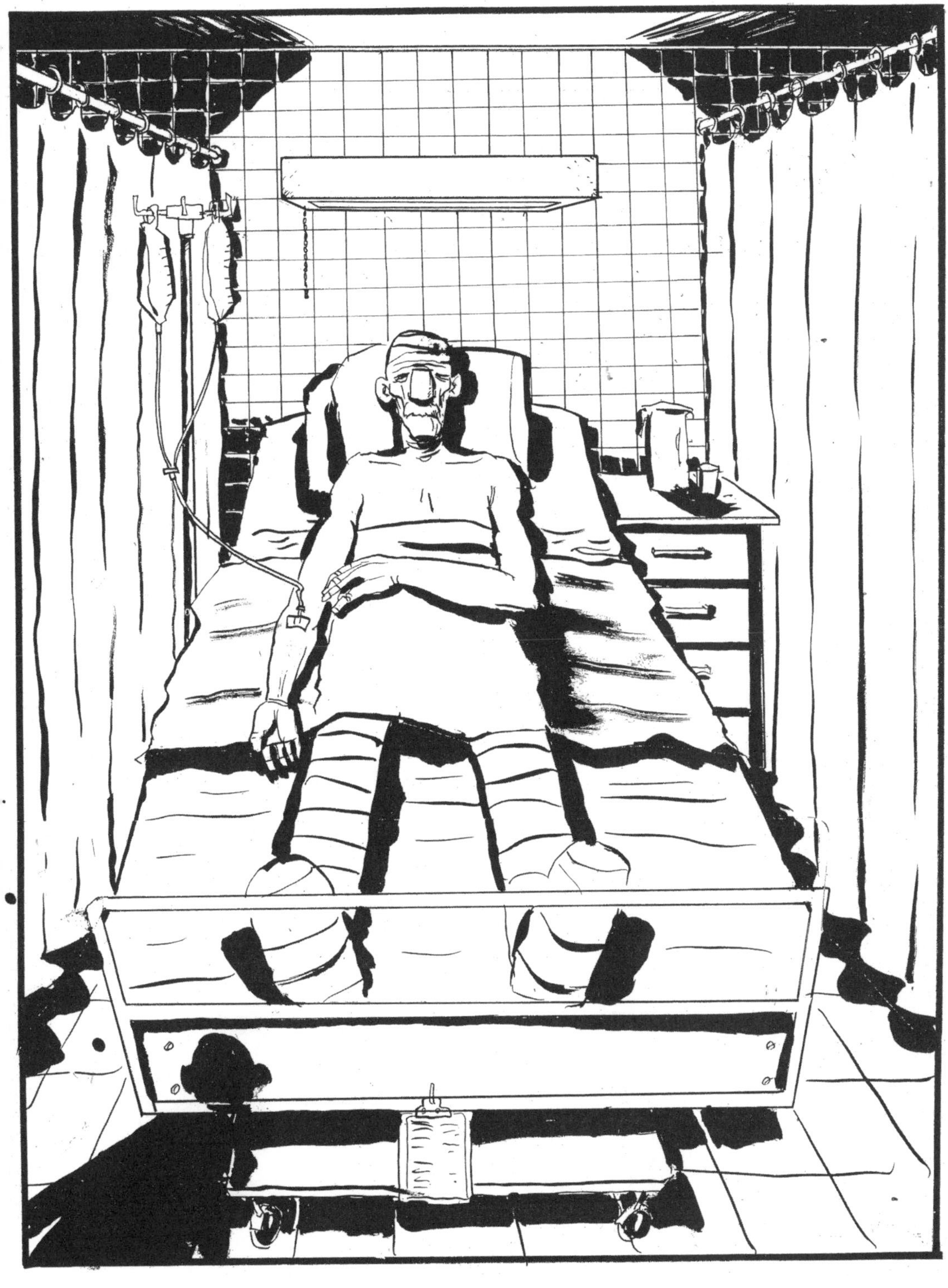

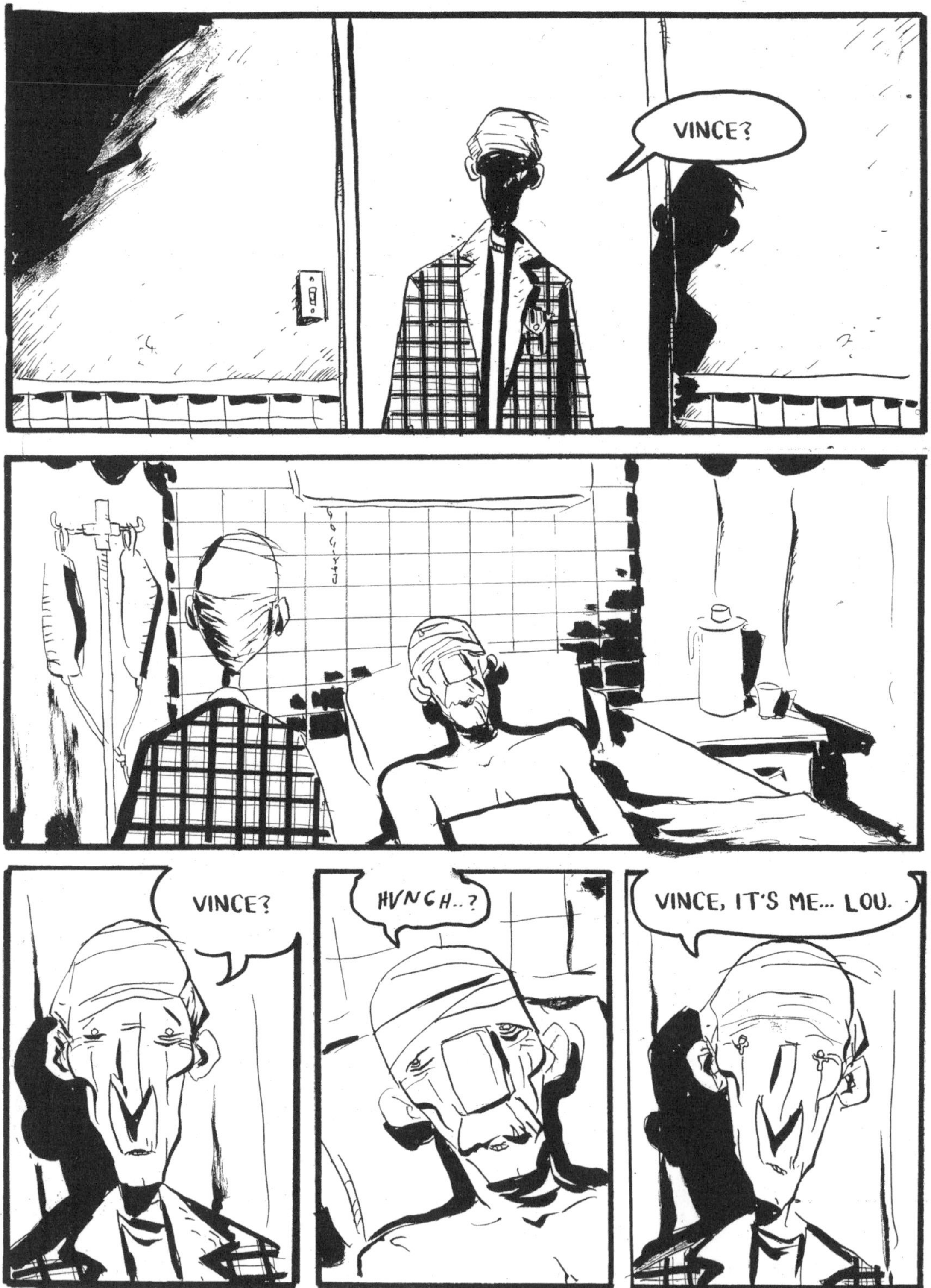

VINCE?
VINCE?
HVNGH..?
VINCE, IT'S ME... LOU.

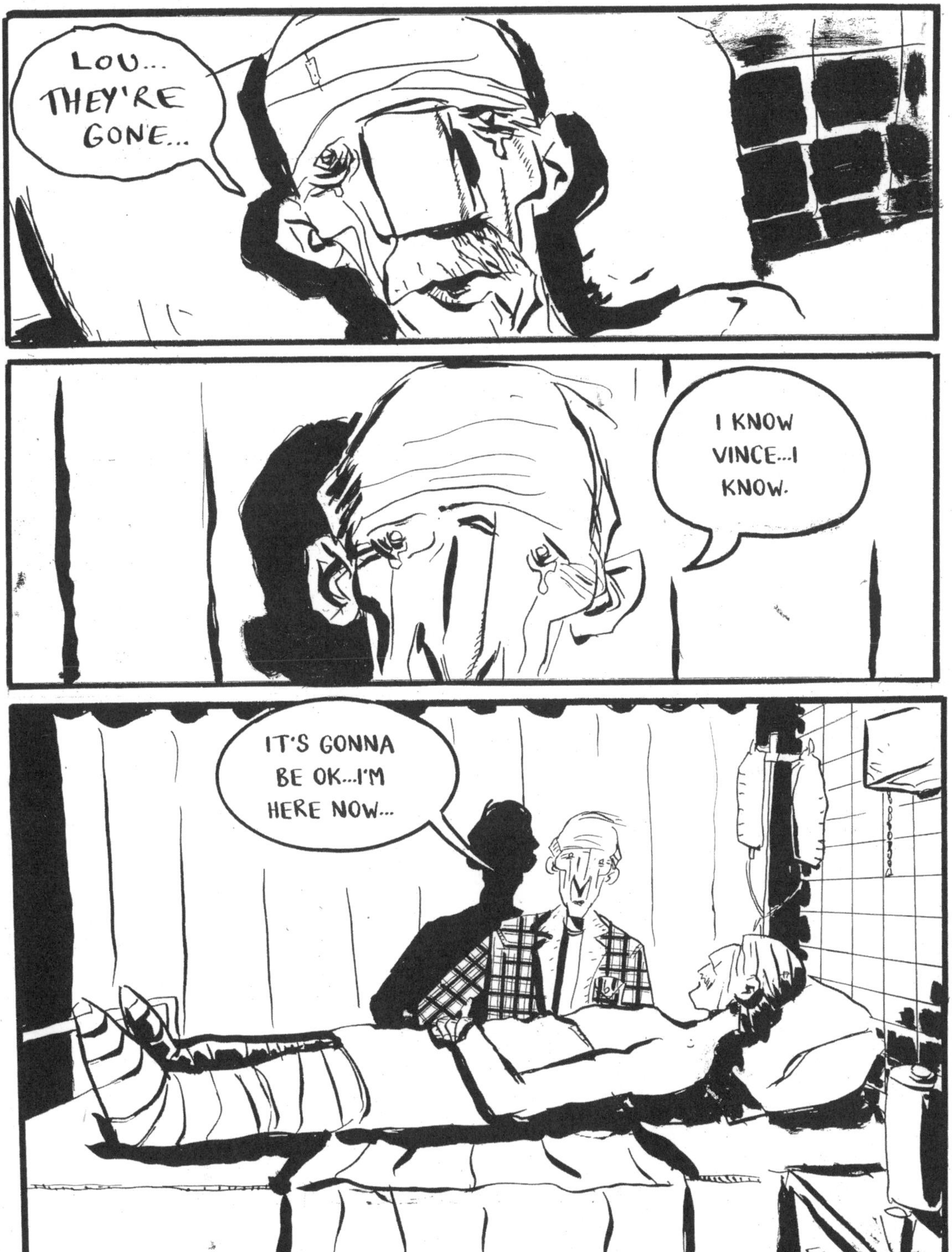
LOU... THEY'RE GONE...
I KNOW VINCE...I KNOW.
IT'S GONNA BE OK...I'M HERE NOW...

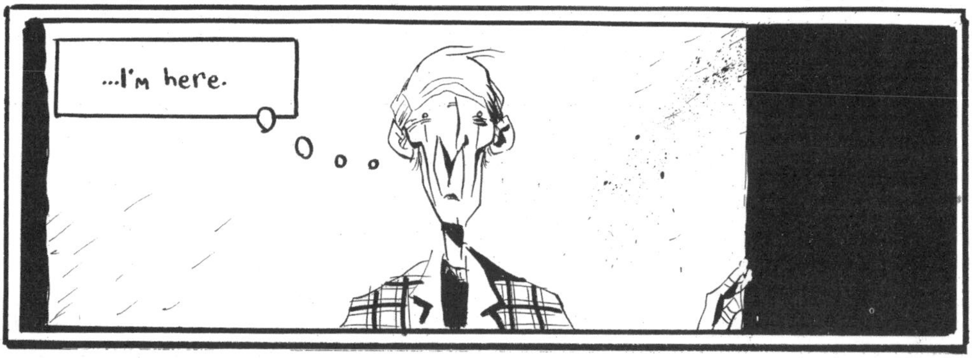
...I'm here.

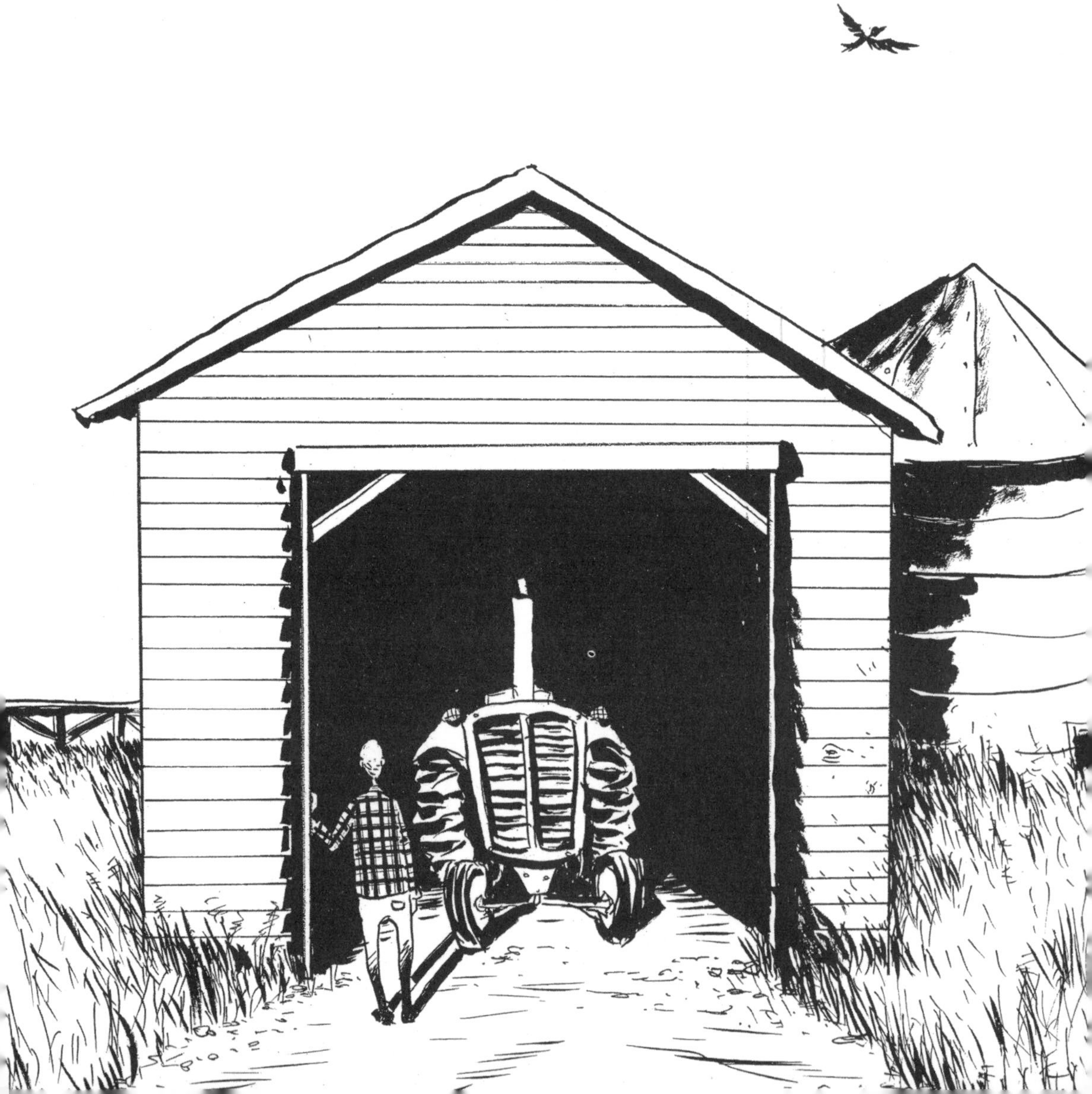

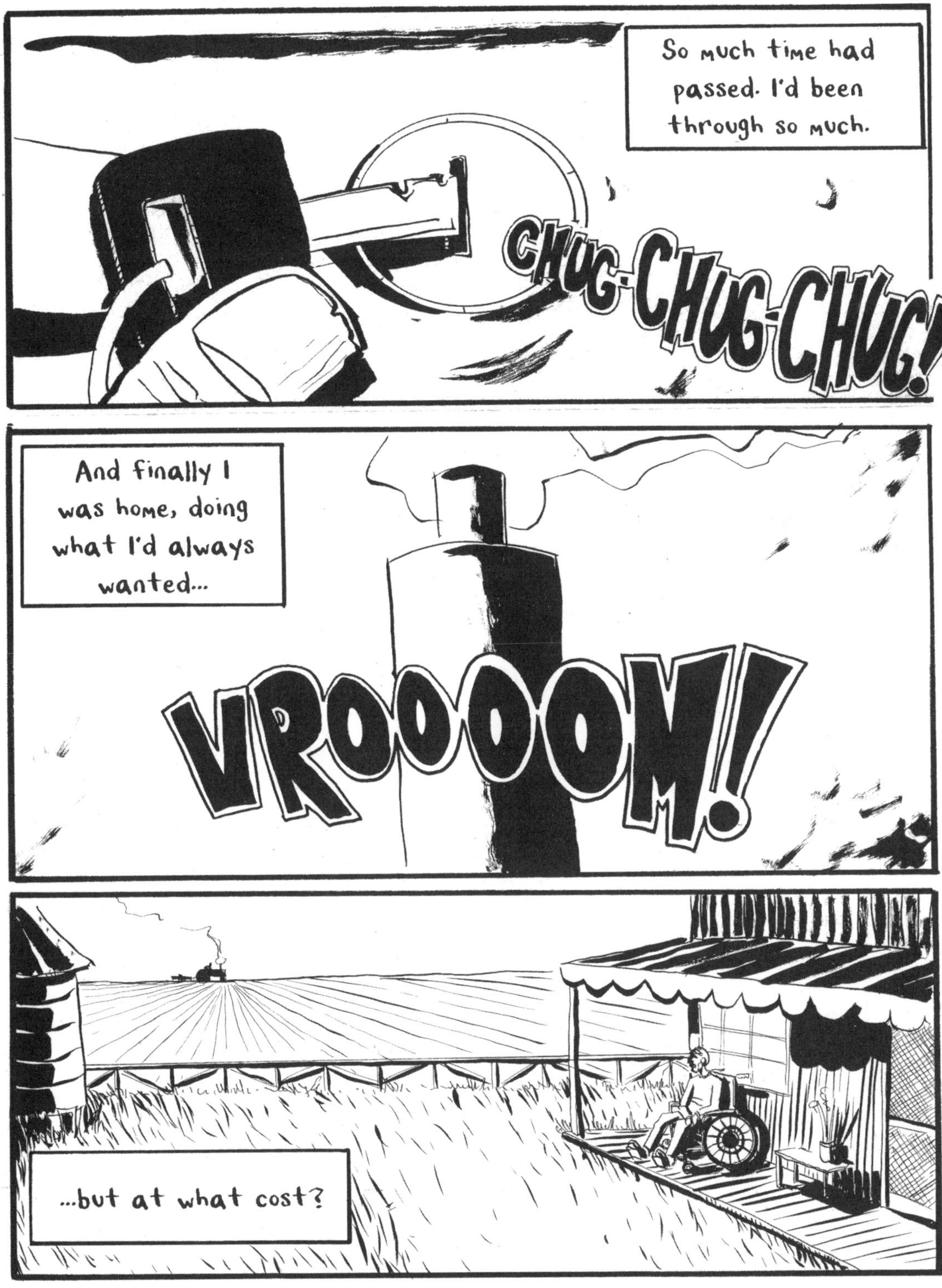
So much time had passed. I'd been through so much.
CHUG-CHUG-CHUG!
And finally I was home, doing what I'd always wanted...
VROOOOM!
...but at what cost?

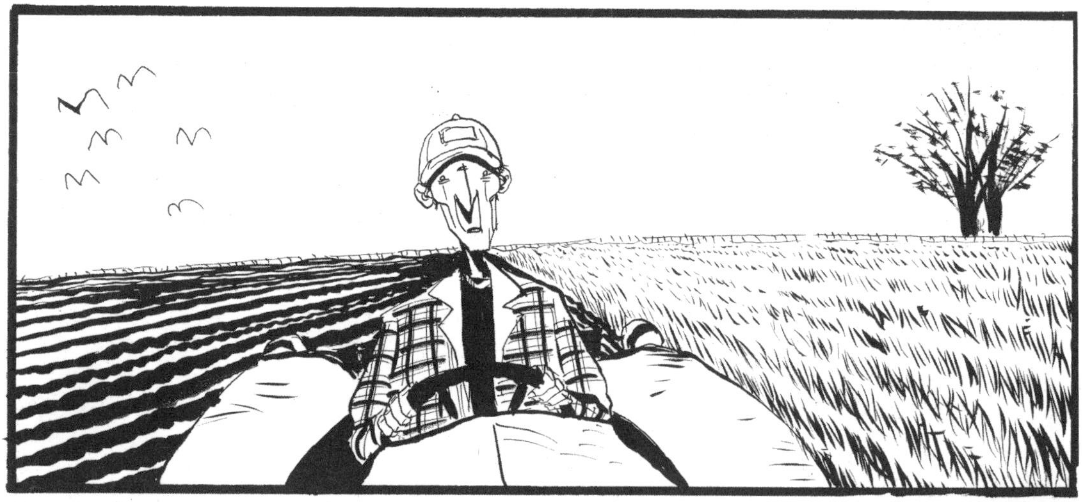

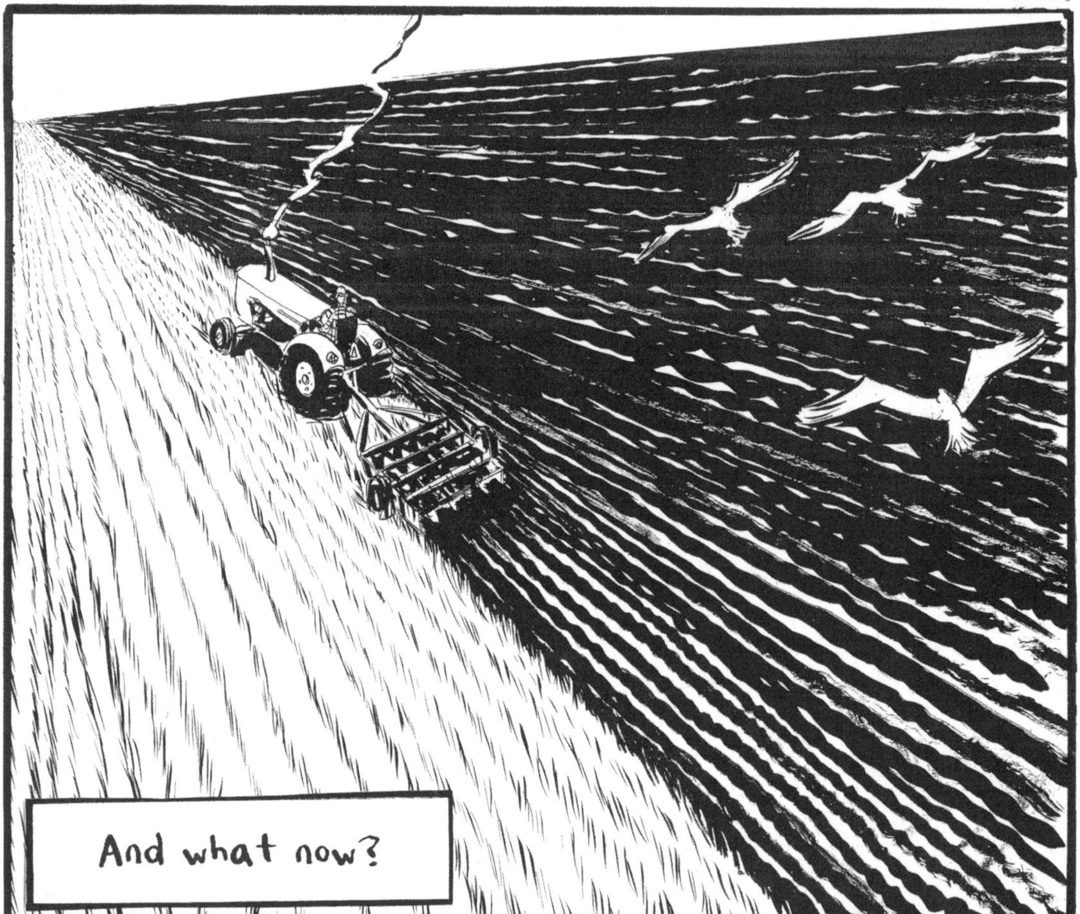
And what now?

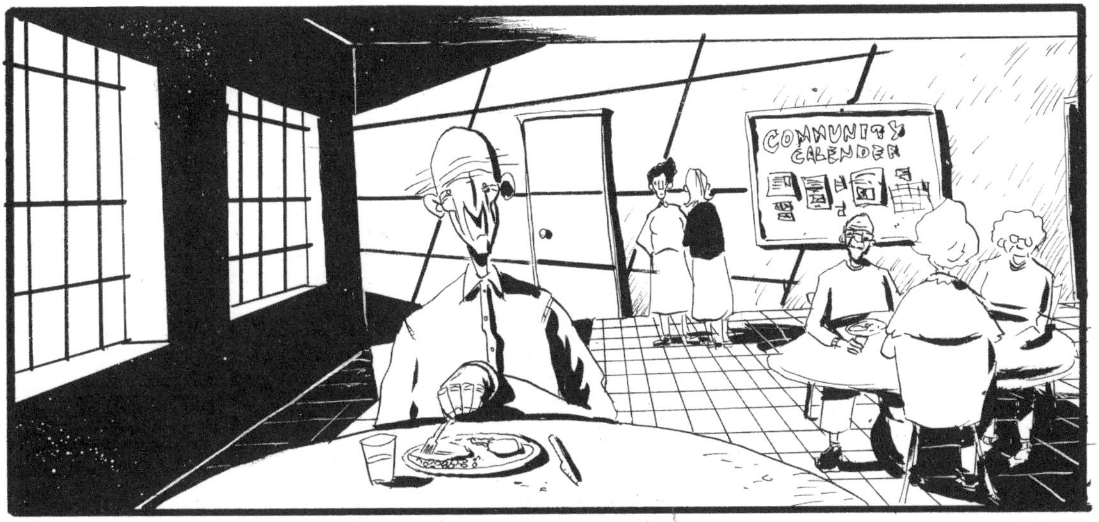
COMMUNITY CALENDER

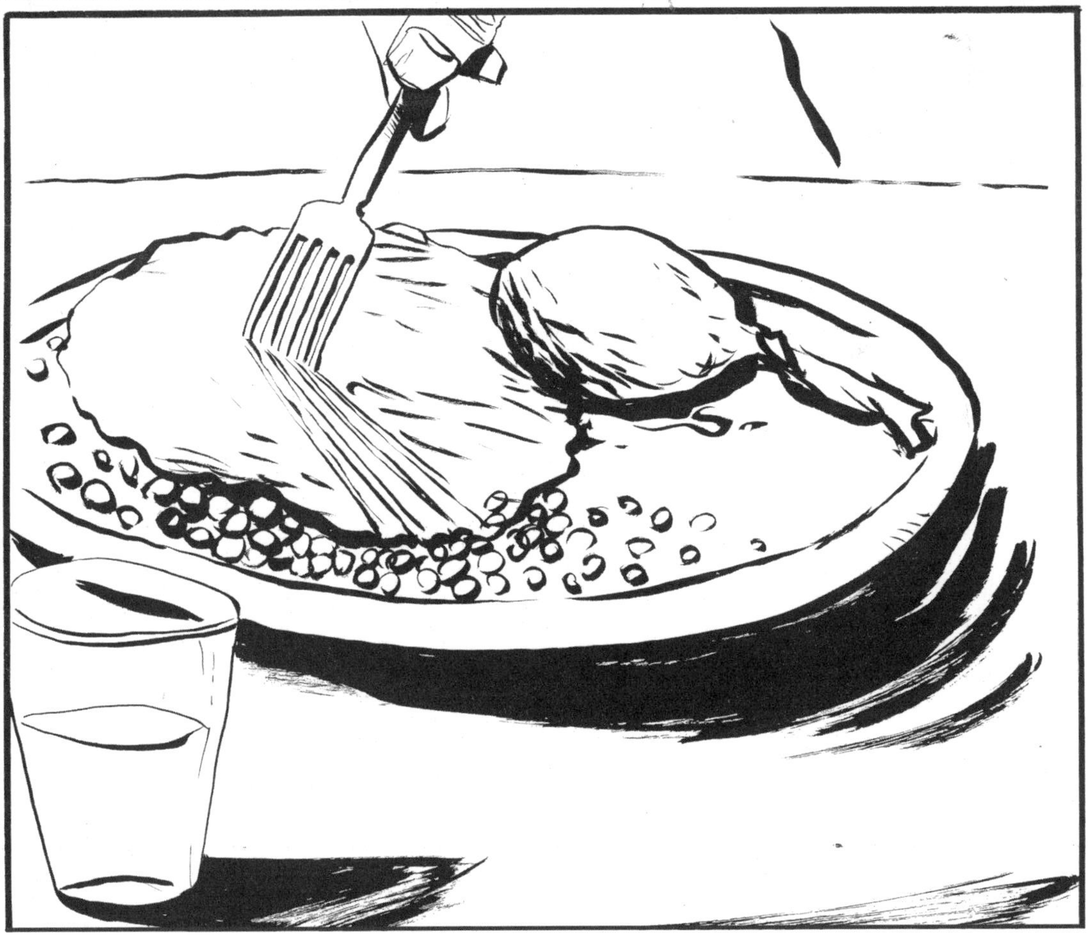

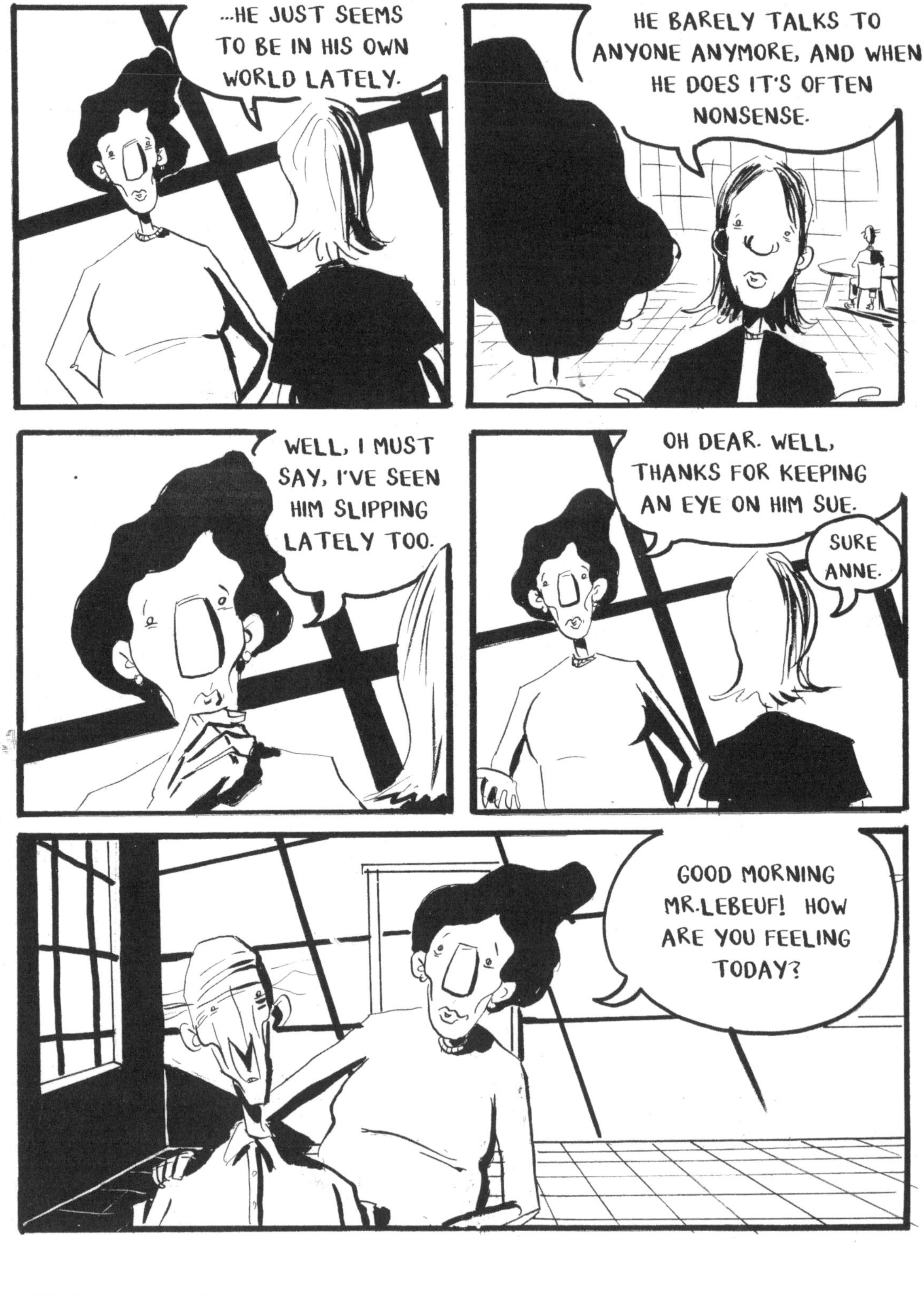

...HE JUST SEEMS TO BE IN HIS OWN WORLD LATELY.
HE BARELY TALKS TO ANYONE ANYMORE, AND WHEN HE DOES IT'S OFTEN NONSENSE.
WELL, I MUST SAY, I'VE SEEN HIM SLIPPING LATELY TOO.
OH DEAR. WELL, THANKS FOR KEEPING AN EYE ON HIM SUE.
SURE ANNE.
GOOD MORNING MR.LEBEUF! HOW ARE YOU FEELING TODAY?

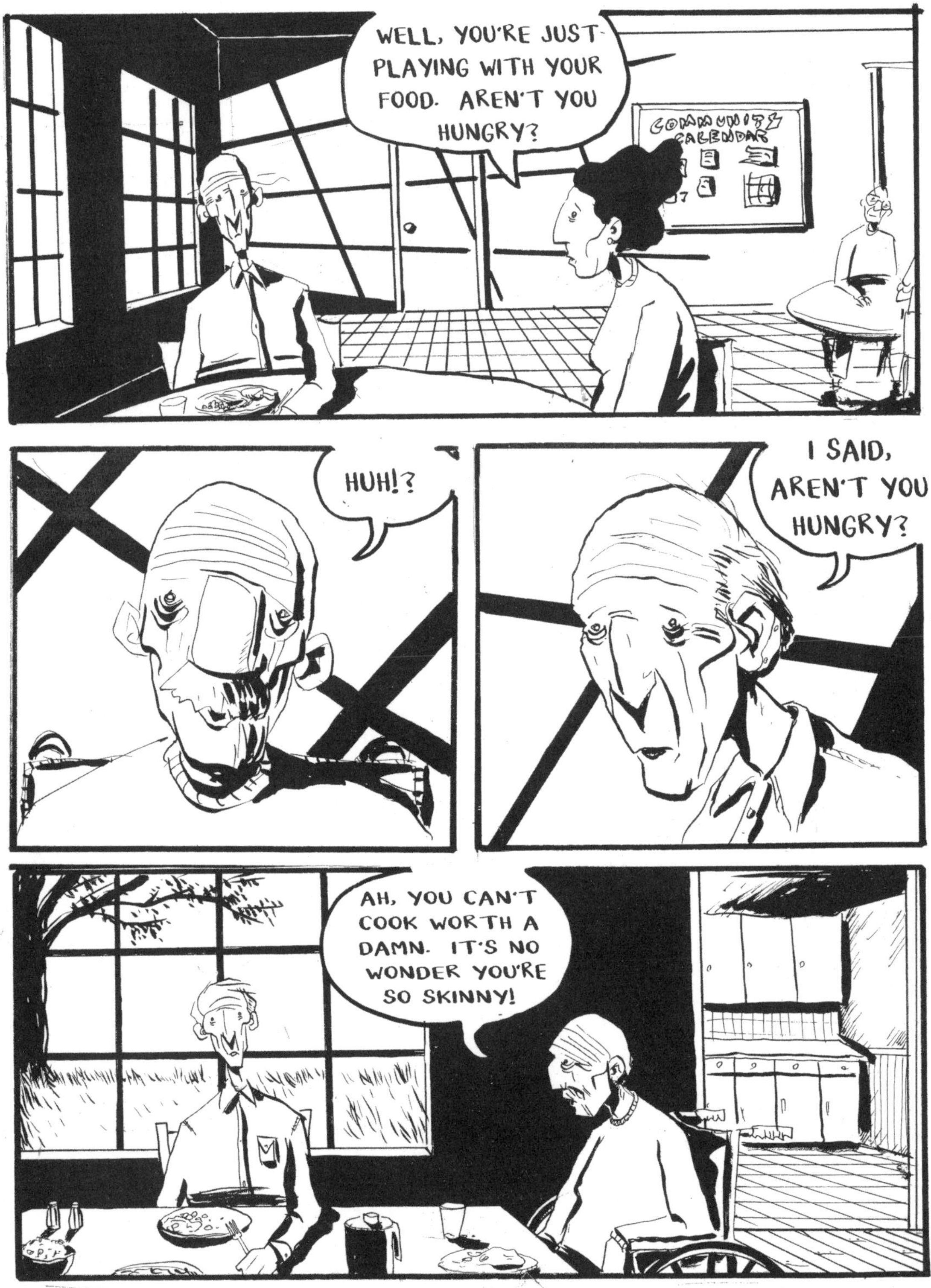
WELL, YOU'RE JUST PLAYING WITH YOUR FOOD. AREN'T YOU HUNGRY?
COMMUNITY CALENDAR
HUH!?
I SAID, AREN'T YOU HUNGRY?
AH, YOU CAN'T COOK WORTH A DAMN. IT'S NO WONDER YOU'RE SO SKINNY!

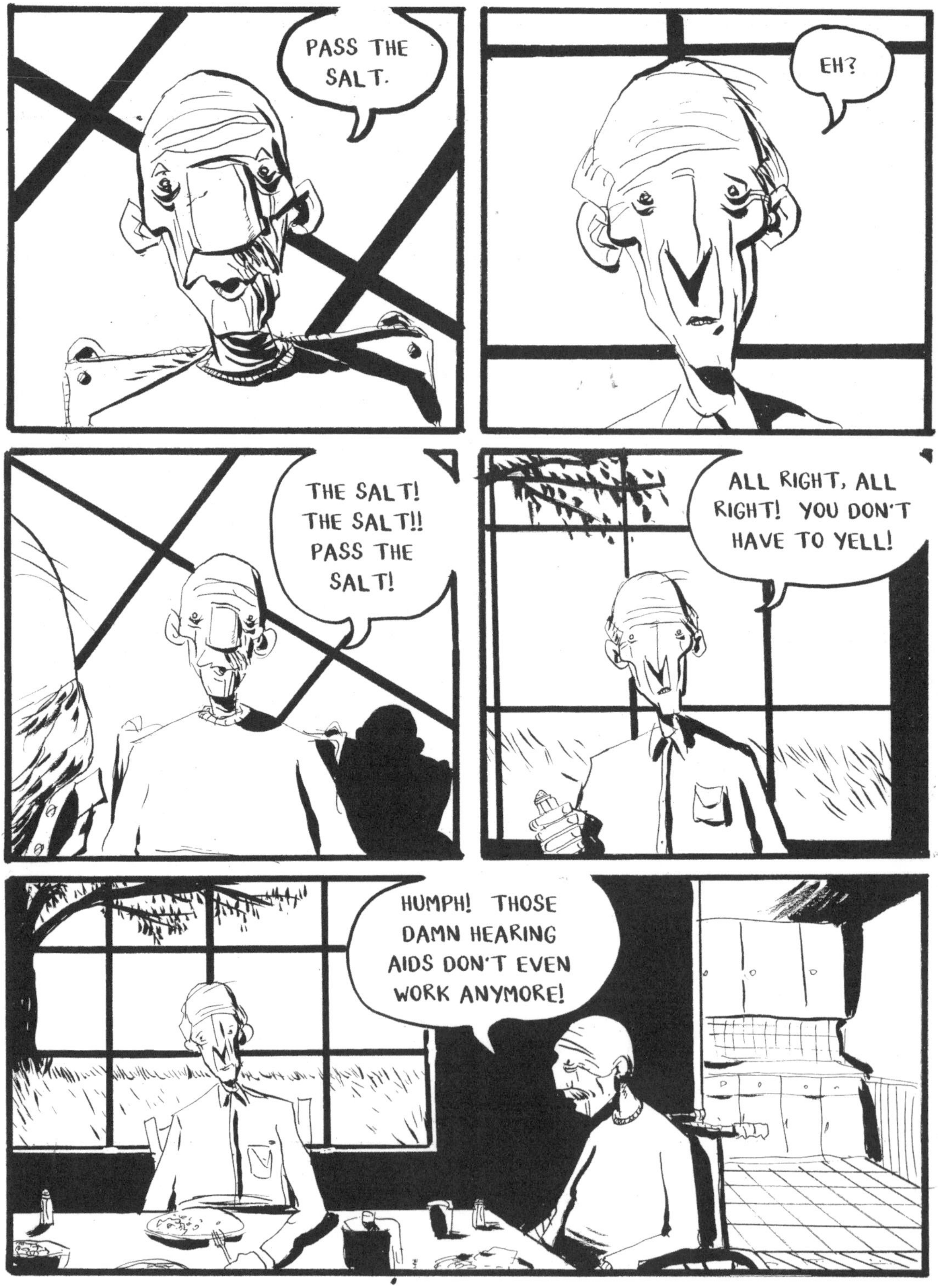
PASS THE SALT.
EH?
THE SALT! THE SALT!! PASS THE SALT!
ALL RIGHT, ALL RIGHT! YOU DON'T HAVE TO YELL!
HUMPH! THOSE DAMN HEARING AIDS DON'T EVEN WORK ANYMORE!

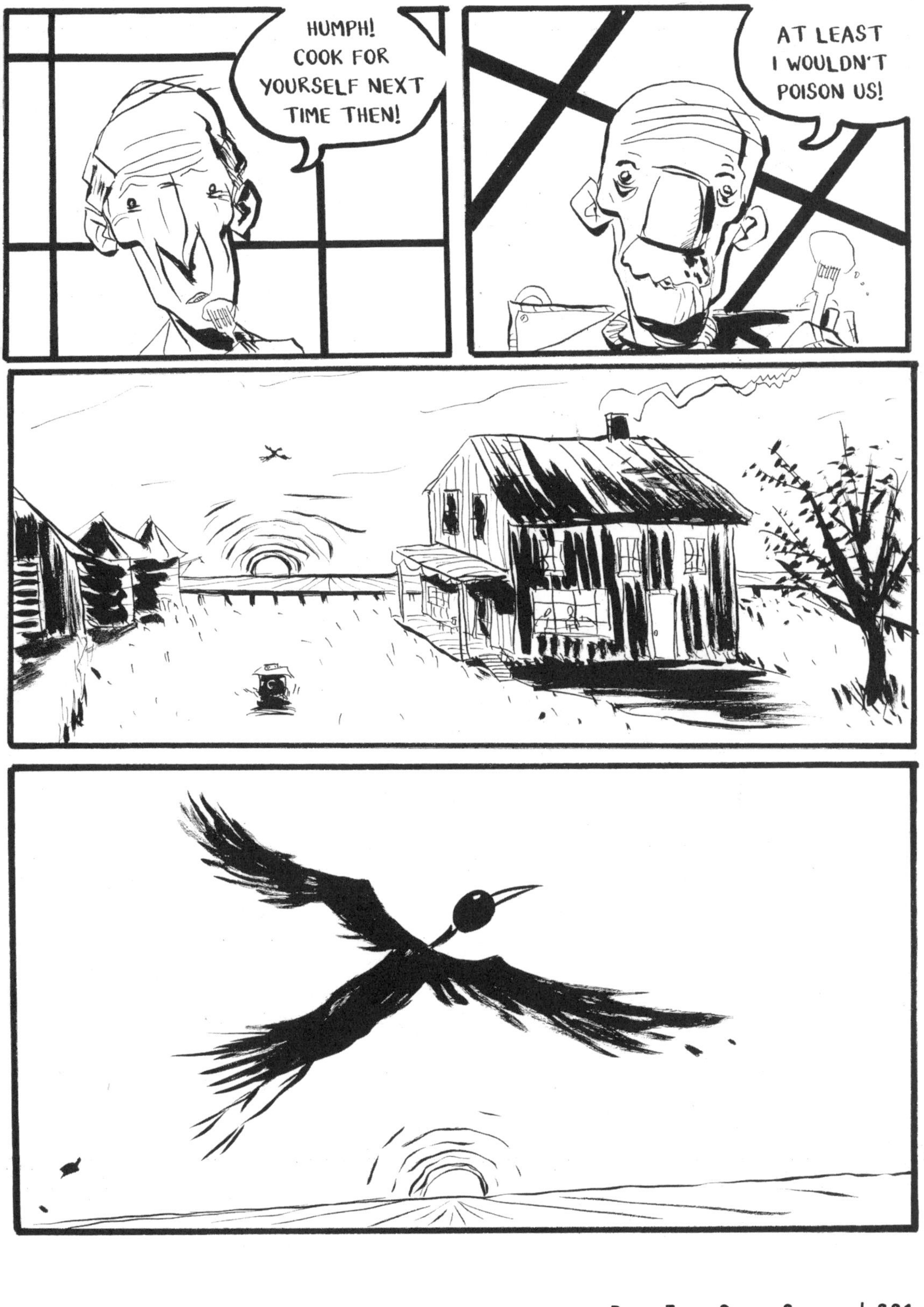
HUMPH! COOK FOR YOURSELF NEXT TIME THEN!
AT LEAST I WOULDN'T POISON US!

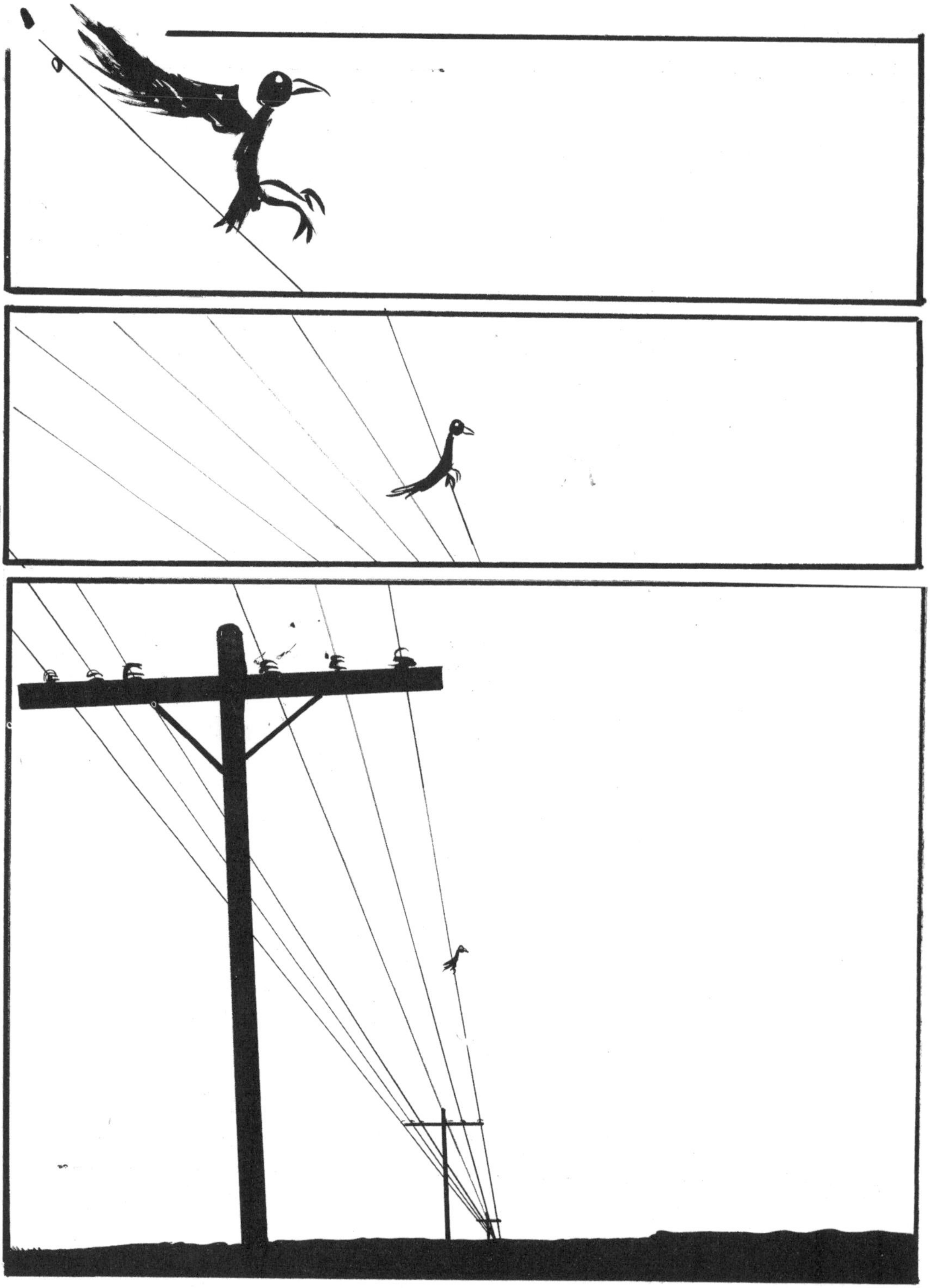

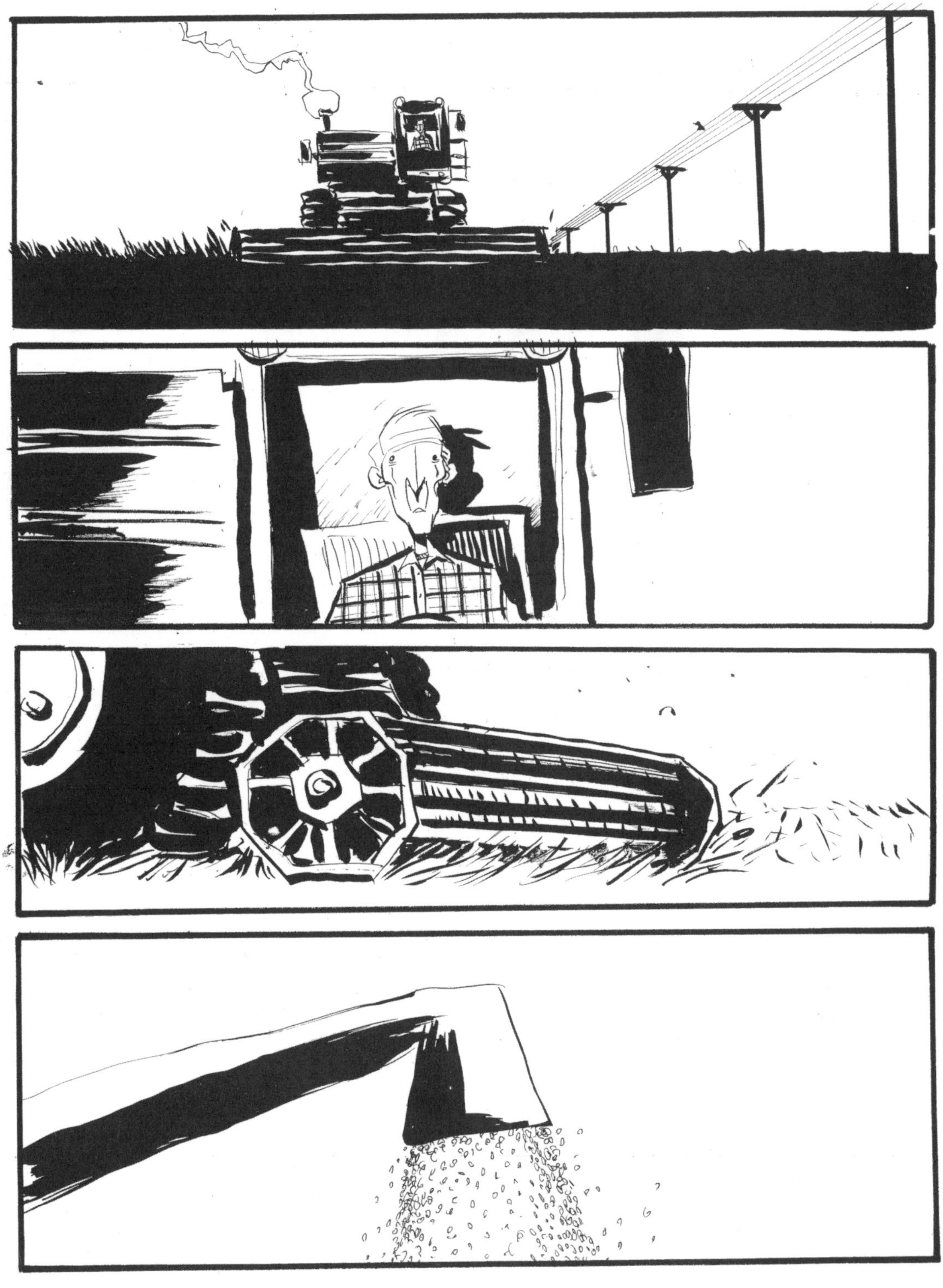

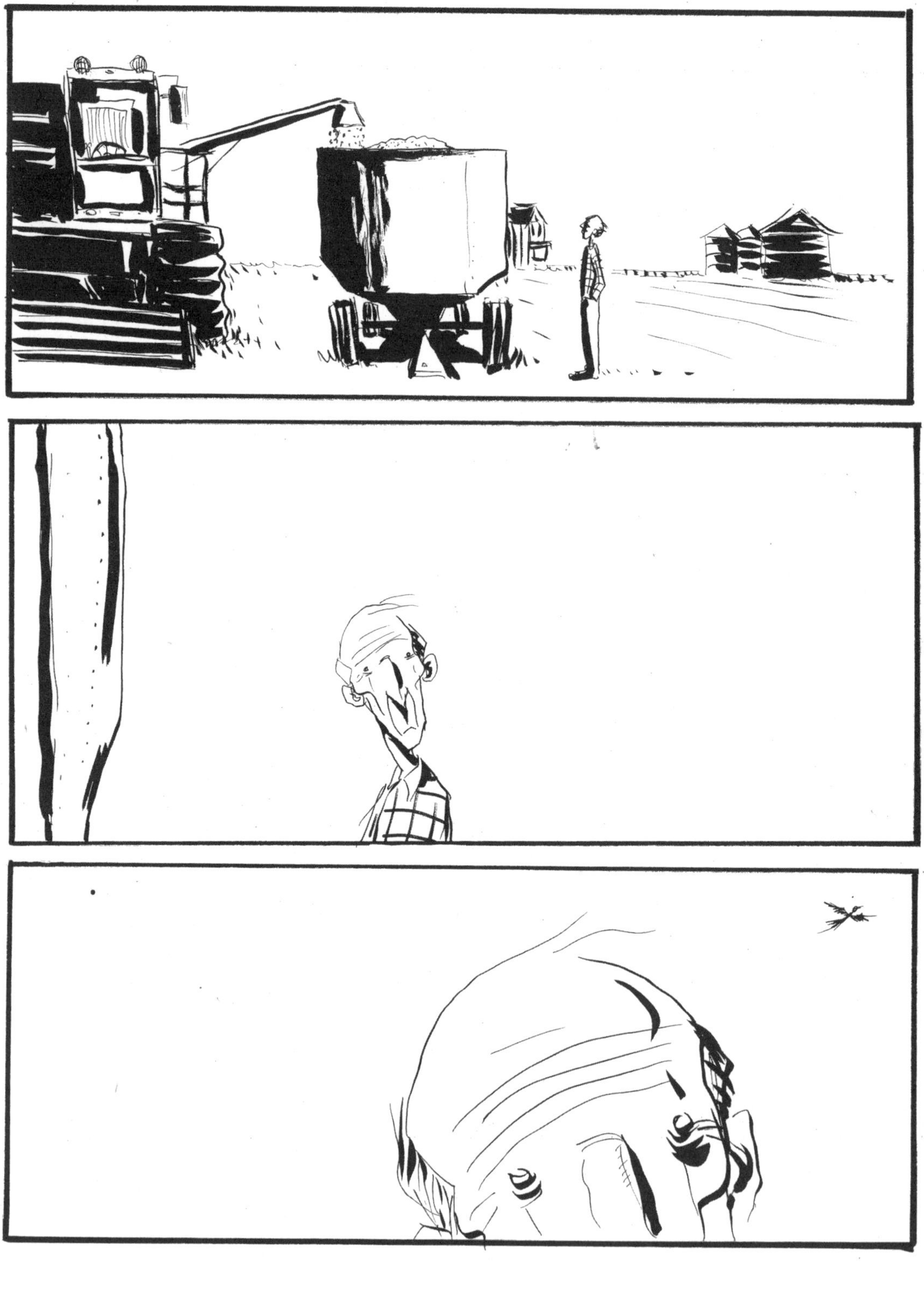

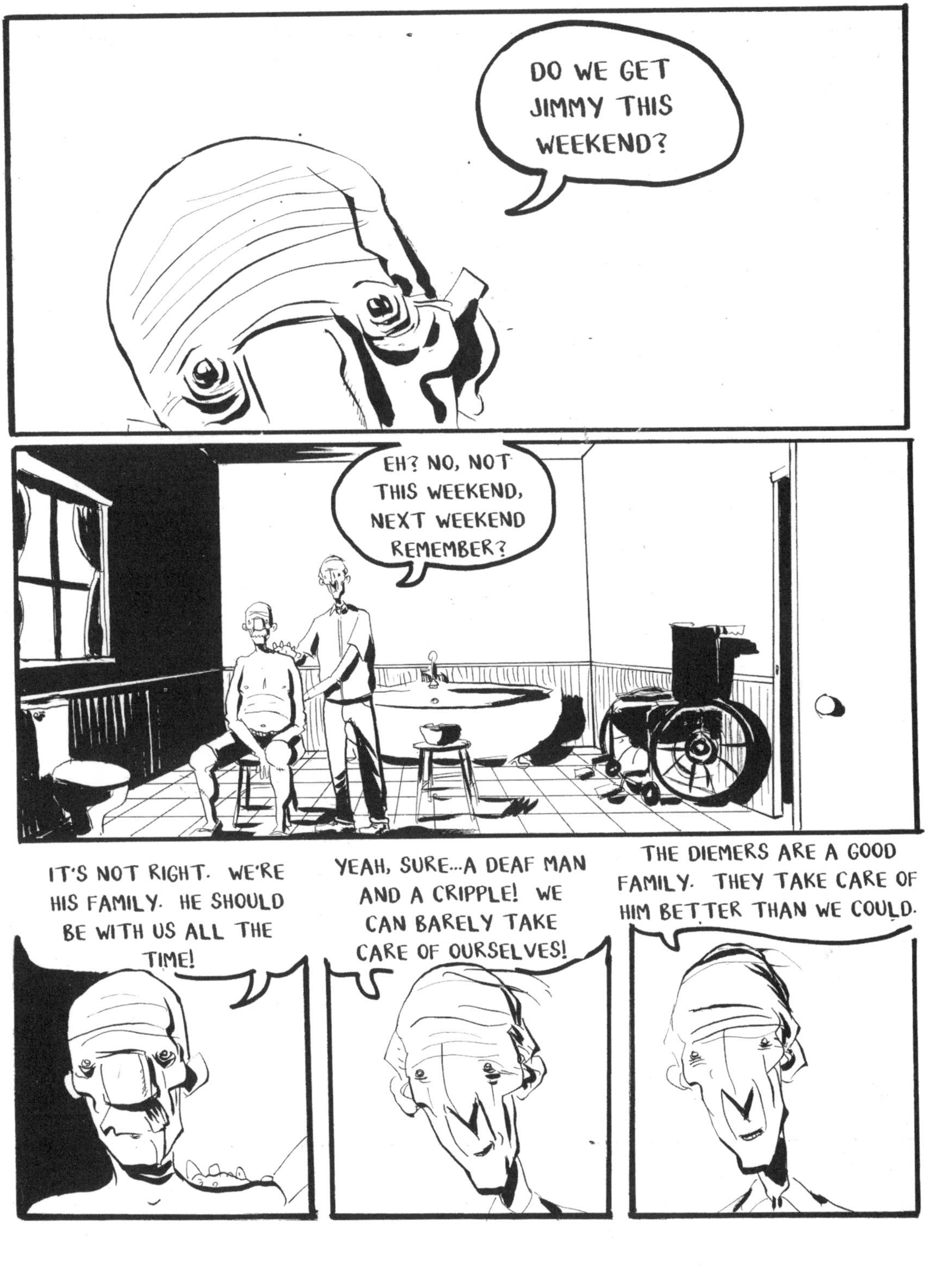
DO WE GET JIMMY THIS WEEKEND?
EH? NO, NOT THIS WEEKEND, NEXT WEEKEND REMEMBER?
IT'S NOT RIGHT. WE'RE HIS FAMILY. HE SHOULD BE WITH US ALL THE TIME!
YEAH, SURE...A DEAF MAN AND A CRIPPLE! WE CAN BARELY TAKE CARE OF OURSELVES!
THE DIEMERS ARE A GOOD FAMILY. THEY TAKE CARE OF HIM BETTER THAN WE COULD.

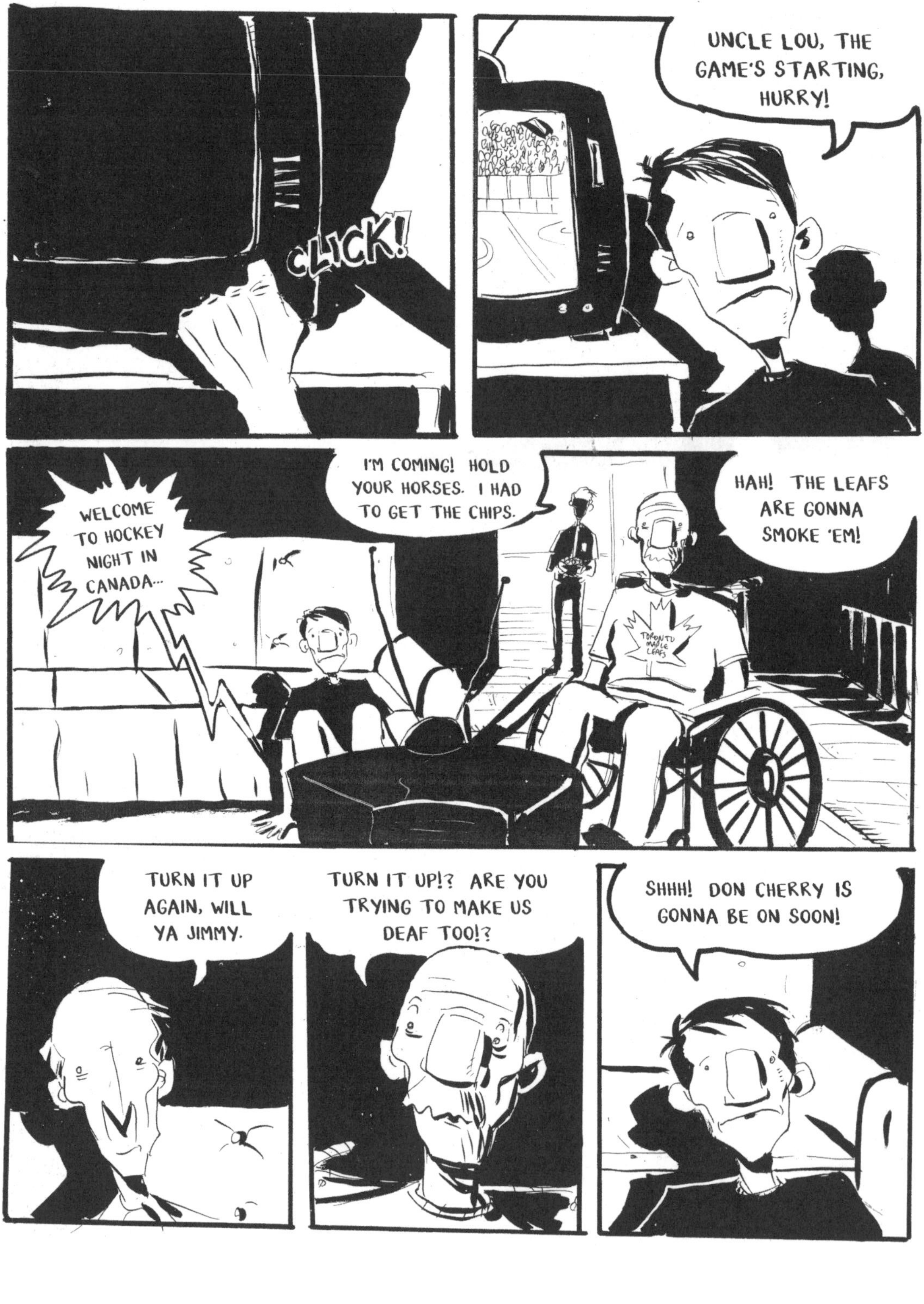
CLICK!
UNCLE LOU, THE GAME'S STARTING, HURRY!
WELCOME TO HOCKEY NIGHT IN CANADA...
I'M COMING! HOLD YOUR HORSES. I HAD TO GET THE CHIPS.
HAH! THE LEAFS ARE GONNA SMOKE 'EM!
TORONTO MAPLE LEAFS
TURN IT UP AGAIN, WILL YA JIMMY.
TURN IT UP!? ARE YOU TRYING TO MAKE US DEAF TOO!?
SHHH! DON CHERRY IS GONNA BE ON SOON!

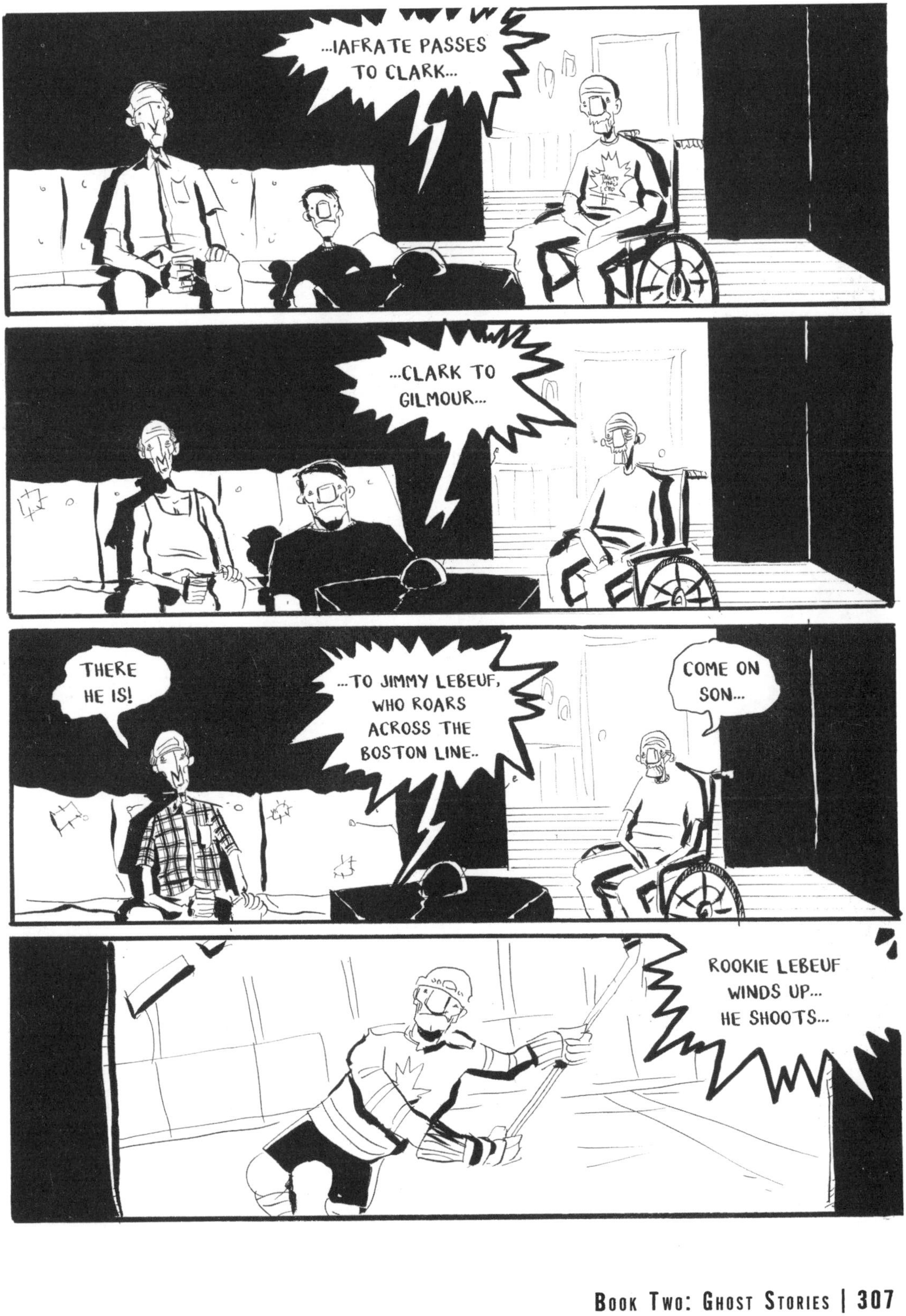
...IAFRATE PASSES TO CLARK...
...CLARK TO GILMOUR...
THERE HE IS!
...TO JIMMY LEBEUF, WHO ROARS ACROSS THE BOSTON LINE..
COME ON SON...
ROOKIE LEBEUF WINDS UP... HE SHOOTS...

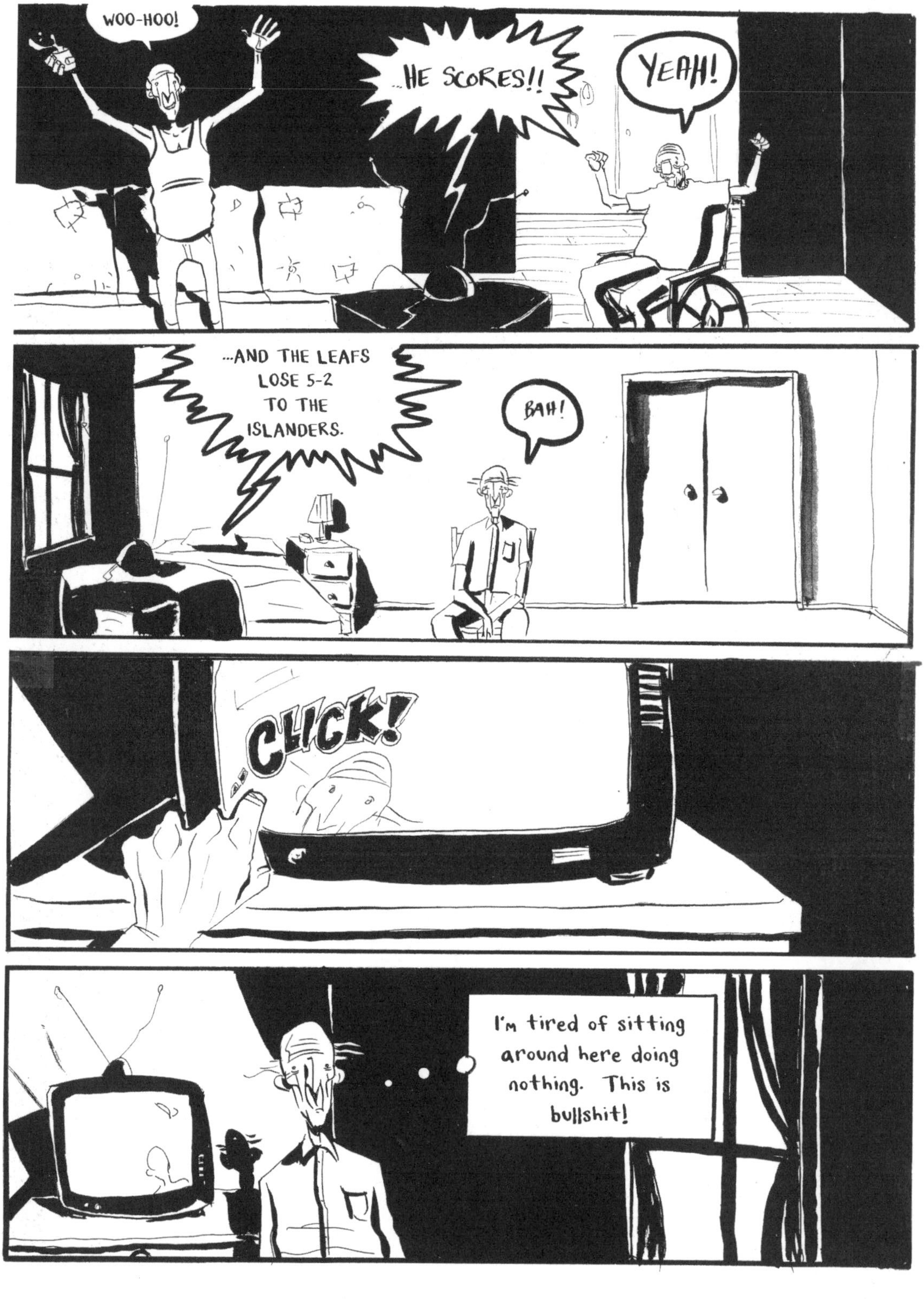
WOO-HOO!
...HE SCORES!!
YEAH!
...AND THE LEAFS LOSE 5-2 TO THE ISLANDERS.
BAH!
CLICK!
I'm tired of sitting around here doing nothing. This is bullshit!

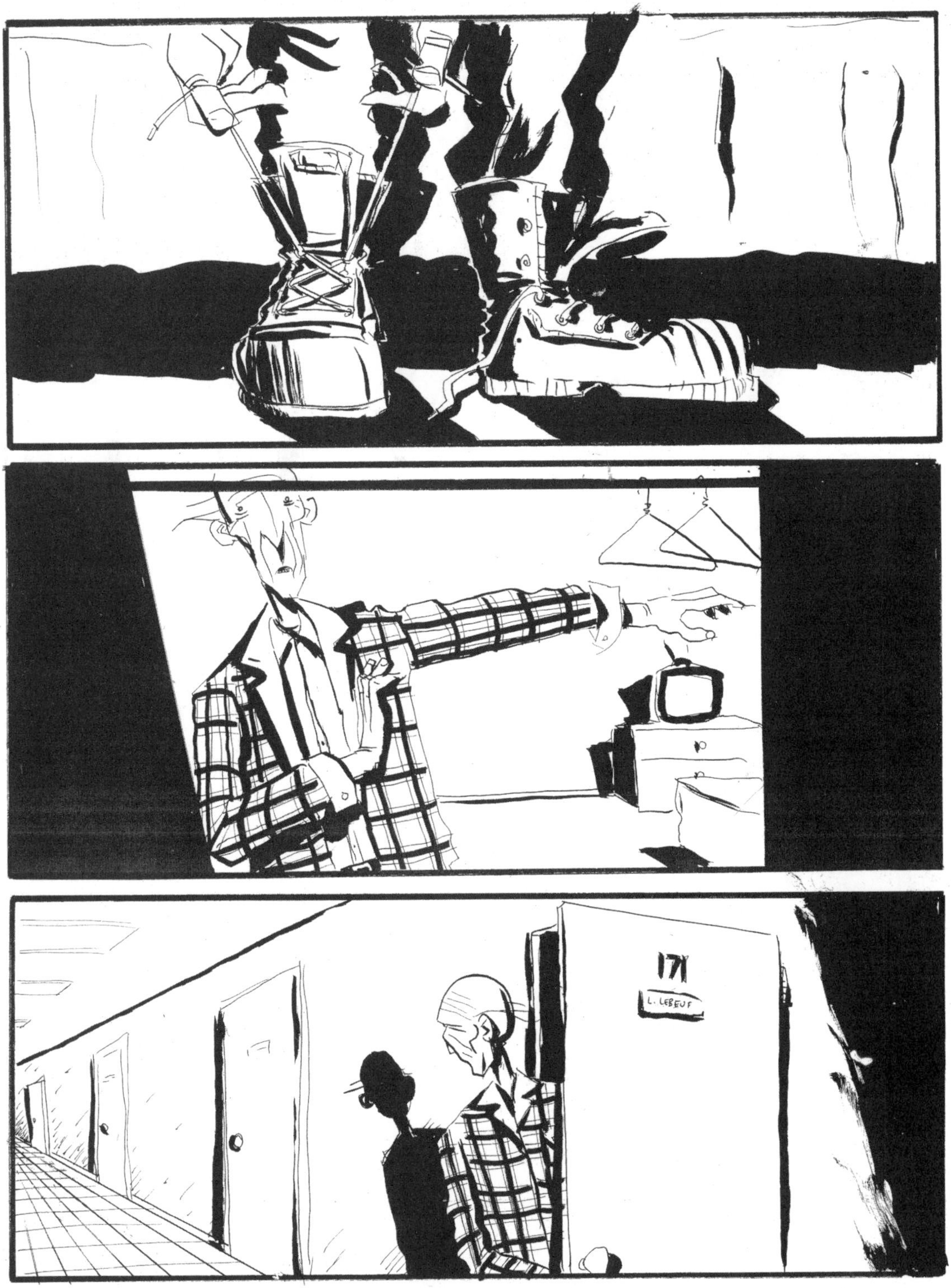
171
L. LEBEUF

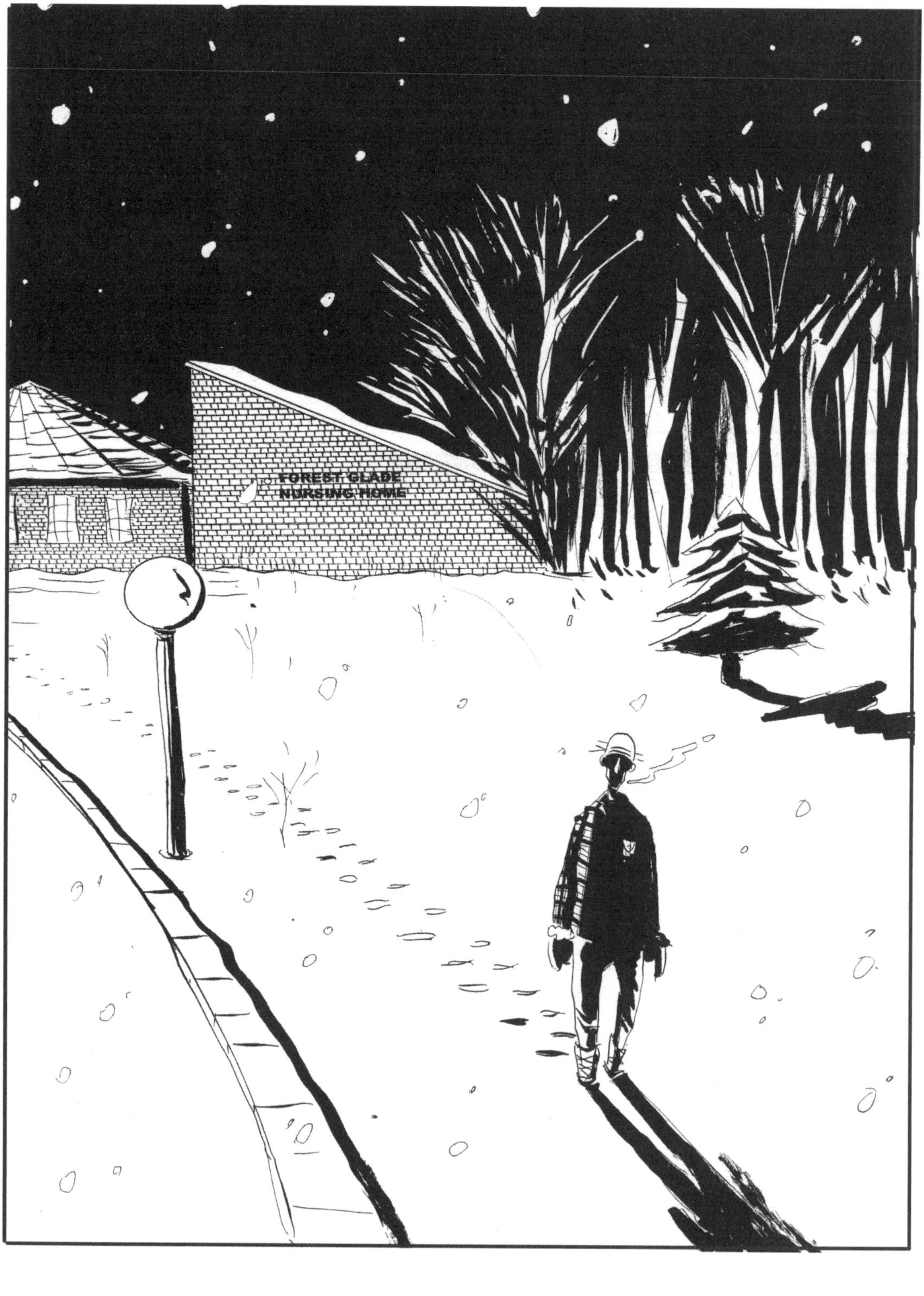
FOREST GLADE
NURSING HOME

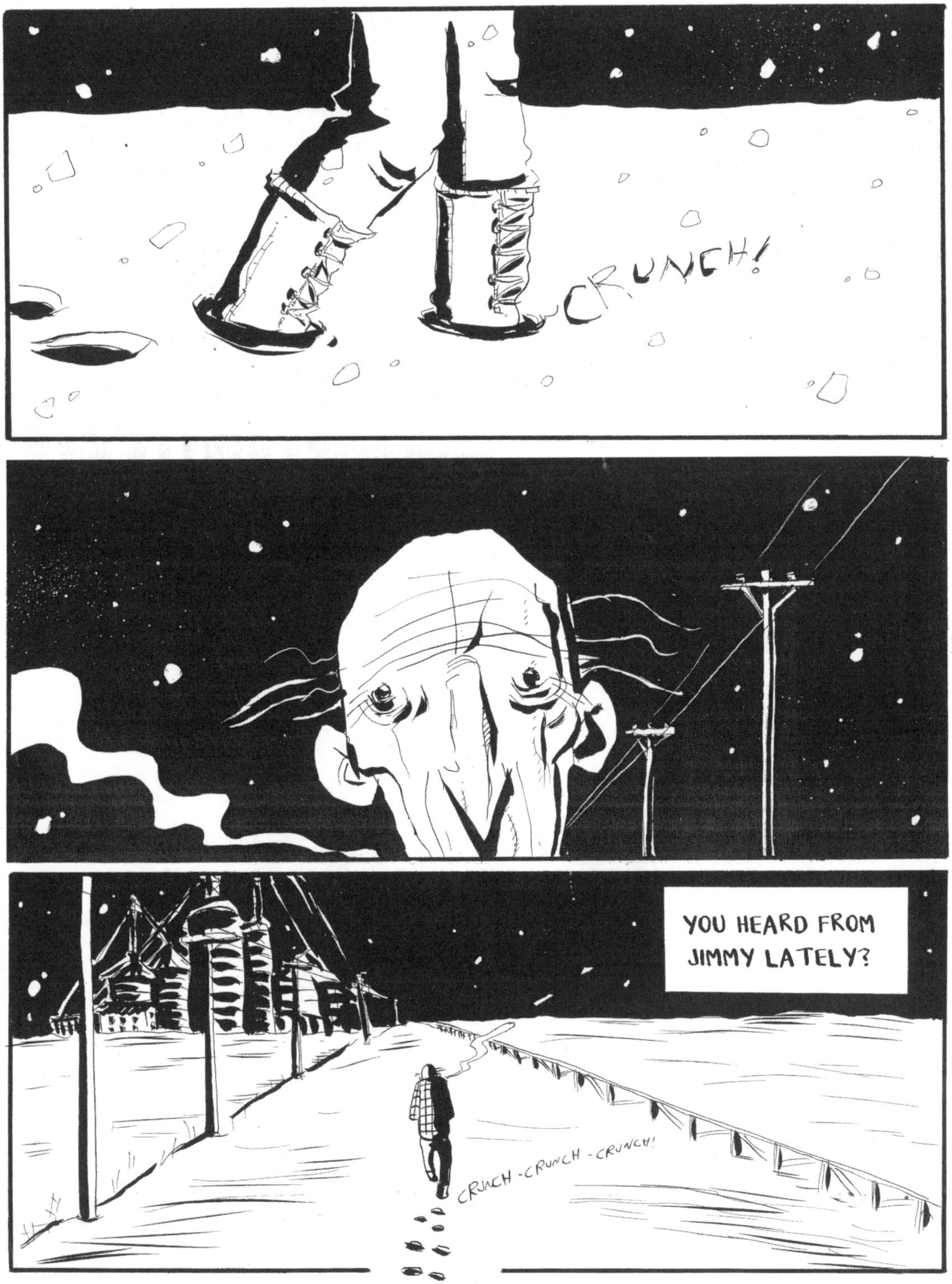
CRUNCH!
YOU HEARD FROM JIMMY LATELY?
CRUNCH -CRUNCH -CRUNCH!

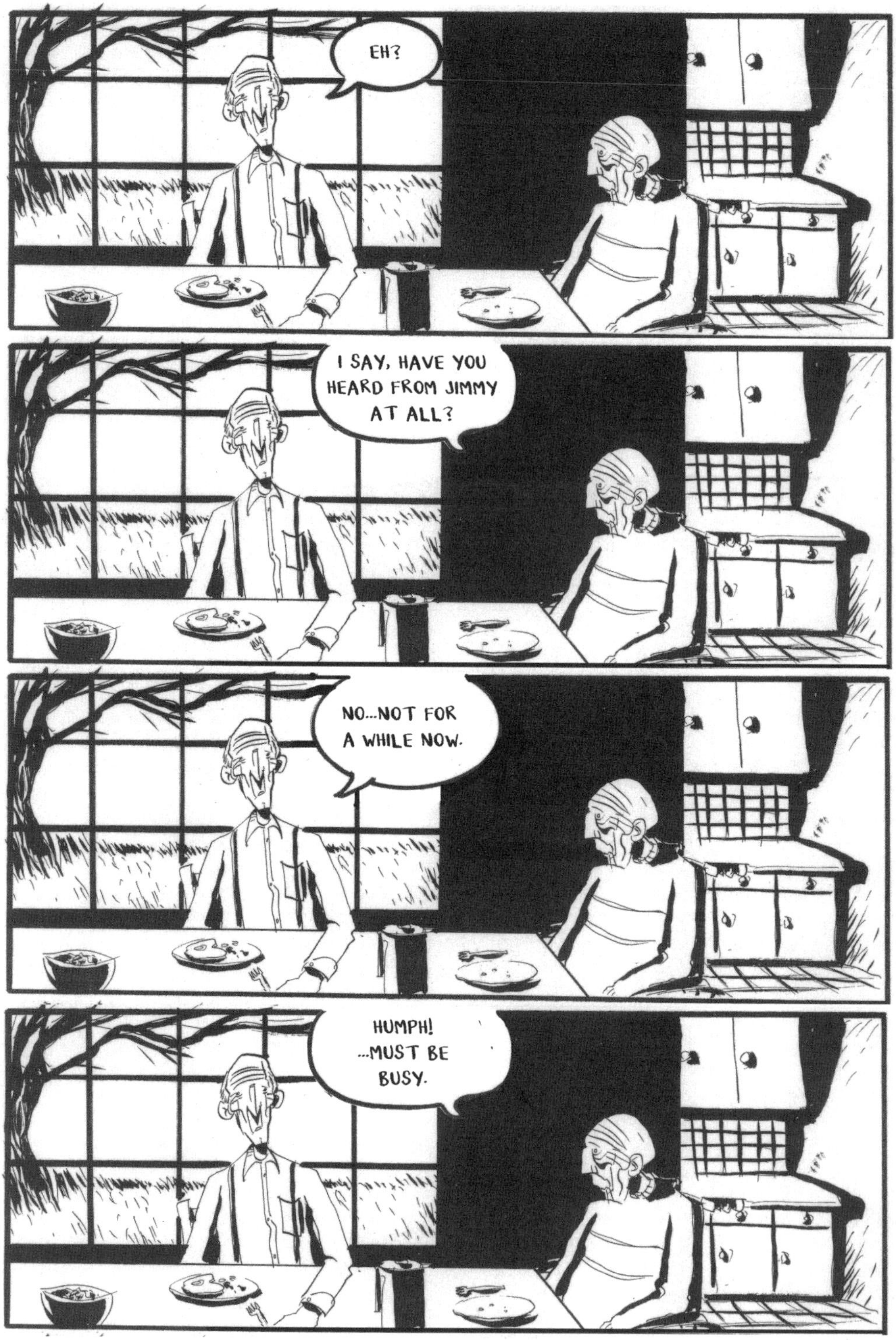
EH?
I SAY, HAVE YOU HEARD FROM JIMMY AT ALL?
NO...NOT FOR A WHILE NOW.
HUMPH! ...MUST BE BUSY.

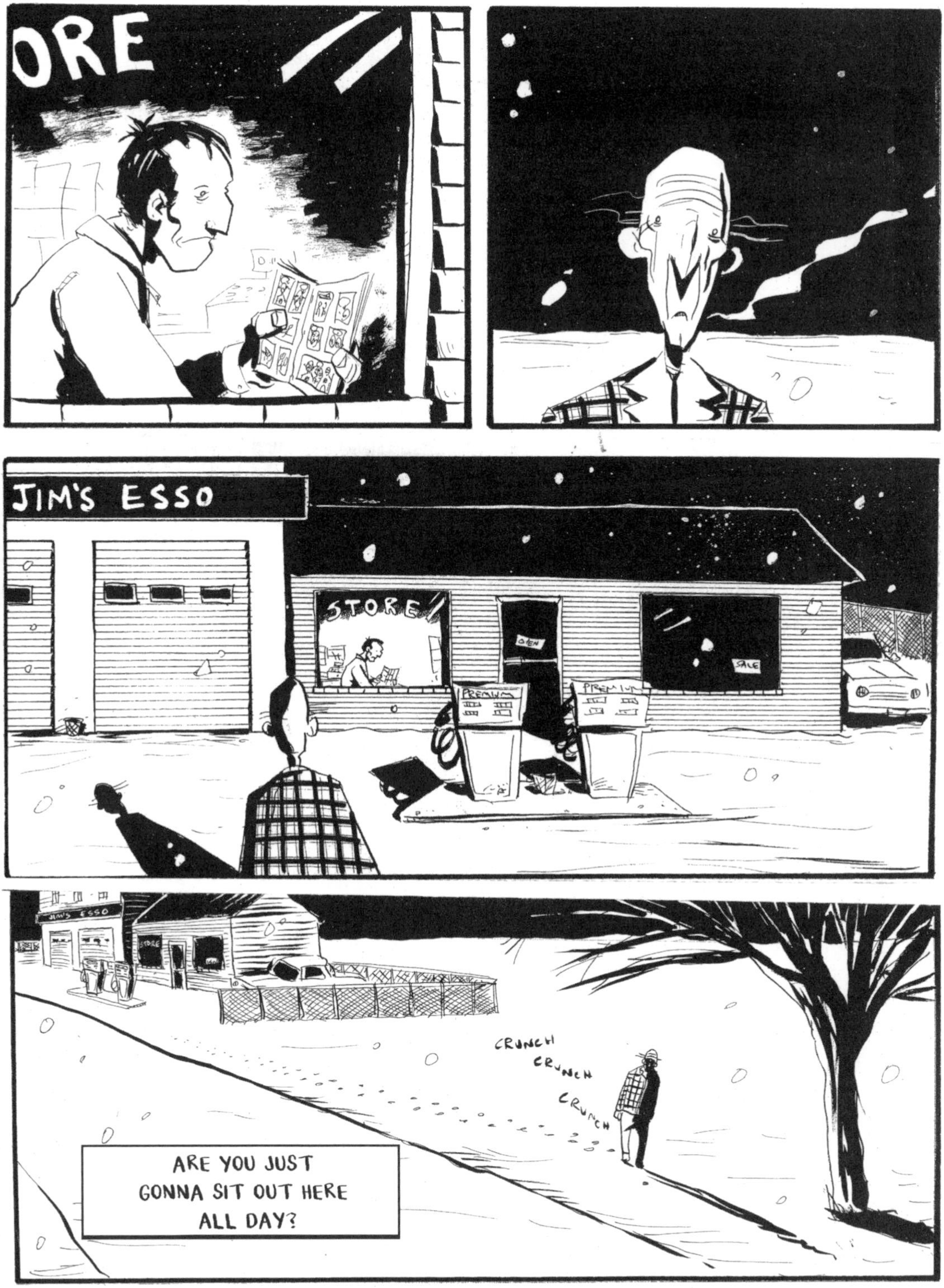
ORE
JIM'S ESSO
STORE
OPEN
SALE
PREMIUM
PREMIUM
JIM'S ESSO
STORE
CRUNCH
CRUNCH
CRUNCH
ARE YOU JUST GONNA SIT OUT HERE ALL DAY?

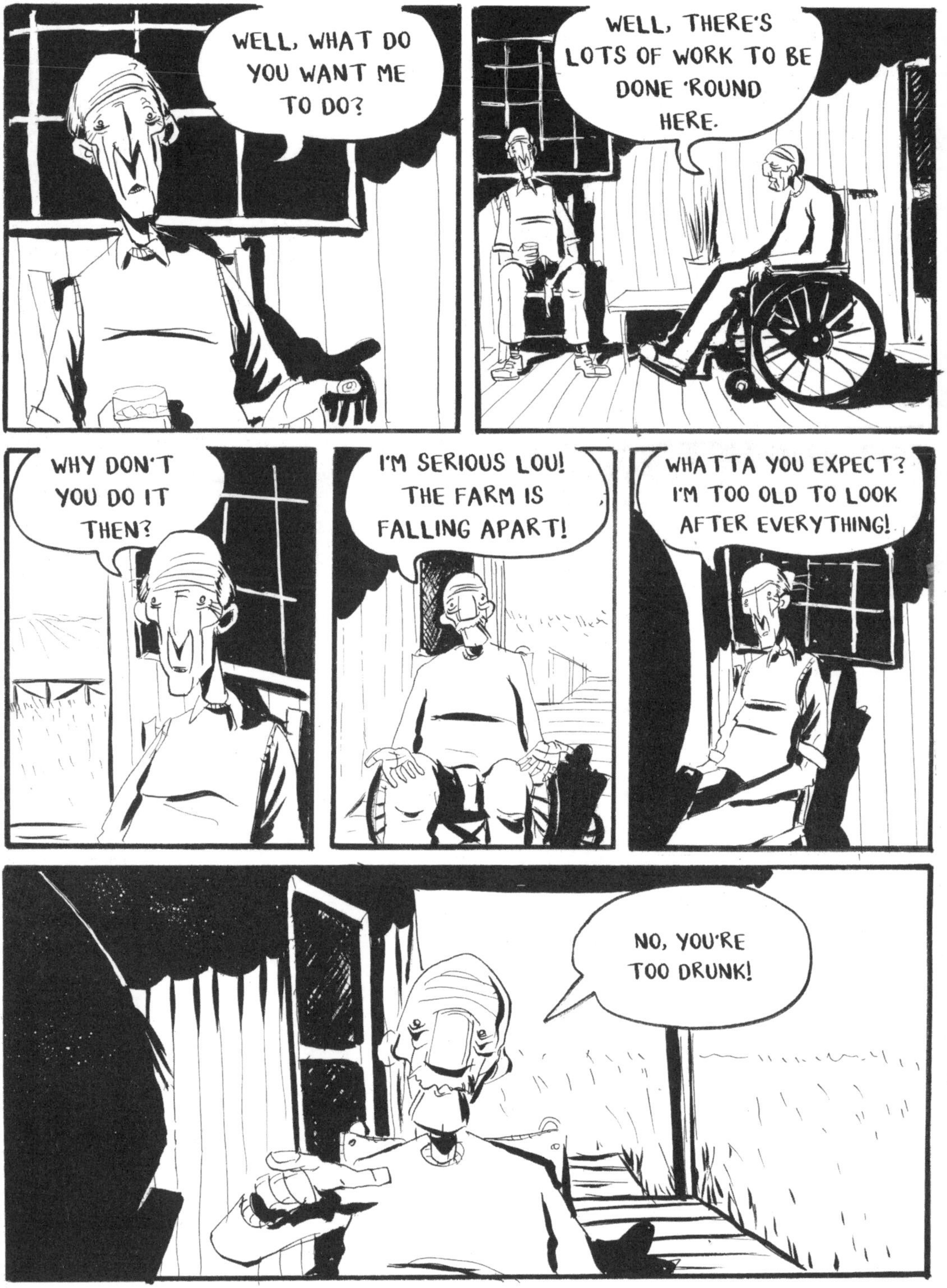
WELL, WHAT DO YOU WANT ME TO DO?
WELL, THERE'S LOTS OF WORK TO BE DONE 'ROUND HERE.
WHY DON'T YOU DO IT THEN?
I'M SERIOUS LOU! THE FARM IS FALLING APART!
WHATTA YOU EXPECT? I'M TOO OLD TO LOOK AFTER EVERYTHING!
NO, YOU'RE TOO DRUNK!

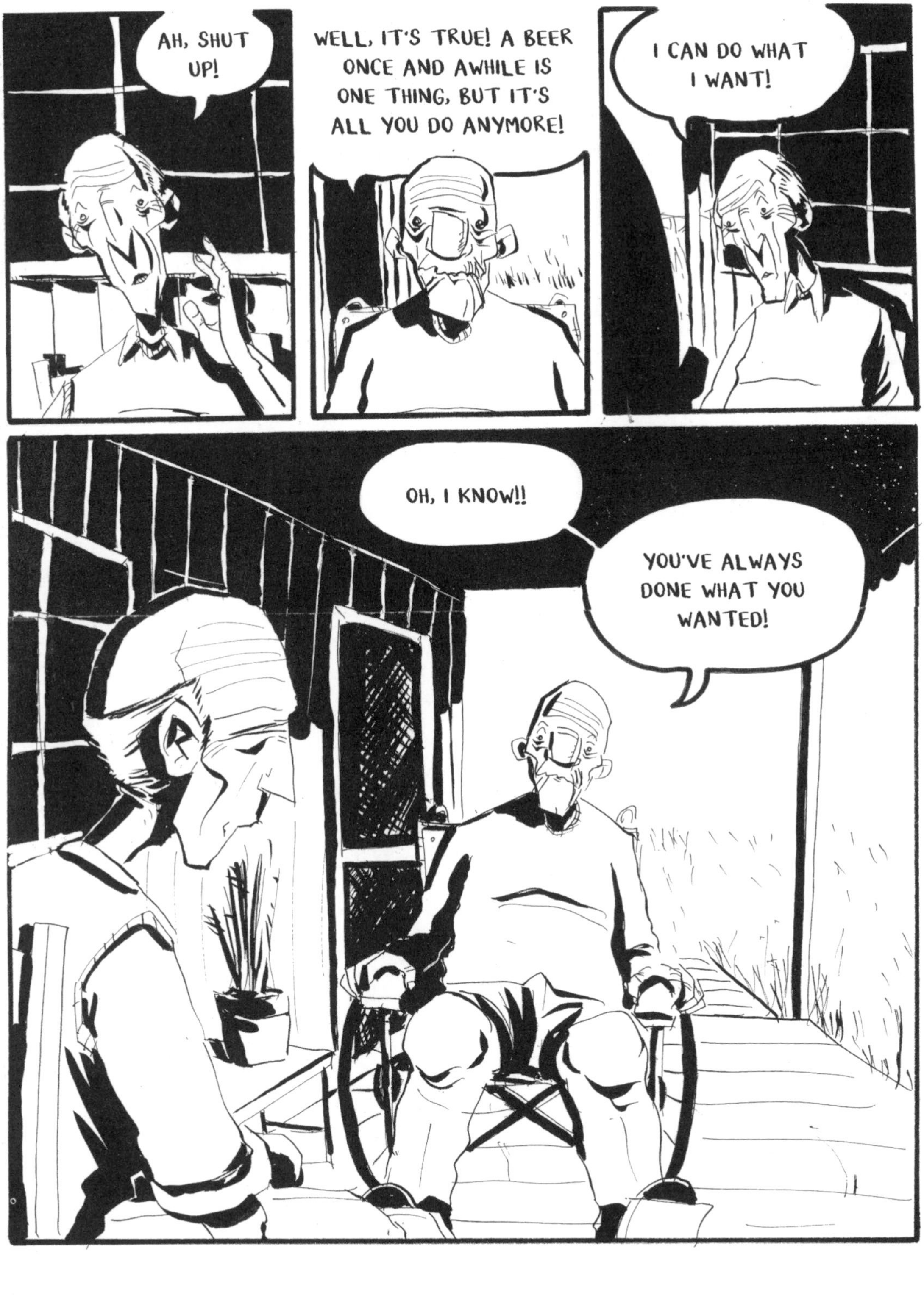
AH, SHUT UP!
WELL, IT'S TRUE! A BEER ONCE AND AWHILE IS ONE THING, BUT IT'S ALL YOU DO ANYMORE!
I CAN DO WHAT I WANT!
OH, I KNOW!!
YOU'VE ALWAYS DONE WHAT YOU WANTED!

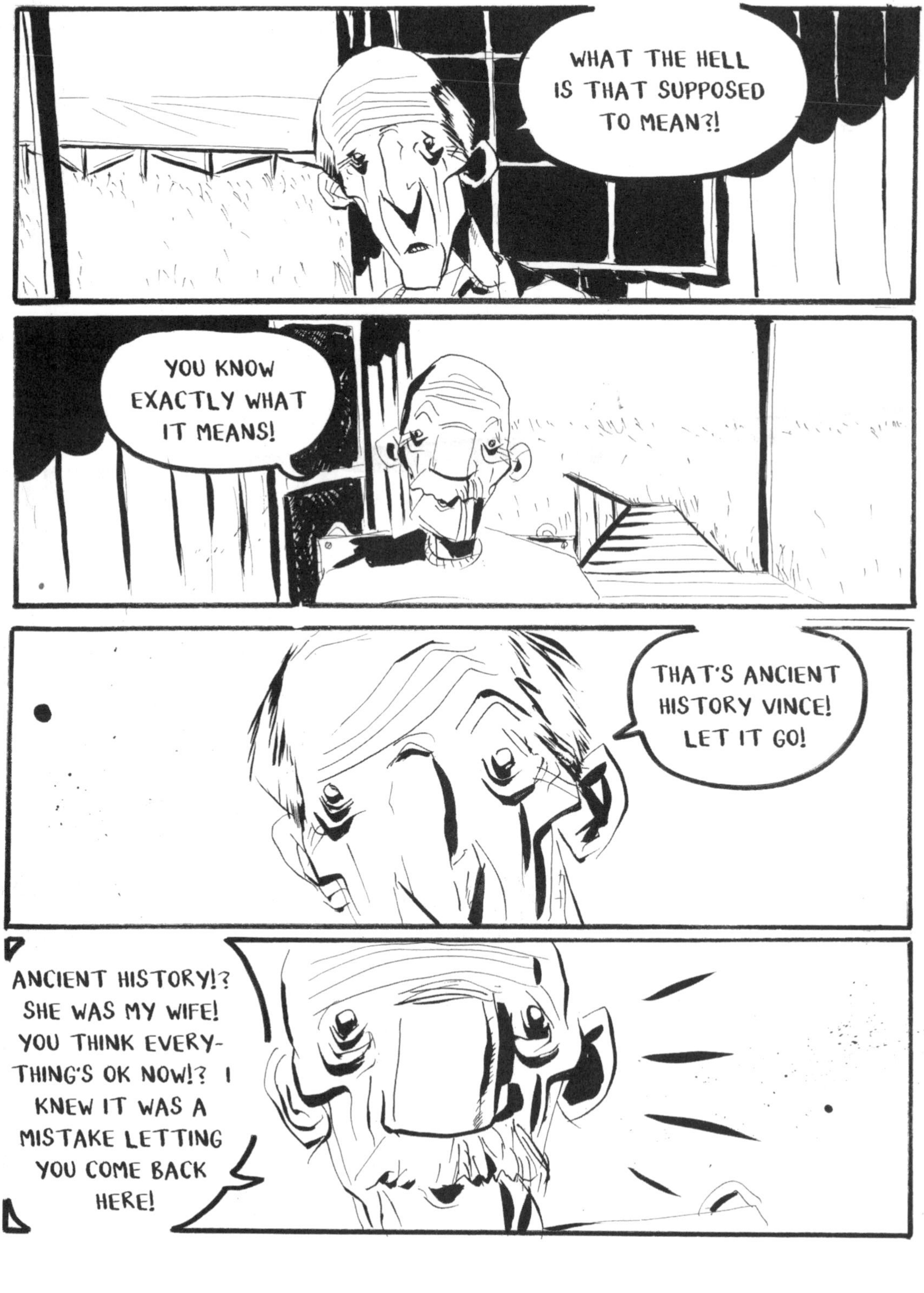
WHAT THE HELL IS THAT SUPPOSED TO MEAN?!
YOU KNOW EXACTLY WHAT IT MEANS!
THAT'S ANCIENT HISTORY VINCE! LET IT GO!
ANCIENT HISTORY!? SHE WAS MY WIFE! YOU THINK EVERY-THING'S OK NOW!? I KNEW IT WAS A MISTAKE LETTING YOU COME BACK HERE!

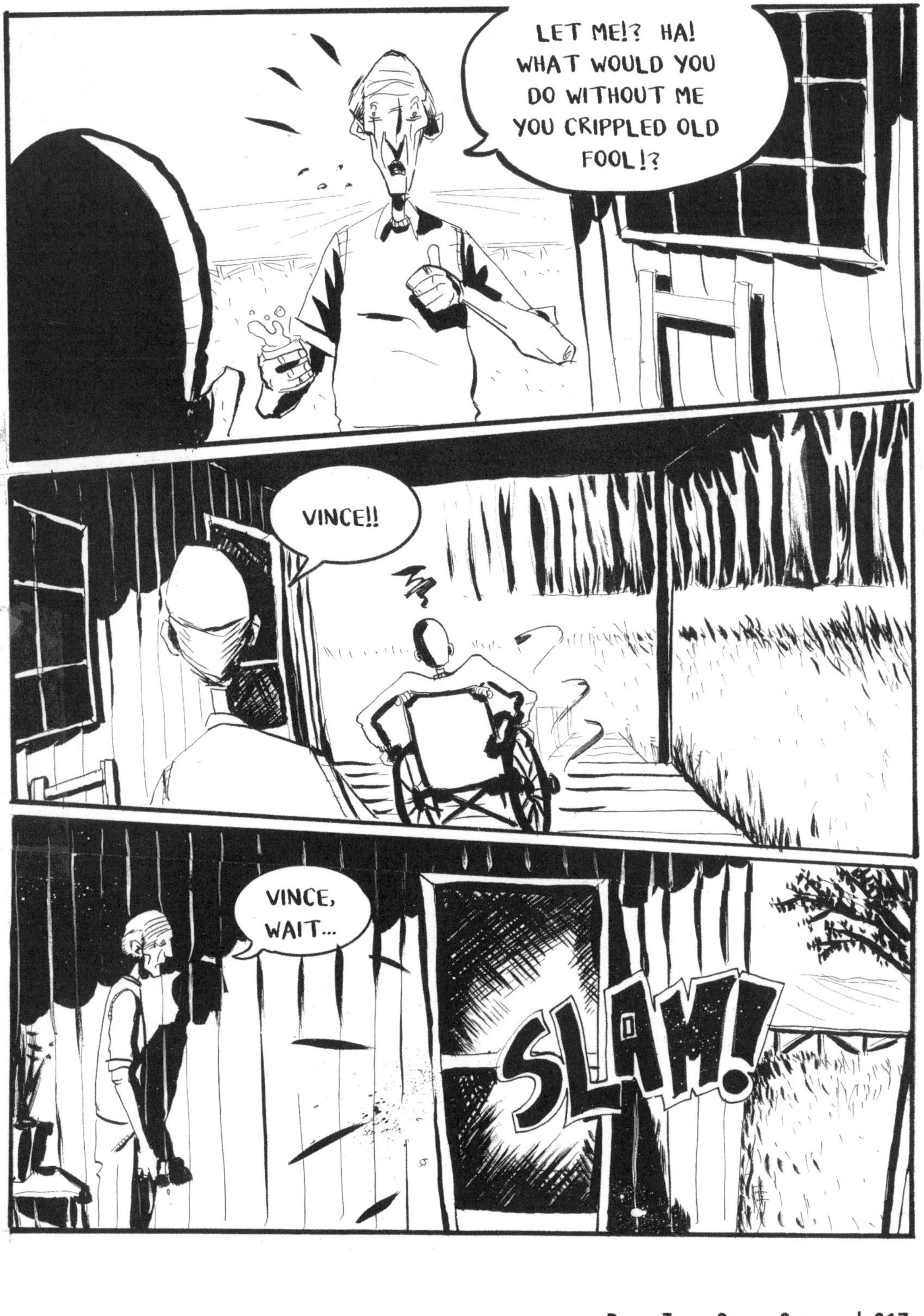
LET ME!? HA! WHAT WOULD YOU DO WITHOUT ME YOU CRIPPLED OLD FOOL!?
VINCE!!
VINCE, WAIT...
SLAM!

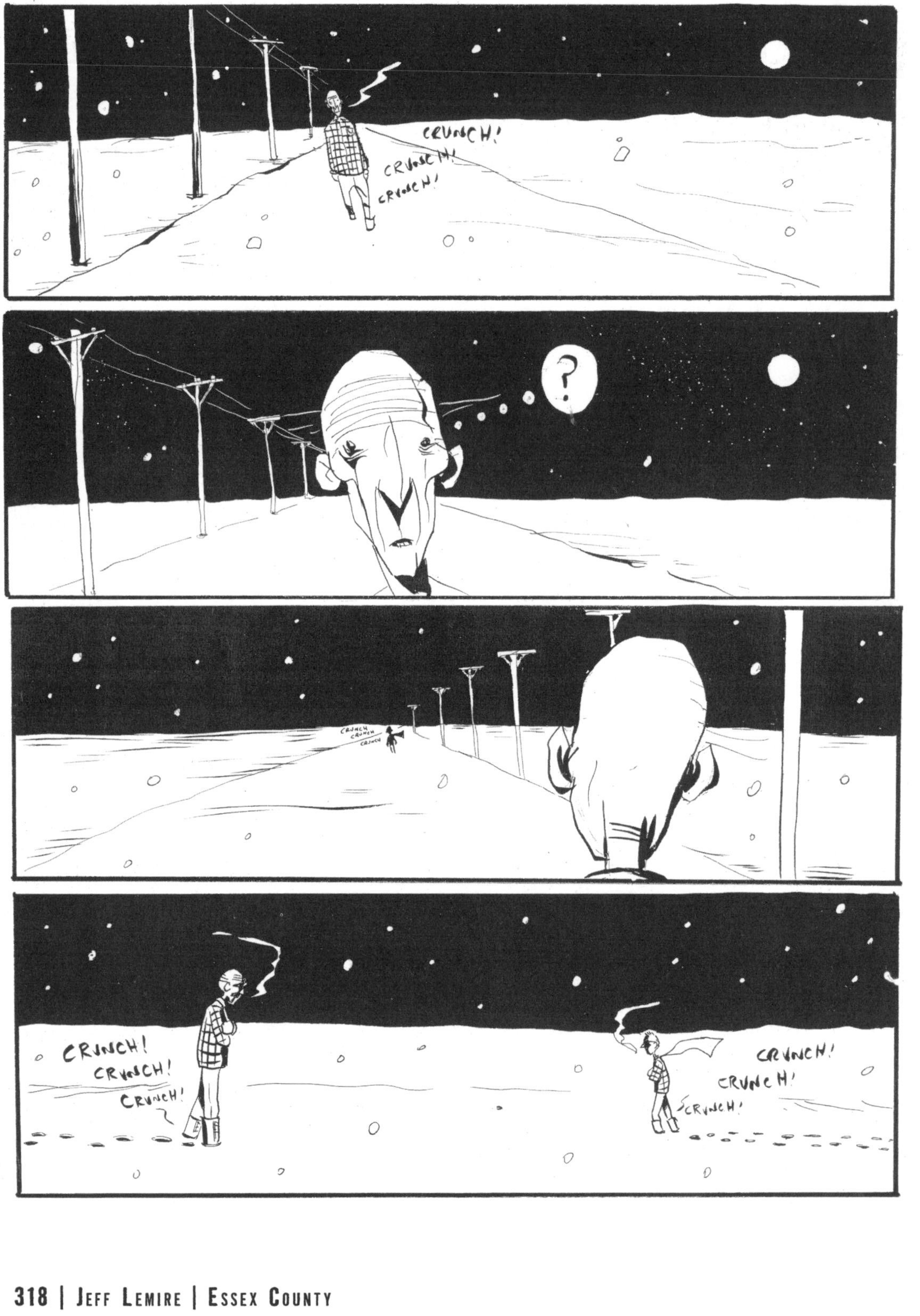
CRUNCH!
CRUNCH!
CRUNCH!
?
CRUNCH!
CRUNCH!
CRUNCH!
CRUNCH!
CRUNCH!
CRUNCH!

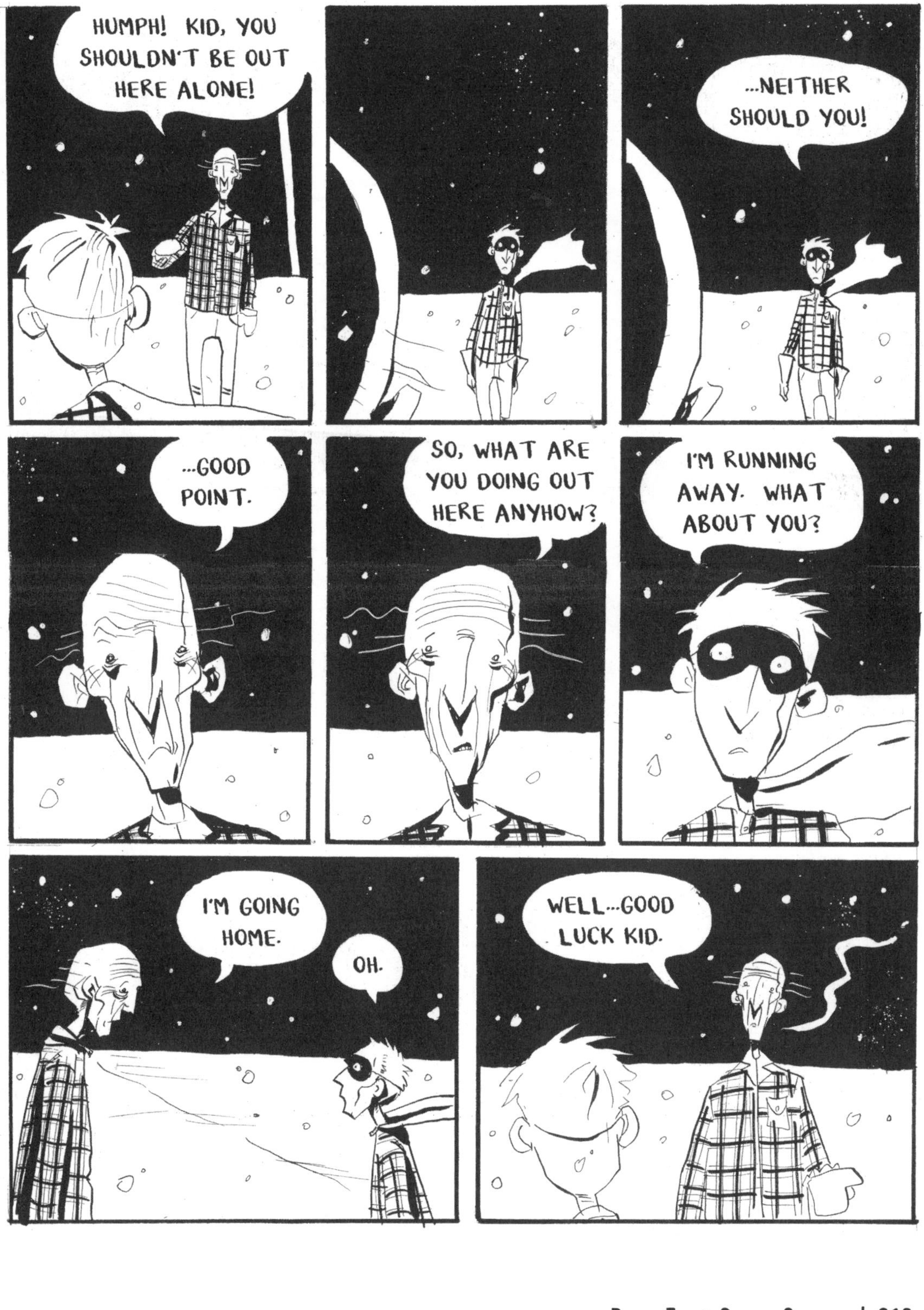
HUMPH! KID, YOU SHOULDN'T BE OUT HERE ALONE!
...NEITHER SHOULD YOU!
...GOOD POINT.
SO, WHAT ARE YOU DOING OUT HERE ANYHOW?
I'M RUNNING AWAY. WHAT ABOUT YOU?
I'M GOING HOME.
OH.
WELL...GOOD LUCK KID.

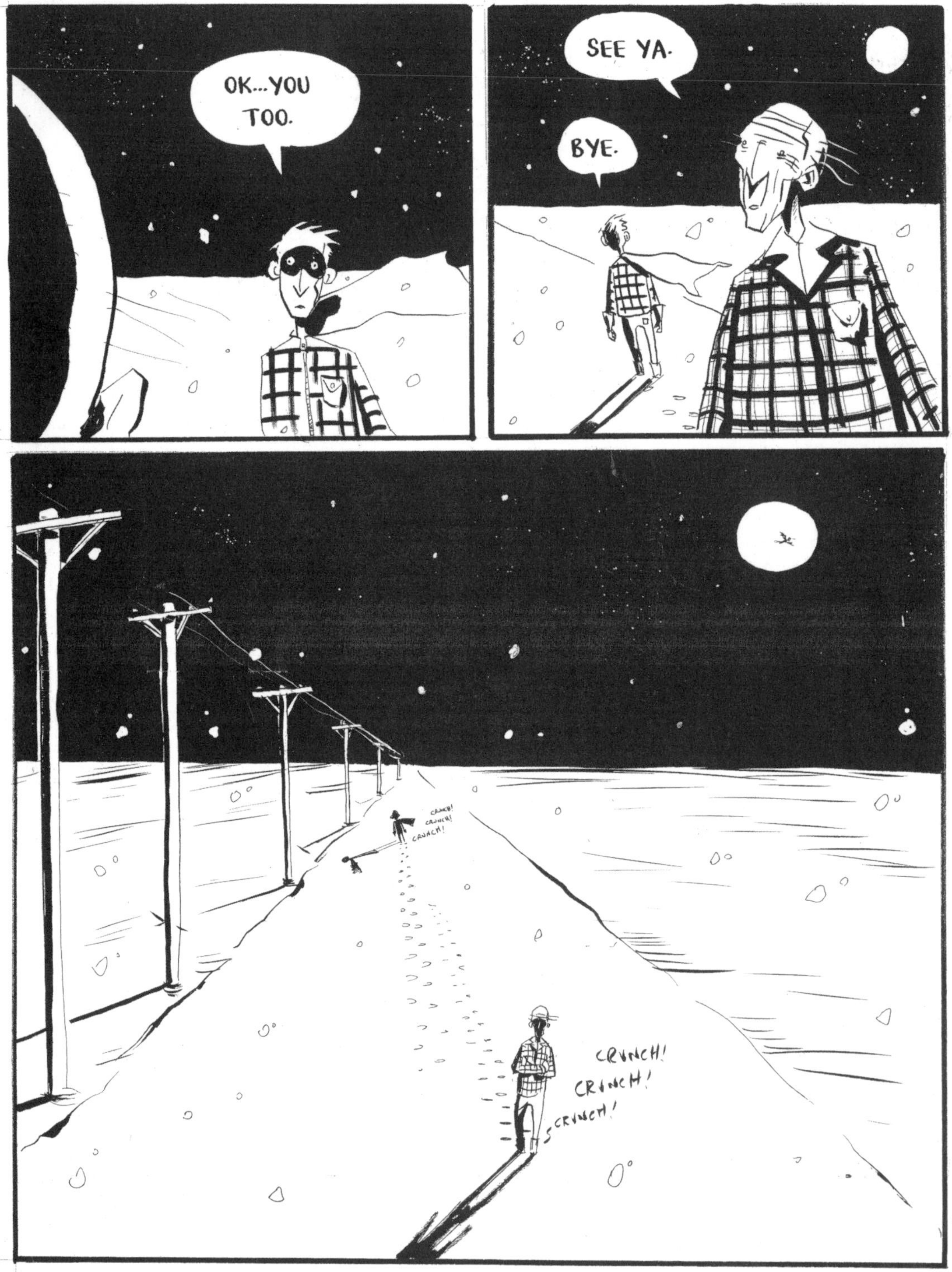
OK...YOU TOO.
SEE YA.
BYE.
CRUNCH!
CRUNCH!
CRUNCH!

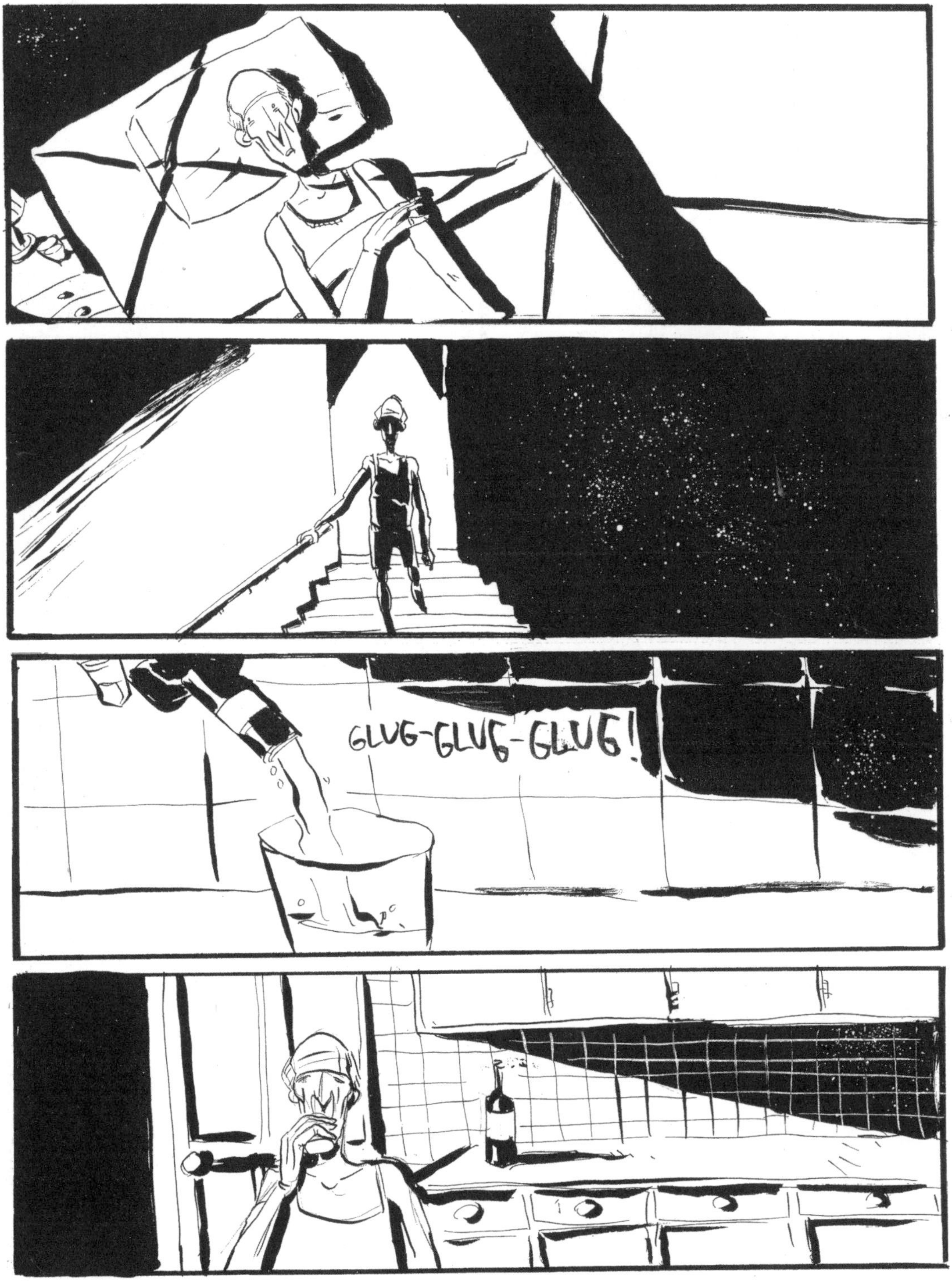
GLUG-GLUG-GLUG!

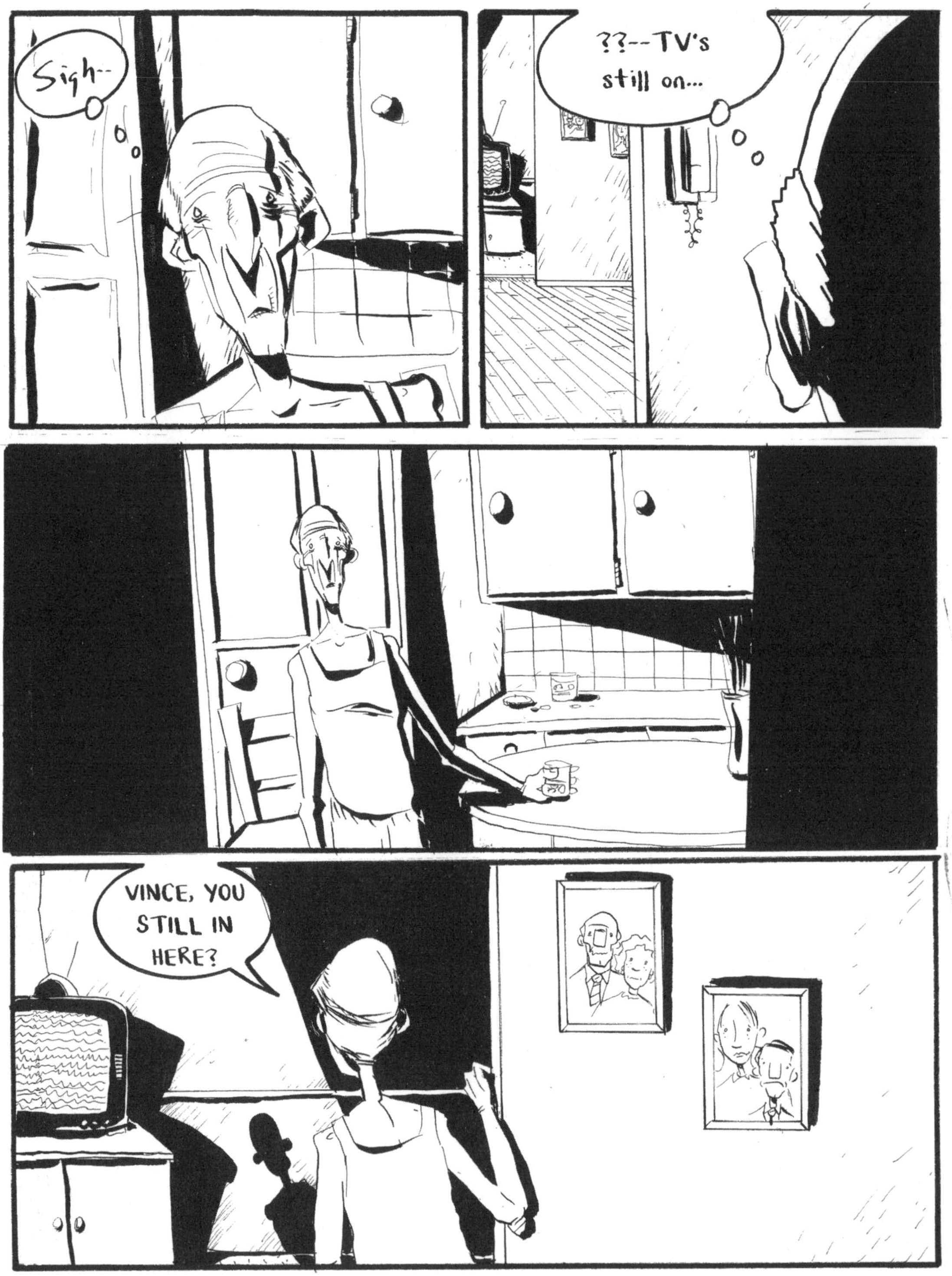
Sigh--
??--TV's still on...
VINCE, YOU STILL IN HERE?

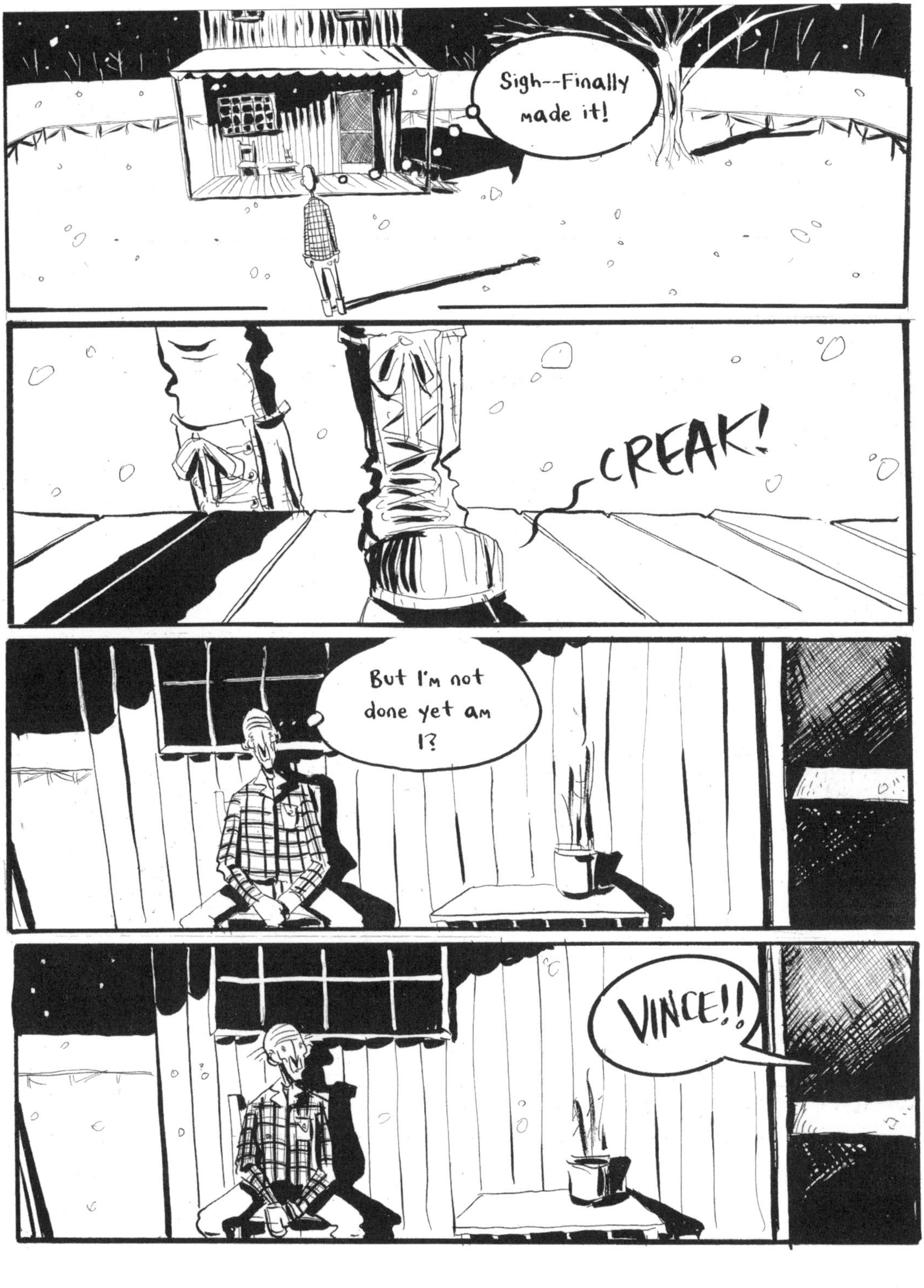
Sigh--Finally made it!
CREAK!
But I'm not done yet am I?
VINCE!!

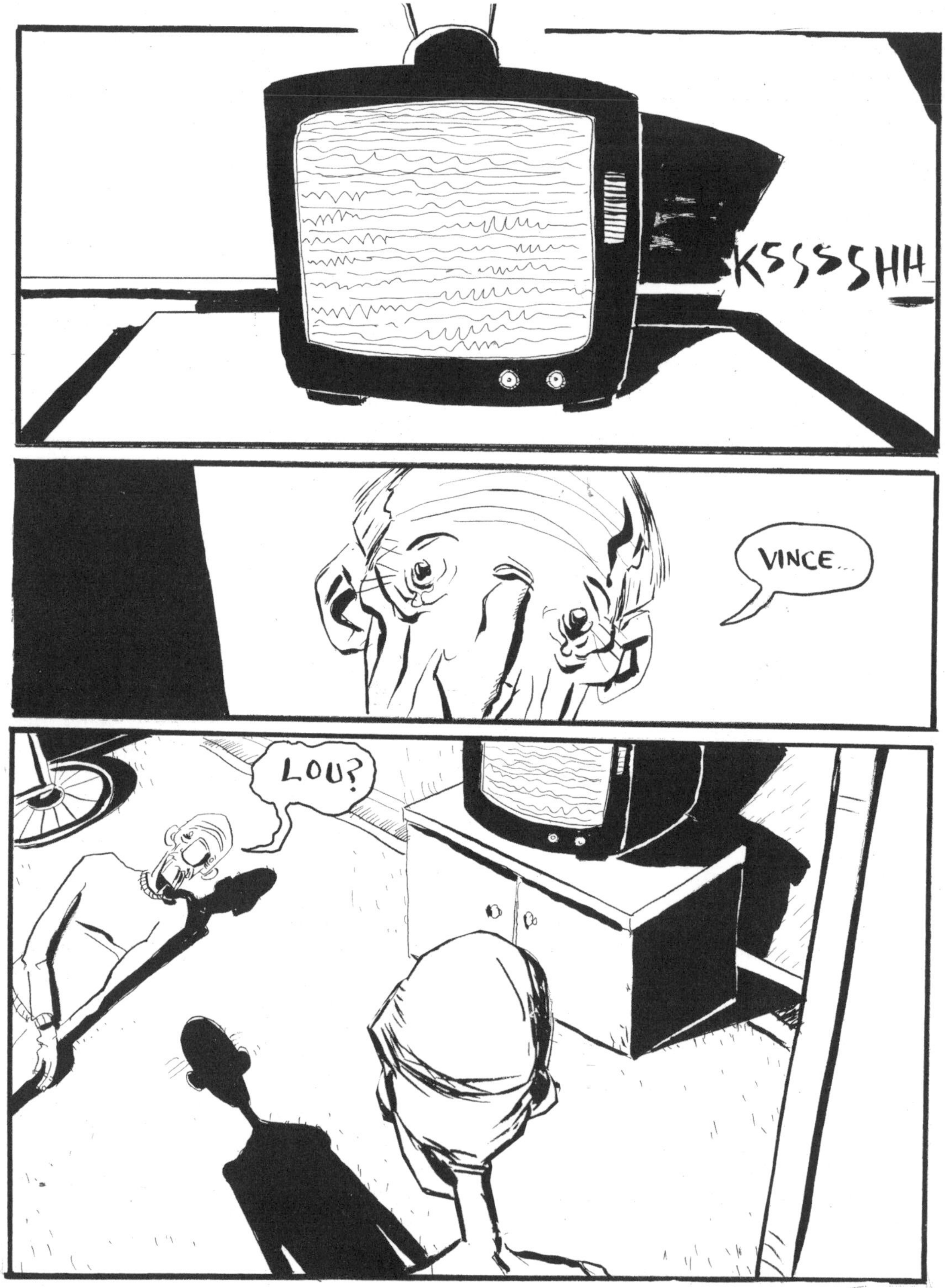
KSSSSHH
VINCE...
LOU?

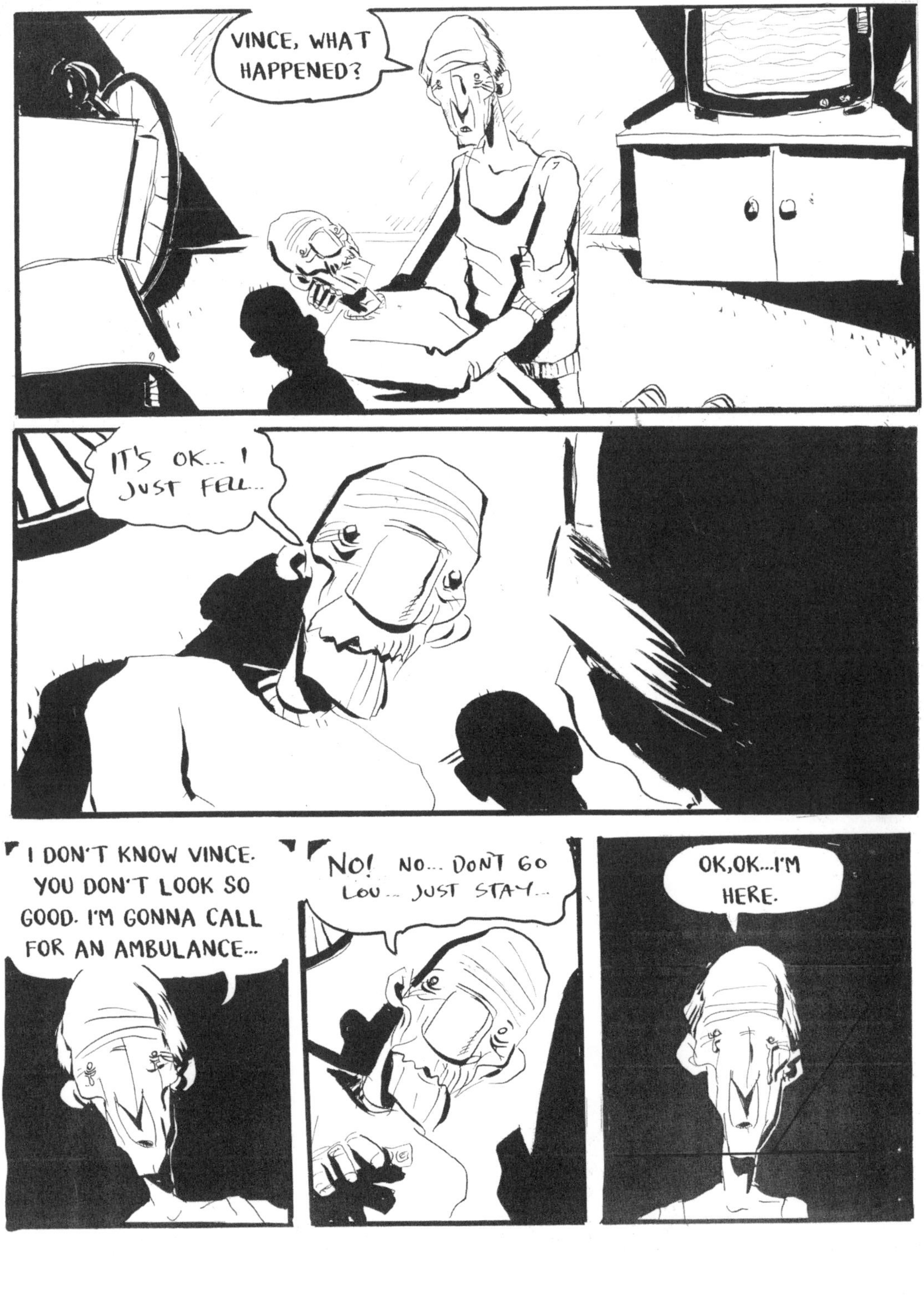
VINCE, WHAT HAPPENED?
IT'S OK... I JUST FELL...
I DON'T KNOW VINCE. YOU DON'T LOOK SO GOOD. I'M GONNA CALL FOR AN AMBULANCE...
NO! NO... DON'T GO LOU... JUST STAY...
OK,OK...I'M HERE.

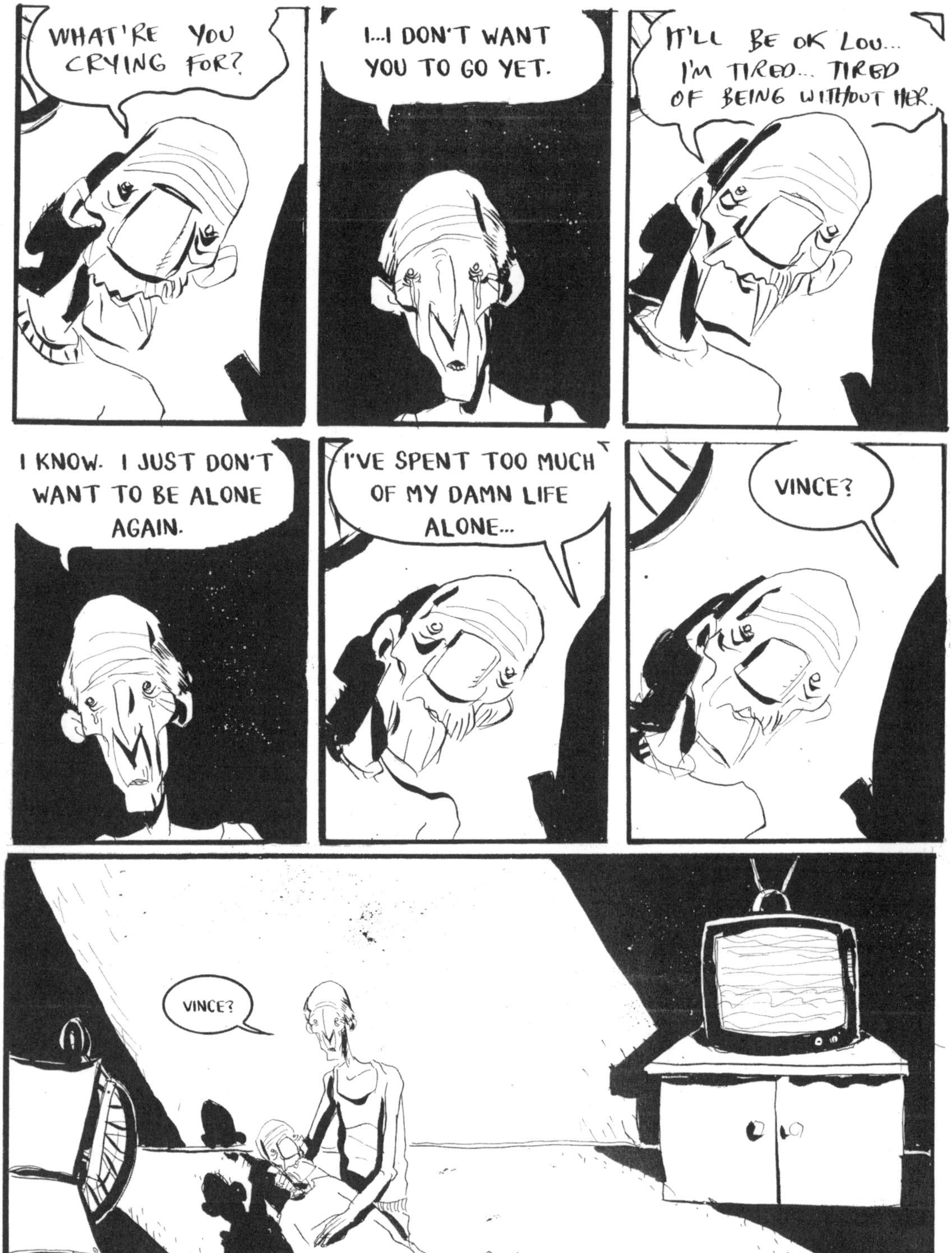
WHAT'RE YOU CRYING FOR?
I...I DON'T WANT YOU TO GO YET.
IT'LL BE OK LOU... I'M TIRED... TIRED OF BEING WITHOUT HER.
I KNOW. I JUST DON'T WANT TO BE ALONE AGAIN.
I'VE SPENT TOO MUCH OF MY DAMN LIFE ALONE...
VINCE?
VINCE?

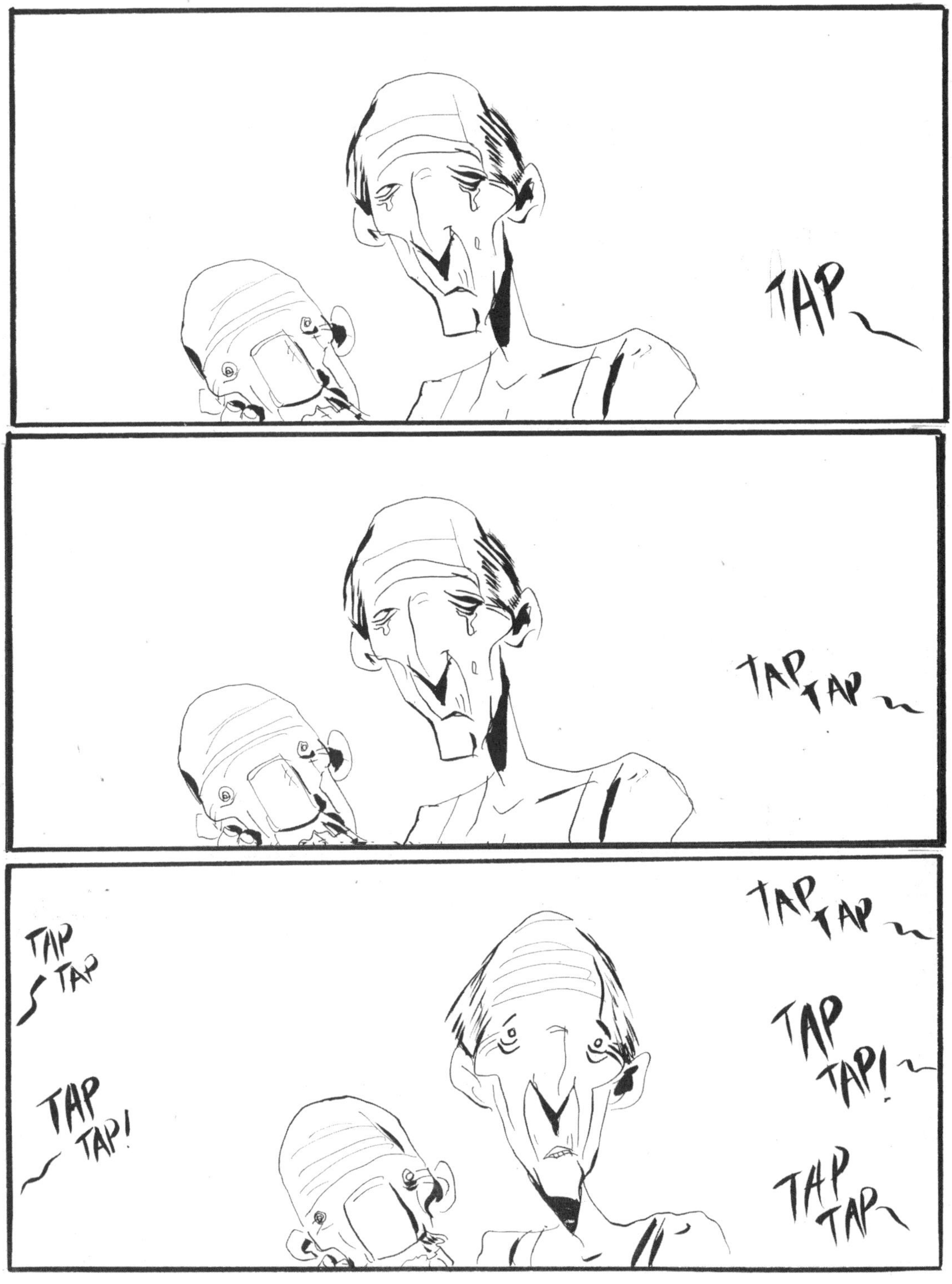
TAP
TAP TAP
TAP TAP
TAP TAP
TAP TAP!
TAP TAP
TAP TAP!
TAP TAP

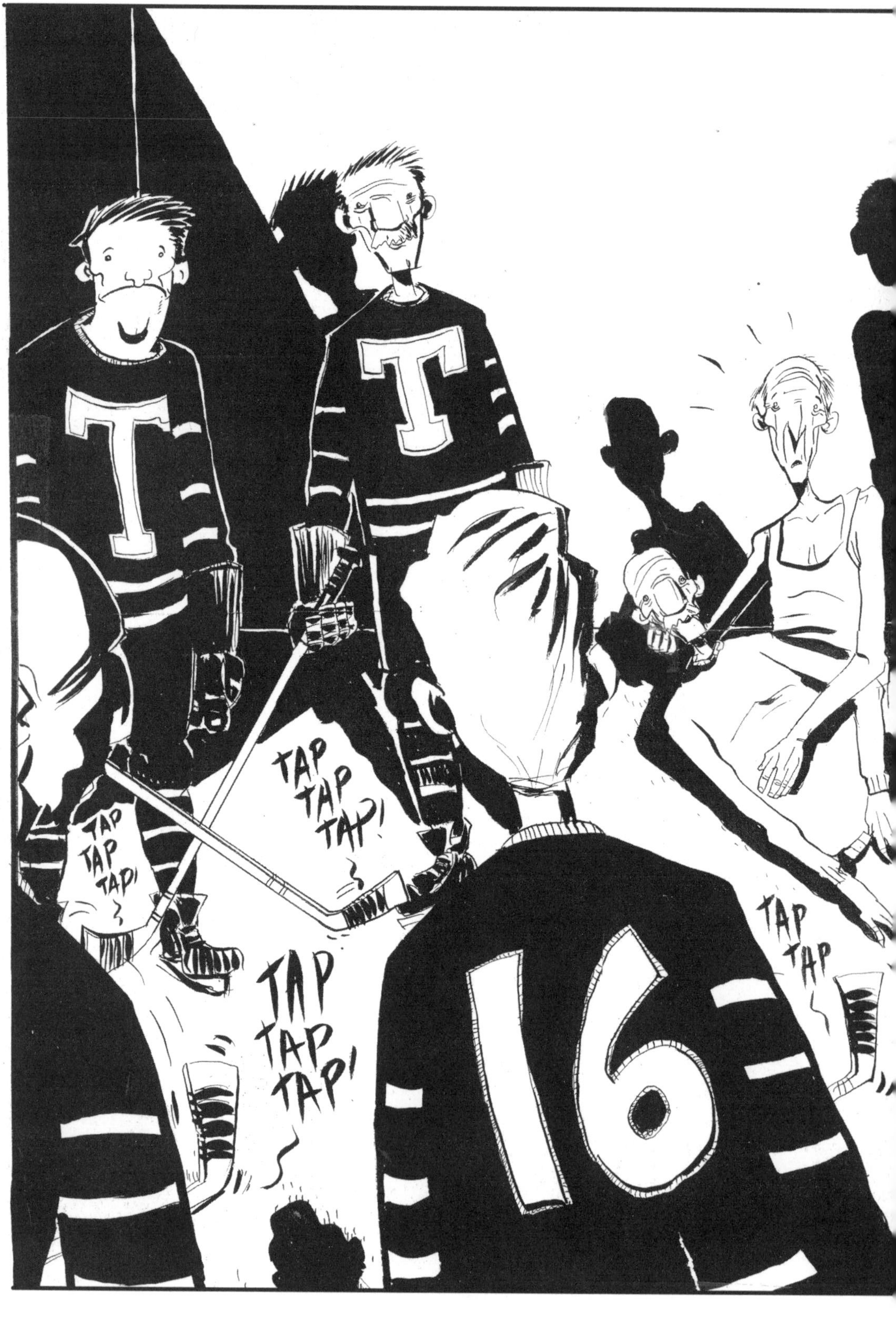
TAP TAP TAP!
TAP TAP TAP!
TAP TAP TAP!
TAP TAP

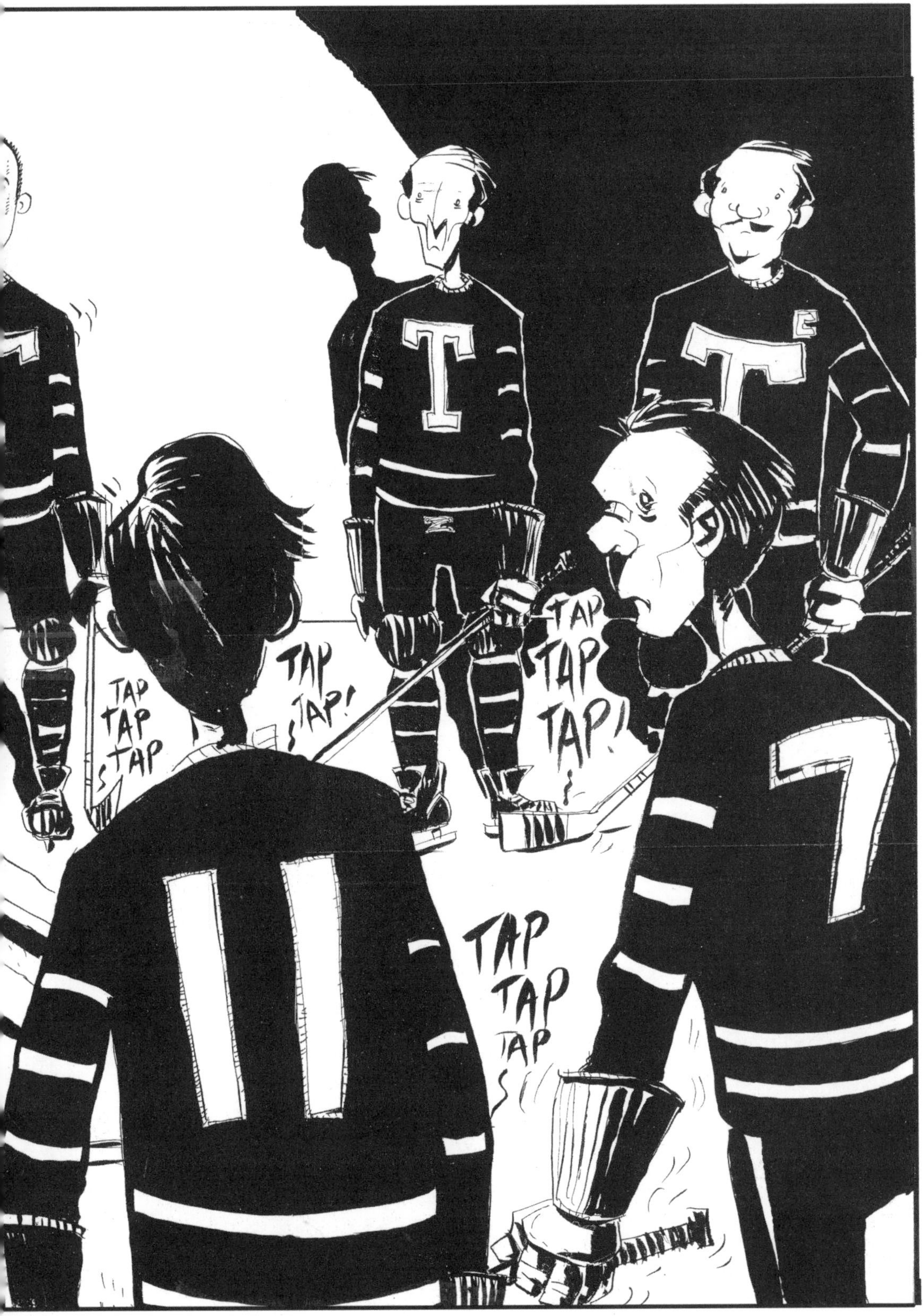
TAP
TAP
TAP
TAP
TAP!
TAP
TAP
TAP!
TAP
TAP
TAP

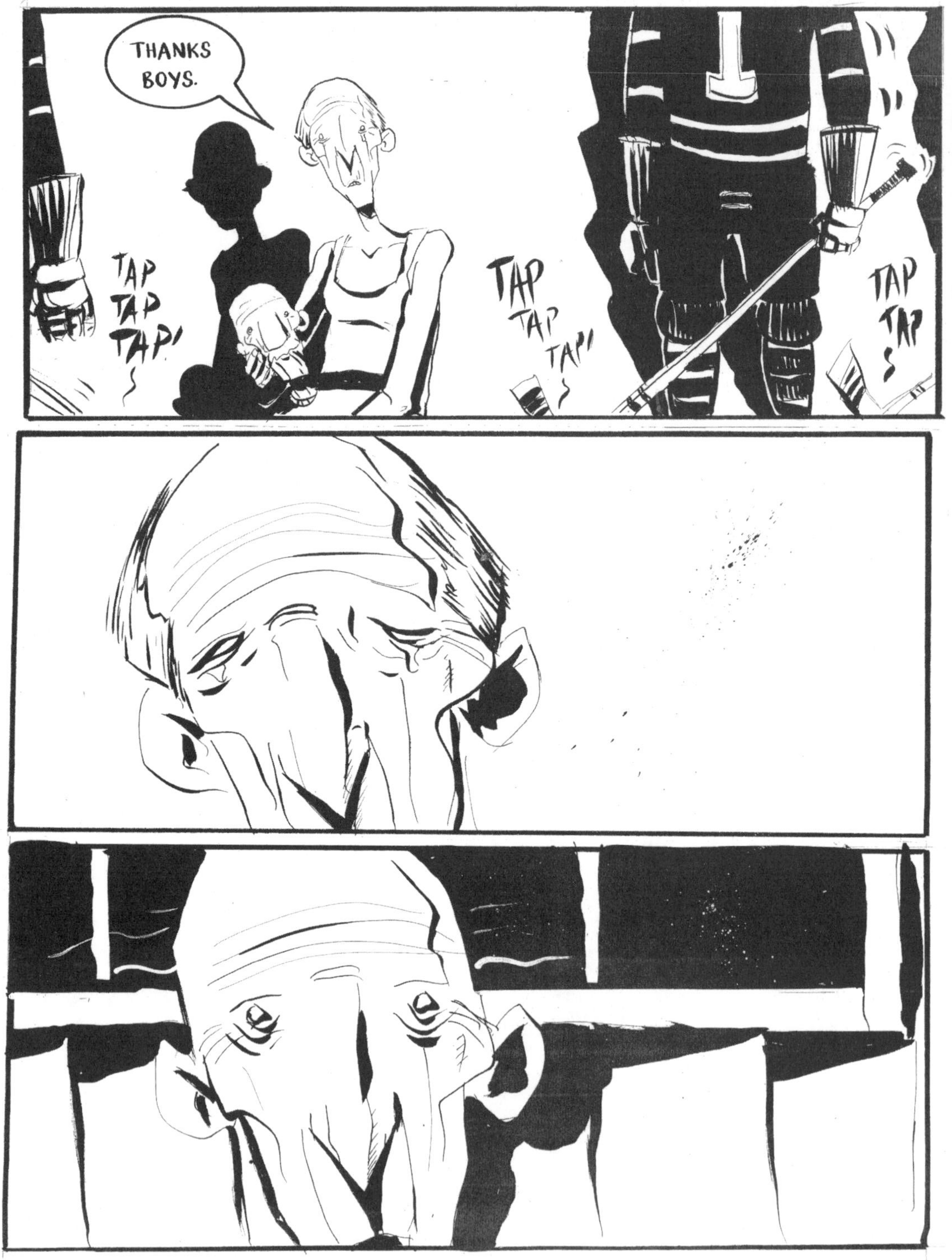
THANKS BOYS.
TAP TAP TAP!
TAP TAP TAP!
TAP TAP S

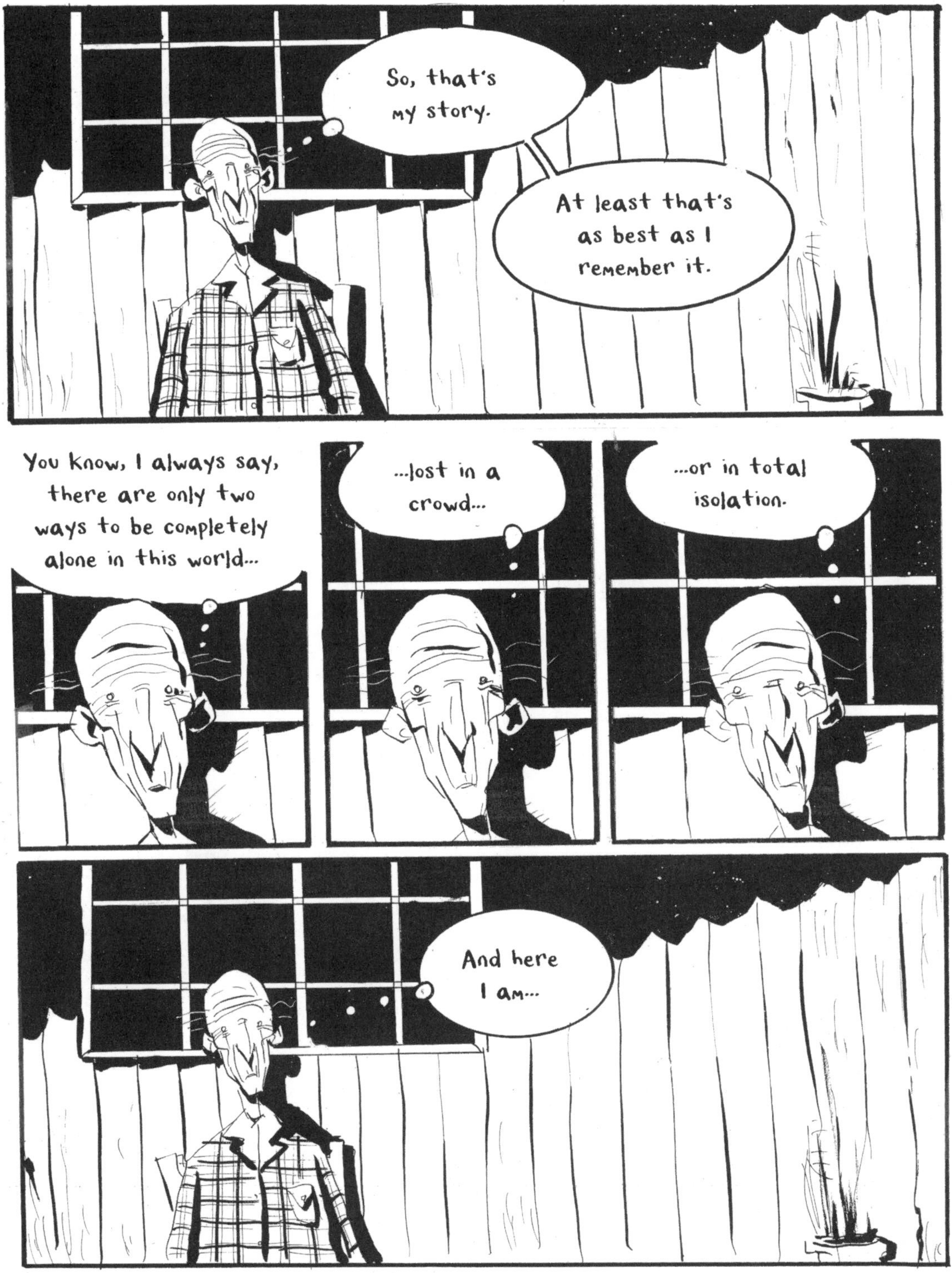
So, that's my story.
At least that's as best as I remember it.
You know, I always say, there are only two ways to be completely alone in this world...
...lost in a crowd...
...or in total isolation.
And here I am...

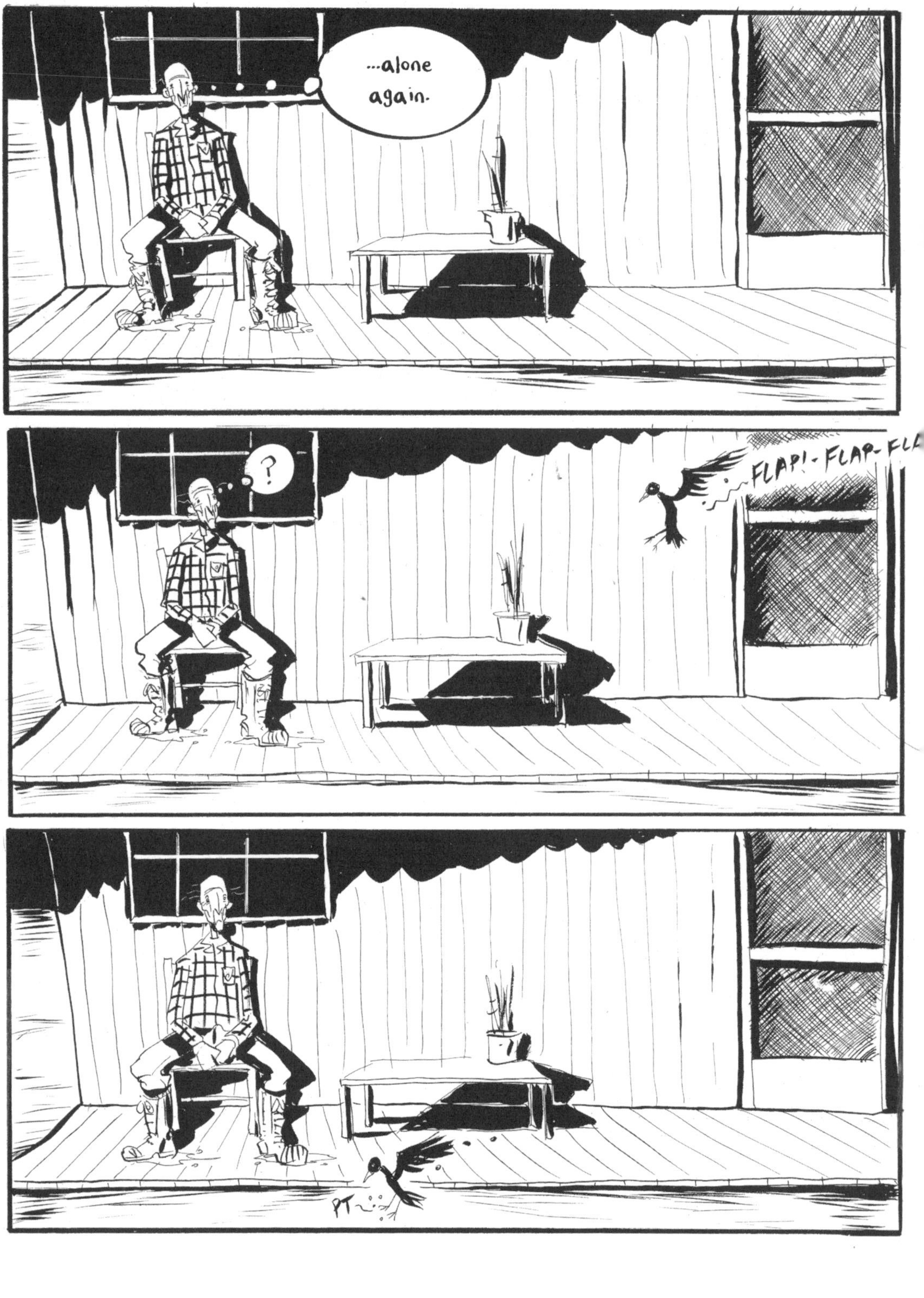
...alone again.
?
FLAP!-FLAP-FL
PT

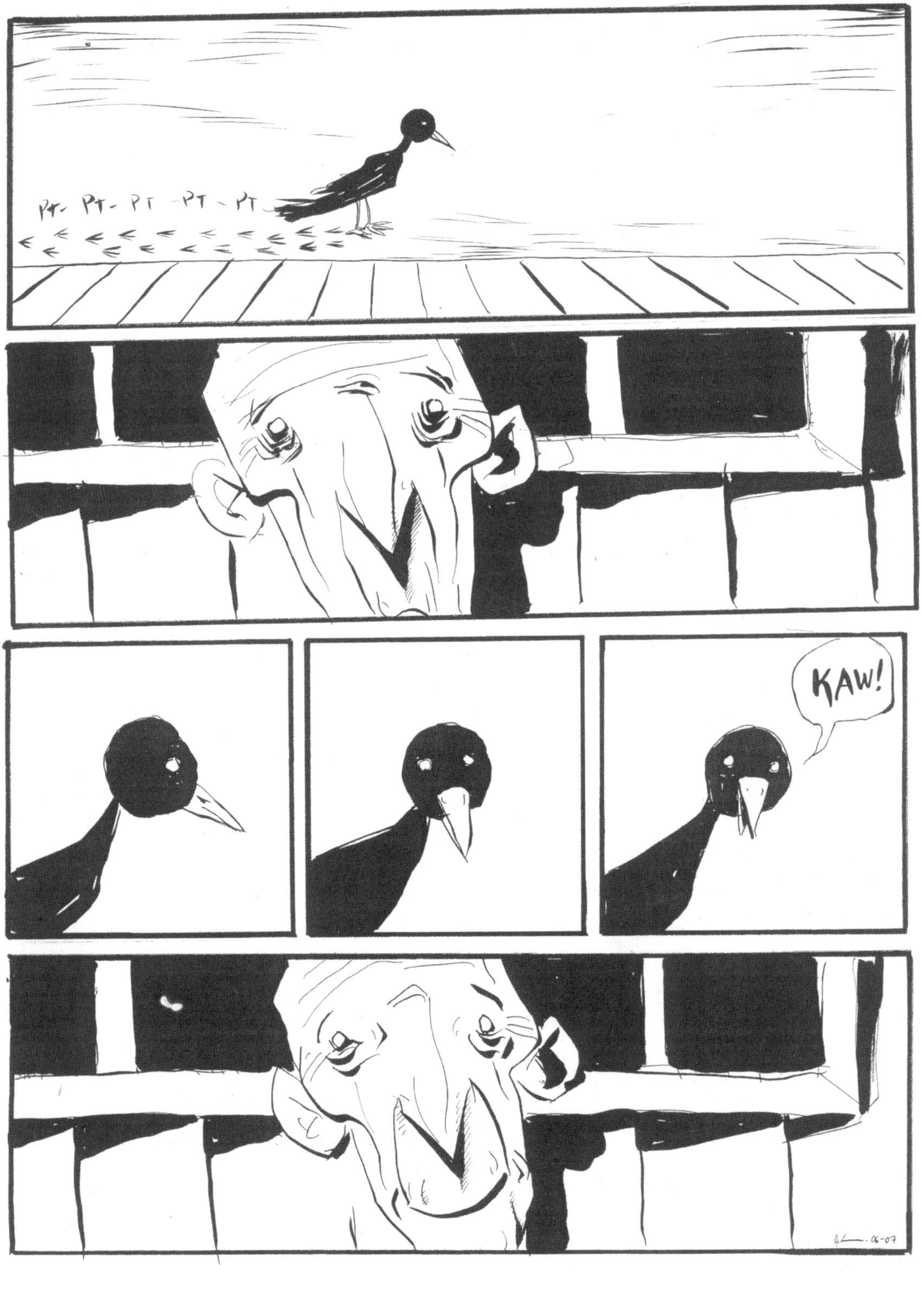
PT- PT- PT -PT -PT
KAW!

BOOK THREE
THE COUNTRY NURSE

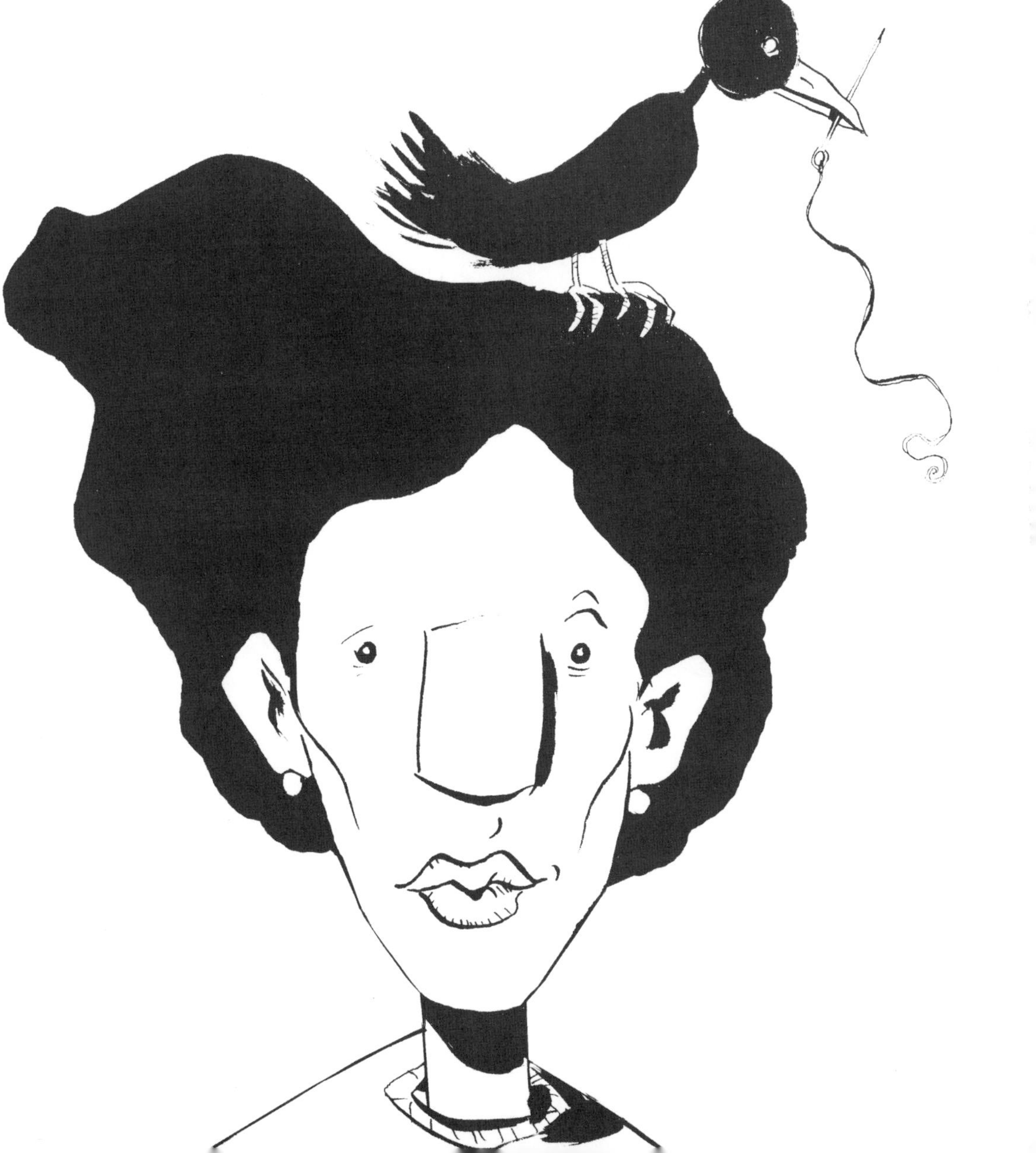

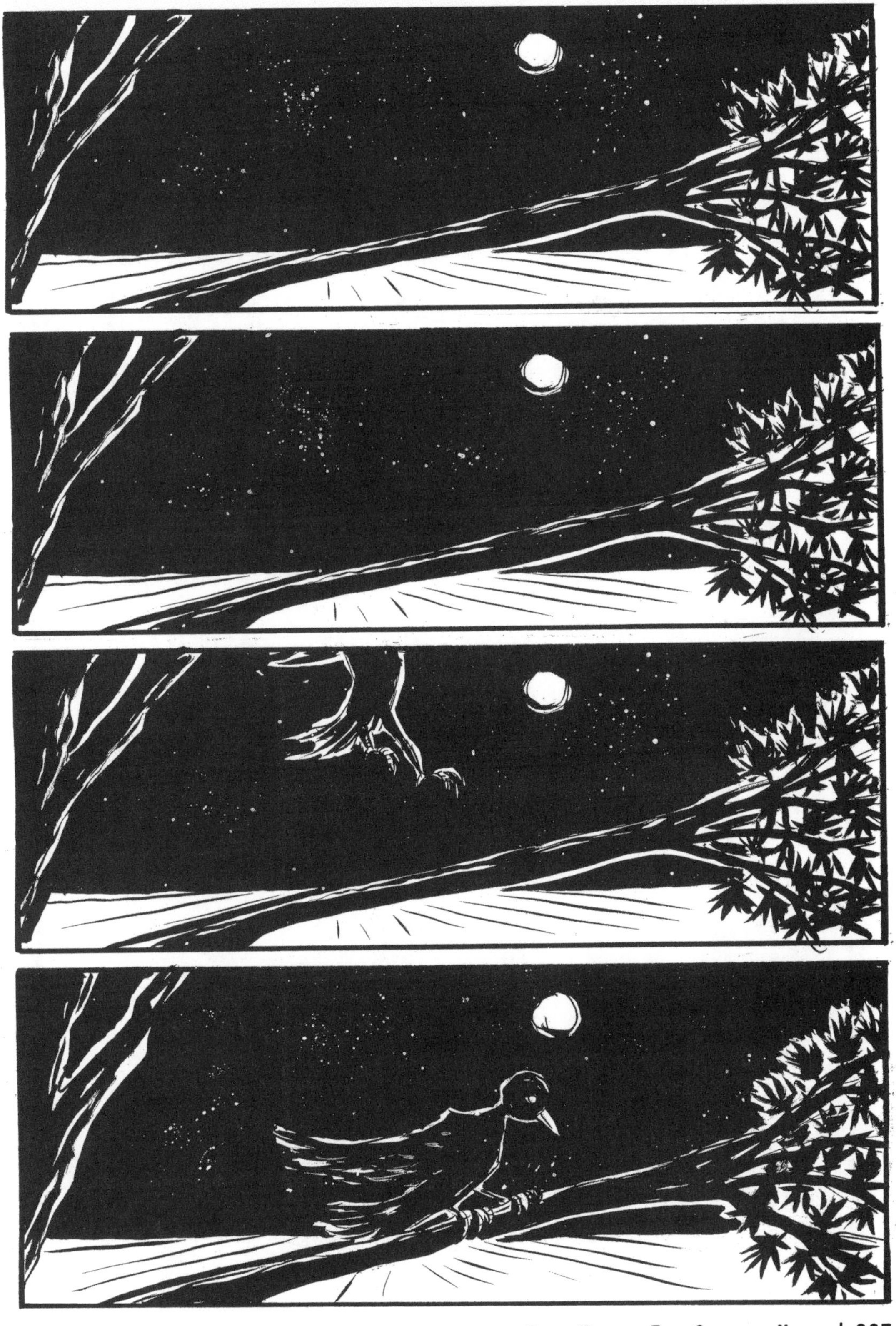

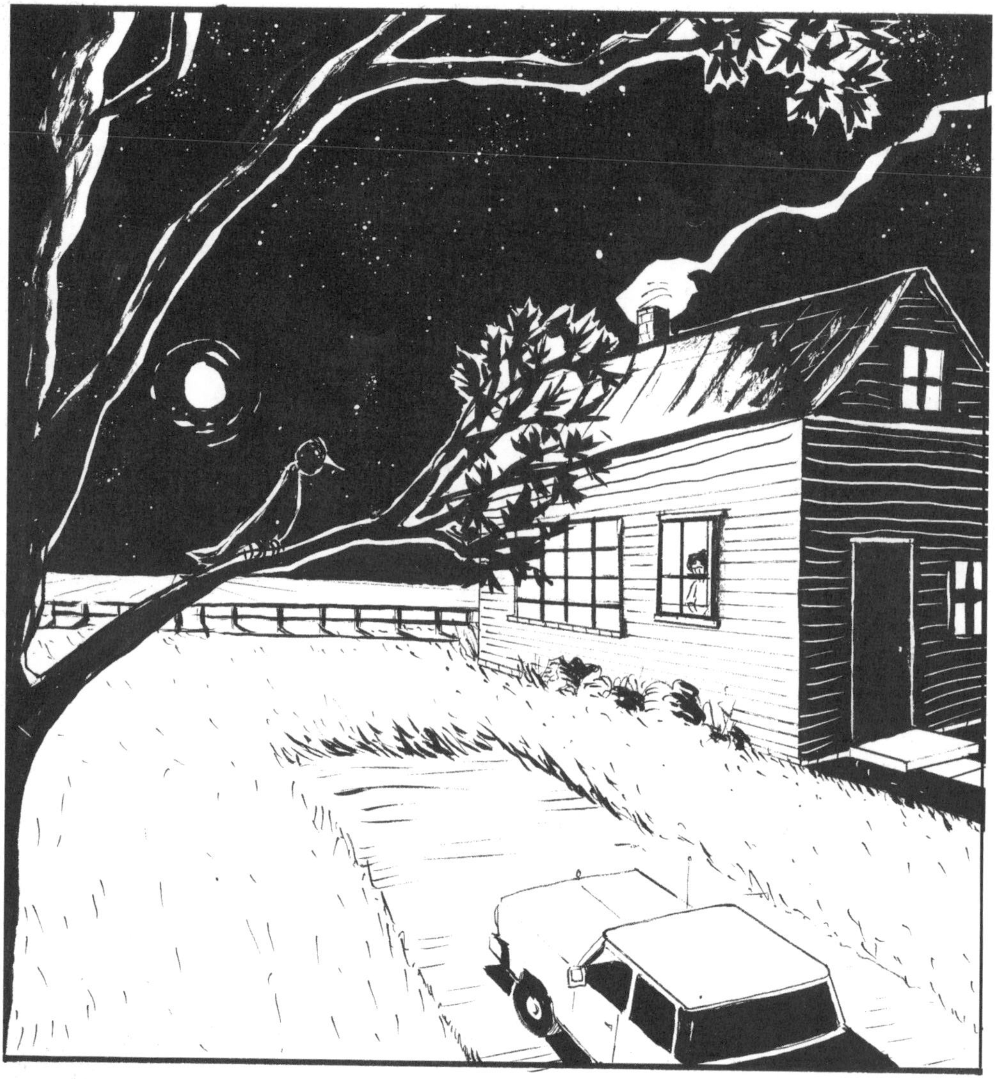

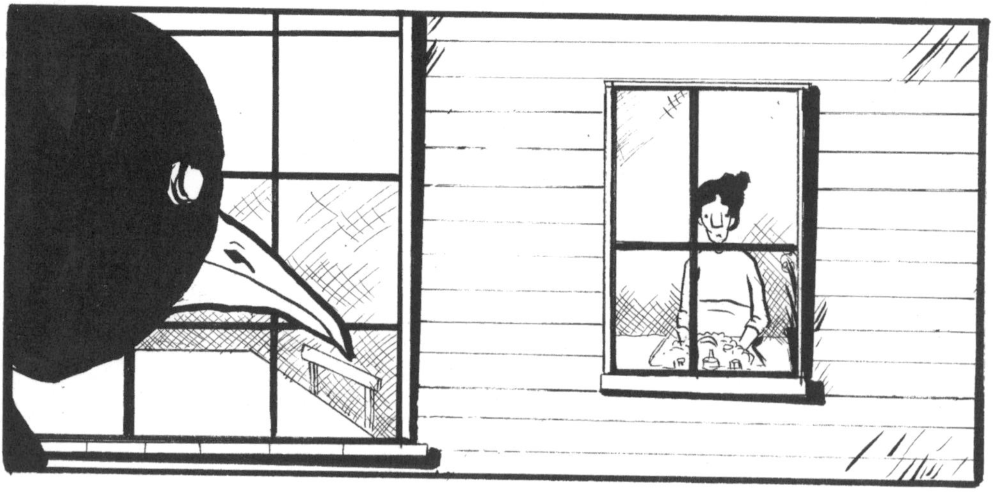

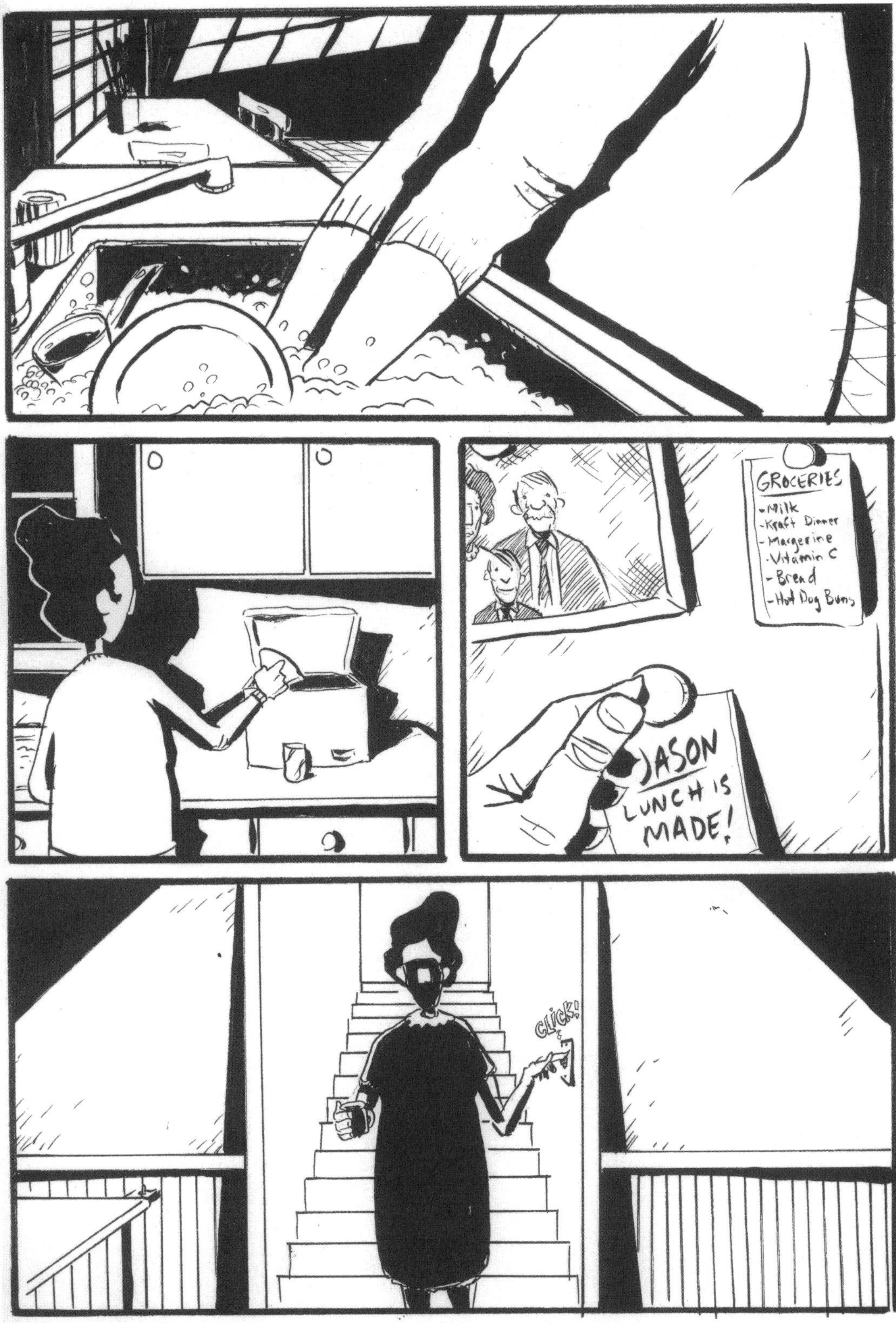
GROCERIES
-Milk
-Kraft Dinner
-Margerine
-Vitamin C
-Bread
-Hot Dog Buns
JASON
LUNCH IS MADE!
CLICK!

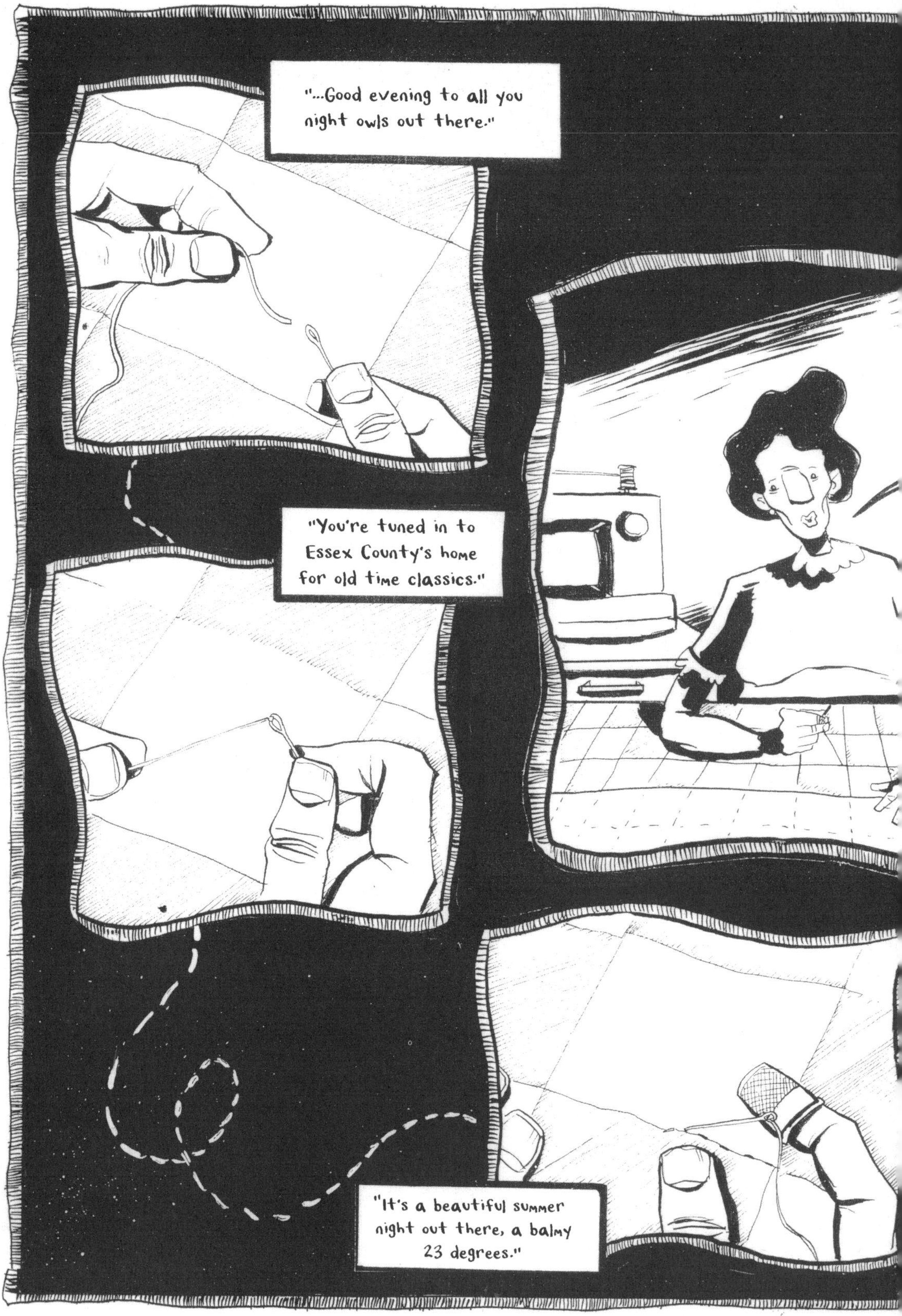
"...Good evening to all you night owls out there."
"You're tuned in to Essex County's home for old time classics."
"It's a beautiful summer night out there, a balmy 23 degrees."

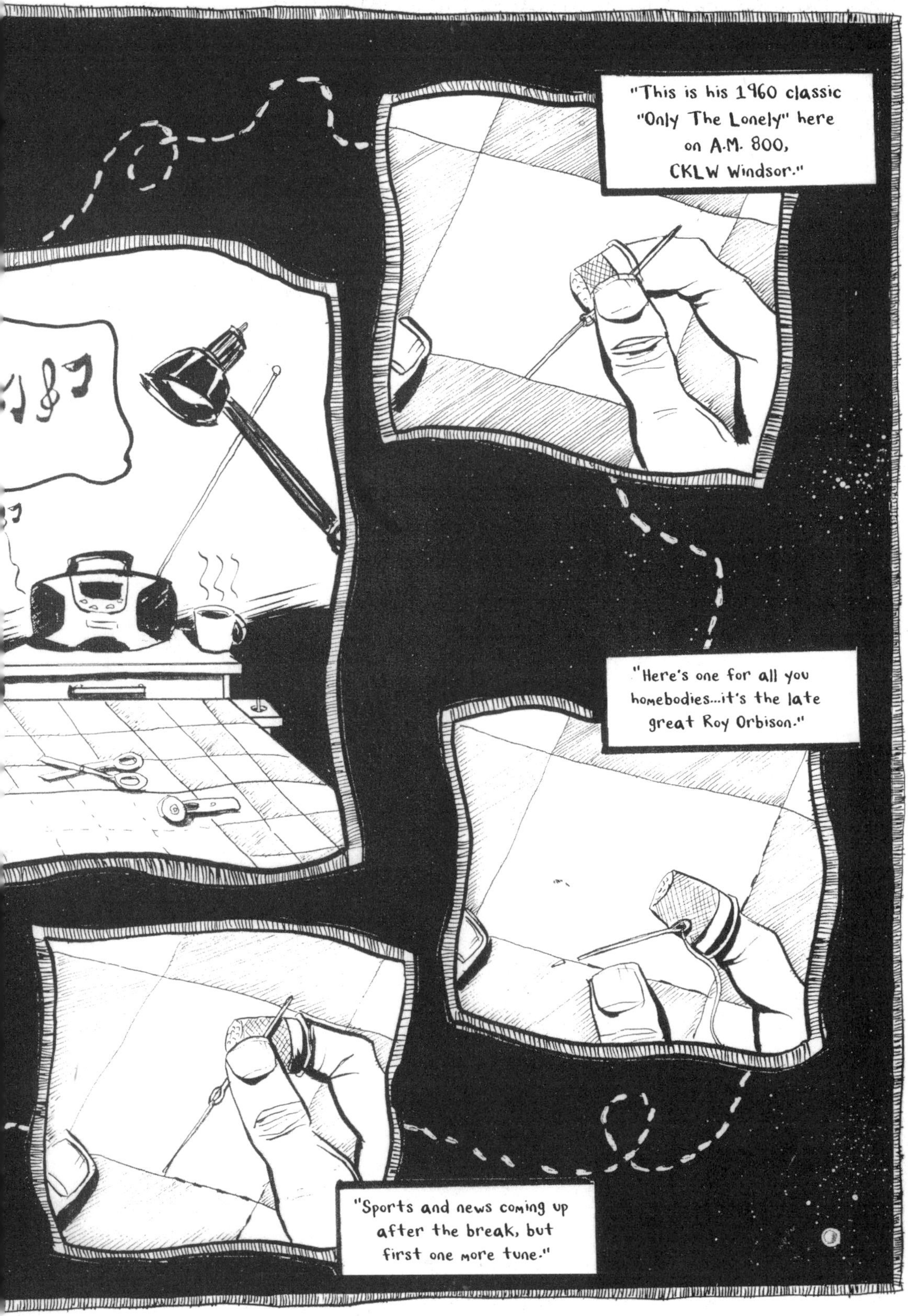
"This is his 1960 classic "Only The Lonely" here on A.M. 800, CKLW Windsor."
"Here's one for all you homebodies...it's the late great Roy Orbison."
"Sports and news coming up after the break, but first one more tune."

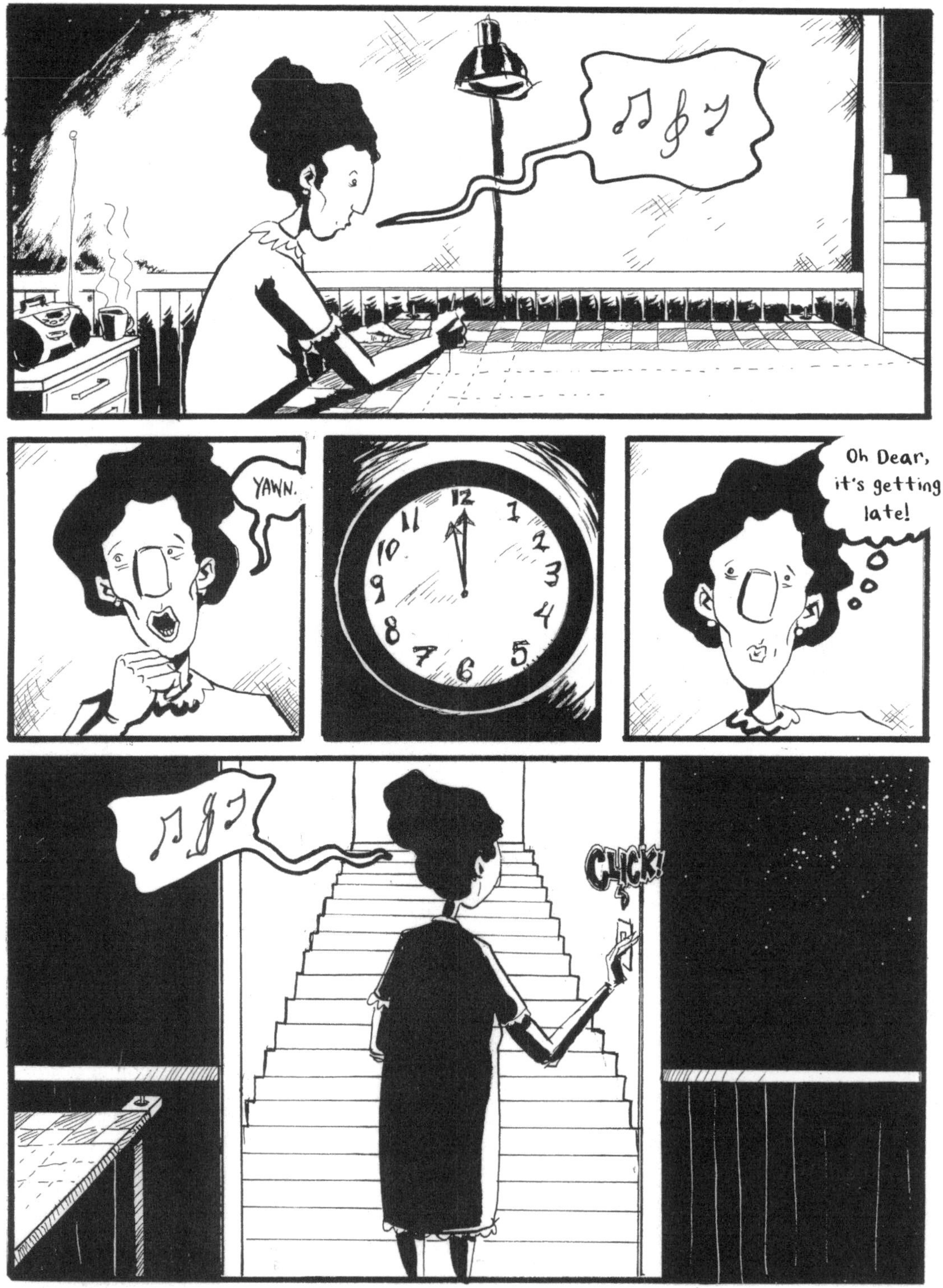
YAWN.
12
1
2
3
4
5
6
7
8
9
10
11
Oh Dear, it's getting late!
CLICK!

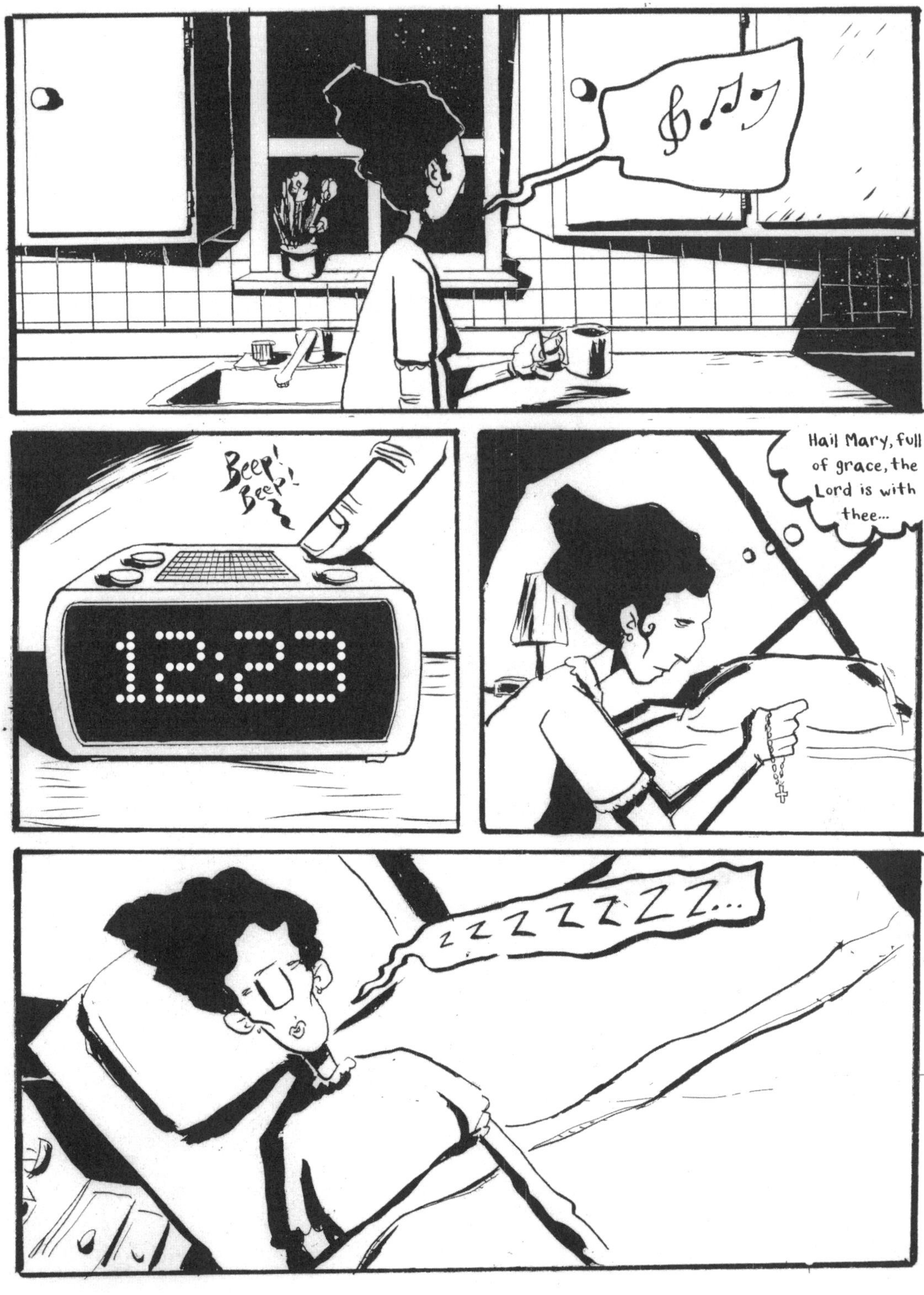
Beep! Beep!
12:23
Hail Mary, full of grace, the Lord is with thee...
ZZZZZZZZZ...

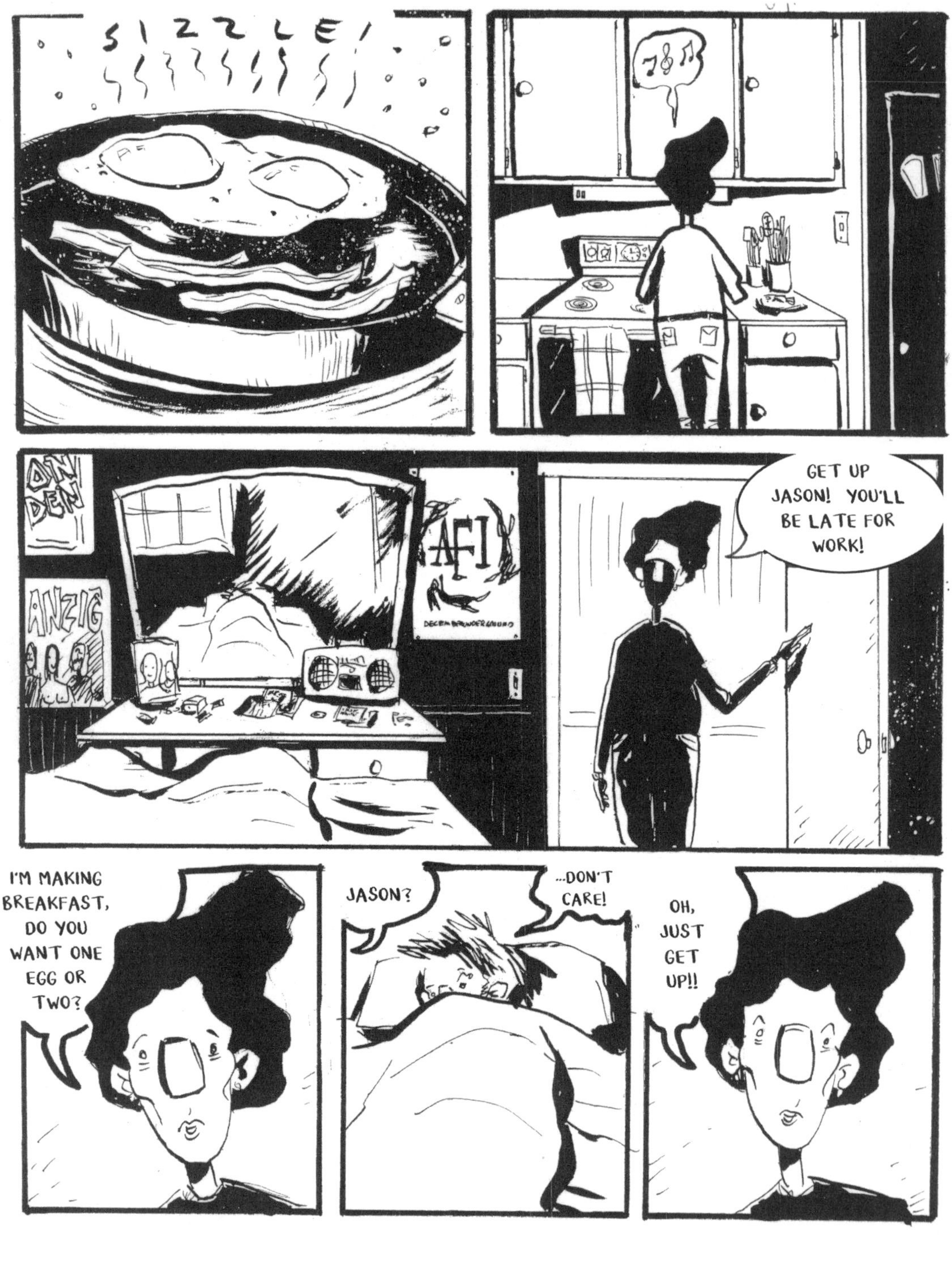
SIZZLE!
GET UP JASON! YOU'LL BE LATE FOR WORK!
I'M MAKING BREAKFAST, DO YOU WANT ONE EGG OR TWO?
JASON?
...DON'T CARE!
OH, JUST GET UP!!

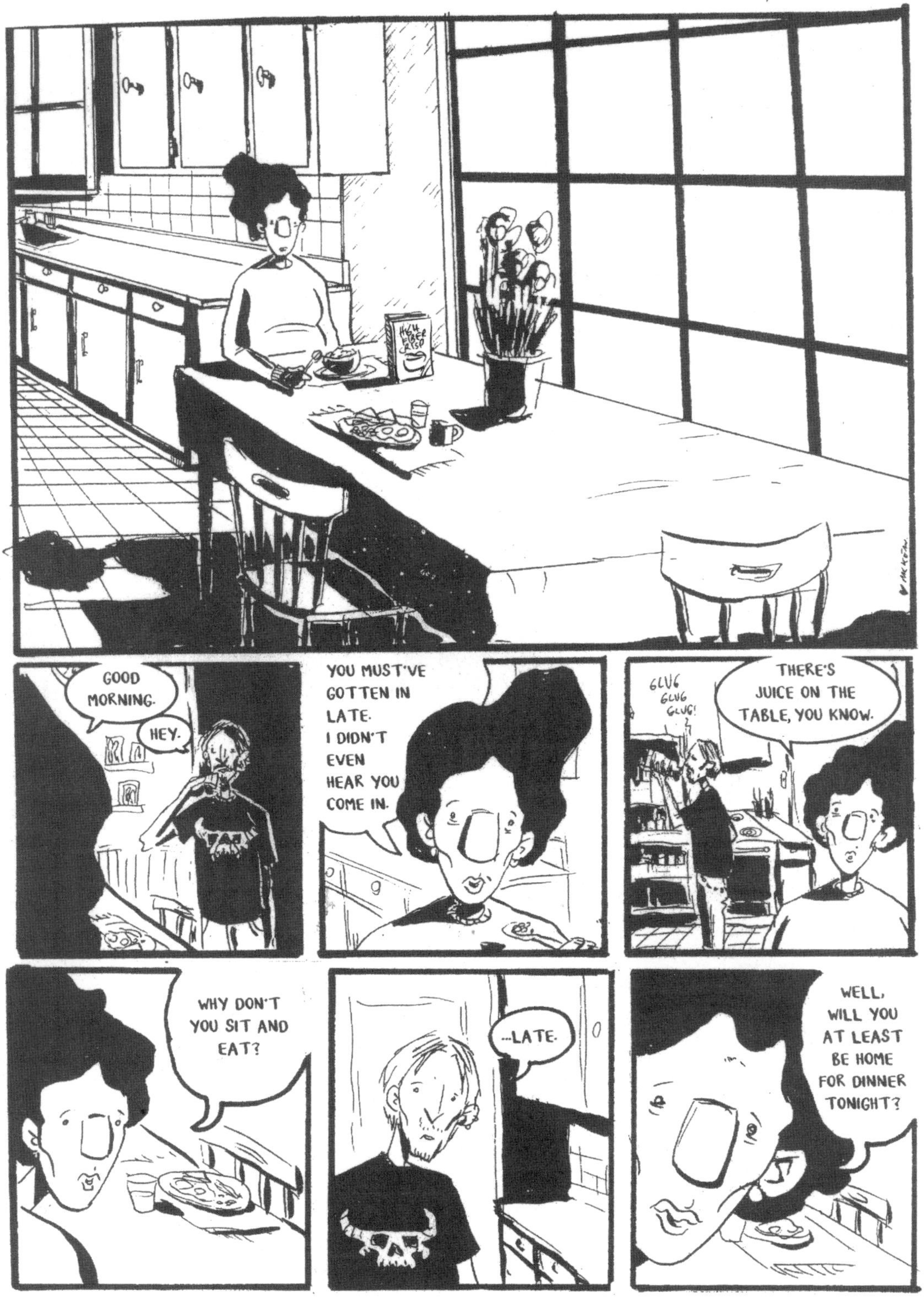
HIGH FIBER CRISP
GOOD MORNING.
HEY.
YOU MUST'VE GOTTEN IN LATE. I DIDN'T EVEN HEAR YOU COME IN.
GLUG GLUG GLUG!
THERE'S JUICE ON THE TABLE, YOU KNOW.
WHY DON'T YOU SIT AND EAT?
...LATE.
WELL, WILL YOU AT LEAST BE HOME FOR DINNER TONIGHT?

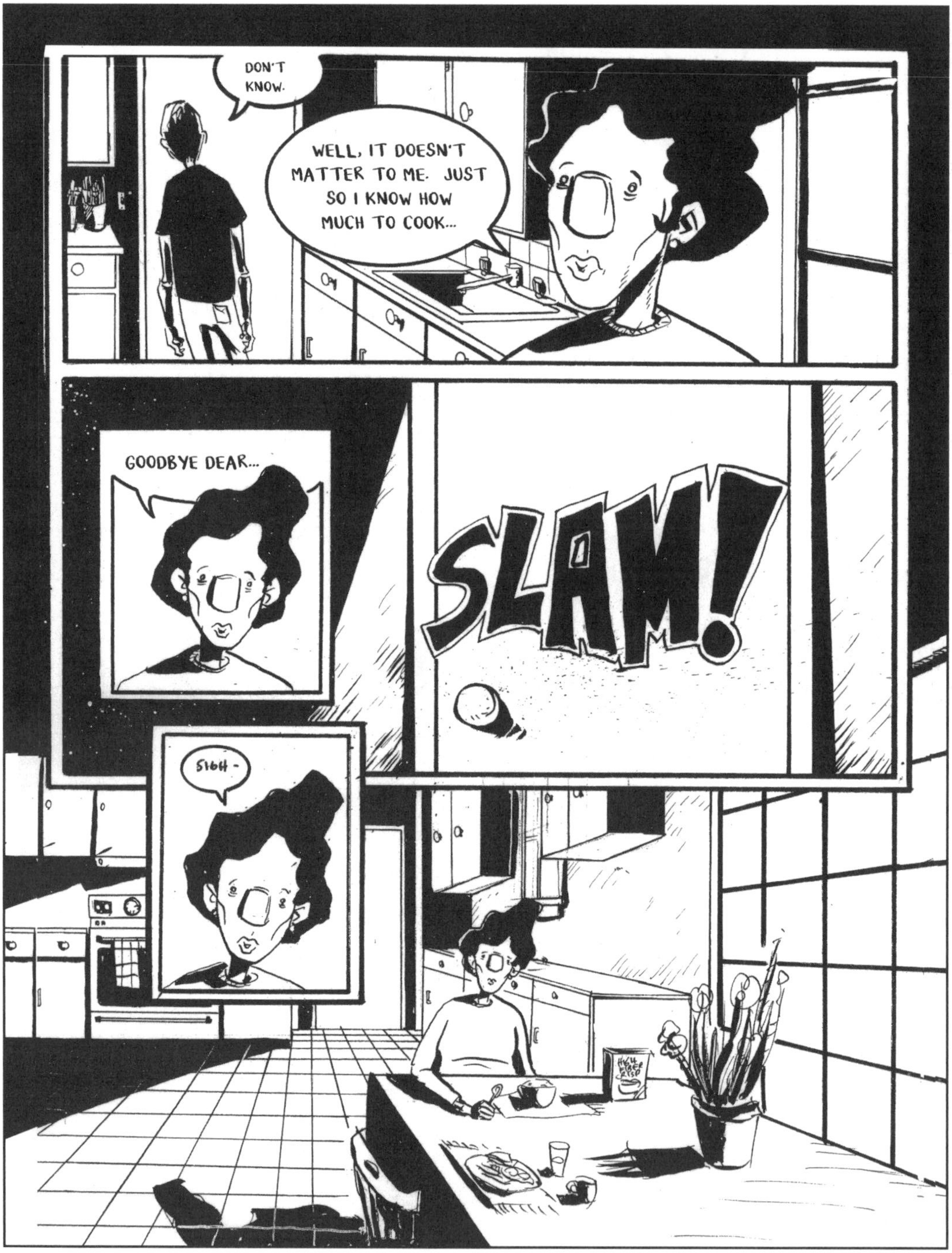
DON'T KNOW.
WELL, IT DOESN'T MATTER TO ME. JUST SO I KNOW HOW MUCH TO COOK...
GOODBYE DEAR...
SLAM!
SIGH -

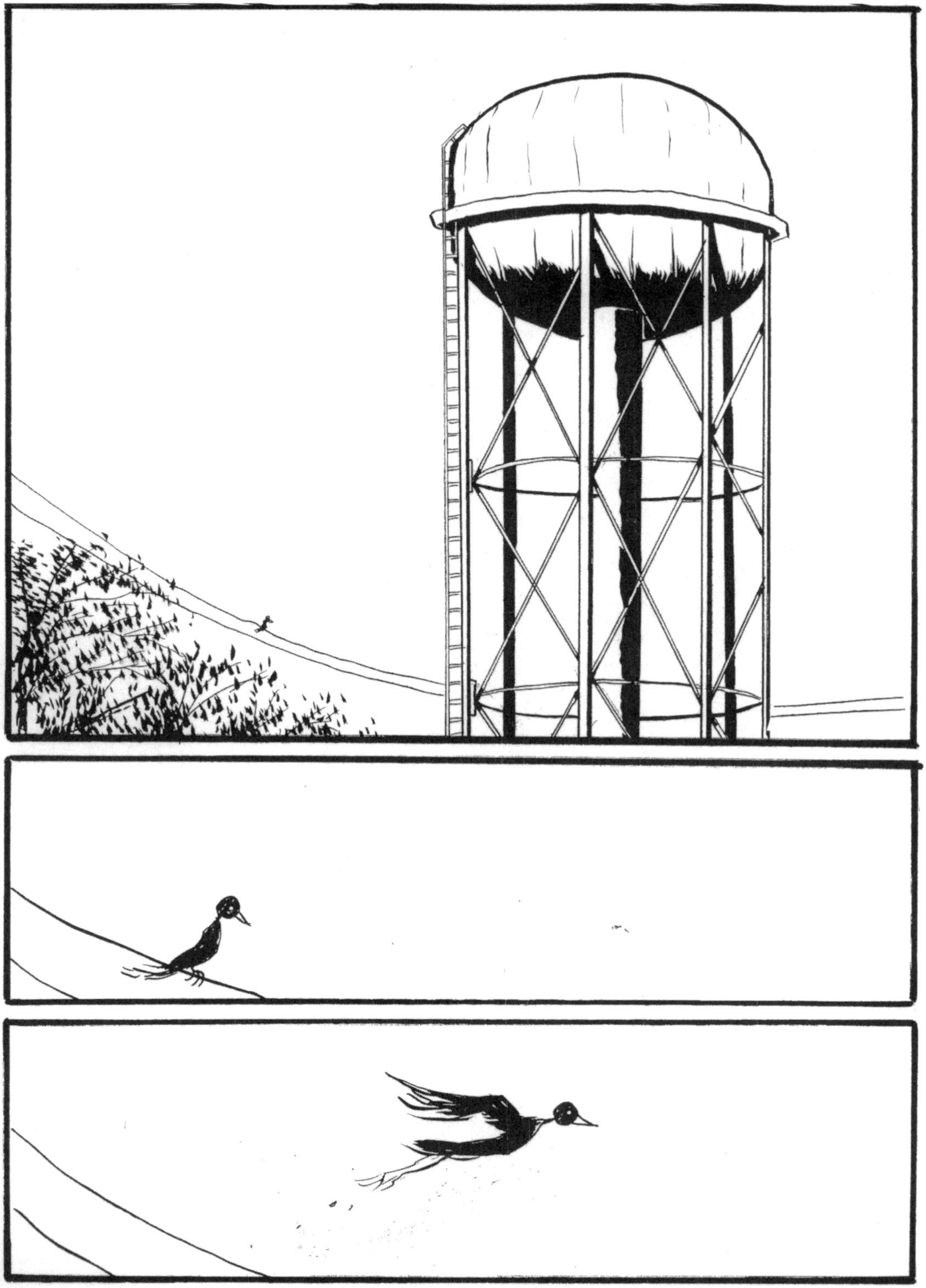

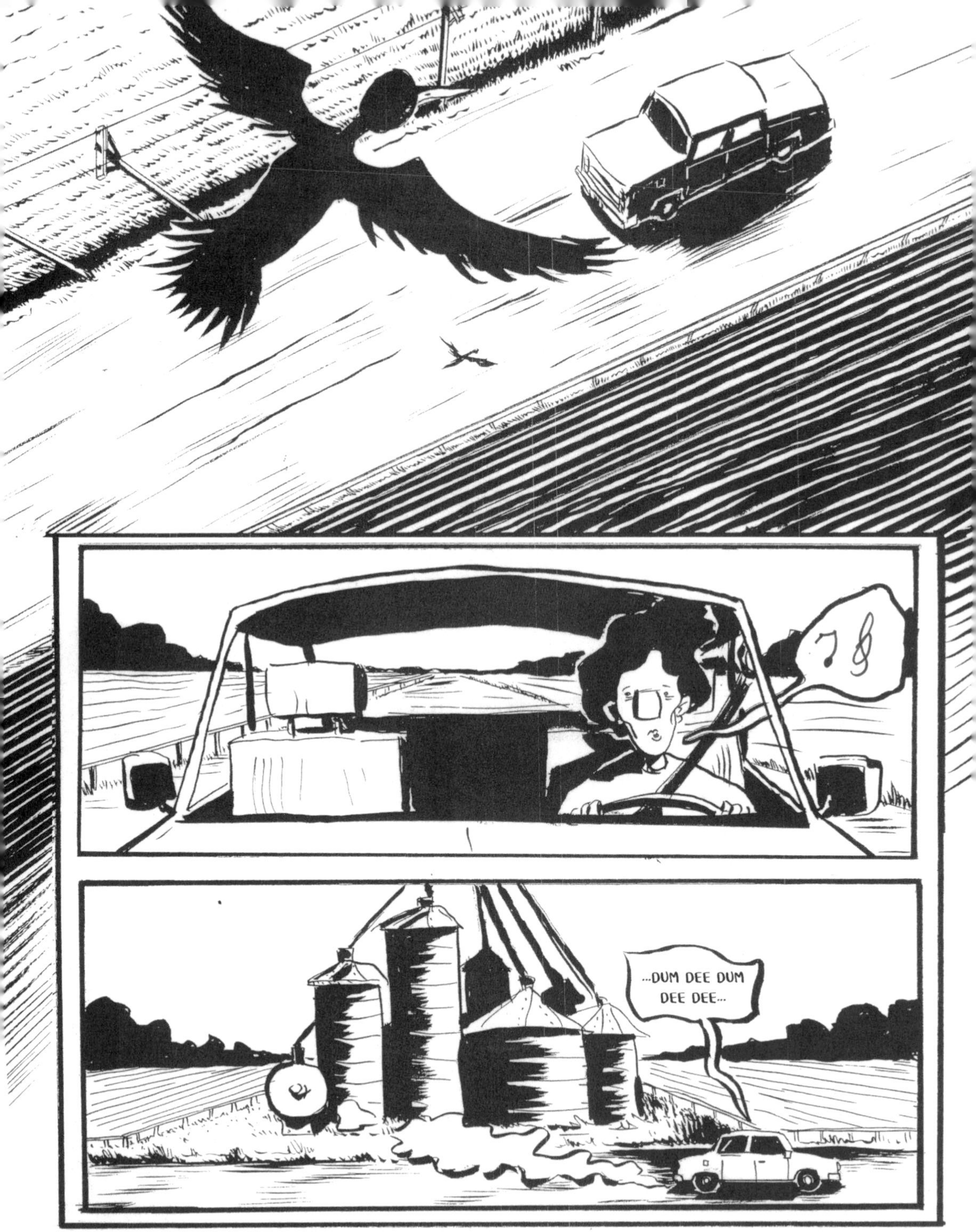
...DUM DEE DUM DEE DEE...

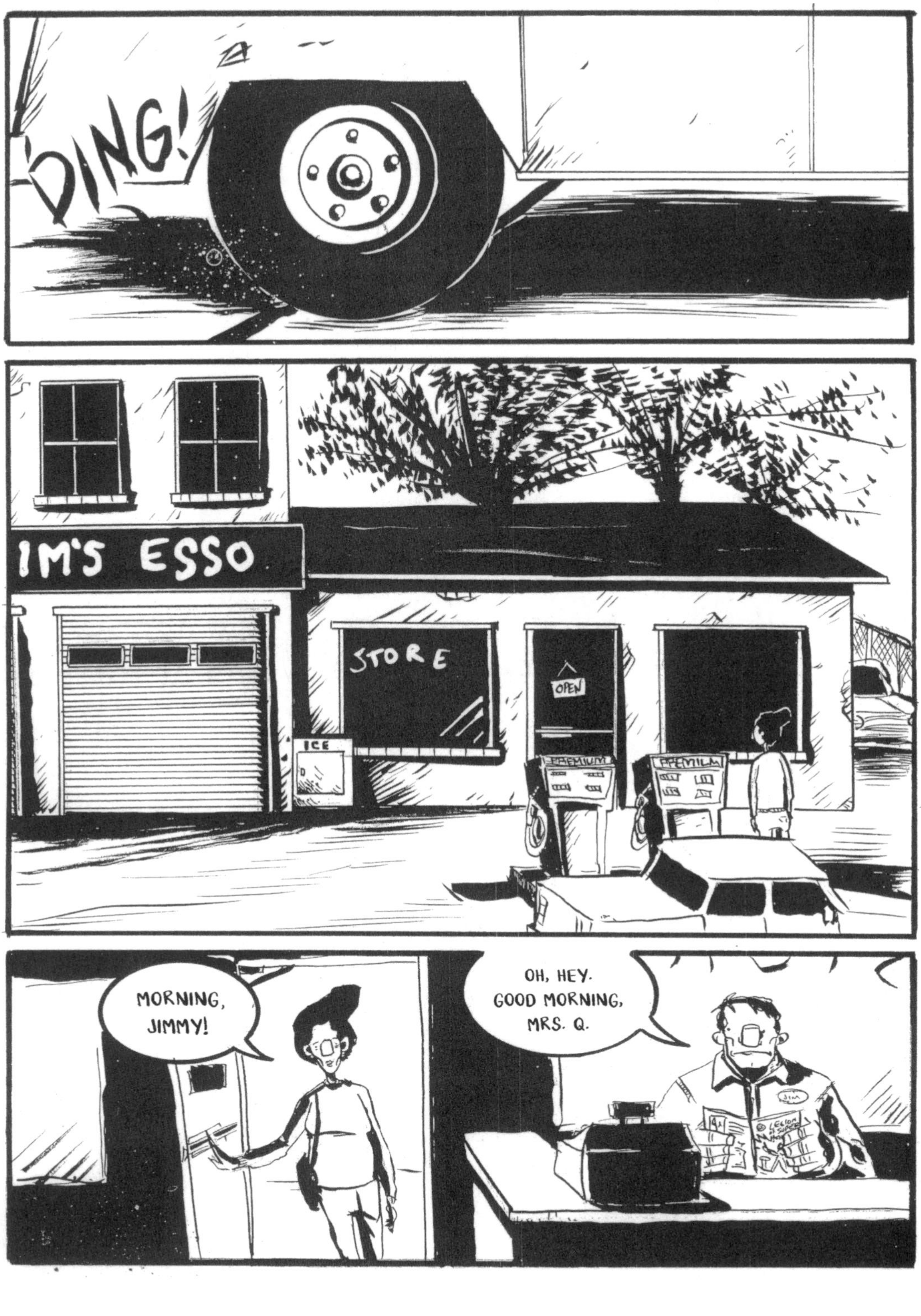
DING!
IM'S ESSO
STORE
OPEN
ICE
PREMIUM
PREMIUM
MORNING, JIMMY!
OH, HEY. GOOD MORNING, MRS. Q.
JIM

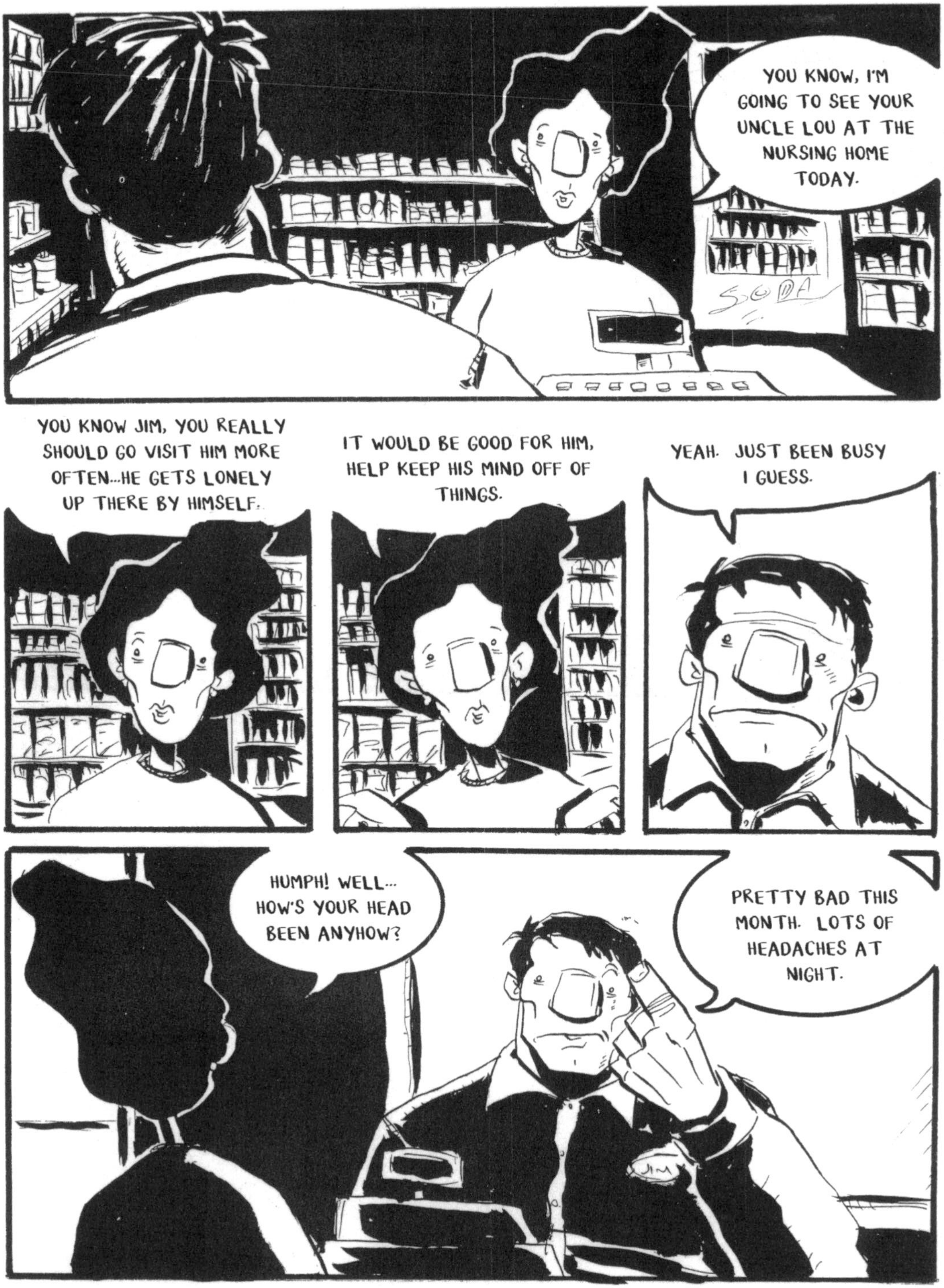
YOU KNOW, I'M GOING TO SEE YOUR UNCLE LOU AT THE NURSING HOME TODAY.
SODA
YOU KNOW JIM, YOU REALLY SHOULD GO VISIT HIM MORE OFTEN...HE GETS LONELY UP THERE BY HIMSELF.
IT WOULD BE GOOD FOR HIM, HELP KEEP HIS MIND OFF OF THINGS.
YEAH. JUST BEEN BUSY I GUESS.
HUMPH! WELL... HOW'S YOUR HEAD BEEN ANYHOW?
PRETTY BAD THIS MONTH. LOTS OF HEADACHES AT NIGHT.
JIM

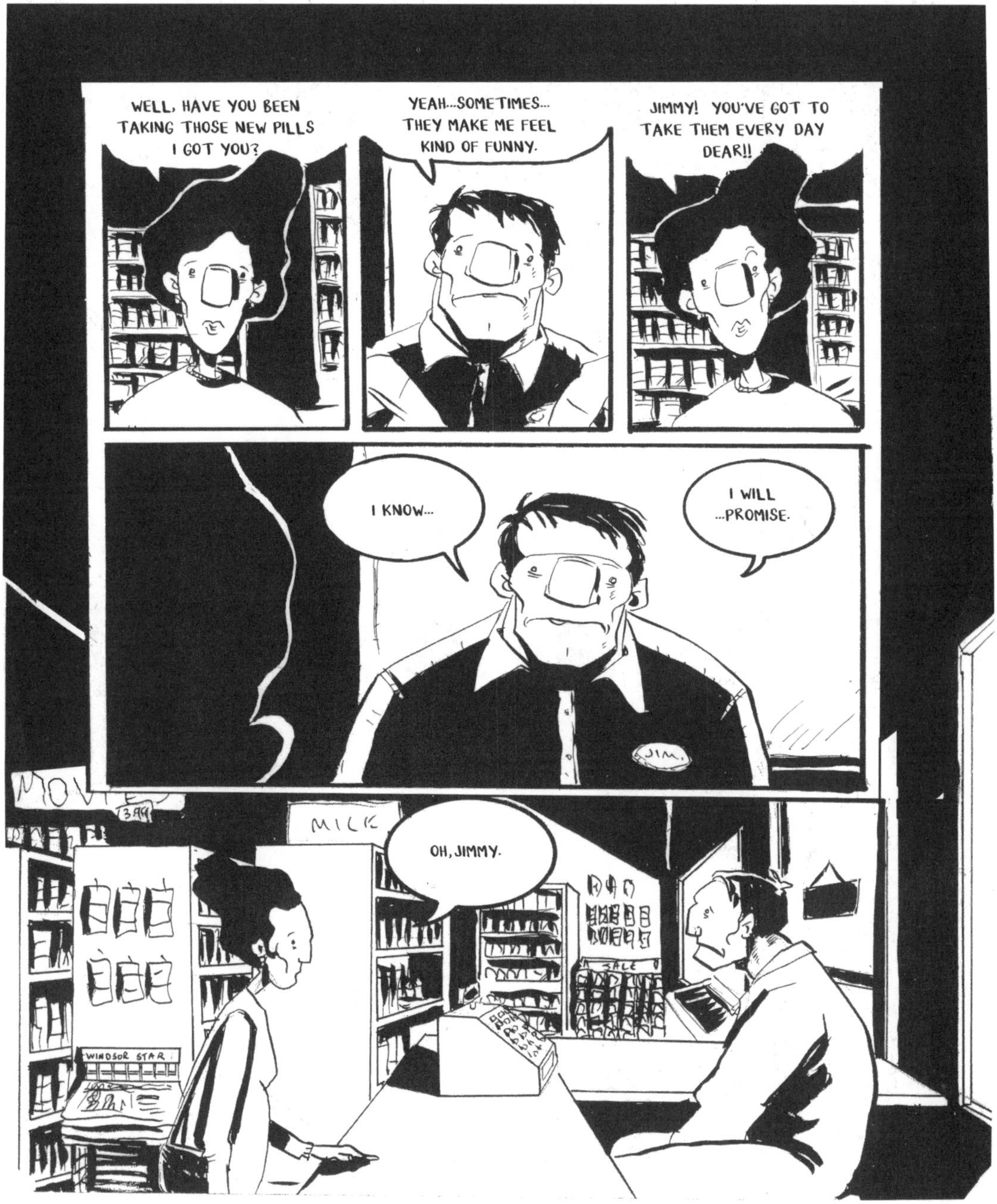
WELL, HAVE YOU BEEN TAKING THOSE NEW PILLS I GOT YOU?
YEAH...SOMETIMES... THEY MAKE ME FEEL KIND OF FUNNY.
JIMMY! YOU'VE GOT TO TAKE THEM EVERY DAY DEAR!!
I KNOW...
I WILL ...PROMISE.
JIM.
MOVIES
MILK
OH, JIMMY.
WINDSOR STAR
SALE

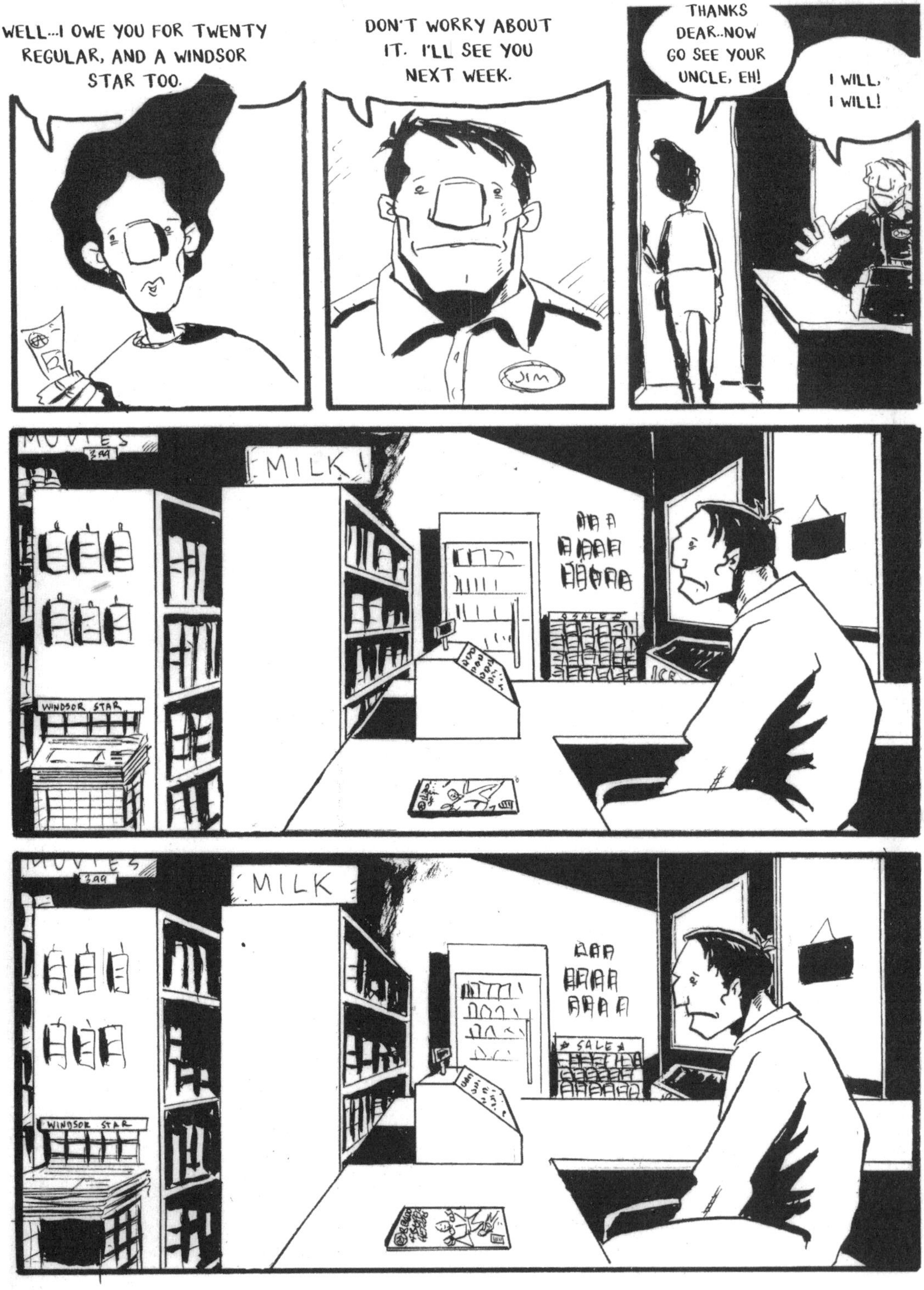
WELL...I OWE YOU FOR TWENTY REGULAR, AND A WINDSOR STAR TOO.
DON'T WORRY ABOUT IT. I'LL SEE YOU NEXT WEEK.
JIM
THANKS DEAR..NOW GO SEE YOUR UNCLE, EH!
I WILL, I WILL!
MILK
WINDSOR STAR
MILK
WINDSOR STAR

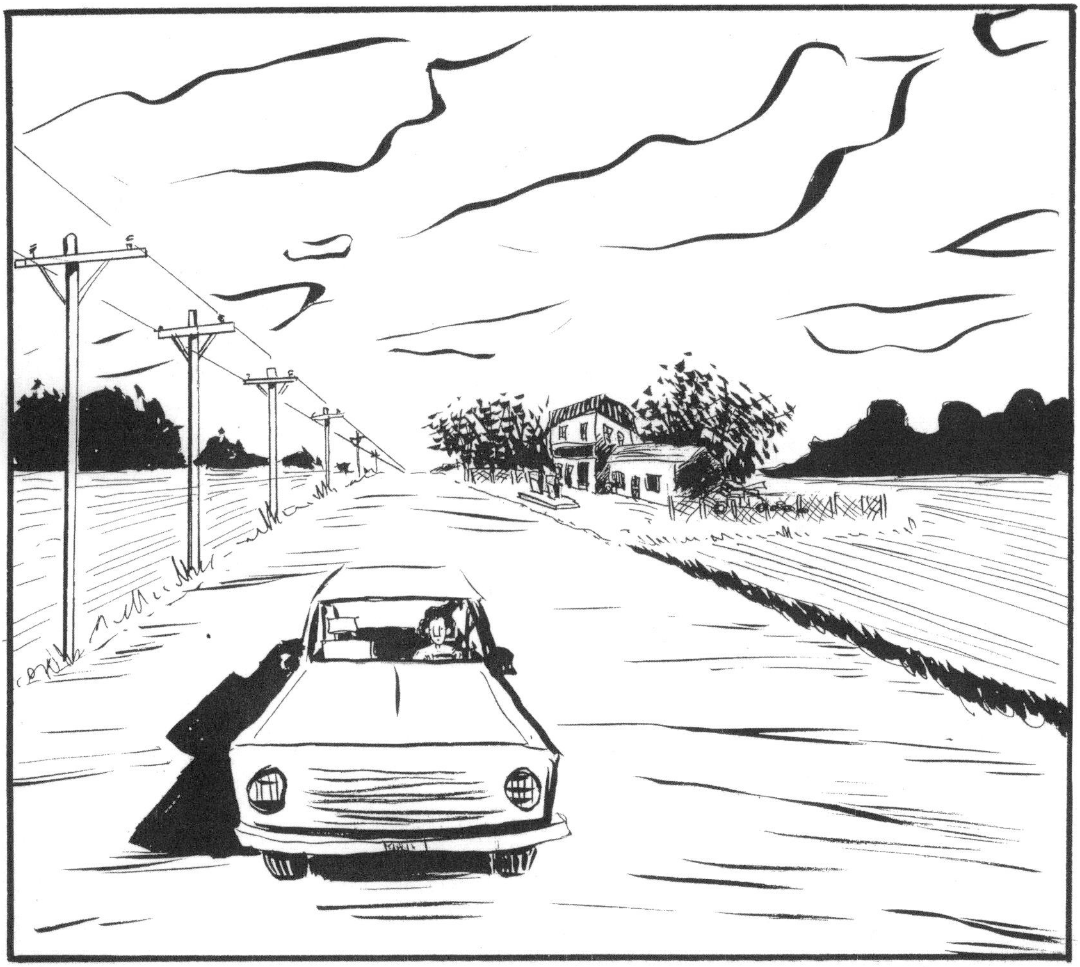

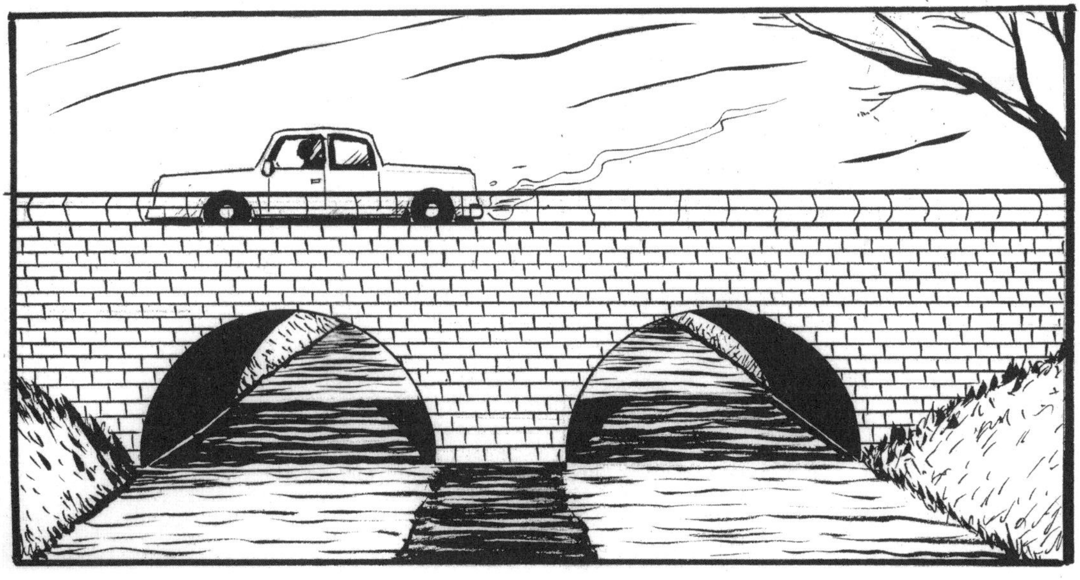

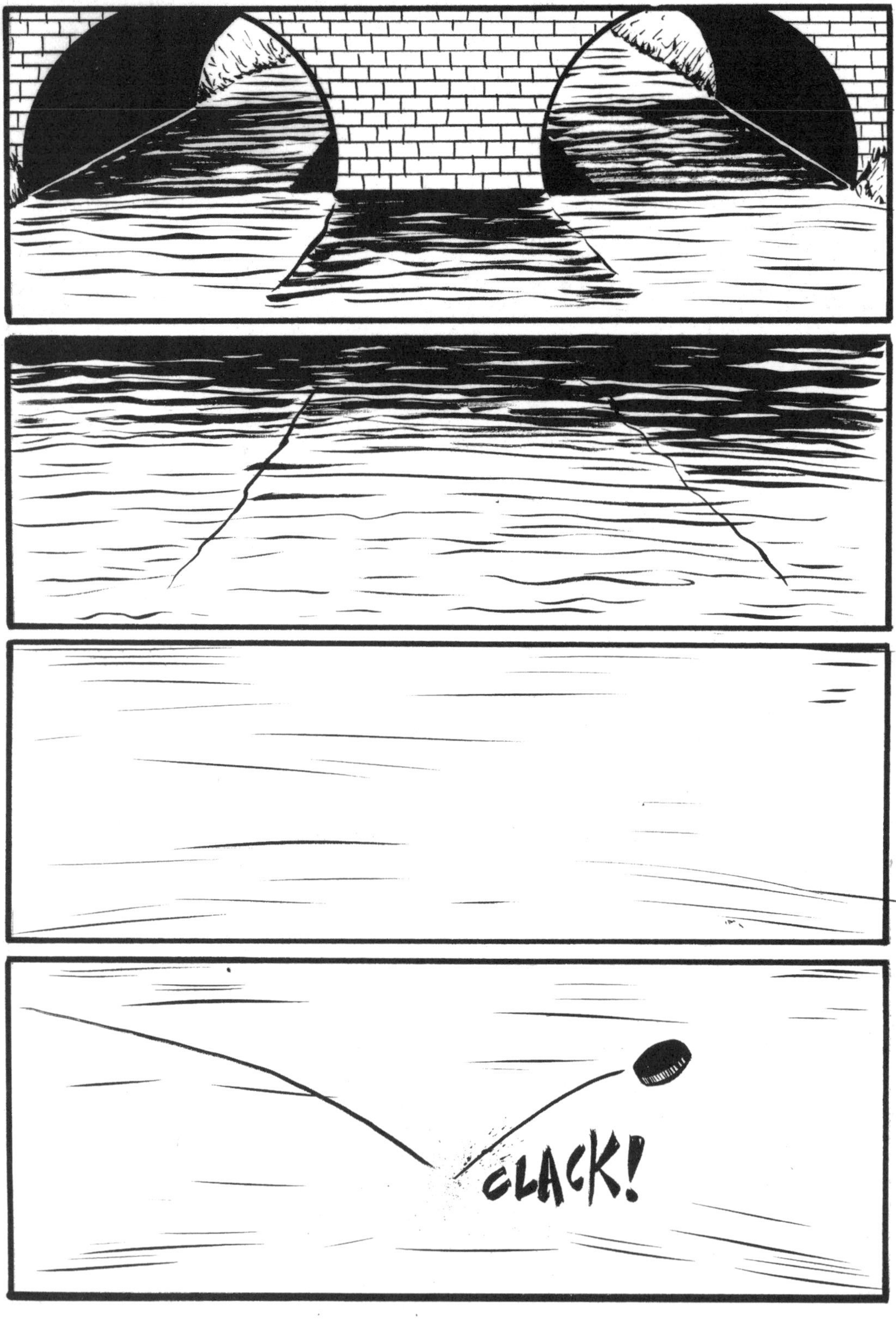
CLACK!

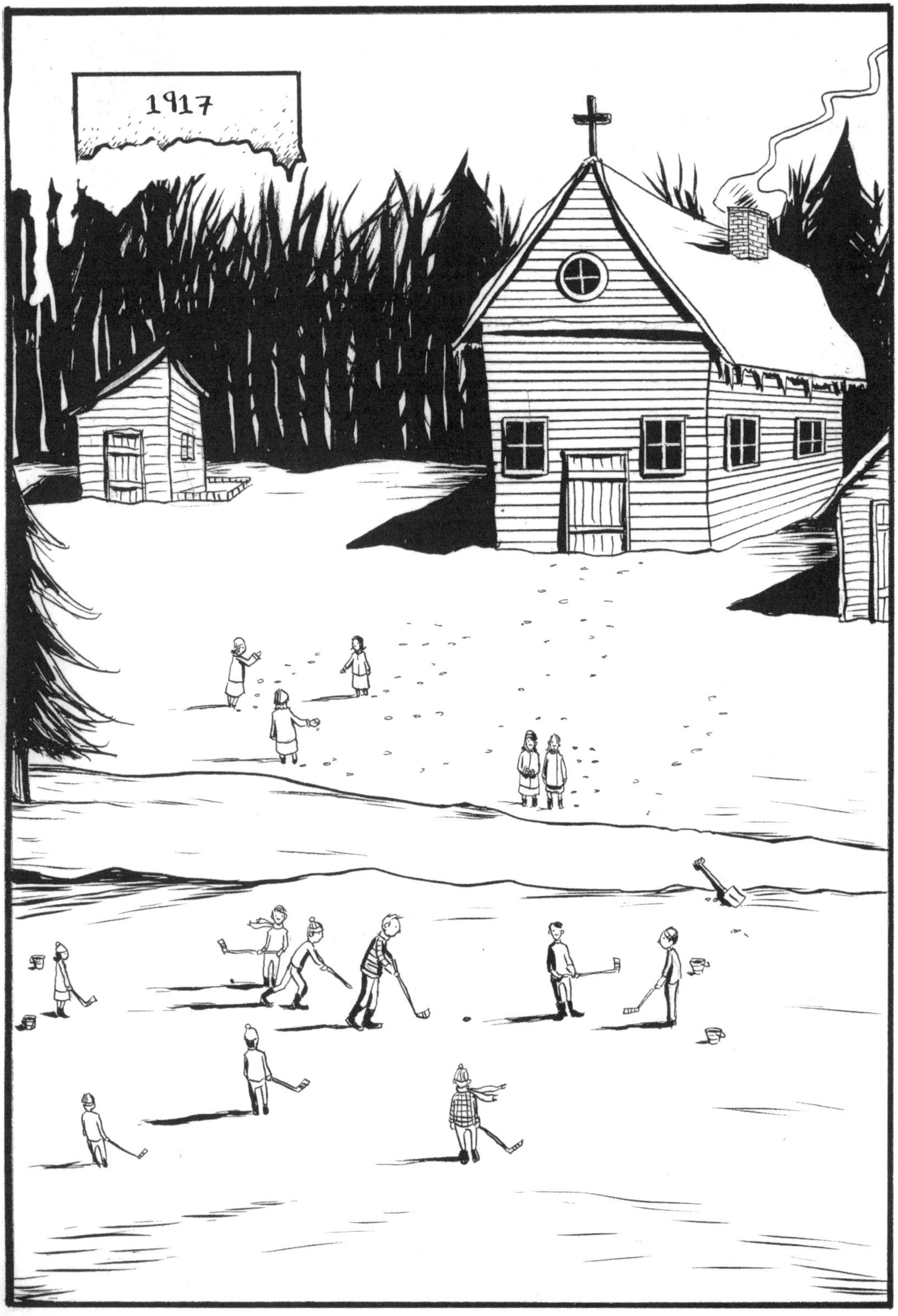
1917

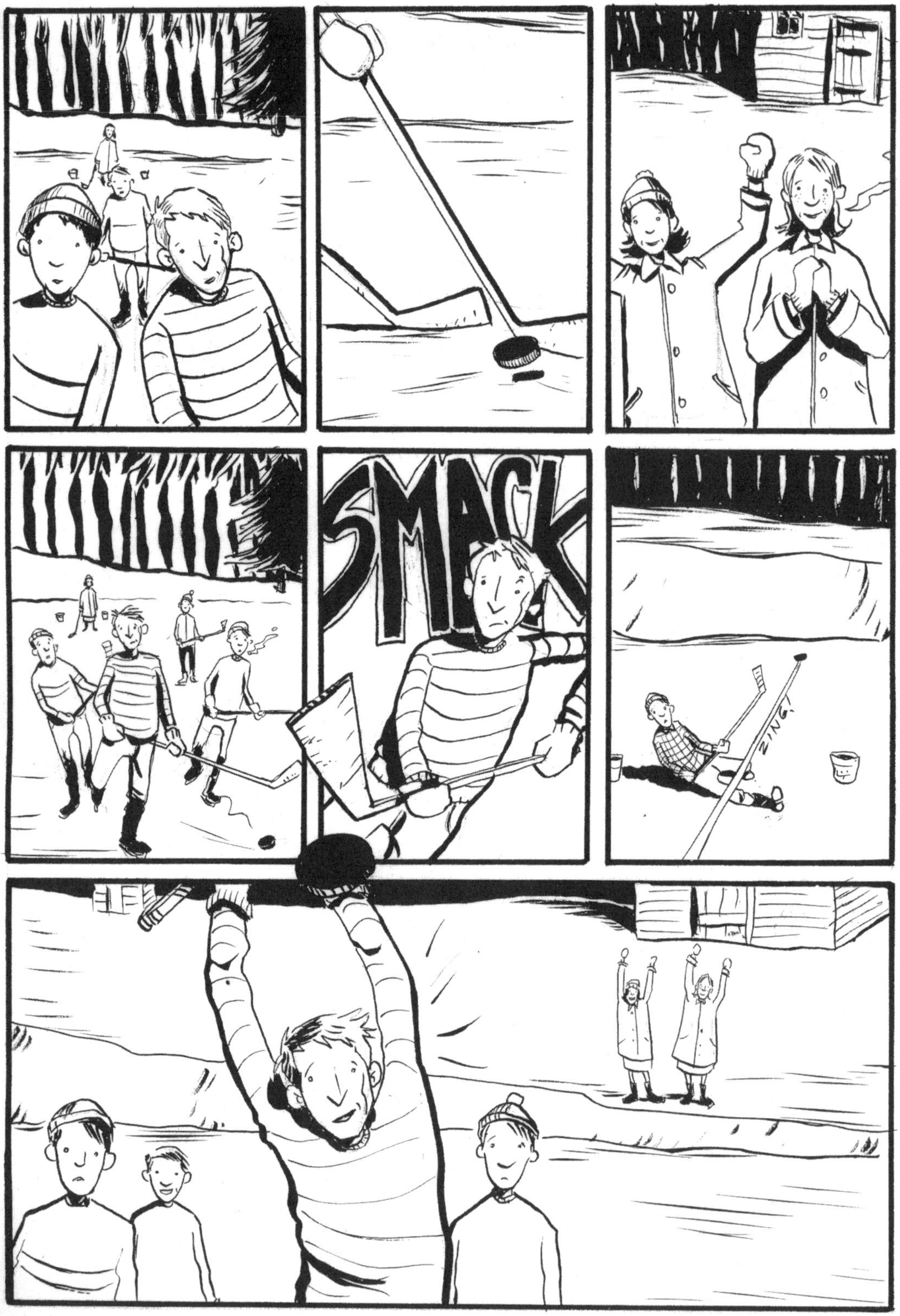
SMACK
ZING!

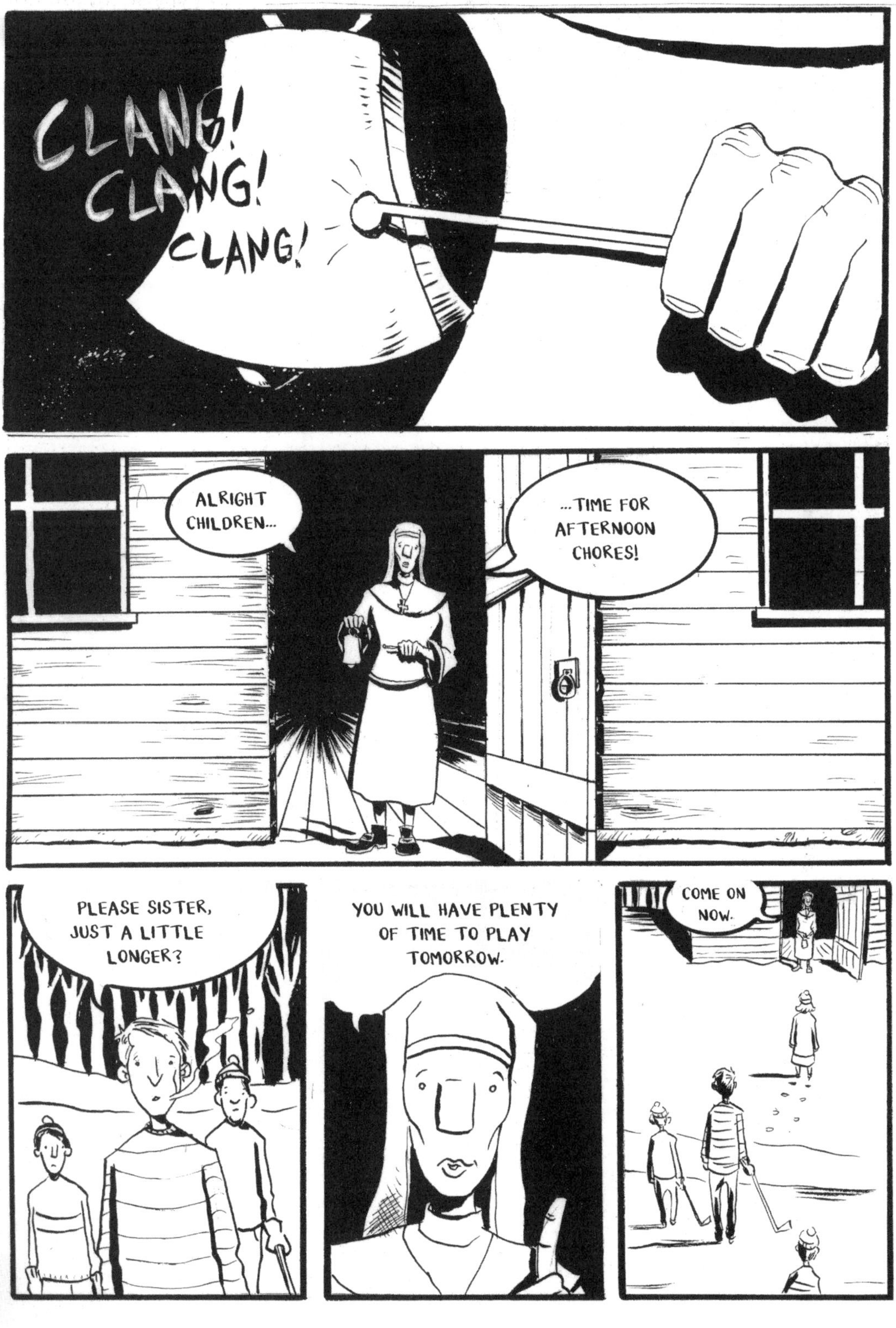
CLANG!
CLANG!
CLANG!
ALRIGHT CHILDREN...
...TIME FOR AFTERNOON CHORES!
PLEASE SISTER, JUST A LITTLE LONGER?
YOU WILL HAVE PLENTY OF TIME TO PLAY TOMORROW.
COME ON NOW.

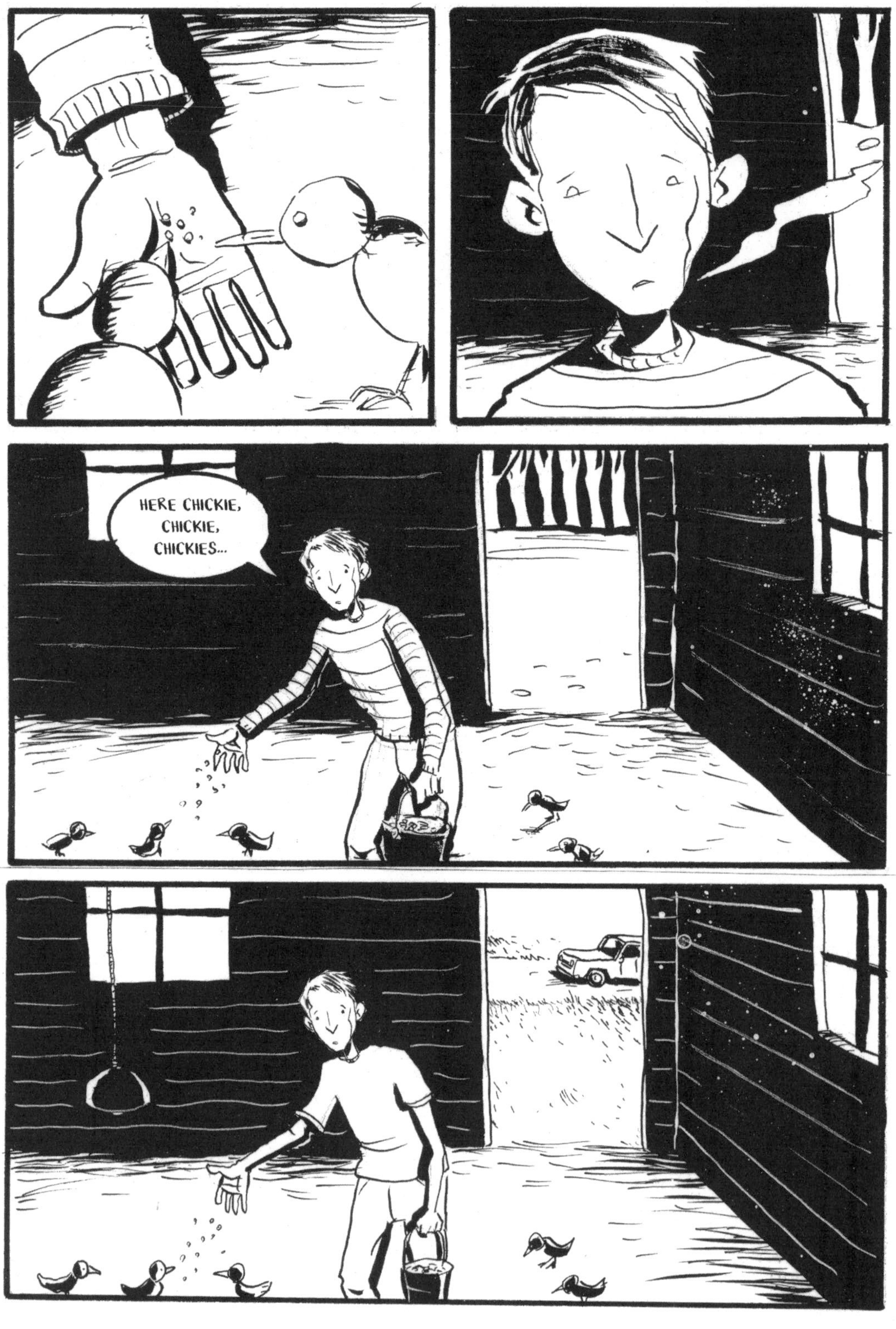
HERE CHICKIE,
CHICKIE,
CHICKIES...

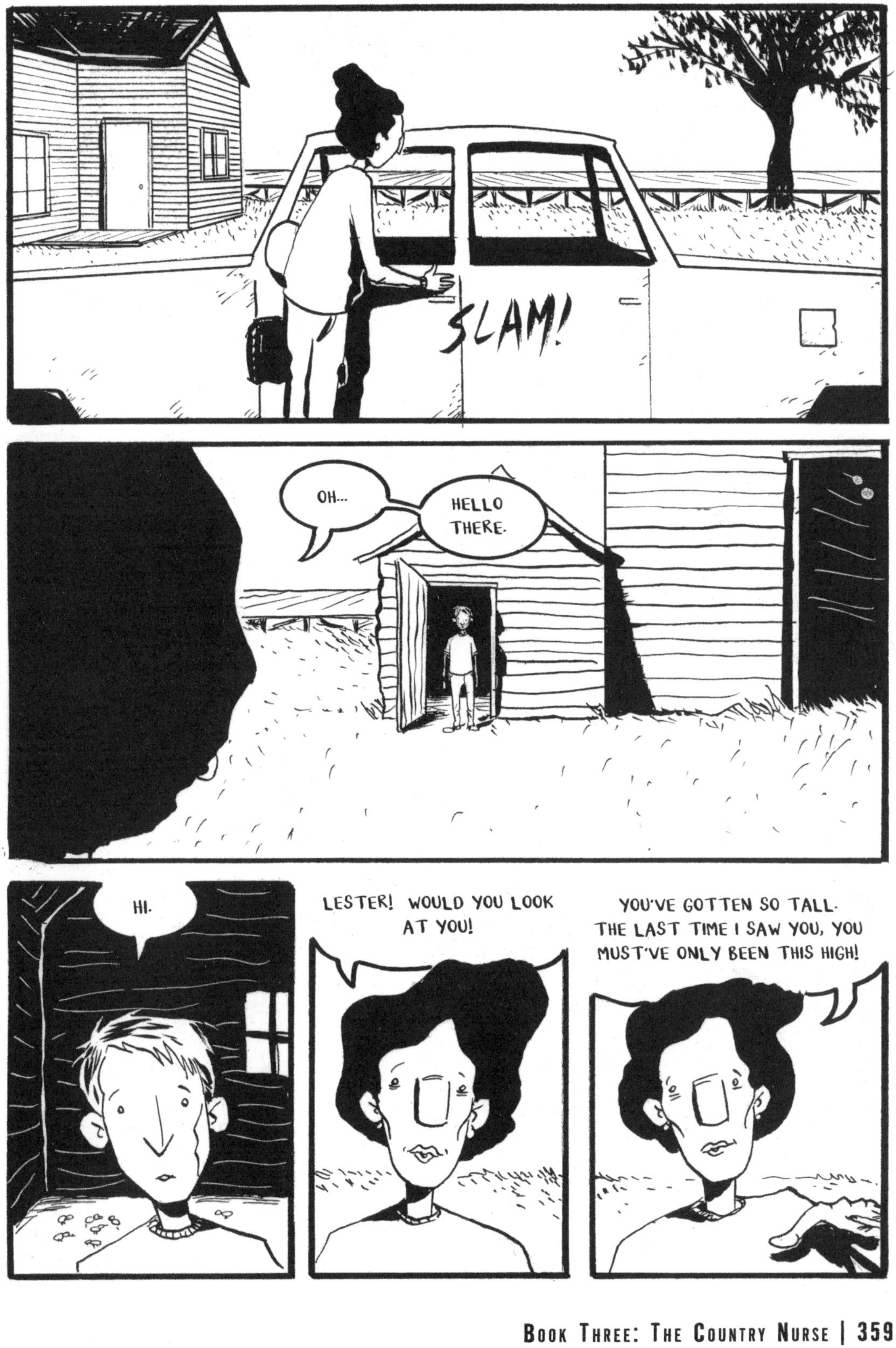
SLAM!
OH...
HELLO THERE.
HI.
LESTER! WOULD YOU LOOK AT YOU!
YOU'VE GOTTEN SO TALL. THE LAST TIME I SAW YOU, YOU MUST'VE ONLY BEEN THIS HIGH!

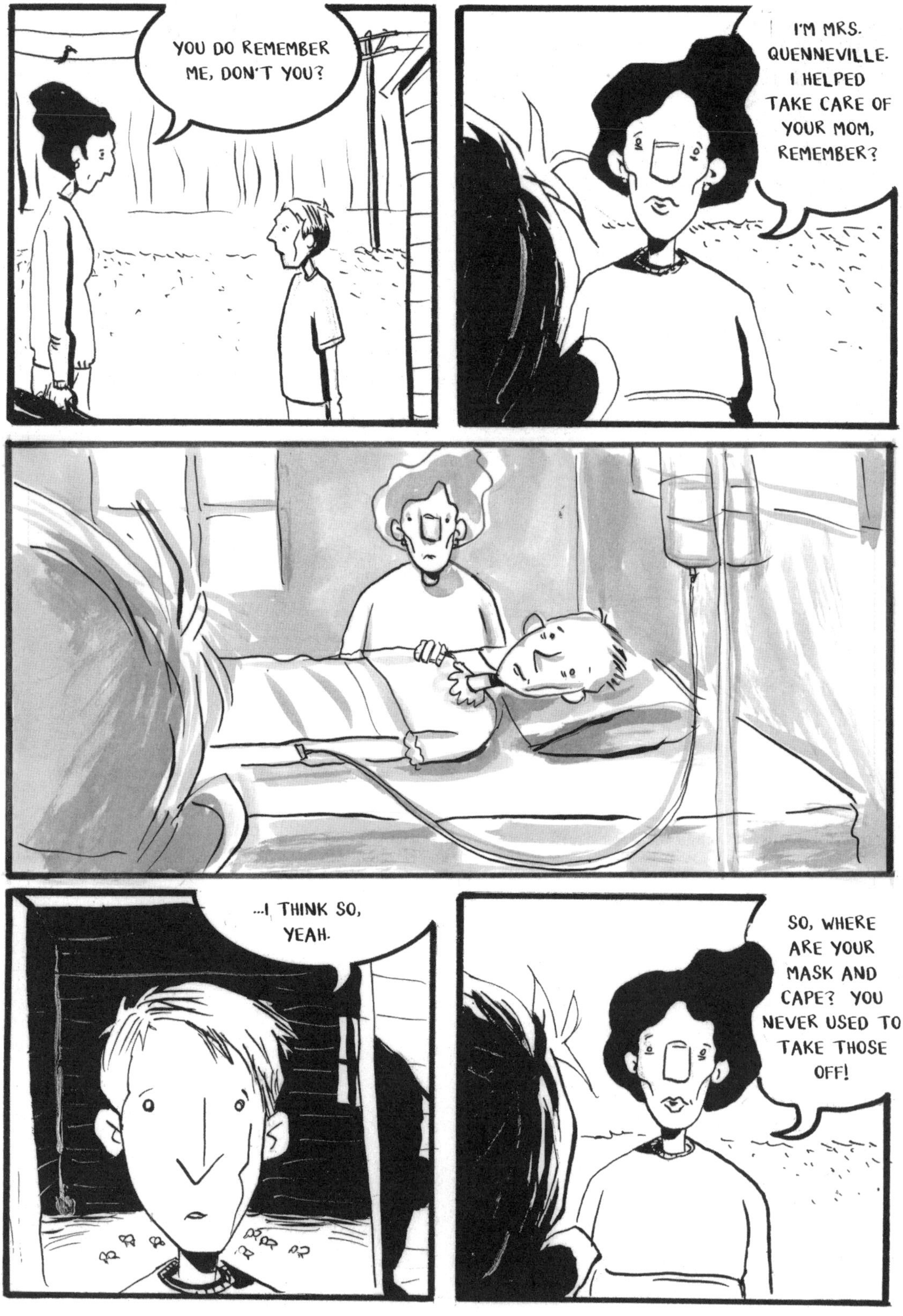

YOU DO REMEMBER ME, DON'T YOU?
I'M MRS. QUENNEVILLE. I HELPED TAKE CARE OF YOUR MOM, REMEMBER?
...I THINK SO, YEAH.
SO, WHERE ARE YOUR MASK AND CAPE? YOU NEVER USED TO TAKE THOSE OFF!

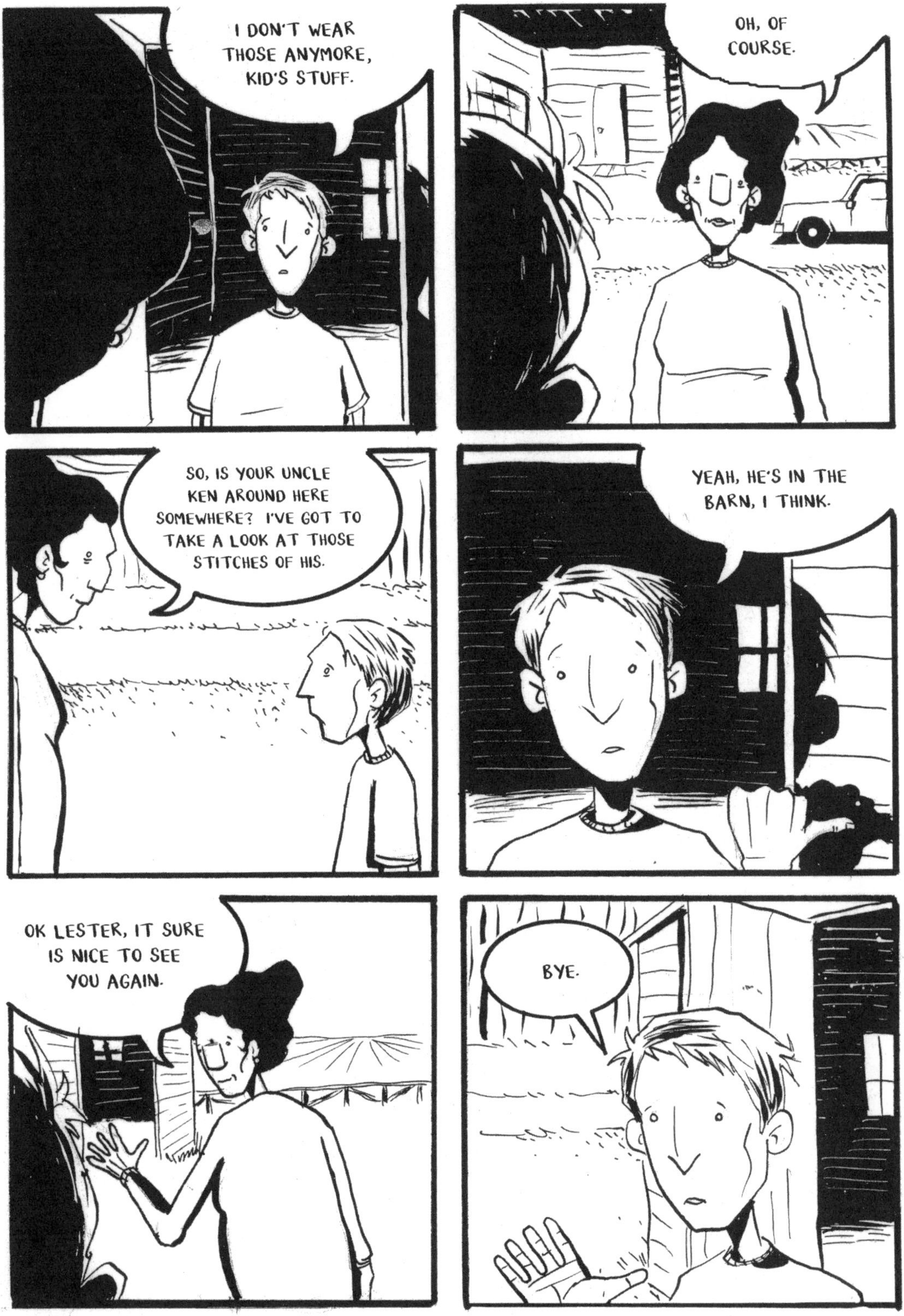
I DON'T WEAR THOSE ANYMORE, KID'S STUFF.
OH, OF COURSE.
SO, IS YOUR UNCLE KEN AROUND HERE SOMEWHERE? I'VE GOT TO TAKE A LOOK AT THOSE STITCHES OF HIS.
YEAH, HE'S IN THE BARN, I THINK.
OK LESTER, IT SURE IS NICE TO SEE YOU AGAIN.
BYE.

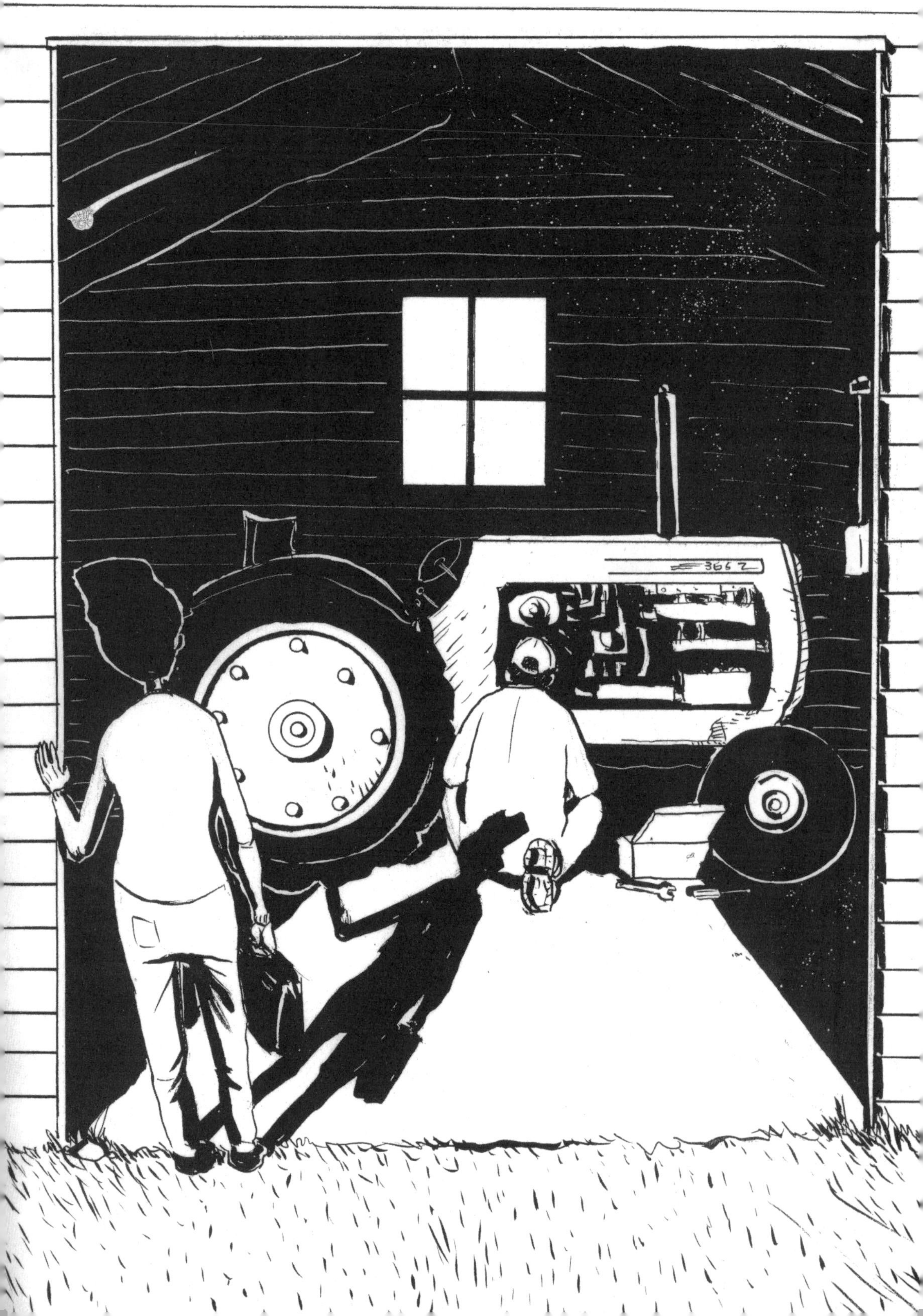
3662

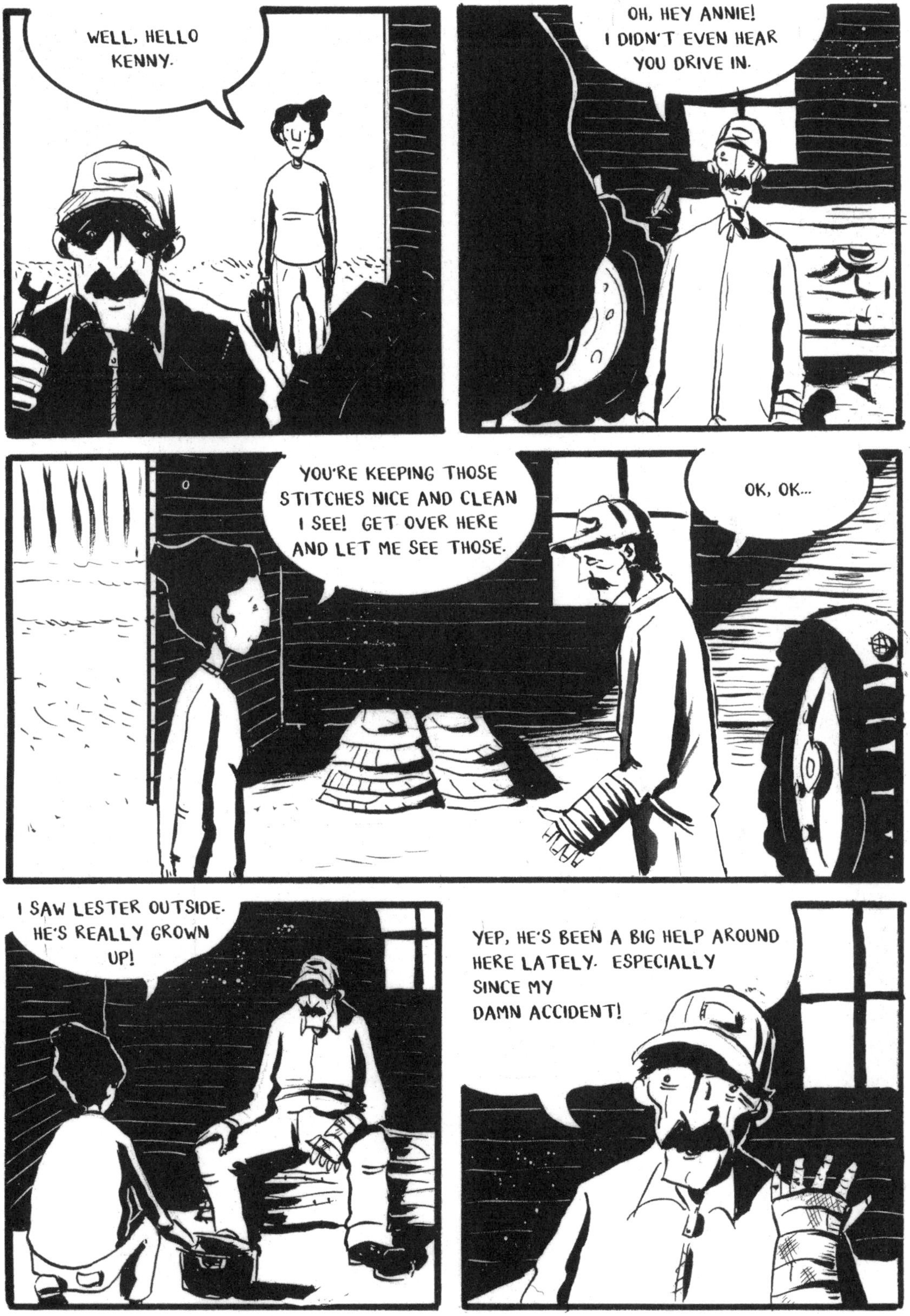
WELL, HELLO KENNY.
OH, HEY ANNIE! I DIDN'T EVEN HEAR YOU DRIVE IN.
YOU'RE KEEPING THOSE STITCHES NICE AND CLEAN I SEE! GET OVER HERE AND LET ME SEE THOSE.
OK, OK...
I SAW LESTER OUTSIDE. HE'S REALLY GROWN UP!
YEP, HE'S BEEN A BIG HELP AROUND HERE LATELY. ESPECIALLY SINCE MY DAMN ACCIDENT!

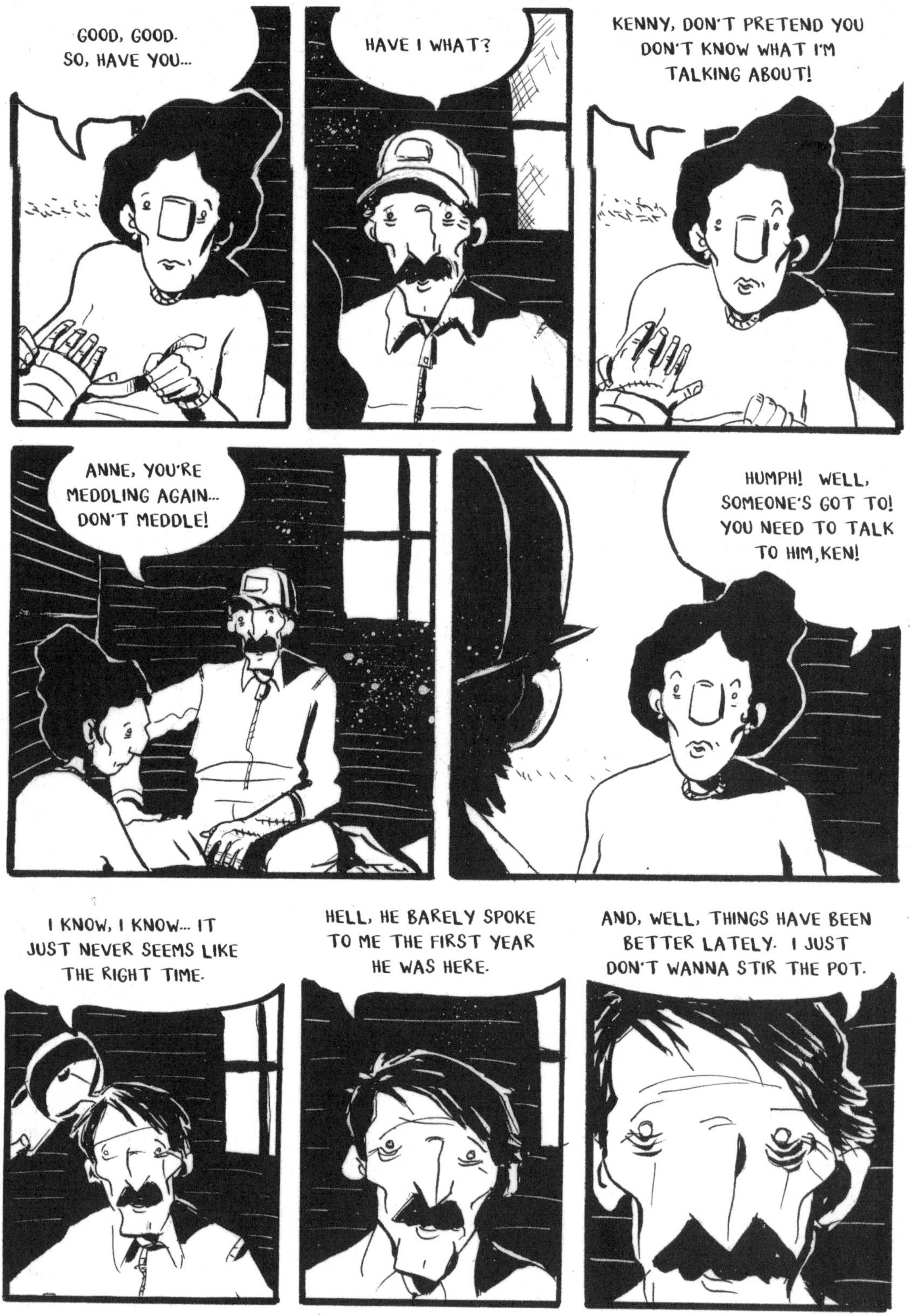
GOOD, GOOD. SO, HAVE YOU...
HAVE I WHAT?
KENNY, DON'T PRETEND YOU DON'T KNOW WHAT I'M TALKING ABOUT!
ANNE, YOU'RE MEDDLING AGAIN... DON'T MEDDLE!
HUMPH! WELL, SOMEONE'S GOT TO! YOU NEED TO TALK TO HIM, KEN!
I KNOW, I KNOW... IT JUST NEVER SEEMS LIKE THE RIGHT TIME.
HELL, HE BARELY SPOKE TO ME THE FIRST YEAR HE WAS HERE.
AND, WELL, THINGS HAVE BEEN BETTER LATELY. I JUST DON'T WANNA STIR THE POT.

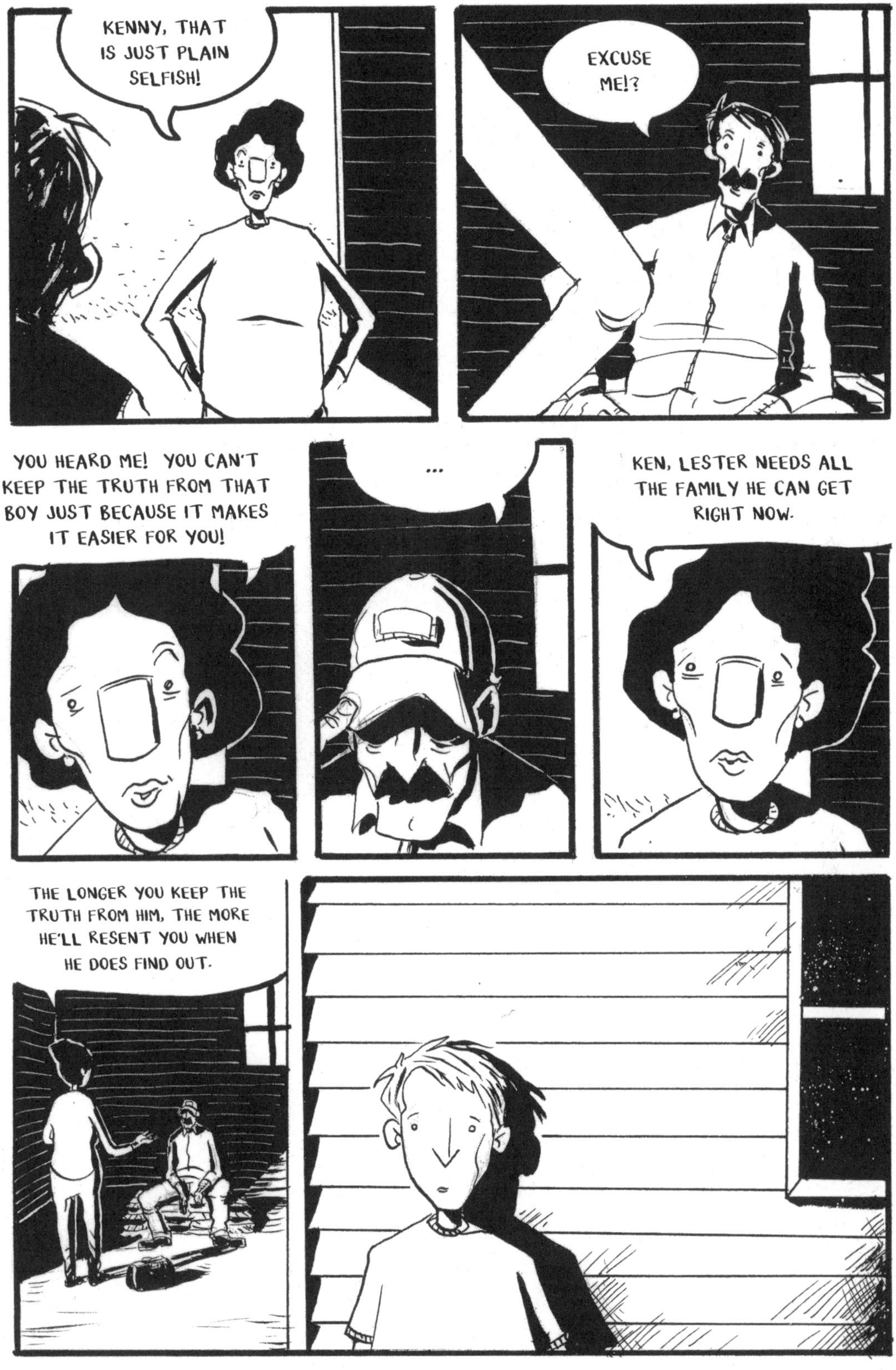
KENNY, THAT IS JUST PLAIN SELFISH!
EXCUSE ME!?
YOU HEARD ME! YOU CAN'T KEEP THE TRUTH FROM THAT BOY JUST BECAUSE IT MAKES IT EASIER FOR YOU!
...
KEN, LESTER NEEDS ALL THE FAMILY HE CAN GET RIGHT NOW.
THE LONGER YOU KEEP THE TRUTH FROM HIM, THE MORE HE'LL RESENT YOU WHEN HE DOES FIND OUT.

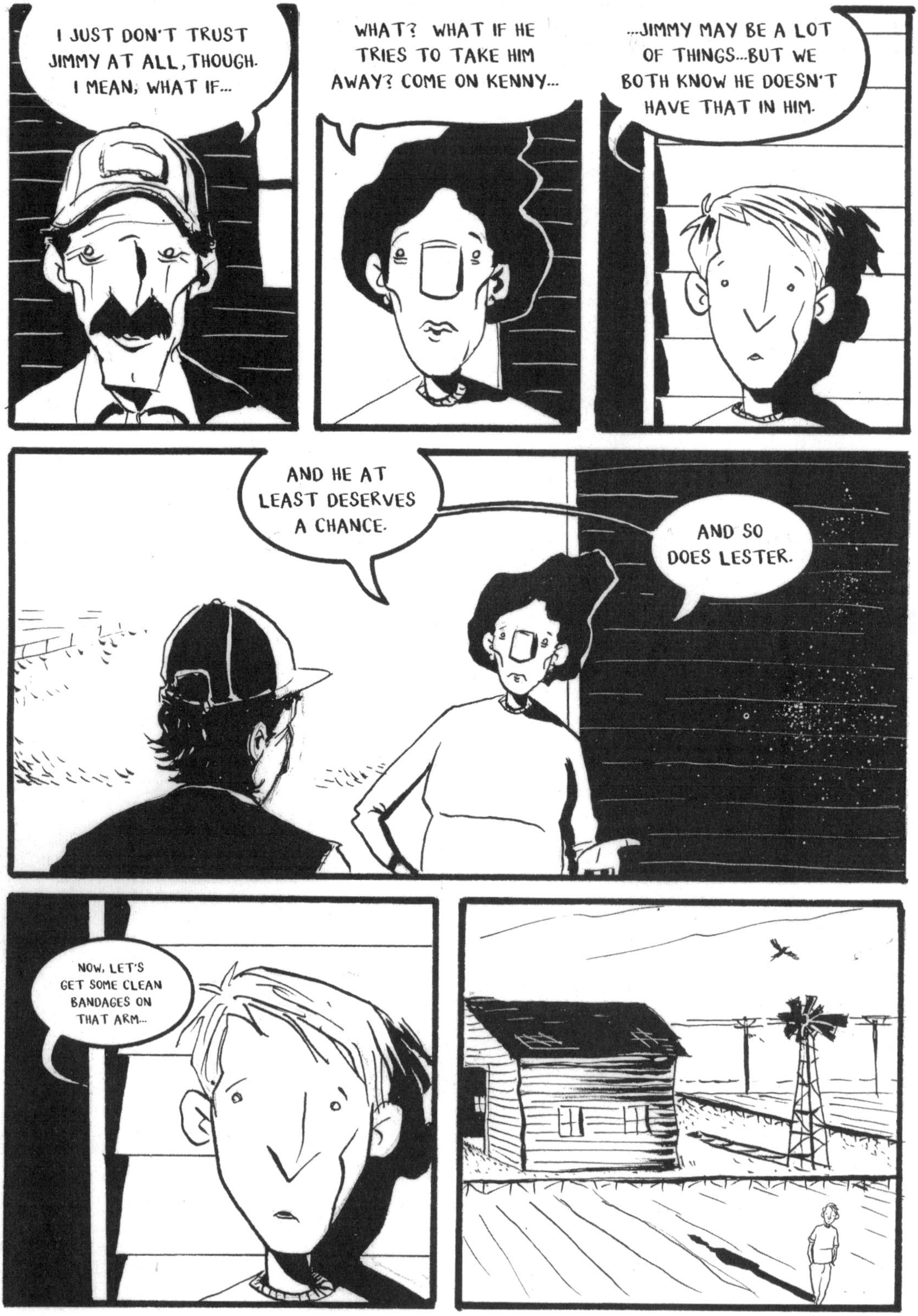
I JUST DON'T TRUST JIMMY AT ALL, THOUGH. I MEAN, WHAT IF...
WHAT? WHAT IF HE TRIES TO TAKE HIM AWAY? COME ON KENNY...
...JIMMY MAY BE A LOT OF THINGS...BUT WE BOTH KNOW HE DOESN'T HAVE THAT IN HIM.
AND HE AT LEAST DESERVES A CHANCE.
AND SO DOES LESTER.
NOW, LET'S GET SOME CLEAN BANDAGES ON THAT ARM...

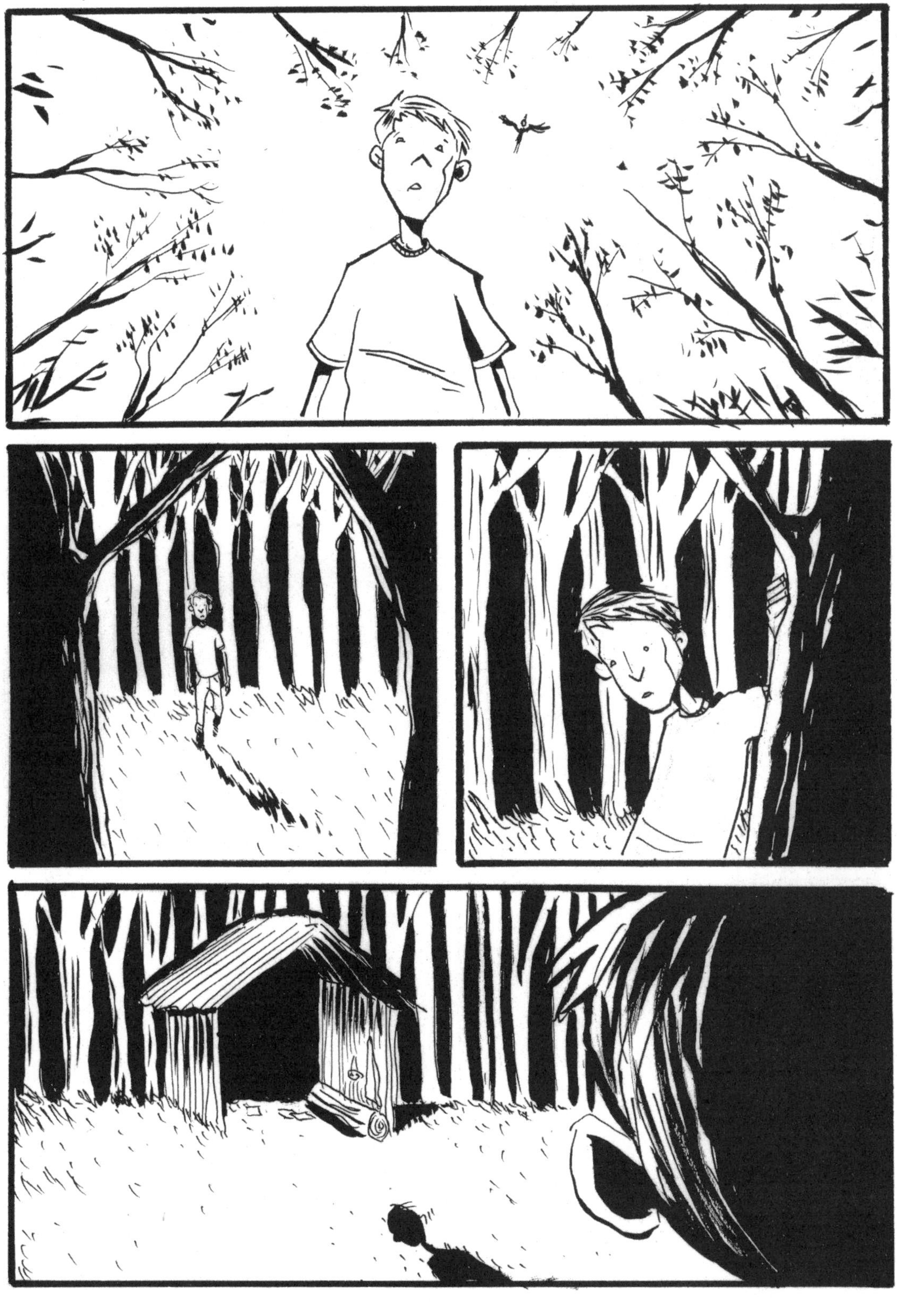

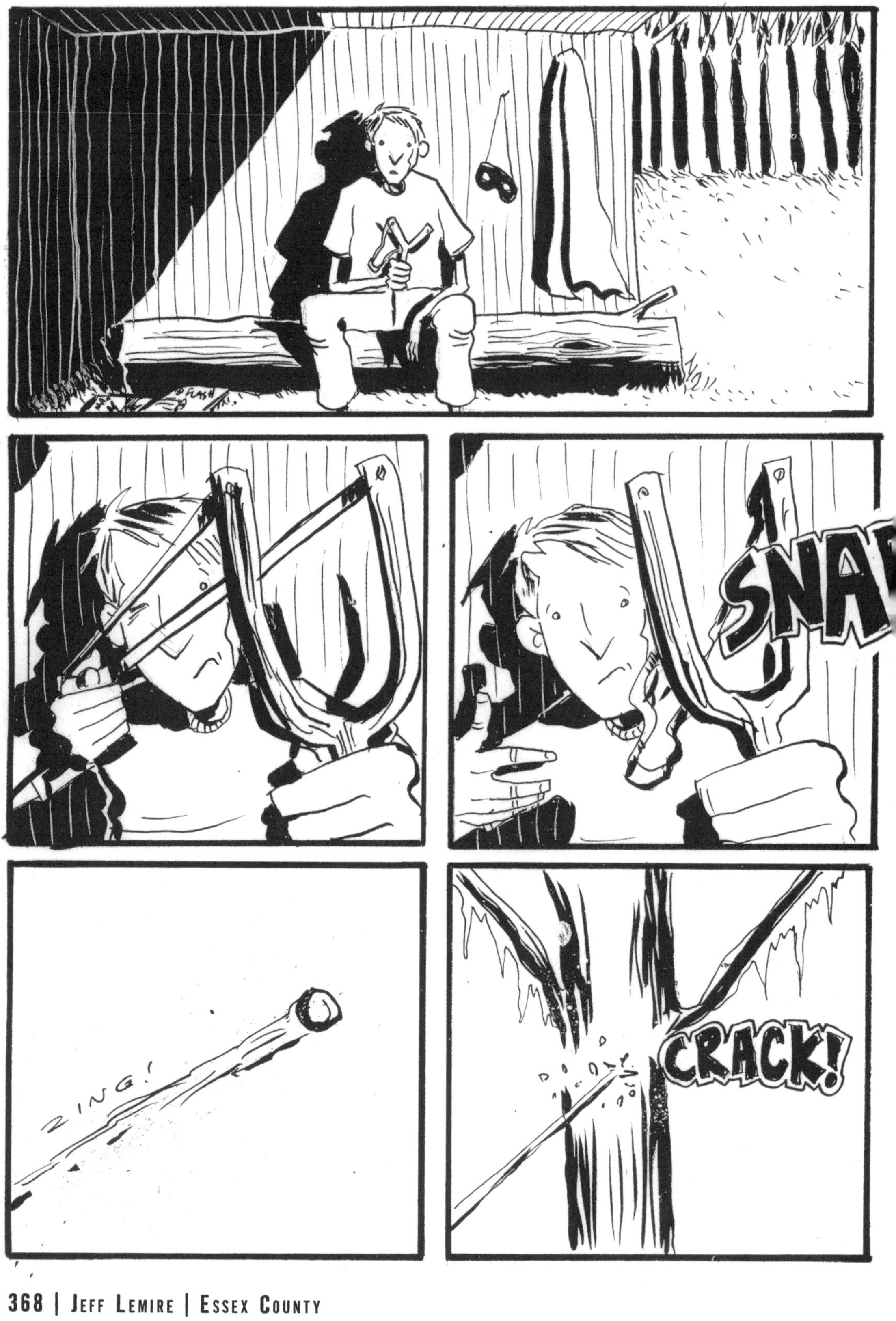
FLASH
SNA
ZING!
CRACK!

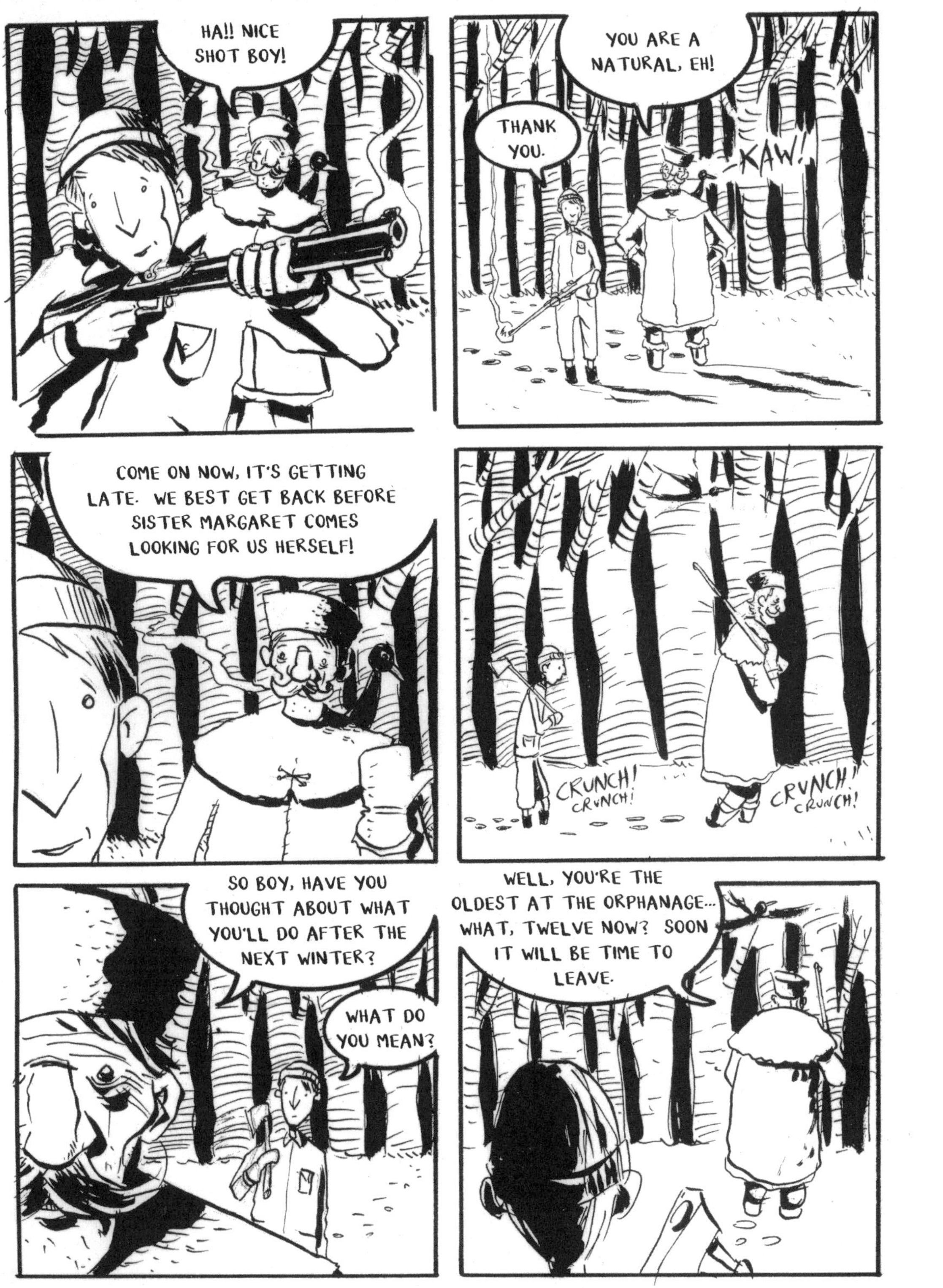
HA!! NICE SHOT BOY!
YOU ARE A NATURAL, EH!
THANK YOU.
KAW!
COME ON NOW, IT'S GETTING LATE. WE BEST GET BACK BEFORE SISTER MARGARET COMES LOOKING FOR US HERSELF!
CRUNCH! CRUNCH!
CRUNCH! CRUNCH!
SO BOY, HAVE YOU THOUGHT ABOUT WHAT YOU'LL DO AFTER THE NEXT WINTER?
WHAT DO YOU MEAN?
WELL, YOU'RE THE OLDEST AT THE ORPHANAGE... WHAT, TWELVE NOW? SOON IT WILL BE TIME TO LEAVE.

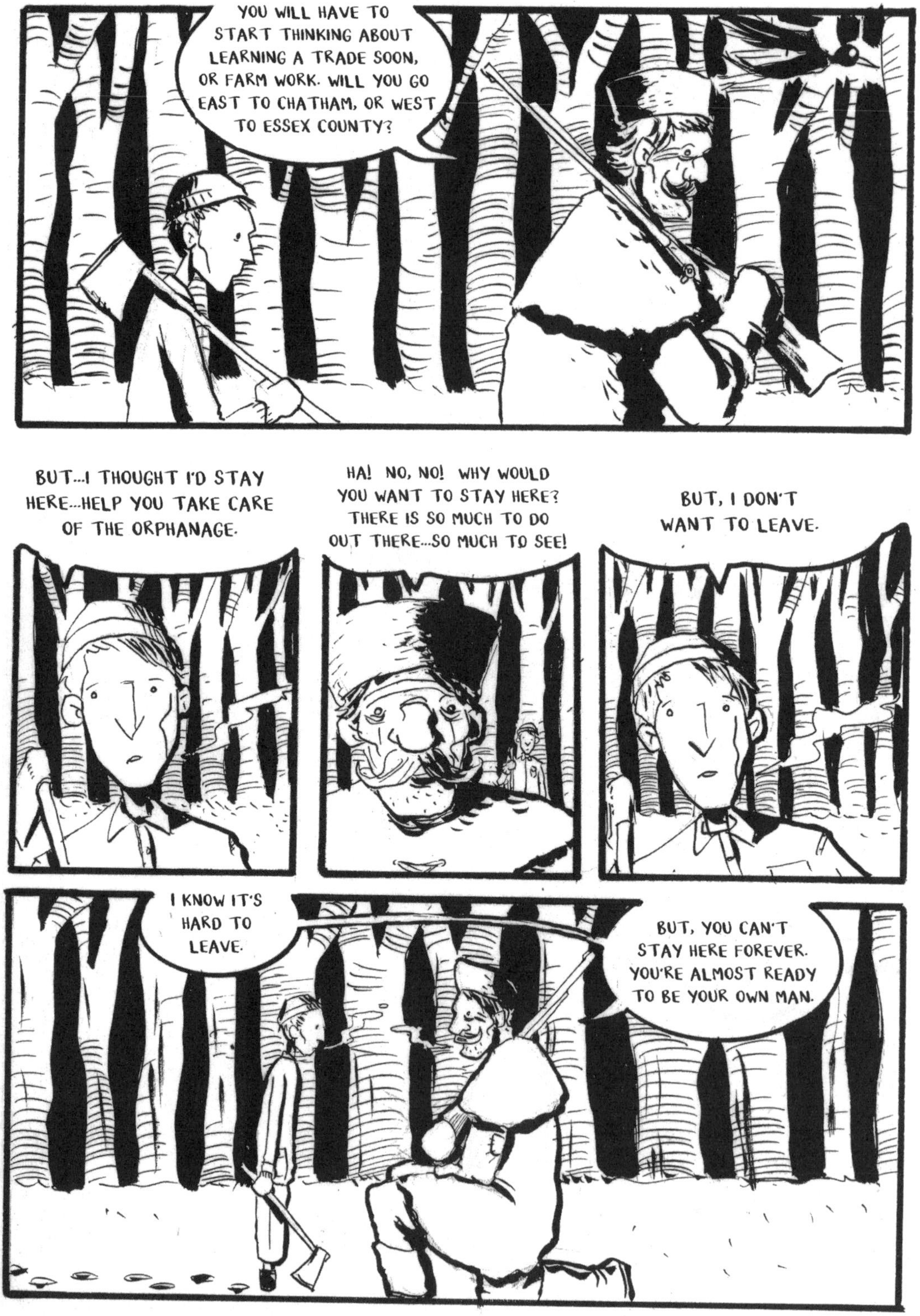
YOU WILL HAVE TO START THINKING ABOUT LEARNING A TRADE SOON, OR FARM WORK. WILL YOU GO EAST TO CHATHAM, OR WEST TO ESSEX COUNTY?
BUT...I THOUGHT I'D STAY HERE...HELP YOU TAKE CARE OF THE ORPHANAGE.
HA! NO, NO! WHY WOULD YOU WANT TO STAY HERE? THERE IS SO MUCH TO DO OUT THERE...SO MUCH TO SEE!
BUT, I DON'T WANT TO LEAVE.
I KNOW IT'S HARD TO LEAVE.
BUT, YOU CAN'T STAY HERE FOREVER. YOU'RE ALMOST READY TO BE YOUR OWN MAN.

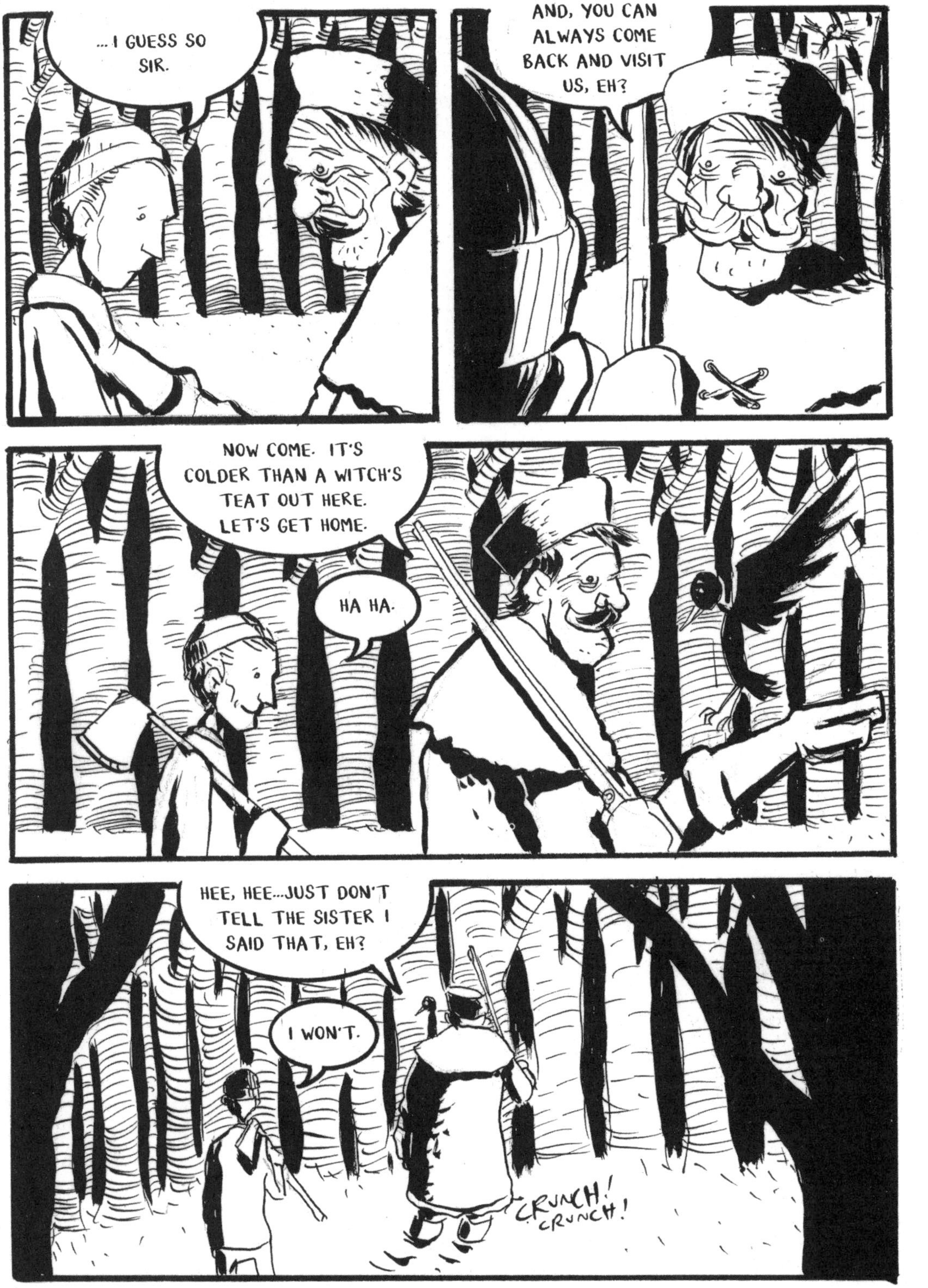

...I GUESS SO SIR.
AND, YOU CAN ALWAYS COME BACK AND VISIT US, EH?
NOW COME. IT'S COLDER THAN A WITCH'S TEAT OUT HERE. LET'S GET HOME.
HA HA.
HEE, HEE...JUST DON'T TELL THE SISTER I SAID THAT, EH?
I WON'T.
CRUNCH! CRUNCH!

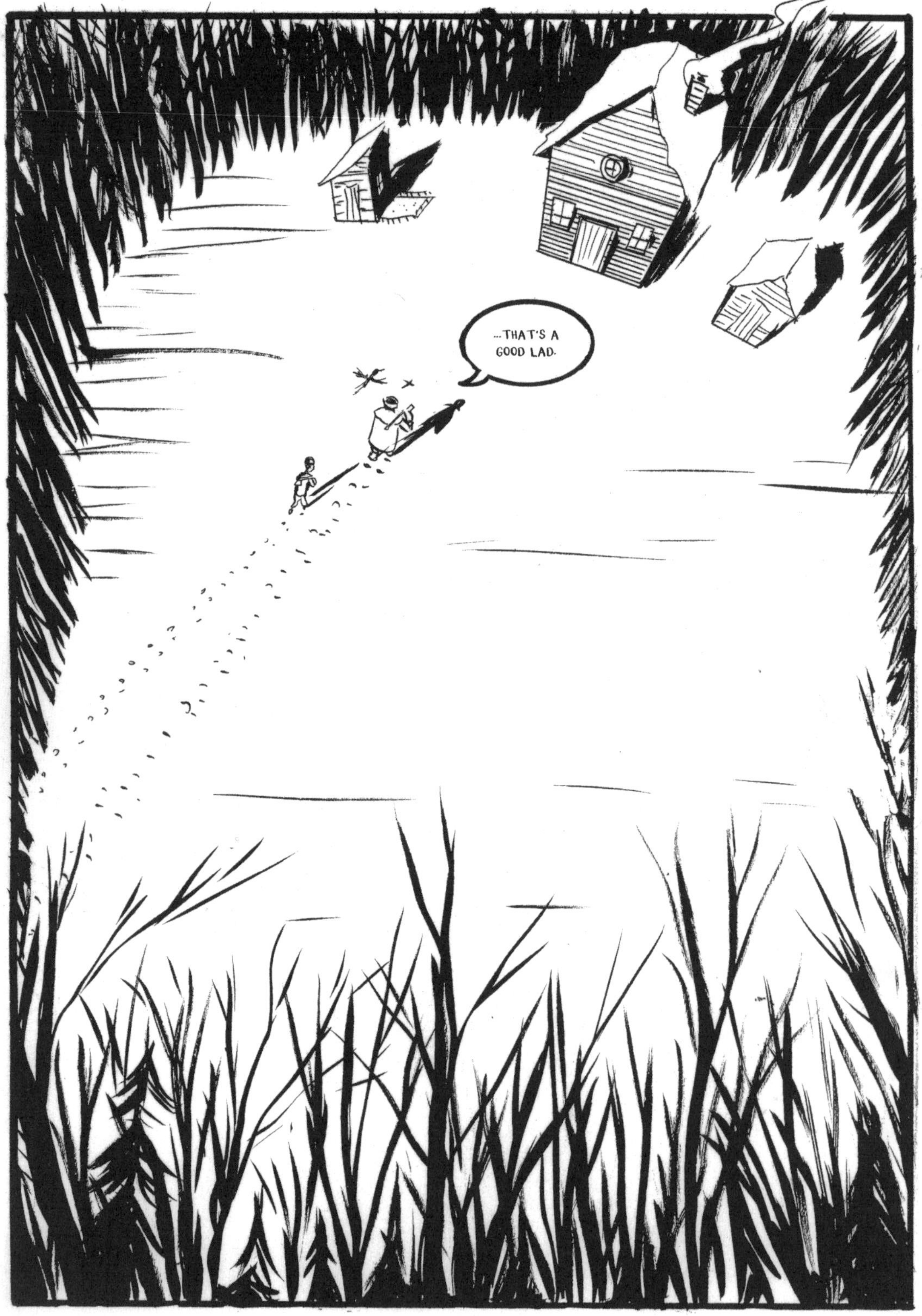
...THAT'S A GOOD LAD.

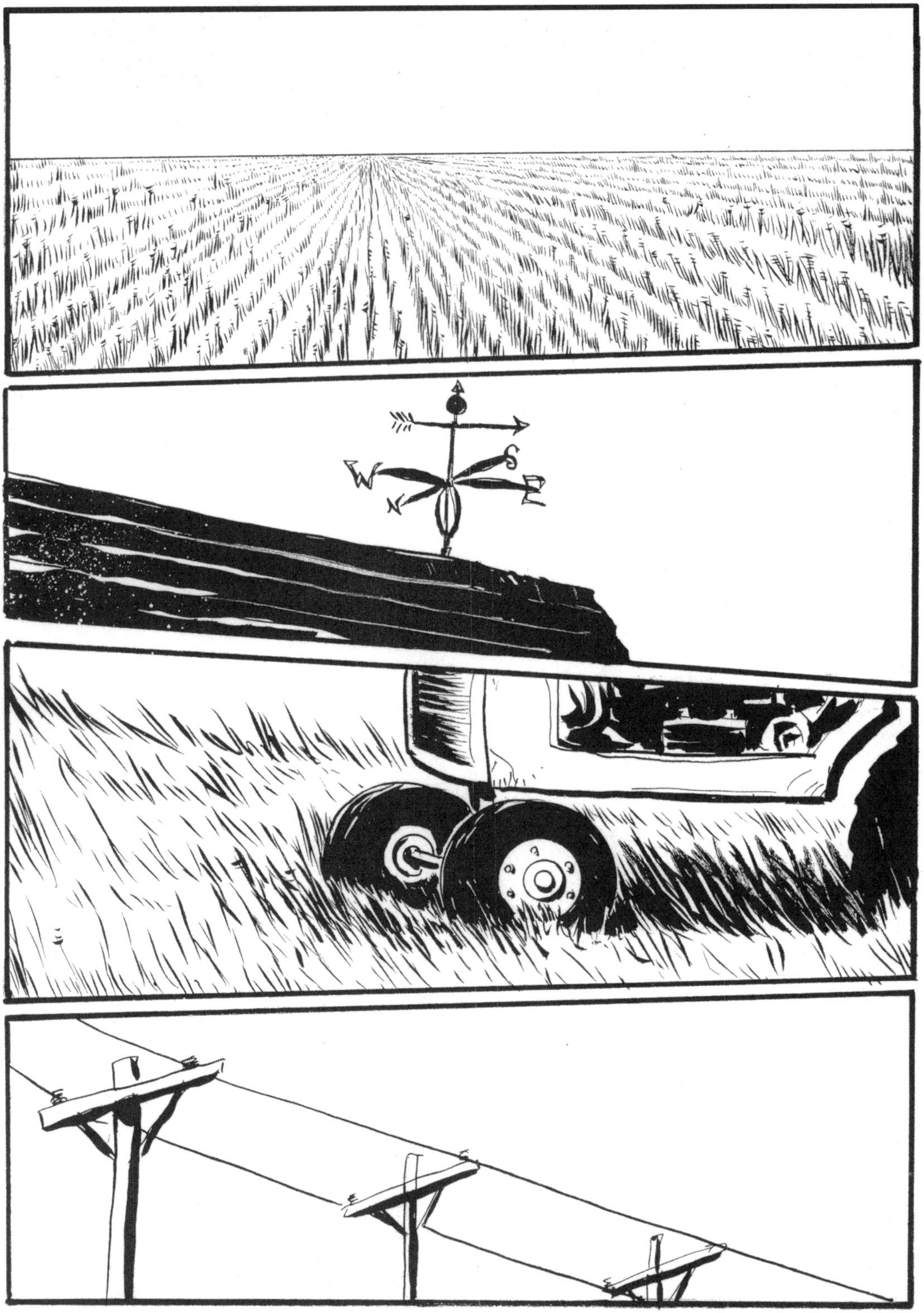
W
S
N
E

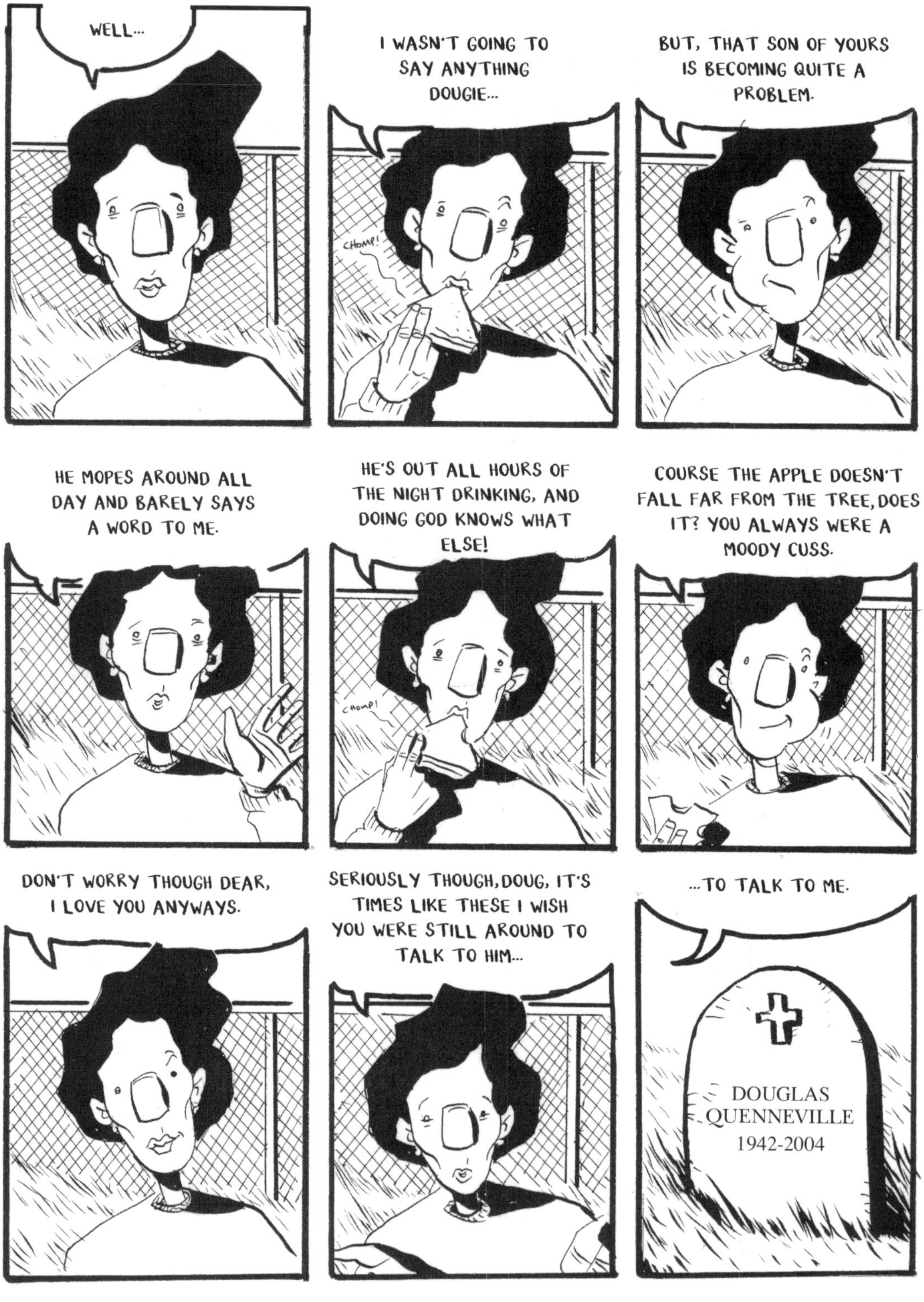
WELL...
I WASN'T GOING TO SAY ANYTHING DOUGIE...
CHOMP!
BUT, THAT SON OF YOURS IS BECOMING QUITE A PROBLEM.
HE MOPES AROUND ALL DAY AND BARELY SAYS A WORD TO ME.
HE'S OUT ALL HOURS OF THE NIGHT DRINKING, AND DOING GOD KNOWS WHAT ELSE!
CHOMP!
COURSE THE APPLE DOESN'T FALL FAR FROM THE TREE, DOES IT? YOU ALWAYS WERE A MOODY CUSS.
DON'T WORRY THOUGH DEAR, I LOVE YOU ANYWAYS.
SERIOUSLY THOUGH, DOUG, IT'S TIMES LIKE THESE I WISH YOU WERE STILL AROUND TO TALK TO HIM...
...TO TALK TO ME.
DOUGLAS QUENNEVILLE
1942-2004

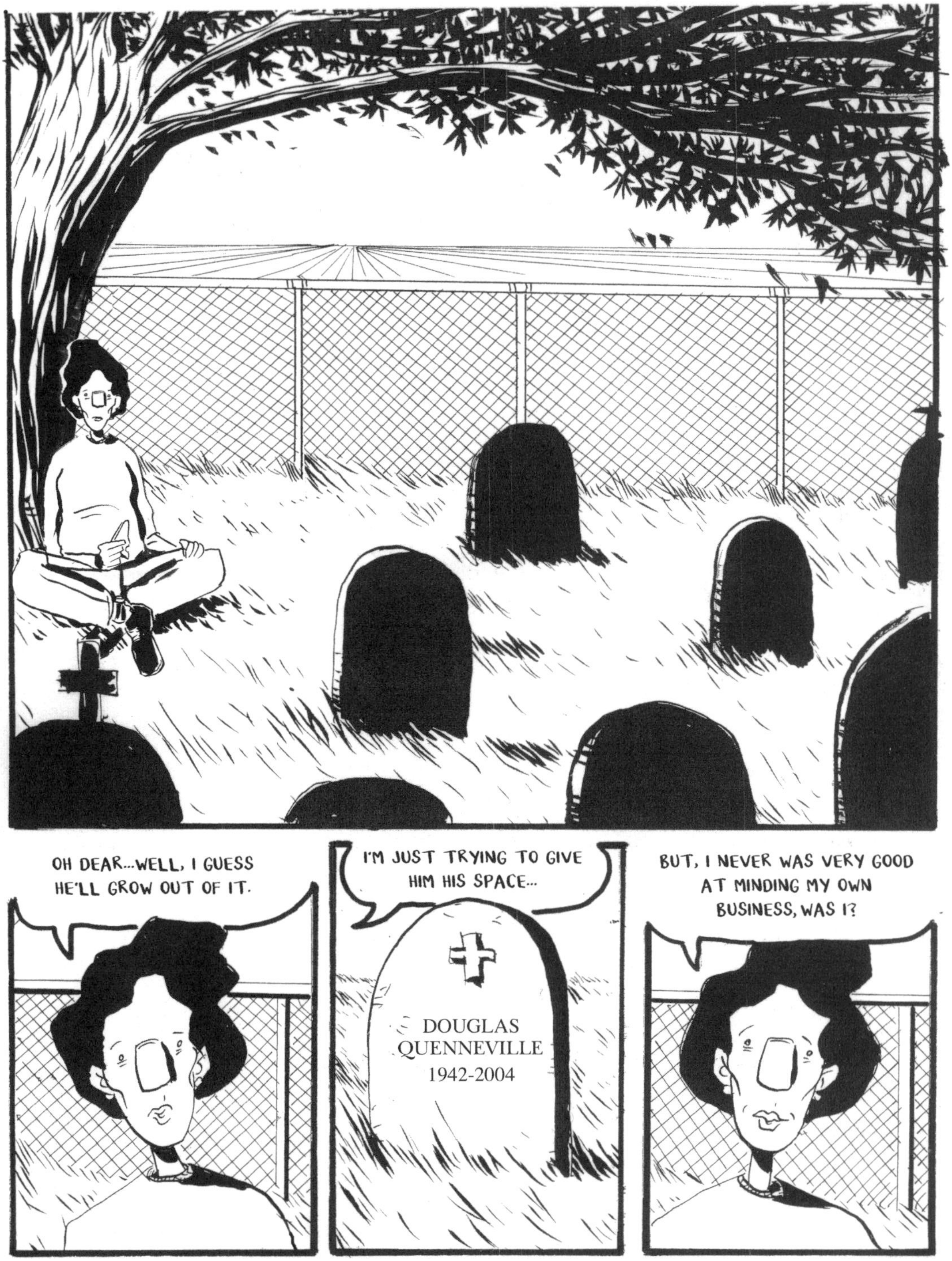
OH DEAR...WELL, I GUESS HE'LL GROW OUT OF IT.
I'M JUST TRYING TO GIVE HIM HIS SPACE...
DOUGLAS QUENNEVILLE 1942-2004
BUT, I NEVER WAS VERY GOOD AT MINDING MY OWN BUSINESS, WAS I?

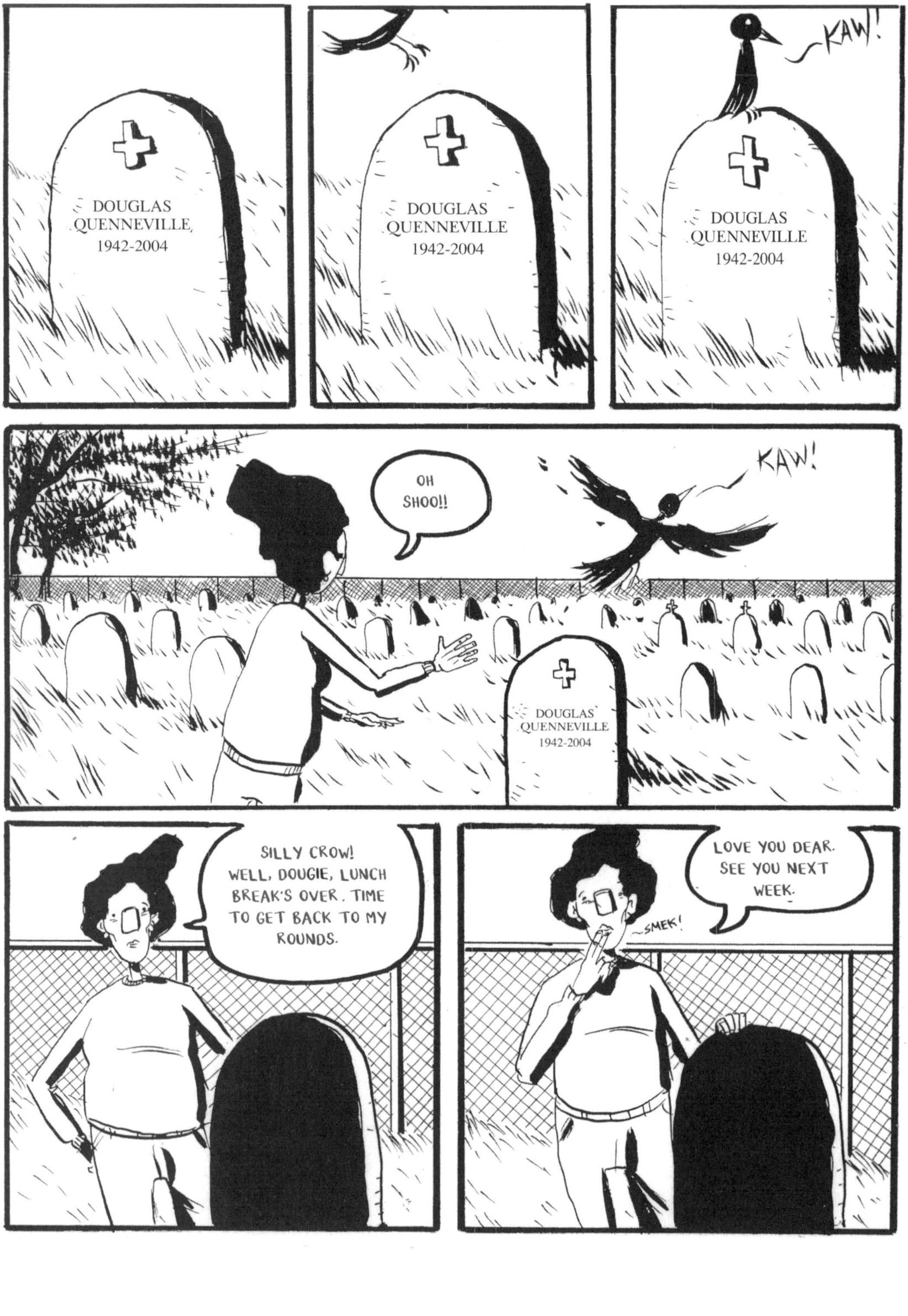
DOUGLAS QUENNEVILLE, 1942-2004
DOUGLAS QUENNEVILLE 1942-2004
DOUGLAS QUENNEVILLE 1942-2004
KAW!
OH SHOO!!
KAW!
DOUGLAS QUENNEVILLE 1942-2004
SILLY CROW! WELL, DOUGIE, LUNCH BREAK'S OVER. TIME TO GET BACK TO MY ROUNDS.
LOVE YOU DEAR. SEE YOU NEXT WEEK.
SMEK!

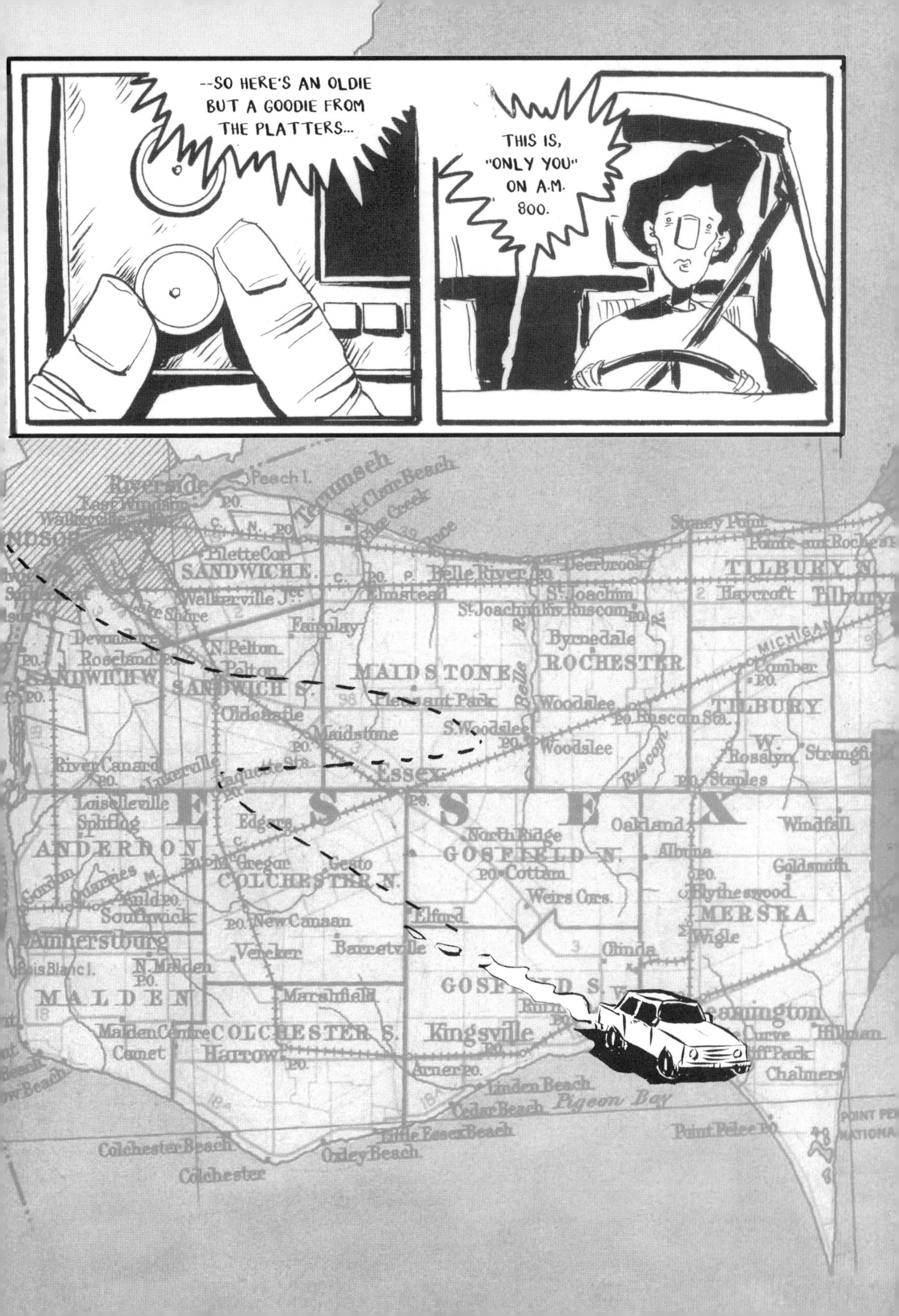
--SO HERE'S AN OLDIE BUT A GOODIE FROM THE PLATTERS...
THIS IS, "ONLY YOU" ON A.M. 800.
Riverside
Peach I.
Tecumseh
St. Clair Beach
SANDWICH E.
Belle River
Deerbrook
TILBURY N.
Haycroft
St. Joachim
Fairplay
Devonshire
N. Pelton
Pelton
Roseland
Byrnedale
ROCHESTER
Comber
MAIDSTONE
Pleasant Park
Woodslee
TILBURY
Oldcastle
Maidstone
S. Woodslee
Ruscom Sta.
W. Rosslyn
River Canard
Essex
Staples
E S S E X
Loiselleville
Edgars
Oakland
Windfall
North Ridge
ANDERDON
GOSFIELD N.
Albuna
McGregar
Gesto
COLCHESTER N.
Cottam
Goldsmith
Weirs Crs.
Blytheswood
Southwick
New Canaan
Elford
MERSEA
Wigle
Amherstburg
Vereker
Barretville
Olinda
Bois Blanc I.
N. Malden
MALDEN
Marshfield
Leamington
Malden Centre
COLCHESTER S.
Kingsville
Hillman
Curve
Cullf Park
Chalmers
Canet
Harrow
Arner
Linden Beach
Pigeon Bay
Cedar Beach
Little Essex Beach
Point Pelee
Colchester Beach
Oxley Beach
Colchester

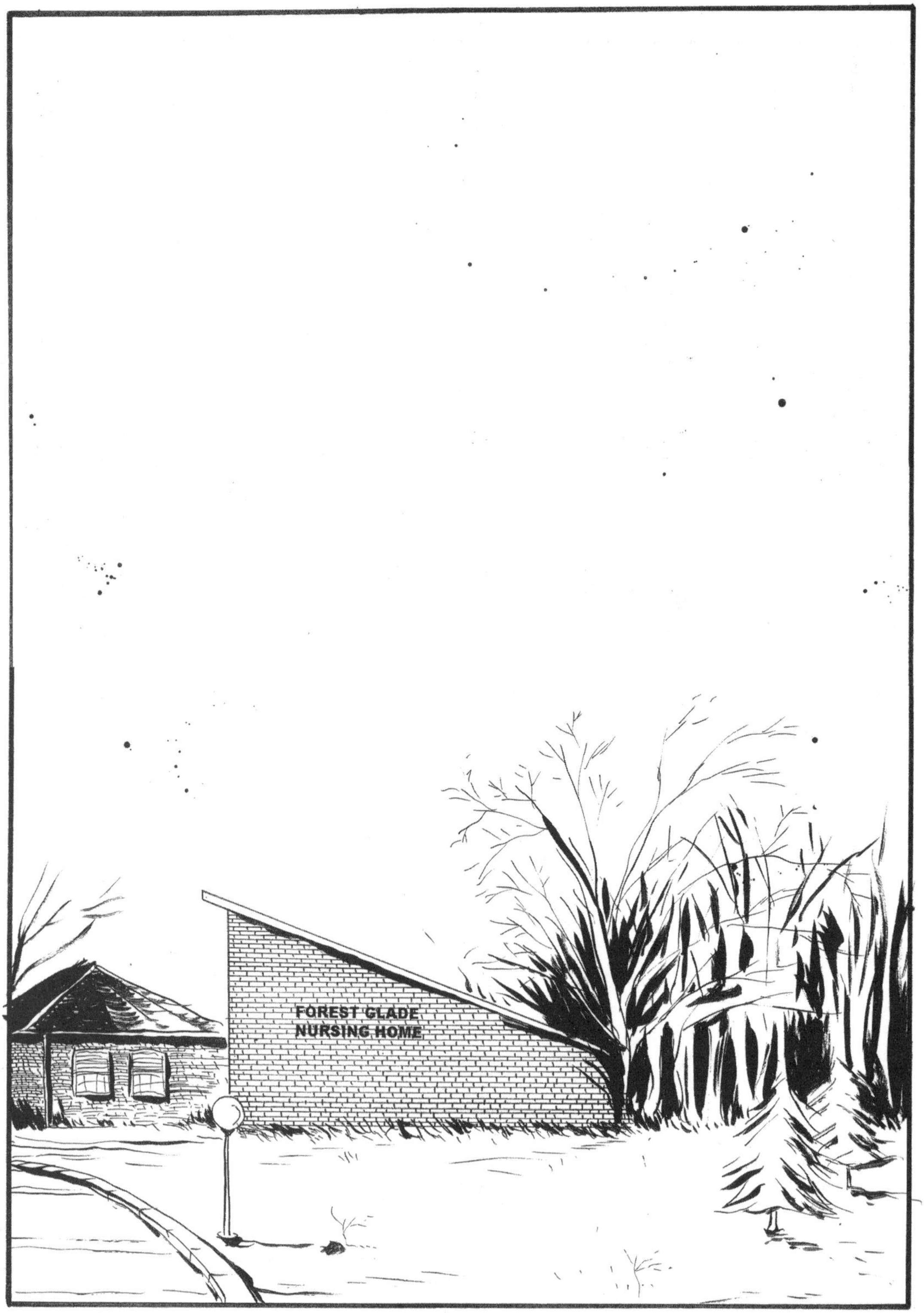
FOREST GLADE
NURSING HOME

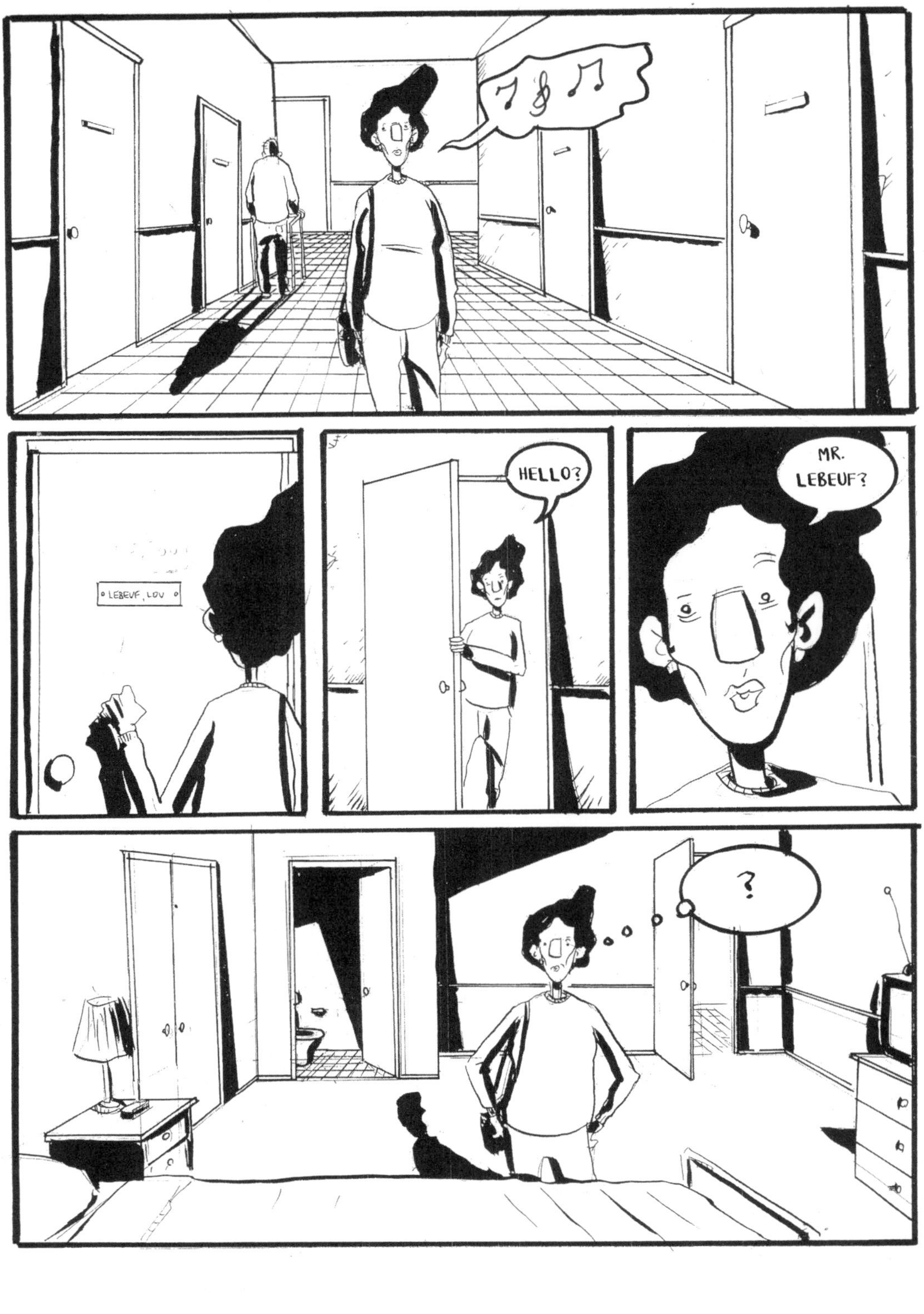
LEBEUF, LOU
HELLO?
MR. LEBEUF?
?

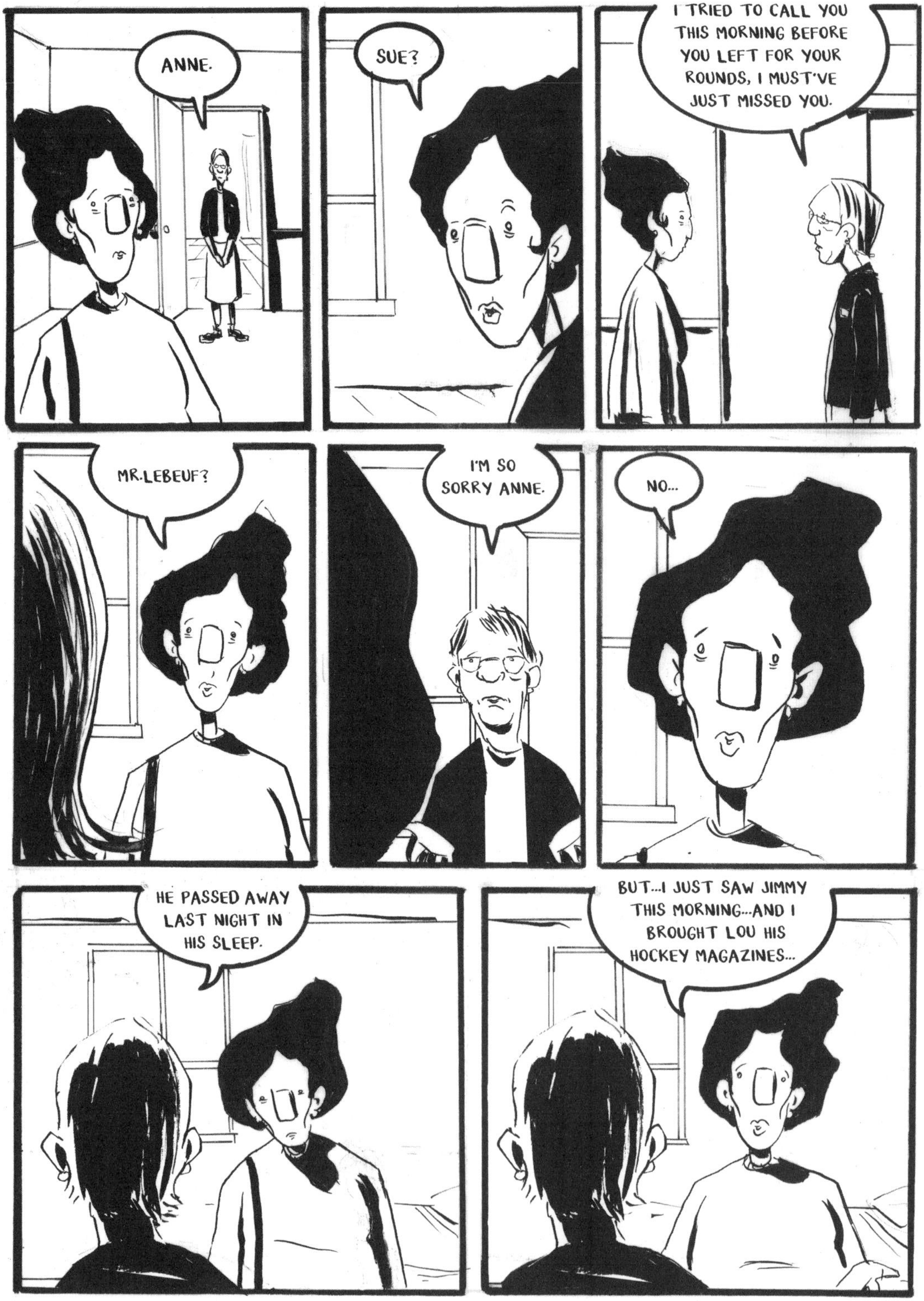
ANNE.
SUE?
I TRIED TO CALL YOU THIS MORNING BEFORE YOU LEFT FOR YOUR ROUNDS, I MUST'VE JUST MISSED YOU.
MR. LEBEUF?
I'M SO SORRY ANNE.
NO...
HE PASSED AWAY LAST NIGHT IN HIS SLEEP.
BUT...I JUST SAW JIMMY THIS MORNING...AND I BROUGHT LOU HIS HOCKEY MAGAZINES...

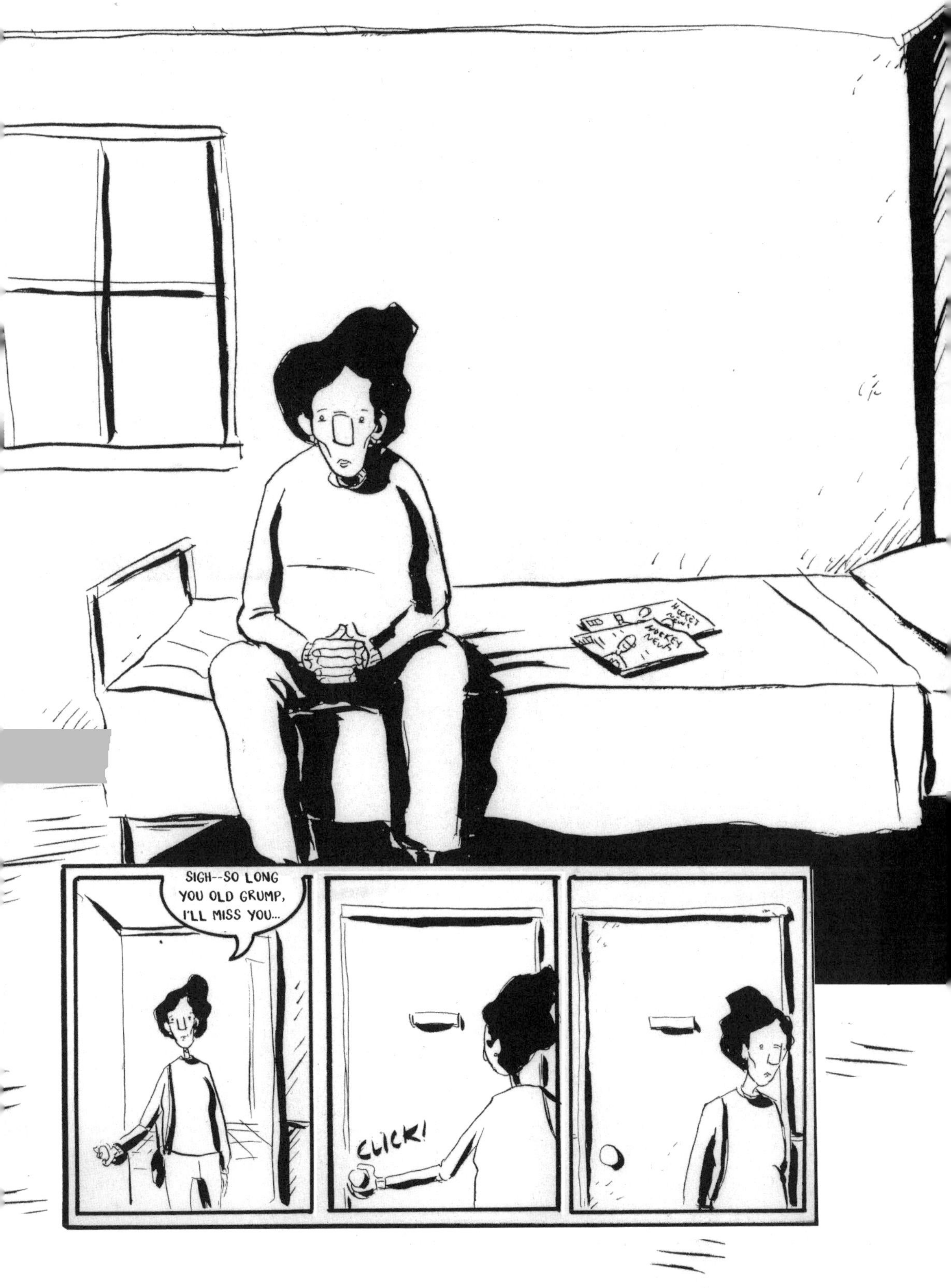
HOCKEY NEWS
HOCKEY NEWS
SIGH--SO LONG YOU OLD GRUMP, I'LL MISS YOU...
CLICK!

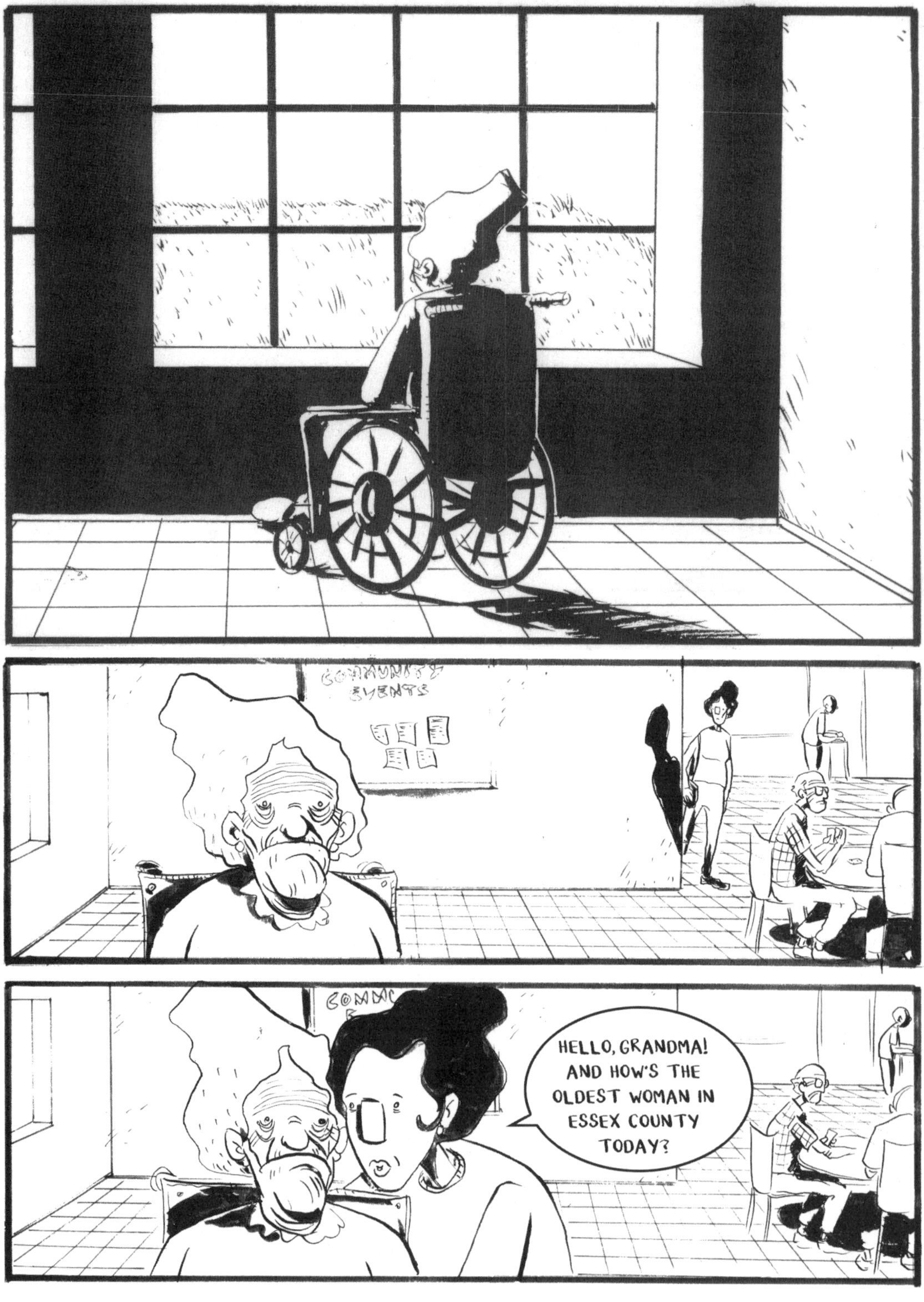
COMMUNITY EVENTS
HELLO, GRANDMA! AND HOW'S THE OLDEST WOMAN IN ESSEX COUNTY TODAY?

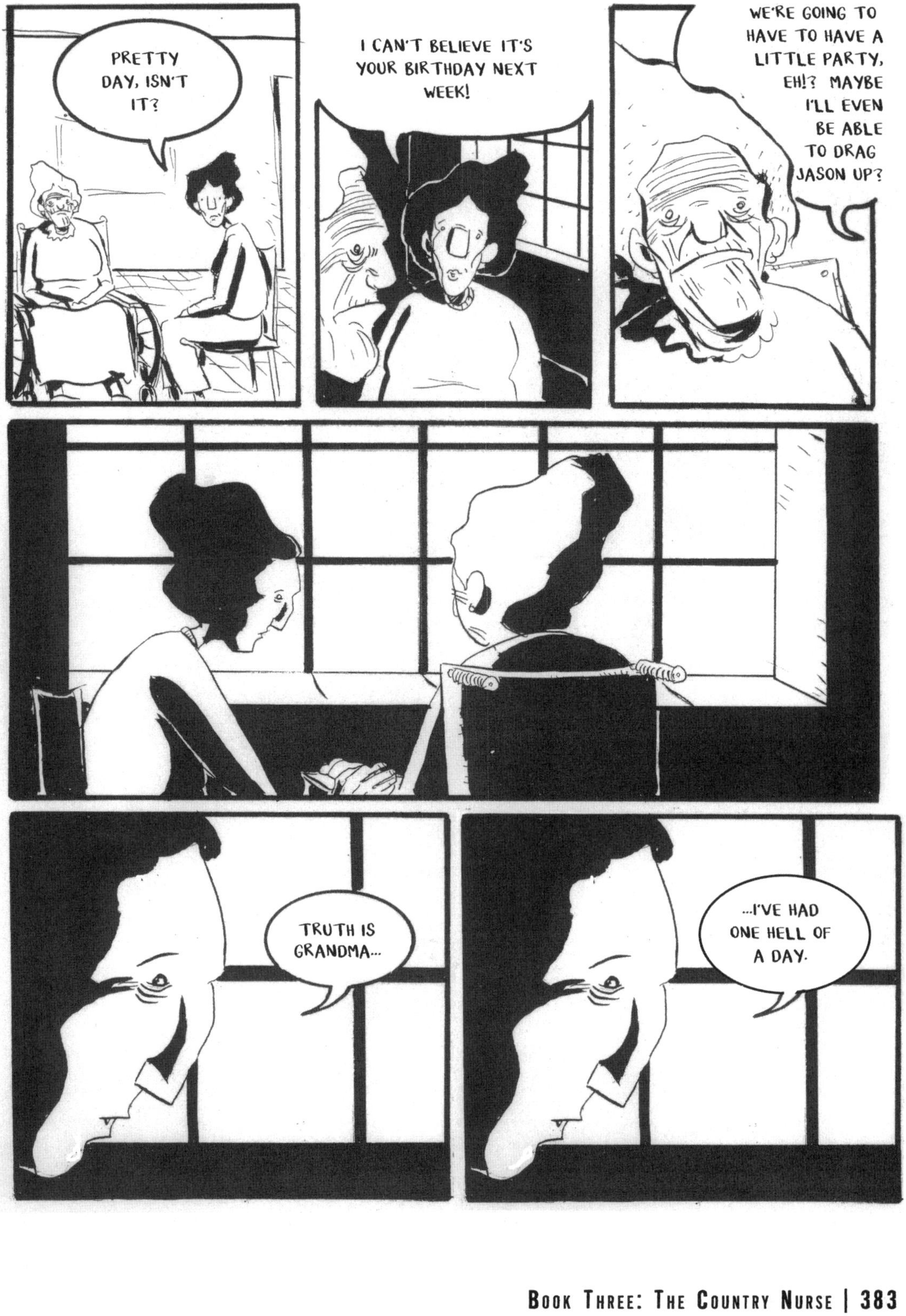
PRETTY DAY, ISN'T IT?
I CAN'T BELIEVE IT'S YOUR BIRTHDAY NEXT WEEK!
WE'RE GOING TO HAVE TO HAVE A LITTLE PARTY, EH!? MAYBE I'LL EVEN BE ABLE TO DRAG JASON UP?
TRUTH IS GRANDMA...
...I'VE HAD ONE HELL OF A DAY.

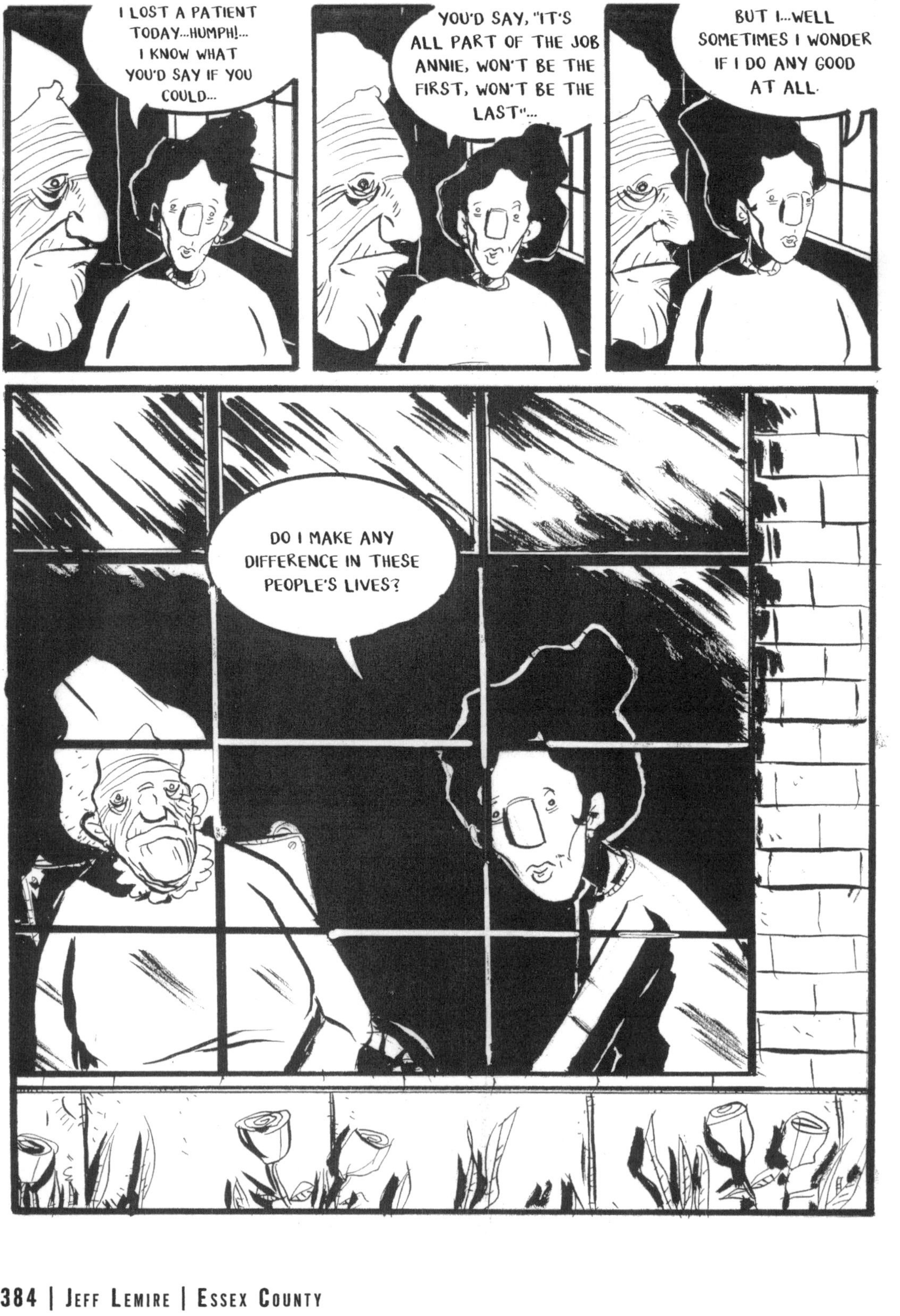
I LOST A PATIENT TODAY...HUMPH!... I KNOW WHAT YOU'D SAY IF YOU COULD...
YOU'D SAY, "IT'S ALL PART OF THE JOB ANNIE, WON'T BE THE FIRST, WON'T BE THE LAST"...
BUT I...WELL SOMETIMES I WONDER IF I DO ANY GOOD AT ALL.
DO I MAKE ANY DIFFERENCE IN THESE PEOPLE'S LIVES?

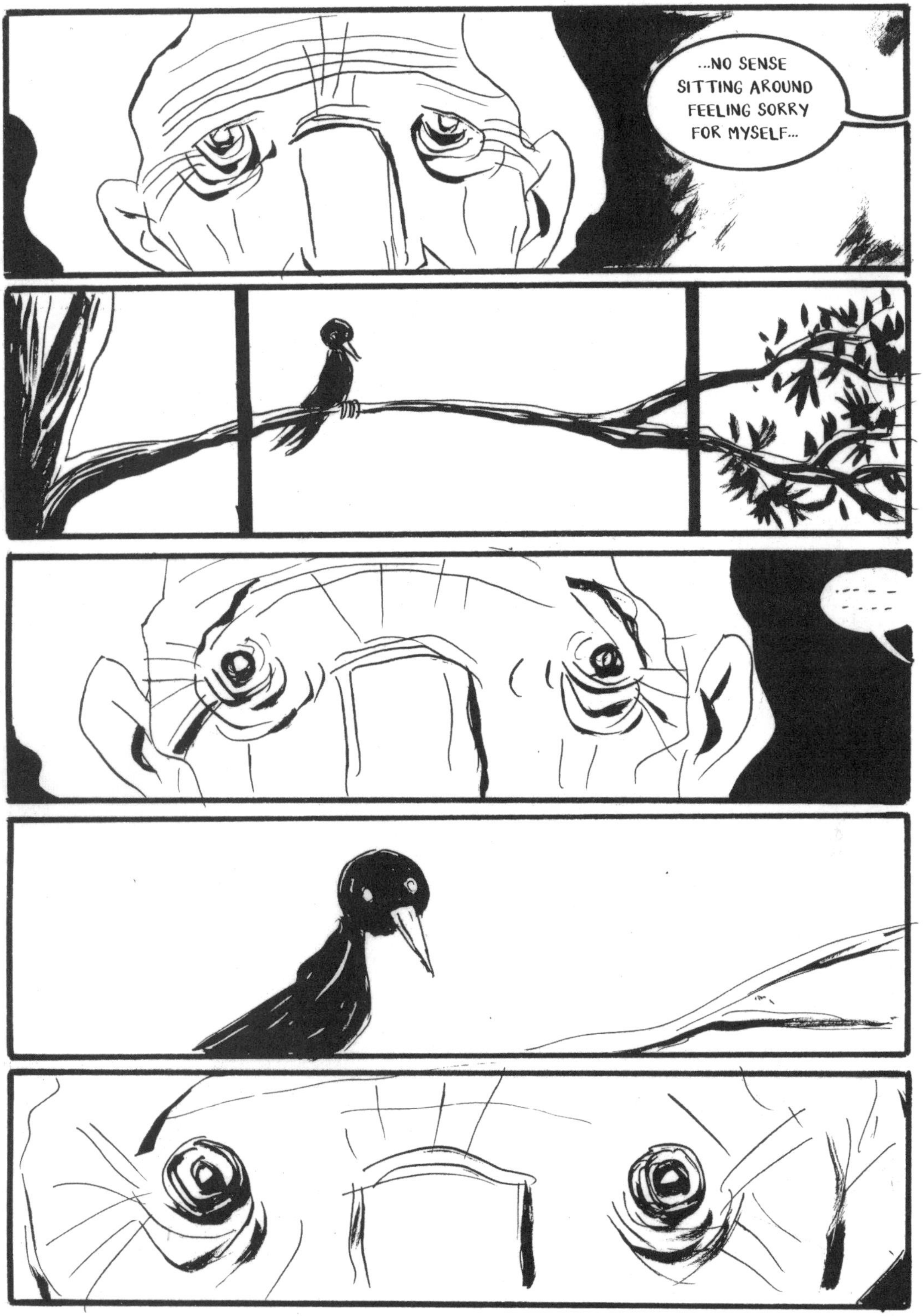
...NO SENSE SITTING AROUND FEELING SORRY FOR MYSELF...

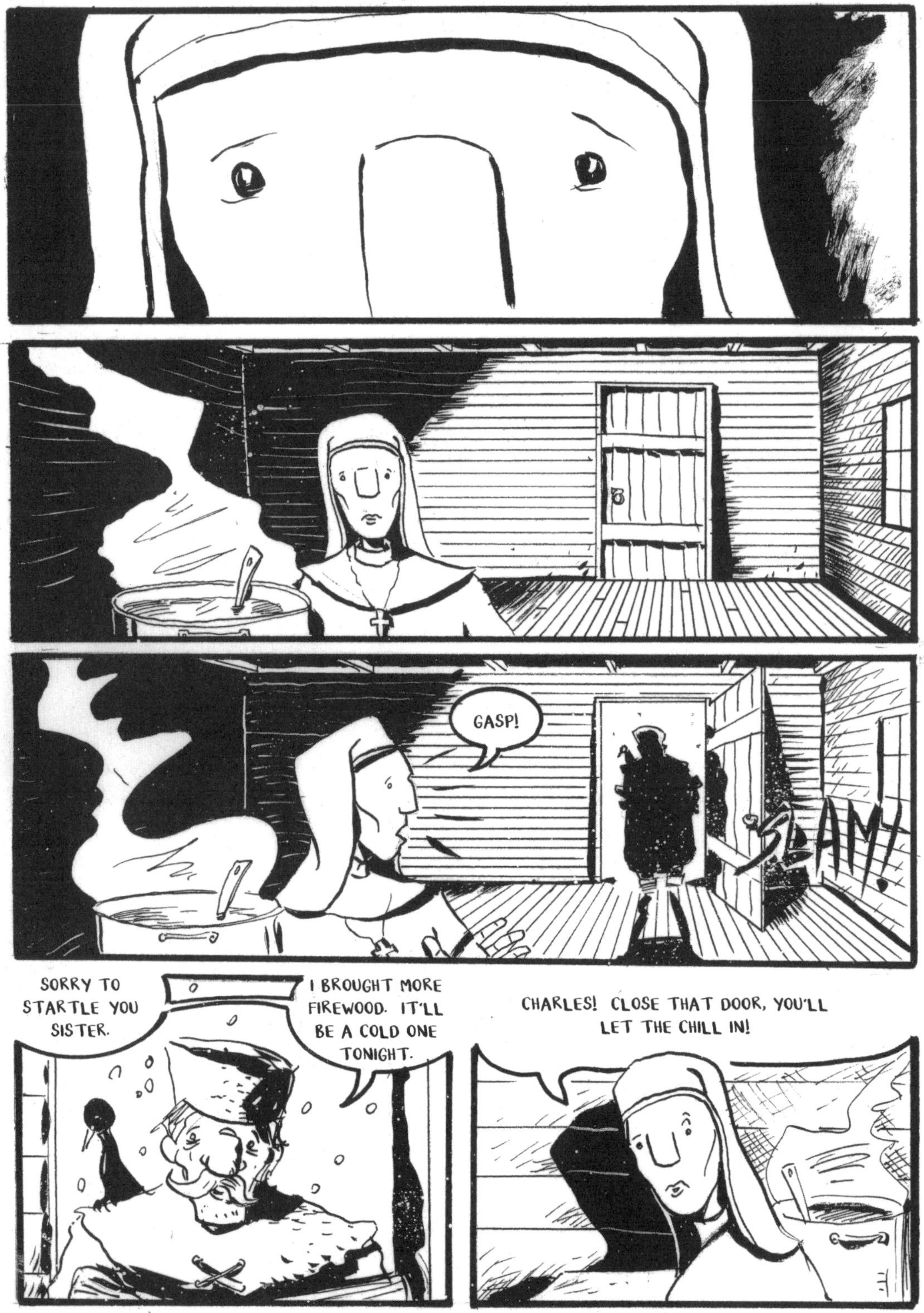
GASP!
SLAM!
SORRY TO STARTLE YOU SISTER.
I BROUGHT MORE FIREWOOD. IT'LL BE A COLD ONE TONIGHT.
CHARLES! CLOSE THAT DOOR, YOU'LL LET THE CHILL IN!

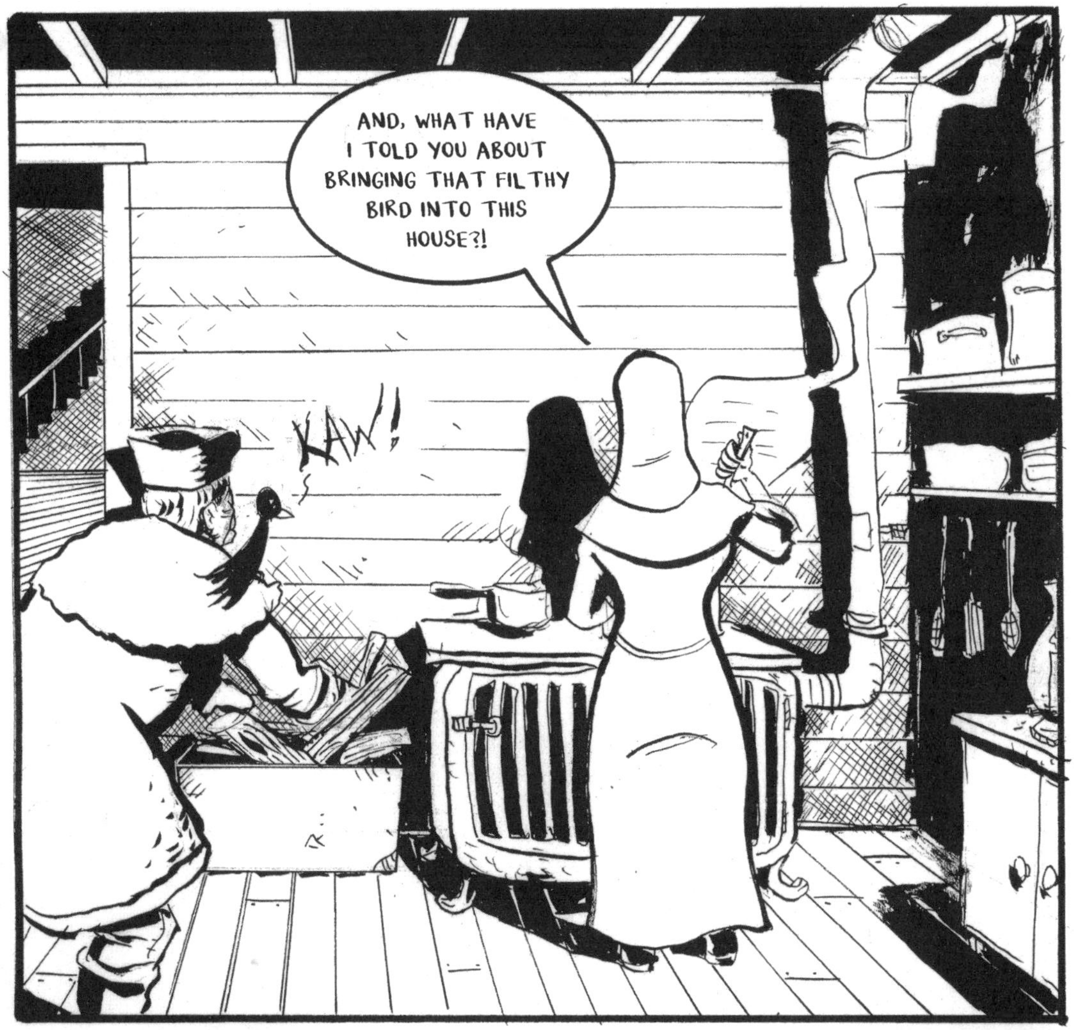
AND, WHAT HAVE I TOLD YOU ABOUT BRINGING THAT FILTHY BIRD INTO THIS HOUSE?!
KAW!

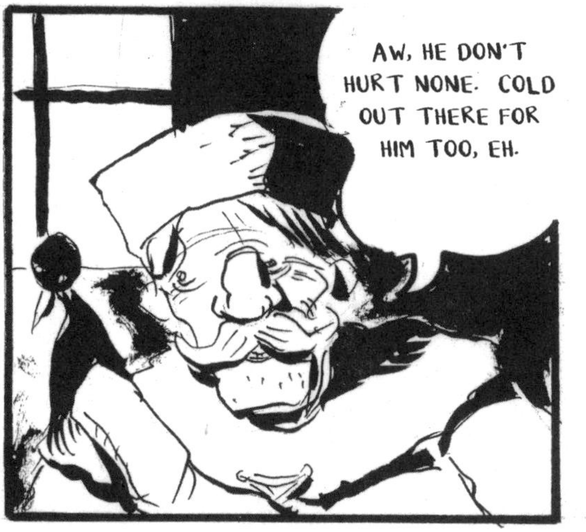
AW, HE DON'T HURT NONE. COLD OUT THERE FOR HIM TOO, EH.

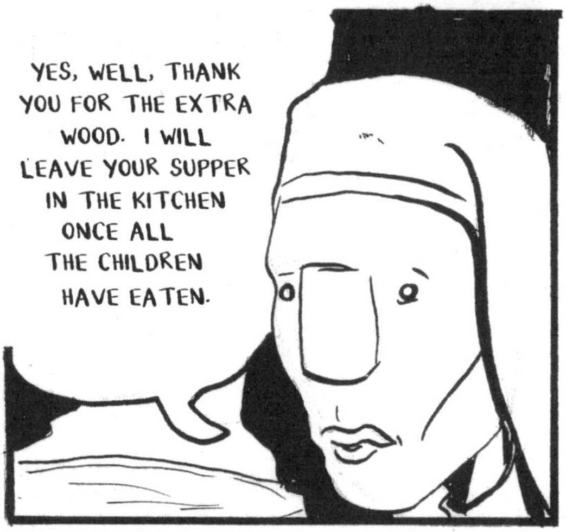
YES, WELL, THANK YOU FOR THE EXTRA WOOD. I WILL LEAVE YOUR SUPPER IN THE KITCHEN ONCE ALL THE CHILDREN HAVE EATEN.

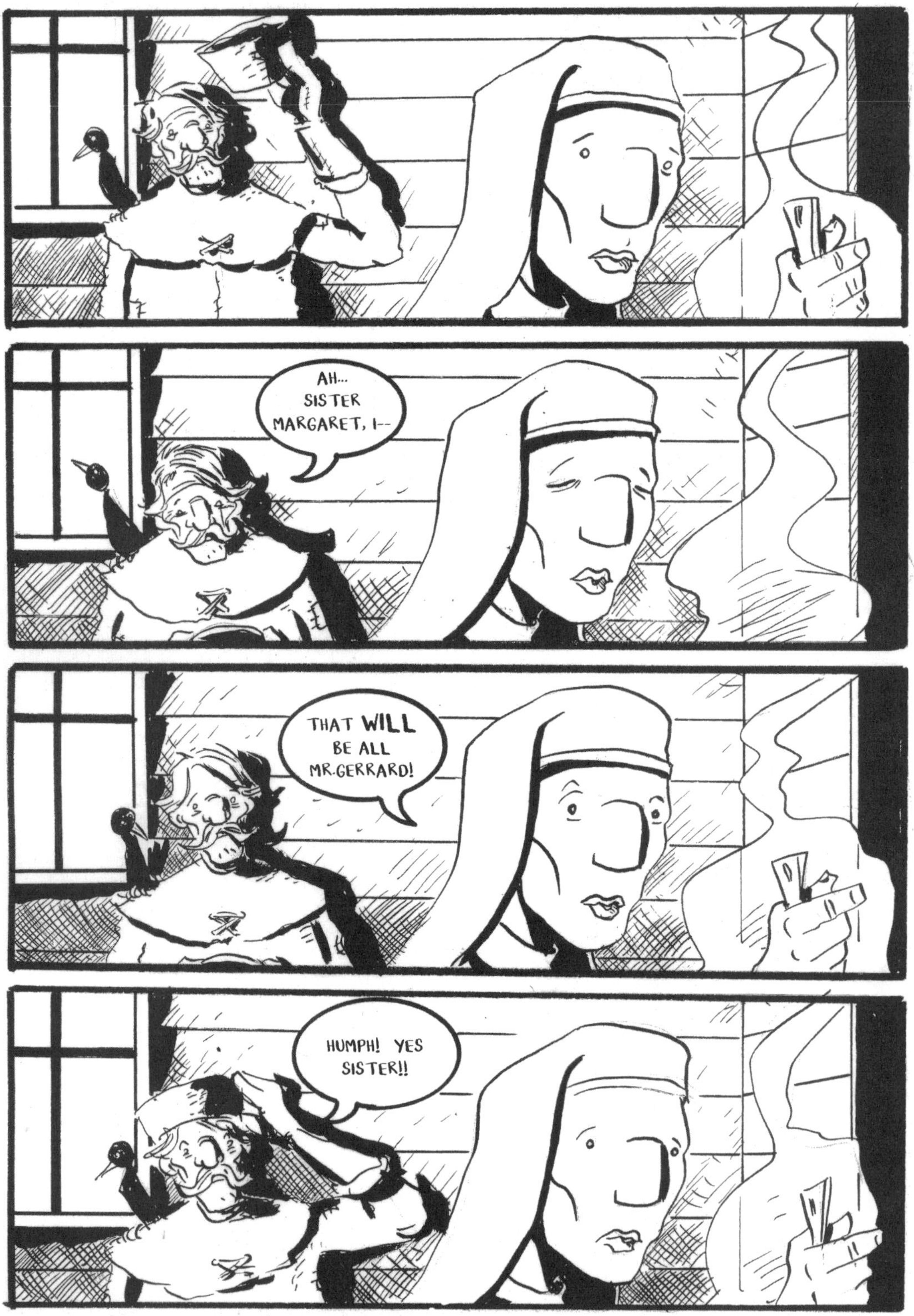
AH... SISTER MARGARET, I--
THAT WILL BE ALL MR.GERRARD!
HUMPH! YES SISTER!!

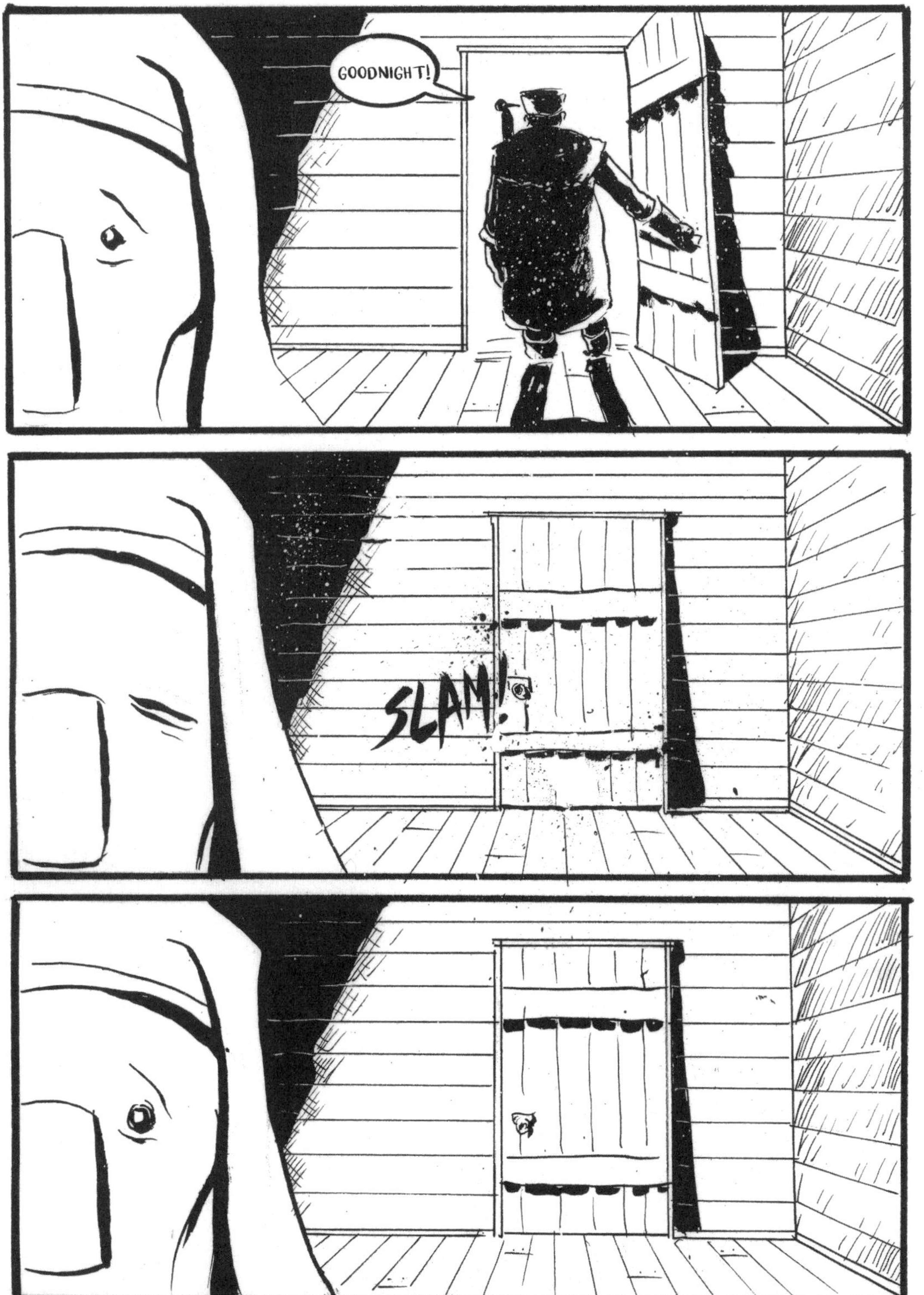
GOODNIGHT!
SLAM!

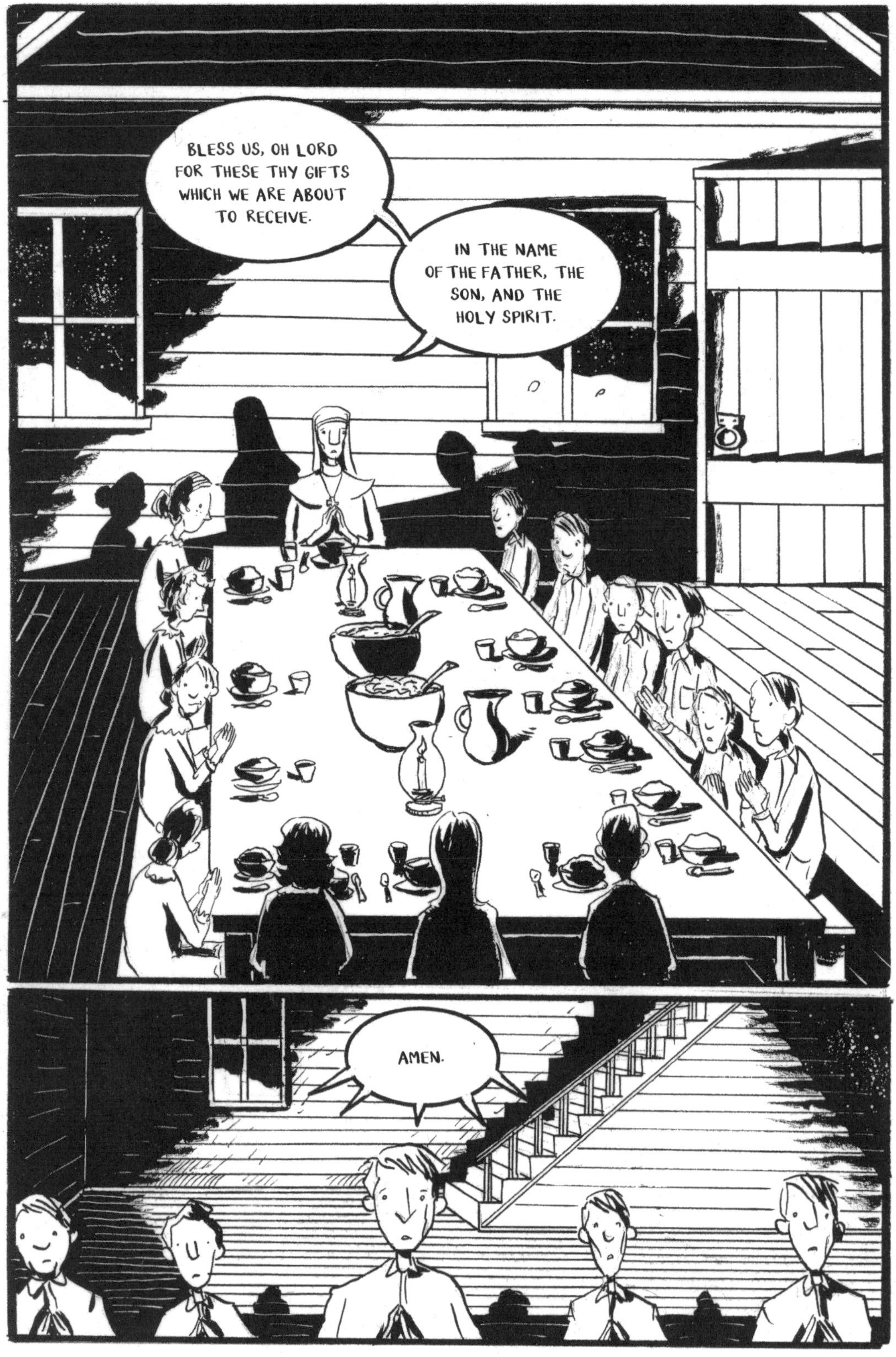
BLESS US, OH LORD FOR THESE THY GIFTS WHICH WE ARE ABOUT TO RECEIVE.
IN THE NAME OF THE FATHER, THE SON, AND THE HOLY SPIRIT.
AMEN.

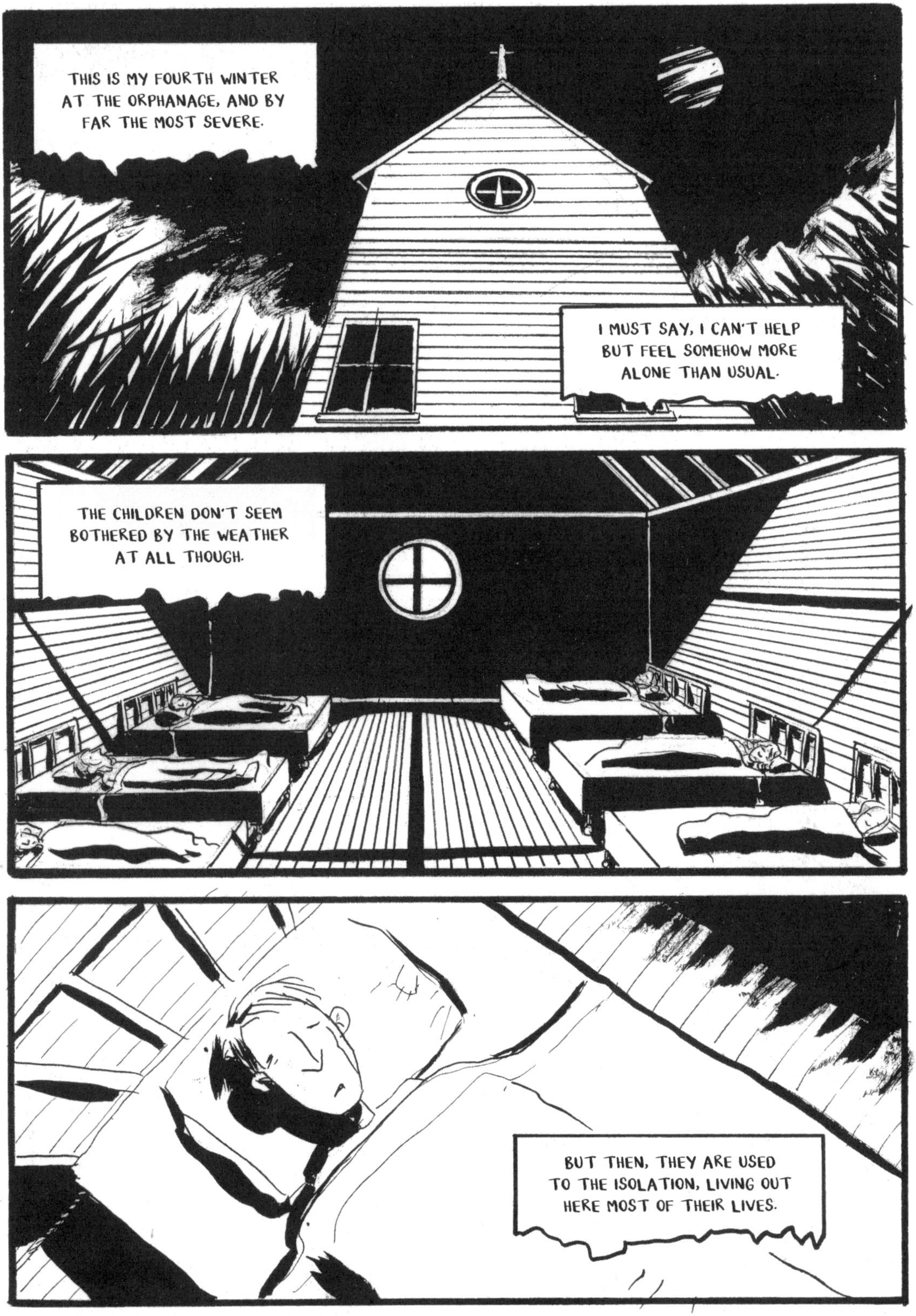
THIS IS MY FOURTH WINTER AT THE ORPHANAGE, AND BY FAR THE MOST SEVERE.
I MUST SAY, I CAN'T HELP BUT FEEL SOMEHOW MORE ALONE THAN USUAL.
THE CHILDREN DON'T SEEM BOTHERED BY THE WEATHER AT ALL THOUGH.
BUT THEN, THEY ARE USED TO THE ISOLATION, LIVING OUT HERE MOST OF THEIR LIVES.

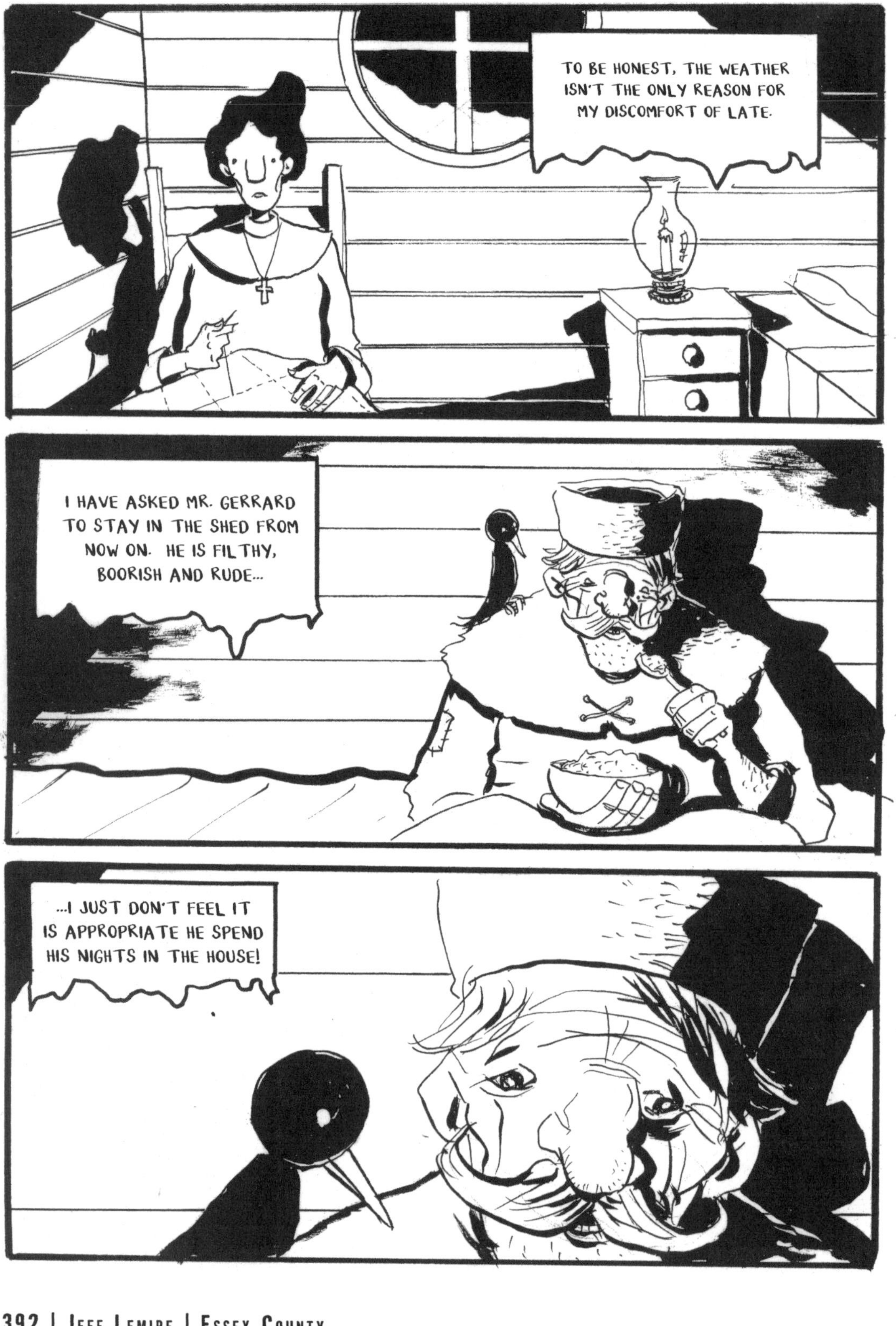
TO BE HONEST, THE WEATHER ISN'T THE ONLY REASON FOR MY DISCOMFORT OF LATE.
I HAVE ASKED MR. GERRARD TO STAY IN THE SHED FROM NOW ON. HE IS FILTHY, BOORISH AND RUDE...
...I JUST DON'T FEEL IT IS APPROPRIATE HE SPEND HIS NIGHTS IN THE HOUSE!

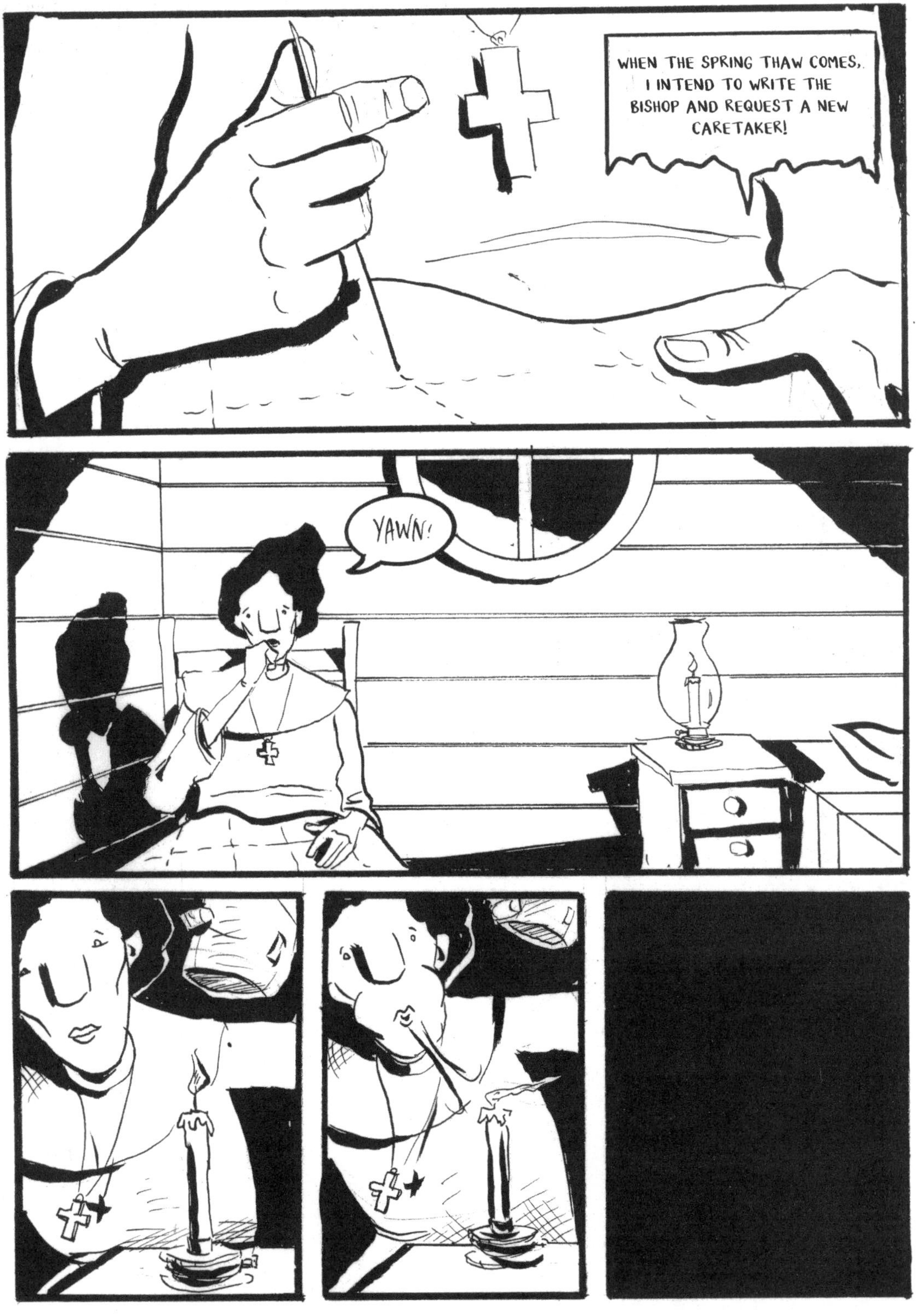
WHEN THE SPRING THAW COMES, I INTEND TO WRITE THE BISHOP AND REQUEST A NEW CARETAKER!
YAWN!

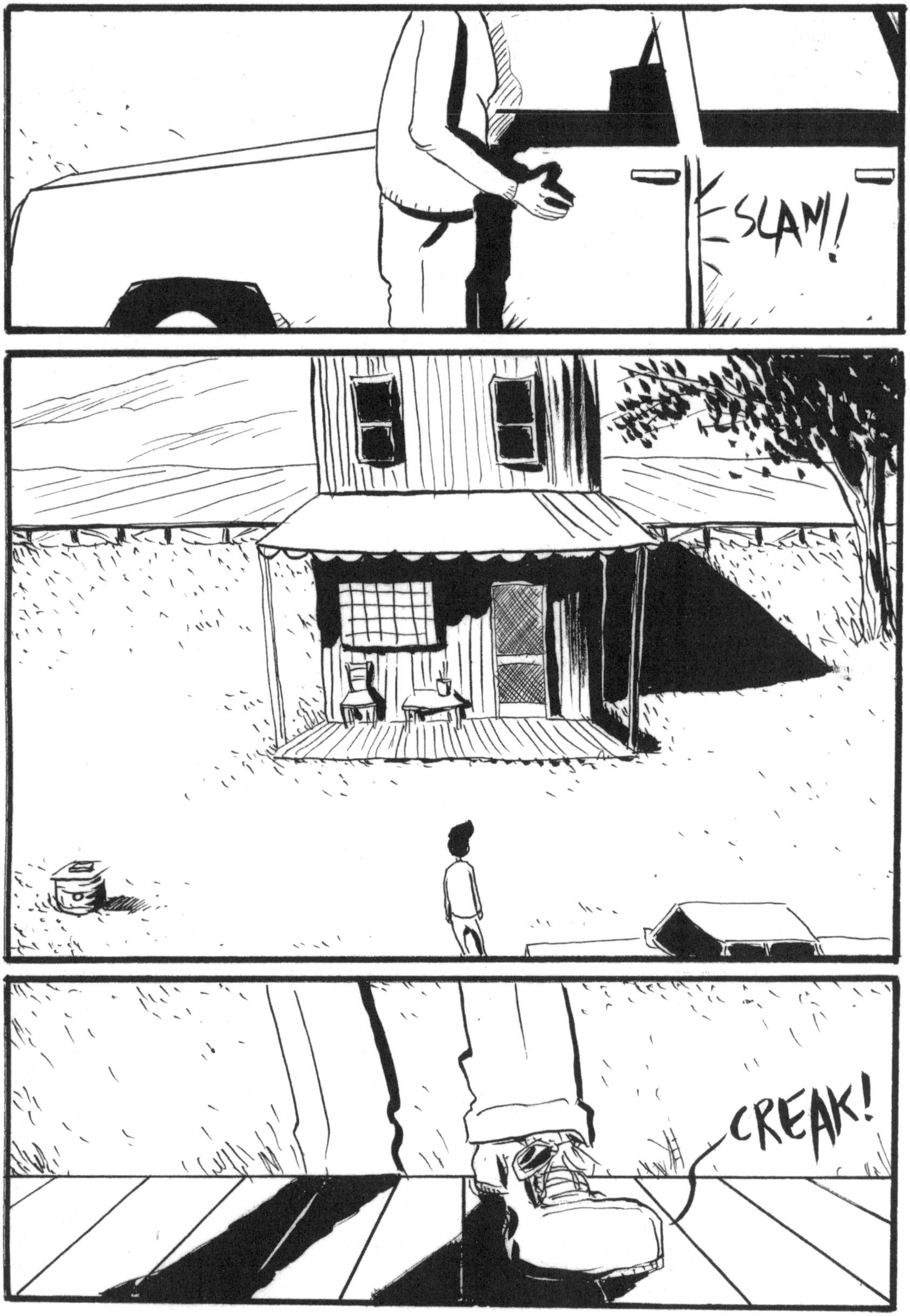
SLAM!
CREAK!

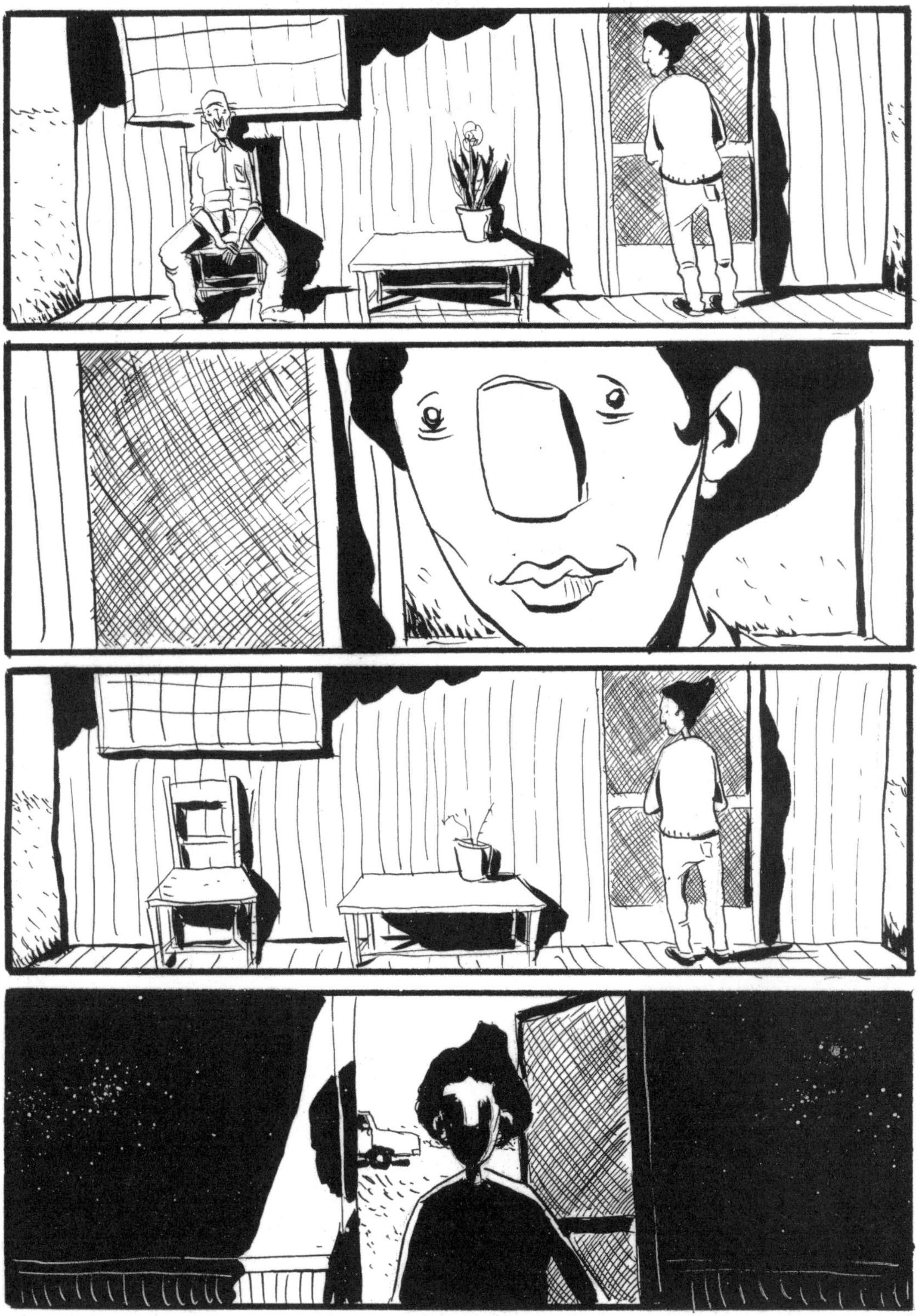

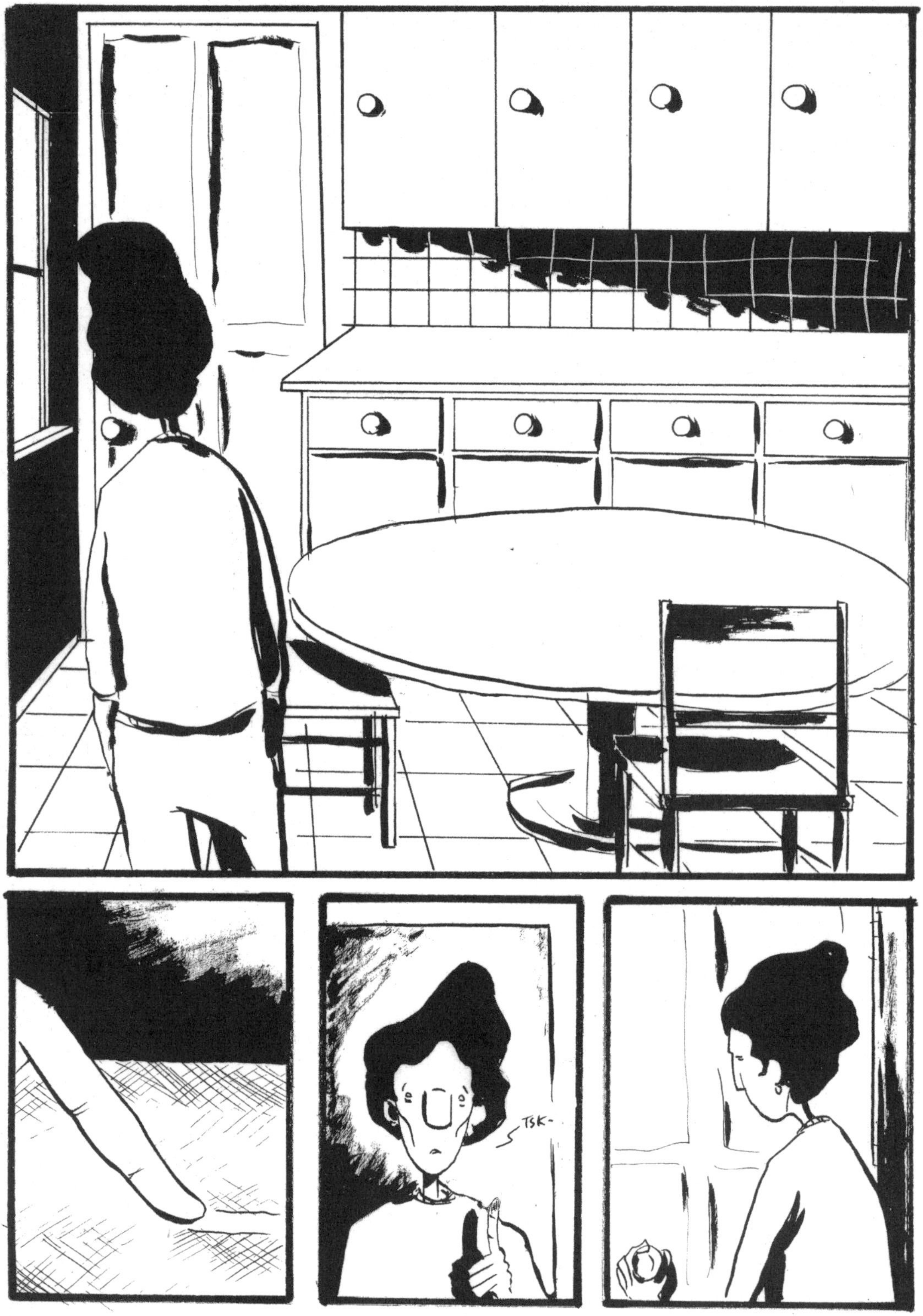
TSK-

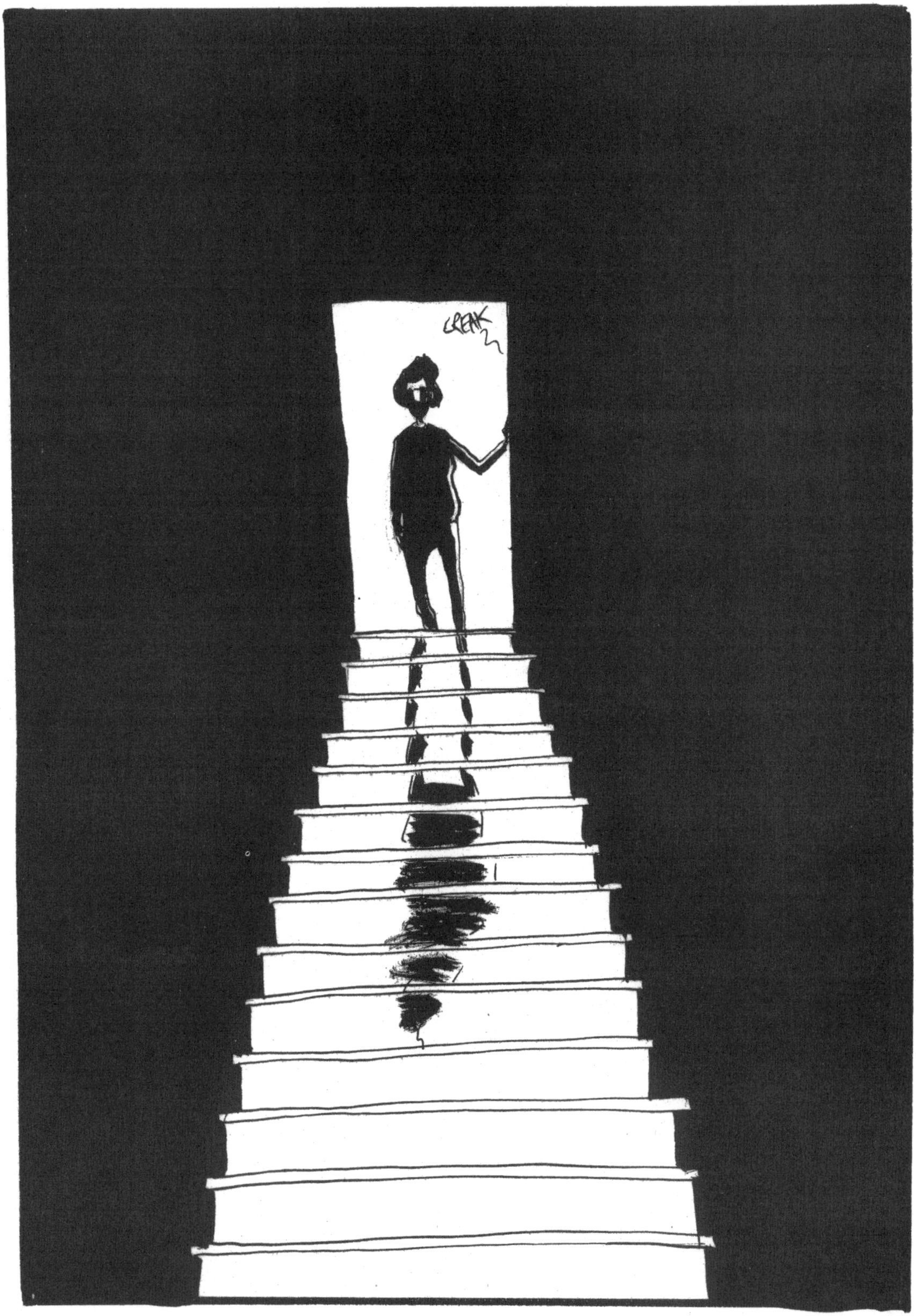
CREAK

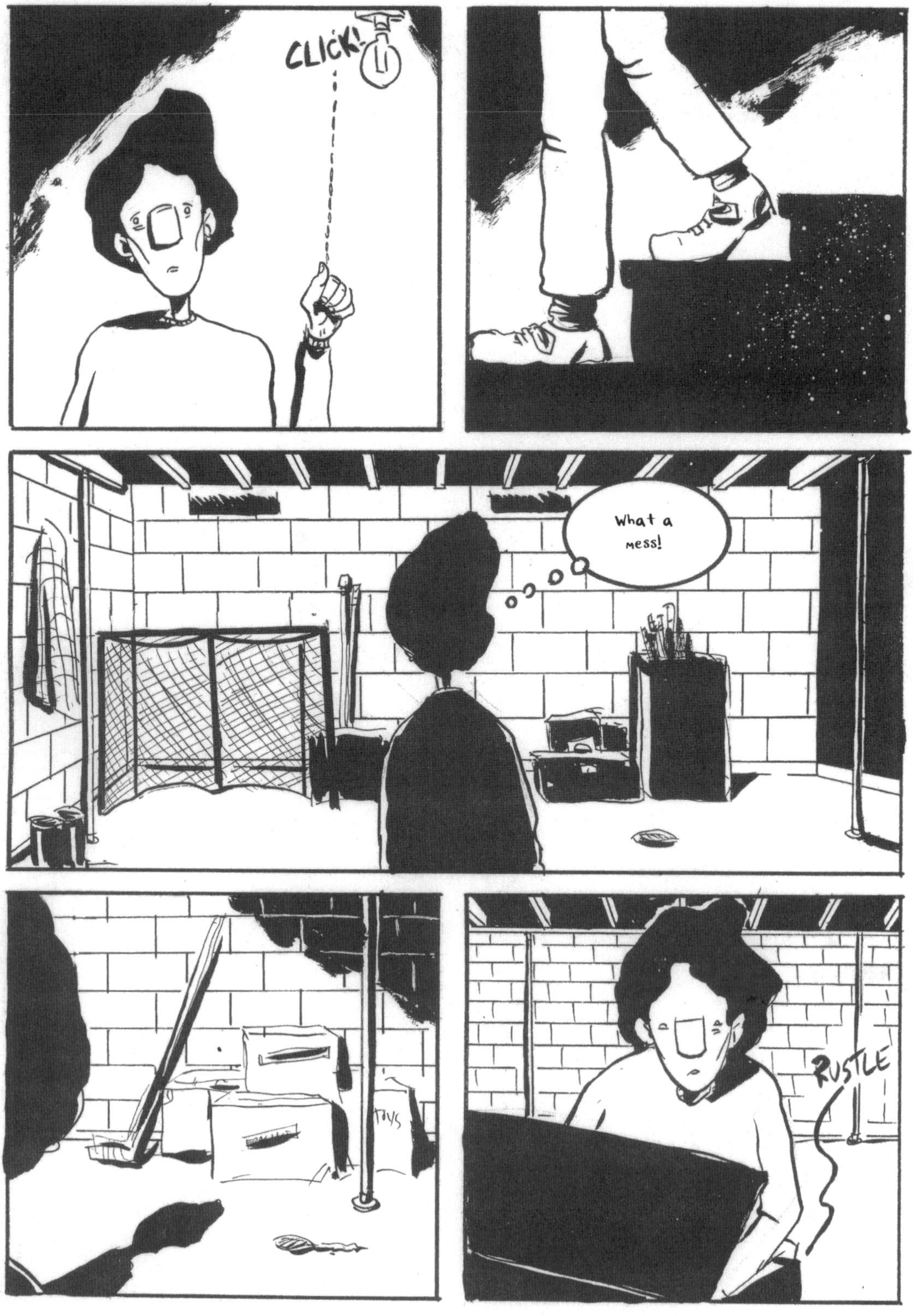
CLICK!
What a mess!
TOYS
RUSTLE

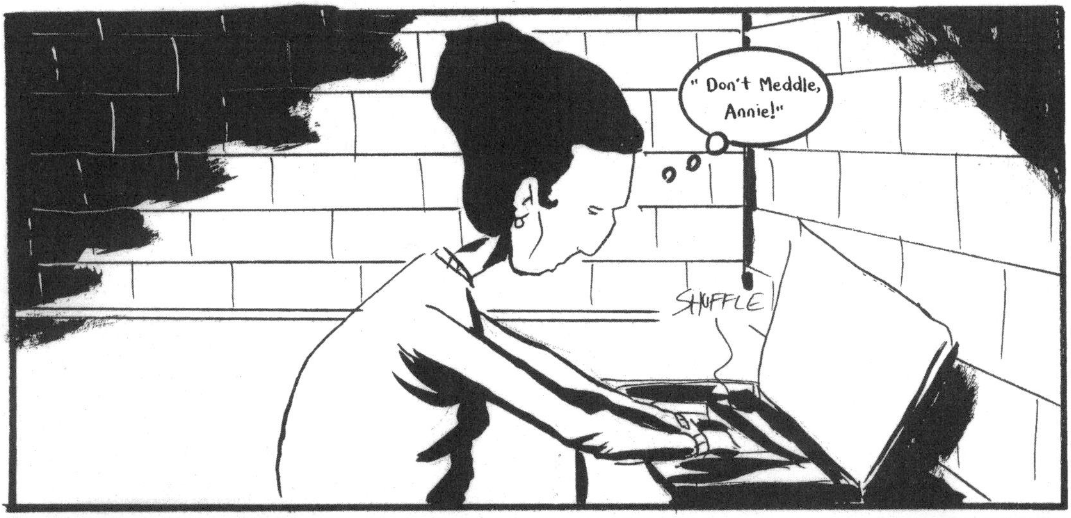
"Don't Meddle, Annie!"
SHUFFLE

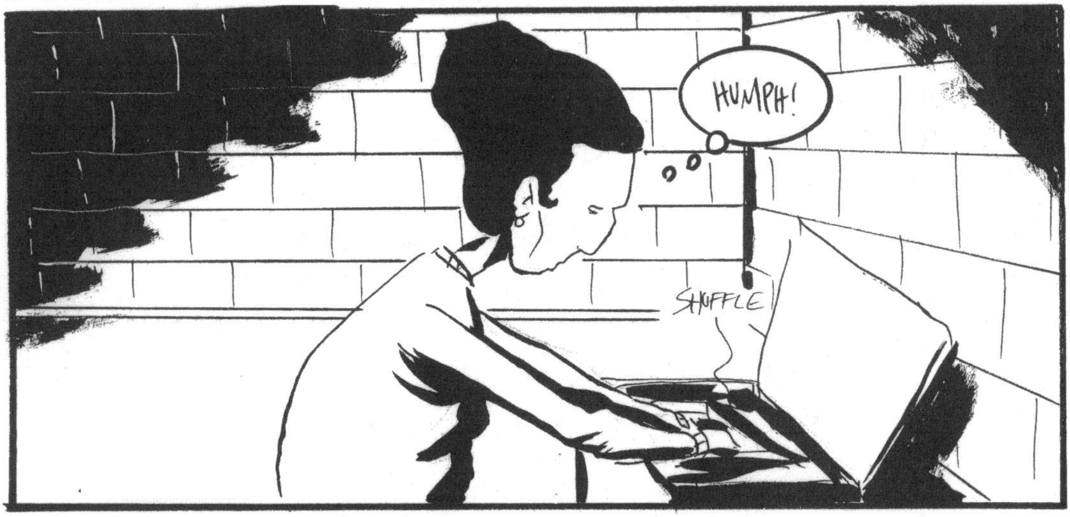
HUMPH!
SHUFFLE

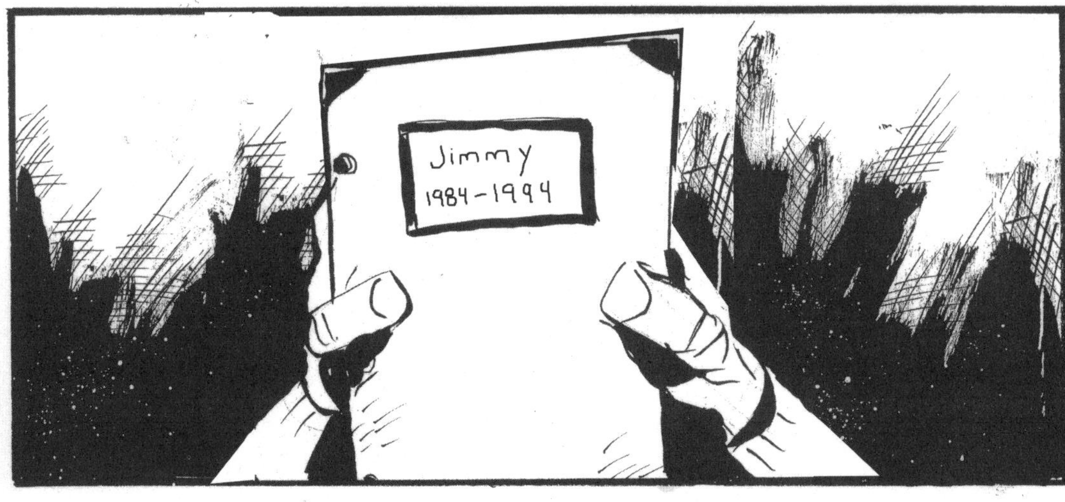
Jimmy
1984-1994

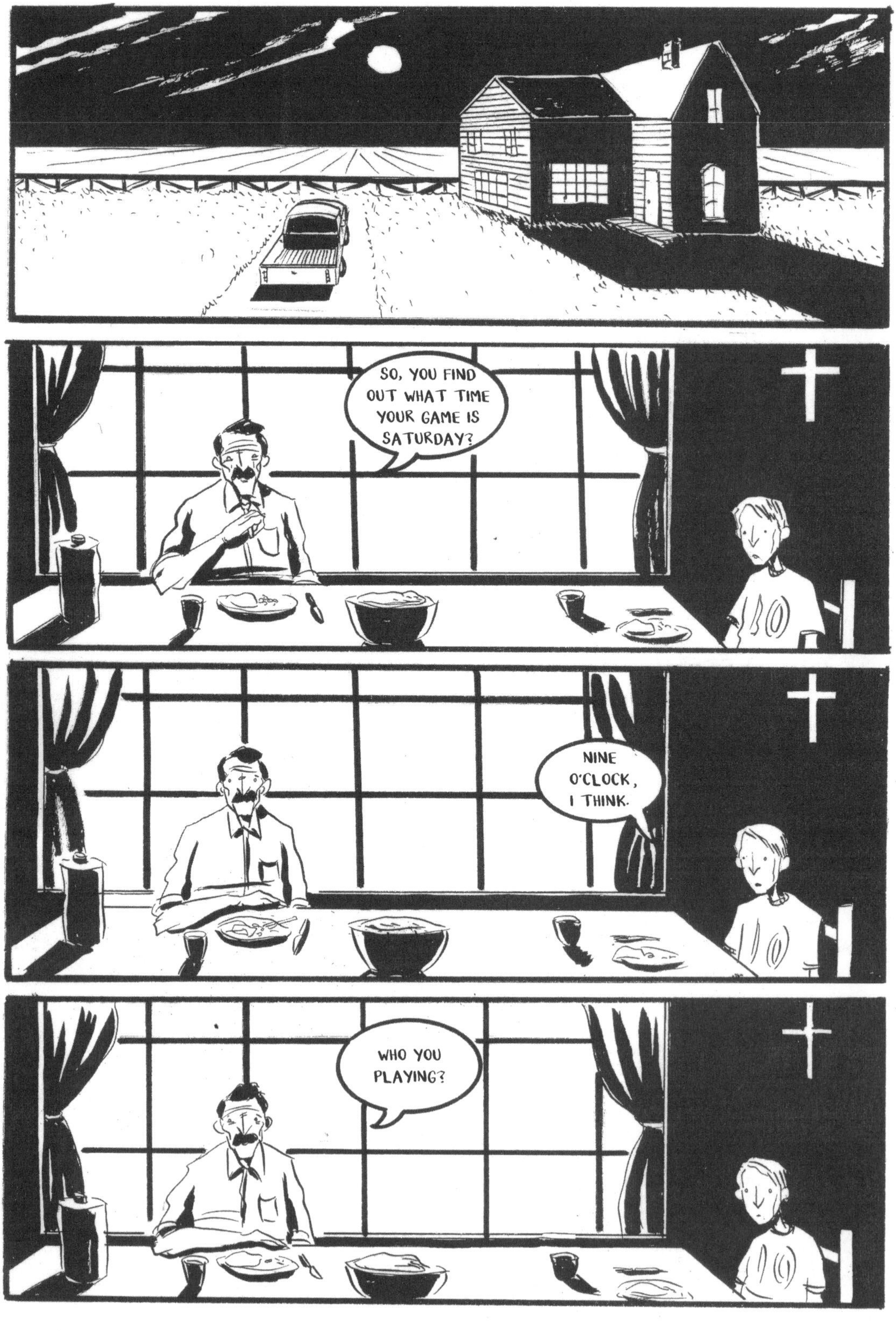
SO, YOU FIND OUT WHAT TIME YOUR GAME IS SATURDAY?
NINE O'CLOCK, I THINK.
WHO YOU PLAYING?

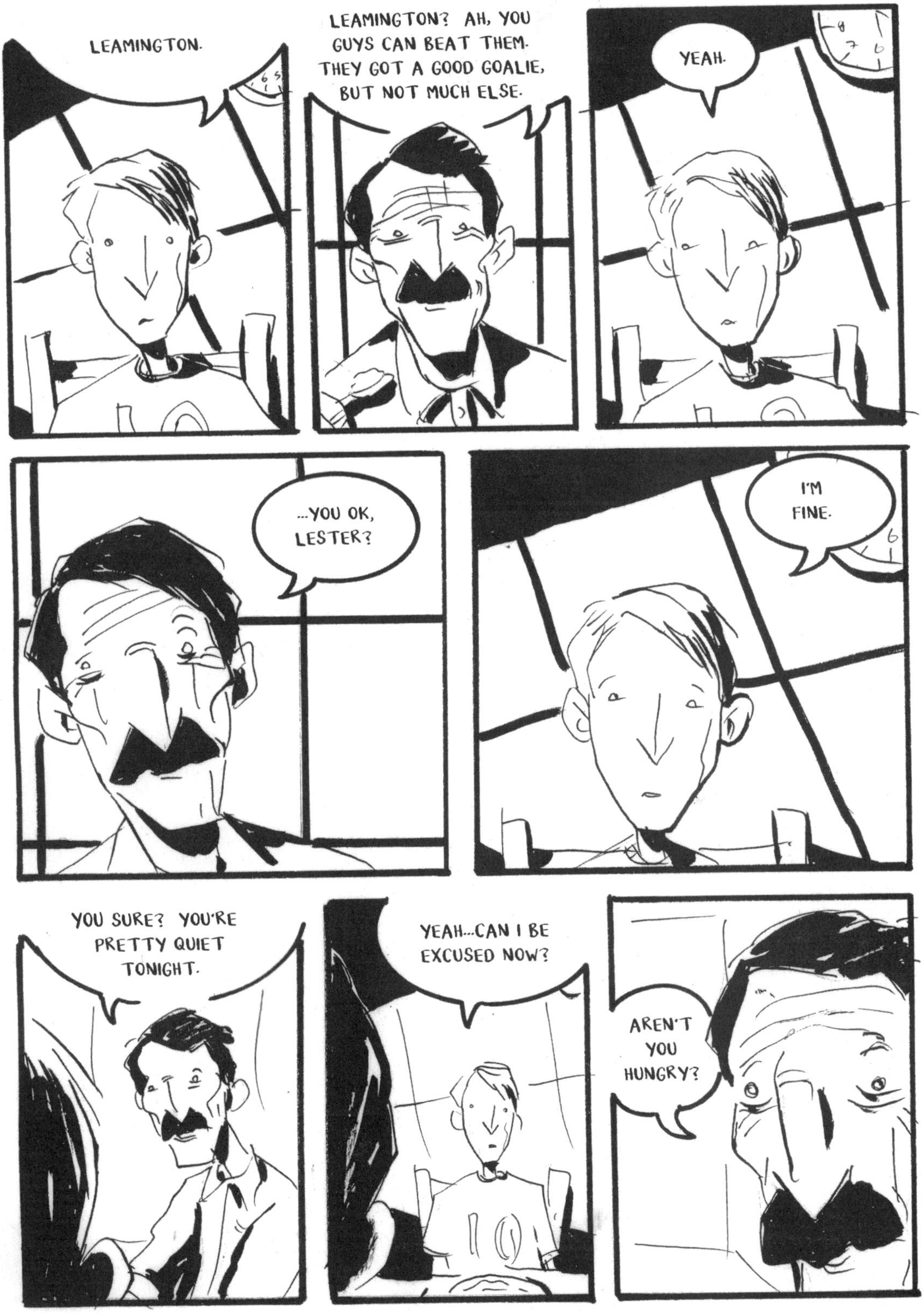
LEAMINGTON.
LEAMINGTON? AH, YOU GUYS CAN BEAT THEM. THEY GOT A GOOD GOALIE, BUT NOT MUCH ELSE.
YEAH.
...YOU OK, LESTER?
I'M FINE.
YOU SURE? YOU'RE PRETTY QUIET TONIGHT.
YEAH...CAN I BE EXCUSED NOW?
AREN'T YOU HUNGRY?

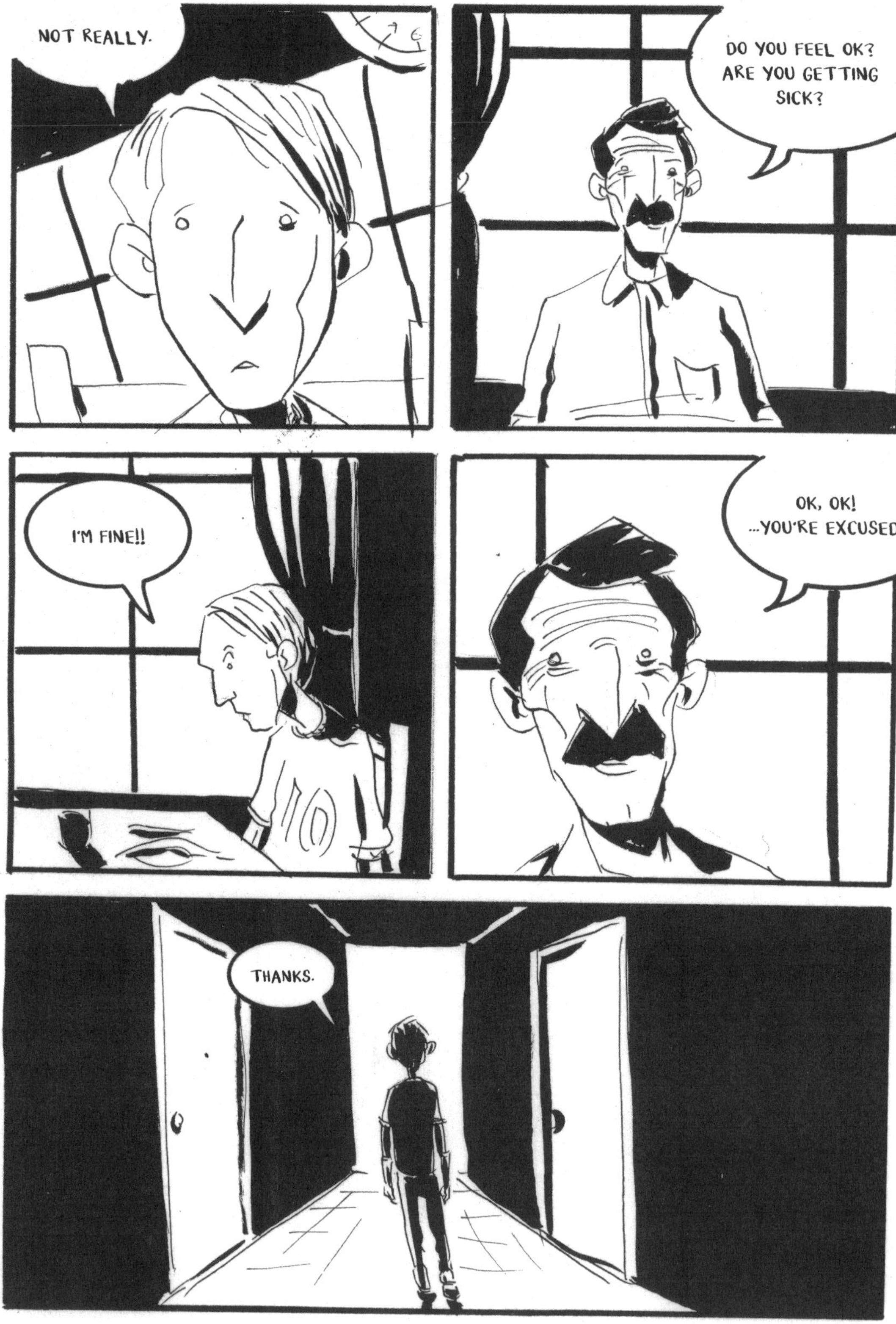
NOT REALLY.
DO YOU FEEL OK? ARE YOU GETTING SICK?
I'M FINE!!
OK, OK! ...YOU'RE EXCUSED.
THANKS.

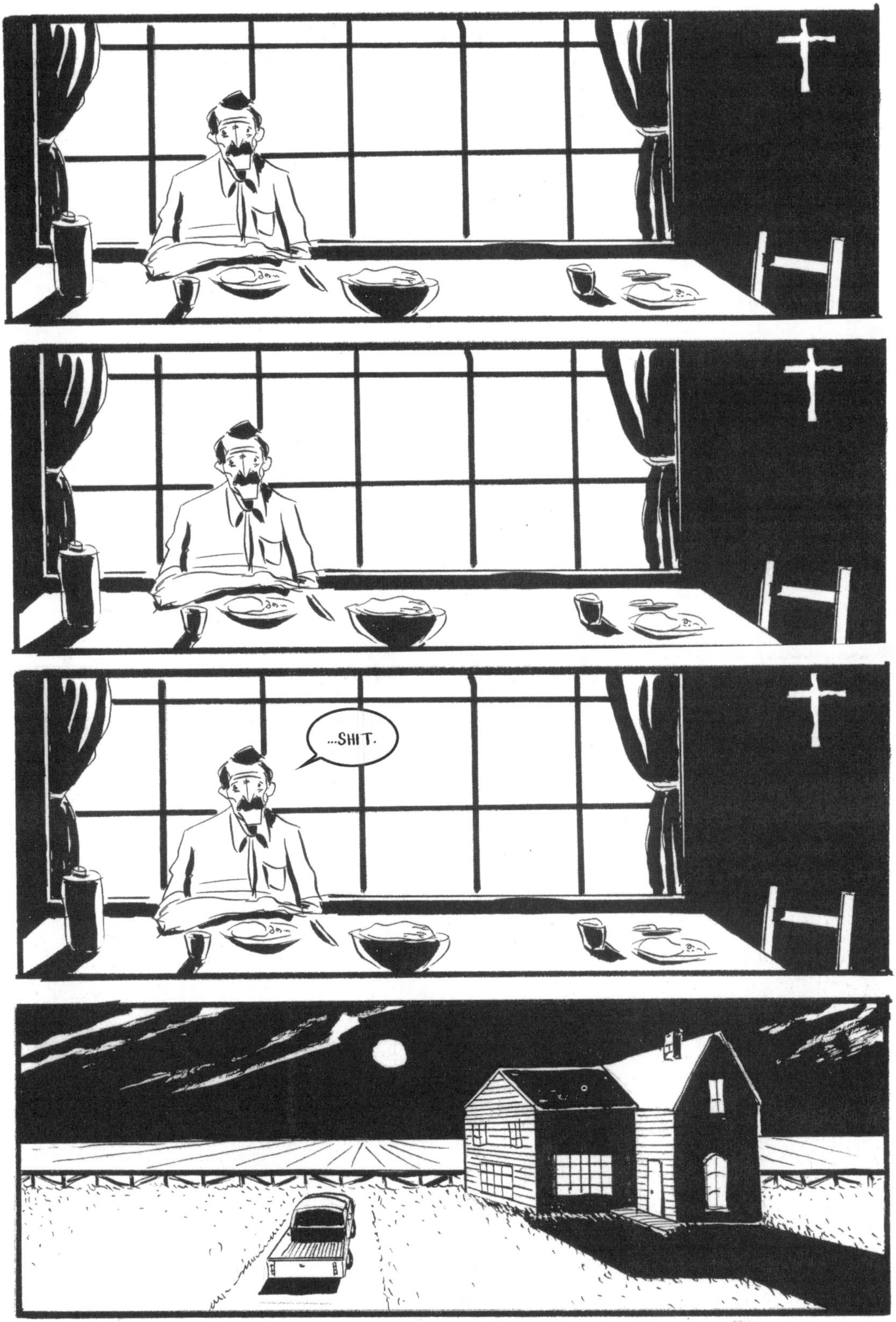
...SHIT.

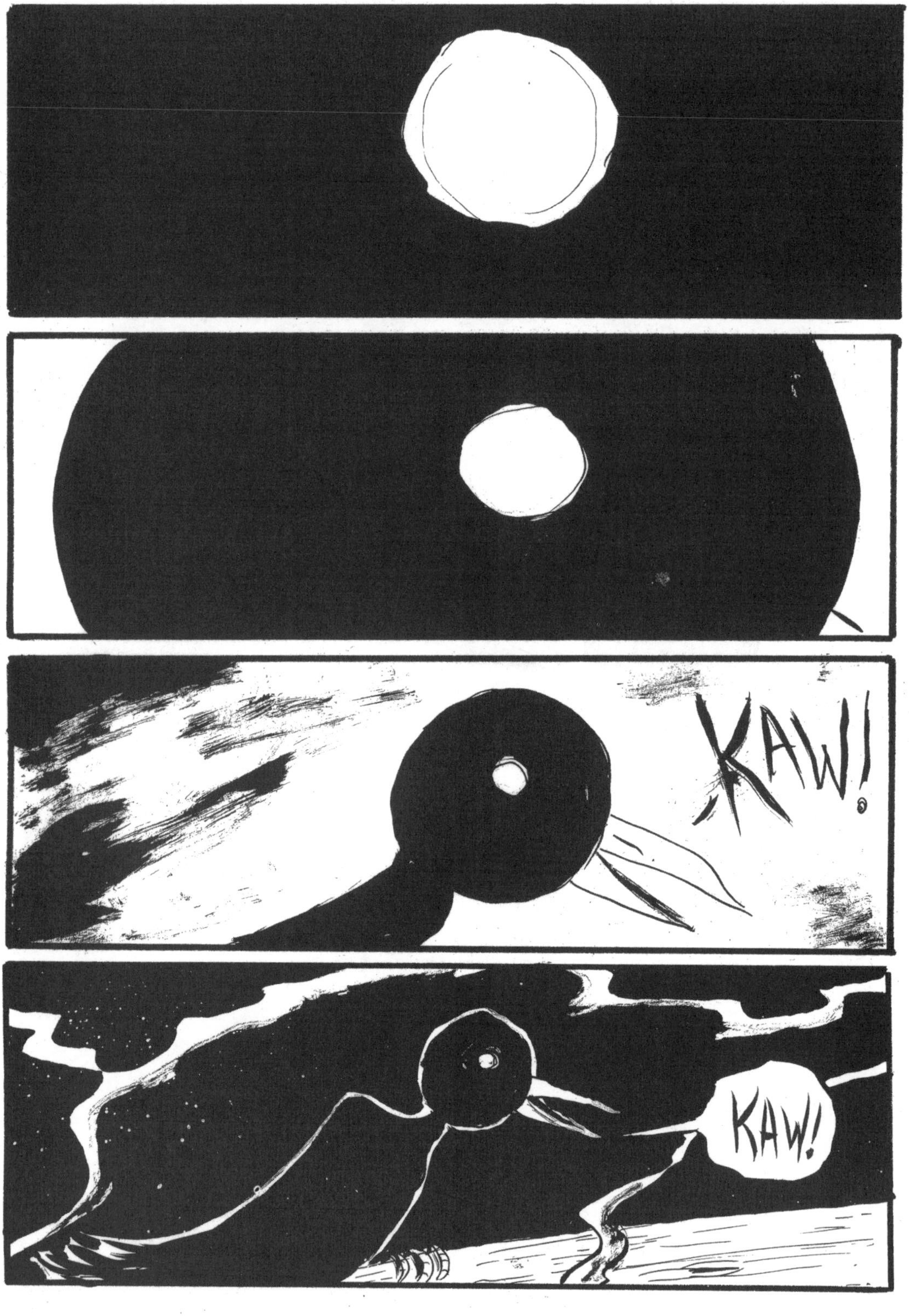
KAW!
KAW!

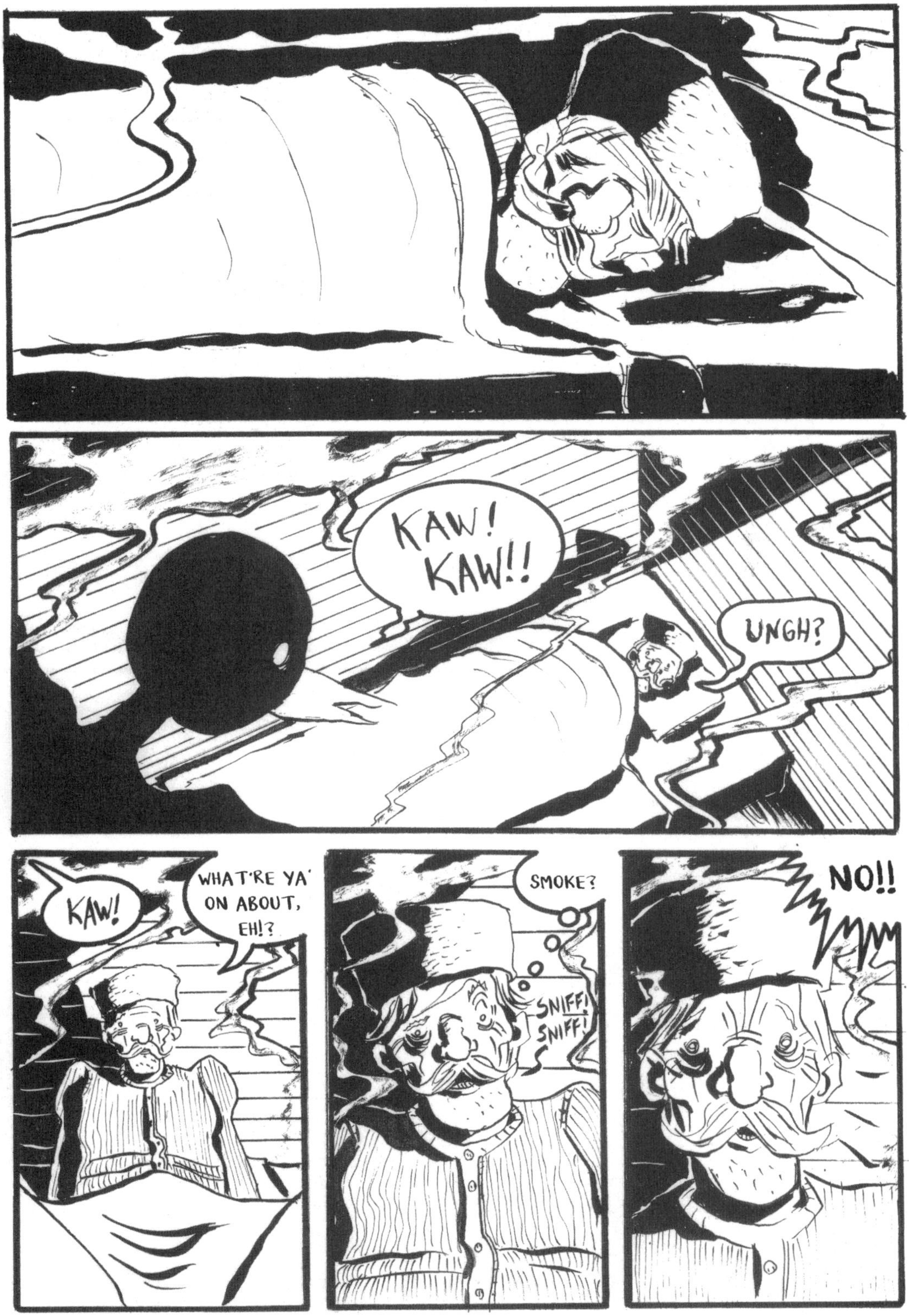
KAW! KAW!!
UNGH?
KAW!
WHAT'RE YA' ON ABOUT, EH!?
SMOKE?
SNIFF! SNIFF!
NO!!

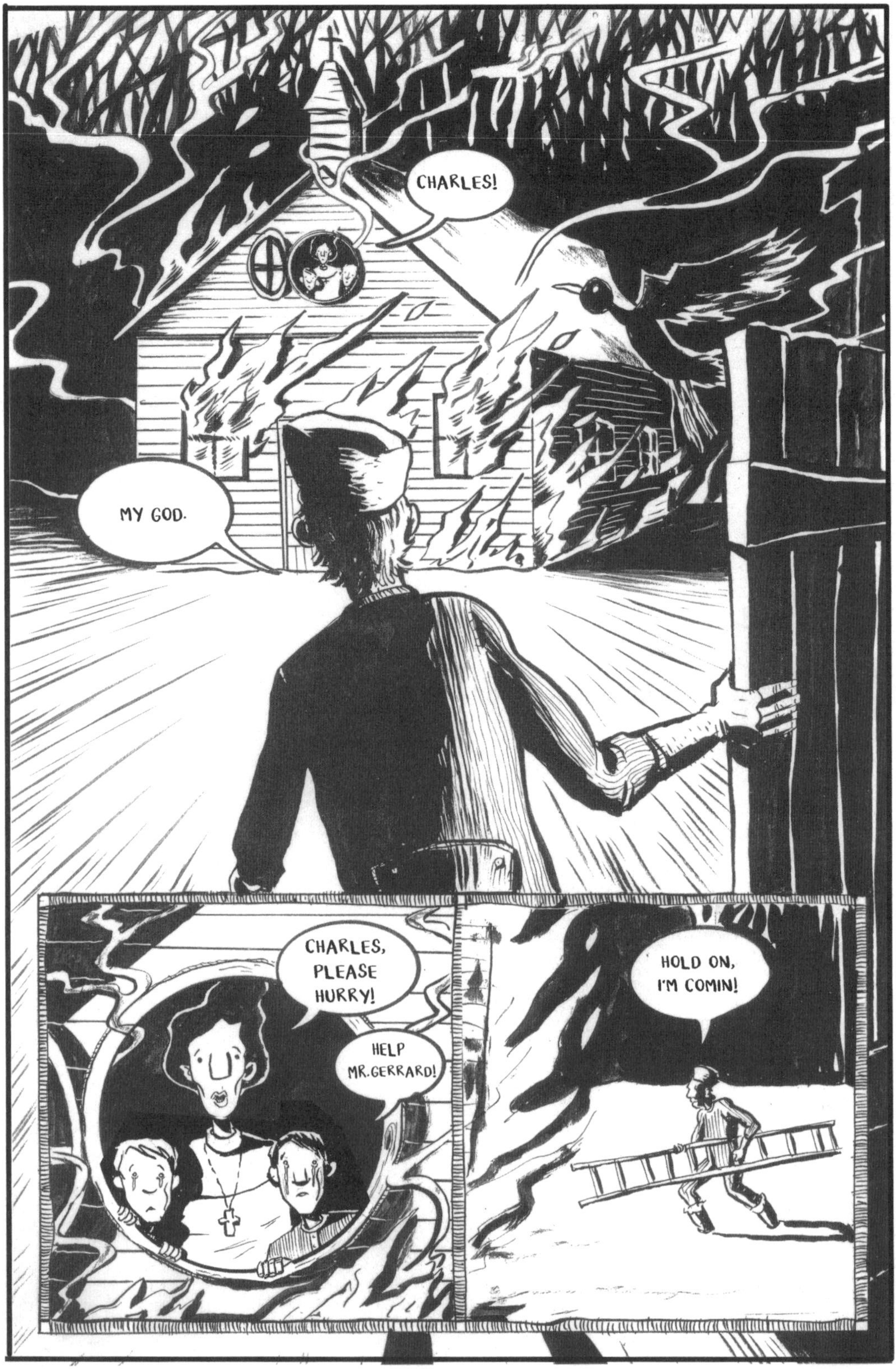
CHARLES!
MY GOD.
CHARLES, PLEASE HURRY!
HELP MR. GERRARD!
HOLD ON, I'M COMIN!

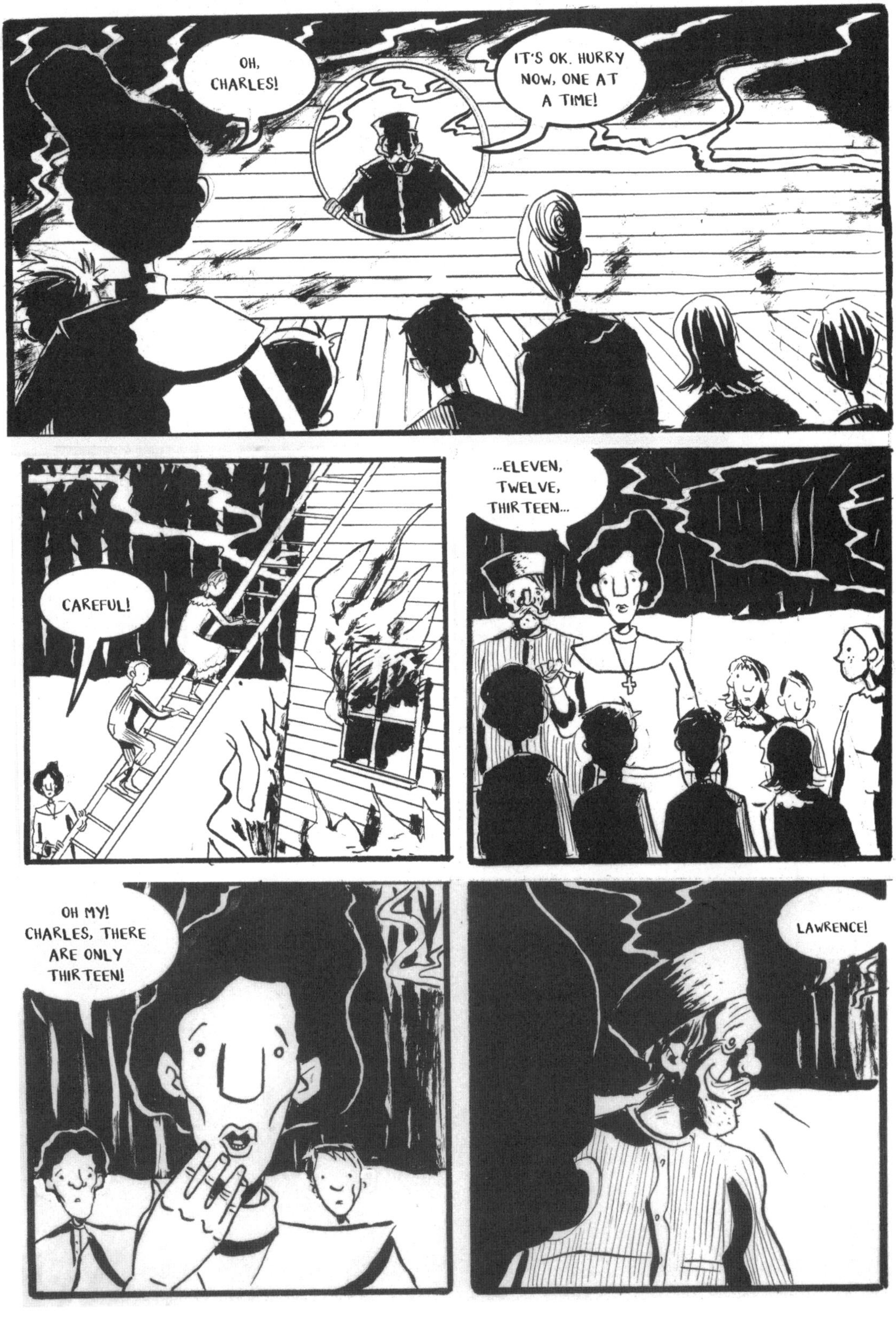
OH, CHARLES!
IT'S OK. HURRY NOW, ONE AT A TIME!
CAREFUL!
...ELEVEN, TWELVE, THIRTEEN...
OH MY! CHARLES, THERE ARE ONLY THIRTEEN!
LAWRENCE!

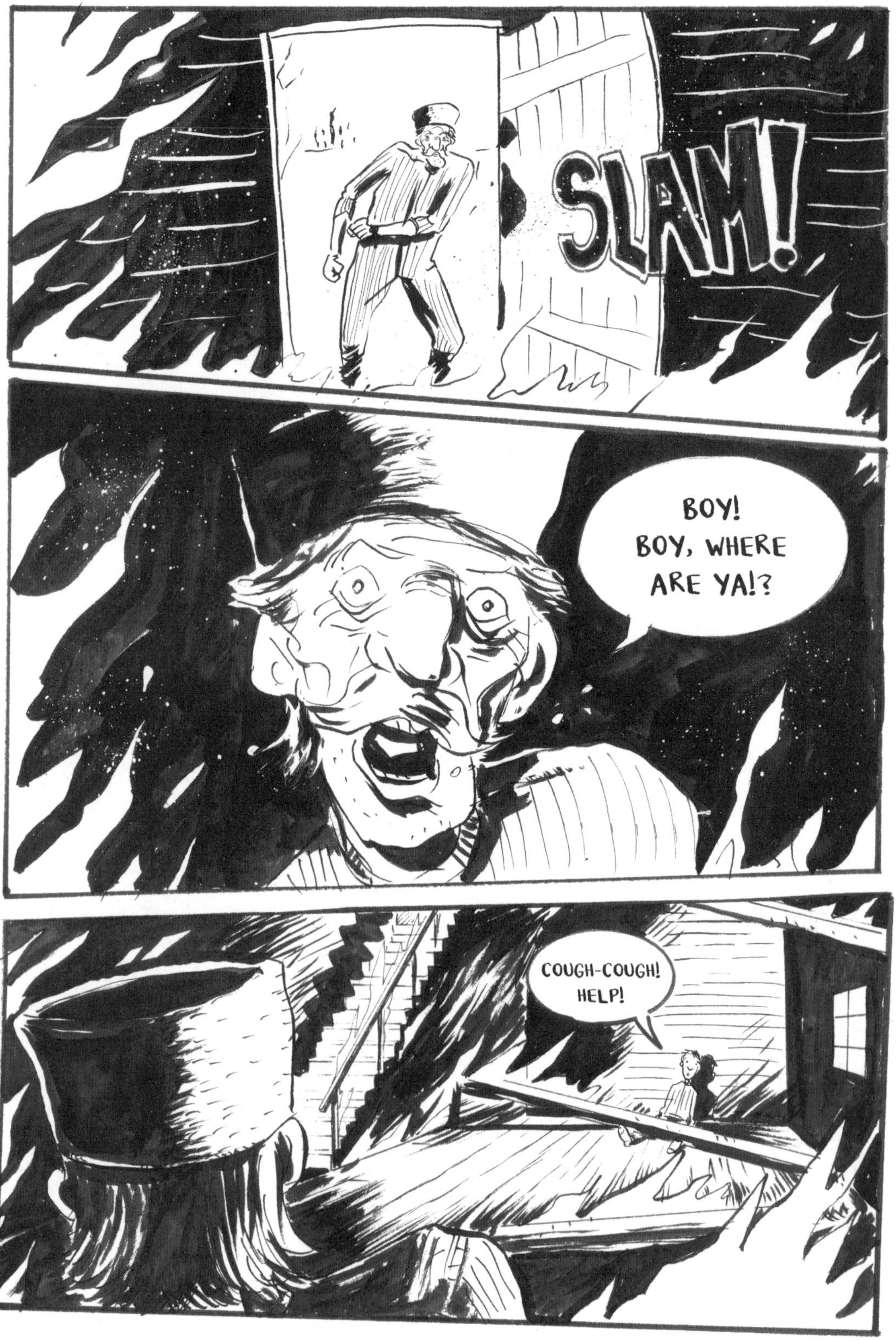
SLAM!
BOY! BOY, WHERE ARE YA!?
COUGH-COUGH! HELP!

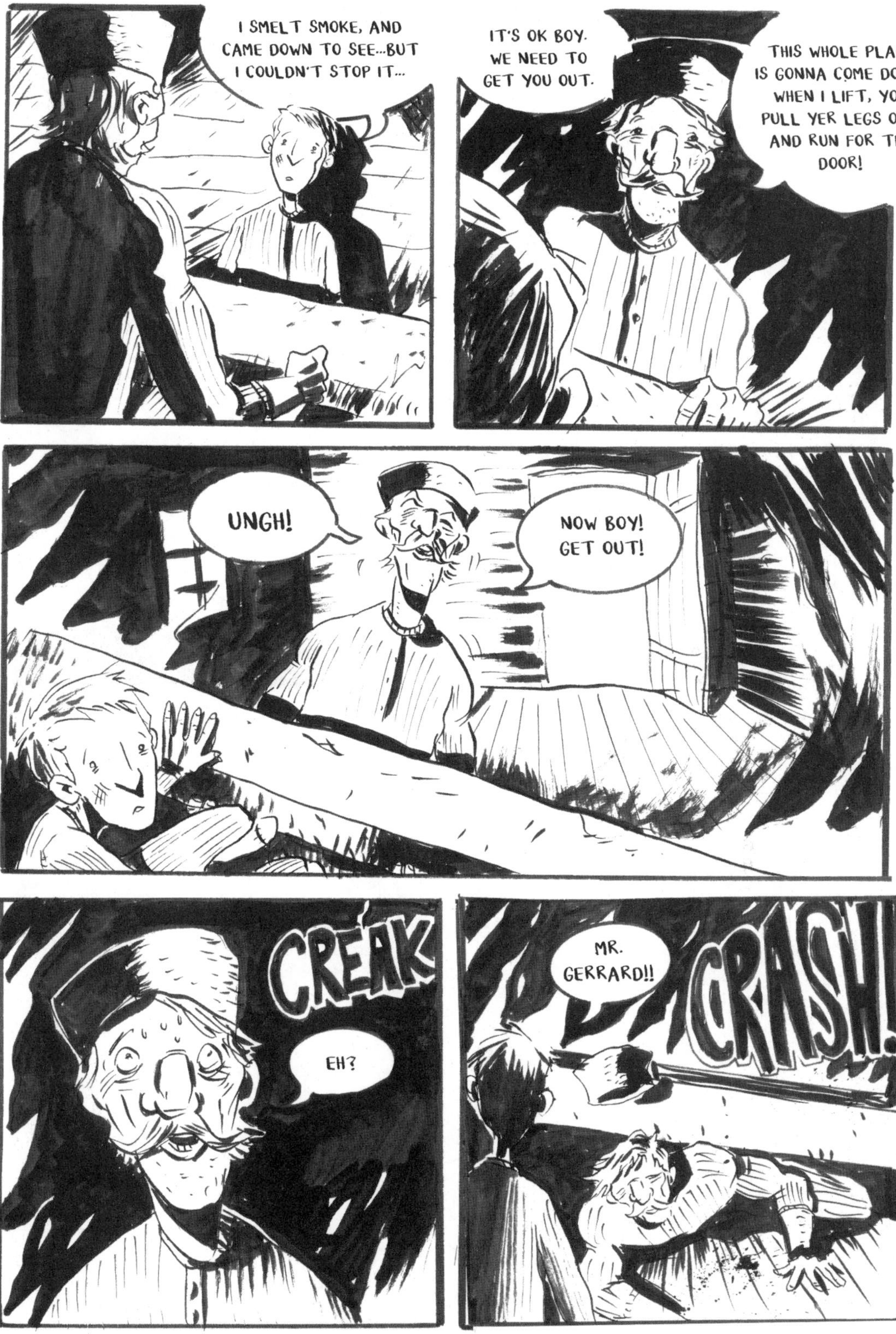
I SMELT SMOKE, AND CAME DOWN TO SEE...BUT I COULDN'T STOP IT...
IT'S OK BOY. WE NEED TO GET YOU OUT.
THIS WHOLE PLACE IS GONNA COME DOWN. WHEN I LIFT, YOU PULL YER LEGS OUT AND RUN FOR THE DOOR!
UNGH!
NOW BOY! GET OUT!
CREAK
EH?
MR. GERRARD!!
CRASH!

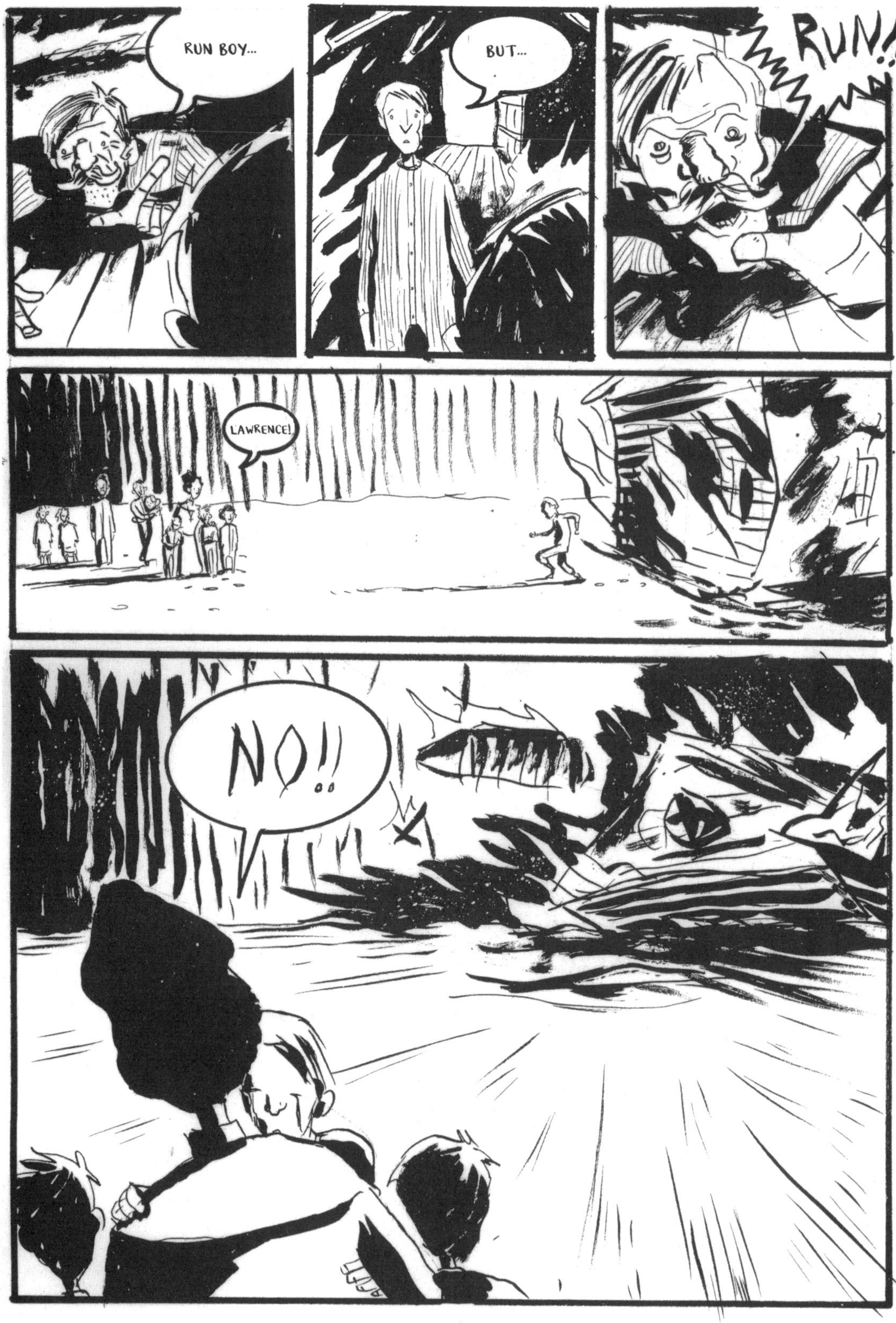
RUN BOY...
BUT...
RUN!!
LAWRENCE!
NO!!

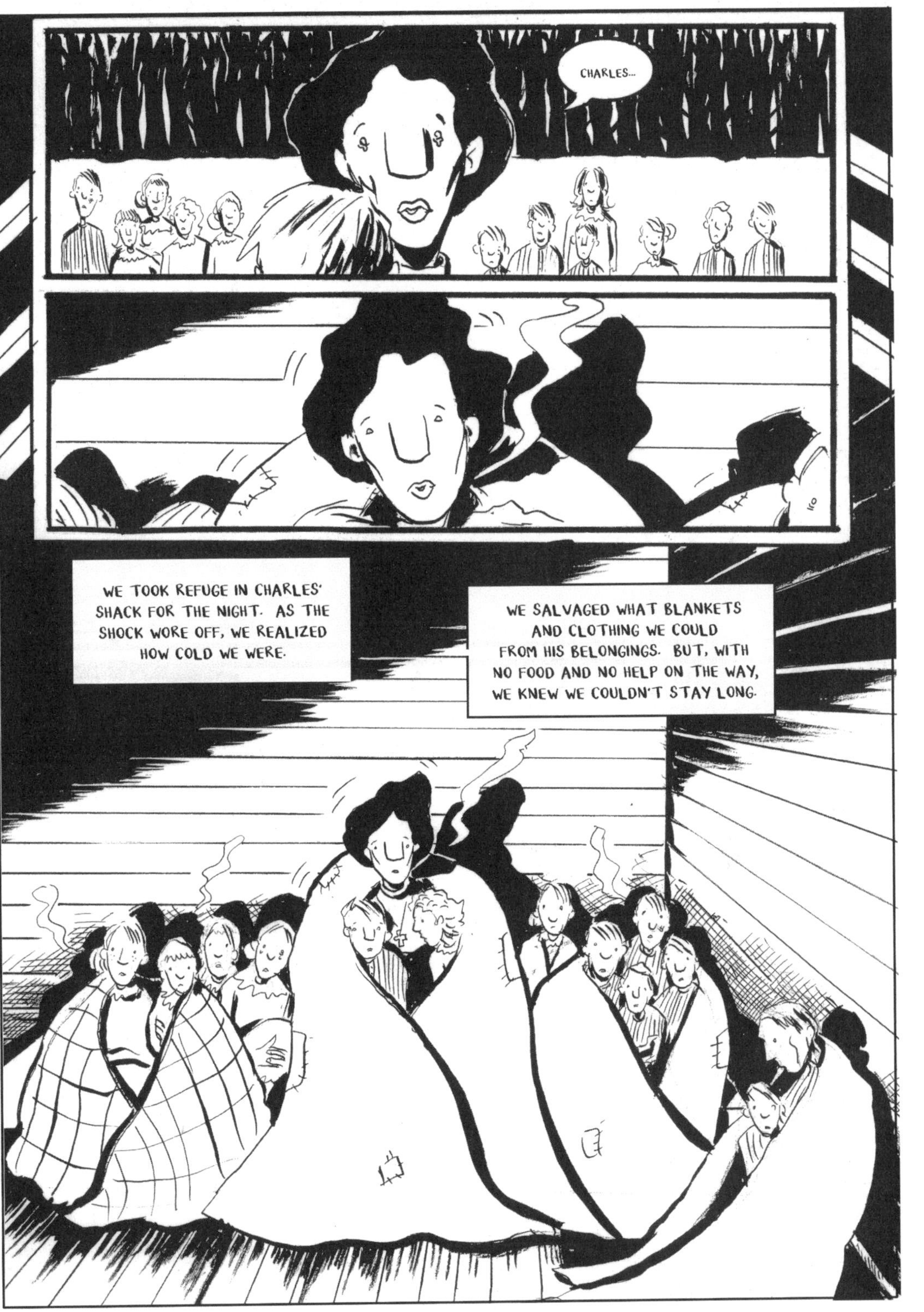
CHARLES...
WE TOOK REFUGE IN CHARLES' SHACK FOR THE NIGHT. AS THE SHOCK WORE OFF, WE REALIZED HOW COLD WE WERE.
WE SALVAGED WHAT BLANKETS AND CLOTHING WE COULD FROM HIS BELONGINGS. BUT, WITH NO FOOD AND NO HELP ON THE WAY, WE KNEW WE COULDN'T STAY LONG.

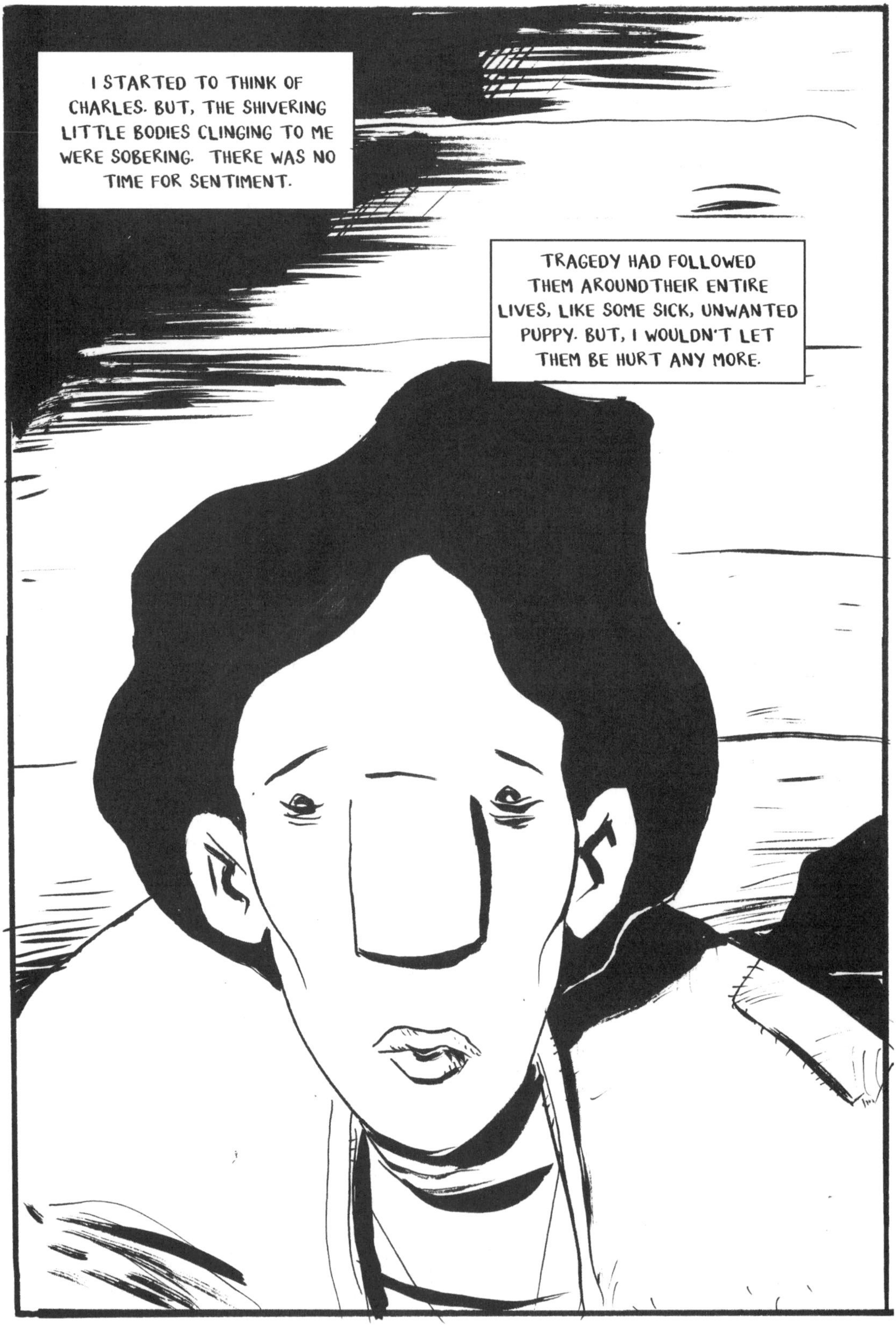
I STARTED TO THINK OF CHARLES. BUT, THE SHIVERING LITTLE BODIES CLINGING TO ME WERE SOBERING. THERE WAS NO TIME FOR SENTIMENT.
TRAGEDY HAD FOLLOWED THEM AROUND THEIR ENTIRE LIVES, LIKE SOME SICK, UNWANTED PUPPY. BUT, I WOULDN'T LET THEM BE HURT ANY MORE.

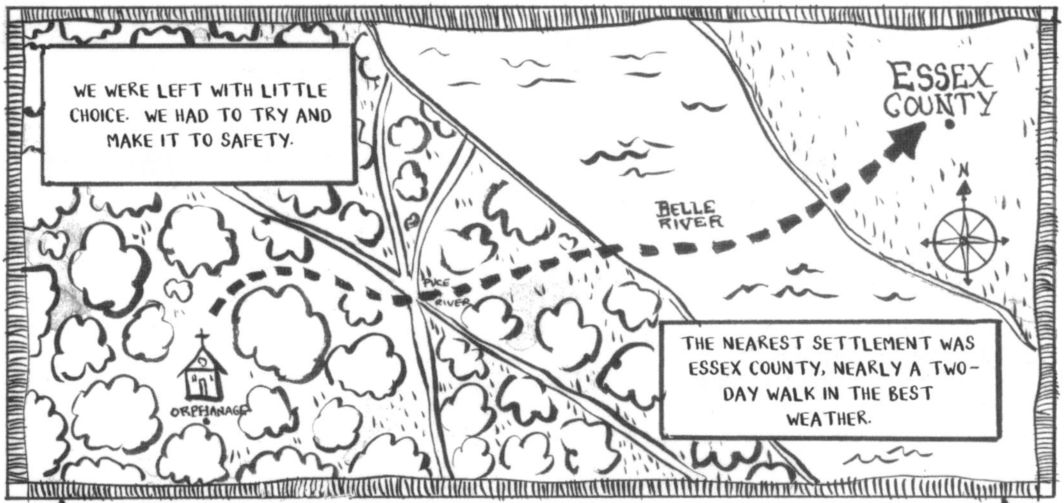
WE WERE LEFT WITH LITTLE CHOICE. WE HAD TO TRY AND MAKE IT TO SAFETY.
ESSEX COUNTY
N
BELLE RIVER
ORPHANAGE
THE NEAREST SETTLEMENT WAS ESSEX COUNTY, NEARLY A TWO-DAY WALK IN THE BEST WEATHER.

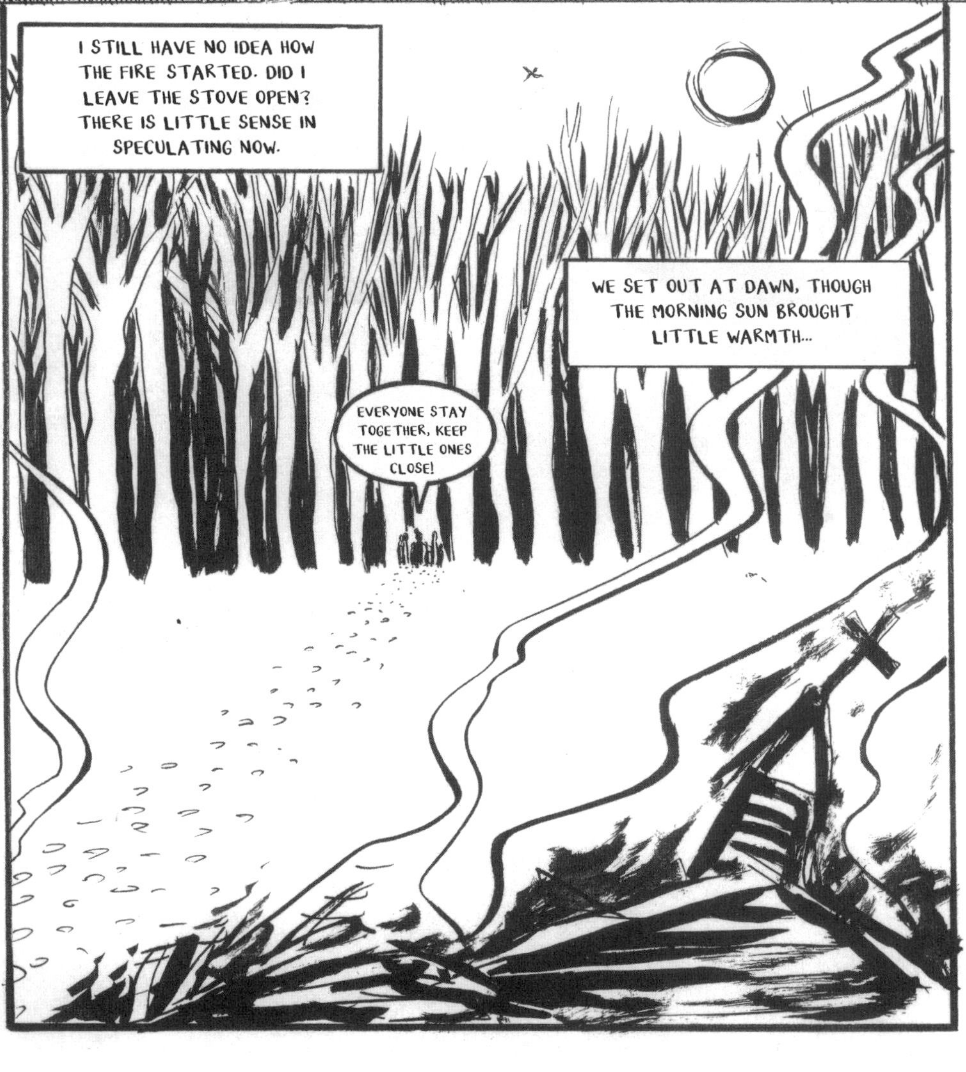
I STILL HAVE NO IDEA HOW THE FIRE STARTED. DID I LEAVE THE STOVE OPEN? THERE IS LITTLE SENSE IN SPECULATING NOW.
WE SET OUT AT DAWN, THOUGH THE MORNING SUN BROUGHT LITTLE WARMTH...
EVERYONE STAY TOGETHER, KEEP THE LITTLE ONES CLOSE!

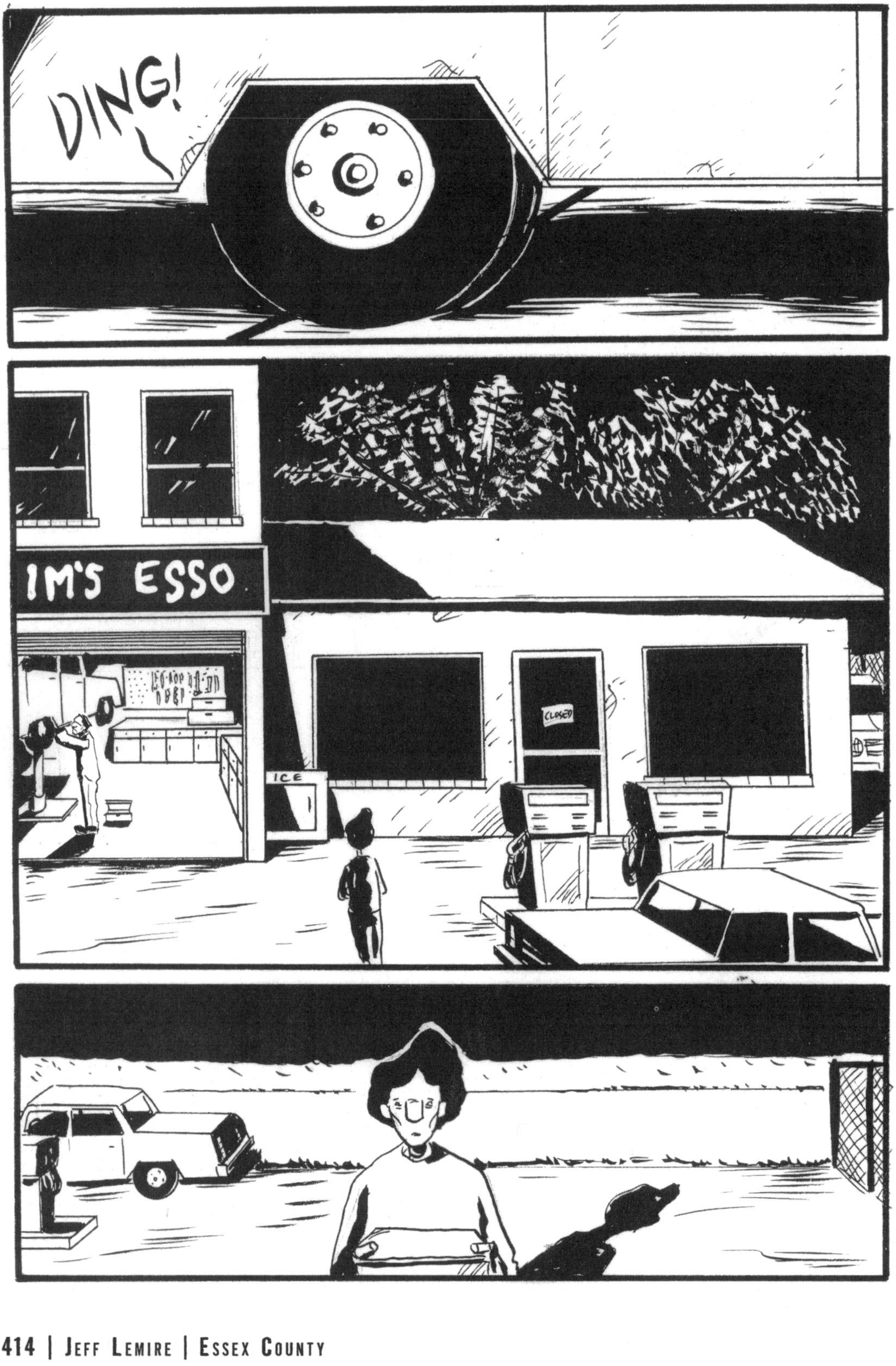
DING!
IM'S ESSO
ICE
CLOSED

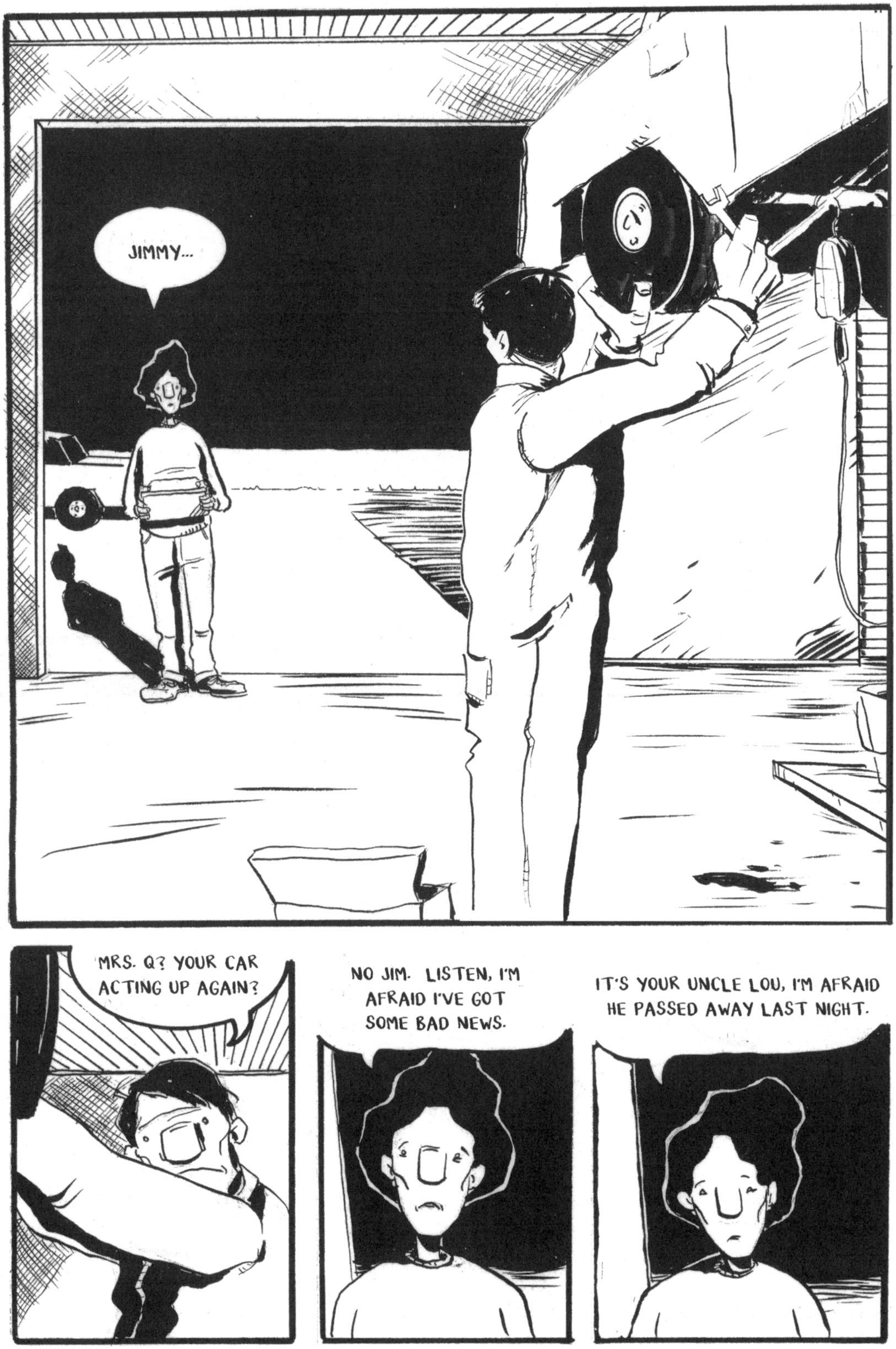
JIMMY...
MRS. Q? YOUR CAR ACTING UP AGAIN?
NO JIM. LISTEN, I'M AFRAID I'VE GOT SOME BAD NEWS.
IT'S YOUR UNCLE LOU, I'M AFRAID HE PASSED AWAY LAST NIGHT.

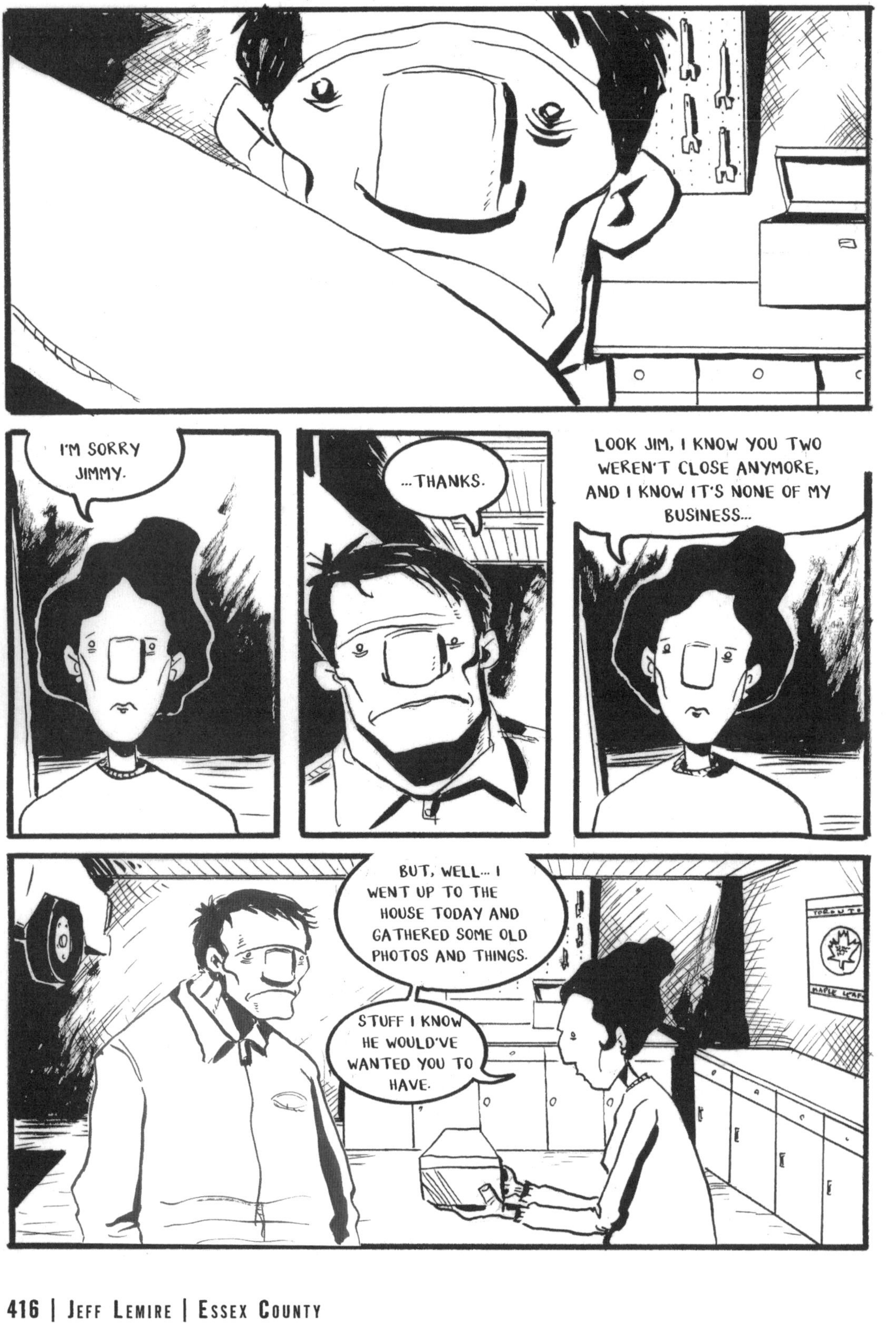
I'M SORRY JIMMY.
...THANKS.
LOOK JIM, I KNOW YOU TWO WEREN'T CLOSE ANYMORE, AND I KNOW IT'S NONE OF MY BUSINESS...
BUT, WELL... I WENT UP TO THE HOUSE TODAY AND GATHERED SOME OLD PHOTOS AND THINGS.
STUFF I KNOW HE WOULD'VE WANTED YOU TO HAVE.

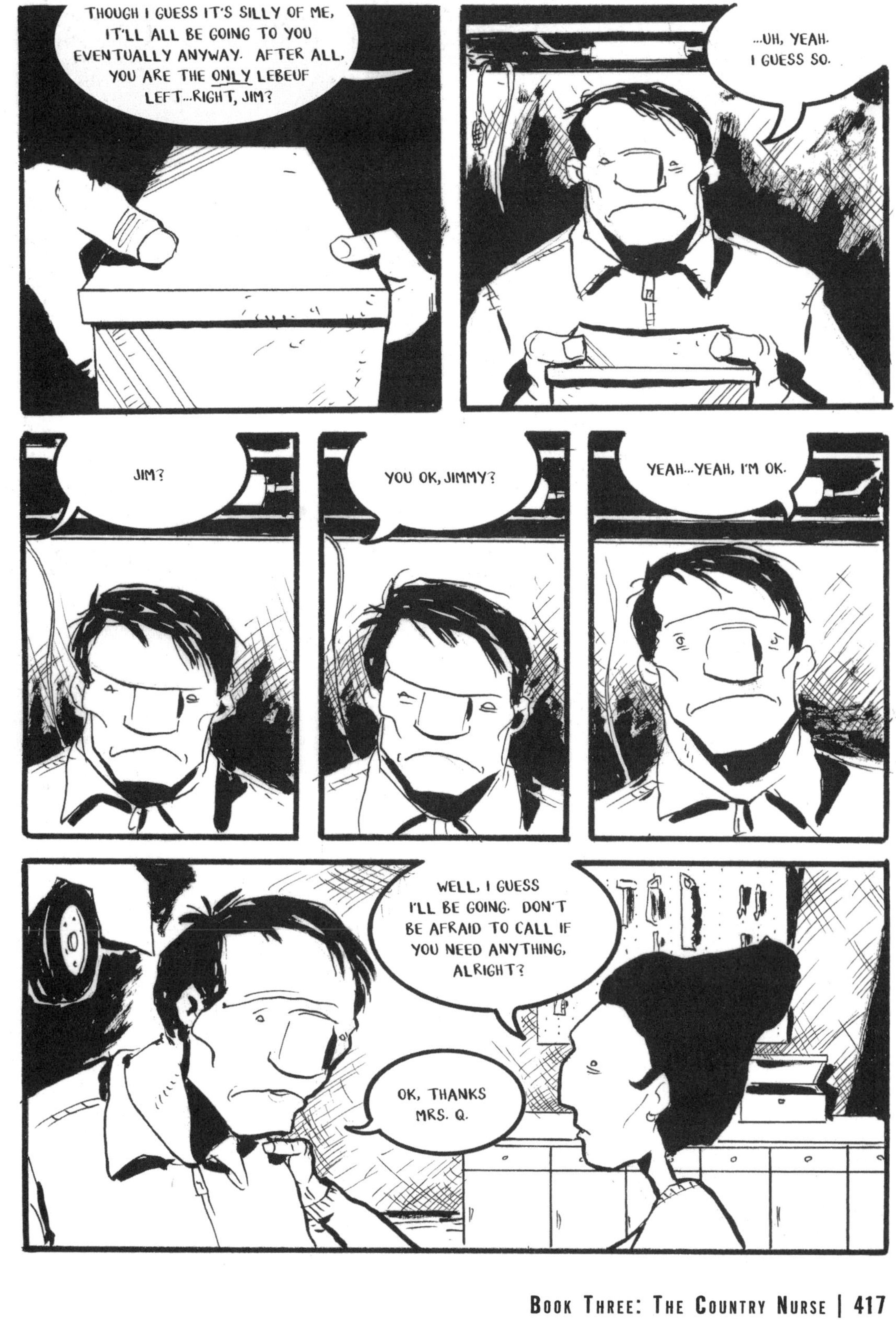
THOUGH I GUESS IT'S SILLY OF ME, IT'LL ALL BE GOING TO YOU EVENTUALLY ANYWAY. AFTER ALL, YOU ARE THE ONLY LEBEUF LEFT...RIGHT, JIM?
...UH, YEAH. I GUESS SO.
JIM?
YOU OK, JIMMY?
YEAH...YEAH, I'M OK.
WELL, I GUESS I'LL BE GOING. DON'T BE AFRAID TO CALL IF YOU NEED ANYTHING, ALRIGHT?
OK, THANKS MRS. Q.

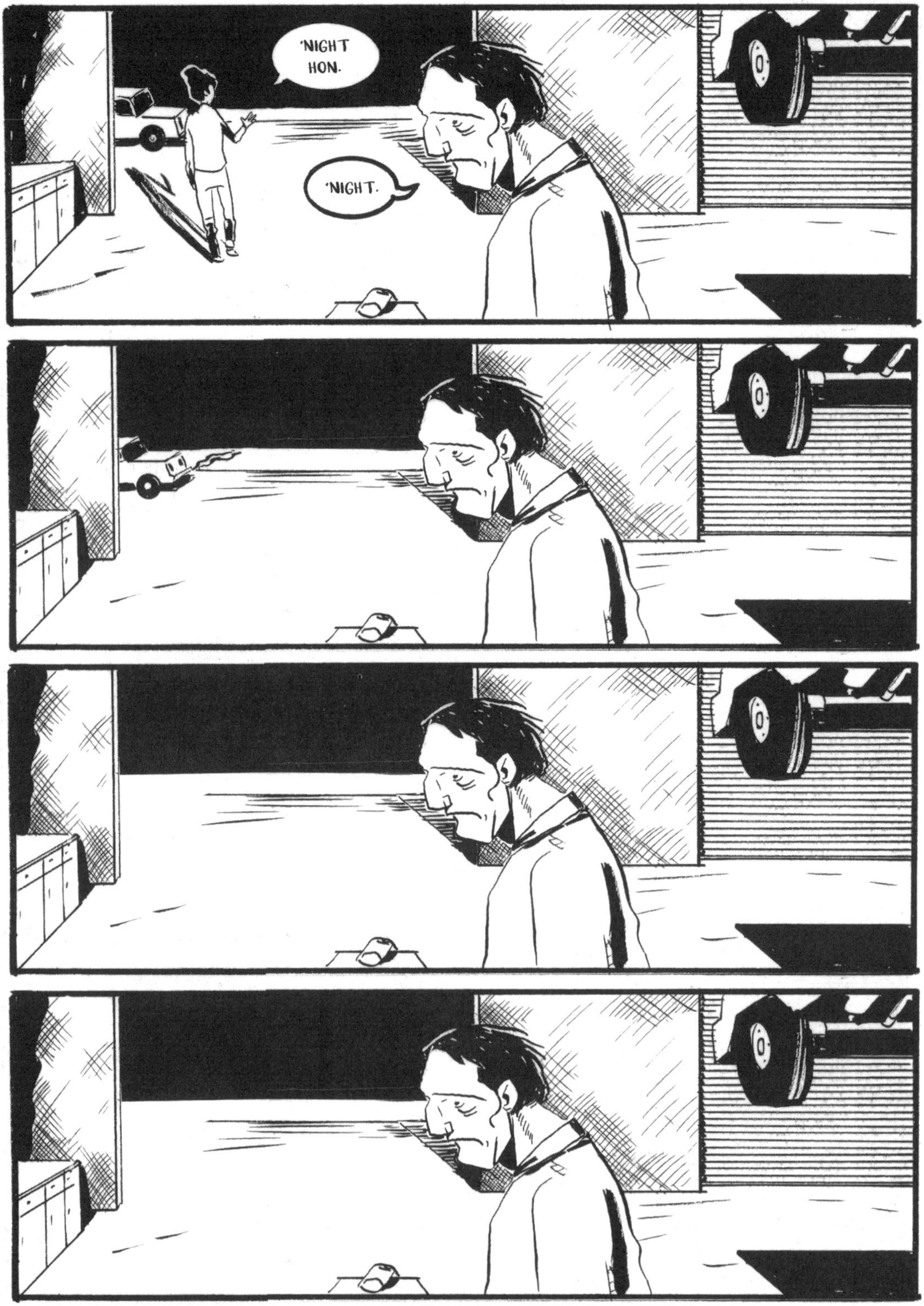
'NIGHT HON.
'NIGHT.

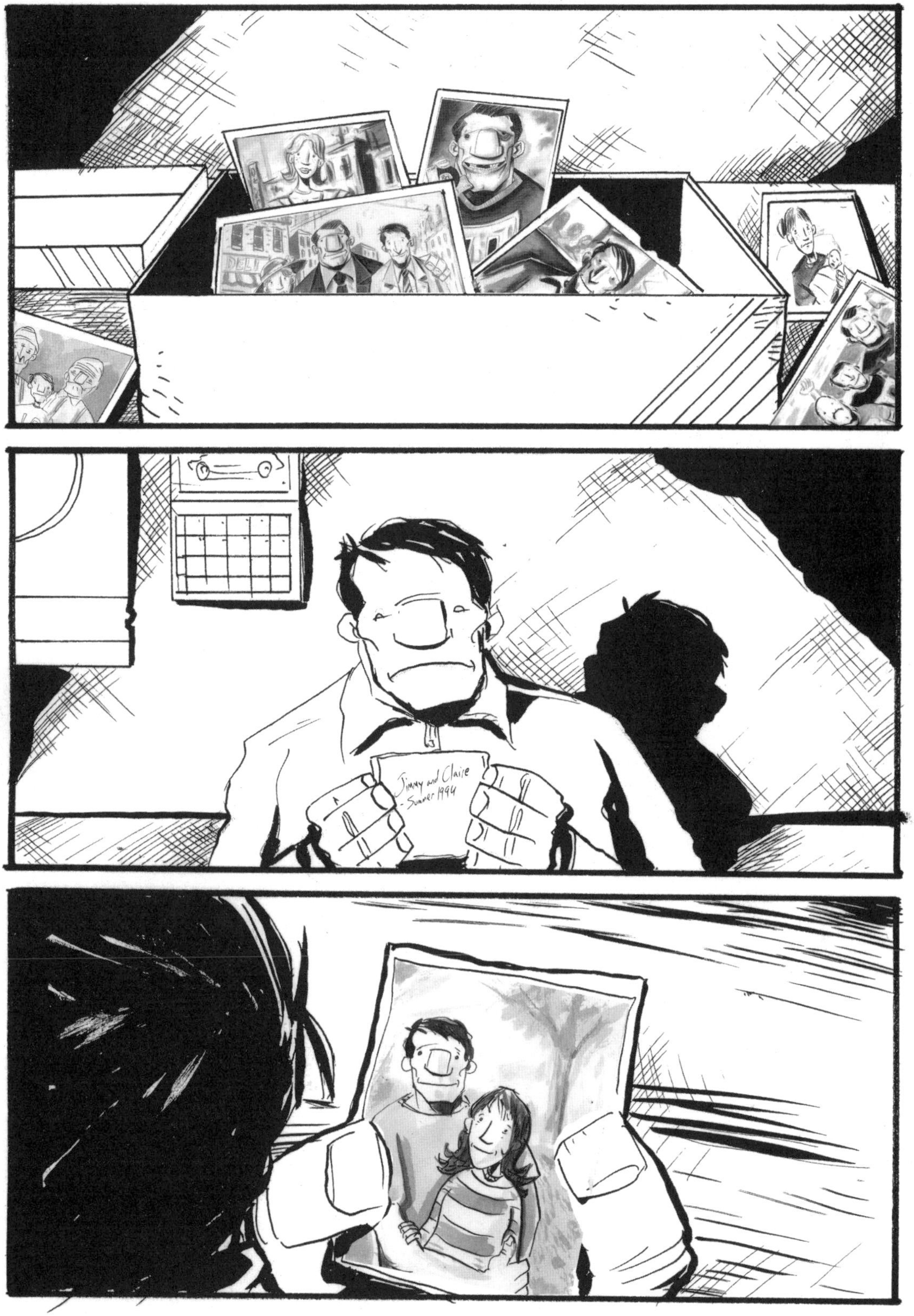
Jimmy and Claire
- Summer 1994

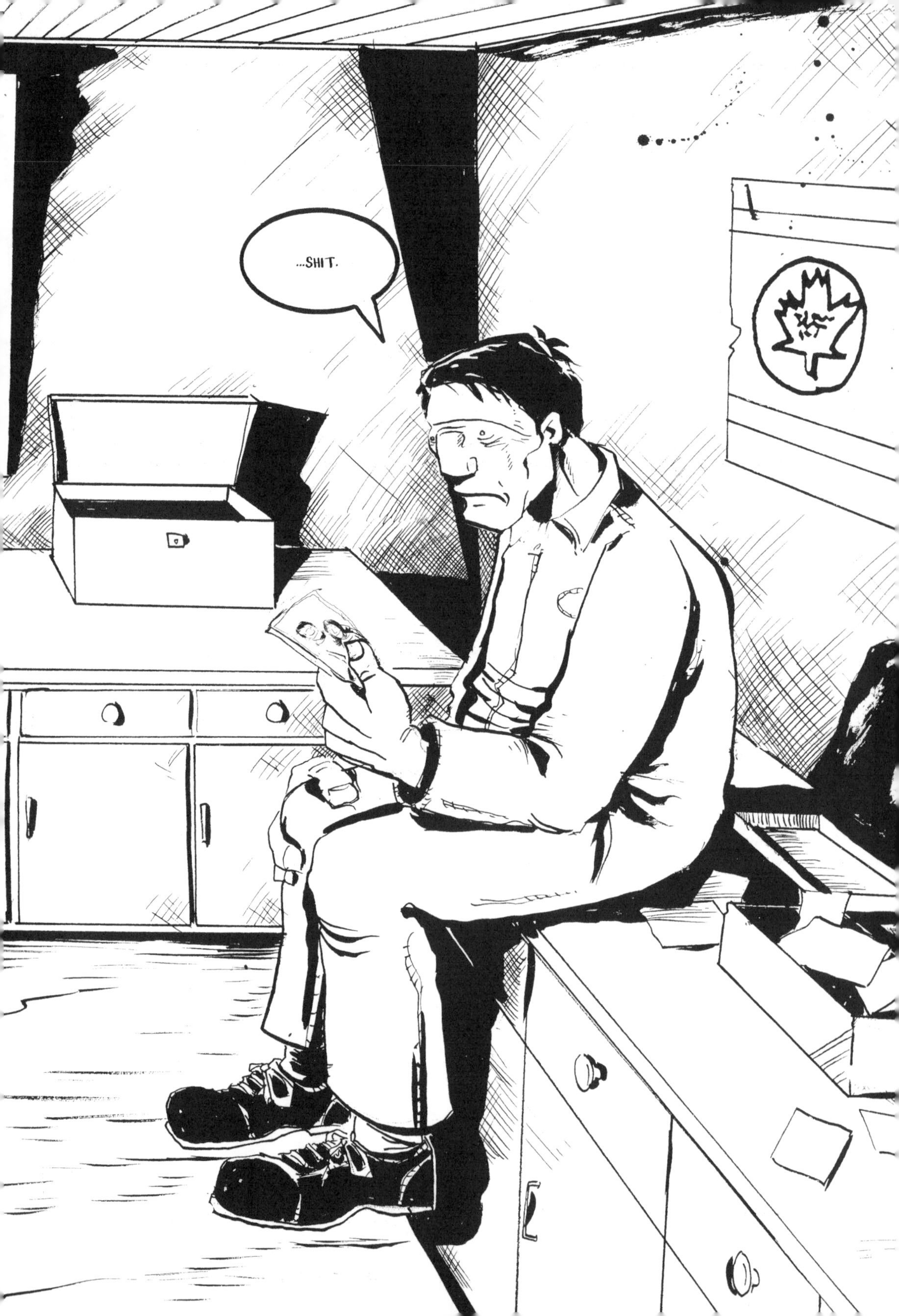
...SHIT.

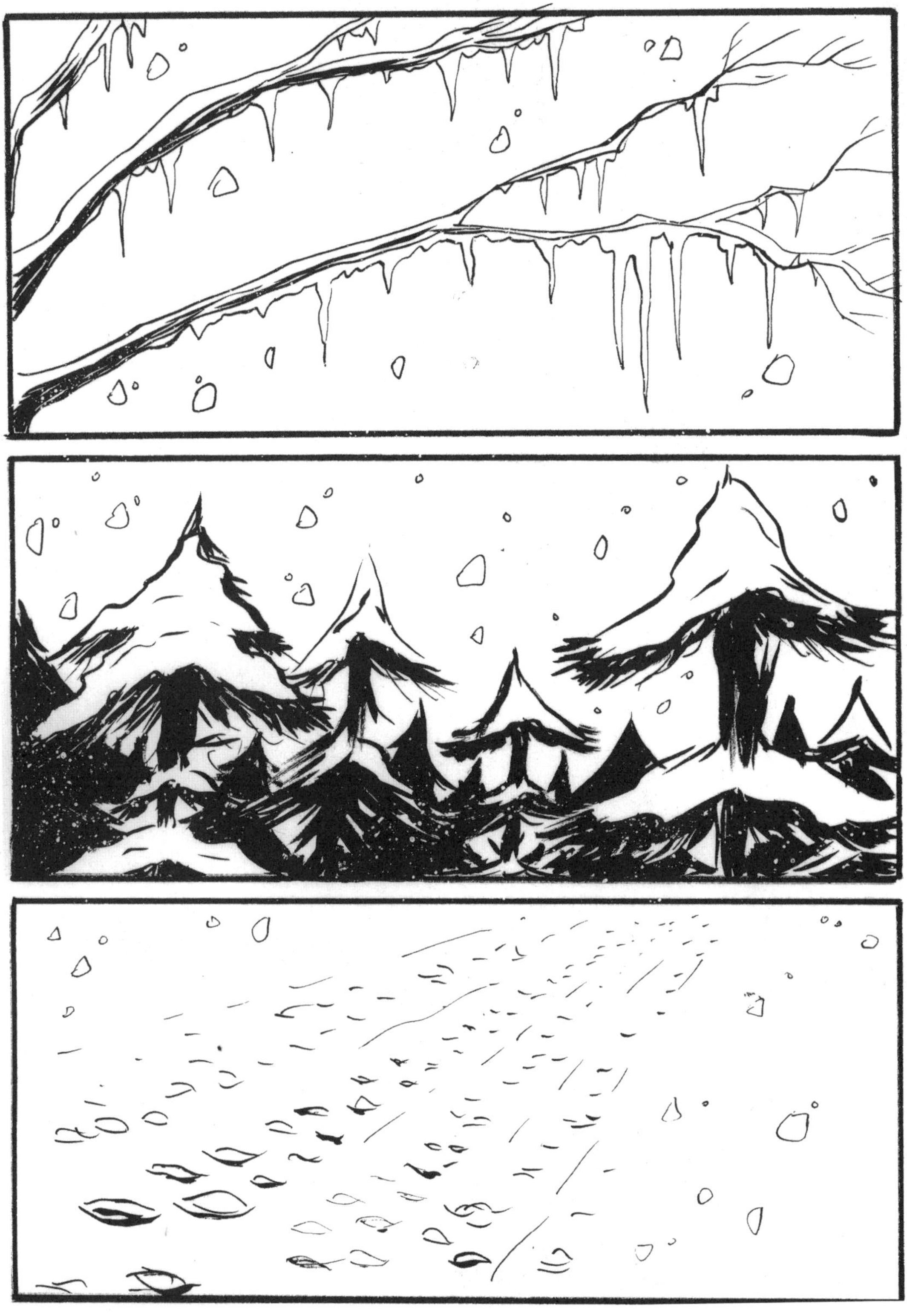

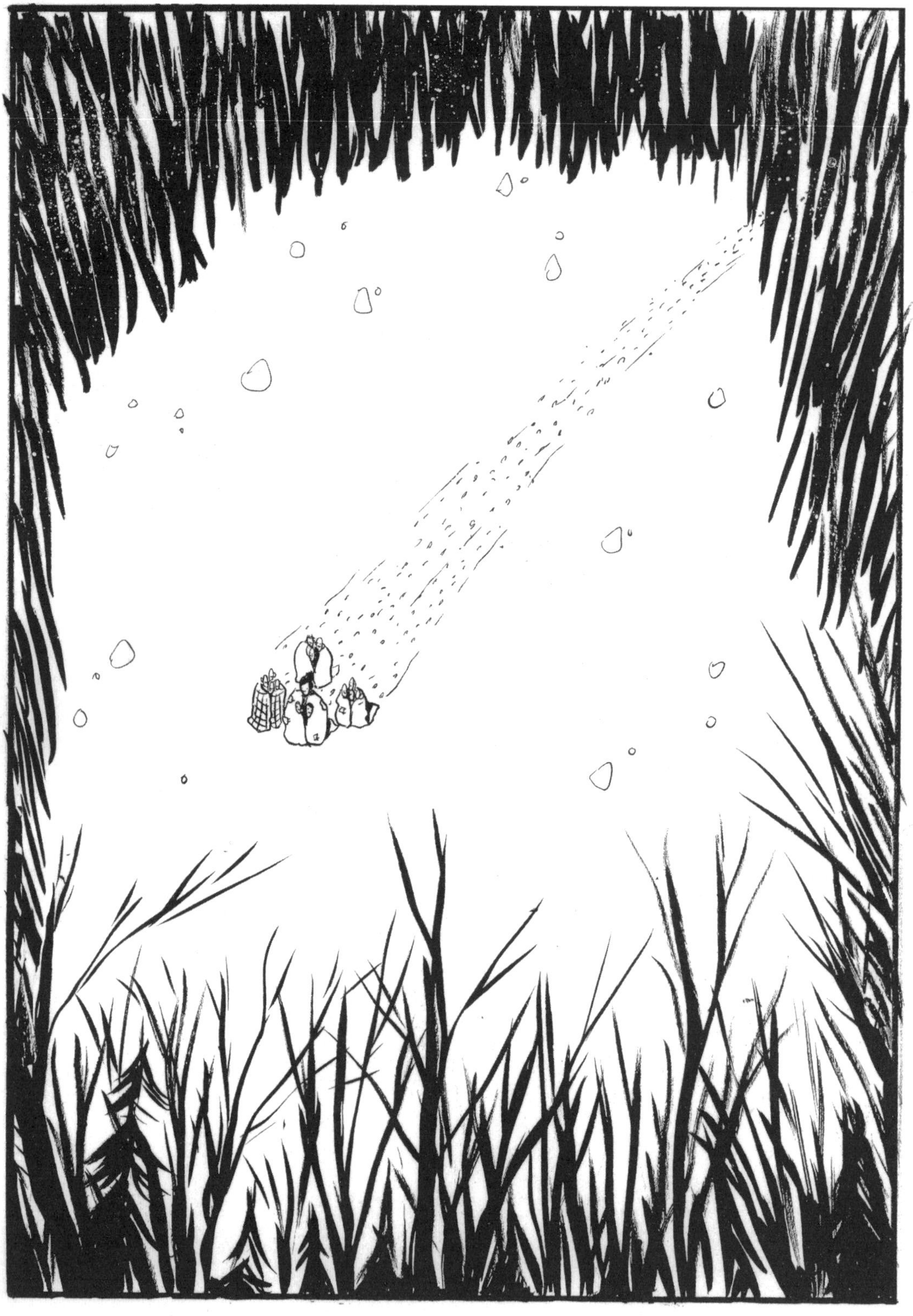

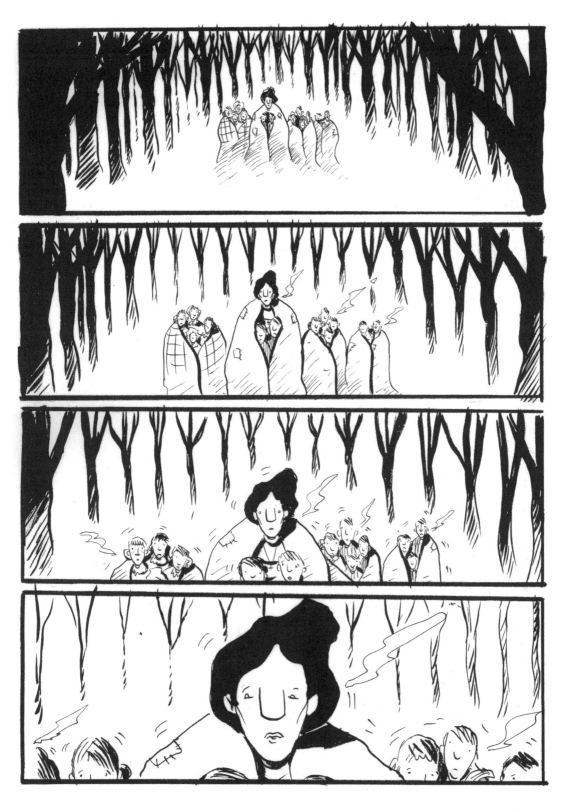

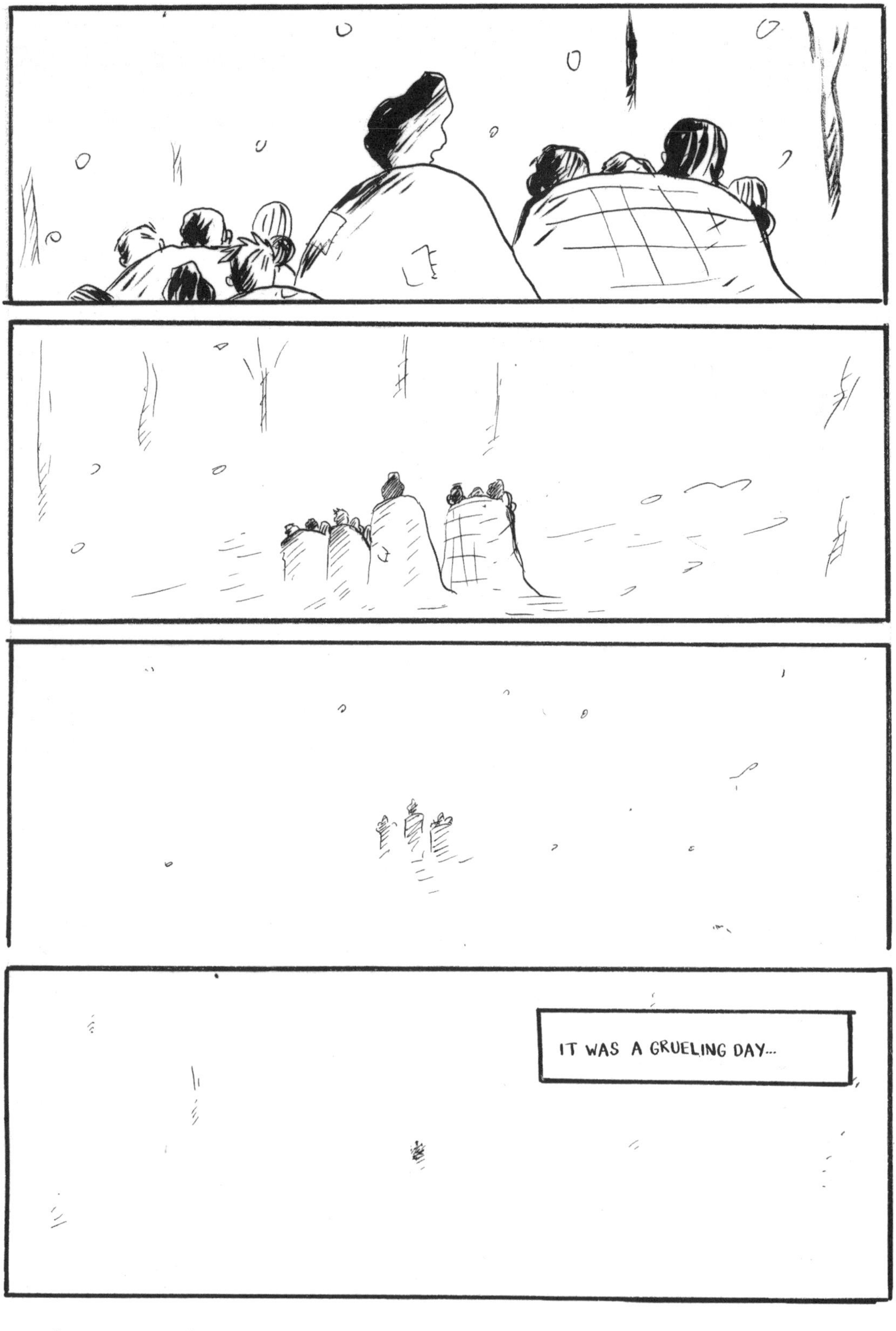
IT WAS A GRUELING DAY...

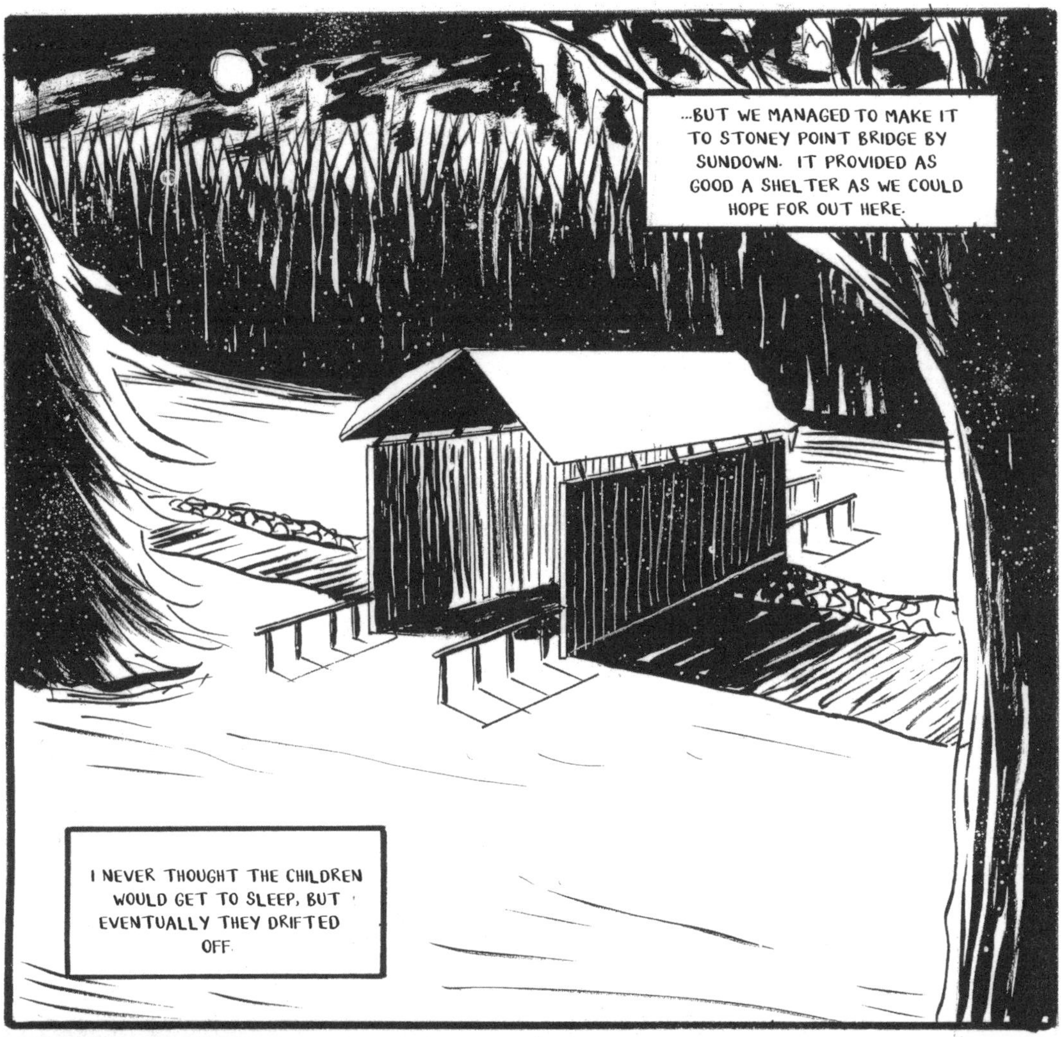
...BUT WE MANAGED TO MAKE IT TO STONEY POINT BRIDGE BY SUNDOWN. IT PROVIDED AS GOOD A SHELTER AS WE COULD HOPE FOR OUT HERE.
I NEVER THOUGHT THE CHILDREN WOULD GET TO SLEEP, BUT EVENTUALLY THEY DRIFTED OFF.

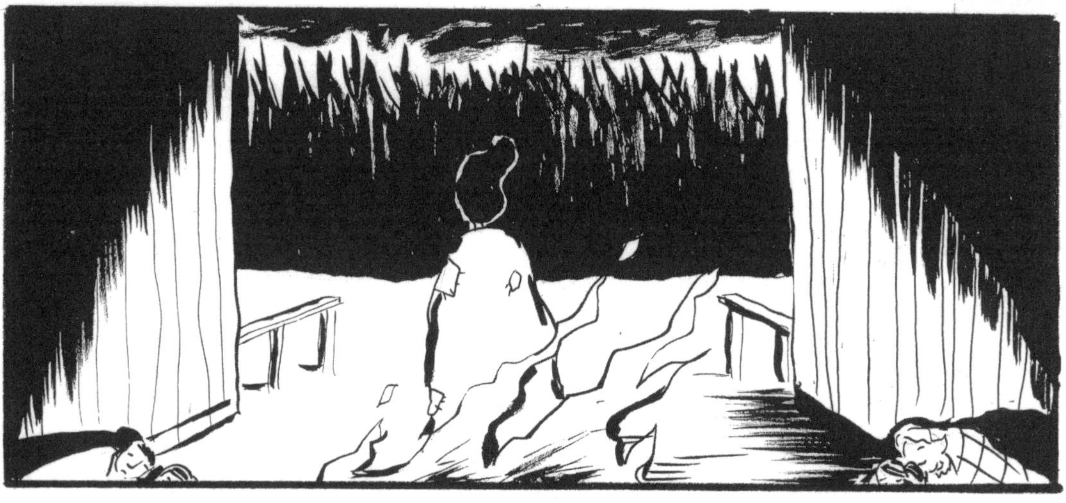

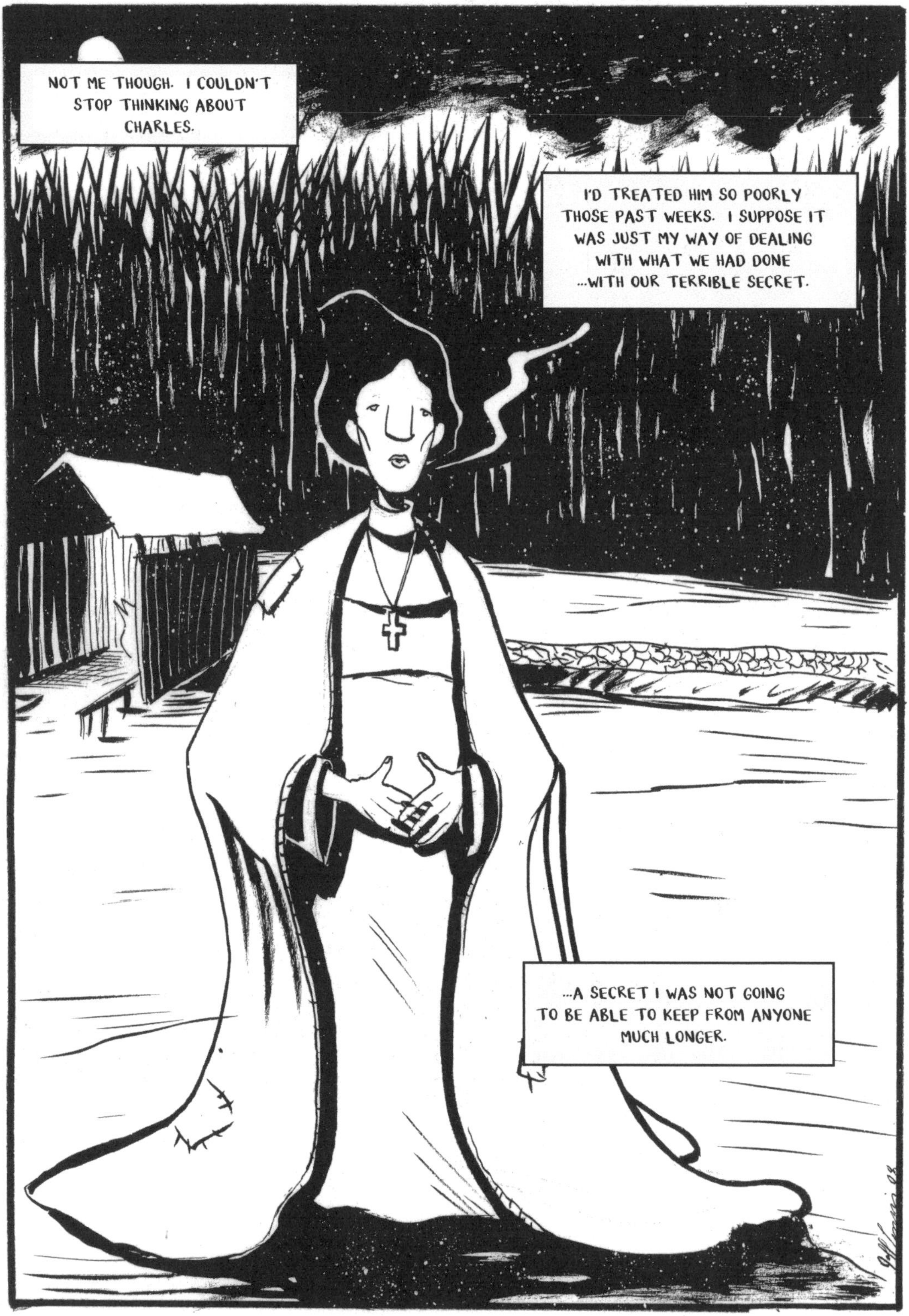
NOT ME THOUGH. I COULDN'T STOP THINKING ABOUT CHARLES.
I'D TREATED HIM SO POORLY THOSE PAST WEEKS. I SUPPOSE IT WAS JUST MY WAY OF DEALING WITH WHAT WE HAD DONE ...WITH OUR TERRIBLE SECRET.
...A SECRET I WAS NOT GOING TO BE ABLE TO KEEP FROM ANYONE MUCH LONGER.

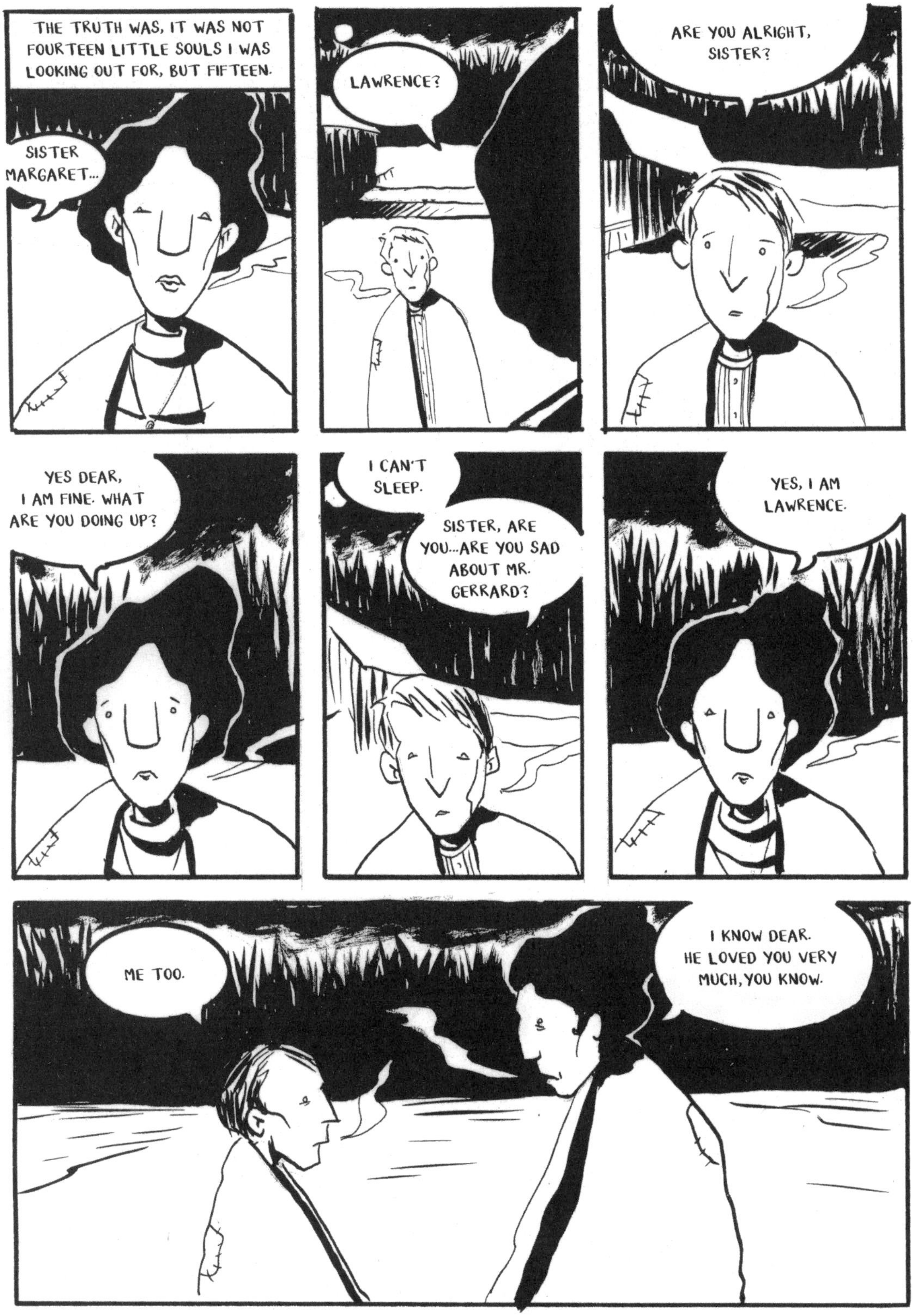
THE TRUTH WAS, IT WAS NOT FOURTEEN LITTLE SOULS I WAS LOOKING OUT FOR, BUT FIFTEEN.
SISTER MARGARET...
LAWRENCE?
ARE YOU ALRIGHT, SISTER?
YES DEAR, I AM FINE. WHAT ARE YOU DOING UP?
I CAN'T SLEEP.
SISTER, ARE YOU...ARE YOU SAD ABOUT MR. GERRARD?
YES, I AM LAWRENCE.
ME TOO.
I KNOW DEAR. HE LOVED YOU VERY MUCH, YOU KNOW.

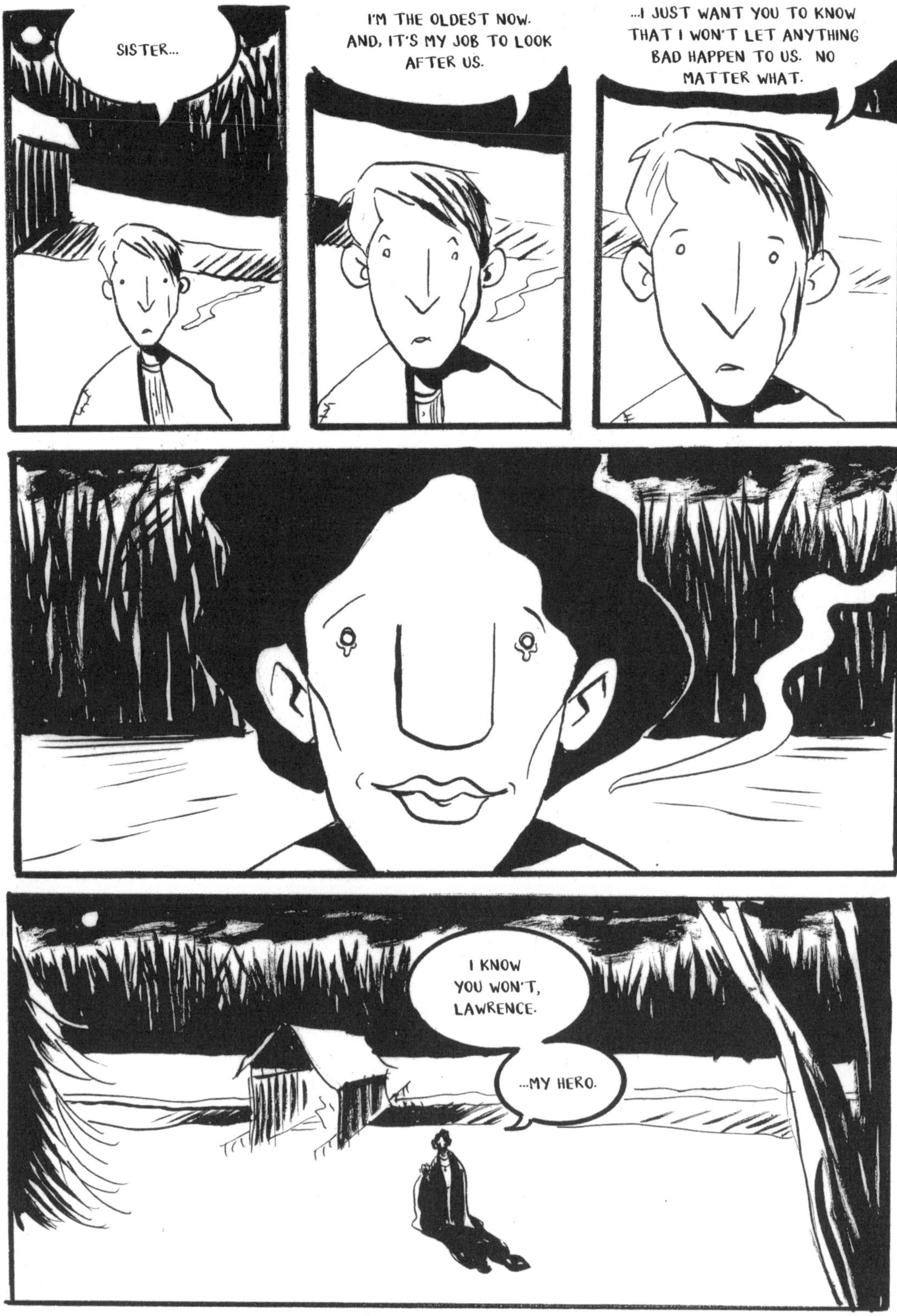
SISTER...
I'M THE OLDEST NOW. AND, IT'S MY JOB TO LOOK AFTER US.
...I JUST WANT YOU TO KNOW THAT I WON'T LET ANYTHING BAD HAPPEN TO US. NO MATTER WHAT.
I KNOW YOU WON'T, LAWRENCE.
...MY HERO.

#1 in a 3 issue mini series
CANADIAN COMICS
THE NEW
CAPTAIN CANADA
INVINCIBLE
#13
SUNDIN
TORONTO MAPLE LEAFS
THE NEW TEEN TITANS
10

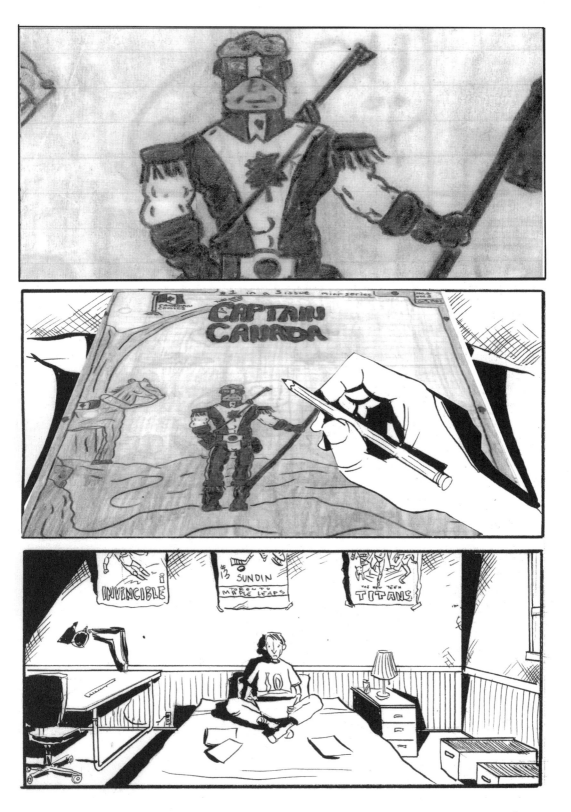

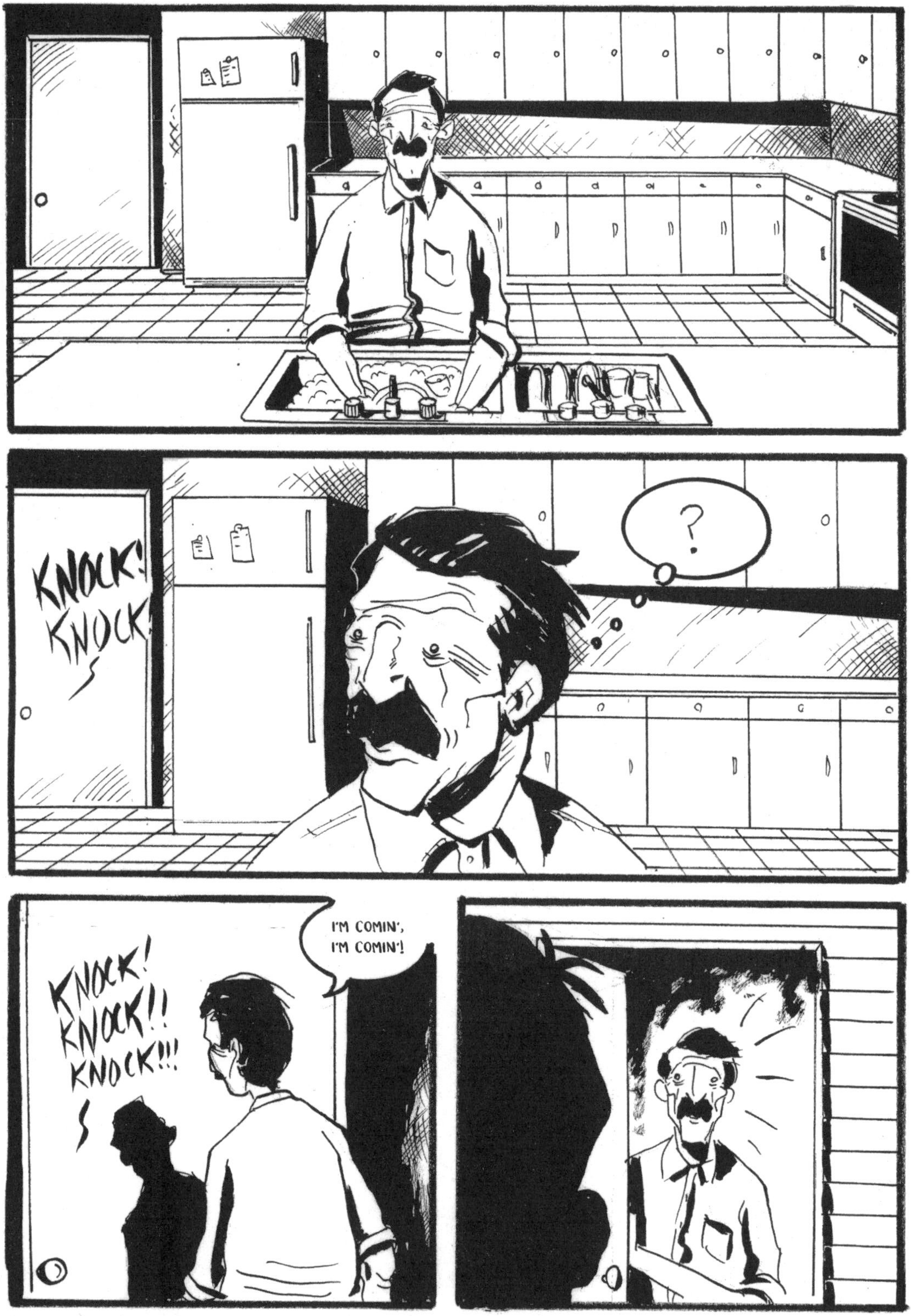
KNOCK!
KNOCK!
I'M COMIN',
I'M COMIN'!
KNOCK!
KNOCK!!
KNOCK!!!

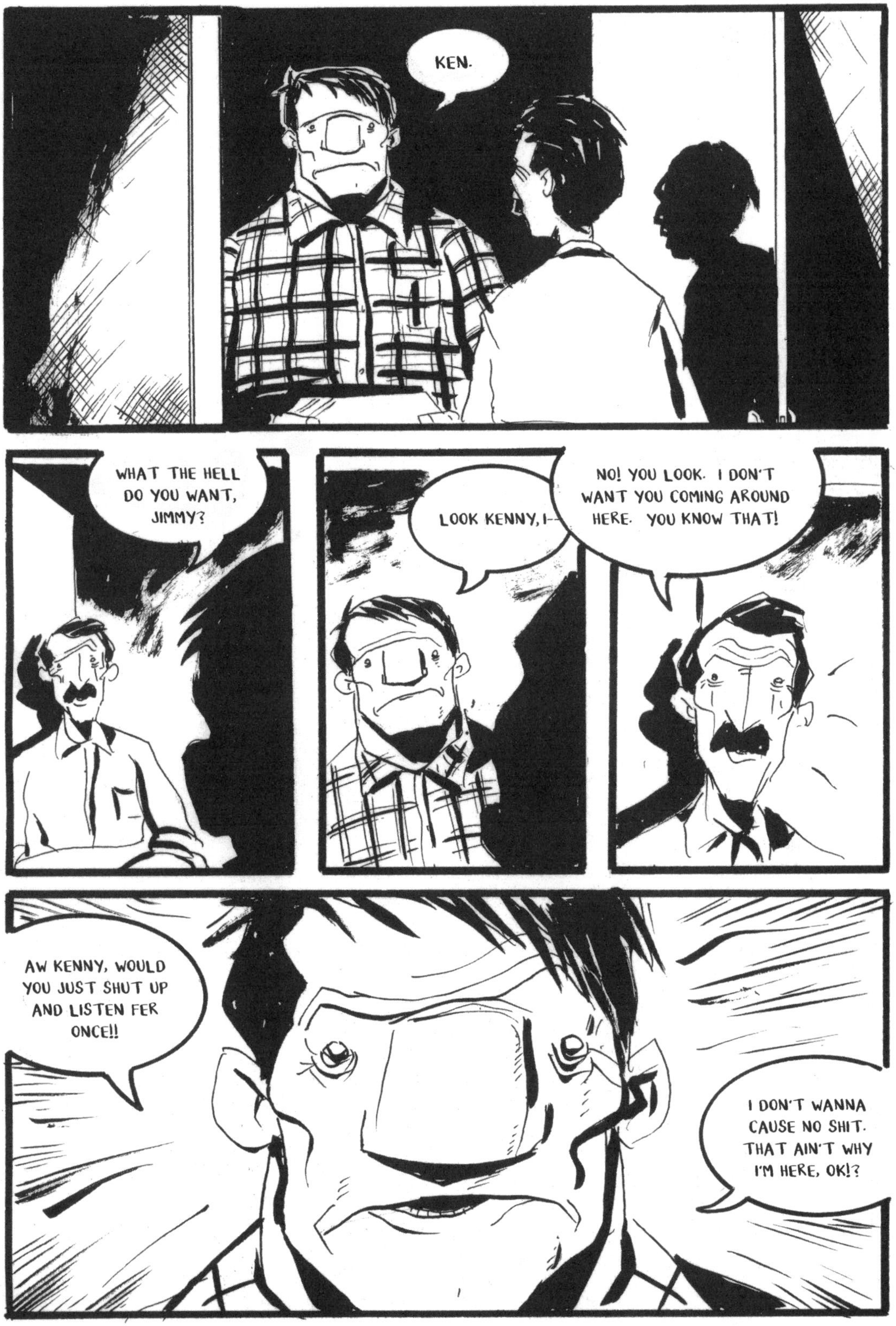
KEN.
WHAT THE HELL DO YOU WANT, JIMMY?
LOOK KENNY, I--
NO! YOU LOOK. I DON'T WANT YOU COMING AROUND HERE. YOU KNOW THAT!
AW KENNY, WOULD YOU JUST SHUT UP AND LISTEN FER ONCE!!
I DON'T WANNA CAUSE NO SHIT. THAT AIN'T WHY I'M HERE, OK!?

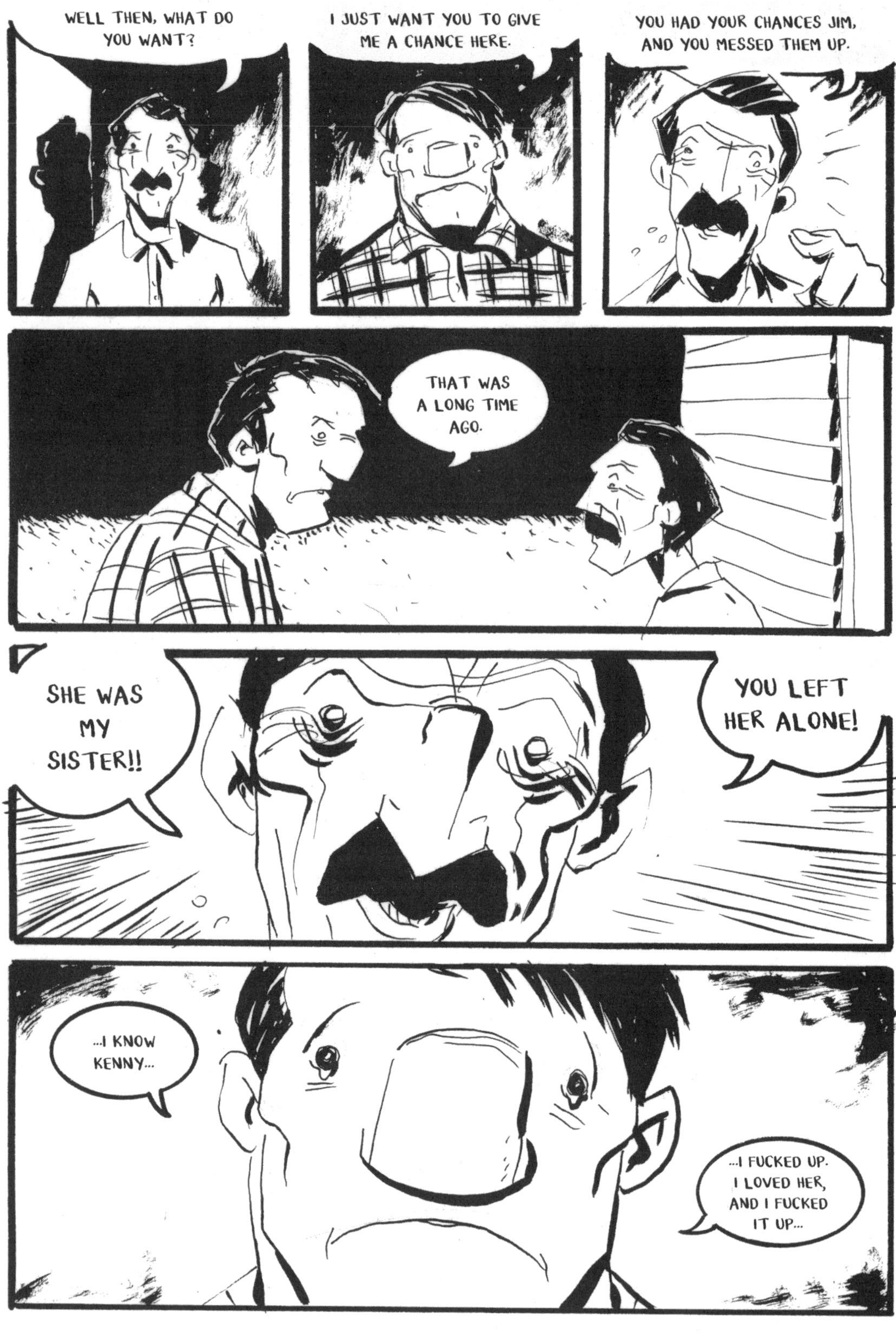
WELL THEN, WHAT DO YOU WANT?
I JUST WANT YOU TO GIVE ME A CHANCE HERE.
YOU HAD YOUR CHANCES JIM, AND YOU MESSED THEM UP.
THAT WAS A LONG TIME AGO.
SHE WAS MY SISTER!!
YOU LEFT HER ALONE!
...I KNOW KENNY...
...I FUCKED UP. I LOVED HER, AND I FUCKED IT UP...

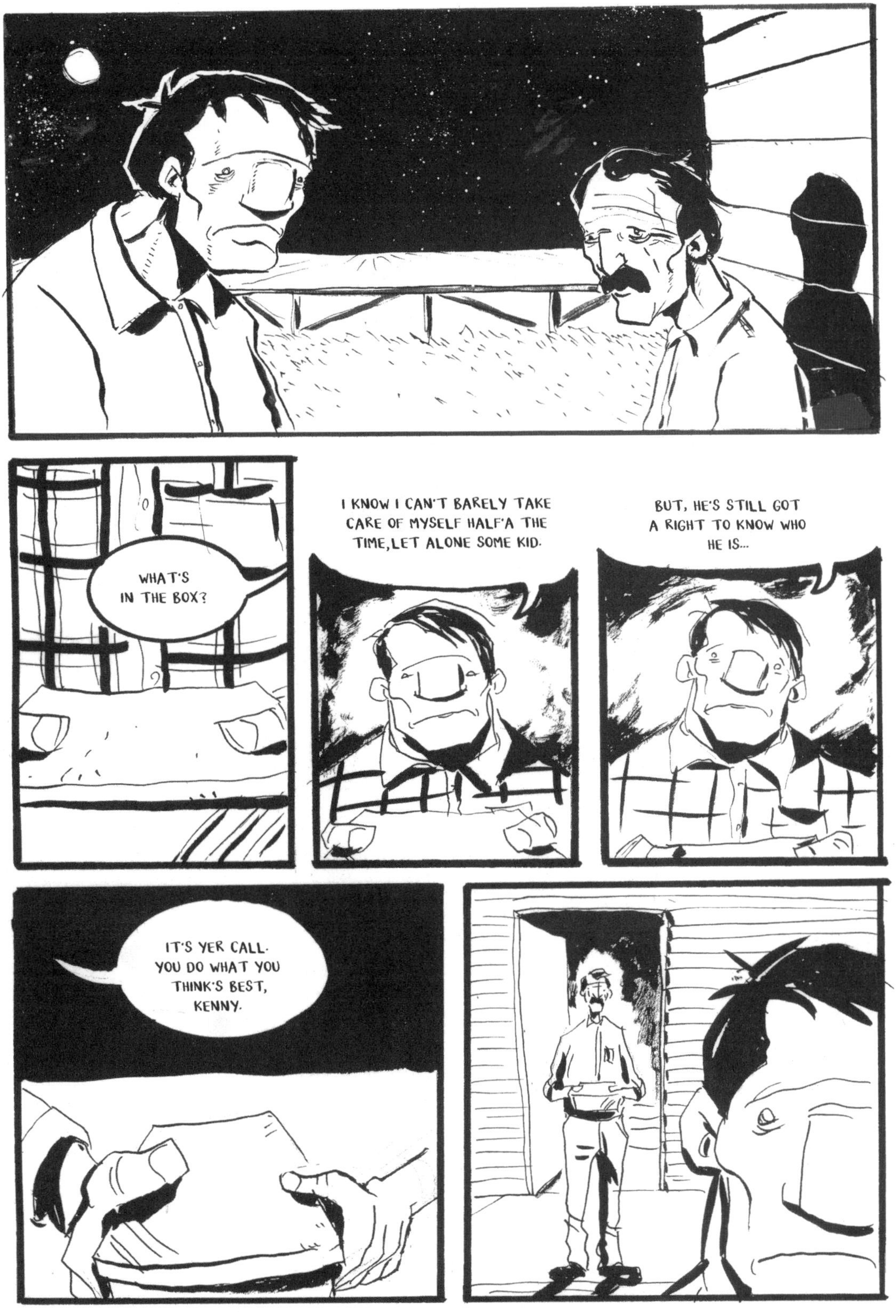
WHAT'S IN THE BOX?
I KNOW I CAN'T BARELY TAKE CARE OF MYSELF HALF'A THE TIME, LET ALONE SOME KID.
BUT, HE'S STILL GOT A RIGHT TO KNOW WHO HE IS...
IT'S YER CALL. YOU DO WHAT YOU THINK'S BEST, KENNY.

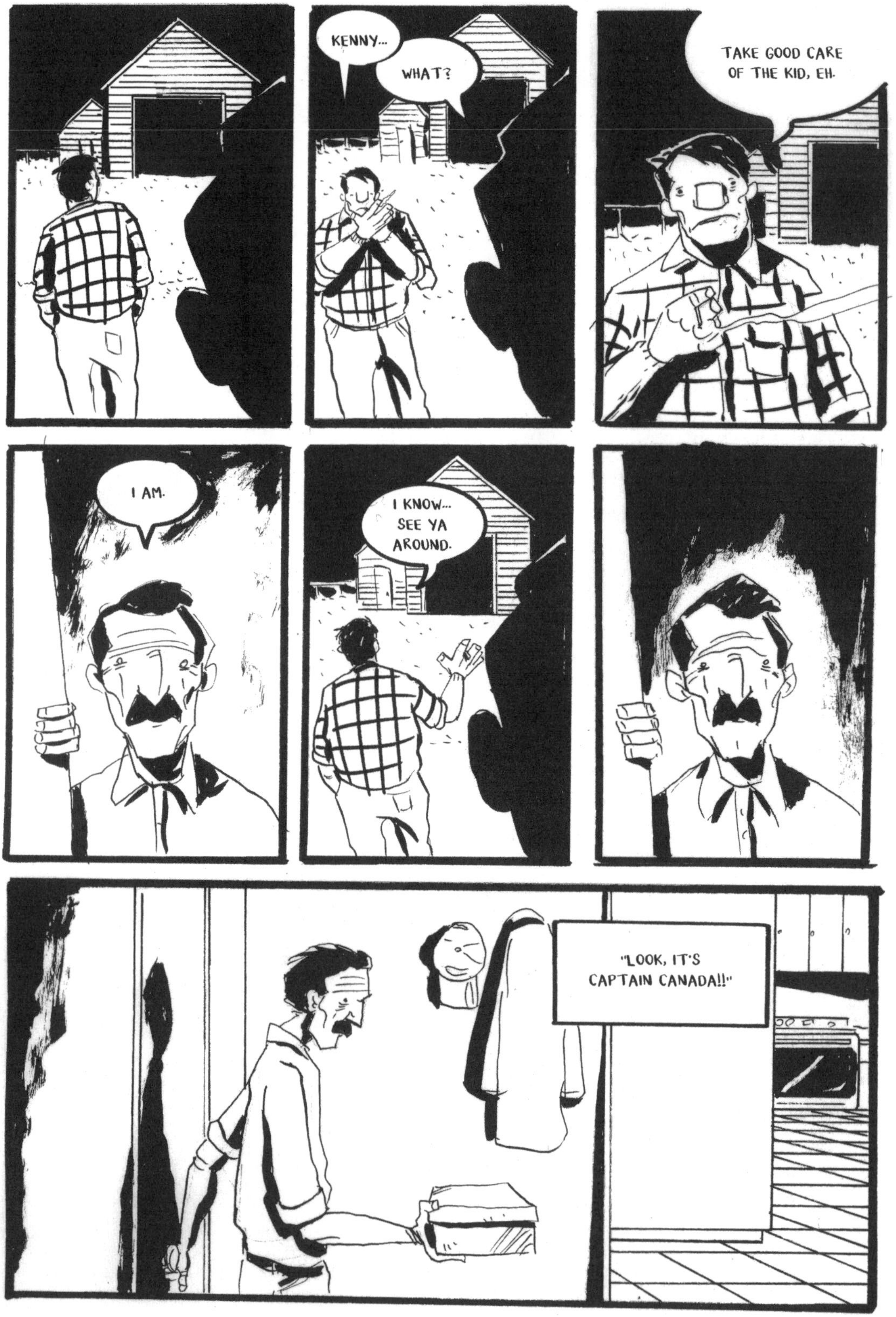
KENNY...
WHAT?
TAKE GOOD CARE OF THE KID, EH.
I AM.
I KNOW... SEE YA AROUND.
"LOOK, IT'S CAPTAIN CANADA!!"

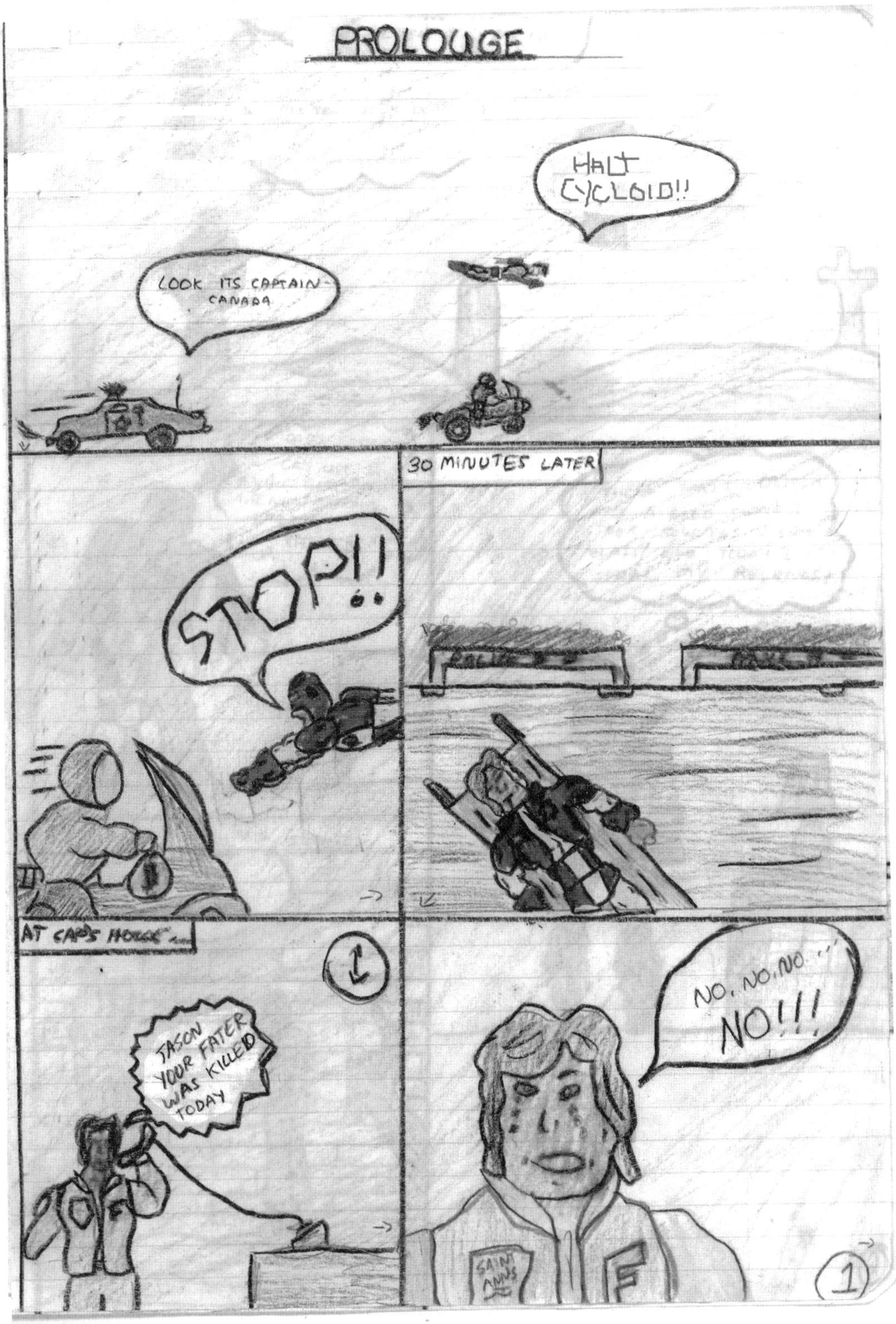
PROLOUGE
HALT CYCLOID!!
LOOK ITS CAPTAIN CANADA
STOP!!
30 MINUTES LATER
AT CAP'S HOUSE....
JASON YOUR FATER WAS KILLED TODAY
NO, NO, NO...
NO!!!
SAINT ANNS
1

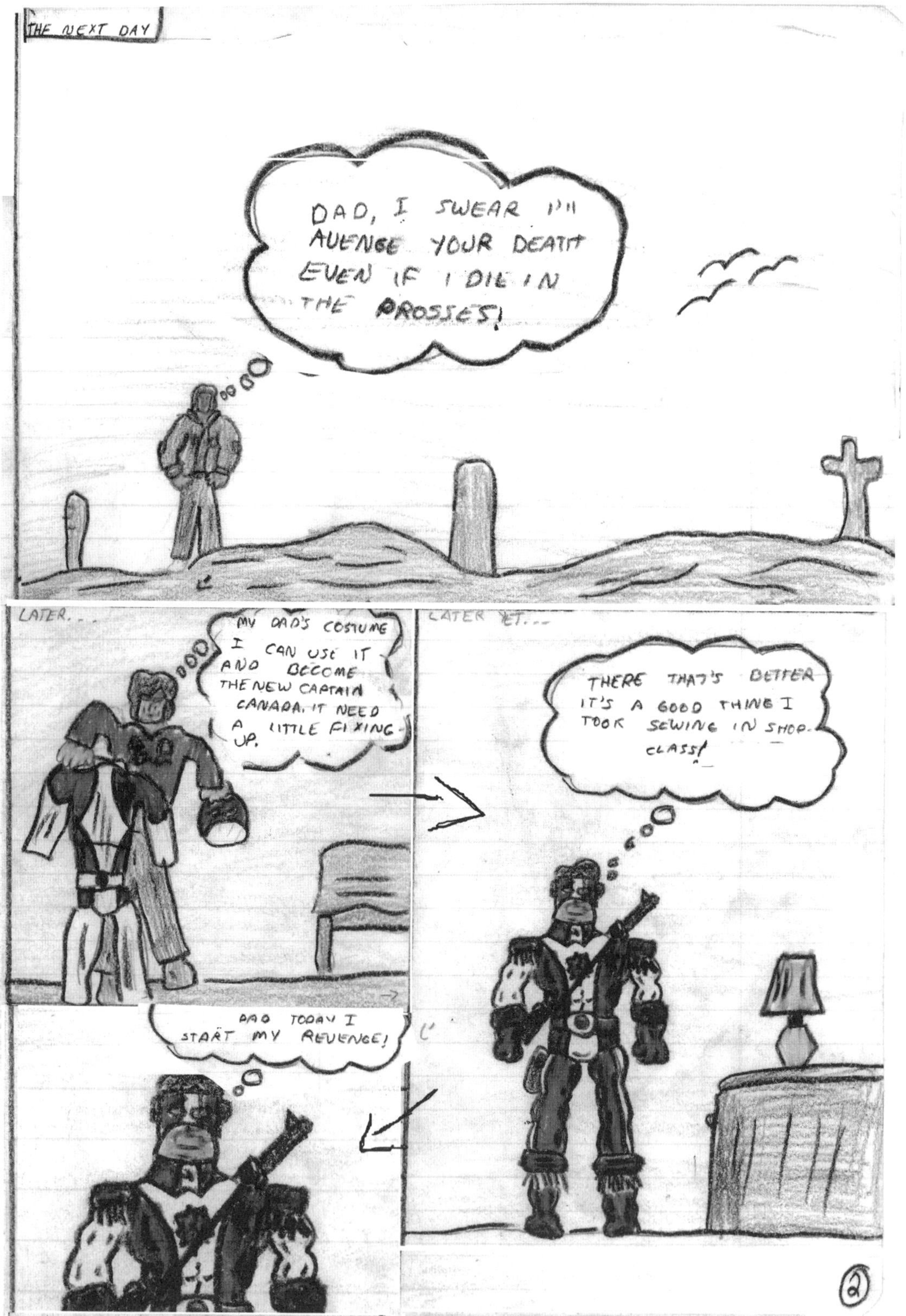
THE NEXT DAY
DAD, I SWEAR I'll AVENGE YOUR DEATH EVEN IF I DIE IN THE PROSSES!
LATER...
MY DAD'S COSTUME I CAN USE IT AND BECOME THE NEW CAPTAIN CANADA. IT NEED A LITTLE FIXING UP.
LATER YET...
THERE THAT'S BETTER IT'S A GOOD THING I TOOK SEWING IN SHOP CLASS!
AND TODAY I START MY REVENGE!
2

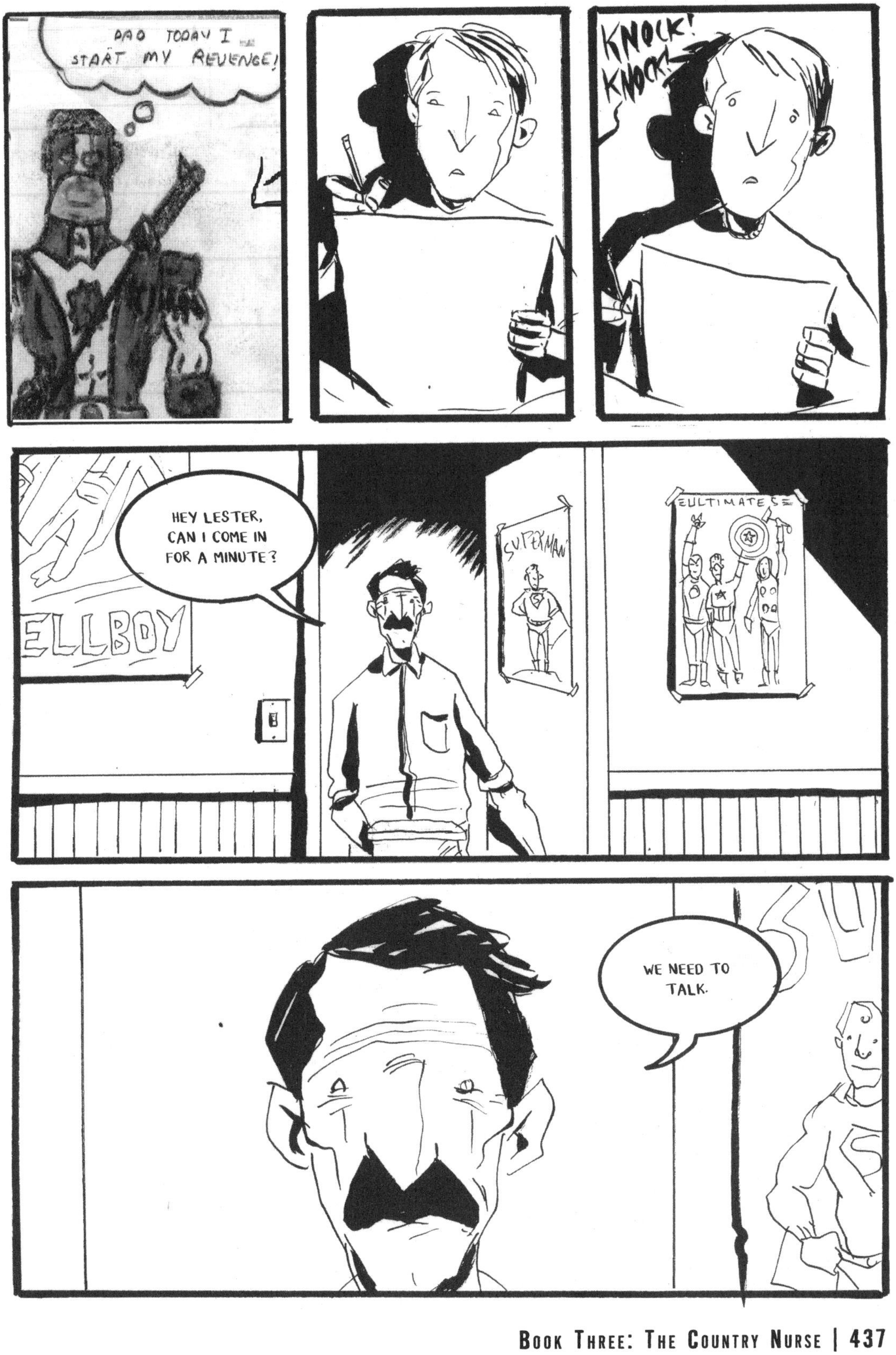
DAD TODAY I START MY REVENGE!
KNOCK! KNOCK!
HEY LESTER, CAN I COME IN FOR A MINUTE?
ELLBOY
SUPERMAN
ULTIMATES
WE NEED TO TALK.

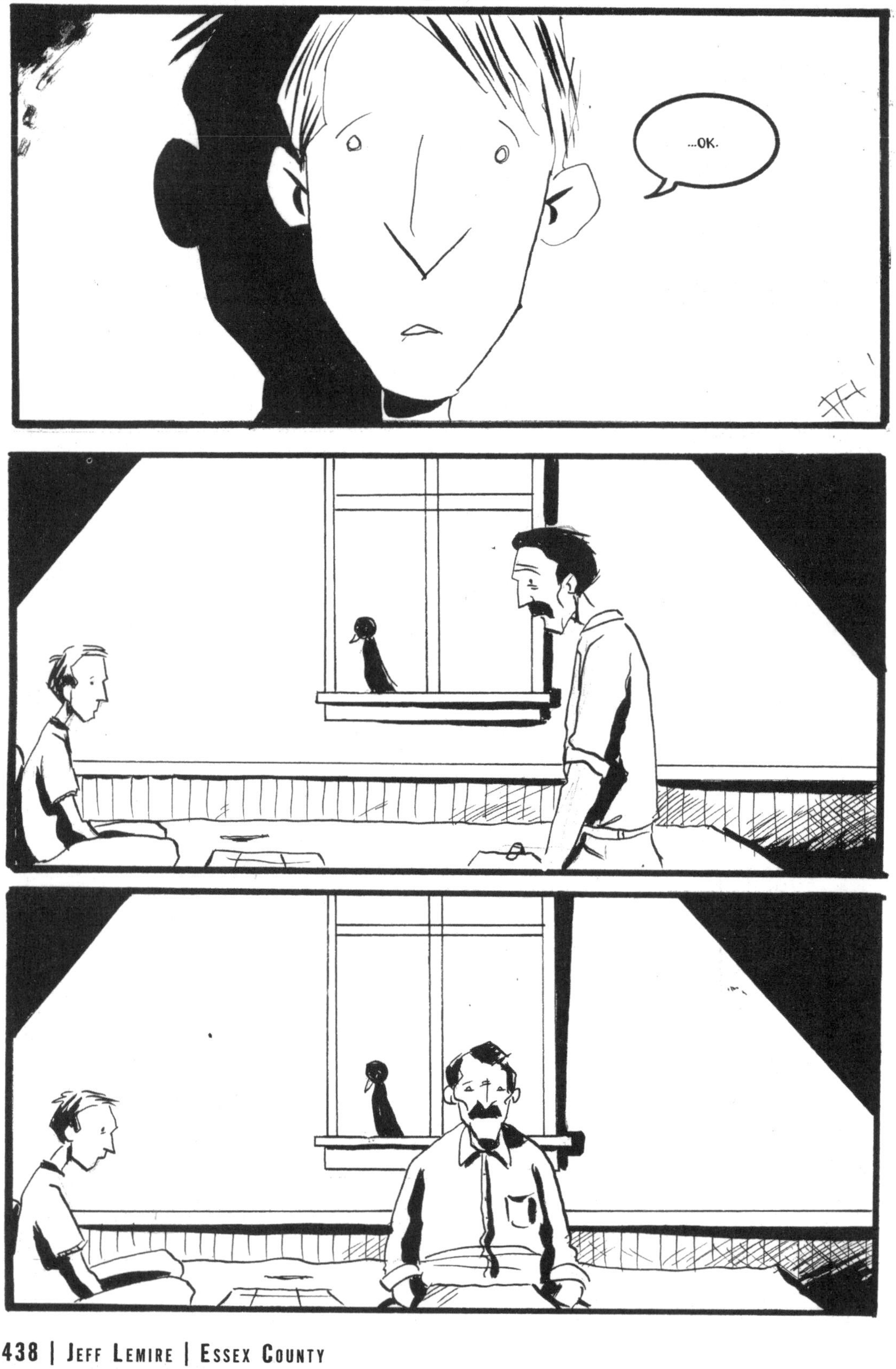
...OK.

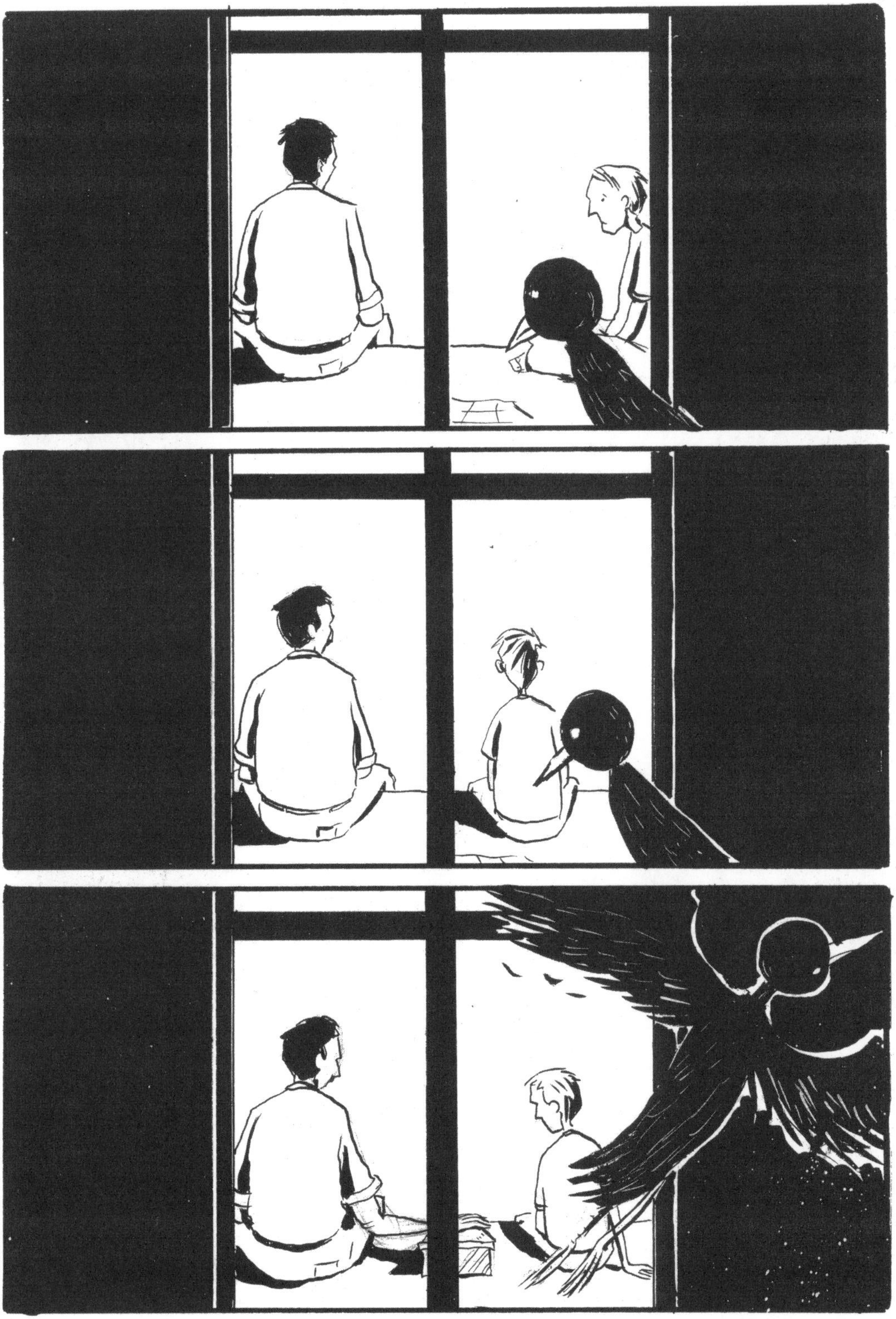

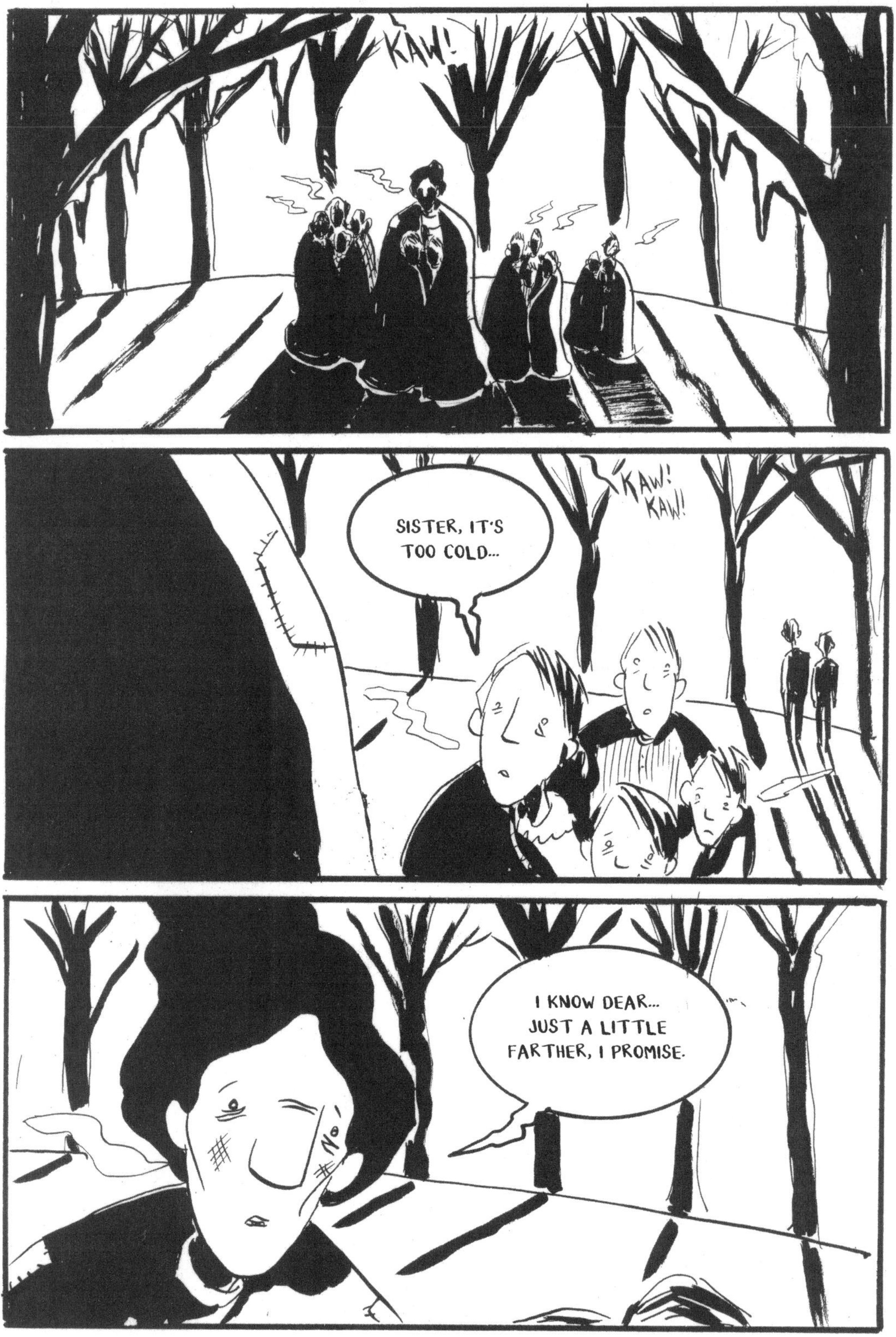
KAW!
SISTER, IT'S TOO COLD...
KAW! KAW!
I KNOW DEAR... JUST A LITTLE FARTHER, I PROMISE.

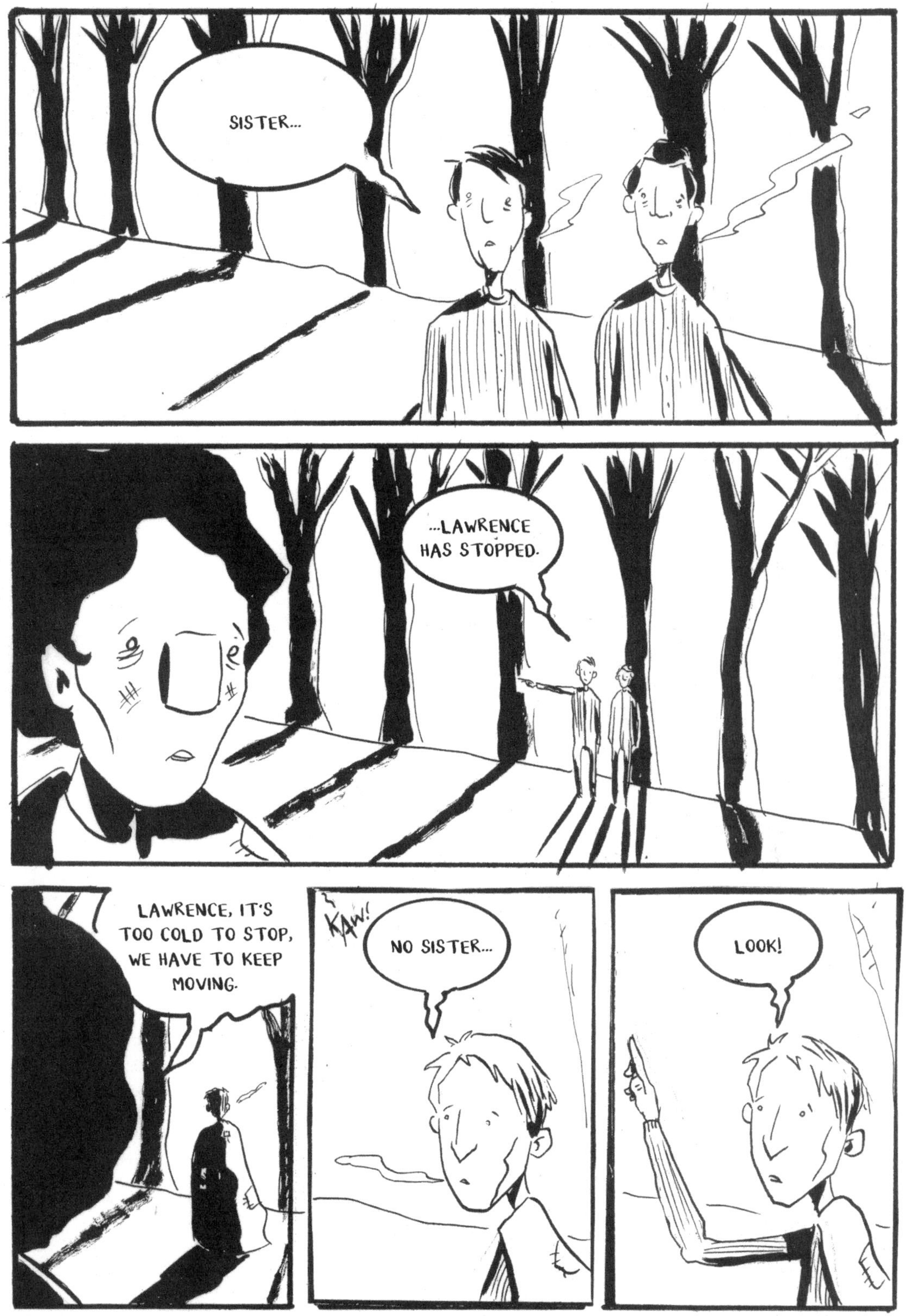
SISTER...
...LAWRENCE HAS STOPPED.
LAWRENCE, IT'S TOO COLD TO STOP, WE HAVE TO KEEP MOVING.
KAW!
NO SISTER...
LOOK!

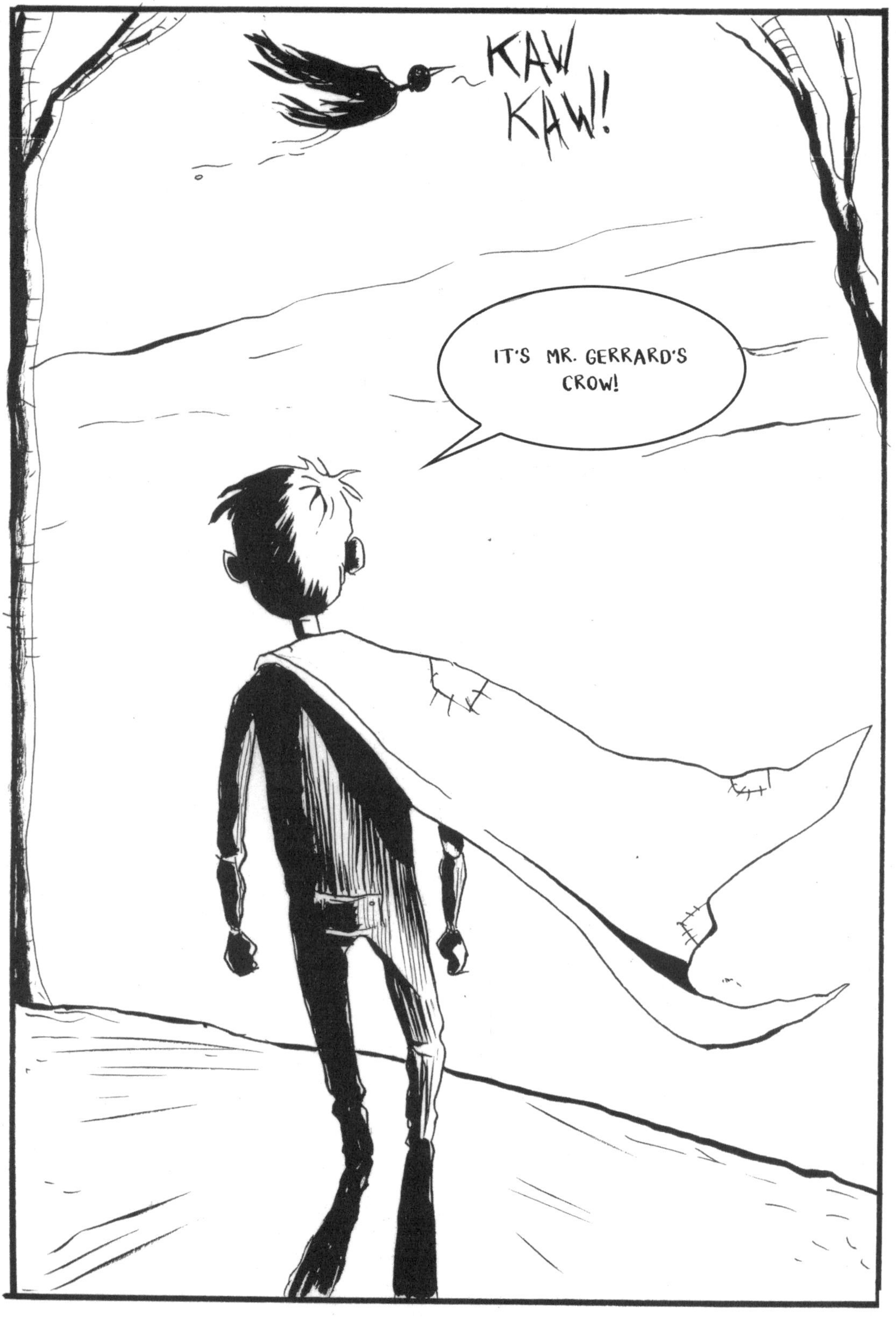
KAW KAW!
IT'S MR. GERRARD'S CROW!

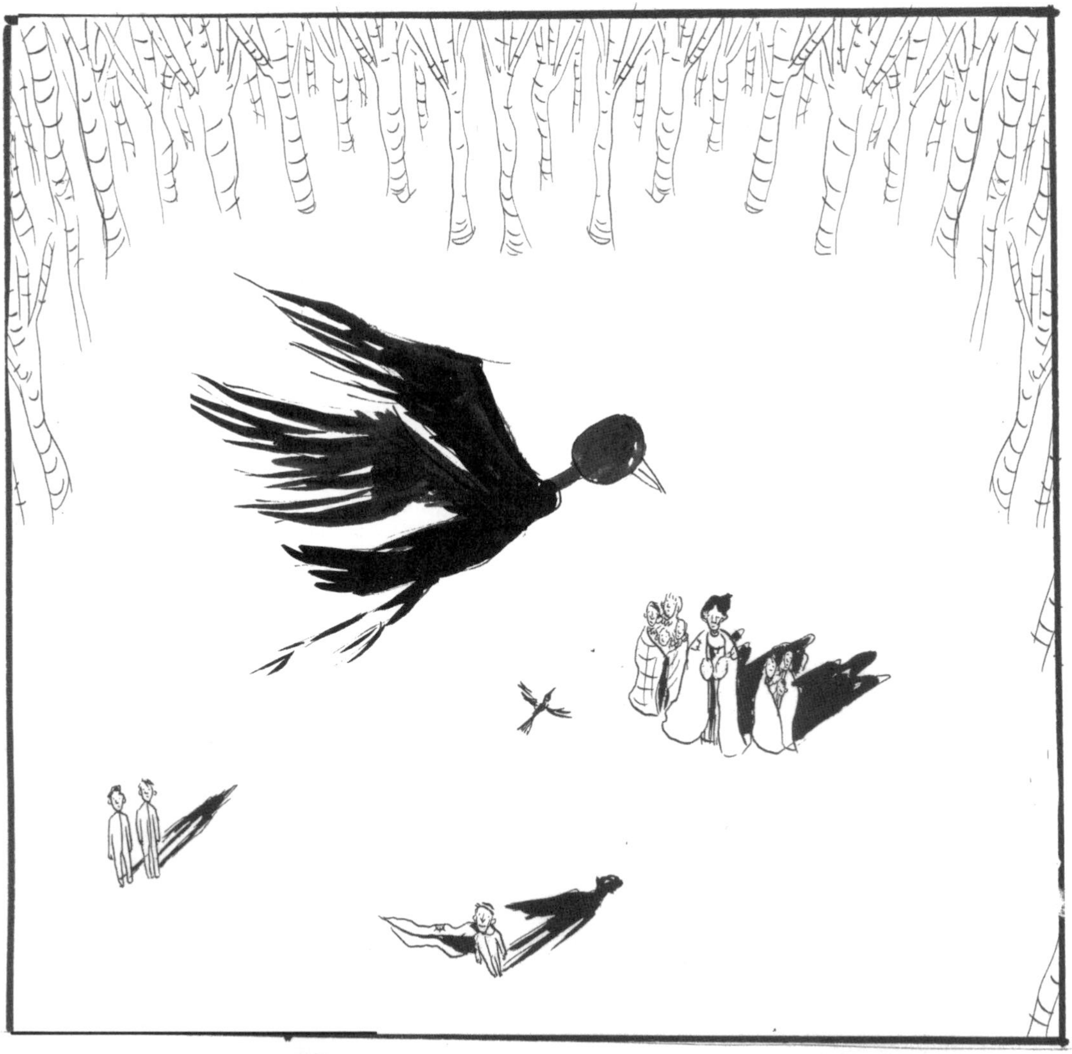

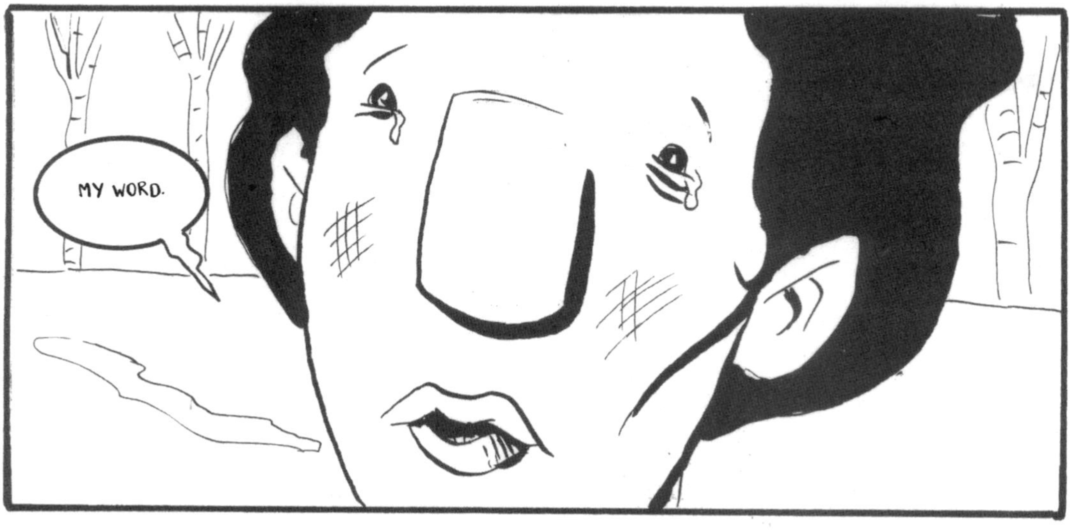
MY WORD.

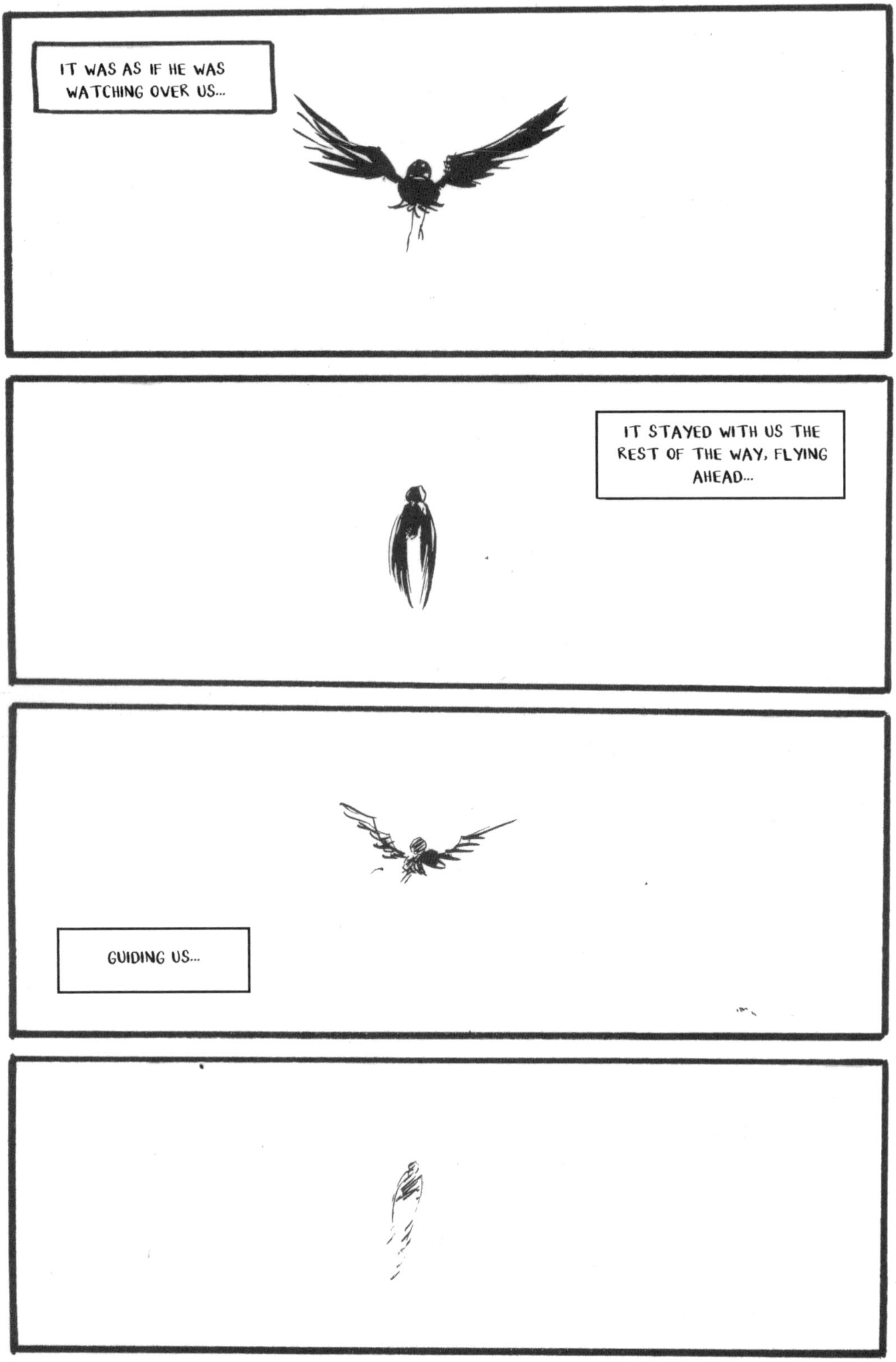
IT WAS AS IF HE WAS WATCHING OVER US...
IT STAYED WITH US THE REST OF THE WAY, FLYING AHEAD...
GUIDING US...

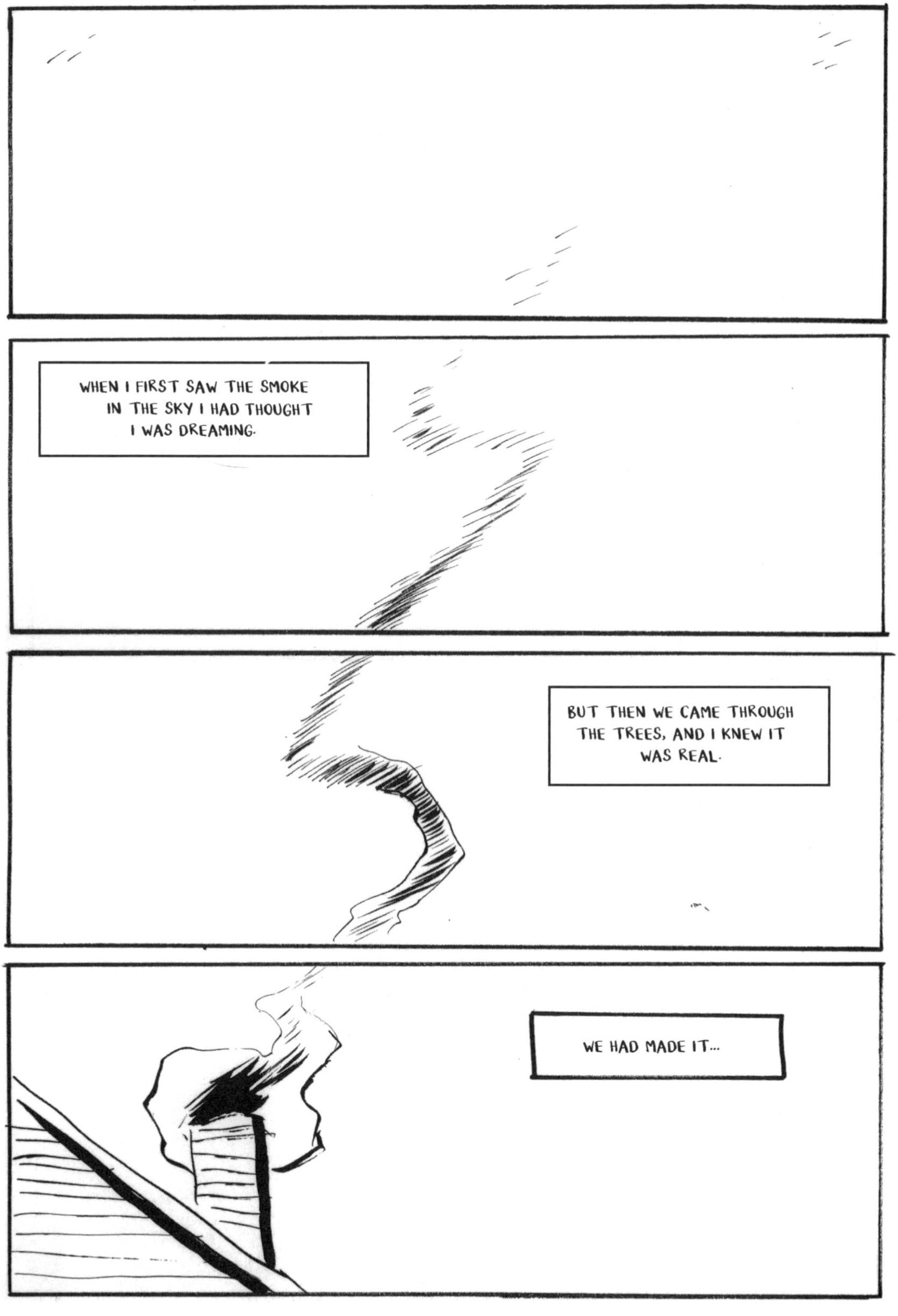
WHEN I FIRST SAW THE SMOKE IN THE SKY I HAD THOUGHT I WAS DREAMING.
BUT THEN WE CAME THROUGH THE TREES, AND I KNEW IT WAS REAL.
WE HAD MADE IT...

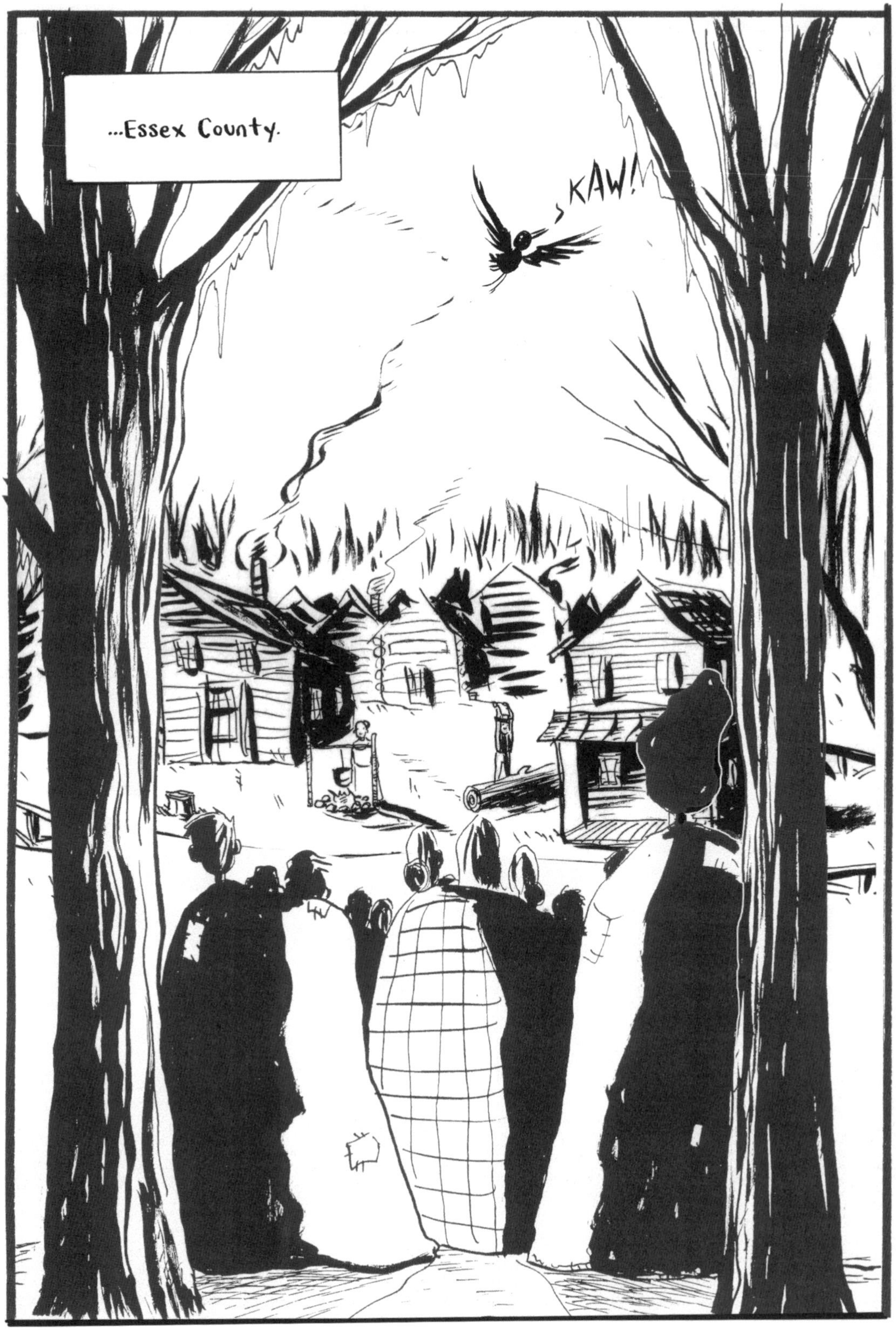
...Essex County.
KAW!

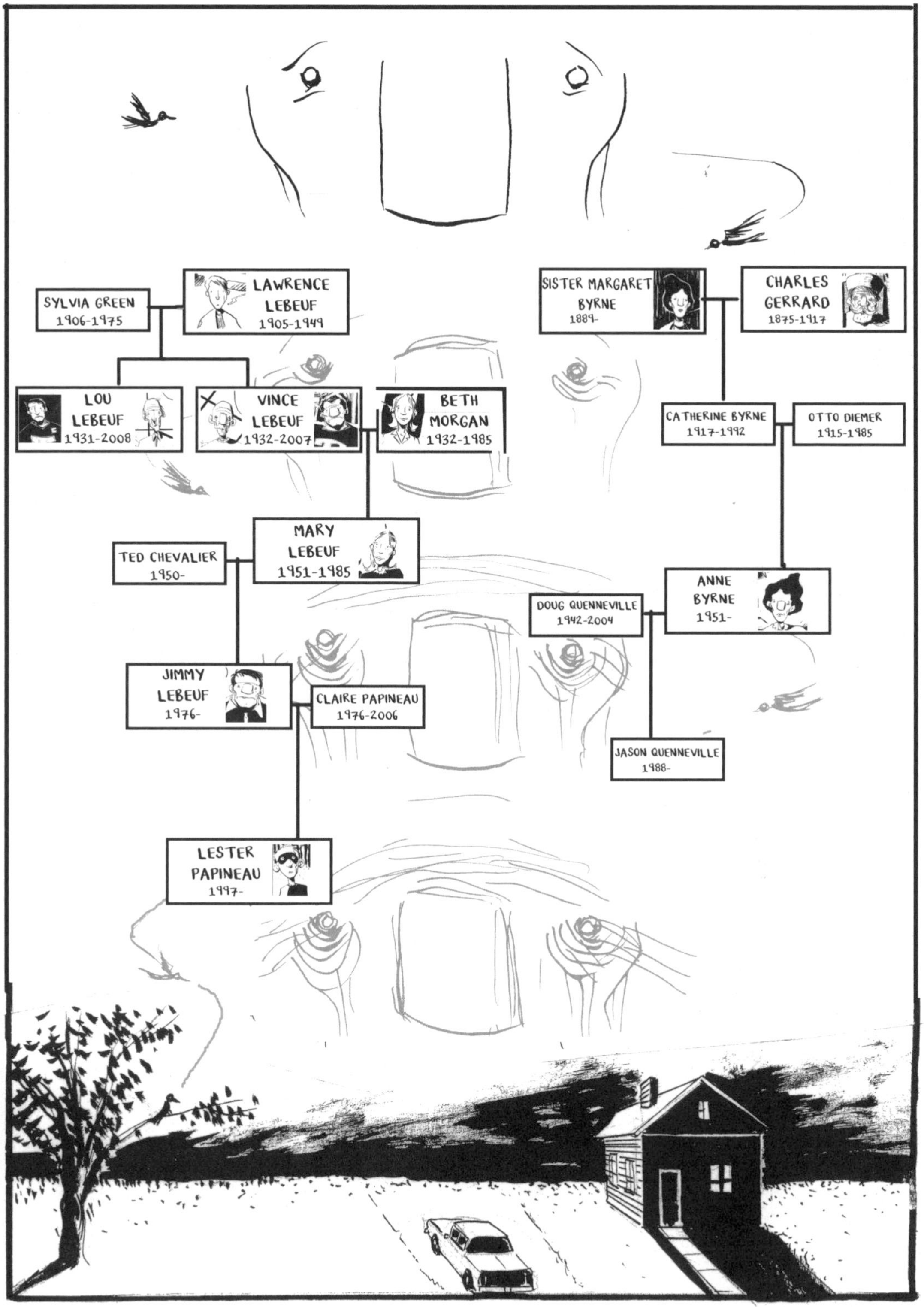
SYLVIA GREEN
1906-1975
LAWRENCE LEBEUF
1905-1949
SISTER MARGARET BYRNE
1889-
CHARLES GERRARD
1875-1917
LOU LEBEUF
1931-2008
VINCE LEBEUF
1932-2007
BETH MORGAN
1932-1985
CATHERINE BYRNE
1917-1992
OTTO DIEMER
1915-1985
TED CHEVALIER
1950-
MARY LEBEUF
1951-1985
ANNE BYRNE
1951-
DOUG QUENNEVILLE
1942-2004
JIMMY LEBEUF
1976-
CLAIRE PAPINEAU
1976-2006
JASON QUENNEVILLE
1988-
LESTER PAPINEAU
1997-

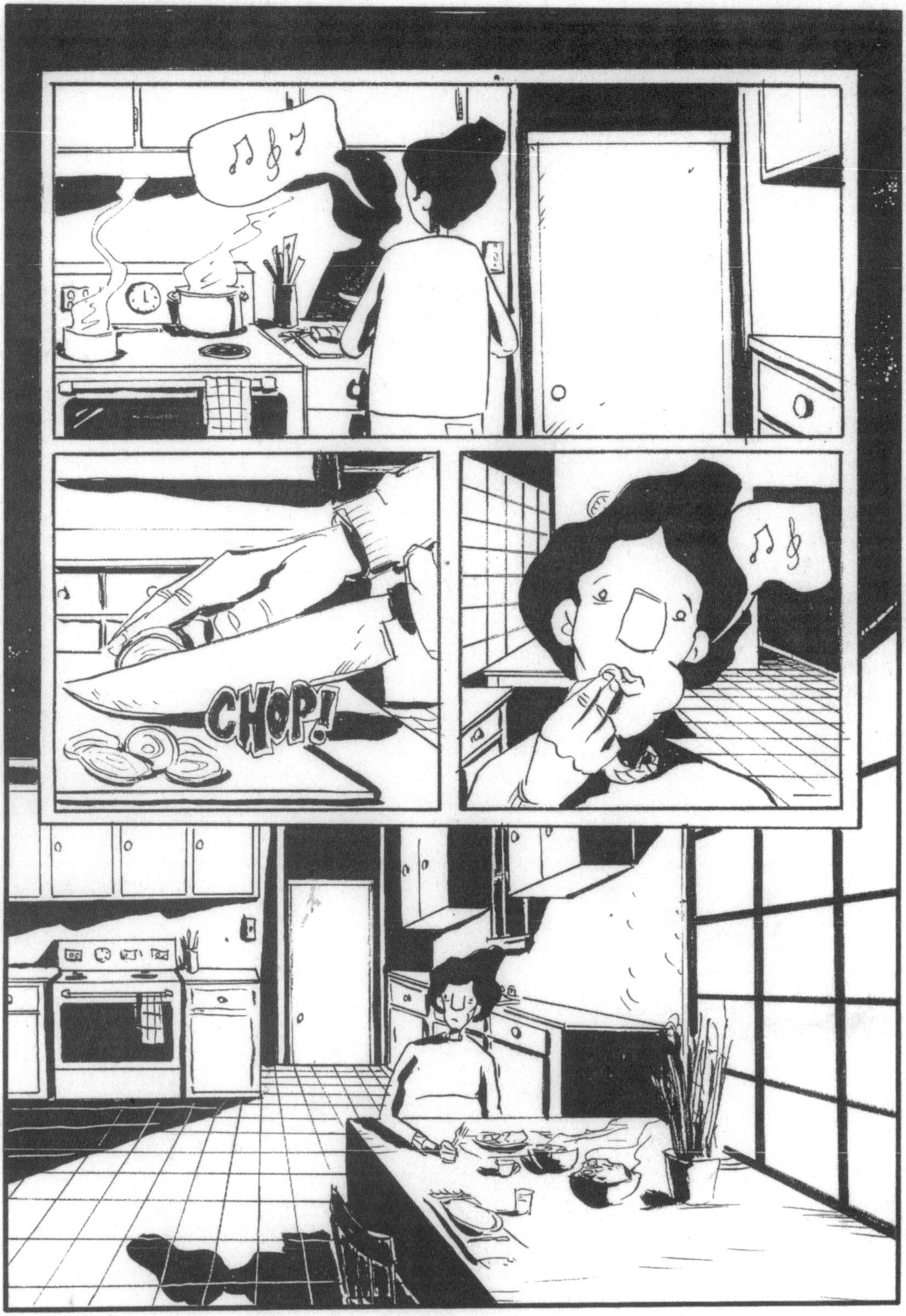
CHOP!

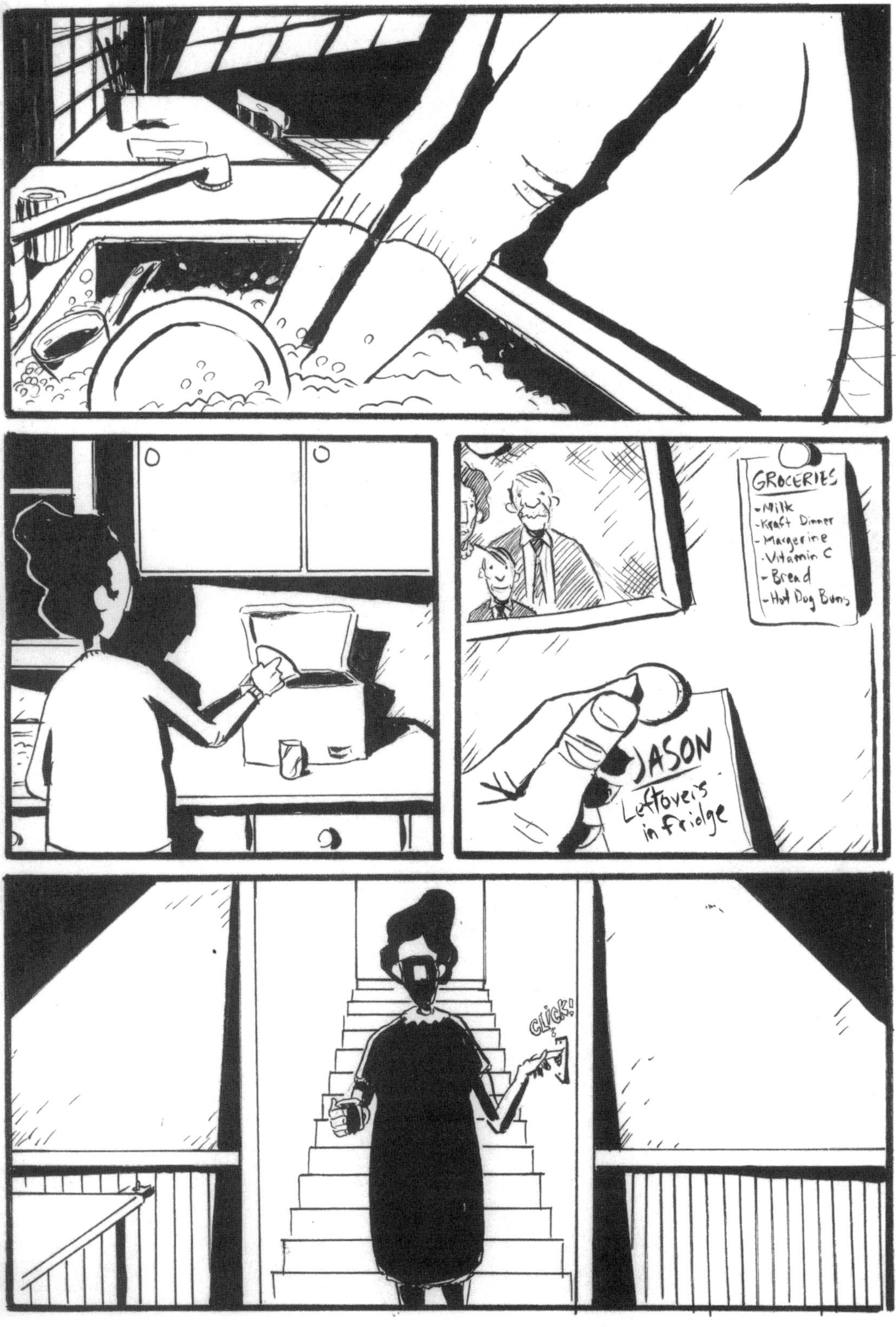
GROCERIES
-Milk
-Kraft Dinner
-Margerine
-Vitamin C
-Bread
-Hot Dog Buns
JASON
Leftovers in Fridge
CLICK!

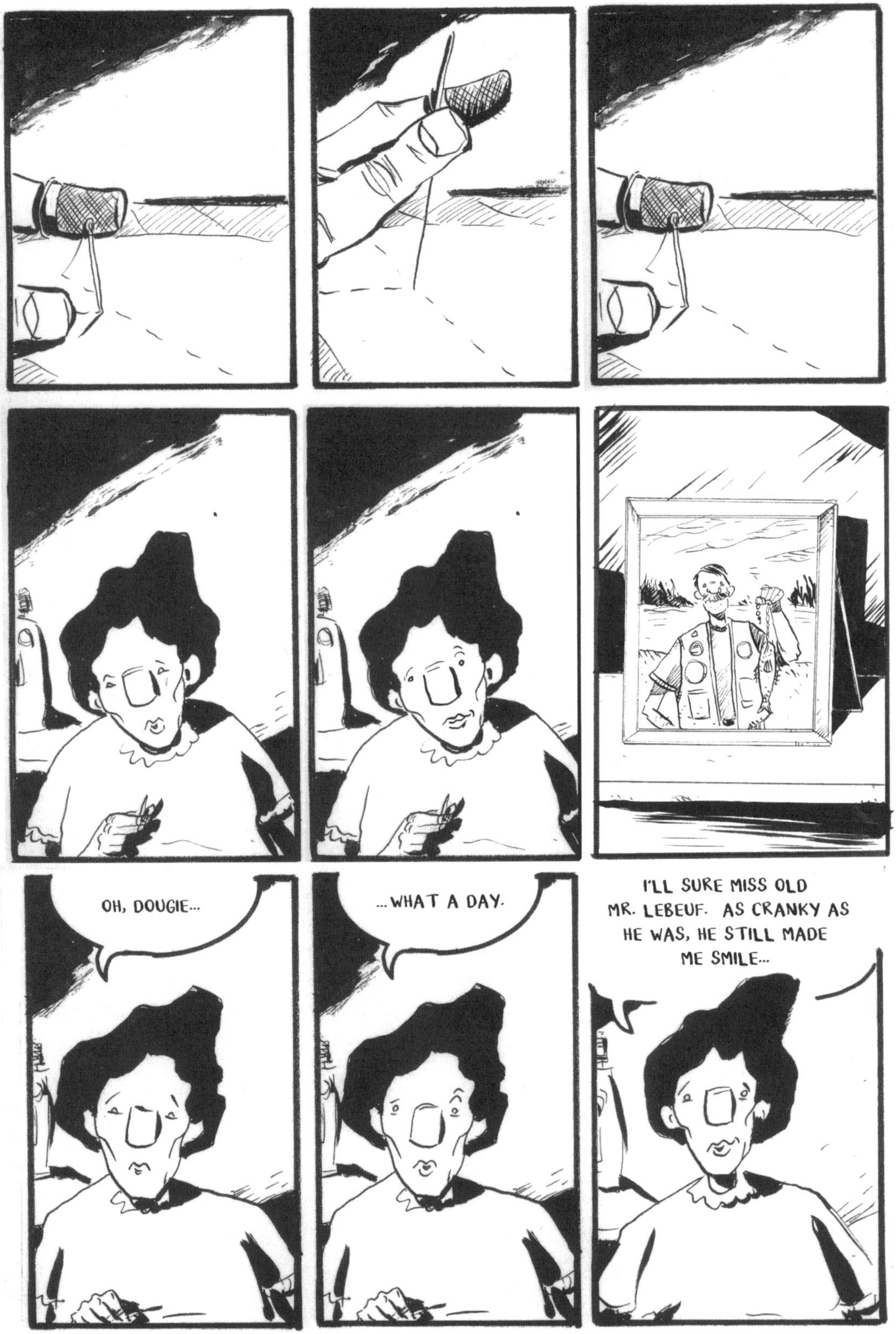
OH, DOUGIE...
...WHAT A DAY.
I'LL SURE MISS OLD MR. LEBEUF. AS CRANKY AS HE WAS, HE STILL MADE ME SMILE...

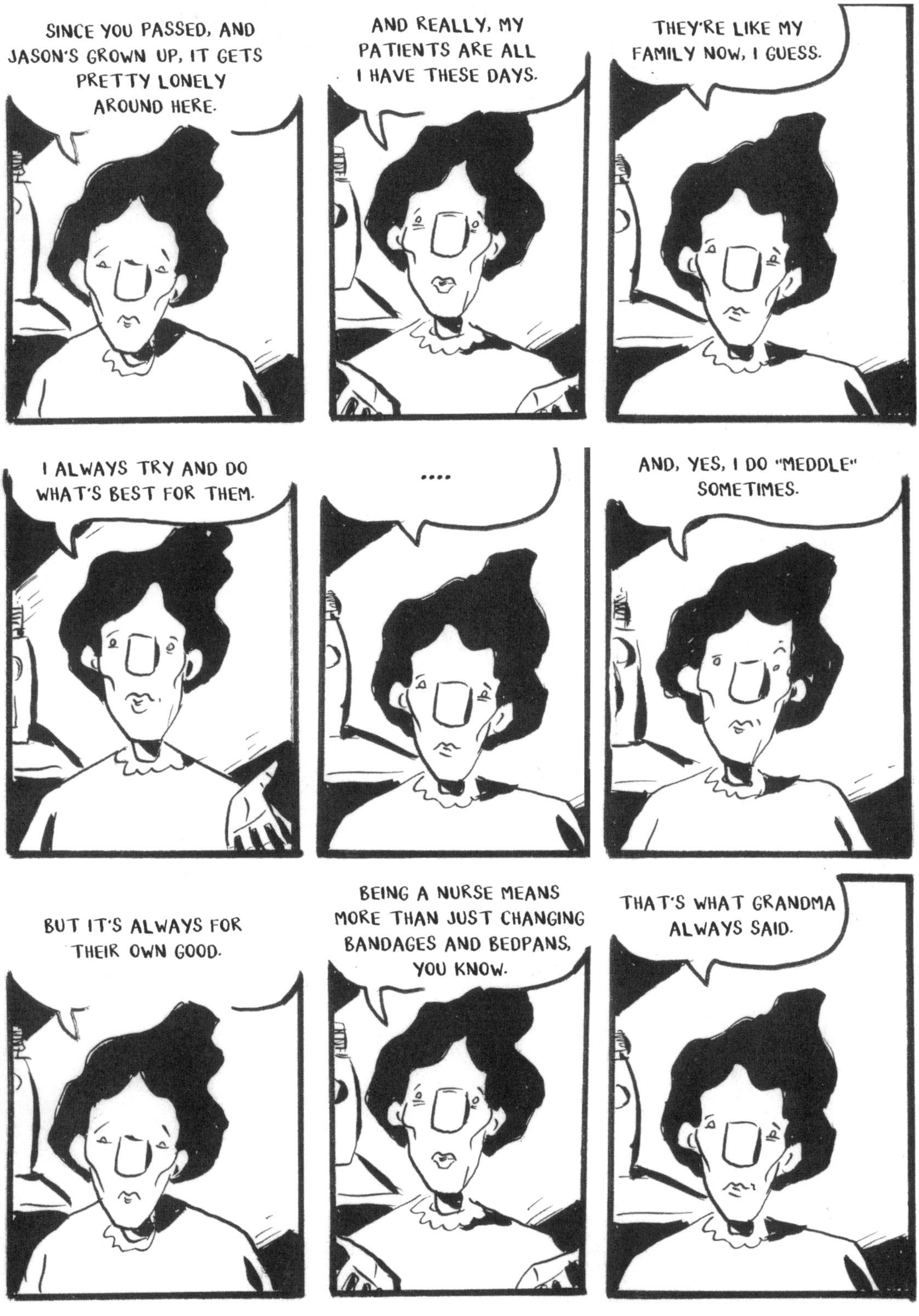
SINCE YOU PASSED, AND JASON'S GROWN UP, IT GETS PRETTY LONELY AROUND HERE.
AND REALLY, MY PATIENTS ARE ALL I HAVE THESE DAYS.
THEY'RE LIKE MY FAMILY NOW, I GUESS.
I ALWAYS TRY AND DO WHAT'S BEST FOR THEM.
....
AND, YES, I DO "MEDDLE" SOMETIMES.
BUT IT'S ALWAYS FOR THEIR OWN GOOD.
BEING A NURSE MEANS MORE THAN JUST CHANGING BANDAGES AND BEDPANS, YOU KNOW.
THAT'S WHAT GRANDMA ALWAYS SAID.

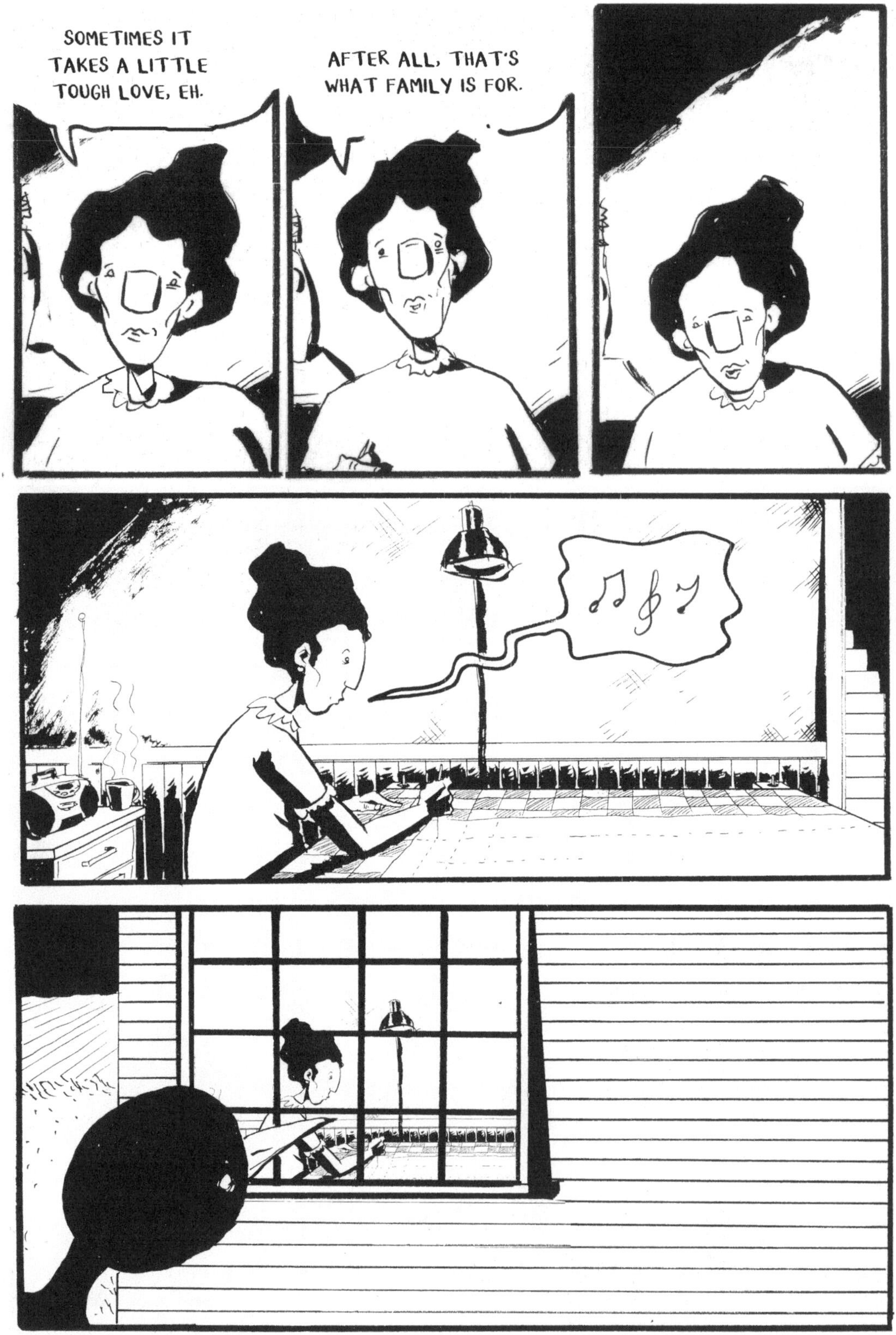
SOMETIMES IT TAKES A LITTLE TOUGH LOVE, EH.
AFTER ALL, THAT'S WHAT FAMILY IS FOR.

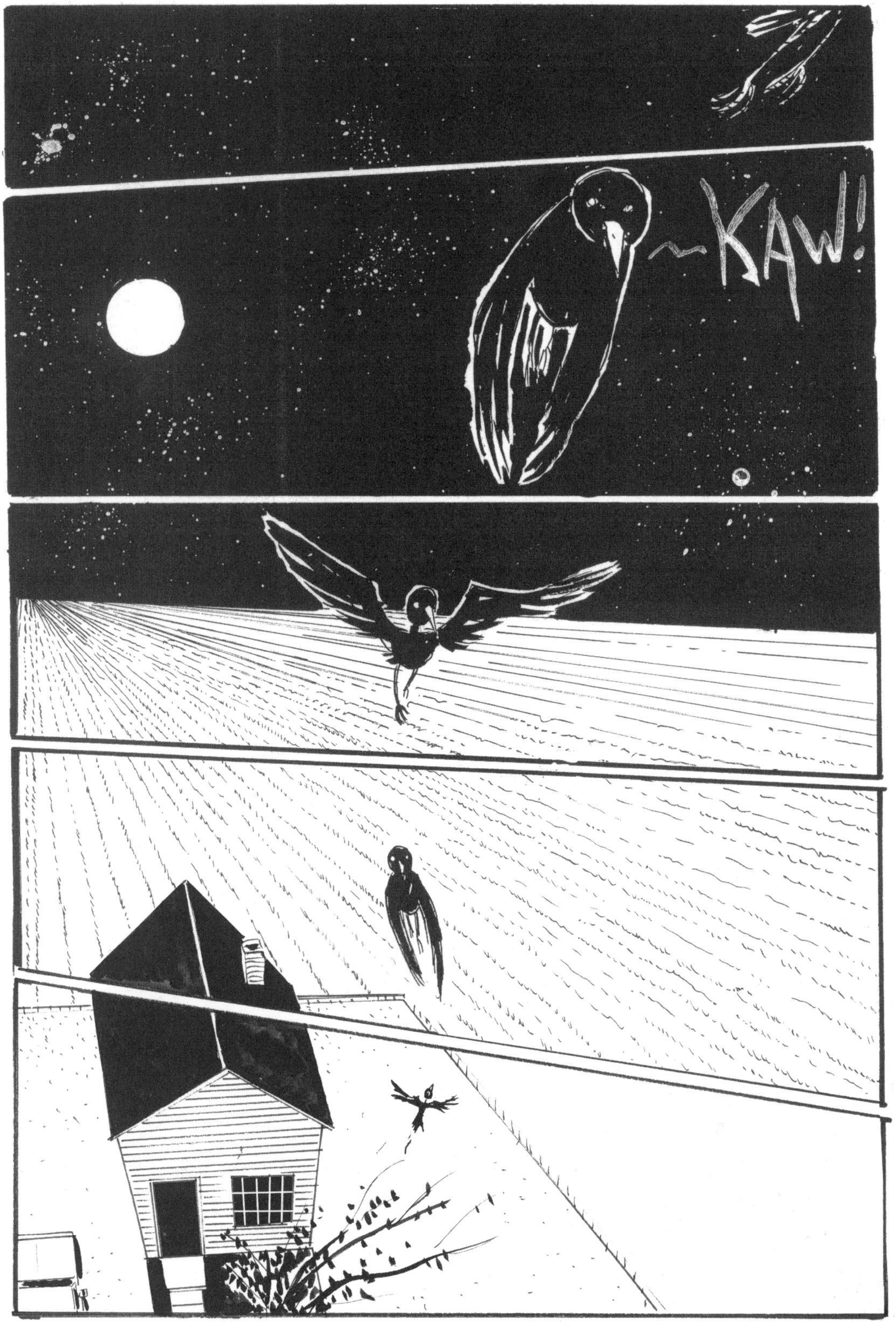
KAW!

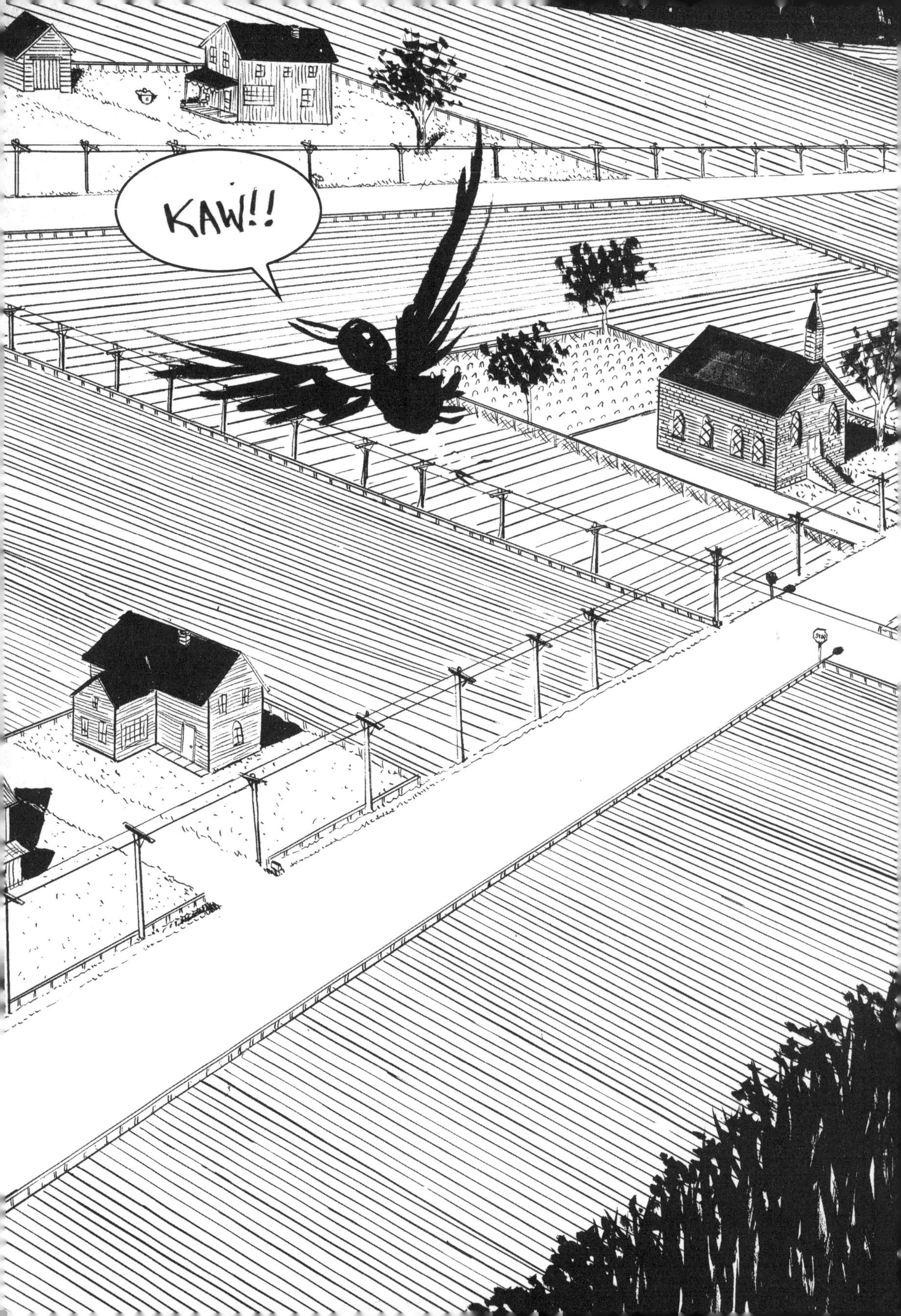
KAW!!

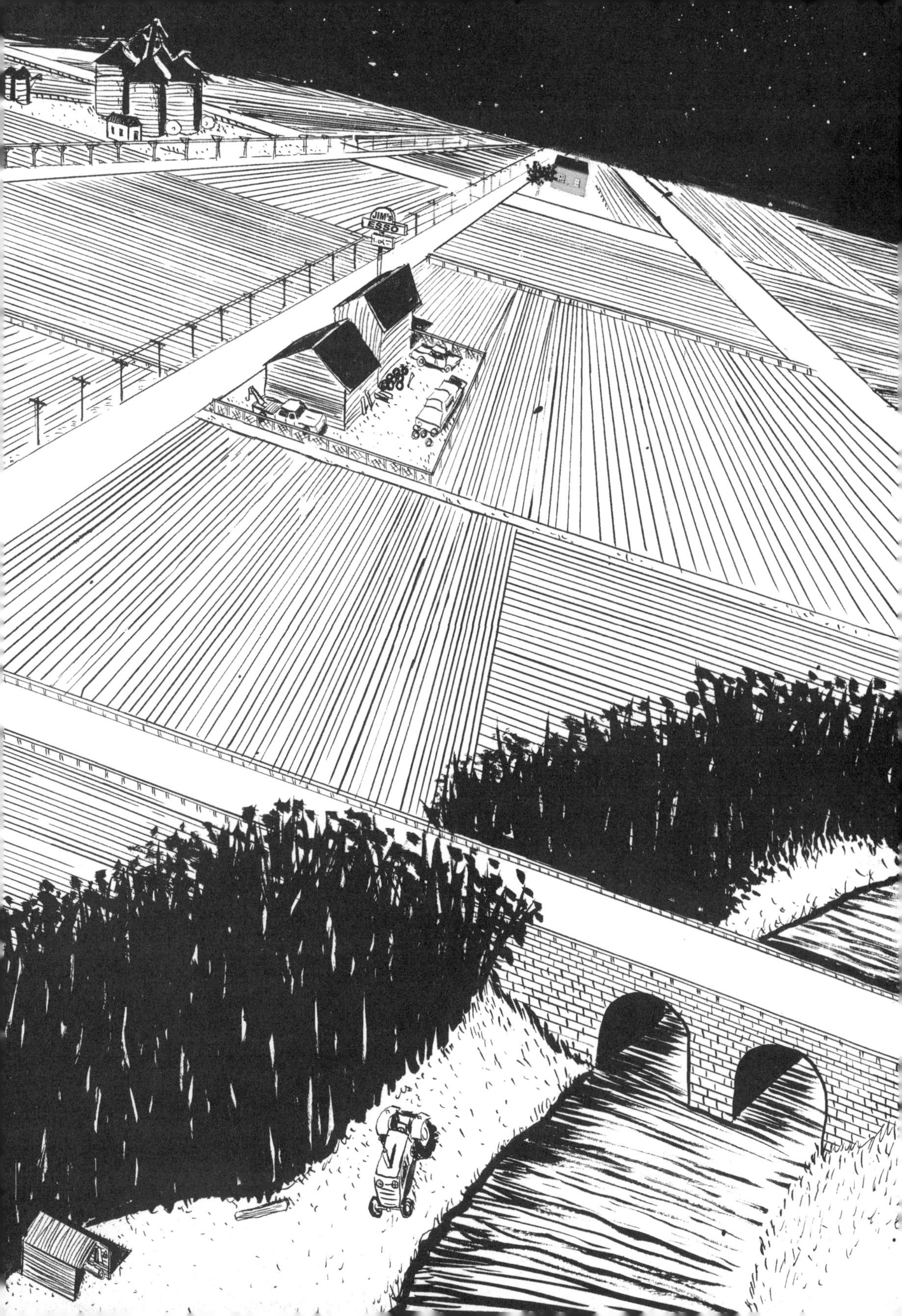
JIM's
ESSO

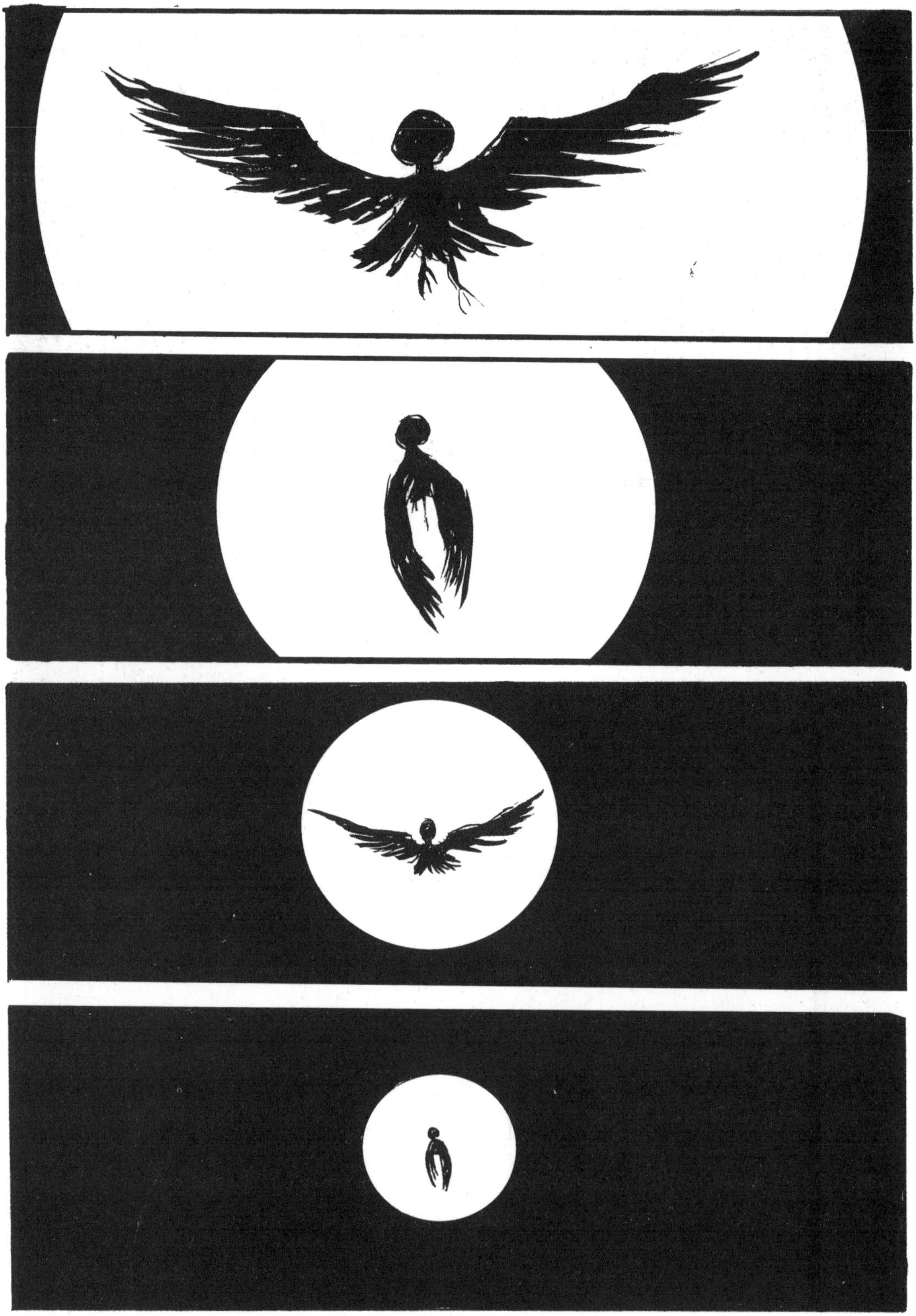

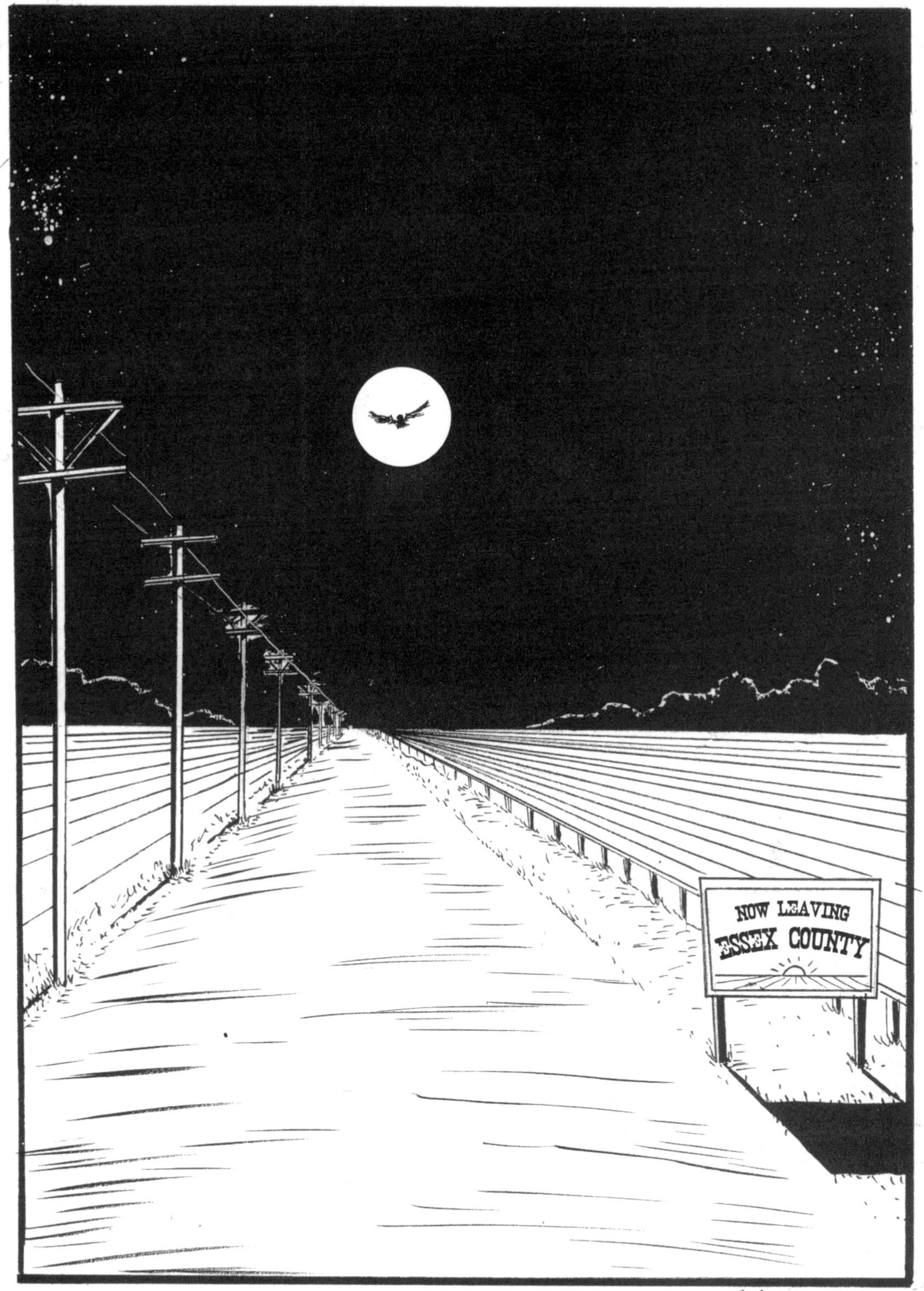
NOW LEAVING
ESSEX COUNTY

J. Lemire 2005 - 2008

THE ESSEX COUNTY BOXING CLUB

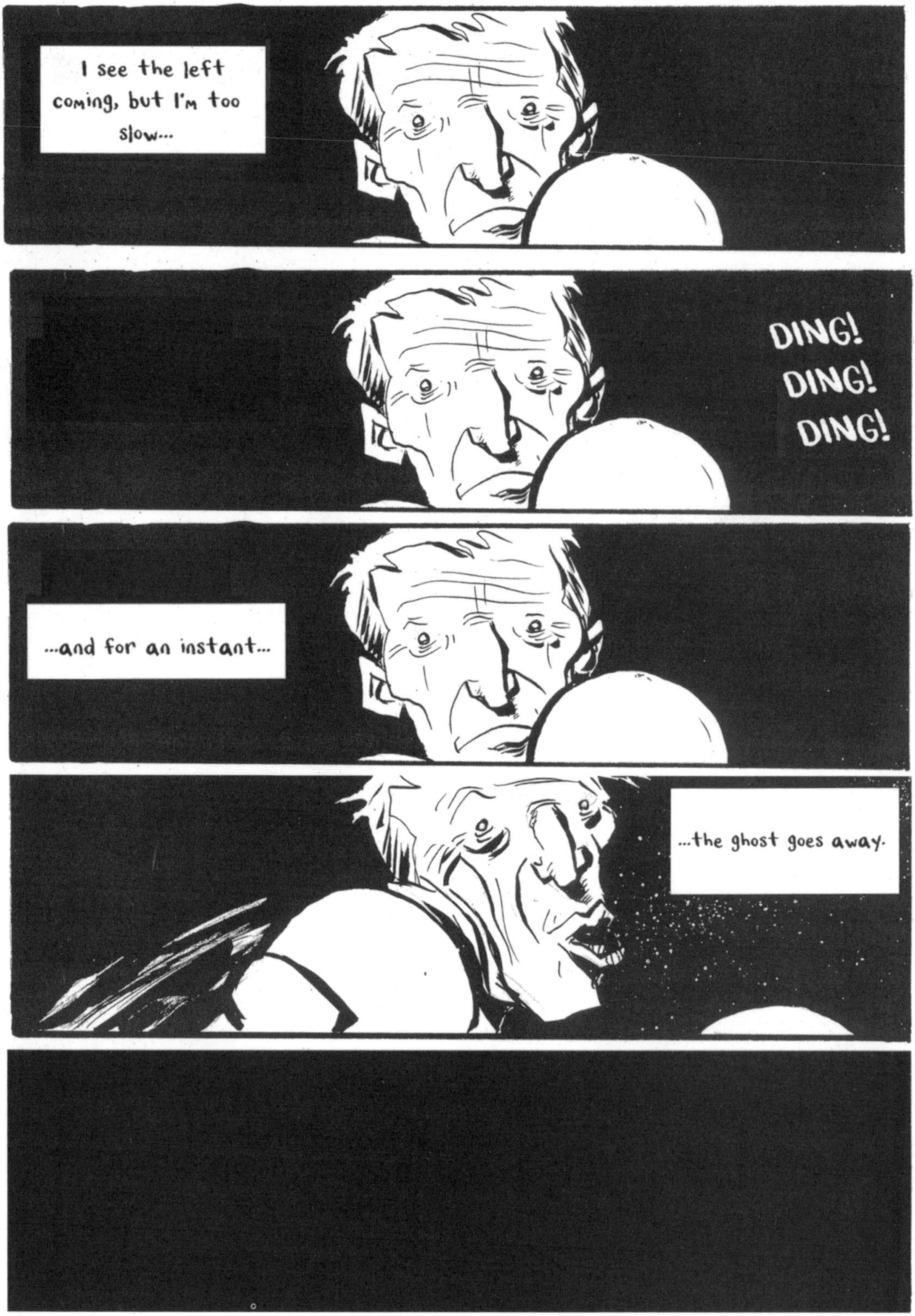
I see the left coming, but I'm too slow...
DING!
DING!
DING!
...and for an instant...
...the ghost goes away.

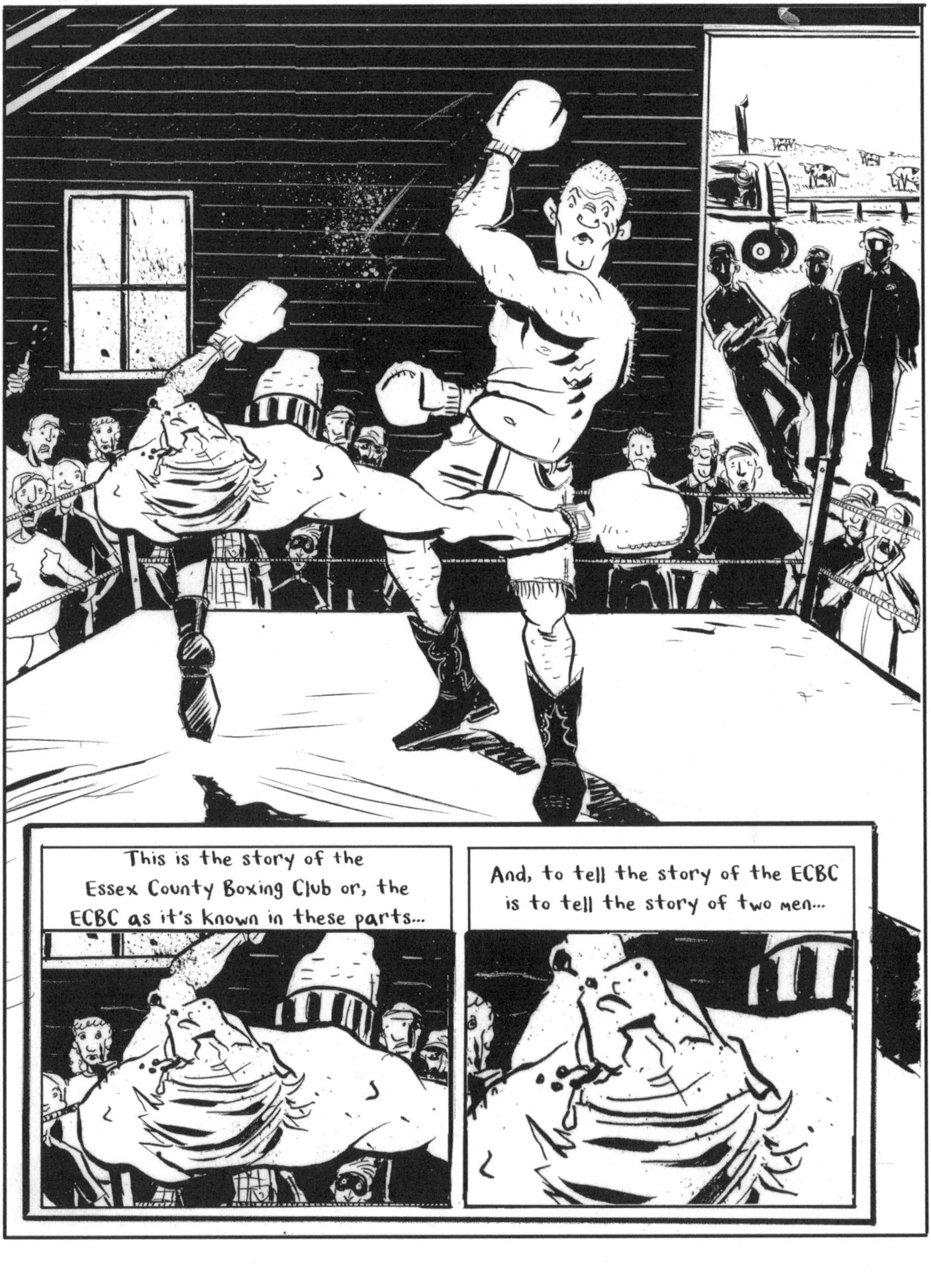
This is the story of the Essex County Boxing Club or, the ECBC as it's known in these parts...
And, to tell the story of the ECBC is to tell the story of two men...

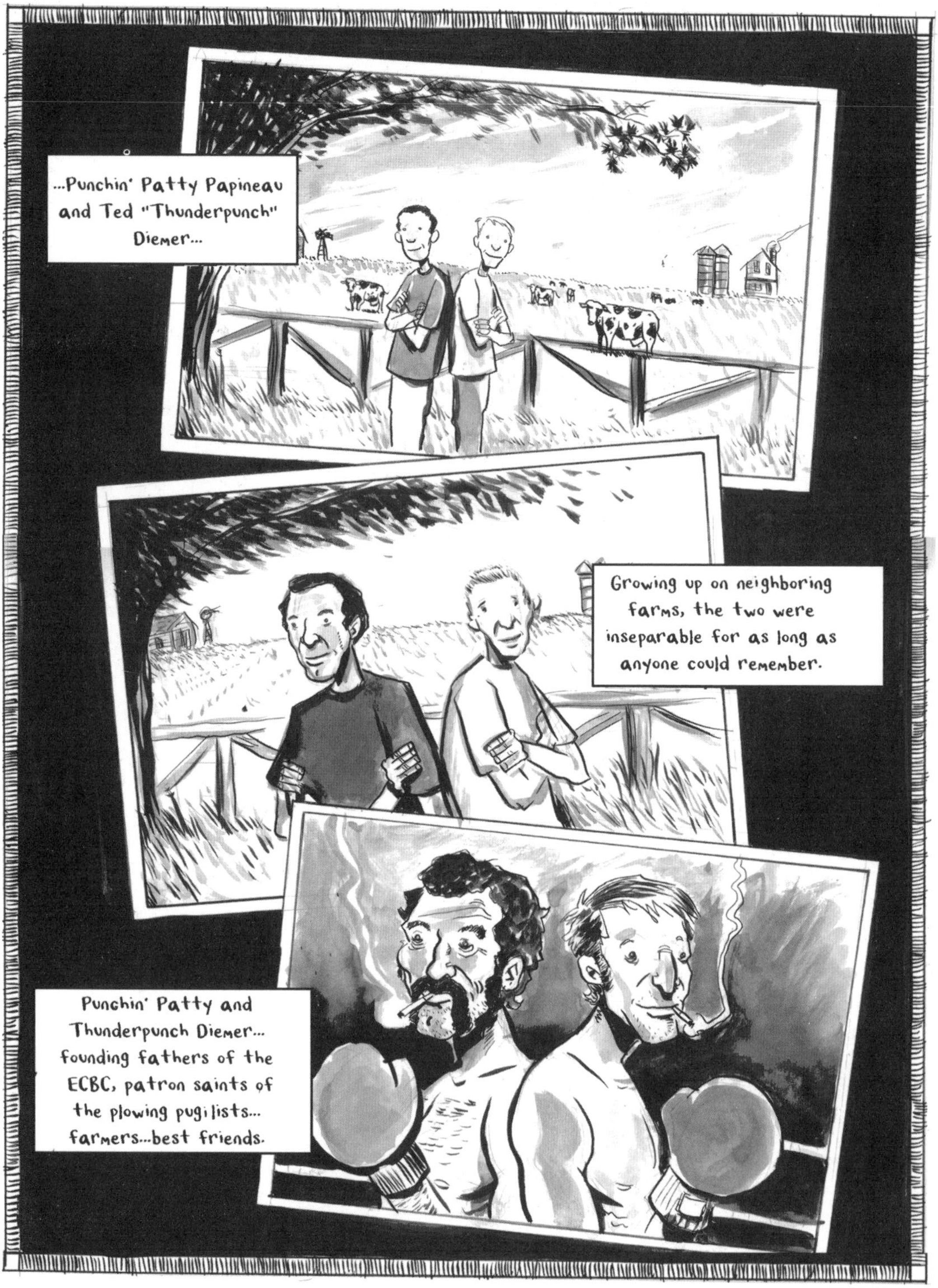
...Punchin' Patty Papineau and Ted "Thunderpunch" Diemer...
Growing up on neighboring farms, the two were inseparable for as long as anyone could remember.
Punchin' Patty and Thunderpunch Diemer... founding fathers of the ECBC, patron saints of the plowing pugilists... farmers...best friends.

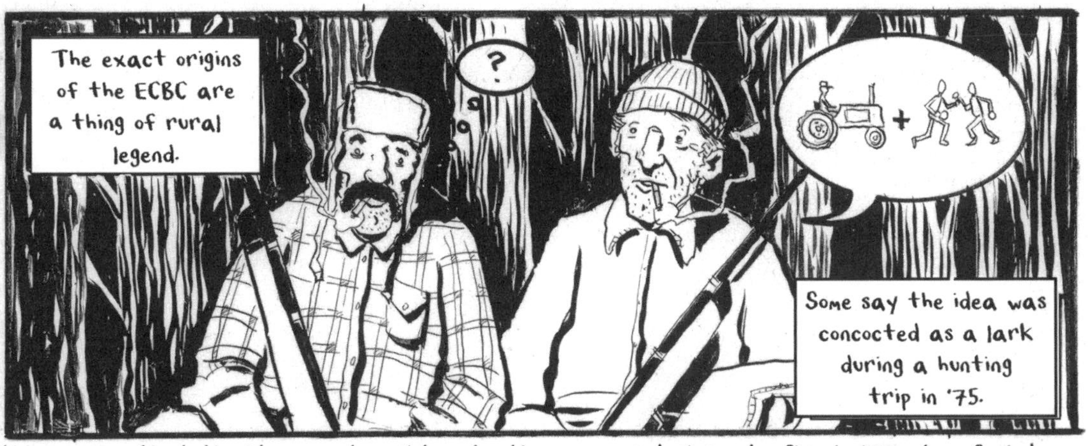

The exact origins of the ECBC are a thing of rural legend.
?
Some say the idea was concocted as a lark during a hunting trip in '75.

Others argue that the idea was brought on by the boredom of an ice-fishing vacation in '76...

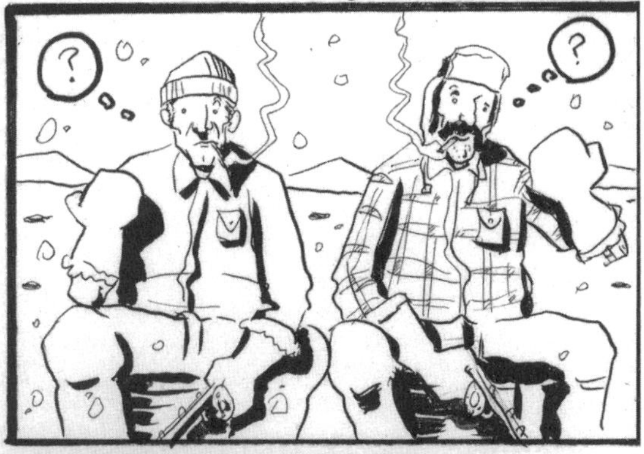

?
?

...or during a bonfire in '77 when, fueled by a few too many Rye and Cokes, things got out of hand between the two young farmers.

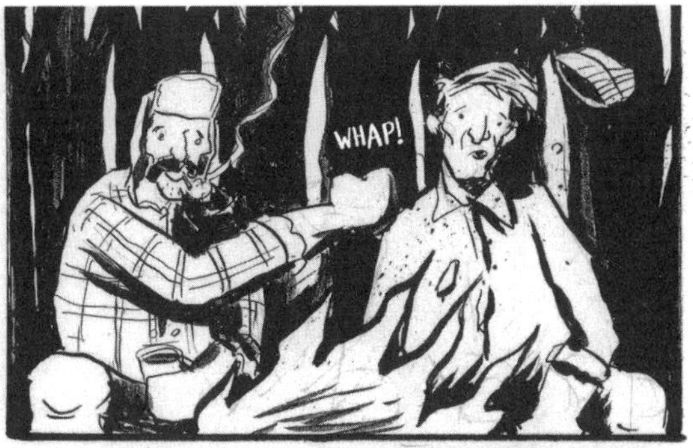

WHAP!

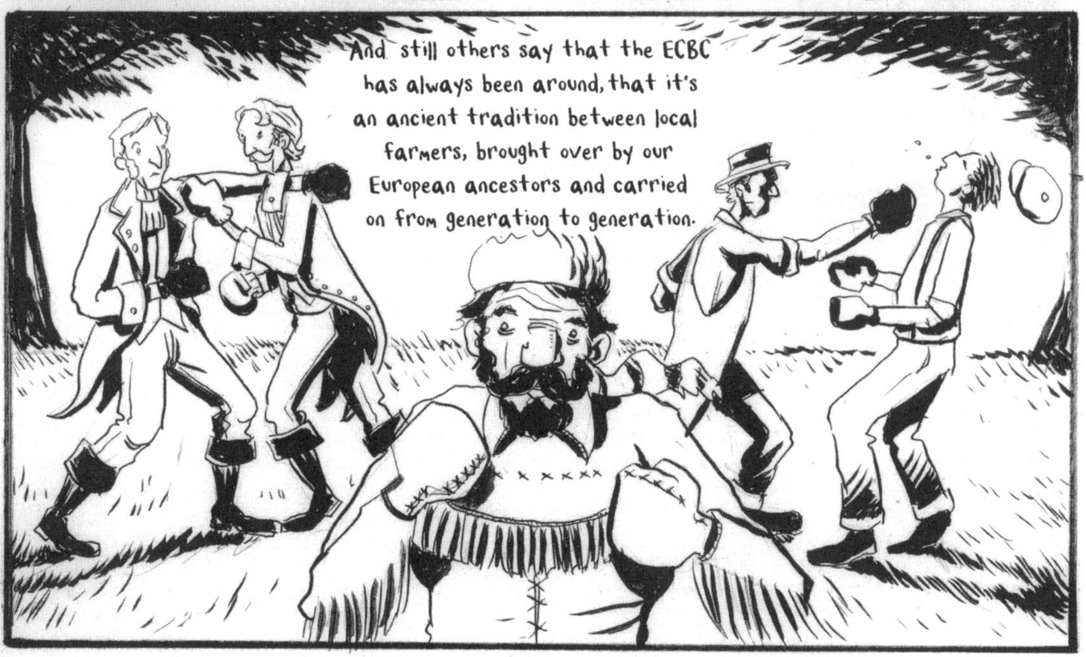

And still others say that the ECBC has always been around, that it's an ancient tradition between local farmers, brought over by our European ancestors and carried on from generation to generation.

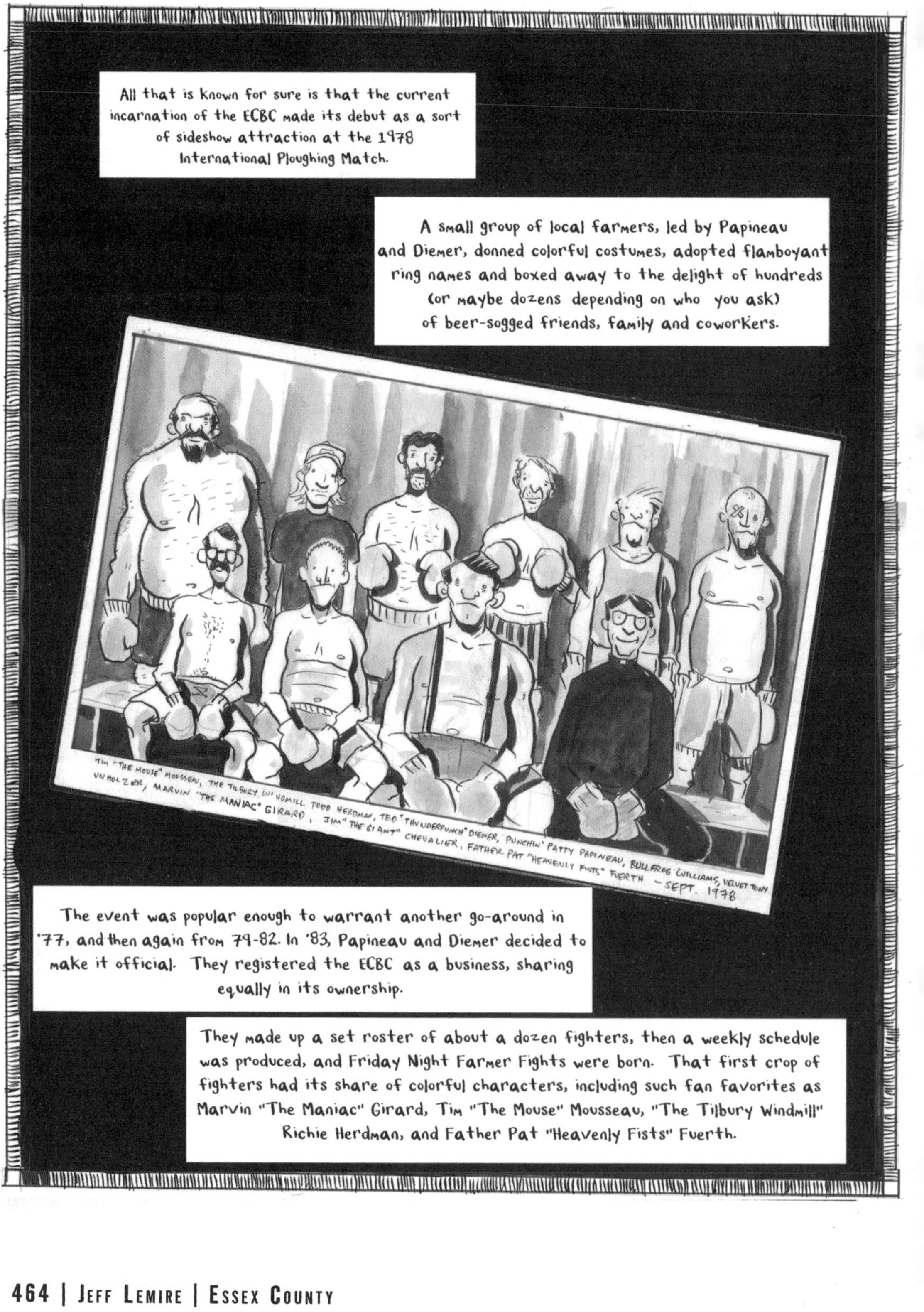
All that is known for sure is that the current incarnation of the ECBC made its debut as a sort of sideshow attraction at the 1978 International Ploughing Match.
A small group of local farmers, led by Papineau and Diemer, donned colorful costumes, adopted flamboyant ring names and boxed away to the delight of hundreds (or maybe dozens depending on who you ask) of beer-sogged friends, family and coworkers.
TIM "THE MOUSE" MOUSSEAU, THE TILBURY WINDMILL TODD HERDMAN, TED "THUNDERPUNCH" DIEMER, PUNCHIN' PATTY PAPINEAU, BULLFROG WILLIAMS, VELVET TONY VNHOLZER, MARVIN "THE MANIAC" GIRARD, JIM "THE GIANT" CHEVALIER, FATHER PAT "HEAVENLY FISTS" FUERTH - SEPT. 1978
The event was popular enough to warrant another go-around in '77, and then again from 79-82. In '83, Papineau and Diemer decided to make it official. They registered the ECBC as a business, sharing equally in its ownership.
They made up a set roster of about a dozen fighters, then a weekly schedule was produced, and Friday Night Farmer Fights were born. That first crop of fighters had its share of colorful characters, including such fan favorites as Marvin "The Maniac" Girard, Tim "The Mouse" Mousseau, "The Tilbury Windmill" Richie Herdman, and Father Pat "Heavenly Fists" Fuerth.

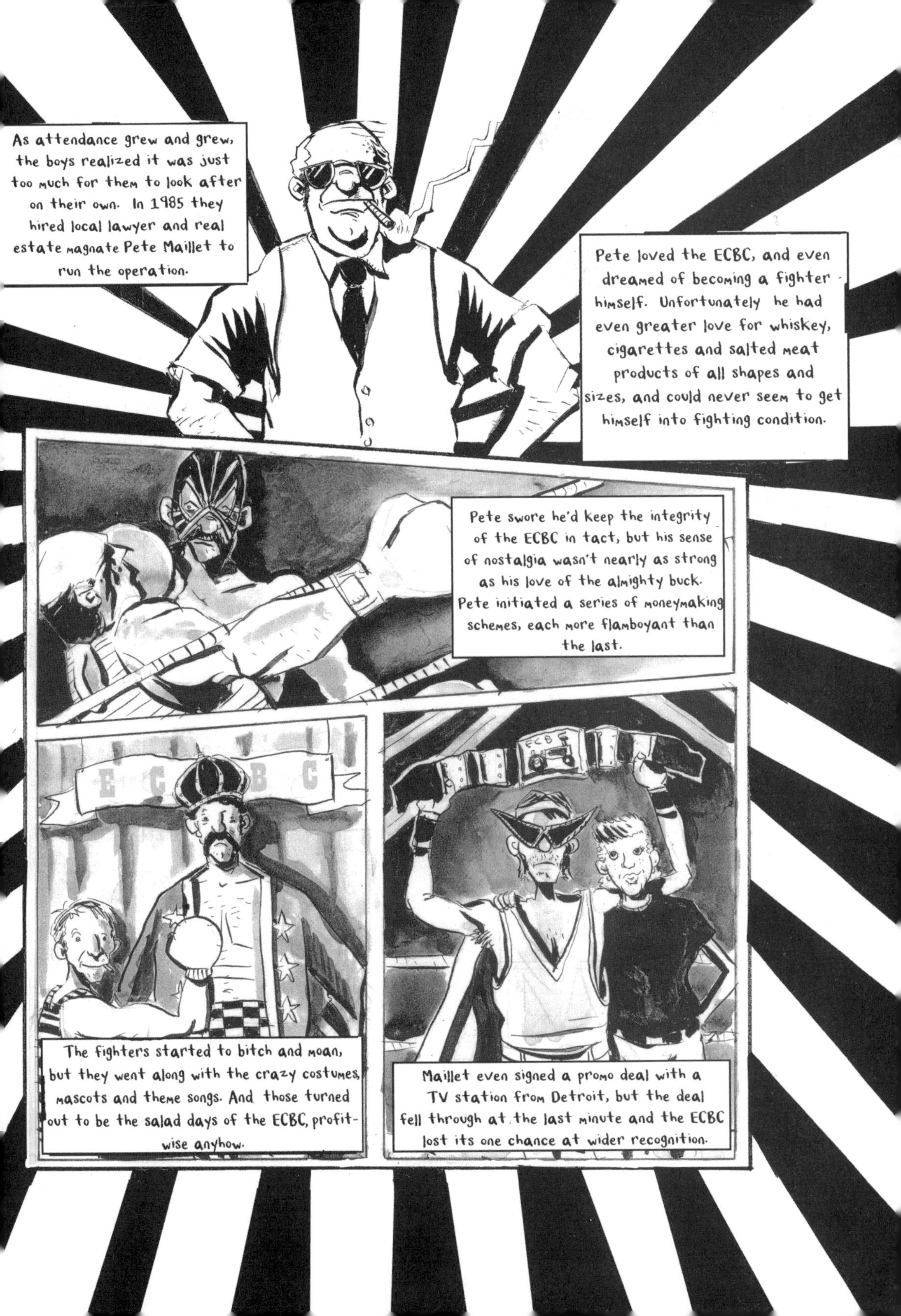
As attendance grew and grew, the boys realized it was just too much for them to look after on their own. In 1985 they hired local lawyer and real estate magnate Pete Maillet to run the operation.
Pete loved the ECBC, and even dreamed of becoming a fighter himself. Unfortunately he had even greater love for whiskey, cigarettes and salted meat products of all shapes and sizes, and could never seem to get himself into fighting condition.
Pete swore he'd keep the integrity of the ECBC in tact, but his sense of nostalgia wasn't nearly as strong as his love of the almighty buck. Pete initiated a series of moneymaking schemes, each more flamboyant than the last.
E C B C
The fighters started to bitch and moan, but they went along with the crazy costumes, mascots and theme songs. And those turned out to be the salad days of the ECBC, profit-wise anyhow.
ECB
Maillet even signed a promo deal with a TV station from Detroit, but the deal fell through at the last minute and the ECBC lost its one chance at wider recognition.

That suited many of the fighters just fine, however. To them the ECBC was fun, an exciting way to escape the daily grind, but they had farms to run, and families to look after, and the ECBC was becoming too big a part of their lives as it was.

After the TV deal fell apart, Pete Maillet lost interest. Without his showbiz touch, attendance dropped and profits started to dry up.

Then, on July 30th, 1989, true tragedy struck the ECBC. Punchin' Patty was helping Thunderpunch put up some new grain bins on Diemer's farm. It was long, hot day, and the two had been working at it since dawn.

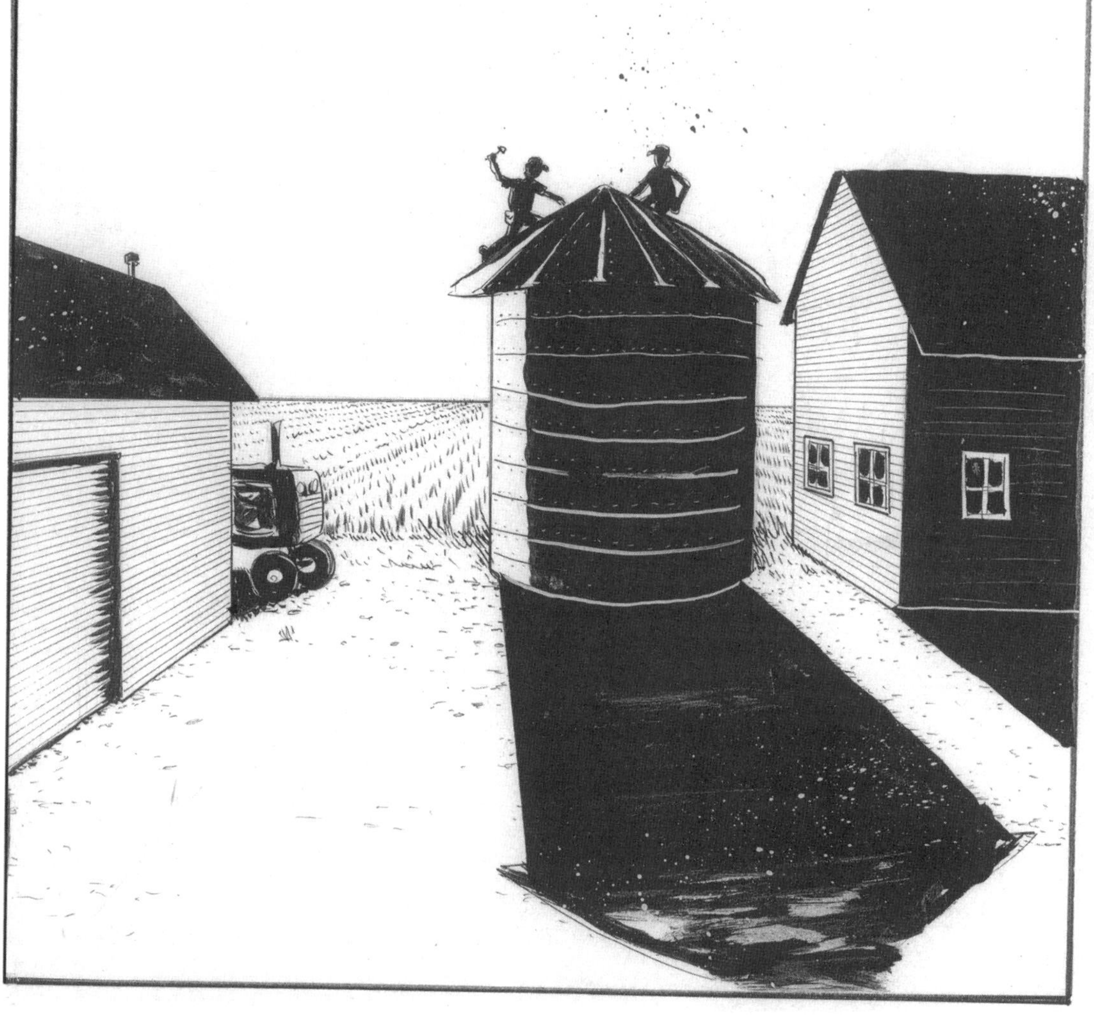

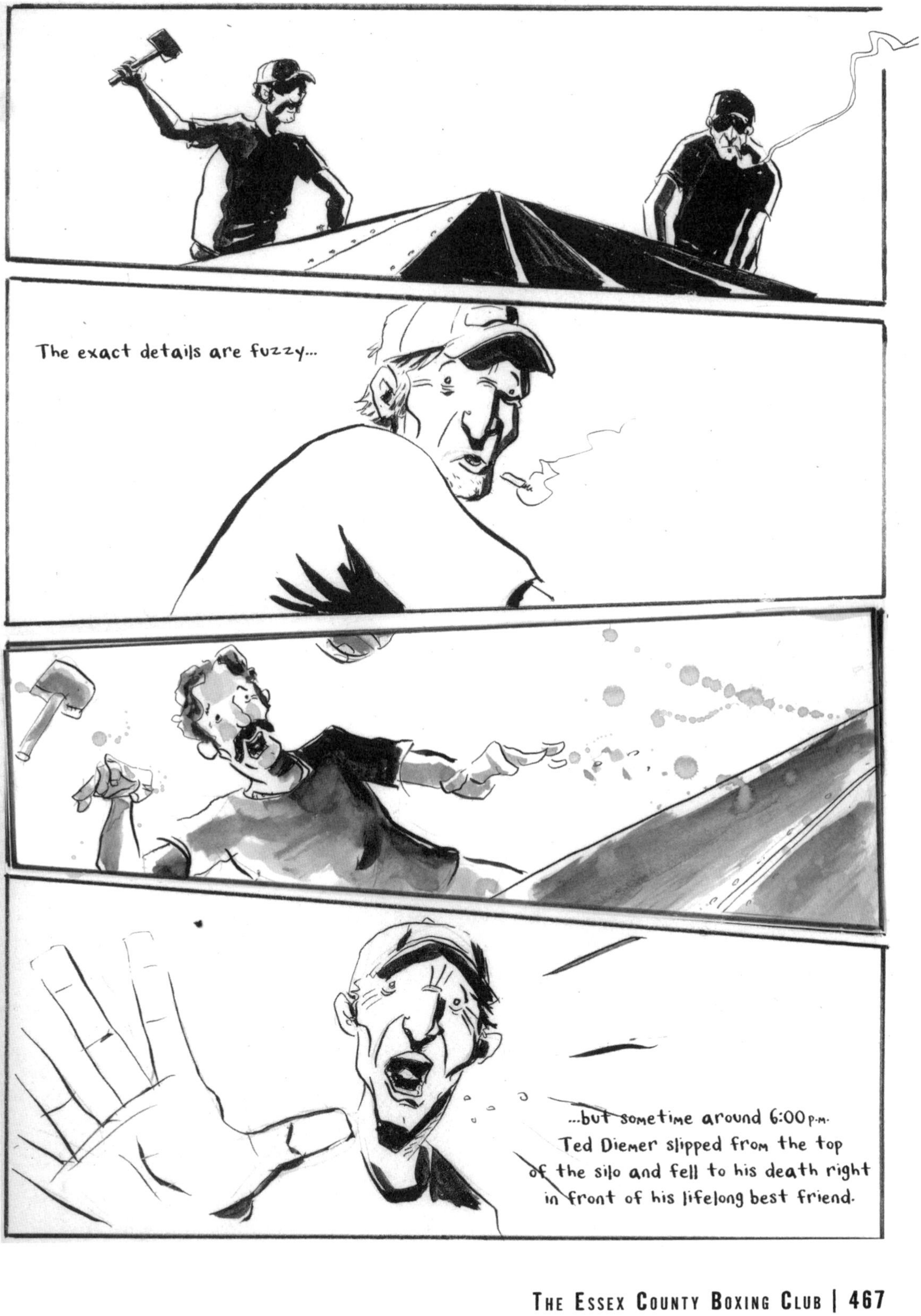
The exact details are fuzzy...
...but sometime around 6:00 p.m. Ted Diemer slipped from the top of the silo and fell to his death right in front of his lifelong best friend.

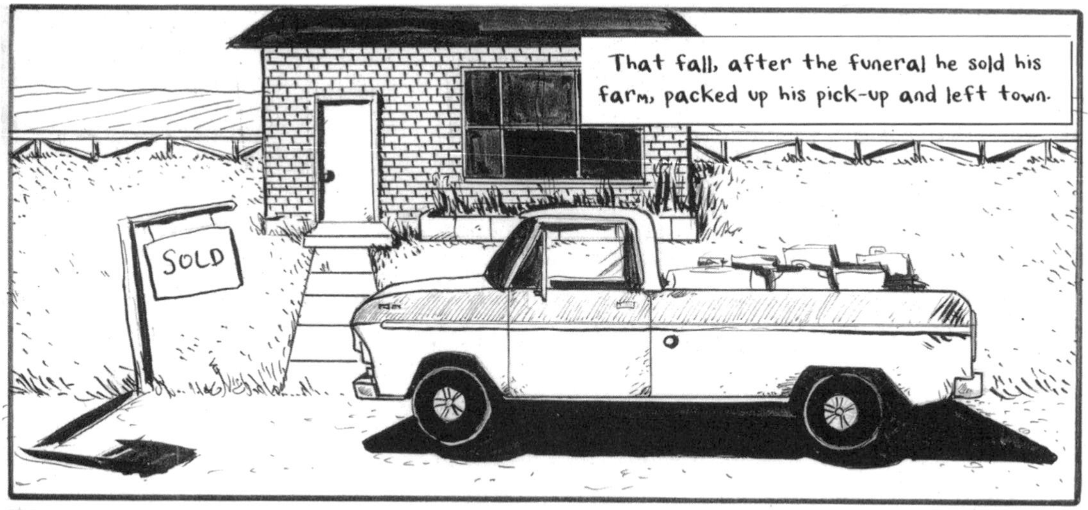
That fall, after the funeral he sold his farm, packed up his pick-up and left town.
SOLD

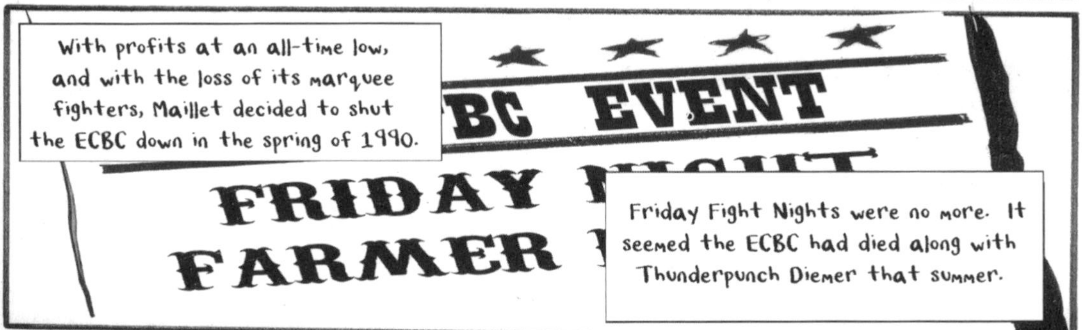
With profits at an all-time low, and with the loss of its marquee fighters, Maillet decided to shut the ECBC down in the spring of 1990.
BC EVENT
FRIDAY
FARMER
Friday Fight Nights were no more. It seemed the ECBC had died along with Thunderpunch Diemer that summer.

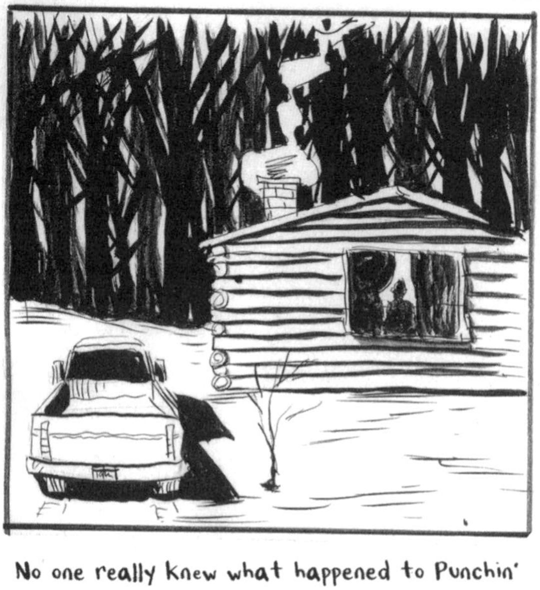

No one really knew what happened to Punchin' Patty for the next five years.

The common belief is that he moved up north away from everything and everyone.

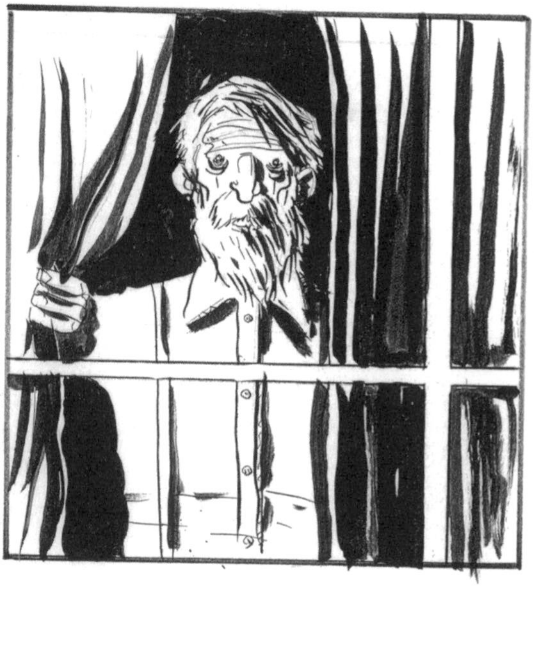

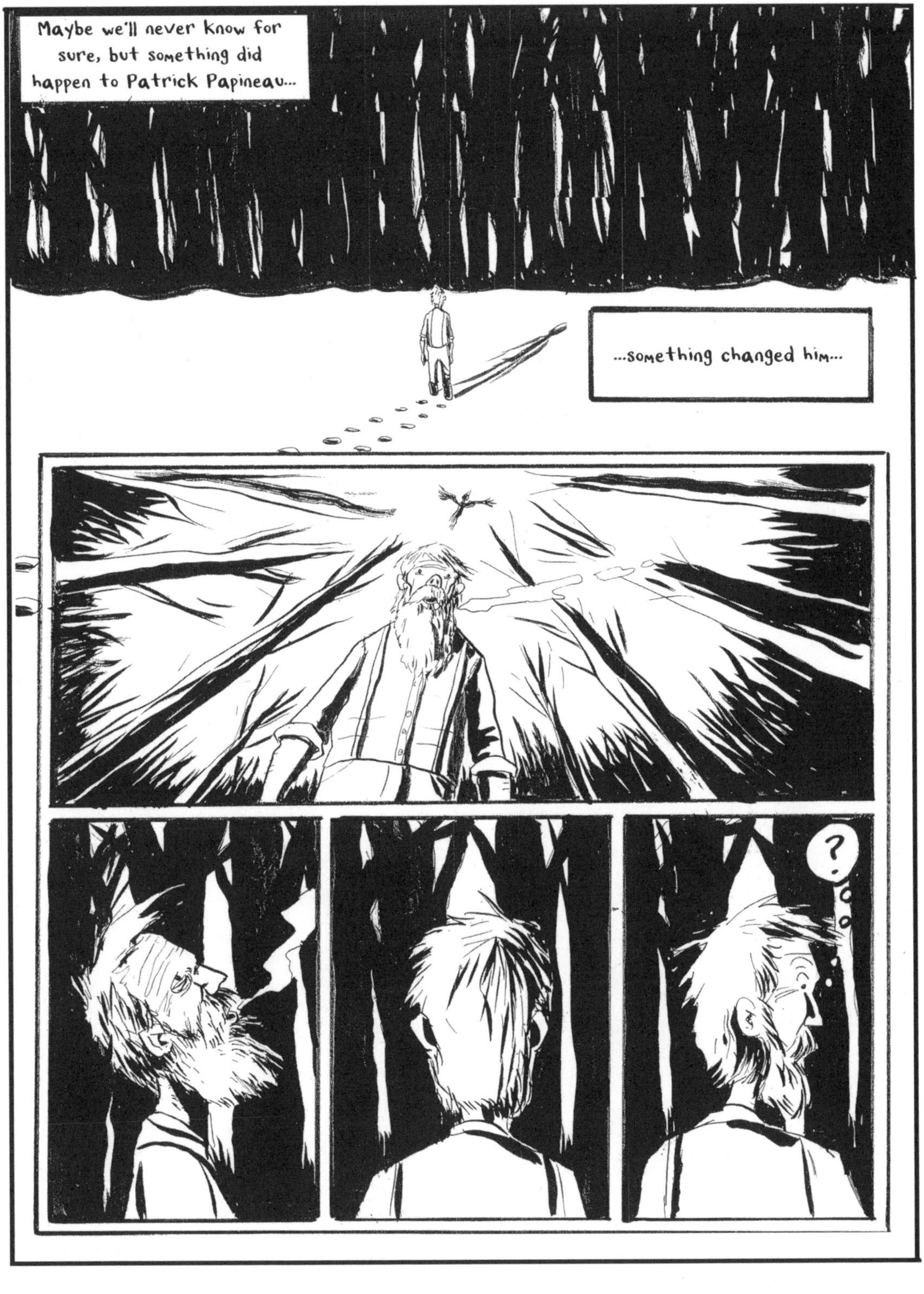
Maybe we'll never know for sure, but something did happen to Patrick Papineau...
...something changed him...
?

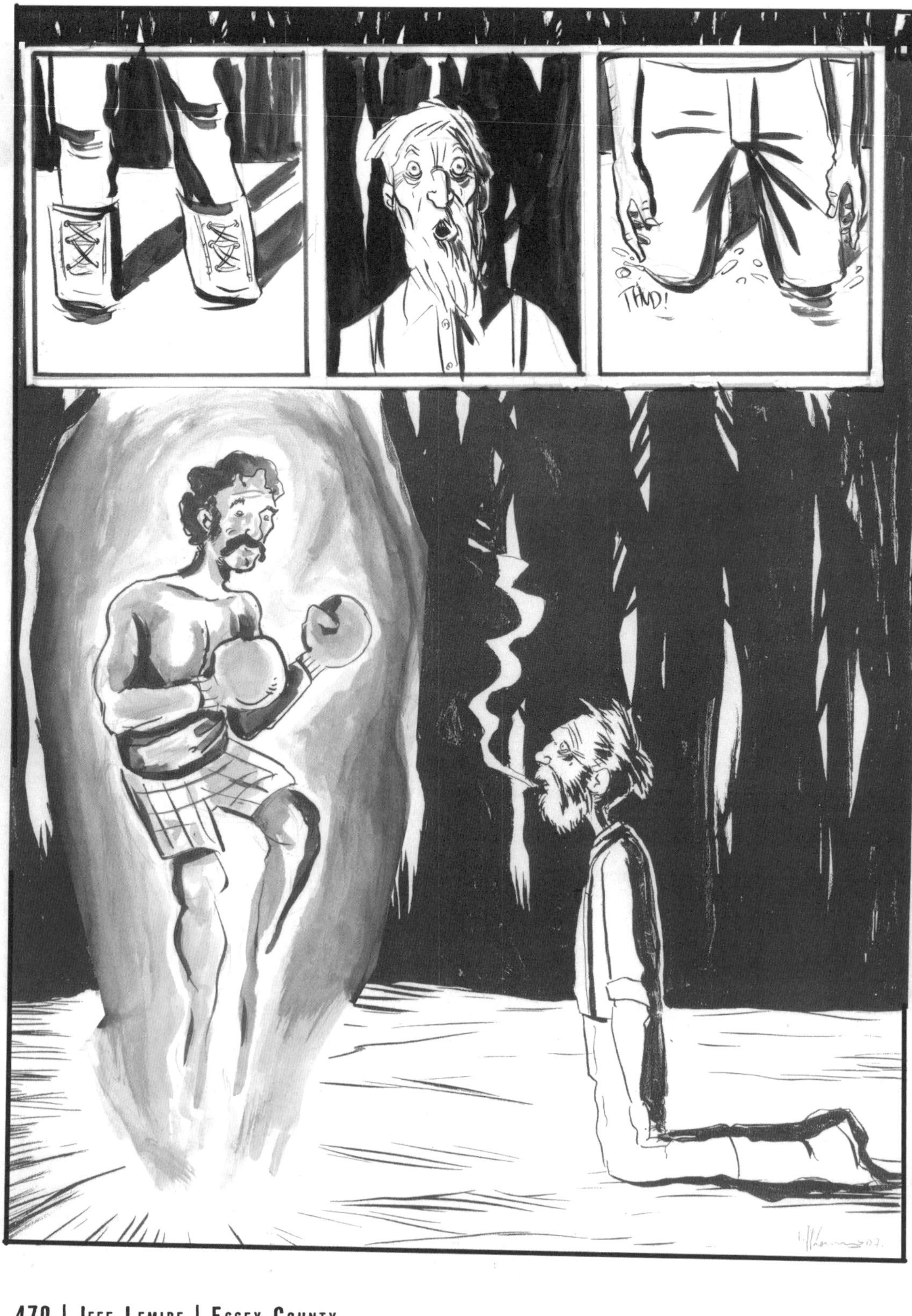
THUD!

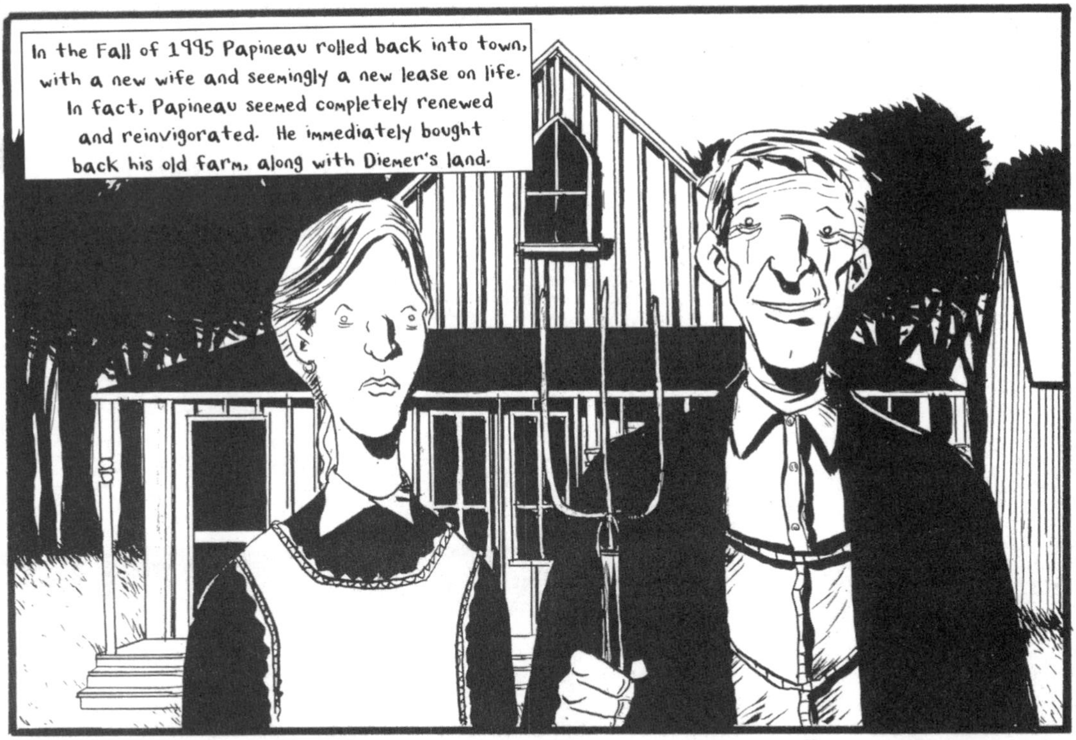
In the Fall of 1995 Papineau rolled back into town, with a new wife and seemingly a new lease on life. In fact, Papineau seemed completely renewed and reinvigorated. He immediately bought back his old farm, along with Diemer's land.

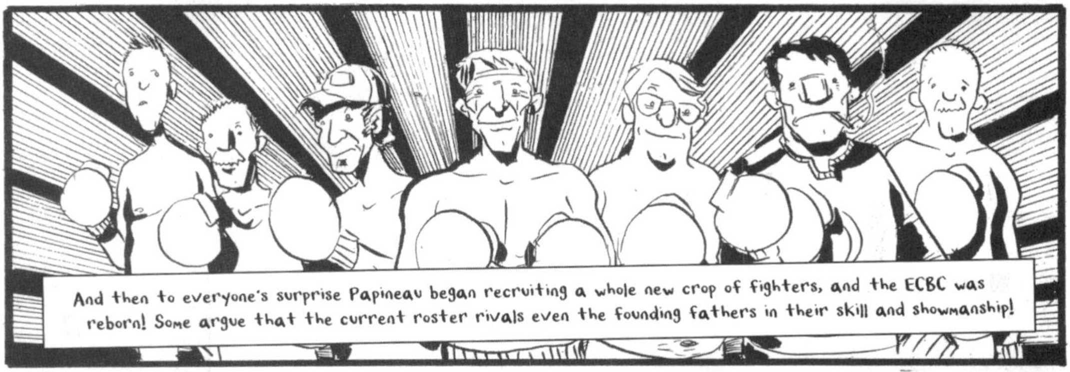
And then to everyone's surprise Papineau began recruiting a whole new crop of fighters, and the ECBC was reborn! Some argue that the current roster rivals even the founding fathers in their skill and showmanship!

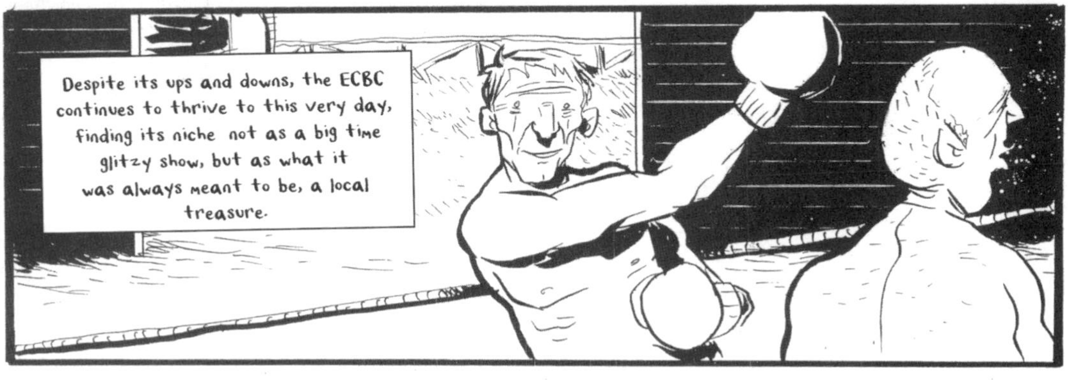
Despite its ups and downs, the ECBC continues to thrive to this very day, finding its niche not as a big time glitzy show, but as what it was always meant to be, a local treasure.

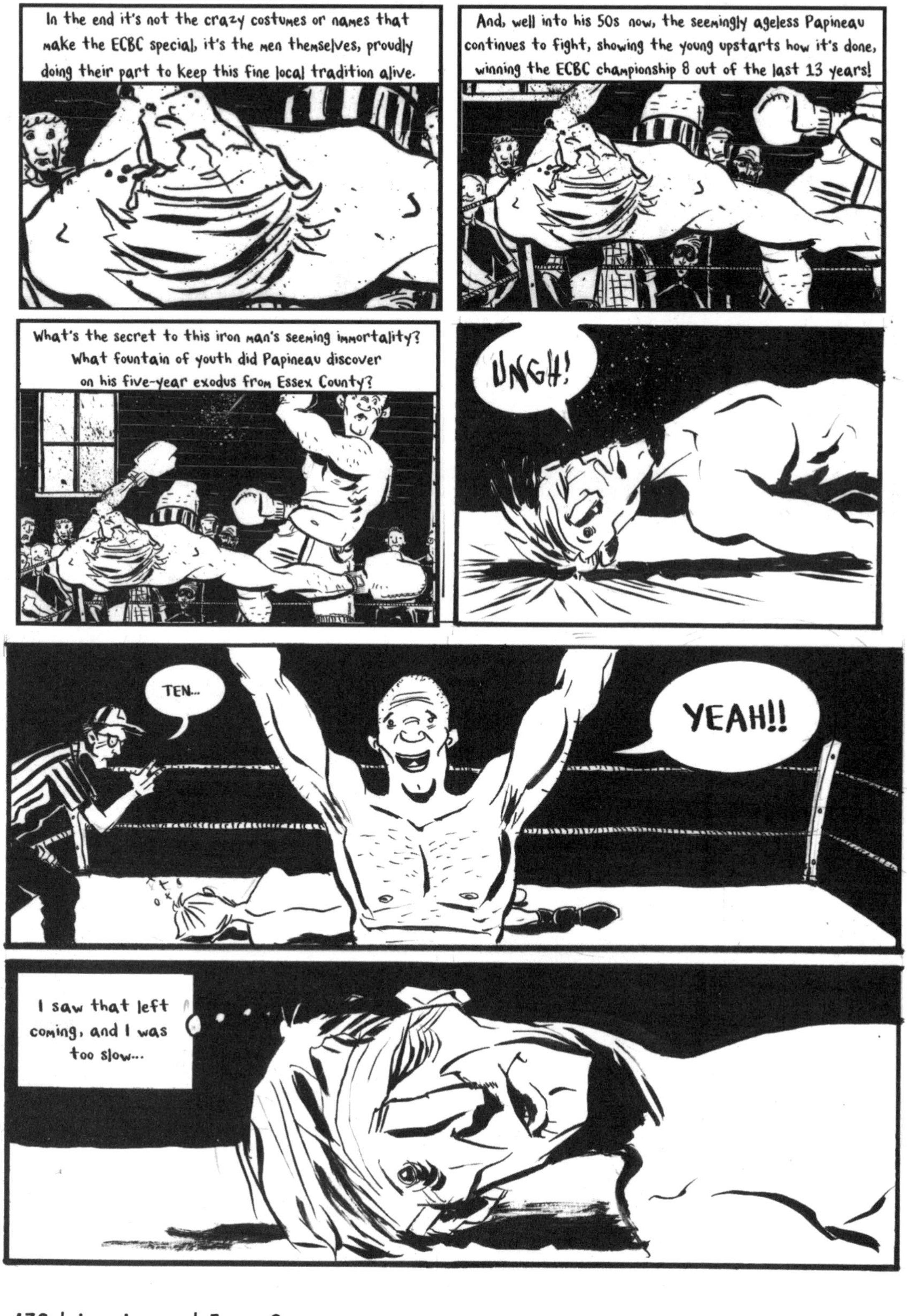
In the end it's not the crazy costumes or names that make the ECBC special, it's the men themselves, proudly doing their part to keep this fine local tradition alive.
And, well into his 50s now, the seemingly ageless Papineau continues to fight, showing the young upstarts how it's done, winning the ECBC championship 8 out of the last 13 years!
What's the secret to this iron man's seeming immortality? What fountain of youth did Papineau discover on his five-year exodus from Essex County?
UNGH!
TEN...
YEAH!!
I saw that left coming, and I was too slow...

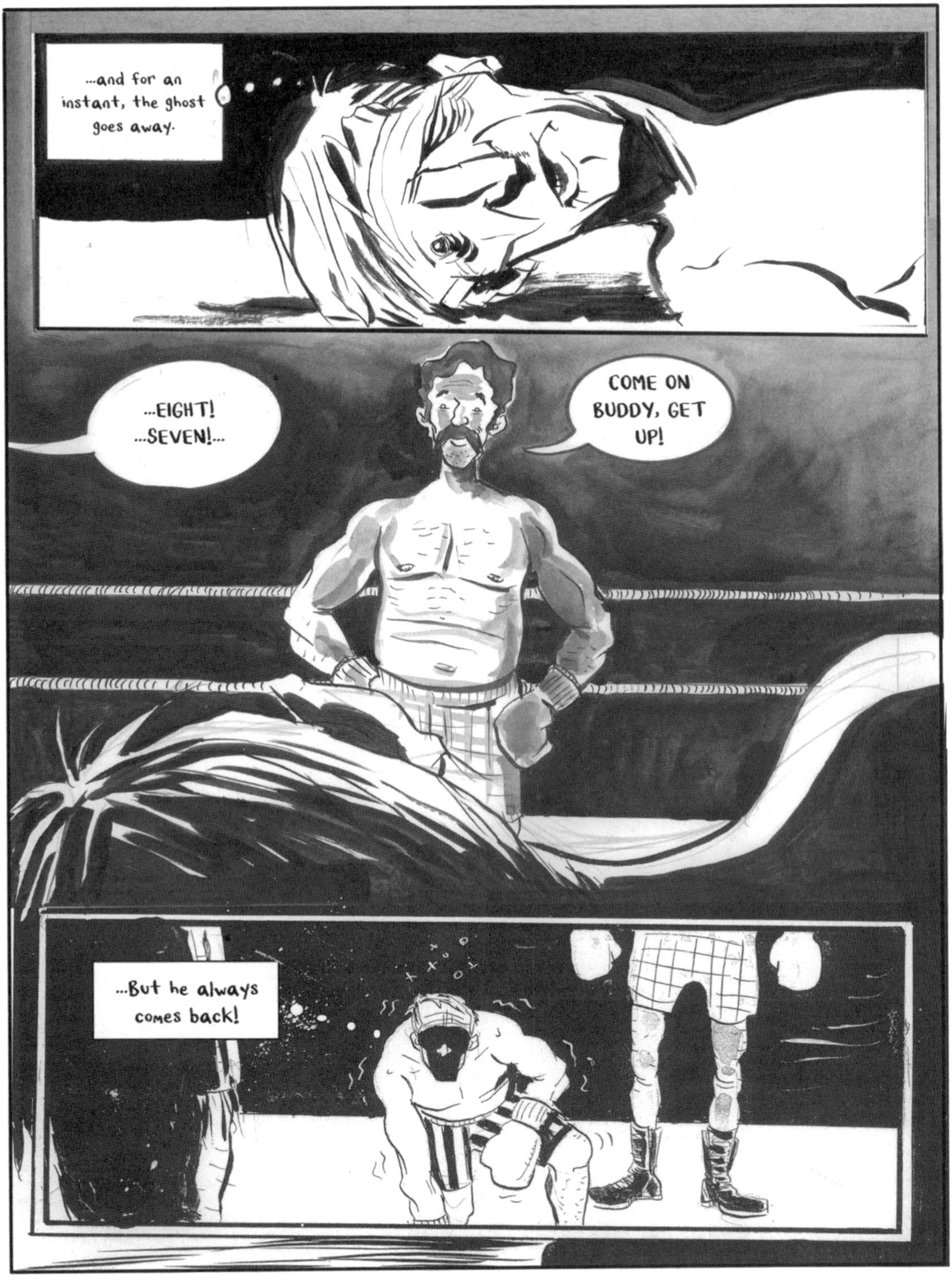
...and for an instant, the ghost goes away.
...EIGHT! ...SEVEN!...
COME ON BUDDY, GET UP!
...But he always comes back!

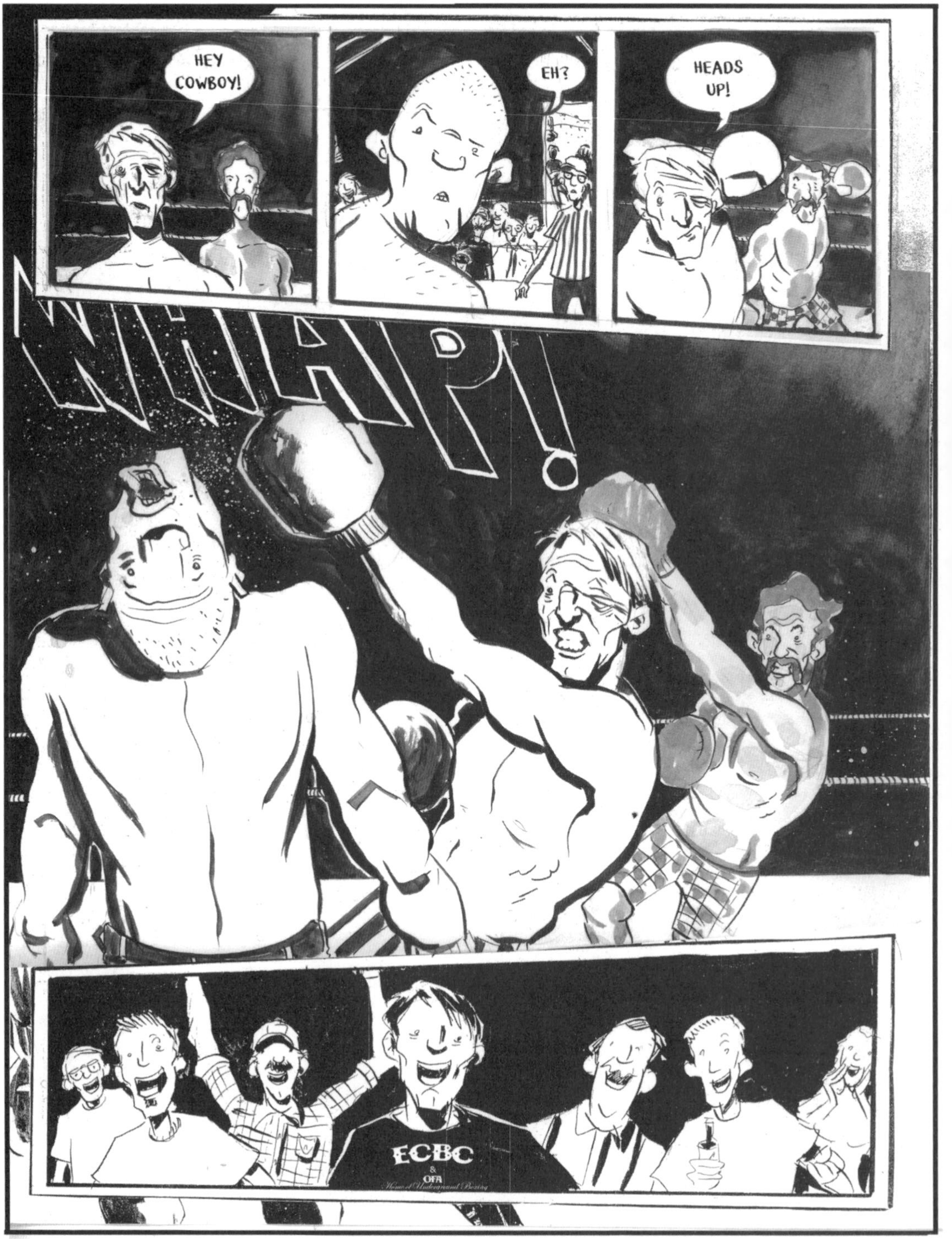
HEY COWBOY!
EH?
HEADS UP!
WHAP!
ECBC

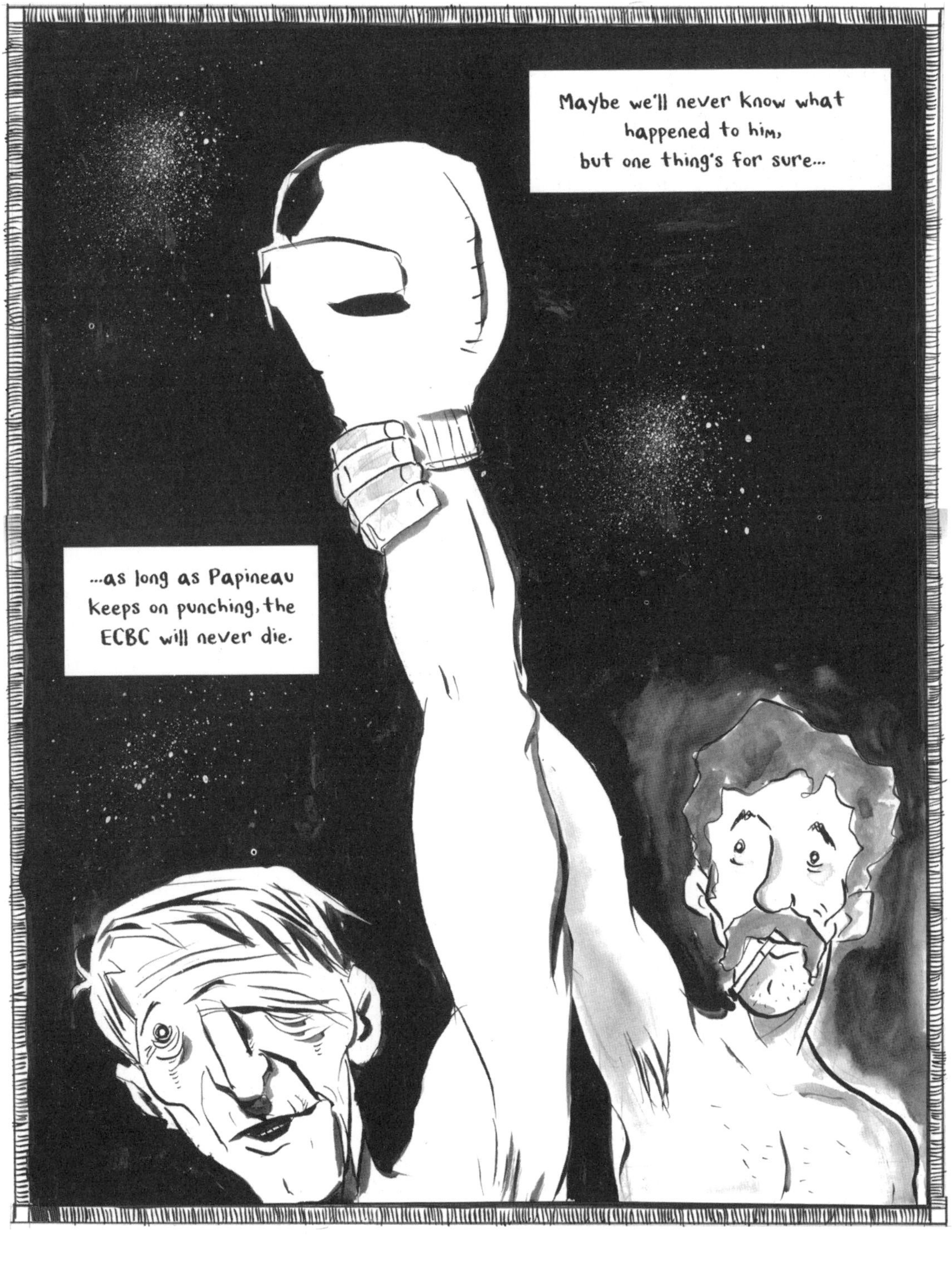
Maybe we'll never know what happened to him, but one thing's for sure...
...as long as Papineau keeps on punching, the ECBC will never die.

The Sad + Lonely Life of Eddie Elephant -Ears

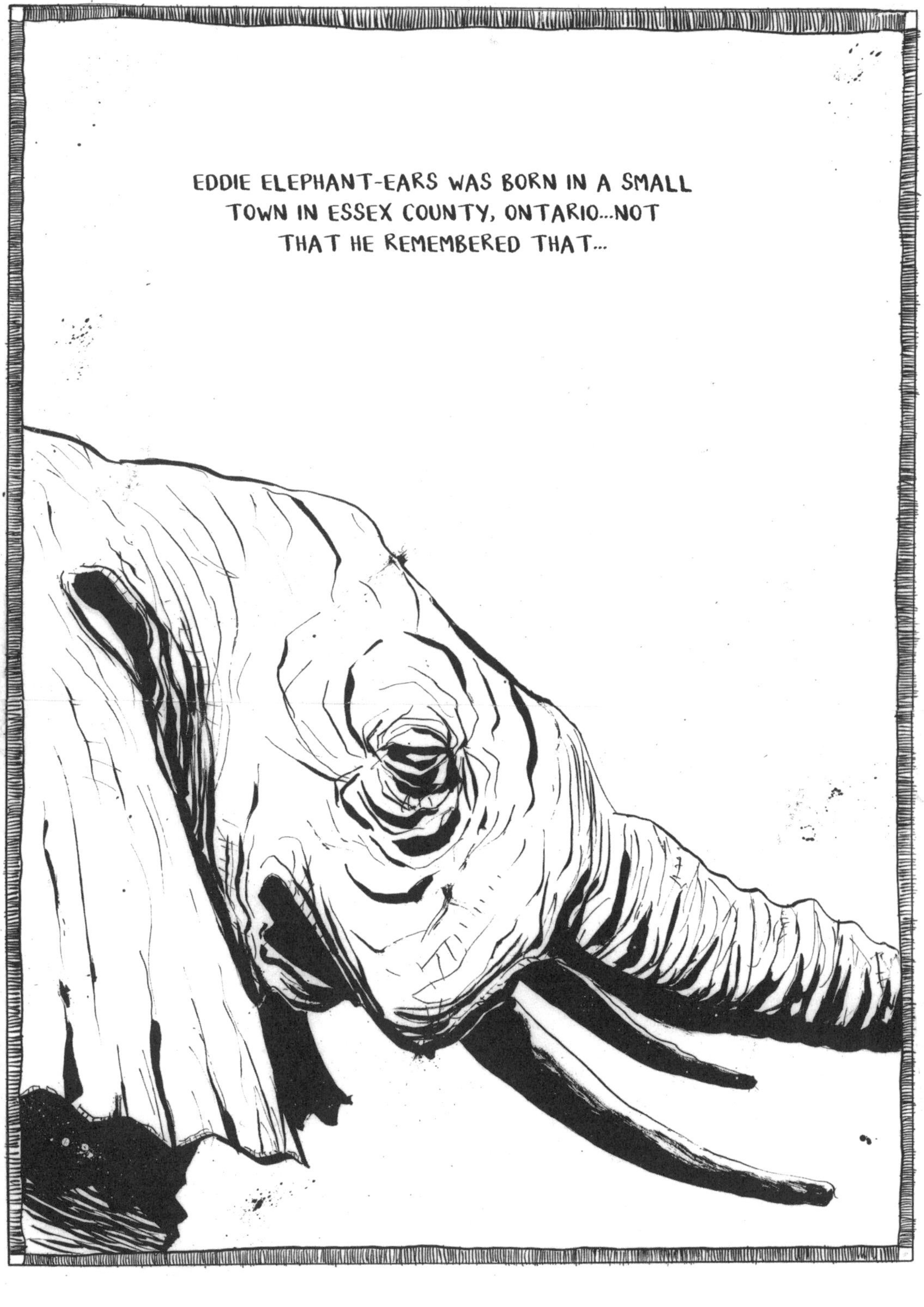
EDDIE ELEPHANT-EARS WAS BORN IN A SMALL TOWN IN ESSEX COUNTY, ONTARIO...NOT THAT HE REMEMBERED THAT...

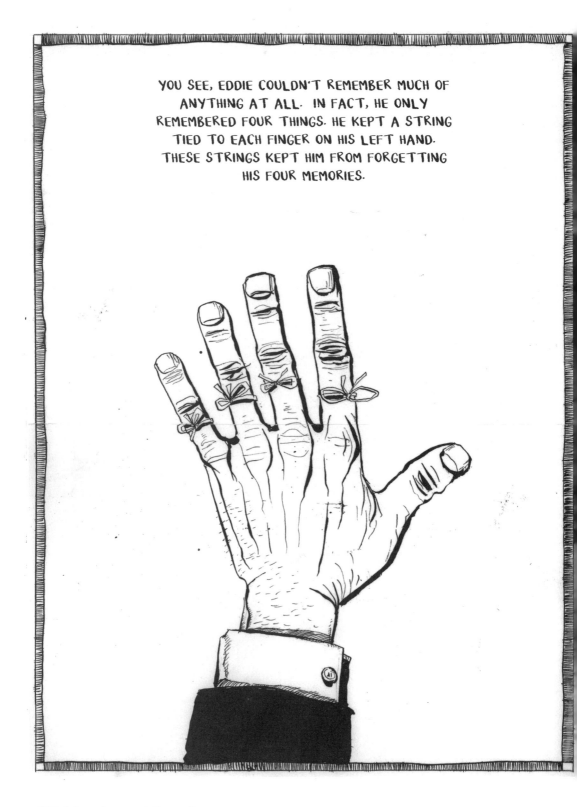

YOU SEE, EDDIE COULDN'T REMEMBER MUCH OF ANYTHING AT ALL. IN FACT, HE ONLY REMEMBERED FOUR THINGS. HE KEPT A STRING TIED TO EACH FINGER ON HIS LEFT HAND. THESE STRINGS KEPT HIM FROM FORGETTING HIS FOUR MEMORIES.

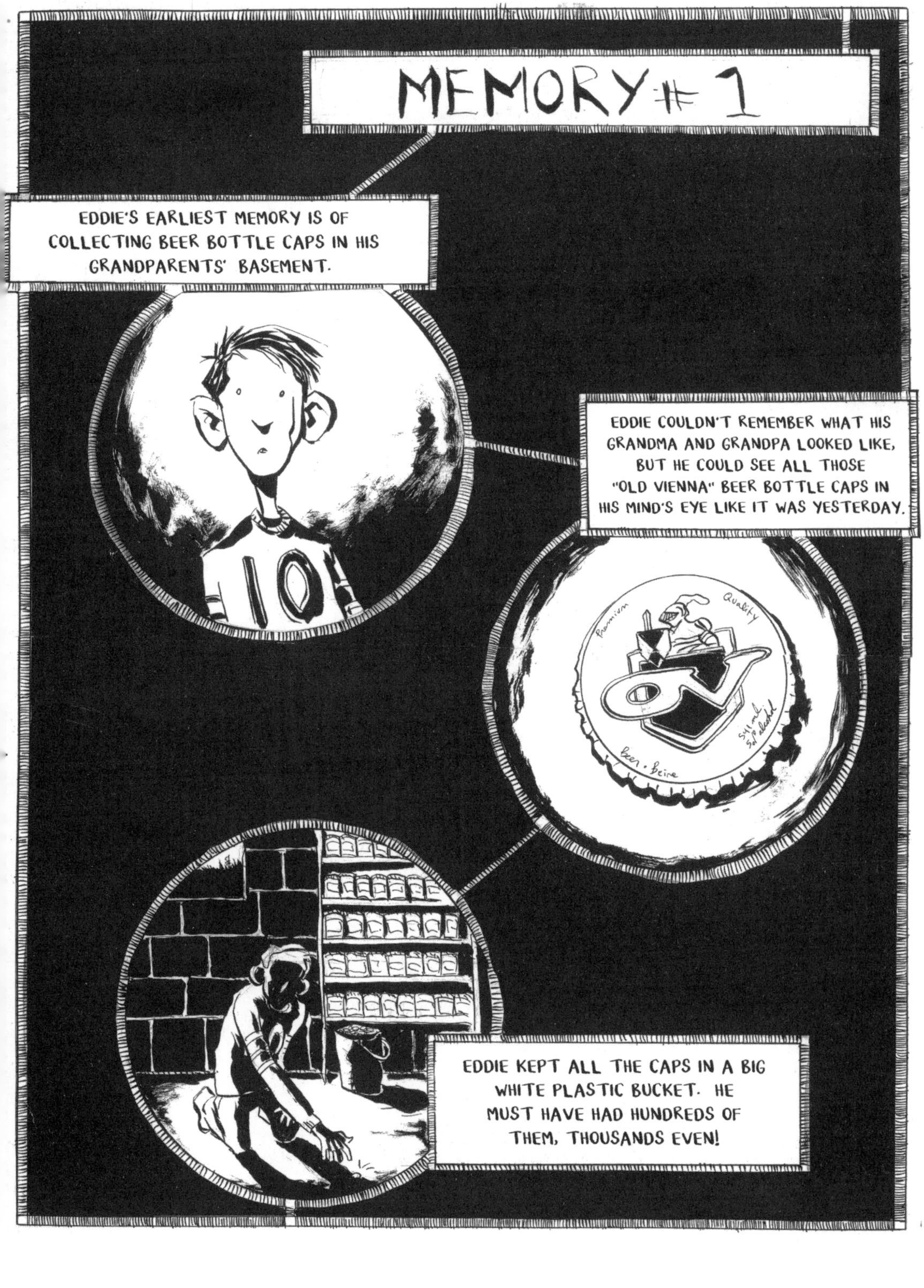
MEMORY #1
EDDIE'S EARLIEST MEMORY IS OF COLLECTING BEER BOTTLE CAPS IN HIS GRANDPARENTS' BASEMENT.
10
EDDIE COULDN'T REMEMBER WHAT HIS GRANDMA AND GRANDPA LOOKED LIKE, BUT HE COULD SEE ALL THOSE "OLD VIENNA" BEER BOTTLE CAPS IN HIS MIND'S EYE LIKE IT WAS YESTERDAY.
Premium
Quality
Beer • Beire
EDDIE KEPT ALL THE CAPS IN A BIG WHITE PLASTIC BUCKET. HE MUST HAVE HAD HUNDREDS OF THEM, THOUSANDS EVEN!

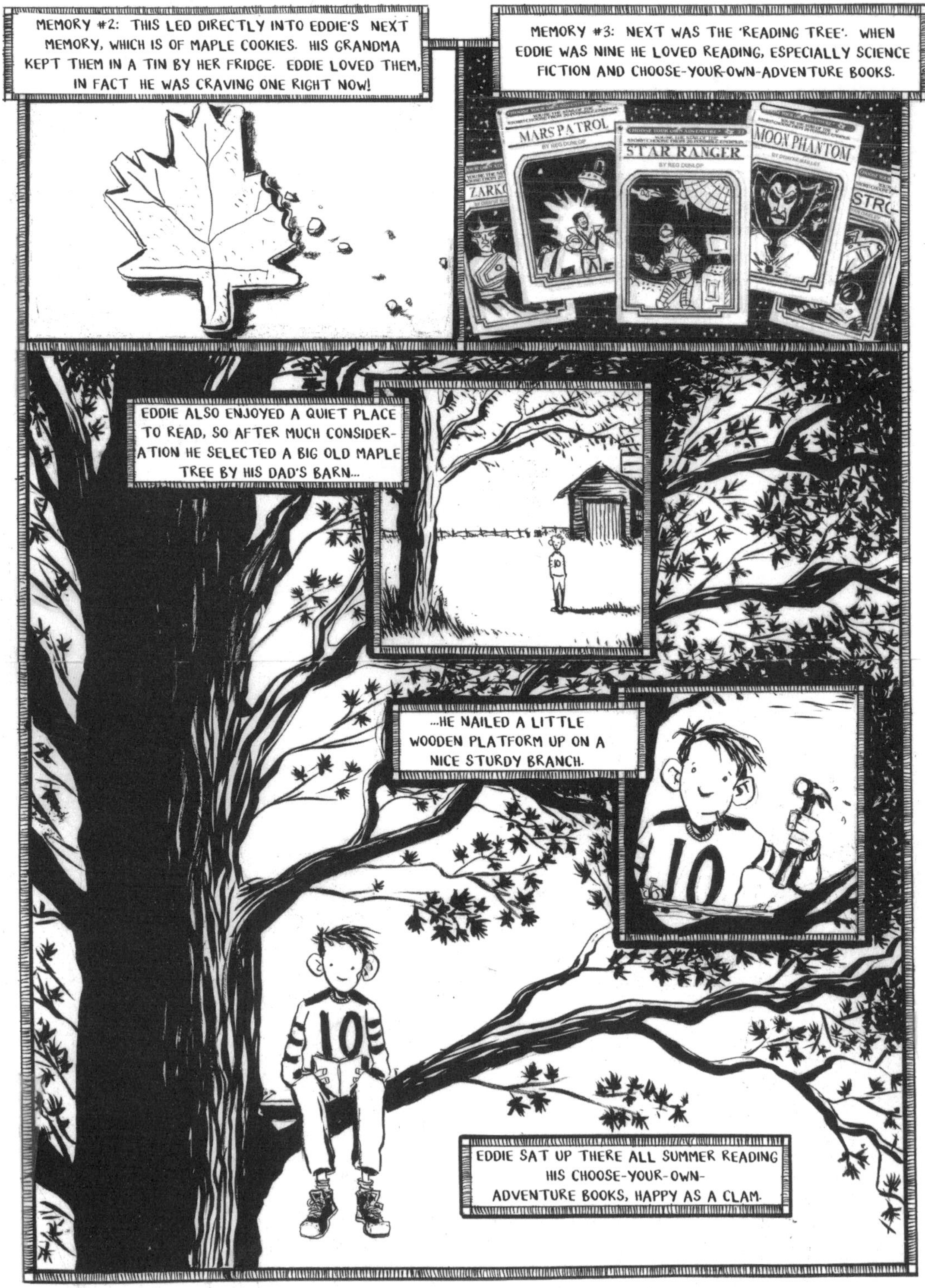
MEMORY #2: THIS LED DIRECTLY INTO EDDIE'S NEXT MEMORY, WHICH IS OF MAPLE COOKIES. HIS GRANDMA KEPT THEM IN A TIN BY HER FRIDGE. EDDIE LOVED THEM, IN FACT HE WAS CRAVING ONE RIGHT NOW!
MEMORY #3: NEXT WAS THE 'READING TREE'. WHEN EDDIE WAS NINE HE LOVED READING, ESPECIALLY SCIENCE FICTION AND CHOOSE-YOUR-OWN-ADVENTURE BOOKS.
MARS PATROL
STAR RANGER
BY REG DUNLOP
MOON PHANTOM
EDDIE ALSO ENJOYED A QUIET PLACE TO READ, SO AFTER MUCH CONSIDER-ATION HE SELECTED A BIG OLD MAPLE TREE BY HIS DAD'S BARN...
...HE NAILED A LITTLE WOODEN PLATFORM UP ON A NICE STURDY BRANCH.
EDDIE SAT UP THERE ALL SUMMER READING HIS CHOOSE-YOUR-OWN-ADVENTURE BOOKS, HAPPY AS A CLAM.

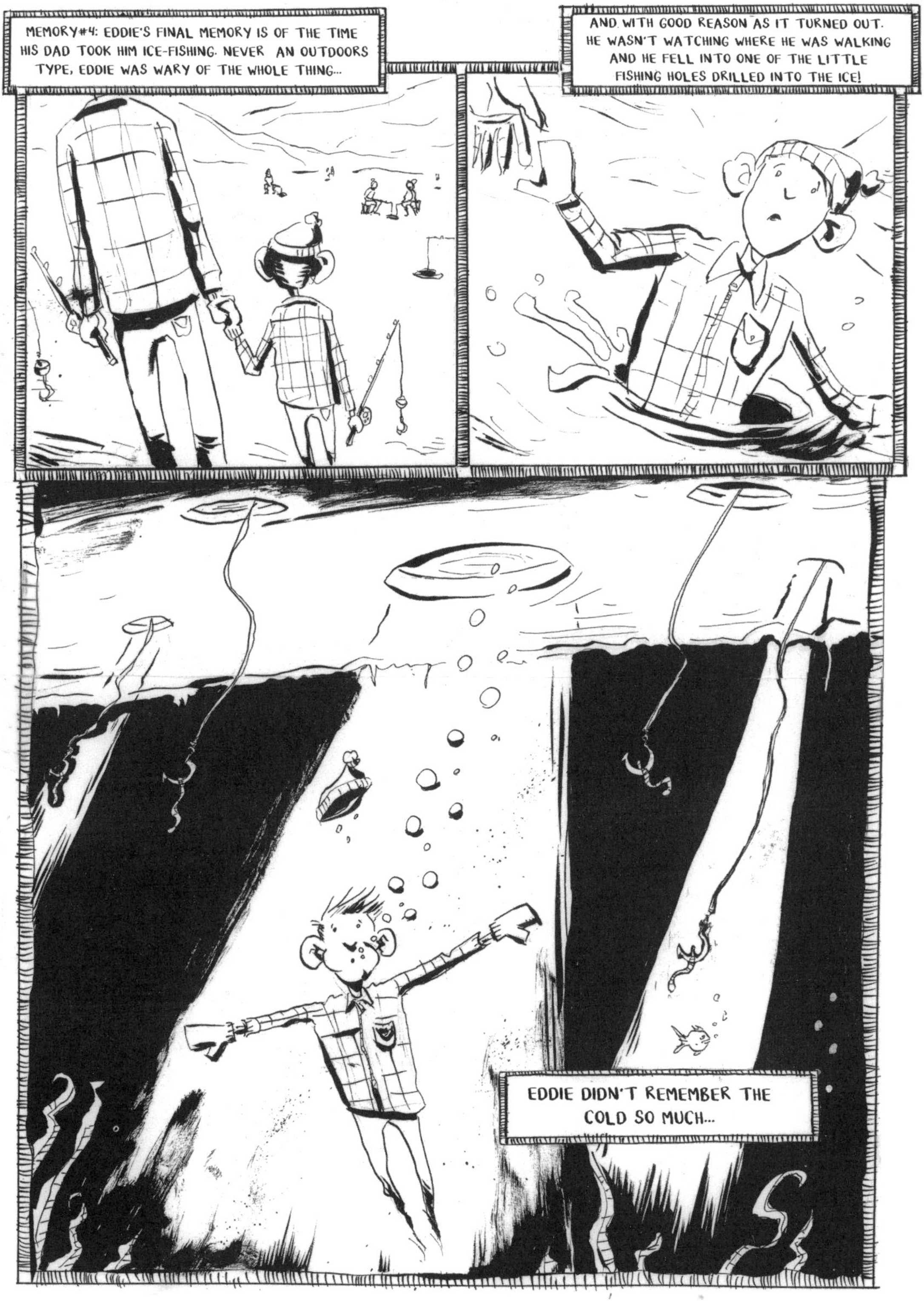
MEMORY#4: EDDIE'S FINAL MEMORY IS OF THE TIME HIS DAD TOOK HIM ICE-FISHING. NEVER AN OUTDOORS TYPE, EDDIE WAS WARY OF THE WHOLE THING...
AND WITH GOOD REASON AS IT TURNED OUT. HE WASN'T WATCHING WHERE HE WAS WALKING AND HE FELL INTO ONE OF THE LITTLE FISHING HOLES DRILLED INTO THE ICE!
EDDIE DIDN'T REMEMBER THE COLD SO MUCH...

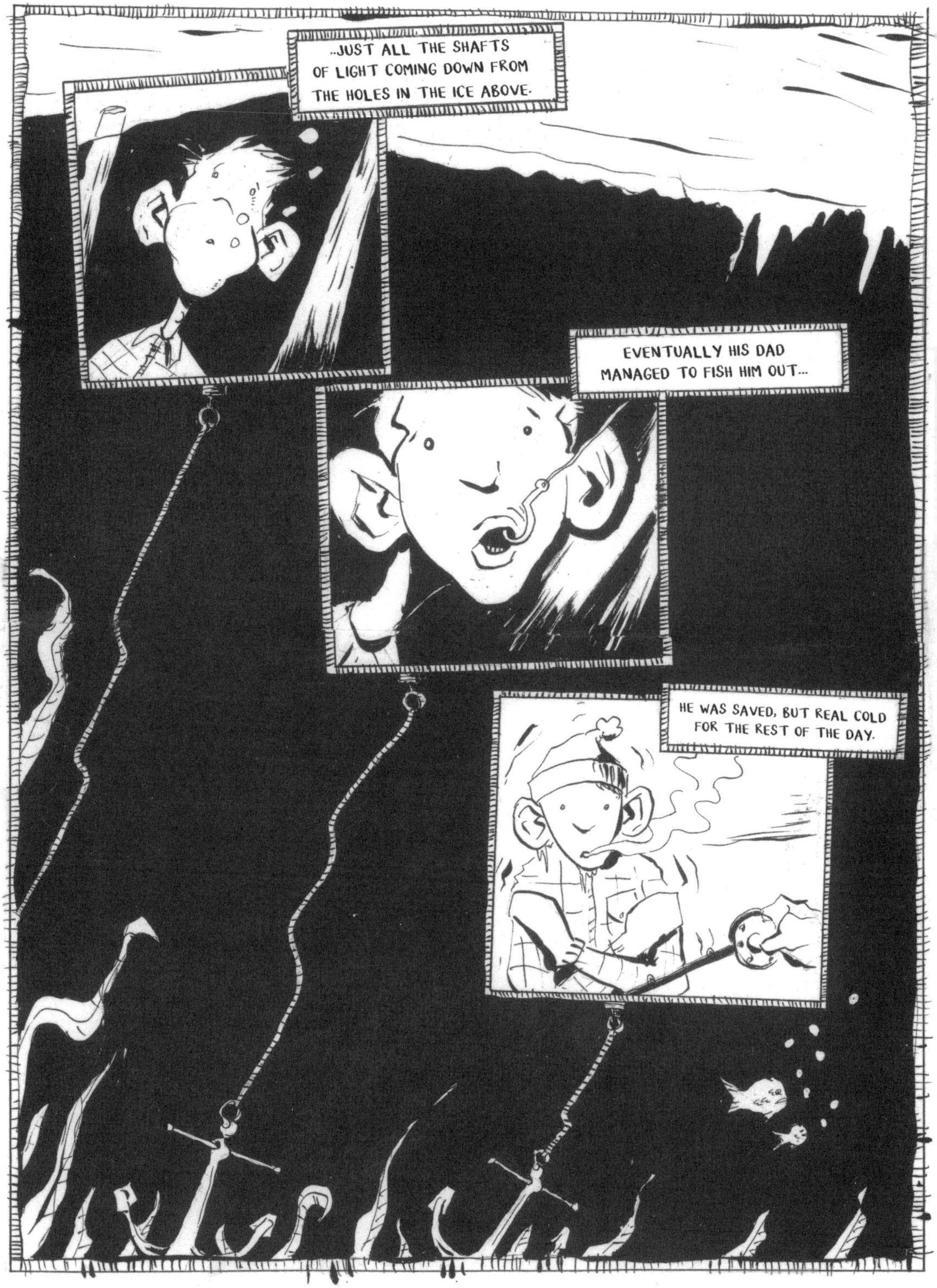
..JUST ALL THE SHAFTS OF LIGHT COMING DOWN FROM THE HOLES IN THE ICE ABOVE.
EVENTUALLY HIS DAD MANAGED TO FISH HIM OUT...
HE WAS SAVED, BUT REAL COLD FOR THE REST OF THE DAY.

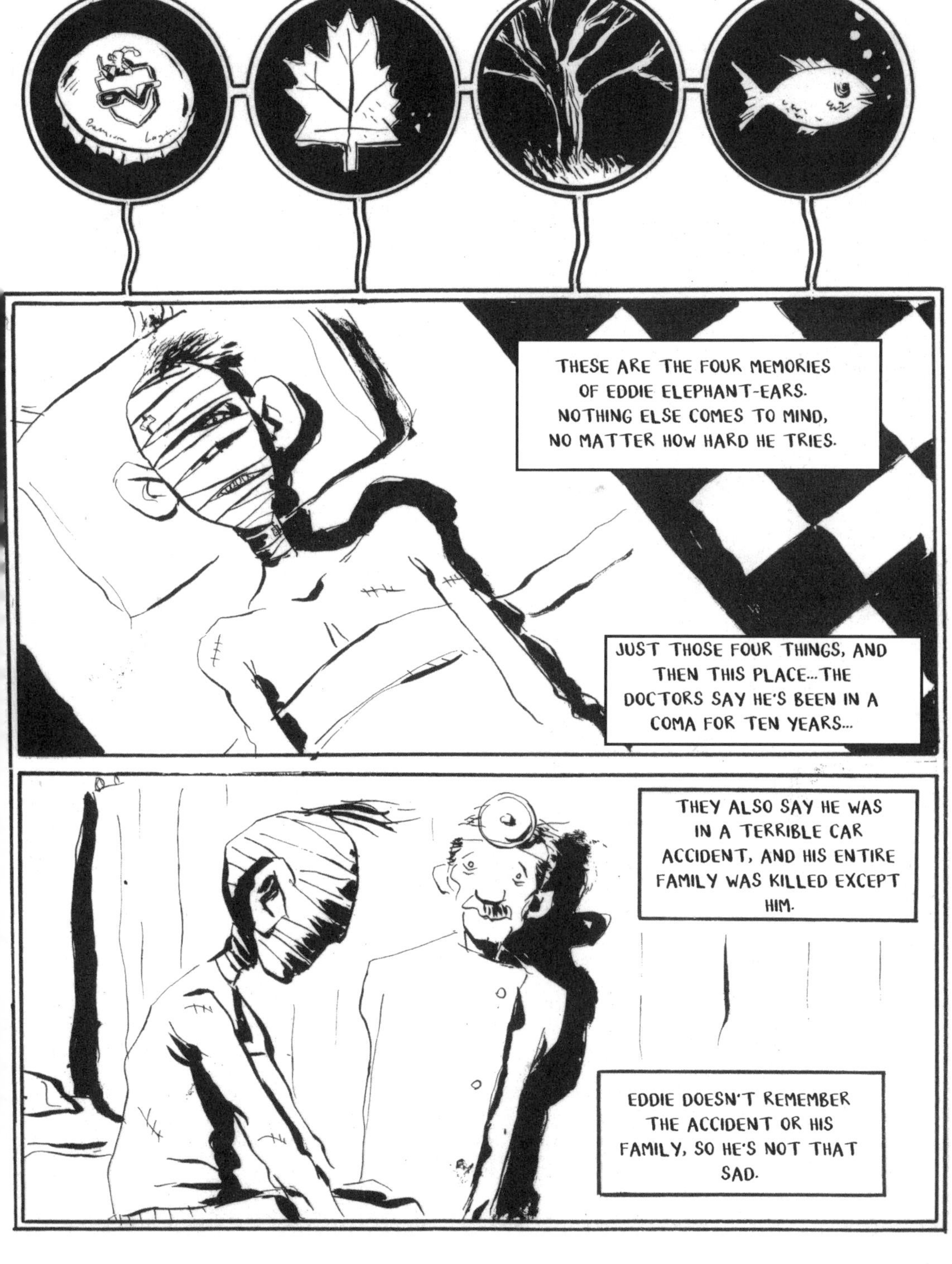
THESE ARE THE FOUR MEMORIES OF EDDIE ELEPHANT-EARS. NOTHING ELSE COMES TO MIND, NO MATTER HOW HARD HE TRIES.
JUST THOSE FOUR THINGS, AND THEN THIS PLACE... THE DOCTORS SAY HE'S BEEN IN A COMA FOR TEN YEARS...
THEY ALSO SAY HE WAS IN A TERRIBLE CAR ACCIDENT, AND HIS ENTIRE FAMILY WAS KILLED EXCEPT HIM.
EDDIE DOESN'T REMEMBER THE ACCIDENT OR HIS FAMILY, SO HE'S NOT THAT SAD.

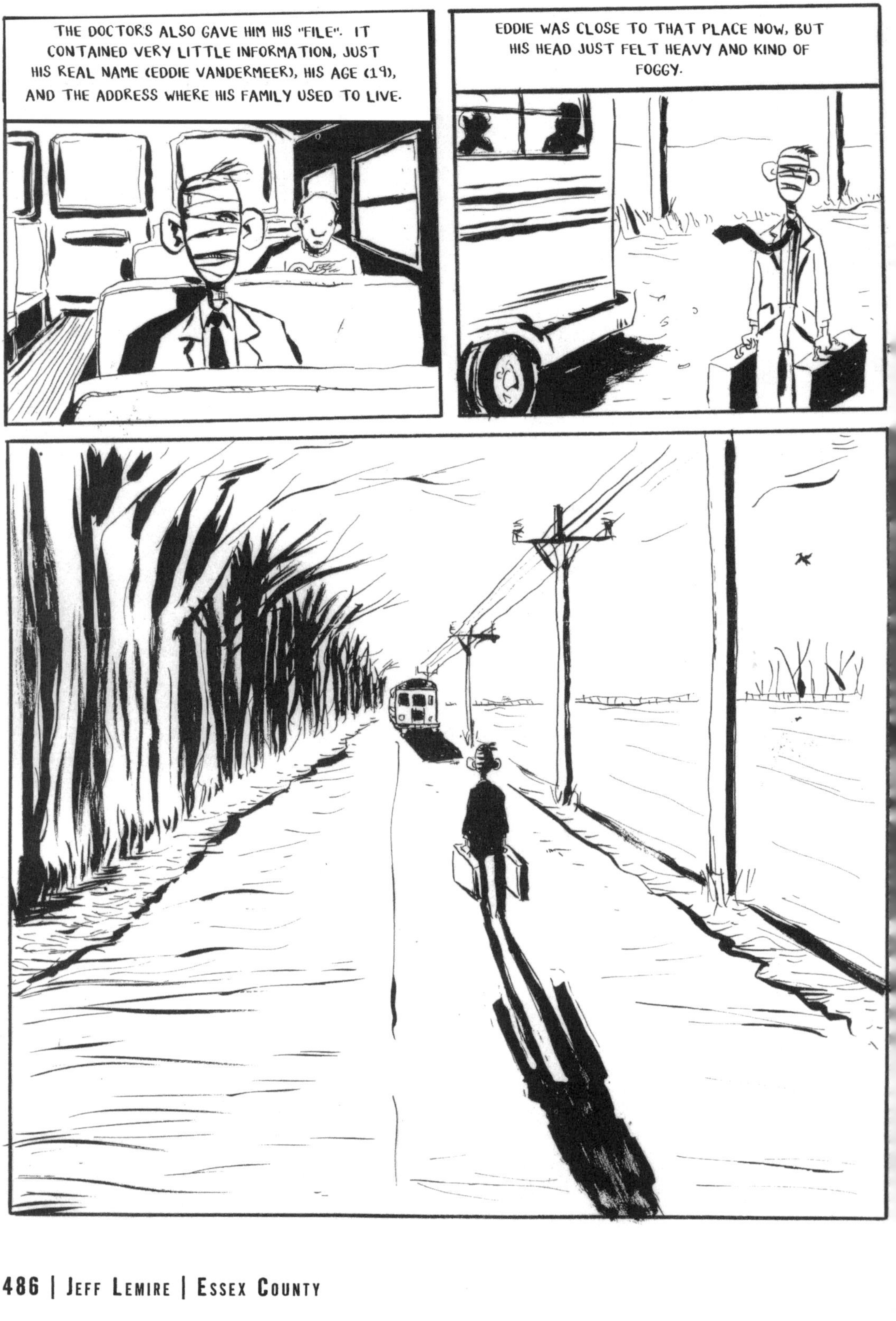
THE DOCTORS ALSO GAVE HIM HIS "FILE". IT CONTAINED VERY LITTLE INFORMATION, JUST HIS REAL NAME (EDDIE VANDERMEER), HIS AGE (19), AND THE ADDRESS WHERE HIS FAMILY USED TO LIVE.
EDDIE WAS CLOSE TO THAT PLACE NOW, BUT HIS HEAD JUST FELT HEAVY AND KIND OF FOGGY.

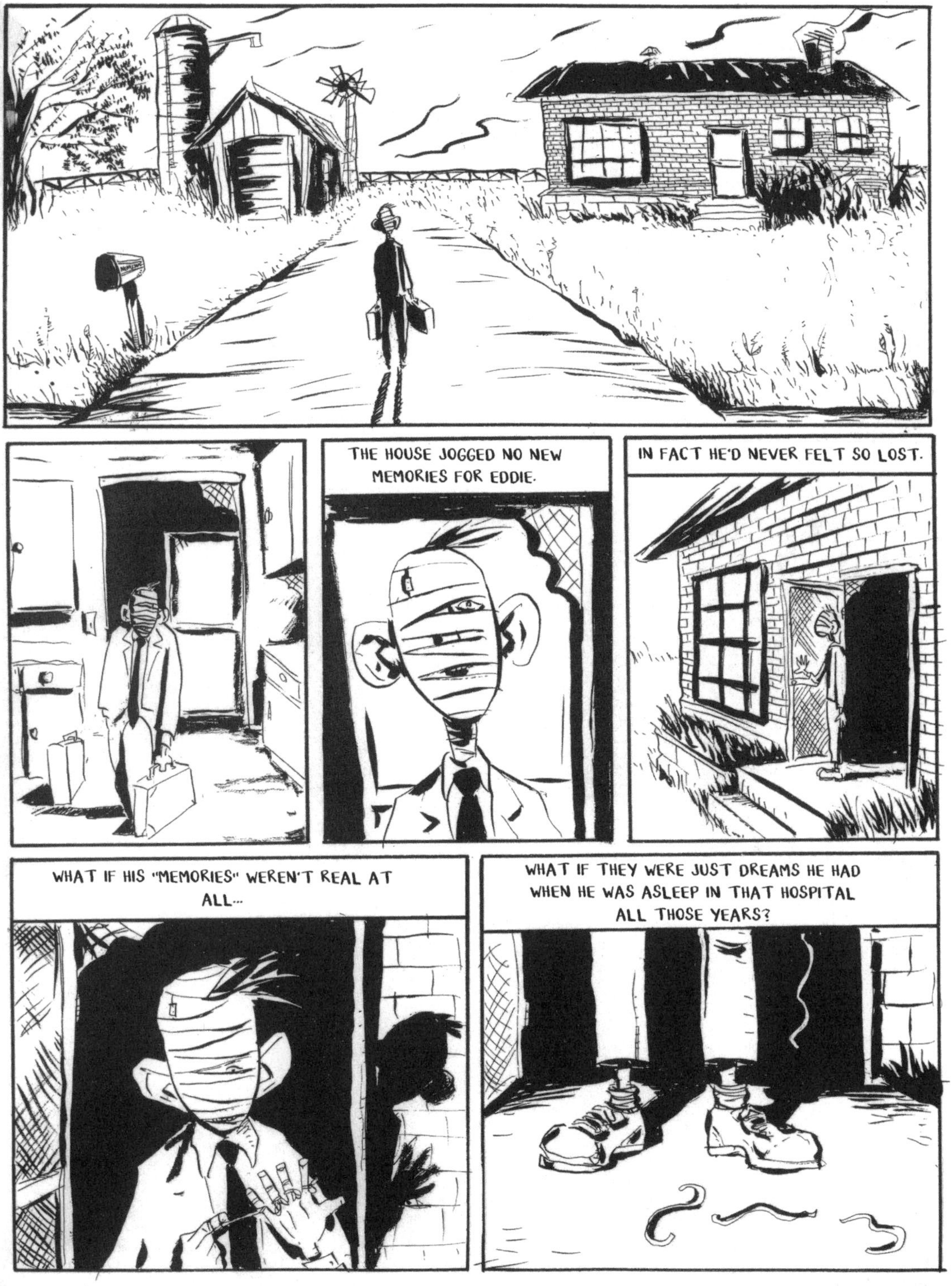
THE HOUSE JOGGED NO NEW MEMORIES FOR EDDIE.
IN FACT HE'D NEVER FELT SO LOST.
WHAT IF HIS "MEMORIES" WEREN'T REAL AT ALL...
WHAT IF THEY WERE JUST DREAMS HE HAD WHEN HE WAS ASLEEP IN THAT HOSPITAL ALL THOSE YEARS?

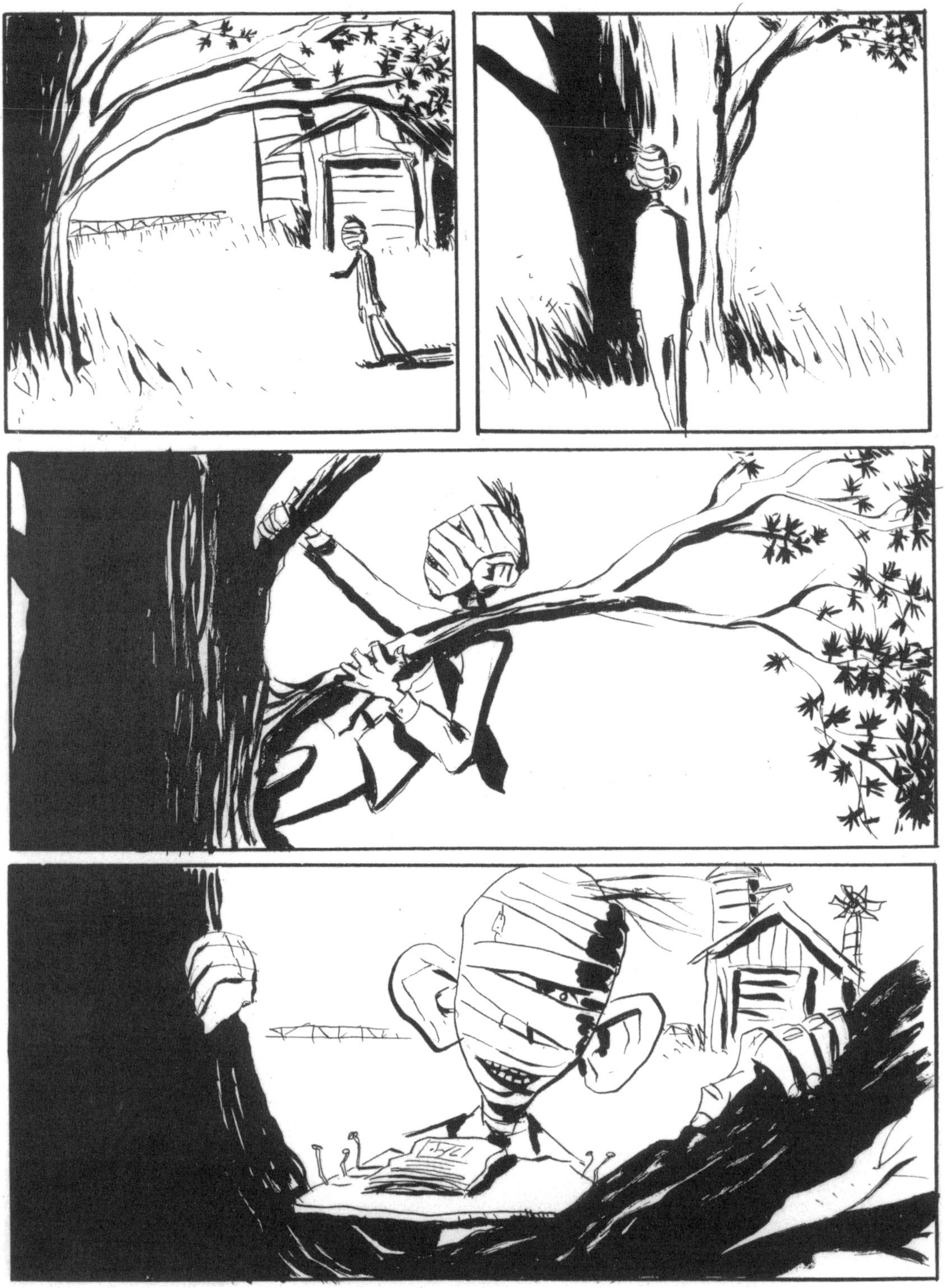

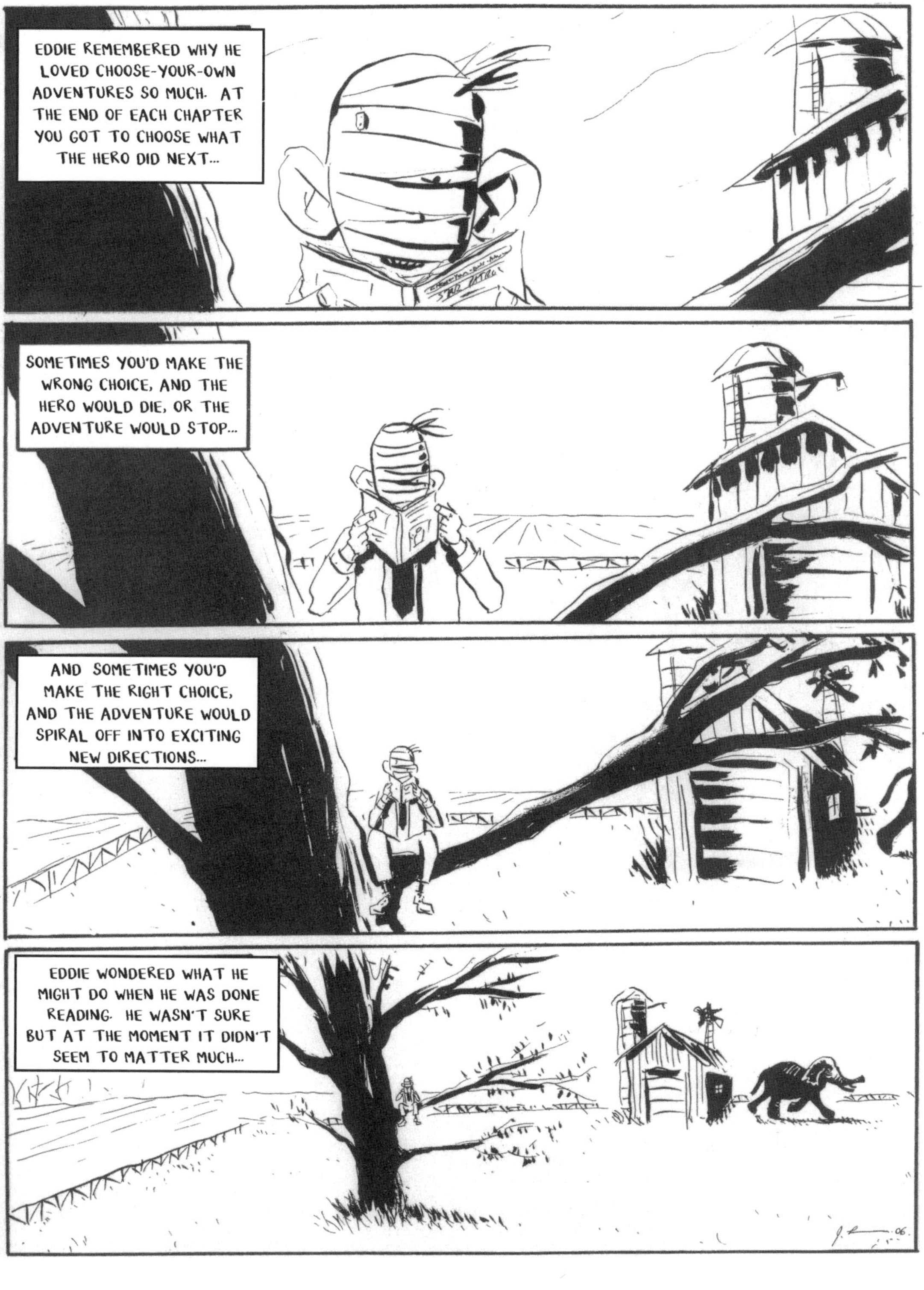
EDDIE REMEMBERED WHY HE LOVED CHOOSE-YOUR-OWN ADVENTURES SO MUCH. AT THE END OF EACH CHAPTER YOU GOT TO CHOOSE WHAT THE HERO DID NEXT...
SOMETIMES YOU'D MAKE THE WRONG CHOICE, AND THE HERO WOULD DIE, OR THE ADVENTURE WOULD STOP...
AND SOMETIMES YOU'D MAKE THE RIGHT CHOICE, AND THE ADVENTURE WOULD SPIRAL OFF INTO EXCITING NEW DIRECTIONS...
EDDIE WONDERED WHAT HE MIGHT DO WHEN HE WAS DONE READING. HE WASN'T SURE BUT AT THE MOMENT IT DIDN'T SEEM TO MATTER MUCH...

BARNYARD SCRAPS
BONUS MATERIAL

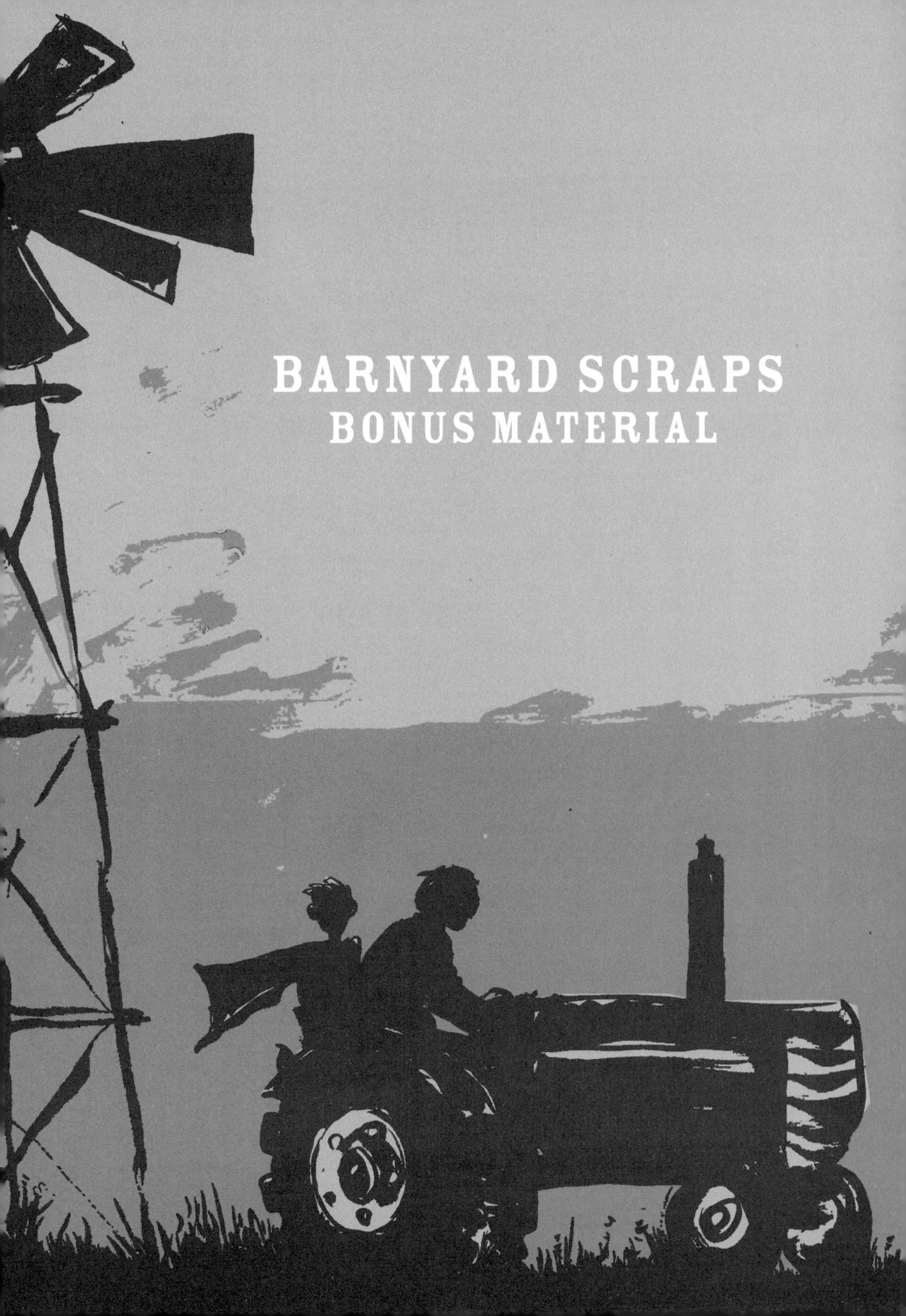

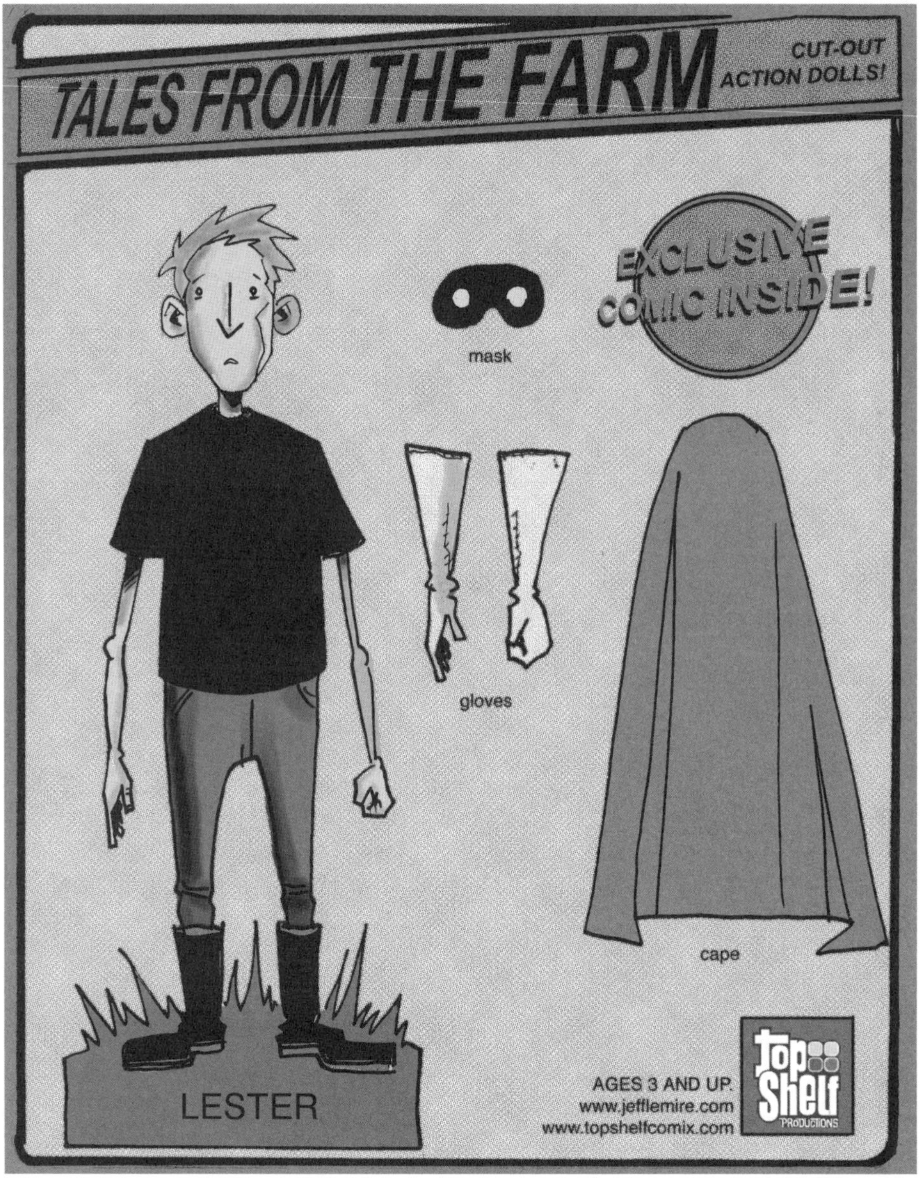
TALES FROM THE FARM
CUT-OUT ACTION DOLLS!
EXCLUSIVE COMIC INSIDE!
mask
gloves
cape
LESTER
AGES 3 AND UP.
www.jefflemire.com
www.topshelfcomix.com
Top Shelf PRODUCTIONS

TALES FROM THE FARM cut-out dolls.

In 2008 I printed a very limited edition run of TALES cut-out dolls featuring fully accessorized Jimmy and Lester figures, printed in full color on card stock. The inside opened into an exclusive 2-page Jimmy and Lester comic (pp. 494–495). In total I think I only printed and sold about 25 copies at conventions.

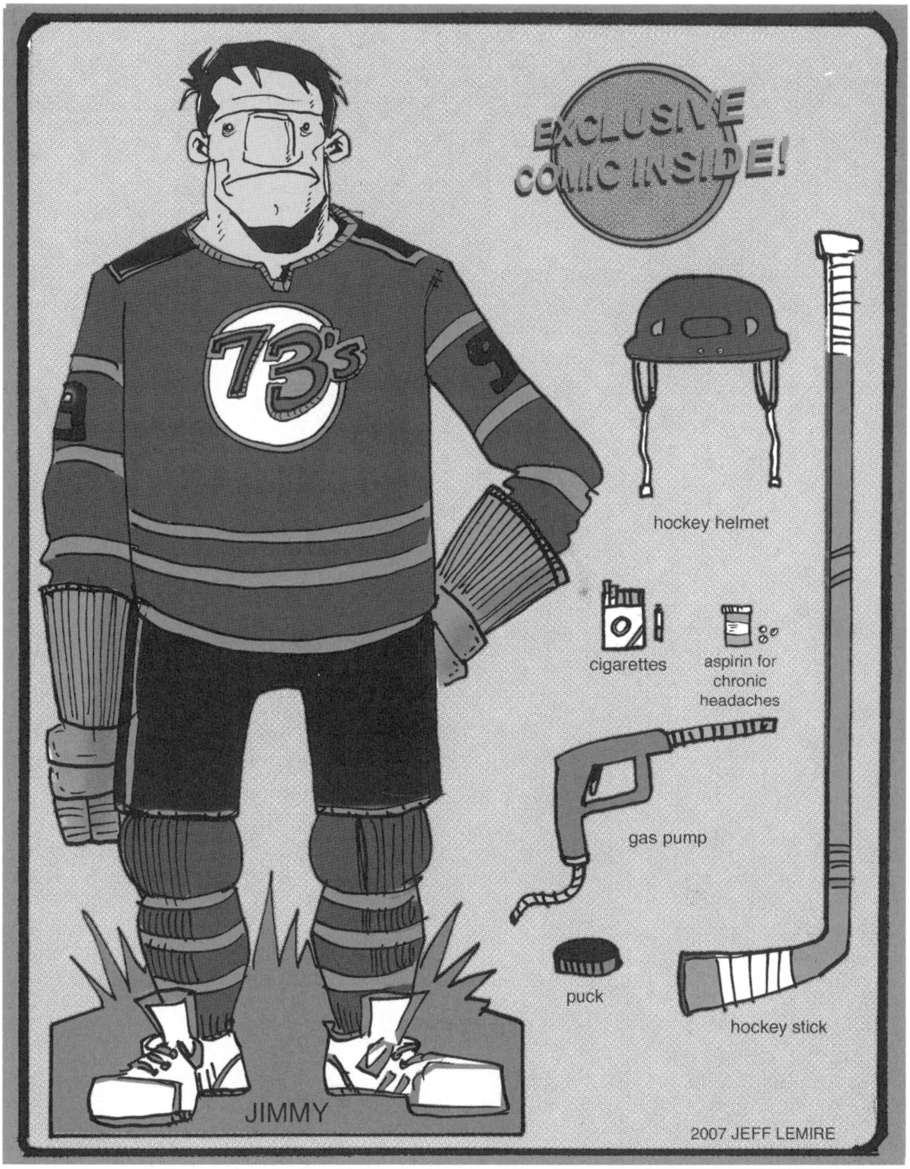
EXCLUSIVE COMIC INSIDE!
73's
hockey helmet
cigarettes
aspirin for chronic headaches
gas pump
puck
hockey stick
JIMMY
2007 JEFF LEMIRE

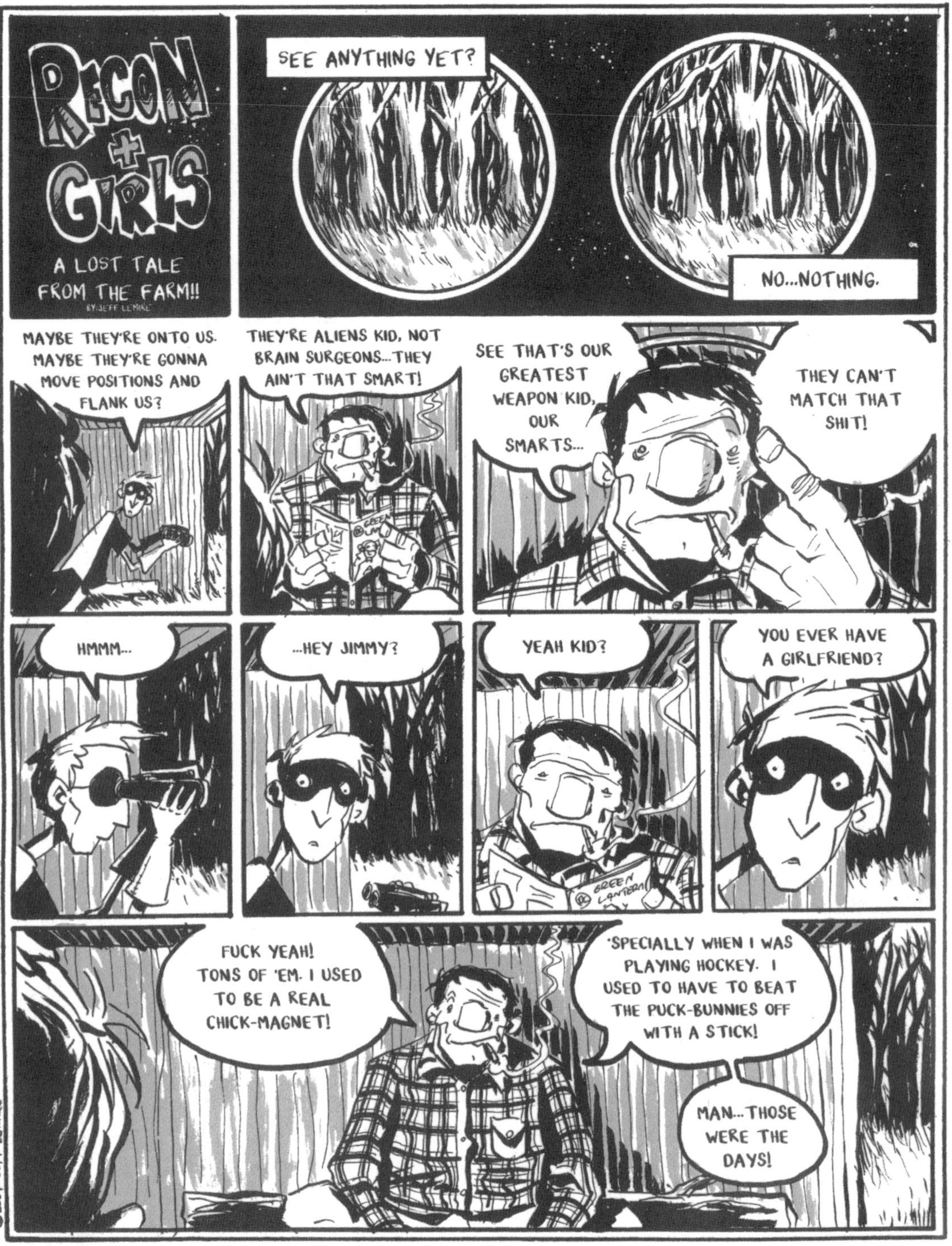
RECON + GIRLS
A LOST TALE FROM THE FARM!!
BY: JEFF LEMIRE
SEE ANYTHING YET?
NO...NOTHING.
MAYBE THEY'RE ONTO US. MAYBE THEY'RE GONNA MOVE POSITIONS AND FLANK US?
THEY'RE ALIENS KID, NOT BRAIN SURGEONS...THEY AIN'T THAT SMART!
SEE THAT'S OUR GREATEST WEAPON KID, OUR SMARTS...
THEY CAN'T MATCH THAT SHIT!
HMMM...
...HEY JIMMY?
YEAH KID?
YOU EVER HAVE A GIRLFRIEND?
FUCK YEAH! TONS OF 'EM. I USED TO BE A REAL CHICK-MAGNET!
'SPECIALLY WHEN I WAS PLAYING HOCKEY. I USED TO HAVE TO BEAT THE PUCK-BUNNIES OFF WITH A STICK!
MAN...THOSE WERE THE DAYS!
©2007 JEFF LEMIRE

TALES FROM THE FARM mini-comic. This was the 2-page comic included with the cut-out dolls. Continuity-wise, it would fit somewhere into Chapter 3 of **TALES FROM THE FARM**.

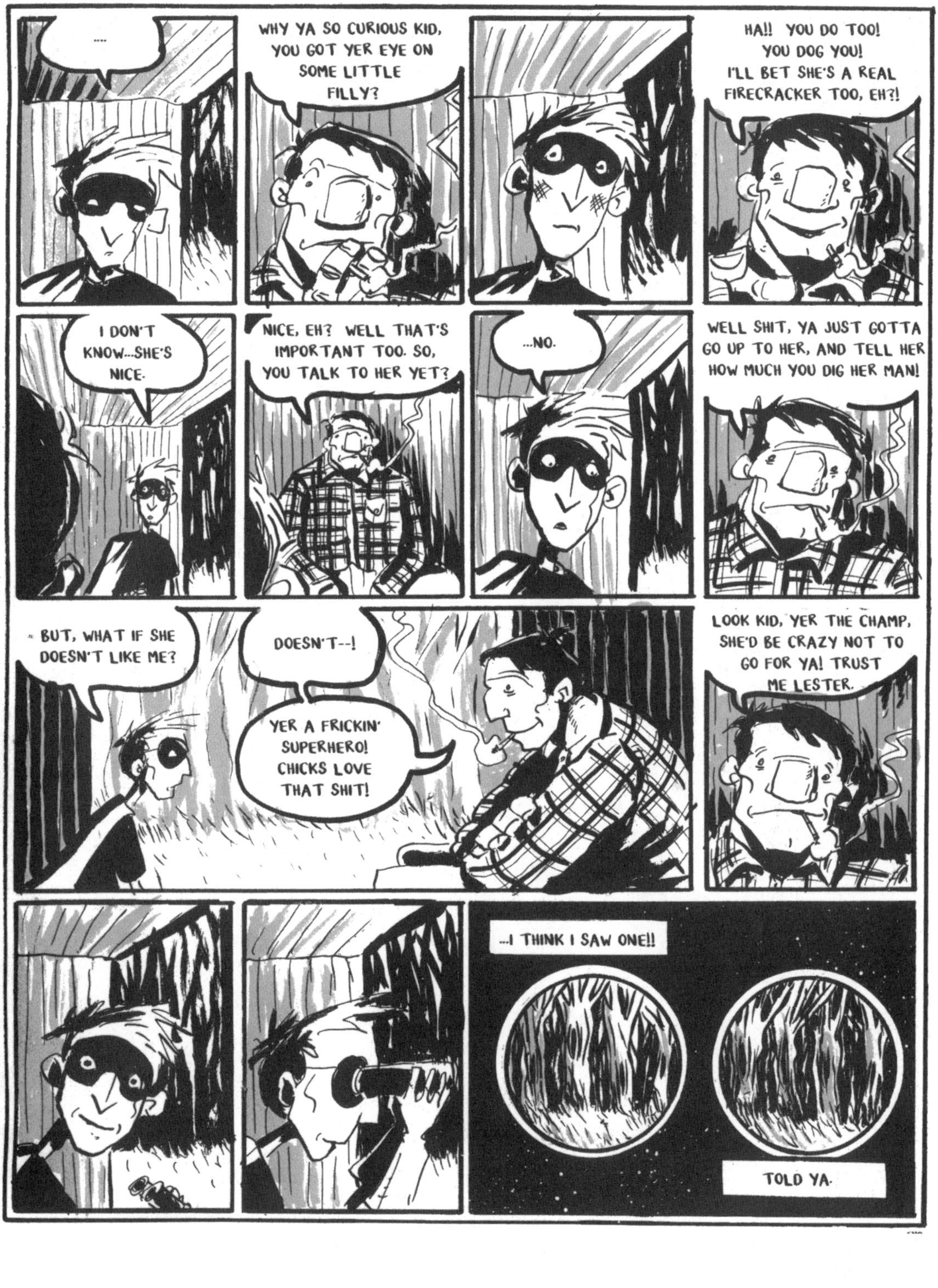
....
WHY YA SO CURIOUS KID, YOU GOT YER EYE ON SOME LITTLE FILLY?
HA!! YOU DO TOO! YOU DOG YOU! I'LL BET SHE'S A REAL FIRECRACKER TOO, EH?!
I DON'T KNOW...SHE'S NICE.
NICE, EH? WELL THAT'S IMPORTANT TOO. SO, YOU TALK TO HER YET?
...NO.
WELL SHIT, YA JUST GOTTA GO UP TO HER, AND TELL HER HOW MUCH YOU DIG HER MAN!
..BUT, WHAT IF SHE DOESN'T LIKE ME?
DOESN'T--!
YER A FRICKIN' SUPERHERO! CHICKS LOVE THAT SHIT!
LOOK KID, YER THE CHAMP, SHE'D BE CRAZY NOT TO GO FOR YA! TRUST ME LESTER.
...I THINK I SAW ONE!!
TOLD YA.

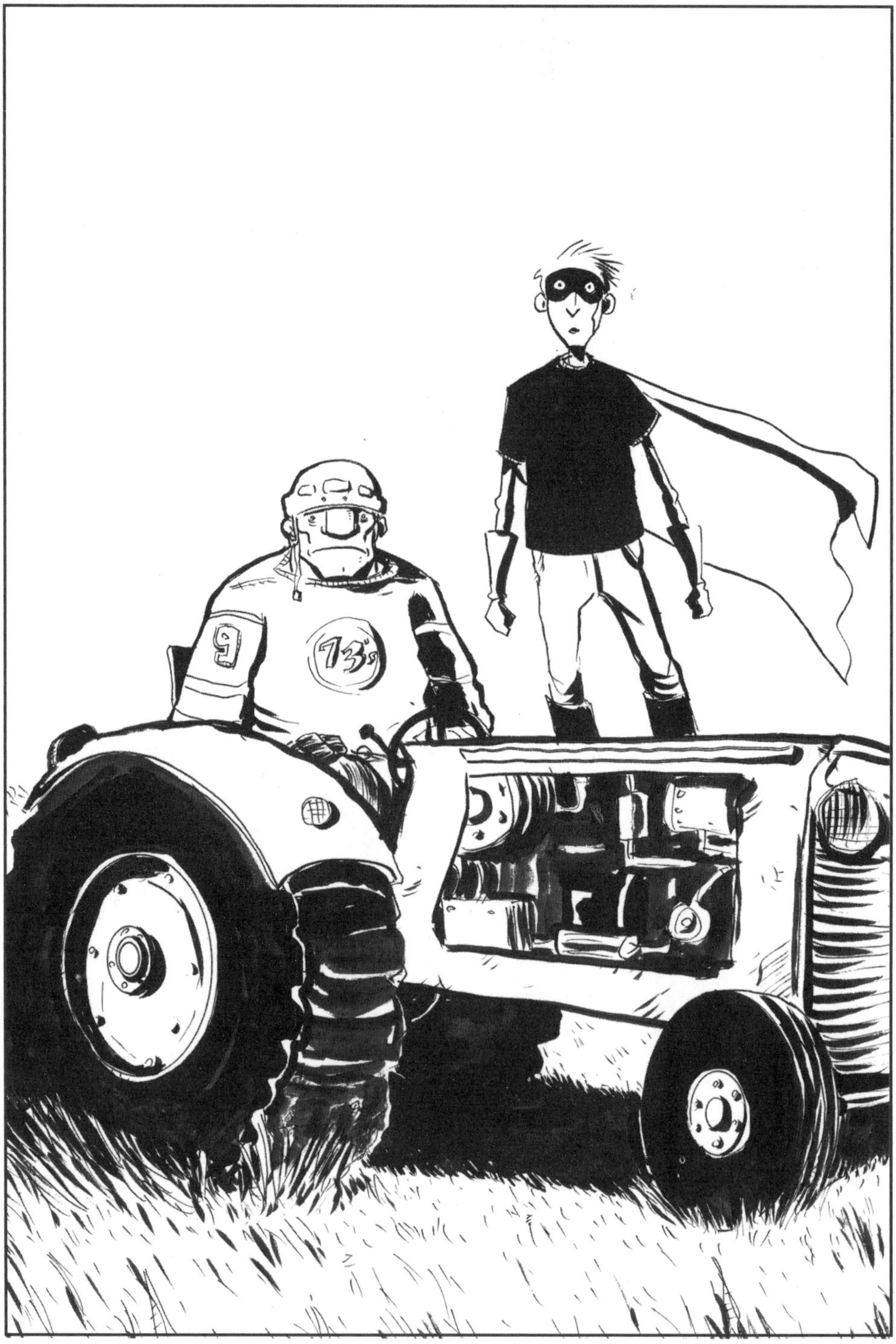
9
73's

Unpublished TALES FROM THE FARM promotional artwork.

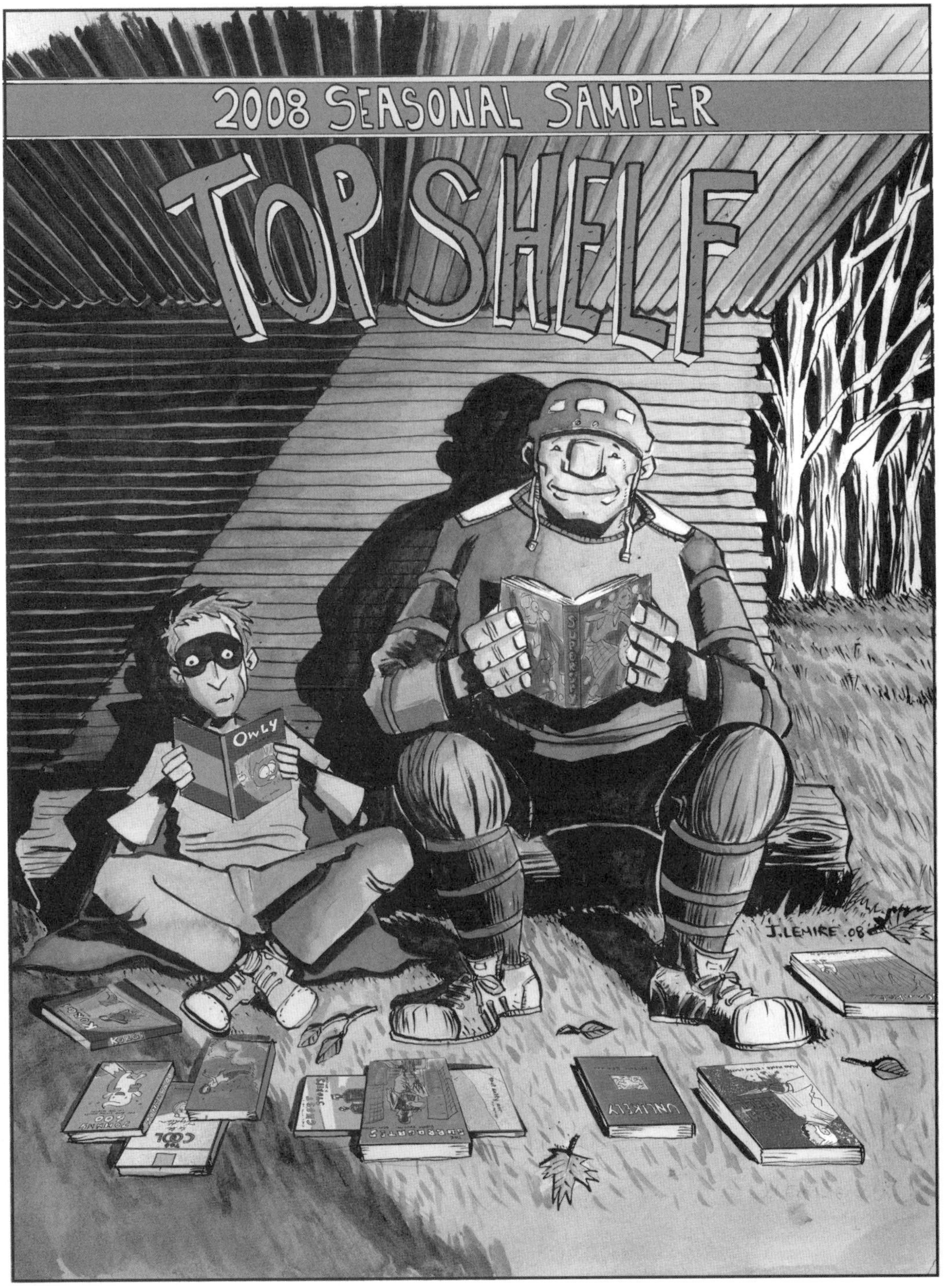
2008 SEASONAL SAMPLER
TOP SHELF
OWLY
UNLIKELY
J. LEMIRE '08

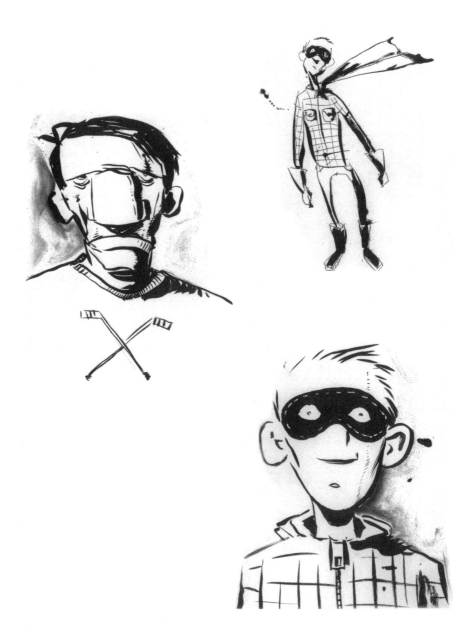

Early Designs: TALES FROM THE FARM.

Here are some of the earliest character designs for Lester and Jimmy. Jimmy isn't quite as imposing as he would become, but that nose is still there even in the first incarnation. Interestingly enough, the early Lester had a nose much more like Jimmy's.

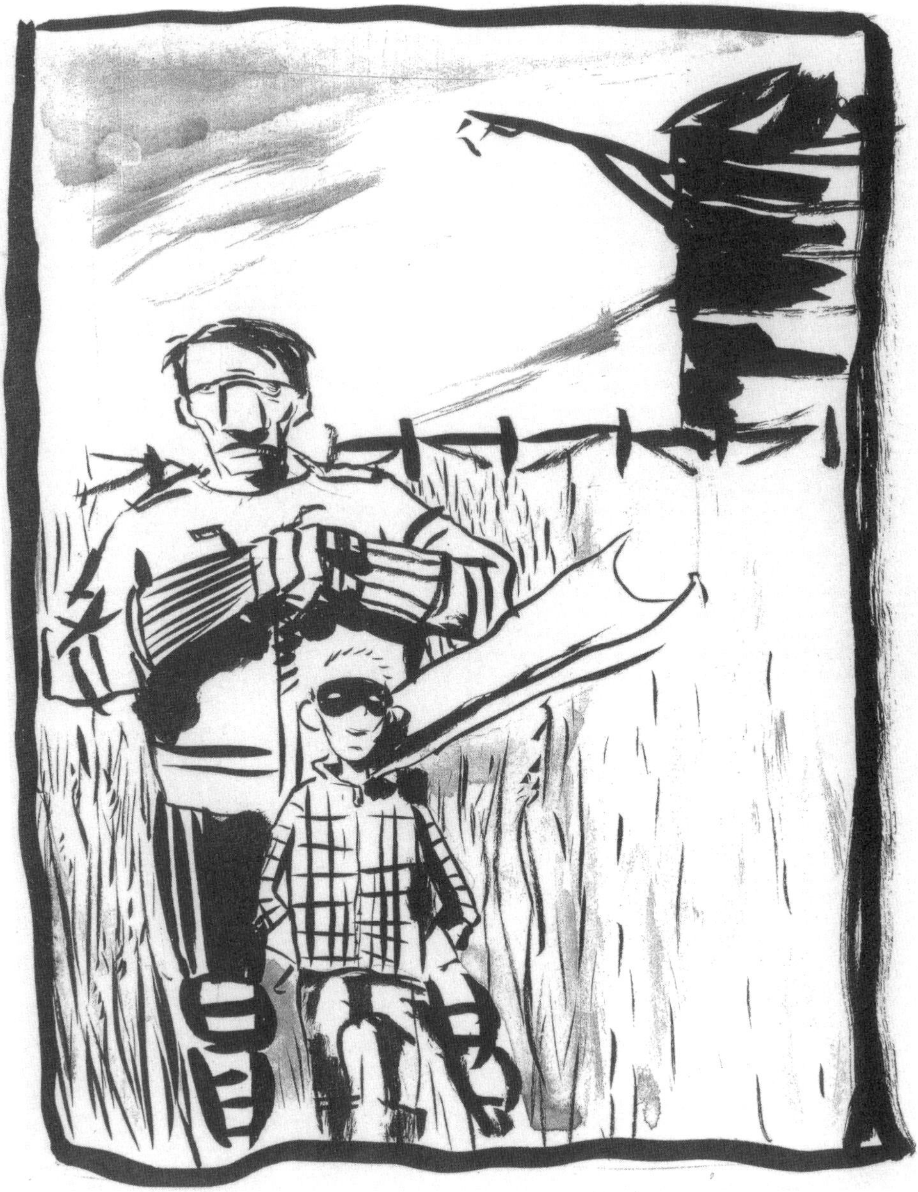

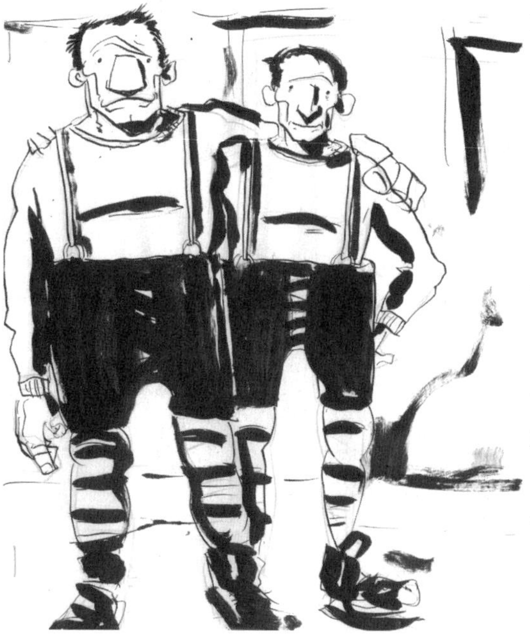

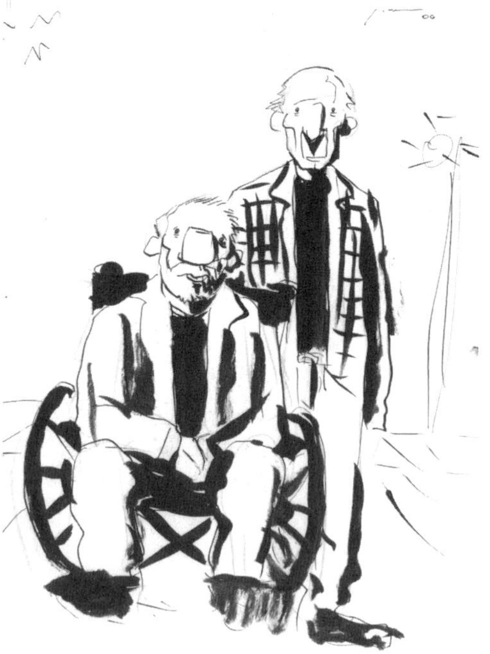

Early Designs: GHOST STORIES.

These are some of the earliest design sketches of the characters from GHOST STORIES. While a bit cruder than the final versions, the early attempts at aging the characters over several decades were pretty successful.

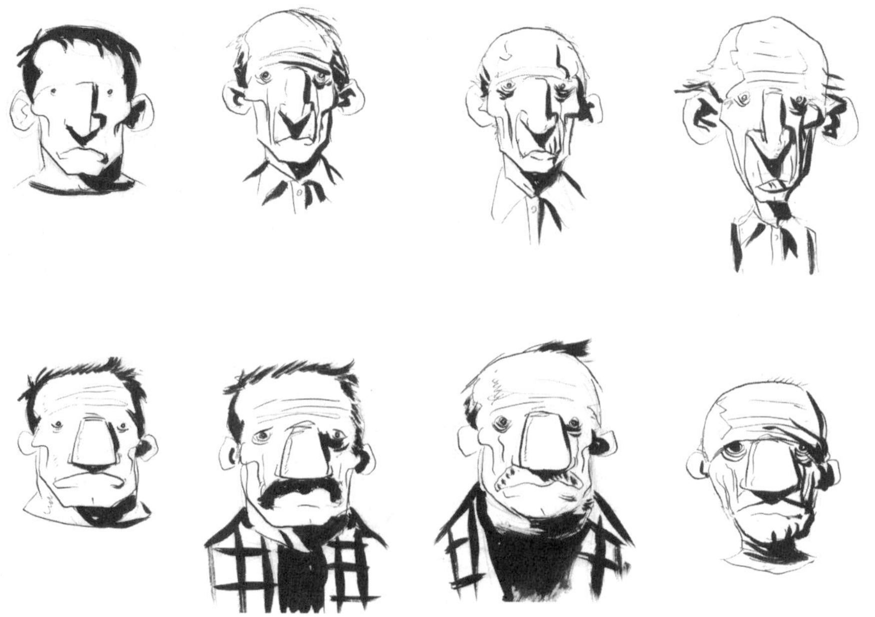

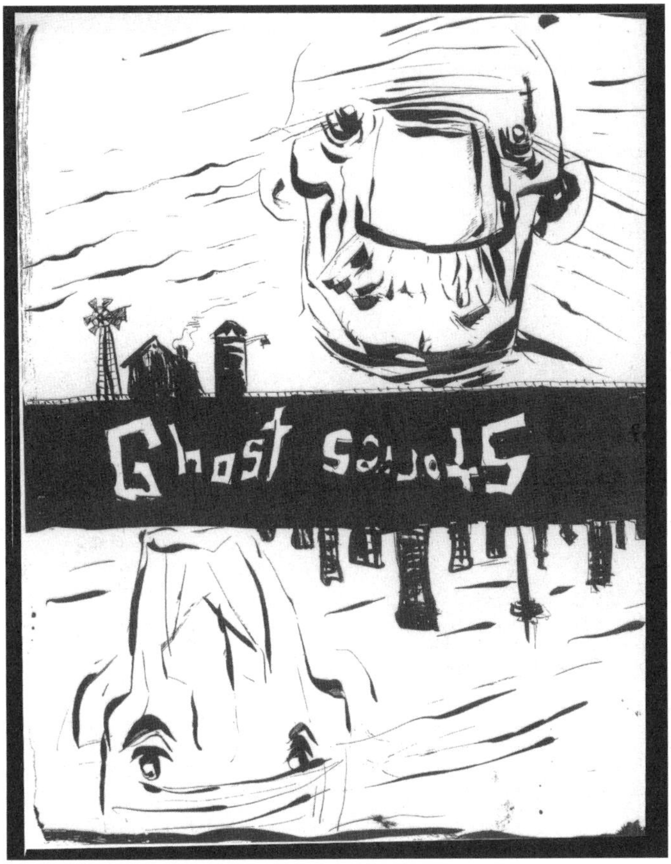
Ghost Stories

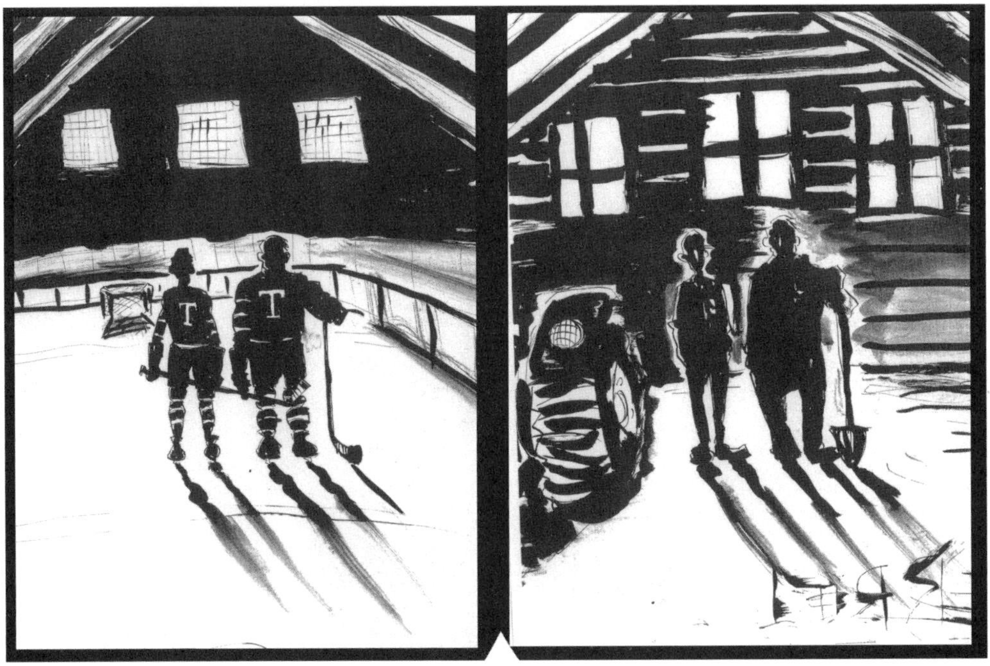

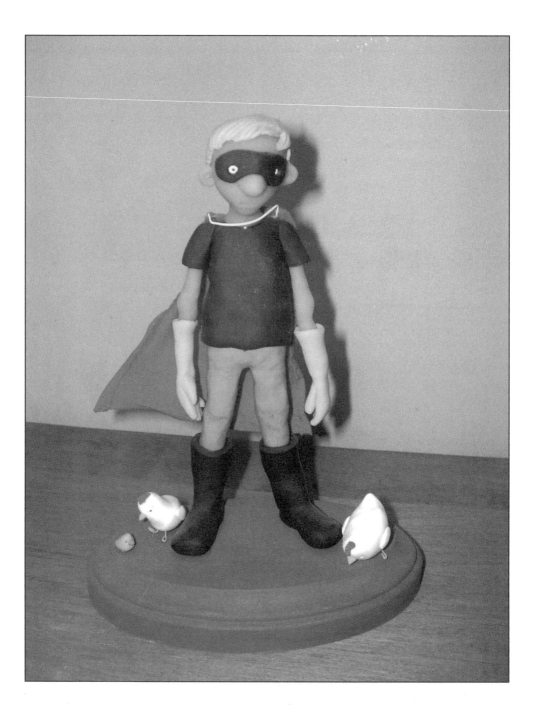

Lester Action Figure:
My Wife Lesley-Anne Green is also a sculpture and doll maker. She made a Lester action figure for Christmas in 2007. He is my most prized possession.

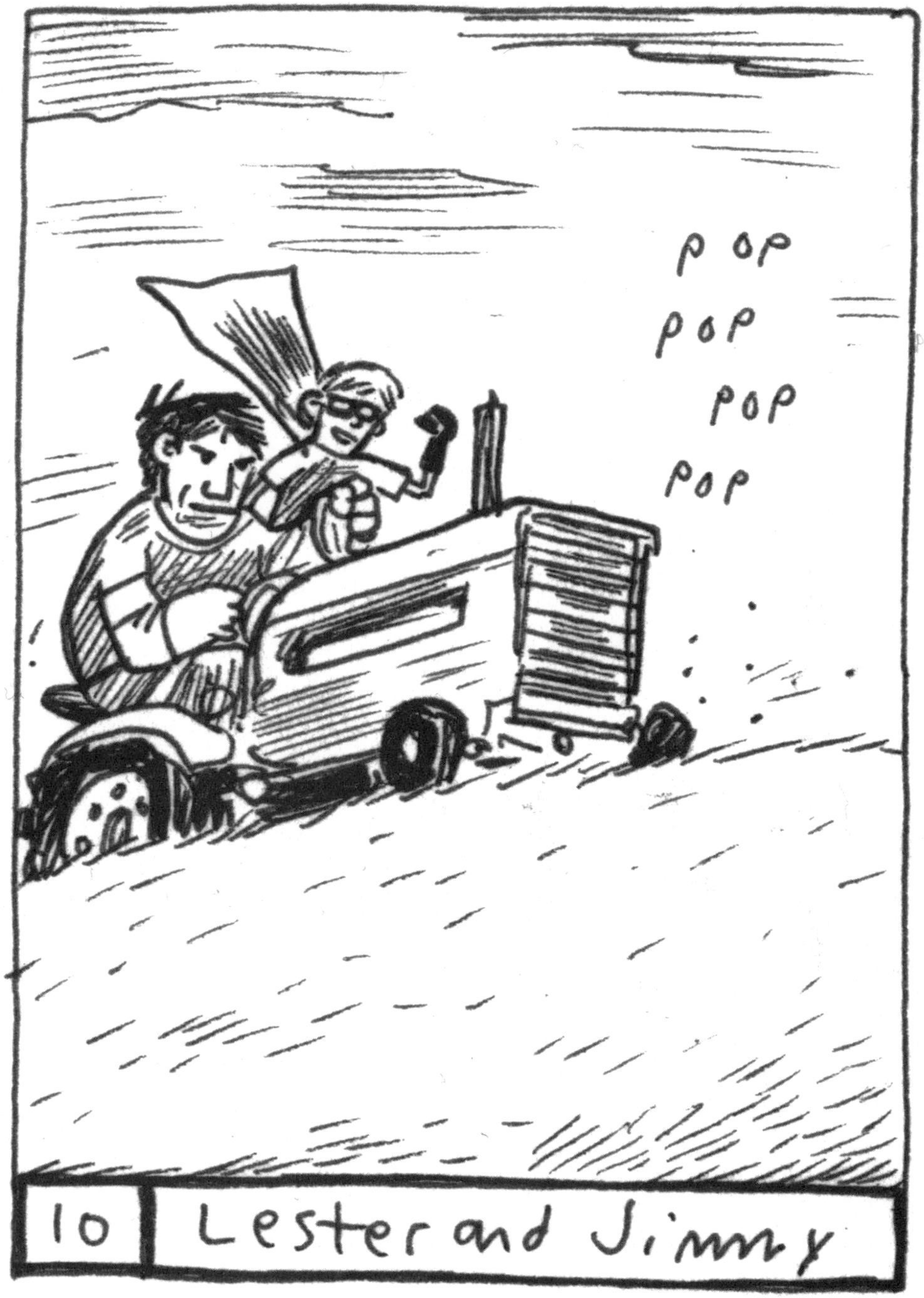
pop
pop
pop
pop
10
Lester and Jimmy

This was the front of a trading card sketch cartoonist and friend Jeffrey Brown drew for me while manning the Top Shelf table at New York Comicon in 2008.

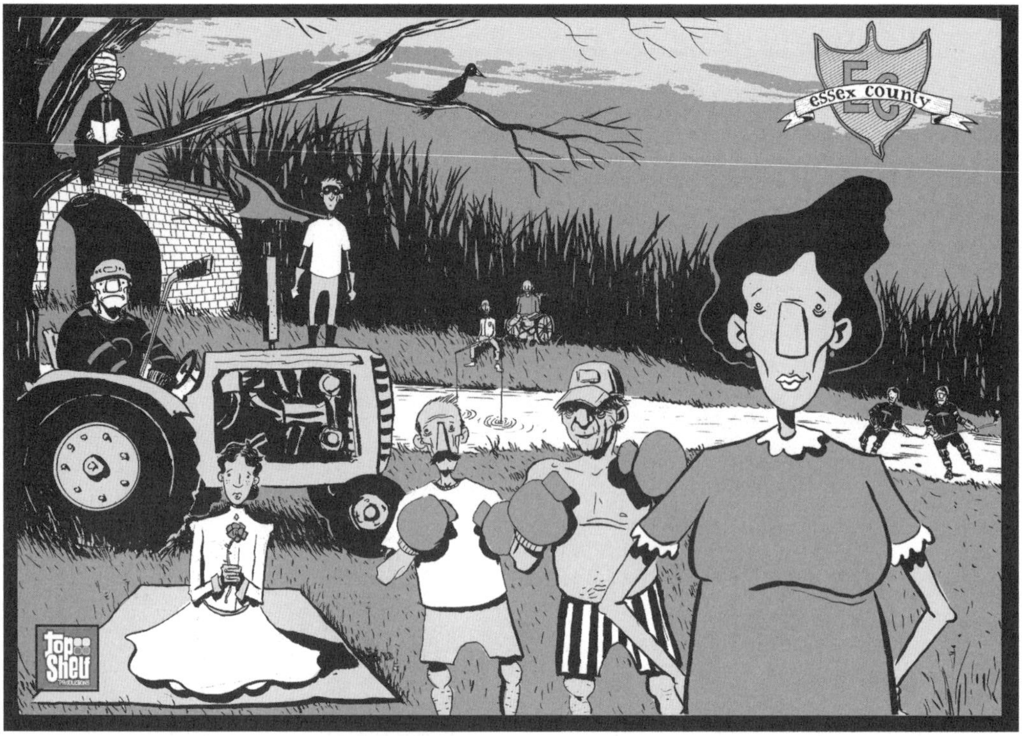
essex county
EC

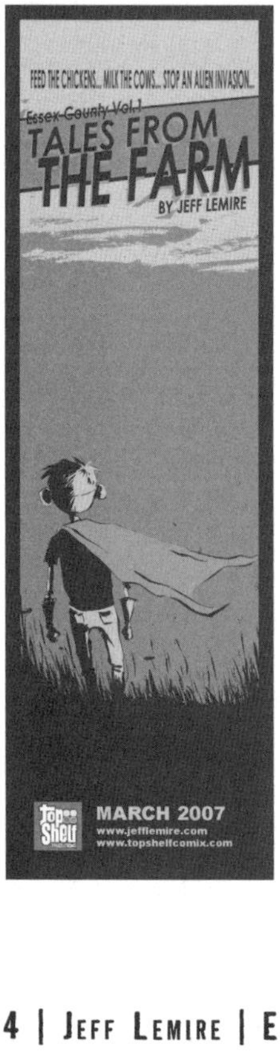
FEED THE CHICKENS... MILK THE COWS... STOP AN ALIEN INVASION...
Essex County Vol.1
TALES FROM THE FARM
BY JEFF LEMIRE
MARCH 2007
www.jefflemire.com
www.topshelfcomix.com

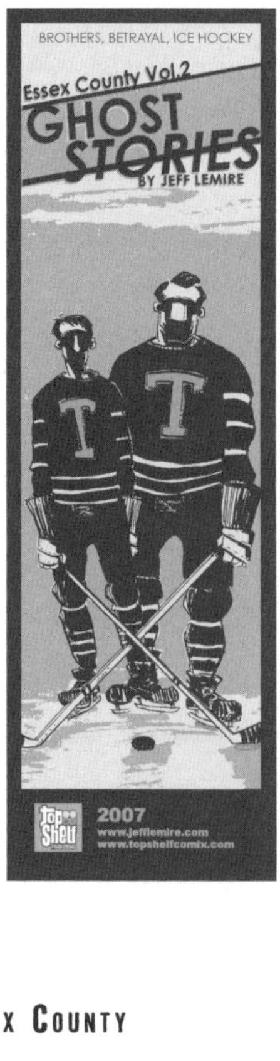
BROTHERS, BETRAYAL, ICE HOCKEY
Essex County Vol.2
GHOST STORIES
BY JEFF LEMIRE
2007
www.jefflemire.com
www.topshelfcomix.com

ESSEX COUNTY Dust Jacket (above): When TALES FROM THE FARM and GHOST STORIES were released Brett Warnock asked me to start thinking about possible cover designs for the eventual collected edition. This was an early attempt. You might notice it features a few characters who never made it into the trilogy, including an ancestor of Beth and Mary from GHOST STORIES. Her role was later replaced by the young nun in COUNTRY NURSE.

ESSEX COUNTY Bookmarks (left): This was a doublesided bookmark which I printed to hand out at conventions and mail to comics shops as promotional material. There were only 1,000 printed. I especially like the two catch phrases I used at the tops of each.

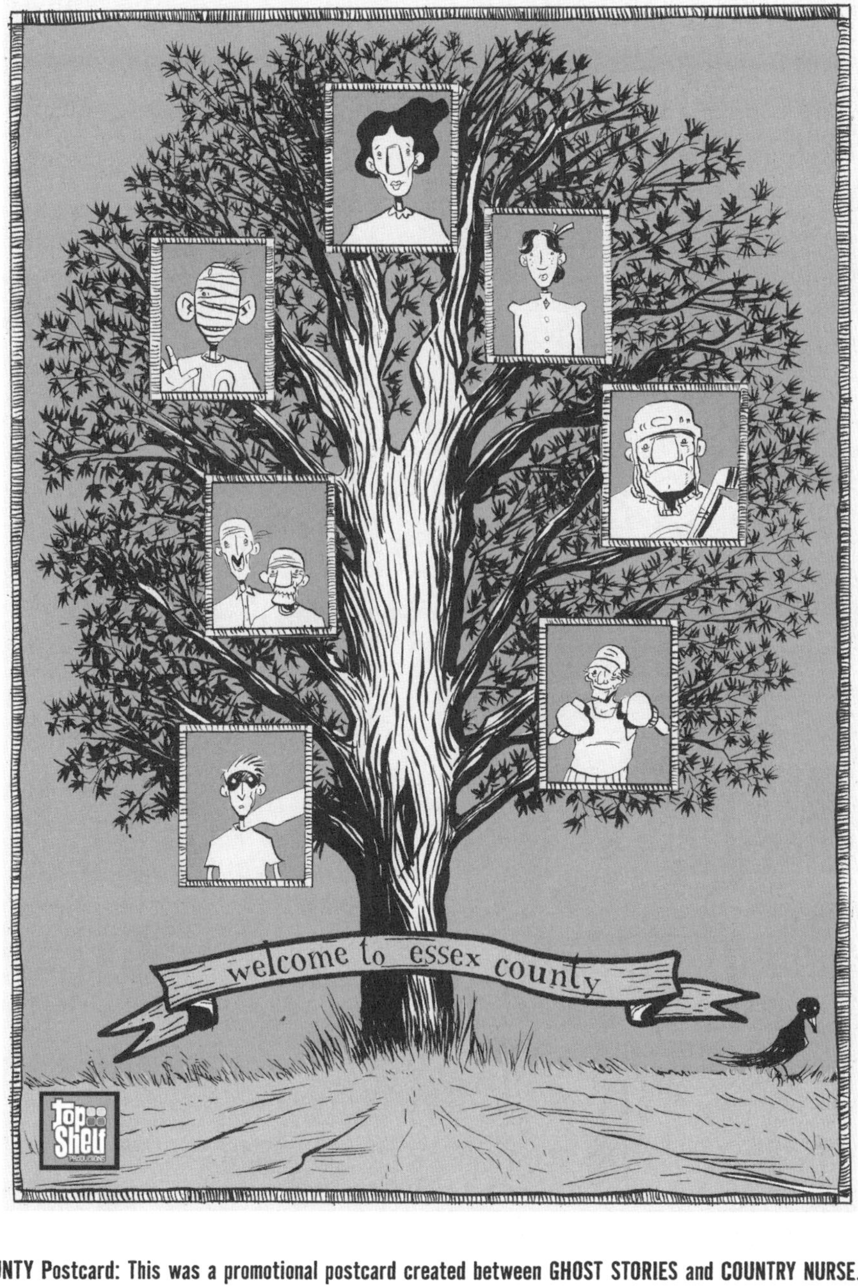
welcome to essex county
Top Shelf Productions

ESSEX COUNTY Postcard: This was a promotional postcard created between GHOST STORIES and COUNTRY NURSE. Again, the mysterious and unused ancestor to Beth and Mary pops up. In my earlier scripts of COUNTRY NURSE, the characters from "The Essex County Boxing Club" and "Eddie Elephant-Ears" were going to be tied into the overall mythology in a much more direct way. Later, Chris Staros and I agreed to focus more on Lester and Jimmy in the finale, and those two stories became separate mini-comics.

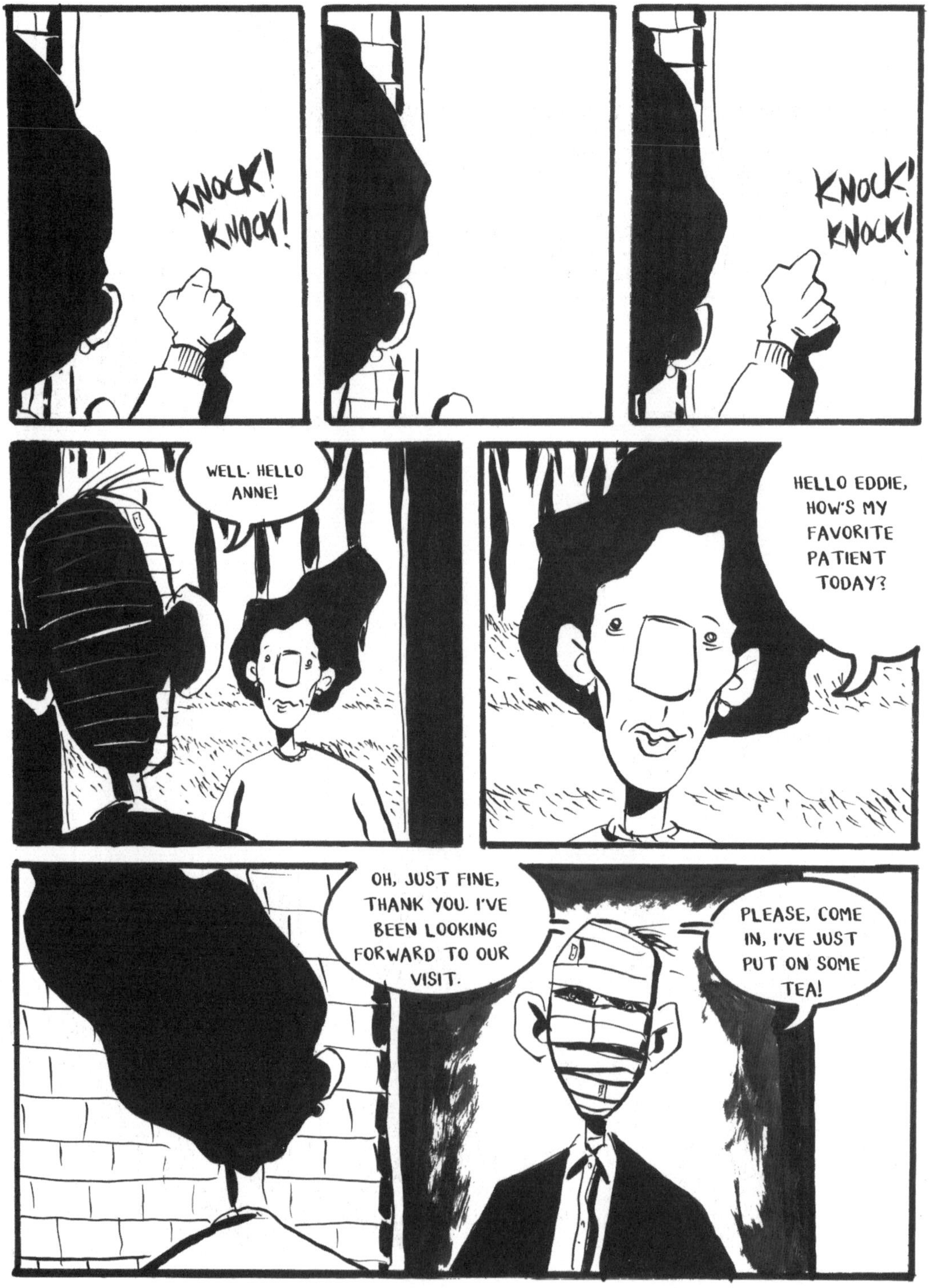
KNOCK! KNOCK!
KNOCK! KNOCK!
WELL. HELLO ANNE!
HELLO EDDIE, HOW'S MY FAVORITE PATIENT TODAY?
OH, JUST FINE, THANK YOU. I'VE BEEN LOOKING FORWARD TO OUR VISIT.
PLEASE, COME IN, I'VE JUST PUT ON SOME TEA!

Anne Meets Eddie Elephant-Ears: As previously mentioned, Eddie and the Boxing Club crew were a much more direct part of the trilogy in my early draft of THE COUNTRY NURSE before being pulled out and made into

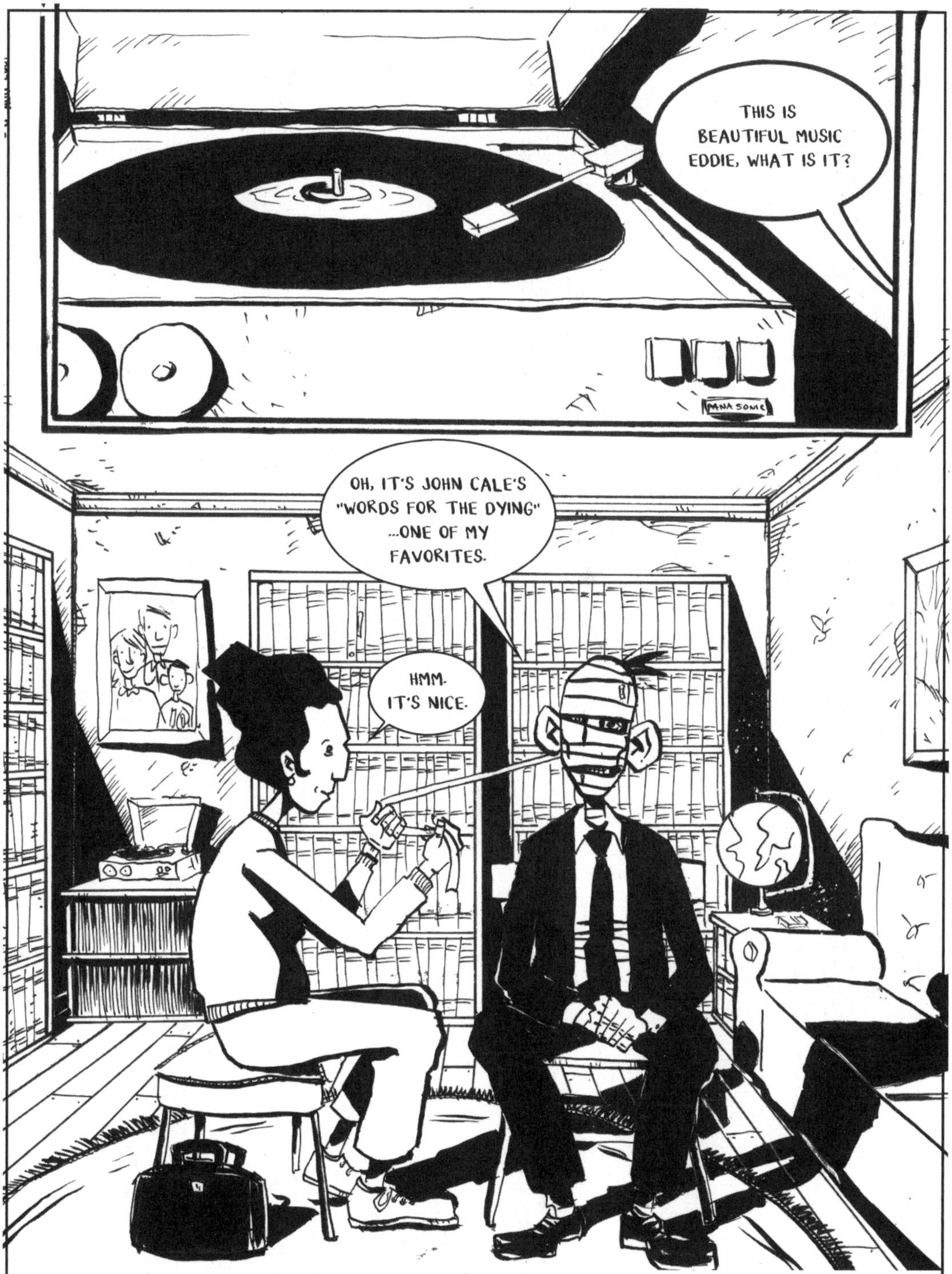
THIS IS BEAUTIFUL MUSIC EDDIE, WHAT IS IT?
OH, IT'S JOHN CALE'S "WORDS FOR THE DYING" ...ONE OF MY FAVORITES.
HMM. IT'S NICE.
PANASONIC

separate stories. This deleted scene, in which Anne visits an adult Eddie on her rounds, originally took place right after she visits Jimmy at the gas station, and before she heads to the cemetery for lunch.

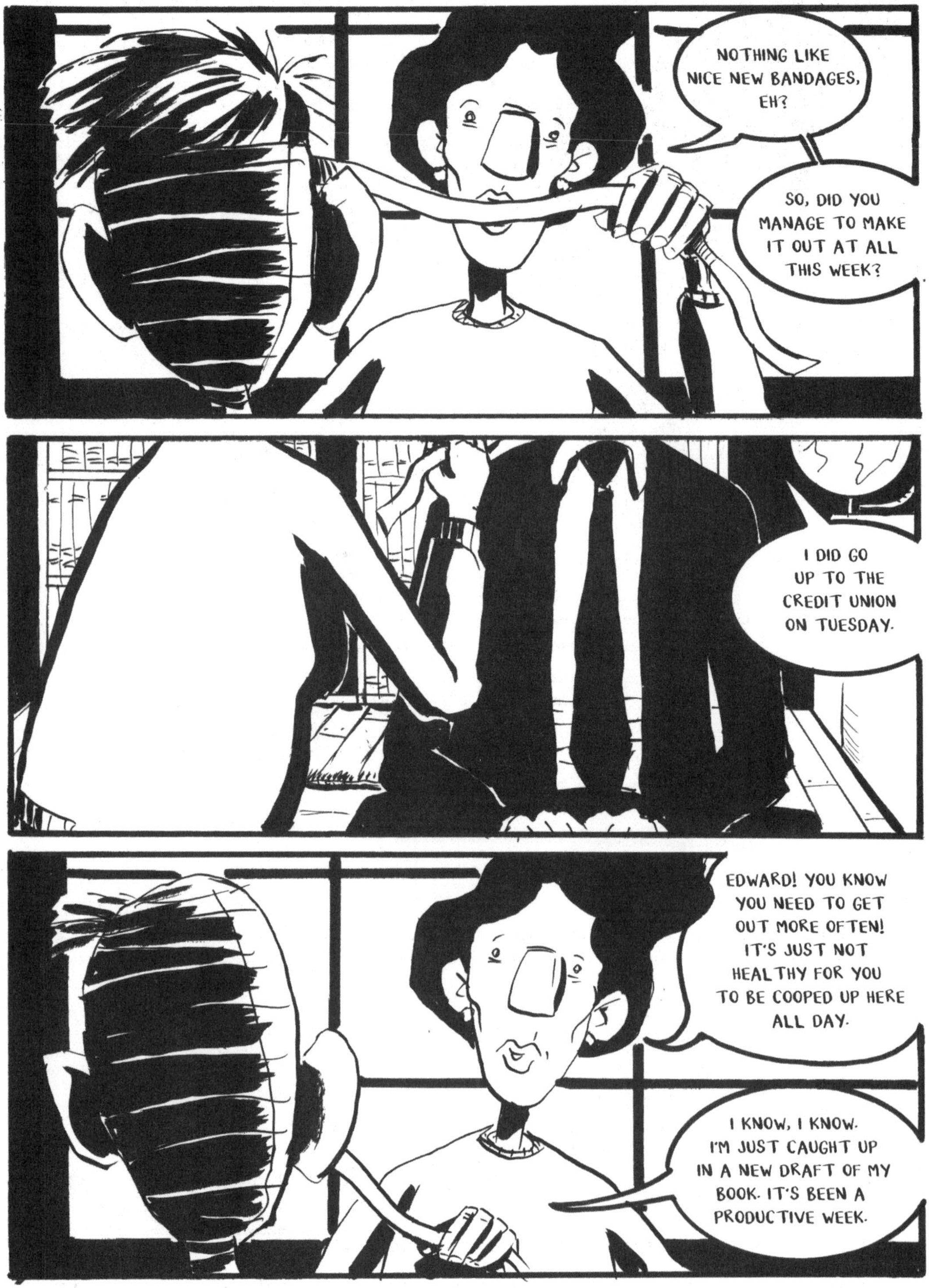
NOTHING LIKE NICE NEW BANDAGES, EH?
SO, DID YOU MANAGE TO MAKE IT OUT AT ALL THIS WEEK?
I DID GO UP TO THE CREDIT UNION ON TUESDAY.
EDWARD! YOU KNOW YOU NEED TO GET OUT MORE OFTEN! IT'S JUST NOT HEALTHY FOR YOU TO BE COOPED UP HERE ALL DAY.
I KNOW, I KNOW. I'M JUST CAUGHT UP IN A NEW DRAFT OF MY BOOK. IT'S BEEN A PRODUCTIVE WEEK.

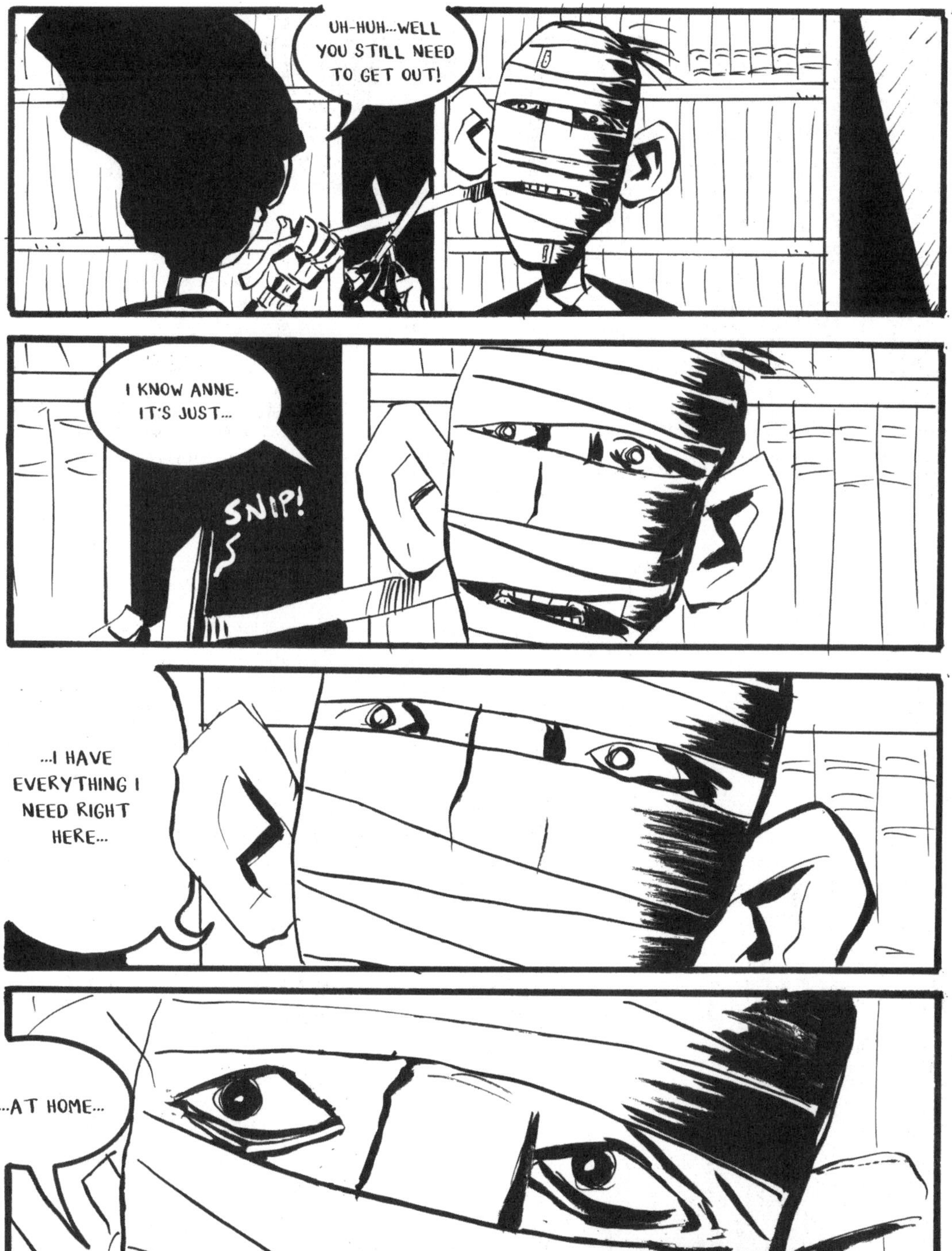
UH-HUH...WELL YOU STILL NEED TO GET OUT!
I KNOW ANNE. IT'S JUST...
SNIP!
...I HAVE EVERYTHING I NEED RIGHT HERE...
...AT HOME...

From here we transitioned into Eddie's backstory, which was later separated and made into one of two very limited edition signed & numbered mini-comics which I sold at conventions and online. It is inlucuded in this volume as one of the LOST TALES FROM THE FARM.

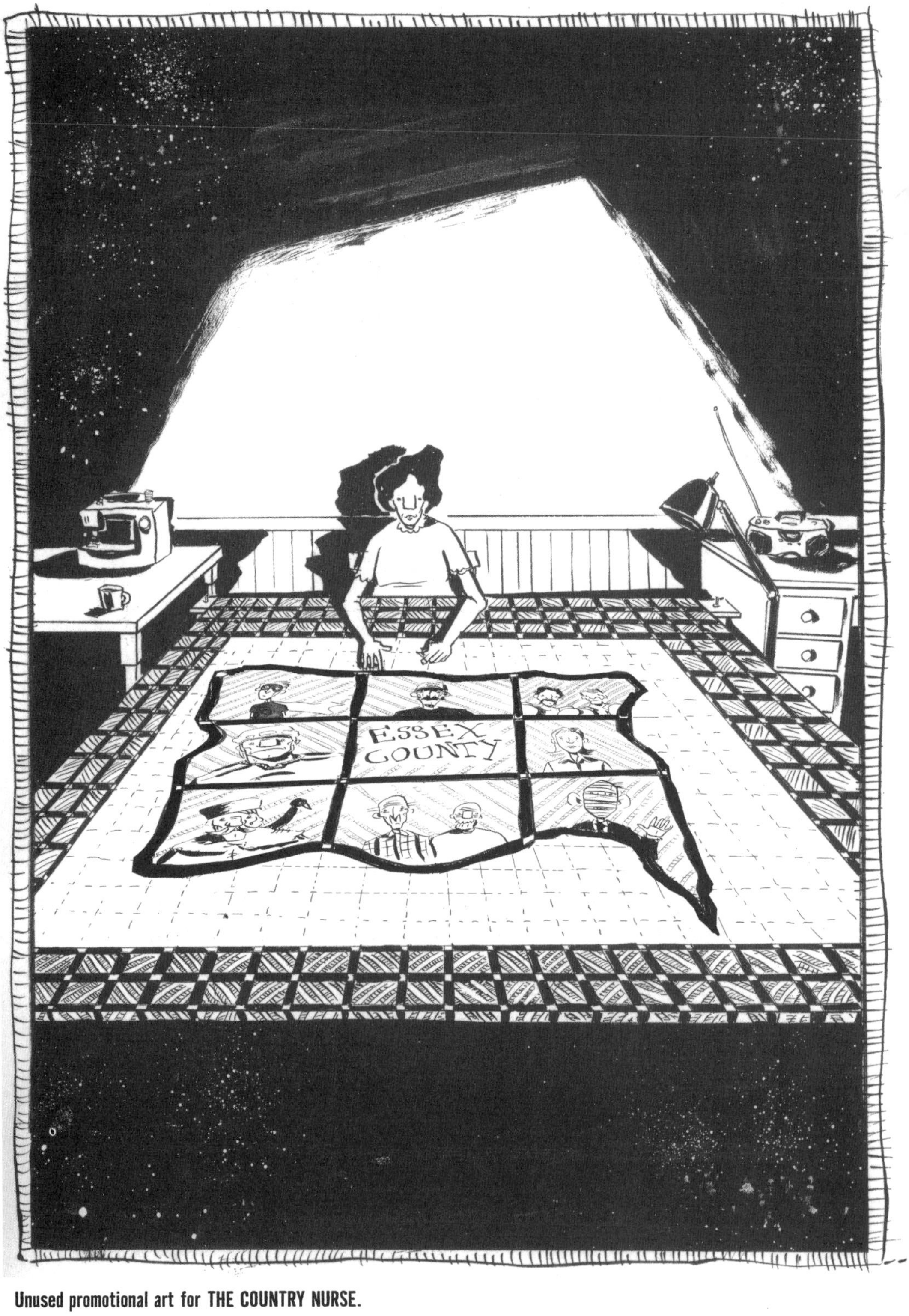
ESSEX COUNTY

Unused promotional art for THE COUNTRY NURSE.

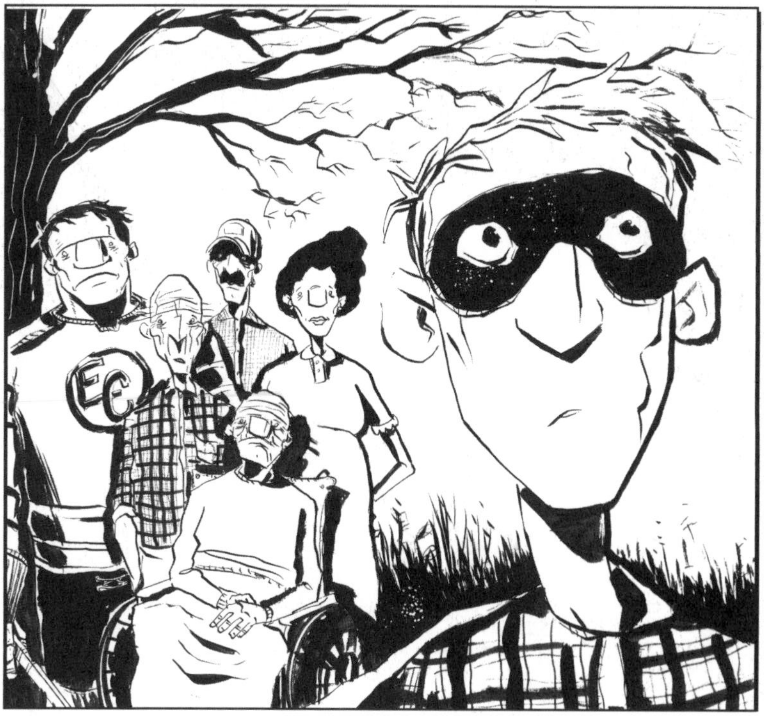
EC

ACKNOWLEDGEMENTS

I would like to thank Chris Staros and Brett Warnock. Without their support and guidance, these books would never have seen the light of day. Also, a big thank you to Matt Kindt for his amazing book design and friendship, Rob Venditti for his tireless proofreading, Jeffrey Brown for letting me include his convention sketch and for being such a great guy (even if he is a Red Wings fan), and to Darwyn Cooke for his introduction, and inspiration.

And special thanks to my main man and fellow Essex County ex-patriot, Dwayne Maillet, for his friendship, constant good humor, and all those nights watching hockey, drinking too much, and talking about comics.

And of course, Lesley-Anne Green, my wife and best friend, whose love and support keeps me at the drawing board every day.

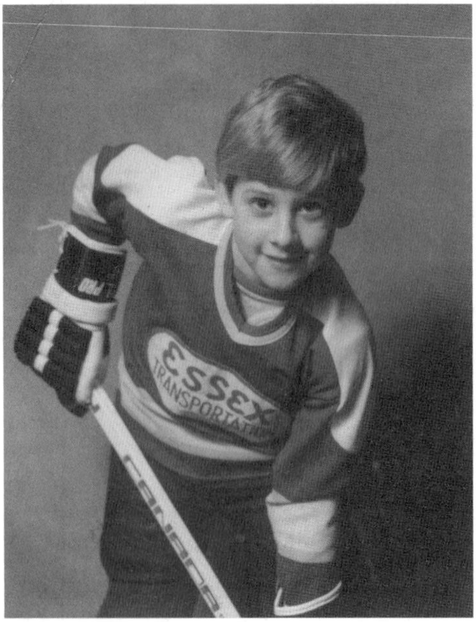
ESSEX

Born and raised on a farm in Essex County, Ontario, Jeff Lemire has been making comics his whole life. His first book, the Xeric award-winning LOST DOGS, debuted in 2005.

His three-part graphic novel ESSEX COUNTY has been nominated for multiple Eisner, Harvey, and Ignatz Awards. In 2008, Jeff won the Shuster Award for Best Canadian Cartoonist and the Doug Wright Award for Best Emerging Talent. He also received the American Library Association's prestigious Alex Award, recognizing books for adults with specific teen appeal. Most recently, ESSEX COUNTY became an official selection of the CBC's Canada Reads program, which declared it one of the Essential Canadian Novels of the Decade.

Jeff has also published the graphic novel THE NOBODY for DC/Vertigo, and is currently hard at work on the monthly ongoing series SWEET TOOTH (DC/Vertigo), the new SUPERBOY and ATOM series for DC Comics, and THE UNDERWATER WELDER, a new graphic novel for Top Shelf.

Jeff lives in Toronto with his wife, sculptor Lesley-Anne Green, and their son, Gus.